MW01006170

Mortgage Loan Monthly Amortization Payment Tables

JULIAN MERITZ

FIRST EDITION

Copyright

Terms of Use and Disclaimer

The information provided in this book is for informational purposes only. It should not be considered legal or financial advice. You should consult with an attorney or other professional to determine what may be best for your individual needs.

This book is offered or sold with the understanding that neither the publisher nor the author is engaged in rendering legal, accounting or other professional service. If legal advice or other expert assistance is required, the services of a competent professional should be sought.

THIS BOOK IS PROVIDED "AS IS". THE AUTHOR AND PUBLISHER MAKE NO GUARANTEES OR WARRANTIES AS TO THE ACCURACY, ADEQUACY OR COMPLETENESS OF OR RESULTS TO BE OBTAINED FROM USING THIS BOOK, AND EXPRESSLY DISCLAIM ANY WARRANTY, EXPRESS OR IMPLIED, INCLUDING BUT NOT LIMITED TO IMPLIED WARRANTIES OF MER-CHANTABILITY OR FITNESS FOR A PARTICULAR PURPOSE. THE AUTHOR AND PUBLISHER DO NOT ASSUME AND HEREBY DISCLAIM ANY LIABILITY TO ANY PARTY FOR ANY LOSS, DAMAGE, OR DISRUPTION CAUSED BY ERRORS OR OMISSIONS, WHETHER SUCH ERRORS OR OMISSIONS RESULT FROM ACCIDENT, NEGLIGENCE, OR ANY OTHER CAUSE.

You are responsible for your own choices, actions, and results.

Contact Info

Web   MeritzPress.com
Facebook MeritzPress
Twitter   @MeritzPress

How To Get Your Bonus Gift

Thank you for buying our book! We worked hard to create it, and we hope you'll find it to be a valuable help that will serve you well.

This book was designed to be a practical tool for anyone who needs to plan and calculate monthly mortgage loan payments, and prefers to do it the old fashioned way. It's inexpensive, it needs no batteries, cannot be hacked, and there's no screen to break. It will last a lifetime or more - you won't need to replace it every year.

Please **submit a positive honest review to book's Amazon page**. More positive reviews mean more eyes on the book's Amazon page and hopefully more readers. Which in turn keeps us in business and preserves book's low price.

After your review to Amazon is submitted, jump to our web site at MeritzPress.com to **request your bonus gift***. Click the contact form, and tell us that you wrote a nice review, and we will reply with a pdf bonus content* that didn't make it to this book.

If you are on Facebook, Twitter, Instagram, or any other social media, and like our book, please tell your friends too. Especially if you think they may find it useful. And follow us to stay in touch.

Finally, if the book didn't work for you, please tell us what we should change or improve. Your feedback makes the next edition and other books better and more useful.

* Standard disclaimer applies - offer is valid for limited time only, and quantities are limited.

Register for Updates and Corrections

Please make a quick trip to MeritzPress.com and register your book. Why? We're not perfect, and we make mistakes. When we do, we admit it, and do our best to correct them. If you are registered, you'll be the first to know. If an updated edition is out, you'll be first to know too.

If you find an error, please report it at the same place. Thank you!

Bulk Orders

If you'd like to order 5 or more copies of this book, we would like to offer you a discount. Please contact us at MeritzPress.com

More from MERITZ PRESS

Look for other books and publications by Meritz Press at MeritzPress.com

About MERITZ PRESS

We are modern ultra-efficient publisher with long-term plans and goals. We seek out and publish books that are unique, and that deliver lasting value to the readers. We create publications and grow our business using our parent company's 25 years of experience in publishing, advertising, and design world, as well as in web and software development area. Taking advantage of that expertise mix allows for faster production of better and less expensive publications.

Sponsor or Advertise in This Book

This reference book is relatively expensive to produce and offers only a very small profit potential in return ... but it delivers real value. It can be an excellent vehicle for a company or business, who would like to promote their brand or product. Sponsorship bylines and display ads are just two of many options.

If you think your company or product could be a good match with what this book offers, please contact us at MeritzPress.com and let's talk.

Customized Books for Your Business

We can produce and deliver a customized version of this book exactly to your specifications. **Banks, mortgage brokers, credit unions, real estate professionals, financial advisors, accounting and law firms, insurance agencies, schools and universities** ... the list goes on. It's a unique promotional item to give out to your customers, who will use and keep it! The books stay with their owners for a long time, and your business promotional benefits are obvious.

The front and back cover can be replaced with your artwork, and the intro pages updated with your language. The content pages typically remain as they are now, but some flexibility is there too.

Very low minimum quantities, quick delivery times, and prices that make it worthwhile for business of any size. Contact us at MeritzPress.com, and let's talk.

How To Use This Book?

Mortgage Loan Monthly Amortization Payment Tables ... what a sexy title! Well, maybe not quite, but the book does exactly what it spells out to do. Combined with very low cost, the fact it IS a book and not a computer or phone application without need for power and battery and updates and charging and security and skills and ... we think it is simply a good old fashioned value, a tool anyone needs and can use.

It does one thing and it does it exactly as you expect. You need to know your monthly mortgage payment? Look up the page that has your **loan amount (1)** at the top, or an amount closest to it, find your **interest rate (2)** row and column with **number of years (3)** the mortgage is going to last for, and your **monthly payment (4)** is where the row and column intersect. If your mortgage amount, interest rate, or term is not exact, the monthly payment will be off, but usually close enough to give you an idea. No clicking, no typing, no turning on and off, it's printed right in front of you.

Look at the numbers next to your payment and start contemplating what would the loan look like with a few less years. Or better interest rate. Flip a page and see what the payment could look like if you borrow more. Or less! It's simple, and intuitive. It lets you focus on getting the best deal without distractions.

The book is a small 5 x 8 paperback format, it fits to any briefcase, purse, and even some pockets. Take it to the bank, mortgage broker, credit union, or real estate agent with you, and use it to quickly find the correct numbers, remove confusion and complexity in negotiations. If you work at a financial institution, real estate office, law or accounting firm, insurance agency, you will find it helpful even more often. It will save your and your clients' time, add transparency to the deal and trust to your reputation.

It is just a tool to help you along the way, you yourself are responsible for the decisions you make. But you already knew that!

$155,000

1.00 - 10.75%

	5	7	8	10	15	20
1.00%	2,649.53	1,911.34	1,680.70	1,357.86	927.67	712.
1.25%	2,666.25	1,928.10	1,697.50	1,374.		
1.50%	2,683.03	1,944.96	1,714.40	1,391.77	962.15	747.95
		1,961.91	1,731.42	1,408.92	979.70	765.90
2.00%	2,716.80	1,978.95	1,748.54	1,426.21	997.44	784.12
2.25%	2,733.79	1,996.09	1,765.76	1,443.63	1,015.38	784.12 (
2.50%	2,750.84	2,013.32	1,783.10	1,461.18	1,033.52	802.60 6
2.75%	2,767.96	2,030.64	1,800.54	1,478.87	1,051.86	821.35 6
						840.36 7
3.00%	2,785.15	2,048.06	1,818.08	1,496.69	1,070.40	859.63 7.
3.25%	2,802.40	2,065.57	1,835.74	1,514.64	1,089.14	879.15 7!
3.50%	2,819.72	2,083.18	1,853.50	1,532.73	1,108.07	898.94 77
3.75%	2,837.11	2,100.87	1,871.36	1,550.95	1,127.19	918.98 79
4.00%	2,854.56	2,118.66	1,889.34	1,569.30	1,146.52	939.27 81.
4.25%	2,872.08	2,136.55	1,907.4	1,587.78	1,166.03	959.81 83!
4.50%	2,889.67	2,154	1,925.60	1,606.40	1,185.74	980.61 861
4.75%	2,907.32	2,172.59	1,943.89	1,625.14	1,2	883
5.00%	2,925.04	2,190	1,962.29	1,644.02	1,22	
5.25%			1,980.79	1,663.02	1,246.01	906
5.50%	2,960.68	2,227.36	1,999.39	1,682.16	1,266.48	1,044.46 928.
5.75%	2,978.60	2,245.80	2,018.11	1,701.42	1,287.14	1,066.23 951.
6.00%	2,996.58	2,264.33	2,036.92	1,720.82	1,307.98	1,088.23 975.
6.25%	3,014.64	2,282.95	2,055.84	1,740.34	1,329.01	1,110.47 998.6
6.50%	3,032.75	2,301.66	2,074.87	1,759.99	1,350.22	1,132.94 1,022.4
6.75%	3,050.94	2,320.47	2,093.99	1,779.77	1,371.61	1,155.64 1,046.5
7.00%	3,069.19	2,339.37	2,113.23	1,799.68	1,393.18	1,178.56 1,070.9
7.25%	3,087.50	2,358.35	2,132.56	1,819.72	1,414.94	1,201.71 1,095.5
7.50%	3,105.88	2,377.43	2,152.00	1,839.88	1,436.87	1,225.08 1,120.35
7.75%						1,248.67 1,145.4

Loan Amount ❶

Interest Rate ❷

Term in Years ❸

Monthly Payment ❹

Mortgage Loan Monthly Payment Amortization Tables

	3	5	7	8	10	15	20	25	30	35
1.00%	564.16	341.87	246.62	216.86	175.21	119.70	91.98	75.37	64.33	56.46
1.25%	566.33	344.03	248.79	219.03	177.39	121.91	94.23	77.66	66.65	58.82
1.50%	568.50	346.20	250.96	221.21	179.58	124.15	96.51	79.99	69.02	61.24
1.75%	570.67	348.37	253.15	223.41	181.80	126.41	98.83	82.36	71.45	63.72
2.00%	572.85	350.56	255.35	225.62	184.03	128.70	101.18	84.77	73.92	66.25
2.25%	575.04	352.75	257.56	227.84	186.27	131.02	103.56	87.23	76.45	68.85
2.50%	577.23	354.95	259.78	230.08	188.54	133.36	105.98	89.72	79.02	71.50
2.75%	579.42	357.16	262.02	232.33	190.82	135.72	108.43	92.26	81.65	74.21
3.00%	581.62	359.37	264.27	234.59	193.12	138.12	110.92	94.84	84.32	76.97
3.25%	583.83	361.60	266.53	236.87	195.44	140.53	113.44	97.46	87.04	79.79
3.50%	586.04	363.83	268.80	239.16	197.77	142.98	115.99	100.12	89.81	82.66
3.75%	588.26	366.08	271.08	241.47	200.12	145.44	118.58	102.83	92.62	85.58
4.00%	590.48	368.33	273.38	243.79	202.49	147.94	121.20	105.57	95.48	88.55
4.25%	592.71	370.59	275.68	246.12	204.88	150.46	123.85	108.35	98.39	91.58
4.50%	594.94	372.86	278.00	248.46	207.28	153.00	126.53	111.17	101.34	94.65
4.75%	597.18	375.14	280.33	250.82	209.70	155.57	129.24	114.02	104.33	97.77
5.00%	599.42	377.42	282.68	253.20	212.13	158.16	131.99	116.92	107.36	100.94
5.25%	601.67	379.72	285.03	255.59	214.58	160.78	134.77	119.85	110.44	104.15
5.50%	603.92	382.02	287.40	257.99	217.05	163.42	137.58	122.82	113.56	107.40
5.75%	606.18	384.34	289.78	260.40	219.54	166.08	140.42	125.82	116.71	110.70
6.00%	608.44	386.66	292.17	262.83	222.04	168.77	143.29	128.86	119.91	114.04
6.25%	610.71	388.99	294.57	265.27	224.56	171.48	146.19	131.93	123.14	117.42
6.50%	612.98	391.32	296.99	267.72	227.10	174.22	149.11	135.04	126.41	120.83
6.75%	615.26	393.67	299.42	270.19	229.65	176.98	152.07	138.18	129.72	124.28
7.00%	617.54	396.02	301.85	272.67	232.22	179.77	155.06	141.36	133.06	127.77
7.25%	619.83	398.39	304.30	275.17	234.80	182.57	158.08	144.56	136.44	131.29
7.50%	622.12	400.76	306.77	277.68	237.40	185.40	161.12	147.80	139.84	134.85
7.75%	624.42	403.14	309.24	280.20	240.02	188.26	164.19	151.07	143.28	138.44
8.00%	626.73	405.53	311.72	282.73	242.66	191.13	167.29	154.36	146.75	142.05
8.25%	629.04	407.93	314.22	285.28	245.31	194.03	170.41	157.69	150.25	145.70
8.50%	631.35	410.33	316.73	287.84	247.97	196.95	173.56	161.05	153.78	149.37
8.75%	633.67	412.74	319.25	290.42	250.65	199.89	176.74	164.43	157.34	153.07
9.00%	635.99	415.17	321.78	293.00	253.35	202.85	179.95	167.84	160.92	156.80
9.25%	638.32	417.60	324.32	295.60	256.07	205.84	183.17	171.28	164.54	160.55
9.50%	640.66	420.04	326.88	298.22	258.80	208.84	186.43	174.74	168.17	164.32
9.75%	643.00	422.48	329.45	300.84	261.54	211.87	189.70	178.23	171.83	168.12
10.00%	645.34	424.94	332.02	303.48	264.30	214.92	193.00	181.74	175.51	171.93
10.25%	647.69	427.41	334.61	306.14	267.08	217.99	196.33	185.28	179.22	175.77
10.50%	650.05	429.88	337.21	308.80	269.87	221.08	199.68	188.84	182.95	179.63
10.75%	652.41	432.36	339.83	311.48	272.68	224.19	203.05	192.42	186.70	183.50

$20,000   11.00 - 20.75%   3 - 35 Years

	3	5	7	8	10	15	20	25	30	35
11.00%	654.77	434.85	342.45	314.17	275.50	227.32	206.44	196.02	190.46	187.39
11.25%	657.14	437.35	345.08	316.87	278.34	230.47	209.85	199.65	194.25	191.30
11.50%	659.52	439.85	347.73	319.59	281.19	233.64	213.29	203.29	198.06	195.22
11.75%	661.90	442.37	350.39	322.32	284.06	236.83	216.74	206.96	201.88	199.16
12.00%	664.29	444.89	353.05	325.06	286.94	240.03	220.22	210.64	205.72	203.11
12.25%	666.68	447.42	355.73	327.81	289.84	243.26	223.71	214.35	209.58	207.07
12.50%	669.07	449.96	358.42	330.58	292.75	246.50	227.23	218.07	213.45	211.05
12.75%	671.47	452.51	361.13	333.35	295.68	249.77	230.76	221.81	217.34	215.04
13.00%	673.88	455.06	363.84	336.15	298.62	253.05	234.32	225.57	221.24	219.04
13.25%	676.29	457.63	366.56	338.95	301.58	256.35	237.89	229.34	225.15	223.05
13.50%	678.71	460.20	369.30	341.76	304.55	259.66	241.47	233.13	229.08	227.07
13.75%	681.13	462.78	372.04	344.59	307.53	263.00	245.08	236.93	233.02	231.10
14.00%	683.55	465.37	374.80	347.43	310.53	266.35	248.70	240.75	236.97	235.13
14.25%	685.98	467.96	377.57	350.28	313.55	269.72	252.34	244.59	240.94	239.18
14.50%	688.42	470.57	380.35	353.15	316.57	273.10	256.00	248.43	244.91	243.23
14.75%	690.86	473.18	383.14	356.02	319.61	276.50	259.67	252.29	248.90	247.29
15.00%	693.31	475.80	385.94	358.91	322.67	279.92	263.36	256.17	252.89	251.36
15.25%	695.76	478.43	388.75	361.81	325.74	283.35	267.06	260.05	256.89	255.44
15.50%	698.21	481.06	391.57	364.72	328.82	286.80	270.78	263.95	260.90	259.52
15.75%	700.67	483.71	394.40	367.64	331.92	290.26	274.51	267.86	264.92	263.60
16.00%	703.14	486.36	397.24	370.58	335.03	293.74	278.25	271.78	268.95	267.69
16.25%	705.61	489.02	400.09	373.52	338.15	297.23	282.01	275.71	272.99	271.79
16.50%	708.09	491.69	402.96	376.48	341.28	300.74	285.78	279.65	277.03	275.89
16.75%	710.57	494.37	405.83	379.45	344.43	304.26	289.56	283.60	281.08	280.00
17.00%	713.05	497.05	408.72	382.43	347.60	307.80	293.36	287.56	285.14	284.11
17.25%	715.55	499.74	411.61	385.42	350.77	311.35	297.17	291.53	289.20	288.22
17.50%	718.04	502.44	414.52	388.42	353.96	314.92	300.99	295.51	293.27	292.34
17.75%	720.54	505.15	417.43	391.44	357.16	318.49	304.82	299.49	297.34	296.46
18.00%	723.05	507.87	420.36	394.46	360.37	322.08	308.66	303.49	301.42	300.58
18.25%	725.56	510.59	423.29	397.50	363.60	325.69	312.52	307.49	305.50	304.70
18.50%	728.07	513.32	426.24	400.55	366.83	329.30	316.38	311.50	309.59	308.83
18.75%	730.59	516.06	429.19	403.61	370.08	332.93	320.25	315.51	313.68	312.97
19.00%	733.12	518.81	432.16	406.68	373.34	336.58	324.14	319.54	317.78	317.10
19.25%	735.65	521.57	435.14	409.76	376.62	340.23	328.03	323.57	321.88	321.24
19.50%	738.19	524.33	438.12	412.85	379.90	343.89	331.93	327.60	325.98	325.37
19.75%	740.73	527.10	441.12	415.95	383.20	347.57	335.84	331.64	330.09	329.51
20.00%	743.27	529.88	444.12	419.06	386.51	351.26	339.76	335.69	334.20	333.66
20.25%	745.82	532.66	447.14	422.19	389.83	354.96	343.69	339.74	338.32	337.80
20.50%	748.38	535.46	450.16	425.32	393.16	358.67	347.63	343.80	342.44	341.94
20.75%	750.94	538.26	453.20	428.47	396.51	362.39	351.58	347.86	346.56	346.09

$22,500   1.00 - 10.75%   3 - 35 Years

	3	5	7	8	10	15	20	25	30	35
1.00%	634.68	384.61	277.45	243.97	197.11	134.66	103.48	84.80	72.37	63.51
1.25%	637.12	387.04	279.89	246.41	199.56	137.15	106.01	87.37	74.98	66.17
1.50%	639.56	389.47	282.33	248.86	202.03	139.67	108.57	89.99	77.65	68.89
1.75%	642.01	391.92	284.79	251.33	204.52	142.21	111.18	92.65	80.38	71.68
2.00%	644.46	394.37	287.27	253.82	207.03	144.79	113.82	95.37	83.16	74.53
2.25%	646.92	396.84	289.75	256.32	209.56	147.39	116.51	98.13	86.01	77.45
2.50%	649.38	399.32	292.26	258.84	212.11	150.03	119.23	100.94	88.90	80.44
2.75%	651.85	401.80	294.77	261.37	214.67	152.69	121.99	103.79	91.85	83.48
3.00%	654.33	404.30	297.30	263.92	217.26	155.38	124.78	106.70	94.86	86.59
3.25%	656.81	406.80	299.84	266.48	219.87	158.10	127.62	109.65	97.92	89.76
3.50%	659.30	409.31	302.40	269.06	222.49	160.85	130.49	112.64	101.04	92.99
3.75%	661.79	411.84	304.97	271.65	225.14	163.63	133.40	115.68	104.20	96.28
4.00%	664.29	414.37	307.55	274.26	227.80	166.43	136.35	118.76	107.42	99.62
4.25%	666.79	416.92	310.14	276.88	230.48	169.26	139.33	121.89	110.69	103.03
4.50%	669.31	419.47	312.75	279.52	233.19	172.12	142.35	125.06	114.00	106.48
4.75%	671.82	422.03	315.38	282.18	235.91	175.01	145.40	128.28	117.37	109.99
5.00%	674.35	424.60	318.01	284.85	238.65	177.93	148.49	131.53	120.78	113.55
5.25%	676.87	427.18	320.66	287.53	241.41	180.87	151.61	134.83	124.25	117.17
5.50%	679.41	429.78	323.33	290.23	244.18	183.84	154.77	138.17	127.75	120.83
5.75%	681.95	432.38	326.00	292.95	246.98	186.84	157.97	141.55	131.30	124.54
6.00%	684.49	434.99	328.69	295.68	249.80	189.87	161.20	144.97	134.90	128.29
6.25%	687.05	437.61	331.40	298.43	252.63	192.92	164.46	148.43	138.54	132.09
6.50%	689.60	440.24	334.11	301.19	255.48	196.00	167.75	151.92	142.22	135.93
6.75%	692.17	442.88	336.84	303.97	258.35	199.10	171.08	155.46	145.93	139.82
7.00%	694.73	445.53	339.59	306.76	261.24	202.24	174.44	159.03	149.69	143.74
7.25%	697.31	448.19	342.34	309.57	264.15	205.39	177.83	162.63	153.49	147.71
7.50%	699.89	450.85	345.11	312.39	267.08	208.58	181.26	166.27	157.32	151.70
7.75%	702.48	453.53	347.89	315.22	270.02	211.79	184.71	169.95	161.19	155.74
8.00%	705.07	456.22	350.69	318.08	272.99	215.02	188.20	173.66	165.10	159.81
8.25%	707.67	458.92	353.50	320.94	275.97	218.28	191.71	177.40	169.03	163.91
8.50%	710.27	461.62	356.32	323.82	278.97	221.57	195.26	181.18	173.01	168.04
8.75%	712.88	464.34	359.16	326.72	281.99	224.88	198.83	184.98	177.01	172.21
9.00%	715.49	467.06	362.00	329.63	285.02	228.21	202.44	188.82	181.04	176.40
9.25%	718.11	469.80	364.87	332.55	288.07	231.57	206.07	192.69	185.10	180.62
9.50%	720.74	472.54	367.74	335.49	291.14	234.95	209.73	196.58	189.19	184.86
9.75%	723.37	475.30	370.63	338.45	294.23	238.36	213.42	200.51	193.31	189.13
10.00%	726.01	478.06	373.53	341.42	297.34	241.79	217.13	204.46	197.45	193.43
10.25%	728.66	480.83	376.44	344.40	300.46	245.24	220.87	208.44	201.62	197.74
10.50%	731.30	483.61	379.37	347.40	303.60	248.71	224.64	212.44	205.82	202.08
10.75%	733.96	486.40	382.30	350.41	306.76	252.21	228.43	216.47	210.03	206.44

$22,500   11.00 - 20.75%   3 - 35 Years

	3	5	7	8	10	15	20	25	30	35
11.00%	736.62	489.20	385.25	353.44	309.94	255.73	232.24	220.53	214.27	210.82
11.25%	739.29	492.01	388.22	356.48	313.13	259.28	236.08	224.60	218.53	215.21
11.50%	741.96	494.83	391.20	359.54	316.34	262.84	239.95	228.71	222.82	219.62
11.75%	744.64	497.66	394.18	362.61	319.57	266.43	243.83	232.83	227.12	224.05
12.00%	747.32	500.50	397.19	365.69	322.81	270.04	247.74	236.98	231.44	228.50
12.25%	750.01	503.35	400.20	368.79	326.07	273.67	251.68	241.14	235.78	232.96
12.50%	752.71	506.20	403.23	371.90	329.35	277.32	255.63	245.33	240.13	237.43
12.75%	755.41	509.07	406.27	375.02	332.64	280.99	259.61	249.54	244.51	241.92
13.00%	758.11	511.94	409.32	378.16	335.95	284.68	263.60	253.76	248.89	246.42
13.25%	760.83	514.83	412.38	381.32	339.28	288.39	267.62	258.01	253.30	250.93
13.50%	763.54	517.72	415.46	384.48	342.62	292.12	271.66	262.27	257.72	255.45
13.75%	766.27	520.62	418.55	387.66	345.98	295.87	275.72	266.55	262.15	259.98
14.00%	769.00	523.54	421.65	390.86	349.35	299.64	279.79	270.85	266.60	264.53
14.25%	771.73	526.46	424.76	394.07	352.74	303.43	283.89	275.16	271.05	269.08
14.50%	774.47	529.39	427.89	397.29	356.15	307.24	288.00	279.49	275.53	273.64
14.75%	777.22	532.33	431.03	400.52	359.57	311.06	292.13	283.83	280.01	278.21
15.00%	779.97	535.27	434.18	403.77	363.00	314.91	296.28	288.19	284.50	282.78
15.25%	782.73	538.23	437.34	407.03	366.46	318.77	300.44	292.56	289.00	287.37
15.50%	785.49	541.20	440.51	410.31	369.92	322.65	304.62	296.94	293.52	291.96
15.75%	788.26	544.17	443.70	413.60	373.41	326.54	308.82	301.34	298.04	296.55
16.00%	791.03	547.16	446.90	416.90	376.90	330.46	313.03	305.75	302.57	301.16
16.25%	793.81	550.15	450.11	420.21	380.42	334.39	317.26	310.17	307.11	305.76
16.50%	796.60	553.15	453.33	423.54	383.95	338.33	321.50	314.61	311.66	310.38
16.75%	799.39	556.16	456.56	426.88	387.49	342.30	325.76	319.05	316.21	315.00
17.00%	802.19	559.18	459.81	430.23	391.04	346.28	330.03	323.50	320.78	319.62
17.25%	804.99	562.21	463.06	433.60	394.62	350.27	334.31	327.97	325.35	324.25
17.50%	807.80	565.25	466.33	436.98	398.20	354.28	338.61	332.44	329.92	328.88
17.75%	810.61	568.30	469.61	440.37	401.80	358.30	342.92	336.93	334.51	333.51
18.00%	813.43	571.35	472.90	443.77	405.42	362.34	347.25	341.42	339.09	338.15
18.25%	816.25	574.42	476.20	447.19	409.05	366.40	351.58	345.92	343.69	342.79
18.50%	819.08	577.49	479.52	450.62	412.69	370.47	355.93	350.43	348.29	347.44
18.75%	821.92	580.57	482.84	454.06	416.34	374.55	360.28	354.95	352.89	352.09
19.00%	824.76	583.66	486.18	457.51	420.01	378.65	364.65	359.48	357.50	356.74
19.25%	827.61	586.76	489.53	460.98	423.70	382.76	369.03	364.01	362.11	361.39
19.50%	830.46	589.87	492.89	464.46	427.39	386.88	373.42	368.55	366.73	366.05
19.75%	833.32	592.99	496.26	467.95	431.10	391.02	377.83	373.10	371.35	370.70
20.00%	836.18	596.11	499.64	471.45	434.83	395.17	382.24	377.65	375.98	375.36
20.25%	839.05	599.25	503.03	474.96	438.56	399.33	386.66	382.21	380.61	380.02
20.50%	841.92	602.39	506.44	478.49	442.31	403.50	391.08	386.78	385.24	384.69
20.75%	844.80	605.54	509.85	482.02	446.07	407.69	395.52	391.35	389.88	389.35

	3	5	7	8	10	15	20	25	30	35
1.00%	705.20	427.34	308.28	271.08	219.01	149.62	114.97	94.22	80.41	70.57
1.25%	707.91	430.04	310.98	273.79	221.73	152.39	117.78	97.07	83.31	73.52
1.50%	710.62	432.75	313.70	276.52	224.48	155.19	120.64	99.98	86.28	76.55
1.75%	713.34	435.47	316.44	279.26	227.25	158.02	123.53	102.95	89.31	79.64
2.00%	716.06	438.19	319.19	282.02	230.03	160.88	126.47	105.96	92.40	82.82
2.25%	718.80	440.93	321.95	284.80	232.84	163.77	129.45	109.03	95.56	86.06
2.50%	721.53	443.68	324.73	287.60	235.67	166.70	132.48	112.15	98.78	89.37
2.75%	724.28	446.45	327.52	290.41	238.53	169.66	135.54	115.33	102.06	92.76
3.00%	727.03	449.22	330.33	293.24	241.40	172.65	138.65	118.55	105.40	96.21
3.25%	729.79	452.00	333.16	296.09	244.30	175.67	141.80	121.83	108.80	99.73
3.50%	732.55	454.79	336.00	298.95	247.21	178.72	144.99	125.16	112.26	103.32
3.75%	735.32	457.60	338.85	301.83	250.15	181.81	148.22	128.53	115.78	106.98
4.00%	738.10	460.41	341.72	304.73	253.11	184.92	151.50	131.96	119.35	110.69
4.25%	740.88	463.24	344.60	307.65	256.09	188.07	154.81	135.43	122.98	114.47
4.50%	743.67	466.08	347.50	310.58	259.10	191.25	158.16	138.96	126.67	118.31
4.75%	746.47	468.92	350.42	313.53	262.12	194.46	161.56	142.53	130.41	122.21
5.00%	749.27	471.78	353.35	316.50	265.16	197.70	164.99	146.15	134.21	126.17
5.25%	752.08	474.65	356.29	319.48	268.23	200.97	168.46	149.81	138.05	130.19
5.50%	754.90	477.53	359.25	322.48	271.32	204.27	171.97	153.52	141.95	134.25
5.75%	757.72	480.42	362.23	325.50	274.42	207.60	175.52	157.28	145.89	138.38
6.00%	760.55	483.32	365.21	328.54	277.55	210.96	179.11	161.08	149.89	142.55
6.25%	763.38	486.23	368.22	331.59	280.70	214.36	182.73	164.92	153.93	146.77
6.50%	766.23	489.15	371.24	334.66	283.87	217.78	186.39	168.80	158.02	151.04
6.75%	769.07	492.09	374.27	337.74	287.06	221.23	190.09	172.73	162.15	155.35
7.00%	771.93	495.03	377.32	340.84	290.27	224.71	193.82	176.69	166.33	159.71
7.25%	774.79	497.98	380.38	343.96	293.50	228.22	197.59	180.70	170.54	164.12
7.50%	777.66	500.95	383.46	347.10	296.75	231.75	201.40	184.75	174.80	168.56
7.75%	780.53	503.92	386.55	350.25	300.03	235.32	205.24	188.83	179.10	173.04
8.00%	783.41	506.91	389.66	353.42	303.32	238.91	209.11	192.95	183.44	177.57
8.25%	786.30	509.91	392.78	356.60	306.63	242.54	213.02	197.11	187.82	182.12
8.50%	789.19	512.91	395.91	359.80	309.96	246.18	216.96	201.31	192.23	186.72
8.75%	792.09	515.93	399.06	363.02	313.32	249.86	220.93	205.54	196.68	191.34
9.00%	794.99	518.96	402.23	366.26	316.69	253.57	224.93	209.80	201.16	196.00
9.25%	797.91	522.00	405.41	369.51	320.08	257.30	228.97	214.10	205.67	200.69
9.50%	800.82	525.05	408.60	372.77	323.49	261.06	233.03	218.42	210.21	205.40
9.75%	803.75	528.11	411.81	376.06	326.93	264.84	237.13	222.78	214.79	210.15
10.00%	806.68	531.18	415.03	379.35	330.38	268.65	241.26	227.18	219.39	214.92
10.25%	809.62	534.26	418.27	382.67	333.85	272.49	245.41	231.60	224.03	219.71
10.50%	812.56	537.35	421.52	386.00	337.34	276.35	249.59	236.05	228.68	224.53
10.75%	815.51	540.45	424.78	389.35	340.85	280.24	253.81	240.52	233.37	229.38

$25,000   11.00 - 20.75%   3 - 35 Years

	3	5	7	8	10	15	20	25	30	35
11.00%	818.47	543.56	428.06	392.71	344.38	284.15	258.05	245.03	238.08	234.24
11.25%	821.43	546.68	431.35	396.09	347.92	288.09	262.31	249.56	242.82	239.12
11.50%	824.40	549.82	434.66	399.48	351.49	292.05	266.61	254.12	247.57	244.03
11.75%	827.38	552.96	437.98	402.89	355.07	296.03	270.93	258.70	252.35	248.95
12.00%	830.36	556.11	441.32	406.32	358.68	300.04	275.27	263.31	257.15	253.89
12.25%	833.35	559.27	444.67	409.76	362.30	304.07	279.64	267.94	261.97	258.84
12.50%	836.34	562.45	448.03	413.22	365.94	308.13	284.04	272.59	266.81	263.81
12.75%	839.34	565.63	451.41	416.69	369.60	312.21	288.45	277.26	271.67	268.80
13.00%	842.35	568.83	454.80	420.18	373.28	316.31	292.89	281.96	276.55	273.80
13.25%	845.36	572.03	458.20	423.69	376.97	320.43	297.36	286.68	281.44	278.81
13.50%	848.38	575.25	461.62	427.20	380.69	324.58	301.84	291.41	286.35	283.84
13.75%	851.41	578.47	465.05	430.74	384.42	328.75	306.35	296.17	291.28	288.87
14.00%	854.44	581.71	468.50	434.29	388.17	332.94	310.88	300.94	296.22	293.92
14.25%	857.48	584.95	471.96	437.85	391.93	337.14	315.43	305.73	301.17	298.98
14.50%	860.52	588.21	475.43	441.43	395.72	341.38	320.00	310.54	306.14	304.04
14.75%	863.58	591.47	478.92	445.03	399.52	345.63	324.59	315.37	311.12	309.12
15.00%	866.63	594.75	482.42	448.64	403.34	349.90	329.20	320.21	316.11	314.20
15.25%	869.70	598.03	485.93	452.26	407.17	354.19	333.82	325.06	321.11	319.30
15.50%	872.77	601.33	489.46	455.90	411.03	358.50	338.47	329.94	326.13	324.40
15.75%	875.84	604.64	493.00	459.55	414.90	362.83	343.13	334.82	331.15	329.50
16.00%	878.93	607.95	496.55	463.22	418.78	367.18	347.81	339.72	336.19	334.62
16.25%	882.01	611.28	500.12	466.90	422.69	371.54	352.51	344.64	341.23	339.74
16.50%	885.11	614.61	503.70	470.60	426.61	375.93	357.23	349.56	346.29	344.86
16.75%	888.21	617.96	507.29	474.31	430.54	380.33	361.95	354.50	351.35	349.99
17.00%	891.32	621.31	510.90	478.04	434.49	384.75	366.70	359.45	356.42	355.13
17.25%	894.43	624.68	514.51	481.78	438.46	389.19	371.46	364.41	361.50	360.27
17.50%	897.55	628.06	518.14	485.53	442.45	393.64	376.24	369.38	366.58	365.42
17.75%	900.68	631.44	521.79	489.30	446.45	398.12	381.02	374.36	371.67	370.57
18.00%	903.81	634.84	525.45	493.08	450.46	402.61	385.83	379.36	376.77	375.72
18.25%	906.95	638.24	529.12	496.88	454.49	407.11	390.64	384.36	381.88	380.88
18.50%	910.09	641.66	532.80	500.69	458.54	411.63	395.47	389.37	386.99	386.04
18.75%	913.24	645.08	536.49	504.51	462.60	416.17	400.32	394.39	392.10	391.21
19.00%	916.40	648.51	540.20	508.35	466.68	420.72	405.17	399.42	397.22	396.37
19.25%	919.56	651.96	543.92	512.20	470.77	425.29	410.04	404.46	402.35	401.54
19.50%	922.73	655.41	547.65	516.06	474.88	429.87	414.92	409.50	407.48	406.72
19.75%	925.91	658.87	551.40	519.94	479.00	434.46	419.81	414.55	412.62	411.89
20.00%	929.09	662.35	555.15	523.83	483.14	439.07	424.71	419.61	417.75	417.07
20.25%	932.28	665.83	558.92	527.73	487.29	443.70	429.62	424.68	422.90	422.25
20.50%	935.47	669.32	562.71	531.65	491.46	448.34	434.54	429.75	428.05	427.43
20.75%	938.67	672.82	566.50	535.58	495.64	452.99	439.47	434.83	433.20	432.61

	3	5	7	8	10	15	20	25	30	35
1.00%	775.72	470.08	339.11	298.19	240.91	164.59	126.47	103.64	88.45	77.63
1.25%	778.70	473.04	342.08	301.17	243.91	167.63	129.56	106.78	91.64	80.87
1.50%	781.68	476.02	345.07	304.17	246.93	170.70	132.70	109.98	94.91	84.20
1.75%	784.67	479.01	348.08	307.19	249.97	173.82	135.89	113.24	98.24	87.61
2.00%	787.67	482.01	351.10	310.22	253.04	176.96	139.12	116.56	101.65	91.10
2.25%	790.68	485.03	354.14	313.28	256.13	180.15	142.40	119.94	105.12	94.67
2.50%	793.69	488.05	357.20	316.36	259.24	183.37	145.72	123.37	108.66	98.31
2.75%	796.71	491.09	360.28	319.45	262.38	186.62	149.10	126.86	112.27	102.03
3.00%	799.73	494.14	363.37	322.56	265.54	189.91	152.51	130.41	115.94	105.83
3.25%	802.77	497.20	366.47	325.70	268.73	193.23	155.98	134.01	119.68	109.71
3.50%	805.81	500.27	369.60	328.85	271.94	196.59	159.49	137.67	123.49	113.65
3.75%	808.85	503.36	372.74	332.02	275.17	199.99	163.04	141.39	127.36	117.67
4.00%	811.91	506.45	375.89	335.21	278.42	203.41	166.64	145.16	131.29	121.76
4.25%	814.97	509.56	379.07	338.41	281.70	206.88	170.29	148.98	135.28	125.92
4.50%	818.04	512.68	382.25	341.64	285.01	210.37	173.98	152.85	139.34	130.15
4.75%	821.12	515.82	385.46	344.88	288.33	213.90	177.71	156.78	143.45	134.44
5.00%	824.20	518.96	388.68	348.15	291.68	217.47	181.49	160.76	147.63	138.79
5.25%	827.29	522.11	391.92	351.43	295.05	221.07	185.31	164.79	151.86	143.20
5.50%	830.39	525.28	395.18	354.73	298.45	224.70	189.17	168.87	156.14	147.68
5.75%	833.49	528.46	398.45	358.05	301.87	228.36	193.07	173.00	160.48	152.21
6.00%	836.60	531.65	401.74	361.39	305.31	232.06	197.02	177.18	164.88	156.80
6.25%	839.72	534.85	405.04	364.75	308.77	235.79	201.01	181.41	169.32	161.45
6.50%	842.85	538.07	408.36	368.12	312.26	239.55	205.03	185.68	173.82	166.14
6.75%	845.98	541.30	411.70	371.52	315.77	243.35	209.10	190.00	178.36	170.89
7.00%	849.12	544.53	415.05	374.93	319.30	247.18	213.21	194.36	182.96	175.69
7.25%	852.27	547.78	418.42	378.36	322.85	251.04	217.35	198.77	187.60	180.53
7.50%	855.42	551.04	421.80	381.81	326.43	254.93	221.54	203.22	192.28	185.42
7.75%	858.58	554.32	425.20	385.27	330.03	258.85	225.76	207.72	197.01	190.35
8.00%	861.75	557.60	428.62	388.76	333.65	262.80	230.02	212.25	201.79	195.32
8.25%	864.93	560.90	432.05	392.26	337.29	266.79	234.32	216.82	206.60	200.34
8.50%	868.11	564.20	435.50	395.78	340.96	270.80	238.65	221.44	211.45	205.39
8.75%	871.30	567.52	438.97	399.32	344.65	274.85	243.02	226.09	216.34	210.47
9.00%	874.49	570.85	442.45	402.88	348.36	278.92	247.42	230.78	221.27	215.60
9.25%	877.70	574.20	445.95	406.46	352.09	283.03	251.86	235.51	226.24	220.75
9.50%	880.91	577.55	449.46	410.05	355.84	287.16	256.34	240.27	231.23	225.94
9.75%	884.12	580.92	452.99	413.66	359.62	291.32	260.84	245.06	236.27	231.16
10.00%	887.35	584.29	456.53	417.29	363.41	295.52	265.38	249.89	241.33	236.41
10.25%	890.58	587.68	460.09	420.94	367.23	299.74	269.95	254.76	246.43	241.69
10.50%	893.82	591.08	463.67	424.60	371.07	303.98	274.55	259.65	251.55	246.99
10.75%	897.06	594.49	467.26	428.28	374.93	308.26	279.19	264.58	256.71	252.31

$27,500

11.00 - 20.75%   3 - 35 Years

	3	5	7	8	10	15	20	25	30	35
11.00%	900.31	597.92	470.87	431.98	378.81	312.56	283.85	269.53	261.89	257.66
11.25%	903.57	601.35	474.49	435.70	382.71	316.89	288.55	274.52	267.10	263.04
11.50%	906.84	604.80	478.13	439.43	386.64	321.25	293.27	279.53	272.33	268.43
11.75%	910.11	608.25	481.78	443.18	390.58	325.64	298.02	284.57	277.59	273.84
12.00%	913.39	611.72	485.45	446.95	394.55	330.05	302.80	289.64	282.87	279.28
12.25%	916.68	615.20	489.13	450.74	398.53	334.48	307.61	294.73	288.17	284.73
12.50%	919.97	618.69	492.83	454.54	402.53	338.94	312.44	299.85	293.50	290.19
12.75%	923.28	622.20	496.55	458.36	406.56	343.43	317.30	304.99	298.84	295.68
13.00%	926.58	625.71	500.28	462.20	410.60	347.94	322.18	310.15	304.20	301.18
13.25%	929.90	629.23	504.02	466.05	414.67	352.48	327.09	315.34	309.59	306.69
13.50%	933.22	632.77	507.78	469.92	418.75	357.04	332.03	320.55	314.99	312.22
13.75%	936.55	636.32	511.56	473.81	422.86	361.62	336.99	325.78	320.41	317.76
14.00%	939.88	639.88	515.35	477.72	426.98	366.23	341.97	331.03	325.84	323.31
14.25%	943.23	643.45	519.16	481.64	431.13	370.86	346.97	336.31	331.29	328.87
14.50%	946.58	647.03	522.98	485.57	435.29	375.51	352.00	341.59	336.75	334.45
14.75%	949.93	650.62	526.81	489.53	439.47	380.19	357.05	346.90	342.23	340.03
15.00%	953.30	654.22	530.66	493.50	443.67	384.89	362.12	352.23	347.72	345.62
15.25%	956.67	657.84	534.53	497.49	447.89	389.61	367.21	357.57	353.23	351.23
15.50%	960.04	661.46	538.40	501.49	452.13	394.35	372.32	362.93	358.74	356.84
15.75%	963.43	665.10	542.30	505.51	456.39	399.11	377.45	368.30	364.27	362.45
16.00%	966.82	668.75	546.21	509.54	460.66	403.89	382.60	373.69	369.81	368.08
16.25%	970.22	672.40	550.13	513.59	464.95	408.70	387.76	379.10	375.36	373.71
16.50%	973.62	676.07	554.07	517.66	469.27	413.52	392.95	384.52	380.92	379.35
16.75%	977.03	679.75	558.02	521.74	473.60	418.36	398.15	389.95	386.48	384.99
17.00%	980.45	683.45	561.98	525.84	477.94	423.23	403.37	395.39	392.06	390.64
17.25%	983.87	687.15	565.96	529.95	482.31	428.11	408.61	400.85	397.65	396.30
17.50%	987.31	690.86	569.96	534.08	486.69	433.01	413.86	406.32	403.24	401.96
17.75%	990.75	694.58	573.97	538.23	491.09	437.93	419.13	411.80	408.84	407.63
18.00%	994.19	698.32	577.99	542.39	495.51	442.87	424.41	417.29	414.45	413.30
18.25%	997.64	702.06	582.03	546.56	499.94	447.82	429.71	422.80	420.06	418.97
18.50%	1,001.10	705.82	586.08	550.75	504.40	452.79	435.02	428.31	425.68	424.65
18.75%	1,004.57	709.59	590.14	554.96	508.86	457.78	440.35	433.83	431.31	430.33
19.00%	1,008.04	713.37	594.22	559.18	513.35	462.79	445.69	439.36	436.95	436.01
19.25%	1,011.52	717.15	598.31	563.42	517.85	467.81	451.04	444.90	442.58	441.70
19.50%	1,015.01	720.95	602.42	567.67	522.37	472.85	456.41	450.45	448.23	447.39
19.75%	1,018.50	724.76	606.54	571.93	526.90	477.91	461.79	456.01	453.88	453.08
20.00%	1,022.00	728.58	610.67	576.21	531.45	482.98	467.18	461.57	459.53	458.78
20.25%	1,025.50	732.41	614.82	580.51	536.02	488.07	472.58	467.15	465.19	464.47
20.50%	1,029.02	736.25	618.98	584.82	540.60	493.17	477.99	472.73	470.85	470.17
20.75%	1,032.54	740.11	623.15	589.14	545.20	498.29	483.42	478.31	476.52	475.88

$30,000   1.00 - 10.75%   3 - 35 Years

	3	5	7	8	10	15	20	25	30	35
1.00%	846.24	512.81	369.94	325.30	262.81	179.55	137.97	113.06	96.49	84.69
1.25%	849.49	516.05	373.18	328.55	266.08	182.87	141.34	116.49	99.98	88.23
1.50%	852.74	519.30	376.44	331.82	269.37	186.22	144.76	119.98	103.54	91.86
1.75%	856.01	522.56	379.72	335.11	272.69	189.62	148.24	123.54	107.17	95.57
2.00%	859.28	525.83	383.02	338.43	276.04	193.05	151.77	127.16	110.89	99.38
2.25%	862.56	529.12	386.34	341.76	279.41	196.53	155.34	130.84	114.67	103.27
2.50%	865.84	532.42	389.67	345.12	282.81	200.04	158.97	134.59	118.54	107.25
2.75%	869.13	535.73	393.03	348.49	286.23	203.59	162.65	138.39	122.47	111.31
3.00%	872.44	539.06	396.40	351.89	289.68	207.17	166.38	142.26	126.48	115.46
3.25%	875.75	542.40	399.79	355.30	293.16	210.80	170.16	146.19	130.56	119.68
3.50%	879.06	545.75	403.20	358.74	296.66	214.46	173.99	150.19	134.71	123.99
3.75%	882.39	549.12	406.62	362.20	300.18	218.17	177.87	154.24	138.93	128.37
4.00%	885.72	552.50	410.06	365.68	303.74	221.91	181.79	158.35	143.22	132.83
4.25%	889.06	555.89	413.53	369.18	307.31	225.68	185.77	162.52	147.58	137.37
4.50%	892.41	559.29	417.00	372.70	310.92	229.50	189.79	166.75	152.01	141.98
4.75%	895.76	562.71	420.50	376.24	314.54	233.35	193.87	171.04	156.49	146.66
5.00%	899.13	566.14	424.02	379.80	318.20	237.24	197.99	175.38	161.05	151.41
5.25%	902.50	569.58	427.55	383.38	321.88	241.16	202.15	179.77	165.66	156.22
5.50%	905.88	573.03	431.10	386.98	325.58	245.13	206.37	184.23	170.34	161.10
5.75%	909.26	576.50	434.67	390.60	329.31	249.12	210.63	188.73	175.07	166.05
6.00%	912.66	579.98	438.26	394.24	333.06	253.16	214.93	193.29	179.87	171.06
6.25%	916.06	583.48	441.86	397.90	336.84	257.23	219.28	197.90	184.72	176.12
6.50%	919.47	586.98	445.48	401.59	340.64	261.33	223.67	202.56	189.62	181.25
6.75%	922.89	590.50	449.12	405.29	344.47	265.47	228.11	207.27	194.58	186.42
7.00%	926.31	594.04	452.78	409.01	348.33	269.65	232.59	212.03	199.59	191.66
7.25%	929.75	597.58	456.46	412.75	352.20	273.86	237.11	216.84	204.65	196.94
7.50%	933.19	601.14	460.15	416.52	356.11	278.10	241.68	221.70	209.76	202.27
7.75%	936.63	604.71	463.86	420.30	360.03	282.38	246.28	226.60	214.92	207.65
8.00%	940.09	608.29	467.59	424.10	363.98	286.70	250.93	231.54	220.13	213.08
8.25%	943.55	611.89	471.33	427.92	367.96	291.04	255.62	236.54	225.38	218.55
8.50%	947.03	615.50	475.09	431.76	371.96	295.42	260.35	241.57	230.67	224.06
8.75%	950.51	619.12	478.87	435.63	375.98	299.83	265.11	246.64	236.01	229.61
9.00%	953.99	622.75	482.67	439.51	380.03	304.28	269.92	251.76	241.39	235.20
9.25%	957.49	626.40	486.49	443.41	384.10	308.76	274.76	256.91	246.80	240.82
9.50%	960.99	630.06	490.32	447.33	388.19	313.27	279.64	262.11	252.26	246.48
9.75%	964.50	633.73	494.17	451.27	392.31	317.81	284.56	267.34	257.75	252.18
10.00%	968.02	637.41	498.04	455.22	396.45	322.38	289.51	272.61	263.27	257.90
10.25%	971.54	641.11	501.92	459.20	400.62	326.99	294.49	277.91	268.83	263.66
10.50%	975.07	644.82	505.82	463.20	404.80	331.62	299.51	283.25	274.42	269.44
10.75%	978.61	648.54	509.74	467.22	409.02	336.28	304.57	288.63	280.04	275.25

$30,000   11.00 - 20.75%   3 - 35 Years

	3	5	7	8	10	15	20	25	30	35
11.00%	982.16	652.27	513.67	471.25	413.25	340.98	309.66	294.03	285.70	281.09
11.25%	985.72	656.02	517.63	475.31	417.51	345.70	314.78	299.47	291.38	286.95
11.50%	989.28	659.78	521.59	479.38	421.79	350.46	319.93	304.94	297.09	292.83
11.75%	992.85	663.55	525.58	483.47	426.09	355.24	325.11	310.44	302.82	298.74
12.00%	996.43	667.33	529.58	487.59	430.41	360.05	330.33	315.97	308.58	304.66
12.25%	1,000.02	671.13	533.60	491.72	434.76	364.89	335.57	321.52	314.37	310.61
12.50%	1,003.61	674.94	537.64	495.86	439.13	369.76	340.84	327.11	320.18	316.58
12.75%	1,007.21	678.76	541.69	500.03	443.52	374.65	346.14	332.72	326.01	322.56
13.00%	1,010.82	682.59	545.76	504.22	447.93	379.57	351.47	338.35	331.86	328.56
13.25%	1,014.43	686.44	549.84	508.42	452.37	384.52	356.83	344.01	337.73	334.57
13.50%	1,018.06	690.30	553.95	512.64	456.82	389.50	362.21	349.69	343.62	340.60
13.75%	1,021.69	694.17	558.07	516.89	461.30	394.50	367.62	355.40	349.53	346.65
14.00%	1,025.33	698.05	562.20	521.15	465.80	399.52	373.06	361.13	355.46	352.70
14.25%	1,028.98	701.94	566.35	525.42	470.32	404.57	378.52	366.88	361.41	358.77
14.50%	1,032.63	705.85	570.52	529.72	474.86	409.65	384.00	372.65	367.37	364.85
14.75%	1,036.29	709.77	574.70	534.03	479.42	414.75	389.51	378.44	373.34	370.94
15.00%	1,039.96	713.70	578.90	538.36	484.00	419.88	395.04	384.25	379.33	377.04
15.25%	1,043.64	717.64	583.12	542.71	488.61	425.02	400.59	390.08	385.34	383.16
15.50%	1,047.32	721.60	587.35	547.08	493.23	430.20	406.16	395.92	391.36	389.28
15.75%	1,051.01	725.56	591.60	551.46	497.88	435.39	411.76	401.79	397.39	395.40
16.00%	1,054.71	729.54	595.86	555.86	502.54	440.61	417.38	407.67	403.43	401.54
16.25%	1,058.42	733.53	600.14	560.28	507.22	445.85	423.01	413.56	409.48	407.68
16.50%	1,062.13	737.54	604.44	564.72	511.93	451.11	428.67	419.47	415.54	413.84
16.75%	1,065.85	741.55	608.75	569.17	516.65	456.40	434.35	425.40	421.62	419.99
17.00%	1,069.58	745.58	613.07	573.64	521.39	461.70	440.04	431.34	427.70	426.16
17.25%	1,073.32	749.62	617.42	578.13	526.16	467.03	445.75	437.29	433.80	432.33
17.50%	1,077.06	753.67	621.77	582.64	530.94	472.37	451.48	443.26	439.90	438.50
17.75%	1,080.81	757.73	626.15	587.16	535.74	477.74	457.23	449.24	446.01	444.68
18.00%	1,084.57	761.80	630.54	591.70	540.56	483.13	462.99	455.23	452.13	450.87
18.25%	1,088.34	765.89	634.94	596.25	545.39	488.53	468.77	461.23	458.25	457.06
18.50%	1,092.11	769.99	639.36	600.82	550.25	493.96	474.57	467.25	464.38	463.25
18.75%	1,095.89	774.10	643.79	605.41	555.12	499.40	480.38	473.27	470.52	469.45
19.00%	1,099.68	778.22	648.24	610.02	560.02	504.86	486.21	479.30	476.67	475.65
19.25%	1,103.48	782.35	652.70	614.64	564.93	510.34	492.05	485.35	482.82	481.85
19.50%	1,107.28	786.49	657.18	619.27	569.86	515.84	497.90	491.40	488.98	488.06
19.75%	1,111.09	790.65	661.68	623.93	574.80	521.36	503.77	497.46	495.14	494.27
20.00%	1,114.91	794.82	666.19	628.60	579.77	526.89	509.65	503.54	501.31	500.48
20.25%	1,118.73	799.00	670.71	633.28	584.75	532.44	515.54	509.61	507.48	506.70
20.50%	1,122.57	803.19	675.25	637.98	589.75	538.00	521.45	515.70	513.65	512.92
20.75%	1,126.40	807.39	679.80	642.70	594.76	543.59	527.36	521.80	519.84	519.14

	3	5	7	8	10	15	20	25	30	35
1.00%	916.76	555.55	400.77	352.40	284.71	194.51	149.47	122.48	104.53	91.74
1.25%	920.28	559.05	404.28	355.93	288.25	198.11	153.12	126.20	108.31	95.58
1.50%	923.81	562.57	407.81	359.47	291.82	201.74	156.83	129.98	112.16	99.51
1.75%	927.34	566.10	411.37	363.04	295.42	205.42	160.59	133.83	116.10	103.54
2.00%	930.88	569.65	414.94	366.63	299.04	209.14	164.41	137.75	120.13	107.66
2.25%	934.44	573.21	418.53	370.24	302.70	212.90	168.29	141.74	124.23	111.88
2.50%	937.99	576.79	422.15	373.87	306.38	216.71	172.22	145.80	128.41	116.19
2.75%	941.56	580.38	425.78	377.53	310.09	220.55	176.20	149.93	132.68	120.59
3.00%	945.14	583.98	429.43	381.21	313.82	224.44	180.24	154.12	137.02	125.08
3.25%	948.72	587.60	433.10	384.91	317.59	228.37	184.34	158.38	141.44	129.65
3.50%	952.32	591.23	436.80	388.64	321.38	232.34	188.49	162.70	145.94	134.32
3.75%	955.92	594.88	440.51	392.38	325.20	236.35	192.69	167.09	150.51	139.07
4.00%	959.53	598.54	444.24	396.15	329.05	240.40	196.94	171.55	155.16	143.90
4.25%	963.15	602.21	447.99	399.94	332.92	244.49	201.25	176.06	159.88	148.82
4.50%	966.78	605.90	451.76	403.76	336.82	248.62	205.61	180.65	164.67	153.81
4.75%	970.41	609.60	455.54	407.59	340.76	252.80	210.02	185.29	169.54	158.88
5.00%	974.05	613.32	459.35	411.45	344.71	257.01	214.49	189.99	174.47	164.02
5.25%	977.71	617.04	463.18	415.33	348.70	261.26	219.00	194.76	179.47	169.24
5.50%	981.37	620.79	467.03	419.23	352.71	265.55	223.56	199.58	184.53	174.53
5.75%	985.04	624.54	470.89	423.15	356.75	269.88	228.18	204.46	189.66	179.89
6.00%	988.71	628.32	474.78	427.10	360.82	274.25	232.84	209.40	194.85	185.31
6.25%	992.40	632.10	478.68	431.06	364.91	278.66	237.55	214.39	200.11	190.80
6.50%	996.09	635.90	482.61	435.05	369.03	283.11	242.31	219.44	205.42	196.35
6.75%	999.79	639.71	486.55	439.06	373.18	287.60	247.12	224.55	210.79	201.96
7.00%	1,003.51	643.54	490.51	443.10	377.35	292.12	251.97	229.70	216.22	207.63
7.25%	1,007.22	647.38	494.49	447.15	381.55	296.68	256.87	234.91	221.71	213.35
7.50%	1,010.95	651.23	498.49	451.23	385.78	301.28	261.82	240.17	227.24	219.13
7.75%	1,014.69	655.10	502.51	455.32	390.03	305.91	266.81	245.48	232.83	224.96
8.00%	1,018.43	658.98	506.55	459.44	394.31	310.59	271.84	250.84	238.47	230.83
8.25%	1,022.18	662.88	510.61	463.58	398.62	315.30	276.92	256.25	244.16	236.76
8.50%	1,025.94	666.79	514.69	467.74	402.95	320.04	282.04	261.70	249.90	242.73
8.75%	1,029.71	670.71	518.78	471.93	407.31	324.82	287.21	267.20	255.68	248.74
9.00%	1,033.49	674.65	522.90	476.13	411.70	329.64	292.41	272.74	261.50	254.80
9.25%	1,037.28	678.60	527.03	480.36	416.11	334.49	297.66	278.32	267.37	260.89
9.50%	1,041.07	682.56	531.18	484.60	420.54	339.37	302.94	283.95	273.28	267.02
9.75%	1,044.87	686.54	535.35	488.87	425.00	344.29	308.27	289.62	279.23	273.19
10.00%	1,048.68	690.53	539.54	493.16	429.49	349.25	313.63	295.33	285.21	279.39
10.25%	1,052.50	694.53	543.75	497.47	434.00	354.23	319.03	301.07	291.23	285.63
10.50%	1,056.33	698.55	547.97	501.80	438.54	359.25	324.47	306.86	297.29	291.89
10.75%	1,060.16	702.58	552.22	506.15	443.10	364.31	329.95	312.68	303.38	298.19

$32,500   11.00 - 20.75%   3 - 35 Years

	3	5	7	8	10	15	20	25	30	35
11.00%	1,064.01	706.63	556.48	510.52	447.69	369.39	335.46	318.54	309.51	304.51
11.25%	1,067.86	710.69	560.76	514.92	452.30	374.51	341.01	324.43	315.66	310.86
11.50%	1,071.72	714.76	565.06	519.33	456.94	379.66	346.59	330.35	321.84	317.23
11.75%	1,075.59	718.85	569.38	523.76	461.60	384.84	352.20	336.31	328.06	323.63
12.00%	1,079.47	722.94	573.71	528.22	466.28	390.05	357.85	342.30	334.30	330.05
12.25%	1,083.35	727.06	578.07	532.69	470.99	395.30	363.53	348.32	340.57	336.50
12.50%	1,087.24	731.18	582.44	537.19	475.72	400.57	369.25	354.37	346.86	342.96
12.75%	1,091.14	735.32	586.83	541.70	480.48	405.87	374.99	360.44	353.18	349.44
13.00%	1,095.05	739.47	591.24	546.24	485.26	411.20	380.76	366.55	359.51	355.94
13.25%	1,098.97	743.64	595.66	550.79	490.06	416.56	386.56	372.68	365.88	362.45
13.50%	1,102.90	747.82	600.11	555.37	494.89	421.95	392.40	378.83	372.26	368.99
13.75%	1,106.83	752.01	604.57	559.96	499.74	427.37	398.26	385.02	378.66	375.53
14.00%	1,110.77	756.22	609.05	564.57	504.62	432.82	404.14	391.22	385.08	382.09
14.25%	1,114.72	760.44	613.55	569.21	509.51	438.29	410.06	397.45	391.52	388.67
14.50%	1,118.68	764.67	618.06	573.86	514.43	443.79	416.00	403.70	397.98	395.26
14.75%	1,122.65	768.91	622.59	578.53	519.37	449.31	421.97	409.98	404.45	401.85
15.00%	1,126.62	773.17	627.14	583.23	524.34	454.87	427.96	416.27	410.94	408.46
15.25%	1,130.61	777.44	631.71	587.94	529.33	460.44	433.97	422.58	417.45	415.08
15.50%	1,134.60	781.73	636.30	592.67	534.33	466.05	440.01	428.92	423.97	421.72
15.75%	1,138.60	786.03	640.90	597.42	539.37	471.68	446.07	435.27	430.50	428.35
16.00%	1,142.60	790.34	645.52	602.19	544.42	477.33	452.16	441.64	437.05	435.00
16.25%	1,146.62	794.66	650.15	606.97	549.49	483.00	458.26	448.03	443.60	441.66
16.50%	1,150.64	799.00	654.81	611.78	554.59	488.71	464.39	454.43	450.17	448.32
16.75%	1,154.67	803.35	659.48	616.60	559.70	494.43	470.54	460.85	456.75	454.99
17.00%	1,158.71	807.71	664.16	621.45	564.84	500.18	476.71	467.28	463.34	461.67
17.25%	1,162.76	812.08	668.87	626.31	570.00	505.95	482.90	473.73	469.95	468.35
17.50%	1,166.82	816.47	673.59	631.19	575.18	511.74	489.11	480.20	476.56	475.04
17.75%	1,170.88	820.87	678.33	636.09	580.38	517.55	495.33	486.67	483.17	481.74
18.00%	1,174.95	825.29	683.08	641.00	585.60	523.39	501.58	493.16	489.80	488.44
18.25%	1,179.03	829.71	687.85	645.94	590.84	529.24	507.84	499.67	496.44	495.14
18.50%	1,183.12	834.15	692.64	650.89	596.10	535.12	514.12	506.18	503.08	501.85
18.75%	1,187.22	838.60	697.44	655.86	601.38	541.02	520.41	512.71	509.73	508.57
19.00%	1,191.32	843.07	702.26	660.85	606.69	546.93	526.72	519.25	516.39	515.29
19.25%	1,195.43	847.54	707.10	665.86	612.01	552.87	533.05	525.79	523.05	522.01
19.50%	1,199.55	852.03	711.95	670.88	617.34	558.83	539.39	532.35	529.72	528.73
19.75%	1,203.68	856.54	716.82	675.92	622.70	564.80	545.75	538.92	536.40	535.46
20.00%	1,207.82	861.05	721.70	680.98	628.08	570.80	552.12	545.50	543.08	542.19
20.25%	1,211.96	865.58	726.60	686.05	633.48	576.81	558.50	552.08	549.77	548.92
20.50%	1,216.11	870.12	731.52	691.15	638.89	582.84	564.90	558.68	556.46	555.66
20.75%	1,220.27	874.67	736.45	696.26	644.33	588.88	571.31	565.28	563.15	562.40

	3	5	7	8	10	15	20	25	30	35
1.00%	987.28	598.28	431.59	379.51	306.61	209.47	160.96	131.91	112.57	98.80
1.25%	991.07	602.06	435.38	383.31	310.43	213.34	164.90	135.90	116.64	102.93
1.50%	994.87	605.85	439.18	387.12	314.27	217.26	168.89	139.98	120.79	107.16
1.75%	998.67	609.65	443.01	390.96	318.14	221.22	172.95	144.13	125.04	111.50
2.00%	1,002.49	613.47	446.86	394.83	322.05	225.23	177.06	148.35	129.37	115.94
2.25%	1,006.31	617.31	450.73	398.72	325.98	229.28	181.23	152.65	133.79	120.48
2.50%	1,010.15	621.16	454.62	402.63	329.94	233.38	185.47	157.02	138.29	125.12
2.75%	1,013.99	625.02	458.53	406.57	333.94	237.52	189.76	161.46	142.88	129.86
3.00%	1,017.84	628.90	462.47	410.54	337.96	241.70	194.11	165.97	147.56	134.70
3.25%	1,021.70	632.80	466.42	414.52	342.02	245.93	198.52	170.56	152.32	139.63
3.50%	1,025.57	636.71	470.39	418.53	346.10	250.21	202.99	175.22	157.17	144.65
3.75%	1,029.45	640.64	474.39	422.57	350.21	254.53	207.51	179.95	162.09	149.77
4.00%	1,033.34	644.58	478.41	426.62	354.36	258.89	212.09	184.74	167.10	154.97
4.25%	1,037.24	648.53	482.45	430.71	358.53	263.30	216.73	189.61	172.18	160.26
4.50%	1,041.14	652.51	486.51	434.81	362.73	267.75	221.43	194.54	177.34	165.64
4.75%	1,045.06	656.49	490.59	438.94	366.97	272.24	226.18	199.54	182.58	171.10
5.00%	1,048.98	660.49	494.69	443.10	371.23	276.78	230.98	204.61	187.89	176.64
5.25%	1,052.91	664.51	498.81	447.27	375.52	281.36	235.85	209.74	193.27	182.26
5.50%	1,056.86	668.54	502.95	451.48	379.84	285.98	240.76	214.93	198.73	187.96
5.75%	1,060.81	672.59	507.12	455.70	384.19	290.64	245.73	220.19	204.25	193.73
6.00%	1,064.77	676.65	511.30	459.95	388.57	295.35	250.75	225.51	209.84	199.57
6.25%	1,068.74	680.72	515.50	464.22	392.98	300.10	255.82	230.88	215.50	205.48
6.50%	1,072.72	684.82	519.73	468.52	397.42	304.89	260.95	236.32	221.22	211.45
6.75%	1,076.70	688.92	523.98	472.84	401.88	309.72	266.13	241.82	227.01	217.50
7.00%	1,080.70	693.04	528.24	477.18	406.38	314.59	271.35	247.37	232.86	223.60
7.25%	1,084.70	697.18	532.53	481.55	410.90	319.50	276.63	252.98	238.76	229.76
7.50%	1,088.72	701.33	536.84	485.94	415.46	324.45	281.96	258.65	244.73	235.98
7.75%	1,092.74	705.49	541.17	490.35	420.04	329.45	287.33	264.37	250.74	242.26
8.00%	1,096.77	709.67	545.52	494.78	424.65	334.48	292.75	270.14	256.82	248.59
8.25%	1,100.81	713.87	549.89	499.24	429.28	339.55	298.22	275.96	262.94	254.97
8.50%	1,104.86	718.08	554.28	503.72	433.95	344.66	303.74	281.83	269.12	261.40
8.75%	1,108.92	722.30	558.69	508.23	438.64	349.81	309.30	287.75	275.35	267.88
9.00%	1,112.99	726.54	563.12	512.76	443.37	354.99	314.90	293.72	281.62	274.40
9.25%	1,117.07	730.80	567.57	517.31	448.11	360.22	320.55	299.73	287.94	280.96
9.50%	1,121.15	735.07	572.04	521.88	452.89	365.48	326.25	305.79	294.30	287.56
9.75%	1,125.25	739.35	576.53	526.48	457.70	370.78	331.98	311.90	300.70	294.21
10.00%	1,129.35	743.65	581.04	531.10	462.53	376.11	337.76	318.05	307.15	300.89
10.25%	1,133.46	747.96	585.57	535.74	467.39	381.48	343.58	324.23	313.64	307.60
10.50%	1,137.59	752.29	590.12	540.40	472.27	386.89	349.43	330.46	320.16	314.35
10.75%	1,141.72	756.63	594.69	545.09	477.19	392.33	355.33	336.73	326.72	321.13

	3	5	7	8	10	15	20	25	30	35
11.00%	1,145.86	760.98	599.29	549.79	482.13	397.81	361.27	343.04	333.31	327.94
11.25%	1,150.00	765.36	603.90	554.53	487.09	403.32	367.24	349.38	339.94	334.77
11.50%	1,154.16	769.74	608.53	559.28	492.08	408.87	373.25	355.76	346.60	341.64
11.75%	1,158.33	774.14	613.18	564.05	497.10	414.45	379.30	362.18	353.29	348.53
12.00%	1,162.50	778.56	617.85	568.85	502.15	420.06	385.38	368.63	360.01	355.44
12.25%	1,166.68	782.98	622.53	573.67	507.22	425.70	391.50	375.11	366.76	362.38
12.50%	1,170.88	787.43	627.24	578.51	512.32	431.38	397.65	381.62	373.54	369.34
12.75%	1,175.08	791.89	631.97	583.37	517.44	437.09	403.83	388.17	380.34	376.32
13.00%	1,179.29	796.36	636.72	588.25	522.59	442.83	410.05	394.74	387.17	383.32
13.25%	1,183.51	800.84	641.49	593.16	527.76	448.61	416.30	401.35	394.02	390.33
13.50%	1,187.74	805.34	646.27	598.09	532.96	454.41	422.58	407.98	400.89	397.37
13.75%	1,191.97	809.86	651.08	603.03	538.18	460.25	428.89	414.63	407.79	404.42
14.00%	1,196.22	814.39	655.90	608.00	543.43	466.11	435.23	421.32	414.71	411.49
14.25%	1,200.47	818.93	660.74	612.99	548.71	472.00	441.60	428.02	421.64	418.57
14.50%	1,204.73	823.49	665.61	618.00	554.00	477.93	448.00	434.76	428.59	425.66
14.75%	1,209.01	828.06	670.49	623.04	559.33	483.88	454.42	441.51	435.57	432.77
15.00%	1,213.29	832.65	675.39	628.09	564.67	489.86	460.88	448.29	442.56	439.88
15.25%	1,217.58	837.25	680.30	633.16	570.04	495.86	467.35	455.09	449.56	447.01
15.50%	1,221.87	841.86	685.24	638.26	575.44	501.90	473.86	461.91	456.58	454.15
15.75%	1,226.18	846.49	690.20	643.37	580.85	507.96	480.39	468.75	463.62	461.30
16.00%	1,230.50	851.13	695.17	648.51	586.30	514.05	486.94	475.61	470.66	468.46
16.25%	1,234.82	855.79	700.16	653.66	591.76	520.16	493.52	482.49	477.73	475.63
16.50%	1,239.15	860.46	705.18	658.84	597.25	526.30	500.12	489.39	484.80	482.81
16.75%	1,243.50	865.14	710.21	664.03	602.76	532.46	506.74	496.30	491.89	489.99
17.00%	1,247.85	869.84	715.25	669.25	608.29	538.65	513.38	503.23	498.99	497.18
17.25%	1,252.20	874.55	720.32	674.49	613.85	544.86	520.04	510.17	506.10	504.38
17.50%	1,256.57	879.28	725.40	679.74	619.43	551.10	526.73	517.14	513.21	511.59
17.75%	1,260.95	884.02	730.50	685.02	625.03	557.36	533.43	524.11	520.34	518.80
18.00%	1,265.33	888.77	735.62	690.31	630.65	563.65	540.16	531.10	527.48	526.01
18.25%	1,269.73	893.54	740.76	695.63	636.29	569.95	546.90	538.10	534.63	533.23
18.50%	1,274.13	898.32	745.92	700.96	641.96	576.28	553.66	545.12	541.78	540.46
18.75%	1,278.54	903.11	751.09	706.31	647.64	582.63	560.44	552.15	548.94	547.69
19.00%	1,282.96	907.92	756.28	711.69	653.35	589.01	567.24	559.19	556.11	554.92
19.25%	1,287.39	912.74	761.49	717.08	659.08	595.40	574.05	566.24	563.29	562.16
19.50%	1,291.83	917.58	766.71	722.49	664.83	601.81	580.88	573.30	570.47	569.40
19.75%	1,296.27	922.42	771.96	727.91	670.60	608.25	587.73	580.38	577.66	576.65
20.00%	1,300.73	927.29	777.22	733.36	676.39	614.70	594.59	587.46	584.86	583.90
20.25%	1,305.19	932.16	782.49	738.83	682.21	621.18	601.46	594.55	592.06	591.15
20.50%	1,309.66	937.05	787.79	744.31	688.04	627.67	608.35	601.65	599.26	598.40
20.75%	1,314.14	941.95	793.10	749.81	693.89	634.18	615.26	608.76	606.47	605.66

$37,500　　1.00 - 10.75%　　3 - 35 Years

	3	5	7	8	10	15	20	25	30	35
1.00%	1,057.80	641.02	462.42	406.62	328.52	224.44	172.46	141.33	120.61	105.86
1.25%	1,061.86	645.06	466.48	410.68	332.60	228.58	176.68	145.61	124.97	110.28
1.50%	1,065.93	649.12	470.55	414.77	336.72	232.78	180.95	149.98	129.42	114.82
1.75%	1,070.01	653.20	474.66	418.89	340.87	237.02	185.30	154.42	133.97	119.47
2.00%	1,074.10	657.29	478.78	423.03	345.05	241.32	189.71	158.95	138.61	124.22
2.25%	1,078.19	661.40	482.92	427.20	349.27	245.66	194.18	163.55	143.34	129.09
2.50%	1,082.30	665.53	487.09	431.39	353.51	250.05	198.71	168.23	148.17	134.06
2.75%	1,086.42	669.67	491.28	435.61	357.79	254.48	203.31	172.99	153.09	139.14
3.00%	1,090.55	673.83	495.50	439.86	362.10	258.97	207.97	177.83	158.10	144.32
3.25%	1,094.68	678.00	499.74	444.13	366.45	263.50	212.70	182.74	163.20	149.60
3.50%	1,098.83	682.19	503.99	448.43	370.82	268.08	217.48	187.73	168.39	154.98
3.75%	1,102.98	686.40	508.28	452.75	375.23	272.71	222.33	192.80	173.67	160.46
4.00%	1,107.15	690.62	512.58	457.10	379.67	277.38	227.24	197.94	179.03	166.04
4.25%	1,111.32	694.86	516.91	461.47	384.14	282.10	232.21	203.15	184.48	171.71
4.50%	1,115.51	699.11	521.26	465.87	388.64	286.87	237.24	208.44	190.01	177.47
4.75%	1,119.70	703.38	525.63	470.30	393.18	291.69	242.33	213.79	195.62	183.32
5.00%	1,123.91	707.67	530.02	474.75	397.75	296.55	247.48	219.22	201.31	189.26
5.25%	1,128.12	711.97	534.44	479.22	402.34	301.45	252.69	224.72	207.08	195.28
5.50%	1,132.35	716.29	538.88	483.72	406.97	306.41	257.96	230.28	212.92	201.38
5.75%	1,136.58	720.63	543.34	488.25	411.63	311.40	263.28	235.91	218.84	207.56
6.00%	1,140.82	724.98	547.82	492.80	416.33	316.45	268.66	241.61	224.83	213.82
6.25%	1,145.08	729.35	552.33	497.38	421.05	321.53	274.10	247.38	230.89	220.15
6.50%	1,149.34	733.73	556.85	501.98	425.80	326.67	279.59	253.20	237.03	226.56
6.75%	1,153.61	738.13	561.40	506.61	430.59	331.84	285.14	259.09	243.22	233.03
7.00%	1,157.89	742.54	565.98	511.26	435.41	337.06	290.74	265.04	249.49	239.57
7.25%	1,162.18	746.98	570.57	515.94	440.25	342.32	296.39	271.05	255.82	246.18
7.50%	1,166.48	751.42	575.19	520.65	445.13	347.63	302.10	277.12	262.21	252.84
7.75%	1,170.79	755.89	579.82	525.37	450.04	352.98	307.86	283.25	268.65	259.57
8.00%	1,175.11	760.36	584.48	530.13	454.98	358.37	313.67	289.43	275.16	266.35
8.25%	1,179.44	764.86	589.16	534.90	459.95	363.80	319.52	295.67	281.72	273.18
8.50%	1,183.78	769.37	593.87	539.70	464.95	369.28	325.43	301.96	288.34	280.07
8.75%	1,188.13	773.90	598.59	544.53	469.98	374.79	331.39	308.30	295.01	287.01
9.00%	1,192.49	778.44	603.34	549.38	475.03	380.35	337.40	314.70	301.73	294.00
9.25%	1,196.86	783.00	608.11	554.26	480.12	385.95	343.45	321.14	308.50	301.03
9.50%	1,201.24	787.57	612.90	559.16	485.24	391.58	349.55	327.64	315.32	308.10
9.75%	1,205.62	792.16	617.71	564.08	490.39	397.26	355.69	334.18	322.18	315.22
10.00%	1,210.02	796.76	622.54	569.03	495.57	402.98	361.88	340.76	329.09	322.38
10.25%	1,214.43	801.38	627.40	574.00	500.77	408.73	368.12	347.39	336.04	329.57
10.50%	1,218.84	806.02	632.28	579.00	506.01	414.52	374.39	354.07	343.03	336.80
10.75%	1,223.27	810.67	637.17	584.02	511.27	420.36	380.71	360.78	350.06	344.06

$37,500   11.00 - 20.75%   3 - 35 Years

	3	5	7	8	10	15	20	25	30	35
11.00%	1,227.70	815.34	642.09	589.07	516.56	426.22	387.07	367.54	357.12	351.36
11.25%	1,232.15	820.02	647.03	594.13	521.88	432.13	393.47	374.34	364.22	358.69
11.50%	1,236.60	824.72	651.99	599.23	527.23	438.07	399.91	381.18	371.36	366.04
11.75%	1,241.06	829.44	656.97	604.34	532.61	444.05	406.39	388.05	378.53	373.42
12.00%	1,245.54	834.17	661.98	609.48	538.02	450.06	412.91	394.96	385.73	380.83
12.25%	1,250.02	838.91	667.00	614.64	543.45	456.11	419.46	401.90	392.96	388.26
12.50%	1,254.51	843.67	672.05	619.83	548.91	462.20	426.05	408.88	400.22	395.72
12.75%	1,259.01	848.45	677.11	625.04	554.40	468.31	432.68	415.89	407.51	403.20
13.00%	1,263.52	853.24	682.20	630.27	559.92	474.47	439.34	422.94	414.82	410.70
13.25%	1,268.04	858.05	687.31	635.53	565.46	480.65	446.04	430.01	422.17	418.22
13.50%	1,272.57	862.87	692.43	640.81	571.03	486.87	452.77	437.12	429.53	425.75
13.75%	1,277.11	867.71	697.58	646.11	576.63	493.12	459.53	444.25	436.92	433.31
14.00%	1,281.66	872.56	702.75	651.43	582.25	499.40	466.32	451.41	444.33	440.88
14.25%	1,286.22	877.43	707.94	656.78	587.90	505.72	473.14	458.60	451.76	448.46
14.50%	1,290.79	882.31	713.15	662.15	593.58	512.06	480.00	465.81	459.21	456.06
14.75%	1,295.36	887.21	718.38	667.54	599.28	518.44	486.88	473.05	466.68	463.68
15.00%	1,299.95	892.12	723.63	672.95	605.01	524.85	493.80	480.31	474.17	471.30
15.25%	1,304.55	897.05	728.90	678.39	610.76	531.28	500.74	487.60	481.67	478.94
15.50%	1,309.15	901.99	734.19	683.85	616.54	537.75	507.71	494.90	489.19	486.59
15.75%	1,313.76	906.95	739.50	689.33	622.34	544.24	514.70	502.23	496.73	494.26
16.00%	1,318.39	911.93	744.83	694.83	628.17	550.76	521.72	509.58	504.28	501.93
16.25%	1,323.02	916.92	750.18	700.35	634.03	557.31	528.77	516.95	511.85	509.61
16.50%	1,327.66	921.92	755.55	705.90	639.91	563.89	535.84	524.34	519.43	517.30
16.75%	1,332.32	926.94	760.93	711.47	645.81	570.50	542.93	531.75	527.02	524.99
17.00%	1,336.98	931.97	766.34	717.05	651.74	577.13	550.05	539.17	534.63	532.70
17.25%	1,341.65	937.02	771.77	722.66	657.69	583.78	557.19	546.62	542.24	540.41
17.50%	1,346.33	942.08	777.22	728.30	663.67	590.47	564.35	554.07	549.87	548.13
17.75%	1,351.02	947.16	782.68	733.95	669.67	597.17	571.54	561.55	557.51	555.85
18.00%	1,355.71	952.25	788.17	739.62	675.69	603.91	578.74	569.04	565.16	563.58
18.25%	1,360.42	957.36	793.67	745.31	681.74	610.67	585.97	576.54	572.81	571.32
18.50%	1,365.14	962.48	799.20	751.03	687.81	617.45	593.21	584.06	580.48	579.06
18.75%	1,369.87	967.62	804.74	756.76	693.91	624.25	600.47	591.59	588.15	586.81
19.00%	1,374.60	972.77	810.30	762.52	700.02	631.08	607.76	599.13	595.83	594.56
19.25%	1,379.35	977.94	815.88	768.30	706.16	637.93	615.06	606.69	603.52	602.32
19.50%	1,384.10	983.12	821.48	774.09	712.32	644.80	622.37	614.25	611.22	610.08
19.75%	1,388.86	988.31	827.10	779.91	718.50	651.70	629.71	621.83	618.92	617.84
20.00%	1,393.63	993.52	832.73	785.75	724.71	658.61	637.06	629.42	626.63	625.60
20.25%	1,398.42	998.74	838.39	791.60	730.94	665.55	644.43	637.02	634.35	633.37
20.50%	1,403.21	1,003.98	844.06	797.48	737.18	672.51	651.81	644.63	642.07	641.15
20.75%	1,408.01	1,009.23	849.75	803.37	743.45	679.48	659.20	652.25	649.79	648.92

	3	5	7	8	10	15	20	25	30	35
1.00%	1,128.32	683.75	493.25	433.73	350.42	239.40	183.96	150.75	128.66	112.91
1.25%	1,132.65	688.06	497.58	438.06	354.77	243.82	188.45	155.32	133.30	117.63
1.50%	1,136.99	692.40	501.93	442.43	359.17	248.30	193.02	159.97	138.05	122.47
1.75%	1,141.34	696.74	506.30	446.82	363.59	252.82	197.65	164.72	142.90	127.43
2.00%	1,145.70	701.11	510.70	451.23	368.05	257.40	202.35	169.54	147.85	132.51
2.25%	1,150.07	705.49	515.12	455.68	372.55	262.03	207.12	174.45	152.90	137.69
2.50%	1,154.46	709.89	519.57	460.15	377.08	266.72	211.96	179.45	158.05	143.00
2.75%	1,158.85	714.31	524.04	464.65	381.64	271.45	216.87	184.52	163.30	148.41
3.00%	1,163.25	718.75	528.53	469.18	386.24	276.23	221.84	189.68	168.64	153.94
3.25%	1,167.66	723.20	533.05	473.74	390.88	281.07	226.88	194.93	174.08	159.57
3.50%	1,172.08	727.67	537.59	478.32	395.54	285.95	231.98	200.25	179.62	165.32
3.75%	1,176.52	732.16	542.16	482.93	400.24	290.89	237.16	205.65	185.25	171.16
4.00%	1,180.96	736.66	546.75	487.57	404.98	295.88	242.39	211.13	190.97	177.11
4.25%	1,185.41	741.18	551.37	492.24	409.75	300.91	247.69	216.70	196.78	183.16
4.50%	1,189.88	745.72	556.01	496.93	414.55	306.00	253.06	222.33	202.67	189.30
4.75%	1,194.35	750.28	560.67	501.65	419.39	311.13	258.49	228.05	208.66	195.54
5.00%	1,198.84	754.85	565.36	506.40	424.26	316.32	263.98	233.84	214.73	201.88
5.25%	1,203.33	759.44	570.07	511.17	429.17	321.55	269.54	239.70	220.88	208.30
5.50%	1,207.84	764.05	574.80	515.97	434.11	326.83	275.15	245.63	227.12	214.81
5.75%	1,212.35	768.67	579.56	520.80	439.08	332.16	280.83	251.64	233.43	221.40
6.00%	1,216.88	773.31	584.34	525.66	444.08	337.54	286.57	257.72	239.82	228.08
6.25%	1,221.41	777.97	589.15	530.54	449.12	342.97	292.37	263.87	246.29	234.83
6.50%	1,225.96	782.65	593.98	535.45	454.19	348.44	298.23	270.08	252.83	241.66
6.75%	1,230.52	787.34	598.83	540.39	459.30	353.96	304.15	276.36	259.44	248.57
7.00%	1,235.08	792.05	603.71	545.35	464.43	359.53	310.12	282.71	266.12	255.54
7.25%	1,239.66	796.77	608.61	550.34	469.60	365.15	316.15	289.12	272.87	262.59
7.50%	1,244.25	801.52	613.53	555.35	474.81	370.80	322.24	295.60	279.69	269.70
7.75%	1,248.85	806.28	618.48	560.40	480.04	376.51	328.38	302.13	286.56	276.87
8.00%	1,253.45	811.06	623.45	565.47	485.31	382.26	334.58	308.73	293.51	284.10
8.25%	1,258.07	815.85	628.44	570.56	490.61	388.06	340.83	315.38	300.51	291.40
8.50%	1,262.70	820.66	633.46	575.69	495.94	393.90	347.13	322.09	307.57	298.74
8.75%	1,267.34	825.49	638.50	580.83	501.31	399.78	353.48	328.86	314.68	306.15
9.00%	1,271.99	830.33	643.56	586.01	506.70	405.71	359.89	335.68	321.85	313.60
9.25%	1,276.65	835.20	648.65	591.21	512.13	411.68	366.35	342.55	329.07	321.10
9.50%	1,281.32	840.07	653.76	596.44	517.59	417.69	372.85	349.48	336.34	328.64
9.75%	1,286.00	844.97	658.89	601.69	523.08	423.75	379.41	356.45	343.66	336.24
10.00%	1,290.69	849.88	664.05	606.97	528.60	429.84	386.01	363.48	351.03	343.87
10.25%	1,295.39	854.81	669.23	612.27	534.16	435.98	392.66	370.55	358.44	351.54
10.50%	1,300.10	859.76	674.43	617.60	539.74	442.16	399.35	377.67	365.90	359.25
10.75%	1,304.82	864.72	679.65	622.96	545.35	448.38	406.09	384.84	373.39	367.00

$40,000　　11.00 - 20.75%　　3 - 35 Years

	3	5	7	8	10	15	20	25	30	35
11.00%	1,309.55	869.70	684.90	628.34	551.00	454.64	412.88	392.05	380.93	374.78
11.25%	1,314.29	874.69	690.17	633.74	556.68	460.94	419.70	399.30	388.50	382.60
11.50%	1,319.04	879.70	695.46	639.17	562.38	467.28	426.57	406.59	396.12	390.44
11.75%	1,323.80	884.73	700.77	644.63	568.12	473.65	433.48	413.92	403.76	398.32
12.00%	1,328.57	889.78	706.11	650.11	573.88	480.07	440.43	421.29	411.45	406.22
12.25%	1,333.35	894.84	711.47	655.62	579.68	486.52	447.43	428.70	419.16	414.15
12.50%	1,338.15	899.92	716.85	661.15	585.50	493.01	454.46	436.14	426.90	422.10
12.75%	1,342.95	905.01	722.25	666.71	591.36	499.53	461.52	443.62	434.68	430.08
13.00%	1,347.76	910.12	727.68	672.29	597.24	506.10	468.63	451.13	442.48	438.08
13.25%	1,352.58	915.25	733.13	677.90	603.16	512.69	475.77	458.68	450.31	446.10
13.50%	1,357.41	920.39	738.60	683.53	609.10	519.33	482.95	466.26	458.16	454.14
13.75%	1,362.25	925.55	744.09	689.18	615.07	525.99	490.16	473.87	466.05	462.19
14.00%	1,367.11	930.73	749.60	694.86	621.07	532.70	497.41	481.50	473.95	470.27
14.25%	1,371.97	935.92	755.14	700.56	627.09	539.43	504.69	489.17	481.87	478.36
14.50%	1,376.84	941.13	760.69	706.29	633.15	546.20	512.00	496.87	489.82	486.47
14.75%	1,381.72	946.36	766.27	712.04	639.23	553.00	519.34	504.59	497.79	494.59
15.00%	1,386.61	951.60	771.87	717.82	645.34	559.83	526.72	512.33	505.78	502.73
15.25%	1,391.52	956.85	777.49	723.61	651.48	566.70	534.12	520.10	513.78	510.87
15.50%	1,396.43	962.13	783.13	729.44	657.64	573.60	541.55	527.90	521.81	519.03
15.75%	1,401.35	967.42	788.80	735.28	663.83	580.52	549.01	535.72	529.85	527.21
16.00%	1,406.28	972.72	794.48	741.15	670.05	587.48	556.50	543.56	537.90	535.39
16.25%	1,411.22	978.04	800.19	747.04	676.30	594.47	564.02	551.42	545.97	543.58
16.50%	1,416.18	983.38	805.92	752.96	682.57	601.48	571.56	559.30	554.06	551.78
16.75%	1,421.14	988.73	811.66	758.90	688.87	608.53	579.13	567.20	562.16	559.99
17.00%	1,426.11	994.10	817.43	764.86	695.19	615.60	586.72	575.12	570.27	568.21
17.25%	1,431.09	999.49	823.22	770.84	701.54	622.70	594.34	583.06	578.39	576.44
17.50%	1,436.08	1,004.89	829.03	776.85	707.92	629.83	601.98	591.01	586.53	584.67
17.75%	1,441.08	1,010.30	834.86	782.88	714.32	636.99	609.64	598.98	594.68	592.91
18.00%	1,446.10	1,015.74	840.71	788.93	720.74	644.17	617.32	606.97	602.83	601.16
18.25%	1,451.12	1,021.18	846.59	795.00	727.19	651.38	625.03	614.98	611.00	609.41
18.50%	1,456.15	1,026.65	852.48	801.10	733.67	658.61	632.76	622.99	619.18	617.67
18.75%	1,461.19	1,032.13	858.39	807.22	740.17	665.87	640.51	631.03	627.36	625.93
19.00%	1,466.24	1,037.62	864.32	813.35	746.69	673.15	648.27	639.07	635.56	634.20
19.25%	1,471.30	1,043.13	870.27	819.52	753.24	680.46	656.06	647.13	643.76	642.47
19.50%	1,476.37	1,048.66	876.24	825.70	759.81	687.79	663.87	655.20	651.97	650.75
19.75%	1,481.45	1,054.20	882.24	831.90	766.40	695.14	671.69	663.29	660.18	659.03
20.00%	1,486.54	1,059.76	888.25	838.13	773.02	702.52	679.53	671.38	668.41	667.31
20.25%	1,491.64	1,065.33	894.28	844.37	779.66	709.92	687.39	679.49	676.64	675.60
20.50%	1,496.75	1,070.91	900.33	850.64	786.33	717.34	695.26	687.60	684.87	683.89
20.75%	1,501.87	1,076.52	906.40	856.93	793.02	724.78	703.15	695.73	693.11	692.18

$42,500   1.00 - 10.75%   3 - 35 Years

	3	5	7	8	10	15	20	25	30	35
1.00%	1,198.84	726.48	524.08	460.84	372.32	254.36	195.46	160.17	136.70	119.97
1.25%	1,203.44	731.07	528.67	465.44	376.95	259.06	200.23	165.03	141.63	124.99
1.50%	1,208.05	735.67	533.30	470.08	381.61	263.82	205.08	169.97	146.68	130.13
1.75%	1,212.68	740.29	537.94	474.74	386.32	268.63	210.00	175.01	151.83	135.40
2.00%	1,217.31	744.93	542.62	479.44	391.06	273.49	215.00	180.14	157.09	140.79
2.25%	1,221.95	749.59	547.31	484.16	395.83	278.41	220.07	185.36	162.45	146.30
2.50%	1,226.61	754.26	552.04	488.91	400.65	283.39	225.21	190.66	167.93	151.94
2.75%	1,231.27	758.96	556.79	493.70	405.50	288.41	230.42	196.06	173.50	157.69
3.00%	1,235.95	763.67	561.57	498.51	410.38	293.50	235.70	201.54	179.18	163.56
3.25%	1,240.64	768.40	566.37	503.35	415.31	298.63	241.06	207.11	184.96	169.55
3.50%	1,245.34	773.15	571.19	508.22	420.26	303.83	246.48	212.77	190.84	175.65
3.75%	1,250.05	777.92	576.05	513.12	425.26	309.07	251.98	218.51	196.82	181.86
4.00%	1,254.77	782.70	580.92	518.04	430.29	314.37	257.54	224.33	202.90	188.18
4.25%	1,259.50	787.51	585.83	523.00	435.36	319.72	263.17	230.24	209.07	194.60
4.50%	1,264.24	792.33	590.76	527.99	440.46	325.12	268.88	236.23	215.34	201.13
4.75%	1,269.00	797.17	595.71	533.00	445.60	330.58	274.65	242.30	221.70	207.76
5.00%	1,273.76	802.03	600.69	538.05	450.78	336.09	280.48	248.45	228.15	214.49
5.25%	1,278.54	806.90	605.70	543.12	455.99	341.65	286.38	254.68	234.69	221.32
5.50%	1,283.33	811.80	610.73	548.22	461.24	347.26	292.35	260.99	241.31	228.23
5.75%	1,288.12	816.71	615.78	553.35	466.52	352.92	298.39	267.37	248.02	235.24
6.00%	1,292.93	821.64	620.86	558.51	471.84	358.64	304.48	273.83	254.81	242.33
6.25%	1,297.75	826.59	625.97	563.70	477.19	364.40	310.64	280.36	261.68	249.51
6.50%	1,302.58	831.56	631.10	568.91	482.58	370.22	316.87	286.96	268.63	256.77
6.75%	1,307.42	836.55	636.26	574.16	488.00	376.09	323.15	293.64	275.65	264.10
7.00%	1,312.28	841.55	641.44	579.43	493.46	382.00	329.50	300.38	282.75	271.51
7.25%	1,317.14	846.57	646.65	584.73	498.95	387.97	335.91	307.19	289.92	279.00
7.50%	1,322.01	851.61	651.88	590.06	504.48	393.98	342.38	314.07	297.17	286.55
7.75%	1,326.90	856.67	657.13	595.42	510.05	400.04	348.90	321.01	304.48	294.17
8.00%	1,331.80	861.75	662.41	600.81	515.64	406.15	355.49	328.02	311.85	301.86
8.25%	1,336.70	866.84	667.72	606.22	521.27	412.31	362.13	335.09	319.29	309.61
8.50%	1,341.62	871.95	673.05	611.67	526.94	418.51	368.82	342.22	326.79	317.42
8.75%	1,346.55	877.08	678.41	617.14	532.64	424.77	375.58	349.41	334.35	325.28
9.00%	1,351.49	882.23	683.79	622.63	538.37	431.06	382.38	356.66	341.96	333.20
9.25%	1,356.44	887.40	689.19	628.16	544.14	437.41	389.24	363.96	349.64	341.17
9.50%	1,361.40	892.58	694.62	633.71	549.94	443.80	396.16	371.32	357.36	349.18
9.75%	1,366.37	897.78	700.07	639.29	555.77	450.23	403.12	378.73	365.14	357.25
10.00%	1,371.36	903.00	705.55	644.90	561.64	456.71	410.13	386.20	372.97	365.36
10.25%	1,376.35	908.24	711.05	650.54	567.54	463.23	417.20	393.71	380.84	373.51
10.50%	1,381.35	913.49	716.58	656.20	573.47	469.79	424.31	401.28	388.76	381.71
10.75%	1,386.37	918.76	722.13	661.89	579.44	476.40	431.47	408.89	396.73	389.94

	3	5	7	8	10	15	20	25	30	35
11.00%	1,391.40	924.05	727.70	667.61	585.44	483.05	438.68	416.55	404.74	398.21
11.25%	1,396.43	929.36	733.30	673.35	591.47	489.75	445.93	424.25	412.79	406.51
11.50%	1,401.48	934.69	738.92	679.12	597.53	496.48	453.23	432.00	420.87	414.85
11.75%	1,406.54	940.03	744.57	684.92	603.63	503.26	460.58	439.79	429.00	423.21
12.00%	1,411.61	945.39	750.24	690.75	609.75	510.07	467.96	447.62	437.16	431.61
12.25%	1,416.69	950.77	755.94	696.60	615.91	516.93	475.39	455.49	445.36	440.03
12.50%	1,421.78	956.16	761.65	702.47	622.10	523.82	482.86	463.40	453.58	448.48
12.75%	1,426.88	961.58	767.39	708.38	628.32	530.76	490.37	471.35	461.84	456.96
13.00%	1,431.99	967.01	773.16	714.31	634.57	537.73	497.92	479.33	470.13	465.46
13.25%	1,437.12	972.45	778.95	720.26	640.85	544.74	505.51	487.35	478.45	473.98
13.50%	1,442.25	977.92	784.76	726.25	647.17	551.79	513.13	495.40	486.80	482.52
13.75%	1,447.39	983.40	790.59	732.25	653.51	558.87	520.80	503.48	495.17	491.08
14.00%	1,452.55	988.90	796.45	738.29	659.88	565.99	528.50	511.60	503.57	499.66
14.25%	1,457.72	994.42	802.33	744.35	666.29	573.15	536.23	519.74	511.99	508.26
14.50%	1,462.89	999.95	808.24	750.43	672.72	580.34	544.00	527.92	520.44	516.87
14.75%	1,468.08	1,005.50	814.16	756.54	679.18	587.56	551.80	536.12	528.90	525.50
15.00%	1,473.28	1,011.07	820.11	762.68	685.67	594.82	559.64	544.35	537.39	534.15
15.25%	1,478.48	1,016.66	826.08	768.84	692.19	602.12	567.50	552.61	545.89	542.80
15.50%	1,483.70	1,022.26	832.08	775.03	698.74	609.45	575.40	560.89	554.42	551.47
15.75%	1,488.93	1,027.88	838.10	781.24	705.32	616.81	583.33	569.20	562.96	560.16
16.00%	1,494.17	1,033.52	844.14	787.47	711.93	624.20	591.28	577.53	571.52	568.85
16.25%	1,499.42	1,039.17	850.20	793.73	718.57	631.62	599.27	585.88	580.10	577.55
16.50%	1,504.69	1,044.84	856.29	800.02	725.23	639.08	607.28	594.25	588.69	586.27
16.75%	1,509.96	1,050.53	862.39	806.33	731.92	646.56	615.32	602.65	597.29	594.99
17.00%	1,515.24	1,056.23	868.52	812.66	738.64	654.08	623.39	611.06	605.91	603.72
17.25%	1,520.53	1,061.96	874.67	819.02	745.39	661.62	631.48	619.50	614.54	612.46
17.50%	1,525.84	1,067.69	880.85	825.40	752.16	669.20	639.60	627.95	623.19	621.21
17.75%	1,531.15	1,073.45	887.04	831.81	758.96	676.80	647.74	636.42	631.84	629.97
18.00%	1,536.48	1,079.22	893.26	838.24	765.79	684.43	655.91	644.91	640.51	638.73
18.25%	1,541.81	1,085.01	899.50	844.69	772.64	692.09	664.10	653.41	649.19	647.50
18.50%	1,547.16	1,090.81	905.76	851.17	779.52	699.77	672.31	661.93	657.88	656.27
18.75%	1,552.51	1,096.64	912.04	857.67	786.43	707.48	680.54	670.47	666.57	665.05
19.00%	1,557.88	1,102.47	918.34	864.19	793.36	715.22	688.79	679.01	675.28	673.84
19.25%	1,563.26	1,108.33	924.66	870.74	800.31	722.99	697.06	687.58	683.99	682.62
19.50%	1,568.65	1,114.20	931.01	877.30	807.30	730.77	705.36	696.15	692.72	691.42
19.75%	1,574.04	1,120.09	937.38	883.90	814.30	738.59	713.67	704.74	701.45	700.22
20.00%	1,579.45	1,125.99	943.76	890.51	821.34	746.43	722.00	713.34	710.18	709.02
20.25%	1,584.87	1,131.91	950.17	897.15	828.39	754.29	730.35	721.95	718.93	717.82
20.50%	1,590.30	1,137.85	956.60	903.81	835.47	762.17	738.72	730.58	727.68	726.63
20.75%	1,595.74	1,143.80	963.05	910.49	842.58	770.08	747.10	739.21	736.43	735.44

	3	5	7	8	10	15	20	25	30	35
1.00%	1,269.36	769.22	554.91	487.95	394.22	269.32	206.95	169.59	144.74	127.03
1.25%	1,274.23	774.07	559.77	492.82	399.12	274.30	212.01	174.73	149.96	132.34
1.50%	1,279.12	778.94	564.67	497.73	404.06	279.33	217.15	179.97	155.30	137.78
1.75%	1,284.01	783.84	569.59	502.67	409.04	284.43	222.36	185.31	160.76	143.36
2.00%	1,288.92	788.75	574.53	507.64	414.06	289.58	227.65	190.73	166.33	149.07
2.25%	1,293.83	793.68	579.51	512.64	419.12	294.79	233.01	196.26	172.01	154.91
2.50%	1,298.76	798.63	584.51	517.67	424.21	300.06	238.46	201.88	177.80	160.87
2.75%	1,303.70	803.60	589.54	522.74	429.35	305.38	243.97	207.59	183.71	166.97
3.00%	1,308.65	808.59	594.60	527.83	434.52	310.76	249.57	213.40	189.72	173.18
3.25%	1,313.62	813.60	599.68	532.96	439.74	316.20	255.24	219.29	195.84	179.52
3.50%	1,318.59	818.63	604.79	538.11	444.99	321.70	260.98	225.28	202.07	185.98
3.75%	1,323.58	823.68	609.93	543.30	450.28	327.25	266.80	231.36	208.40	192.56
4.00%	1,328.58	828.74	615.10	548.52	455.60	332.86	272.69	237.53	214.84	199.25
4.25%	1,333.59	833.83	620.29	553.77	460.97	338.53	278.66	243.78	221.37	206.05
4.50%	1,338.61	838.94	625.51	559.05	466.37	344.25	284.69	250.12	228.01	212.97
4.75%	1,343.65	844.06	630.75	564.36	471.81	350.02	290.80	256.55	234.74	219.99
5.00%	1,348.69	849.21	636.03	569.70	477.29	355.86	296.98	263.07	241.57	227.11
5.25%	1,353.75	854.37	641.33	575.07	482.81	361.74	303.23	269.66	248.49	234.33
5.50%	1,358.82	859.55	646.65	580.47	488.37	367.69	309.55	276.34	255.51	241.66
5.75%	1,363.90	864.75	652.01	585.90	493.96	373.68	315.94	283.10	262.61	249.08
6.00%	1,368.99	869.98	657.38	591.36	499.59	379.74	322.39	289.94	269.80	256.59
6.25%	1,374.09	875.22	662.79	596.86	505.26	385.84	328.92	296.85	277.07	264.18
6.50%	1,379.21	880.48	668.22	602.38	510.97	392.00	335.51	303.84	284.43	271.87
6.75%	1,384.33	885.76	673.68	607.93	516.71	398.21	342.16	310.91	291.87	279.64
7.00%	1,389.47	891.05	679.17	613.52	522.49	404.47	348.88	318.05	299.39	287.49
7.25%	1,394.62	896.37	684.68	619.13	528.30	410.79	355.67	325.26	306.98	295.41
7.50%	1,399.78	901.71	690.22	624.77	534.16	417.16	362.52	332.55	314.65	303.41
7.75%	1,404.95	907.06	695.79	630.45	540.05	423.57	369.43	339.90	322.39	311.48
8.00%	1,410.14	912.44	701.38	636.15	545.97	430.04	376.40	347.32	330.19	319.62
8.25%	1,415.33	917.83	707.00	641.88	551.94	436.56	383.43	354.80	338.07	327.82
8.50%	1,420.54	923.24	712.64	647.65	557.94	443.13	390.52	362.35	346.01	336.09
8.75%	1,425.76	928.68	718.31	653.44	563.97	449.75	397.67	369.96	354.02	344.41
9.00%	1,430.99	934.13	724.01	659.26	570.04	456.42	404.88	377.64	362.08	352.80
9.25%	1,436.23	939.60	729.73	665.11	576.15	463.14	412.14	385.37	370.20	361.23
9.50%	1,441.48	945.08	735.48	670.99	582.29	469.90	419.46	393.16	378.38	369.73
9.75%	1,446.75	950.59	741.25	676.90	588.47	476.71	426.83	401.01	386.62	378.27
10.00%	1,452.02	956.12	747.05	682.84	594.68	483.57	434.26	408.92	394.91	386.85
10.25%	1,457.31	961.66	752.88	688.80	600.93	490.48	441.74	416.87	403.25	395.49
10.50%	1,462.61	967.23	758.73	694.80	607.21	497.43	449.27	424.88	411.63	404.16
10.75%	1,467.92	972.81	764.61	700.83	613.52	504.43	456.85	432.94	420.07	412.88

$45,000   11.00 - 20.75%   3 - 35 Years

	3	5	7	8	10	15	20	25	30	35
11.00%	1,473.24	978.41	770.51	706.88	619.88	511.47	464.48	441.05	428.55	421.63
11.25%	1,478.58	984.03	776.44	712.96	626.26	518.56	472.17	449.21	437.07	430.42
11.50%	1,483.92	989.67	782.39	719.07	632.68	525.69	479.89	457.41	445.63	439.25
11.75%	1,489.28	995.32	788.37	725.21	639.13	532.86	487.67	465.66	454.23	448.11
12.00%	1,494.64	1,001.00	794.37	731.38	645.62	540.08	495.49	473.95	462.88	457.00
12.25%	1,500.02	1,006.69	800.40	737.57	652.14	547.33	503.35	482.28	471.55	465.92
12.50%	1,505.41	1,012.41	806.46	743.80	658.69	554.63	511.26	490.66	480.27	474.86
12.75%	1,510.81	1,018.14	812.53	750.05	665.28	561.98	519.22	499.07	489.01	483.84
13.00%	1,516.23	1,023.89	818.64	756.33	671.90	569.36	527.21	507.53	497.79	492.84
13.25%	1,521.65	1,029.66	824.77	762.63	678.55	576.78	535.24	516.02	506.60	501.86
13.50%	1,527.09	1,035.44	830.92	768.97	685.23	584.24	543.32	524.54	515.44	510.90
13.75%	1,532.53	1,041.25	837.10	775.33	691.95	591.74	551.43	533.10	524.30	519.97
14.00%	1,537.99	1,047.07	843.30	781.72	698.70	599.28	559.58	541.69	533.19	529.05
14.25%	1,543.46	1,052.91	849.53	788.13	705.48	606.86	567.77	550.32	542.11	538.16
14.50%	1,548.94	1,058.77	855.78	794.58	712.29	614.48	576.00	558.97	551.05	547.28
14.75%	1,554.44	1,064.65	862.05	801.05	719.13	622.13	584.26	567.66	560.01	556.41
15.00%	1,559.94	1,070.55	868.35	807.54	726.01	629.81	592.56	576.37	569.00	565.57
15.25%	1,565.45	1,076.46	874.68	814.07	732.91	637.54	600.88	585.12	578.01	574.73
15.50%	1,570.98	1,082.39	881.03	820.62	739.85	645.30	609.25	593.89	587.03	583.91
15.75%	1,576.52	1,088.34	887.40	827.19	746.81	653.09	617.64	602.68	596.08	593.11
16.00%	1,582.07	1,094.31	893.79	833.80	753.81	660.92	626.07	611.50	605.14	602.31
16.25%	1,587.63	1,100.30	900.21	840.42	760.83	668.78	634.52	620.34	614.22	611.53
16.50%	1,593.20	1,106.30	906.66	847.08	767.89	676.67	643.01	629.21	623.32	620.75
16.75%	1,598.78	1,112.33	913.12	853.76	774.98	684.59	651.52	638.10	632.43	629.99
17.00%	1,604.37	1,118.37	919.61	860.47	782.09	692.55	660.06	647.01	641.55	639.24
17.25%	1,609.98	1,124.42	926.12	867.20	789.23	700.54	668.63	655.94	650.69	648.49
17.50%	1,615.59	1,130.50	932.66	873.95	796.40	708.56	677.22	664.89	659.85	657.75
17.75%	1,621.22	1,136.59	939.22	880.74	803.60	716.61	685.84	673.86	669.01	667.02
18.00%	1,626.86	1,142.70	945.80	887.54	810.83	724.69	694.49	682.84	678.19	676.30
18.25%	1,632.51	1,148.83	952.41	894.38	818.09	732.80	703.16	691.85	687.38	685.59
18.50%	1,638.17	1,154.98	959.04	901.23	825.37	740.94	711.85	700.87	696.58	694.88
18.75%	1,643.84	1,161.14	965.69	908.12	832.69	749.10	720.57	709.90	705.78	704.17
19.00%	1,649.52	1,167.32	972.36	915.02	840.03	757.29	729.31	718.96	715.00	713.47
19.25%	1,655.21	1,173.52	979.06	921.96	847.39	765.51	738.07	728.02	724.23	722.78
19.50%	1,660.92	1,179.74	985.78	928.91	854.78	773.76	746.85	737.10	733.46	732.09
19.75%	1,666.63	1,185.97	992.52	935.89	862.20	782.03	755.65	746.20	742.71	741.41
20.00%	1,672.36	1,192.22	999.28	942.89	869.65	790.33	764.47	755.30	751.96	750.73
20.25%	1,678.10	1,198.49	1,006.06	949.92	877.12	798.66	773.31	764.42	761.22	760.05
20.50%	1,683.85	1,204.78	1,012.87	956.97	884.62	807.01	782.17	773.55	770.48	769.38
20.75%	1,689.61	1,211.08	1,019.70	964.05	892.14	815.38	791.05	782.70	779.75	778.71

	3	5	7	8	10	15	20	25	30	35
1.00%	1,339.88	811.95	585.73	515.05	416.12	284.28	218.45	179.01	152.78	134.09
1.25%	1,345.03	817.08	590.87	520.20	421.29	289.54	223.79	184.44	158.29	139.69
1.50%	1,350.18	822.22	596.04	525.38	426.51	294.85	229.21	189.97	163.93	145.44
1.75%	1,355.34	827.38	601.23	530.60	431.77	300.23	234.71	195.60	169.69	151.32
2.00%	1,360.52	832.57	606.45	535.84	437.06	305.67	240.29	201.33	175.57	157.35
2.25%	1,365.71	837.77	611.70	541.12	442.40	311.17	245.96	207.16	181.57	163.51
2.50%	1,370.92	843.00	616.99	546.43	447.78	316.72	251.70	213.09	187.68	169.81
2.75%	1,376.13	848.25	622.29	551.78	453.20	322.35	257.53	219.12	193.91	176.24
3.00%	1,381.36	853.51	627.63	557.15	458.66	328.03	263.43	225.25	200.26	182.80
3.25%	1,386.60	858.80	633.00	562.56	464.17	333.77	269.42	231.48	206.72	189.50
3.50%	1,391.85	864.11	638.39	568.01	469.71	339.57	275.48	237.80	213.30	196.31
3.75%	1,397.11	869.44	643.82	573.48	475.29	345.43	281.62	244.21	219.98	203.25
4.00%	1,402.39	874.78	649.27	578.99	480.91	351.35	287.84	250.72	226.77	210.32
4.25%	1,407.68	880.15	654.75	584.53	486.58	357.33	294.14	257.33	233.67	217.50
4.50%	1,412.98	885.54	660.26	590.10	492.28	363.37	300.51	264.02	240.68	224.80
4.75%	1,418.29	890.95	665.79	595.71	498.03	369.47	306.96	270.81	247.78	232.21
5.00%	1,423.62	896.38	671.36	601.35	503.81	375.63	313.48	277.68	254.99	239.73
5.25%	1,428.96	901.83	676.95	607.02	509.64	381.84	320.08	284.64	262.30	247.35
5.50%	1,434.31	907.31	682.58	612.72	515.50	388.11	326.75	291.69	269.70	255.08
5.75%	1,439.67	912.80	688.23	618.45	521.40	394.44	333.49	298.83	277.20	262.91
6.00%	1,445.04	918.31	693.91	624.22	527.35	400.83	340.30	306.04	284.79	270.84
6.25%	1,450.43	923.84	699.61	630.02	533.33	407.28	347.19	313.34	292.47	278.86
6.50%	1,455.83	929.39	705.35	635.85	539.35	413.78	354.15	320.72	300.23	286.97
6.75%	1,461.24	934.96	711.11	641.71	545.41	420.33	361.17	328.18	308.08	295.17
7.00%	1,466.66	940.56	716.90	647.60	551.52	426.94	368.27	335.72	316.02	303.46
7.25%	1,472.10	946.17	722.72	653.53	557.65	433.61	375.43	343.33	324.03	311.82
7.50%	1,477.55	951.80	728.57	659.48	563.83	440.33	382.66	351.02	332.13	320.27
7.75%	1,483.01	957.46	734.44	665.47	570.05	447.11	389.95	358.78	340.30	328.78
8.00%	1,488.48	963.13	740.35	671.49	576.31	453.93	397.31	366.61	348.54	337.37
8.25%	1,493.96	968.82	746.28	677.54	582.60	460.82	404.73	374.51	356.85	346.03
8.50%	1,499.46	974.54	752.23	683.63	588.93	467.75	412.22	382.48	365.23	354.76
8.75%	1,504.97	980.27	758.22	689.74	595.30	474.74	419.76	390.52	373.68	363.55
9.00%	1,510.49	986.02	764.23	695.88	601.71	481.78	427.37	398.62	382.20	372.40
9.25%	1,516.02	991.80	770.27	702.06	608.16	488.87	435.04	406.78	390.77	381.30
9.50%	1,521.57	997.59	776.34	708.27	614.64	496.01	442.76	415.01	399.41	390.27
9.75%	1,527.12	1,003.40	782.43	714.50	621.16	503.20	450.55	423.29	408.10	399.28
10.00%	1,532.69	1,009.23	788.56	720.77	627.72	510.44	458.39	431.63	416.85	408.34
10.25%	1,538.27	1,015.09	794.71	727.07	634.31	517.73	466.28	440.03	425.65	417.46
10.50%	1,543.87	1,020.96	800.88	733.40	640.94	525.06	474.23	448.49	434.50	426.61
10.75%	1,549.47	1,026.85	807.09	739.76	647.61	532.45	482.23	456.99	443.40	435.81

$47,500　　　11.00 - 20.75%　　　3 - 35 Years

	3	5	7	8	10	15	20	25	30	35
11.00%	1,555.09	1,032.77	813.32	746.15	654.31	539.88	490.29	465.55	452.35	445.05
11.25%	1,560.72	1,038.70	819.57	752.57	661.05	547.36	498.40	474.16	461.35	454.33
11.50%	1,566.36	1,044.65	825.86	759.02	667.83	554.89	506.55	482.82	470.39	463.65
11.75%	1,572.01	1,050.62	832.17	765.50	674.64	562.46	514.76	491.53	479.47	473.00
12.00%	1,577.68	1,056.61	838.50	772.01	681.49	570.08	523.02	500.28	488.59	482.39
12.25%	1,583.36	1,062.62	844.87	778.55	688.37	577.74	531.32	509.08	497.75	491.80
12.50%	1,589.05	1,068.65	851.26	785.12	695.29	585.45	539.67	517.92	506.95	501.25
12.75%	1,594.75	1,074.70	857.68	791.72	702.24	593.20	548.06	526.80	516.18	510.72
13.00%	1,600.46	1,080.77	864.12	798.34	709.23	600.99	556.50	535.72	525.44	520.22
13.25%	1,606.19	1,086.86	870.59	805.00	716.25	608.82	564.98	544.68	534.74	529.74
13.50%	1,611.93	1,092.97	877.08	811.69	723.30	616.70	573.50	553.68	544.07	539.29
13.75%	1,617.68	1,099.10	883.60	818.40	730.39	624.62	582.07	562.72	553.43	548.86
14.00%	1,623.44	1,105.24	890.15	825.15	737.52	632.58	590.67	571.79	562.81	558.44
14.25%	1,629.21	1,111.41	896.72	831.92	744.67	640.58	599.32	580.89	572.23	568.05
14.50%	1,635.00	1,117.59	903.32	838.72	751.86	648.61	608.00	590.03	581.66	577.68
14.75%	1,640.79	1,123.80	909.95	845.55	759.09	656.69	616.72	599.20	591.13	587.33
15.00%	1,646.60	1,130.02	916.60	852.41	766.34	664.80	625.48	608.39	600.61	596.99
15.25%	1,652.42	1,136.26	923.27	859.29	773.63	672.96	634.27	617.62	610.12	606.66
15.50%	1,658.26	1,142.53	929.97	866.21	780.95	681.15	643.09	626.88	619.65	616.35
15.75%	1,664.10	1,148.81	936.70	873.15	788.30	689.37	651.95	636.16	629.19	626.06
16.00%	1,669.96	1,155.11	943.45	880.12	795.69	697.63	660.85	645.47	638.76	635.77
16.25%	1,675.83	1,161.43	950.22	887.11	803.10	705.93	669.77	654.81	648.34	645.50
16.50%	1,681.71	1,167.76	957.02	894.14	810.55	714.26	678.73	664.17	657.95	655.24
16.75%	1,687.60	1,174.12	963.85	901.19	818.03	722.63	687.71	673.55	667.56	664.99
17.00%	1,693.50	1,180.50	970.70	908.27	825.54	731.03	696.73	682.95	677.20	674.75
17.25%	1,699.42	1,186.89	977.58	915.37	833.08	739.46	705.77	692.38	686.84	684.52
17.50%	1,705.35	1,193.31	984.48	922.51	840.65	747.92	714.85	701.83	696.50	694.30
17.75%	1,711.29	1,199.74	991.40	929.67	848.25	756.42	723.95	711.29	706.18	704.08
18.00%	1,717.24	1,206.19	998.35	936.85	855.88	764.95	733.07	720.78	715.87	713.87
18.25%	1,723.20	1,212.66	1,005.32	944.06	863.54	773.51	742.22	730.28	725.56	723.67
18.50%	1,729.18	1,219.14	1,012.32	951.30	871.23	782.10	751.40	739.80	735.27	733.48
18.75%	1,735.16	1,225.65	1,019.34	958.57	878.95	790.72	760.60	749.34	744.99	743.29
19.00%	1,741.16	1,232.18	1,026.38	965.86	886.69	799.37	769.83	758.90	754.72	753.11
19.25%	1,747.17	1,238.72	1,033.45	973.17	894.47	808.04	779.07	768.47	764.46	762.93
19.50%	1,753.19	1,245.28	1,040.54	980.52	902.27	816.75	788.34	778.05	774.21	772.76
19.75%	1,759.23	1,251.86	1,047.66	987.88	910.10	825.48	797.63	787.65	783.97	782.59
20.00%	1,765.27	1,258.46	1,054.79	995.28	917.96	834.24	806.94	797.26	793.73	792.43
20.25%	1,771.33	1,265.08	1,061.96	1,002.69	925.85	843.03	816.27	806.89	803.51	802.27
20.50%	1,777.39	1,271.71	1,069.14	1,010.14	933.77	851.84	825.62	816.53	813.29	812.12
20.75%	1,783.47	1,278.36	1,076.35	1,017.61	941.71	860.68	834.99	826.18	823.07	821.97

	3	5	7	8	10	15	20	25	30	35
1.00%	1,410.40	854.69	616.56	542.16	438.02	299.25	229.95	188.44	160.82	141.14
1.25%	1,415.82	860.08	621.97	547.58	443.47	304.78	235.57	194.15	166.63	147.04
1.50%	1,421.24	865.49	627.41	553.03	448.96	310.37	241.27	199.97	172.56	153.09
1.75%	1,426.68	870.93	632.87	558.52	454.49	316.03	247.06	205.89	178.62	159.29
2.00%	1,432.13	876.39	638.37	564.04	460.07	321.75	252.94	211.93	184.81	165.63
2.25%	1,437.59	881.87	643.90	569.60	465.69	327.54	258.90	218.07	191.12	172.12
2.50%	1,443.07	887.37	649.46	575.19	471.35	333.39	264.95	224.31	197.56	178.75
2.75%	1,448.56	892.89	655.05	580.82	477.06	339.31	271.08	230.66	204.12	185.52
3.00%	1,454.06	898.43	660.67	586.48	482.80	345.29	277.30	237.11	210.80	192.43
3.25%	1,459.58	904.00	666.31	592.17	488.60	351.33	283.60	243.66	217.60	199.47
3.50%	1,465.10	909.59	671.99	597.90	494.43	357.44	289.98	250.31	224.52	206.65
3.75%	1,470.65	915.20	677.70	603.67	500.31	363.61	296.44	257.07	231.56	213.95
4.00%	1,476.20	920.83	683.44	609.46	506.23	369.84	302.99	263.92	238.71	221.39
4.25%	1,481.77	926.48	689.21	615.30	512.19	376.14	309.62	270.87	245.97	228.95
4.50%	1,487.35	932.15	695.01	621.16	518.19	382.50	316.32	277.92	253.34	236.63
4.75%	1,492.94	937.85	700.84	627.06	524.24	388.92	323.11	285.06	260.82	244.43
5.00%	1,498.54	943.56	706.70	633.00	530.33	395.40	329.98	292.30	268.41	252.34
5.25%	1,504.16	949.30	712.58	638.96	536.46	401.94	336.92	299.62	276.10	260.37
5.50%	1,509.80	955.06	718.50	644.97	542.63	408.54	343.94	307.04	283.89	268.51
5.75%	1,515.44	960.84	724.45	651.00	548.85	415.21	351.04	314.55	291.79	276.75
6.00%	1,521.10	966.64	730.43	657.07	555.10	421.93	358.22	322.15	299.78	285.09
6.25%	1,526.77	972.46	736.43	663.17	561.40	428.71	365.46	329.83	307.86	293.54
6.50%	1,532.45	978.31	742.47	669.31	567.74	435.55	372.79	337.60	316.03	302.08
6.75%	1,538.15	984.17	748.54	675.48	574.12	442.45	380.18	345.46	324.30	310.71
7.00%	1,543.85	990.06	754.63	681.69	580.54	449.41	387.65	353.39	332.65	319.43
7.25%	1,549.58	995.97	760.76	687.92	587.01	456.43	395.19	361.40	341.09	328.23
7.50%	1,555.31	1,001.90	766.91	694.19	593.51	463.51	402.80	369.50	349.61	337.12
7.75%	1,561.06	1,007.85	773.10	700.50	600.05	470.64	410.47	377.66	358.21	346.09
8.00%	1,566.82	1,013.82	779.31	706.83	606.64	477.83	418.22	385.91	366.88	355.13
8.25%	1,572.59	1,019.81	785.55	713.20	613.26	485.07	426.03	394.23	375.63	364.25
8.50%	1,578.38	1,025.83	791.82	719.61	619.93	492.37	433.91	402.61	384.46	373.43
8.75%	1,584.18	1,031.86	798.12	726.04	626.63	499.72	441.86	411.07	393.35	382.68
9.00%	1,589.99	1,037.92	804.45	732.51	633.38	507.13	449.86	419.60	402.31	392.00
9.25%	1,595.81	1,043.99	810.81	739.01	640.16	514.60	457.93	428.19	411.34	401.37
9.50%	1,601.65	1,050.09	817.20	745.54	646.99	522.11	466.07	436.85	420.43	410.81
9.75%	1,607.50	1,056.21	823.61	752.11	653.85	529.68	474.26	445.57	429.58	420.29
10.00%	1,613.36	1,062.35	830.06	758.71	660.75	537.30	482.51	454.35	438.79	429.84
10.25%	1,619.23	1,068.51	836.53	765.34	667.70	544.98	490.82	463.19	448.05	439.43
10.50%	1,625.12	1,074.70	843.03	772.00	674.67	552.70	499.19	472.09	457.37	449.07
10.75%	1,631.02	1,080.90	849.56	778.70	681.69	560.47	507.61	481.05	466.74	458.75

$50,000   11.00 - 20.75%   3 - 35 Years

	3	5	7	8	10	15	20	25	30	35
11.00%	1,636.94	1,087.12	856.12	785.42	688.75	568.30	516.09	490.06	476.16	468.48
11.25%	1,642.86	1,093.37	862.71	792.18	695.84	576.17	524.63	499.12	485.63	478.25
11.50%	1,648.80	1,099.63	869.32	798.97	702.98	584.09	533.21	508.23	495.15	488.05
11.75%	1,654.75	1,105.92	875.97	805.79	710.15	592.07	541.85	517.40	504.70	497.90
12.00%	1,660.72	1,112.22	882.64	812.64	717.35	600.08	550.54	526.61	514.31	507.77
12.25%	1,666.69	1,118.55	889.34	819.53	724.60	608.15	559.28	535.87	523.95	517.69
12.50%	1,672.68	1,124.90	896.06	826.44	731.88	616.26	568.07	545.18	533.63	527.63
12.75%	1,678.68	1,131.27	902.82	833.39	739.20	624.42	576.91	554.53	543.35	537.60
13.00%	1,684.70	1,137.65	909.60	840.36	746.55	632.62	585.79	563.92	553.10	547.60
13.25%	1,690.72	1,144.06	916.41	847.37	753.94	640.87	594.72	573.35	562.89	557.62
13.50%	1,696.76	1,150.49	923.24	854.41	761.37	649.16	603.69	582.82	572.71	567.67
13.75%	1,702.82	1,156.94	930.11	861.48	768.83	657.49	612.70	592.33	582.56	577.74
14.00%	1,708.88	1,163.41	937.00	868.58	776.33	665.87	621.76	601.88	592.44	587.84
14.25%	1,714.96	1,169.90	943.92	875.70	783.87	674.29	630.86	611.46	602.34	597.95
14.50%	1,721.05	1,176.41	950.87	882.86	791.43	682.75	640.00	621.08	612.28	608.09
14.75%	1,727.15	1,182.95	957.84	890.05	799.04	691.25	649.18	630.73	622.24	618.24
15.00%	1,733.27	1,189.50	964.84	897.27	806.67	699.79	658.39	640.42	632.22	628.41
15.25%	1,739.39	1,196.07	971.86	904.52	814.35	708.37	667.65	650.13	642.23	638.59
15.50%	1,745.53	1,202.66	978.92	911.80	822.05	717.00	676.94	659.87	652.26	648.79
15.75%	1,751.69	1,209.27	986.00	919.10	829.79	725.65	686.27	669.64	662.31	659.01
16.00%	1,757.85	1,215.90	993.10	926.44	837.57	734.35	695.63	679.44	672.38	669.23
16.25%	1,764.03	1,222.55	1,000.24	933.80	845.37	743.08	705.02	689.27	682.47	679.47
16.50%	1,770.22	1,229.23	1,007.39	941.20	853.21	751.85	714.45	699.12	692.57	689.73
16.75%	1,776.42	1,235.92	1,014.58	948.62	861.08	760.66	723.91	709.00	702.70	699.99
17.00%	1,782.64	1,242.63	1,021.79	956.07	868.99	769.50	733.40	718.90	712.84	710.26
17.25%	1,788.86	1,249.36	1,029.03	963.55	876.93	778.38	742.92	728.82	722.99	720.55
17.50%	1,795.10	1,256.11	1,036.29	971.06	884.89	787.29	752.47	738.76	733.16	730.84
17.75%	1,801.36	1,262.88	1,043.58	978.60	892.89	796.23	762.05	748.73	743.35	741.14
18.00%	1,807.62	1,269.67	1,050.89	986.16	900.93	805.21	771.66	758.71	753.54	751.45
18.25%	1,813.90	1,276.48	1,058.23	993.75	908.99	814.22	781.29	768.72	763.75	761.76
18.50%	1,820.19	1,283.31	1,065.60	1,001.37	917.08	823.26	790.95	778.74	773.97	772.08
18.75%	1,826.49	1,290.16	1,072.99	1,009.02	925.21	832.33	800.63	788.78	784.20	782.41
19.00%	1,832.80	1,297.03	1,080.40	1,016.69	933.36	841.44	810.34	798.84	794.45	792.75
19.25%	1,839.13	1,303.92	1,087.84	1,024.39	941.55	850.57	820.08	808.91	804.70	803.09
19.50%	1,845.47	1,310.82	1,095.31	1,032.12	949.76	859.74	829.83	819.00	814.96	813.43
19.75%	1,851.82	1,317.75	1,102.80	1,039.88	958.01	868.93	839.61	829.11	825.23	823.78
20.00%	1,858.18	1,324.69	1,110.31	1,047.66	966.28	878.15	849.41	839.23	835.51	834.14
20.25%	1,864.55	1,331.66	1,117.85	1,055.47	974.58	887.40	859.23	849.36	845.80	844.50
20.50%	1,870.94	1,338.64	1,125.41	1,063.30	982.91	896.67	869.08	859.50	856.09	854.86
20.75%	1,877.34	1,345.65	1,133.00	1,071.16	991.27	905.98	878.94	869.66	866.39	865.23

	3	5	7	8	10	15	20	25	30	35
1.00%	1,480.93	897.42	647.39	569.27	459.92	314.21	241.44	197.86	168.86	148.20
1.25%	1,486.61	903.08	653.07	574.96	465.64	320.02	247.35	203.86	174.96	154.40
1.50%	1,492.30	908.77	658.78	580.68	471.41	325.89	253.34	209.97	181.19	160.75
1.75%	1,498.01	914.48	664.52	586.45	477.22	331.83	259.42	216.19	187.55	167.25
2.00%	1,503.74	920.21	670.29	592.25	483.07	337.84	265.59	222.52	194.05	173.91
2.25%	1,509.47	925.96	676.09	598.08	488.97	343.92	271.85	228.97	200.68	180.72
2.50%	1,515.22	931.74	681.93	603.95	494.92	350.06	278.20	235.52	207.44	187.68
2.75%	1,520.99	937.54	687.80	609.86	500.91	356.28	284.64	242.19	214.33	194.79
3.00%	1,526.76	943.36	693.70	615.80	506.94	362.56	291.16	248.96	221.34	202.05
3.25%	1,532.55	949.20	699.63	621.78	513.02	368.90	297.78	255.84	228.48	209.44
3.50%	1,538.36	955.07	705.59	627.80	519.15	375.31	304.48	262.83	235.75	216.98
3.75%	1,544.18	960.96	711.59	633.85	525.32	381.79	311.27	269.92	243.14	224.65
4.00%	1,550.01	966.87	717.61	639.94	531.54	388.34	318.14	277.11	250.64	232.46
4.25%	1,555.85	972.80	723.67	646.06	537.80	394.95	325.10	284.41	258.27	240.39
4.50%	1,561.71	978.76	729.76	652.22	544.10	401.62	332.14	291.81	266.01	248.46
4.75%	1,567.59	984.74	735.88	658.41	550.45	408.36	339.27	299.31	273.86	256.65
5.00%	1,573.47	990.74	742.03	664.65	556.84	415.17	346.48	306.91	281.83	264.96
5.25%	1,579.37	996.76	748.21	670.91	563.28	422.04	353.77	314.61	289.91	273.39
5.50%	1,585.28	1,002.81	754.43	677.21	569.76	428.97	361.14	322.40	298.09	281.93
5.75%	1,591.21	1,008.88	760.67	683.55	576.29	435.97	368.59	330.28	306.38	290.59
6.00%	1,597.15	1,014.97	766.95	689.93	582.86	443.02	376.13	338.26	314.76	299.35
6.25%	1,603.11	1,021.09	773.26	696.33	589.47	450.15	383.74	346.33	323.25	308.22
6.50%	1,609.07	1,027.22	779.60	702.78	596.13	457.33	391.43	354.48	331.84	317.18
6.75%	1,615.05	1,033.38	785.97	709.26	602.83	464.58	399.19	362.73	340.51	326.24
7.00%	1,621.05	1,039.56	792.37	715.77	609.57	471.88	407.03	371.06	349.28	335.40
7.25%	1,627.06	1,045.77	798.80	722.32	616.36	479.25	414.95	379.47	358.14	344.65
7.50%	1,633.08	1,051.99	805.26	728.90	623.18	486.68	422.94	387.97	367.09	353.98
7.75%	1,639.11	1,058.24	811.75	735.52	630.06	494.17	431.00	396.55	376.12	363.39
8.00%	1,645.16	1,064.51	818.28	742.18	636.97	501.72	439.13	405.20	385.23	372.89
8.25%	1,651.22	1,070.80	824.83	748.86	643.93	509.32	447.33	413.94	394.41	382.46
8.50%	1,657.30	1,077.12	831.42	755.59	650.92	516.99	455.61	422.74	403.68	392.10
8.75%	1,663.38	1,083.45	838.03	762.34	657.97	524.71	463.95	431.63	413.02	401.82
9.00%	1,669.49	1,089.81	844.68	769.14	665.05	532.49	472.36	440.58	422.43	411.60
9.25%	1,675.60	1,096.19	851.35	775.96	672.17	540.33	480.83	449.60	431.90	421.44
9.50%	1,681.73	1,102.60	858.06	782.82	679.34	548.22	489.37	458.69	441.45	431.35
9.75%	1,687.87	1,109.02	864.80	789.72	686.54	556.17	497.97	467.85	451.06	441.31
10.00%	1,694.03	1,115.47	871.56	796.64	693.79	564.17	506.64	477.07	460.73	451.33
10.25%	1,700.20	1,121.94	878.36	803.61	701.08	572.22	515.36	486.35	470.45	461.40
10.50%	1,706.38	1,128.43	885.19	810.60	708.41	580.33	524.15	495.70	480.24	471.52
10.75%	1,712.57	1,134.94	892.04	817.63	715.78	588.50	533.00	505.10	490.08	481.69

$52,500   11.00 - 20.75%   3 - 35 Years

	3	5	7	8	10	15	20	25	30	35
11.00%	1,718.78	1,141.48	898.93	824.69	723.19	596.71	541.90	514.56	499.97	491.90
11.25%	1,725.00	1,148.03	905.84	831.79	730.64	604.98	550.86	524.08	509.91	502.16
11.50%	1,731.24	1,154.61	912.79	838.92	738.13	613.30	559.88	533.65	519.90	512.46
11.75%	1,737.49	1,161.21	919.76	846.08	745.65	621.67	568.95	543.27	529.94	522.79
12.00%	1,743.75	1,167.83	926.77	853.27	753.22	630.09	578.07	552.94	540.02	533.16
12.25%	1,750.03	1,174.48	933.80	860.50	760.83	638.56	587.25	562.67	550.15	543.57
12.50%	1,756.32	1,181.14	940.87	867.76	768.47	647.07	596.47	572.44	560.31	554.01
12.75%	1,762.62	1,187.83	947.96	875.06	776.16	655.64	605.75	582.25	570.51	564.48
13.00%	1,768.93	1,194.54	955.08	882.38	783.88	664.25	615.08	592.11	580.75	574.98
13.25%	1,775.26	1,201.27	962.23	889.74	791.64	672.91	624.45	602.02	591.03	585.50
13.50%	1,781.60	1,208.02	969.41	897.13	799.44	681.62	633.87	611.96	601.34	596.05
13.75%	1,787.96	1,214.79	976.61	904.55	807.28	690.37	643.34	621.95	611.68	606.63
14.00%	1,794.33	1,221.58	983.85	912.00	815.15	699.16	652.85	631.97	622.06	617.23
14.25%	1,800.71	1,228.40	991.12	919.49	823.06	708.00	662.40	642.04	632.46	627.85
14.50%	1,807.10	1,235.23	998.41	927.01	831.01	716.89	672.00	652.14	642.89	638.49
14.75%	1,813.51	1,242.09	1,005.73	934.55	838.99	725.81	681.64	662.27	653.35	649.15
15.00%	1,819.93	1,248.97	1,013.08	942.13	847.01	734.78	691.31	672.44	663.83	659.83
15.25%	1,826.36	1,255.87	1,020.46	949.74	855.06	743.79	701.03	682.64	674.34	670.52
15.50%	1,832.81	1,262.79	1,027.86	957.39	863.16	752.84	710.79	692.87	684.87	681.23
15.75%	1,839.27	1,269.73	1,035.30	965.06	871.28	761.94	720.58	703.13	695.42	691.96
16.00%	1,845.74	1,276.70	1,042.76	972.76	879.44	771.07	730.41	713.42	706.00	702.70
16.25%	1,852.23	1,283.68	1,050.25	980.49	887.64	780.24	740.27	723.73	716.59	713.45
16.50%	1,858.73	1,290.69	1,057.76	988.26	895.87	789.45	750.17	734.08	727.20	724.21
16.75%	1,865.24	1,297.71	1,065.31	996.05	904.14	798.69	760.11	744.45	737.83	734.99
17.00%	1,871.77	1,304.76	1,072.88	1,003.88	912.44	807.98	770.07	754.84	748.48	745.78
17.25%	1,878.31	1,311.83	1,080.48	1,011.73	920.77	817.30	780.07	765.26	759.14	756.57
17.50%	1,884.86	1,318.92	1,088.10	1,019.61	929.14	826.65	790.09	775.70	769.82	767.38
17.75%	1,891.42	1,326.03	1,095.76	1,027.53	937.54	836.04	800.15	786.17	780.51	778.19
18.00%	1,898.00	1,333.15	1,103.44	1,035.47	945.97	845.47	810.24	796.65	791.22	789.02
18.25%	1,904.59	1,340.31	1,111.14	1,043.44	954.44	854.93	820.35	807.16	801.94	799.85
18.50%	1,911.20	1,347.48	1,118.88	1,051.44	962.94	864.42	830.50	817.68	812.67	810.69
18.75%	1,917.81	1,354.67	1,126.64	1,059.47	971.47	873.95	840.66	828.22	823.41	821.53
19.00%	1,924.44	1,361.88	1,134.42	1,067.53	980.03	883.51	850.86	838.78	834.17	832.38
19.25%	1,931.08	1,369.11	1,142.23	1,075.61	988.62	893.10	861.08	849.36	844.93	843.24
19.50%	1,937.74	1,376.36	1,150.07	1,083.73	997.25	902.72	871.32	859.95	855.71	854.11
19.75%	1,944.41	1,383.64	1,157.94	1,091.87	1,005.91	912.37	881.59	870.56	866.49	864.97
20.00%	1,951.09	1,390.93	1,165.83	1,100.04	1,014.59	922.06	891.88	881.19	877.28	875.85
20.25%	1,957.78	1,398.24	1,173.74	1,108.24	1,023.31	931.77	902.20	891.83	888.09	886.72
20.50%	1,964.49	1,405.58	1,181.68	1,116.47	1,032.06	941.51	912.53	902.48	898.90	897.61
20.75%	1,971.21	1,412.93	1,189.65	1,124.72	1,040.83	951.28	922.89	913.14	909.71	908.49

	3	5	7	8	10	15	20	25	30	35
1.00%	1,551.45	940.16	678.22	596.38	481.82	329.17	252.94	207.28	176.90	155.26
1.25%	1,557.40	946.09	684.17	602.34	487.81	335.25	259.12	213.56	183.29	161.75
1.50%	1,563.37	952.04	690.15	608.34	493.85	341.41	265.40	219.96	189.82	168.40
1.75%	1,569.35	958.02	696.16	614.37	499.94	347.63	271.77	226.48	196.48	175.22
2.00%	1,575.34	964.03	702.21	620.45	506.07	353.93	278.24	233.12	203.29	182.19
2.25%	1,581.35	970.05	708.29	626.56	512.26	360.30	284.79	239.87	210.24	189.33
2.50%	1,587.38	976.10	714.40	632.71	518.48	366.73	291.45	246.74	217.32	196.62
2.75%	1,593.41	982.18	720.55	638.90	524.76	373.24	298.19	253.72	224.53	204.07
3.00%	1,599.47	988.28	726.73	645.13	531.08	379.82	305.03	260.82	231.88	211.67
3.25%	1,605.53	994.40	732.95	651.39	537.45	386.47	311.96	268.02	239.36	219.42
3.50%	1,611.61	1,000.55	739.19	657.69	543.87	393.19	318.98	275.34	246.97	227.31
3.75%	1,617.71	1,006.72	745.47	664.03	550.34	399.97	326.09	282.77	254.71	235.35
4.00%	1,623.82	1,012.91	751.78	670.41	556.85	406.83	333.29	290.31	262.58	243.53
4.25%	1,629.94	1,019.13	758.13	676.83	563.41	413.75	340.58	297.96	270.57	251.84
4.50%	1,636.08	1,025.37	764.51	683.28	570.01	420.75	347.96	305.71	278.68	260.29
4.75%	1,642.23	1,031.63	770.92	689.77	576.66	427.81	355.42	313.56	286.91	268.87
5.00%	1,648.40	1,037.92	777.36	696.30	583.36	434.94	362.98	321.52	295.25	277.58
5.25%	1,654.58	1,044.23	783.84	702.86	590.10	442.13	370.61	329.59	303.71	286.41
5.50%	1,660.77	1,050.56	790.35	709.46	596.89	449.40	378.34	337.75	312.28	295.36
5.75%	1,666.98	1,056.92	796.90	716.10	603.73	456.73	386.15	346.01	320.97	304.43
6.00%	1,673.21	1,063.30	803.47	722.78	610.61	464.12	394.04	354.37	329.75	313.60
6.25%	1,679.44	1,069.71	810.08	729.49	617.54	471.58	402.01	362.82	338.64	322.89
6.50%	1,685.70	1,076.14	816.72	736.24	624.51	479.11	410.07	371.36	347.64	332.28
6.75%	1,691.96	1,082.59	823.39	743.03	631.53	486.70	418.20	380.00	356.73	341.78
7.00%	1,698.24	1,089.07	830.10	749.85	638.60	494.36	426.41	388.73	365.92	351.37
7.25%	1,704.53	1,095.56	836.84	756.72	645.71	502.07	434.71	397.54	375.20	361.06
7.50%	1,710.84	1,102.09	843.61	763.61	652.86	509.86	443.08	406.45	384.57	370.83
7.75%	1,717.16	1,108.63	850.41	770.55	660.06	517.70	451.52	415.43	394.03	380.70
8.00%	1,723.50	1,115.20	857.24	777.52	667.30	525.61	460.04	424.50	403.57	390.64
8.25%	1,729.85	1,121.79	864.11	784.52	674.59	533.58	468.64	433.65	413.20	400.67
8.50%	1,736.21	1,128.41	871.01	791.57	681.92	541.61	477.30	442.87	422.90	410.77
8.75%	1,742.59	1,135.05	877.94	798.65	689.30	549.70	486.04	452.18	432.69	420.95
9.00%	1,748.99	1,141.71	884.90	805.76	696.72	557.85	494.85	461.56	442.54	431.20
9.25%	1,755.39	1,148.39	891.89	812.91	704.18	566.06	503.73	471.01	452.47	441.51
9.50%	1,761.81	1,155.10	898.92	820.10	711.69	574.32	512.67	480.53	462.47	451.89
9.75%	1,768.25	1,161.83	905.98	827.32	719.24	582.65	521.68	490.13	472.53	462.32
10.00%	1,774.70	1,168.59	913.07	834.58	726.83	591.03	530.76	499.79	482.66	472.82
10.25%	1,781.16	1,175.36	920.19	841.87	734.46	599.47	539.90	509.51	492.86	483.37
10.50%	1,787.63	1,182.16	927.34	849.20	742.14	607.97	549.11	519.30	503.11	493.97
10.75%	1,794.12	1,188.99	934.52	856.56	749.86	616.52	558.38	529.15	513.41	504.63

$55,000   11.00 - 20.75%   3 - 35 Years

	3	5	7	8	10	15	20	25	30	35
11.00%	1,800.63	1,195.83	941.73	863.96	757.63	625.13	567.70	539.06	523.78	515.33
11.25%	1,807.15	1,202.70	948.98	871.40	765.43	633.79	577.09	549.03	534.19	526.07
11.50%	1,813.68	1,209.59	956.26	878.87	773.27	642.50	586.54	559.06	544.66	536.86
11.75%	1,820.23	1,216.51	963.56	886.37	781.16	651.27	596.04	569.14	555.18	547.69
12.00%	1,826.79	1,223.44	970.90	893.91	789.09	660.09	605.60	579.27	565.74	558.55
12.25%	1,833.36	1,230.40	978.27	901.48	797.06	668.96	615.21	589.46	576.34	569.45
12.50%	1,839.95	1,237.39	985.67	909.08	805.07	677.89	624.88	599.69	586.99	580.39
12.75%	1,846.55	1,244.39	993.10	916.72	813.12	686.86	634.60	609.98	597.68	591.36
13.00%	1,853.17	1,251.42	1,000.56	924.40	821.21	695.88	644.37	620.31	608.41	602.36
13.25%	1,859.80	1,258.47	1,008.05	932.11	829.34	704.96	654.19	630.69	619.18	613.38
13.50%	1,866.44	1,265.54	1,015.57	939.85	837.51	714.08	664.06	641.10	629.98	624.44
13.75%	1,873.10	1,272.64	1,023.12	947.62	845.72	723.24	673.97	651.57	640.81	635.52
14.00%	1,879.77	1,279.75	1,030.70	955.43	853.97	732.46	683.94	662.07	651.68	646.62
14.25%	1,886.45	1,286.89	1,038.31	963.27	862.25	741.72	693.95	672.61	662.58	657.75
14.50%	1,893.15	1,294.06	1,045.95	971.15	870.58	751.03	704.00	683.19	673.51	668.89
14.75%	1,899.87	1,301.24	1,053.62	979.06	878.94	760.38	714.10	693.81	684.46	680.06
15.00%	1,906.59	1,308.45	1,061.32	987.00	887.34	769.77	724.23	704.46	695.44	691.25
15.25%	1,913.33	1,315.67	1,069.05	994.97	895.78	779.21	734.41	715.14	706.45	702.45
15.50%	1,920.09	1,322.93	1,076.81	1,002.98	904.26	788.69	744.63	725.86	717.48	713.67
15.75%	1,926.86	1,330.20	1,084.60	1,011.01	912.77	798.22	754.89	736.61	728.54	724.91
16.00%	1,933.64	1,337.49	1,092.41	1,019.08	921.32	807.79	765.19	747.39	739.62	736.16
16.25%	1,940.43	1,344.81	1,100.26	1,027.18	929.91	817.39	775.53	758.20	750.71	747.42
16.50%	1,947.24	1,352.15	1,108.13	1,035.32	938.53	827.04	785.90	769.03	761.83	758.70
16.75%	1,954.06	1,359.51	1,116.04	1,043.48	947.19	836.73	796.30	779.90	772.97	769.99
17.00%	1,960.90	1,366.89	1,123.97	1,051.68	955.89	846.45	806.74	790.79	784.12	781.29
17.25%	1,967.75	1,374.30	1,131.93	1,059.91	964.62	856.22	817.21	801.70	795.29	792.60
17.50%	1,974.61	1,381.72	1,139.92	1,068.17	973.38	866.02	827.72	812.64	806.48	803.92
17.75%	1,981.49	1,389.17	1,147.94	1,076.46	982.18	875.86	838.25	823.60	817.68	815.25
18.00%	1,988.38	1,396.64	1,155.98	1,084.78	991.02	885.73	848.82	834.59	828.90	826.59
18.25%	1,995.29	1,404.13	1,164.05	1,093.13	999.89	895.64	859.42	845.59	840.13	837.94
18.50%	2,002.20	1,411.64	1,172.16	1,101.51	1,008.79	905.59	870.04	856.62	851.37	849.29
18.75%	2,009.14	1,419.18	1,180.28	1,109.92	1,017.73	915.57	880.70	867.66	862.62	860.65
19.00%	2,016.08	1,426.73	1,188.44	1,118.36	1,026.70	925.58	891.38	878.72	873.89	872.02
19.25%	2,023.04	1,434.31	1,196.63	1,126.83	1,035.70	935.63	902.08	889.81	885.17	883.40
19.50%	2,030.01	1,441.90	1,204.84	1,135.34	1,044.74	945.71	912.82	900.90	896.46	894.78
19.75%	2,037.00	1,449.52	1,213.08	1,143.87	1,053.81	955.82	923.57	912.02	907.75	906.16
20.00%	2,044.00	1,457.16	1,221.34	1,152.43	1,062.91	965.96	934.35	923.15	919.06	917.55
20.25%	2,051.01	1,464.82	1,229.63	1,161.02	1,072.04	976.14	945.16	934.29	930.38	928.95
20.50%	2,058.04	1,472.51	1,237.95	1,169.63	1,081.20	986.34	955.98	945.45	941.70	940.35
20.75%	2,065.08	1,480.21	1,246.30	1,178.28	1,090.40	996.57	966.83	956.63	953.03	951.75

	3	5	7	8	10	15	20	25	30	35
1.00%	1,621.97	982.89	709.05	623.49	503.72	344.13	264.44	216.70	184.94	162.31
1.25%	1,628.19	989.09	715.26	629.72	509.99	350.49	270.90	223.27	191.62	169.10
1.50%	1,634.43	995.32	721.52	635.99	516.30	356.93	277.46	229.96	198.44	176.06
1.75%	1,640.68	1,001.57	727.81	642.30	522.66	363.44	284.12	236.78	205.41	183.18
2.00%	1,646.95	1,007.85	734.13	648.65	529.08	370.02	290.88	243.72	212.53	190.48
2.25%	1,653.23	1,014.15	740.48	655.04	535.54	376.67	297.74	250.78	219.79	197.94
2.50%	1,659.53	1,020.47	746.88	661.47	542.05	383.40	304.69	257.95	227.19	205.56
2.75%	1,665.84	1,026.82	753.30	667.94	548.61	390.21	311.75	265.25	234.74	213.34
3.00%	1,672.17	1,033.20	759.76	674.45	555.22	397.08	318.89	272.67	242.42	221.29
3.25%	1,678.51	1,039.60	766.26	681.00	561.88	404.03	326.14	280.21	250.24	229.39
3.50%	1,684.87	1,046.03	772.79	687.59	568.59	411.06	333.48	287.86	258.20	237.64
3.75%	1,691.24	1,052.48	779.36	694.22	575.35	418.15	340.91	295.63	266.29	246.05
4.00%	1,697.63	1,058.95	785.96	700.88	582.16	425.32	348.44	303.51	274.51	254.60
4.25%	1,704.03	1,065.45	792.59	707.59	589.02	432.56	356.06	311.50	282.87	263.29
4.50%	1,710.45	1,071.97	799.26	714.34	595.92	439.87	363.77	319.60	291.34	272.12
4.75%	1,716.88	1,078.52	805.96	721.12	602.87	447.25	371.58	327.82	299.95	281.09
5.00%	1,723.33	1,085.10	812.70	727.95	609.88	454.71	379.47	336.14	308.67	290.20
5.25%	1,729.79	1,091.69	819.47	734.81	616.93	462.23	387.46	344.57	317.52	299.43
5.50%	1,736.26	1,098.32	826.28	741.71	624.03	469.82	395.54	353.10	326.48	308.78
5.75%	1,742.76	1,104.96	833.12	748.65	631.17	477.49	403.70	361.74	335.55	318.26
6.00%	1,749.26	1,111.64	839.99	755.63	638.37	485.22	411.95	370.47	344.74	327.86
6.25%	1,755.78	1,118.33	846.90	762.65	645.61	493.02	420.28	379.31	354.04	337.57
6.50%	1,762.32	1,125.05	853.84	769.71	652.90	500.89	428.70	388.24	363.44	347.39
6.75%	1,768.87	1,131.80	860.82	776.80	660.24	508.82	437.21	397.27	372.94	357.31
7.00%	1,775.43	1,138.57	867.83	783.94	667.62	516.83	445.80	406.40	382.55	367.34
7.25%	1,782.01	1,145.36	874.87	791.11	675.06	524.90	454.47	415.61	392.25	377.47
7.50%	1,788.61	1,152.18	881.95	798.32	682.54	533.03	463.22	424.92	402.05	387.69
7.75%	1,795.22	1,159.03	889.06	805.57	690.06	541.23	472.05	434.31	411.94	398.00
8.00%	1,801.84	1,165.89	896.21	812.86	697.63	549.50	480.95	443.79	421.91	408.40
8.25%	1,808.48	1,172.78	903.39	820.18	705.25	557.83	489.94	453.36	431.98	418.88
8.50%	1,815.13	1,179.70	910.60	827.55	712.92	566.23	499.00	463.01	442.13	429.44
8.75%	1,821.80	1,186.64	917.84	834.95	720.63	574.68	508.13	472.73	452.35	440.08
9.00%	1,828.48	1,193.61	925.12	842.39	728.39	583.20	517.34	482.54	462.66	450.80
9.25%	1,835.18	1,200.59	932.43	849.86	736.19	591.79	526.62	492.42	473.04	461.58
9.50%	1,841.89	1,207.61	939.78	857.38	744.04	600.43	535.98	502.38	483.49	472.43
9.75%	1,848.62	1,214.64	947.16	864.93	751.93	609.13	545.40	512.40	494.01	483.34
10.00%	1,855.36	1,221.71	954.57	872.51	759.87	617.90	554.89	522.50	504.60	494.31
10.25%	1,862.12	1,228.79	962.01	880.14	767.85	626.72	564.44	532.67	515.26	505.34
10.50%	1,868.89	1,235.90	969.49	887.80	775.88	635.60	574.07	542.90	525.98	516.43
10.75%	1,875.68	1,243.03	977.00	895.50	783.95	644.55	583.76	553.20	536.75	527.56

	3	5	7	8	10	15	20	25	30	35
11.00%	1,882.48	1,250.19	984.54	903.23	792.06	653.54	593.51	563.57	547.59	538.75
11.25%	1,889.29	1,257.37	992.11	911.01	800.22	662.60	603.32	573.99	558.48	549.98
11.50%	1,896.12	1,264.57	999.72	918.81	808.42	671.71	613.20	584.47	569.42	561.26
11.75%	1,902.96	1,271.80	1,007.36	926.66	816.67	680.88	623.13	595.01	580.41	572.58
12.00%	1,909.82	1,279.06	1,015.03	934.54	824.96	690.10	633.12	605.60	591.45	583.94
12.25%	1,916.70	1,286.33	1,022.74	942.45	833.29	699.37	643.17	616.25	602.54	595.34
12.50%	1,923.58	1,293.63	1,030.47	950.41	841.66	708.70	653.28	626.95	613.67	606.77
12.75%	1,930.49	1,300.95	1,038.24	958.39	850.08	718.08	663.44	637.71	624.85	618.24
13.00%	1,937.40	1,308.30	1,046.04	966.42	858.54	727.51	673.66	648.51	636.06	629.74
13.25%	1,944.33	1,315.67	1,053.87	974.48	867.04	737.00	683.92	659.35	647.32	641.26
13.50%	1,951.28	1,323.07	1,061.73	982.57	875.58	746.53	694.24	670.25	658.61	652.82
13.75%	1,958.24	1,330.48	1,069.63	990.70	884.16	756.12	704.61	681.18	669.94	664.40
14.00%	1,965.21	1,337.92	1,077.55	998.86	892.78	765.75	715.02	692.16	681.30	676.01
14.25%	1,972.20	1,345.39	1,085.51	1,007.06	901.45	775.43	725.49	703.18	692.70	687.64
14.50%	1,979.21	1,352.88	1,093.49	1,015.29	910.15	785.16	736.00	714.24	704.12	699.30
14.75%	1,986.22	1,360.39	1,101.51	1,023.56	918.89	794.94	746.55	725.34	715.57	710.97
15.00%	1,993.26	1,367.92	1,109.56	1,031.86	927.68	804.76	757.15	736.48	727.06	722.67
15.25%	2,000.30	1,375.48	1,117.64	1,040.20	936.50	814.63	767.80	747.65	738.56	734.38
15.50%	2,007.36	1,383.06	1,125.75	1,048.57	945.36	824.54	778.48	758.85	750.10	746.11
15.75%	2,014.44	1,390.66	1,133.90	1,056.97	954.26	834.50	789.21	770.09	761.65	757.86
16.00%	2,021.53	1,398.29	1,142.07	1,065.41	963.20	844.50	799.97	781.36	773.24	769.62
16.25%	2,028.63	1,405.94	1,150.27	1,073.88	972.18	854.55	810.78	792.66	784.84	781.40
16.50%	2,035.75	1,413.61	1,158.50	1,082.38	981.19	864.63	821.62	803.99	796.46	793.19
16.75%	2,042.88	1,421.31	1,166.77	1,090.91	990.25	874.76	832.50	815.35	808.10	804.99
17.00%	2,050.03	1,429.02	1,175.06	1,099.48	999.34	884.93	843.41	826.73	819.76	816.80
17.25%	2,057.19	1,436.76	1,183.38	1,108.09	1,008.46	895.14	854.36	838.14	831.44	828.63
17.50%	2,064.37	1,444.53	1,191.73	1,116.72	1,017.63	905.38	865.34	849.58	843.14	840.46
17.75%	2,071.56	1,452.31	1,200.11	1,125.39	1,026.83	915.67	876.36	861.04	854.85	852.31
18.00%	2,078.76	1,460.12	1,208.53	1,134.08	1,036.06	925.99	887.40	872.52	866.57	864.16
18.25%	2,085.98	1,467.95	1,216.97	1,142.82	1,045.34	936.35	898.48	884.03	878.31	876.03
18.50%	2,093.21	1,475.81	1,225.44	1,151.58	1,054.65	946.75	909.59	895.55	890.07	887.90
18.75%	2,100.46	1,483.68	1,233.93	1,160.37	1,063.99	957.18	920.73	907.10	901.83	899.77
19.00%	2,107.72	1,491.58	1,242.46	1,169.20	1,073.37	967.65	931.89	918.67	913.61	911.66
19.25%	2,115.00	1,499.50	1,251.02	1,178.05	1,082.78	978.16	943.09	930.25	925.40	923.55
19.50%	2,122.29	1,507.45	1,259.60	1,186.94	1,092.23	988.70	954.31	941.85	937.20	935.45
19.75%	2,129.59	1,515.41	1,268.21	1,195.86	1,101.71	999.27	965.55	953.47	949.02	947.35
20.00%	2,136.91	1,523.40	1,276.86	1,204.81	1,111.22	1,009.87	976.82	965.11	960.84	959.26
20.25%	2,144.24	1,531.41	1,285.53	1,213.79	1,120.77	1,020.51	988.12	976.76	972.67	971.17
20.50%	2,151.58	1,539.44	1,294.22	1,222.80	1,130.35	1,031.17	999.44	988.43	984.50	983.09
20.75%	2,158.94	1,547.49	1,302.95	1,231.84	1,139.96	1,041.87	1,010.78	1,000.11	996.35	995.01

	3	5	7	8	10	15	20	25	30	35
1.00%	1,692.49	1,025.62	739.87	650.59	525.62	359.10	275.94	226.12	192.98	169.37
1.25%	1,698.98	1,032.10	746.36	657.10	532.16	365.73	282.68	232.98	199.95	176.45
1.50%	1,705.49	1,038.59	752.89	663.64	538.75	372.45	289.53	239.96	207.07	183.71
1.75%	1,712.01	1,045.12	759.45	670.23	545.39	379.24	296.48	247.07	214.35	191.15
2.00%	1,718.55	1,051.67	766.05	676.85	552.08	386.11	303.53	254.31	221.77	198.76
2.25%	1,725.11	1,058.24	772.68	683.52	558.82	393.05	310.68	261.68	229.35	206.54
2.50%	1,731.68	1,064.84	779.35	690.23	565.62	400.07	317.94	269.17	237.07	214.50
2.75%	1,738.27	1,071.47	786.06	696.98	572.47	407.17	325.30	276.79	244.94	222.62
3.00%	1,744.87	1,078.12	792.80	703.77	579.36	414.35	332.76	284.53	252.96	230.91
3.25%	1,751.49	1,084.80	799.58	710.61	586.31	421.60	340.32	292.39	261.12	239.36
3.50%	1,758.12	1,091.50	806.39	717.48	593.32	428.93	347.98	300.37	269.43	247.97
3.75%	1,764.77	1,098.24	813.24	724.40	600.37	436.33	355.73	308.48	277.87	256.74
4.00%	1,771.44	1,104.99	820.13	731.36	607.47	443.81	363.59	316.70	286.45	265.66
4.25%	1,778.12	1,111.77	827.05	738.35	614.63	451.37	371.54	325.04	295.16	274.74
4.50%	1,784.82	1,118.58	834.01	745.39	621.83	459.00	379.59	333.50	304.01	283.95
4.75%	1,791.53	1,125.41	841.00	752.47	629.09	466.70	387.73	342.07	312.99	293.31
5.00%	1,798.25	1,132.27	848.03	759.60	636.39	474.48	395.97	350.75	322.09	302.81
5.25%	1,805.00	1,139.16	855.10	766.76	643.75	482.33	404.31	359.55	331.32	312.45
5.50%	1,811.75	1,146.07	862.20	773.96	651.16	490.25	412.73	368.45	340.67	322.21
5.75%	1,818.53	1,153.01	869.34	781.20	658.62	498.25	421.25	377.46	350.14	332.10
6.00%	1,825.32	1,159.97	876.51	788.49	666.12	506.31	429.86	386.58	359.73	342.11
6.25%	1,832.12	1,166.96	883.72	795.81	673.68	514.45	438.56	395.80	369.43	352.25
6.50%	1,838.94	1,173.97	890.97	803.17	681.29	522.66	447.34	405.12	379.24	362.49
6.75%	1,845.78	1,181.01	898.25	810.58	688.94	530.95	456.22	414.55	389.16	372.85
7.00%	1,852.63	1,188.07	905.56	818.02	696.65	539.30	465.18	424.07	399.18	383.31
7.25%	1,859.49	1,195.16	912.91	825.51	704.41	547.72	474.23	433.68	409.31	393.88
7.50%	1,866.37	1,202.28	920.30	833.03	712.21	556.21	483.36	443.39	419.53	404.55
7.75%	1,873.27	1,209.42	927.72	840.60	720.06	564.77	492.57	453.20	429.85	415.31
8.00%	1,880.18	1,216.58	935.17	848.20	727.97	573.39	501.86	463.09	440.26	426.16
8.25%	1,887.11	1,223.78	942.66	855.84	735.92	582.08	511.24	473.07	450.76	437.09
8.50%	1,894.05	1,230.99	950.19	863.53	743.91	590.84	520.69	483.14	461.35	448.12
8.75%	1,901.01	1,238.23	957.75	871.25	751.96	599.67	530.23	493.29	472.02	459.22
9.00%	1,907.98	1,245.50	965.34	879.01	760.05	608.56	539.84	503.52	482.77	470.40
9.25%	1,914.97	1,252.79	972.97	886.81	768.20	617.52	549.52	513.83	493.61	481.65
9.50%	1,921.98	1,260.11	980.64	894.65	776.39	626.53	559.28	524.22	504.51	492.97
9.75%	1,929.00	1,267.45	988.34	902.53	784.62	635.62	569.11	534.68	515.49	504.35
10.00%	1,936.03	1,274.82	996.07	910.45	792.90	644.76	579.01	545.22	526.54	515.80
10.25%	1,943.08	1,282.22	1,003.84	918.41	801.23	653.97	588.99	555.83	537.66	527.31
10.50%	1,950.15	1,289.63	1,011.64	926.40	809.61	663.24	599.03	566.51	548.84	538.88
10.75%	1,957.23	1,297.08	1,019.48	934.43	818.03	672.57	609.14	577.26	560.09	550.50

$60,000   11.00 - 20.75%   3 - 35 Years

	3	5	7	8	10	15	20	25	30	35
11.00%	1,964.32	1,304.55	1,027.35	942.51	826.50	681.96	619.31	588.07	571.39	562.17
11.25%	1,971.43	1,312.04	1,035.25	950.62	835.01	691.41	629.55	598.94	582.76	573.90
11.50%	1,978.56	1,319.56	1,043.19	958.76	843.57	700.91	639.86	609.88	594.17	585.66
11.75%	1,985.70	1,327.10	1,051.16	966.95	852.18	710.48	650.22	620.88	605.65	597.48
12.00%	1,992.86	1,334.67	1,059.16	975.17	860.83	720.10	660.65	631.93	617.17	609.33
12.25%	2,000.03	1,342.26	1,067.20	983.43	869.52	729.78	671.14	643.05	628.74	621.22
12.50%	2,007.22	1,349.88	1,075.27	991.73	878.26	739.51	681.68	654.21	640.35	633.15
12.75%	2,014.42	1,357.52	1,083.38	1,000.06	887.04	749.30	692.29	665.43	652.02	645.12
13.00%	2,021.64	1,365.18	1,091.52	1,008.44	895.86	759.15	702.95	676.70	663.72	657.12
13.25%	2,028.87	1,372.88	1,099.69	1,016.84	904.73	769.04	713.66	688.02	675.46	669.15
13.50%	2,036.12	1,380.59	1,107.89	1,025.29	913.65	778.99	724.42	699.39	687.25	681.20
13.75%	2,043.38	1,388.33	1,116.13	1,033.77	922.60	788.99	735.24	710.80	699.07	693.29
14.00%	2,050.66	1,396.10	1,124.40	1,042.29	931.60	799.04	746.11	722.26	710.92	705.40
14.25%	2,057.95	1,403.88	1,132.70	1,050.84	940.64	809.15	757.03	733.76	722.81	717.54
14.50%	2,065.26	1,411.70	1,141.04	1,059.44	949.72	819.30	768.00	745.30	734.73	729.70
14.75%	2,072.58	1,419.53	1,149.41	1,068.06	958.84	829.50	779.01	756.88	746.69	741.88
15.00%	2,079.92	1,427.40	1,157.81	1,076.72	968.01	839.75	790.07	768.50	758.67	754.09
15.25%	2,087.27	1,435.28	1,166.24	1,085.42	977.22	850.05	801.18	780.15	770.68	766.31
15.50%	2,094.64	1,443.19	1,174.70	1,094.16	986.46	860.39	812.33	791.85	782.71	778.55
15.75%	2,102.02	1,451.13	1,183.20	1,102.92	995.75	870.78	823.52	803.57	794.77	790.81
16.00%	2,109.42	1,459.08	1,191.72	1,111.73	1,005.08	881.22	834.75	815.33	806.85	803.08
16.25%	2,116.83	1,467.07	1,200.28	1,120.57	1,014.45	891.70	846.03	827.12	818.96	815.37
16.50%	2,124.26	1,475.07	1,208.87	1,129.44	1,023.85	902.23	857.34	838.95	831.09	827.67
16.75%	2,131.71	1,483.10	1,217.50	1,138.35	1,033.30	912.79	868.69	850.80	843.24	839.99
17.00%	2,139.16	1,491.15	1,226.15	1,147.29	1,042.79	923.40	880.08	862.68	855.41	852.32
17.25%	2,146.64	1,499.23	1,234.83	1,156.26	1,052.31	934.05	891.51	874.58	867.59	864.66
17.50%	2,154.12	1,507.33	1,243.55	1,165.27	1,061.87	944.75	902.97	886.52	879.80	877.01
17.75%	2,161.63	1,515.46	1,252.29	1,174.32	1,071.47	955.48	914.46	898.48	892.02	889.37
18.00%	2,169.14	1,523.61	1,261.07	1,183.39	1,081.11	966.25	925.99	910.46	904.25	901.74
18.25%	2,176.68	1,531.78	1,269.88	1,192.50	1,090.79	977.06	937.55	922.46	916.50	914.11
18.50%	2,184.22	1,539.97	1,278.72	1,201.65	1,100.50	987.91	949.14	934.49	928.77	926.50
18.75%	2,191.78	1,548.19	1,287.58	1,210.82	1,110.25	998.80	960.76	946.54	941.04	938.90
19.00%	2,199.36	1,556.43	1,296.48	1,220.03	1,120.03	1,009.73	972.41	958.61	953.34	951.30
19.25%	2,206.95	1,564.70	1,305.41	1,229.27	1,129.86	1,020.69	984.09	970.70	965.64	963.71
19.50%	2,214.56	1,572.99	1,314.37	1,238.55	1,139.71	1,031.68	995.80	982.80	977.95	976.12
19.75%	2,222.18	1,581.30	1,323.35	1,247.85	1,149.61	1,042.71	1,007.53	994.93	990.28	988.54
20.00%	2,229.82	1,589.63	1,332.37	1,257.19	1,159.53	1,053.78	1,019.29	1,007.07	1,002.61	1,000.97
20.25%	2,237.47	1,597.99	1,341.42	1,266.56	1,169.50	1,064.88	1,031.08	1,019.23	1,014.96	1,013.40
20.50%	2,245.13	1,606.37	1,350.49	1,275.96	1,179.49	1,076.01	1,042.89	1,031.40	1,027.31	1,025.83
20.75%	2,252.81	1,614.78	1,359.60	1,285.40	1,189.53	1,087.17	1,054.73	1,043.59	1,039.67	1,038.27

$62,500   1.00 - 10.75%   3 - 35 Years

	3	5	7	8	10	15	20	25	30	35
1.00%	1,763.01	1,068.36	770.70	677.70	547.53	374.06	287.43	235.55	201.02	176.43
1.25%	1,769.77	1,075.10	777.46	684.47	554.33	380.97	294.46	242.69	208.28	183.80
1.50%	1,776.55	1,081.87	784.26	691.29	561.20	387.96	301.59	249.96	215.70	191.37
1.75%	1,783.35	1,088.66	791.09	698.15	568.11	395.04	308.83	257.37	223.28	199.11
2.00%	1,790.16	1,095.49	797.96	705.05	575.08	402.19	316.18	264.91	231.01	207.04
2.25%	1,796.99	1,102.33	804.87	712.00	582.11	409.43	323.63	272.58	238.90	215.15
2.50%	1,803.84	1,109.21	811.82	718.99	589.19	416.74	331.19	280.39	246.95	223.43
2.75%	1,810.70	1,116.11	818.81	726.02	596.32	424.14	338.85	288.32	255.15	231.90
3.00%	1,817.58	1,123.04	825.83	733.10	603.50	431.61	346.62	296.38	263.50	240.53
3.25%	1,824.47	1,130.00	832.89	740.22	610.74	439.17	354.50	304.57	272.00	249.34
3.50%	1,831.38	1,136.98	839.99	747.38	618.04	446.80	362.47	312.89	280.65	258.31
3.75%	1,838.31	1,143.99	847.13	754.58	625.38	454.51	370.56	321.33	289.45	267.44
4.00%	1,845.25	1,151.03	854.30	761.83	632.78	462.30	378.74	329.90	298.38	276.73
4.25%	1,852.21	1,158.10	861.51	769.12	640.23	470.17	387.02	338.59	307.46	286.18
4.50%	1,859.18	1,165.19	868.76	776.45	647.74	478.12	395.41	347.40	316.68	295.79
4.75%	1,866.17	1,172.31	876.05	783.83	655.30	486.14	403.89	356.32	326.03	305.54
5.00%	1,873.18	1,179.45	883.37	791.25	662.91	494.25	412.47	365.37	335.51	315.43
5.25%	1,880.20	1,186.62	890.73	798.71	670.57	502.42	421.15	374.53	345.13	325.46
5.50%	1,887.24	1,193.82	898.13	806.21	678.29	510.68	429.93	383.80	354.87	335.64
5.75%	1,894.30	1,201.05	905.56	813.75	686.06	519.01	438.80	393.19	364.73	345.94
6.00%	1,901.37	1,208.30	913.03	821.34	693.88	527.41	447.77	402.69	374.72	356.37
6.25%	1,908.46	1,215.58	920.54	828.97	701.75	535.89	456.83	412.29	384.82	366.92
6.50%	1,915.56	1,222.88	928.09	836.64	709.67	544.44	465.98	422.00	395.04	377.60
6.75%	1,922.68	1,230.22	935.67	844.35	717.65	553.07	475.23	431.82	405.37	388.39
7.00%	1,929.82	1,237.57	943.29	852.11	725.68	561.77	484.56	441.74	415.81	399.29
7.25%	1,936.97	1,244.96	950.95	859.90	733.76	570.54	493.98	451.75	426.36	410.29
7.50%	1,944.14	1,252.37	958.64	867.74	741.89	579.38	503.50	461.87	437.01	421.40
7.75%	1,951.32	1,259.81	966.37	875.62	750.07	588.30	513.09	472.08	447.76	432.61
8.00%	1,958.52	1,267.27	974.14	883.54	758.30	597.28	522.78	482.39	458.60	443.91
8.25%	1,965.74	1,274.77	981.94	891.50	766.58	606.34	532.54	492.78	469.54	455.31
8.50%	1,972.97	1,282.28	989.78	899.51	774.91	615.46	542.39	503.27	480.57	466.79
8.75%	1,980.22	1,289.83	997.66	907.55	783.29	624.66	552.32	513.84	491.69	478.35
9.00%	1,987.48	1,297.40	1,005.57	915.64	791.72	633.92	562.33	524.50	502.89	490.00
9.25%	1,994.76	1,304.99	1,013.52	923.76	800.20	643.25	572.42	535.24	514.17	501.72
9.50%	2,002.06	1,312.62	1,021.50	931.93	808.73	652.64	582.58	546.06	525.53	513.51
9.75%	2,009.37	1,320.27	1,029.52	940.14	817.31	662.10	592.82	556.96	536.97	525.37
10.00%	2,016.70	1,327.94	1,037.57	948.39	825.94	671.63	603.14	567.94	548.48	537.30
10.25%	2,024.04	1,335.64	1,045.67	956.67	834.62	681.22	613.53	578.99	560.06	549.28
10.50%	2,031.40	1,343.37	1,053.79	965.00	843.34	690.87	623.99	590.11	571.71	561.33
10.75%	2,038.78	1,351.12	1,061.95	973.37	852.12	700.59	634.52	601.31	583.43	573.44

$62,500   11.00 - 20.75%   3 - 35 Years

	3	5	7	8	10	15	20	25	30	35
11.00%	2,046.17	1,358.90	1,070.15	981.78	860.94	710.37	645.12	612.57	595.20	585.60
11.25%	2,053.58	1,366.71	1,078.39	990.22	869.81	720.22	655.79	623.90	607.04	597.81
11.50%	2,061.00	1,374.54	1,086.65	998.71	878.72	730.12	666.52	635.29	618.93	610.07
11.75%	2,068.44	1,382.40	1,094.96	1,007.24	887.68	740.08	677.32	646.75	630.88	622.37
12.00%	2,075.89	1,390.28	1,103.30	1,015.80	896.69	750.11	688.18	658.27	642.88	634.72
12.25%	2,083.37	1,398.19	1,111.67	1,024.41	905.75	760.19	699.10	669.84	654.94	647.11
12.50%	2,090.85	1,406.12	1,120.08	1,033.05	914.85	770.33	710.09	681.47	667.04	659.53
12.75%	2,098.35	1,414.08	1,128.52	1,041.73	924.00	780.52	721.13	693.16	679.18	672.00
13.00%	2,105.87	1,422.07	1,137.00	1,050.45	933.19	790.78	732.23	704.90	691.37	684.50
13.25%	2,113.41	1,430.08	1,145.51	1,059.21	942.43	801.09	743.39	716.69	703.61	697.03
13.50%	2,120.96	1,438.12	1,154.06	1,068.01	951.71	811.45	754.61	728.53	715.88	709.59
13.75%	2,128.52	1,446.18	1,162.64	1,076.85	961.04	821.87	765.88	740.42	728.20	722.18
14.00%	2,136.10	1,454.27	1,171.25	1,085.72	970.42	832.34	777.20	752.35	740.54	734.80
14.25%	2,143.70	1,462.38	1,179.90	1,094.63	979.83	842.86	788.57	764.33	752.93	747.44
14.50%	2,151.31	1,470.52	1,188.58	1,103.58	989.29	853.44	800.00	776.35	765.35	760.11
14.75%	2,158.94	1,478.68	1,197.30	1,112.56	998.80	864.06	811.47	788.42	777.80	772.80
15.00%	2,166.58	1,486.87	1,206.05	1,121.59	1,008.34	874.74	822.99	800.52	790.28	785.51
15.25%	2,174.24	1,495.08	1,214.83	1,130.65	1,017.93	885.47	834.56	812.66	802.79	798.24
15.50%	2,181.92	1,503.32	1,223.65	1,139.75	1,027.57	896.24	846.18	824.84	815.32	810.99
15.75%	2,189.61	1,511.59	1,232.50	1,148.88	1,037.24	907.07	857.83	837.06	827.89	823.76
16.00%	2,197.31	1,519.88	1,241.38	1,158.05	1,046.96	917.94	869.53	849.31	840.47	836.54
16.25%	2,205.04	1,528.19	1,250.29	1,167.26	1,056.72	928.86	881.28	861.59	853.08	849.34
16.50%	2,212.77	1,536.53	1,259.24	1,176.50	1,066.51	939.82	893.06	873.90	865.72	862.16
16.75%	2,220.53	1,544.90	1,268.22	1,185.78	1,076.35	950.83	904.89	886.25	878.37	874.99
17.00%	2,228.30	1,553.29	1,277.24	1,195.09	1,086.24	961.88	916.75	898.62	891.05	887.83
17.25%	2,236.08	1,561.70	1,286.28	1,204.44	1,096.16	972.97	928.65	911.03	903.74	900.68
17.50%	2,243.88	1,570.14	1,295.36	1,213.83	1,106.12	984.11	940.59	923.46	916.45	913.55
17.75%	2,251.69	1,578.60	1,304.47	1,223.25	1,116.12	995.29	952.56	935.91	929.18	926.42
18.00%	2,259.52	1,587.09	1,313.61	1,232.70	1,126.16	1,006.51	964.57	948.39	941.93	939.31
18.25%	2,267.37	1,595.60	1,322.79	1,242.19	1,136.24	1,017.78	976.61	960.90	954.69	952.20
18.50%	2,275.23	1,604.14	1,331.99	1,251.72	1,146.35	1,029.08	988.69	973.43	967.47	965.10
18.75%	2,283.11	1,612.70	1,341.23	1,261.27	1,156.51	1,040.42	1,000.79	985.98	980.26	978.02
19.00%	2,291.00	1,621.28	1,350.50	1,270.87	1,166.70	1,051.80	1,012.93	998.55	993.06	990.93
19.25%	2,298.91	1,629.89	1,359.80	1,280.49	1,176.93	1,063.21	1,025.09	1,011.14	1,005.87	1,003.86
19.50%	2,306.83	1,638.53	1,369.13	1,290.15	1,187.20	1,074.67	1,037.29	1,023.75	1,018.70	1,016.79
19.75%	2,314.77	1,647.19	1,378.49	1,299.85	1,197.51	1,086.16	1,049.51	1,036.38	1,031.54	1,029.73
20.00%	2,322.72	1,655.87	1,387.89	1,309.58	1,207.85	1,097.69	1,061.77	1,049.03	1,044.39	1,042.67
20.25%	2,330.69	1,664.57	1,397.31	1,319.34	1,218.23	1,109.25	1,074.04	1,061.70	1,057.25	1,055.62
20.50%	2,338.68	1,673.30	1,406.77	1,329.13	1,228.64	1,120.84	1,086.35	1,074.38	1,070.11	1,068.58
20.75%	2,346.68	1,682.06	1,416.25	1,338.95	1,239.09	1,132.47	1,098.67	1,087.08	1,082.99	1,081.54

	3	5	7	8	10	15	20	25	30	35
1.00%	1,833.53	1,111.09	801.53	704.81	569.43	389.02	298.93	244.97	209.07	183.49
1.25%	1,840.56	1,118.10	808.56	711.85	576.51	396.21	306.24	252.39	216.61	191.16
1.50%	1,847.61	1,125.14	815.63	718.94	583.64	403.48	313.65	259.96	224.33	199.02
1.75%	1,854.68	1,132.21	822.74	726.08	590.84	410.84	321.18	267.66	232.21	207.08
2.00%	1,861.77	1,139.30	829.88	733.26	598.09	418.28	328.82	275.51	240.25	215.32
2.25%	1,868.87	1,146.43	837.07	740.48	605.39	425.81	336.58	283.48	248.46	223.75
2.50%	1,875.99	1,153.58	844.30	747.75	612.75	433.41	344.44	291.60	256.83	232.37
2.75%	1,883.13	1,160.76	851.56	755.06	620.17	441.10	352.41	299.85	265.36	241.17
3.00%	1,890.28	1,167.96	858.86	762.42	627.64	448.88	360.49	308.24	274.04	250.15
3.25%	1,897.45	1,175.20	866.21	769.83	635.17	456.73	368.68	316.76	282.88	259.31
3.50%	1,904.64	1,182.46	873.59	777.27	642.76	464.67	376.97	325.41	291.88	268.64
3.75%	1,911.84	1,189.75	881.01	784.77	650.40	472.69	385.38	334.19	301.03	278.14
4.00%	1,919.06	1,197.07	888.47	792.30	658.09	480.80	393.89	343.09	310.32	287.80
4.25%	1,926.30	1,204.42	895.97	799.88	665.84	488.98	402.50	352.13	319.76	297.63
4.50%	1,933.55	1,211.80	903.51	807.51	673.65	497.25	411.22	361.29	329.35	307.62
4.75%	1,940.82	1,219.20	911.09	815.18	681.51	505.59	420.05	370.58	339.07	317.76
5.00%	1,948.11	1,226.63	918.70	822.89	689.43	514.02	428.97	379.98	348.93	328.05
5.25%	1,955.41	1,234.09	926.36	830.65	697.40	522.52	438.00	389.51	358.93	338.48
5.50%	1,962.73	1,241.58	934.05	838.46	705.42	531.10	447.13	399.16	369.06	349.06
5.75%	1,970.07	1,249.09	941.79	846.30	713.50	539.77	456.35	408.92	379.32	359.78
6.00%	1,977.43	1,256.63	949.56	854.19	721.63	548.51	465.68	418.80	389.71	370.62
6.25%	1,984.80	1,264.20	957.37	862.13	729.82	557.32	475.10	428.79	400.22	381.60
6.50%	1,992.19	1,271.80	965.21	870.11	738.06	566.22	484.62	438.88	410.84	392.70
6.75%	1,999.59	1,279.42	973.10	878.13	746.36	575.19	494.24	449.09	421.59	403.92
7.00%	2,007.01	1,287.08	981.02	886.19	754.71	584.24	503.94	459.41	432.45	415.26
7.25%	2,014.45	1,294.76	988.99	894.30	763.11	593.36	513.74	469.82	443.41	426.70
7.50%	2,021.90	1,302.47	996.99	902.45	771.56	602.56	523.64	480.34	454.49	438.26
7.75%	2,029.38	1,310.20	1,005.03	910.65	780.07	611.83	533.62	490.96	465.67	449.91
8.00%	2,036.86	1,317.97	1,013.10	918.88	788.63	621.17	543.69	501.68	476.95	461.67
8.25%	2,044.37	1,325.76	1,021.22	927.16	797.24	630.59	553.84	512.49	488.32	473.52
8.50%	2,051.89	1,333.57	1,029.37	935.49	805.91	640.08	564.09	523.40	499.79	485.46
8.75%	2,059.43	1,341.42	1,037.56	943.85	814.62	649.64	574.41	534.39	511.36	497.49
9.00%	2,066.98	1,349.29	1,045.79	952.26	823.39	659.27	584.82	545.48	523.00	509.60
9.25%	2,074.55	1,357.19	1,054.06	960.71	832.21	668.97	595.31	556.65	534.74	521.78
9.50%	2,082.14	1,365.12	1,062.36	969.21	841.08	678.75	605.89	567.90	546.56	534.05
9.75%	2,089.75	1,373.08	1,070.70	977.74	850.01	688.59	616.54	579.24	558.45	546.38
10.00%	2,097.37	1,381.06	1,079.08	986.32	858.98	698.49	627.26	590.66	570.42	558.79
10.25%	2,105.00	1,389.07	1,087.49	994.94	868.00	708.47	638.07	602.15	582.47	571.26
10.50%	2,112.66	1,397.10	1,095.94	1,003.60	877.08	718.51	648.95	613.72	594.58	583.79
10.75%	2,120.33	1,405.17	1,104.43	1,012.30	886.20	728.62	659.90	625.36	606.76	596.38

$65,000   11.00 - 20.75%   3 - 35 Years

	3	5	7	8	10	15	20	25	30	35
11.00%	2,128.02	1,413.26	1,112.96	1,021.05	895.38	738.79	670.92	637.07	619.01	609.02
11.25%	2,135.72	1,421.38	1,121.52	1,029.83	904.60	749.02	682.02	648.86	631.32	621.72
11.50%	2,143.44	1,429.52	1,130.12	1,038.66	913.87	759.32	693.18	660.70	643.69	634.47
11.75%	2,151.18	1,437.69	1,138.76	1,047.53	923.19	769.69	704.41	672.62	656.12	647.27
12.00%	2,158.93	1,445.89	1,147.43	1,056.43	932.56	780.11	715.71	684.60	668.60	660.11
12.25%	2,166.70	1,454.11	1,156.14	1,065.38	941.98	790.59	727.07	696.63	681.13	672.99
12.50%	2,174.49	1,462.37	1,164.88	1,074.37	951.45	801.14	738.49	708.73	693.72	685.92
12.75%	2,182.29	1,470.64	1,173.66	1,083.40	960.96	811.74	749.98	720.88	706.35	698.88
13.00%	2,190.11	1,478.95	1,182.48	1,092.47	970.52	822.41	761.52	733.09	719.03	711.88
13.25%	2,197.94	1,487.28	1,191.33	1,101.58	980.13	833.13	773.13	745.36	731.75	724.91
13.50%	2,205.79	1,495.64	1,200.22	1,110.73	989.78	843.91	784.79	757.67	744.52	737.97
13.75%	2,213.66	1,504.02	1,209.14	1,119.92	999.48	854.74	796.51	770.03	757.32	751.07
14.00%	2,221.55	1,512.44	1,218.10	1,129.15	1,009.23	865.63	808.29	782.44	770.17	764.19
14.25%	2,229.45	1,520.87	1,227.10	1,138.42	1,019.03	876.58	820.12	794.90	783.05	777.34
14.50%	2,237.36	1,529.34	1,236.12	1,147.72	1,028.86	887.58	832.00	807.41	795.96	790.51
14.75%	2,245.30	1,537.83	1,245.19	1,157.07	1,038.75	898.63	843.93	819.95	808.91	803.71
15.00%	2,253.25	1,546.35	1,254.29	1,166.45	1,048.68	909.73	855.91	832.54	821.89	816.93
15.25%	2,261.21	1,554.89	1,263.42	1,175.87	1,058.65	920.89	867.94	845.17	834.90	830.17
15.50%	2,269.19	1,563.46	1,272.59	1,185.33	1,068.67	932.09	880.02	857.83	847.94	843.43
15.75%	2,277.19	1,572.05	1,281.80	1,194.83	1,078.73	943.35	892.15	870.54	861.00	856.71
16.00%	2,285.21	1,580.67	1,291.03	1,204.37	1,088.84	954.66	904.32	883.28	874.09	870.01
16.25%	2,293.24	1,589.32	1,300.31	1,213.95	1,098.98	966.01	916.53	896.05	887.21	883.32
16.50%	2,301.28	1,597.99	1,309.61	1,223.56	1,109.17	977.41	928.79	908.86	900.35	896.65
16.75%	2,309.35	1,606.69	1,318.95	1,233.21	1,119.41	988.86	941.08	921.70	913.51	909.99
17.00%	2,317.43	1,615.42	1,328.33	1,242.89	1,129.68	1,000.35	953.42	934.57	926.69	923.34
17.25%	2,325.52	1,624.17	1,337.74	1,252.62	1,140.00	1,011.89	965.80	947.47	939.89	936.71
17.50%	2,333.63	1,632.94	1,347.18	1,262.38	1,150.36	1,023.48	978.21	960.39	953.11	950.09
17.75%	2,341.76	1,641.75	1,356.65	1,272.18	1,160.76	1,035.10	990.66	973.35	966.35	963.48
18.00%	2,349.91	1,650.57	1,366.16	1,282.01	1,171.20	1,046.77	1,003.15	986.33	979.61	976.88
18.25%	2,358.07	1,659.43	1,375.70	1,291.88	1,181.69	1,058.49	1,015.68	999.34	992.88	990.29
18.50%	2,366.24	1,668.30	1,385.27	1,301.78	1,192.21	1,070.24	1,028.23	1,012.36	1,006.16	1,003.71
18.75%	2,374.43	1,677.21	1,394.88	1,311.72	1,202.77	1,082.03	1,040.82	1,025.42	1,019.47	1,017.14
19.00%	2,382.64	1,686.14	1,404.52	1,321.70	1,213.37	1,093.87	1,053.45	1,038.49	1,032.78	1,030.57
19.25%	2,390.87	1,695.09	1,414.19	1,331.71	1,224.01	1,105.74	1,066.10	1,051.59	1,046.11	1,044.01
19.50%	2,399.11	1,704.07	1,423.90	1,341.76	1,234.69	1,117.66	1,078.78	1,064.70	1,059.45	1,057.46
19.75%	2,407.36	1,713.07	1,433.63	1,351.84	1,245.41	1,129.61	1,091.49	1,077.84	1,072.80	1,070.92
20.00%	2,415.63	1,722.10	1,443.40	1,361.96	1,256.16	1,141.59	1,104.24	1,090.99	1,086.16	1,084.38
20.25%	2,423.92	1,731.16	1,453.20	1,372.11	1,266.95	1,153.62	1,117.00	1,104.17	1,099.54	1,097.85
20.50%	2,432.22	1,740.24	1,463.04	1,382.29	1,277.78	1,165.68	1,129.80	1,117.35	1,112.92	1,111.32
20.75%	2,440.54	1,749.34	1,472.90	1,392.51	1,288.65	1,177.77	1,142.62	1,130.56	1,126.31	1,124.80

	3	5	7	8	10	15	20	25	30	35
1.00%	1,904.05	1,153.83	832.36	731.92	591.33	403.98	310.43	254.39	217.11	190.54
1.25%	1,911.35	1,161.11	839.66	739.23	598.68	411.45	318.02	262.10	224.94	198.51
1.50%	1,918.68	1,168.42	847.00	746.59	606.09	419.00	325.72	269.96	232.96	206.67
1.75%	1,926.02	1,175.76	854.38	754.00	613.56	426.64	333.54	277.96	241.14	215.04
2.00%	1,933.37	1,183.12	861.80	761.46	621.09	434.37	341.47	286.10	249.49	223.60
2.25%	1,940.75	1,190.52	869.26	768.96	628.68	442.18	349.52	294.39	258.02	232.36
2.50%	1,948.14	1,197.95	876.77	776.51	636.32	450.08	357.68	302.82	266.71	241.31
2.75%	1,955.55	1,205.40	884.31	784.10	644.02	458.07	365.96	311.38	275.56	250.45
3.00%	1,962.98	1,212.89	891.90	791.75	651.79	466.14	374.35	320.09	284.58	259.77
3.25%	1,970.43	1,220.40	899.52	799.43	659.60	474.30	382.86	328.94	293.76	269.28
3.50%	1,977.89	1,227.94	907.19	807.17	667.48	482.55	391.47	337.92	303.11	278.97
3.75%	1,985.37	1,235.51	914.90	814.95	675.41	490.88	400.20	347.04	312.60	288.84
4.00%	1,992.87	1,243.12	922.64	822.78	683.40	499.29	409.04	356.29	322.26	298.87
4.25%	2,000.38	1,250.75	930.43	830.65	691.45	507.79	417.98	365.67	332.06	309.08
4.50%	2,007.92	1,258.40	938.26	838.57	699.56	516.37	427.04	375.19	342.01	319.45
4.75%	2,015.47	1,266.09	946.13	846.53	707.72	525.04	436.20	384.83	352.11	329.98
5.00%	2,023.04	1,273.81	954.04	854.54	715.94	533.79	445.47	394.60	362.35	340.66
5.25%	2,030.62	1,281.55	961.99	862.60	724.22	542.62	454.84	404.49	372.74	351.50
5.50%	2,038.22	1,289.33	969.98	870.70	732.55	551.53	464.32	414.51	383.26	362.49
5.75%	2,045.84	1,297.13	978.01	878.85	740.94	560.53	473.91	424.65	393.91	373.61
6.00%	2,053.48	1,304.96	986.08	887.05	749.39	569.60	483.59	434.90	404.70	384.88
6.25%	2,061.14	1,312.83	994.19	895.29	757.89	578.76	493.38	445.28	415.61	396.28
6.50%	2,068.81	1,320.72	1,002.34	903.57	766.45	588.00	503.26	455.76	426.65	407.80
6.75%	2,076.50	1,328.63	1,010.53	911.90	775.06	597.31	513.25	466.37	437.80	419.46
7.00%	2,084.20	1,336.58	1,018.76	920.28	783.73	606.71	523.33	477.08	449.08	431.23
7.25%	2,091.93	1,344.56	1,027.02	928.70	792.46	616.18	533.50	487.89	460.47	443.12
7.50%	2,099.67	1,352.56	1,035.33	937.16	801.24	625.73	543.78	498.82	471.97	455.11
7.75%	2,107.43	1,360.59	1,043.68	945.67	810.07	635.36	554.14	509.85	483.58	467.22
8.00%	2,115.20	1,368.66	1,052.07	954.23	818.96	645.07	564.60	520.98	495.29	479.43
8.25%	2,123.00	1,376.75	1,060.50	962.83	827.91	654.84	575.14	532.20	507.10	491.73
8.50%	2,130.81	1,384.87	1,068.96	971.47	836.90	664.70	585.78	543.53	519.02	504.13
8.75%	2,138.64	1,393.01	1,077.47	980.16	845.96	674.63	596.50	554.95	531.02	516.62
9.00%	2,146.48	1,401.19	1,086.01	988.89	855.06	684.63	607.32	566.46	543.12	529.20
9.25%	2,154.34	1,409.39	1,094.60	997.66	864.22	694.70	618.21	578.06	555.31	541.85
9.50%	2,162.22	1,417.63	1,103.22	1,006.48	873.43	704.85	629.19	589.75	567.58	554.59
9.75%	2,170.12	1,425.89	1,111.88	1,015.35	882.70	715.07	640.25	601.52	579.93	567.40
10.00%	2,178.04	1,434.18	1,120.58	1,024.26	892.02	725.36	651.39	613.37	592.36	580.28
10.25%	2,185.97	1,442.49	1,129.32	1,033.21	901.39	735.72	662.61	625.31	604.87	593.23
10.50%	2,193.91	1,450.84	1,138.10	1,042.20	910.81	746.14	673.91	637.32	617.45	606.24
10.75%	2,201.88	1,459.21	1,146.91	1,051.24	920.29	756.64	685.28	649.41	630.10	619.31

$67,500   11.00 - 20.75%   3 - 35 Years

	3	5	7	8	10	15	20	25	30	35
11.00%	2,209.86	1,467.61	1,155.76	1,060.32	929.81	767.20	696.73	661.58	642.82	632.45
11.25%	2,217.86	1,476.04	1,164.66	1,069.44	939.39	777.83	708.25	673.81	655.60	645.63
11.50%	2,225.88	1,484.50	1,173.59	1,078.61	949.02	788.53	719.84	686.12	668.45	658.87
11.75%	2,233.91	1,492.99	1,182.55	1,087.82	958.70	799.29	731.50	698.49	681.35	672.16
12.00%	2,241.97	1,501.50	1,191.56	1,097.07	968.43	810.11	743.23	710.93	694.31	685.50
12.25%	2,250.03	1,510.04	1,200.60	1,106.36	978.21	821.00	755.03	723.43	707.33	698.88
12.50%	2,258.12	1,518.61	1,209.68	1,115.69	988.04	831.95	766.89	735.99	720.40	712.30
12.75%	2,266.22	1,527.21	1,218.80	1,125.07	997.92	842.96	778.82	748.61	733.52	725.76
13.00%	2,274.34	1,535.83	1,227.96	1,134.49	1,007.85	854.04	790.81	761.29	746.68	739.26
13.25%	2,282.48	1,544.48	1,237.15	1,143.95	1,017.83	865.17	802.87	774.02	759.90	752.79
13.50%	2,290.63	1,553.16	1,246.38	1,153.45	1,027.85	876.37	814.98	786.81	773.15	766.35
13.75%	2,298.80	1,561.87	1,255.65	1,162.99	1,037.93	887.62	827.15	799.65	786.45	779.95
14.00%	2,306.99	1,570.61	1,264.95	1,172.58	1,048.05	898.93	839.38	812.54	799.79	793.58
14.25%	2,315.19	1,579.37	1,274.29	1,182.20	1,058.22	910.29	851.66	825.48	813.16	807.23
14.50%	2,323.42	1,588.16	1,283.67	1,191.86	1,068.44	921.71	864.00	838.46	826.58	820.92
14.75%	2,331.65	1,596.98	1,293.08	1,201.57	1,078.70	933.19	876.39	851.49	840.02	834.62
15.00%	2,339.91	1,605.82	1,302.53	1,211.31	1,089.01	944.72	888.83	864.56	853.50	848.35
15.25%	2,348.18	1,614.69	1,312.02	1,221.10	1,099.37	956.31	901.33	877.67	867.01	862.10
15.50%	2,356.47	1,623.59	1,321.54	1,230.92	1,109.77	967.94	913.87	890.83	880.55	875.87
15.75%	2,364.78	1,632.52	1,331.10	1,240.79	1,120.22	979.63	926.46	904.02	894.12	889.66
16.00%	2,373.10	1,641.47	1,340.69	1,250.69	1,130.71	991.37	939.10	917.25	907.71	903.47
16.25%	2,381.44	1,650.45	1,350.32	1,260.64	1,141.25	1,003.16	951.78	930.52	921.33	917.29
16.50%	2,389.80	1,659.46	1,359.98	1,270.62	1,151.84	1,015.00	964.51	943.82	934.97	931.13
16.75%	2,398.17	1,668.49	1,369.68	1,280.64	1,162.46	1,026.89	977.28	957.15	948.64	944.99
17.00%	2,406.56	1,677.55	1,379.42	1,290.70	1,173.13	1,038.83	990.09	970.51	962.33	958.86
17.25%	2,414.97	1,686.64	1,389.19	1,300.80	1,183.85	1,050.81	1,002.94	983.91	976.04	972.74
17.50%	2,423.39	1,695.75	1,398.99	1,310.93	1,194.61	1,062.84	1,015.84	997.33	989.77	986.63
17.75%	2,431.83	1,704.89	1,408.83	1,321.11	1,205.41	1,074.91	1,028.77	1,010.79	1,003.52	1,000.54
18.00%	2,440.29	1,714.06	1,418.70	1,331.32	1,216.25	1,087.03	1,041.74	1,024.27	1,017.28	1,014.45
18.25%	2,448.76	1,723.25	1,428.61	1,341.57	1,227.14	1,099.20	1,054.74	1,037.77	1,031.06	1,028.38
18.50%	2,457.25	1,732.47	1,438.55	1,351.85	1,238.06	1,111.40	1,067.78	1,051.30	1,044.86	1,042.31
18.75%	2,465.76	1,741.72	1,448.53	1,362.18	1,249.03	1,123.65	1,080.85	1,064.86	1,058.68	1,056.26
19.00%	2,474.28	1,750.99	1,458.54	1,372.54	1,260.04	1,135.94	1,093.96	1,078.43	1,072.50	1,070.21
19.25%	2,482.82	1,760.29	1,468.59	1,382.93	1,271.09	1,148.27	1,107.10	1,092.03	1,086.34	1,084.17
19.50%	2,491.38	1,769.61	1,478.66	1,393.37	1,282.18	1,160.64	1,120.27	1,105.65	1,100.20	1,098.14
19.75%	2,499.95	1,778.96	1,488.77	1,403.84	1,293.31	1,173.05	1,133.48	1,119.29	1,114.06	1,112.11
20.00%	2,508.54	1,788.34	1,498.92	1,414.34	1,304.48	1,185.50	1,146.71	1,132.95	1,127.94	1,126.09
20.25%	2,517.15	1,797.74	1,509.10	1,424.88	1,315.68	1,197.99	1,159.97	1,146.63	1,141.82	1,140.07
20.50%	2,525.77	1,807.17	1,519.31	1,435.46	1,326.93	1,210.51	1,173.25	1,160.33	1,155.72	1,154.06
20.75%	2,534.41	1,816.62	1,529.55	1,446.07	1,338.22	1,223.07	1,186.57	1,174.04	1,169.63	1,168.06

$70,000   1.00 - 10.75%   3 - 35 Years

	3	5	7	8	10	15	20	25	30	35
1.00%	1,974.57	1,196.56	863.19	759.03	613.23	418.95	321.93	263.81	225.15	197.60
1.25%	1,982.14	1,204.11	870.76	766.61	620.85	426.69	329.79	271.81	233.28	205.86
1.50%	1,989.74	1,211.69	878.37	774.25	628.54	434.52	337.78	279.96	241.58	214.33
1.75%	1,997.35	1,219.30	886.02	781.93	636.29	442.44	345.89	288.25	250.07	223.00
2.00%	2,004.98	1,226.94	893.72	789.66	644.09	450.46	354.12	296.70	258.73	231.88
2.25%	2,012.63	1,234.61	901.46	797.44	651.96	458.56	362.47	305.29	267.57	240.97
2.50%	2,020.30	1,242.32	909.24	805.27	659.89	466.75	370.93	314.03	276.58	250.25
2.75%	2,027.98	1,250.05	917.06	813.15	667.88	475.04	379.52	322.92	285.77	259.72
3.00%	2,035.68	1,257.81	924.93	821.07	675.93	483.41	388.22	331.95	295.12	269.40
3.25%	2,043.41	1,265.60	932.84	829.04	684.03	491.87	397.04	341.12	304.64	279.26
3.50%	2,051.15	1,273.42	940.79	837.06	692.20	500.42	405.97	350.44	314.33	289.30
3.75%	2,058.90	1,281.27	948.78	845.13	700.43	509.06	415.02	359.89	324.18	299.53
4.00%	2,066.68	1,289.16	956.82	853.25	708.72	517.78	424.19	369.49	334.19	309.94
4.25%	2,074.47	1,297.07	964.89	861.41	717.06	526.59	433.46	379.22	344.36	320.53
4.50%	2,082.28	1,305.01	973.01	869.63	725.47	535.50	442.85	389.08	354.68	331.28
4.75%	2,090.11	1,312.98	981.17	877.89	733.93	544.48	452.36	399.08	365.15	342.20
5.00%	2,097.96	1,320.99	989.37	886.19	742.46	553.56	461.97	409.21	375.78	353.28
5.25%	2,105.83	1,329.02	997.62	894.55	751.04	562.71	471.69	419.47	386.54	364.52
5.50%	2,113.71	1,337.08	1,005.90	902.95	759.68	571.96	481.52	429.86	397.45	375.91
5.75%	2,121.62	1,345.17	1,014.23	911.40	768.38	581.29	491.46	440.37	408.50	387.45
6.00%	2,129.54	1,353.30	1,022.60	919.90	777.14	590.70	501.50	451.01	419.69	399.13
6.25%	2,137.47	1,361.45	1,031.01	928.44	785.96	600.20	511.65	461.77	431.00	410.95
6.50%	2,145.43	1,369.63	1,039.46	937.04	794.84	609.78	521.90	472.65	442.45	422.91
6.75%	2,153.40	1,377.84	1,047.95	945.67	803.77	619.44	532.25	483.64	454.02	434.99
7.00%	2,161.40	1,386.08	1,056.49	954.36	812.76	629.18	542.71	494.75	465.71	447.20
7.25%	2,169.41	1,394.36	1,065.06	963.09	821.81	639.00	553.26	505.96	477.52	459.53
7.50%	2,177.44	1,402.66	1,073.68	971.87	830.91	648.91	563.92	517.29	489.45	471.97
7.75%	2,185.48	1,410.99	1,082.34	980.70	840.07	658.89	574.66	528.73	501.49	484.52
8.00%	2,193.55	1,419.35	1,091.04	989.57	849.29	668.96	585.51	540.27	513.64	497.18
8.25%	2,201.63	1,427.74	1,099.77	998.49	858.57	679.10	596.45	551.92	525.89	509.94
8.50%	2,209.73	1,436.16	1,108.55	1,007.45	867.90	689.32	607.48	563.66	538.24	522.80
8.75%	2,217.85	1,444.61	1,117.37	1,016.46	877.29	699.61	618.60	575.50	550.69	535.75
9.00%	2,225.98	1,453.08	1,126.24	1,025.51	886.73	709.99	629.81	587.44	563.24	548.80
9.25%	2,234.13	1,461.59	1,135.14	1,034.62	896.23	720.43	641.11	599.47	575.87	561.92
9.50%	2,242.31	1,470.13	1,144.08	1,043.76	905.78	730.96	652.49	611.59	588.60	575.13
9.75%	2,250.50	1,478.70	1,153.06	1,052.95	915.39	741.55	663.96	623.80	601.41	588.41
10.00%	2,258.70	1,487.29	1,162.08	1,062.19	925.06	752.22	675.52	636.09	614.30	601.77
10.25%	2,266.93	1,495.92	1,171.15	1,071.47	934.77	762.97	687.15	648.47	627.27	615.20
10.50%	2,275.17	1,504.57	1,180.25	1,080.80	944.54	773.78	698.87	660.93	640.32	628.69
10.75%	2,283.43	1,513.26	1,189.39	1,090.17	954.37	784.66	710.66	673.46	653.44	642.25

$70,000   11.00 - 20.75%   3 - 35 Years

	3	5	7	8	10	15	20	25	30	35
11.00%	2,291.71	1,521.97	1,198.57	1,099.59	964.25	795.62	722.53	686.08	666.63	655.87
11.25%	2,300.01	1,530.71	1,207.79	1,109.05	974.18	806.64	734.48	698.77	679.88	669.55
11.50%	2,308.32	1,539.48	1,217.05	1,118.56	984.17	817.73	746.50	711.53	693.20	683.28
11.75%	2,316.65	1,548.28	1,226.35	1,128.11	994.21	828.89	758.59	724.36	706.59	697.06
12.00%	2,325.00	1,557.11	1,235.69	1,137.70	1,004.30	840.12	770.76	737.26	720.03	710.88
12.25%	2,333.37	1,565.97	1,245.07	1,147.34	1,014.44	851.41	783.00	750.22	733.53	724.76
12.50%	2,341.75	1,574.86	1,254.49	1,157.02	1,024.63	862.77	795.30	763.25	747.08	738.68
12.75%	2,350.16	1,583.77	1,263.94	1,166.74	1,034.88	874.19	807.67	776.34	760.69	752.64
13.00%	2,358.58	1,592.72	1,273.44	1,176.51	1,045.18	885.67	820.10	789.48	774.34	766.64
13.25%	2,367.01	1,601.69	1,282.97	1,186.32	1,055.52	897.22	832.60	802.69	788.04	780.67
13.50%	2,375.47	1,610.69	1,292.54	1,196.17	1,065.92	908.82	845.16	815.95	801.79	794.74
13.75%	2,383.94	1,619.72	1,302.15	1,206.07	1,076.37	920.49	857.78	829.27	815.58	808.84
14.00%	2,392.43	1,628.78	1,311.80	1,216.01	1,086.87	932.22	870.46	842.63	829.41	822.97
14.25%	2,400.94	1,637.86	1,321.49	1,225.99	1,097.41	944.01	883.20	856.05	843.28	837.13
14.50%	2,409.47	1,646.98	1,331.21	1,236.01	1,108.01	955.85	896.00	869.51	857.19	851.32
14.75%	2,418.01	1,656.12	1,340.97	1,246.07	1,118.65	967.75	908.85	883.03	871.13	865.53
15.00%	2,426.57	1,665.30	1,350.77	1,256.18	1,129.34	979.71	921.75	896.58	885.11	879.77
15.25%	2,435.15	1,674.50	1,360.61	1,266.33	1,140.09	991.72	934.71	910.18	899.12	894.03
15.50%	2,443.75	1,683.72	1,370.48	1,276.51	1,150.87	1,003.79	947.72	923.82	913.16	908.31
15.75%	2,452.36	1,692.98	1,380.40	1,286.74	1,161.71	1,015.92	960.77	937.50	927.23	922.61
16.00%	2,460.99	1,702.26	1,390.34	1,297.02	1,172.59	1,028.09	973.88	951.22	941.33	936.93
16.25%	2,469.64	1,711.58	1,400.33	1,307.33	1,183.52	1,040.32	987.03	964.98	955.45	951.26
16.50%	2,478.31	1,720.92	1,410.35	1,317.68	1,194.50	1,052.60	1,000.23	978.77	969.60	965.62
16.75%	2,486.99	1,730.28	1,420.41	1,328.07	1,205.52	1,064.92	1,013.47	992.60	983.78	979.99
17.00%	2,495.69	1,739.68	1,430.51	1,338.50	1,216.58	1,077.30	1,026.76	1,006.46	997.97	994.37
17.25%	2,504.41	1,749.10	1,440.64	1,348.97	1,227.70	1,089.73	1,040.09	1,020.35	1,012.19	1,008.76
17.50%	2,513.14	1,758.55	1,450.81	1,359.48	1,238.85	1,102.20	1,053.46	1,034.27	1,026.43	1,023.17
17.75%	2,521.90	1,768.03	1,461.01	1,370.04	1,250.05	1,114.73	1,066.87	1,048.22	1,040.68	1,037.59
18.00%	2,530.67	1,777.54	1,471.25	1,380.62	1,261.30	1,127.29	1,080.32	1,062.20	1,054.96	1,052.02
18.25%	2,539.46	1,787.07	1,481.52	1,391.25	1,272.58	1,139.91	1,093.80	1,076.21	1,069.25	1,066.47
18.50%	2,548.26	1,796.63	1,491.83	1,401.92	1,283.92	1,152.57	1,107.33	1,090.24	1,083.56	1,080.92
18.75%	2,557.08	1,806.22	1,502.18	1,412.63	1,295.29	1,165.27	1,120.89	1,104.30	1,097.89	1,095.38
19.00%	2,565.92	1,815.84	1,512.56	1,423.37	1,306.71	1,178.01	1,134.48	1,118.38	1,112.22	1,109.85
19.25%	2,574.78	1,825.48	1,522.98	1,434.15	1,318.17	1,190.80	1,148.11	1,132.48	1,126.58	1,124.32
19.50%	2,583.65	1,835.15	1,533.43	1,444.97	1,329.67	1,203.63	1,161.77	1,146.60	1,140.94	1,138.81
19.75%	2,592.54	1,844.85	1,543.91	1,455.83	1,341.21	1,216.50	1,175.46	1,160.75	1,155.32	1,153.30
20.00%	2,601.45	1,854.57	1,554.43	1,466.72	1,352.79	1,229.41	1,189.18	1,174.92	1,169.71	1,167.79
20.25%	2,610.38	1,864.32	1,564.99	1,477.66	1,364.41	1,242.36	1,202.93	1,189.10	1,184.11	1,182.30
20.50%	2,619.32	1,874.10	1,575.58	1,488.62	1,376.08	1,255.34	1,216.71	1,203.30	1,198.53	1,196.81
20.75%	2,628.28	1,883.90	1,586.20	1,499.63	1,387.78	1,268.37	1,230.52	1,217.53	1,212.95	1,211.32

	3	5	7	8	10	15	20	25	30	35
1.00%	2,045.09	1,239.30	894.02	786.13	635.13	433.91	333.42	273.23	233.19	204.66
1.25%	2,052.93	1,247.12	901.86	793.99	643.03	441.93	341.57	281.52	241.61	213.21
1.50%	2,060.80	1,254.97	909.74	801.90	650.99	450.04	349.85	289.95	250.21	221.98
1.75%	2,068.68	1,262.85	917.67	809.86	659.01	458.24	358.24	298.55	259.00	230.97
2.00%	2,076.59	1,270.76	925.64	817.86	667.10	466.54	366.77	307.29	267.97	240.17
2.25%	2,084.51	1,278.71	933.65	825.92	675.25	474.94	375.41	316.19	277.13	249.57
2.50%	2,092.45	1,286.68	941.71	834.03	683.46	483.42	384.18	325.25	286.46	259.18
2.75%	2,100.41	1,294.69	949.82	842.19	691.73	492.00	393.07	334.45	295.97	269.00
3.00%	2,108.39	1,302.73	957.96	850.39	700.07	500.67	402.08	343.80	305.66	279.02
3.25%	2,116.38	1,310.80	966.15	858.65	708.46	509.43	411.22	353.30	315.52	289.23
3.50%	2,124.40	1,318.90	974.39	866.96	716.92	518.29	420.47	362.95	325.56	299.64
3.75%	2,132.44	1,327.03	982.67	875.32	725.44	527.24	429.84	372.75	335.76	310.23
4.00%	2,140.49	1,335.20	990.99	883.72	734.03	536.27	439.34	382.68	346.13	321.01
4.25%	2,148.56	1,343.39	999.35	892.18	742.67	545.40	448.94	392.76	356.66	331.97
4.50%	2,156.65	1,351.62	1,007.76	900.68	751.38	554.62	458.67	402.98	367.35	343.11
4.75%	2,164.76	1,359.88	1,016.21	909.24	760.15	563.93	468.51	413.34	378.19	354.42
5.00%	2,172.89	1,368.16	1,024.71	917.84	768.97	573.33	478.47	423.83	389.20	365.90
5.25%	2,181.04	1,376.48	1,033.25	926.50	777.86	582.81	488.54	434.45	400.35	377.54
5.50%	2,189.20	1,384.83	1,041.83	935.20	786.82	592.39	498.72	445.21	411.65	389.34
5.75%	2,197.39	1,393.22	1,050.45	943.95	795.83	602.05	509.01	456.10	423.09	401.29
6.00%	2,205.59	1,401.63	1,059.12	952.75	804.90	611.80	519.41	467.12	434.67	413.39
6.25%	2,213.81	1,410.07	1,067.83	961.60	814.03	621.63	529.92	478.26	446.39	425.63
6.50%	2,222.05	1,418.55	1,076.58	970.50	823.22	631.55	540.54	489.53	458.25	438.01
6.75%	2,230.31	1,427.05	1,085.38	979.45	832.47	641.56	551.26	500.91	470.23	450.53
7.00%	2,238.59	1,435.59	1,094.22	988.44	841.79	651.65	562.09	512.41	482.34	463.17
7.25%	2,246.89	1,444.15	1,103.10	997.49	851.16	661.83	573.02	524.03	494.58	475.94
7.50%	2,255.20	1,452.75	1,112.02	1,006.58	860.59	672.08	584.06	535.77	506.93	488.83
7.75%	2,263.53	1,461.38	1,120.99	1,015.72	870.08	682.42	595.19	547.61	519.40	501.83
8.00%	2,271.89	1,470.04	1,130.00	1,024.91	879.63	692.85	606.42	559.57	531.98	514.94
8.25%	2,280.26	1,478.73	1,139.05	1,034.15	889.23	703.35	617.75	571.63	544.67	528.16
8.50%	2,288.65	1,487.45	1,148.15	1,043.43	898.90	713.94	629.17	583.79	557.46	541.47
8.75%	2,297.05	1,496.20	1,157.28	1,052.76	908.62	724.60	640.69	596.05	570.36	554.89
9.00%	2,305.48	1,504.98	1,166.46	1,062.14	918.40	735.34	652.30	608.42	583.35	568.39
9.25%	2,313.93	1,513.79	1,175.68	1,071.57	928.24	746.16	664.00	620.88	596.44	581.99
9.50%	2,322.39	1,522.63	1,184.94	1,081.04	938.13	757.06	675.80	633.43	609.62	595.67
9.75%	2,330.87	1,531.51	1,194.24	1,090.56	948.08	768.04	687.67	646.07	622.89	609.43
10.00%	2,339.37	1,540.41	1,203.59	1,100.13	958.09	779.09	699.64	658.81	636.24	623.26
10.25%	2,347.89	1,549.34	1,212.97	1,109.74	968.16	790.21	711.69	671.63	649.67	637.17
10.50%	2,356.43	1,558.31	1,222.40	1,119.40	978.28	801.41	723.83	684.53	663.19	651.15
10.75%	2,364.98	1,567.30	1,231.87	1,129.11	988.46	812.69	736.04	697.52	676.77	665.19

$72,500   11.00 - 20.75%   3 - 35 Years

	3	5	7	8	10	15	20	25	30	35
11.00%	2,373.56	1,576.33	1,241.38	1,138.86	998.69	824.03	748.34	710.58	690.43	679.29
11.25%	2,382.15	1,585.38	1,250.93	1,148.66	1,008.97	835.45	760.71	723.72	704.16	693.46
11.50%	2,390.76	1,594.46	1,260.52	1,158.50	1,019.32	846.94	773.16	736.94	717.96	707.68
11.75%	2,399.39	1,603.58	1,270.15	1,168.40	1,029.71	858.50	785.69	750.23	731.82	721.95
12.00%	2,408.04	1,612.72	1,279.82	1,178.33	1,040.16	870.12	798.29	763.59	745.74	736.27
12.25%	2,416.70	1,621.90	1,289.54	1,188.31	1,050.67	881.82	810.96	777.01	759.72	750.64
12.50%	2,425.39	1,631.10	1,299.29	1,198.34	1,061.23	893.58	823.70	790.51	773.76	765.06
12.75%	2,434.09	1,640.33	1,309.08	1,208.41	1,071.84	905.41	836.51	804.06	787.85	779.52
13.00%	2,442.81	1,649.60	1,318.92	1,218.53	1,082.50	917.30	849.39	817.68	801.99	794.02
13.25%	2,451.55	1,658.89	1,328.79	1,228.69	1,093.22	929.26	862.34	831.36	816.19	808.55
13.50%	2,460.31	1,668.21	1,338.70	1,238.89	1,103.99	941.28	875.35	845.09	830.42	823.12
13.75%	2,469.08	1,677.57	1,348.66	1,249.14	1,114.81	953.37	888.42	858.88	844.71	837.73
14.00%	2,477.88	1,686.95	1,358.65	1,259.43	1,125.68	965.51	901.55	872.73	859.03	852.36
14.25%	2,486.69	1,696.36	1,368.68	1,269.77	1,136.61	977.72	914.75	886.62	873.40	867.03
14.50%	2,495.52	1,705.80	1,378.75	1,280.15	1,147.58	989.99	928.00	900.57	887.80	881.72
14.75%	2,504.37	1,715.27	1,388.87	1,290.57	1,158.60	1,002.32	941.31	914.56	902.24	896.44
15.00%	2,513.24	1,724.77	1,399.01	1,301.04	1,169.68	1,014.70	954.67	928.60	916.72	911.19
15.25%	2,522.12	1,734.30	1,409.20	1,311.55	1,180.80	1,027.14	968.09	942.69	931.23	925.96
15.50%	2,531.02	1,743.86	1,419.43	1,322.10	1,191.98	1,039.64	981.56	956.82	945.77	940.75
15.75%	2,539.95	1,753.44	1,429.70	1,332.70	1,203.20	1,052.20	995.09	970.98	960.35	955.56
16.00%	2,548.88	1,763.06	1,440.00	1,343.34	1,214.47	1,064.81	1,008.66	985.19	974.95	970.39
16.25%	2,557.84	1,772.70	1,450.34	1,354.02	1,225.79	1,077.47	1,022.28	999.44	989.58	985.24
16.50%	2,566.82	1,782.38	1,460.72	1,364.74	1,237.16	1,090.19	1,035.95	1,013.73	1,004.23	1,000.10
16.75%	2,575.81	1,792.08	1,471.14	1,375.50	1,248.57	1,102.96	1,049.67	1,028.05	1,018.91	1,014.99
17.00%	2,584.82	1,801.81	1,481.60	1,386.31	1,260.03	1,115.78	1,063.43	1,042.40	1,033.61	1,029.88
17.25%	2,593.85	1,811.57	1,492.09	1,397.15	1,271.54	1,128.65	1,077.24	1,056.79	1,048.34	1,044.79
17.50%	2,602.90	1,821.36	1,502.62	1,408.04	1,283.10	1,141.57	1,091.08	1,071.21	1,063.09	1,059.71
17.75%	2,611.97	1,831.18	1,513.19	1,418.97	1,294.70	1,154.54	1,104.97	1,085.66	1,077.85	1,074.65
18.00%	2,621.05	1,841.02	1,523.79	1,429.93	1,306.34	1,167.56	1,118.90	1,100.14	1,092.64	1,089.60
18.25%	2,630.15	1,850.90	1,534.44	1,440.94	1,318.03	1,180.62	1,132.87	1,114.64	1,107.44	1,104.55
18.50%	2,639.27	1,860.80	1,545.11	1,451.99	1,329.77	1,193.73	1,146.88	1,129.18	1,122.26	1,119.52
18.75%	2,648.41	1,870.73	1,555.83	1,463.08	1,341.55	1,206.89	1,160.92	1,143.73	1,137.10	1,134.50
19.00%	2,657.56	1,880.69	1,566.58	1,474.21	1,353.37	1,220.09	1,175.00	1,158.32	1,151.95	1,149.48
19.25%	2,666.73	1,890.68	1,577.37	1,485.37	1,365.24	1,233.33	1,189.11	1,172.92	1,166.81	1,164.48
19.50%	2,675.93	1,900.69	1,588.19	1,496.58	1,377.15	1,246.62	1,203.26	1,187.55	1,181.69	1,179.48
19.75%	2,685.13	1,910.74	1,599.05	1,507.82	1,389.11	1,259.94	1,217.44	1,202.21	1,196.58	1,194.49
20.00%	2,694.36	1,920.81	1,609.95	1,519.11	1,401.10	1,273.31	1,231.65	1,216.88	1,211.49	1,209.50
20.25%	2,703.60	1,930.91	1,620.88	1,530.43	1,413.14	1,286.73	1,245.89	1,231.57	1,226.40	1,224.52
20.50%	2,712.87	1,941.03	1,631.85	1,541.79	1,425.22	1,300.18	1,260.16	1,246.28	1,241.33	1,239.55
20.75%	2,722.15	1,951.19	1,642.85	1,553.19	1,437.34	1,313.67	1,274.46	1,261.01	1,256.27	1,254.58

	3	5	7	8	10	15	20	25	30	35
1.00%	2,115.61	1,282.03	924.84	813.24	657.03	448.87	344.92	282.65	241.23	211.71
1.25%	2,123.72	1,290.12	932.95	821.37	665.20	457.17	353.35	291.22	249.94	220.56
1.50%	2,131.86	1,298.24	941.11	829.55	673.44	465.56	361.91	299.95	258.84	229.64
1.75%	2,140.02	1,306.40	949.31	837.78	681.74	474.05	370.60	308.84	267.93	238.93
2.00%	2,148.19	1,314.58	957.56	846.07	690.10	482.63	379.41	317.89	277.21	248.45
2.25%	2,156.39	1,322.80	965.85	854.40	698.53	491.31	388.36	327.10	286.68	258.18
2.50%	2,164.60	1,331.05	974.19	862.79	707.02	500.09	397.43	336.46	296.34	268.12
2.75%	2,172.84	1,339.34	982.57	871.23	715.58	508.97	406.62	345.98	306.18	278.28
3.00%	2,181.09	1,347.65	991.00	879.72	724.21	517.94	415.95	355.66	316.20	288.64
3.25%	2,189.36	1,356.00	999.47	888.26	732.89	527.00	425.40	365.49	326.40	299.20
3.50%	2,197.66	1,364.38	1,007.99	896.85	741.64	536.16	434.97	375.47	336.78	309.97
3.75%	2,205.97	1,372.79	1,016.55	905.50	750.46	545.42	444.67	385.60	347.34	320.93
4.00%	2,214.30	1,381.24	1,025.16	914.20	759.34	554.77	454.49	395.88	358.06	332.08
4.25%	2,222.65	1,389.72	1,033.81	922.94	768.28	564.21	464.43	406.30	368.95	343.42
4.50%	2,231.02	1,398.23	1,042.51	931.74	777.29	573.74	474.49	416.87	380.01	354.94
4.75%	2,239.41	1,406.77	1,051.26	940.59	786.36	583.37	484.67	427.59	391.24	366.64
5.00%	2,247.82	1,415.34	1,060.04	949.49	795.49	593.10	494.97	438.44	402.62	378.52
5.25%	2,256.25	1,423.95	1,068.88	958.45	804.69	602.91	505.38	449.44	414.15	390.56
5.50%	2,264.69	1,432.59	1,077.75	967.45	813.95	612.81	515.92	460.57	425.84	402.76
5.75%	2,273.16	1,441.26	1,086.68	976.50	823.27	622.81	526.56	471.83	437.68	415.13
6.00%	2,281.65	1,449.96	1,095.64	985.61	832.65	632.89	537.32	483.23	449.66	427.64
6.25%	2,290.15	1,458.69	1,104.65	994.76	842.10	643.07	548.20	494.75	461.79	440.31
6.50%	2,298.68	1,467.46	1,113.71	1,003.97	851.61	653.33	559.18	506.41	474.05	453.12
6.75%	2,307.22	1,476.26	1,122.81	1,013.22	861.18	663.68	570.27	518.18	486.45	466.06
7.00%	2,315.78	1,485.09	1,131.95	1,022.53	870.81	674.12	581.47	530.08	498.98	479.14
7.25%	2,324.36	1,493.95	1,141.14	1,031.88	880.51	684.65	592.78	542.11	511.63	492.35
7.50%	2,332.97	1,502.85	1,150.37	1,041.29	890.26	695.26	604.19	554.24	524.41	505.68
7.75%	2,341.59	1,511.77	1,159.65	1,050.75	900.08	705.96	615.71	566.50	537.31	519.13
8.00%	2,350.23	1,520.73	1,168.97	1,060.25	909.96	716.74	627.33	578.86	550.32	532.70
8.25%	2,358.89	1,529.72	1,178.33	1,069.81	919.89	727.61	639.05	591.34	563.45	546.37
8.50%	2,367.57	1,538.74	1,187.74	1,079.41	929.89	738.55	650.87	603.92	576.69	560.15
8.75%	2,376.26	1,547.79	1,197.19	1,089.06	939.95	749.59	662.78	616.61	590.03	574.02
9.00%	2,384.98	1,556.88	1,206.68	1,098.77	950.07	760.70	674.79	629.40	603.47	587.99
9.25%	2,393.72	1,565.99	1,216.22	1,108.52	960.25	771.89	686.90	642.29	617.01	602.06
9.50%	2,402.47	1,575.14	1,225.80	1,118.32	970.48	783.17	699.10	655.27	630.64	616.21
9.75%	2,411.25	1,584.32	1,235.42	1,128.17	980.78	794.52	711.39	668.35	644.37	630.44
10.00%	2,420.04	1,593.53	1,245.09	1,138.06	991.13	805.95	723.77	681.53	658.18	644.75
10.25%	2,428.85	1,602.77	1,254.80	1,148.01	1,001.54	817.46	736.23	694.79	672.08	659.14
10.50%	2,437.68	1,612.04	1,264.55	1,158.00	1,012.01	829.05	748.78	708.14	686.05	673.60
10.75%	2,446.53	1,621.35	1,274.35	1,168.04	1,022.54	840.71	761.42	721.57	700.11	688.13

$75,000   11.00 - 20.75%   3 - 35 Years

	3	5	7	8	10	15	20	25	30	35
11.00%	2,455.40	1,630.68	1,284.18	1,178.13	1,033.13	852.45	774.14	735.08	714.24	702.72
11.25%	2,464.29	1,640.05	1,294.06	1,188.27	1,043.77	864.26	786.94	748.68	728.45	717.37
11.50%	2,473.20	1,649.45	1,303.98	1,198.45	1,054.47	876.14	799.82	762.35	742.72	732.08
11.75%	2,482.13	1,658.87	1,313.95	1,208.68	1,065.22	888.10	812.78	776.10	757.06	746.85
12.00%	2,491.07	1,668.33	1,323.95	1,218.96	1,076.03	900.13	825.81	789.92	771.46	761.66
12.25%	2,500.04	1,677.82	1,334.00	1,229.29	1,086.90	912.22	838.92	803.81	785.92	776.53
12.50%	2,509.02	1,687.35	1,344.09	1,239.66	1,097.82	924.39	852.11	817.77	800.44	791.44
12.75%	2,518.02	1,696.90	1,354.22	1,250.08	1,108.80	936.63	865.36	831.79	815.02	806.40
13.00%	2,527.05	1,706.48	1,364.40	1,260.54	1,119.83	948.93	878.68	845.88	829.65	821.39
13.25%	2,536.09	1,716.09	1,374.61	1,271.06	1,130.92	961.30	892.07	860.03	844.33	836.43
13.50%	2,545.15	1,725.74	1,384.87	1,281.61	1,142.06	973.74	905.53	874.23	859.06	851.51
13.75%	2,554.22	1,735.41	1,395.16	1,292.21	1,153.25	986.24	919.05	888.50	873.83	866.61
14.00%	2,563.32	1,745.12	1,405.50	1,302.86	1,164.50	998.81	932.64	902.82	888.65	881.75
14.25%	2,572.44	1,754.85	1,415.88	1,313.56	1,175.80	1,011.43	946.29	917.20	903.52	896.93
14.50%	2,581.57	1,764.62	1,426.30	1,324.29	1,187.15	1,024.13	960.00	931.62	918.42	912.13
14.75%	2,590.73	1,774.42	1,436.76	1,335.08	1,198.56	1,036.88	973.77	946.10	933.36	927.36
15.00%	2,599.90	1,784.24	1,447.26	1,345.91	1,210.01	1,049.69	987.59	960.62	948.33	942.61
15.25%	2,609.09	1,794.10	1,457.80	1,356.78	1,221.52	1,062.56	1,001.47	975.19	963.34	957.89
15.50%	2,618.30	1,803.99	1,468.38	1,367.69	1,233.08	1,075.49	1,015.41	989.81	978.39	973.19
15.75%	2,627.53	1,813.91	1,479.00	1,378.65	1,244.69	1,088.48	1,029.40	1,004.47	993.46	988.51
16.00%	2,636.78	1,823.85	1,489.65	1,389.66	1,256.35	1,101.53	1,043.44	1,019.17	1,008.57	1,003.85
16.25%	2,646.04	1,833.83	1,500.35	1,400.71	1,268.06	1,114.63	1,057.53	1,033.91	1,023.70	1,019.21
16.50%	2,655.33	1,843.84	1,511.09	1,411.80	1,279.82	1,127.78	1,071.68	1,048.68	1,038.86	1,034.59
16.75%	2,664.63	1,853.88	1,521.87	1,422.93	1,291.63	1,140.99	1,085.86	1,063.50	1,054.05	1,049.98
17.00%	2,673.95	1,863.94	1,532.69	1,434.11	1,303.48	1,154.25	1,100.10	1,078.35	1,069.26	1,065.39
17.25%	2,683.30	1,874.04	1,543.54	1,445.33	1,315.39	1,167.57	1,114.38	1,093.23	1,084.49	1,080.82
17.50%	2,692.65	1,884.17	1,554.43	1,456.59	1,327.34	1,180.93	1,128.71	1,108.15	1,099.74	1,096.26
17.75%	2,702.03	1,894.32	1,565.37	1,467.89	1,339.34	1,194.35	1,143.07	1,123.09	1,115.02	1,111.71
18.00%	2,711.43	1,904.51	1,576.34	1,479.24	1,351.39	1,207.82	1,157.48	1,138.07	1,130.31	1,127.17
18.25%	2,720.84	1,914.72	1,587.35	1,490.63	1,363.48	1,221.33	1,171.93	1,153.08	1,145.63	1,142.64
18.50%	2,730.28	1,924.97	1,598.39	1,502.06	1,375.62	1,234.89	1,186.42	1,168.11	1,160.96	1,158.13
18.75%	2,739.73	1,935.24	1,609.48	1,513.53	1,387.81	1,248.50	1,200.95	1,183.17	1,176.31	1,173.62
19.00%	2,749.20	1,945.54	1,620.60	1,525.04	1,400.04	1,262.16	1,215.51	1,198.26	1,191.67	1,189.12
19.25%	2,758.69	1,955.87	1,631.76	1,536.59	1,412.32	1,275.86	1,230.11	1,213.37	1,207.05	1,204.63
19.50%	2,768.20	1,966.23	1,642.96	1,548.18	1,424.64	1,289.60	1,244.75	1,228.50	1,222.44	1,220.15
19.75%	2,777.72	1,976.62	1,654.19	1,559.82	1,437.01	1,303.39	1,259.42	1,243.66	1,237.85	1,235.68
20.00%	2,787.27	1,987.04	1,665.46	1,571.49	1,449.42	1,317.22	1,274.12	1,258.84	1,253.26	1,251.21
20.25%	2,796.83	1,997.49	1,676.77	1,583.20	1,461.87	1,331.10	1,288.85	1,274.04	1,268.69	1,266.75
20.50%	2,806.41	2,007.96	1,688.12	1,594.95	1,474.37	1,345.01	1,303.62	1,289.26	1,284.14	1,282.29
20.75%	2,816.01	2,018.47	1,699.50	1,606.75	1,486.91	1,358.96	1,318.41	1,304.49	1,299.59	1,297.84

$77,500 1.00 - 10.75% 3 - 35 Years

	3	5	7	8	10	15	20	25	30	35
1.00%	2,186.13	1,324.77	955.67	840.35	678.93	463.83	356.42	292.08	249.27	218.77
1.25%	2,194.52	1,333.12	964.05	848.75	687.37	472.40	365.13	300.93	258.27	227.92
1.50%	2,202.92	1,341.52	972.48	857.20	695.88	481.08	373.97	309.95	267.47	237.29
1.75%	2,211.35	1,349.94	980.95	865.71	704.46	489.85	382.95	319.14	276.86	246.90
2.00%	2,219.80	1,358.40	989.48	874.27	713.10	498.72	392.06	328.49	286.46	256.73
2.25%	2,228.27	1,366.89	998.04	882.88	721.81	507.69	401.30	338.00	296.24	266.78
2.50%	2,236.76	1,375.42	1,006.66	891.55	730.59	516.76	410.67	347.68	306.22	277.06
2.75%	2,245.27	1,383.98	1,015.32	900.27	739.44	525.93	420.18	357.52	316.39	287.55
3.00%	2,253.79	1,392.57	1,024.03	909.04	748.35	535.20	429.81	367.51	326.74	298.26
3.25%	2,262.34	1,401.20	1,032.79	917.87	757.32	544.57	439.58	377.67	337.28	309.18
3.50%	2,270.91	1,409.86	1,041.59	926.75	766.37	554.03	449.47	387.98	348.01	320.30
3.75%	2,279.50	1,418.55	1,050.44	935.68	775.47	563.60	459.49	398.45	358.91	331.63
4.00%	2,288.11	1,427.28	1,059.33	944.67	784.65	573.26	469.63	409.07	370.00	343.15
4.25%	2,296.74	1,436.04	1,068.27	953.71	793.89	583.02	479.91	419.85	381.25	354.87
4.50%	2,305.39	1,444.83	1,077.26	962.80	803.20	592.87	490.30	430.77	392.68	366.77
4.75%	2,314.06	1,453.66	1,086.30	971.95	812.57	602.82	500.82	441.84	404.28	378.86
5.00%	2,322.74	1,462.52	1,095.38	981.14	822.01	612.87	511.47	453.06	416.04	391.13
5.25%	2,331.45	1,471.41	1,104.51	990.39	831.51	623.01	522.23	464.42	427.96	403.58
5.50%	2,340.18	1,480.34	1,113.68	999.70	841.08	633.24	533.11	475.92	440.04	416.19
5.75%	2,348.93	1,489.30	1,122.90	1,009.05	850.71	643.57	544.11	487.56	452.27	428.96
6.00%	2,357.70	1,498.29	1,132.16	1,018.46	860.41	653.99	555.23	499.33	464.65	441.90
6.25%	2,366.49	1,507.32	1,141.47	1,027.92	870.17	664.50	566.47	511.24	477.18	454.98
6.50%	2,375.30	1,516.38	1,150.83	1,037.43	880.00	675.11	577.82	523.29	489.85	468.22
6.75%	2,384.13	1,525.47	1,160.23	1,047.00	889.89	685.80	589.28	535.46	502.66	481.60
7.00%	2,392.98	1,534.59	1,169.68	1,056.61	899.84	696.59	600.86	547.75	515.61	495.11
7.25%	2,401.84	1,543.75	1,179.18	1,066.28	909.86	707.47	612.54	560.18	528.69	508.76
7.50%	2,410.73	1,552.94	1,188.72	1,076.00	919.94	718.43	624.33	572.72	541.89	522.54
7.75%	2,419.64	1,562.16	1,198.30	1,085.77	930.08	729.49	636.24	585.38	555.22	536.44
8.00%	2,428.57	1,571.42	1,207.93	1,095.59	940.29	740.63	648.24	598.16	568.67	550.45
8.25%	2,437.52	1,580.71	1,217.61	1,105.47	950.56	751.86	660.35	611.05	582.23	564.58
8.50%	2,446.48	1,590.03	1,227.33	1,115.39	960.89	763.17	672.56	624.05	595.91	578.82
8.75%	2,455.47	1,599.39	1,237.09	1,125.37	971.28	774.57	684.88	637.16	609.69	593.16
9.00%	2,464.48	1,608.77	1,246.90	1,135.39	981.74	786.06	697.29	650.38	623.58	607.59
9.25%	2,473.51	1,618.19	1,256.76	1,145.47	992.25	797.62	709.80	663.70	637.57	622.13
9.50%	2,482.55	1,627.64	1,266.66	1,155.59	1,002.83	809.27	722.40	677.11	651.66	636.75
9.75%	2,491.62	1,637.13	1,276.60	1,165.77	1,013.47	821.01	735.10	690.63	665.84	651.46
10.00%	2,500.71	1,646.65	1,286.59	1,176.00	1,024.17	832.82	747.89	704.24	680.12	666.25
10.25%	2,509.81	1,656.20	1,296.62	1,186.27	1,034.93	844.71	760.77	717.95	694.48	681.11
10.50%	2,518.94	1,665.78	1,306.70	1,196.60	1,045.75	856.68	773.74	731.74	708.92	696.05
10.75%	2,528.09	1,675.39	1,316.82	1,206.98	1,056.62	868.73	786.80	745.62	723.45	711.06

	3	5	7	8	10	15	20	25	30	35
11.00%	2,537.25	1,685.04	1,326.99	1,217.40	1,067.56	880.86	799.95	759.59	738.05	726.14
11.25%	2,546.44	1,694.72	1,337.20	1,227.88	1,078.56	893.07	813.17	773.64	752.73	741.28
11.50%	2,555.64	1,704.43	1,347.45	1,238.40	1,089.61	905.35	826.48	787.76	767.48	756.48
11.75%	2,564.86	1,714.17	1,357.75	1,248.97	1,100.73	917.70	839.87	801.97	782.29	771.74
12.00%	2,574.11	1,723.94	1,368.09	1,259.60	1,111.90	930.13	853.34	816.25	797.17	787.05
12.25%	2,583.37	1,733.75	1,378.47	1,270.26	1,123.13	942.63	866.89	830.60	812.12	802.41
12.50%	2,592.66	1,743.59	1,388.90	1,280.98	1,134.42	955.20	880.51	845.02	827.12	817.82
12.75%	2,601.96	1,753.46	1,399.37	1,291.75	1,145.76	967.85	894.20	859.52	842.19	833.28
13.00%	2,611.28	1,763.36	1,409.88	1,302.56	1,157.16	980.56	907.97	874.07	857.30	848.77
13.25%	2,620.62	1,773.30	1,420.43	1,313.42	1,168.61	993.35	921.81	888.69	872.47	864.31
13.50%	2,629.98	1,783.26	1,431.03	1,324.33	1,180.13	1,006.20	935.72	903.37	887.69	879.89
13.75%	2,639.37	1,793.26	1,441.67	1,335.29	1,191.69	1,019.12	949.69	918.12	902.96	895.50
14.00%	2,648.77	1,803.29	1,452.35	1,346.29	1,203.31	1,032.10	963.73	932.91	918.28	911.15
14.25%	2,658.19	1,813.35	1,463.08	1,357.34	1,214.99	1,045.15	977.83	947.77	933.63	926.82
14.50%	2,667.63	1,823.44	1,473.84	1,368.44	1,226.72	1,058.26	992.00	962.68	949.03	942.53
14.75%	2,677.08	1,833.57	1,484.65	1,379.58	1,238.51	1,071.44	1,006.23	977.64	964.47	958.27
15.00%	2,686.56	1,843.72	1,495.50	1,390.77	1,250.35	1,084.68	1,020.51	992.64	979.94	974.03
15.25%	2,696.06	1,853.91	1,506.39	1,402.00	1,262.24	1,097.98	1,034.86	1,007.70	995.46	989.82
15.50%	2,705.58	1,864.12	1,517.32	1,413.28	1,274.18	1,111.34	1,049.26	1,022.80	1,011.00	1,005.63
15.75%	2,715.11	1,874.37	1,528.30	1,424.61	1,286.18	1,124.76	1,063.71	1,037.95	1,026.58	1,021.46
16.00%	2,724.67	1,884.65	1,539.31	1,435.98	1,298.23	1,138.24	1,078.22	1,053.14	1,042.19	1,037.31
16.25%	2,734.25	1,894.96	1,550.37	1,447.40	1,310.33	1,151.78	1,092.79	1,068.37	1,057.82	1,053.19
16.50%	2,743.84	1,905.30	1,561.46	1,458.86	1,322.48	1,165.37	1,107.40	1,083.64	1,073.49	1,069.08
16.75%	2,753.45	1,915.67	1,572.60	1,470.36	1,334.68	1,179.02	1,122.06	1,098.95	1,089.18	1,084.98
17.00%	2,763.09	1,926.07	1,583.77	1,481.91	1,346.93	1,192.73	1,136.77	1,114.29	1,104.90	1,100.91
17.25%	2,772.74	1,936.51	1,594.99	1,493.51	1,359.23	1,206.49	1,151.53	1,129.67	1,120.64	1,116.85
17.50%	2,782.41	1,946.97	1,606.25	1,505.14	1,371.59	1,220.30	1,166.33	1,145.09	1,136.40	1,132.80
17.75%	2,792.10	1,957.47	1,617.55	1,516.82	1,383.99	1,234.16	1,181.18	1,160.53	1,152.19	1,148.76
18.00%	2,801.81	1,967.99	1,628.88	1,528.55	1,396.44	1,248.08	1,196.07	1,176.01	1,167.99	1,164.74
18.25%	2,811.54	1,978.55	1,640.26	1,540.32	1,408.93	1,262.04	1,211.00	1,191.51	1,183.82	1,180.73
18.50%	2,821.29	1,989.13	1,651.67	1,552.13	1,421.48	1,276.06	1,225.97	1,207.05	1,199.66	1,196.73
18.75%	2,831.06	1,999.75	1,663.13	1,563.98	1,434.07	1,290.12	1,240.98	1,222.61	1,215.52	1,212.74
19.00%	2,840.84	2,010.39	1,674.62	1,575.87	1,446.71	1,304.23	1,256.03	1,238.20	1,231.39	1,228.76
19.25%	2,850.65	2,021.07	1,686.15	1,587.81	1,459.40	1,318.39	1,271.12	1,253.82	1,247.28	1,244.79
19.50%	2,860.47	2,031.77	1,697.72	1,599.79	1,472.13	1,332.59	1,286.24	1,269.45	1,263.19	1,260.82
19.75%	2,870.32	2,042.51	1,709.33	1,611.81	1,484.91	1,346.84	1,301.40	1,285.12	1,279.11	1,276.87
20.00%	2,880.18	2,053.28	1,720.98	1,623.87	1,497.73	1,361.13	1,316.59	1,300.80	1,295.04	1,292.92
20.25%	2,890.06	2,064.07	1,732.67	1,635.98	1,510.60	1,375.47	1,331.81	1,316.51	1,310.98	1,308.97
20.50%	2,899.96	2,074.90	1,744.39	1,648.12	1,523.51	1,389.84	1,347.07	1,332.23	1,326.94	1,325.04
20.75%	2,909.88	2,085.75	1,756.15	1,660.30	1,536.47	1,404.26	1,362.36	1,347.98	1,342.91	1,341.10

	3	5	7	8	10	15	20	25	30	35
1.00%	2,256.65	1,367.50	986.50	867.46	700.83	478.80	367.92	301.50	257.31	225.83
1.25%	2,265.31	1,376.13	995.15	876.13	709.55	487.64	376.91	310.64	266.60	235.27
1.50%	2,273.99	1,384.79	1,003.85	884.85	718.33	496.59	386.04	319.95	276.10	244.95
1.75%	2,282.69	1,393.49	1,012.60	893.63	727.19	505.65	395.30	329.43	285.79	254.86
2.00%	2,291.41	1,402.22	1,021.39	902.47	736.11	514.81	404.71	339.08	295.70	265.01
2.25%	2,300.15	1,410.99	1,030.24	911.36	745.10	524.07	414.25	348.90	305.80	275.39
2.50%	2,308.91	1,419.79	1,039.13	920.31	754.16	533.43	423.92	358.89	316.10	286.00
2.75%	2,317.69	1,428.62	1,048.07	929.31	763.29	542.90	433.73	369.05	326.59	296.83
3.00%	2,326.50	1,437.50	1,057.06	938.37	772.49	552.47	443.68	379.37	337.28	307.88
3.25%	2,335.32	1,446.40	1,066.10	947.48	781.75	562.14	453.76	389.85	348.17	319.15
3.50%	2,344.17	1,455.34	1,075.19	956.64	791.09	571.91	463.97	400.50	359.24	330.63
3.75%	2,353.03	1,464.31	1,084.32	965.87	800.49	581.78	474.31	411.30	370.49	342.32
4.00%	2,361.92	1,473.32	1,093.50	975.14	809.96	591.75	484.78	422.27	381.93	354.22
4.25%	2,370.83	1,482.36	1,102.73	984.47	819.50	601.82	495.39	433.39	393.55	366.32
4.50%	2,379.75	1,491.44	1,112.01	993.86	829.11	611.99	506.12	444.67	405.35	378.61
4.75%	2,388.70	1,500.55	1,121.34	1,003.30	838.78	622.27	516.98	456.09	417.32	391.09
5.00%	2,397.67	1,509.70	1,130.71	1,012.79	848.52	632.63	527.96	467.67	429.46	403.75
5.25%	2,406.66	1,518.88	1,140.13	1,022.34	858.33	643.10	539.08	479.40	441.76	416.59
5.50%	2,415.67	1,528.09	1,149.60	1,031.95	868.21	653.67	550.31	491.27	454.23	429.61
5.75%	2,424.70	1,537.34	1,159.12	1,041.60	878.15	664.33	561.67	503.29	466.86	442.80
6.00%	2,433.75	1,546.62	1,168.68	1,051.31	888.16	675.09	573.14	515.44	479.64	456.15
6.25%	2,442.83	1,555.94	1,178.30	1,061.08	898.24	685.94	584.74	527.74	492.57	469.66
6.50%	2,451.92	1,565.29	1,187.95	1,070.90	908.38	696.89	596.46	540.17	505.65	483.32
6.75%	2,461.03	1,574.68	1,197.66	1,080.77	918.59	707.93	608.29	552.73	518.88	497.13
7.00%	2,470.17	1,584.10	1,207.41	1,090.70	928.87	719.06	620.24	565.42	532.24	511.09
7.25%	2,479.32	1,593.55	1,217.21	1,100.68	939.21	730.29	632.30	578.25	545.74	525.17
7.50%	2,488.50	1,603.04	1,227.06	1,110.71	949.61	741.61	644.47	591.19	559.37	539.39
7.75%	2,497.69	1,612.56	1,236.96	1,120.80	960.09	753.02	656.76	604.26	573.13	553.74
8.00%	2,506.91	1,622.11	1,246.90	1,130.93	970.62	764.52	669.15	617.45	587.01	568.21
8.25%	2,516.15	1,631.70	1,256.88	1,141.13	981.22	776.11	681.65	630.76	601.01	582.79
8.50%	2,525.40	1,641.32	1,266.92	1,151.37	991.89	787.79	694.26	644.18	615.13	597.49
8.75%	2,534.68	1,650.98	1,277.00	1,161.67	1,002.61	799.56	706.97	657.71	629.36	612.29
9.00%	2,543.98	1,660.67	1,287.13	1,172.02	1,013.41	811.41	719.78	671.36	643.70	627.19
9.25%	2,553.30	1,670.39	1,297.30	1,182.42	1,024.26	823.35	732.69	685.11	658.14	642.20
9.50%	2,562.64	1,680.15	1,307.52	1,192.87	1,035.18	835.38	745.70	698.96	672.68	657.29
9.75%	2,572.00	1,689.94	1,317.78	1,203.38	1,046.16	847.49	758.81	712.91	687.32	672.47
10.00%	2,581.37	1,699.76	1,328.09	1,213.93	1,057.21	859.68	772.02	726.96	702.06	687.74
10.25%	2,590.78	1,709.62	1,338.45	1,224.54	1,068.31	871.96	785.31	741.11	716.88	703.08
10.50%	2,600.20	1,719.51	1,348.85	1,235.20	1,079.48	884.32	798.70	755.35	731.79	718.51
10.75%	2,609.64	1,729.44	1,359.30	1,245.91	1,090.71	896.76	812.18	769.67	746.79	734.00

	3	5	7	8	10	15	20	25	30	35
11.00%	2,619.10	1,739.39	1,369.79	1,256.67	1,102.00	909.28	825.75	784.09	761.86	749.57
11.25%	2,628.58	1,749.38	1,380.33	1,267.49	1,113.35	921.88	839.40	798.59	777.01	765.20
11.50%	2,638.08	1,759.41	1,390.92	1,278.35	1,124.76	934.55	853.14	813.18	792.23	780.89
11.75%	2,647.60	1,769.47	1,401.55	1,289.26	1,136.24	947.31	866.97	827.84	807.53	796.64
12.00%	2,657.14	1,779.56	1,412.22	1,300.23	1,147.77	960.13	880.87	842.58	822.89	812.44
12.25%	2,666.71	1,789.68	1,422.94	1,311.24	1,159.36	973.04	894.85	857.40	838.32	828.30
12.50%	2,676.29	1,799.84	1,433.70	1,322.30	1,171.01	986.02	908.91	872.28	853.81	844.20
12.75%	2,685.89	1,810.02	1,444.51	1,333.42	1,182.72	999.07	923.05	887.24	869.35	860.16
13.00%	2,695.52	1,820.25	1,455.36	1,344.58	1,194.49	1,012.19	937.26	902.27	884.96	876.15
13.25%	2,705.16	1,830.50	1,466.25	1,355.79	1,206.31	1,025.39	951.54	917.36	900.62	892.19
13.50%	2,714.82	1,840.79	1,477.19	1,367.05	1,218.19	1,038.65	965.90	932.52	916.33	908.27
13.75%	2,724.51	1,851.11	1,488.17	1,378.36	1,230.13	1,051.99	980.32	947.73	932.09	924.39
14.00%	2,734.21	1,861.46	1,499.20	1,389.72	1,242.13	1,065.39	994.82	963.01	947.90	940.54
14.25%	2,743.93	1,871.85	1,510.27	1,401.13	1,254.18	1,078.86	1,009.38	978.34	963.75	956.72
14.50%	2,753.68	1,882.26	1,521.38	1,412.58	1,266.29	1,092.40	1,024.00	993.73	979.64	972.94
14.75%	2,763.44	1,892.71	1,532.54	1,424.08	1,278.46	1,106.00	1,038.68	1,009.17	995.58	989.18
15.00%	2,773.23	1,903.19	1,543.74	1,435.63	1,290.68	1,119.67	1,053.43	1,024.66	1,011.56	1,005.45
15.25%	2,783.03	1,913.71	1,554.98	1,447.23	1,302.95	1,133.40	1,068.24	1,040.21	1,027.57	1,021.75
15.50%	2,792.85	1,924.26	1,566.27	1,458.87	1,315.28	1,147.19	1,083.10	1,055.80	1,043.61	1,038.07
15.75%	2,802.70	1,934.83	1,577.60	1,470.57	1,327.67	1,161.05	1,098.03	1,071.43	1,059.69	1,054.41
16.00%	2,812.56	1,945.44	1,588.97	1,482.30	1,340.10	1,174.96	1,113.00	1,087.11	1,075.81	1,070.78
16.25%	2,822.45	1,956.09	1,600.38	1,494.09	1,352.60	1,188.93	1,128.04	1,102.83	1,091.95	1,087.16
16.50%	2,832.35	1,966.76	1,611.83	1,505.92	1,365.14	1,202.97	1,143.12	1,118.60	1,108.12	1,103.56
16.75%	2,842.27	1,977.47	1,623.33	1,517.79	1,377.73	1,217.06	1,158.26	1,134.40	1,124.32	1,119.98
17.00%	2,852.22	1,988.21	1,634.86	1,529.72	1,390.38	1,231.20	1,173.44	1,150.24	1,140.54	1,136.42
17.25%	2,862.18	1,998.98	1,646.44	1,541.68	1,403.08	1,245.41	1,188.67	1,166.11	1,156.79	1,152.87
17.50%	2,872.17	2,009.78	1,658.06	1,553.70	1,415.83	1,259.66	1,203.95	1,182.02	1,173.06	1,169.34
17.75%	2,882.17	2,020.61	1,669.72	1,565.75	1,428.63	1,273.97	1,219.28	1,197.97	1,189.35	1,185.82
18.00%	2,892.19	2,031.47	1,681.43	1,577.86	1,441.48	1,288.34	1,234.65	1,213.94	1,205.67	1,202.31
18.25%	2,902.23	2,042.37	1,693.17	1,590.00	1,454.38	1,302.75	1,250.06	1,229.95	1,222.00	1,218.82
18.50%	2,912.30	2,053.30	1,704.95	1,602.20	1,467.33	1,317.22	1,265.52	1,245.99	1,238.36	1,235.33
18.75%	2,922.38	2,064.25	1,716.78	1,614.43	1,480.33	1,331.74	1,281.01	1,262.05	1,254.73	1,251.86
19.00%	2,932.48	2,075.24	1,728.64	1,626.71	1,493.38	1,346.30	1,296.55	1,278.14	1,271.11	1,268.40
19.25%	2,942.60	2,086.26	1,740.55	1,639.03	1,506.47	1,360.91	1,312.12	1,294.26	1,287.52	1,284.94
19.50%	2,952.74	2,097.32	1,752.49	1,651.40	1,519.62	1,375.58	1,327.73	1,310.40	1,303.94	1,301.49
19.75%	2,962.91	2,108.40	1,764.47	1,663.81	1,532.81	1,390.28	1,343.38	1,326.57	1,320.37	1,318.05
20.00%	2,973.09	2,119.51	1,776.50	1,676.26	1,546.05	1,405.04	1,359.06	1,342.76	1,336.81	1,334.62
20.25%	2,983.29	2,130.65	1,788.56	1,688.75	1,559.33	1,419.84	1,374.78	1,358.97	1,353.27	1,351.20
20.50%	2,993.51	2,141.83	1,800.66	1,701.28	1,572.66	1,434.68	1,390.52	1,375.21	1,369.74	1,367.78
20.75%	3,003.75	2,153.03	1,812.80	1,713.86	1,586.03	1,449.56	1,406.30	1,391.46	1,386.23	1,384.37

	3	5	7	8	10	15	20	25	30	35
1.00%	2,327.17	1,410.23	1,017.33	894.57	722.73	493.76	379.41	310.92	265.35	232.89
1.25%	2,336.10	1,419.13	1,026.25	903.51	731.72	502.88	388.69	320.35	274.93	242.62
1.50%	2,345.05	1,428.07	1,035.22	912.50	740.78	512.11	398.10	329.95	284.72	252.60
1.75%	2,354.02	1,437.04	1,044.24	921.56	749.91	521.45	407.66	339.73	294.73	262.83
2.00%	2,363.01	1,446.04	1,053.31	930.67	759.11	530.89	417.35	349.68	304.94	273.29
2.25%	2,372.03	1,455.08	1,062.43	939.84	768.38	540.44	427.19	359.81	315.35	284.00
2.50%	2,381.06	1,464.16	1,071.61	949.07	777.73	550.10	437.17	370.11	325.97	294.93
2.75%	2,390.12	1,473.27	1,080.83	958.35	787.14	559.86	447.29	380.58	336.80	306.10
3.00%	2,399.20	1,482.42	1,090.10	967.69	796.63	569.73	457.54	391.22	347.82	317.50
3.25%	2,408.30	1,491.60	1,099.42	977.09	806.18	579.70	467.94	402.04	359.05	329.12
3.50%	2,417.42	1,500.82	1,108.79	986.54	815.81	589.78	478.47	413.01	370.46	340.96
3.75%	2,426.56	1,510.07	1,118.21	996.05	825.51	599.96	489.13	424.16	382.07	353.02
4.00%	2,435.73	1,519.36	1,127.68	1,005.62	835.27	610.24	499.93	435.47	393.87	365.29
4.25%	2,444.91	1,528.69	1,137.20	1,015.24	845.11	620.63	510.87	446.93	405.85	377.76
4.50%	2,454.12	1,538.05	1,146.76	1,024.92	855.02	631.12	521.94	458.56	418.02	390.44
4.75%	2,463.35	1,547.45	1,156.38	1,034.65	864.99	641.71	533.13	470.35	430.36	403.31
5.00%	2,472.60	1,556.88	1,166.05	1,044.44	875.04	652.40	544.46	482.29	442.88	416.37
5.25%	2,481.87	1,566.34	1,175.76	1,054.29	885.16	663.20	555.92	494.38	455.57	429.61
5.50%	2,491.16	1,575.85	1,185.53	1,064.19	895.34	674.09	567.51	506.62	468.43	443.04
5.75%	2,500.48	1,585.38	1,195.34	1,074.15	905.60	685.09	579.22	519.01	481.45	456.64
6.00%	2,509.81	1,594.96	1,205.21	1,084.17	915.92	696.18	591.06	531.55	494.63	470.41
6.25%	2,519.17	1,604.56	1,215.12	1,094.24	926.31	707.37	603.02	544.23	507.97	484.34
6.50%	2,528.54	1,614.21	1,225.08	1,104.36	936.77	718.66	615.10	557.05	521.46	498.43
6.75%	2,537.94	1,623.89	1,235.09	1,114.55	947.30	730.05	627.30	570.00	535.09	512.67
7.00%	2,547.36	1,633.60	1,245.15	1,124.78	957.89	741.53	639.62	583.09	548.87	527.06
7.25%	2,556.80	1,643.35	1,255.25	1,135.07	968.56	753.11	652.06	596.32	562.80	541.59
7.50%	2,566.26	1,653.13	1,265.41	1,145.42	979.29	764.79	664.61	609.67	576.85	556.25
7.75%	2,575.75	1,662.95	1,275.61	1,155.82	990.09	776.55	677.28	623.15	591.04	571.05
8.00%	2,585.25	1,672.80	1,285.86	1,166.28	1,000.95	788.41	690.06	636.75	605.36	585.97
8.25%	2,594.78	1,682.69	1,296.16	1,176.79	1,011.88	800.37	702.95	650.47	619.79	601.01
8.50%	2,604.32	1,692.61	1,306.51	1,187.35	1,022.88	812.41	715.95	664.31	634.35	616.16
8.75%	2,613.89	1,702.57	1,316.91	1,197.97	1,033.95	824.55	729.06	678.27	649.03	631.42
9.00%	2,623.48	1,712.56	1,327.35	1,208.64	1,045.08	836.77	742.27	692.34	663.81	646.79
9.25%	2,633.09	1,722.59	1,337.84	1,219.37	1,056.27	849.08	755.59	706.52	678.71	662.26
9.50%	2,642.72	1,732.65	1,348.38	1,230.15	1,067.53	861.49	769.01	720.80	693.70	677.83
9.75%	2,652.37	1,742.75	1,358.96	1,240.98	1,078.85	873.97	782.53	735.19	708.80	693.49
10.00%	2,662.04	1,752.88	1,369.60	1,251.87	1,090.24	886.55	796.14	749.68	724.00	709.23
10.25%	2,671.74	1,763.05	1,380.28	1,262.81	1,101.70	899.21	809.86	764.27	739.28	725.06
10.50%	2,681.45	1,773.25	1,391.01	1,273.80	1,113.21	911.95	823.66	778.95	754.66	740.96
10.75%	2,691.19	1,783.48	1,401.78	1,284.85	1,124.79	924.78	837.56	793.73	770.12	756.94

$82,500   11.00 - 20.75%   3 - 35 Years

	3	5	7	8	10	15	20	25	30	35
11.00%	2,700.94	1,793.75	1,412.60	1,295.95	1,136.44	937.69	851.56	808.59	785.67	772.99
11.25%	2,710.72	1,804.05	1,423.47	1,307.10	1,148.14	950.68	865.64	823.55	801.29	789.11
11.50%	2,720.52	1,814.39	1,434.38	1,318.30	1,159.91	963.76	879.80	838.59	816.99	805.29
11.75%	2,730.34	1,824.76	1,445.34	1,329.55	1,171.74	976.91	894.06	853.71	832.76	821.53
12.00%	2,740.18	1,835.17	1,456.35	1,340.86	1,183.64	990.14	908.40	868.91	848.61	837.83
12.25%	2,750.04	1,845.61	1,467.40	1,352.22	1,195.59	1,003.45	922.82	884.19	864.51	854.18
12.50%	2,759.92	1,856.08	1,478.50	1,363.63	1,207.60	1,016.83	937.32	899.54	880.49	870.58
12.75%	2,769.83	1,866.59	1,489.65	1,375.09	1,219.68	1,030.29	951.89	914.97	896.52	887.04
13.00%	2,779.75	1,877.13	1,500.84	1,386.60	1,231.81	1,043.82	966.55	930.46	912.61	903.53
13.25%	2,789.70	1,887.70	1,512.07	1,398.16	1,244.01	1,057.43	981.28	946.03	928.76	920.07
13.50%	2,799.66	1,898.31	1,523.35	1,409.77	1,256.26	1,071.11	996.08	961.66	944.97	936.66
13.75%	2,809.65	1,908.95	1,534.68	1,421.44	1,268.58	1,084.86	1,010.96	977.35	961.22	953.28
14.00%	2,819.65	1,919.63	1,546.05	1,433.15	1,280.95	1,098.69	1,025.90	993.10	977.52	969.93
14.25%	2,829.68	1,930.34	1,557.47	1,444.91	1,293.38	1,112.58	1,040.92	1,008.92	993.87	986.62
14.50%	2,839.73	1,941.08	1,568.93	1,456.72	1,305.87	1,126.54	1,056.00	1,024.78	1,010.26	1,003.34
14.75%	2,849.80	1,951.86	1,580.43	1,468.59	1,318.41	1,140.57	1,071.14	1,040.71	1,026.69	1,020.09
15.00%	2,859.89	1,962.67	1,591.98	1,480.50	1,331.01	1,154.66	1,086.35	1,056.69	1,043.17	1,036.87
15.25%	2,870.00	1,973.51	1,603.58	1,492.46	1,343.67	1,168.82	1,101.62	1,072.71	1,059.68	1,053.68
15.50%	2,880.13	1,984.39	1,615.21	1,504.46	1,356.39	1,183.04	1,116.95	1,088.79	1,076.23	1,070.51
15.75%	2,890.28	1,995.30	1,626.90	1,516.52	1,369.16	1,197.33	1,132.34	1,104.91	1,092.81	1,087.36
16.00%	2,900.46	2,006.24	1,638.62	1,528.62	1,381.98	1,211.68	1,147.79	1,121.08	1,109.42	1,104.24
16.25%	2,910.65	2,017.21	1,650.39	1,540.78	1,394.86	1,226.09	1,163.29	1,137.30	1,126.07	1,121.13
16.50%	2,920.86	2,028.22	1,662.20	1,552.98	1,407.80	1,240.56	1,178.84	1,153.55	1,142.75	1,138.05
16.75%	2,931.10	2,039.26	1,674.06	1,565.23	1,420.79	1,255.09	1,194.45	1,169.85	1,159.45	1,154.98
17.00%	2,941.35	2,050.34	1,685.95	1,577.52	1,433.83	1,269.68	1,210.11	1,186.18	1,176.18	1,171.93
17.25%	2,951.62	2,061.44	1,697.89	1,589.86	1,446.93	1,284.32	1,225.82	1,202.55	1,192.94	1,188.90
17.50%	2,961.92	2,072.58	1,709.88	1,602.25	1,460.07	1,299.03	1,241.58	1,218.96	1,209.72	1,205.88
17.75%	2,972.24	2,083.75	1,721.90	1,614.68	1,473.28	1,313.78	1,257.38	1,235.40	1,226.52	1,222.88
18.00%	2,982.57	2,094.96	1,733.97	1,627.17	1,486.53	1,328.60	1,273.23	1,251.88	1,243.35	1,239.89
18.25%	2,992.93	2,106.19	1,746.08	1,639.69	1,499.83	1,343.46	1,289.13	1,268.39	1,260.19	1,256.91
18.50%	3,003.31	2,117.46	1,758.23	1,652.26	1,513.19	1,358.38	1,305.06	1,284.92	1,277.05	1,273.94
18.75%	3,013.70	2,128.76	1,770.43	1,664.88	1,526.59	1,373.35	1,321.04	1,301.49	1,293.94	1,290.98
19.00%	3,024.12	2,140.10	1,782.66	1,677.54	1,540.05	1,388.37	1,337.07	1,318.09	1,310.84	1,308.03
19.25%	3,034.56	2,151.46	1,794.94	1,690.25	1,553.55	1,403.44	1,353.12	1,334.71	1,327.75	1,325.09
19.50%	3,045.02	2,162.86	1,807.25	1,703.00	1,567.11	1,418.56	1,369.22	1,351.36	1,344.68	1,342.17
19.75%	3,055.50	2,174.29	1,819.61	1,715.80	1,580.71	1,433.73	1,385.36	1,368.03	1,361.63	1,359.24
20.00%	3,066.00	2,185.75	1,832.01	1,728.64	1,594.36	1,448.94	1,401.53	1,384.72	1,378.59	1,376.33
20.25%	3,076.51	2,197.24	1,844.45	1,741.52	1,608.06	1,464.21	1,417.74	1,401.44	1,395.56	1,393.42
20.50%	3,087.05	2,208.76	1,856.93	1,754.45	1,621.80	1,479.51	1,433.98	1,418.18	1,412.55	1,410.52
20.75%	3,097.61	2,220.32	1,869.45	1,767.42	1,635.60	1,494.86	1,450.25	1,434.94	1,429.55	1,427.63

	3	5	7	8	10	15	20	25	30	35
1.00%	2,397.69	1,452.97	1,048.16	921.67	744.64	508.72	390.91	320.34	273.39	239.94
1.25%	2,406.89	1,462.14	1,057.35	930.89	753.89	518.12	400.46	330.05	283.26	249.97
1.50%	2,416.11	1,471.34	1,066.59	940.16	763.23	527.63	410.16	339.95	293.35	260.26
1.75%	2,425.35	1,480.58	1,075.89	949.49	772.63	537.25	420.01	350.02	303.66	270.79
2.00%	2,434.62	1,489.86	1,085.23	958.87	782.11	546.98	430.00	360.28	314.18	281.57
2.25%	2,443.91	1,499.17	1,094.63	968.32	791.67	556.82	440.14	370.71	324.91	292.60
2.50%	2,453.22	1,508.53	1,104.08	977.83	801.29	566.77	450.42	381.32	335.85	303.87
2.75%	2,462.55	1,517.91	1,113.58	987.39	810.99	576.83	460.84	392.11	347.01	315.38
3.00%	2,471.90	1,527.34	1,123.13	997.01	820.77	586.99	471.41	403.08	358.36	327.12
3.25%	2,481.28	1,536.80	1,132.73	1,006.69	830.61	597.27	482.12	414.22	369.93	339.10
3.50%	2,490.68	1,546.30	1,142.39	1,016.43	840.53	607.65	492.97	425.53	381.69	351.30
3.75%	2,500.10	1,555.83	1,152.09	1,026.23	850.52	618.14	503.96	437.01	393.65	363.72
4.00%	2,509.54	1,565.40	1,161.85	1,036.09	860.58	628.73	515.08	448.66	405.80	376.36
4.25%	2,519.00	1,575.01	1,171.66	1,046.00	870.72	639.44	526.35	460.48	418.15	389.21
4.50%	2,528.49	1,584.66	1,181.51	1,055.97	880.93	650.24	537.75	472.46	430.68	402.27
4.75%	2,538.00	1,594.34	1,191.42	1,066.01	891.21	661.16	549.29	484.60	443.40	415.53
5.00%	2,547.53	1,604.05	1,201.38	1,076.09	901.56	672.17	560.96	496.90	456.30	428.98
5.25%	2,557.08	1,613.81	1,211.39	1,086.24	911.98	683.30	572.77	509.36	469.37	442.63
5.50%	2,566.65	1,623.60	1,221.45	1,096.44	922.47	694.52	584.70	521.97	482.62	456.46
5.75%	2,576.25	1,633.43	1,231.57	1,106.70	933.04	705.85	596.77	534.74	496.04	470.48
6.00%	2,585.86	1,643.29	1,241.73	1,117.02	943.67	717.28	608.97	547.66	509.62	484.66
6.25%	2,595.50	1,653.19	1,251.94	1,127.40	954.38	728.81	621.29	560.72	523.36	499.02
6.50%	2,605.17	1,663.12	1,262.20	1,137.83	965.16	740.44	633.74	573.93	537.26	513.53
6.75%	2,614.85	1,673.09	1,272.51	1,148.32	976.00	752.17	646.31	587.27	551.31	528.20
7.00%	2,624.55	1,683.10	1,282.88	1,158.87	986.92	764.00	659.00	600.76	565.51	543.03
7.25%	2,634.28	1,693.15	1,293.29	1,169.47	997.91	775.93	671.82	614.39	579.85	558.00
7.50%	2,644.03	1,703.23	1,303.75	1,180.13	1,008.97	787.96	684.75	628.14	594.33	573.11
7.75%	2,653.80	1,713.34	1,314.27	1,190.85	1,020.09	800.08	697.81	642.03	608.95	588.35
8.00%	2,663.59	1,723.49	1,324.83	1,201.62	1,031.28	812.30	710.97	656.04	623.70	603.72
8.25%	2,673.40	1,733.68	1,335.44	1,212.45	1,042.55	824.62	724.26	670.18	638.58	619.22
8.50%	2,683.24	1,743.91	1,346.10	1,223.33	1,053.88	837.03	737.65	684.44	653.58	634.83
8.75%	2,693.10	1,754.16	1,356.81	1,234.27	1,065.28	849.53	751.15	698.82	668.70	650.56
9.00%	2,702.98	1,764.46	1,367.57	1,245.27	1,076.74	862.13	764.77	713.32	683.93	666.39
9.25%	2,712.88	1,774.79	1,378.38	1,256.32	1,088.28	874.81	778.49	727.92	699.27	682.33
9.50%	2,722.80	1,785.16	1,389.24	1,267.43	1,099.88	887.59	792.31	742.64	714.73	698.37
9.75%	2,732.74	1,795.56	1,400.15	1,278.59	1,111.55	900.46	806.24	757.47	730.28	714.50
10.00%	2,742.71	1,806.00	1,411.10	1,289.80	1,123.28	913.41	820.27	772.40	745.94	730.72
10.25%	2,752.70	1,816.47	1,422.10	1,301.08	1,135.08	926.46	834.40	787.43	761.69	747.03
10.50%	2,762.71	1,826.98	1,433.16	1,312.40	1,146.95	939.59	848.62	802.55	777.53	763.41
10.75%	2,772.74	1,837.53	1,444.26	1,323.78	1,158.88	952.81	862.94	817.78	793.46	779.88

$85,000   11.00 - 20.75%   3 - 35 Years

	3	5	7	8	10	15	20	25	30	35
11.00%	2,782.79	1,848.11	1,455.41	1,335.22	1,170.88	966.11	877.36	833.10	809.47	796.41
11.25%	2,792.86	1,858.72	1,466.60	1,346.70	1,182.94	979.49	891.87	848.50	825.57	813.02
11.50%	2,802.96	1,869.37	1,477.85	1,358.25	1,195.06	992.96	906.47	864.00	841.75	829.69
11.75%	2,813.08	1,880.06	1,489.14	1,369.84	1,207.25	1,006.51	921.15	879.58	858.00	846.42
12.00%	2,823.22	1,890.78	1,500.48	1,381.49	1,219.50	1,020.14	935.92	895.24	874.32	863.22
12.25%	2,833.38	1,901.53	1,511.87	1,393.19	1,231.82	1,033.85	950.78	910.98	890.71	880.07
12.50%	2,843.56	1,912.32	1,523.31	1,404.95	1,244.20	1,047.64	965.72	926.80	907.17	896.97
12.75%	2,853.76	1,923.15	1,534.79	1,416.76	1,256.64	1,061.51	980.74	942.69	923.69	913.92
13.00%	2,863.99	1,934.01	1,546.32	1,428.62	1,269.14	1,075.46	995.84	958.66	940.27	930.91
13.25%	2,874.23	1,944.91	1,557.89	1,440.53	1,281.71	1,089.48	1,011.02	974.70	956.91	947.96
13.50%	2,884.50	1,955.84	1,569.52	1,452.49	1,294.33	1,103.57	1,026.27	990.80	973.60	965.04
13.75%	2,894.79	1,966.80	1,581.19	1,464.51	1,307.02	1,117.74	1,041.59	1,006.97	990.35	982.16
14.00%	2,905.10	1,977.80	1,592.90	1,476.58	1,319.76	1,131.98	1,056.99	1,023.20	1,007.14	999.32
14.25%	2,915.43	1,988.84	1,604.66	1,488.70	1,332.57	1,146.29	1,072.46	1,039.49	1,023.98	1,016.52
14.50%	2,925.78	1,999.90	1,616.47	1,500.87	1,345.44	1,160.68	1,088.00	1,055.84	1,040.87	1,033.74
14.75%	2,936.16	2,011.01	1,628.32	1,513.09	1,358.36	1,175.13	1,103.60	1,072.25	1,057.80	1,051.00
15.00%	2,946.55	2,022.14	1,640.22	1,525.36	1,371.35	1,189.65	1,119.27	1,088.71	1,074.78	1,068.29
15.25%	2,956.97	2,033.32	1,652.17	1,537.68	1,384.39	1,204.24	1,135.00	1,105.22	1,091.79	1,085.61
15.50%	2,967.41	2,044.52	1,664.16	1,550.05	1,397.49	1,218.89	1,150.80	1,121.78	1,108.84	1,102.95
15.75%	2,977.87	2,055.76	1,676.19	1,562.48	1,410.65	1,233.61	1,166.65	1,138.40	1,125.92	1,120.31
16.00%	2,988.35	2,067.03	1,688.28	1,574.95	1,423.86	1,248.40	1,182.57	1,155.06	1,143.04	1,137.70
16.25%	2,998.85	2,078.34	1,700.40	1,587.47	1,437.13	1,263.24	1,198.54	1,171.76	1,160.19	1,155.11
16.50%	3,009.37	2,089.68	1,712.57	1,600.04	1,450.46	1,278.15	1,214.57	1,188.51	1,177.38	1,172.54
16.75%	3,019.92	2,101.06	1,724.78	1,612.66	1,463.84	1,293.12	1,230.65	1,205.30	1,194.59	1,189.98
17.00%	3,030.48	2,112.47	1,737.04	1,625.32	1,477.28	1,308.15	1,246.78	1,222.13	1,211.82	1,207.45
17.25%	3,041.07	2,123.91	1,749.35	1,638.04	1,490.77	1,323.24	1,262.97	1,239.00	1,229.09	1,224.93
17.50%	3,051.68	2,135.39	1,761.69	1,650.80	1,504.32	1,338.39	1,279.20	1,255.90	1,246.38	1,242.42
17.75%	3,062.30	2,146.90	1,774.08	1,663.61	1,517.92	1,353.60	1,295.48	1,272.84	1,263.69	1,259.93
18.00%	3,072.95	2,158.44	1,786.52	1,676.47	1,531.57	1,368.86	1,311.81	1,289.82	1,281.02	1,277.46
18.25%	3,083.62	2,170.02	1,798.99	1,689.38	1,545.28	1,384.17	1,328.19	1,306.82	1,298.38	1,294.99
18.50%	3,094.32	2,181.63	1,811.51	1,702.33	1,559.04	1,399.54	1,344.61	1,323.86	1,315.75	1,312.54
18.75%	3,105.03	2,193.27	1,824.08	1,715.33	1,572.85	1,414.97	1,361.08	1,340.93	1,333.15	1,330.10
19.00%	3,115.76	2,204.95	1,836.68	1,728.38	1,586.72	1,430.44	1,377.58	1,358.03	1,350.56	1,347.67
19.25%	3,126.52	2,216.66	1,849.33	1,741.47	1,600.63	1,445.97	1,394.13	1,375.15	1,367.99	1,365.25
19.50%	3,137.29	2,228.40	1,862.02	1,754.61	1,614.59	1,461.55	1,410.71	1,392.31	1,385.43	1,382.84
19.75%	3,148.09	2,240.17	1,874.75	1,767.79	1,628.61	1,477.18	1,427.34	1,409.48	1,402.89	1,400.43
20.00%	3,158.90	2,251.98	1,887.53	1,781.02	1,642.67	1,492.85	1,444.00	1,426.68	1,420.37	1,418.04
20.25%	3,169.74	2,263.82	1,900.34	1,794.30	1,656.79	1,508.58	1,460.70	1,443.91	1,437.85	1,435.65
20.50%	3,180.60	2,275.69	1,913.20	1,807.62	1,670.95	1,524.34	1,477.43	1,461.16	1,455.35	1,453.27
20.75%	3,191.48	2,287.60	1,926.10	1,820.98	1,685.16	1,540.16	1,494.20	1,478.42	1,472.87	1,470.89

$87,500 1.00 - 10.75% 3 - 35 Years

	3	5	7	8	10	15	20	25	30	35
1.00%	2,468.21	1,495.70	1,078.98	948.78	766.54	523.68	402.41	329.76	281.43	247.00
1.25%	2,477.68	1,505.14	1,088.45	958.26	776.07	533.36	412.24	339.76	291.60	257.33
1.50%	2,487.17	1,514.62	1,097.96	967.81	785.68	543.15	422.23	349.94	301.98	267.91
1.75%	2,496.69	1,524.13	1,107.53	977.41	795.36	553.05	432.36	360.32	312.59	278.76
2.00%	2,506.23	1,533.68	1,117.15	987.08	805.12	563.07	442.65	370.87	323.42	289.85
2.25%	2,515.79	1,543.27	1,126.82	996.80	814.95	573.20	453.08	381.61	334.47	301.21
2.50%	2,525.37	1,552.89	1,136.55	1,006.59	824.86	583.44	463.67	392.54	345.73	312.81
2.75%	2,534.98	1,562.56	1,146.33	1,016.43	834.85	593.79	474.40	403.65	357.21	324.66
3.00%	2,544.61	1,572.26	1,156.16	1,026.34	844.91	604.26	485.27	414.93	368.90	336.74
3.25%	2,554.26	1,582.00	1,166.05	1,036.30	855.04	614.84	496.30	426.40	380.81	349.07
3.50%	2,563.93	1,591.78	1,175.99	1,046.33	865.25	625.52	507.46	438.05	392.91	361.63
3.75%	2,573.63	1,601.59	1,185.98	1,056.42	875.54	636.32	518.78	449.86	405.23	374.42
4.00%	2,583.35	1,611.45	1,196.02	1,066.56	885.89	647.23	530.23	461.86	417.74	387.43
4.25%	2,593.09	1,621.34	1,206.12	1,076.77	896.33	658.24	541.83	474.02	430.45	400.66
4.50%	2,602.86	1,631.26	1,216.26	1,087.03	906.84	669.37	553.57	486.35	443.35	414.10
4.75%	2,612.64	1,641.23	1,226.46	1,097.36	917.42	680.60	565.45	498.85	456.44	427.75
5.00%	2,622.45	1,651.23	1,236.72	1,107.74	928.07	691.94	577.46	511.52	469.72	441.60
5.25%	2,632.29	1,661.27	1,247.02	1,118.19	938.80	703.39	589.61	524.34	483.18	455.65
5.50%	2,642.14	1,671.35	1,257.38	1,128.69	949.60	714.95	601.90	537.33	496.82	469.89
5.75%	2,652.02	1,681.47	1,267.79	1,139.25	960.48	726.61	614.32	550.47	510.63	484.31
6.00%	2,661.92	1,691.62	1,278.25	1,149.88	971.43	738.37	626.88	563.76	524.61	498.92
6.25%	2,671.84	1,701.81	1,288.76	1,160.56	982.45	750.25	639.56	577.21	538.75	513.69
6.50%	2,681.79	1,712.04	1,299.33	1,171.30	993.54	762.22	652.38	590.81	553.06	528.64
6.75%	2,691.76	1,722.30	1,309.94	1,182.09	1,004.71	774.30	665.32	604.55	567.52	543.74
7.00%	2,701.75	1,732.60	1,320.61	1,192.95	1,015.95	786.47	678.39	618.43	582.14	559.00
7.25%	2,711.76	1,742.94	1,331.33	1,203.87	1,027.26	798.76	691.58	632.46	596.90	574.41
7.50%	2,721.79	1,753.32	1,342.10	1,214.84	1,038.64	811.14	704.89	646.62	611.81	589.96
7.75%	2,731.85	1,763.73	1,352.92	1,225.87	1,050.09	823.62	718.33	660.91	626.86	605.65
8.00%	2,741.93	1,774.18	1,363.79	1,236.96	1,061.62	836.20	731.89	675.34	642.04	621.48
8.25%	2,752.03	1,784.67	1,374.72	1,248.11	1,073.21	848.87	745.56	689.89	657.36	637.43
8.50%	2,762.16	1,795.20	1,385.69	1,259.31	1,084.87	861.65	759.35	704.57	672.80	653.50
8.75%	2,772.31	1,805.76	1,396.72	1,270.57	1,096.61	874.52	773.25	719.38	688.36	669.69
9.00%	2,782.48	1,816.36	1,407.79	1,281.89	1,108.41	887.48	787.26	734.30	704.04	685.99
9.25%	2,792.67	1,826.99	1,418.92	1,293.27	1,120.29	900.54	801.38	749.33	719.84	702.40
9.50%	2,802.88	1,837.66	1,430.10	1,304.70	1,132.23	913.70	815.61	764.48	735.75	718.91
9.75%	2,813.12	1,848.37	1,441.33	1,316.19	1,144.24	926.94	829.95	779.75	751.76	735.52
10.00%	2,823.38	1,859.12	1,452.60	1,327.74	1,156.32	940.28	844.39	795.11	767.88	752.21
10.25%	2,833.66	1,869.90	1,463.93	1,339.34	1,168.47	953.71	858.94	810.59	784.09	769.00
10.50%	2,843.96	1,880.72	1,475.31	1,351.00	1,180.68	967.22	873.58	826.16	800.40	785.87
10.75%	2,854.29	1,891.57	1,486.74	1,362.72	1,192.96	980.83	888.33	841.83	816.80	802.82

$87,500   11.00 - 20.75%   3 - 35 Years

	3	5	7	8	10	15	20	25	30	35
11.00%	2,864.64	1,902.46	1,498.21	1,374.49	1,205.31	994.52	903.16	857.60	833.28	819.84
11.25%	2,875.01	1,913.39	1,509.74	1,386.31	1,217.73	1,008.30	918.10	873.46	849.85	836.93
11.50%	2,885.40	1,924.35	1,521.32	1,398.20	1,230.21	1,022.17	933.13	889.41	866.51	854.09
11.75%	2,895.82	1,935.35	1,532.94	1,410.13	1,242.76	1,036.11	948.24	905.45	883.23	871.32
12.00%	2,906.25	1,946.39	1,544.61	1,422.12	1,255.37	1,050.15	963.45	921.57	900.04	888.61
12.25%	2,916.71	1,957.46	1,556.34	1,434.17	1,268.05	1,064.26	978.74	937.78	916.91	905.95
12.50%	2,927.19	1,968.57	1,568.11	1,446.27	1,280.79	1,078.46	994.12	954.06	933.85	923.35
12.75%	2,937.70	1,979.71	1,579.93	1,458.43	1,293.60	1,092.73	1,009.59	970.42	950.86	940.80
13.00%	2,948.22	1,990.89	1,591.80	1,470.63	1,306.47	1,107.09	1,025.13	986.86	967.92	958.29
13.25%	2,958.77	2,002.11	1,603.71	1,482.90	1,319.40	1,121.52	1,040.75	1,003.36	985.05	975.84
13.50%	2,969.34	2,013.36	1,615.68	1,495.21	1,332.40	1,136.03	1,056.45	1,019.94	1,002.24	993.42
13.75%	2,979.93	2,024.65	1,627.69	1,507.58	1,345.46	1,150.61	1,072.23	1,036.58	1,019.47	1,011.05
14.00%	2,990.54	2,035.97	1,639.75	1,520.01	1,358.58	1,165.27	1,088.08	1,053.29	1,036.76	1,028.71
14.25%	3,001.18	2,047.33	1,651.86	1,532.48	1,371.76	1,180.01	1,104.00	1,070.06	1,054.10	1,046.41
14.50%	3,011.84	2,058.72	1,664.01	1,545.01	1,385.01	1,194.81	1,120.00	1,086.89	1,071.49	1,064.15
14.75%	3,022.51	2,070.15	1,676.22	1,557.59	1,398.31	1,209.69	1,136.06	1,103.78	1,088.92	1,081.92
15.00%	3,033.22	2,081.62	1,688.47	1,570.22	1,411.68	1,224.64	1,152.19	1,120.73	1,106.39	1,099.71
15.25%	3,043.94	2,093.12	1,700.76	1,582.91	1,425.11	1,239.66	1,168.39	1,137.73	1,123.90	1,117.54
15.50%	3,054.68	2,104.65	1,713.11	1,595.64	1,438.59	1,254.74	1,184.65	1,154.78	1,141.45	1,135.39
15.75%	3,065.45	2,116.22	1,725.49	1,608.43	1,452.14	1,269.89	1,200.97	1,171.88	1,159.04	1,153.26
16.00%	3,076.24	2,127.83	1,737.93	1,621.27	1,465.74	1,285.11	1,217.35	1,189.03	1,176.66	1,171.16
16.25%	3,087.05	2,139.47	1,750.41	1,634.16	1,479.40	1,300.40	1,233.79	1,206.22	1,194.32	1,189.08
16.50%	3,097.88	2,151.15	1,762.94	1,647.10	1,493.12	1,315.75	1,250.29	1,223.46	1,212.00	1,207.02
16.75%	3,108.74	2,162.86	1,775.51	1,660.09	1,506.90	1,331.16	1,266.84	1,240.75	1,229.72	1,224.98
17.00%	3,119.61	2,174.60	1,788.13	1,673.13	1,520.73	1,346.63	1,283.45	1,258.07	1,247.47	1,242.96
17.25%	3,130.51	2,186.38	1,800.80	1,686.22	1,534.62	1,362.16	1,300.11	1,275.44	1,265.24	1,260.96
17.50%	3,141.43	2,198.19	1,813.51	1,699.36	1,548.56	1,377.76	1,316.82	1,292.84	1,283.03	1,278.97
17.75%	3,152.37	2,210.04	1,826.26	1,712.54	1,562.56	1,393.41	1,333.59	1,310.28	1,300.86	1,296.99
18.00%	3,163.33	2,221.92	1,839.06	1,725.78	1,576.62	1,409.12	1,350.40	1,327.75	1,318.70	1,315.03
18.25%	3,174.32	2,233.84	1,851.90	1,739.07	1,590.73	1,424.89	1,367.26	1,345.26	1,336.57	1,333.08
18.50%	3,185.33	2,245.79	1,864.79	1,752.40	1,604.89	1,440.71	1,384.16	1,362.80	1,354.45	1,351.15
18.75%	3,196.35	2,257.78	1,877.73	1,765.78	1,619.11	1,456.59	1,401.11	1,380.37	1,372.36	1,369.22
19.00%	3,207.40	2,269.80	1,890.70	1,779.21	1,633.38	1,472.52	1,418.10	1,397.97	1,390.28	1,387.31
19.25%	3,218.47	2,281.85	1,903.72	1,792.69	1,647.71	1,488.50	1,435.13	1,415.60	1,408.22	1,405.40
19.50%	3,229.56	2,293.94	1,916.79	1,806.22	1,662.08	1,504.54	1,452.21	1,433.26	1,426.18	1,423.51
19.75%	3,240.68	2,306.06	1,929.89	1,819.79	1,676.51	1,520.62	1,469.32	1,450.94	1,444.15	1,441.62
20.00%	3,251.81	2,318.21	1,943.04	1,833.41	1,690.99	1,536.76	1,486.47	1,468.65	1,462.14	1,459.74
20.25%	3,262.97	2,330.40	1,956.24	1,847.07	1,705.52	1,552.94	1,503.66	1,486.38	1,480.14	1,477.87
20.50%	3,274.15	2,342.63	1,969.47	1,860.78	1,720.10	1,569.18	1,520.88	1,504.13	1,498.16	1,496.01
20.75%	3,285.35	2,354.88	1,982.75	1,874.54	1,734.72	1,585.46	1,538.14	1,521.91	1,516.19	1,514.15

	3	5	7	8	10	15	20	25	30	35
1.00%	2,538.73	1,538.44	1,109.81	975.89	788.44	538.65	413.90	339.19	289.48	254.06
1.25%	2,548.47	1,548.14	1,119.54	985.64	798.24	548.60	424.02	349.47	299.93	264.68
1.50%	2,558.23	1,557.89	1,129.33	995.46	808.12	558.67	434.29	359.94	310.61	275.57
1.75%	2,568.02	1,567.67	1,139.17	1,005.34	818.08	568.86	444.72	370.61	321.52	286.72
2.00%	2,577.83	1,577.50	1,149.07	1,015.28	828.12	579.16	455.30	381.47	332.66	298.14
2.25%	2,587.67	1,587.36	1,159.02	1,025.28	838.24	589.58	466.03	392.52	344.02	309.81
2.50%	2,597.52	1,597.26	1,169.02	1,035.35	848.43	600.11	476.91	403.76	355.61	321.75
2.75%	2,607.40	1,607.20	1,179.08	1,045.47	858.70	610.76	487.95	415.18	367.42	333.93
3.00%	2,617.31	1,617.18	1,189.20	1,055.66	869.05	621.52	499.14	426.79	379.44	346.37
3.25%	2,627.24	1,627.20	1,199.36	1,065.91	879.47	632.40	510.48	438.58	391.69	359.04
3.50%	2,637.19	1,637.26	1,209.59	1,076.22	889.97	643.39	521.96	450.56	404.14	371.96
3.75%	2,647.16	1,647.35	1,219.86	1,086.60	900.55	654.50	533.60	462.72	416.80	385.11
4.00%	2,657.16	1,657.49	1,230.19	1,097.03	911.21	665.72	545.38	475.05	429.67	398.50
4.25%	2,667.18	1,667.66	1,240.58	1,107.53	921.94	677.05	557.31	487.56	442.75	412.10
4.50%	2,677.22	1,677.87	1,251.01	1,118.09	932.75	688.49	569.38	500.25	456.02	425.93
4.75%	2,687.29	1,688.12	1,261.51	1,128.71	943.63	700.05	581.60	513.11	469.48	439.97
5.00%	2,697.38	1,698.41	1,272.05	1,139.39	954.59	711.71	593.96	526.13	483.14	454.22
5.25%	2,707.49	1,708.74	1,282.65	1,150.14	965.63	723.49	606.46	539.32	496.98	468.67
5.50%	2,717.63	1,719.10	1,293.30	1,160.94	976.74	735.38	619.10	552.68	511.01	483.31
5.75%	2,727.79	1,729.51	1,304.01	1,171.80	987.92	747.37	631.88	566.20	525.22	498.15
6.00%	2,737.97	1,739.95	1,314.77	1,182.73	999.18	759.47	644.79	579.87	539.60	513.17
6.25%	2,748.18	1,750.43	1,325.58	1,193.71	1,010.52	771.68	657.84	593.70	554.15	528.37
6.50%	2,758.41	1,760.95	1,336.45	1,204.76	1,021.93	784.00	671.02	607.69	568.86	543.74
6.75%	2,768.66	1,771.51	1,347.37	1,215.87	1,033.42	796.42	684.33	621.82	583.74	559.27
7.00%	2,778.94	1,782.11	1,358.34	1,227.03	1,044.98	808.95	697.77	636.10	598.77	574.97
7.25%	2,789.24	1,792.74	1,369.37	1,238.26	1,056.61	821.58	711.34	650.53	613.96	590.82
7.50%	2,799.56	1,803.42	1,380.44	1,249.55	1,068.32	834.31	725.03	665.09	629.29	606.82
7.75%	2,809.90	1,814.13	1,391.58	1,260.89	1,080.10	847.15	738.85	679.80	644.77	622.96
8.00%	2,820.27	1,824.88	1,402.76	1,272.30	1,091.95	860.09	752.80	694.63	660.39	639.23
8.25%	2,830.66	1,835.66	1,414.00	1,283.77	1,103.87	873.13	766.86	709.61	676.14	655.64
8.50%	2,841.08	1,846.49	1,425.28	1,295.29	1,115.87	886.27	781.04	724.70	692.02	672.17
8.75%	2,851.52	1,857.35	1,436.62	1,306.88	1,127.94	899.50	795.34	739.93	708.03	688.83
9.00%	2,861.98	1,868.25	1,448.02	1,318.52	1,140.08	912.84	809.75	755.28	724.16	705.59
9.25%	2,872.46	1,879.19	1,459.46	1,330.22	1,152.29	926.27	824.28	770.74	740.41	722.47
9.50%	2,882.97	1,890.17	1,470.96	1,341.98	1,164.58	939.80	838.92	786.33	756.77	739.45
9.75%	2,893.49	1,901.18	1,482.51	1,353.80	1,176.93	953.43	853.67	802.02	773.24	756.53
10.00%	2,904.05	1,912.23	1,494.11	1,365.67	1,189.36	967.14	868.52	817.83	789.81	773.71
10.25%	2,914.62	1,923.32	1,505.76	1,377.61	1,201.85	980.96	883.48	833.74	806.49	790.97
10.50%	2,925.22	1,934.45	1,517.46	1,389.60	1,214.41	994.86	898.54	849.76	823.27	808.32
10.75%	2,935.84	1,945.62	1,529.21	1,401.65	1,227.05	1,008.85	913.71	865.88	840.13	825.75

$90,000   11.00 - 20.75%   3 - 35 Years

	3	5	7	8	10	15	20	25	30	35
11.00%	2,946.48	1,956.82	1,541.02	1,413.76	1,239.75	1,022.94	928.97	882.10	857.09	843.26
11.25%	2,957.15	1,968.06	1,552.88	1,425.92	1,252.52	1,037.11	944.33	898.42	874.14	860.84
11.50%	2,967.84	1,979.33	1,564.78	1,438.14	1,265.36	1,051.37	959.79	914.82	891.26	878.50
11.75%	2,978.55	1,990.65	1,576.74	1,450.42	1,278.27	1,065.72	975.34	931.32	908.47	896.21
12.00%	2,989.29	2,002.00	1,588.75	1,462.76	1,291.24	1,080.15	990.98	947.90	925.75	913.99
12.25%	3,000.05	2,013.39	1,600.80	1,475.15	1,304.28	1,094.67	1,006.71	964.57	943.11	931.83
12.50%	3,010.83	2,024.81	1,612.91	1,487.59	1,317.39	1,109.27	1,022.53	981.32	960.53	949.73
12.75%	3,021.63	2,036.28	1,625.07	1,500.10	1,330.56	1,123.95	1,038.43	998.15	978.02	967.68
13.00%	3,032.46	2,047.78	1,637.28	1,512.65	1,343.80	1,138.72	1,054.42	1,015.05	995.58	985.67
13.25%	3,043.30	2,059.31	1,649.53	1,525.27	1,357.10	1,153.56	1,070.49	1,032.03	1,013.20	1,003.72
13.50%	3,054.18	2,070.89	1,661.84	1,537.93	1,370.47	1,168.49	1,086.64	1,049.08	1,030.87	1,021.81
13.75%	3,065.07	2,082.50	1,674.20	1,550.66	1,383.90	1,183.49	1,102.86	1,066.20	1,048.60	1,039.94
14.00%	3,075.99	2,094.14	1,686.60	1,563.44	1,397.40	1,198.57	1,119.17	1,083.38	1,066.38	1,058.11
14.25%	3,086.93	2,105.83	1,699.05	1,576.27	1,410.96	1,213.72	1,135.55	1,100.63	1,084.22	1,076.31
14.50%	3,097.89	2,117.55	1,711.56	1,589.15	1,424.58	1,228.95	1,152.00	1,117.95	1,102.10	1,094.55
14.75%	3,108.87	2,129.30	1,724.11	1,602.09	1,438.27	1,244.25	1,168.52	1,135.32	1,120.03	1,112.83
15.00%	3,119.88	2,141.09	1,736.71	1,615.09	1,452.01	1,259.63	1,185.11	1,152.75	1,138.00	1,131.13
15.25%	3,130.91	2,152.92	1,749.36	1,628.13	1,465.82	1,275.07	1,201.77	1,170.23	1,156.01	1,149.47
15.50%	3,141.96	2,164.79	1,762.05	1,641.23	1,479.69	1,290.59	1,218.49	1,187.77	1,174.07	1,167.83
15.75%	3,153.04	2,176.69	1,774.79	1,654.39	1,493.63	1,306.18	1,235.28	1,205.36	1,192.16	1,186.21
16.00%	3,164.13	2,188.63	1,787.59	1,667.59	1,507.62	1,321.83	1,252.13	1,223.00	1,210.28	1,204.62
16.25%	3,175.25	2,200.60	1,800.42	1,680.85	1,521.67	1,337.55	1,269.04	1,240.69	1,228.44	1,223.05
16.50%	3,186.39	2,212.61	1,813.31	1,694.16	1,535.78	1,353.34	1,286.01	1,258.42	1,246.63	1,241.51
16.75%	3,197.56	2,224.65	1,826.24	1,707.52	1,549.95	1,369.19	1,303.04	1,276.20	1,264.86	1,259.98
17.00%	3,208.75	2,236.73	1,839.22	1,720.93	1,564.18	1,385.10	1,320.12	1,294.02	1,283.11	1,278.47
17.25%	3,219.95	2,248.85	1,852.25	1,734.39	1,578.47	1,401.08	1,337.26	1,311.88	1,301.39	1,296.98
17.50%	3,231.19	2,261.00	1,865.32	1,747.91	1,592.81	1,417.12	1,354.45	1,329.78	1,319.69	1,315.51
17.75%	3,242.44	2,273.19	1,878.44	1,761.47	1,607.21	1,433.22	1,371.69	1,347.71	1,338.02	1,334.05
18.00%	3,253.72	2,285.41	1,891.61	1,775.09	1,621.67	1,449.38	1,388.98	1,365.69	1,356.38	1,352.60
18.25%	3,265.01	2,297.67	1,904.82	1,788.75	1,636.18	1,465.60	1,406.32	1,383.69	1,374.75	1,371.17
18.50%	3,276.33	2,309.96	1,918.07	1,802.47	1,650.75	1,481.87	1,423.71	1,401.74	1,393.15	1,389.75
18.75%	3,287.68	2,322.29	1,931.37	1,816.23	1,665.37	1,498.20	1,441.14	1,419.81	1,411.57	1,408.34
19.00%	3,299.04	2,334.65	1,944.72	1,830.05	1,680.05	1,514.59	1,458.62	1,437.91	1,430.00	1,426.95
19.25%	3,310.43	2,347.05	1,958.11	1,843.91	1,694.78	1,531.03	1,476.14	1,456.04	1,448.46	1,445.56
19.50%	3,321.84	2,359.48	1,971.55	1,857.82	1,709.57	1,547.52	1,493.70	1,474.21	1,466.93	1,464.18
19.75%	3,333.27	2,371.95	1,985.03	1,871.78	1,724.41	1,564.07	1,511.30	1,492.39	1,485.41	1,482.81
20.00%	3,344.72	2,384.45	1,998.56	1,885.79	1,739.30	1,580.67	1,528.94	1,510.61	1,503.92	1,501.45
20.25%	3,356.20	2,396.99	2,012.13	1,899.84	1,754.25	1,597.31	1,546.62	1,528.84	1,522.43	1,520.10
20.50%	3,367.70	2,409.56	2,025.74	1,913.95	1,769.24	1,614.01	1,564.34	1,547.11	1,540.96	1,538.75
20.75%	3,379.21	2,422.16	2,039.40	1,928.09	1,784.29	1,630.76	1,582.09	1,565.39	1,559.51	1,557.41

	3	5	7	8	10	15	20	25	30	35
1.00%	2,609.25	1,581.17	1,140.64	1,003.00	810.34	553.61	425.40	348.61	297.52	261.11
1.25%	2,619.26	1,591.15	1,150.64	1,013.02	820.41	563.84	435.80	359.17	308.26	272.03
1.50%	2,629.30	1,601.16	1,160.70	1,023.11	830.57	574.19	446.35	369.94	319.24	283.22
1.75%	2,639.36	1,611.22	1,170.82	1,033.26	840.81	584.66	457.07	380.90	330.45	294.68
2.00%	2,649.44	1,621.32	1,180.99	1,043.48	851.12	595.25	467.94	392.07	341.90	306.42
2.25%	2,659.55	1,631.45	1,191.21	1,053.76	861.52	605.95	478.97	403.42	353.58	318.42
2.50%	2,669.68	1,641.63	1,201.50	1,064.11	872.00	616.78	490.16	414.97	365.49	330.68
2.75%	2,679.83	1,651.85	1,211.84	1,074.51	882.55	627.73	501.50	426.71	377.62	343.21
3.00%	2,690.01	1,662.10	1,222.23	1,084.99	893.19	638.79	513.00	438.65	389.98	355.99
3.25%	2,700.22	1,672.40	1,232.68	1,095.52	903.90	649.97	524.66	450.77	402.57	369.02
3.50%	2,710.44	1,682.74	1,243.19	1,106.12	914.69	661.27	536.46	463.08	415.37	382.29
3.75%	2,720.69	1,693.11	1,253.75	1,116.78	925.57	672.68	548.42	475.57	428.38	395.81
4.00%	2,730.97	1,703.53	1,264.36	1,127.51	936.52	684.21	560.53	488.25	441.61	409.57
4.25%	2,741.27	1,713.98	1,275.04	1,138.30	947.55	695.86	572.79	501.11	455.04	423.55
4.50%	2,751.59	1,724.48	1,285.76	1,149.15	958.66	707.62	585.20	514.15	468.68	437.76
4.75%	2,761.94	1,735.01	1,296.55	1,160.06	969.84	719.49	597.76	527.36	482.52	452.19
5.00%	2,772.31	1,745.59	1,307.39	1,171.04	981.11	731.48	610.46	540.75	496.56	466.84
5.25%	2,782.70	1,756.20	1,318.28	1,182.08	992.45	743.59	623.31	554.30	510.79	481.69
5.50%	2,793.12	1,766.86	1,329.23	1,193.19	1,003.87	755.80	636.30	568.03	525.20	496.74
5.75%	2,803.56	1,777.55	1,340.23	1,204.35	1,015.37	768.13	649.43	581.92	539.80	511.99
6.00%	2,814.03	1,788.28	1,351.29	1,215.58	1,026.94	780.57	662.70	595.98	554.58	527.43
6.25%	2,824.52	1,799.06	1,362.40	1,226.87	1,038.59	793.12	676.11	610.19	569.54	543.05
6.50%	2,835.03	1,809.87	1,373.57	1,238.23	1,050.32	805.77	689.66	624.57	584.66	558.84
6.75%	2,845.57	1,820.72	1,384.80	1,249.64	1,062.12	818.54	703.34	639.09	599.95	574.81
7.00%	2,856.13	1,831.61	1,396.07	1,261.12	1,074.00	831.42	717.15	653.77	615.40	590.94
7.25%	2,866.72	1,842.54	1,407.40	1,272.66	1,085.96	844.40	731.10	668.60	631.01	607.23
7.50%	2,877.33	1,853.51	1,418.79	1,284.26	1,097.99	857.49	745.17	683.57	646.77	623.67
7.75%	2,887.96	1,864.52	1,430.23	1,295.92	1,110.10	870.68	759.38	698.69	662.68	640.26
8.00%	2,898.61	1,875.57	1,441.72	1,307.64	1,122.28	883.98	773.71	713.93	678.73	656.99
8.25%	2,909.29	1,886.65	1,453.27	1,319.43	1,134.54	897.38	788.16	729.32	694.92	673.85
8.50%	2,920.00	1,897.78	1,464.87	1,331.27	1,146.87	910.88	802.74	744.84	711.24	690.85
8.75%	2,930.72	1,908.94	1,476.53	1,343.18	1,159.27	924.49	817.43	760.48	727.70	707.96
9.00%	2,941.48	1,920.15	1,488.24	1,355.14	1,171.75	938.20	832.25	776.26	744.28	725.19
9.25%	2,952.25	1,931.39	1,500.00	1,367.17	1,184.30	952.00	847.18	792.15	760.97	742.54
9.50%	2,963.05	1,942.67	1,511.82	1,379.26	1,196.93	965.91	862.22	808.17	777.79	759.99
9.75%	2,973.87	1,953.99	1,523.69	1,391.40	1,209.62	979.91	877.38	824.30	794.72	777.55
10.00%	2,984.71	1,965.35	1,535.61	1,403.61	1,222.39	994.01	892.65	840.55	811.75	795.20
10.25%	2,995.58	1,976.75	1,547.58	1,415.88	1,235.24	1,008.20	908.02	856.90	828.89	812.94
10.50%	3,006.48	1,988.19	1,559.61	1,428.20	1,248.15	1,022.49	923.50	873.37	846.13	830.77
10.75%	3,017.39	1,999.66	1,571.69	1,440.59	1,261.13	1,036.88	939.09	889.94	863.47	848.69

$92,500   11.00 - 20.75%   3 - 35 Years

	3	5	7	8	10	15	20	25	30	35
11.00%	3,028.33	2,011.17	1,583.83	1,453.03	1,274.19	1,051.35	954.77	906.60	880.90	866.69
11.25%	3,039.29	2,022.73	1,596.01	1,465.53	1,287.31	1,065.92	970.56	923.37	898.42	884.76
11.50%	3,050.28	2,034.32	1,608.25	1,478.09	1,300.51	1,080.58	986.45	940.23	916.02	902.90
11.75%	3,061.29	2,045.94	1,620.54	1,490.71	1,313.77	1,095.32	1,002.43	957.19	933.70	921.11
12.00%	3,072.32	2,057.61	1,632.88	1,503.39	1,327.11	1,110.16	1,018.50	974.23	951.47	939.38
12.25%	3,083.38	2,069.32	1,645.27	1,516.12	1,340.51	1,125.08	1,034.67	991.36	969.30	957.72
12.50%	3,094.46	2,081.06	1,657.71	1,528.91	1,353.98	1,140.08	1,050.93	1,008.58	987.21	976.11
12.75%	3,105.56	2,092.84	1,670.21	1,541.76	1,367.52	1,155.17	1,067.28	1,025.87	1,005.19	994.56
13.00%	3,116.69	2,104.66	1,682.76	1,554.67	1,381.12	1,170.35	1,083.71	1,043.25	1,023.23	1,013.05
13.25%	3,127.84	2,116.52	1,695.35	1,567.63	1,394.80	1,185.61	1,100.22	1,060.70	1,041.34	1,031.60
13.50%	3,139.01	2,128.41	1,708.00	1,580.65	1,408.54	1,200.94	1,116.82	1,078.22	1,059.51	1,050.19
13.75%	3,150.21	2,140.34	1,720.70	1,593.73	1,422.34	1,216.36	1,133.50	1,095.82	1,077.73	1,068.82
14.00%	3,161.43	2,152.31	1,733.45	1,606.86	1,436.21	1,231.86	1,150.26	1,113.48	1,096.01	1,087.50
14.25%	3,172.67	2,164.32	1,746.25	1,620.05	1,450.15	1,247.44	1,167.09	1,131.21	1,114.34	1,106.21
14.50%	3,183.94	2,176.37	1,759.10	1,633.30	1,464.15	1,263.09	1,184.00	1,149.00	1,132.71	1,124.96
14.75%	3,195.23	2,188.45	1,772.00	1,646.60	1,478.22	1,278.82	1,200.98	1,166.85	1,151.14	1,143.74
15.00%	3,206.54	2,200.57	1,784.95	1,659.95	1,492.35	1,294.62	1,218.03	1,184.77	1,169.61	1,162.55
15.25%	3,217.88	2,212.73	1,797.95	1,673.36	1,506.54	1,310.49	1,235.15	1,202.74	1,188.12	1,181.40
15.50%	3,229.24	2,224.92	1,811.00	1,686.82	1,520.80	1,326.44	1,252.34	1,220.76	1,206.68	1,200.27
15.75%	3,240.62	2,237.15	1,824.09	1,700.34	1,535.12	1,342.46	1,269.59	1,238.84	1,225.27	1,219.16
16.00%	3,252.03	2,249.42	1,837.24	1,713.91	1,549.50	1,358.55	1,286.91	1,256.97	1,243.90	1,238.08
16.25%	3,263.45	2,261.73	1,850.44	1,727.54	1,563.94	1,374.71	1,304.29	1,275.15	1,262.56	1,257.03
16.50%	3,274.91	2,274.07	1,863.68	1,741.22	1,578.44	1,390.93	1,321.73	1,293.38	1,281.26	1,275.99
16.75%	3,286.38	2,286.45	1,876.97	1,754.95	1,593.00	1,407.22	1,339.23	1,311.65	1,299.99	1,294.98
17.00%	3,297.88	2,298.86	1,890.31	1,768.73	1,607.63	1,423.58	1,356.79	1,329.96	1,318.75	1,313.99
17.25%	3,309.40	2,311.32	1,903.70	1,782.57	1,622.31	1,440.00	1,374.40	1,348.32	1,337.54	1,333.01
17.50%	3,320.94	2,323.80	1,917.14	1,796.46	1,637.05	1,456.48	1,392.07	1,366.71	1,356.35	1,352.05
17.75%	3,332.51	2,336.33	1,930.62	1,810.40	1,651.85	1,473.03	1,409.79	1,385.15	1,375.19	1,371.11
18.00%	3,344.10	2,348.89	1,944.15	1,824.40	1,666.71	1,489.64	1,427.56	1,403.62	1,394.05	1,390.18
18.25%	3,355.71	2,361.49	1,957.73	1,838.44	1,681.63	1,506.31	1,445.38	1,422.13	1,412.94	1,409.26
18.50%	3,367.34	2,374.12	1,971.35	1,852.54	1,696.60	1,523.03	1,463.25	1,440.67	1,431.85	1,428.35
18.75%	3,379.00	2,386.79	1,985.02	1,866.69	1,711.63	1,539.82	1,481.17	1,459.25	1,450.78	1,447.46
19.00%	3,390.68	2,399.50	1,998.74	1,880.88	1,726.72	1,556.66	1,499.13	1,477.85	1,469.73	1,466.58
19.25%	3,402.39	2,412.24	2,012.51	1,895.13	1,741.86	1,573.56	1,517.14	1,496.49	1,488.69	1,485.71
19.50%	3,414.11	2,425.02	2,026.32	1,909.43	1,757.06	1,590.51	1,535.19	1,515.16	1,507.68	1,504.85
19.75%	3,425.86	2,437.83	2,040.17	1,923.77	1,772.31	1,607.52	1,553.28	1,533.85	1,526.68	1,524.00
20.00%	3,437.63	2,450.68	2,054.07	1,938.17	1,787.61	1,624.57	1,571.41	1,552.57	1,545.69	1,543.16
20.25%	3,449.43	2,463.57	2,068.02	1,952.62	1,802.97	1,641.68	1,589.58	1,571.31	1,564.72	1,562.32
20.50%	3,461.24	2,476.49	2,082.01	1,967.11	1,818.39	1,658.85	1,607.79	1,590.08	1,583.77	1,581.49
20.75%	3,473.08	2,489.44	2,096.05	1,981.65	1,833.85	1,676.06	1,626.04	1,608.87	1,602.83	1,600.67

	3	5	7	8	10	15	20	25	30	35
1.00%	2,679.77	1,623.91	1,171.47	1,030.11	832.24	568.57	436.90	358.03	305.56	268.17
1.25%	2,690.05	1,634.15	1,181.74	1,040.40	842.59	579.08	447.58	368.88	316.59	279.38
1.50%	2,700.36	1,644.44	1,192.07	1,050.76	853.02	589.71	458.42	379.94	327.86	290.88
1.75%	2,710.69	1,654.77	1,202.46	1,061.19	863.53	600.46	469.42	391.20	339.38	302.65
2.00%	2,721.04	1,665.14	1,212.91	1,071.68	874.13	611.33	480.59	402.66	351.14	314.70
2.25%	2,731.43	1,675.55	1,223.41	1,082.24	884.81	622.33	491.92	414.32	363.13	327.02
2.50%	2,741.83	1,686.00	1,233.97	1,092.87	895.56	633.45	503.41	426.19	375.36	339.62
2.75%	2,752.26	1,696.49	1,244.59	1,103.55	906.40	644.69	515.06	438.25	387.83	352.48
3.00%	2,762.71	1,707.03	1,255.26	1,114.31	917.33	656.05	526.87	450.50	400.52	365.61
3.25%	2,773.19	1,717.60	1,266.00	1,125.13	928.33	667.54	538.84	462.95	413.45	378.99
3.50%	2,783.70	1,728.22	1,276.79	1,136.01	939.42	679.14	550.96	475.59	426.59	392.63
3.75%	2,794.23	1,738.87	1,287.63	1,146.97	950.58	690.86	563.24	488.42	439.96	406.51
4.00%	2,804.78	1,749.57	1,298.54	1,157.98	961.83	702.70	575.68	501.44	453.54	420.64
4.25%	2,815.36	1,760.31	1,309.50	1,169.06	973.16	714.66	588.27	514.65	467.34	435.00
4.50%	2,825.96	1,771.09	1,320.52	1,180.21	984.56	726.74	601.02	528.04	481.35	449.59
4.75%	2,836.58	1,781.91	1,331.59	1,191.42	996.05	738.94	613.91	541.61	495.56	464.41
5.00%	2,847.24	1,792.77	1,342.72	1,202.69	1,007.62	751.25	626.96	555.36	509.98	479.45
5.25%	2,857.91	1,803.67	1,353.91	1,214.03	1,019.27	763.68	640.15	569.29	524.59	494.71
5.50%	2,868.61	1,814.61	1,365.15	1,225.44	1,031.00	776.23	653.49	583.38	539.40	510.17
5.75%	2,879.34	1,825.59	1,376.46	1,236.90	1,042.81	788.89	666.98	597.65	554.39	525.83
6.00%	2,890.08	1,836.62	1,387.81	1,248.44	1,054.69	801.66	680.61	612.09	569.57	541.68
6.25%	2,900.86	1,847.68	1,399.23	1,260.03	1,066.66	814.55	694.38	626.69	584.93	557.72
6.50%	2,911.66	1,858.78	1,410.70	1,271.69	1,078.71	827.55	708.29	641.45	600.46	573.95
6.75%	2,922.48	1,869.93	1,422.22	1,283.42	1,090.83	840.66	722.35	656.37	616.17	590.35
7.00%	2,933.32	1,881.11	1,433.80	1,295.20	1,103.03	853.89	736.53	671.44	632.04	606.91
7.25%	2,944.20	1,892.34	1,445.44	1,307.05	1,115.31	867.22	750.86	686.67	648.07	623.64
7.50%	2,955.09	1,903.61	1,457.14	1,318.97	1,127.67	880.66	765.31	702.04	664.25	640.53
7.75%	2,966.01	1,914.91	1,468.89	1,330.94	1,140.10	894.21	779.90	717.56	680.59	657.57
8.00%	2,976.95	1,926.26	1,480.69	1,342.98	1,152.61	907.87	794.62	733.23	697.08	674.75
8.25%	2,987.92	1,937.64	1,492.55	1,355.09	1,165.20	921.63	809.46	749.03	713.70	692.07
8.50%	2,998.92	1,949.07	1,504.47	1,367.25	1,177.86	935.50	824.43	764.97	730.47	709.52
8.75%	3,009.93	1,960.54	1,516.44	1,379.48	1,190.60	949.48	839.53	781.04	747.37	727.09
9.00%	3,020.97	1,972.04	1,528.46	1,391.77	1,203.42	963.55	854.74	797.24	764.39	744.79
9.25%	3,032.04	1,983.59	1,540.54	1,404.12	1,216.31	977.73	870.07	813.56	781.54	762.61
9.50%	3,043.13	1,995.18	1,552.68	1,416.53	1,229.28	992.01	885.52	830.01	798.81	780.53
9.75%	3,054.24	2,006.80	1,564.87	1,429.01	1,242.32	1,006.39	901.09	846.58	816.20	798.56
10.00%	3,065.38	2,018.47	1,577.11	1,441.55	1,255.43	1,020.87	916.77	863.27	833.69	816.69
10.25%	3,076.55	2,030.18	1,589.41	1,454.14	1,268.62	1,035.45	932.56	880.06	851.30	834.91
10.50%	3,087.73	2,041.92	1,601.76	1,466.80	1,281.88	1,050.13	948.46	896.97	869.00	853.23
10.75%	3,098.94	2,053.71	1,614.17	1,479.52	1,295.22	1,064.90	964.47	913.99	886.81	871.63

$95,000   11.00 - 20.75%   3 - 35 Years

	3	5	7	8	10	15	20	25	30	35
11.00%	3,110.18	2,065.53	1,626.63	1,492.30	1,308.63	1,079.77	980.58	931.11	904.71	890.11
11.25%	3,121.44	2,077.39	1,639.15	1,505.14	1,322.10	1,094.73	996.79	948.33	922.70	908.67
11.50%	3,132.72	2,089.30	1,651.71	1,518.04	1,335.66	1,109.78	1,013.11	965.65	940.78	927.30
11.75%	3,144.03	2,101.24	1,664.34	1,531.00	1,349.28	1,124.92	1,029.52	983.06	958.94	946.00
12.00%	3,155.36	2,113.22	1,677.01	1,544.02	1,362.97	1,140.16	1,046.03	1,000.56	977.18	964.77
12.25%	3,166.71	2,125.24	1,689.74	1,557.10	1,376.74	1,155.48	1,062.64	1,018.16	995.50	983.60
12.50%	3,178.09	2,137.30	1,702.52	1,570.24	1,390.57	1,170.90	1,079.33	1,035.84	1,013.89	1,002.49
12.75%	3,189.50	2,149.40	1,715.35	1,583.43	1,404.48	1,186.40	1,096.12	1,053.60	1,032.36	1,021.44
13.00%	3,200.93	2,161.54	1,728.24	1,596.69	1,418.45	1,201.98	1,113.00	1,071.44	1,050.89	1,040.43
13.25%	3,212.38	2,173.72	1,741.17	1,610.00	1,432.49	1,217.65	1,129.96	1,089.37	1,069.48	1,059.48
13.50%	3,223.85	2,185.94	1,754.16	1,623.38	1,446.61	1,233.40	1,147.01	1,107.36	1,088.14	1,078.57
13.75%	3,235.35	2,198.19	1,767.21	1,636.81	1,460.78	1,249.24	1,164.14	1,125.43	1,106.86	1,097.71
14.00%	3,246.87	2,210.48	1,780.30	1,650.29	1,475.03	1,265.15	1,181.34	1,143.57	1,125.63	1,116.89
14.25%	3,258.42	2,222.82	1,793.45	1,663.84	1,489.34	1,281.15	1,198.63	1,161.78	1,144.45	1,136.11
14.50%	3,269.99	2,235.19	1,806.64	1,677.44	1,503.72	1,297.23	1,216.00	1,180.05	1,163.33	1,155.36
14.75%	3,281.59	2,247.60	1,819.89	1,691.10	1,518.17	1,313.38	1,233.44	1,198.39	1,182.25	1,174.65
15.00%	3,293.21	2,260.04	1,833.19	1,704.81	1,532.68	1,329.61	1,250.95	1,216.79	1,201.22	1,193.97
15.25%	3,304.85	2,272.53	1,846.54	1,718.59	1,547.26	1,345.91	1,268.53	1,235.25	1,220.24	1,213.32
15.50%	3,316.51	2,285.05	1,859.94	1,732.41	1,561.90	1,362.29	1,286.19	1,253.76	1,239.29	1,232.71
15.75%	3,328.20	2,297.62	1,873.39	1,746.30	1,576.61	1,378.74	1,303.91	1,272.33	1,258.39	1,252.11
16.00%	3,339.92	2,310.22	1,886.90	1,760.23	1,591.37	1,395.27	1,321.69	1,290.94	1,277.52	1,271.55
16.25%	3,351.66	2,322.85	1,900.45	1,774.23	1,606.21	1,411.86	1,339.54	1,309.61	1,296.69	1,291.00
16.50%	3,363.42	2,335.53	1,914.05	1,788.28	1,621.10	1,428.52	1,357.46	1,328.33	1,315.89	1,310.48
16.75%	3,375.20	2,348.24	1,927.70	1,802.38	1,636.06	1,445.26	1,375.43	1,347.10	1,335.13	1,329.98
17.00%	3,387.01	2,360.99	1,941.40	1,816.54	1,651.08	1,462.05	1,393.46	1,365.91	1,354.39	1,349.50
17.25%	3,398.84	2,373.78	1,955.15	1,830.75	1,666.16	1,478.92	1,411.55	1,384.76	1,373.69	1,369.04
17.50%	3,410.70	2,386.61	1,968.95	1,845.01	1,681.30	1,495.85	1,429.69	1,403.65	1,393.01	1,388.59
17.75%	3,422.58	2,399.47	1,982.80	1,859.33	1,696.50	1,512.84	1,447.89	1,422.59	1,412.36	1,408.16
18.00%	3,434.48	2,412.38	1,996.69	1,873.71	1,711.76	1,529.90	1,466.15	1,441.56	1,431.73	1,427.75
18.25%	3,446.40	2,425.31	2,010.64	1,888.13	1,727.08	1,547.02	1,484.45	1,460.57	1,451.13	1,447.35
18.50%	3,458.35	2,438.29	2,024.63	1,902.61	1,742.46	1,564.20	1,502.80	1,479.61	1,470.55	1,466.96
18.75%	3,470.33	2,451.30	2,038.67	1,917.14	1,757.89	1,581.44	1,521.20	1,498.69	1,489.99	1,486.58
19.00%	3,482.32	2,464.35	2,052.76	1,931.72	1,773.39	1,598.73	1,539.65	1,517.80	1,509.45	1,506.22
19.25%	3,494.34	2,477.44	2,066.90	1,946.35	1,788.94	1,616.09	1,558.14	1,536.94	1,528.93	1,525.87
19.50%	3,506.38	2,490.56	2,081.08	1,961.03	1,804.55	1,633.50	1,576.68	1,556.11	1,548.42	1,545.52
19.75%	3,518.45	2,503.72	2,095.31	1,975.77	1,820.21	1,650.96	1,595.26	1,575.30	1,567.94	1,565.19
20.00%	3,530.54	2,516.92	2,109.59	1,990.55	1,835.93	1,668.48	1,613.88	1,594.53	1,587.47	1,584.86
20.25%	3,542.65	2,530.15	2,123.91	2,005.39	1,851.70	1,686.05	1,632.55	1,613.78	1,607.01	1,604.55
20.50%	3,554.79	2,543.42	2,138.28	2,020.28	1,867.53	1,703.68	1,651.25	1,633.06	1,626.57	1,624.24
20.75%	3,566.95	2,556.73	2,152.70	2,035.21	1,883.41	1,721.36	1,669.99	1,652.36	1,646.14	1,643.94

	3	5	7	8	10	15	20	25	30	35
1.00%	2,750.29	1,666.64	1,202.30	1,057.21	854.14	583.53	448.40	367.45	313.60	275.23
1.25%	2,760.84	1,677.16	1,212.84	1,067.78	864.76	594.32	459.36	378.59	324.92	286.73
1.50%	2,771.42	1,687.71	1,223.44	1,078.41	875.47	605.22	470.48	389.94	336.49	298.53
1.75%	2,782.02	1,698.31	1,234.10	1,089.12	886.26	616.26	481.78	401.49	348.31	310.61
2.00%	2,792.65	1,708.96	1,244.82	1,099.89	897.13	627.42	493.24	413.26	360.38	322.98
2.25%	2,803.31	1,719.64	1,255.60	1,110.72	908.09	638.71	504.86	425.23	372.69	335.63
2.50%	2,813.98	1,730.37	1,266.44	1,121.62	919.13	650.12	516.66	437.40	385.24	348.56
2.75%	2,824.69	1,741.14	1,277.34	1,132.60	930.26	661.66	528.61	449.78	398.04	361.76
3.00%	2,835.42	1,751.95	1,288.30	1,143.63	941.47	673.32	540.73	462.36	411.06	375.23
3.25%	2,846.17	1,762.80	1,299.31	1,154.74	952.76	685.10	553.02	475.13	424.33	388.96
3.50%	2,856.95	1,773.70	1,310.39	1,165.91	964.14	697.01	565.46	488.11	437.82	402.96
3.75%	2,867.76	1,784.63	1,321.52	1,177.15	975.60	709.04	578.07	501.28	451.54	417.21
4.00%	2,878.59	1,795.61	1,332.71	1,188.45	987.14	721.20	590.83	514.64	465.48	431.71
4.25%	2,889.44	1,806.63	1,343.96	1,199.83	998.77	733.47	603.75	528.19	479.64	446.45
4.50%	2,900.33	1,817.69	1,355.27	1,211.27	1,010.47	745.87	616.83	541.94	494.02	461.43
4.75%	2,911.23	1,828.80	1,366.63	1,222.77	1,022.27	758.39	630.07	555.86	508.61	476.64
5.00%	2,922.16	1,839.95	1,378.06	1,234.34	1,034.14	771.02	643.46	569.98	523.40	492.07
5.25%	2,933.12	1,851.13	1,389.54	1,245.98	1,046.09	783.78	657.00	584.27	538.40	507.72
5.50%	2,944.10	1,862.36	1,401.08	1,257.68	1,058.13	796.66	670.69	598.74	553.59	523.59
5.75%	2,955.11	1,873.63	1,412.68	1,269.45	1,070.25	809.65	684.53	613.38	568.98	539.66
6.00%	2,966.14	1,884.95	1,424.33	1,281.29	1,082.45	822.76	698.52	628.19	584.56	555.93
6.25%	2,977.20	1,896.30	1,436.05	1,293.19	1,094.73	835.99	712.65	643.18	600.32	572.40
6.50%	2,988.28	1,907.70	1,447.82	1,305.16	1,107.09	849.33	726.93	658.33	616.27	589.05
6.75%	2,999.38	1,919.14	1,459.65	1,317.19	1,119.54	862.79	741.35	673.64	632.38	605.88
7.00%	3,010.52	1,930.62	1,471.54	1,329.29	1,132.06	876.36	755.92	689.11	648.67	622.88
7.25%	3,021.67	1,942.14	1,483.48	1,341.45	1,144.66	890.04	770.62	704.74	665.12	640.06
7.50%	3,032.86	1,953.70	1,495.48	1,353.68	1,157.34	903.84	785.45	720.52	681.73	657.39
7.75%	3,044.06	1,965.30	1,507.54	1,365.97	1,170.10	917.74	800.42	736.45	698.50	674.87
8.00%	3,055.30	1,976.95	1,519.66	1,378.33	1,182.94	931.76	815.53	752.52	715.42	692.50
8.25%	3,066.55	1,988.63	1,531.83	1,390.75	1,195.86	945.89	830.76	768.74	732.48	710.28
8.50%	3,077.83	2,000.36	1,544.06	1,403.23	1,208.86	960.12	846.13	785.10	749.69	728.19
8.75%	3,089.14	2,012.13	1,556.34	1,415.78	1,221.94	974.46	861.62	801.59	767.03	746.23
9.00%	3,100.47	2,023.94	1,568.69	1,428.39	1,235.09	988.91	877.23	818.22	784.51	764.39
9.25%	3,111.83	2,035.79	1,581.08	1,441.07	1,248.32	1,003.46	892.97	834.97	802.11	782.68
9.50%	3,123.21	2,047.68	1,593.54	1,453.81	1,261.63	1,018.12	908.83	851.85	819.83	801.07
9.75%	3,134.62	2,059.61	1,606.05	1,466.61	1,275.01	1,032.88	924.80	868.86	837.68	819.57
10.00%	3,146.05	2,071.59	1,618.62	1,479.48	1,288.47	1,047.74	940.90	885.98	855.63	838.18
10.25%	3,157.51	2,083.60	1,631.24	1,492.41	1,302.01	1,062.70	957.10	903.22	873.70	856.88
10.50%	3,168.99	2,095.66	1,643.92	1,505.40	1,315.62	1,077.76	973.42	920.58	891.87	875.68
10.75%	3,180.49	2,107.75	1,656.65	1,518.46	1,329.30	1,092.92	989.85	938.04	910.14	894.57

	3	5	7	8	10	15	20	25	30	35
11.00%	3,192.02	2,119.89	1,669.44	1,531.57	1,343.06	1,108.18	1,006.38	955.61	928.52	913.53
11.25%	3,203.58	2,132.06	1,682.28	1,544.75	1,356.90	1,123.54	1,023.02	973.28	946.98	932.58
11.50%	3,215.16	2,144.28	1,695.18	1,557.99	1,370.81	1,138.99	1,039.77	991.06	965.53	951.70
11.75%	3,226.77	2,156.54	1,708.13	1,571.29	1,384.79	1,154.53	1,056.61	1,008.93	984.17	970.90
12.00%	3,238.40	2,168.83	1,721.14	1,584.65	1,398.84	1,170.16	1,073.56	1,026.89	1,002.90	990.16
12.25%	3,250.05	2,181.17	1,734.20	1,598.08	1,412.97	1,185.89	1,090.60	1,044.95	1,021.70	1,009.49
12.50%	3,261.73	2,193.55	1,747.32	1,611.56	1,427.17	1,201.71	1,107.74	1,063.10	1,040.58	1,028.87
12.75%	3,273.43	2,205.97	1,760.49	1,625.10	1,441.44	1,217.62	1,124.97	1,081.33	1,059.53	1,048.32
13.00%	3,285.16	2,218.42	1,773.72	1,638.71	1,455.78	1,233.61	1,142.29	1,099.64	1,078.54	1,067.81
13.25%	3,296.91	2,230.92	1,786.99	1,652.37	1,470.19	1,249.69	1,159.69	1,118.03	1,097.63	1,087.36
13.50%	3,308.69	2,243.46	1,800.33	1,666.10	1,484.67	1,265.86	1,177.19	1,136.50	1,116.78	1,106.96
13.75%	3,320.49	2,256.04	1,813.71	1,679.88	1,499.23	1,282.11	1,194.77	1,155.05	1,135.98	1,126.60
14.00%	3,332.32	2,268.65	1,827.15	1,693.72	1,513.85	1,298.45	1,212.43	1,173.67	1,155.25	1,146.28
14.25%	3,344.17	2,281.31	1,840.64	1,707.62	1,528.54	1,314.87	1,230.18	1,192.35	1,174.57	1,166.01
14.50%	3,356.05	2,294.01	1,854.19	1,721.58	1,543.30	1,331.36	1,248.00	1,211.11	1,193.94	1,185.77
14.75%	3,367.95	2,306.74	1,867.78	1,735.60	1,558.12	1,347.94	1,265.90	1,229.93	1,213.36	1,205.56
15.00%	3,379.87	2,319.52	1,881.43	1,749.68	1,573.02	1,364.60	1,283.87	1,248.81	1,232.83	1,225.39
15.25%	3,391.82	2,332.33	1,895.14	1,763.81	1,587.98	1,381.33	1,301.92	1,267.75	1,252.35	1,245.25
15.50%	3,403.79	2,345.19	1,908.89	1,778.00	1,603.00	1,398.14	1,320.03	1,286.75	1,271.90	1,265.15
15.75%	3,415.79	2,358.08	1,922.69	1,792.25	1,618.10	1,415.03	1,338.22	1,305.81	1,291.50	1,285.06
16.00%	3,427.81	2,371.01	1,936.55	1,806.56	1,633.25	1,431.98	1,356.47	1,324.92	1,311.14	1,305.01
16.25%	3,439.86	2,383.98	1,950.46	1,820.92	1,648.48	1,449.01	1,374.79	1,344.08	1,330.81	1,324.98
16.50%	3,451.93	2,396.99	1,964.42	1,835.34	1,663.76	1,466.12	1,393.18	1,363.29	1,350.52	1,344.97
16.75%	3,464.02	2,410.04	1,978.43	1,849.81	1,679.11	1,483.29	1,411.62	1,382.55	1,370.26	1,364.98
17.00%	3,476.14	2,423.13	1,992.49	1,864.34	1,694.53	1,500.53	1,430.13	1,401.85	1,390.03	1,385.01
17.25%	3,488.28	2,436.25	2,006.60	1,878.93	1,710.00	1,517.84	1,448.70	1,421.20	1,409.84	1,405.06
17.50%	3,500.45	2,449.42	2,020.76	1,893.57	1,725.54	1,535.21	1,467.32	1,440.59	1,429.67	1,425.13
17.75%	3,512.64	2,462.62	2,034.98	1,908.26	1,741.14	1,552.65	1,486.00	1,460.02	1,449.52	1,445.22
18.00%	3,524.86	2,475.86	2,049.24	1,923.01	1,756.81	1,570.16	1,504.73	1,479.49	1,469.41	1,465.32
18.25%	3,537.10	2,489.14	2,063.55	1,937.82	1,772.53	1,587.73	1,523.51	1,499.00	1,489.32	1,485.43
18.50%	3,549.36	2,502.46	2,077.91	1,952.68	1,788.31	1,605.36	1,542.35	1,518.55	1,509.25	1,505.56
18.75%	3,561.65	2,515.81	2,092.32	1,967.59	1,804.15	1,623.05	1,561.23	1,538.13	1,529.20	1,525.70
19.00%	3,573.96	2,529.20	2,106.78	1,982.55	1,820.06	1,640.80	1,580.17	1,557.74	1,549.17	1,545.86
19.25%	3,586.30	2,542.63	2,121.29	1,997.57	1,836.02	1,658.61	1,599.15	1,577.38	1,569.16	1,566.02
19.50%	3,598.66	2,556.10	2,135.85	2,012.64	1,852.03	1,676.48	1,618.17	1,597.06	1,589.17	1,586.20
19.75%	3,611.04	2,569.61	2,150.45	2,027.76	1,868.11	1,694.41	1,637.24	1,616.76	1,609.20	1,606.38
20.00%	3,623.45	2,583.15	2,165.10	2,042.94	1,884.24	1,712.39	1,656.35	1,636.49	1,629.24	1,626.57
20.25%	3,635.88	2,596.73	2,179.81	2,058.16	1,900.43	1,730.42	1,675.51	1,656.25	1,649.30	1,646.77
20.50%	3,648.34	2,610.35	2,194.55	2,073.44	1,916.68	1,748.51	1,694.70	1,676.03	1,669.38	1,666.98
20.75%	3,660.82	2,624.01	2,209.35	2,088.77	1,932.98	1,766.65	1,713.93	1,695.84	1,689.46	1,687.20

	3	5	7	8	10	15	20	25	30	35
1.00%	2,820.81	1,709.37	1,233.12	1,084.32	876.04	598.49	459.89	376.87	321.64	282.29
1.25%	2,831.63	1,720.16	1,243.94	1,095.16	886.93	609.55	471.13	388.30	333.25	294.09
1.50%	2,842.48	1,730.99	1,254.81	1,106.07	897.91	620.74	482.55	399.94	345.12	306.18
1.75%	2,853.36	1,741.86	1,265.75	1,117.04	908.98	632.06	494.13	411.79	357.24	318.58
2.00%	2,864.26	1,752.78	1,276.74	1,128.09	920.13	643.51	505.88	423.85	369.62	331.26
2.25%	2,875.18	1,763.73	1,287.80	1,139.20	931.37	655.08	517.81	436.13	382.25	344.24
2.50%	2,886.14	1,774.74	1,298.92	1,150.38	942.70	666.79	529.90	448.62	395.12	357.50
2.75%	2,897.12	1,785.78	1,310.09	1,161.64	954.11	678.62	542.17	461.31	408.24	371.03
3.00%	2,908.12	1,796.87	1,321.33	1,172.96	965.61	690.58	554.60	474.21	421.60	384.85
3.25%	2,919.15	1,808.00	1,332.63	1,184.35	977.19	702.67	567.20	487.32	435.21	398.94
3.50%	2,930.21	1,819.17	1,343.99	1,195.81	988.86	714.88	579.96	500.62	449.04	413.29
3.75%	2,941.29	1,830.39	1,355.40	1,207.33	1,000.61	727.22	592.89	514.13	463.12	427.91
4.00%	2,952.40	1,841.65	1,366.88	1,218.93	1,012.45	739.69	605.98	527.84	477.42	442.77
4.25%	2,963.53	1,852.96	1,378.42	1,230.59	1,024.38	752.28	619.23	541.74	491.94	457.89
4.50%	2,974.69	1,864.30	1,390.02	1,242.32	1,036.38	764.99	632.65	555.83	506.69	473.26
4.75%	2,985.88	1,875.69	1,401.67	1,254.12	1,048.48	777.83	646.22	570.12	521.65	488.86
5.00%	2,997.09	1,887.12	1,413.39	1,265.99	1,060.66	790.79	659.96	584.59	536.82	504.69
5.25%	3,008.33	1,898.60	1,425.17	1,277.93	1,072.92	803.88	673.84	599.25	552.20	520.74
5.50%	3,019.59	1,910.12	1,437.00	1,289.93	1,085.26	817.08	687.89	614.09	567.79	537.02
5.75%	3,030.88	1,921.68	1,448.90	1,302.00	1,097.69	830.41	702.08	629.11	583.57	553.50
6.00%	3,042.19	1,933.28	1,460.86	1,314.14	1,110.21	843.86	716.43	644.30	599.55	570.19
6.25%	3,053.53	1,944.93	1,472.87	1,326.35	1,122.80	857.42	730.93	659.67	615.72	587.08
6.50%	3,064.90	1,956.61	1,484.94	1,338.62	1,135.48	871.11	745.57	675.21	632.07	604.15
6.75%	3,076.29	1,968.35	1,497.08	1,350.96	1,148.24	884.91	760.36	690.91	648.60	621.42
7.00%	3,087.71	1,980.12	1,509.27	1,363.37	1,161.08	898.83	775.30	706.78	665.30	638.86
7.25%	3,099.15	1,991.94	1,521.52	1,375.85	1,174.01	912.86	790.38	722.81	682.18	656.47
7.50%	3,110.62	2,003.79	1,533.83	1,388.39	1,187.02	927.01	805.59	738.99	699.21	674.24
7.75%	3,122.12	2,015.70	1,546.20	1,400.99	1,200.11	941.28	820.95	755.33	716.41	692.18
8.00%	3,133.64	2,027.64	1,558.62	1,413.67	1,213.28	955.65	836.44	771.82	733.76	710.26
8.25%	3,145.18	2,039.63	1,571.11	1,426.41	1,226.53	970.14	852.07	788.45	751.27	728.49
8.50%	3,156.75	2,051.65	1,583.65	1,439.21	1,239.86	984.74	867.82	805.23	768.91	746.86
8.75%	3,168.35	2,063.72	1,596.25	1,452.08	1,253.27	999.45	883.71	822.14	786.70	765.36
9.00%	3,179.97	2,075.84	1,608.91	1,465.02	1,266.76	1,014.27	899.73	839.20	804.62	783.99
9.25%	3,191.62	2,087.99	1,621.62	1,478.02	1,280.33	1,029.19	915.87	856.38	822.68	802.74
9.50%	3,203.29	2,100.19	1,634.40	1,491.09	1,293.98	1,044.22	932.13	873.70	840.85	821.61
9.75%	3,214.99	2,112.42	1,647.23	1,504.22	1,307.70	1,059.36	948.52	891.14	859.15	840.59
10.00%	3,226.72	2,124.70	1,660.12	1,517.42	1,321.51	1,074.61	965.02	908.70	877.57	859.67
10.25%	3,238.47	2,137.03	1,673.06	1,530.68	1,335.39	1,089.95	981.64	926.38	896.10	878.86
10.50%	3,250.24	2,149.39	1,686.07	1,544.00	1,349.35	1,105.40	998.38	944.18	914.74	898.13
10.75%	3,262.05	2,161.80	1,699.13	1,557.39	1,363.39	1,120.95	1,015.23	962.09	933.48	917.50

$100,000   11.00 - 20.75%   3 - 35 Years

	3	5	7	8	10	15	20	25	30	35
11.00%	3,273.87	2,174.24	1,712.24	1,570.84	1,377.50	1,136.60	1,032.19	980.11	952.32	936.96
11.25%	3,285.72	2,186.73	1,725.42	1,584.36	1,391.69	1,152.34	1,049.26	998.24	971.26	956.49
11.50%	3,297.60	2,199.26	1,738.65	1,597.94	1,405.95	1,168.19	1,066.43	1,016.47	990.29	976.11
11.75%	3,309.50	2,211.83	1,751.93	1,611.58	1,420.29	1,184.13	1,083.71	1,034.80	1,009.41	995.79
12.00%	3,321.43	2,224.44	1,765.27	1,625.28	1,434.71	1,200.17	1,101.09	1,053.22	1,028.61	1,015.55
12.25%	3,333.38	2,237.10	1,778.67	1,639.05	1,449.20	1,216.30	1,118.56	1,071.74	1,047.90	1,035.37
12.50%	3,345.36	2,249.79	1,792.12	1,652.88	1,463.76	1,232.52	1,136.14	1,090.35	1,067.26	1,055.25
12.75%	3,357.37	2,262.53	1,805.63	1,666.77	1,478.40	1,248.84	1,153.81	1,109.05	1,086.69	1,075.20
13.00%	3,369.40	2,275.31	1,819.20	1,680.73	1,493.11	1,265.24	1,171.58	1,127.84	1,106.20	1,095.19
13.25%	3,381.45	2,288.13	1,832.82	1,694.74	1,507.89	1,281.74	1,189.43	1,146.70	1,125.77	1,115.24
13.50%	3,393.53	2,300.98	1,846.49	1,708.82	1,522.74	1,298.32	1,207.37	1,165.64	1,145.41	1,135.34
13.75%	3,405.63	2,313.88	1,860.22	1,722.95	1,537.67	1,314.99	1,225.41	1,184.67	1,165.11	1,155.49
14.00%	3,417.76	2,326.83	1,874.00	1,737.15	1,552.66	1,331.74	1,243.52	1,203.76	1,184.87	1,175.67
14.25%	3,429.92	2,339.81	1,887.84	1,751.41	1,567.73	1,348.58	1,261.72	1,222.93	1,204.69	1,195.90
14.50%	3,442.10	2,352.83	1,901.73	1,765.73	1,582.87	1,365.50	1,280.00	1,242.16	1,224.56	1,216.17
14.75%	3,454.30	2,365.89	1,915.68	1,780.10	1,598.07	1,382.50	1,298.36	1,261.46	1,244.48	1,236.47
15.00%	3,466.53	2,378.99	1,929.68	1,794.54	1,613.35	1,399.59	1,316.79	1,280.83	1,264.44	1,256.81
15.25%	3,478.79	2,392.14	1,943.73	1,809.04	1,628.69	1,416.75	1,335.30	1,300.26	1,284.46	1,277.18
15.50%	3,491.07	2,405.32	1,957.83	1,823.59	1,644.11	1,433.99	1,353.88	1,319.75	1,304.52	1,297.58
15.75%	3,503.37	2,418.54	1,971.99	1,838.21	1,659.58	1,451.31	1,372.53	1,339.29	1,324.62	1,318.01
16.00%	3,515.70	2,431.81	1,986.21	1,852.88	1,675.13	1,468.70	1,391.26	1,358.89	1,344.76	1,338.47
16.25%	3,528.06	2,445.11	2,000.47	1,867.61	1,690.74	1,486.17	1,410.05	1,378.54	1,364.93	1,358.95
16.50%	3,540.44	2,458.45	2,014.79	1,882.40	1,706.42	1,503.71	1,428.90	1,398.24	1,385.15	1,379.45
16.75%	3,552.84	2,471.84	2,029.16	1,897.24	1,722.17	1,521.32	1,447.82	1,418.00	1,405.40	1,399.98
17.00%	3,565.27	2,485.26	2,043.58	1,912.15	1,737.98	1,539.00	1,466.80	1,437.80	1,425.68	1,420.53
17.25%	3,577.73	2,498.72	2,058.05	1,927.10	1,753.85	1,556.76	1,485.84	1,457.64	1,445.99	1,441.09
17.50%	3,590.21	2,512.22	2,072.58	1,942.12	1,769.79	1,574.58	1,504.94	1,477.53	1,466.33	1,461.68
17.75%	3,602.71	2,525.76	2,087.16	1,957.19	1,785.79	1,592.47	1,524.10	1,497.46	1,486.69	1,482.28
18.00%	3,615.24	2,539.34	2,101.78	1,972.32	1,801.85	1,610.42	1,543.31	1,517.43	1,507.09	1,502.89
18.25%	3,627.79	2,552.96	2,116.46	1,987.51	1,817.98	1,628.44	1,562.58	1,537.44	1,527.50	1,523.52
18.50%	3,640.37	2,566.62	2,131.19	2,002.74	1,834.17	1,646.52	1,581.90	1,557.48	1,547.94	1,544.17
18.75%	3,652.97	2,580.32	2,145.97	2,018.04	1,850.41	1,664.67	1,601.27	1,577.57	1,568.41	1,564.83
19.00%	3,665.60	2,594.06	2,160.80	2,033.39	1,866.72	1,682.88	1,620.68	1,597.68	1,588.89	1,585.49
19.25%	3,678.25	2,607.83	2,175.68	2,048.79	1,883.09	1,701.14	1,640.15	1,617.83	1,609.40	1,606.18
19.50%	3,690.93	2,621.64	2,190.61	2,064.25	1,899.52	1,719.47	1,659.66	1,638.01	1,629.92	1,626.87
19.75%	3,703.63	2,635.50	2,205.59	2,079.76	1,916.01	1,737.85	1,679.22	1,658.21	1,650.46	1,647.57
20.00%	3,716.36	2,649.39	2,220.62	2,095.32	1,932.56	1,756.30	1,698.82	1,678.45	1,671.02	1,668.28
20.25%	3,729.11	2,663.32	2,235.70	2,110.94	1,949.16	1,774.79	1,718.47	1,698.72	1,691.59	1,689.00
20.50%	3,741.88	2,677.29	2,250.82	2,126.61	1,965.82	1,793.35	1,738.15	1,719.01	1,712.18	1,709.72
20.75%	3,754.68	2,691.29	2,266.00	2,142.33	1,982.54	1,811.95	1,757.88	1,739.32	1,732.78	1,730.46

$102,500   1.00 - 10.75%   3 - 35 Years

	3	5	7	8	10	15	20	25	30	35
1.00%	2,891.33	1,752.11	1,263.95	1,111.43	897.94	613.46	471.39	386.29	329.68	289.34
1.25%	2,902.42	1,763.16	1,275.04	1,122.54	909.11	624.79	482.91	398.00	341.58	301.44
1.50%	2,913.54	1,774.26	1,286.18	1,133.72	920.36	636.26	494.61	409.93	353.75	313.84
1.75%	2,924.69	1,785.41	1,297.39	1,144.97	931.71	647.86	506.48	422.08	366.17	326.54
2.00%	2,935.86	1,796.60	1,308.66	1,156.29	943.14	659.60	518.53	434.45	378.86	339.54
2.25%	2,947.06	1,807.83	1,319.99	1,167.68	954.66	671.46	530.75	447.03	391.80	352.84
2.50%	2,958.29	1,819.10	1,331.39	1,179.14	966.27	683.46	543.15	459.83	405.00	366.43
2.75%	2,969.54	1,830.43	1,342.85	1,190.68	977.96	695.59	555.72	472.84	418.45	380.31
3.00%	2,980.82	1,841.79	1,354.36	1,202.28	989.75	707.85	568.46	486.07	432.14	394.47
3.25%	2,992.13	1,853.20	1,365.94	1,213.96	1,001.62	720.24	581.38	499.50	446.09	408.91
3.50%	3,003.46	1,864.65	1,377.58	1,225.70	1,013.58	732.75	594.46	513.14	460.27	423.62
3.75%	3,014.82	1,876.15	1,389.29	1,237.52	1,025.63	745.40	607.71	526.98	474.69	438.60
4.00%	3,026.21	1,887.69	1,401.05	1,249.40	1,037.76	758.18	621.13	541.03	489.35	453.84
4.25%	3,037.62	1,899.28	1,412.88	1,261.36	1,049.98	771.09	634.72	555.28	504.24	469.34
4.50%	3,049.06	1,910.91	1,424.77	1,273.38	1,062.29	784.12	648.47	569.73	519.35	485.09
4.75%	3,060.53	1,922.58	1,436.72	1,285.48	1,074.69	797.28	662.38	584.37	534.69	501.08
5.00%	3,072.02	1,934.30	1,448.73	1,297.64	1,087.17	810.56	676.45	599.20	550.24	517.30
5.25%	3,083.54	1,946.06	1,460.80	1,309.88	1,099.74	823.97	690.69	614.23	566.01	533.76
5.50%	3,095.08	1,957.87	1,472.93	1,322.18	1,112.39	837.51	705.08	629.44	581.98	550.44
5.75%	3,106.65	1,969.72	1,485.12	1,334.55	1,125.13	851.17	719.64	644.83	598.16	567.34
6.00%	3,118.25	1,981.61	1,497.38	1,347.00	1,137.96	864.95	734.34	660.41	614.54	584.44
6.25%	3,129.87	1,993.55	1,509.69	1,359.51	1,150.87	878.86	749.20	676.16	631.11	601.75
6.50%	3,141.52	2,005.53	1,522.07	1,372.09	1,163.87	892.89	764.21	692.09	647.87	619.26
6.75%	3,153.20	2,017.55	1,534.50	1,384.74	1,176.95	907.03	779.37	708.18	664.81	636.95
7.00%	3,164.90	2,029.62	1,547.00	1,397.46	1,190.11	921.30	794.68	724.45	681.94	654.83
7.25%	3,176.63	2,041.73	1,559.56	1,410.24	1,203.36	935.68	810.14	740.88	699.23	672.88
7.50%	3,188.39	2,053.89	1,572.17	1,423.10	1,216.69	950.19	825.73	757.47	716.69	691.10
7.75%	3,200.17	2,066.09	1,584.85	1,436.02	1,230.11	964.81	841.47	774.21	734.32	709.48
8.00%	3,211.98	2,078.33	1,597.59	1,449.01	1,243.61	979.54	857.35	791.11	752.11	728.02
8.25%	3,223.81	2,090.62	1,610.38	1,462.07	1,257.19	994.39	873.37	808.16	770.05	746.70
8.50%	3,235.67	2,102.94	1,623.24	1,475.19	1,270.85	1,009.36	889.52	825.36	788.14	765.53
8.75%	3,247.56	2,115.32	1,636.16	1,488.39	1,284.60	1,024.43	905.80	842.70	806.37	784.50
9.00%	3,259.47	2,127.73	1,649.13	1,501.65	1,298.43	1,039.62	922.22	860.18	824.74	803.59
9.25%	3,271.41	2,140.19	1,662.16	1,514.97	1,312.34	1,054.92	938.76	877.79	843.24	822.81
9.50%	3,283.38	2,152.69	1,675.26	1,528.37	1,326.32	1,070.33	955.43	895.54	861.88	842.15
9.75%	3,295.37	2,165.23	1,688.41	1,541.83	1,340.39	1,085.85	972.23	913.42	880.63	861.60
10.00%	3,307.39	2,177.82	1,701.62	1,555.35	1,354.55	1,101.47	989.15	931.42	899.51	881.16
10.25%	3,319.43	2,190.45	1,714.89	1,568.94	1,368.77	1,117.20	1,006.18	949.54	918.50	900.83
10.50%	3,331.50	2,203.12	1,728.22	1,582.60	1,383.08	1,133.03	1,023.34	967.79	937.61	920.59
10.75%	3,343.60	2,215.84	1,741.61	1,596.32	1,397.47	1,148.97	1,040.61	986.15	956.82	940.44

$102,500   11.00 - 20.75%   3 - 35 Years

	3	5	7	8	10	15	20	25	30	35
11.00%	3,355.72	2,228.60	1,755.05	1,610.11	1,411.94	1,165.01	1,057.99	1,004.62	976.13	960.38
11.25%	3,367.87	2,241.40	1,768.55	1,623.97	1,426.48	1,181.15	1,075.49	1,023.20	995.54	980.41
11.50%	3,380.04	2,254.24	1,782.11	1,637.89	1,441.10	1,197.39	1,093.09	1,041.88	1,015.05	1,000.51
11.75%	3,392.24	2,267.13	1,795.73	1,651.87	1,455.80	1,213.73	1,110.80	1,060.67	1,034.64	1,020.69
12.00%	3,404.47	2,280.06	1,809.41	1,665.92	1,470.58	1,230.17	1,128.61	1,079.55	1,054.33	1,040.94
12.25%	3,416.72	2,293.03	1,823.14	1,680.03	1,485.43	1,246.71	1,146.53	1,098.54	1,074.09	1,061.26
12.50%	3,429.00	2,306.04	1,836.93	1,694.20	1,500.36	1,263.34	1,164.54	1,117.61	1,093.94	1,081.64
12.75%	3,441.30	2,319.09	1,850.77	1,708.44	1,515.36	1,280.06	1,182.66	1,136.78	1,113.86	1,102.08
13.00%	3,453.63	2,332.19	1,864.68	1,722.74	1,530.44	1,296.87	1,200.87	1,156.03	1,133.85	1,122.57
13.25%	3,465.99	2,345.33	1,878.64	1,737.11	1,545.59	1,313.78	1,219.17	1,175.37	1,153.92	1,143.12
13.50%	3,478.37	2,358.51	1,892.65	1,751.54	1,560.81	1,330.78	1,237.56	1,194.79	1,174.05	1,163.72
13.75%	3,490.77	2,371.73	1,906.72	1,766.03	1,576.11	1,347.86	1,256.04	1,214.28	1,194.24	1,184.37
14.00%	3,503.21	2,385.00	1,920.85	1,780.58	1,591.48	1,365.03	1,274.61	1,233.86	1,214.49	1,205.07
14.25%	3,515.67	2,398.30	1,935.03	1,795.19	1,606.92	1,382.29	1,293.26	1,253.50	1,234.80	1,225.80
14.50%	3,528.15	2,411.65	1,949.27	1,809.87	1,622.44	1,399.64	1,312.00	1,273.22	1,255.17	1,246.57
14.75%	3,540.66	2,425.04	1,963.57	1,824.61	1,638.03	1,417.07	1,330.81	1,293.00	1,275.59	1,267.39
15.00%	3,553.20	2,438.47	1,977.92	1,839.40	1,653.68	1,434.58	1,349.71	1,312.85	1,296.06	1,288.23
15.25%	3,565.76	2,451.94	1,992.32	1,854.26	1,669.41	1,452.17	1,368.68	1,332.76	1,316.57	1,309.11
15.50%	3,578.34	2,465.45	2,006.78	1,869.18	1,685.21	1,469.84	1,387.73	1,352.74	1,337.13	1,330.02
15.75%	3,590.96	2,479.01	2,021.29	1,884.16	1,701.07	1,487.59	1,406.85	1,372.77	1,357.73	1,350.96
16.00%	3,603.60	2,492.60	2,035.86	1,899.20	1,717.01	1,505.42	1,426.04	1,392.86	1,378.38	1,371.93
16.25%	3,616.26	2,506.24	2,050.48	1,914.30	1,733.01	1,523.32	1,445.30	1,413.00	1,399.06	1,392.92
16.50%	3,628.95	2,519.91	2,065.16	1,929.46	1,749.08	1,541.30	1,464.62	1,433.20	1,419.78	1,413.94
16.75%	3,641.66	2,533.63	2,079.89	1,944.67	1,765.22	1,559.35	1,484.02	1,453.45	1,440.53	1,434.98
17.00%	3,654.40	2,547.39	2,094.67	1,959.95	1,781.43	1,577.48	1,503.47	1,473.74	1,461.32	1,456.04
17.25%	3,667.17	2,561.19	2,109.51	1,975.28	1,797.70	1,595.68	1,522.99	1,494.08	1,482.14	1,477.12
17.50%	3,679.96	2,575.03	2,124.39	1,990.67	1,814.03	1,613.94	1,542.57	1,514.47	1,502.98	1,498.22
17.75%	3,692.78	2,588.91	2,139.33	2,006.12	1,830.43	1,632.28	1,562.20	1,534.90	1,523.86	1,519.33
18.00%	3,705.62	2,602.83	2,154.33	2,021.63	1,846.90	1,650.68	1,581.89	1,555.37	1,544.76	1,540.46
18.25%	3,718.49	2,616.79	2,169.37	2,037.19	1,863.43	1,669.15	1,601.64	1,575.87	1,565.69	1,561.61
18.50%	3,731.38	2,630.79	2,184.47	2,052.81	1,880.02	1,687.69	1,621.44	1,596.42	1,586.64	1,582.77
18.75%	3,744.30	2,644.83	2,199.62	2,068.49	1,896.67	1,706.29	1,641.30	1,617.00	1,607.62	1,603.95
19.00%	3,757.24	2,658.91	2,214.82	2,084.22	1,913.39	1,724.95	1,661.20	1,637.62	1,628.61	1,625.13
19.25%	3,770.21	2,673.03	2,230.07	2,100.01	1,930.17	1,743.67	1,681.16	1,658.27	1,649.63	1,646.33
19.50%	3,783.20	2,687.19	2,245.38	2,115.85	1,947.01	1,762.46	1,701.16	1,678.96	1,670.67	1,667.54
19.75%	3,796.22	2,701.38	2,260.73	2,131.75	1,963.91	1,781.30	1,721.20	1,699.67	1,691.72	1,688.76
20.00%	3,809.27	2,715.62	2,276.14	2,147.70	1,980.87	1,800.20	1,741.30	1,720.41	1,712.79	1,709.99
20.25%	3,822.34	2,729.90	2,291.59	2,163.71	1,997.89	1,819.16	1,761.43	1,741.18	1,733.88	1,731.22
20.50%	3,835.43	2,744.22	2,307.09	2,179.77	2,014.97	1,838.18	1,781.61	1,761.98	1,754.99	1,752.47
20.75%	3,848.55	2,758.57	2,322.65	2,195.89	2,032.11	1,857.25	1,801.83	1,782.81	1,776.10	1,773.72

	3	5	7	8	10	15	20	25	30	35
1.00%	2,961.85	1,794.84	1,294.78	1,138.54	919.84	628.42	482.89	395.72	337.72	296.40
1.25%	2,973.21	1,806.17	1,306.14	1,149.92	931.28	640.03	494.69	407.71	349.91	308.79
1.50%	2,984.61	1,817.54	1,317.55	1,161.37	942.81	651.78	506.67	419.93	362.38	321.49
1.75%	2,996.02	1,828.95	1,329.04	1,172.89	954.43	663.66	518.84	432.38	375.11	334.51
2.00%	3,007.47	1,840.41	1,340.58	1,184.49	966.14	675.68	531.18	445.05	388.10	347.83
2.25%	3,018.94	1,851.92	1,352.19	1,196.16	977.94	687.84	543.70	457.94	401.36	361.45
2.50%	3,030.44	1,863.47	1,363.86	1,207.90	989.83	700.13	556.40	471.05	414.88	375.37
2.75%	3,041.97	1,875.07	1,375.60	1,219.72	1,001.82	712.55	569.27	484.38	428.65	389.59
3.00%	3,053.53	1,886.71	1,387.40	1,231.61	1,013.89	725.11	582.33	497.92	442.68	404.09
3.25%	3,065.11	1,898.40	1,399.26	1,243.56	1,026.05	737.80	595.56	511.68	456.97	418.88
3.50%	3,076.72	1,910.13	1,411.18	1,255.60	1,038.30	750.63	608.96	525.65	471.50	433.96
3.75%	3,088.35	1,921.91	1,423.17	1,267.70	1,050.64	763.58	622.53	539.84	486.27	449.30
4.00%	3,100.02	1,933.73	1,435.22	1,279.87	1,063.07	776.67	636.28	554.23	501.29	464.91
4.25%	3,111.71	1,945.60	1,447.34	1,292.12	1,075.59	789.89	650.20	568.83	516.54	480.79
4.50%	3,123.43	1,957.52	1,459.52	1,304.44	1,088.20	803.24	664.28	583.62	532.02	496.92
4.75%	3,135.17	1,969.48	1,471.76	1,316.83	1,100.90	816.72	678.53	598.62	547.73	513.30
5.00%	3,146.94	1,981.48	1,484.06	1,329.29	1,113.69	830.33	692.95	613.82	563.66	529.92
5.25%	3,158.74	1,993.53	1,496.43	1,341.82	1,126.56	844.07	707.54	629.21	579.81	546.78
5.50%	3,170.57	2,005.62	1,508.85	1,354.43	1,139.53	857.94	722.28	644.79	596.18	563.87
5.75%	3,182.42	2,017.76	1,521.35	1,367.10	1,152.58	871.93	737.19	660.56	612.75	581.18
6.00%	3,194.30	2,029.94	1,533.90	1,379.85	1,165.72	886.05	752.25	676.52	629.53	598.70
6.25%	3,206.21	2,042.17	1,546.51	1,392.67	1,178.94	900.29	767.47	692.65	646.50	616.43
6.50%	3,218.15	2,054.45	1,559.19	1,405.55	1,192.25	914.66	782.85	708.97	663.67	634.36
6.75%	3,230.11	2,066.76	1,571.93	1,418.51	1,205.65	929.15	798.38	725.46	681.03	652.49
7.00%	3,242.10	2,079.13	1,584.73	1,431.54	1,219.14	943.77	814.06	742.12	698.57	670.80
7.25%	3,254.11	2,091.53	1,597.59	1,444.64	1,232.71	958.51	829.89	758.95	716.29	689.29
7.50%	3,266.15	2,103.98	1,610.52	1,457.81	1,246.37	973.36	845.87	775.94	734.18	707.95
7.75%	3,278.22	2,116.48	1,623.51	1,471.04	1,260.11	988.34	862.00	793.10	752.23	726.78
8.00%	3,290.32	2,129.02	1,636.55	1,484.35	1,273.94	1,003.43	878.26	810.41	770.45	745.77
8.25%	3,302.44	2,141.61	1,649.66	1,497.73	1,287.85	1,018.65	894.67	827.87	788.83	764.92
8.50%	3,314.59	2,154.24	1,662.83	1,511.17	1,301.85	1,033.98	911.21	845.49	807.36	784.20
8.75%	3,326.77	2,166.91	1,676.06	1,524.69	1,315.93	1,049.42	927.90	863.25	826.04	803.63
9.00%	3,338.97	2,179.63	1,689.35	1,538.27	1,330.10	1,064.98	944.71	881.16	844.85	823.19
9.25%	3,351.20	2,192.39	1,702.71	1,551.92	1,344.34	1,080.65	961.66	899.20	863.81	842.88
9.50%	3,363.46	2,205.20	1,716.12	1,565.64	1,358.67	1,096.44	978.74	917.38	882.90	862.69
9.75%	3,375.74	2,218.05	1,729.59	1,579.43	1,373.09	1,112.33	995.94	935.69	902.11	882.62
10.00%	3,388.05	2,230.94	1,743.12	1,593.29	1,387.58	1,128.34	1,013.27	954.14	921.45	902.66
10.25%	3,400.39	2,243.88	1,756.72	1,607.21	1,402.16	1,144.45	1,030.73	972.70	940.91	922.80
10.50%	3,412.76	2,256.86	1,770.37	1,621.20	1,416.82	1,160.67	1,048.30	991.39	960.48	943.04
10.75%	3,425.15	2,269.89	1,784.08	1,635.26	1,431.56	1,177.00	1,065.99	1,010.20	980.16	963.38

$105,000   11.00 - 20.75%   3 - 35 Years

	3	5	7	8	10	15	20	25	30	35
11.00%	3,437.57	2,282.95	1,797.86	1,649.38	1,446.38	1,193.43	1,083.80	1,029.12	999.94	983.81
11.25%	3,450.01	2,296.07	1,811.69	1,663.58	1,461.27	1,209.96	1,101.72	1,048.15	1,019.82	1,004.32
11.50%	3,462.48	2,309.22	1,825.58	1,677.83	1,476.25	1,226.60	1,119.75	1,067.29	1,039.81	1,024.91
11.75%	3,474.98	2,322.42	1,839.53	1,692.16	1,491.31	1,243.34	1,137.89	1,086.54	1,059.88	1,045.58
12.00%	3,487.50	2,335.67	1,853.54	1,706.55	1,506.44	1,260.18	1,156.14	1,105.89	1,080.04	1,066.33
12.25%	3,500.05	2,348.95	1,867.60	1,721.00	1,521.66	1,277.11	1,174.49	1,125.33	1,100.29	1,087.14
12.50%	3,512.63	2,362.28	1,881.73	1,735.52	1,536.95	1,294.15	1,192.95	1,144.87	1,120.62	1,108.02
12.75%	3,525.23	2,375.66	1,895.91	1,750.11	1,552.32	1,311.28	1,211.50	1,164.50	1,141.03	1,128.96
13.00%	3,537.86	2,389.07	1,910.16	1,764.76	1,567.76	1,328.50	1,230.15	1,184.23	1,161.51	1,149.95
13.25%	3,550.52	2,402.53	1,924.46	1,779.48	1,583.28	1,345.82	1,248.90	1,204.04	1,182.06	1,171.00
13.50%	3,563.21	2,416.03	1,938.81	1,794.26	1,598.88	1,363.23	1,267.74	1,223.93	1,202.68	1,192.11
13.75%	3,575.91	2,429.58	1,953.23	1,809.10	1,614.55	1,380.74	1,286.68	1,243.90	1,223.37	1,213.26
14.00%	3,588.65	2,443.17	1,967.70	1,824.01	1,630.30	1,398.33	1,305.70	1,263.95	1,244.12	1,234.46
14.25%	3,601.41	2,456.80	1,982.23	1,838.98	1,646.12	1,416.01	1,324.80	1,284.07	1,264.92	1,255.70
14.50%	3,614.20	2,470.47	1,996.82	1,854.01	1,662.01	1,433.78	1,344.00	1,304.27	1,285.78	1,276.98
14.75%	3,627.02	2,484.18	2,011.46	1,869.11	1,677.98	1,451.63	1,363.27	1,324.54	1,306.70	1,298.30
15.00%	3,639.86	2,497.94	2,026.16	1,884.27	1,694.02	1,469.57	1,382.63	1,344.87	1,327.67	1,319.65
15.25%	3,652.73	2,511.74	2,040.91	1,899.49	1,710.13	1,487.59	1,402.06	1,365.27	1,348.68	1,341.04
15.50%	3,665.62	2,525.59	2,055.73	1,914.77	1,726.31	1,505.69	1,421.57	1,385.73	1,369.74	1,362.46
15.75%	3,678.54	2,539.47	2,070.59	1,930.12	1,742.56	1,523.87	1,441.16	1,406.25	1,390.85	1,383.91
16.00%	3,691.49	2,553.40	2,085.52	1,945.52	1,758.89	1,542.14	1,460.82	1,426.83	1,411.99	1,405.39
16.25%	3,704.46	2,567.36	2,100.49	1,960.99	1,775.28	1,560.48	1,480.55	1,447.47	1,433.18	1,426.90
16.50%	3,717.46	2,581.37	2,115.53	1,976.52	1,791.74	1,578.89	1,500.35	1,468.16	1,454.41	1,448.43
16.75%	3,730.49	2,595.43	2,130.62	1,992.10	1,808.28	1,597.39	1,520.21	1,488.90	1,475.67	1,469.98
17.00%	3,743.54	2,609.52	2,145.76	2,007.75	1,824.88	1,615.95	1,540.14	1,509.69	1,496.96	1,491.55
17.25%	3,756.61	2,623.66	2,160.96	2,023.46	1,841.54	1,634.59	1,560.13	1,530.52	1,518.29	1,513.15
17.50%	3,769.72	2,637.83	2,176.21	2,039.23	1,858.28	1,653.31	1,580.19	1,551.41	1,539.64	1,534.76
17.75%	3,782.85	2,652.05	2,191.51	2,055.05	1,875.08	1,672.09	1,600.30	1,572.33	1,561.03	1,556.39
18.00%	3,796.00	2,666.31	2,206.87	2,070.94	1,891.94	1,690.94	1,620.48	1,593.30	1,582.44	1,578.04
18.25%	3,809.18	2,680.61	2,222.29	2,086.88	1,908.88	1,709.86	1,640.71	1,614.31	1,603.88	1,599.70
18.50%	3,822.39	2,694.95	2,237.75	2,102.88	1,925.87	1,728.85	1,660.99	1,635.36	1,625.34	1,621.38
18.75%	3,835.62	2,709.33	2,253.27	2,118.94	1,942.93	1,747.90	1,681.33	1,656.44	1,646.83	1,643.07
19.00%	3,848.88	2,723.76	2,268.84	2,135.06	1,960.06	1,767.02	1,701.72	1,677.56	1,668.34	1,664.77
19.25%	3,862.17	2,738.22	2,284.47	2,151.23	1,977.25	1,786.20	1,722.16	1,698.72	1,689.87	1,686.48
19.50%	3,875.48	2,752.73	2,300.14	2,167.46	1,994.50	1,805.44	1,742.65	1,719.91	1,711.42	1,708.21
19.75%	3,888.81	2,767.27	2,315.87	2,183.74	2,011.81	1,824.75	1,763.18	1,741.13	1,732.98	1,729.95
20.00%	3,902.18	2,781.86	2,331.65	2,200.09	2,029.18	1,844.11	1,783.77	1,762.37	1,754.57	1,751.69
20.25%	3,915.56	2,796.48	2,347.48	2,216.48	2,046.62	1,863.53	1,804.39	1,783.65	1,776.17	1,773.45
20.50%	3,928.98	2,811.15	2,363.37	2,232.94	2,064.11	1,883.01	1,825.06	1,804.96	1,797.79	1,795.21
20.75%	3,942.42	2,825.86	2,379.30	2,249.44	2,081.67	1,902.55	1,845.77	1,826.29	1,819.42	1,816.98

$107,500   1.00 - 10.75%   3 - 35 Years

	3	5	7	8	10	15	20	25	30	35
1.00%	3,032.37	1,837.58	1,325.61	1,165.65	941.74	643.38	494.39	405.14	345.76	303.46
1.25%	3,044.01	1,849.17	1,337.23	1,177.30	953.45	655.27	506.47	417.42	358.25	316.14
1.50%	3,055.67	1,860.81	1,348.92	1,189.02	965.26	667.30	518.74	429.93	371.00	329.15
1.75%	3,067.36	1,872.50	1,360.68	1,200.82	977.16	679.47	531.19	442.67	384.04	342.47
2.00%	3,079.08	1,884.23	1,372.50	1,212.69	989.14	691.77	543.82	455.64	397.34	356.11
2.25%	3,090.82	1,896.01	1,384.38	1,224.64	1,001.23	704.22	556.64	468.84	410.91	370.05
2.50%	3,102.60	1,907.84	1,396.33	1,236.66	1,013.40	716.80	569.65	482.26	424.75	384.31
2.75%	3,114.40	1,919.71	1,408.35	1,248.76	1,025.67	729.52	582.83	495.91	438.86	398.86
3.00%	3,126.23	1,931.63	1,420.43	1,260.93	1,038.03	742.38	596.19	509.78	453.22	413.71
3.25%	3,138.09	1,943.60	1,432.57	1,273.17	1,050.48	755.37	609.74	523.86	467.85	428.86
3.50%	3,149.97	1,955.61	1,444.78	1,285.49	1,063.02	768.50	623.46	538.17	482.72	444.29
3.75%	3,161.89	1,967.67	1,457.06	1,297.88	1,075.66	781.76	637.35	552.69	497.85	460.00
4.00%	3,173.83	1,979.78	1,469.40	1,310.35	1,088.39	795.16	651.43	567.42	513.22	475.98
4.25%	3,185.80	1,991.93	1,481.80	1,322.89	1,101.20	808.70	665.68	582.37	528.84	492.24
4.50%	3,197.79	2,004.12	1,494.27	1,335.50	1,114.11	822.37	680.10	597.52	544.69	508.75
4.75%	3,209.82	2,016.37	1,506.80	1,348.18	1,127.11	836.17	694.69	612.88	560.77	525.52
5.00%	3,221.87	2,028.66	1,519.40	1,360.94	1,140.20	850.10	709.45	628.43	577.08	542.54
5.25%	3,233.95	2,040.99	1,532.06	1,373.77	1,153.39	864.17	724.38	644.19	593.62	559.80
5.50%	3,246.06	2,053.37	1,544.78	1,386.68	1,166.66	878.36	739.48	660.14	610.37	577.29
5.75%	3,258.20	2,065.80	1,557.57	1,399.65	1,180.02	892.69	754.74	676.29	627.34	595.01
6.00%	3,270.36	2,078.28	1,570.42	1,412.70	1,193.47	907.15	770.16	692.62	644.52	612.95
6.25%	3,282.55	2,090.80	1,583.34	1,425.83	1,207.01	921.73	785.75	709.14	661.90	631.11
6.50%	3,294.77	2,103.36	1,596.31	1,439.02	1,220.64	936.44	801.49	725.85	679.47	649.47
6.75%	3,307.01	2,115.97	1,609.36	1,452.29	1,234.36	951.28	817.39	742.73	697.24	668.02
7.00%	3,319.29	2,128.63	1,622.46	1,465.62	1,248.17	966.24	833.45	759.79	715.20	686.77
7.25%	3,331.59	2,141.33	1,635.63	1,479.03	1,262.06	981.33	849.65	777.02	733.34	705.70
7.50%	3,343.92	2,154.08	1,648.86	1,492.52	1,276.04	996.54	866.01	794.42	751.66	724.81
7.75%	3,356.28	2,166.87	1,662.16	1,506.07	1,290.11	1,011.87	882.52	811.98	770.14	744.09
8.00%	3,368.66	2,179.71	1,675.52	1,519.69	1,304.27	1,027.33	899.17	829.70	788.80	763.53
8.25%	3,381.07	2,192.60	1,688.94	1,533.39	1,318.52	1,042.90	915.97	847.58	807.61	783.13
8.50%	3,393.51	2,205.53	1,702.42	1,547.15	1,332.85	1,058.60	932.91	865.62	826.58	802.88
8.75%	3,405.98	2,218.50	1,715.97	1,560.99	1,347.26	1,074.41	949.99	883.80	845.70	822.77
9.00%	3,418.47	2,231.52	1,729.58	1,574.90	1,361.76	1,090.34	967.21	902.14	864.97	842.79
9.25%	3,430.99	2,244.59	1,743.25	1,588.87	1,376.35	1,106.38	984.56	920.61	884.38	862.95
9.50%	3,443.54	2,257.70	1,756.98	1,602.92	1,391.02	1,122.54	1,002.04	939.22	903.92	883.23
9.75%	3,456.12	2,270.86	1,770.77	1,617.04	1,405.78	1,138.81	1,019.66	957.97	923.59	903.63
10.00%	3,468.72	2,284.06	1,784.63	1,631.22	1,420.62	1,155.20	1,037.40	976.85	943.39	924.15
10.25%	3,481.35	2,297.30	1,798.54	1,645.48	1,435.54	1,171.70	1,055.27	995.86	963.31	944.77
10.50%	3,494.01	2,310.59	1,812.52	1,659.80	1,450.55	1,188.30	1,073.26	1,015.00	983.34	965.49
10.75%	3,506.70	2,323.93	1,826.56	1,674.19	1,465.64	1,205.02	1,091.37	1,034.25	1,003.49	986.32

$107,500   11.00 - 20.75%   3 - 35 Years

	3	5	7	8	10	15	20	25	30	35
11.00%	3,519.41	2,337.31	1,840.66	1,688.66	1,480.81	1,221.84	1,109.60	1,053.62	1,023.75	1,007.23
11.25%	3,532.15	2,350.74	1,854.82	1,703.19	1,496.07	1,238.77	1,127.95	1,073.11	1,044.11	1,028.23
11.50%	3,544.92	2,364.21	1,869.04	1,717.78	1,511.40	1,255.80	1,146.41	1,092.70	1,064.56	1,049.32
11.75%	3,557.72	2,377.72	1,883.33	1,732.45	1,526.82	1,272.94	1,164.99	1,112.41	1,085.12	1,070.48
12.00%	3,570.54	2,391.28	1,897.67	1,747.18	1,542.31	1,290.18	1,183.67	1,132.22	1,105.76	1,091.72
12.25%	3,583.39	2,404.88	1,912.07	1,761.98	1,557.89	1,307.52	1,202.46	1,152.12	1,126.49	1,113.02
12.50%	3,596.26	2,418.53	1,926.53	1,776.85	1,573.54	1,324.96	1,221.35	1,172.13	1,147.30	1,134.40
12.75%	3,609.17	2,432.22	1,941.05	1,791.78	1,589.28	1,342.50	1,240.35	1,192.23	1,168.20	1,155.84
13.00%	3,622.10	2,445.96	1,955.64	1,806.78	1,605.09	1,360.14	1,259.44	1,212.42	1,189.16	1,177.33
13.25%	3,635.06	2,459.73	1,970.28	1,821.85	1,620.98	1,377.87	1,278.64	1,232.70	1,210.21	1,198.89
13.50%	3,648.04	2,473.56	1,984.98	1,836.98	1,636.95	1,395.69	1,297.93	1,253.07	1,231.32	1,220.49
13.75%	3,661.06	2,487.43	1,999.73	1,852.17	1,652.99	1,413.61	1,317.31	1,273.52	1,252.50	1,242.15
14.00%	3,674.10	2,501.34	2,014.55	1,867.44	1,669.11	1,431.62	1,336.78	1,294.04	1,273.74	1,263.85
14.25%	3,687.16	2,515.29	2,029.43	1,882.76	1,685.31	1,449.72	1,356.35	1,314.65	1,295.04	1,285.60
14.50%	3,700.26	2,529.29	2,044.36	1,898.16	1,701.58	1,467.91	1,376.00	1,335.33	1,316.40	1,307.38
14.75%	3,713.38	2,543.33	2,059.35	1,913.61	1,717.93	1,486.19	1,395.73	1,356.07	1,337.81	1,329.21
15.00%	3,726.52	2,557.42	2,074.40	1,929.13	1,734.35	1,504.56	1,415.55	1,376.89	1,359.28	1,351.07
15.25%	3,739.70	2,571.55	2,089.51	1,944.71	1,750.85	1,523.01	1,435.45	1,397.78	1,380.79	1,372.97
15.50%	3,752.90	2,585.72	2,104.67	1,960.36	1,767.41	1,541.54	1,455.42	1,418.73	1,402.36	1,394.90
15.75%	3,766.13	2,599.93	2,119.89	1,976.07	1,784.05	1,560.16	1,475.47	1,439.74	1,423.96	1,416.86
16.00%	3,779.38	2,614.19	2,135.17	1,991.84	1,800.77	1,578.85	1,495.60	1,460.81	1,445.61	1,438.85
16.25%	3,792.66	2,628.49	2,150.51	2,007.68	1,817.55	1,597.63	1,515.80	1,481.93	1,467.30	1,460.87
16.50%	3,805.97	2,642.84	2,165.90	2,023.58	1,834.40	1,616.49	1,536.07	1,503.11	1,489.03	1,482.91
16.75%	3,819.31	2,657.22	2,181.35	2,039.54	1,851.33	1,635.42	1,556.41	1,524.35	1,510.80	1,504.98
17.00%	3,832.67	2,671.65	2,196.85	2,055.56	1,868.32	1,654.43	1,576.81	1,545.63	1,532.60	1,527.07
17.25%	3,846.06	2,686.12	2,212.41	2,071.64	1,885.39	1,673.51	1,597.28	1,566.96	1,554.43	1,549.17
17.50%	3,859.47	2,700.64	2,228.02	2,087.78	1,902.52	1,692.67	1,617.81	1,588.34	1,576.30	1,571.30
17.75%	3,872.91	2,715.19	2,243.69	2,103.98	1,919.72	1,711.90	1,638.41	1,609.77	1,598.19	1,593.45
18.00%	3,886.38	2,729.79	2,259.42	2,120.25	1,936.99	1,731.20	1,659.06	1,631.24	1,620.12	1,615.61
18.25%	3,899.88	2,744.43	2,275.20	2,136.57	1,954.33	1,750.57	1,679.77	1,652.75	1,642.07	1,637.79
18.50%	3,913.40	2,759.12	2,291.03	2,152.95	1,971.73	1,770.01	1,700.54	1,674.30	1,664.04	1,659.98
18.75%	3,926.95	2,773.84	2,306.92	2,169.39	1,989.20	1,789.52	1,721.36	1,695.88	1,686.04	1,682.19
19.00%	3,940.52	2,788.61	2,322.86	2,185.89	2,006.73	1,809.09	1,742.24	1,717.51	1,708.06	1,704.41
19.25%	3,954.12	2,803.42	2,338.86	2,202.45	2,024.33	1,828.73	1,763.16	1,739.16	1,730.10	1,726.64
19.50%	3,967.75	2,818.27	2,354.91	2,219.06	2,041.99	1,848.43	1,784.14	1,760.86	1,752.16	1,748.88
19.75%	3,981.40	2,833.16	2,371.01	2,235.74	2,059.71	1,868.19	1,805.16	1,782.58	1,774.25	1,771.14
20.00%	3,995.09	2,848.09	2,387.17	2,252.47	2,077.50	1,888.02	1,826.24	1,804.34	1,796.35	1,793.40
20.25%	4,008.79	2,863.07	2,403.37	2,269.26	2,095.35	1,907.90	1,847.35	1,826.12	1,818.46	1,815.67
20.50%	4,022.52	2,878.08	2,419.64	2,286.10	2,113.26	1,927.85	1,868.52	1,847.93	1,840.59	1,837.95
20.75%	4,036.28	2,893.14	2,435.95	2,303.00	2,131.23	1,947.85	1,889.72	1,869.77	1,862.74	1,860.24

	3	5	7	8	10	15	20	25	30	35
1.00%	3,102.89	1,880.31	1,356.44	1,192.75	963.65	658.34	505.88	414.56	353.80	310.51
1.25%	3,114.80	1,892.18	1,368.33	1,204.68	975.63	670.51	518.25	427.13	366.58	323.49
1.50%	3,126.73	1,904.09	1,380.29	1,216.67	987.71	682.82	530.80	439.93	379.63	336.80
1.75%	3,138.69	1,916.05	1,392.32	1,228.75	999.88	695.27	543.54	452.97	392.97	350.44
2.00%	3,150.68	1,928.05	1,404.42	1,240.90	1,012.15	707.86	556.47	466.24	406.58	364.39
2.25%	3,162.70	1,940.11	1,416.58	1,253.12	1,024.51	720.59	569.59	479.74	420.47	378.66
2.50%	3,174.75	1,952.21	1,428.81	1,265.42	1,036.97	733.47	582.89	493.48	434.63	393.24
2.75%	3,186.83	1,964.36	1,441.10	1,277.80	1,049.52	746.48	596.38	507.44	449.07	408.14
3.00%	3,198.93	1,976.56	1,453.46	1,290.25	1,062.17	759.64	610.06	521.63	463.76	423.34
3.25%	3,211.07	1,988.80	1,465.89	1,302.78	1,074.91	772.94	623.92	536.05	478.73	438.83
3.50%	3,223.23	2,001.09	1,478.38	1,315.39	1,087.74	786.37	637.96	550.69	493.95	454.62
3.75%	3,235.42	2,013.43	1,490.94	1,328.07	1,100.67	799.94	652.18	565.54	509.43	470.70
4.00%	3,247.64	2,025.82	1,503.57	1,340.82	1,113.70	813.66	666.58	580.62	525.16	487.05
4.25%	3,259.89	2,038.25	1,516.26	1,353.65	1,126.81	827.51	681.16	595.91	541.13	503.68
4.50%	3,272.16	2,050.73	1,529.02	1,366.56	1,140.02	841.49	695.91	611.42	557.35	520.58
4.75%	3,284.47	2,063.26	1,541.84	1,379.54	1,153.33	855.62	710.85	627.13	573.81	537.74
5.00%	3,296.80	2,075.84	1,554.73	1,392.59	1,166.72	869.87	725.95	643.05	590.50	555.16
5.25%	3,309.16	2,088.46	1,567.68	1,405.72	1,180.21	884.27	741.23	659.17	607.42	572.82
5.50%	3,321.55	2,101.13	1,580.70	1,418.93	1,193.79	898.79	756.68	675.50	624.57	590.72
5.75%	3,333.97	2,113.84	1,593.79	1,432.20	1,207.46	913.45	772.29	692.02	641.93	608.85
6.00%	3,346.41	2,126.61	1,606.94	1,445.56	1,221.23	928.24	788.07	708.73	659.51	627.21
6.25%	3,358.89	2,139.42	1,620.16	1,458.98	1,235.08	943.17	804.02	725.64	677.29	645.78
6.50%	3,371.39	2,152.28	1,633.44	1,472.49	1,249.03	958.22	820.13	742.73	695.27	664.57
6.75%	3,383.92	2,165.18	1,646.78	1,486.06	1,263.07	973.40	836.40	760.00	713.46	683.56
7.00%	3,396.48	2,178.13	1,660.19	1,499.71	1,277.19	988.71	852.83	777.46	731.83	702.74
7.25%	3,409.07	2,191.13	1,673.67	1,513.43	1,291.41	1,004.15	869.41	795.09	750.39	722.11
7.50%	3,421.68	2,204.17	1,687.21	1,527.23	1,305.72	1,019.71	886.15	812.89	769.14	741.67
7.75%	3,434.33	2,217.27	1,700.81	1,541.09	1,320.12	1,035.40	903.04	830.86	788.05	761.39
8.00%	3,447.00	2,230.40	1,714.48	1,555.03	1,334.60	1,051.22	920.08	849.00	807.14	781.29
8.25%	3,459.70	2,243.59	1,728.22	1,569.05	1,349.18	1,067.15	937.27	867.30	826.39	801.34
8.50%	3,472.43	2,256.82	1,742.01	1,583.13	1,363.84	1,083.21	954.61	885.75	845.80	821.55
8.75%	3,485.19	2,270.10	1,755.87	1,597.29	1,378.59	1,099.39	972.08	904.36	865.37	841.90
9.00%	3,497.97	2,283.42	1,769.80	1,611.52	1,393.43	1,115.69	989.70	923.12	885.08	862.39
9.25%	3,510.78	2,296.79	1,783.79	1,625.82	1,408.36	1,132.11	1,007.45	942.02	904.94	883.02
9.50%	3,523.62	2,310.20	1,797.84	1,640.20	1,423.37	1,148.65	1,025.34	961.07	924.94	903.77
9.75%	3,536.49	2,323.67	1,811.95	1,654.64	1,438.47	1,165.30	1,043.37	980.25	945.07	924.65
10.00%	3,549.39	2,337.17	1,826.13	1,669.16	1,453.66	1,182.07	1,061.52	999.57	965.33	945.64
10.25%	3,562.32	2,350.73	1,840.37	1,683.74	1,468.93	1,198.95	1,079.81	1,019.02	985.71	966.74
10.50%	3,575.27	2,364.33	1,854.67	1,698.40	1,484.28	1,215.94	1,098.22	1,038.60	1,006.21	987.95
10.75%	3,588.25	2,377.97	1,869.04	1,713.13	1,499.73	1,233.04	1,116.75	1,058.30	1,026.83	1,009.25

$110,000   11.00 - 20.75%   3 - 35 Years

	3	5	7	8	10	15	20	25	30	35
11.00%	3,601.26	2,391.67	1,883.47	1,727.93	1,515.25	1,250.26	1,135.41	1,078.12	1,047.56	1,030.65
11.25%	3,614.30	2,405.40	1,897.96	1,742.79	1,530.86	1,267.58	1,154.18	1,098.06	1,068.39	1,052.14
11.50%	3,627.36	2,419.19	1,912.51	1,757.73	1,546.55	1,285.01	1,173.07	1,118.12	1,089.32	1,073.72
11.75%	3,640.45	2,433.02	1,927.12	1,772.74	1,562.32	1,302.54	1,192.08	1,138.28	1,110.35	1,095.37
12.00%	3,653.57	2,446.89	1,941.80	1,787.81	1,578.18	1,320.18	1,211.19	1,158.55	1,131.47	1,117.10
12.25%	3,666.72	2,460.81	1,956.54	1,802.96	1,594.12	1,337.93	1,230.42	1,178.92	1,152.69	1,138.91
12.50%	3,679.90	2,474.77	1,971.34	1,818.17	1,610.14	1,355.77	1,249.75	1,199.39	1,173.98	1,160.78
12.75%	3,693.10	2,488.78	1,986.20	1,833.45	1,626.24	1,373.72	1,269.19	1,219.96	1,195.36	1,182.72
13.00%	3,706.33	2,502.84	2,001.12	1,848.80	1,642.42	1,391.77	1,288.73	1,240.62	1,216.82	1,204.71
13.25%	3,719.59	2,516.94	2,016.10	1,864.21	1,658.68	1,409.91	1,308.37	1,261.37	1,238.35	1,226.77
13.50%	3,732.88	2,531.08	2,031.14	1,879.70	1,675.02	1,428.15	1,328.11	1,282.21	1,259.95	1,248.87
13.75%	3,746.20	2,545.27	2,046.24	1,895.25	1,691.43	1,446.49	1,347.95	1,303.13	1,281.62	1,271.03
14.00%	3,759.54	2,559.51	2,061.40	1,910.87	1,707.93	1,464.92	1,367.87	1,324.14	1,303.36	1,293.24
14.25%	3,772.91	2,573.79	2,076.62	1,926.55	1,724.50	1,483.44	1,387.89	1,345.22	1,325.16	1,315.49
14.50%	3,786.31	2,588.11	2,091.90	1,942.30	1,741.15	1,502.05	1,408.00	1,366.38	1,347.01	1,337.79
14.75%	3,799.73	2,602.48	2,107.24	1,958.11	1,757.88	1,520.75	1,428.19	1,387.61	1,368.92	1,360.12
15.00%	3,813.19	2,616.89	2,122.64	1,973.99	1,774.68	1,539.55	1,448.47	1,408.91	1,390.89	1,382.49
15.25%	3,826.67	2,631.35	2,138.10	1,989.94	1,791.56	1,558.42	1,468.83	1,430.28	1,412.90	1,404.90
15.50%	3,840.17	2,645.85	2,153.62	2,005.95	1,808.52	1,577.39	1,489.27	1,451.72	1,434.97	1,427.34
15.75%	3,853.71	2,660.40	2,169.19	2,022.03	1,825.54	1,596.44	1,509.79	1,473.22	1,457.08	1,449.82
16.00%	3,867.27	2,674.99	2,184.83	2,038.17	1,842.64	1,615.57	1,530.38	1,494.78	1,479.23	1,472.32
16.25%	3,880.86	2,689.62	2,200.52	2,054.37	1,859.82	1,634.78	1,551.05	1,516.40	1,501.43	1,494.84
16.50%	3,894.48	2,704.30	2,216.27	2,070.64	1,877.07	1,654.08	1,571.79	1,538.07	1,523.66	1,517.40
16.75%	3,908.13	2,719.02	2,232.07	2,086.97	1,894.38	1,673.45	1,592.60	1,559.80	1,545.94	1,539.98
17.00%	3,921.80	2,733.78	2,247.94	2,103.36	1,911.77	1,692.90	1,613.48	1,581.58	1,568.24	1,562.58
17.25%	3,935.50	2,748.59	2,263.86	2,119.82	1,929.24	1,712.43	1,634.43	1,603.41	1,590.58	1,585.20
17.50%	3,949.23	2,763.44	2,279.84	2,136.33	1,946.77	1,732.04	1,655.44	1,625.28	1,612.96	1,607.84
17.75%	3,962.98	2,778.34	2,295.87	2,152.91	1,964.37	1,751.71	1,676.51	1,647.21	1,635.36	1,630.50
18.00%	3,976.76	2,793.28	2,311.96	2,169.55	1,982.04	1,771.46	1,697.64	1,669.17	1,657.79	1,653.18
18.25%	3,990.57	2,808.26	2,328.11	2,186.26	1,999.78	1,791.28	1,718.84	1,691.18	1,680.25	1,675.88
18.50%	4,004.41	2,823.28	2,344.31	2,203.02	2,017.58	1,811.18	1,740.09	1,713.23	1,702.74	1,698.58
18.75%	4,018.27	2,838.35	2,360.57	2,219.84	2,035.46	1,831.14	1,761.39	1,735.32	1,725.25	1,721.31
19.00%	4,032.16	2,853.46	2,376.88	2,236.73	2,053.40	1,851.16	1,782.75	1,757.45	1,747.78	1,744.04
19.25%	4,046.08	2,868.61	2,393.25	2,253.67	2,071.40	1,871.26	1,804.17	1,779.61	1,770.34	1,766.79
19.50%	4,060.02	2,883.81	2,409.67	2,270.67	2,089.47	1,891.42	1,825.63	1,801.81	1,792.91	1,789.55
19.75%	4,074.00	2,899.05	2,426.15	2,287.73	2,107.61	1,911.64	1,847.15	1,824.04	1,815.51	1,812.32
20.00%	4,087.99	2,914.33	2,442.68	2,304.85	2,125.81	1,931.93	1,868.71	1,846.30	1,838.12	1,835.11
20.25%	4,102.02	2,929.65	2,459.27	2,322.03	2,144.08	1,952.27	1,890.32	1,868.59	1,860.75	1,857.90
20.50%	4,116.07	2,945.01	2,475.91	2,339.27	2,162.41	1,972.68	1,911.97	1,890.91	1,883.40	1,880.70
20.75%	4,130.15	2,960.42	2,492.60	2,356.56	2,180.80	1,993.15	1,933.67	1,913.26	1,906.06	1,903.50

	3	5	7	8	10	15	20	25	30	35
1.00%	3,173.41	1,923.05	1,387.27	1,219.86	985.55	673.31	517.38	423.98	361.84	317.57
1.25%	3,185.59	1,935.18	1,399.43	1,232.05	997.80	685.75	530.03	436.83	374.91	330.85
1.50%	3,197.79	1,947.36	1,411.66	1,244.32	1,010.15	698.34	542.86	449.93	388.26	344.46
1.75%	3,210.03	1,959.59	1,423.97	1,256.67	1,022.60	711.07	555.89	463.26	401.90	358.40
2.00%	3,222.29	1,971.87	1,436.34	1,269.10	1,035.15	723.95	569.12	476.84	415.82	372.67
2.25%	3,234.58	1,984.20	1,448.77	1,281.60	1,047.80	736.97	582.53	490.65	430.03	387.27
2.50%	3,246.90	1,996.58	1,461.28	1,294.18	1,060.54	750.14	596.14	504.69	444.51	402.18
2.75%	3,259.26	2,009.00	1,473.85	1,306.84	1,073.37	763.45	609.94	518.97	459.27	417.41
3.00%	3,271.64	2,021.48	1,486.50	1,319.58	1,086.31	776.90	623.92	533.49	474.30	432.96
3.25%	3,284.05	2,034.00	1,499.21	1,332.39	1,099.34	790.50	638.10	548.23	489.61	448.80
3.50%	3,296.48	2,046.57	1,511.98	1,345.28	1,112.47	804.24	652.45	563.20	505.18	464.95
3.75%	3,308.95	2,059.19	1,524.83	1,358.25	1,125.69	818.13	667.00	578.40	521.01	481.39
4.00%	3,321.45	2,071.86	1,537.74	1,371.29	1,139.01	832.15	681.73	593.82	537.09	498.12
4.25%	3,333.97	2,084.58	1,550.72	1,384.42	1,152.42	846.31	696.64	609.46	553.43	515.13
4.50%	3,346.53	2,097.34	1,563.77	1,397.61	1,165.93	860.62	711.73	625.31	570.02	532.41
4.75%	3,359.11	2,110.15	1,576.88	1,410.89	1,179.54	875.06	727.00	641.38	586.85	549.96
5.00%	3,371.73	2,123.01	1,590.06	1,424.24	1,193.24	889.64	742.45	657.66	603.92	567.77
5.25%	3,384.37	2,135.92	1,603.31	1,437.67	1,207.03	904.36	758.07	674.15	621.23	585.84
5.50%	3,397.04	2,148.88	1,616.63	1,451.17	1,220.92	919.22	773.87	690.85	638.76	604.14
5.75%	3,409.74	2,161.89	1,630.01	1,464.75	1,234.90	934.21	789.84	707.74	656.52	622.69
6.00%	3,422.47	2,174.94	1,643.46	1,478.41	1,248.98	949.34	805.98	724.84	674.49	641.46
6.25%	3,435.23	2,188.04	1,656.98	1,492.14	1,263.15	964.60	822.29	742.13	692.68	660.46
6.50%	3,448.01	2,201.19	1,670.56	1,505.95	1,277.41	980.00	838.77	759.61	711.08	679.67
6.75%	3,460.83	2,214.39	1,684.21	1,519.83	1,291.77	995.52	855.41	777.28	729.67	699.09
7.00%	3,473.67	2,227.63	1,697.93	1,533.79	1,306.22	1,011.18	872.21	795.13	748.47	718.71
7.25%	3,486.55	2,240.93	1,711.71	1,547.83	1,320.76	1,026.97	889.17	813.16	767.45	738.53
7.50%	3,499.45	2,254.27	1,725.56	1,561.94	1,335.39	1,042.89	906.29	831.37	786.62	758.52
7.75%	3,512.38	2,267.66	1,739.47	1,576.12	1,350.12	1,058.94	923.57	849.74	805.96	778.70
8.00%	3,525.34	2,281.09	1,753.45	1,590.38	1,364.94	1,075.11	941.00	868.29	825.49	799.04
8.25%	3,538.33	2,294.58	1,767.49	1,604.71	1,379.84	1,091.41	958.57	887.01	845.17	819.55
8.50%	3,551.35	2,308.11	1,781.60	1,619.11	1,394.84	1,107.83	976.30	905.88	865.03	840.22
8.75%	3,564.39	2,321.69	1,795.78	1,633.59	1,409.93	1,124.38	994.17	924.91	885.04	861.03
9.00%	3,577.47	2,335.31	1,810.02	1,648.15	1,425.10	1,141.05	1,012.19	944.10	905.20	881.99
9.25%	3,590.57	2,348.99	1,824.33	1,662.77	1,440.37	1,157.84	1,030.35	963.43	925.51	903.09
9.50%	3,603.71	2,362.71	1,838.70	1,677.47	1,455.72	1,174.75	1,048.65	982.91	945.96	924.31
9.75%	3,616.87	2,376.48	1,853.13	1,692.25	1,471.17	1,191.78	1,067.08	1,002.53	966.55	945.66
10.00%	3,630.06	2,390.29	1,867.63	1,707.09	1,486.70	1,208.93	1,085.65	1,022.29	987.27	967.13
10.25%	3,643.28	2,404.15	1,882.20	1,722.01	1,502.31	1,226.19	1,104.35	1,042.18	1,008.11	988.71
10.50%	3,656.52	2,418.06	1,896.83	1,737.00	1,518.02	1,243.57	1,123.18	1,062.20	1,029.08	1,010.40
10.75%	3,669.80	2,432.02	1,911.52	1,752.06	1,533.81	1,261.07	1,142.13	1,082.35	1,050.17	1,032.19

$112,500   11.00 - 20.75%   3 - 35 Years

	3	5	7	8	10	15	20	25	30	35
11.00%	3,683.11	2,446.02	1,926.27	1,767.20	1,549.69	1,278.67	1,161.21	1,102.63	1,071.36	1,054.08
11.25%	3,696.44	2,460.07	1,941.09	1,782.40	1,565.65	1,296.39	1,180.41	1,123.02	1,092.67	1,076.06
11.50%	3,709.80	2,474.17	1,955.98	1,797.68	1,581.70	1,314.21	1,199.73	1,143.53	1,114.08	1,098.12
11.75%	3,723.19	2,488.31	1,970.92	1,813.03	1,597.83	1,332.15	1,219.17	1,164.15	1,135.59	1,120.27
12.00%	3,736.61	2,502.50	1,985.93	1,828.44	1,614.05	1,350.19	1,238.72	1,184.88	1,157.19	1,142.49
12.25%	3,750.06	2,516.74	2,001.00	1,843.93	1,630.35	1,368.34	1,258.39	1,205.71	1,178.88	1,164.79
12.50%	3,763.53	2,531.02	2,016.14	1,859.49	1,646.73	1,386.59	1,278.16	1,226.65	1,200.66	1,187.16
12.75%	3,777.04	2,545.35	2,031.34	1,875.12	1,663.20	1,404.94	1,298.04	1,247.68	1,222.53	1,209.60
13.00%	3,790.57	2,559.72	2,046.60	1,890.82	1,679.75	1,423.40	1,318.02	1,268.81	1,244.47	1,232.09
13.25%	3,804.13	2,574.14	2,061.92	1,906.58	1,696.38	1,441.95	1,338.11	1,290.04	1,266.50	1,254.65
13.50%	3,817.72	2,588.61	2,077.30	1,922.42	1,713.09	1,460.61	1,358.30	1,311.35	1,288.59	1,277.26
13.75%	3,831.34	2,603.12	2,092.75	1,938.32	1,729.88	1,479.36	1,378.58	1,332.75	1,310.75	1,299.92
14.00%	3,844.98	2,617.68	2,108.25	1,954.29	1,746.75	1,498.21	1,398.96	1,354.23	1,332.98	1,322.63
14.25%	3,858.66	2,632.28	2,123.82	1,970.33	1,763.70	1,517.15	1,419.43	1,375.79	1,355.27	1,345.39
14.50%	3,872.36	2,646.93	2,139.45	1,986.44	1,780.73	1,536.19	1,440.00	1,397.43	1,377.63	1,368.19
14.75%	3,886.09	2,661.63	2,155.14	2,002.62	1,797.83	1,555.32	1,460.65	1,419.15	1,400.04	1,391.03
15.00%	3,899.85	2,676.37	2,170.88	2,018.86	1,815.02	1,574.54	1,481.39	1,440.93	1,422.50	1,413.91
15.25%	3,913.64	2,691.15	2,186.69	2,035.17	1,832.28	1,593.84	1,502.21	1,462.79	1,445.02	1,436.83
15.50%	3,927.45	2,705.98	2,202.56	2,051.54	1,849.62	1,613.24	1,523.12	1,484.71	1,467.58	1,459.78
15.75%	3,941.29	2,720.86	2,218.49	2,067.98	1,867.03	1,632.72	1,544.10	1,506.70	1,490.19	1,482.77
16.00%	3,955.17	2,735.78	2,234.48	2,084.49	1,884.52	1,652.29	1,565.16	1,528.75	1,512.85	1,505.78
16.25%	3,969.07	2,750.75	2,250.53	2,101.06	1,902.09	1,671.94	1,586.30	1,550.86	1,535.55	1,528.82
16.50%	3,982.99	2,765.76	2,266.64	2,117.70	1,919.73	1,691.67	1,607.51	1,573.03	1,558.29	1,551.89
16.75%	3,996.95	2,780.81	2,282.80	2,134.40	1,937.44	1,711.49	1,628.80	1,595.25	1,581.07	1,574.98
17.00%	4,010.93	2,795.91	2,299.03	2,151.16	1,955.22	1,731.38	1,650.15	1,617.52	1,603.88	1,598.09
17.25%	4,024.94	2,811.06	2,315.31	2,167.99	1,973.08	1,751.35	1,671.57	1,639.85	1,626.73	1,621.23
17.50%	4,038.98	2,826.25	2,331.65	2,184.89	1,991.01	1,771.40	1,693.06	1,662.22	1,649.62	1,644.38
17.75%	4,053.05	2,841.48	2,348.05	2,201.84	2,009.01	1,791.52	1,714.61	1,684.64	1,672.53	1,667.56
18.00%	4,067.14	2,856.76	2,364.51	2,218.86	2,027.08	1,811.72	1,736.23	1,707.11	1,695.47	1,690.75
18.25%	4,081.27	2,872.08	2,381.02	2,235.94	2,045.23	1,832.00	1,757.90	1,729.62	1,718.44	1,713.96
18.50%	4,095.42	2,887.45	2,397.59	2,253.09	2,063.44	1,852.34	1,779.63	1,752.17	1,741.44	1,737.19
18.75%	4,109.60	2,902.86	2,414.22	2,270.29	2,081.72	1,872.75	1,801.42	1,774.76	1,764.46	1,760.43
19.00%	4,123.80	2,918.31	2,430.90	2,287.56	2,100.06	1,893.24	1,823.27	1,797.39	1,787.50	1,783.68
19.25%	4,138.04	2,933.81	2,447.64	2,304.89	2,118.48	1,913.79	1,845.17	1,820.06	1,810.57	1,806.95
19.50%	4,152.30	2,949.35	2,464.44	2,322.28	2,136.96	1,934.40	1,867.12	1,842.76	1,833.66	1,830.23
19.75%	4,166.59	2,964.93	2,481.29	2,339.73	2,155.51	1,955.09	1,889.13	1,865.49	1,856.77	1,853.51
20.00%	4,180.90	2,980.56	2,498.20	2,357.24	2,174.13	1,975.83	1,911.18	1,888.26	1,879.90	1,876.81
20.25%	4,195.25	2,996.23	2,515.16	2,374.80	2,192.81	1,996.64	1,933.28	1,911.06	1,903.04	1,900.12
20.50%	4,209.62	3,011.95	2,532.18	2,392.43	2,211.55	2,017.52	1,955.42	1,933.88	1,926.20	1,923.44
20.75%	4,224.02	3,027.70	2,549.25	2,410.12	2,230.36	2,038.45	1,977.61	1,956.74	1,949.38	1,946.77

$115,000   1.00 - 10.75%   3 - 35 Years

	3	5	7	8	10	15	20	25	30	35
1.00%	3,243.93	1,965.78	1,418.09	1,246.97	1,007.45	688.27	528.88	433.40	369.89	324.63
1.25%	3,256.38	1,978.18	1,430.53	1,259.43	1,019.98	700.99	541.80	446.54	383.24	338.20
1.50%	3,268.85	1,990.64	1,443.03	1,271.98	1,032.60	713.85	554.93	459.93	396.89	352.11
1.75%	3,281.36	2,003.14	1,455.61	1,284.60	1,045.33	726.87	568.25	473.56	410.83	366.36
2.00%	3,293.90	2,015.69	1,468.26	1,297.30	1,058.15	740.04	581.77	487.43	425.06	380.95
2.25%	3,306.46	2,028.29	1,480.97	1,310.08	1,071.08	753.35	595.48	501.55	439.58	395.87
2.50%	3,319.06	2,040.95	1,493.75	1,322.94	1,084.10	766.81	609.39	515.91	454.39	411.12
2.75%	3,331.68	2,053.65	1,506.61	1,335.88	1,097.23	780.41	623.49	530.51	469.48	426.69
3.00%	3,344.34	2,066.40	1,519.53	1,348.90	1,110.45	794.17	637.79	545.34	484.84	442.58
3.25%	3,357.02	2,079.20	1,532.52	1,362.00	1,123.77	808.07	652.28	560.41	500.49	458.78
3.50%	3,369.74	2,092.05	1,545.58	1,375.18	1,137.19	822.11	666.95	575.72	516.40	475.28
3.75%	3,382.48	2,104.95	1,558.71	1,388.43	1,150.70	836.31	681.82	591.25	532.58	492.09
4.00%	3,395.26	2,117.90	1,571.91	1,401.77	1,164.32	850.64	696.88	607.01	549.03	509.19
4.25%	3,408.06	2,130.90	1,585.18	1,415.18	1,178.03	865.12	712.12	623.00	565.73	526.58
4.50%	3,420.90	2,143.95	1,598.52	1,428.67	1,191.84	879.74	727.55	639.21	582.69	544.25
4.75%	3,433.76	2,157.04	1,611.92	1,442.24	1,205.75	894.51	743.16	655.63	599.89	562.19
5.00%	3,446.65	2,170.19	1,625.40	1,455.89	1,219.75	909.41	758.95	672.28	617.34	580.39
5.25%	3,459.58	2,183.39	1,638.94	1,469.62	1,233.85	924.46	774.92	689.13	635.03	598.85
5.50%	3,472.53	2,196.63	1,652.55	1,483.42	1,248.05	939.65	791.07	706.20	652.96	617.57
5.75%	3,485.51	2,209.93	1,666.24	1,497.30	1,262.35	954.97	807.40	723.47	671.11	636.53
6.00%	3,498.52	2,223.27	1,679.98	1,511.26	1,276.74	970.44	823.90	740.95	689.48	655.72
6.25%	3,511.56	2,236.67	1,693.80	1,525.30	1,291.22	986.04	840.57	758.62	708.07	675.14
6.50%	3,524.64	2,250.11	1,707.69	1,539.42	1,305.80	1,001.77	857.41	776.49	726.88	694.78
6.75%	3,537.74	2,263.60	1,721.64	1,553.61	1,320.48	1,017.65	874.42	794.55	745.89	714.63
7.00%	3,550.87	2,277.14	1,735.66	1,567.88	1,335.25	1,033.65	891.59	812.80	765.10	734.68
7.25%	3,564.03	2,290.73	1,749.75	1,582.22	1,350.11	1,049.79	908.93	831.23	784.50	754.94
7.50%	3,577.22	2,304.36	1,763.90	1,596.65	1,365.07	1,066.06	926.43	849.84	804.10	775.38
7.75%	3,590.43	2,318.05	1,778.12	1,611.14	1,380.12	1,082.47	944.09	868.63	823.87	796.00
8.00%	3,603.68	2,331.79	1,792.41	1,625.72	1,395.27	1,099.00	961.91	887.59	843.83	816.80
8.25%	3,616.96	2,345.57	1,806.77	1,640.37	1,410.51	1,115.66	979.88	906.72	863.96	837.76
8.50%	3,630.27	2,359.40	1,821.20	1,655.09	1,425.84	1,132.45	998.00	926.01	884.25	858.89
8.75%	3,643.60	2,373.28	1,835.69	1,669.90	1,441.26	1,149.37	1,016.27	945.47	904.71	880.17
9.00%	3,656.97	2,387.21	1,850.24	1,684.77	1,456.77	1,166.41	1,034.68	965.08	925.32	901.59
9.25%	3,670.36	2,401.19	1,864.87	1,699.73	1,472.38	1,183.57	1,053.25	984.84	946.08	923.16
9.50%	3,683.79	2,415.21	1,879.56	1,714.75	1,488.07	1,200.86	1,071.95	1,004.75	966.98	944.85
9.75%	3,697.24	2,429.29	1,894.31	1,729.85	1,503.86	1,218.27	1,090.79	1,024.81	988.03	966.68
10.00%	3,710.73	2,443.41	1,909.14	1,745.03	1,519.73	1,235.80	1,109.77	1,045.01	1,009.21	988.62
10.25%	3,724.24	2,457.58	1,924.02	1,760.28	1,535.70	1,253.44	1,128.89	1,065.34	1,030.52	1,010.68
10.50%	3,737.78	2,471.80	1,938.98	1,775.60	1,551.75	1,271.21	1,148.14	1,085.81	1,051.95	1,032.85
10.75%	3,751.35	2,486.06	1,954.00	1,791.00	1,567.89	1,289.09	1,167.51	1,106.41	1,073.50	1,055.13

$115,000   11.00 - 20.75%   3 - 35 Years

	3	5	7	8	10	15	20	25	30	35
11.00%	3,764.95	2,500.38	1,969.08	1,806.47	1,584.13	1,307.09	1,187.02	1,127.13	1,095.17	1,077.50
11.25%	3,778.58	2,514.74	1,984.23	1,822.01	1,600.44	1,325.20	1,206.64	1,147.98	1,116.95	1,099.97
11.50%	3,792.24	2,529.15	1,999.44	1,837.63	1,616.85	1,343.42	1,226.39	1,168.94	1,138.84	1,122.52
11.75%	3,805.93	2,543.61	2,014.72	1,853.32	1,633.34	1,361.75	1,246.26	1,190.02	1,160.82	1,145.16
12.00%	3,819.65	2,558.11	2,030.06	1,869.08	1,649.92	1,380.19	1,266.25	1,211.21	1,182.90	1,167.88
12.25%	3,833.39	2,572.66	2,045.47	1,884.91	1,666.58	1,398.74	1,286.35	1,232.51	1,205.08	1,190.68
12.50%	3,847.17	2,587.26	2,060.94	1,900.81	1,683.33	1,417.40	1,306.56	1,253.91	1,227.35	1,213.54
12.75%	3,860.97	2,601.91	2,076.48	1,916.79	1,700.16	1,436.16	1,326.88	1,275.41	1,249.70	1,236.48
13.00%	3,874.80	2,616.60	2,092.08	1,932.83	1,717.07	1,455.03	1,347.31	1,297.01	1,272.13	1,259.47
13.25%	3,888.67	2,631.34	2,107.74	1,948.95	1,734.07	1,474.00	1,367.85	1,318.71	1,294.64	1,282.53
13.50%	3,902.56	2,646.13	2,123.46	1,965.14	1,751.15	1,493.07	1,388.48	1,340.49	1,317.22	1,305.64
13.75%	3,916.48	2,660.97	2,139.25	1,981.40	1,768.32	1,512.24	1,409.22	1,362.37	1,339.88	1,328.81
14.00%	3,930.43	2,675.85	2,155.10	1,997.72	1,785.56	1,531.50	1,430.05	1,384.33	1,362.60	1,352.02
14.25%	3,944.41	2,690.78	2,171.01	2,014.12	1,802.89	1,550.87	1,450.98	1,406.37	1,385.39	1,375.29
14.50%	3,958.41	2,705.75	2,186.99	2,030.58	1,820.30	1,570.33	1,472.00	1,428.49	1,408.24	1,398.60
14.75%	3,972.45	2,720.77	2,203.03	2,047.12	1,837.79	1,589.88	1,493.11	1,450.68	1,431.15	1,421.95
15.00%	3,986.51	2,735.84	2,219.13	2,063.72	1,855.35	1,609.53	1,514.31	1,472.96	1,454.11	1,445.34
15.25%	4,000.61	2,750.96	2,235.29	2,080.39	1,873.00	1,629.26	1,535.59	1,495.30	1,477.13	1,468.76
15.50%	4,014.73	2,766.12	2,251.51	2,097.13	1,890.72	1,649.09	1,556.96	1,517.71	1,500.19	1,492.22
15.75%	4,028.88	2,781.32	2,267.79	2,113.94	1,908.52	1,669.00	1,578.41	1,540.18	1,523.31	1,515.72
16.00%	4,043.06	2,796.58	2,284.14	2,130.81	1,926.40	1,689.01	1,599.94	1,562.72	1,546.47	1,539.24
16.25%	4,057.27	2,811.88	2,300.54	2,147.75	1,944.36	1,709.09	1,621.55	1,585.32	1,569.67	1,562.79
16.50%	4,071.50	2,827.22	2,317.01	2,164.76	1,962.39	1,729.26	1,643.24	1,607.98	1,592.92	1,586.37
16.75%	4,085.77	2,842.61	2,333.53	2,181.83	1,980.49	1,749.52	1,664.99	1,630.70	1,616.20	1,609.98
17.00%	4,100.06	2,858.05	2,350.12	2,198.97	1,998.67	1,769.85	1,686.82	1,653.47	1,639.53	1,633.61
17.25%	4,114.39	2,873.53	2,366.76	2,216.17	2,016.93	1,790.27	1,708.72	1,676.29	1,662.88	1,657.26
17.50%	4,128.74	2,889.05	2,383.47	2,233.44	2,035.26	1,810.76	1,730.68	1,699.16	1,686.27	1,680.93
17.75%	4,143.12	2,904.63	2,400.23	2,250.77	2,053.66	1,831.34	1,752.71	1,722.08	1,709.70	1,704.62
18.00%	4,157.53	2,920.24	2,417.05	2,268.17	2,072.13	1,851.98	1,774.81	1,745.04	1,733.15	1,728.33
18.25%	4,171.96	2,935.91	2,433.93	2,285.63	2,090.67	1,872.71	1,796.96	1,768.05	1,756.63	1,752.05
18.50%	4,186.43	2,951.61	2,450.87	2,303.16	2,109.29	1,893.50	1,819.18	1,791.11	1,780.14	1,775.79
18.75%	4,200.92	2,967.37	2,467.87	2,320.74	2,127.98	1,914.37	1,841.46	1,814.20	1,803.67	1,799.55
19.00%	4,215.44	2,983.16	2,484.92	2,338.39	2,146.73	1,935.31	1,863.79	1,837.33	1,827.23	1,823.32
19.25%	4,229.99	2,999.01	2,502.03	2,356.11	2,165.56	1,956.31	1,886.17	1,860.50	1,850.81	1,847.10
19.50%	4,244.57	3,014.89	2,519.20	2,373.88	2,184.45	1,977.39	1,908.61	1,883.71	1,874.41	1,870.90
19.75%	4,259.18	3,030.82	2,536.43	2,391.72	2,203.41	1,998.53	1,931.11	1,906.95	1,898.03	1,894.70
20.00%	4,273.81	3,046.80	2,553.71	2,409.62	2,222.44	2,019.74	1,953.65	1,930.22	1,921.67	1,918.52
20.25%	4,288.48	3,062.82	2,571.05	2,427.58	2,241.54	2,041.01	1,976.24	1,953.52	1,945.33	1,942.35
20.50%	4,303.17	3,078.88	2,588.45	2,445.60	2,260.70	2,062.35	1,998.88	1,976.86	1,969.01	1,966.18
20.75%	4,317.89	3,094.99	2,605.90	2,463.68	2,279.92	2,083.75	2,021.56	2,000.22	1,992.70	1,990.03

	3	5	7	8	10	15	20	25	30	35
1.00%	3,314.45	2,008.52	1,448.92	1,274.08	1,029.35	703.23	540.38	442.83	377.93	331.69
1.25%	3,327.17	2,021.19	1,461.63	1,286.81	1,042.15	716.23	553.58	456.25	391.57	345.55
1.50%	3,339.92	2,033.91	1,474.41	1,299.63	1,055.05	729.37	566.99	469.93	405.52	359.77
1.75%	3,352.69	2,046.69	1,487.25	1,312.52	1,068.05	742.67	580.60	483.85	419.76	374.33
2.00%	3,365.50	2,059.51	1,500.17	1,325.50	1,081.16	756.12	594.41	498.03	434.30	389.23
2.25%	3,378.34	2,072.39	1,513.16	1,338.56	1,094.36	769.72	608.42	512.45	449.14	404.48
2.50%	3,391.21	2,085.31	1,526.23	1,351.70	1,107.67	783.48	622.64	527.12	464.27	420.06
2.75%	3,404.11	2,098.29	1,539.36	1,364.92	1,121.08	797.38	637.05	542.04	479.68	435.97
3.00%	3,417.04	2,111.32	1,552.56	1,378.22	1,134.59	811.43	651.65	557.20	495.38	452.20
3.25%	3,430.00	2,124.40	1,565.84	1,391.61	1,148.20	825.64	666.46	572.60	511.37	468.75
3.50%	3,442.99	2,137.53	1,579.18	1,405.07	1,161.91	839.99	681.45	588.23	527.63	485.62
3.75%	3,456.02	2,150.71	1,592.60	1,418.62	1,175.72	854.49	696.64	604.10	544.16	502.79
4.00%	3,469.07	2,163.94	1,606.08	1,432.24	1,189.63	869.13	712.03	620.21	560.96	520.26
4.25%	3,482.15	2,177.22	1,619.64	1,445.94	1,203.64	883.93	727.60	636.54	578.03	538.03
4.50%	3,495.26	2,190.55	1,633.27	1,459.73	1,217.75	898.87	743.36	653.10	595.36	556.08
4.75%	3,508.41	2,203.94	1,646.97	1,473.60	1,231.96	913.95	759.31	669.89	612.94	574.41
5.00%	3,521.58	2,217.37	1,660.73	1,487.54	1,246.27	929.18	775.45	686.89	630.77	593.01
5.25%	3,534.78	2,230.85	1,674.57	1,501.57	1,260.68	944.56	791.77	704.12	648.84	611.87
5.50%	3,548.02	2,244.39	1,688.48	1,515.67	1,275.18	960.07	808.27	721.55	667.15	630.99
5.75%	3,561.28	2,257.97	1,702.46	1,529.85	1,289.79	975.73	824.95	739.20	685.70	650.36
6.00%	3,574.58	2,271.60	1,716.51	1,544.12	1,304.49	991.53	841.81	757.05	704.47	669.97
6.25%	3,587.90	2,285.29	1,730.62	1,558.46	1,319.29	1,007.47	858.84	775.11	723.47	689.81
6.50%	3,601.26	2,299.02	1,744.81	1,572.88	1,334.19	1,023.55	876.05	793.37	742.68	709.88
6.75%	3,614.64	2,312.81	1,759.06	1,587.38	1,349.18	1,039.77	893.43	811.82	762.10	730.16
7.00%	3,628.06	2,326.64	1,773.39	1,601.96	1,364.27	1,056.12	910.98	830.47	781.73	750.66
7.25%	3,641.50	2,340.52	1,787.78	1,616.62	1,379.46	1,072.61	928.69	849.30	801.56	771.35
7.50%	3,654.98	2,354.46	1,802.25	1,631.35	1,394.75	1,089.24	946.57	868.31	821.58	792.24
7.75%	3,668.49	2,368.44	1,816.78	1,646.17	1,410.12	1,106.00	964.61	887.51	841.78	813.31
8.00%	3,682.02	2,382.48	1,831.38	1,661.06	1,425.60	1,122.89	982.82	906.88	862.17	834.56
8.25%	3,695.59	2,396.56	1,846.05	1,676.03	1,441.17	1,139.91	1,001.18	926.43	882.74	855.98
8.50%	3,709.19	2,410.69	1,860.79	1,691.08	1,456.83	1,157.07	1,019.69	946.14	903.47	877.56
8.75%	3,722.81	2,424.87	1,875.59	1,706.20	1,472.59	1,174.35	1,038.36	966.02	924.37	899.30
9.00%	3,736.47	2,439.11	1,890.47	1,721.40	1,488.44	1,191.76	1,057.18	986.06	945.43	921.19
9.25%	3,750.16	2,453.39	1,905.41	1,736.68	1,504.38	1,209.30	1,076.14	1,006.25	966.64	943.22
9.50%	3,763.87	2,467.72	1,920.42	1,752.03	1,520.42	1,226.96	1,095.25	1,026.59	988.00	965.39
9.75%	3,777.62	2,482.10	1,935.49	1,767.46	1,536.55	1,244.75	1,114.51	1,047.09	1,009.51	987.69
10.00%	3,791.39	2,496.53	1,950.64	1,782.96	1,552.77	1,262.66	1,133.90	1,067.72	1,031.15	1,010.12
10.25%	3,805.20	2,511.01	1,965.85	1,798.55	1,569.08	1,280.69	1,153.43	1,088.50	1,052.92	1,032.66
10.50%	3,819.04	2,525.53	1,981.13	1,814.20	1,585.49	1,298.84	1,173.10	1,109.41	1,074.82	1,055.31
10.75%	3,832.90	2,540.11	1,996.47	1,829.93	1,601.98	1,317.11	1,192.89	1,130.46	1,096.84	1,078.07

$117,500   11.00 - 20.75%   3 - 35 Years

	3	5	7	8	10	15	20	25	30	35
11.00%	3,846.80	2,554.73	2,011.89	1,845.74	1,618.56	1,335.50	1,212.82	1,151.63	1,118.98	1,100.93
11.25%	3,860.73	2,569.41	2,027.36	1,861.62	1,635.24	1,354.00	1,232.88	1,172.93	1,141.23	1,123.88
11.50%	3,874.68	2,584.13	2,042.91	1,877.58	1,652.00	1,372.62	1,253.05	1,194.35	1,163.59	1,146.93
11.75%	3,888.67	2,598.90	2,058.52	1,893.61	1,668.85	1,391.35	1,273.36	1,215.89	1,186.06	1,170.06
12.00%	3,902.68	2,613.72	2,074.20	1,909.71	1,685.78	1,410.20	1,293.78	1,237.54	1,208.62	1,193.27
12.25%	3,916.73	2,628.59	2,089.94	1,925.89	1,702.81	1,429.15	1,314.31	1,259.30	1,231.28	1,216.56
12.50%	3,930.80	2,643.51	2,105.75	1,942.14	1,719.92	1,448.21	1,334.97	1,281.17	1,254.03	1,239.92
12.75%	3,944.91	2,658.47	2,121.62	1,958.46	1,737.12	1,467.38	1,355.73	1,303.14	1,276.86	1,263.36
13.00%	3,959.04	2,673.49	2,137.56	1,974.85	1,754.40	1,486.66	1,376.60	1,325.21	1,299.78	1,286.85
13.25%	3,973.20	2,688.55	2,153.56	1,991.32	1,771.77	1,506.04	1,397.58	1,347.37	1,322.78	1,310.41
13.50%	3,987.40	2,703.66	2,169.62	2,007.86	1,789.22	1,525.52	1,418.67	1,369.63	1,345.86	1,334.03
13.75%	4,001.62	2,718.81	2,185.76	2,024.47	1,806.76	1,545.11	1,439.85	1,391.98	1,369.01	1,357.69
14.00%	4,015.87	2,734.02	2,201.95	2,041.15	1,824.38	1,564.80	1,461.14	1,414.42	1,392.22	1,381.42
14.25%	4,030.15	2,749.27	2,218.21	2,057.90	1,842.08	1,584.58	1,482.52	1,436.94	1,415.51	1,405.19
14.50%	4,044.46	2,764.57	2,234.53	2,074.73	1,859.87	1,604.46	1,504.00	1,459.54	1,438.85	1,429.00
14.75%	4,058.81	2,779.92	2,250.92	2,091.62	1,877.74	1,624.44	1,525.57	1,482.22	1,462.26	1,452.86
15.00%	4,073.18	2,795.32	2,267.37	2,108.59	1,895.69	1,644.51	1,547.23	1,504.98	1,485.72	1,476.76
15.25%	4,087.58	2,810.76	2,283.88	2,125.62	1,913.71	1,664.68	1,568.98	1,527.80	1,509.24	1,500.69
15.50%	4,102.01	2,826.25	2,300.46	2,142.72	1,931.82	1,684.94	1,590.81	1,550.70	1,532.81	1,524.66
15.75%	4,116.46	2,841.79	2,317.09	2,159.89	1,950.01	1,705.29	1,612.73	1,573.67	1,556.43	1,548.67
16.00%	4,130.95	2,857.37	2,333.79	2,177.13	1,968.28	1,725.72	1,634.73	1,596.69	1,580.09	1,572.70
16.25%	4,145.47	2,873.00	2,350.55	2,194.44	1,986.62	1,746.25	1,656.80	1,619.79	1,603.80	1,596.77
16.50%	4,160.01	2,888.68	2,367.38	2,211.82	2,005.05	1,766.86	1,678.96	1,642.94	1,627.55	1,620.86
16.75%	4,174.59	2,904.41	2,384.26	2,229.26	2,023.55	1,787.55	1,701.19	1,666.15	1,651.34	1,644.98
17.00%	4,189.20	2,920.18	2,401.21	2,246.77	2,042.12	1,808.33	1,723.49	1,689.41	1,675.17	1,669.12
17.25%	4,203.83	2,936.00	2,418.21	2,264.35	2,060.77	1,829.19	1,745.86	1,712.73	1,699.03	1,693.28
17.50%	4,218.49	2,951.86	2,435.28	2,281.99	2,079.50	1,850.13	1,768.31	1,736.10	1,722.93	1,717.47
17.75%	4,233.19	2,967.77	2,452.41	2,299.70	2,098.30	1,871.15	1,790.82	1,759.52	1,746.86	1,741.67
18.00%	4,247.91	2,983.73	2,469.60	2,317.48	2,117.18	1,892.24	1,813.39	1,782.98	1,770.83	1,765.90
18.25%	4,262.66	2,999.73	2,486.84	2,335.32	2,136.12	1,913.42	1,836.03	1,806.49	1,794.82	1,790.14
18.50%	4,277.44	3,015.78	2,504.15	2,353.22	2,155.14	1,934.66	1,858.73	1,830.04	1,818.83	1,814.40
18.75%	4,292.24	3,031.87	2,521.52	2,371.19	2,174.24	1,955.99	1,881.49	1,853.64	1,842.88	1,838.67
19.00%	4,307.08	3,048.01	2,538.94	2,389.23	2,193.40	1,977.38	1,904.30	1,877.27	1,866.95	1,862.96
19.25%	4,321.95	3,064.20	2,556.43	2,407.33	2,212.63	1,998.84	1,927.18	1,900.95	1,891.04	1,887.26
19.50%	4,336.84	3,080.43	2,573.97	2,425.49	2,231.94	2,020.38	1,950.11	1,924.66	1,915.16	1,911.57
19.75%	4,351.77	3,096.71	2,591.57	2,443.71	2,251.31	2,041.98	1,973.09	1,948.40	1,939.29	1,935.89
20.00%	4,366.72	3,113.03	2,609.23	2,462.00	2,270.75	2,063.65	1,996.12	1,972.18	1,963.45	1,960.23
20.25%	4,381.70	3,129.40	2,626.94	2,480.35	2,290.26	2,085.38	2,019.20	1,995.99	1,987.62	1,984.57
20.50%	4,396.71	3,145.81	2,644.72	2,498.76	2,309.84	2,107.18	2,042.33	2,019.83	2,011.81	2,008.93
20.75%	4,411.75	3,162.27	2,662.55	2,517.23	2,329.49	2,129.04	2,065.51	2,043.70	2,036.02	2,033.29

$120,000   1.00 - 10.75%   3 - 35 Years

	3	5	7	8	10	15	20	25	30	35
1.00%	3,384.97	2,051.25	1,479.75	1,301.19	1,051.25	718.19	551.87	452.25	385.97	338.74
1.25%	3,397.96	2,064.19	1,492.73	1,314.19	1,064.32	731.46	565.36	465.96	399.90	352.90
1.50%	3,410.98	2,077.19	1,505.78	1,327.28	1,077.50	744.89	579.05	479.92	414.14	367.42
1.75%	3,424.03	2,090.23	1,518.90	1,340.45	1,090.78	758.47	592.95	494.15	428.69	382.29
2.00%	3,437.11	2,103.33	1,532.09	1,353.70	1,104.16	772.21	607.06	508.63	443.54	397.52
2.25%	3,450.22	2,116.48	1,545.36	1,367.04	1,117.65	786.10	621.37	523.36	458.70	413.08
2.50%	3,463.37	2,129.68	1,558.70	1,380.46	1,131.24	800.15	635.88	538.34	474.15	428.99
2.75%	3,476.54	2,142.94	1,572.11	1,393.96	1,144.93	814.35	650.60	553.57	489.89	445.24
3.00%	3,489.75	2,156.24	1,585.60	1,407.55	1,158.73	828.70	665.52	569.05	505.92	461.82
3.25%	3,502.98	2,169.60	1,599.15	1,421.22	1,172.63	843.20	680.63	584.78	522.25	478.72
3.50%	3,516.25	2,183.01	1,612.78	1,434.97	1,186.63	857.86	695.95	600.75	538.85	495.95
3.75%	3,529.55	2,196.47	1,626.48	1,448.80	1,200.73	872.67	711.47	616.96	555.74	513.49
4.00%	3,542.88	2,209.98	1,640.26	1,462.71	1,214.94	887.63	727.18	633.40	572.90	531.33
4.25%	3,556.24	2,223.55	1,654.10	1,476.71	1,229.25	902.73	743.08	650.09	590.33	549.47
4.50%	3,569.63	2,237.16	1,668.02	1,490.79	1,243.66	917.99	759.18	667.00	608.02	567.91
4.75%	3,583.05	2,250.83	1,682.01	1,504.95	1,258.17	933.40	775.47	684.14	625.98	586.63
5.00%	3,596.51	2,264.55	1,696.07	1,519.19	1,272.79	948.95	791.95	701.51	644.19	605.63
5.25%	3,609.99	2,278.32	1,710.20	1,533.51	1,287.50	964.65	808.61	719.10	662.64	624.89
5.50%	3,623.51	2,292.14	1,724.41	1,547.92	1,302.32	980.50	825.46	736.90	681.35	644.42
5.75%	3,637.05	2,306.01	1,738.68	1,562.40	1,317.23	996.49	842.50	754.93	700.29	664.20
6.00%	3,650.63	2,319.94	1,753.03	1,576.97	1,332.25	1,012.63	859.72	773.16	719.46	684.23
6.25%	3,664.24	2,333.91	1,767.44	1,591.62	1,347.36	1,028.91	877.11	791.60	738.86	704.49
6.50%	3,677.88	2,347.94	1,781.93	1,606.35	1,362.58	1,045.33	894.69	810.25	758.48	724.99
6.75%	3,691.55	2,362.02	1,796.49	1,621.16	1,377.89	1,061.89	912.44	829.09	778.32	745.70
7.00%	3,705.25	2,376.14	1,811.12	1,636.05	1,393.30	1,078.59	930.36	848.14	798.36	766.63
7.25%	3,718.98	2,390.32	1,825.82	1,651.02	1,408.81	1,095.44	948.45	867.37	818.61	787.76
7.50%	3,732.75	2,404.55	1,840.59	1,666.06	1,424.42	1,112.41	966.71	886.79	839.06	809.09
7.75%	3,746.54	2,418.84	1,855.43	1,681.19	1,440.13	1,129.53	985.14	906.39	859.69	830.61
8.00%	3,760.36	2,433.17	1,870.35	1,696.40	1,455.93	1,146.78	1,003.73	926.18	880.52	852.31
8.25%	3,774.22	2,447.55	1,885.33	1,711.69	1,471.83	1,164.17	1,022.48	946.14	901.52	874.19
8.50%	3,788.10	2,461.98	1,900.38	1,727.06	1,487.83	1,181.69	1,041.39	966.27	922.70	896.23
8.75%	3,802.02	2,476.47	1,915.50	1,742.50	1,503.92	1,199.34	1,060.45	986.57	944.04	918.44
9.00%	3,815.97	2,491.00	1,930.69	1,758.02	1,520.11	1,217.12	1,079.67	1,007.04	965.55	940.79
9.25%	3,829.95	2,505.59	1,945.95	1,773.63	1,536.39	1,235.03	1,099.04	1,027.66	987.21	963.29
9.50%	3,843.95	2,520.22	1,961.28	1,789.31	1,552.77	1,253.07	1,118.56	1,048.44	1,009.03	985.93
9.75%	3,857.99	2,534.91	1,976.68	1,805.06	1,569.24	1,271.24	1,138.22	1,069.36	1,030.99	1,008.71
10.00%	3,872.06	2,549.65	1,992.14	1,820.90	1,585.81	1,289.53	1,158.03	1,090.44	1,053.09	1,031.61
10.25%	3,886.16	2,564.43	2,007.68	1,836.81	1,602.47	1,307.94	1,177.97	1,111.66	1,075.32	1,054.63
10.50%	3,900.29	2,579.27	2,023.28	1,852.80	1,619.22	1,326.48	1,198.06	1,133.02	1,097.69	1,077.76
10.75%	3,914.45	2,594.15	2,038.95	1,868.87	1,636.06	1,345.14	1,218.27	1,154.51	1,120.18	1,101.00

	3	5	7	8	10	15	20	25	30	35
11.00%	3,928.65	2,609.09	2,054.69	1,885.01	1,653.00	1,363.92	1,238.63	1,176.14	1,142.79	1,124.35
11.25%	3,942.87	2,624.08	2,070.50	1,901.23	1,670.03	1,382.81	1,259.11	1,197.89	1,165.51	1,147.79
11.50%	3,957.12	2,639.11	2,086.38	1,917.52	1,687.15	1,401.83	1,279.72	1,219.76	1,188.35	1,171.33
11.75%	3,971.40	2,654.20	2,102.32	1,933.90	1,704.35	1,420.96	1,300.45	1,241.76	1,211.29	1,194.95
12.00%	3,985.72	2,669.33	2,118.33	1,950.34	1,721.65	1,440.20	1,321.30	1,263.87	1,234.34	1,218.66
12.25%	4,000.06	2,684.52	2,134.40	1,966.86	1,739.04	1,459.56	1,342.28	1,286.09	1,257.48	1,242.45
12.50%	4,014.44	2,699.75	2,150.55	1,983.46	1,756.51	1,479.03	1,363.37	1,308.42	1,280.71	1,266.31
12.75%	4,028.84	2,715.04	2,166.76	2,000.13	1,774.08	1,498.60	1,384.57	1,330.86	1,304.03	1,290.24
13.00%	4,043.27	2,730.37	2,183.04	2,016.87	1,791.73	1,518.29	1,405.89	1,353.40	1,327.44	1,314.23
13.25%	4,057.74	2,745.75	2,199.38	2,033.69	1,809.47	1,538.08	1,427.32	1,376.04	1,350.93	1,338.29
13.50%	4,072.23	2,761.18	2,215.79	2,050.58	1,827.29	1,557.98	1,448.85	1,398.77	1,374.49	1,362.41
13.75%	4,086.76	2,776.66	2,232.26	2,067.54	1,845.20	1,577.98	1,470.49	1,421.60	1,398.14	1,386.58
14.00%	4,101.32	2,792.19	2,248.80	2,084.58	1,863.20	1,598.09	1,492.22	1,444.51	1,421.85	1,410.81
14.25%	4,115.90	2,807.77	2,265.41	2,101.69	1,881.28	1,618.30	1,514.06	1,467.51	1,445.62	1,435.08
14.50%	4,130.52	2,823.39	2,282.08	2,118.87	1,899.44	1,638.60	1,536.00	1,490.60	1,469.47	1,459.40
14.75%	4,145.16	2,839.07	2,298.81	2,136.12	1,917.69	1,659.00	1,558.03	1,513.76	1,493.37	1,483.77
15.00%	4,159.84	2,854.79	2,315.61	2,153.45	1,936.02	1,679.50	1,580.15	1,537.00	1,517.33	1,508.18
15.25%	4,174.55	2,870.56	2,332.47	2,170.84	1,954.43	1,700.10	1,602.36	1,560.31	1,541.35	1,532.62
15.50%	4,189.28	2,886.38	2,349.40	2,188.31	1,972.93	1,720.79	1,624.66	1,583.69	1,565.42	1,557.10
15.75%	4,204.05	2,902.25	2,366.39	2,205.85	1,991.50	1,741.57	1,647.04	1,607.15	1,589.54	1,581.62
16.00%	4,218.84	2,918.17	2,383.45	2,223.45	2,010.16	1,762.44	1,669.51	1,630.67	1,613.71	1,606.16
16.25%	4,233.67	2,934.13	2,400.57	2,241.13	2,028.89	1,783.40	1,692.05	1,654.25	1,637.92	1,630.74
16.50%	4,248.53	2,950.14	2,417.75	2,258.88	2,047.71	1,804.45	1,714.68	1,677.89	1,662.18	1,655.34
16.75%	4,263.41	2,966.20	2,434.99	2,276.69	2,066.60	1,825.59	1,737.38	1,701.60	1,686.47	1,679.98
17.00%	4,278.33	2,982.31	2,452.30	2,294.57	2,085.57	1,846.81	1,760.16	1,725.36	1,710.81	1,704.63
17.25%	4,293.27	2,998.46	2,469.66	2,312.53	2,104.62	1,868.11	1,783.01	1,749.17	1,735.18	1,729.31
17.50%	4,308.25	3,014.67	2,487.10	2,330.55	2,123.75	1,889.49	1,805.93	1,773.04	1,759.59	1,754.01
17.75%	4,323.25	3,030.91	2,504.59	2,348.63	2,142.95	1,910.96	1,828.92	1,796.95	1,784.03	1,778.73
18.00%	4,338.29	3,047.21	2,522.14	2,366.79	2,162.22	1,932.51	1,851.97	1,820.92	1,808.50	1,803.47
18.25%	4,353.35	3,063.55	2,539.76	2,385.01	2,181.57	1,954.13	1,875.09	1,844.93	1,833.00	1,828.23
18.50%	4,368.45	3,079.95	2,557.43	2,403.29	2,201.00	1,975.83	1,898.28	1,868.98	1,857.53	1,853.00
18.75%	4,383.57	3,096.38	2,575.17	2,421.65	2,220.50	1,997.60	1,921.52	1,893.08	1,882.09	1,877.79
19.00%	4,398.72	3,112.87	2,592.96	2,440.06	2,240.07	2,019.45	1,944.82	1,917.22	1,906.67	1,902.59
19.25%	4,413.91	3,129.40	2,610.82	2,458.55	2,259.71	2,041.37	1,968.18	1,941.39	1,931.28	1,927.41
19.50%	4,429.12	3,145.97	2,628.73	2,477.10	2,279.43	2,063.36	1,991.60	1,965.61	1,955.90	1,952.24
19.75%	4,444.36	3,162.60	2,646.71	2,495.71	2,299.21	2,085.43	2,015.07	1,989.86	1,980.55	1,977.08
20.00%	4,459.63	3,179.27	2,664.74	2,514.38	2,319.07	2,107.56	2,038.59	2,014.14	2,005.22	2,001.93
20.25%	4,474.93	3,195.98	2,682.84	2,533.12	2,338.99	2,129.75	2,062.16	2,038.46	2,029.91	2,026.80
20.50%	4,490.26	3,212.74	2,700.99	2,551.93	2,358.99	2,152.02	2,085.78	2,062.81	2,054.62	2,051.67
20.75%	4,505.62	3,229.55	2,719.20	2,570.79	2,379.05	2,174.34	2,109.46	2,087.19	2,079.34	2,076.55

	3	5	7	8	10	15	20	25	30	35
1.00%	3,455.49	2,093.98	1,510.58	1,328.30	1,073.15	733.16	563.37	461.67	394.01	345.80
1.25%	3,468.75	2,107.20	1,523.82	1,341.57	1,086.50	746.70	577.14	475.66	408.23	360.26
1.50%	3,482.04	2,120.46	1,537.15	1,354.93	1,099.95	760.41	591.12	489.92	422.77	375.08
1.75%	3,495.36	2,133.78	1,550.54	1,368.38	1,113.50	774.28	605.31	504.44	437.62	390.26
2.00%	3,508.72	2,147.15	1,564.01	1,381.91	1,127.16	788.30	619.71	519.22	452.78	405.80
2.25%	3,522.10	2,160.57	1,577.55	1,395.52	1,140.93	802.48	634.32	534.26	468.25	421.69
2.50%	3,535.52	2,174.05	1,591.17	1,409.22	1,154.81	816.82	649.13	549.56	484.02	437.93
2.75%	3,548.97	2,187.58	1,604.86	1,423.00	1,168.79	831.31	664.15	565.11	500.10	454.52
3.00%	3,562.45	2,201.16	1,618.63	1,436.87	1,182.87	845.96	679.38	580.91	516.46	471.44
3.25%	3,575.96	2,214.80	1,632.47	1,450.82	1,197.06	860.77	694.81	596.96	533.13	488.70
3.50%	3,589.50	2,228.49	1,646.38	1,464.86	1,211.35	875.73	710.45	613.26	550.08	506.28
3.75%	3,603.08	2,242.23	1,660.37	1,478.98	1,225.75	890.85	726.29	629.81	567.32	524.18
4.00%	3,616.69	2,256.02	1,674.43	1,493.19	1,240.25	906.12	742.33	646.60	584.83	542.40
4.25%	3,630.33	2,269.87	1,688.56	1,507.47	1,254.86	921.54	758.56	663.63	602.63	560.92
4.50%	3,644.00	2,283.77	1,702.77	1,521.85	1,269.57	937.12	775.00	680.89	620.69	579.74
4.75%	3,657.70	2,297.72	1,717.05	1,536.30	1,284.38	952.84	791.62	698.39	639.02	598.85
5.00%	3,671.43	2,311.73	1,731.40	1,550.84	1,299.30	968.72	808.45	716.12	657.61	618.24
5.25%	3,685.20	2,325.78	1,745.83	1,565.46	1,314.32	984.75	825.46	734.08	676.45	637.91
5.50%	3,699.00	2,339.89	1,760.33	1,580.17	1,329.45	1,000.93	842.66	752.26	695.54	657.84
5.75%	3,712.83	2,354.05	1,774.90	1,594.95	1,344.67	1,017.25	860.05	770.66	714.88	678.04
6.00%	3,726.69	2,368.27	1,789.55	1,609.83	1,360.00	1,033.72	877.63	789.27	734.45	698.48
6.25%	3,740.58	2,382.53	1,804.27	1,624.78	1,375.43	1,050.34	895.39	808.09	754.25	719.17
6.50%	3,754.50	2,396.85	1,819.06	1,639.81	1,390.96	1,067.11	913.33	827.13	774.28	740.09
6.75%	3,768.46	2,411.22	1,833.92	1,654.93	1,406.60	1,084.01	931.45	846.37	794.53	761.24
7.00%	3,782.44	2,425.65	1,848.85	1,670.13	1,422.33	1,101.06	949.74	865.80	815.00	782.60
7.25%	3,796.46	2,440.12	1,863.86	1,685.41	1,438.16	1,118.26	968.21	885.44	835.67	804.17
7.50%	3,810.51	2,454.65	1,878.94	1,700.77	1,454.10	1,135.59	986.85	905.26	856.54	825.95
7.75%	3,824.59	2,469.23	1,894.09	1,716.22	1,470.13	1,153.06	1,005.66	925.28	877.61	847.92
8.00%	3,838.70	2,483.86	1,909.31	1,731.74	1,486.26	1,170.67	1,024.64	945.47	898.86	870.07
8.25%	3,852.85	2,498.54	1,924.60	1,747.35	1,502.49	1,188.42	1,043.78	965.85	920.30	892.40
8.50%	3,867.02	2,513.28	1,939.97	1,763.04	1,518.82	1,206.31	1,063.08	986.40	941.92	914.90
8.75%	3,881.23	2,528.06	1,955.41	1,778.80	1,535.25	1,224.32	1,082.55	1,007.13	963.71	937.57
9.00%	3,895.47	2,542.90	1,970.91	1,794.65	1,551.78	1,242.48	1,102.16	1,028.02	985.66	960.39
9.25%	3,909.74	2,557.79	1,986.49	1,810.58	1,568.40	1,260.76	1,121.94	1,049.07	1,007.78	983.36
9.50%	3,924.04	2,572.73	2,002.14	1,826.58	1,585.12	1,279.18	1,141.86	1,070.28	1,030.05	1,006.47
9.75%	3,938.37	2,587.72	2,017.86	1,842.67	1,601.94	1,297.72	1,161.93	1,091.64	1,052.46	1,029.72
10.00%	3,952.73	2,602.76	2,033.65	1,858.84	1,618.85	1,316.39	1,182.15	1,113.16	1,075.03	1,053.10
10.25%	3,967.12	2,617.86	2,049.50	1,875.08	1,635.85	1,335.19	1,202.51	1,134.82	1,097.72	1,076.60
10.50%	3,981.55	2,633.00	2,065.43	1,891.40	1,652.95	1,354.11	1,223.02	1,156.62	1,120.56	1,100.21
10.75%	3,996.01	2,648.20	2,081.43	1,907.80	1,670.15	1,373.16	1,243.66	1,178.56	1,143.51	1,123.94

$122,500   11.00 - 20.75%   3 - 35 Years

	3	5	7	8	10	15	20	25	30	35
11.00%	4,010.49	2,663.45	2,097.50	1,924.28	1,687.44	1,392.33	1,264.43	1,200.64	1,166.60	1,147.77
11.25%	4,025.01	2,678.75	2,113.64	1,940.84	1,704.82	1,411.62	1,285.34	1,222.84	1,189.80	1,171.71
11.50%	4,039.56	2,694.09	2,129.84	1,957.47	1,722.29	1,431.03	1,306.38	1,245.17	1,213.11	1,195.73
11.75%	4,054.14	2,709.49	2,146.12	1,974.18	1,739.86	1,450.56	1,327.54	1,267.63	1,236.53	1,219.85
12.00%	4,068.75	2,724.94	2,162.46	1,990.97	1,757.52	1,470.21	1,348.83	1,290.20	1,260.05	1,244.05
12.25%	4,083.40	2,740.45	2,178.87	2,007.84	1,775.27	1,489.97	1,370.24	1,312.89	1,283.67	1,268.33
12.50%	4,098.07	2,756.00	2,195.35	2,024.78	1,793.11	1,509.84	1,391.77	1,335.68	1,307.39	1,292.69
12.75%	4,112.77	2,771.60	2,211.90	2,041.80	1,811.04	1,529.83	1,413.42	1,358.59	1,331.20	1,317.12
13.00%	4,127.51	2,787.25	2,228.52	2,058.89	1,829.06	1,549.92	1,435.18	1,381.60	1,355.09	1,341.61
13.25%	4,142.28	2,802.95	2,245.20	2,076.06	1,847.16	1,570.13	1,457.05	1,404.71	1,379.07	1,366.17
13.50%	4,157.07	2,818.71	2,261.95	2,093.30	1,865.36	1,590.44	1,479.03	1,427.91	1,403.13	1,390.79
13.75%	4,171.90	2,834.51	2,278.77	2,110.62	1,883.64	1,610.86	1,501.12	1,451.22	1,427.26	1,415.47
14.00%	4,186.76	2,850.36	2,295.65	2,128.01	1,902.01	1,631.38	1,523.31	1,474.61	1,451.47	1,440.20
14.25%	4,201.65	2,866.26	2,312.60	2,145.47	1,920.47	1,652.01	1,545.61	1,498.09	1,475.74	1,464.98
14.50%	4,216.57	2,882.21	2,329.62	2,163.01	1,939.01	1,672.74	1,568.00	1,521.65	1,500.08	1,489.81
14.75%	4,231.52	2,898.22	2,346.70	2,180.63	1,957.64	1,693.57	1,590.49	1,545.29	1,524.48	1,514.68
15.00%	4,246.50	2,914.27	2,363.85	2,198.31	1,976.35	1,714.49	1,613.07	1,569.02	1,548.94	1,539.60
15.25%	4,261.52	2,930.37	2,381.07	2,216.07	1,995.15	1,735.52	1,635.74	1,592.82	1,573.46	1,564.55
15.50%	4,276.56	2,946.52	2,398.35	2,233.90	2,014.03	1,756.64	1,658.50	1,616.69	1,598.03	1,589.54
15.75%	4,291.63	2,962.71	2,415.69	2,251.80	2,032.99	1,777.85	1,681.35	1,640.63	1,622.66	1,614.57
16.00%	4,306.74	2,978.96	2,433.10	2,269.78	2,052.04	1,799.16	1,704.29	1,664.64	1,647.33	1,639.63
16.25%	4,321.87	2,995.26	2,450.58	2,287.82	2,071.16	1,820.56	1,727.31	1,688.71	1,672.04	1,664.71
16.50%	4,337.04	3,011.60	2,468.12	2,305.94	2,090.37	1,842.04	1,750.40	1,712.85	1,696.81	1,689.83
16.75%	4,352.23	3,028.00	2,485.72	2,324.12	2,109.65	1,863.62	1,773.58	1,737.05	1,721.61	1,714.98
17.00%	4,367.46	3,044.44	2,503.39	2,342.38	2,129.02	1,885.28	1,796.83	1,761.30	1,746.45	1,740.14
17.25%	4,382.72	3,060.93	2,521.12	2,360.70	2,148.47	1,907.03	1,820.16	1,785.61	1,771.33	1,765.34
17.50%	4,398.00	3,077.47	2,538.91	2,379.10	2,167.99	1,928.86	1,843.55	1,809.97	1,796.25	1,790.55
17.75%	4,413.32	3,094.06	2,556.77	2,397.56	2,187.59	1,950.77	1,867.02	1,834.39	1,821.20	1,815.79
18.00%	4,428.67	3,110.69	2,574.69	2,416.09	2,207.27	1,972.77	1,890.56	1,858.85	1,846.18	1,841.04
18.25%	4,444.05	3,127.38	2,592.67	2,434.69	2,227.02	1,994.84	1,914.16	1,883.36	1,871.19	1,866.32
18.50%	4,459.46	3,144.11	2,610.71	2,453.36	2,246.85	2,016.99	1,937.82	1,907.92	1,896.23	1,891.61
18.75%	4,474.89	3,160.89	2,628.82	2,472.10	2,266.76	2,039.22	1,961.55	1,932.52	1,921.30	1,916.91
19.00%	4,490.36	3,177.72	2,646.98	2,490.90	2,286.74	2,061.52	1,985.34	1,957.16	1,946.39	1,942.23
19.25%	4,505.86	3,194.59	2,665.21	2,509.77	2,306.79	2,083.90	2,009.19	1,981.84	1,971.51	1,967.57
19.50%	4,521.39	3,211.51	2,683.50	2,528.70	2,326.91	2,106.35	2,033.09	2,006.56	1,996.65	1,992.91
19.75%	4,536.95	3,228.48	2,701.85	2,547.70	2,347.11	2,128.87	2,057.05	2,031.31	2,021.81	2,018.27
20.00%	4,552.54	3,245.50	2,720.26	2,566.77	2,367.38	2,151.46	2,081.06	2,056.10	2,047.00	2,043.64
20.25%	4,568.16	3,262.56	2,738.73	2,585.90	2,387.72	2,174.12	2,105.12	2,080.93	2,072.20	2,069.02
20.50%	4,583.81	3,279.68	2,757.26	2,605.09	2,408.13	2,196.85	2,129.24	2,105.78	2,097.42	2,094.41
20.75%	4,599.49	3,296.83	2,775.85	2,624.35	2,428.61	2,219.64	2,153.40	2,130.67	2,122.66	2,119.81

	3	5	7	8	10	15	20	25	30	35
1.00%	3,526.01	2,136.72	1,541.41	1,355.40	1,095.05	748.12	574.87	471.09	402.05	352.86
1.25%	3,539.54	2,150.20	1,554.92	1,368.95	1,108.67	761.94	588.92	485.37	416.56	367.61
1.50%	3,553.10	2,163.74	1,568.52	1,382.58	1,122.39	775.93	603.18	499.92	431.40	382.73
1.75%	3,566.70	2,177.33	1,582.18	1,396.30	1,136.23	790.08	617.66	514.74	446.55	398.22
2.00%	3,580.32	2,190.97	1,595.93	1,410.11	1,150.17	804.39	632.35	529.82	462.02	414.08
2.25%	3,593.98	2,204.67	1,609.75	1,424.00	1,164.22	818.86	647.26	545.16	477.81	430.30
2.50%	3,607.67	2,218.42	1,623.64	1,437.98	1,178.37	833.49	662.38	560.77	493.90	446.87
2.75%	3,621.40	2,232.23	1,637.62	1,452.05	1,192.64	848.28	677.71	576.64	510.30	463.79
3.00%	3,635.15	2,246.09	1,651.66	1,466.20	1,207.01	863.23	693.25	592.76	527.01	481.06
3.25%	3,648.94	2,260.00	1,665.78	1,480.43	1,221.49	878.34	708.99	609.15	544.01	498.67
3.50%	3,662.76	2,273.97	1,679.98	1,494.76	1,236.07	893.60	724.95	625.78	561.31	516.61
3.75%	3,676.61	2,287.99	1,694.25	1,509.17	1,250.77	909.03	741.11	642.66	578.89	534.88
4.00%	3,690.50	2,302.07	1,708.60	1,523.66	1,265.56	924.61	757.48	659.80	596.77	553.47
4.25%	3,704.42	2,316.19	1,723.02	1,538.24	1,280.47	940.35	774.04	677.17	614.92	572.37
4.50%	3,718.37	2,330.38	1,737.52	1,552.90	1,295.48	956.24	790.81	694.79	633.36	591.57
4.75%	3,732.35	2,344.61	1,752.09	1,567.65	1,310.60	972.29	807.78	712.65	652.06	611.07
5.00%	3,746.36	2,358.90	1,766.74	1,582.49	1,325.82	988.49	824.94	730.74	671.03	630.86
5.25%	3,760.41	2,373.25	1,781.46	1,597.41	1,341.15	1,004.85	842.31	749.06	690.25	650.93
5.50%	3,774.49	2,387.65	1,796.26	1,612.42	1,356.58	1,021.35	859.86	767.61	709.74	671.27
5.75%	3,788.60	2,402.10	1,811.13	1,627.50	1,372.12	1,038.01	877.60	786.38	729.47	691.88
6.00%	3,802.74	2,416.60	1,826.07	1,642.68	1,387.76	1,054.82	895.54	805.38	749.44	712.74
6.25%	3,816.92	2,431.16	1,841.09	1,657.94	1,403.50	1,071.78	913.66	824.59	769.65	733.85
6.50%	3,831.13	2,445.77	1,856.18	1,673.28	1,419.35	1,088.88	931.97	844.01	790.09	755.19
6.75%	3,845.37	2,460.43	1,871.35	1,688.71	1,435.30	1,106.14	950.46	863.64	810.75	776.77
7.00%	3,859.64	2,475.15	1,886.58	1,704.21	1,451.36	1,123.54	969.12	883.47	831.63	798.57
7.25%	3,873.94	2,489.92	1,901.90	1,719.81	1,467.51	1,141.08	987.97	903.51	852.72	820.58
7.50%	3,888.28	2,504.74	1,917.28	1,735.48	1,483.77	1,158.77	1,006.99	923.74	874.02	842.80
7.75%	3,902.65	2,519.62	1,932.74	1,751.24	1,500.13	1,176.59	1,026.19	944.16	895.52	865.22
8.00%	3,917.05	2,534.55	1,948.28	1,767.08	1,516.59	1,194.57	1,045.55	964.77	917.21	887.83
8.25%	3,931.48	2,549.53	1,963.88	1,783.01	1,533.16	1,212.68	1,065.08	985.56	939.08	910.61
8.50%	3,945.94	2,564.57	1,979.56	1,799.02	1,549.82	1,230.92	1,084.78	1,006.53	961.14	933.58
8.75%	3,960.44	2,579.65	1,995.31	1,815.10	1,566.58	1,249.31	1,104.64	1,027.68	983.38	956.70
9.00%	3,974.97	2,594.79	2,011.13	1,831.28	1,583.45	1,267.83	1,124.66	1,049.00	1,005.78	979.99
9.25%	3,989.53	2,609.99	2,027.03	1,847.53	1,600.41	1,286.49	1,144.83	1,070.48	1,028.34	1,003.43
9.50%	4,004.12	2,625.23	2,043.00	1,863.86	1,617.47	1,305.28	1,165.16	1,092.12	1,051.07	1,027.01
9.75%	4,018.74	2,640.53	2,059.04	1,880.28	1,634.63	1,324.20	1,185.65	1,113.92	1,073.94	1,050.74
10.00%	4,033.40	2,655.88	2,075.15	1,896.77	1,651.88	1,343.26	1,206.28	1,135.88	1,096.96	1,074.59
10.25%	4,048.09	2,671.28	2,091.33	1,913.35	1,669.24	1,362.44	1,227.05	1,157.98	1,120.13	1,098.57
10.50%	4,062.81	2,686.74	2,107.58	1,930.00	1,686.69	1,381.75	1,247.97	1,180.23	1,143.42	1,122.67
10.75%	4,077.56	2,702.24	2,123.91	1,946.74	1,704.23	1,401.18	1,269.04	1,202.62	1,166.85	1,146.88

$125,000   11.00 - 20.75%   3 - 35 Years

	3	5	7	8	10	15	20	25	30	35
11.00%	4,092.34	2,717.80	2,140.30	1,963.55	1,721.88	1,420.75	1,290.24	1,225.14	1,190.40	1,171.20
11.25%	4,107.15	2,733.41	2,156.77	1,980.45	1,739.61	1,440.43	1,311.57	1,247.80	1,214.08	1,195.62
11.50%	4,122.00	2,749.08	2,173.31	1,997.42	1,757.44	1,460.24	1,333.04	1,270.59	1,237.86	1,220.13
11.75%	4,136.88	2,764.79	2,189.91	2,014.47	1,775.37	1,480.16	1,354.63	1,293.50	1,261.76	1,244.74
12.00%	4,151.79	2,780.56	2,206.59	2,031.61	1,793.39	1,500.21	1,376.36	1,316.53	1,285.77	1,269.44
12.25%	4,166.73	2,796.37	2,223.34	2,048.81	1,811.50	1,520.37	1,398.21	1,339.68	1,309.87	1,294.21
12.50%	4,181.70	2,812.24	2,240.15	2,066.10	1,829.70	1,540.65	1,420.18	1,362.94	1,334.07	1,319.07
12.75%	4,196.71	2,828.16	2,257.04	2,083.47	1,848.00	1,561.05	1,442.26	1,386.32	1,358.37	1,344.00
13.00%	4,211.74	2,844.13	2,274.00	2,100.91	1,866.38	1,581.55	1,464.47	1,409.79	1,382.75	1,368.99
13.25%	4,226.81	2,860.16	2,291.02	2,118.43	1,884.86	1,602.17	1,486.79	1,433.38	1,407.22	1,394.05
13.50%	4,241.91	2,876.23	2,308.11	2,136.02	1,903.43	1,622.90	1,509.22	1,457.06	1,431.77	1,419.18
13.75%	4,257.04	2,892.36	2,325.27	2,153.69	1,922.09	1,643.73	1,531.76	1,480.83	1,456.39	1,444.36
14.00%	4,272.20	2,908.53	2,342.50	2,171.44	1,940.83	1,664.68	1,554.40	1,504.70	1,481.09	1,469.59
14.25%	4,287.40	2,924.76	2,359.80	2,189.26	1,959.66	1,685.72	1,577.15	1,528.66	1,505.86	1,494.88
14.50%	4,302.62	2,941.04	2,377.16	2,207.16	1,978.58	1,706.88	1,600.00	1,552.70	1,530.69	1,520.21
14.75%	4,317.88	2,957.36	2,394.60	2,225.13	1,997.59	1,728.13	1,622.94	1,576.83	1,555.59	1,545.59
15.00%	4,333.17	2,973.74	2,412.09	2,243.18	2,016.69	1,749.48	1,645.99	1,601.04	1,580.56	1,571.02
15.25%	4,348.48	2,990.17	2,429.66	2,261.30	2,035.87	1,770.94	1,669.12	1,625.32	1,605.57	1,596.48
15.50%	4,363.84	3,006.65	2,447.29	2,279.49	2,055.13	1,792.49	1,692.35	1,649.68	1,630.65	1,621.98
15.75%	4,379.22	3,023.18	2,464.99	2,297.76	2,074.48	1,814.13	1,715.67	1,674.11	1,655.77	1,647.52
16.00%	4,394.63	3,039.76	2,482.76	2,316.10	2,093.91	1,835.88	1,739.07	1,698.61	1,680.95	1,673.09
16.25%	4,410.07	3,056.39	2,500.59	2,334.51	2,113.43	1,857.71	1,762.56	1,723.18	1,706.17	1,698.69
16.50%	4,425.55	3,073.07	2,518.49	2,353.00	2,133.03	1,879.64	1,786.13	1,747.81	1,731.44	1,724.32
16.75%	4,441.05	3,089.79	2,536.45	2,371.55	2,152.71	1,901.65	1,809.77	1,772.50	1,756.74	1,749.97
17.00%	4,456.59	3,106.57	2,554.48	2,390.18	2,172.47	1,923.76	1,833.50	1,797.25	1,782.09	1,775.66
17.25%	4,472.16	3,123.40	2,572.57	2,408.88	2,192.31	1,945.95	1,857.30	1,822.05	1,807.48	1,801.36
17.50%	4,487.76	3,140.28	2,590.72	2,427.65	2,212.23	1,968.22	1,881.18	1,846.91	1,832.91	1,827.09
17.75%	4,503.39	3,157.20	2,608.95	2,446.49	2,232.24	1,990.58	1,905.12	1,871.82	1,858.37	1,852.84
18.00%	4,519.05	3,174.18	2,627.23	2,465.40	2,252.31	2,013.03	1,929.14	1,896.79	1,883.86	1,878.61
18.25%	4,534.74	3,191.20	2,645.58	2,484.38	2,272.47	2,035.55	1,953.22	1,921.80	1,909.38	1,904.40
18.50%	4,550.46	3,208.28	2,663.99	2,503.43	2,292.71	2,058.15	1,977.37	1,946.86	1,934.93	1,930.21
18.75%	4,566.22	3,225.40	2,682.46	2,522.55	2,313.02	2,080.84	2,001.58	1,971.96	1,960.51	1,956.03
19.00%	4,582.00	3,242.57	2,701.00	2,541.73	2,333.40	2,103.60	2,025.86	1,997.10	1,986.12	1,981.87
19.25%	4,597.82	3,259.79	2,719.60	2,560.99	2,353.87	2,126.43	2,050.19	2,022.28	2,011.75	2,007.72
19.50%	4,613.66	3,277.06	2,738.26	2,580.31	2,374.40	2,149.34	2,074.58	2,047.51	2,037.40	2,033.58
19.75%	4,629.54	3,294.37	2,756.99	2,599.70	2,395.01	2,172.32	2,099.03	2,072.77	2,063.08	2,059.46
20.00%	4,645.45	3,311.74	2,775.77	2,619.15	2,415.70	2,195.37	2,123.53	2,098.06	2,088.77	2,085.35
20.25%	4,661.39	3,329.15	2,794.62	2,638.67	2,436.45	2,218.49	2,148.09	2,123.40	2,114.49	2,111.25
20.50%	4,677.35	3,346.61	2,813.53	2,658.26	2,457.28	2,241.68	2,172.69	2,148.76	2,140.23	2,137.15
20.75%	4,693.35	3,364.11	2,832.50	2,677.91	2,478.18	2,264.94	2,197.35	2,174.15	2,165.98	2,163.07

	3	5	7	8	10	15	20	25	30	35
1.00%	3,596.53	2,179.45	1,572.23	1,382.51	1,116.95	763.08	586.37	480.51	410.09	359.91
1.25%	3,610.33	2,193.20	1,586.02	1,396.33	1,130.84	777.18	600.70	495.08	424.90	374.96
1.50%	3,624.16	2,207.01	1,599.89	1,410.23	1,144.84	791.45	615.25	509.92	440.03	390.39
1.75%	3,638.03	2,220.87	1,613.83	1,424.23	1,158.95	805.88	630.01	525.03	455.49	406.19
2.00%	3,651.93	2,234.79	1,627.85	1,438.31	1,173.17	820.47	645.00	540.41	471.26	422.36
2.25%	3,665.86	2,248.76	1,641.94	1,452.48	1,187.50	835.23	660.21	556.07	487.36	438.90
2.50%	3,679.83	2,262.79	1,656.12	1,466.74	1,201.94	850.16	675.63	571.99	503.78	455.81
2.75%	3,693.82	2,276.87	1,670.37	1,481.09	1,216.49	865.24	691.26	588.17	520.51	473.07
3.00%	3,707.85	2,291.01	1,684.70	1,495.52	1,231.15	880.49	707.11	604.62	537.55	490.68
3.25%	3,721.92	2,305.20	1,699.10	1,510.04	1,245.92	895.90	723.17	621.33	554.89	508.64
3.50%	3,736.02	2,319.45	1,713.58	1,524.65	1,260.79	911.48	739.45	638.30	572.53	526.95
3.75%	3,750.15	2,333.75	1,728.14	1,539.35	1,275.78	927.21	755.93	655.52	590.47	545.58
4.00%	3,764.31	2,348.11	1,742.77	1,554.13	1,290.88	943.10	772.62	672.99	608.70	564.54
4.25%	3,778.50	2,362.52	1,757.48	1,569.00	1,306.08	959.15	789.52	690.72	627.22	583.81
4.50%	3,792.73	2,376.98	1,772.27	1,583.96	1,321.39	975.37	806.63	708.69	646.02	603.40
4.75%	3,806.99	2,391.51	1,787.13	1,599.01	1,336.81	991.74	823.94	726.90	665.10	623.29
5.00%	3,821.29	2,406.08	1,802.07	1,614.14	1,352.34	1,008.26	841.44	745.35	684.45	643.48
5.25%	3,835.62	2,420.71	1,817.09	1,629.36	1,367.97	1,024.94	859.15	764.04	704.06	663.95
5.50%	3,849.98	2,435.40	1,832.18	1,644.66	1,383.71	1,041.78	877.06	782.96	723.93	684.70
5.75%	3,864.37	2,450.14	1,847.35	1,660.05	1,399.56	1,058.77	895.16	802.11	744.06	705.71
6.00%	3,878.80	2,464.93	1,862.59	1,675.53	1,415.51	1,075.92	913.45	821.48	764.43	726.99
6.25%	3,893.26	2,479.78	1,877.91	1,691.10	1,431.57	1,093.21	931.93	841.08	785.04	748.52
6.50%	3,907.75	2,494.68	1,893.30	1,706.74	1,447.74	1,110.66	950.61	860.89	805.89	770.30
6.75%	3,922.27	2,509.64	1,908.77	1,722.48	1,464.01	1,128.26	969.46	880.91	826.96	792.31
7.00%	3,936.83	2,524.65	1,924.32	1,738.30	1,480.38	1,146.01	988.51	901.14	848.26	814.54
7.25%	3,951.42	2,539.72	1,939.94	1,754.20	1,496.86	1,163.90	1,007.73	921.58	869.77	837.00
7.50%	3,966.04	2,554.84	1,955.63	1,770.19	1,513.45	1,181.94	1,027.13	942.21	891.50	859.66
7.75%	3,980.70	2,570.01	1,971.40	1,786.27	1,530.14	1,200.13	1,046.71	963.04	913.43	882.52
8.00%	3,995.39	2,585.24	1,987.24	1,802.43	1,546.93	1,218.46	1,066.46	984.07	935.55	905.58
8.25%	4,010.11	2,600.52	2,003.16	1,818.67	1,563.82	1,236.93	1,086.38	1,005.27	957.86	928.83
8.50%	4,024.86	2,615.86	2,019.15	1,835.00	1,580.82	1,255.54	1,106.47	1,026.66	980.36	952.25
8.75%	4,039.65	2,631.25	2,035.22	1,851.41	1,597.92	1,274.30	1,126.73	1,048.23	1,003.04	975.84
9.00%	4,054.47	2,646.69	2,051.36	1,867.90	1,615.12	1,293.19	1,147.15	1,069.98	1,025.89	999.59
9.25%	4,069.32	2,662.19	2,067.57	1,884.48	1,632.42	1,312.22	1,167.73	1,091.89	1,048.91	1,023.50
9.50%	4,084.20	2,677.74	2,083.86	1,901.14	1,649.82	1,331.39	1,188.47	1,113.96	1,072.09	1,047.55
9.75%	4,099.12	2,693.34	2,100.22	1,917.88	1,667.32	1,350.69	1,209.36	1,136.20	1,095.42	1,071.75
10.00%	4,114.07	2,709.00	2,116.65	1,934.71	1,684.92	1,370.12	1,230.40	1,158.59	1,118.90	1,096.08
10.25%	4,129.05	2,724.71	2,133.16	1,951.61	1,702.62	1,389.69	1,251.60	1,181.14	1,142.53	1,120.54
10.50%	4,144.06	2,740.47	2,149.74	1,968.60	1,720.42	1,409.38	1,272.93	1,203.83	1,166.29	1,145.12
10.75%	4,159.11	2,756.29	2,166.39	1,985.67	1,738.32	1,429.21	1,294.42	1,226.67	1,190.19	1,169.82

$127,500   11.00 - 20.75%   3 - 35 Years

	3	5	7	8	10	15	20	25	30	35
11.00%	4,174.19	2,772.16	2,183.11	2,002.82	1,756.31	1,449.16	1,316.04	1,249.64	1,214.21	1,194.62
11.25%	4,189.30	2,788.08	2,199.91	2,020.06	1,774.40	1,469.24	1,337.80	1,272.76	1,238.36	1,219.53
11.50%	4,204.44	2,804.06	2,216.77	2,037.37	1,792.59	1,489.44	1,359.70	1,296.00	1,262.62	1,244.54
11.75%	4,219.62	2,820.09	2,233.71	2,054.76	1,810.88	1,509.77	1,381.73	1,319.37	1,287.00	1,269.64
12.00%	4,234.82	2,836.17	2,250.72	2,072.24	1,829.25	1,530.21	1,403.88	1,342.86	1,311.48	1,294.83
12.25%	4,250.06	2,852.30	2,267.81	2,089.79	1,847.73	1,550.78	1,426.17	1,366.47	1,336.07	1,320.10
12.50%	4,265.34	2,868.49	2,284.96	2,107.42	1,866.30	1,571.47	1,448.58	1,390.20	1,360.75	1,345.45
12.75%	4,280.64	2,884.73	2,302.18	2,125.13	1,884.96	1,592.27	1,471.11	1,414.04	1,385.53	1,370.88
13.00%	4,295.98	2,901.02	2,319.48	2,142.93	1,903.71	1,613.18	1,493.76	1,437.99	1,410.40	1,396.37
13.25%	4,311.35	2,917.36	2,336.84	2,160.79	1,922.56	1,634.21	1,516.52	1,462.04	1,435.36	1,421.93
13.50%	4,326.75	2,933.76	2,354.27	2,178.74	1,941.50	1,655.36	1,539.40	1,486.20	1,460.40	1,447.56
13.75%	4,342.18	2,950.20	2,371.78	2,196.76	1,960.53	1,676.61	1,562.39	1,510.45	1,485.52	1,473.24
14.00%	4,357.65	2,966.70	2,389.35	2,214.87	1,979.65	1,697.97	1,585.49	1,534.80	1,510.71	1,498.98
14.25%	4,373.15	2,983.25	2,406.99	2,233.05	1,998.86	1,719.44	1,608.69	1,559.23	1,535.98	1,524.78
14.50%	4,388.67	2,999.86	2,424.71	2,251.30	2,018.16	1,741.01	1,632.00	1,583.76	1,561.31	1,550.62
14.75%	4,404.24	3,016.51	2,442.49	2,269.63	2,037.54	1,762.69	1,655.40	1,608.37	1,586.71	1,576.51
15.00%	4,419.83	3,033.22	2,460.34	2,288.04	2,057.02	1,784.47	1,678.91	1,633.06	1,612.17	1,602.44
15.25%	4,435.45	3,049.97	2,478.25	2,306.52	2,076.58	1,806.36	1,702.51	1,657.83	1,637.68	1,628.41
15.50%	4,451.11	3,066.78	2,496.24	2,325.08	2,096.23	1,828.34	1,726.20	1,682.68	1,663.26	1,654.42
15.75%	4,466.80	3,083.64	2,514.29	2,343.71	2,115.97	1,850.42	1,749.98	1,707.59	1,688.89	1,680.47
16.00%	4,482.52	3,100.55	2,532.41	2,362.42	2,135.79	1,872.59	1,773.85	1,732.58	1,714.57	1,706.55
16.25%	4,498.27	3,117.51	2,550.60	2,381.20	2,155.70	1,894.86	1,797.81	1,757.64	1,740.29	1,732.66
16.50%	4,514.06	3,134.53	2,568.86	2,400.06	2,175.69	1,917.23	1,821.85	1,782.76	1,766.06	1,758.80
16.75%	4,529.87	3,151.59	2,587.18	2,418.98	2,195.76	1,939.68	1,845.97	1,807.95	1,791.88	1,784.97
17.00%	4,545.72	3,168.70	2,605.57	2,437.99	2,215.92	1,962.23	1,870.17	1,833.19	1,817.74	1,811.17
17.25%	4,561.60	3,185.87	2,624.02	2,457.06	2,236.16	1,984.87	1,894.45	1,858.49	1,843.63	1,837.39
17.50%	4,577.51	3,203.08	2,642.54	2,476.20	2,256.48	2,007.59	1,918.80	1,883.85	1,869.56	1,863.64
17.75%	4,593.46	3,220.35	2,661.12	2,495.42	2,276.88	2,030.39	1,943.23	1,909.26	1,895.53	1,889.90
18.00%	4,609.43	3,237.66	2,679.77	2,514.71	2,297.36	2,053.29	1,967.72	1,934.72	1,921.53	1,916.19
18.25%	4,625.44	3,255.03	2,698.49	2,534.07	2,317.92	2,076.26	1,992.29	1,960.23	1,947.57	1,942.49
18.50%	4,641.47	3,272.44	2,717.27	2,553.50	2,338.56	2,099.32	2,016.92	1,985.79	1,973.63	1,968.81
18.75%	4,657.54	3,289.91	2,736.11	2,573.00	2,359.28	2,122.45	2,041.61	2,011.40	1,999.72	1,995.15
19.00%	4,673.64	3,307.42	2,755.02	2,592.57	2,380.07	2,145.67	2,066.37	2,037.04	2,025.84	2,021.51
19.25%	4,689.77	3,324.98	2,773.99	2,612.21	2,400.94	2,168.96	2,091.19	2,062.73	2,051.98	2,047.87
19.50%	4,705.94	3,342.60	2,793.03	2,631.91	2,421.89	2,192.32	2,116.07	2,088.46	2,078.15	2,074.26
19.75%	4,722.13	3,360.26	2,812.13	2,651.69	2,442.91	2,215.76	2,141.01	2,114.22	2,104.34	2,100.65
20.00%	4,738.36	3,377.97	2,831.29	2,671.53	2,464.01	2,239.28	2,166.00	2,140.03	2,130.55	2,127.05
20.25%	4,754.61	3,395.73	2,850.51	2,691.44	2,485.18	2,262.86	2,191.05	2,165.86	2,156.78	2,153.47
20.50%	4,770.90	3,413.54	2,869.80	2,711.42	2,506.42	2,286.52	2,216.15	2,191.73	2,183.03	2,179.90
20.75%	4,787.22	3,431.40	2,889.15	2,731.47	2,527.74	2,310.24	2,241.30	2,217.64	2,209.30	2,206.33

	3	5	7	8	10	15	20	25	30	35
1.00%	3,667.05	2,222.19	1,603.06	1,409.62	1,138.85	778.04	597.86	489.93	418.13	366.97
1.25%	3,681.12	2,236.21	1,617.12	1,423.71	1,153.02	792.42	612.47	504.79	433.23	382.31
1.50%	3,695.23	2,250.29	1,631.26	1,437.89	1,167.29	806.97	627.31	519.92	448.66	398.04
1.75%	3,709.36	2,264.42	1,645.47	1,452.15	1,181.68	821.68	642.37	535.33	464.42	414.15
2.00%	3,723.54	2,278.61	1,659.77	1,466.51	1,196.17	836.56	657.65	551.01	480.51	430.64
2.25%	3,737.74	2,292.85	1,674.14	1,480.96	1,210.79	851.61	673.15	566.97	496.92	447.51
2.50%	3,751.98	2,307.16	1,688.59	1,495.50	1,225.51	866.83	688.87	583.20	513.66	464.74
2.75%	3,766.25	2,321.52	1,703.12	1,510.13	1,240.34	882.21	704.82	599.70	530.71	482.34
3.00%	3,780.56	2,335.93	1,717.73	1,524.84	1,255.29	897.76	720.98	616.47	548.09	500.31
3.25%	3,794.90	2,350.40	1,732.42	1,539.65	1,270.35	913.47	737.35	633.51	565.77	518.62
3.50%	3,809.27	2,364.93	1,747.18	1,554.55	1,285.52	929.35	753.95	650.81	583.76	537.28
3.75%	3,823.68	2,379.51	1,762.02	1,569.53	1,300.80	945.39	770.75	668.37	602.05	556.28
4.00%	3,838.12	2,394.15	1,776.94	1,584.61	1,316.19	961.59	787.77	686.19	620.64	575.61
4.25%	3,852.59	2,408.84	1,791.94	1,599.77	1,331.69	977.96	805.00	704.26	639.52	595.26
4.50%	3,867.10	2,423.59	1,807.02	1,615.02	1,347.30	994.49	822.44	722.58	658.69	615.23
4.75%	3,881.64	2,438.40	1,822.18	1,630.36	1,363.02	1,011.18	840.09	741.15	678.14	635.51
5.00%	3,896.22	2,453.26	1,837.41	1,645.79	1,378.85	1,028.03	857.94	759.97	697.87	656.09
5.25%	3,910.83	2,468.18	1,852.72	1,661.31	1,394.79	1,045.04	876.00	779.02	717.86	676.97
5.50%	3,925.47	2,483.15	1,868.11	1,676.91	1,410.84	1,062.21	894.25	798.31	738.13	698.12
5.75%	3,940.14	2,498.18	1,883.57	1,692.61	1,427.00	1,079.53	912.71	817.84	758.64	719.55
6.00%	3,954.85	2,513.26	1,899.11	1,708.39	1,443.27	1,097.01	931.36	837.59	779.42	741.25
6.25%	3,969.59	2,528.40	1,914.73	1,724.25	1,459.64	1,114.65	950.21	857.57	800.43	763.20
6.50%	3,984.37	2,543.60	1,930.43	1,740.21	1,476.12	1,132.44	969.25	877.77	821.69	785.40
6.75%	3,999.18	2,558.85	1,946.20	1,756.25	1,492.71	1,150.38	988.47	898.18	843.18	807.84
7.00%	4,014.02	2,574.16	1,962.05	1,772.38	1,509.41	1,168.48	1,007.89	918.81	864.89	830.51
7.25%	4,028.90	2,589.52	1,977.97	1,788.60	1,526.21	1,186.72	1,027.49	939.65	886.83	853.41
7.50%	4,043.81	2,604.93	1,993.98	1,804.90	1,543.12	1,205.12	1,047.27	960.69	908.98	876.52
7.75%	4,058.75	2,620.40	2,010.05	1,821.29	1,560.14	1,223.66	1,067.23	981.93	931.34	899.83
8.00%	4,073.73	2,635.93	2,026.21	1,837.77	1,577.26	1,242.35	1,087.37	1,003.36	953.89	923.34
8.25%	4,088.74	2,651.51	2,042.44	1,854.33	1,594.48	1,261.18	1,107.69	1,024.99	976.65	947.04
8.50%	4,103.78	2,667.15	2,058.74	1,870.98	1,611.81	1,280.16	1,128.17	1,046.80	999.59	970.92
8.75%	4,118.86	2,682.84	2,075.12	1,887.71	1,629.25	1,299.28	1,148.82	1,068.79	1,022.71	994.97
9.00%	4,133.97	2,698.59	2,091.58	1,904.53	1,646.79	1,318.55	1,169.64	1,090.96	1,046.01	1,019.19
9.25%	4,149.11	2,714.39	2,108.11	1,921.43	1,664.43	1,337.95	1,190.63	1,113.30	1,069.48	1,043.57
9.50%	4,164.28	2,730.24	2,124.72	1,938.42	1,682.17	1,357.49	1,211.77	1,135.81	1,093.11	1,068.10
9.75%	4,179.49	2,746.15	2,141.40	1,955.49	1,700.01	1,377.17	1,233.07	1,158.48	1,116.90	1,092.77
10.00%	4,194.73	2,762.12	2,158.15	1,972.64	1,717.96	1,396.99	1,254.53	1,181.31	1,140.84	1,117.57
10.25%	4,210.01	2,778.13	2,174.98	1,989.88	1,736.01	1,416.94	1,276.14	1,204.30	1,164.93	1,142.51
10.50%	4,225.32	2,794.21	2,191.89	2,007.20	1,754.15	1,437.02	1,297.89	1,227.44	1,189.16	1,167.57
10.75%	4,240.66	2,810.33	2,208.87	2,024.61	1,772.40	1,457.23	1,319.80	1,250.72	1,213.53	1,192.75

$130,000   11.00 - 20.75%   3 - 35 Years

	3	5	7	8	10	15	20	25	30	35
11.00%	4,256.03	2,826.51	2,225.92	2,042.10	1,790.75	1,477.58	1,341.84	1,274.15	1,238.02	1,218.04
11.25%	4,271.44	2,842.75	2,243.04	2,059.67	1,809.20	1,498.05	1,364.03	1,297.71	1,262.64	1,243.44
11.50%	4,286.88	2,859.04	2,260.24	2,077.32	1,827.74	1,518.65	1,386.36	1,321.41	1,287.38	1,268.94
11.75%	4,302.35	2,875.38	2,277.51	2,095.05	1,846.38	1,539.37	1,408.82	1,345.24	1,312.23	1,294.53
12.00%	4,317.86	2,891.78	2,294.86	2,112.87	1,865.12	1,560.22	1,431.41	1,369.19	1,337.20	1,320.21
12.25%	4,333.40	2,908.23	2,312.27	2,130.77	1,883.96	1,581.19	1,454.13	1,393.27	1,362.27	1,345.98
12.50%	4,348.97	2,924.73	2,329.76	2,148.75	1,902.89	1,602.28	1,476.98	1,417.46	1,387.44	1,371.83
12.75%	4,364.58	2,941.29	2,347.32	2,166.80	1,921.92	1,623.49	1,499.96	1,441.77	1,412.70	1,397.75
13.00%	4,380.21	2,957.90	2,364.96	2,184.94	1,941.04	1,644.81	1,523.05	1,466.19	1,438.06	1,423.75
13.25%	4,395.88	2,974.56	2,382.66	2,203.16	1,960.26	1,666.26	1,546.26	1,490.71	1,463.51	1,449.81
13.50%	4,411.59	2,991.28	2,400.44	2,221.46	1,979.57	1,687.81	1,569.59	1,515.34	1,489.04	1,475.94
13.75%	4,427.32	3,008.05	2,418.28	2,239.84	1,998.97	1,709.48	1,593.03	1,540.07	1,514.65	1,502.13
14.00%	4,443.09	3,024.87	2,436.20	2,258.30	2,018.46	1,731.26	1,616.58	1,564.89	1,540.33	1,528.38
14.25%	4,458.89	3,041.75	2,454.19	2,276.83	2,038.05	1,753.15	1,640.23	1,589.81	1,566.09	1,554.67
14.50%	4,474.73	3,058.68	2,472.25	2,295.44	2,057.73	1,775.15	1,664.00	1,614.81	1,591.92	1,581.02
14.75%	4,490.59	3,075.66	2,490.38	2,314.13	2,077.50	1,797.25	1,687.86	1,639.90	1,617.82	1,607.42
15.00%	4,506.49	3,092.69	2,508.58	2,332.90	2,097.35	1,819.46	1,711.83	1,665.08	1,643.78	1,633.86
15.25%	4,522.42	3,109.78	2,526.85	2,351.75	2,117.30	1,841.77	1,735.89	1,690.34	1,669.80	1,660.34
15.50%	4,538.39	3,126.91	2,545.19	2,370.67	2,137.34	1,864.19	1,760.04	1,715.67	1,695.87	1,686.86
15.75%	4,554.39	3,144.11	2,563.59	2,389.67	2,157.46	1,886.70	1,784.29	1,741.08	1,722.00	1,713.42
16.00%	4,570.41	3,161.35	2,582.07	2,408.74	2,177.67	1,909.31	1,808.63	1,766.56	1,748.18	1,740.01
16.25%	4,586.48	3,178.64	2,600.61	2,427.89	2,197.97	1,932.02	1,833.06	1,792.10	1,774.42	1,766.63
16.50%	4,602.57	3,195.99	2,619.23	2,447.12	2,218.35	1,954.82	1,857.57	1,817.72	1,800.69	1,793.29
16.75%	4,618.70	3,213.39	2,637.91	2,466.42	2,238.82	1,977.72	1,882.17	1,843.40	1,827.01	1,819.97
17.00%	4,634.85	3,230.83	2,656.65	2,485.79	2,259.37	2,000.71	1,906.84	1,869.14	1,853.38	1,846.68
17.25%	4,651.05	3,248.34	2,675.47	2,505.24	2,280.01	2,023.78	1,931.59	1,894.93	1,879.78	1,873.42
17.50%	4,667.27	3,265.89	2,694.35	2,524.76	2,300.72	2,046.95	1,956.42	1,920.79	1,906.22	1,900.18
17.75%	4,683.52	3,283.49	2,713.30	2,544.35	2,321.52	2,070.21	1,981.33	1,946.70	1,932.70	1,926.96
18.00%	4,699.81	3,301.15	2,732.32	2,564.02	2,342.41	2,093.55	2,006.30	1,972.66	1,959.21	1,953.76
18.25%	4,716.13	3,318.85	2,751.40	2,583.76	2,363.37	2,116.97	2,031.35	1,998.67	1,985.75	1,980.58
18.50%	4,732.48	3,336.61	2,770.55	2,603.57	2,384.42	2,140.48	2,056.47	2,024.73	2,012.33	2,007.42
18.75%	4,748.87	3,354.41	2,789.76	2,623.45	2,405.54	2,164.07	2,081.65	2,050.83	2,038.93	2,034.27
19.00%	4,765.28	3,372.27	2,809.04	2,643.40	2,426.74	2,187.74	2,106.89	2,076.98	2,065.56	2,061.14
19.25%	4,781.73	3,390.18	2,828.39	2,663.43	2,448.02	2,211.49	2,132.20	2,103.18	2,092.22	2,088.03
19.50%	4,798.21	3,408.14	2,847.80	2,683.52	2,469.38	2,235.31	2,157.56	2,129.41	2,118.90	2,114.93
19.75%	4,814.72	3,426.15	2,867.27	2,703.68	2,490.81	2,259.21	2,182.99	2,155.68	2,145.60	2,141.84
20.00%	4,831.27	3,444.20	2,886.81	2,723.92	2,512.32	2,283.19	2,208.47	2,181.99	2,172.32	2,168.76
20.25%	4,847.84	3,462.31	2,906.41	2,744.22	2,533.91	2,307.23	2,234.01	2,208.33	2,199.07	2,195.70
20.50%	4,864.45	3,480.47	2,926.07	2,764.59	2,555.57	2,331.35	2,259.60	2,234.71	2,225.84	2,222.64
20.75%	4,881.09	3,498.68	2,945.80	2,785.03	2,577.30	2,355.54	2,285.24	2,261.12	2,252.62	2,249.60

	3	5	7	8	10	15	20	25	30	35
1.00%	3,737.57	2,264.92	1,633.89	1,436.73	1,160.75	793.01	609.36	499.36	426.17	374.03
1.25%	3,751.91	2,279.21	1,648.22	1,451.09	1,175.19	807.66	624.25	514.49	441.56	389.66
1.50%	3,766.29	2,293.56	1,662.63	1,465.54	1,189.74	822.48	639.37	529.92	457.28	405.69
1.75%	3,780.70	2,307.97	1,677.12	1,480.08	1,204.40	837.48	654.72	545.62	473.35	422.12
2.00%	3,795.14	2,322.43	1,691.69	1,494.72	1,219.18	852.65	670.30	561.61	489.75	438.92
2.25%	3,809.62	2,336.95	1,706.33	1,509.44	1,234.07	867.99	686.10	577.87	506.48	456.11
2.50%	3,824.13	2,351.53	1,721.06	1,524.26	1,249.08	883.50	702.12	594.42	523.54	473.68
2.75%	3,838.68	2,366.16	1,735.87	1,539.17	1,264.20	899.17	718.37	611.24	540.92	491.62
3.00%	3,853.26	2,380.85	1,750.76	1,554.17	1,279.43	915.02	734.84	628.33	558.63	509.93
3.25%	3,867.88	2,395.60	1,765.73	1,569.26	1,294.78	931.04	751.53	645.69	576.65	528.59
3.50%	3,882.53	2,410.41	1,780.78	1,584.44	1,310.24	947.22	768.45	663.33	594.98	547.61
3.75%	3,897.21	2,425.27	1,795.91	1,599.72	1,325.81	963.57	785.58	681.22	613.63	566.97
4.00%	3,911.93	2,440.19	1,811.12	1,615.08	1,341.50	980.09	802.92	699.38	632.58	586.68
4.25%	3,926.68	2,455.17	1,826.40	1,630.53	1,357.30	996.77	820.49	717.80	651.82	606.71
4.50%	3,941.47	2,470.20	1,841.77	1,646.08	1,373.21	1,013.62	838.26	736.48	671.36	627.07
4.75%	3,956.29	2,485.29	1,857.22	1,661.71	1,389.23	1,030.63	856.25	755.41	691.18	647.74
5.00%	3,971.14	2,500.44	1,872.74	1,677.44	1,405.37	1,047.80	874.44	774.58	711.29	668.71
5.25%	3,986.03	2,515.64	1,888.35	1,693.25	1,421.62	1,065.14	892.84	794.00	731.67	689.98
5.50%	4,000.96	2,530.90	1,904.03	1,709.16	1,437.97	1,082.64	911.45	813.67	752.32	711.55
5.75%	4,015.91	2,546.22	1,919.79	1,725.16	1,454.44	1,100.29	930.26	833.57	773.23	733.39
6.00%	4,030.91	2,561.60	1,935.63	1,741.24	1,471.02	1,118.11	949.27	853.70	794.40	755.50
6.25%	4,045.93	2,577.03	1,951.55	1,757.41	1,487.71	1,136.09	968.48	874.06	815.83	777.88
6.50%	4,060.99	2,592.51	1,967.55	1,773.68	1,504.51	1,154.22	987.88	894.65	837.49	800.50
6.75%	4,076.09	2,608.06	1,983.63	1,790.03	1,521.42	1,172.51	1,007.48	915.46	859.39	823.38
7.00%	4,091.22	2,623.66	1,999.78	1,806.47	1,538.44	1,190.95	1,027.27	936.48	881.53	846.48
7.25%	4,106.38	2,639.32	2,016.01	1,823.00	1,555.56	1,209.54	1,047.25	957.72	903.88	869.82
7.50%	4,121.57	2,655.03	2,032.32	1,839.61	1,572.80	1,228.29	1,067.41	979.16	926.46	893.37
7.75%	4,136.80	2,670.80	2,048.71	1,856.32	1,590.14	1,247.19	1,087.76	1,000.81	949.25	917.13
8.00%	4,152.07	2,686.62	2,065.17	1,873.11	1,607.59	1,266.24	1,108.28	1,022.66	972.24	941.10
8.25%	4,167.37	2,702.50	2,081.72	1,889.99	1,625.15	1,285.44	1,128.99	1,044.70	995.43	965.25
8.50%	4,182.70	2,718.44	2,098.33	1,906.96	1,642.81	1,304.78	1,149.87	1,066.93	1,018.81	989.59
8.75%	4,198.06	2,734.43	2,115.03	1,924.01	1,660.58	1,324.27	1,170.92	1,089.34	1,042.38	1,014.11
9.00%	4,213.46	2,750.48	2,131.80	1,941.15	1,678.45	1,343.90	1,192.14	1,111.94	1,066.12	1,038.79
9.25%	4,228.90	2,766.59	2,148.65	1,958.38	1,696.43	1,363.68	1,213.52	1,134.71	1,090.04	1,063.64
9.50%	4,244.37	2,782.75	2,165.58	1,975.69	1,714.52	1,383.60	1,235.07	1,157.65	1,114.13	1,088.64
9.75%	4,259.87	2,798.96	2,182.58	1,993.09	1,732.71	1,403.66	1,256.78	1,180.76	1,138.38	1,113.78
10.00%	4,275.40	2,815.23	2,199.66	2,010.58	1,751.00	1,423.85	1,278.65	1,204.03	1,162.78	1,139.07
10.25%	4,290.97	2,831.56	2,216.81	2,028.15	1,769.39	1,444.18	1,300.68	1,227.46	1,187.33	1,164.48
10.50%	4,306.57	2,847.94	2,234.04	2,045.80	1,787.89	1,464.65	1,322.85	1,251.04	1,212.03	1,190.03
10.75%	4,322.21	2,864.38	2,251.34	2,063.54	1,806.49	1,485.26	1,345.18	1,274.77	1,236.86	1,215.69

$132,500   11.00 - 20.75%   3 - 35 Years

	3	5	7	8	10	15	20	25	30	35
11.00%	4,337.88	2,880.87	2,268.72	2,081.37	1,825.19	1,505.99	1,367.65	1,298.65	1,261.83	1,241.47
11.25%	4,353.58	2,897.42	2,286.18	2,099.27	1,843.99	1,526.86	1,390.26	1,322.67	1,286.92	1,267.35
11.50%	4,369.32	2,914.02	2,303.71	2,117.27	1,862.89	1,547.85	1,413.02	1,346.82	1,312.14	1,293.34
11.75%	4,385.09	2,930.68	2,321.31	2,135.34	1,881.89	1,568.97	1,435.91	1,371.11	1,337.47	1,319.43
12.00%	4,400.90	2,947.39	2,338.99	2,153.50	1,900.99	1,590.22	1,458.94	1,395.52	1,362.91	1,345.60
12.25%	4,416.73	2,964.16	2,356.74	2,171.74	1,920.19	1,611.60	1,482.10	1,420.06	1,388.46	1,371.87
12.50%	4,432.61	2,980.98	2,374.56	2,190.07	1,939.48	1,633.09	1,505.39	1,444.72	1,414.12	1,398.21
12.75%	4,448.51	2,997.85	2,392.46	2,208.47	1,958.88	1,654.71	1,528.80	1,469.49	1,439.87	1,424.63
13.00%	4,464.45	3,014.78	2,410.44	2,226.96	1,978.37	1,676.45	1,552.34	1,494.38	1,465.71	1,451.13
13.25%	4,480.42	3,031.77	2,428.48	2,245.53	1,997.95	1,698.30	1,576.00	1,519.38	1,491.65	1,477.70
13.50%	4,496.43	3,048.80	2,446.60	2,264.18	2,017.63	1,720.27	1,599.77	1,544.48	1,517.67	1,504.33
13.75%	4,512.46	3,065.90	2,464.79	2,282.91	2,037.41	1,742.36	1,623.66	1,569.68	1,543.77	1,531.02
14.00%	4,528.54	3,083.04	2,483.05	2,301.72	2,057.28	1,764.56	1,647.67	1,594.98	1,569.96	1,557.77
14.25%	4,544.64	3,100.24	2,501.39	2,320.62	2,077.24	1,786.87	1,671.78	1,620.38	1,596.21	1,584.57
14.50%	4,560.78	3,117.50	2,519.79	2,339.59	2,097.30	1,809.29	1,696.00	1,645.87	1,622.54	1,611.43
14.75%	4,576.95	3,134.80	2,538.27	2,358.64	2,117.45	1,831.82	1,720.32	1,671.44	1,648.93	1,638.33
15.00%	4,593.16	3,152.17	2,556.82	2,377.77	2,137.69	1,854.45	1,744.75	1,697.10	1,675.39	1,665.28
15.25%	4,609.39	3,169.58	2,575.44	2,396.97	2,158.02	1,877.19	1,769.27	1,722.84	1,701.91	1,692.27
15.50%	4,625.67	3,187.05	2,594.13	2,416.26	2,178.44	1,900.04	1,793.89	1,748.66	1,728.48	1,719.30
15.75%	4,641.97	3,204.57	2,612.89	2,435.62	2,198.95	1,922.98	1,818.61	1,774.56	1,755.12	1,746.37
16.00%	4,658.31	3,222.14	2,631.72	2,455.06	2,219.55	1,946.03	1,843.41	1,800.53	1,781.80	1,773.47
16.25%	4,674.68	3,239.77	2,650.62	2,474.58	2,240.24	1,969.17	1,868.31	1,826.57	1,808.54	1,800.61
16.50%	4,691.08	3,257.45	2,669.60	2,494.18	2,261.01	1,992.41	1,893.29	1,852.67	1,835.32	1,827.78
16.75%	4,707.52	3,275.18	2,688.64	2,513.85	2,281.87	2,015.75	1,918.36	1,878.85	1,862.15	1,854.97
17.00%	4,723.99	3,292.97	2,707.74	2,533.59	2,302.82	2,039.18	1,943.51	1,905.08	1,889.02	1,882.20
17.25%	4,740.49	3,310.80	2,726.92	2,553.41	2,323.85	2,062.70	1,968.74	1,931.37	1,915.93	1,909.45
17.50%	4,757.02	3,328.69	2,746.17	2,573.31	2,344.97	2,086.32	1,994.05	1,957.73	1,942.88	1,936.72
17.75%	4,773.59	3,346.64	2,765.48	2,593.28	2,366.17	2,110.02	2,019.43	1,984.13	1,969.87	1,964.00
18.00%	4,790.19	3,364.63	2,784.86	2,613.33	2,387.45	2,133.81	2,044.89	2,010.59	1,996.89	1,991.33
18.25%	4,806.83	3,382.68	2,804.31	2,633.44	2,408.82	2,157.68	2,070.42	2,037.11	2,023.94	2,018.67
18.50%	4,823.49	3,400.77	2,823.83	2,653.64	2,430.27	2,181.64	2,096.01	2,063.67	2,051.03	2,046.02
18.75%	4,840.19	3,418.92	2,843.41	2,673.90	2,451.80	2,205.69	2,121.68	2,090.27	2,078.14	2,073.39
19.00%	4,856.92	3,437.12	2,863.06	2,694.24	2,473.41	2,229.81	2,147.41	2,116.93	2,105.28	2,100.78
19.25%	4,873.69	3,455.38	2,882.78	2,714.65	2,495.10	2,254.02	2,173.20	2,143.62	2,132.45	2,128.18
19.50%	4,890.48	3,473.68	2,902.56	2,735.13	2,516.87	2,278.30	2,199.06	2,170.36	2,159.64	2,155.60
19.75%	4,907.31	3,492.03	2,922.41	2,755.68	2,538.71	2,302.66	2,224.97	2,197.13	2,186.86	2,183.03
20.00%	4,924.17	3,510.44	2,942.32	2,776.30	2,560.64	2,327.09	2,250.94	2,223.95	2,214.10	2,210.47
20.25%	4,941.07	3,528.90	2,962.30	2,796.99	2,582.64	2,351.60	2,276.97	2,250.80	2,241.36	2,237.92
20.50%	4,958.00	3,547.40	2,982.34	2,817.75	2,604.72	2,376.18	2,303.05	2,277.68	2,268.64	2,265.38
20.75%	4,974.95	3,565.96	3,002.45	2,838.58	2,626.87	2,400.84	2,329.19	2,304.60	2,295.94	2,292.86

	3	5	7	8	10	15	20	25	30	35
1.00%	3,808.09	2,307.66	1,664.72	1,463.84	1,182.66	807.97	620.86	508.78	434.21	381.09
1.25%	3,822.70	2,322.22	1,679.32	1,478.47	1,197.36	822.90	636.03	524.20	449.89	397.02
1.50%	3,837.35	2,336.83	1,694.00	1,493.19	1,212.19	838.00	651.44	539.91	465.91	413.35
1.75%	3,852.03	2,351.51	1,708.76	1,508.01	1,227.13	853.28	667.07	555.92	482.28	430.08
2.00%	3,866.75	2,366.25	1,723.60	1,522.92	1,242.18	868.74	682.94	572.20	498.99	447.20
2.25%	3,881.50	2,381.04	1,738.53	1,537.92	1,257.35	884.36	699.04	588.78	516.03	464.72
2.50%	3,896.29	2,395.89	1,753.54	1,553.02	1,272.64	900.17	715.37	605.63	533.41	482.62
2.75%	3,911.11	2,410.80	1,768.63	1,568.21	1,288.05	916.14	731.92	622.77	551.13	500.90
3.00%	3,925.96	2,425.77	1,783.80	1,583.49	1,303.57	932.29	748.71	640.19	569.17	519.55
3.25%	3,940.85	2,440.80	1,799.05	1,598.87	1,319.21	948.60	765.71	657.88	587.53	538.57
3.50%	3,955.78	2,455.89	1,814.38	1,614.34	1,334.96	965.09	782.95	675.84	606.21	557.94
3.75%	3,970.74	2,471.03	1,829.79	1,629.90	1,350.83	981.75	800.40	694.08	625.21	577.67
4.00%	3,985.74	2,486.23	1,845.29	1,645.55	1,366.81	998.58	818.07	712.58	644.51	597.75
4.25%	4,000.77	2,501.49	1,860.86	1,661.30	1,382.91	1,015.58	835.97	731.35	664.12	618.16
4.50%	4,015.83	2,516.81	1,876.52	1,677.14	1,399.12	1,032.74	854.08	750.37	684.03	638.90
4.75%	4,030.94	2,532.18	1,892.26	1,693.07	1,415.44	1,050.07	872.40	769.66	704.22	659.96
5.00%	4,046.07	2,547.62	1,908.08	1,709.09	1,431.88	1,067.57	890.94	789.20	724.71	681.33
5.25%	4,061.24	2,563.11	1,923.98	1,725.20	1,448.44	1,085.23	909.69	808.98	745.47	703.00
5.50%	4,076.45	2,578.66	1,939.96	1,741.41	1,465.10	1,103.06	928.65	829.02	766.52	724.97
5.75%	4,091.69	2,594.26	1,956.02	1,757.71	1,481.88	1,121.05	947.81	849.29	787.82	747.23
6.00%	4,106.96	2,609.93	1,972.15	1,774.09	1,498.78	1,139.21	967.18	869.81	809.39	769.76
6.25%	4,122.27	2,625.65	1,988.37	1,790.57	1,515.78	1,157.52	986.75	890.55	831.22	792.55
6.50%	4,137.62	2,641.43	2,004.67	1,807.14	1,532.90	1,175.99	1,006.52	911.53	853.29	815.61
6.75%	4,152.99	2,657.27	2,021.05	1,823.80	1,550.13	1,194.63	1,026.49	932.73	875.61	838.91
7.00%	4,168.41	2,673.16	2,037.51	1,840.55	1,567.46	1,213.42	1,046.65	954.15	898.16	862.46
7.25%	4,183.86	2,689.11	2,054.05	1,857.39	1,584.91	1,232.36	1,067.01	975.79	920.94	886.23
7.50%	4,199.34	2,705.12	2,070.67	1,874.32	1,602.47	1,251.47	1,087.55	997.64	943.94	910.23
7.75%	4,214.86	2,721.19	2,087.36	1,891.34	1,620.14	1,270.72	1,108.28	1,019.69	967.16	934.44
8.00%	4,230.41	2,737.31	2,104.14	1,908.45	1,637.92	1,290.13	1,129.19	1,041.95	990.58	958.85
8.25%	4,246.00	2,753.49	2,120.99	1,925.65	1,655.81	1,309.69	1,150.29	1,064.41	1,014.21	983.46
8.50%	4,261.62	2,769.73	2,137.93	1,942.94	1,673.81	1,329.40	1,171.56	1,087.06	1,038.03	1,008.26
8.75%	4,277.27	2,786.03	2,154.94	1,960.31	1,691.91	1,349.26	1,193.01	1,109.89	1,062.05	1,033.24
9.00%	4,292.96	2,802.38	2,172.03	1,977.78	1,710.12	1,369.26	1,214.63	1,132.92	1,086.24	1,058.39
9.25%	4,308.69	2,818.79	2,189.19	1,995.33	1,728.44	1,389.41	1,236.42	1,156.12	1,110.61	1,083.70
9.50%	4,324.45	2,835.25	2,206.44	2,012.97	1,746.87	1,409.70	1,258.38	1,179.49	1,135.15	1,109.18
9.75%	4,340.24	2,851.77	2,223.76	2,030.70	1,765.40	1,430.14	1,280.50	1,203.04	1,159.86	1,134.80
10.00%	4,356.07	2,868.35	2,241.16	2,048.51	1,784.03	1,450.72	1,302.78	1,226.75	1,184.72	1,160.56
10.25%	4,371.93	2,884.99	2,258.64	2,066.41	1,802.78	1,471.43	1,325.22	1,250.62	1,209.74	1,186.46
10.50%	4,387.83	2,901.68	2,276.19	2,084.40	1,821.62	1,492.29	1,347.81	1,274.65	1,234.90	1,212.48
10.75%	4,403.76	2,918.42	2,293.82	2,102.48	1,840.57	1,513.28	1,370.56	1,298.83	1,260.20	1,238.63

$135,000   11.00 - 20.75%   3 - 35 Years

	3	5	7	8	10	15	20	25	30	35
11.00%	4,419.73	2,935.23	2,311.53	2,120.64	1,859.63	1,534.41	1,393.45	1,323.15	1,285.64	1,264.89
11.25%	4,435.73	2,952.09	2,329.31	2,138.88	1,878.78	1,555.67	1,416.50	1,347.62	1,311.20	1,291.27
11.50%	4,451.76	2,969.00	2,347.17	2,157.22	1,898.04	1,577.06	1,439.68	1,372.23	1,336.89	1,317.74
11.75%	4,467.83	2,985.97	2,365.11	2,175.63	1,917.40	1,598.58	1,463.00	1,396.98	1,362.70	1,344.32
12.00%	4,483.93	3,003.00	2,383.12	2,194.13	1,936.86	1,620.23	1,486.47	1,421.85	1,388.63	1,370.99
12.25%	4,500.07	3,020.08	2,401.21	2,212.72	1,956.42	1,642.00	1,510.06	1,446.85	1,414.66	1,397.75
12.50%	4,516.24	3,037.22	2,419.37	2,231.39	1,976.08	1,663.90	1,533.79	1,471.98	1,440.80	1,424.59
12.75%	4,532.44	3,054.42	2,437.60	2,250.14	1,995.84	1,685.93	1,557.65	1,497.22	1,467.04	1,451.51
13.00%	4,548.68	3,071.66	2,455.92	2,268.98	2,015.69	1,708.08	1,581.63	1,522.58	1,493.37	1,478.51
13.25%	4,564.96	3,088.97	2,474.30	2,287.90	2,035.65	1,730.34	1,605.73	1,548.05	1,519.79	1,505.58
13.50%	4,581.26	3,106.33	2,492.76	2,306.90	2,055.70	1,752.73	1,629.96	1,573.62	1,546.31	1,532.71
13.75%	4,597.60	3,123.74	2,511.29	2,325.99	2,075.85	1,775.23	1,654.30	1,599.30	1,572.90	1,559.90
14.00%	4,613.98	3,141.21	2,529.90	2,345.15	2,096.10	1,797.85	1,678.75	1,625.08	1,599.58	1,587.16
14.25%	4,630.39	3,158.74	2,548.58	2,364.40	2,116.44	1,820.58	1,703.32	1,650.95	1,626.33	1,614.47
14.50%	4,646.83	3,176.32	2,567.34	2,383.73	2,136.87	1,843.43	1,728.00	1,676.92	1,653.15	1,641.83
14.75%	4,663.31	3,193.95	2,586.16	2,403.14	2,157.40	1,866.38	1,752.78	1,702.98	1,680.04	1,669.24
15.00%	4,679.82	3,211.64	2,605.06	2,422.63	2,178.02	1,889.44	1,777.67	1,729.12	1,707.00	1,696.70
15.25%	4,696.36	3,229.38	2,624.03	2,442.20	2,198.74	1,912.61	1,802.65	1,755.35	1,734.02	1,724.20
15.50%	4,712.94	3,247.18	2,643.08	2,461.85	2,219.54	1,935.89	1,827.74	1,781.66	1,761.10	1,751.74
15.75%	4,729.55	3,265.03	2,662.19	2,481.58	2,240.44	1,959.27	1,852.92	1,808.04	1,788.23	1,779.32
16.00%	4,746.20	3,282.94	2,681.38	2,501.39	2,261.43	1,982.75	1,878.20	1,834.50	1,815.42	1,806.93
16.25%	4,762.88	3,300.90	2,700.64	2,521.27	2,282.50	2,006.33	1,903.56	1,861.03	1,842.66	1,834.58
16.50%	4,779.59	3,318.91	2,719.97	2,541.24	2,303.67	2,030.01	1,929.02	1,887.63	1,869.95	1,862.26
16.75%	4,796.34	3,336.98	2,739.36	2,561.28	2,324.93	2,053.78	1,954.56	1,914.30	1,897.28	1,889.97
17.00%	4,813.12	3,355.10	2,758.83	2,581.40	2,346.27	2,077.66	1,980.18	1,941.03	1,924.66	1,917.71
17.25%	4,829.93	3,373.27	2,778.37	2,601.59	2,367.70	2,101.62	2,005.89	1,967.82	1,952.08	1,945.47
17.50%	4,846.78	3,391.50	2,797.98	2,621.86	2,389.21	2,125.68	2,031.67	1,994.67	1,979.54	1,973.26
17.75%	4,863.66	3,409.78	2,817.66	2,642.21	2,410.81	2,149.83	2,057.53	2,021.57	2,007.03	2,001.07
18.00%	4,880.57	3,428.11	2,837.41	2,662.63	2,432.50	2,174.07	2,083.47	2,048.53	2,034.57	2,028.90
18.25%	4,897.52	3,446.50	2,857.22	2,683.13	2,454.27	2,198.39	2,109.48	2,075.54	2,062.13	2,056.76
18.50%	4,914.50	3,464.94	2,877.11	2,703.70	2,476.12	2,222.81	2,135.56	2,102.60	2,089.73	2,084.63
18.75%	4,931.52	3,483.43	2,897.06	2,724.35	2,498.06	2,247.30	2,161.71	2,129.71	2,117.35	2,112.51
19.00%	4,948.56	3,501.97	2,917.08	2,745.07	2,520.08	2,271.88	2,187.92	2,156.87	2,145.00	2,140.42
19.25%	4,965.64	3,520.57	2,937.17	2,765.87	2,542.18	2,296.54	2,214.20	2,184.07	2,172.69	2,168.34
19.50%	4,982.76	3,539.22	2,957.33	2,786.73	2,564.35	2,321.28	2,240.55	2,211.31	2,200.39	2,196.27
19.75%	4,999.90	3,557.92	2,977.55	2,807.67	2,586.61	2,346.10	2,266.95	2,238.59	2,228.12	2,224.22
20.00%	5,017.08	3,576.67	2,997.84	2,828.68	2,608.95	2,371.00	2,293.41	2,265.91	2,255.88	2,252.18
20.25%	5,034.30	3,595.48	3,018.19	2,849.76	2,631.37	2,395.97	2,319.93	2,293.27	2,283.65	2,280.15
20.50%	5,051.54	3,614.34	3,038.61	2,870.92	2,653.86	2,421.02	2,346.51	2,320.66	2,311.44	2,308.13
20.75%	5,068.82	3,633.24	3,059.10	2,892.14	2,676.43	2,446.14	2,373.14	2,348.09	2,339.26	2,336.12

$137,500   1.00 - 10.75%   3 - 35 Years

	3	5	7	8	10	15	20	25	30	35
1.00%	3,878.61	2,350.39	1,695.55	1,490.94	1,204.56	822.93	632.35	518.20	442.25	388.14
1.25%	3,893.50	2,365.22	1,710.42	1,505.84	1,219.54	838.14	647.81	533.91	458.22	404.37
1.50%	3,908.41	2,380.11	1,725.37	1,520.84	1,234.63	853.52	663.50	549.91	474.54	421.00
1.75%	3,923.37	2,395.06	1,740.40	1,535.93	1,249.85	869.08	679.43	566.21	491.21	438.04
2.00%	3,938.35	2,410.07	1,755.52	1,551.12	1,265.18	884.82	695.59	582.80	508.23	455.49
2.25%	3,953.38	2,425.13	1,770.72	1,566.40	1,280.64	900.74	711.99	599.68	525.59	473.33
2.50%	3,968.44	2,440.26	1,786.01	1,581.78	1,296.21	916.84	728.62	616.85	543.29	491.56
2.75%	3,983.53	2,455.45	1,801.38	1,597.25	1,311.90	933.10	745.48	634.30	561.33	510.17
3.00%	3,998.67	2,470.69	1,816.83	1,612.82	1,327.71	949.55	762.57	652.04	579.71	529.17
3.25%	4,013.83	2,486.00	1,832.36	1,628.48	1,343.64	966.17	779.89	670.06	598.41	548.54
3.50%	4,029.04	2,501.36	1,847.98	1,644.23	1,359.68	982.96	797.44	688.36	617.44	568.27
3.75%	4,044.27	2,516.79	1,863.68	1,660.08	1,375.84	999.93	815.22	706.93	636.78	588.37
4.00%	4,059.55	2,532.27	1,879.46	1,676.03	1,392.12	1,017.07	833.22	725.78	656.45	608.82
4.25%	4,074.86	2,547.81	1,895.33	1,692.06	1,408.52	1,034.38	851.45	744.89	676.42	629.60
4.50%	4,090.20	2,563.42	1,911.27	1,708.19	1,425.03	1,051.87	869.89	764.27	696.69	650.73
4.75%	4,105.58	2,579.08	1,927.30	1,724.42	1,441.66	1,069.52	888.56	783.91	717.27	672.18
5.00%	4,121.00	2,594.79	1,943.41	1,740.74	1,458.40	1,087.34	907.44	803.81	738.13	693.95
5.25%	4,136.45	2,610.57	1,959.61	1,757.15	1,475.26	1,105.33	926.54	823.97	759.28	716.02
5.50%	4,151.94	2,626.41	1,975.88	1,773.66	1,492.24	1,123.49	945.85	844.37	780.71	738.40
5.75%	4,167.46	2,642.31	1,992.24	1,790.26	1,509.33	1,141.81	965.36	865.02	802.41	761.06
6.00%	4,183.02	2,658.26	2,008.68	1,806.95	1,526.53	1,160.30	985.09	885.91	824.38	784.01
6.25%	4,198.61	2,674.27	2,025.20	1,823.73	1,543.85	1,178.96	1,005.03	907.05	846.61	807.23
6.50%	4,214.24	2,690.35	2,041.80	1,840.61	1,561.28	1,197.77	1,025.16	928.41	869.09	830.71
6.75%	4,229.90	2,706.48	2,058.48	1,857.58	1,578.83	1,216.75	1,045.50	950.00	891.82	854.45
7.00%	4,245.60	2,722.66	2,075.24	1,874.64	1,596.49	1,235.89	1,066.04	971.82	914.79	878.43
7.25%	4,261.34	2,738.91	2,092.09	1,891.79	1,614.26	1,255.19	1,086.77	993.86	937.99	902.64
7.50%	4,277.10	2,755.22	2,109.01	1,909.03	1,632.15	1,274.64	1,107.69	1,016.11	961.42	927.08
7.75%	4,292.91	2,771.58	2,126.02	1,926.37	1,650.15	1,294.25	1,128.80	1,038.58	985.07	951.74
8.00%	4,308.75	2,788.00	2,143.10	1,943.79	1,668.25	1,314.02	1,150.11	1,061.25	1,008.93	976.61
8.25%	4,324.63	2,804.48	2,160.27	1,961.31	1,686.47	1,333.94	1,171.59	1,084.12	1,032.99	1,001.68
8.50%	4,340.54	2,821.02	2,177.52	1,978.92	1,704.80	1,354.02	1,193.26	1,107.19	1,057.26	1,026.93
8.75%	4,356.48	2,837.62	2,194.84	1,996.62	1,723.24	1,374.24	1,215.10	1,130.45	1,081.71	1,052.37
9.00%	4,372.46	2,854.27	2,212.25	2,014.40	1,741.79	1,394.62	1,237.12	1,153.89	1,106.36	1,077.99
9.25%	4,388.48	2,870.99	2,229.73	2,032.28	1,760.45	1,415.14	1,259.32	1,177.53	1,131.18	1,103.77
9.50%	4,404.53	2,887.76	2,247.30	2,050.25	1,779.22	1,435.81	1,281.68	1,201.33	1,156.17	1,129.72
9.75%	4,420.62	2,904.58	2,264.94	2,068.30	1,798.09	1,456.62	1,304.21	1,225.31	1,181.34	1,155.81
10.00%	4,436.74	2,921.47	2,282.66	2,086.45	1,817.07	1,477.58	1,326.90	1,249.46	1,206.66	1,182.05
10.25%	4,452.89	2,938.41	2,300.46	2,104.68	1,836.16	1,498.68	1,349.76	1,273.78	1,232.14	1,208.43
10.50%	4,469.09	2,955.41	2,318.34	2,123.00	1,855.36	1,519.92	1,372.77	1,298.25	1,257.77	1,234.93
10.75%	4,485.31	2,972.47	2,336.30	2,141.41	1,874.66	1,541.30	1,395.94	1,322.88	1,283.54	1,261.57

$137,500   11.00 - 20.75%   3 - 35 Years

	3	5	7	8	10	15	20	25	30	35
11.00%	4,501.57	2,989.58	2,354.34	2,159.91	1,894.06	1,562.82	1,419.26	1,347.66	1,309.44	1,288.32
11.25%	4,517.87	3,006.75	2,372.45	2,178.49	1,913.57	1,584.47	1,442.73	1,372.58	1,335.48	1,315.18
11.50%	4,534.20	3,023.98	2,390.64	2,197.16	1,933.19	1,606.26	1,466.34	1,397.64	1,361.65	1,342.15
11.75%	4,550.57	3,041.27	2,408.91	2,215.92	1,952.91	1,628.18	1,490.10	1,422.85	1,387.94	1,369.22
12.00%	4,566.97	3,058.61	2,427.25	2,234.77	1,972.73	1,650.23	1,513.99	1,448.18	1,414.34	1,396.38
12.25%	4,583.40	3,076.01	2,445.67	2,253.70	1,992.65	1,672.41	1,538.03	1,473.65	1,440.86	1,423.64
12.50%	4,599.87	3,093.47	2,464.17	2,272.71	2,012.67	1,694.72	1,562.19	1,499.24	1,467.48	1,450.97
12.75%	4,616.38	3,110.98	2,482.74	2,291.81	2,032.80	1,717.15	1,586.49	1,524.95	1,494.20	1,478.39
13.00%	4,632.92	3,128.55	2,501.39	2,311.00	2,053.02	1,739.71	1,610.92	1,550.77	1,521.02	1,505.89
13.25%	4,649.49	3,146.17	2,520.12	2,330.27	2,073.35	1,762.39	1,635.47	1,576.71	1,547.94	1,533.46
13.50%	4,666.10	3,163.85	2,538.92	2,349.62	2,093.77	1,785.19	1,660.14	1,602.76	1,574.94	1,561.09
13.75%	4,682.75	3,181.59	2,557.80	2,369.06	2,114.29	1,808.11	1,684.93	1,628.92	1,602.03	1,588.79
14.00%	4,699.42	3,199.38	2,576.75	2,388.58	2,134.91	1,831.14	1,709.84	1,655.17	1,629.20	1,616.55
14.25%	4,716.14	3,217.23	2,595.78	2,408.19	2,155.63	1,854.30	1,734.86	1,681.53	1,656.44	1,644.37
14.50%	4,732.88	3,235.14	2,614.88	2,427.87	2,176.44	1,877.56	1,760.00	1,707.97	1,683.76	1,672.23
14.75%	4,749.67	3,253.10	2,634.05	2,447.64	2,197.35	1,900.94	1,785.24	1,734.51	1,711.15	1,700.15
15.00%	4,766.48	3,271.12	2,653.30	2,467.49	2,218.36	1,924.43	1,810.59	1,761.14	1,738.61	1,728.12
15.25%	4,783.33	3,289.19	2,672.63	2,487.43	2,239.45	1,948.03	1,836.04	1,787.86	1,766.13	1,756.13
15.50%	4,800.22	3,307.31	2,692.02	2,507.44	2,260.64	1,971.74	1,861.59	1,814.65	1,793.71	1,784.18
15.75%	4,817.14	3,325.50	2,711.49	2,527.53	2,281.93	1,995.55	1,887.23	1,841.52	1,821.35	1,812.27
16.00%	4,834.09	3,343.73	2,731.03	2,547.71	2,303.31	2,019.46	1,912.98	1,868.47	1,849.04	1,840.40
16.25%	4,851.08	3,362.02	2,750.65	2,567.96	2,324.77	2,043.48	1,938.81	1,895.49	1,876.79	1,868.56
16.50%	4,868.10	3,380.37	2,770.33	2,588.30	2,346.33	2,067.60	1,964.74	1,922.59	1,904.58	1,896.75
16.75%	4,885.16	3,398.77	2,790.09	2,608.71	2,367.98	2,091.82	1,990.75	1,949.75	1,932.42	1,924.97
17.00%	4,902.25	3,417.23	2,809.92	2,629.20	2,389.72	2,116.13	2,016.85	1,976.97	1,960.30	1,953.22
17.25%	4,919.37	3,435.74	2,829.82	2,649.77	2,411.54	2,140.54	2,043.03	2,004.26	1,988.23	1,981.50
17.50%	4,936.53	3,454.30	2,849.80	2,670.42	2,433.46	2,165.05	2,069.30	2,031.60	2,016.20	2,009.80
17.75%	4,953.73	3,472.92	2,869.84	2,691.14	2,455.46	2,189.64	2,095.64	2,059.01	2,044.20	2,038.13
18.00%	4,970.95	3,491.60	2,889.95	2,711.94	2,477.55	2,214.33	2,122.05	2,086.47	2,072.24	2,066.48
18.25%	4,988.22	3,510.32	2,910.14	2,732.82	2,499.72	2,239.11	2,148.54	2,113.98	2,100.32	2,094.84
18.50%	5,005.51	3,529.10	2,930.39	2,753.77	2,521.98	2,263.97	2,175.11	2,141.54	2,128.42	2,123.23
18.75%	5,022.84	3,547.94	2,950.71	2,774.80	2,544.32	2,288.92	2,201.74	2,169.15	2,156.56	2,151.63
19.00%	5,040.20	3,566.83	2,971.10	2,795.91	2,566.74	2,313.95	2,228.44	2,196.81	2,184.73	2,180.06
19.25%	5,057.60	3,585.77	2,991.56	2,817.09	2,589.25	2,339.07	2,255.21	2,224.51	2,212.92	2,208.49
19.50%	5,075.03	3,604.76	3,012.09	2,838.34	2,611.84	2,364.27	2,282.04	2,252.26	2,241.14	2,236.94
19.75%	5,092.49	3,623.81	3,032.69	2,859.67	2,634.51	2,389.55	2,308.93	2,280.05	2,269.38	2,265.41
20.00%	5,109.99	3,642.91	3,053.35	2,881.07	2,657.27	2,414.91	2,335.88	2,307.87	2,297.65	2,293.88
20.25%	5,127.52	3,662.06	3,074.08	2,902.54	2,680.10	2,440.34	2,362.89	2,335.73	2,325.94	2,322.37
20.50%	5,145.09	3,681.27	3,094.88	2,924.08	2,703.01	2,465.85	2,389.96	2,363.63	2,354.25	2,350.87
20.75%	5,162.69	3,700.53	3,115.75	2,945.70	2,725.99	2,491.44	2,417.08	2,391.57	2,382.58	2,379.38

	3	5	7	8	10	15	20	25	30	35
1.00%	3,949.13	2,393.12	1,726.37	1,518.05	1,226.46	837.89	643.85	527.62	450.30	395.20
1.25%	3,964.29	2,408.22	1,741.51	1,533.22	1,241.71	853.38	659.59	543.62	466.55	411.72
1.50%	3,979.47	2,423.38	1,756.74	1,548.49	1,257.08	869.04	675.56	559.91	483.17	428.66
1.75%	3,994.70	2,438.61	1,772.05	1,563.86	1,272.57	884.89	691.78	576.50	500.14	446.01
2.00%	4,009.96	2,453.89	1,787.44	1,579.32	1,288.19	900.91	708.24	593.40	517.47	463.77
2.25%	4,025.26	2,469.23	1,802.92	1,594.88	1,303.92	917.12	724.93	610.58	535.14	481.93
2.50%	4,040.59	2,484.63	1,818.48	1,610.54	1,319.78	933.50	741.86	628.06	553.17	500.49
2.75%	4,055.96	2,500.09	1,834.13	1,626.29	1,335.75	950.07	759.03	645.84	571.54	519.45
3.00%	4,071.37	2,515.62	1,849.86	1,642.14	1,351.85	966.81	776.44	663.90	590.25	538.79
3.25%	4,086.81	2,531.20	1,865.68	1,658.09	1,368.07	983.74	794.07	682.24	609.29	558.51
3.50%	4,102.29	2,546.84	1,881.58	1,674.13	1,384.40	1,000.84	811.94	700.87	628.66	578.61
3.75%	4,117.81	2,562.55	1,897.56	1,690.26	1,400.86	1,018.11	830.04	719.78	648.36	599.07
4.00%	4,133.36	2,578.31	1,913.63	1,706.50	1,417.43	1,035.56	848.37	738.97	668.38	619.88
4.25%	4,148.95	2,594.14	1,929.79	1,722.83	1,434.13	1,053.19	866.93	758.43	688.72	641.05
4.50%	4,164.57	2,610.02	1,946.02	1,739.25	1,450.94	1,070.99	885.71	778.17	709.36	662.56
4.75%	4,180.23	2,625.97	1,962.34	1,755.77	1,467.87	1,088.96	904.71	798.16	730.31	684.40
5.00%	4,195.93	2,641.97	1,978.75	1,772.39	1,484.92	1,107.11	923.94	818.43	751.55	706.56
5.25%	4,211.66	2,658.04	1,995.23	1,789.10	1,502.08	1,125.43	943.38	838.95	773.09	729.04
5.50%	4,227.43	2,674.16	2,011.81	1,805.91	1,519.37	1,143.92	963.04	859.72	794.90	751.82
5.75%	4,243.23	2,690.35	2,028.46	1,822.81	1,536.77	1,162.57	982.92	880.75	817.00	774.90
6.00%	4,259.07	2,706.59	2,045.20	1,839.80	1,554.29	1,181.40	1,003.00	902.02	839.37	798.27
6.25%	4,274.95	2,722.90	2,062.02	1,856.89	1,571.92	1,200.39	1,023.30	923.54	862.00	821.91
6.50%	4,290.86	2,739.26	2,078.92	1,874.07	1,589.67	1,219.55	1,043.80	945.29	884.90	845.82
6.75%	4,306.81	2,755.68	2,095.91	1,891.35	1,607.54	1,238.87	1,064.51	967.28	908.04	869.98
7.00%	4,322.79	2,772.17	2,112.98	1,908.72	1,625.52	1,258.36	1,085.42	989.49	931.42	894.40
7.25%	4,338.81	2,788.71	2,130.13	1,926.18	1,643.61	1,278.01	1,106.53	1,011.93	955.05	919.05
7.50%	4,354.87	2,805.31	2,147.36	1,943.74	1,661.82	1,297.82	1,127.83	1,034.59	978.90	943.94
7.75%	4,370.96	2,821.97	2,164.67	1,961.39	1,680.15	1,317.79	1,149.33	1,057.46	1,002.98	969.05
8.00%	4,387.09	2,838.70	2,182.07	1,979.14	1,698.59	1,337.91	1,171.02	1,080.54	1,027.27	994.37
8.25%	4,403.26	2,855.48	2,199.55	1,996.97	1,717.14	1,358.20	1,192.89	1,103.83	1,051.77	1,019.89
8.50%	4,419.46	2,872.31	2,217.11	2,014.90	1,735.80	1,378.64	1,214.95	1,127.32	1,076.48	1,045.60
8.75%	4,435.69	2,889.21	2,234.75	2,032.92	1,754.57	1,399.23	1,237.19	1,151.00	1,101.38	1,071.51
9.00%	4,451.96	2,906.17	2,252.47	2,051.03	1,773.46	1,419.97	1,259.62	1,174.87	1,126.47	1,097.59
9.25%	4,468.27	2,923.19	2,270.27	2,069.23	1,792.46	1,440.87	1,282.21	1,198.93	1,151.75	1,123.84
9.50%	4,484.61	2,940.26	2,288.16	2,087.52	1,811.57	1,461.91	1,304.98	1,223.18	1,177.20	1,150.26
9.75%	4,500.99	2,957.39	2,306.12	2,105.91	1,830.78	1,483.11	1,327.92	1,247.59	1,202.82	1,176.83
10.00%	4,517.41	2,974.59	2,324.17	2,124.38	1,850.11	1,504.45	1,351.03	1,272.18	1,228.60	1,203.54
10.25%	4,533.86	2,991.84	2,342.29	2,142.95	1,869.55	1,525.93	1,374.30	1,296.94	1,254.54	1,230.40
10.50%	4,550.34	3,009.15	2,360.49	2,161.60	1,889.09	1,547.56	1,397.73	1,321.85	1,280.64	1,257.39
10.75%	4,566.86	3,026.51	2,378.78	2,180.35	1,908.74	1,569.33	1,421.32	1,346.93	1,306.87	1,284.50

	3	5	7	8	10	15	20	25	30	35
11.00%	4,583.42	3,043.94	2,397.14	2,199.18	1,928.50	1,591.24	1,445.06	1,372.16	1,333.25	1,311.74
11.25%	4,600.01	3,061.42	2,415.58	2,218.10	1,948.37	1,613.28	1,468.96	1,397.54	1,359.77	1,339.09
11.50%	4,616.64	3,078.97	2,434.10	2,237.11	1,968.34	1,635.47	1,493.00	1,423.06	1,386.41	1,366.55
11.75%	4,633.30	3,096.56	2,452.70	2,256.21	1,988.41	1,657.78	1,517.19	1,448.72	1,413.17	1,394.11
12.00%	4,650.00	3,114.22	2,471.38	2,275.40	2,008.59	1,680.24	1,541.52	1,474.51	1,440.06	1,421.77
12.25%	4,666.74	3,131.94	2,490.14	2,294.67	2,028.88	1,702.82	1,565.99	1,500.44	1,467.06	1,449.52
12.50%	4,683.51	3,149.71	2,508.97	2,314.03	2,049.27	1,725.53	1,590.60	1,526.50	1,494.16	1,477.36
12.75%	4,700.31	3,167.54	2,527.89	2,333.48	2,069.76	1,748.37	1,615.34	1,552.67	1,521.37	1,505.27
13.00%	4,717.15	3,185.43	2,546.87	2,353.02	2,090.35	1,771.34	1,640.21	1,578.97	1,548.68	1,533.27
13.25%	4,734.03	3,203.38	2,565.94	2,372.64	2,111.04	1,794.43	1,665.20	1,605.38	1,576.08	1,561.34
13.50%	4,750.94	3,221.38	2,585.08	2,392.34	2,131.84	1,817.65	1,690.32	1,631.90	1,603.58	1,589.48
13.75%	4,767.89	3,239.44	2,604.31	2,412.13	2,152.74	1,840.98	1,715.57	1,658.53	1,631.16	1,617.68
14.00%	4,784.87	3,257.56	2,623.60	2,432.01	2,173.73	1,864.44	1,740.93	1,685.27	1,658.82	1,645.94
14.25%	4,801.88	3,275.73	2,642.97	2,451.97	2,194.82	1,888.01	1,766.41	1,712.10	1,686.56	1,674.26
14.50%	4,818.94	3,293.96	2,662.42	2,472.02	2,216.02	1,911.70	1,792.00	1,739.03	1,714.38	1,702.64
14.75%	4,836.02	3,312.25	2,681.95	2,492.14	2,237.30	1,935.51	1,817.70	1,766.05	1,742.27	1,731.06
15.00%	4,853.15	3,330.59	2,701.55	2,512.36	2,258.69	1,959.42	1,843.51	1,793.16	1,770.22	1,759.54
15.25%	4,870.30	3,348.99	2,721.22	2,532.65	2,280.17	1,983.45	1,869.42	1,820.36	1,798.24	1,788.06
15.50%	4,887.50	3,367.45	2,740.97	2,553.03	2,301.75	2,007.59	1,895.43	1,847.64	1,826.32	1,816.62
15.75%	4,904.72	3,385.96	2,760.79	2,573.49	2,323.42	2,031.83	1,921.55	1,875.01	1,854.46	1,845.22
16.00%	4,921.98	3,404.53	2,780.69	2,594.03	2,345.18	2,056.18	1,947.76	1,902.44	1,882.66	1,873.86
16.25%	4,939.28	3,423.15	2,800.66	2,614.65	2,367.04	2,080.64	1,974.06	1,929.96	1,910.91	1,902.53
16.50%	4,956.61	3,441.83	2,820.70	2,635.36	2,388.99	2,105.19	2,000.46	1,957.54	1,939.21	1,931.24
16.75%	4,973.98	3,460.57	2,840.82	2,656.14	2,411.03	2,129.85	2,026.95	1,985.20	1,967.55	1,959.97
17.00%	4,991.38	3,479.36	2,861.01	2,677.00	2,433.17	2,154.61	2,053.52	2,012.92	1,995.95	1,988.74
17.25%	5,008.82	3,498.21	2,881.28	2,697.95	2,455.39	2,179.46	2,080.18	2,040.70	2,024.38	2,017.53
17.50%	5,026.29	3,517.11	2,901.61	2,718.97	2,477.70	2,204.41	2,106.92	2,068.54	2,052.86	2,046.35
17.75%	5,043.79	3,536.07	2,922.02	2,740.07	2,500.10	2,229.45	2,133.74	2,096.44	2,081.37	2,075.19
18.00%	5,061.34	3,555.08	2,942.50	2,761.25	2,522.59	2,254.59	2,160.64	2,124.40	2,109.92	2,104.05
18.25%	5,078.91	3,574.15	2,963.05	2,782.51	2,545.17	2,279.82	2,187.61	2,152.41	2,138.50	2,132.93
18.50%	5,096.52	3,593.27	2,983.67	2,803.84	2,567.83	2,305.13	2,214.66	2,180.48	2,167.12	2,161.83
18.75%	5,114.16	3,612.45	3,004.36	2,825.25	2,590.58	2,330.54	2,241.77	2,208.59	2,195.77	2,190.76
19.00%	5,131.84	3,631.68	3,025.12	2,846.74	2,613.41	2,356.03	2,268.96	2,236.75	2,224.45	2,219.69
19.25%	5,149.56	3,650.96	3,045.95	2,868.30	2,636.33	2,381.60	2,296.21	2,264.96	2,253.16	2,248.65
19.50%	5,167.30	3,670.30	3,066.86	2,889.94	2,659.33	2,407.26	2,323.53	2,293.21	2,281.89	2,277.61
19.75%	5,185.09	3,689.70	3,087.83	2,911.66	2,682.41	2,433.00	2,350.91	2,321.50	2,310.65	2,306.60
20.00%	5,202.90	3,709.14	3,108.87	2,933.45	2,705.58	2,458.82	2,378.35	2,349.83	2,339.43	2,335.59
20.25%	5,220.75	3,728.65	3,129.98	2,955.31	2,728.83	2,484.71	2,405.86	2,378.20	2,368.23	2,364.60
20.50%	5,238.64	3,748.20	3,151.15	2,977.25	2,752.15	2,510.69	2,433.42	2,406.61	2,397.05	2,393.61
20.75%	5,256.56	3,767.81	3,172.40	2,999.26	2,775.56	2,536.73	2,461.03	2,435.05	2,425.90	2,422.64

	3	5	7	8	10	15	20	25	30	35
1.00%	4,019.65	2,435.86	1,757.20	1,545.16	1,248.36	852.85	655.35	537.04	458.34	402.26
1.25%	4,035.08	2,451.23	1,772.61	1,560.60	1,263.88	868.61	671.37	553.32	474.88	419.07
1.50%	4,050.54	2,466.66	1,788.11	1,576.14	1,279.53	884.56	687.63	569.91	491.80	436.31
1.75%	4,066.03	2,482.15	1,803.69	1,591.79	1,295.30	900.69	704.13	586.80	509.07	453.97
2.00%	4,081.57	2,497.71	1,819.36	1,607.52	1,311.19	917.00	720.88	603.99	526.71	472.05
2.25%	4,097.14	2,513.32	1,835.11	1,623.36	1,327.21	933.50	737.88	621.49	544.70	490.54
2.50%	4,112.75	2,529.00	1,850.96	1,639.30	1,343.35	950.17	755.11	639.28	563.05	509.43
2.75%	4,128.39	2,544.74	1,866.88	1,655.33	1,359.61	967.04	772.59	657.37	581.74	528.72
3.00%	4,144.07	2,560.54	1,882.90	1,671.46	1,375.99	984.08	790.30	675.75	600.79	548.41
3.25%	4,159.79	2,576.40	1,898.99	1,687.69	1,392.50	1,001.30	808.25	694.43	620.17	568.49
3.50%	4,175.55	2,592.32	1,915.18	1,704.02	1,409.12	1,018.71	826.44	713.39	639.89	588.94
3.75%	4,191.34	2,608.31	1,931.45	1,720.45	1,425.87	1,036.29	844.87	732.64	659.94	609.76
4.00%	4,207.17	2,624.35	1,947.80	1,736.97	1,442.74	1,054.06	863.52	752.17	680.32	630.95
4.25%	4,223.03	2,640.46	1,964.25	1,753.59	1,459.73	1,072.00	882.41	771.98	701.01	652.50
4.50%	4,238.94	2,656.63	1,980.77	1,770.31	1,476.85	1,090.12	901.53	792.06	722.03	674.39
4.75%	4,254.88	2,672.86	1,997.38	1,787.13	1,494.08	1,108.41	920.87	812.42	743.35	696.62
5.00%	4,270.85	2,689.15	2,014.08	1,804.04	1,511.43	1,126.88	940.44	833.04	764.97	719.18
5.25%	4,286.87	2,705.50	2,030.86	1,821.05	1,528.91	1,145.53	960.23	853.93	786.89	742.06
5.50%	4,302.92	2,721.92	2,047.73	1,838.15	1,546.50	1,164.34	980.24	875.07	809.10	765.25
5.75%	4,319.00	2,738.39	2,064.68	1,855.36	1,564.21	1,183.33	1,000.47	896.48	831.59	788.74
6.00%	4,335.13	2,754.92	2,081.72	1,872.65	1,582.04	1,202.50	1,020.91	918.13	854.36	812.52
6.25%	4,351.29	2,771.52	2,098.84	1,890.05	1,599.99	1,221.83	1,041.57	940.03	877.40	836.58
6.50%	4,367.48	2,788.18	2,116.04	1,907.54	1,618.06	1,241.33	1,062.44	962.17	900.70	860.92
6.75%	4,383.72	2,804.89	2,133.33	1,925.12	1,636.24	1,261.00	1,083.52	984.55	924.25	885.52
7.00%	4,399.99	2,821.67	2,150.71	1,942.80	1,654.55	1,280.83	1,104.80	1,007.16	948.06	910.37
7.25%	4,416.29	2,838.51	2,168.16	1,960.58	1,672.96	1,300.83	1,126.29	1,030.00	972.10	935.47
7.50%	4,432.64	2,855.41	2,185.70	1,978.45	1,691.50	1,320.99	1,147.97	1,053.06	996.38	960.80
7.75%	4,449.02	2,872.37	2,203.33	1,996.42	1,710.15	1,341.32	1,169.85	1,076.34	1,020.89	986.35
8.00%	4,465.43	2,889.39	2,221.04	2,014.48	1,728.92	1,361.80	1,191.93	1,099.84	1,045.61	1,012.12
8.25%	4,481.88	2,906.47	2,238.83	2,032.63	1,747.80	1,382.45	1,214.19	1,123.54	1,070.55	1,038.10
8.50%	4,498.37	2,923.61	2,256.70	2,050.88	1,766.80	1,403.25	1,236.65	1,147.45	1,095.70	1,064.28
8.75%	4,514.90	2,940.81	2,274.66	2,069.22	1,785.91	1,424.21	1,259.29	1,171.55	1,121.05	1,090.64
9.00%	4,531.46	2,958.07	2,292.69	2,087.65	1,805.13	1,445.33	1,282.11	1,195.85	1,146.59	1,117.19
9.25%	4,548.06	2,975.39	2,310.81	2,106.18	1,824.47	1,466.60	1,305.11	1,220.34	1,172.31	1,143.91
9.50%	4,564.70	2,992.77	2,329.02	2,124.80	1,843.92	1,488.02	1,328.29	1,245.02	1,198.22	1,170.80
9.75%	4,581.37	3,010.20	2,347.30	2,143.51	1,863.48	1,509.59	1,351.64	1,269.87	1,224.30	1,197.84
10.00%	4,598.07	3,027.70	2,365.67	2,162.32	1,883.15	1,531.31	1,375.16	1,294.90	1,250.54	1,225.03
10.25%	4,614.82	3,045.26	2,384.12	2,181.21	1,902.93	1,553.18	1,398.84	1,320.10	1,276.94	1,252.37
10.50%	4,631.60	3,062.88	2,402.65	2,200.20	1,922.82	1,575.19	1,422.69	1,345.46	1,303.50	1,279.84
10.75%	4,648.41	3,080.56	2,421.26	2,219.28	1,942.83	1,597.35	1,446.70	1,370.98	1,330.21	1,307.44

$142,500   11.00 - 20.75%   3 - 35 Years

	3	5	7	8	10	15	20	25	30	35
11.00%	4,665.27	3,098.30	2,439.95	2,238.45	1,962.94	1,619.65	1,470.87	1,396.66	1,357.06	1,335.16
11.25%	4,682.16	3,116.09	2,458.72	2,257.71	1,983.16	1,642.09	1,495.19	1,422.49	1,384.05	1,363.00
11.50%	4,699.08	3,133.95	2,477.57	2,277.06	2,003.49	1,664.67	1,519.66	1,448.47	1,411.17	1,390.95
11.75%	4,716.04	3,151.86	2,496.50	2,296.50	2,023.92	1,687.39	1,544.28	1,474.59	1,438.41	1,419.01
12.00%	4,733.04	3,169.83	2,515.51	2,316.03	2,044.46	1,710.24	1,569.05	1,500.84	1,465.77	1,447.16
12.25%	4,750.07	3,187.87	2,534.61	2,335.65	2,065.11	1,733.23	1,593.95	1,527.23	1,493.25	1,475.40
12.50%	4,767.14	3,205.96	2,553.78	2,355.36	2,085.86	1,756.34	1,619.00	1,553.75	1,520.84	1,503.74
12.75%	4,784.25	3,224.11	2,573.03	2,375.15	2,106.72	1,779.59	1,644.18	1,580.40	1,548.54	1,532.15
13.00%	4,801.39	3,242.31	2,592.35	2,395.03	2,127.68	1,802.97	1,669.50	1,607.17	1,576.33	1,560.65
13.25%	4,818.57	3,260.58	2,611.76	2,415.00	2,148.74	1,826.47	1,694.94	1,634.05	1,604.23	1,589.22
13.50%	4,835.78	3,278.90	2,631.25	2,435.06	2,169.91	1,850.10	1,720.51	1,661.04	1,632.21	1,617.86
13.75%	4,853.03	3,297.29	2,650.81	2,455.21	2,191.18	1,873.86	1,746.20	1,688.15	1,660.29	1,646.57
14.00%	4,870.31	3,315.73	2,670.45	2,475.44	2,212.55	1,897.73	1,772.02	1,715.36	1,688.44	1,675.33
14.25%	4,887.63	3,334.22	2,690.17	2,495.76	2,234.02	1,921.73	1,797.95	1,742.67	1,716.68	1,704.16
14.50%	4,904.99	3,352.78	2,709.97	2,516.16	2,255.59	1,945.84	1,824.00	1,770.08	1,744.99	1,733.04
14.75%	4,922.38	3,371.39	2,729.84	2,536.65	2,277.26	1,970.07	1,850.16	1,797.59	1,773.38	1,761.98
15.00%	4,939.81	3,390.07	2,749.79	2,557.22	2,299.02	1,994.41	1,876.43	1,825.18	1,801.83	1,790.96
15.25%	4,957.27	3,408.79	2,769.81	2,577.88	2,320.89	2,018.87	1,902.80	1,852.87	1,830.35	1,819.99
15.50%	4,974.77	3,427.58	2,789.91	2,598.62	2,342.85	2,043.44	1,929.28	1,880.64	1,858.94	1,849.06
15.75%	4,992.31	3,446.42	2,810.09	2,619.44	2,364.91	2,068.11	1,955.86	1,908.49	1,887.58	1,878.17
16.00%	5,009.88	3,465.32	2,830.34	2,640.35	2,387.06	2,092.90	1,982.54	1,936.42	1,916.28	1,907.32
16.25%	5,027.48	3,484.28	2,850.67	2,661.34	2,409.31	2,117.79	2,009.31	1,964.42	1,945.03	1,936.50
16.50%	5,045.12	3,503.29	2,871.07	2,682.42	2,431.65	2,142.78	2,036.18	1,992.50	1,973.84	1,965.72
16.75%	5,062.80	3,522.36	2,891.55	2,703.57	2,454.09	2,167.88	2,063.14	2,020.65	2,002.69	1,994.97
17.00%	5,080.51	3,541.49	2,912.10	2,724.81	2,476.62	2,193.08	2,090.19	2,048.86	2,031.59	2,024.25
17.25%	5,098.26	3,560.68	2,932.73	2,746.12	2,499.24	2,218.38	2,117.32	2,077.14	2,060.53	2,053.56
17.50%	5,116.04	3,579.92	2,953.43	2,767.52	2,521.95	2,243.77	2,144.54	2,105.48	2,089.51	2,082.89
17.75%	5,133.86	3,599.21	2,974.20	2,789.00	2,544.75	2,269.26	2,171.84	2,133.88	2,118.54	2,112.24
18.00%	5,151.72	3,618.56	2,995.04	2,810.56	2,567.64	2,294.85	2,199.22	2,162.34	2,147.60	2,141.62
18.25%	5,169.61	3,637.97	3,015.96	2,832.19	2,590.62	2,320.53	2,226.67	2,190.85	2,176.69	2,171.02
18.50%	5,187.53	3,657.43	3,036.95	2,853.91	2,613.69	2,346.30	2,254.20	2,219.41	2,205.82	2,200.44
18.75%	5,205.49	3,676.95	3,058.01	2,875.70	2,636.84	2,372.15	2,281.80	2,248.03	2,234.98	2,229.88
19.00%	5,223.48	3,696.53	3,079.14	2,897.58	2,660.08	2,398.10	2,309.48	2,276.69	2,264.17	2,259.33
19.25%	5,241.51	3,716.16	3,100.35	2,919.52	2,683.41	2,424.13	2,337.22	2,305.40	2,293.39	2,288.80
19.50%	5,259.58	3,735.84	3,121.62	2,941.55	2,706.82	2,450.24	2,365.02	2,334.16	2,322.64	2,318.29
19.75%	5,277.68	3,755.58	3,142.97	2,963.65	2,730.31	2,476.44	2,392.89	2,362.96	2,351.91	2,347.78
20.00%	5,295.81	3,775.38	3,164.38	2,985.83	2,753.89	2,502.72	2,420.83	2,391.79	2,381.20	2,377.30
20.25%	5,313.98	3,795.23	3,185.87	3,008.08	2,777.55	2,529.08	2,448.82	2,420.67	2,410.52	2,406.82
20.50%	5,332.18	3,815.13	3,207.42	3,030.41	2,801.30	2,555.52	2,476.87	2,449.59	2,439.86	2,436.36
20.75%	5,350.42	3,835.09	3,229.05	3,052.82	2,825.12	2,582.03	2,504.98	2,478.54	2,469.22	2,465.90

$145,000   1.00 - 10.75%   3 - 35 Years

	3	5	7	8	10	15	20	25	30	35
1.00%	4,090.17	2,478.59	1,788.03	1,572.27	1,270.26	867.82	666.85	546.47	466.38	409.31
1.25%	4,105.87	2,494.23	1,803.71	1,587.98	1,286.06	883.85	683.14	563.03	483.21	426.43
1.50%	4,121.60	2,509.93	1,819.48	1,603.80	1,301.98	900.08	699.69	579.91	500.42	443.97
1.75%	4,137.37	2,525.70	1,835.33	1,619.71	1,318.02	916.49	716.49	597.09	518.00	461.94
2.00%	4,153.17	2,541.53	1,851.28	1,635.73	1,334.20	933.09	733.53	614.59	535.95	480.33
2.25%	4,169.02	2,557.41	1,867.31	1,651.84	1,350.49	949.87	750.82	632.39	554.26	499.14
2.50%	4,184.90	2,573.37	1,883.43	1,668.06	1,366.91	966.84	768.36	650.49	572.93	518.37
2.75%	4,200.82	2,589.38	1,899.63	1,684.37	1,383.46	984.00	786.14	668.90	591.95	538.00
3.00%	4,216.78	2,605.46	1,915.93	1,700.79	1,400.13	1,001.34	804.17	687.61	611.33	558.03
3.25%	4,232.77	2,621.60	1,932.31	1,717.30	1,416.93	1,018.87	822.43	706.61	631.05	578.46
3.50%	4,248.80	2,637.80	1,948.78	1,733.92	1,433.85	1,036.58	840.94	725.90	651.11	599.27
3.75%	4,264.87	2,654.07	1,965.33	1,750.63	1,450.89	1,054.47	859.69	745.49	671.52	620.46
4.00%	4,280.98	2,670.40	1,981.98	1,767.44	1,468.05	1,072.55	878.67	765.36	692.25	642.02
4.25%	4,297.12	2,686.79	1,998.71	1,784.36	1,485.34	1,090.80	897.89	785.52	713.31	663.95
4.50%	4,313.30	2,703.24	2,015.52	1,801.37	1,502.76	1,109.24	917.34	805.96	734.69	686.22
4.75%	4,329.52	2,719.75	2,032.43	1,818.48	1,520.29	1,127.86	937.02	826.67	756.39	708.84
5.00%	4,345.78	2,736.33	2,049.42	1,835.69	1,537.95	1,146.65	956.94	847.66	778.39	731.80
5.25%	4,362.07	2,752.97	2,066.49	1,853.00	1,555.73	1,165.62	977.07	868.91	800.70	755.08
5.50%	4,378.41	2,769.67	2,083.66	1,870.40	1,573.63	1,184.77	997.44	890.43	823.29	778.67
5.75%	4,394.77	2,786.43	2,100.91	1,887.91	1,591.65	1,204.09	1,018.02	912.20	846.18	802.58
6.00%	4,411.18	2,803.26	2,118.24	1,905.51	1,609.80	1,223.59	1,038.83	934.24	869.35	826.78
6.25%	4,427.62	2,820.14	2,135.66	1,923.21	1,628.06	1,243.26	1,059.85	956.52	892.79	851.26
6.50%	4,444.11	2,837.09	2,153.17	1,941.00	1,646.45	1,263.11	1,081.08	979.05	916.50	876.02
6.75%	4,460.62	2,854.10	2,170.76	1,958.90	1,664.95	1,283.12	1,102.53	1,001.82	940.47	901.05
7.00%	4,477.18	2,871.17	2,188.44	1,976.89	1,683.57	1,303.30	1,124.18	1,024.83	964.69	926.34
7.25%	4,493.77	2,888.31	2,206.20	1,994.98	1,702.32	1,323.65	1,146.05	1,048.07	989.16	951.88
7.50%	4,510.40	2,905.50	2,224.05	2,013.16	1,721.18	1,344.17	1,168.11	1,071.54	1,013.86	977.65
7.75%	4,527.07	2,922.76	2,241.98	2,031.44	1,740.15	1,364.85	1,190.38	1,095.23	1,038.80	1,003.66
8.00%	4,543.77	2,940.08	2,260.00	2,049.82	1,759.25	1,385.70	1,212.84	1,119.13	1,063.96	1,029.88
8.25%	4,560.51	2,957.46	2,278.10	2,068.29	1,778.46	1,406.70	1,235.50	1,143.25	1,089.34	1,056.31
8.50%	4,577.29	2,974.90	2,296.29	2,086.86	1,797.79	1,427.87	1,258.34	1,167.58	1,114.92	1,082.95
8.75%	4,594.11	2,992.40	2,314.56	2,105.52	1,817.24	1,449.20	1,281.38	1,192.11	1,140.72	1,109.78
9.00%	4,610.96	3,009.96	2,332.92	2,124.28	1,836.80	1,470.69	1,304.60	1,216.83	1,166.70	1,136.79
9.25%	4,627.85	3,027.59	2,351.36	2,143.13	1,856.47	1,492.33	1,328.01	1,241.75	1,192.88	1,163.98
9.50%	4,644.78	3,045.27	2,369.88	2,162.08	1,876.26	1,514.13	1,351.59	1,266.86	1,219.24	1,191.34
9.75%	4,661.74	3,063.02	2,388.48	2,181.12	1,896.17	1,536.08	1,375.35	1,292.15	1,245.77	1,218.85
10.00%	4,678.74	3,080.82	2,407.17	2,200.25	1,916.19	1,558.18	1,399.28	1,317.62	1,272.48	1,246.53
10.25%	4,695.78	3,098.69	2,425.94	2,219.48	1,936.32	1,580.43	1,423.38	1,343.26	1,299.35	1,274.34
10.50%	4,712.85	3,116.62	2,444.80	2,238.80	1,956.56	1,602.83	1,447.65	1,369.06	1,326.37	1,302.29
10.75%	4,729.97	3,134.60	2,463.73	2,258.22	1,976.91	1,625.37	1,472.08	1,395.03	1,353.55	1,330.38

$145,000   11.00 - 20.75%   3 - 35 Years

	3	5	7	8	10	15	20	25	30	35
11.00%	4,747.11	3,152.65	2,482.75	2,277.72	1,997.38	1,648.07	1,496.67	1,421.16	1,380.87	1,358.59
11.25%	4,764.30	3,170.76	2,501.85	2,297.32	2,017.95	1,670.90	1,521.42	1,447.45	1,408.33	1,386.92
11.50%	4,781.52	3,188.93	2,521.04	2,317.01	2,038.63	1,693.88	1,546.32	1,473.88	1,435.92	1,415.36
11.75%	4,798.78	3,207.16	2,540.30	2,336.79	2,059.43	1,716.99	1,571.38	1,500.46	1,463.64	1,443.90
12.00%	4,816.07	3,225.44	2,559.65	2,356.66	2,080.33	1,740.24	1,596.57	1,527.18	1,491.49	1,472.55
12.25%	4,833.41	3,243.79	2,579.07	2,376.62	2,101.34	1,763.63	1,621.92	1,554.03	1,519.45	1,501.29
12.50%	4,850.78	3,262.20	2,598.58	2,396.68	2,122.45	1,787.16	1,647.40	1,581.01	1,547.52	1,530.12
12.75%	4,868.18	3,280.67	2,618.17	2,416.82	2,143.68	1,810.81	1,673.03	1,608.13	1,575.71	1,559.03
13.00%	4,885.62	3,299.20	2,637.83	2,437.05	2,165.01	1,834.60	1,698.78	1,635.36	1,603.99	1,588.03
13.25%	4,903.10	3,317.78	2,657.58	2,457.37	2,186.44	1,858.52	1,724.67	1,662.72	1,632.37	1,617.10
13.50%	4,920.62	3,336.43	2,677.41	2,477.78	2,207.98	1,882.56	1,750.69	1,690.19	1,660.85	1,646.24
13.75%	4,938.17	3,355.13	2,697.32	2,498.28	2,229.62	1,906.73	1,776.84	1,717.77	1,689.41	1,675.45
14.00%	4,955.76	3,373.90	2,717.30	2,518.87	2,251.36	1,931.03	1,803.11	1,745.45	1,718.06	1,704.73
14.25%	4,973.38	3,392.72	2,737.37	2,539.54	2,273.21	1,955.44	1,829.49	1,773.24	1,746.80	1,734.06
14.50%	4,991.04	3,411.60	2,757.51	2,560.30	2,295.16	1,979.98	1,856.00	1,801.14	1,775.61	1,763.45
14.75%	5,008.74	3,430.54	2,777.73	2,581.15	2,317.21	2,004.63	1,882.62	1,829.12	1,804.49	1,792.89
15.00%	5,026.47	3,449.54	2,798.03	2,602.08	2,339.36	2,029.40	1,909.34	1,857.20	1,833.44	1,822.38
15.25%	5,044.24	3,468.60	2,818.41	2,623.10	2,361.61	2,054.29	1,936.18	1,885.37	1,862.46	1,851.92
15.50%	5,062.05	3,487.71	2,838.86	2,644.21	2,383.95	2,079.29	1,963.13	1,913.63	1,891.55	1,881.50
15.75%	5,079.89	3,506.89	2,859.39	2,665.40	2,406.40	2,104.40	1,990.17	1,941.97	1,920.69	1,911.12
16.00%	5,097.77	3,526.12	2,880.00	2,686.67	2,428.94	2,129.62	2,017.32	1,970.39	1,949.90	1,940.78
16.25%	5,115.68	3,545.41	2,900.68	2,708.03	2,451.58	2,154.94	2,044.57	1,998.88	1,979.16	1,970.48
16.50%	5,133.64	3,564.76	2,921.44	2,729.48	2,474.31	2,180.38	2,071.91	2,027.45	2,008.46	2,000.21
16.75%	5,151.62	3,584.16	2,942.28	2,751.00	2,497.14	2,205.92	2,099.34	2,056.10	2,037.82	2,029.97
17.00%	5,169.65	3,603.62	2,963.19	2,772.61	2,520.07	2,231.56	2,126.86	2,084.81	2,067.23	2,059.76
17.25%	5,187.70	3,623.14	2,984.18	2,794.30	2,543.08	2,257.30	2,154.47	2,113.58	2,096.68	2,089.58
17.50%	5,205.80	3,642.72	3,005.24	2,816.08	2,566.19	2,283.14	2,182.17	2,142.42	2,126.17	2,119.43
17.75%	5,223.93	3,662.36	3,026.38	2,837.93	2,589.39	2,309.08	2,209.94	2,171.32	2,155.70	2,149.30
18.00%	5,242.10	3,682.05	3,047.59	2,859.87	2,612.69	2,335.11	2,237.80	2,200.27	2,185.27	2,179.19
18.25%	5,260.30	3,701.80	3,068.87	2,881.88	2,636.07	2,361.24	2,265.74	2,229.29	2,214.88	2,209.11
18.50%	5,278.54	3,721.60	3,090.23	2,903.98	2,659.54	2,387.46	2,293.75	2,258.35	2,244.52	2,239.04
18.75%	5,296.81	3,741.46	3,111.66	2,926.16	2,683.10	2,413.77	2,321.84	2,287.47	2,274.19	2,269.00
19.00%	5,315.12	3,761.38	3,133.16	2,948.41	2,706.75	2,440.17	2,349.99	2,316.64	2,303.89	2,298.97
19.25%	5,333.47	3,781.35	3,154.74	2,970.74	2,730.48	2,466.66	2,378.22	2,345.85	2,333.63	2,328.95
19.50%	5,351.85	3,801.38	3,176.39	2,993.16	2,754.31	2,493.23	2,406.51	2,375.11	2,363.38	2,358.96
19.75%	5,370.27	3,821.47	3,198.11	3,015.65	2,778.21	2,519.89	2,434.87	2,404.41	2,393.17	2,388.97
20.00%	5,388.72	3,841.61	3,219.90	3,038.21	2,802.21	2,546.63	2,463.30	2,433.76	2,422.98	2,419.00
20.25%	5,407.21	3,861.81	3,241.76	3,060.86	2,826.28	2,573.45	2,491.78	2,463.14	2,452.81	2,449.05
20.50%	5,425.73	3,882.06	3,263.70	3,083.58	2,850.44	2,600.35	2,520.32	2,492.56	2,482.66	2,479.10
20.75%	5,444.29	3,902.37	3,285.70	3,106.37	2,874.69	2,627.33	2,548.92	2,522.02	2,512.54	2,509.16

	3	5	7	8	10	15	20	25	30	35
1.00%	4,160.69	2,521.33	1,818.86	1,599.38	1,292.16	882.78	678.34	555.89	474.42	416.37
1.25%	4,176.66	2,537.24	1,834.81	1,615.36	1,308.23	899.09	694.92	572.74	491.55	433.78
1.50%	4,192.66	2,553.21	1,850.85	1,631.45	1,324.42	915.60	711.75	589.91	509.05	451.62
1.75%	4,208.70	2,569.24	1,866.98	1,647.64	1,340.75	932.29	728.84	607.39	526.93	469.90
2.00%	4,224.78	2,585.34	1,883.20	1,663.93	1,357.20	949.18	746.18	625.19	545.19	488.61
2.25%	4,240.90	2,601.51	1,899.50	1,680.32	1,373.78	966.25	763.77	643.29	563.81	507.75
2.50%	4,257.05	2,617.74	1,915.90	1,696.82	1,390.48	983.51	781.61	661.71	582.80	527.31
2.75%	4,273.25	2,634.03	1,932.39	1,713.41	1,407.31	1,000.97	799.70	680.43	602.16	547.28
3.00%	4,289.48	2,650.38	1,948.96	1,730.11	1,424.27	1,018.61	818.03	699.46	621.87	567.65
3.25%	4,305.75	2,666.80	1,965.63	1,746.91	1,441.36	1,036.44	836.61	718.79	641.93	588.43
3.50%	4,322.06	2,683.28	1,982.38	1,763.81	1,458.57	1,054.45	855.44	738.42	662.34	609.60
3.75%	4,338.40	2,699.83	1,999.22	1,780.81	1,475.90	1,072.65	874.51	758.34	683.10	631.16
4.00%	4,354.79	2,716.44	2,016.15	1,797.92	1,493.37	1,091.04	893.82	778.56	704.19	653.09
4.25%	4,371.21	2,733.11	2,033.17	1,815.12	1,510.95	1,109.61	913.37	799.06	725.61	675.39
4.50%	4,387.67	2,749.85	2,050.27	1,832.43	1,528.67	1,128.37	933.16	819.85	747.36	698.05
4.75%	4,404.17	2,766.64	2,067.47	1,849.83	1,546.50	1,147.30	953.18	840.92	769.43	721.06
5.00%	4,420.71	2,783.51	2,084.75	1,867.34	1,564.47	1,166.42	973.43	862.27	791.81	744.41
5.25%	4,437.28	2,800.43	2,102.12	1,884.94	1,582.55	1,185.72	993.92	883.89	814.50	768.10
5.50%	4,453.90	2,817.42	2,119.58	1,902.65	1,600.76	1,205.20	1,014.63	905.78	837.49	792.10
5.75%	4,470.55	2,834.47	2,137.13	1,920.46	1,619.10	1,224.85	1,035.57	927.93	860.77	816.41
6.00%	4,487.24	2,851.59	2,154.76	1,938.36	1,637.55	1,244.69	1,056.74	950.34	884.34	841.03
6.25%	4,503.96	2,868.77	2,172.48	1,956.37	1,656.13	1,264.70	1,078.12	973.01	908.18	865.94
6.50%	4,520.73	2,886.01	2,190.29	1,974.47	1,674.83	1,284.88	1,099.72	995.93	932.30	891.13
6.75%	4,537.53	2,903.31	2,208.19	1,992.67	1,693.66	1,305.24	1,121.54	1,019.09	956.68	916.59
7.00%	4,554.37	2,920.68	2,226.17	2,010.97	1,712.60	1,325.77	1,143.57	1,042.50	981.32	942.31
7.25%	4,571.25	2,938.11	2,244.24	2,029.37	1,731.67	1,346.47	1,165.80	1,066.14	1,006.21	968.29
7.50%	4,588.17	2,955.60	2,262.40	2,047.87	1,750.85	1,367.34	1,188.25	1,090.01	1,031.34	994.51
7.75%	4,605.12	2,973.15	2,280.64	2,066.47	1,770.16	1,388.38	1,210.90	1,114.11	1,056.71	1,020.96
8.00%	4,622.11	2,990.77	2,298.97	2,085.16	1,789.58	1,409.59	1,233.75	1,138.43	1,082.30	1,047.63
8.25%	4,639.14	3,008.45	2,317.38	2,103.95	1,809.13	1,430.96	1,256.80	1,162.96	1,108.12	1,074.52
8.50%	4,656.21	3,026.19	2,335.88	2,122.84	1,828.79	1,452.49	1,280.04	1,187.71	1,134.15	1,101.62
8.75%	4,673.32	3,043.99	2,354.47	2,141.82	1,848.57	1,474.19	1,303.47	1,212.66	1,160.38	1,128.91
9.00%	4,690.46	3,061.86	2,373.14	2,160.90	1,868.47	1,496.04	1,327.10	1,237.81	1,186.82	1,156.39
9.25%	4,707.64	3,079.78	2,391.90	2,180.08	1,888.48	1,518.06	1,350.90	1,263.16	1,213.45	1,184.05
9.50%	4,724.86	3,097.77	2,410.74	2,199.36	1,908.61	1,540.23	1,374.89	1,288.70	1,240.26	1,211.88
9.75%	4,742.12	3,115.83	2,429.66	2,218.72	1,928.86	1,562.56	1,399.06	1,314.43	1,267.25	1,239.87
10.00%	4,759.41	3,133.94	2,448.67	2,238.19	1,949.22	1,585.04	1,423.41	1,340.33	1,294.42	1,268.02
10.25%	4,776.74	3,152.11	2,467.77	2,257.75	1,969.70	1,607.68	1,447.92	1,366.42	1,321.75	1,296.31
10.50%	4,794.11	3,170.35	2,486.95	2,277.40	1,990.29	1,630.46	1,472.61	1,392.67	1,349.24	1,324.75
10.75%	4,811.52	3,188.65	2,506.21	2,297.15	2,011.00	1,653.40	1,497.46	1,419.09	1,376.89	1,353.32

$147,500　11.00 - 20.75%　3 - 35 Years

	3	5	7	8	10	15	20	25	30	35
11.00%	4,828.96	3,207.01	2,525.56	2,316.99	2,031.81	1,676.48	1,522.48	1,445.67	1,404.68	1,382.01
11.25%	4,846.44	3,225.43	2,544.99	2,336.93	2,052.74	1,699.71	1,547.65	1,472.40	1,432.61	1,410.83
11.50%	4,863.96	3,243.91	2,564.50	2,356.96	2,073.78	1,723.08	1,572.98	1,499.29	1,460.68	1,439.76
11.75%	4,881.52	3,262.45	2,584.10	2,377.08	2,094.93	1,746.59	1,598.47	1,526.33	1,488.88	1,468.80
12.00%	4,899.11	3,281.06	2,603.78	2,397.29	2,116.20	1,770.25	1,624.10	1,553.51	1,517.20	1,497.94
12.25%	4,916.74	3,299.72	2,623.54	2,417.60	2,137.57	1,794.04	1,649.88	1,580.82	1,545.65	1,527.17
12.50%	4,934.41	3,318.45	2,643.38	2,438.00	2,159.05	1,817.97	1,675.81	1,608.27	1,574.21	1,556.50
12.75%	4,952.12	3,337.23	2,663.31	2,458.49	2,180.64	1,842.03	1,701.87	1,635.85	1,602.87	1,585.91
13.00%	4,969.86	3,356.08	2,683.31	2,479.07	2,202.33	1,866.23	1,728.07	1,663.56	1,631.64	1,615.41
13.25%	4,987.64	3,374.99	2,703.40	2,499.74	2,224.14	1,890.56	1,754.41	1,691.38	1,660.52	1,644.98
13.50%	5,005.45	3,393.95	2,723.57	2,520.50	2,246.05	1,915.02	1,780.88	1,719.33	1,689.48	1,674.63
13.75%	5,023.31	3,412.98	2,743.82	2,541.36	2,268.06	1,939.61	1,807.47	1,747.38	1,718.54	1,704.34
14.00%	5,041.20	3,432.07	2,764.15	2,562.30	2,290.18	1,964.32	1,834.19	1,775.55	1,747.69	1,734.12
14.25%	5,059.13	3,451.21	2,784.56	2,583.33	2,312.40	1,989.16	1,861.04	1,803.82	1,776.91	1,763.96
14.50%	5,077.09	3,470.42	2,805.05	2,604.45	2,334.73	2,014.11	1,888.00	1,832.19	1,806.22	1,793.85
14.75%	5,095.10	3,489.69	2,825.62	2,625.65	2,357.16	2,039.19	1,915.07	1,860.66	1,835.60	1,823.80
15.00%	5,113.14	3,509.01	2,846.27	2,646.95	2,379.69	2,064.39	1,942.26	1,889.23	1,865.05	1,853.80
15.25%	5,131.21	3,528.40	2,867.00	2,668.33	2,402.32	2,089.71	1,969.57	1,917.88	1,894.58	1,883.85
15.50%	5,149.33	3,547.85	2,887.81	2,689.80	2,425.06	2,115.14	1,996.97	1,946.62	1,924.16	1,913.94
15.75%	5,167.48	3,567.35	2,908.69	2,711.35	2,447.89	2,140.68	2,024.49	1,975.45	1,953.81	1,944.07
16.00%	5,185.66	3,586.91	2,929.65	2,733.00	2,470.82	2,166.33	2,052.10	2,004.36	1,983.52	1,974.24
16.25%	5,203.89	3,606.54	2,950.70	2,754.72	2,493.85	2,192.10	2,079.82	2,033.35	2,013.28	2,004.45
16.50%	5,222.15	3,626.22	2,971.81	2,776.54	2,516.97	2,217.97	2,107.63	2,062.41	2,043.09	2,034.69
16.75%	5,240.44	3,645.96	2,993.01	2,798.43	2,540.20	2,243.95	2,135.53	2,091.55	2,072.96	2,064.97
17.00%	5,258.78	3,665.75	3,014.28	2,820.41	2,563.52	2,270.03	2,163.53	2,120.75	2,102.87	2,095.28
17.25%	5,277.15	3,685.61	3,035.63	2,842.48	2,586.93	2,296.22	2,191.62	2,150.02	2,132.83	2,125.61
17.50%	5,295.55	3,705.53	3,057.05	2,864.63	2,610.44	2,322.50	2,219.79	2,179.36	2,162.83	2,155.97
17.75%	5,314.00	3,725.50	3,078.56	2,886.86	2,634.04	2,348.89	2,248.05	2,208.75	2,192.87	2,186.36
18.00%	5,332.48	3,745.53	3,100.13	2,909.17	2,657.73	2,375.37	2,276.38	2,238.21	2,222.95	2,216.77
18.25%	5,350.99	3,765.62	3,121.78	2,931.57	2,681.52	2,401.95	2,304.80	2,267.72	2,253.07	2,247.20
18.50%	5,369.55	3,785.77	3,143.51	2,954.05	2,705.39	2,428.62	2,333.30	2,297.29	2,283.22	2,277.65
18.75%	5,388.14	3,805.97	3,165.31	2,976.61	2,729.36	2,455.39	2,361.87	2,326.91	2,313.40	2,308.12
19.00%	5,406.76	3,826.23	3,187.18	2,999.25	2,753.42	2,482.24	2,390.51	2,356.58	2,343.62	2,338.60
19.25%	5,425.42	3,846.55	3,209.13	3,021.96	2,777.56	2,509.19	2,419.22	2,386.30	2,373.86	2,369.11
19.50%	5,444.12	3,866.93	3,231.15	3,044.76	2,801.80	2,536.22	2,448.01	2,416.06	2,404.13	2,399.63
19.75%	5,462.86	3,887.36	3,253.25	3,067.64	2,826.12	2,563.34	2,476.85	2,445.87	2,434.43	2,430.16
20.00%	5,481.63	3,907.85	3,275.41	3,090.60	2,850.52	2,590.54	2,505.77	2,475.72	2,464.75	2,460.71
20.25%	5,500.44	3,928.39	3,297.65	3,113.63	2,875.01	2,617.82	2,534.74	2,505.61	2,495.10	2,491.27
20.50%	5,519.28	3,949.00	3,319.97	3,136.74	2,899.59	2,645.19	2,563.78	2,535.54	2,525.47	2,521.84
20.75%	5,538.16	3,969.66	3,342.35	3,159.93	2,924.25	2,672.63	2,592.87	2,565.50	2,555.86	2,552.43

$150,000   1.00 - 10.75%   3 - 35 Years

	3	5	7	8	10	15	20	25	30	35
1.00%	4,231.21	2,564.06	1,849.69	1,626.48	1,314.06	897.74	689.84	565.31	482.46	423.43
1.25%	4,247.45	2,580.24	1,865.91	1,642.74	1,330.40	914.33	706.70	582.45	499.88	441.13
1.50%	4,263.72	2,596.48	1,882.22	1,659.10	1,346.87	931.11	723.82	599.90	517.68	459.28
1.75%	4,280.04	2,612.79	1,898.62	1,675.56	1,363.47	948.09	741.19	617.68	535.87	477.87
2.00%	4,296.39	2,629.16	1,915.12	1,692.13	1,380.20	965.26	758.83	635.78	554.43	496.89
2.25%	4,312.78	2,645.60	1,931.70	1,708.80	1,397.06	982.63	776.71	654.20	573.37	516.35
2.50%	4,329.21	2,662.10	1,948.37	1,725.58	1,414.05	1,000.18	794.85	672.93	592.68	536.24
2.75%	4,345.67	2,678.67	1,965.14	1,742.45	1,431.17	1,017.93	813.25	691.97	612.36	556.55
3.00%	4,362.18	2,695.30	1,982.00	1,759.44	1,448.41	1,035.87	831.90	711.32	632.41	577.28
3.25%	4,378.73	2,712.00	1,998.94	1,776.52	1,465.79	1,054.00	850.79	730.97	652.81	598.41
3.50%	4,395.31	2,728.76	2,015.98	1,793.71	1,483.29	1,072.32	869.94	750.94	673.57	619.94
3.75%	4,411.94	2,745.59	2,033.10	1,811.00	1,500.92	1,090.83	889.33	771.20	694.67	641.86
4.00%	4,428.60	2,762.48	2,050.32	1,828.39	1,518.68	1,109.53	908.97	791.76	716.12	664.16
4.25%	4,445.30	2,779.43	2,067.63	1,845.89	1,536.56	1,128.42	928.85	812.61	737.91	686.84
4.50%	4,462.04	2,796.45	2,085.02	1,863.49	1,554.58	1,147.49	948.97	833.75	760.03	709.89
4.75%	4,478.82	2,813.54	2,102.51	1,881.19	1,572.72	1,166.75	969.34	855.18	782.47	733.29
5.00%	4,495.63	2,830.69	2,120.09	1,898.99	1,590.98	1,186.19	989.93	876.89	805.23	757.03
5.25%	4,512.49	2,847.90	2,137.75	1,916.89	1,609.38	1,205.82	1,010.77	898.87	828.31	781.11
5.50%	4,529.39	2,865.17	2,155.51	1,934.90	1,627.89	1,225.63	1,031.83	921.13	851.68	805.52
5.75%	4,546.32	2,882.52	2,173.35	1,953.01	1,646.54	1,245.62	1,053.13	943.66	875.36	830.25
6.00%	4,563.29	2,899.92	2,191.28	1,971.21	1,665.31	1,265.79	1,074.65	966.45	899.33	855.28
6.25%	4,580.30	2,917.39	2,209.30	1,989.52	1,684.20	1,286.13	1,096.39	989.50	923.58	880.61
6.50%	4,597.35	2,934.92	2,227.42	2,007.93	1,703.22	1,306.66	1,118.36	1,012.81	948.10	906.23
6.75%	4,614.44	2,952.52	2,245.61	2,026.45	1,722.36	1,327.36	1,140.55	1,036.37	972.90	932.12
7.00%	4,631.56	2,970.18	2,263.90	2,045.06	1,741.63	1,348.24	1,162.95	1,060.17	997.95	958.28
7.25%	4,648.73	2,987.90	2,282.28	2,063.77	1,761.02	1,369.29	1,185.56	1,084.21	1,023.26	984.70
7.50%	4,665.93	3,005.69	2,300.74	2,082.58	1,780.53	1,390.52	1,208.39	1,108.49	1,048.82	1,011.36
7.75%	4,683.17	3,023.54	2,319.29	2,101.49	1,800.16	1,411.91	1,231.42	1,132.99	1,074.62	1,038.26
8.00%	4,700.45	3,041.46	2,337.93	2,120.50	1,819.91	1,433.48	1,254.66	1,157.72	1,100.65	1,065.39
8.25%	4,717.77	3,059.44	2,356.66	2,139.61	1,839.79	1,455.21	1,278.10	1,182.68	1,126.90	1,092.74
8.50%	4,735.13	3,077.48	2,375.47	2,158.82	1,859.79	1,477.11	1,301.73	1,207.84	1,153.37	1,120.29
8.75%	4,752.53	3,095.58	2,394.37	2,178.13	1,879.90	1,499.17	1,325.57	1,233.22	1,180.05	1,148.04
9.00%	4,769.96	3,113.75	2,413.36	2,197.53	1,900.14	1,521.40	1,349.59	1,258.79	1,206.93	1,175.99
9.25%	4,787.43	3,131.98	2,432.44	2,217.03	1,920.49	1,543.79	1,373.80	1,284.57	1,234.01	1,204.12
9.50%	4,804.94	3,150.28	2,451.60	2,236.63	1,940.96	1,566.34	1,398.20	1,310.54	1,261.28	1,232.42
9.75%	4,822.49	3,168.64	2,470.84	2,256.33	1,961.55	1,589.04	1,422.78	1,336.71	1,288.73	1,260.88
10.00%	4,840.08	3,187.06	2,490.18	2,276.12	1,982.26	1,611.91	1,447.53	1,363.05	1,316.36	1,289.51
10.25%	4,857.70	3,205.54	2,509.60	2,296.02	2,003.09	1,634.93	1,472.47	1,389.57	1,344.15	1,318.28
10.50%	4,875.37	3,224.09	2,529.10	2,316.00	2,024.02	1,658.10	1,497.57	1,416.27	1,372.11	1,347.20
10.75%	4,893.07	3,242.69	2,548.69	2,336.09	2,045.08	1,681.42	1,522.84	1,443.14	1,400.22	1,376.25

$150,000   11.00 - 20.75%   3 - 35 Years

	3	5	7	8	10	15	20	25	30	35
11.00%	4,910.81	3,261.36	2,568.37	2,356.26	2,066.25	1,704.90	1,548.28	1,470.17	1,428.49	1,405.44
11.25%	4,928.59	3,280.10	2,588.13	2,376.54	2,087.53	1,728.52	1,573.88	1,497.36	1,456.89	1,434.74
11.50%	4,946.40	3,298.89	2,607.97	2,396.91	2,108.93	1,752.28	1,599.64	1,524.70	1,485.44	1,464.16
11.75%	4,964.25	3,317.75	2,627.90	2,417.37	2,130.44	1,776.20	1,625.56	1,552.20	1,514.11	1,493.69
12.00%	4,982.15	3,336.67	2,647.91	2,437.93	2,152.06	1,800.25	1,651.63	1,579.84	1,542.92	1,523.32
12.25%	5,000.08	3,355.65	2,668.01	2,458.58	2,173.80	1,824.45	1,677.85	1,607.62	1,571.84	1,553.06
12.50%	5,018.04	3,374.69	2,688.19	2,479.32	2,195.64	1,848.78	1,704.21	1,635.53	1,600.89	1,582.88
12.75%	5,036.05	3,393.80	2,708.45	2,500.16	2,217.60	1,873.26	1,730.72	1,663.58	1,630.04	1,612.79
13.00%	5,054.09	3,412.96	2,728.79	2,521.09	2,239.66	1,897.86	1,757.36	1,691.75	1,659.30	1,642.79
13.25%	5,072.17	3,432.19	2,749.22	2,542.11	2,261.83	1,922.60	1,784.15	1,720.05	1,688.66	1,672.86
13.50%	5,090.29	3,451.48	2,769.73	2,563.22	2,284.11	1,947.48	1,811.06	1,748.47	1,718.12	1,703.01
13.75%	5,108.45	3,470.83	2,790.33	2,584.43	2,306.50	1,972.48	1,838.11	1,777.00	1,747.67	1,733.23
14.00%	5,126.64	3,490.24	2,811.00	2,605.73	2,329.00	1,997.61	1,865.28	1,805.64	1,777.31	1,763.51
14.25%	5,144.88	3,509.71	2,831.76	2,627.11	2,351.60	2,022.87	1,892.58	1,834.39	1,807.03	1,793.85
14.50%	5,163.15	3,529.24	2,852.60	2,648.59	2,374.30	2,048.25	1,920.00	1,863.24	1,836.83	1,824.26
14.75%	5,181.45	3,548.84	2,873.51	2,670.16	2,397.11	2,073.76	1,947.53	1,892.20	1,866.71	1,854.71
15.00%	5,199.80	3,568.49	2,894.51	2,691.81	2,420.02	2,099.38	1,975.18	1,921.25	1,896.67	1,885.22
15.25%	5,218.18	3,588.20	2,915.59	2,713.56	2,443.04	2,125.12	2,002.95	1,950.39	1,926.69	1,915.78
15.50%	5,236.60	3,607.98	2,936.75	2,735.39	2,466.16	2,150.99	2,030.82	1,979.62	1,956.78	1,946.38
15.75%	5,255.06	3,627.81	2,957.99	2,757.31	2,489.38	2,176.96	2,058.80	2,008.93	1,986.93	1,977.01
16.00%	5,273.55	3,647.71	2,979.31	2,779.32	2,512.70	2,203.05	2,086.88	2,038.33	2,017.14	2,007.70
16.25%	5,292.09	3,667.66	3,000.71	2,801.41	2,536.12	2,229.25	2,115.07	2,067.81	2,047.40	2,038.42
16.50%	5,310.66	3,687.68	3,022.18	2,823.60	2,559.63	2,255.56	2,143.35	2,097.37	2,077.72	2,069.18
16.75%	5,329.26	3,707.75	3,043.74	2,845.86	2,583.25	2,281.98	2,171.73	2,127.00	2,108.09	2,099.97
17.00%	5,347.91	3,727.89	3,065.37	2,868.22	2,606.96	2,308.51	2,200.20	2,156.69	2,138.51	2,130.79
17.25%	5,366.59	3,748.08	3,087.08	2,890.66	2,630.78	2,335.14	2,228.76	2,186.46	2,168.98	2,161.64
17.50%	5,385.31	3,768.33	3,108.87	2,913.18	2,654.68	2,361.87	2,257.41	2,216.29	2,199.49	2,192.51
17.75%	5,404.07	3,788.64	3,130.73	2,935.79	2,678.68	2,388.70	2,286.15	2,246.19	2,230.04	2,223.41
18.00%	5,422.86	3,809.01	3,152.68	2,958.48	2,702.78	2,415.63	2,314.97	2,276.14	2,260.63	2,254.34
18.25%	5,441.69	3,829.44	3,174.69	2,981.26	2,726.97	2,442.66	2,343.87	2,306.16	2,291.25	2,285.28
18.50%	5,460.56	3,849.93	3,196.79	3,004.12	2,751.25	2,469.79	2,372.84	2,336.23	2,321.92	2,316.25
18.75%	5,479.46	3,870.48	3,218.96	3,027.06	2,775.62	2,497.00	2,401.90	2,366.35	2,352.61	2,347.24
19.00%	5,498.40	3,891.08	3,241.20	3,050.08	2,800.09	2,524.31	2,431.03	2,396.52	2,383.34	2,378.24
19.25%	5,517.38	3,911.75	3,263.52	3,073.18	2,824.64	2,551.72	2,460.23	2,426.74	2,414.10	2,409.26
19.50%	5,536.40	3,932.47	3,285.92	3,096.37	2,849.28	2,579.21	2,489.50	2,457.01	2,444.88	2,440.30
19.75%	5,555.45	3,953.25	3,308.39	3,119.63	2,874.02	2,606.78	2,518.83	2,487.32	2,475.69	2,471.35
20.00%	5,574.54	3,974.08	3,330.93	3,142.98	2,898.84	2,634.44	2,548.24	2,517.68	2,506.53	2,502.42
20.25%	5,593.66	3,994.98	3,353.55	3,166.40	2,923.74	2,662.19	2,577.70	2,548.07	2,537.39	2,533.50
20.50%	5,612.83	4,015.93	3,376.24	3,189.91	2,948.73	2,690.02	2,607.23	2,578.51	2,568.27	2,564.59
20.75%	5,632.02	4,036.94	3,399.00	3,213.49	2,973.81	2,717.93	2,636.82	2,608.98	2,599.18	2,595.69

	5	7	8	10	15	20	25	30	35	40
1.00%	2,649.53	1,911.34	1,680.70	1,357.86	927.67	712.84	584.15	498.54	437.54	391.93
1.25%	2,666.25	1,928.10	1,697.50	1,374.75	944.81	730.26	601.86	516.54	455.83	410.51
1.50%	2,683.03	1,944.96	1,714.40	1,391.77	962.15	747.95	619.90	534.94	474.59	429.62
1.75%	2,699.88	1,961.91	1,731.42	1,408.92	979.70	765.90	638.27	553.73	493.80	449.24
2.00%	2,716.80	1,978.95	1,748.54	1,426.21	997.44	784.12	656.97	572.91	513.46	469.38
2.25%	2,733.79	1,996.09	1,765.76	1,443.63	1,015.38	802.60	676.00	592.48	533.57	490.02
2.50%	2,750.84	2,013.32	1,783.10	1,461.18	1,033.52	821.35	695.36	612.44	554.12	511.16
2.75%	2,767.96	2,030.64	1,800.54	1,478.87	1,051.86	840.36	715.03	632.77	575.10	532.78
3.00%	2,785.15	2,048.06	1,818.08	1,496.69	1,070.40	859.63	735.03	653.49	596.52	554.88
3.25%	2,802.40	2,065.57	1,835.74	1,514.64	1,089.14	879.15	755.34	674.57	618.35	577.44
3.50%	2,819.72	2,083.18	1,853.50	1,532.73	1,108.07	898.94	775.97	696.02	640.60	600.46
3.75%	2,837.11	2,100.87	1,871.36	1,550.95	1,127.19	918.98	796.90	717.83	663.25	623.92
4.00%	2,854.56	2,118.66	1,889.34	1,569.30	1,146.52	939.27	818.15	739.99	686.30	647.80
4.25%	2,872.08	2,136.55	1,907.42	1,587.78	1,166.03	959.81	839.69	762.51	709.74	672.11
4.50%	2,889.67	2,154.53	1,925.60	1,606.40	1,185.74	980.61	861.54	785.36	733.55	696.82
4.75%	2,907.32	2,172.59	1,943.89	1,625.14	1,205.64	1,001.65	883.68	808.55	757.73	721.92
5.00%	2,925.04	2,190.76	1,962.29	1,644.02	1,225.73	1,022.93	906.11	832.07	782.27	747.40
5.25%	2,942.83	2,209.01	1,980.79	1,663.02	1,246.01	1,044.46	928.83	855.92	807.15	773.25
5.50%	2,960.68	2,227.36	1,999.39	1,682.16	1,266.48	1,066.23	951.84	880.07	832.38	799.44
5.75%	2,978.60	2,245.80	2,018.11	1,701.42	1,287.14	1,088.23	975.11	904.54	857.93	825.98
6.00%	2,996.58	2,264.33	2,036.92	1,720.82	1,307.98	1,110.47	998.67	929.30	883.79	852.83
6.25%	3,014.64	2,282.95	2,055.84	1,740.34	1,329.01	1,132.94	1,022.49	954.36	909.97	880.00
6.50%	3,032.75	2,301.66	2,074.87	1,759.99	1,350.22	1,155.64	1,046.57	979.71	936.44	907.46
6.75%	3,050.94	2,320.47	2,093.99	1,779.77	1,371.61	1,178.56	1,070.91	1,005.33	963.20	935.20
7.00%	3,069.19	2,339.37	2,113.23	1,799.68	1,393.18	1,201.71	1,095.51	1,031.22	990.23	963.22
7.25%	3,087.50	2,358.35	2,132.56	1,819.72	1,414.94	1,225.08	1,120.35	1,057.37	1,017.52	991.49
7.50%	3,105.88	2,377.43	2,152.00	1,839.88	1,436.87	1,248.67	1,145.44	1,083.78	1,045.08	1,020.01
7.75%	3,124.33	2,396.60	2,171.54	1,860.16	1,458.98	1,272.47	1,170.76	1,110.44	1,072.87	1,048.76
8.00%	3,142.84	2,415.86	2,191.19	1,880.58	1,481.26	1,296.48	1,196.32	1,137.34	1,100.90	1,077.73
8.25%	3,161.42	2,435.21	2,210.93	1,901.12	1,503.72	1,320.70	1,222.10	1,164.46	1,129.16	1,106.92
8.50%	3,180.06	2,454.66	2,230.78	1,921.78	1,526.35	1,345.13	1,248.10	1,191.82	1,157.63	1,136.30
8.75%	3,198.77	2,474.19	2,250.73	1,942.56	1,549.15	1,369.75	1,274.32	1,219.39	1,186.31	1,165.86
9.00%	3,217.55	2,493.81	2,270.78	1,963.47	1,572.11	1,394.58	1,300.75	1,247.17	1,215.19	1,195.61
9.25%	3,236.38	2,513.52	2,290.93	1,984.51	1,595.25	1,419.59	1,327.39	1,275.15	1,244.25	1,225.52
9.50%	3,255.29	2,533.32	2,311.19	2,005.66	1,618.55	1,444.80	1,354.23	1,303.32	1,273.50	1,255.60
9.75%	3,274.26	2,553.21	2,331.54	2,026.94	1,642.01	1,470.20	1,381.26	1,331.69	1,302.91	1,285.82
10.00%	3,293.29	2,573.18	2,352.00	2,048.34	1,665.64	1,495.78	1,408.49	1,360.24	1,332.49	1,316.18
10.25%	3,312.39	2,593.25	2,372.55	2,069.85	1,689.42	1,521.55	1,435.89	1,388.96	1,362.23	1,346.67
10.50%	3,331.55	2,613.40	2,393.20	2,091.49	1,713.37	1,547.49	1,463.48	1,417.85	1,392.11	1,377.28
10.75%	3,350.78	2,633.65	2,413.95	2,113.25	1,737.47	1,573.60	1,491.24	1,446.90	1,422.13	1,408.02

$155,000   11.00 - 20.75%   5 - 40 Years

	5	7	8	10	15	20	25	30	35	40
11.00%	3,370.08	2,653.98	2,434.81	2,135.13	1,761.73	1,599.89	1,519.18	1,476.10	1,452.28	1,438.86
11.25%	3,389.43	2,674.40	2,455.76	2,157.12	1,786.13	1,626.35	1,547.27	1,505.46	1,482.57	1,469.80
11.50%	3,408.85	2,694.90	2,476.80	2,179.23	1,810.69	1,652.97	1,575.53	1,534.95	1,512.97	1,500.84
11.75%	3,428.34	2,715.49	2,497.95	2,201.46	1,835.40	1,679.75	1,603.94	1,564.59	1,543.48	1,531.96
12.00%	3,447.89	2,736.17	2,519.19	2,223.80	1,860.26	1,706.68	1,632.50	1,594.35	1,574.10	1,563.17
12.25%	3,467.50	2,756.94	2,540.53	2,246.26	1,885.26	1,733.78	1,661.20	1,624.24	1,604.83	1,594.46
12.50%	3,487.18	2,777.79	2,561.97	2,268.83	1,910.41	1,761.02	1,690.05	1,654.25	1,635.64	1,625.83
12.75%	3,506.92	2,798.73	2,583.50	2,291.52	1,935.70	1,788.41	1,719.03	1,684.37	1,666.55	1,657.25
13.00%	3,526.73	2,819.75	2,605.12	2,314.32	1,961.13	1,815.94	1,748.14	1,714.61	1,697.55	1,688.75
13.25%	3,546.59	2,840.86	2,626.85	2,337.23	1,986.69	1,843.62	1,777.39	1,744.95	1,728.63	1,720.30
13.50%	3,566.53	2,862.06	2,648.66	2,360.25	2,012.39	1,871.43	1,806.75	1,775.39	1,759.78	1,751.90
13.75%	3,586.52	2,883.34	2,670.58	2,383.39	2,038.23	1,899.38	1,836.23	1,805.92	1,791.00	1,783.56
14.00%	3,606.58	2,904.70	2,692.58	2,406.63	2,064.20	1,927.46	1,865.83	1,836.55	1,822.29	1,815.27
14.25%	3,626.70	2,926.15	2,714.68	2,429.98	2,090.30	1,955.66	1,895.54	1,867.26	1,853.65	1,847.02
14.50%	3,646.88	2,947.68	2,736.87	2,453.45	2,116.53	1,984.00	1,925.35	1,898.06	1,885.06	1,878.81
14.75%	3,667.13	2,969.30	2,759.16	2,477.02	2,142.88	2,012.45	1,955.27	1,928.94	1,916.54	1,910.63
15.00%	3,687.44	2,991.00	2,781.54	2,500.69	2,169.36	2,041.02	1,985.29	1,959.89	1,948.06	1,942.50
15.25%	3,707.81	3,012.78	2,804.01	2,524.47	2,195.96	2,069.71	2,015.40	1,990.91	1,979.64	1,974.39
15.50%	3,728.24	3,034.64	2,826.57	2,548.36	2,222.69	2,098.52	2,045.61	2,022.00	2,011.26	2,006.32
15.75%	3,748.74	3,056.59	2,849.22	2,572.36	2,249.53	2,127.43	2,075.90	2,053.16	2,042.92	2,038.27
16.00%	3,769.30	3,078.62	2,871.96	2,596.45	2,276.49	2,156.45	2,106.28	2,084.37	2,074.63	2,070.26
16.25%	3,789.92	3,100.73	2,894.79	2,620.65	2,303.56	2,185.57	2,136.74	2,115.65	2,106.37	2,102.26
16.50%	3,810.60	3,122.92	2,917.72	2,644.96	2,330.75	2,214.80	2,167.28	2,146.98	2,138.15	2,134.29
16.75%	3,831.34	3,145.20	2,940.73	2,669.36	2,358.05	2,244.12	2,197.90	2,178.36	2,169.97	2,166.33
17.00%	3,852.15	3,167.55	2,963.83	2,693.86	2,385.46	2,273.54	2,228.58	2,209.80	2,201.82	2,198.40
17.25%	3,873.02	3,189.98	2,987.01	2,718.47	2,412.97	2,303.05	2,259.34	2,241.28	2,233.69	2,230.49
17.50%	3,893.94	3,212.50	3,010.29	2,743.17	2,440.60	2,332.66	2,290.17	2,272.80	2,265.60	2,262.59
17.75%	3,914.93	3,235.09	3,033.65	2,767.97	2,468.32	2,362.35	2,321.06	2,304.37	2,297.53	2,294.70
18.00%	3,935.98	3,257.76	3,057.10	2,792.87	2,496.15	2,392.13	2,352.02	2,335.98	2,329.48	2,326.83
18.25%	3,957.09	3,280.52	3,080.63	2,817.87	2,524.08	2,422.00	2,383.03	2,367.63	2,361.46	2,358.98
18.50%	3,978.26	3,303.35	3,104.25	2,842.96	2,552.11	2,451.94	2,414.10	2,399.31	2,393.46	2,391.13
18.75%	3,999.49	3,326.26	3,127.96	2,868.14	2,580.24	2,481.96	2,445.23	2,431.03	2,425.48	2,423.30
19.00%	4,020.79	3,349.24	3,151.75	2,893.42	2,608.46	2,512.06	2,476.40	2,462.78	2,457.52	2,455.47
19.25%	4,042.14	3,372.31	3,175.62	2,918.79	2,636.77	2,542.23	2,507.63	2,494.57	2,489.57	2,487.66
19.50%	4,063.55	3,395.45	3,199.58	2,944.26	2,665.18	2,572.48	2,538.91	2,526.38	2,521.64	2,519.85
19.75%	4,085.02	3,418.67	3,223.62	2,969.82	2,693.67	2,602.80	2,570.23	2,558.21	2,553.73	2,552.05
20.00%	4,106.55	3,441.96	3,247.75	2,995.46	2,722.26	2,633.18	2,601.60	2,590.08	2,585.83	2,584.26
20.25%	4,128.14	3,465.33	3,271.95	3,021.20	2,750.93	2,663.63	2,633.01	2,621.97	2,617.95	2,616.47
20.50%	4,149.79	3,488.78	3,296.24	3,047.03	2,779.69	2,694.14	2,664.46	2,653.88	2,650.07	2,648.70
20.75%	4,171.50	3,512.30	3,320.61	3,072.94	2,808.53	2,724.71	2,695.95	2,685.81	2,682.21	2,680.92

$160,000   1.00 - 10.75%   5 - 40 Years

	5	7	8	10	15	20	25	30	35	40
1.00%	2,735.00	1,973.00	1,734.92	1,401.67	957.59	735.83	603.00	514.62	451.66	404.57
1.25%	2,752.24	1,990.30	1,752.26	1,419.10	975.29	753.81	621.28	533.20	470.54	423.75
1.50%	2,769.58	2,007.70	1,769.71	1,436.66	993.19	772.07	639.90	552.19	489.90	443.48
1.75%	2,786.98	2,025.20	1,787.27	1,454.37	1,011.30	790.61	658.86	571.59	509.72	463.73
2.00%	2,804.44	2,042.79	1,804.94	1,472.22	1,029.61	809.41	678.17	591.39	530.02	484.52
2.25%	2,821.98	2,060.48	1,822.72	1,490.20	1,048.14	828.49	697.81	611.59	550.78	505.83
2.50%	2,839.58	2,078.27	1,840.61	1,508.32	1,066.86	847.84	717.79	632.19	571.99	527.65
2.75%	2,857.25	2,096.15	1,858.62	1,526.58	1,085.79	867.47	738.10	653.19	593.66	549.96
3.00%	2,874.99	2,114.13	1,876.73	1,544.97	1,104.93	887.36	758.74	674.57	615.76	572.78
3.25%	2,892.80	2,132.20	1,894.95	1,563.50	1,124.27	907.51	779.71	696.33	638.30	596.07
3.50%	2,910.68	2,150.38	1,913.29	1,582.17	1,143.81	927.94	801.00	718.47	661.27	619.83
3.75%	2,928.63	2,168.64	1,931.73	1,600.98	1,163.56	948.62	822.61	740.98	684.65	644.04
4.00%	2,946.64	2,187.01	1,950.28	1,619.92	1,183.50	969.57	844.54	763.86	708.44	668.70
4.25%	2,964.73	2,205.47	1,968.95	1,639.00	1,203.65	990.78	866.78	787.10	732.63	693.79
4.50%	2,982.88	2,224.03	1,987.72	1,658.21	1,223.99	1,012.24	889.33	810.70	757.21	719.30
4.75%	3,001.11	2,242.68	2,006.60	1,677.56	1,244.53	1,033.96	912.19	834.64	782.17	745.21
5.00%	3,019.40	2,261.43	2,025.59	1,697.05	1,265.27	1,055.93	935.34	858.91	807.50	771.51
5.25%	3,037.76	2,280.27	2,044.69	1,716.67	1,286.20	1,078.15	958.80	883.53	833.19	798.19
5.50%	3,056.19	2,299.21	2,063.89	1,736.42	1,307.33	1,100.62	982.54	908.46	859.23	825.23
5.75%	3,074.68	2,318.24	2,083.21	1,756.31	1,328.66	1,123.33	1,006.57	933.72	885.60	852.62
6.00%	3,093.25	2,337.37	2,102.63	1,776.33	1,350.17	1,146.29	1,030.88	959.28	912.30	880.34
6.25%	3,111.88	2,356.59	2,122.16	1,796.48	1,371.88	1,169.49	1,055.47	985.15	939.32	908.38
6.50%	3,130.58	2,375.91	2,141.80	1,816.77	1,393.77	1,192.92	1,080.33	1,011.31	966.65	936.73
6.75%	3,149.35	2,395.32	2,161.54	1,837.19	1,415.86	1,216.58	1,105.46	1,037.76	994.27	965.37
7.00%	3,168.19	2,414.83	2,181.39	1,857.74	1,438.13	1,240.48	1,130.85	1,064.48	1,022.17	994.29
7.25%	3,187.10	2,434.43	2,201.35	1,878.42	1,460.58	1,264.60	1,156.49	1,091.48	1,050.35	1,023.48
7.50%	3,206.07	2,454.12	2,221.42	1,899.23	1,483.22	1,288.95	1,182.39	1,118.74	1,078.79	1,052.91
7.75%	3,225.11	2,473.91	2,241.59	1,920.17	1,506.04	1,313.52	1,208.53	1,146.26	1,107.48	1,082.59
8.00%	3,244.22	2,493.79	2,261.87	1,941.24	1,529.04	1,338.30	1,234.91	1,174.02	1,136.42	1,112.50
8.25%	3,263.40	2,513.77	2,282.25	1,962.44	1,552.22	1,363.31	1,261.52	1,202.03	1,165.59	1,142.62
8.50%	3,282.65	2,533.84	2,302.74	1,983.77	1,575.58	1,388.52	1,288.36	1,230.26	1,194.98	1,172.95
8.75%	3,301.96	2,554.00	2,323.33	2,005.23	1,599.12	1,413.94	1,315.43	1,258.72	1,224.58	1,203.47
9.00%	3,321.34	2,574.25	2,344.03	2,026.81	1,622.83	1,439.56	1,342.71	1,287.40	1,254.39	1,234.18
9.25%	3,340.78	2,594.60	2,364.84	2,048.52	1,646.71	1,465.39	1,370.21	1,316.28	1,284.39	1,265.06
9.50%	3,360.30	2,615.04	2,385.74	2,070.36	1,670.76	1,491.41	1,397.91	1,345.37	1,314.58	1,296.10
9.75%	3,379.88	2,635.57	2,406.75	2,092.32	1,694.98	1,517.63	1,425.82	1,374.65	1,344.94	1,327.29
10.00%	3,399.53	2,656.19	2,427.87	2,114.41	1,719.37	1,544.03	1,453.92	1,404.11	1,375.48	1,358.63
10.25%	3,419.24	2,676.90	2,449.08	2,136.62	1,743.92	1,570.63	1,482.21	1,433.76	1,406.17	1,390.11
10.50%	3,439.02	2,697.71	2,470.40	2,158.96	1,768.64	1,597.41	1,510.69	1,463.58	1,437.01	1,421.71
10.75%	3,458.87	2,718.60	2,491.82	2,181.42	1,793.52	1,624.37	1,539.35	1,493.57	1,468.00	1,453.44

	5	7	8	10	15	20	25	30	35	40
11.00%	3,478.79	2,739.59	2,513.35	2,204.00	1,818.56	1,651.50	1,568.18	1,523.72	1,499.13	1,485.27
11.25%	3,498.77	2,760.67	2,534.97	2,226.70	1,843.75	1,678.81	1,597.18	1,554.02	1,530.39	1,517.21
11.50%	3,518.82	2,781.83	2,556.70	2,249.53	1,869.10	1,706.29	1,626.35	1,584.47	1,561.77	1,549.25
11.75%	3,538.93	2,803.09	2,578.53	2,272.47	1,894.61	1,733.93	1,655.68	1,615.06	1,593.27	1,581.38
12.00%	3,559.11	2,824.44	2,600.45	2,295.54	1,920.27	1,761.74	1,685.16	1,645.78	1,624.88	1,613.60
12.25%	3,579.36	2,845.87	2,622.48	2,318.72	1,946.08	1,789.70	1,714.79	1,676.63	1,656.59	1,645.90
12.50%	3,599.67	2,867.40	2,644.61	2,342.02	1,972.04	1,817.82	1,744.57	1,707.61	1,688.41	1,678.27
12.75%	3,620.05	2,889.01	2,666.84	2,365.44	1,998.14	1,846.10	1,774.48	1,738.71	1,720.31	1,710.71
13.00%	3,640.49	2,910.71	2,689.16	2,388.97	2,024.39	1,874.52	1,804.54	1,769.92	1,752.31	1,743.22
13.25%	3,661.00	2,932.50	2,711.58	2,412.62	2,050.78	1,903.09	1,834.72	1,801.24	1,784.39	1,775.79
13.50%	3,681.58	2,954.38	2,734.11	2,436.39	2,077.31	1,931.80	1,865.03	1,832.66	1,816.54	1,808.42
13.75%	3,702.22	2,976.35	2,756.72	2,460.27	2,103.98	1,960.65	1,895.47	1,864.18	1,848.78	1,841.10
14.00%	3,722.92	2,998.40	2,779.44	2,484.26	2,130.79	1,989.63	1,926.02	1,895.79	1,881.08	1,873.82
14.25%	3,743.69	3,020.54	2,802.25	2,508.37	2,157.73	2,018.75	1,956.68	1,927.50	1,913.44	1,906.60
14.50%	3,764.52	3,042.77	2,825.16	2,532.59	2,184.80	2,048.00	1,987.46	1,959.29	1,945.87	1,939.41
14.75%	3,785.42	3,065.08	2,848.17	2,556.92	2,212.01	2,077.37	2,018.34	1,991.16	1,978.36	1,972.27
15.00%	3,806.39	3,087.48	2,871.26	2,581.36	2,239.34	2,106.86	2,049.33	2,023.11	2,010.90	2,005.16
15.25%	3,827.42	3,109.97	2,894.46	2,605.91	2,266.80	2,136.48	2,080.41	2,055.13	2,043.49	2,038.08
15.50%	3,848.51	3,132.54	2,917.75	2,630.57	2,294.38	2,166.21	2,111.59	2,087.23	2,076.14	2,071.04
15.75%	3,869.67	3,155.19	2,941.13	2,655.34	2,322.09	2,196.05	2,142.86	2,119.39	2,108.82	2,104.03
16.00%	3,890.89	3,177.93	2,964.61	2,680.21	2,349.92	2,226.01	2,174.22	2,151.61	2,141.55	2,137.04
16.25%	3,912.17	3,200.75	2,988.17	2,705.19	2,377.87	2,256.07	2,205.67	2,183.90	2,174.32	2,170.07
16.50%	3,933.52	3,223.66	3,011.84	2,730.28	2,405.93	2,286.24	2,237.19	2,216.24	2,207.13	2,203.13
16.75%	3,954.94	3,246.65	3,035.59	2,755.47	2,434.11	2,316.51	2,268.80	2,248.63	2,239.97	2,236.22
17.00%	3,976.41	3,269.73	3,059.43	2,780.76	2,462.41	2,346.88	2,300.47	2,281.08	2,272.84	2,269.32
17.25%	3,997.95	3,292.89	3,083.37	2,806.16	2,490.81	2,377.35	2,332.23	2,313.58	2,305.75	2,302.44
17.50%	4,019.55	3,316.13	3,107.39	2,831.66	2,519.33	2,407.91	2,364.05	2,346.12	2,338.68	2,335.57
17.75%	4,041.22	3,339.45	3,131.51	2,857.26	2,547.95	2,438.56	2,395.94	2,378.71	2,371.64	2,368.73
18.00%	4,062.95	3,362.85	3,155.71	2,882.96	2,576.67	2,469.30	2,427.89	2,411.34	2,404.63	2,401.89
18.25%	4,084.74	3,386.34	3,180.01	2,908.76	2,605.50	2,500.12	2,459.90	2,444.01	2,437.64	2,435.07
18.50%	4,106.59	3,409.91	3,204.39	2,934.66	2,634.44	2,531.03	2,491.97	2,476.71	2,470.67	2,468.26
18.75%	4,128.51	3,433.55	3,228.86	2,960.66	2,663.47	2,562.03	2,524.10	2,509.45	2,503.72	2,501.47
19.00%	4,150.49	3,457.28	3,253.42	2,986.76	2,692.60	2,593.10	2,556.29	2,542.23	2,536.79	2,534.69
19.25%	4,172.53	3,481.09	3,278.06	3,012.95	2,721.83	2,624.24	2,588.52	2,575.03	2,569.88	2,567.90
19.50%	4,194.63	3,504.98	3,302.79	3,039.24	2,751.15	2,655.46	2,620.81	2,607.87	2,602.99	2,601.13
19.75%	4,216.80	3,528.95	3,327.61	3,065.62	2,780.57	2,686.76	2,653.14	2,640.74	2,636.11	2,634.37
20.00%	4,239.02	3,552.99	3,352.51	3,092.09	2,810.07	2,718.12	2,685.52	2,673.63	2,669.25	2,667.62
20.25%	4,261.31	3,577.12	3,377.50	3,118.66	2,839.67	2,749.55	2,717.95	2,706.55	2,702.40	2,700.88
20.50%	4,283.66	3,601.32	3,402.57	3,145.32	2,869.35	2,781.05	2,750.41	2,739.49	2,735.56	2,734.14
20.75%	4,306.07	3,625.60	3,427.72	3,172.07	2,899.13	2,812.61	2,782.92	2,772.45	2,768.73	2,767.40

$165,000   1.00 - 10.75%   5 - 40 Years

	5	7	8	10	15	20	25	30	35	40
1.00%	2,820.47	2,034.66	1,789.13	1,445.47	987.52	758.83	621.84	530.71	465.77	417.21
1.25%	2,838.26	2,052.50	1,807.01	1,463.44	1,005.76	777.37	640.69	549.87	485.24	436.99
1.50%	2,856.13	2,070.44	1,825.01	1,481.56	1,024.23	796.20	659.89	569.45	505.20	457.33
1.75%	2,874.07	2,088.48	1,843.12	1,499.82	1,042.90	815.31	679.45	589.45	525.65	478.23
2.00%	2,892.08	2,106.63	1,861.34	1,518.22	1,061.79	834.71	699.36	609.87	546.58	499.66
2.25%	2,910.16	2,124.87	1,879.68	1,536.77	1,080.89	854.38	719.62	630.71	567.99	521.63
2.50%	2,928.31	2,143.21	1,898.13	1,555.45	1,100.20	874.34	740.22	651.95	589.87	544.13
2.75%	2,946.54	2,161.65	1,916.70	1,574.28	1,119.73	894.57	761.16	673.60	612.21	567.15
3.00%	2,964.83	2,180.19	1,935.38	1,593.25	1,139.46	915.09	782.45	695.65	635.00	590.67
3.25%	2,983.20	2,198.84	1,954.17	1,612.36	1,159.40	935.87	804.07	718.09	658.25	614.69
3.50%	3,001.64	2,217.58	1,973.08	1,631.62	1,179.56	956.93	826.03	740.92	681.93	639.20
3.75%	3,020.15	2,236.41	1,992.10	1,651.01	1,199.92	978.27	848.32	764.14	706.04	664.17
4.00%	3,038.73	2,255.35	2,011.23	1,670.54	1,220.49	999.87	870.93	787.74	730.58	689.60
4.25%	3,057.38	2,274.39	2,030.48	1,690.22	1,241.26	1,021.74	893.87	811.70	755.53	715.47
4.50%	3,076.10	2,293.53	2,049.83	1,710.03	1,262.24	1,043.87	917.12	836.03	780.87	741.78
4.75%	3,094.89	2,312.76	2,069.30	1,729.99	1,283.42	1,066.27	940.69	860.72	806.61	768.50
5.00%	3,113.75	2,332.09	2,088.89	1,750.08	1,304.81	1,088.93	964.57	885.76	832.73	795.62
5.25%	3,132.69	2,351.53	2,108.58	1,770.31	1,326.40	1,111.84	988.76	911.14	859.23	823.14
5.50%	3,151.69	2,371.06	2,128.39	1,790.68	1,348.19	1,135.01	1,013.24	936.85	886.08	851.02
5.75%	3,170.77	2,390.69	2,148.31	1,811.19	1,370.18	1,158.44	1,038.03	962.90	913.28	879.26
6.00%	3,189.91	2,410.41	2,168.34	1,831.84	1,392.36	1,182.11	1,063.10	989.26	940.81	907.85
6.25%	3,209.13	2,430.24	2,188.48	1,852.62	1,414.75	1,206.03	1,088.45	1,015.93	968.68	936.77
6.50%	3,228.41	2,450.16	2,208.73	1,873.54	1,437.33	1,230.20	1,114.09	1,042.91	996.85	966.00
6.75%	3,247.77	2,470.18	2,229.09	1,894.60	1,460.10	1,254.60	1,140.00	1,070.19	1,025.34	995.54
7.00%	3,267.20	2,490.29	2,249.56	1,915.79	1,483.07	1,279.24	1,166.19	1,097.75	1,054.11	1,025.36
7.25%	3,286.69	2,510.51	2,270.15	1,937.12	1,506.22	1,304.12	1,192.63	1,125.59	1,083.17	1,055.46
7.50%	3,306.26	2,530.82	2,290.84	1,958.58	1,529.57	1,329.23	1,219.34	1,153.70	1,112.50	1,085.82
7.75%	3,325.90	2,551.22	2,311.64	1,980.18	1,553.10	1,354.57	1,246.29	1,182.08	1,142.09	1,116.42
8.00%	3,345.61	2,571.73	2,332.55	2,001.91	1,576.83	1,380.13	1,273.50	1,210.71	1,171.93	1,147.26
8.25%	3,365.38	2,592.32	2,353.57	2,023.77	1,600.73	1,405.91	1,300.94	1,239.59	1,202.01	1,178.33
8.50%	3,385.23	2,613.02	2,374.70	2,045.76	1,624.82	1,431.91	1,328.62	1,268.71	1,232.32	1,209.61
8.75%	3,405.14	2,633.81	2,395.94	2,067.89	1,649.09	1,458.12	1,356.54	1,298.06	1,262.85	1,241.08
9.00%	3,425.13	2,654.70	2,417.28	2,090.15	1,673.54	1,484.55	1,384.67	1,327.63	1,293.59	1,272.75
9.25%	3,445.18	2,675.68	2,438.74	2,112.54	1,698.17	1,511.18	1,413.03	1,357.41	1,324.53	1,304.59
9.50%	3,465.31	2,696.76	2,460.30	2,135.06	1,722.97	1,538.02	1,441.60	1,387.41	1,355.66	1,336.60
9.75%	3,485.50	2,717.93	2,481.96	2,157.71	1,747.95	1,565.05	1,470.38	1,417.60	1,386.97	1,368.77
10.00%	3,505.76	2,739.20	2,503.74	2,180.49	1,773.10	1,592.29	1,499.36	1,447.99	1,418.46	1,401.09
10.25%	3,526.09	2,760.56	2,525.62	2,203.39	1,798.42	1,619.71	1,528.53	1,478.57	1,450.11	1,433.55
10.50%	3,546.49	2,782.01	2,547.60	2,226.43	1,823.91	1,647.33	1,557.90	1,509.32	1,481.92	1,466.14
10.75%	3,566.96	2,803.56	2,569.69	2,249.59	1,849.56	1,675.13	1,587.45	1,540.24	1,513.88	1,498.86

$165,000   11.00 - 20.75%   5 - 40 Years

	5	7	8	10	15	20	25	30	35	40
11.00%	3,587.50	2,825.20	2,591.89	2,272.88	1,875.38	1,703.11	1,617.19	1,571.33	1,545.98	1,531.69
11.25%	3,608.11	2,846.94	2,614.19	2,296.29	1,901.37	1,731.27	1,647.10	1,602.58	1,578.21	1,564.62
11.50%	3,628.78	2,868.77	2,636.60	2,319.82	1,927.51	1,759.61	1,677.17	1,633.98	1,610.58	1,597.67
11.75%	3,649.52	2,890.69	2,659.11	2,343.49	1,953.82	1,788.12	1,707.42	1,665.53	1,643.06	1,630.80
12.00%	3,670.33	2,912.70	2,681.72	2,367.27	1,980.28	1,816.79	1,737.82	1,697.21	1,675.66	1,664.02
12.25%	3,691.21	2,934.81	2,704.43	2,391.18	2,006.89	1,845.63	1,768.38	1,729.03	1,708.36	1,697.33
12.50%	3,712.16	2,957.00	2,727.25	2,415.21	2,033.66	1,874.63	1,799.08	1,760.98	1,741.17	1,730.72
12.75%	3,733.17	2,979.29	2,750.17	2,439.36	2,060.58	1,903.79	1,829.94	1,793.04	1,774.07	1,764.17
13.00%	3,754.26	3,001.67	2,773.20	2,463.63	2,087.65	1,933.10	1,860.93	1,825.23	1,807.07	1,797.70
13.25%	3,775.41	3,024.15	2,796.32	2,488.02	2,114.87	1,962.56	1,892.06	1,857.53	1,840.15	1,831.29
13.50%	3,796.62	3,046.71	2,819.55	2,512.53	2,142.23	1,992.17	1,923.31	1,889.93	1,873.31	1,864.93
13.75%	3,817.91	3,069.36	2,842.87	2,537.15	2,169.73	2,021.92	1,954.70	1,922.44	1,906.55	1,898.63
14.00%	3,839.26	3,092.10	2,866.30	2,561.90	2,197.37	2,051.81	1,986.21	1,955.04	1,939.86	1,932.38
14.25%	3,860.68	3,114.93	2,889.82	2,586.76	2,225.16	2,081.84	2,017.83	1,987.73	1,973.24	1,966.18
14.50%	3,882.17	3,137.86	2,913.45	2,611.73	2,253.08	2,112.00	2,049.57	2,020.52	2,006.68	2,000.02
14.75%	3,903.72	3,160.87	2,937.17	2,636.82	2,281.13	2,142.29	2,081.42	2,053.38	2,040.18	2,033.90
15.00%	3,925.34	3,183.96	2,960.99	2,662.03	2,309.32	2,172.70	2,113.37	2,086.33	2,073.74	2,067.82
15.25%	3,947.02	3,207.15	2,984.91	2,687.34	2,337.64	2,203.24	2,145.43	2,119.36	2,107.35	2,101.77
15.50%	3,968.78	3,230.43	3,008.93	2,712.77	2,366.08	2,233.90	2,177.58	2,152.45	2,141.01	2,135.76
15.75%	3,990.59	3,253.79	3,033.04	2,738.31	2,394.66	2,264.68	2,209.83	2,185.62	2,174.72	2,169.78
16.00%	4,012.48	3,277.24	3,057.25	2,763.97	2,423.36	2,295.57	2,242.17	2,218.85	2,208.47	2,203.82
16.25%	4,034.43	3,300.78	3,081.55	2,789.73	2,452.18	2,326.58	2,274.59	2,252.14	2,242.27	2,237.89
16.50%	4,056.45	3,324.40	3,105.96	2,815.60	2,481.12	2,357.69	2,307.10	2,285.49	2,276.10	2,271.98
16.75%	4,078.53	3,348.11	3,130.45	2,841.58	2,510.18	2,388.90	2,339.70	2,318.90	2,309.97	2,306.10
17.00%	4,100.68	3,371.91	3,155.04	2,867.66	2,539.36	2,420.22	2,372.36	2,352.36	2,343.87	2,340.23
17.25%	4,122.89	3,395.79	3,179.72	2,893.85	2,568.65	2,451.64	2,405.11	2,385.88	2,377.80	2,374.39
17.50%	4,145.17	3,419.76	3,204.50	2,920.15	2,598.05	2,483.15	2,437.92	2,419.44	2,411.76	2,408.56
17.75%	4,167.51	3,443.81	3,229.37	2,946.55	2,627.57	2,514.76	2,470.81	2,453.04	2,445.76	2,442.75
18.00%	4,189.92	3,467.94	3,254.33	2,973.06	2,657.19	2,546.46	2,503.76	2,486.69	2,479.77	2,476.95
18.25%	4,212.39	3,492.16	3,279.38	2,999.66	2,686.93	2,578.25	2,536.77	2,520.38	2,513.81	2,511.17
18.50%	4,234.92	3,516.47	3,304.53	3,026.37	2,716.76	2,610.13	2,569.85	2,554.11	2,547.88	2,545.40
18.75%	4,257.53	3,540.85	3,329.76	3,053.18	2,746.70	2,642.09	2,602.98	2,587.87	2,581.96	2,579.64
19.00%	4,280.19	3,565.32	3,355.09	3,080.09	2,776.75	2,674.13	2,636.17	2,621.67	2,616.07	2,613.89
19.25%	4,302.92	3,589.88	3,380.50	3,107.10	2,806.89	2,706.25	2,669.42	2,655.50	2,650.19	2,648.15
19.50%	4,325.71	3,614.51	3,406.01	3,134.21	2,837.13	2,738.45	2,702.71	2,689.37	2,684.33	2,682.42
19.75%	4,348.57	3,639.23	3,431.60	3,161.42	2,867.46	2,770.72	2,736.05	2,723.26	2,718.49	2,716.70
20.00%	4,371.49	3,664.02	3,457.28	3,188.72	2,897.89	2,803.06	2,769.45	2,757.18	2,752.66	2,750.99
20.25%	4,394.47	3,688.90	3,483.05	3,216.12	2,928.41	2,835.47	2,802.88	2,791.13	2,786.85	2,785.28
20.50%	4,417.52	3,713.86	3,508.90	3,243.61	2,959.02	2,867.95	2,836.36	2,825.10	2,821.04	2,819.58
20.75%	4,440.63	3,738.90	3,534.84	3,271.19	2,989.72	2,900.50	2,869.88	2,859.09	2,855.26	2,853.89

	5	7	8	10	15	20	25	30	35	40
1.00%	2,905.94	2,096.31	1,843.35	1,489.27	1,017.44	781.82	640.68	546.79	479.89	429.86
1.25%	2,924.27	2,114.70	1,861.77	1,507.79	1,036.24	800.93	660.11	566.53	499.95	450.24
1.50%	2,942.68	2,133.18	1,880.31	1,526.46	1,055.26	820.33	679.89	586.70	520.51	471.19
1.75%	2,961.16	2,151.77	1,898.97	1,545.27	1,074.50	840.02	700.04	607.31	541.58	492.72
2.00%	2,979.72	2,170.46	1,917.75	1,564.23	1,093.96	860.00	720.55	628.35	563.15	514.80
2.25%	2,998.35	2,189.26	1,936.64	1,583.34	1,113.64	880.27	741.42	649.82	585.20	537.44
2.50%	3,017.05	2,208.16	1,955.65	1,602.59	1,133.54	900.83	762.65	671.71	607.74	560.62
2.75%	3,035.83	2,227.16	1,974.78	1,621.99	1,153.66	921.68	784.23	694.01	630.76	584.34
3.00%	3,054.68	2,246.26	1,994.03	1,641.53	1,173.99	942.82	806.16	716.73	654.25	608.57
3.25%	3,073.60	2,265.47	2,013.39	1,661.22	1,194.54	964.23	828.44	739.85	678.19	633.32
3.50%	3,092.60	2,284.77	2,032.87	1,681.06	1,215.30	985.93	851.06	763.38	702.59	658.56
3.75%	3,111.67	2,304.18	2,052.46	1,701.04	1,236.28	1,007.91	874.02	787.30	727.44	684.29
4.00%	3,130.81	2,323.70	2,072.18	1,721.17	1,257.47	1,030.17	897.32	811.61	752.72	710.50
4.25%	3,150.02	2,343.31	2,092.01	1,741.44	1,278.87	1,052.70	920.95	836.30	778.42	737.15
4.50%	3,169.31	2,363.03	2,111.95	1,761.85	1,300.49	1,075.50	944.92	861.37	804.54	764.26
4.75%	3,188.68	2,382.85	2,132.01	1,782.41	1,322.31	1,098.58	969.20	886.80	831.06	791.79
5.00%	3,208.11	2,402.76	2,152.19	1,803.11	1,344.35	1,121.92	993.80	912.60	857.97	819.73
5.25%	3,227.62	2,422.79	2,172.48	1,823.96	1,366.59	1,145.54	1,018.72	938.75	885.26	848.08
5.50%	3,247.20	2,442.91	2,192.88	1,844.95	1,389.04	1,169.41	1,043.95	965.24	912.93	876.81
5.75%	3,266.85	2,463.13	2,213.41	1,866.08	1,411.70	1,193.54	1,069.48	992.07	940.95	905.91
6.00%	3,286.58	2,483.45	2,234.04	1,887.35	1,434.56	1,217.93	1,095.31	1,019.24	969.32	935.36
6.25%	3,306.37	2,503.88	2,254.79	1,908.76	1,457.62	1,242.58	1,121.44	1,046.72	998.03	965.16
6.50%	3,326.25	2,524.40	2,275.66	1,930.32	1,480.88	1,267.47	1,147.85	1,074.52	1,027.06	995.28
6.75%	3,346.19	2,545.03	2,296.64	1,952.01	1,504.35	1,292.62	1,174.55	1,102.62	1,056.41	1,025.71
7.00%	3,366.20	2,565.76	2,317.73	1,973.84	1,528.01	1,318.01	1,201.52	1,131.01	1,086.06	1,056.43
7.25%	3,386.29	2,586.58	2,338.94	1,995.82	1,551.87	1,343.64	1,228.77	1,159.70	1,115.99	1,087.44
7.50%	3,406.45	2,607.51	2,360.26	2,017.93	1,575.92	1,369.51	1,256.29	1,188.66	1,146.21	1,118.72
7.75%	3,426.68	2,628.53	2,381.69	2,040.18	1,600.17	1,395.61	1,284.06	1,217.90	1,176.70	1,150.25
8.00%	3,446.99	2,649.66	2,403.24	2,062.57	1,624.61	1,421.95	1,312.09	1,247.40	1,207.44	1,182.03
8.25%	3,467.36	2,670.88	2,424.89	2,085.09	1,649.24	1,448.51	1,340.37	1,277.15	1,238.43	1,214.04
8.50%	3,487.81	2,692.20	2,446.66	2,107.76	1,674.06	1,475.30	1,368.89	1,307.15	1,269.66	1,246.26
8.75%	3,508.33	2,713.62	2,468.54	2,130.55	1,699.06	1,502.31	1,397.64	1,337.39	1,301.12	1,278.69
9.00%	3,528.92	2,735.14	2,490.53	2,153.49	1,724.25	1,529.53	1,426.63	1,367.86	1,332.79	1,311.31
9.25%	3,549.58	2,756.76	2,512.64	2,176.56	1,749.63	1,556.97	1,455.85	1,398.55	1,364.67	1,344.12
9.50%	3,570.32	2,778.48	2,534.85	2,199.76	1,775.18	1,584.62	1,485.28	1,429.45	1,396.74	1,377.10
9.75%	3,591.12	2,800.29	2,557.17	2,223.09	1,800.92	1,612.48	1,514.93	1,460.56	1,429.00	1,410.25
10.00%	3,612.00	2,822.20	2,579.61	2,246.56	1,826.83	1,640.54	1,544.79	1,491.87	1,461.44	1,443.55
10.25%	3,632.94	2,844.21	2,602.15	2,270.16	1,852.92	1,668.79	1,574.85	1,523.37	1,494.05	1,476.99
10.50%	3,653.96	2,866.31	2,624.80	2,293.89	1,879.18	1,697.25	1,605.11	1,555.06	1,526.83	1,510.57
10.75%	3,675.05	2,888.52	2,647.56	2,317.76	1,905.61	1,725.89	1,635.56	1,586.92	1,559.75	1,544.28

	5	7	8	10	15	20	25	30	35	40
11.00%	3,696.21	2,910.81	2,670.43	2,341.75	1,932.21	1,754.72	1,666.19	1,618.95	1,592.83	1,578.10
11.25%	3,717.44	2,933.21	2,693.41	2,365.87	1,958.99	1,783.74	1,697.01	1,651.14	1,626.04	1,612.04
11.50%	3,738.74	2,955.70	2,716.49	2,390.12	1,985.92	1,812.93	1,728.00	1,683.50	1,659.38	1,646.08
11.75%	3,760.11	2,978.28	2,739.68	2,414.50	2,013.02	1,842.30	1,759.16	1,716.00	1,692.85	1,680.22
12.00%	3,781.56	3,000.96	2,762.98	2,439.01	2,040.29	1,871.85	1,790.48	1,748.64	1,726.43	1,714.45
12.25%	3,803.07	3,023.74	2,786.39	2,463.64	2,067.71	1,901.56	1,821.96	1,781.42	1,760.13	1,748.77
12.50%	3,824.65	3,046.61	2,809.90	2,488.39	2,095.29	1,931.44	1,853.60	1,814.34	1,793.93	1,783.16
12.75%	3,846.30	3,069.58	2,833.51	2,513.28	2,123.02	1,961.48	1,885.39	1,847.38	1,827.83	1,817.63
13.00%	3,868.02	3,092.63	2,857.23	2,538.28	2,150.91	1,991.68	1,917.32	1,880.54	1,861.83	1,852.17
13.25%	3,889.81	3,115.79	2,881.06	2,563.41	2,178.95	2,022.03	1,949.39	1,913.81	1,895.91	1,886.78
13.50%	3,911.67	3,139.03	2,904.99	2,588.66	2,207.14	2,052.54	1,981.60	1,947.20	1,930.08	1,921.44
13.75%	3,933.60	3,162.37	2,929.02	2,614.04	2,235.48	2,083.19	2,013.93	1,980.69	1,964.32	1,956.17
14.00%	3,955.60	3,185.80	2,953.16	2,639.53	2,263.96	2,113.99	2,046.39	2,014.28	1,998.64	1,990.94
14.25%	3,977.67	3,209.33	2,977.39	2,665.14	2,292.59	2,144.92	2,078.98	2,047.97	2,033.03	2,025.76
14.50%	3,999.81	3,232.94	3,001.73	2,690.88	2,321.35	2,176.00	2,111.68	2,081.75	2,067.49	2,060.63
14.75%	4,022.01	3,256.65	3,026.18	2,716.73	2,350.26	2,207.20	2,144.49	2,115.61	2,102.01	2,095.53
15.00%	4,044.29	3,280.45	3,050.72	2,742.69	2,379.30	2,238.54	2,177.41	2,149.55	2,136.58	2,130.48
15.25%	4,066.63	3,304.34	3,075.36	2,768.78	2,408.47	2,270.01	2,210.44	2,183.58	2,171.21	2,165.46
15.50%	4,089.04	3,328.32	3,100.11	2,794.98	2,437.78	2,301.60	2,243.57	2,217.68	2,205.89	2,200.48
15.75%	4,111.52	3,352.39	3,124.95	2,821.29	2,467.22	2,333.31	2,276.79	2,251.85	2,240.62	2,235.53
16.00%	4,134.07	3,376.55	3,149.89	2,847.72	2,496.79	2,365.14	2,310.11	2,286.09	2,275.40	2,270.60
16.25%	4,156.69	3,400.80	3,174.94	2,874.27	2,526.49	2,397.08	2,343.52	2,320.39	2,310.21	2,305.70
16.50%	4,179.37	3,425.14	3,200.08	2,900.92	2,556.30	2,429.13	2,377.02	2,354.75	2,345.07	2,340.83
16.75%	4,202.12	3,449.57	3,225.31	2,927.68	2,586.25	2,461.29	2,410.59	2,389.17	2,379.97	2,375.98
17.00%	4,224.94	3,474.09	3,250.65	2,954.56	2,616.31	2,493.56	2,444.25	2,423.65	2,414.89	2,411.15
17.25%	4,247.82	3,498.69	3,276.08	2,981.55	2,646.49	2,525.93	2,477.99	2,458.18	2,449.86	2,446.34
17.50%	4,270.78	3,523.38	3,301.61	3,008.64	2,676.78	2,558.40	2,511.80	2,492.75	2,484.85	2,481.55
17.75%	4,293.80	3,548.17	3,327.23	3,035.84	2,707.19	2,590.97	2,545.68	2,527.38	2,519.87	2,516.77
18.00%	4,316.88	3,573.03	3,352.95	3,063.15	2,737.72	2,623.63	2,579.63	2,562.05	2,554.92	2,552.01
18.25%	4,340.04	3,597.99	3,378.76	3,090.56	2,768.35	2,656.38	2,613.65	2,596.76	2,589.99	2,587.26
18.50%	4,363.26	3,623.03	3,404.66	3,118.08	2,799.09	2,689.22	2,647.72	2,631.51	2,625.08	2,622.53
18.75%	4,386.54	3,648.15	3,430.66	3,145.70	2,829.94	2,722.15	2,681.86	2,666.29	2,660.20	2,657.81
19.00%	4,409.89	3,673.36	3,456.76	3,173.43	2,860.89	2,755.16	2,716.06	2,701.12	2,695.34	2,693.10
19.25%	4,433.31	3,698.66	3,482.94	3,201.26	2,891.94	2,788.26	2,750.31	2,735.97	2,730.50	2,728.40
19.50%	4,456.80	3,724.04	3,509.22	3,229.19	2,923.10	2,821.43	2,784.61	2,770.86	2,765.67	2,763.71
19.75%	4,480.35	3,749.51	3,535.59	3,257.22	2,954.35	2,854.68	2,818.96	2,805.78	2,800.87	2,799.02
20.00%	4,503.96	3,775.05	3,562.04	3,285.35	2,985.70	2,888.00	2,853.37	2,840.73	2,836.07	2,834.35
20.25%	4,527.64	3,800.69	3,588.59	3,313.57	3,017.15	2,921.40	2,887.82	2,875.71	2,871.30	2,869.68
20.50%	4,551.39	3,826.40	3,615.23	3,341.90	3,048.69	2,954.86	2,922.31	2,910.71	2,906.53	2,905.02
20.75%	4,575.20	3,852.20	3,641.96	3,370.32	3,080.32	2,988.39	2,956.85	2,945.73	2,941.78	2,940.37

$175,000   1.00 - 10.75%   5 - 40 Years

	5	7	8	10	15	20	25	30	35	40
1.00%	2,991.41	2,157.97	1,897.56	1,533.07	1,047.37	804.82	659.53	562.87	494.00	442.50
1.25%	3,010.28	2,176.89	1,916.53	1,552.14	1,066.72	824.48	679.52	583.19	514.65	463.48
1.50%	3,029.23	2,195.92	1,935.62	1,571.35	1,086.30	844.45	699.89	603.96	535.82	485.05
1.75%	3,048.26	2,215.06	1,954.82	1,590.72	1,106.11	864.73	720.63	625.18	557.51	507.21
2.00%	3,067.36	2,234.30	1,974.15	1,610.24	1,126.14	885.30	741.75	646.83	579.71	529.94
2.25%	3,086.54	2,253.65	1,993.60	1,629.90	1,146.40	906.16	763.23	668.93	602.41	553.25
2.50%	3,105.79	2,273.10	2,013.17	1,649.72	1,166.88	927.33	785.08	691.46	625.62	577.11
2.75%	3,125.12	2,292.66	2,032.86	1,669.69	1,187.59	948.79	807.29	714.42	649.31	601.52
3.00%	3,144.52	2,312.33	2,052.68	1,689.81	1,208.52	970.55	829.87	737.81	673.49	626.47
3.25%	3,164.00	2,332.10	2,072.61	1,710.08	1,229.67	992.59	852.80	761.61	698.14	651.95
3.50%	3,183.56	2,351.97	2,092.66	1,730.50	1,251.04	1,014.93	876.09	785.83	723.26	677.93
3.75%	3,203.19	2,371.95	2,112.83	1,751.07	1,272.64	1,037.55	899.73	810.45	748.83	704.42
4.00%	3,222.89	2,392.04	2,133.12	1,771.79	1,294.45	1,060.47	923.71	835.48	774.86	731.39
4.25%	3,242.67	2,412.23	2,153.53	1,792.66	1,316.49	1,083.66	948.04	860.89	801.31	758.84
4.50%	3,262.53	2,432.53	2,174.07	1,813.67	1,338.74	1,107.14	972.71	886.70	828.20	786.73
4.75%	3,282.46	2,452.93	2,194.72	1,834.84	1,361.21	1,130.89	997.71	912.88	855.50	815.08
5.00%	3,302.47	2,473.43	2,215.49	1,856.15	1,383.89	1,154.92	1,023.03	939.44	883.20	843.84
5.25%	3,322.55	2,494.04	2,236.37	1,877.60	1,406.79	1,179.23	1,048.68	966.36	911.30	873.02
5.50%	3,342.70	2,514.76	2,257.38	1,899.21	1,429.90	1,203.80	1,074.65	993.63	939.78	902.60
5.75%	3,362.93	2,535.58	2,278.51	1,920.96	1,453.22	1,228.65	1,100.94	1,021.25	968.63	932.55
6.00%	3,383.24	2,556.50	2,299.75	1,942.86	1,476.75	1,253.75	1,127.53	1,049.21	997.83	962.87
6.25%	3,403.62	2,577.52	2,321.11	1,964.90	1,500.49	1,279.12	1,154.42	1,077.51	1,027.38	993.54
6.50%	3,424.08	2,598.65	2,342.59	1,987.09	1,524.44	1,304.75	1,181.61	1,106.12	1,057.27	1,024.55
6.75%	3,444.61	2,619.88	2,364.19	2,009.42	1,548.59	1,330.64	1,209.10	1,135.05	1,087.48	1,055.87
7.00%	3,465.21	2,641.22	2,385.90	2,031.90	1,572.95	1,356.77	1,236.86	1,164.28	1,118.00	1,087.50
7.25%	3,485.89	2,662.66	2,407.73	2,054.52	1,597.51	1,383.16	1,264.91	1,193.81	1,148.82	1,119.43
7.50%	3,506.64	2,684.20	2,429.68	2,077.28	1,622.27	1,409.79	1,293.23	1,223.63	1,179.92	1,151.62
7.75%	3,527.47	2,705.84	2,451.74	2,100.19	1,647.23	1,436.66	1,321.83	1,253.72	1,211.31	1,184.08
8.00%	3,548.37	2,727.59	2,473.92	2,123.23	1,672.39	1,463.77	1,350.68	1,284.09	1,242.96	1,216.80
8.25%	3,569.34	2,749.44	2,496.21	2,146.42	1,697.75	1,491.11	1,379.79	1,314.72	1,274.86	1,249.74
8.50%	3,590.39	2,771.38	2,518.62	2,169.75	1,723.29	1,518.69	1,409.15	1,345.60	1,307.01	1,282.91
8.75%	3,611.52	2,793.44	2,541.15	2,193.22	1,749.04	1,546.49	1,438.75	1,376.73	1,339.39	1,316.30
9.00%	3,632.71	2,815.59	2,563.79	2,216.83	1,774.97	1,574.52	1,468.59	1,408.09	1,371.99	1,349.88
9.25%	3,653.98	2,837.84	2,586.54	2,240.57	1,801.09	1,602.77	1,498.67	1,439.68	1,404.80	1,383.66
9.50%	3,675.33	2,860.20	2,609.41	2,264.46	1,827.39	1,631.23	1,528.97	1,471.49	1,437.82	1,417.61
9.75%	3,696.74	2,882.65	2,632.39	2,288.48	1,853.88	1,659.90	1,559.49	1,503.52	1,471.03	1,451.73
10.00%	3,718.23	2,905.21	2,655.48	2,312.64	1,880.56	1,688.79	1,590.23	1,535.75	1,504.43	1,486.01
10.25%	3,739.80	2,927.86	2,678.68	2,336.93	1,907.41	1,717.88	1,621.17	1,568.18	1,538.00	1,520.43
10.50%	3,761.43	2,950.62	2,702.00	2,361.36	1,934.45	1,747.16	1,652.32	1,600.79	1,571.73	1,555.00
10.75%	3,783.14	2,973.47	2,725.43	2,385.93	1,961.66	1,776.65	1,683.66	1,633.59	1,605.63	1,589.70

$175,000   11.00 - 20.75%   5 - 40 Years

	5	7	8	10	15	20	25	30	35	40
11.00%	3,804.92	2,996.43	2,748.97	2,410.63	1,989.04	1,806.33	1,715.20	1,666.57	1,639.68	1,624.52
11.25%	3,826.78	3,019.48	2,772.63	2,435.46	2,016.60	1,836.20	1,746.92	1,699.71	1,673.86	1,659.45
11.50%	3,848.71	3,042.63	2,796.39	2,460.42	2,044.33	1,866.25	1,778.82	1,733.01	1,708.19	1,694.49
11.75%	3,870.71	3,065.88	2,820.26	2,485.52	2,072.23	1,896.49	1,810.90	1,766.47	1,742.64	1,729.64
12.00%	3,892.78	3,089.23	2,844.25	2,510.74	2,100.29	1,926.90	1,843.14	1,800.07	1,777.21	1,764.87
12.25%	3,914.92	3,112.67	2,868.34	2,536.10	2,128.52	1,957.49	1,875.55	1,833.82	1,811.90	1,800.20
12.50%	3,937.14	3,136.22	2,892.54	2,561.58	2,156.91	1,988.25	1,908.12	1,867.70	1,846.70	1,835.61
12.75%	3,959.43	3,159.86	2,916.85	2,587.20	2,185.46	2,019.17	1,940.84	1,901.71	1,881.59	1,871.09
13.00%	3,981.79	3,183.59	2,941.27	2,612.94	2,214.17	2,050.26	1,973.71	1,935.85	1,916.59	1,906.65
13.25%	4,004.22	3,207.43	2,965.80	2,638.81	2,243.04	2,081.50	2,006.73	1,970.10	1,951.67	1,942.27
13.50%	4,026.72	3,231.36	2,990.43	2,664.80	2,272.06	2,112.91	2,039.88	2,004.47	1,986.85	1,977.96
13.75%	4,049.30	3,255.38	3,015.17	2,690.92	2,301.23	2,144.46	2,073.17	2,038.95	2,022.10	2,013.70
14.00%	4,071.94	3,279.50	3,040.01	2,717.16	2,330.55	2,176.16	2,106.58	2,073.53	2,057.43	2,049.50
14.25%	4,094.66	3,303.72	3,064.96	2,743.53	2,360.01	2,208.01	2,140.12	2,108.20	2,092.83	2,085.34
14.50%	4,117.45	3,328.03	3,090.02	2,770.02	2,389.63	2,240.00	2,173.79	2,142.97	2,128.30	2,121.23
14.75%	4,140.31	3,352.43	3,115.18	2,796.63	2,419.38	2,272.12	2,207.56	2,177.83	2,163.83	2,157.17
15.00%	4,163.24	3,376.93	3,140.45	2,823.36	2,449.28	2,304.38	2,241.45	2,212.78	2,199.42	2,193.14
15.25%	4,186.24	3,401.52	3,165.81	2,850.21	2,479.31	2,336.77	2,275.45	2,247.80	2,235.07	2,229.15
15.50%	4,209.31	3,426.21	3,191.29	2,877.18	2,509.48	2,369.29	2,309.55	2,282.90	2,270.77	2,265.20
15.75%	4,232.45	3,450.99	3,216.86	2,904.27	2,539.79	2,401.93	2,343.76	2,318.08	2,306.52	2,301.28
16.00%	4,255.66	3,475.86	3,242.54	2,931.48	2,570.23	2,434.70	2,378.06	2,353.32	2,342.32	2,337.38
16.25%	4,278.94	3,500.82	3,268.32	2,958.80	2,600.79	2,467.58	2,412.45	2,388.64	2,378.16	2,373.52
16.50%	4,302.29	3,525.88	3,294.19	2,986.24	2,631.49	2,500.58	2,446.93	2,424.01	2,414.04	2,409.68
16.75%	4,325.71	3,551.03	3,320.17	3,013.79	2,662.31	2,533.68	2,481.49	2,459.44	2,449.96	2,445.86
17.00%	4,349.20	3,576.27	3,346.25	3,041.46	2,693.26	2,566.90	2,516.14	2,494.93	2,485.92	2,482.07
17.25%	4,372.76	3,601.59	3,372.43	3,069.24	2,724.32	2,600.22	2,550.87	2,530.48	2,521.91	2,518.29
17.50%	4,396.39	3,627.01	3,398.71	3,097.13	2,755.51	2,633.65	2,585.68	2,566.07	2,557.93	2,554.53
17.75%	4,420.08	3,652.52	3,425.09	3,125.13	2,786.82	2,667.17	2,620.55	2,601.71	2,593.98	2,590.79
18.00%	4,443.85	3,678.12	3,451.56	3,153.24	2,818.24	2,700.80	2,655.50	2,637.40	2,630.06	2,627.07
18.25%	4,467.68	3,703.81	3,478.13	3,181.46	2,849.77	2,734.51	2,690.52	2,673.13	2,666.17	2,663.36
18.50%	4,491.59	3,729.59	3,504.80	3,209.79	2,881.42	2,768.32	2,725.60	2,708.90	2,702.29	2,699.66
18.75%	4,515.56	3,755.45	3,531.57	3,238.22	2,913.17	2,802.22	2,760.74	2,744.71	2,738.44	2,735.98
19.00%	4,539.60	3,781.40	3,558.43	3,266.77	2,945.03	2,836.20	2,795.94	2,780.56	2,774.62	2,772.31
19.25%	4,563.70	3,807.44	3,585.38	3,295.41	2,977.00	2,870.27	2,831.20	2,816.44	2,810.81	2,808.64
19.50%	4,587.88	3,833.57	3,612.43	3,324.16	3,009.07	2,904.41	2,866.51	2,852.36	2,847.02	2,844.99
19.75%	4,612.12	3,859.78	3,639.57	3,353.02	3,041.25	2,938.64	2,901.88	2,888.31	2,883.24	2,881.35
20.00%	4,636.43	3,886.08	3,666.81	3,381.97	3,073.52	2,972.94	2,937.29	2,924.28	2,919.49	2,917.71
20.25%	4,660.81	3,912.47	3,694.14	3,411.03	3,105.89	3,007.32	2,972.75	2,960.29	2,955.74	2,954.08
20.50%	4,685.25	3,938.94	3,721.56	3,440.19	3,138.36	3,041.77	3,008.26	2,996.32	2,992.02	2,990.46
20.75%	4,709.76	3,965.50	3,749.07	3,469.45	3,170.92	3,076.29	3,043.82	3,032.37	3,028.30	3,026.85

	5	7	8	10	15	20	25	30	35	40
1.00%	3,076.87	2,219.62	1,951.78	1,576.87	1,077.29	827.81	678.37	578.95	508.11	455.14
1.25%	3,096.29	2,239.09	1,971.29	1,596.48	1,097.20	848.04	698.93	599.85	529.36	476.72
1.50%	3,115.78	2,258.66	1,990.92	1,616.25	1,117.34	868.58	719.89	621.22	551.13	498.91
1.75%	3,135.35	2,278.35	2,010.68	1,636.17	1,137.71	889.43	741.22	643.04	573.44	521.70
2.00%	3,155.00	2,298.14	2,030.56	1,656.24	1,158.32	910.59	762.94	665.32	596.27	545.09
2.25%	3,174.72	2,318.04	2,050.56	1,676.47	1,179.15	932.05	785.04	688.04	619.63	569.06
2.50%	3,194.53	2,338.05	2,070.69	1,696.86	1,200.22	953.83	807.51	711.22	643.49	593.60
2.75%	3,214.41	2,358.17	2,090.95	1,717.40	1,221.52	975.90	830.36	734.83	667.86	618.71
3.00%	3,234.36	2,378.39	2,111.32	1,738.09	1,243.05	998.28	853.58	758.89	692.73	644.37
3.25%	3,254.40	2,398.73	2,131.82	1,758.94	1,264.80	1,020.95	877.17	783.37	718.09	670.57
3.50%	3,274.51	2,419.17	2,152.45	1,779.95	1,286.79	1,043.93	901.12	808.28	743.92	697.30
3.75%	3,294.71	2,439.73	2,173.20	1,801.10	1,309.00	1,067.20	925.44	833.61	770.23	724.55
4.00%	3,314.97	2,460.39	2,194.07	1,822.41	1,331.44	1,090.76	950.11	859.35	796.99	752.29
4.25%	3,335.32	2,481.15	2,215.06	1,843.88	1,354.10	1,114.62	975.13	885.49	824.21	780.52
4.50%	3,355.74	2,502.03	2,236.18	1,865.49	1,376.99	1,138.77	1,000.50	912.03	851.86	809.21
4.75%	3,376.24	2,523.01	2,257.42	1,887.26	1,400.10	1,163.20	1,026.21	938.97	879.94	838.36
5.00%	3,396.82	2,544.10	2,278.79	1,909.18	1,423.43	1,187.92	1,052.26	966.28	908.44	867.95
5.25%	3,417.48	2,565.30	2,300.27	1,931.25	1,446.98	1,212.92	1,078.65	993.97	937.34	897.97
5.50%	3,438.21	2,586.61	2,321.88	1,953.47	1,470.75	1,238.20	1,105.36	1,022.02	966.63	928.39
5.75%	3,459.02	2,608.02	2,343.61	1,975.85	1,494.74	1,263.75	1,132.39	1,050.43	996.30	959.20
6.00%	3,479.90	2,629.54	2,365.46	1,998.37	1,518.94	1,289.58	1,159.74	1,079.19	1,026.34	990.38
6.25%	3,500.87	2,651.17	2,387.43	2,021.04	1,543.36	1,315.67	1,187.40	1,108.29	1,056.74	1,021.93
6.50%	3,521.91	2,672.90	2,409.52	2,043.86	1,567.99	1,342.03	1,215.37	1,137.72	1,087.48	1,053.82
6.75%	3,543.02	2,694.74	2,431.74	2,066.83	1,592.84	1,368.66	1,243.64	1,167.48	1,118.55	1,086.04
7.00%	3,564.22	2,716.68	2,454.07	2,089.95	1,617.89	1,395.54	1,272.20	1,197.54	1,149.94	1,118.58
7.25%	3,585.49	2,738.73	2,476.52	2,113.22	1,643.15	1,422.68	1,301.05	1,227.92	1,181.64	1,151.41
7.50%	3,606.83	2,760.89	2,499.10	2,136.63	1,668.62	1,450.07	1,330.18	1,258.59	1,213.64	1,184.53
7.75%	3,628.25	2,783.15	2,521.79	2,160.19	1,694.30	1,477.71	1,359.59	1,289.54	1,245.92	1,217.92
8.00%	3,649.75	2,805.52	2,544.60	2,183.90	1,720.17	1,505.59	1,389.27	1,320.78	1,278.47	1,251.56
8.25%	3,671.33	2,827.99	2,567.53	2,207.75	1,746.25	1,533.72	1,419.21	1,352.28	1,311.28	1,285.45
8.50%	3,692.98	2,850.57	2,590.58	2,231.74	1,772.53	1,562.08	1,449.41	1,384.04	1,344.35	1,319.57
8.75%	3,714.70	2,873.25	2,613.75	2,255.88	1,799.01	1,590.68	1,479.86	1,416.06	1,377.65	1,353.91
9.00%	3,736.50	2,896.03	2,637.04	2,280.16	1,825.68	1,619.51	1,510.55	1,448.32	1,411.19	1,388.45
9.25%	3,758.38	2,918.92	2,660.44	2,304.59	1,852.55	1,648.56	1,541.49	1,480.82	1,444.94	1,423.19
9.50%	3,780.34	2,941.92	2,683.96	2,329.16	1,879.60	1,677.84	1,572.65	1,513.54	1,478.90	1,458.11
9.75%	3,802.36	2,965.01	2,707.60	2,353.86	1,906.85	1,707.33	1,604.05	1,546.48	1,513.06	1,493.21
10.00%	3,824.47	2,988.21	2,731.35	2,378.71	1,934.29	1,737.04	1,635.66	1,579.63	1,547.41	1,528.46
10.25%	3,846.65	3,011.52	2,755.22	2,403.70	1,961.91	1,766.96	1,667.49	1,612.98	1,581.94	1,563.87
10.50%	3,868.90	3,034.92	2,779.20	2,428.83	1,989.72	1,797.08	1,699.53	1,646.53	1,616.64	1,599.43
10.75%	3,891.23	3,058.43	2,803.30	2,454.10	2,017.71	1,827.41	1,731.77	1,680.27	1,651.51	1,635.12

$180,000   11.00 - 20.75%   5 - 40 Years

	5	7	8	10	15	20	25	30	35	40
11.00%	3,913.64	3,082.04	2,827.52	2,479.50	2,045.87	1,857.94	1,764.20	1,714.18	1,686.52	1,670.93
11.25%	3,936.12	3,105.75	2,851.85	2,505.04	2,074.22	1,888.66	1,796.83	1,748.27	1,721.69	1,706.86
11.50%	3,958.67	3,129.56	2,876.29	2,530.72	2,102.74	1,919.57	1,829.64	1,782.52	1,756.99	1,742.91
11.75%	3,981.30	3,153.48	2,900.84	2,556.53	2,131.44	1,950.67	1,862.64	1,816.94	1,792.43	1,779.06
12.00%	4,004.00	3,177.49	2,925.51	2,582.48	2,160.30	1,981.96	1,895.80	1,851.50	1,827.99	1,815.30
12.25%	4,026.78	3,201.61	2,950.29	2,608.56	2,189.34	2,013.42	1,929.14	1,886.21	1,863.67	1,851.64
12.50%	4,049.63	3,225.82	2,975.19	2,634.77	2,218.54	2,045.05	1,962.64	1,921.06	1,899.46	1,888.05
12.75%	4,072.55	3,250.14	3,000.19	2,661.12	2,247.91	2,076.86	1,996.29	1,956.05	1,935.35	1,924.55
13.00%	4,095.55	3,274.55	3,025.31	2,687.59	2,277.44	2,108.84	2,030.10	1,991.16	1,971.35	1,961.13
13.25%	4,118.63	3,299.07	3,050.53	2,714.20	2,307.13	2,140.98	2,064.06	2,026.39	2,007.44	1,997.77
13.50%	4,141.77	3,323.68	3,075.87	2,740.94	2,336.97	2,173.27	2,098.16	2,061.74	2,043.61	2,034.47
13.75%	4,164.99	3,348.39	3,101.31	2,767.80	2,366.98	2,205.73	2,132.40	2,097.20	2,079.87	2,071.23
14.00%	4,188.29	3,373.20	3,126.87	2,794.80	2,397.13	2,238.34	2,166.77	2,132.77	2,116.21	2,108.05
14.25%	4,211.65	3,398.11	3,152.53	2,821.92	2,427.44	2,271.09	2,201.27	2,168.44	2,152.62	2,144.92
14.50%	4,235.09	3,423.11	3,178.31	2,849.16	2,457.90	2,304.00	2,235.89	2,204.20	2,189.11	2,181.84
14.75%	4,258.60	3,448.22	3,204.19	2,876.53	2,488.51	2,337.04	2,270.64	2,240.06	2,225.65	2,218.80
15.00%	4,282.19	3,473.42	3,230.17	2,904.03	2,519.26	2,370.22	2,305.50	2,276.00	2,262.26	2,255.80
15.25%	4,305.84	3,498.71	3,256.27	2,931.65	2,550.15	2,403.54	2,340.46	2,312.03	2,298.93	2,292.84
15.50%	4,329.57	3,524.10	3,282.47	2,959.39	2,581.18	2,436.99	2,375.54	2,348.13	2,335.65	2,329.92
15.75%	4,353.38	3,549.59	3,308.77	2,987.25	2,612.35	2,470.56	2,410.72	2,384.31	2,372.42	2,367.03
16.00%	4,377.25	3,575.17	3,335.18	3,015.24	2,643.66	2,504.26	2,446.00	2,420.56	2,409.24	2,404.17
16.25%	4,401.20	3,600.85	3,361.70	3,043.34	2,675.10	2,538.08	2,481.37	2,456.88	2,446.11	2,441.33
16.50%	4,425.21	3,626.62	3,388.31	3,071.56	2,706.68	2,572.02	2,516.84	2,493.27	2,483.02	2,478.53
16.75%	4,449.30	3,652.49	3,415.04	3,099.90	2,738.38	2,606.08	2,552.39	2,529.71	2,519.96	2,515.74
17.00%	4,473.46	3,678.44	3,441.86	3,128.36	2,770.21	2,640.24	2,588.03	2,566.22	2,556.95	2,552.98
17.25%	4,497.70	3,704.50	3,468.79	3,156.93	2,802.16	2,674.52	2,623.75	2,602.77	2,593.97	2,590.24
17.50%	4,522.00	3,730.64	3,495.82	3,185.62	2,834.24	2,708.90	2,659.55	2,639.39	2,631.02	2,627.52
17.75%	4,546.37	3,756.88	3,522.95	3,214.42	2,866.44	2,743.38	2,695.43	2,676.05	2,668.10	2,664.82
18.00%	4,570.82	3,783.21	3,550.18	3,243.33	2,898.76	2,777.96	2,731.37	2,712.75	2,705.21	2,702.13
18.25%	4,595.33	3,809.63	3,577.51	3,272.36	2,931.19	2,812.64	2,767.39	2,749.51	2,742.34	2,739.46
18.50%	4,619.92	3,836.15	3,604.94	3,301.50	2,963.74	2,847.41	2,803.47	2,786.30	2,779.50	2,776.80
18.75%	4,644.57	3,862.75	3,632.47	3,330.75	2,996.40	2,882.28	2,839.62	2,823.13	2,816.69	2,814.15
19.00%	4,669.30	3,889.44	3,660.10	3,360.10	3,029.18	2,917.23	2,875.82	2,860.01	2,853.89	2,851.51
19.25%	4,694.09	3,916.23	3,687.82	3,389.57	3,062.06	2,952.27	2,912.09	2,896.91	2,891.12	2,888.89
19.50%	4,718.96	3,943.10	3,715.64	3,419.14	3,095.05	2,987.40	2,948.41	2,933.86	2,928.36	2,926.28
19.75%	4,743.89	3,970.06	3,743.56	3,448.82	3,128.14	3,022.60	2,984.79	2,970.83	2,965.62	2,963.67
20.00%	4,768.90	3,997.12	3,771.58	3,478.60	3,161.33	3,057.88	3,021.21	3,007.83	3,002.90	3,001.08
20.25%	4,793.97	4,024.26	3,799.69	3,508.49	3,194.63	3,093.24	3,057.69	3,044.87	3,040.19	3,038.49
20.50%	4,819.11	4,051.48	3,827.89	3,538.48	3,228.02	3,128.68	3,094.21	3,081.93	3,077.50	3,075.91
20.75%	4,844.33	4,078.80	3,856.19	3,568.58	3,261.52	3,164.18	3,130.78	3,119.01	3,114.82	3,113.33

$185,000   1.00 - 10.75%   5 - 40 Years

	5	7	8	10	15	20	25	30	35	40
1.00%	3,162.34	2,281.28	2,006.00	1,620.68	1,107.21	850.80	697.21	595.03	522.23	467.78
1.25%	3,182.30	2,301.29	2,026.05	1,640.83	1,127.67	871.60	718.35	616.52	544.06	489.96
1.50%	3,202.33	2,321.40	2,046.22	1,661.14	1,148.37	892.71	739.88	638.47	566.44	512.77
1.75%	3,222.44	2,341.63	2,066.53	1,681.62	1,169.31	914.14	761.81	660.90	589.37	536.19
2.00%	3,242.64	2,361.98	2,086.96	1,702.25	1,190.49	935.88	784.13	683.80	612.84	560.23
2.25%	3,262.91	2,382.43	2,107.52	1,723.04	1,211.91	957.95	806.84	707.16	636.84	584.86
2.50%	3,283.26	2,402.99	2,128.21	1,743.99	1,233.56	980.32	829.94	730.97	661.37	610.09
2.75%	3,303.69	2,423.67	2,149.03	1,765.10	1,255.45	1,003.01	853.43	755.25	686.41	635.90
3.00%	3,324.21	2,444.46	2,169.97	1,786.37	1,277.58	1,026.01	877.29	779.97	711.97	662.27
3.25%	3,344.80	2,465.36	2,191.04	1,807.80	1,299.94	1,049.31	901.54	805.13	738.03	689.20
3.50%	3,365.47	2,486.37	2,212.24	1,829.39	1,322.53	1,072.93	926.15	830.73	764.59	716.67
3.75%	3,386.22	2,507.50	2,233.56	1,851.13	1,345.36	1,096.84	951.14	856.76	791.62	744.67
4.00%	3,407.06	2,528.73	2,255.02	1,873.04	1,368.42	1,121.06	976.50	883.22	819.13	773.19
4.25%	3,427.97	2,550.07	2,276.59	1,895.09	1,391.72	1,145.58	1,002.22	910.09	847.10	802.20
4.50%	3,448.96	2,571.53	2,298.30	1,917.31	1,415.24	1,170.40	1,028.29	937.37	875.52	831.69
4.75%	3,470.03	2,593.10	2,320.13	1,939.68	1,438.99	1,195.51	1,054.72	965.05	904.38	861.65
5.00%	3,491.18	2,614.77	2,342.09	1,962.21	1,462.97	1,220.92	1,081.49	993.12	933.67	892.06
5.25%	3,512.41	2,636.56	2,364.17	1,984.90	1,487.17	1,246.61	1,108.61	1,021.58	963.37	922.91
5.50%	3,533.72	2,658.46	2,386.37	2,007.74	1,511.60	1,272.59	1,136.06	1,050.41	993.48	954.18
5.75%	3,555.10	2,680.47	2,408.71	2,030.73	1,536.26	1,298.85	1,163.85	1,079.61	1,023.98	985.84
6.00%	3,576.57	2,702.58	2,431.16	2,053.88	1,561.14	1,325.40	1,191.96	1,109.17	1,054.85	1,017.90
6.25%	3,598.11	2,724.81	2,453.75	2,077.18	1,586.23	1,352.22	1,220.39	1,139.08	1,086.09	1,050.32
6.50%	3,619.74	2,747.15	2,476.45	2,100.64	1,611.55	1,379.31	1,249.13	1,169.33	1,117.69	1,083.10
6.75%	3,641.44	2,769.59	2,499.28	2,124.25	1,637.08	1,406.67	1,278.19	1,199.91	1,149.62	1,116.21
7.00%	3,663.22	2,792.15	2,522.24	2,148.01	1,662.83	1,434.30	1,307.54	1,230.81	1,181.88	1,149.65
7.25%	3,685.08	2,814.81	2,545.32	2,171.92	1,688.80	1,462.20	1,337.19	1,262.03	1,214.46	1,183.39
7.50%	3,707.02	2,837.58	2,568.52	2,195.98	1,714.97	1,490.35	1,367.13	1,293.55	1,247.35	1,217.43
7.75%	3,729.04	2,860.46	2,591.84	2,220.20	1,741.36	1,518.75	1,397.36	1,325.36	1,280.53	1,251.75
8.00%	3,751.13	2,883.45	2,615.29	2,244.56	1,767.96	1,547.41	1,427.86	1,357.46	1,313.98	1,286.33
8.25%	3,773.31	2,906.55	2,638.85	2,269.07	1,794.76	1,576.32	1,458.63	1,389.84	1,347.71	1,321.16
8.50%	3,795.56	2,929.75	2,662.54	2,293.74	1,821.77	1,605.47	1,489.67	1,422.49	1,381.69	1,356.22
8.75%	3,817.89	2,953.06	2,686.36	2,318.54	1,848.98	1,634.86	1,520.97	1,455.40	1,415.92	1,391.52
9.00%	3,840.30	2,976.48	2,710.29	2,343.50	1,876.39	1,664.49	1,552.51	1,488.55	1,450.39	1,427.02
9.25%	3,862.78	3,000.00	2,734.34	2,368.61	1,904.01	1,694.35	1,584.31	1,521.95	1,485.08	1,462.72
9.50%	3,885.34	3,023.64	2,758.51	2,393.85	1,931.82	1,724.44	1,616.34	1,555.58	1,519.98	1,498.61
9.75%	3,907.99	3,047.37	2,782.81	2,419.25	1,959.82	1,754.76	1,648.60	1,589.44	1,555.09	1,534.68
10.00%	3,930.70	3,071.22	2,807.22	2,444.79	1,988.02	1,785.29	1,681.10	1,623.51	1,590.39	1,570.92
10.25%	3,953.50	3,095.17	2,831.75	2,470.47	2,016.41	1,816.04	1,713.81	1,657.79	1,625.88	1,607.31
10.50%	3,976.37	3,119.22	2,856.40	2,496.30	2,044.99	1,847.00	1,746.74	1,692.27	1,661.55	1,643.86
10.75%	3,999.32	3,143.39	2,881.17	2,522.27	2,073.75	1,878.17	1,779.87	1,726.94	1,697.38	1,680.53

$185,000   11.00 - 20.75%   5 - 40 Years

	5	7	8	10	15	20	25	30	35	40
11.00%	4,022.35	3,167.65	2,906.06	2,548.38	2,102.70	1,909.55	1,813.21	1,761.80	1,733.37	1,717.34
11.25%	4,045.45	3,192.02	2,931.06	2,574.63	2,131.84	1,941.12	1,846.74	1,796.83	1,769.51	1,754.28
11.50%	4,068.63	3,216.50	2,956.18	2,601.02	2,161.15	1,972.89	1,880.47	1,832.04	1,805.80	1,791.32
11.75%	4,091.89	3,241.07	2,981.42	2,627.54	2,190.64	2,004.86	1,914.38	1,867.41	1,842.22	1,828.47
12.00%	4,115.22	3,265.76	3,006.78	2,654.21	2,220.31	2,037.01	1,948.46	1,902.93	1,878.77	1,865.72
12.25%	4,138.63	3,290.54	3,032.25	2,681.02	2,250.15	2,069.34	1,982.73	1,938.61	1,915.44	1,903.07
12.50%	4,162.12	3,315.43	3,057.83	2,707.96	2,280.17	2,101.86	2,017.16	1,974.43	1,952.22	1,940.50
12.75%	4,185.68	3,340.42	3,083.53	2,735.04	2,310.35	2,134.55	2,051.75	2,010.38	1,989.11	1,978.01
13.00%	4,209.32	3,365.51	3,109.34	2,762.25	2,340.70	2,167.42	2,086.50	2,046.47	2,026.11	2,015.60
13.25%	4,233.03	3,390.71	3,135.27	2,789.59	2,371.21	2,200.45	2,121.40	2,082.68	2,063.20	2,053.26
13.50%	4,256.82	3,416.01	3,161.31	2,817.07	2,401.89	2,233.64	2,156.44	2,119.01	2,100.38	2,090.98
13.75%	4,280.69	3,441.40	3,187.46	2,844.69	2,432.73	2,267.00	2,191.63	2,155.46	2,137.65	2,128.77
14.00%	4,304.63	3,466.90	3,213.73	2,872.43	2,463.72	2,300.51	2,226.96	2,192.01	2,175.00	2,166.61
14.25%	4,328.64	3,492.50	3,240.10	2,900.30	2,494.87	2,334.18	2,262.42	2,228.67	2,212.42	2,204.50
14.50%	4,352.73	3,518.20	3,266.59	2,928.31	2,526.18	2,368.00	2,298.00	2,265.43	2,249.92	2,242.45
14.75%	4,376.90	3,544.00	3,293.19	2,956.44	2,557.63	2,401.96	2,333.71	2,302.28	2,287.48	2,280.43
15.00%	4,401.14	3,569.90	3,319.90	2,984.70	2,589.24	2,436.06	2,369.54	2,339.22	2,325.10	2,318.46
15.25%	4,425.45	3,595.90	3,346.72	3,013.08	2,620.99	2,470.30	2,405.48	2,376.25	2,362.79	2,356.53
15.50%	4,449.84	3,621.99	3,373.65	3,041.59	2,652.88	2,504.68	2,441.53	2,413.36	2,400.53	2,394.64
15.75%	4,474.30	3,648.19	3,400.68	3,070.23	2,684.92	2,539.19	2,477.69	2,450.54	2,438.33	2,432.78
16.00%	4,498.84	3,674.48	3,427.83	3,098.99	2,717.10	2,573.82	2,513.94	2,487.80	2,476.17	2,470.95
16.25%	4,523.45	3,700.87	3,455.08	3,127.88	2,749.41	2,608.58	2,550.30	2,525.13	2,514.06	2,509.15
16.50%	4,548.14	3,727.36	3,482.43	3,156.88	2,781.86	2,643.47	2,586.75	2,562.52	2,551.99	2,547.37
16.75%	4,572.89	3,753.94	3,509.90	3,186.01	2,814.44	2,678.47	2,623.29	2,599.98	2,589.96	2,585.63
17.00%	4,597.73	3,780.62	3,537.47	3,215.26	2,847.16	2,713.58	2,659.92	2,637.50	2,627.97	2,623.90
17.25%	4,622.63	3,807.40	3,565.14	3,244.62	2,880.00	2,748.81	2,696.64	2,675.07	2,666.02	2,662.19
17.50%	4,647.61	3,834.27	3,592.92	3,274.11	2,912.97	2,784.14	2,733.43	2,712.70	2,704.10	2,700.51
17.75%	4,672.66	3,861.24	3,620.81	3,303.71	2,946.06	2,819.58	2,770.30	2,750.38	2,742.21	2,738.84
18.00%	4,697.78	3,888.30	3,648.79	3,333.43	2,979.28	2,855.13	2,807.25	2,788.11	2,780.35	2,777.19
18.25%	4,722.98	3,915.46	3,676.88	3,363.26	3,012.61	2,890.77	2,844.26	2,825.88	2,818.52	2,815.55
18.50%	4,748.25	3,942.71	3,705.08	3,393.21	3,046.07	2,926.51	2,881.35	2,863.70	2,856.71	2,853.93
18.75%	4,773.59	3,970.05	3,733.37	3,423.27	3,079.64	2,962.34	2,918.50	2,901.55	2,894.93	2,892.32
19.00%	4,799.00	3,997.48	3,761.77	3,453.44	3,113.32	2,998.27	2,955.71	2,939.45	2,933.17	2,930.72
19.25%	4,824.49	4,025.01	3,790.26	3,483.72	3,147.12	3,034.28	2,992.98	2,977.38	2,971.42	2,969.14
19.50%	4,850.04	4,052.63	3,818.86	3,514.12	3,181.02	3,070.38	3,030.31	3,015.35	3,009.70	3,007.56
19.75%	4,875.67	4,080.34	3,847.55	3,544.62	3,215.03	3,106.56	3,067.70	3,053.35	3,048.00	3,046.00
20.00%	4,901.37	4,108.15	3,876.34	3,575.23	3,249.15	3,142.83	3,105.14	3,091.38	3,086.31	3,084.46
20.25%	4,927.14	4,136.04	3,905.23	3,605.95	3,283.37	3,179.17	3,142.63	3,129.45	3,124.64	3,122.89
20.50%	4,952.98	4,164.02	3,934.22	3,636.77	3,317.69	3,215.59	3,180.16	3,167.53	3,162.99	3,161.35
20.75%	4,978.89	4,192.10	3,963.31	3,667.70	3,352.11	3,252.08	3,217.75	3,205.65	3,201.35	3,199.81

	5	7	8	10	15	20	25	30	35	40
1.00%	3,247.81	2,342.94	2,060.21	1,664.48	1,137.14	873.80	716.06	611.12	536.34	480.43
1.25%	3,268.30	2,363.48	2,080.80	1,685.18	1,158.15	895.15	737.76	633.18	558.76	503.21
1.50%	3,288.88	2,384.14	2,101.53	1,706.04	1,179.41	916.84	759.88	655.73	581.75	526.63
1.75%	3,309.54	2,404.92	2,122.38	1,727.07	1,200.92	938.84	782.40	678.76	605.30	550.68
2.00%	3,330.27	2,425.81	2,143.37	1,748.26	1,222.67	961.18	805.32	702.28	629.40	575.37
2.25%	3,351.10	2,446.82	2,164.48	1,769.61	1,244.66	983.84	828.65	726.27	654.05	600.67
2.50%	3,372.00	2,467.94	2,185.73	1,791.13	1,266.90	1,006.82	852.37	750.73	679.24	626.58
2.75%	3,392.98	2,489.18	2,207.11	1,812.81	1,289.38	1,030.12	876.49	775.66	704.97	653.08
3.00%	3,414.05	2,510.53	2,228.62	1,834.65	1,312.11	1,053.74	901.00	801.05	731.22	680.17
3.25%	3,435.20	2,531.99	2,250.26	1,856.66	1,335.07	1,077.67	925.90	826.89	757.98	707.83
3.50%	3,456.43	2,553.57	2,272.03	1,878.83	1,358.28	1,101.92	951.18	853.18	785.25	736.04
3.75%	3,477.74	2,575.27	2,293.93	1,901.16	1,381.72	1,126.49	976.85	879.92	813.02	764.80
4.00%	3,499.14	2,597.07	2,315.96	1,923.66	1,405.41	1,151.36	1,002.89	907.09	841.27	794.08
4.25%	3,520.62	2,619.00	2,338.12	1,946.31	1,429.33	1,176.55	1,029.30	934.69	870.00	823.88
4.50%	3,542.17	2,641.03	2,360.41	1,969.13	1,453.49	1,202.03	1,056.08	962.70	899.19	854.17
4.75%	3,563.81	2,663.18	2,382.84	1,992.11	1,477.88	1,227.82	1,083.22	991.13	928.83	884.94
5.00%	3,585.53	2,685.44	2,405.38	2,015.24	1,502.51	1,253.92	1,110.72	1,019.96	958.91	916.17
5.25%	3,607.34	2,707.82	2,428.06	2,038.54	1,527.37	1,280.30	1,138.57	1,049.19	989.41	947.85
5.50%	3,629.22	2,730.31	2,450.87	2,062.00	1,552.46	1,306.99	1,166.77	1,078.80	1,020.33	979.96
5.75%	3,651.19	2,752.91	2,473.81	2,085.62	1,577.78	1,333.96	1,195.30	1,108.79	1,051.65	1,012.49
6.00%	3,673.23	2,775.63	2,496.87	2,109.39	1,603.33	1,361.22	1,224.17	1,139.15	1,083.36	1,045.41
6.25%	3,695.36	2,798.45	2,520.06	2,133.32	1,629.10	1,388.76	1,253.37	1,169.86	1,115.45	1,078.71
6.50%	3,717.57	2,821.39	2,543.38	2,157.41	1,655.10	1,416.59	1,282.89	1,200.93	1,147.89	1,112.37
6.75%	3,739.86	2,844.45	2,566.83	2,181.66	1,681.33	1,444.69	1,312.73	1,232.34	1,180.69	1,146.38
7.00%	3,762.23	2,867.61	2,590.41	2,206.06	1,707.77	1,473.07	1,342.88	1,264.07	1,213.83	1,180.72
7.25%	3,784.68	2,890.89	2,614.11	2,230.62	1,734.44	1,501.71	1,373.33	1,296.13	1,247.29	1,215.38
7.50%	3,807.21	2,914.27	2,637.94	2,255.33	1,761.32	1,530.63	1,404.08	1,328.51	1,281.06	1,250.33
7.75%	3,829.82	2,937.77	2,661.89	2,280.20	1,788.42	1,559.80	1,435.12	1,361.18	1,315.13	1,285.58
8.00%	3,852.51	2,961.38	2,685.97	2,305.22	1,815.74	1,589.24	1,466.45	1,394.15	1,349.50	1,321.09
8.25%	3,875.29	2,985.10	2,710.17	2,330.40	1,843.27	1,618.92	1,498.06	1,427.41	1,384.13	1,356.86
8.50%	3,898.14	3,008.93	2,734.50	2,355.73	1,871.01	1,648.86	1,529.93	1,460.94	1,419.04	1,392.88
8.75%	3,921.07	3,032.87	2,758.96	2,381.21	1,898.95	1,679.05	1,562.07	1,494.73	1,454.19	1,429.12
9.00%	3,944.09	3,056.92	2,783.54	2,406.84	1,927.11	1,709.48	1,594.47	1,528.78	1,489.59	1,465.59
9.25%	3,967.18	3,081.09	2,808.24	2,432.62	1,955.47	1,740.15	1,627.13	1,563.08	1,525.21	1,502.26
9.50%	3,990.35	3,105.36	2,833.07	2,458.55	1,984.03	1,771.05	1,660.02	1,597.62	1,561.06	1,539.12
9.75%	4,013.61	3,129.74	2,858.02	2,484.63	2,012.79	1,802.18	1,693.16	1,632.39	1,597.12	1,576.16
10.00%	4,036.94	3,154.22	2,883.09	2,510.86	2,041.75	1,833.54	1,726.53	1,667.39	1,633.38	1,613.38
10.25%	4,060.35	3,178.82	2,908.29	2,537.24	2,070.91	1,865.12	1,760.13	1,702.59	1,669.83	1,650.75
10.50%	4,083.84	3,203.53	2,933.60	2,563.76	2,100.26	1,896.92	1,793.95	1,738.00	1,706.45	1,688.28
10.75%	4,107.41	3,228.34	2,959.04	2,590.43	2,129.80	1,928.94	1,827.98	1,773.61	1,743.26	1,725.95

$190,000   11.00 - 20.75%   5 - 40 Years

	5	7	8	10	15	20	25	30	35	40
11.00%	4,131.06	3,253.26	2,984.60	2,617.25	2,159.53	1,961.16	1,862.21	1,809.41	1,780.22	1,763.76
11.25%	4,154.79	3,278.29	3,010.28	2,644.21	2,189.45	1,993.59	1,896.66	1,845.40	1,817.34	1,801.69
11.50%	4,178.60	3,303.43	3,036.08	2,671.31	2,219.56	2,026.22	1,931.29	1,881.55	1,854.60	1,839.74
11.75%	4,202.48	3,328.67	3,062.00	2,698.56	2,249.85	2,059.04	1,966.12	1,917.88	1,892.01	1,877.89
12.00%	4,226.45	3,354.02	3,088.04	2,725.95	2,280.32	2,092.06	2,001.13	1,954.36	1,929.54	1,916.15
12.25%	4,250.49	3,379.47	3,114.20	2,753.48	2,310.97	2,125.27	2,036.31	1,991.00	1,967.21	1,954.50
12.50%	4,274.61	3,405.04	3,140.47	2,781.15	2,341.79	2,158.67	2,071.67	2,027.79	2,004.98	1,992.95
12.75%	4,298.81	3,430.70	3,166.87	2,808.96	2,372.79	2,192.24	2,107.20	2,064.72	2,042.87	2,031.47
13.00%	4,323.08	3,456.47	3,193.38	2,836.90	2,403.96	2,225.99	2,142.89	2,101.78	2,080.87	2,070.08
13.25%	4,347.44	3,482.35	3,220.01	2,864.99	2,435.30	2,259.92	2,178.73	2,138.97	2,118.96	2,108.75
13.50%	4,371.87	3,508.33	3,246.75	2,893.21	2,466.81	2,294.01	2,214.73	2,176.28	2,157.15	2,147.50
13.75%	4,396.38	3,534.41	3,273.61	2,921.57	2,498.48	2,328.27	2,250.87	2,213.71	2,195.42	2,186.30
14.00%	4,420.97	3,560.60	3,300.59	2,950.06	2,530.31	2,362.69	2,287.15	2,251.26	2,233.78	2,225.17
14.25%	4,445.63	3,586.89	3,327.67	2,978.69	2,562.30	2,397.27	2,323.56	2,288.91	2,272.21	2,264.08
14.50%	4,470.37	3,613.29	3,354.88	3,007.45	2,594.45	2,432.00	2,360.11	2,326.66	2,310.72	2,303.05
14.75%	4,495.19	3,639.78	3,382.20	3,036.34	2,626.76	2,466.88	2,396.78	2,364.50	2,349.30	2,342.07
15.00%	4,520.09	3,666.38	3,409.63	3,065.36	2,659.22	2,501.90	2,433.58	2,402.44	2,387.95	2,381.13
15.25%	4,545.06	3,693.08	3,437.17	3,094.52	2,691.82	2,537.07	2,470.49	2,440.47	2,426.65	2,420.22
15.50%	4,570.11	3,719.89	3,464.83	3,123.80	2,724.58	2,572.37	2,507.52	2,478.58	2,465.41	2,459.36
15.75%	4,595.23	3,746.79	3,492.59	3,153.21	2,757.48	2,607.81	2,544.65	2,516.77	2,504.23	2,498.53
16.00%	4,620.43	3,773.79	3,520.47	3,182.75	2,790.53	2,643.39	2,581.89	2,555.04	2,543.09	2,537.73
16.25%	4,645.71	3,800.90	3,548.46	3,212.41	2,823.72	2,679.09	2,619.23	2,593.38	2,582.00	2,576.96
16.50%	4,671.06	3,828.10	3,576.55	3,242.20	2,857.05	2,714.91	2,656.66	2,631.78	2,620.96	2,616.22
16.75%	4,696.49	3,855.40	3,604.76	3,272.12	2,890.51	2,750.86	2,694.19	2,670.25	2,659.96	2,655.51
17.00%	4,721.99	3,882.80	3,633.08	3,302.16	2,924.11	2,786.92	2,731.81	2,708.78	2,699.00	2,694.81
17.25%	4,747.57	3,910.30	3,661.50	3,332.32	2,957.84	2,823.10	2,769.52	2,747.37	2,738.07	2,734.14
17.50%	4,773.22	3,937.90	3,690.03	3,362.60	2,991.70	2,859.39	2,807.31	2,786.02	2,777.18	2,773.49
17.75%	4,798.95	3,965.60	3,718.67	3,393.00	3,025.69	2,895.79	2,845.17	2,824.72	2,816.32	2,812.86
18.00%	4,824.75	3,993.39	3,747.41	3,423.52	3,059.80	2,932.29	2,883.12	2,863.46	2,855.49	2,852.25
18.25%	4,850.63	4,021.28	3,776.26	3,454.16	3,094.04	2,968.90	2,921.13	2,902.26	2,894.69	2,891.65
18.50%	4,876.58	4,049.26	3,805.21	3,484.91	3,128.39	3,005.60	2,959.22	2,941.09	2,933.92	2,931.06
18.75%	4,902.61	4,077.35	3,834.27	3,515.79	3,162.87	3,042.41	2,997.37	2,979.98	2,973.17	2,970.49
19.00%	4,928.70	4,105.52	3,863.43	3,546.77	3,197.46	3,079.30	3,035.59	3,018.90	3,012.44	3,009.93
19.25%	4,954.88	4,133.80	3,892.70	3,577.88	3,232.17	3,116.29	3,073.87	3,057.85	3,051.73	3,049.38
19.50%	4,981.12	4,162.16	3,922.07	3,609.09	3,266.99	3,153.36	3,112.21	3,096.85	3,091.05	3,088.85
19.75%	5,007.44	4,190.62	3,951.54	3,640.42	3,301.92	3,190.52	3,150.61	3,135.88	3,130.38	3,128.32
20.00%	5,033.84	4,219.18	3,981.11	3,671.86	3,336.96	3,227.77	3,189.06	3,174.94	3,169.73	3,167.80
20.25%	5,060.30	4,247.83	4,010.78	3,703.41	3,372.11	3,265.09	3,227.56	3,214.03	3,209.09	3,207.29
20.50%	5,086.84	4,276.57	4,040.55	3,735.06	3,407.36	3,302.49	3,266.11	3,253.14	3,248.48	3,246.79
20.75%	5,113.45	4,305.40	4,070.42	3,766.83	3,442.71	3,339.97	3,304.71	3,292.29	3,287.87	3,286.29

	5	7	8	10	15	20	25	30	35	40
1.00%	3,333.28	2,404.59	2,114.43	1,708.28	1,167.06	896.79	734.90	627.20	550.46	493.07
1.25%	3,354.31	2,425.68	2,135.56	1,729.52	1,188.63	918.71	757.18	649.84	573.47	516.45
1.50%	3,375.43	2,446.89	2,156.83	1,750.93	1,210.45	940.96	779.88	672.98	597.06	540.49
1.75%	3,396.63	2,468.21	2,178.23	1,772.51	1,232.52	963.55	802.99	696.62	621.23	565.18
2.00%	3,417.91	2,489.65	2,199.77	1,794.26	1,254.84	986.47	826.52	720.76	645.96	590.51
2.25%	3,439.28	2,511.21	2,221.44	1,816.18	1,277.42	1,009.73	850.45	745.38	671.26	616.48
2.50%	3,460.74	2,532.89	2,243.25	1,838.26	1,300.24	1,033.31	874.80	770.49	697.12	643.07
2.75%	3,482.27	2,554.68	2,265.19	1,860.52	1,323.31	1,057.22	899.56	796.07	723.52	670.27
3.00%	3,503.89	2,576.59	2,287.27	1,882.93	1,346.63	1,081.47	924.71	822.13	750.46	698.07
3.25%	3,525.60	2,598.62	2,309.48	1,905.52	1,370.20	1,106.03	950.27	848.65	777.93	726.46
3.50%	3,547.39	2,620.77	2,331.82	1,928.27	1,394.02	1,130.92	976.22	875.64	805.92	755.41
3.75%	3,569.26	2,643.04	2,354.30	1,951.19	1,418.08	1,156.13	1,002.56	903.08	834.41	784.93
4.00%	3,591.22	2,665.42	2,376.91	1,974.28	1,442.39	1,181.66	1,029.28	930.96	863.41	814.98
4.25%	3,613.26	2,687.92	2,399.65	1,997.53	1,466.94	1,207.51	1,056.39	959.28	892.89	845.56
4.50%	3,635.39	2,710.53	2,422.53	2,020.95	1,491.74	1,233.67	1,083.87	988.04	922.85	876.65
4.75%	3,657.60	2,733.26	2,445.54	2,044.53	1,516.77	1,260.14	1,111.73	1,017.21	953.27	908.23
5.00%	3,679.89	2,756.11	2,468.68	2,068.28	1,542.05	1,286.91	1,139.95	1,046.80	984.14	940.28
5.25%	3,702.27	2,779.08	2,491.96	2,092.19	1,567.56	1,314.00	1,168.53	1,076.80	1,015.45	972.80
5.50%	3,724.73	2,802.16	2,515.37	2,116.26	1,593.31	1,341.38	1,197.47	1,107.19	1,047.18	1,005.75
5.75%	3,747.27	2,825.36	2,538.91	2,140.50	1,619.30	1,369.06	1,226.76	1,137.97	1,079.33	1,039.13
6.00%	3,769.90	2,848.67	2,562.58	2,164.90	1,645.52	1,397.04	1,256.39	1,169.12	1,111.87	1,072.92
6.25%	3,792.61	2,872.10	2,586.38	2,189.46	1,671.97	1,425.31	1,286.36	1,200.65	1,144.80	1,107.09
6.50%	3,815.40	2,895.64	2,610.32	2,214.19	1,698.66	1,453.87	1,316.65	1,232.53	1,178.10	1,141.64
6.75%	3,838.27	2,919.30	2,634.38	2,239.07	1,725.57	1,482.71	1,347.28	1,264.77	1,211.76	1,176.55
7.00%	3,861.23	2,943.07	2,658.57	2,264.12	1,752.72	1,511.83	1,378.22	1,297.34	1,245.77	1,211.79
7.25%	3,884.28	2,966.96	2,682.90	2,289.32	1,780.08	1,541.23	1,409.47	1,330.24	1,280.11	1,247.36
7.50%	3,907.40	2,990.96	2,707.35	2,314.68	1,807.67	1,570.91	1,441.03	1,363.47	1,314.77	1,283.24
7.75%	3,930.61	3,015.08	2,731.94	2,340.21	1,835.49	1,600.85	1,472.89	1,397.00	1,349.74	1,319.41
8.00%	3,953.90	3,039.31	2,756.65	2,365.89	1,863.52	1,631.06	1,505.04	1,430.84	1,385.01	1,355.86
8.25%	3,977.27	3,063.66	2,781.49	2,391.73	1,891.77	1,661.53	1,537.48	1,464.97	1,420.56	1,392.57
8.50%	4,000.72	3,088.11	2,806.47	2,417.72	1,920.24	1,692.26	1,570.19	1,499.38	1,456.38	1,429.53
8.75%	4,024.26	3,112.69	2,831.56	2,443.87	1,948.92	1,723.24	1,603.18	1,534.07	1,492.46	1,466.73
9.00%	4,047.88	3,137.37	2,856.79	2,470.18	1,977.82	1,754.47	1,636.43	1,569.01	1,528.79	1,504.15
9.25%	4,071.58	3,162.17	2,882.14	2,496.64	2,006.92	1,785.94	1,669.94	1,604.22	1,565.35	1,541.79
9.50%	4,095.36	3,187.08	2,907.62	2,523.25	2,036.24	1,817.66	1,703.71	1,639.67	1,602.14	1,579.62
9.75%	4,119.23	3,212.10	2,933.23	2,550.02	2,065.76	1,849.61	1,737.72	1,675.35	1,639.15	1,617.64
10.00%	4,143.17	3,237.23	2,958.96	2,576.94	2,095.48	1,881.79	1,771.97	1,711.26	1,676.36	1,655.83
10.25%	4,167.20	3,262.48	2,984.82	2,604.01	2,125.40	1,914.20	1,806.45	1,747.40	1,713.77	1,694.20
10.50%	4,191.31	3,287.83	3,010.80	2,631.23	2,155.53	1,946.84	1,841.15	1,783.74	1,751.36	1,732.71
10.75%	4,215.50	3,313.30	3,036.91	2,658.60	2,185.85	1,979.70	1,876.08	1,820.29	1,789.13	1,771.37

$195,000   11.00 - 20.75%   5 - 40 Years

	5	7	8	10	15	20	25	30	35	40
11.00%	4,239.77	3,338.88	3,063.14	2,686.13	2,216.36	2,012.77	1,911.22	1,857.03	1,827.07	1,810.17
11.25%	4,264.13	3,364.56	3,089.50	2,713.79	2,247.07	2,046.05	1,946.57	1,893.96	1,865.16	1,849.10
11.50%	4,288.56	3,390.36	3,115.98	2,741.61	2,277.97	2,079.54	1,982.11	1,931.07	1,903.41	1,888.15
11.75%	4,313.07	3,416.27	3,142.58	2,769.57	2,309.06	2,113.23	2,017.86	1,968.35	1,941.80	1,927.31
12.00%	4,337.67	3,442.28	3,169.30	2,797.68	2,340.33	2,147.12	2,053.79	2,005.79	1,980.32	1,966.57
12.25%	4,362.34	3,468.41	3,196.15	2,825.94	2,371.78	2,181.20	2,089.90	2,043.40	2,018.97	2,005.94
12.50%	4,387.10	3,494.64	3,223.12	2,854.34	2,403.42	2,215.47	2,126.19	2,081.15	2,057.75	2,045.39
12.75%	4,411.93	3,520.98	3,250.21	2,882.88	2,435.23	2,249.93	2,162.65	2,119.05	2,096.63	2,084.93
13.00%	4,436.85	3,547.43	3,277.41	2,911.56	2,467.22	2,284.57	2,199.28	2,157.09	2,135.63	2,124.55
13.25%	4,461.84	3,573.99	3,304.74	2,940.38	2,499.39	2,319.39	2,236.07	2,195.26	2,174.72	2,164.25
13.50%	4,486.92	3,600.65	3,332.19	2,969.35	2,531.72	2,354.38	2,273.01	2,233.55	2,213.91	2,204.01
13.75%	4,512.07	3,627.43	3,359.76	2,998.45	2,564.23	2,389.54	2,310.10	2,271.97	2,253.20	2,243.84
14.00%	4,537.31	3,654.30	3,387.44	3,027.70	2,596.90	2,424.87	2,347.33	2,310.50	2,292.56	2,283.72
14.25%	4,562.62	3,681.29	3,415.25	3,057.08	2,629.73	2,460.35	2,384.71	2,349.14	2,332.01	2,323.67
14.50%	4,588.01	3,708.37	3,443.17	3,086.59	2,662.73	2,496.00	2,422.22	2,387.88	2,371.53	2,363.66
14.75%	4,613.49	3,735.57	3,471.20	3,116.24	2,695.88	2,531.79	2,459.86	2,426.73	2,411.13	2,403.70
15.00%	4,639.04	3,762.87	3,499.35	3,146.03	2,729.19	2,567.74	2,497.62	2,465.67	2,450.79	2,443.79
15.25%	4,664.67	3,790.27	3,527.62	3,175.95	2,762.66	2,603.83	2,535.50	2,504.69	2,490.51	2,483.91
15.50%	4,690.37	3,817.78	3,556.00	3,206.01	2,796.28	2,640.07	2,573.50	2,543.81	2,530.29	2,524.08
15.75%	4,716.16	3,845.39	3,584.50	3,236.19	2,830.05	2,676.44	2,611.61	2,583.00	2,570.13	2,564.28
16.00%	4,742.02	3,873.10	3,613.11	3,266.51	2,863.97	2,712.95	2,649.83	2,622.28	2,610.02	2,604.51
16.25%	4,767.96	3,900.92	3,641.84	3,296.95	2,898.03	2,749.59	2,688.16	2,661.62	2,649.95	2,644.78
16.50%	4,793.98	3,928.84	3,670.67	3,327.52	2,932.23	2,786.36	2,726.58	2,701.04	2,689.94	2,685.07
16.75%	4,820.08	3,956.86	3,699.62	3,358.23	2,966.58	2,823.25	2,765.09	2,740.52	2,729.96	2,725.39
17.00%	4,846.25	3,984.98	3,728.68	3,389.05	3,001.06	2,860.26	2,803.70	2,780.07	2,770.03	2,765.73
17.25%	4,872.50	4,013.21	3,757.85	3,420.01	3,035.68	2,897.39	2,842.40	2,819.67	2,810.13	2,806.10
17.50%	4,898.83	4,041.53	3,787.14	3,451.09	3,070.43	2,934.64	2,881.18	2,859.33	2,850.27	2,846.48
17.75%	4,925.24	4,069.95	3,816.53	3,482.29	3,105.31	2,971.99	2,920.05	2,899.05	2,890.44	2,886.88
18.00%	4,951.72	4,098.48	3,846.03	3,513.61	3,140.32	3,009.46	2,958.99	2,938.82	2,930.64	2,927.31
18.25%	4,978.28	4,127.10	3,875.63	3,545.06	3,175.46	3,047.03	2,998.01	2,978.63	2,970.87	2,967.74
18.50%	5,004.91	4,155.82	3,905.35	3,576.62	3,210.72	3,084.70	3,037.09	3,018.49	3,011.13	3,008.20
18.75%	5,031.62	4,184.64	3,935.17	3,608.31	3,246.10	3,122.47	3,076.25	3,058.40	3,051.41	3,048.66
19.00%	5,058.41	4,213.56	3,965.10	3,640.11	3,281.61	3,160.34	3,115.48	3,098.34	3,091.71	3,089.14
19.25%	5,085.27	4,242.58	3,995.14	3,672.03	3,317.23	3,198.30	3,154.76	3,138.32	3,132.04	3,129.63
19.50%	5,112.21	4,271.69	4,025.28	3,704.07	3,352.97	3,236.35	3,194.11	3,178.34	3,172.39	3,170.13
19.75%	5,139.22	4,300.90	4,055.52	3,736.22	3,388.82	3,274.48	3,233.52	3,218.40	3,212.76	3,210.64
20.00%	5,166.31	4,330.21	4,085.87	3,768.49	3,424.78	3,312.71	3,272.98	3,258.49	3,253.14	3,251.16
20.25%	5,193.47	4,359.61	4,116.33	3,800.86	3,460.85	3,351.01	3,312.50	3,298.61	3,293.54	3,291.69
20.50%	5,220.71	4,389.11	4,146.88	3,833.35	3,497.03	3,389.40	3,352.06	3,338.75	3,333.96	3,332.23
20.75%	5,248.02	4,418.70	4,177.54	3,865.96	3,533.31	3,427.86	3,391.68	3,378.93	3,374.39	3,372.77

$200,000　　1.00 - 10.75%　　5 - 40 Years

	5	7	8	10	15	20	25	30	35	40
1.00%	3,418.75	2,466.25	2,168.65	1,752.08	1,196.99	919.79	753.74	643.28	564.57	505.71
1.25%	3,440.32	2,487.88	2,190.32	1,773.87	1,219.11	942.27	776.59	666.50	588.17	529.69
1.50%	3,461.98	2,509.63	2,212.13	1,795.83	1,241.49	965.09	799.87	690.24	612.37	554.34
1.75%	3,483.72	2,531.50	2,234.08	1,817.96	1,264.12	988.26	823.58	714.49	637.16	579.67
2.00%	3,505.55	2,553.49	2,256.17	1,840.27	1,287.02	1,011.77	847.71	739.24	662.53	605.65
2.25%	3,527.47	2,575.60	2,278.40	1,862.75	1,310.17	1,035.62	872.26	764.49	688.47	632.28
2.50%	3,549.47	2,597.83	2,300.77	1,885.40	1,333.58	1,059.81	897.23	790.24	714.99	659.56
2.75%	3,571.56	2,620.19	2,323.27	1,908.22	1,357.24	1,084.33	922.62	816.48	742.07	687.46
3.00%	3,593.74	2,642.66	2,345.91	1,931.21	1,381.16	1,109.20	948.42	843.21	769.70	715.97
3.25%	3,616.00	2,665.25	2,368.69	1,954.38	1,405.34	1,134.39	974.63	870.41	797.87	745.08
3.50%	3,638.35	2,687.97	2,391.61	1,977.72	1,429.77	1,159.92	1,001.25	898.09	826.58	774.78
3.75%	3,660.78	2,710.81	2,414.66	2,001.22	1,454.44	1,185.78	1,028.26	926.23	855.81	805.05
4.00%	3,683.30	2,733.76	2,437.86	2,024.90	1,479.38	1,211.96	1,055.67	954.83	885.55	835.88
4.25%	3,705.91	2,756.84	2,461.18	2,048.75	1,504.56	1,238.47	1,083.48	983.88	915.79	867.24
4.50%	3,728.60	2,780.03	2,484.65	2,072.77	1,529.99	1,265.30	1,111.66	1,013.37	946.51	899.13
4.75%	3,751.38	2,803.35	2,508.25	2,096.95	1,555.66	1,292.45	1,140.23	1,043.29	977.71	931.52
5.00%	3,774.25	2,826.78	2,531.98	2,121.31	1,581.59	1,319.91	1,169.18	1,073.64	1,009.38	964.39
5.25%	3,797.20	2,850.34	2,555.86	2,145.83	1,607.76	1,347.69	1,198.50	1,104.41	1,041.49	997.74
5.50%	3,820.23	2,874.01	2,579.86	2,170.53	1,634.17	1,375.77	1,228.17	1,135.58	1,074.03	1,031.54
5.75%	3,843.35	2,897.80	2,604.01	2,195.38	1,660.82	1,404.17	1,258.21	1,167.15	1,107.00	1,065.78
6.00%	3,866.56	2,921.71	2,628.29	2,220.41	1,687.71	1,432.86	1,288.60	1,199.10	1,140.38	1,100.43
6.25%	3,889.85	2,945.74	2,652.70	2,245.60	1,714.85	1,461.86	1,319.34	1,231.43	1,174.15	1,135.48
6.50%	3,913.23	2,969.89	2,677.25	2,270.96	1,742.21	1,491.15	1,350.41	1,264.14	1,208.31	1,170.91
6.75%	3,936.69	2,994.15	2,701.93	2,296.48	1,769.82	1,520.73	1,381.82	1,297.20	1,242.83	1,206.71
7.00%	3,960.24	3,018.54	2,726.74	2,322.17	1,797.66	1,550.60	1,413.56	1,330.60	1,277.71	1,242.86
7.25%	3,983.87	3,043.04	2,751.69	2,348.02	1,825.73	1,580.75	1,445.61	1,364.35	1,312.93	1,279.34
7.50%	4,007.59	3,067.66	2,776.77	2,374.04	1,854.02	1,611.19	1,477.98	1,398.43	1,348.49	1,316.14
7.75%	4,031.39	3,092.39	2,801.99	2,400.21	1,882.55	1,641.90	1,510.66	1,432.82	1,384.35	1,353.24
8.00%	4,055.28	3,117.24	2,827.34	2,426.55	1,911.30	1,672.88	1,543.63	1,467.53	1,420.52	1,390.62
8.25%	4,079.25	3,142.21	2,852.81	2,453.05	1,940.28	1,704.13	1,576.90	1,502.53	1,456.98	1,428.28
8.50%	4,103.31	3,167.30	2,878.43	2,479.71	1,969.48	1,735.65	1,610.45	1,537.83	1,493.72	1,466.19
8.75%	4,127.45	3,192.50	2,904.17	2,506.54	1,998.90	1,767.42	1,644.29	1,573.40	1,530.73	1,504.34
9.00%	4,151.67	3,217.82	2,930.04	2,533.52	2,028.53	1,799.45	1,678.39	1,609.25	1,567.99	1,542.72
9.25%	4,175.98	3,243.25	2,956.04	2,560.65	2,058.38	1,831.73	1,712.76	1,645.35	1,605.49	1,581.32
9.50%	4,200.37	3,268.80	2,982.18	2,587.95	2,088.45	1,864.26	1,747.39	1,681.71	1,643.22	1,620.12
9.75%	4,224.85	3,294.46	3,008.44	2,615.40	2,118.73	1,897.03	1,782.27	1,718.31	1,681.18	1,659.12
10.00%	4,249.41	3,320.24	3,034.83	2,643.01	2,149.21	1,930.04	1,817.40	1,755.14	1,719.34	1,698.29
10.25%	4,274.05	3,346.13	3,061.35	2,670.78	2,179.90	1,963.29	1,852.77	1,792.20	1,757.71	1,737.64
10.50%	4,298.78	3,372.13	3,088.00	2,698.70	2,210.80	1,996.76	1,888.36	1,829.48	1,796.27	1,777.14
10.75%	4,323.59	3,398.25	3,114.78	2,726.77	2,241.90	2,030.46	1,924.19	1,866.96	1,835.01	1,816.79

	5	7	8	10	15	20	25	30	35	40
11.00%	4,348.48	3,424.49	3,141.69	2,755.00	2,273.19	2,064.38	1,960.23	1,904.65	1,873.92	1,856.59
11.25%	4,373.46	3,450.83	3,168.72	2,783.38	2,304.69	2,098.51	1,996.48	1,942.52	1,912.99	1,896.51
11.50%	4,398.52	3,477.29	3,195.87	2,811.91	2,336.38	2,132.86	2,032.94	1,980.58	1,952.21	1,936.56
11.75%	4,423.66	3,503.86	3,223.16	2,840.59	2,368.26	2,167.41	2,069.60	2,018.82	1,991.59	1,976.73
12.00%	4,448.89	3,530.55	3,250.57	2,869.42	2,400.34	2,202.17	2,106.45	2,057.23	2,031.10	2,017.00
12.25%	4,474.20	3,557.34	3,278.10	2,898.40	2,432.60	2,237.13	2,143.49	2,095.79	2,070.74	2,057.37
12.50%	4,499.59	3,584.25	3,305.76	2,927.52	2,465.04	2,272.28	2,180.71	2,134.52	2,110.51	2,097.84
12.75%	4,525.06	3,611.26	3,333.54	2,956.80	2,497.67	2,307.62	2,218.10	2,173.39	2,150.39	2,138.39
13.00%	4,550.61	3,638.39	3,361.45	2,986.21	2,530.48	2,343.15	2,255.67	2,212.40	2,190.39	2,179.03
13.25%	4,576.25	3,665.63	3,389.48	3,015.78	2,563.47	2,378.86	2,293.40	2,251.55	2,230.48	2,219.74
13.50%	4,601.97	3,692.98	3,417.63	3,045.49	2,596.64	2,414.75	2,331.29	2,290.82	2,270.68	2,260.52
13.75%	4,627.77	3,720.44	3,445.91	3,075.34	2,629.97	2,450.81	2,369.33	2,330.23	2,310.97	2,301.37
14.00%	4,653.65	3,748.00	3,474.30	3,105.33	2,663.48	2,487.04	2,407.52	2,369.74	2,351.35	2,342.28
14.25%	4,679.61	3,775.68	3,502.82	3,135.46	2,697.16	2,523.44	2,445.86	2,409.37	2,391.81	2,383.25
14.50%	4,705.66	3,803.46	3,531.45	3,165.74	2,731.00	2,560.00	2,484.33	2,449.11	2,432.34	2,424.27
14.75%	4,731.78	3,831.35	3,560.21	3,196.15	2,765.01	2,596.71	2,522.93	2,488.95	2,472.95	2,465.33
15.00%	4,757.99	3,859.35	3,589.08	3,226.70	2,799.17	2,633.58	2,561.66	2,528.89	2,513.63	2,506.45
15.25%	4,784.27	3,887.46	3,618.07	3,257.39	2,833.50	2,670.60	2,600.52	2,568.92	2,554.37	2,547.60
15.50%	4,810.64	3,915.67	3,647.18	3,288.21	2,867.98	2,707.76	2,639.49	2,609.03	2,595.17	2,588.80
15.75%	4,837.08	3,943.99	3,676.41	3,319.17	2,902.62	2,745.07	2,678.58	2,649.23	2,636.03	2,630.03
16.00%	4,863.61	3,972.41	3,705.76	3,350.26	2,937.40	2,782.51	2,717.78	2,689.51	2,676.94	2,671.30
16.25%	4,890.22	4,000.94	3,735.22	3,381.49	2,972.34	2,820.09	2,757.08	2,729.87	2,717.90	2,712.59
16.50%	4,916.90	4,029.58	3,764.79	3,412.85	3,007.42	2,857.80	2,796.49	2,770.30	2,758.91	2,753.92
16.75%	4,943.67	4,058.32	3,794.49	3,444.33	3,042.64	2,895.64	2,835.99	2,810.79	2,799.96	2,795.27
17.00%	4,970.52	4,087.16	3,824.29	3,475.95	3,078.01	2,933.60	2,875.59	2,851.35	2,841.05	2,836.65
17.25%	4,997.44	4,116.11	3,854.21	3,507.70	3,113.51	2,971.68	2,915.28	2,891.97	2,882.18	2,878.05
17.50%	5,024.44	4,145.16	3,884.24	3,539.58	3,149.16	3,009.88	2,955.06	2,932.65	2,923.35	2,919.47
17.75%	5,051.52	4,174.31	3,914.39	3,571.58	3,184.93	3,048.20	2,994.92	2,973.38	2,964.55	2,960.91
18.00%	5,078.69	4,203.57	3,944.64	3,603.70	3,220.84	3,086.62	3,034.86	3,014.17	3,005.78	3,002.36
18.25%	5,105.92	4,232.93	3,975.01	3,635.96	3,256.88	3,125.16	3,074.88	3,055.01	3,047.05	3,043.84
18.50%	5,133.24	4,262.38	4,005.49	3,668.33	3,293.05	3,163.79	3,114.97	3,095.89	3,088.34	3,085.33
18.75%	5,160.64	4,291.94	4,036.08	3,700.83	3,329.34	3,202.53	3,155.13	3,136.82	3,129.65	3,126.83
19.00%	5,188.11	4,321.60	4,066.77	3,733.45	3,365.75	3,241.37	3,195.36	3,177.78	3,170.99	3,168.35
19.25%	5,215.66	4,351.36	4,097.58	3,766.19	3,402.29	3,280.30	3,235.65	3,218.79	3,212.35	3,209.88
19.50%	5,243.29	4,381.22	4,128.49	3,799.04	3,438.94	3,319.33	3,276.01	3,259.84	3,253.73	3,251.42
19.75%	5,270.99	4,411.18	4,159.51	3,832.02	3,475.71	3,358.45	3,316.43	3,300.92	3,295.14	3,292.97
20.00%	5,298.78	4,441.24	4,190.64	3,865.11	3,512.59	3,397.65	3,356.90	3,342.04	3,336.56	3,334.53
20.25%	5,326.64	4,471.40	4,221.87	3,898.32	3,549.59	3,436.94	3,397.43	3,383.18	3,377.99	3,376.10
20.50%	5,354.57	4,501.65	4,253.21	3,931.65	3,586.69	3,476.31	3,438.01	3,424.36	3,419.45	3,417.67
20.75%	5,382.58	4,532.00	4,284.65	3,965.08	3,623.91	3,515.76	3,478.65	3,465.57	3,460.92	3,459.26

$205,000   1.00 - 10.75%   5 - 40 Years

	5	7	8	10	15	20	25	30	35	40
1.00%	3,504.22	2,527.91	2,222.86	1,795.88	1,226.91	942.78	772.59	659.36	578.69	518.35
1.25%	3,526.33	2,550.07	2,245.08	1,818.22	1,249.59	965.82	796.01	683.17	602.88	542.93
1.50%	3,548.53	2,572.37	2,267.44	1,840.73	1,272.52	989.22	819.87	707.50	627.68	568.20
1.75%	3,570.81	2,594.78	2,289.94	1,863.41	1,295.73	1,012.96	844.17	732.35	653.08	594.16
2.00%	3,593.19	2,617.32	2,312.58	1,886.28	1,319.19	1,037.06	868.90	757.72	679.09	620.79
2.25%	3,615.66	2,639.99	2,335.36	1,909.32	1,342.92	1,061.51	894.07	783.60	705.68	648.09
2.50%	3,638.21	2,662.78	2,358.29	1,932.53	1,366.92	1,086.30	919.66	810.00	732.87	676.05
2.75%	3,660.85	2,685.69	2,381.35	1,955.93	1,391.17	1,111.44	945.69	836.89	760.62	704.64
3.00%	3,683.58	2,708.73	2,404.56	1,979.50	1,415.69	1,136.93	972.13	864.29	788.94	733.87
3.25%	3,706.40	2,731.89	2,427.91	2,003.24	1,440.47	1,162.75	999.00	892.17	817.82	763.71
3.50%	3,729.31	2,755.17	2,451.40	2,027.16	1,465.51	1,188.92	1,026.28	920.54	847.25	794.15
3.75%	3,752.30	2,778.58	2,475.03	2,051.26	1,490.81	1,215.42	1,053.97	949.39	877.21	825.18
4.00%	3,775.39	2,802.11	2,498.80	2,075.53	1,516.36	1,242.26	1,082.07	978.70	907.69	856.77
4.25%	3,798.56	2,825.76	2,522.71	2,099.97	1,542.17	1,269.43	1,110.56	1,008.48	938.68	888.92
4.50%	3,821.82	2,849.53	2,546.76	2,124.59	1,568.24	1,296.93	1,139.46	1,038.70	970.18	921.60
4.75%	3,845.17	2,873.43	2,570.95	2,149.38	1,594.56	1,324.76	1,168.74	1,069.38	1,002.16	954.80
5.00%	3,868.60	2,897.45	2,595.28	2,174.34	1,621.13	1,352.91	1,198.41	1,100.48	1,034.61	988.50
5.25%	3,892.13	2,921.59	2,619.75	2,199.48	1,647.95	1,381.38	1,228.46	1,132.02	1,067.52	1,022.68
5.50%	3,915.74	2,945.86	2,644.36	2,224.79	1,675.02	1,410.17	1,258.88	1,163.97	1,100.88	1,057.33
5.75%	3,939.44	2,970.25	2,669.11	2,250.27	1,702.34	1,439.27	1,289.67	1,196.32	1,134.68	1,092.42
6.00%	3,963.22	2,994.75	2,693.99	2,275.92	1,729.91	1,468.68	1,320.82	1,229.08	1,168.89	1,127.94
6.25%	3,987.10	3,019.38	2,719.02	2,301.74	1,757.72	1,498.40	1,352.32	1,262.22	1,203.51	1,163.87
6.50%	4,011.06	3,044.13	2,744.18	2,327.73	1,785.77	1,528.42	1,384.17	1,295.74	1,238.52	1,200.19
6.75%	4,035.11	3,069.01	2,769.48	2,353.89	1,814.06	1,558.75	1,416.37	1,329.63	1,273.90	1,236.88
7.00%	4,059.25	3,094.00	2,794.91	2,380.22	1,842.60	1,589.36	1,448.90	1,363.87	1,309.66	1,273.93
7.25%	4,083.47	3,119.11	2,820.48	2,406.72	1,871.37	1,620.27	1,481.75	1,398.46	1,345.76	1,311.33
7.50%	4,107.78	3,144.35	2,846.19	2,433.39	1,900.38	1,651.47	1,514.93	1,433.39	1,382.20	1,349.04
7.75%	4,132.18	3,169.70	2,872.04	2,460.22	1,929.62	1,682.94	1,548.42	1,468.65	1,418.96	1,387.07
8.00%	4,156.66	3,195.17	2,898.02	2,487.22	1,959.09	1,714.70	1,582.22	1,504.22	1,456.03	1,425.39
8.25%	4,181.23	3,220.77	2,924.14	2,514.38	1,988.79	1,746.73	1,616.32	1,540.10	1,493.41	1,463.98
8.50%	4,205.89	3,246.48	2,950.39	2,541.71	2,018.72	1,779.04	1,650.72	1,576.27	1,531.06	1,502.84
8.75%	4,230.63	3,272.31	2,976.77	2,569.20	2,048.87	1,811.61	1,685.39	1,612.74	1,568.99	1,541.95
9.00%	4,255.46	3,298.26	3,003.29	2,596.85	2,079.25	1,844.44	1,720.35	1,649.48	1,607.19	1,581.29
9.25%	4,280.38	3,324.33	3,029.95	2,624.67	2,109.84	1,877.53	1,755.58	1,686.48	1,645.63	1,620.85
9.50%	4,305.38	3,350.52	3,056.73	2,652.65	2,140.66	1,910.87	1,791.08	1,723.75	1,684.30	1,660.63
9.75%	4,330.47	3,376.82	3,083.65	2,680.79	2,171.69	1,944.46	1,826.83	1,761.27	1,723.21	1,700.60
10.00%	4,355.64	3,403.24	3,110.70	2,709.09	2,202.94	1,978.29	1,862.84	1,799.02	1,762.33	1,740.75
10.25%	4,380.90	3,429.78	3,137.89	2,737.55	2,234.40	2,012.37	1,899.09	1,837.01	1,801.65	1,781.08
10.50%	4,406.25	3,456.44	3,165.20	2,766.17	2,266.07	2,046.68	1,935.57	1,875.22	1,841.17	1,821.57
10.75%	4,431.68	3,483.21	3,192.65	2,794.94	2,297.94	2,081.22	1,972.29	1,913.64	1,880.88	1,862.21

$205,000   11.00 - 20.75%   5 - 40 Years

	5	7	8	10	15	20	25	30	35	40
11.00%	4,457.20	3,510.10	3,220.23	2,823.88	2,330.02	2,115.99	2,009.23	1,952.26	1,920.76	1,903.00
11.25%	4,482.80	3,537.10	3,247.93	2,852.96	2,362.31	2,150.97	2,046.39	1,991.09	1,960.81	1,943.93
11.50%	4,508.48	3,564.22	3,275.77	2,882.21	2,394.79	2,186.18	2,083.76	2,030.10	2,001.02	1,984.98
11.75%	4,534.26	3,591.46	3,303.74	2,911.60	2,427.47	2,221.60	2,121.34	2,069.29	2,041.38	2,026.15
12.00%	4,560.11	3,618.81	3,331.83	2,941.15	2,460.34	2,257.23	2,159.11	2,108.66	2,081.88	2,067.42
12.25%	4,586.05	3,646.27	3,360.06	2,970.86	2,493.41	2,293.06	2,197.07	2,148.19	2,122.51	2,108.81
12.50%	4,612.08	3,673.85	3,388.41	3,000.71	2,526.67	2,329.09	2,235.23	2,187.88	2,163.27	2,150.28
12.75%	4,638.19	3,701.55	3,416.88	3,030.72	2,560.12	2,365.31	2,273.56	2,227.72	2,204.15	2,191.85
13.00%	4,664.38	3,729.35	3,445.49	3,060.87	2,593.75	2,401.73	2,312.06	2,267.71	2,245.15	2,233.50
13.25%	4,690.66	3,757.27	3,474.22	3,091.17	2,627.56	2,438.33	2,350.74	2,307.84	2,286.25	2,275.23
13.50%	4,717.02	3,785.30	3,503.07	3,121.62	2,661.55	2,475.12	2,389.57	2,348.09	2,327.45	2,317.04
13.75%	4,743.46	3,813.45	3,532.05	3,152.22	2,695.72	2,512.08	2,428.57	2,388.48	2,368.74	2,358.90
14.00%	4,769.99	3,841.70	3,561.16	3,182.96	2,730.07	2,549.22	2,467.71	2,428.99	2,410.13	2,400.84
14.25%	4,796.60	3,870.07	3,590.39	3,213.85	2,764.59	2,586.52	2,507.00	2,469.61	2,451.60	2,442.83
14.50%	4,823.30	3,898.55	3,619.74	3,244.88	2,799.28	2,624.00	2,546.43	2,510.34	2,493.15	2,484.87
14.75%	4,850.08	3,927.14	3,649.21	3,276.05	2,834.13	2,661.63	2,586.00	2,551.18	2,534.77	2,526.97
15.00%	4,876.94	3,955.83	3,678.81	3,307.37	2,869.15	2,699.42	2,625.70	2,592.11	2,576.47	2,569.11
15.25%	4,903.88	3,984.64	3,708.53	3,338.82	2,904.34	2,737.36	2,665.53	2,633.14	2,618.23	2,611.29
15.50%	4,930.90	4,013.56	3,738.36	3,370.42	2,939.68	2,775.46	2,705.48	2,674.26	2,660.05	2,653.52
15.75%	4,958.01	4,042.59	3,768.32	3,402.15	2,975.18	2,813.69	2,745.54	2,715.47	2,701.93	2,695.78
16.00%	4,985.20	4,071.72	3,798.40	3,434.02	3,010.84	2,852.07	2,785.72	2,756.75	2,743.86	2,738.08
16.25%	5,012.47	4,100.97	3,828.60	3,466.03	3,046.64	2,890.59	2,826.01	2,798.12	2,785.85	2,780.41
16.50%	5,039.83	4,130.32	3,858.91	3,498.17	3,082.60	2,929.25	2,866.40	2,839.55	2,827.88	2,822.77
16.75%	5,067.26	4,159.78	3,889.35	3,530.44	3,118.71	2,968.03	2,906.89	2,881.06	2,869.96	2,865.15
17.00%	5,094.78	4,189.34	3,919.90	3,562.85	3,154.96	3,006.94	2,947.48	2,922.63	2,912.08	2,907.56
17.25%	5,122.38	4,219.01	3,950.57	3,595.39	3,191.35	3,045.98	2,988.16	2,964.27	2,954.24	2,950.00
17.50%	5,150.05	4,248.79	3,981.35	3,628.06	3,227.89	3,085.13	3,028.94	3,005.97	2,996.43	2,992.45
17.75%	5,177.81	4,278.67	4,012.25	3,660.87	3,264.56	3,124.40	3,069.79	3,047.72	3,038.67	3,034.93
18.00%	5,205.65	4,308.66	4,043.26	3,693.80	3,301.36	3,163.79	3,110.73	3,089.53	3,080.93	3,077.42
18.25%	5,233.57	4,338.75	4,074.39	3,726.85	3,338.30	3,203.28	3,151.75	3,131.38	3,123.22	3,119.94
18.50%	5,261.57	4,368.94	4,105.63	3,760.04	3,375.37	3,242.89	3,192.84	3,173.29	3,165.54	3,162.46
18.75%	5,289.65	4,399.24	4,136.98	3,793.35	3,412.57	3,282.60	3,234.01	3,215.24	3,207.89	3,205.00
19.00%	5,317.81	4,429.64	4,168.44	3,826.78	3,449.90	3,322.40	3,275.24	3,257.23	3,250.26	3,247.56
19.25%	5,346.05	4,460.15	4,200.02	3,860.34	3,487.34	3,362.31	3,316.55	3,299.26	3,292.66	3,290.13
19.50%	5,374.37	4,490.75	4,231.70	3,894.02	3,524.91	3,402.31	3,357.91	3,341.34	3,335.08	3,332.70
19.75%	5,402.77	4,521.46	4,263.50	3,927.82	3,562.60	3,442.41	3,399.34	3,383.44	3,377.51	3,375.29
20.00%	5,431.25	4,552.27	4,295.41	3,961.74	3,600.41	3,482.59	3,440.83	3,425.59	3,419.97	3,417.89
20.25%	5,459.80	4,583.18	4,327.42	3,995.78	3,638.33	3,522.86	3,482.37	3,467.76	3,462.44	3,460.50
20.50%	5,488.44	4,614.19	4,359.54	4,029.94	3,676.36	3,563.22	3,523.96	3,509.97	3,504.93	3,503.11
20.75%	5,517.15	4,645.30	4,391.77	4,064.21	3,714.50	3,603.65	3,565.61	3,552.21	3,547.44	3,545.74

$210,000   1.00 - 10.75%   5 - 40 Years

	5	7	8	10	15	20	25	30	35	40
1.00%	3,589.69	2,589.56	2,277.08	1,839.69	1,256.84	965.78	791.43	675.44	592.80	531.00
1.25%	3,612.34	2,612.27	2,299.84	1,862.56	1,280.06	989.38	815.42	699.83	617.58	556.17
1.50%	3,635.08	2,635.11	2,322.74	1,885.62	1,303.56	1,013.35	839.87	724.75	642.99	582.06
1.75%	3,657.91	2,658.07	2,345.79	1,908.86	1,327.33	1,037.67	864.76	750.21	669.01	608.65
2.00%	3,680.83	2,681.16	2,368.98	1,932.28	1,351.37	1,062.36	890.09	776.20	695.65	635.93
2.25%	3,703.84	2,704.38	2,392.32	1,955.88	1,375.68	1,087.40	915.87	802.72	722.90	663.90
2.50%	3,726.95	2,727.72	2,415.81	1,979.67	1,400.26	1,112.80	942.10	829.75	750.74	692.53
2.75%	3,750.14	2,751.19	2,439.44	2,003.63	1,425.11	1,138.55	968.75	857.31	779.17	721.83
3.00%	3,773.43	2,774.79	2,463.21	2,027.78	1,450.22	1,164.65	995.84	885.37	808.19	751.77
3.25%	3,796.80	2,798.52	2,487.13	2,052.10	1,475.60	1,191.11	1,023.36	913.93	837.77	782.34
3.50%	3,820.27	2,822.37	2,511.19	2,076.60	1,501.25	1,217.92	1,051.31	942.99	867.91	813.52
3.75%	3,843.82	2,846.35	2,535.40	2,101.29	1,527.17	1,245.07	1,079.68	972.54	898.60	845.30
4.00%	3,867.47	2,870.45	2,559.75	2,126.15	1,553.34	1,272.56	1,108.46	1,002.57	929.83	877.67
4.25%	3,891.21	2,894.68	2,584.24	2,151.19	1,579.78	1,300.39	1,137.65	1,033.07	961.58	910.60
4.50%	3,915.03	2,919.03	2,608.88	2,176.41	1,606.49	1,328.56	1,167.25	1,064.04	993.84	944.08
4.75%	3,938.95	2,943.51	2,633.66	2,201.80	1,633.45	1,357.07	1,197.25	1,095.46	1,026.60	978.09
5.00%	3,962.96	2,968.12	2,658.58	2,227.38	1,660.67	1,385.91	1,227.64	1,127.33	1,059.84	1,012.61
5.25%	3,987.06	2,992.85	2,683.65	2,253.13	1,688.14	1,415.07	1,258.42	1,159.63	1,093.56	1,047.63
5.50%	4,011.24	3,017.71	2,708.86	2,279.05	1,715.88	1,444.56	1,289.58	1,192.36	1,127.73	1,083.12
5.75%	4,035.52	3,042.69	2,734.21	2,305.15	1,743.86	1,474.38	1,321.12	1,225.50	1,162.35	1,119.06
6.00%	4,059.89	3,067.80	2,759.70	2,331.43	1,772.10	1,504.51	1,353.03	1,259.06	1,197.40	1,155.45
6.25%	4,084.34	3,093.03	2,785.33	2,357.88	1,800.59	1,534.95	1,385.31	1,293.01	1,232.86	1,192.25
6.50%	4,108.89	3,118.38	2,811.11	2,384.51	1,829.33	1,565.70	1,417.94	1,327.34	1,268.72	1,229.46
6.75%	4,133.53	3,143.86	2,837.02	2,411.31	1,858.31	1,596.76	1,450.91	1,362.06	1,304.97	1,267.05
7.00%	4,158.25	3,169.46	2,863.08	2,438.28	1,887.54	1,628.13	1,484.24	1,397.14	1,341.60	1,305.01
7.25%	4,183.07	3,195.19	2,889.28	2,465.42	1,917.01	1,659.79	1,517.89	1,432.57	1,378.58	1,343.31
7.50%	4,207.97	3,221.04	2,915.61	2,492.74	1,946.73	1,691.75	1,551.88	1,468.35	1,415.91	1,381.95
7.75%	4,232.96	3,247.01	2,942.09	2,520.22	1,976.68	1,723.99	1,586.19	1,504.47	1,453.57	1,420.90
8.00%	4,258.04	3,273.11	2,968.70	2,547.88	2,006.87	1,756.52	1,620.81	1,540.91	1,491.55	1,460.15
8.25%	4,283.21	3,299.32	2,995.46	2,575.71	2,037.29	1,789.34	1,655.75	1,577.66	1,529.83	1,499.69
8.50%	4,308.47	3,325.66	3,022.35	2,603.70	2,067.95	1,822.43	1,690.98	1,614.72	1,568.41	1,539.50
8.75%	4,333.82	3,352.12	3,049.38	2,631.86	2,098.84	1,855.79	1,726.50	1,652.07	1,607.26	1,579.56
9.00%	4,359.25	3,378.71	3,076.54	2,660.19	2,129.96	1,889.42	1,762.31	1,689.71	1,646.39	1,619.86
9.25%	4,384.78	3,405.41	3,103.85	2,688.69	2,161.30	1,923.32	1,798.40	1,727.62	1,685.76	1,660.39
9.50%	4,410.39	3,432.24	3,131.29	2,717.35	2,192.87	1,957.48	1,834.76	1,765.79	1,725.38	1,701.13
9.75%	4,436.09	3,459.18	3,158.86	2,746.18	2,224.66	1,991.89	1,871.39	1,804.22	1,765.24	1,742.07
10.00%	4,461.88	3,486.25	3,186.57	2,775.17	2,256.67	2,026.55	1,908.27	1,842.90	1,805.31	1,783.21
10.25%	4,487.76	3,513.44	3,214.42	2,804.32	2,288.90	2,061.45	1,945.40	1,881.81	1,845.60	1,824.52
10.50%	4,513.72	3,540.74	3,242.40	2,833.63	2,321.34	2,096.60	1,982.78	1,920.95	1,886.08	1,866.00
10.75%	4,539.77	3,568.17	3,270.52	2,863.11	2,353.99	2,131.98	2,020.39	1,960.31	1,926.76	1,907.63

$210,000   11.00 - 20.75%   5 - 40 Years

	5	7	8	10	15	20	25	30	35	40
11.00%	4,565.91	3,595.71	3,298.77	2,892.75	2,386.85	2,167.60	2,058.24	1,999.88	1,967.61	1,949.42
11.25%	4,592.13	3,623.38	3,327.15	2,922.55	2,419.92	2,203.44	2,096.30	2,039.65	2,008.64	1,991.34
11.50%	4,618.45	3,651.16	3,355.67	2,952.50	2,453.20	2,239.50	2,134.58	2,079.61	2,049.83	2,033.39
11.75%	4,644.85	3,679.06	3,384.32	2,982.62	2,486.68	2,275.78	2,173.08	2,119.76	2,091.17	2,075.56
12.00%	4,671.33	3,707.07	3,413.10	3,012.89	2,520.35	2,312.28	2,211.77	2,160.09	2,132.65	2,117.85
12.25%	4,697.91	3,735.21	3,442.01	3,043.32	2,554.23	2,348.99	2,250.66	2,200.58	2,174.28	2,160.24
12.50%	4,724.57	3,763.46	3,471.05	3,073.90	2,588.30	2,385.90	2,289.74	2,241.24	2,216.03	2,202.73
12.75%	4,751.31	3,791.83	3,500.22	3,104.64	2,622.56	2,423.00	2,329.01	2,282.06	2,257.91	2,245.31
13.00%	4,778.15	3,820.31	3,529.52	3,135.53	2,657.01	2,460.31	2,368.45	2,323.02	2,299.91	2,287.98
13.25%	4,805.06	3,848.91	3,558.95	3,166.57	2,691.65	2,497.80	2,408.07	2,364.12	2,342.01	2,330.73
13.50%	4,832.07	3,877.63	3,588.51	3,197.76	2,726.47	2,535.49	2,447.85	2,405.37	2,384.22	2,373.55
13.75%	4,859.16	3,906.46	3,618.20	3,229.10	2,761.47	2,573.35	2,487.80	2,446.74	2,426.52	2,416.44
14.00%	4,886.33	3,935.40	3,648.02	3,260.60	2,796.66	2,611.39	2,527.90	2,488.23	2,468.91	2,459.39
14.25%	4,913.59	3,964.46	3,677.96	3,292.24	2,832.02	2,649.61	2,568.15	2,529.84	2,511.40	2,502.41
14.50%	4,940.94	3,993.63	3,708.02	3,324.02	2,867.55	2,688.00	2,608.54	2,571.57	2,553.96	2,545.48
14.75%	4,968.37	4,022.92	3,738.22	3,355.96	2,903.26	2,726.55	2,649.08	2,613.40	2,596.60	2,588.60
15.00%	4,995.89	4,052.32	3,768.54	3,388.03	2,939.13	2,765.26	2,689.74	2,655.33	2,639.31	2,631.77
15.25%	5,023.49	4,081.83	3,798.98	3,420.26	2,975.17	2,804.13	2,730.54	2,697.36	2,682.09	2,674.98
15.50%	5,051.17	4,111.45	3,829.54	3,452.62	3,011.38	2,843.15	2,771.46	2,739.49	2,724.93	2,718.24
15.75%	5,078.94	4,141.19	3,860.23	3,485.13	3,047.75	2,882.32	2,812.51	2,781.70	2,767.83	2,761.53
16.00%	5,106.79	4,171.03	3,891.05	3,517.78	3,084.27	2,921.64	2,853.67	2,823.99	2,810.79	2,804.86
16.25%	5,134.73	4,200.99	3,921.98	3,550.56	3,120.95	2,961.10	2,894.94	2,866.36	2,853.79	2,848.22
16.50%	5,162.75	4,231.06	3,953.03	3,583.49	3,157.79	3,000.69	2,936.31	2,908.81	2,896.85	2,891.61
16.75%	5,190.85	4,261.23	3,984.21	3,616.55	3,194.77	3,040.42	2,977.79	2,951.33	2,939.96	2,935.03
17.00%	5,219.04	4,291.52	4,015.51	3,649.75	3,231.91	3,080.28	3,019.37	2,993.92	2,983.10	2,978.48
17.25%	5,247.31	4,321.91	4,046.92	3,683.09	3,269.19	3,120.27	3,061.05	3,036.57	3,026.29	3,021.95
17.50%	5,275.66	4,352.42	4,078.45	3,716.55	3,306.61	3,160.38	3,102.81	3,079.28	3,069.52	3,065.44
17.75%	5,304.10	4,383.03	4,110.11	3,750.16	3,344.18	3,200.61	3,144.67	3,122.05	3,112.78	3,108.95
18.00%	5,332.62	4,413.75	4,141.87	3,783.89	3,381.88	3,240.95	3,186.60	3,164.88	3,156.07	3,152.48
18.25%	5,361.22	4,444.57	4,173.76	3,817.75	3,419.72	3,281.41	3,228.62	3,207.76	3,199.40	3,196.03
18.50%	5,389.90	4,475.50	4,205.76	3,851.75	3,457.70	3,321.98	3,270.72	3,250.68	3,242.75	3,239.60
18.75%	5,418.67	4,506.54	4,237.88	3,885.87	3,495.80	3,362.66	3,312.89	3,293.66	3,286.13	3,283.17
19.00%	5,447.52	4,537.68	4,270.11	3,920.12	3,534.04	3,403.44	3,355.13	3,336.67	3,329.54	3,326.77
19.25%	5,476.44	4,568.93	4,302.46	3,954.50	3,572.40	3,444.32	3,397.44	3,379.73	3,372.97	3,370.37
19.50%	5,505.45	4,600.28	4,334.92	3,989.00	3,610.89	3,485.30	3,439.81	3,422.83	3,416.42	3,413.99
19.75%	5,534.54	4,631.74	4,367.49	4,023.62	3,649.49	3,526.37	3,482.25	3,465.97	3,459.89	3,457.62
20.00%	5,563.72	4,663.30	4,400.17	4,058.37	3,688.22	3,567.53	3,524.75	3,509.14	3,503.38	3,501.25
20.25%	5,592.97	4,694.97	4,432.97	4,093.24	3,727.07	3,608.78	3,567.30	3,552.34	3,546.89	3,544.90
20.50%	5,622.30	4,726.73	4,465.87	4,128.23	3,766.03	3,650.12	3,609.91	3,595.58	3,590.42	3,588.56
20.75%	5,651.71	4,758.60	4,498.89	4,163.34	3,805.10	3,691.55	3,652.58	3,638.85	3,633.96	3,632.22

$215,000 1.00 - 10.75% 5 - 40 Years

	5	7	8	10	15	20	25	30	35	40
1.00%	3,675.16	2,651.22	2,331.29	1,883.49	1,286.76	988.77	810.28	691.52	606.91	543.64
1.25%	3,698.34	2,674.47	2,354.59	1,906.91	1,310.54	1,012.94	834.84	716.49	632.29	569.42
1.50%	3,721.63	2,697.85	2,378.04	1,930.52	1,334.60	1,037.47	859.86	742.01	658.30	595.92
1.75%	3,745.00	2,721.36	2,401.64	1,954.31	1,358.93	1,062.38	885.35	768.07	684.94	623.14
2.00%	3,768.47	2,745.00	2,425.39	1,978.29	1,383.54	1,087.65	911.29	794.68	712.21	651.08
2.25%	3,792.03	2,768.77	2,449.28	2,002.45	1,408.43	1,113.29	937.68	821.83	740.11	679.71
2.50%	3,815.68	2,792.67	2,473.33	2,026.80	1,433.60	1,139.29	964.53	849.51	768.61	709.02
2.75%	3,839.43	2,816.70	2,497.52	2,051.34	1,459.04	1,165.66	991.82	877.72	797.72	739.01
3.00%	3,863.27	2,840.86	2,521.86	2,076.06	1,484.75	1,192.38	1,019.55	906.45	827.43	769.67
3.25%	3,887.20	2,865.15	2,546.35	2,100.96	1,510.74	1,219.47	1,047.73	935.69	857.72	800.96
3.50%	3,911.23	2,889.57	2,570.98	2,126.05	1,537.00	1,246.91	1,076.34	965.45	888.57	832.89
3.75%	3,935.34	2,914.12	2,595.76	2,151.32	1,563.53	1,274.71	1,105.38	995.70	920.00	865.43
4.00%	3,959.55	2,938.79	2,620.69	2,176.77	1,590.33	1,302.86	1,134.85	1,026.44	951.97	898.57
4.25%	3,983.85	2,963.60	2,645.77	2,202.41	1,617.40	1,331.35	1,164.74	1,057.67	984.47	932.28
4.50%	4,008.25	2,988.53	2,671.00	2,228.23	1,644.74	1,360.20	1,195.04	1,089.37	1,017.50	966.56
4.75%	4,032.74	3,013.60	2,696.37	2,254.23	1,672.34	1,389.38	1,225.75	1,121.54	1,051.04	1,001.38
5.00%	4,057.32	3,038.79	2,721.88	2,280.41	1,700.21	1,418.90	1,256.87	1,154.17	1,085.08	1,036.72
5.25%	4,081.99	3,064.11	2,747.55	2,306.77	1,728.34	1,448.76	1,288.38	1,187.24	1,119.60	1,072.57
5.50%	4,106.75	3,089.56	2,773.35	2,333.31	1,756.73	1,478.96	1,320.29	1,220.75	1,154.59	1,108.91
5.75%	4,131.61	3,115.14	2,799.31	2,360.04	1,785.38	1,509.48	1,352.58	1,254.68	1,190.03	1,145.71
6.00%	4,156.55	3,140.84	2,825.41	2,386.94	1,814.29	1,540.33	1,385.25	1,289.03	1,225.91	1,182.96
6.25%	4,181.59	3,166.67	2,851.65	2,414.02	1,843.46	1,571.50	1,418.29	1,323.79	1,262.21	1,220.64
6.50%	4,206.72	3,192.63	2,878.04	2,441.28	1,872.88	1,602.98	1,451.70	1,358.95	1,298.93	1,258.73
6.75%	4,231.94	3,218.71	2,904.57	2,468.72	1,902.56	1,634.78	1,485.46	1,394.49	1,336.05	1,297.22
7.00%	4,257.26	3,244.93	2,931.25	2,496.33	1,932.48	1,666.89	1,519.58	1,430.40	1,373.54	1,336.08
7.25%	4,282.66	3,271.26	2,958.07	2,524.12	1,962.66	1,699.31	1,554.03	1,466.68	1,411.40	1,375.29
7.50%	4,308.16	3,297.73	2,985.03	2,552.09	1,993.08	1,732.03	1,588.83	1,503.31	1,449.62	1,414.85
7.75%	4,333.75	3,324.32	3,012.14	2,580.23	2,023.74	1,765.04	1,623.96	1,540.29	1,488.18	1,454.73
8.00%	4,359.42	3,351.04	3,039.39	2,608.54	2,054.65	1,798.35	1,659.40	1,577.59	1,527.06	1,494.92
8.25%	4,385.19	3,377.88	3,066.78	2,637.03	2,085.80	1,831.94	1,695.17	1,615.22	1,566.26	1,535.40
8.50%	4,411.05	3,404.84	3,094.31	2,665.69	2,117.19	1,865.82	1,731.24	1,653.16	1,605.75	1,576.15
8.75%	4,437.01	3,431.94	3,121.98	2,694.53	2,148.81	1,899.98	1,767.61	1,691.41	1,645.53	1,617.17
9.00%	4,463.05	3,459.15	3,149.79	2,723.53	2,180.67	1,934.41	1,804.27	1,729.94	1,685.58	1,658.43
9.25%	4,489.18	3,486.49	3,177.75	2,752.70	2,212.76	1,969.11	1,841.22	1,768.75	1,725.90	1,699.92
9.50%	4,515.40	3,513.96	3,205.84	2,782.05	2,245.08	2,004.08	1,878.45	1,807.84	1,766.46	1,741.63
9.75%	4,541.71	3,541.54	3,234.07	2,811.56	2,277.63	2,039.31	1,915.95	1,847.18	1,807.27	1,783.55
10.00%	4,568.11	3,569.25	3,262.45	2,841.24	2,310.40	2,074.80	1,953.71	1,886.78	1,848.30	1,825.66
10.25%	4,594.61	3,597.09	3,290.96	2,871.09	2,343.39	2,110.53	1,991.72	1,926.62	1,889.54	1,867.96
10.50%	4,621.19	3,625.04	3,319.60	2,901.10	2,376.61	2,146.52	2,029.99	1,966.69	1,930.99	1,910.43
10.75%	4,647.86	3,653.12	3,348.39	2,931.28	2,410.04	2,182.74	2,068.50	2,006.98	1,972.63	1,953.05

MeritzPress.com

$215,000   11.00 - 20.75%   5 - 40 Years

	5	7	8	10	15	20	25	30	35	40
11.00%	4,674.62	3,681.32	3,377.31	2,961.63	2,443.68	2,219.21	2,107.24	2,047.50	2,014.46	1,995.83
11.25%	4,701.47	3,709.65	3,406.37	2,992.13	2,477.54	2,255.90	2,146.22	2,088.21	2,056.46	2,038.75
11.50%	4,728.41	3,738.09	3,435.57	3,022.80	2,511.61	2,292.82	2,185.41	2,129.13	2,098.63	2,081.81
11.75%	4,755.44	3,766.65	3,464.90	3,053.63	2,545.88	2,329.97	2,224.82	2,170.23	2,140.96	2,124.98
12.00%	4,782.56	3,795.34	3,494.36	3,084.63	2,580.36	2,367.34	2,264.43	2,211.52	2,183.43	2,168.27
12.25%	4,809.76	3,824.14	3,523.96	3,115.78	2,615.04	2,404.91	2,304.25	2,252.98	2,226.05	2,211.68
12.50%	4,837.06	3,853.07	3,553.69	3,147.09	2,649.92	2,442.70	2,344.26	2,294.60	2,268.80	2,255.18
12.75%	4,864.44	3,882.11	3,583.56	3,178.56	2,685.00	2,480.69	2,384.46	2,336.39	2,311.67	2,298.77
13.00%	4,891.91	3,911.27	3,613.56	3,210.18	2,720.27	2,518.89	2,424.85	2,378.33	2,354.67	2,342.46
13.25%	4,919.47	3,940.55	3,643.69	3,241.96	2,755.73	2,557.28	2,465.41	2,420.41	2,397.77	2,386.22
13.50%	4,947.12	3,969.95	3,673.95	3,273.90	2,791.38	2,595.86	2,506.14	2,462.64	2,440.98	2,430.06
13.75%	4,974.85	3,999.47	3,704.35	3,305.99	2,827.22	2,634.62	2,547.03	2,504.99	2,484.29	2,473.97
14.00%	5,002.67	4,029.10	3,734.87	3,338.23	2,863.24	2,673.57	2,588.09	2,547.47	2,527.70	2,517.95
14.25%	5,030.58	4,058.85	3,765.53	3,370.62	2,899.45	2,712.70	2,629.29	2,590.08	2,571.19	2,561.99
14.50%	5,058.58	4,088.72	3,796.31	3,403.17	2,935.83	2,752.00	2,670.65	2,632.80	2,614.77	2,606.09
14.75%	5,086.66	4,118.70	3,827.22	3,435.86	2,972.38	2,791.46	2,712.15	2,675.62	2,658.42	2,650.23
15.00%	5,114.83	4,148.80	3,858.26	3,468.70	3,009.11	2,831.10	2,753.79	2,718.55	2,702.15	2,694.43
15.25%	5,143.09	4,179.02	3,889.43	3,501.69	3,046.01	2,870.89	2,795.56	2,761.59	2,745.95	2,738.67
15.50%	5,171.44	4,209.34	3,920.72	3,534.83	3,083.08	2,910.84	2,837.45	2,804.71	2,789.81	2,782.96
15.75%	5,199.87	4,239.79	3,952.14	3,568.11	3,120.31	2,950.95	2,879.47	2,847.93	2,833.73	2,827.28
16.00%	5,228.38	4,270.34	3,983.69	3,601.53	3,157.71	2,991.20	2,921.61	2,891.23	2,877.71	2,871.64
16.25%	5,256.98	4,301.01	4,015.36	3,635.10	3,195.26	3,031.60	2,963.86	2,934.61	2,921.74	2,916.04
16.50%	5,285.67	4,331.80	4,047.15	3,668.81	3,232.97	3,072.14	3,006.23	2,978.07	2,965.83	2,960.46
16.75%	5,314.45	4,362.69	4,079.07	3,702.66	3,270.84	3,112.81	3,048.69	3,021.60	3,009.96	3,004.92
17.00%	5,343.30	4,393.70	4,111.11	3,736.65	3,308.86	3,153.62	3,091.26	3,065.20	3,054.13	3,049.40
17.25%	5,372.25	4,424.82	4,143.28	3,770.78	3,347.03	3,194.56	3,133.93	3,108.87	3,098.35	3,093.90
17.50%	5,401.28	4,456.05	4,175.56	3,805.04	3,385.34	3,235.63	3,176.69	3,152.60	3,142.60	3,138.43
17.75%	5,430.39	4,487.39	4,207.97	3,839.45	3,423.80	3,276.81	3,219.54	3,196.39	3,186.89	3,182.97
18.00%	5,459.59	4,518.84	4,240.49	3,873.98	3,462.41	3,318.12	3,262.47	3,240.23	3,231.22	3,227.54
18.25%	5,488.87	4,550.39	4,273.14	3,908.65	3,501.15	3,359.54	3,305.49	3,284.13	3,275.57	3,272.13
18.50%	5,518.23	4,582.06	4,305.90	3,943.46	3,540.03	3,401.08	3,348.59	3,328.08	3,319.96	3,316.73
18.75%	5,547.68	4,613.84	4,338.78	3,978.39	3,579.04	3,442.72	3,391.77	3,372.08	3,364.37	3,361.35
19.00%	5,577.22	4,645.72	4,371.78	4,013.46	3,618.18	3,484.47	3,435.01	3,416.12	3,408.81	3,405.98
19.25%	5,606.84	4,677.72	4,404.90	4,048.65	3,657.46	3,526.33	3,478.33	3,460.20	3,453.28	3,450.62
19.50%	5,636.54	4,709.82	4,438.13	4,083.97	3,696.86	3,568.28	3,521.71	3,504.33	3,497.76	3,495.27
19.75%	5,666.32	4,742.02	4,471.48	4,119.42	3,736.39	3,610.33	3,565.16	3,548.49	3,542.27	3,539.94
20.00%	5,696.18	4,774.33	4,504.94	4,155.00	3,776.04	3,652.47	3,608.67	3,592.69	3,586.80	3,584.62
20.25%	5,726.13	4,806.75	4,538.51	4,190.70	3,815.81	3,694.71	3,652.24	3,636.92	3,631.34	3,629.30
20.50%	5,756.16	4,839.27	4,572.20	4,226.52	3,855.70	3,737.03	3,695.87	3,681.19	3,675.91	3,674.00
20.75%	5,786.28	4,871.90	4,606.00	4,262.46	3,895.70	3,779.44	3,739.54	3,725.49	3,720.48	3,718.70

$220,000   1.00 - 10.75%   5 - 40 Years

	5	7	8	10	15	20	25	30	35	40
1.00%	3,760.62	2,712.87	2,385.51	1,927.29	1,316.69	1,011.77	829.12	707.61	621.03	556.28
1.25%	3,784.35	2,736.66	2,409.35	1,951.26	1,341.02	1,036.49	854.25	733.15	646.99	582.66
1.50%	3,808.18	2,760.59	2,433.35	1,975.41	1,365.63	1,061.60	879.86	759.26	673.61	609.78
1.75%	3,832.09	2,784.65	2,457.49	1,999.76	1,390.53	1,087.08	905.94	785.94	700.87	637.64
2.00%	3,856.11	2,808.84	2,481.79	2,024.30	1,415.72	1,112.94	932.48	813.16	728.78	666.22
2.25%	3,880.22	2,833.16	2,506.24	2,049.02	1,441.19	1,139.18	959.49	840.94	757.32	695.51
2.50%	3,904.42	2,857.62	2,530.85	2,073.94	1,466.94	1,165.79	986.96	869.27	786.49	725.51
2.75%	3,928.72	2,882.20	2,555.60	2,099.04	1,492.97	1,192.77	1,014.88	898.13	816.28	756.20
3.00%	3,953.11	2,906.93	2,580.51	2,124.34	1,519.28	1,220.11	1,043.26	927.53	846.67	787.57
3.25%	3,977.60	2,931.78	2,605.56	2,149.82	1,545.87	1,247.83	1,072.10	957.45	877.66	819.59
3.50%	4,002.18	2,956.77	2,630.77	2,175.49	1,572.74	1,275.91	1,101.37	987.90	909.24	852.26
3.75%	4,026.86	2,981.89	2,656.13	2,201.35	1,599.89	1,304.35	1,131.09	1,018.85	941.39	885.56
4.00%	4,051.63	3,007.14	2,681.64	2,227.39	1,627.31	1,333.16	1,161.24	1,050.31	974.10	919.46
4.25%	4,076.50	3,032.52	2,707.30	2,253.63	1,655.01	1,362.32	1,191.82	1,082.27	1,007.37	953.96
4.50%	4,101.46	3,058.04	2,733.11	2,280.04	1,682.99	1,391.83	1,222.83	1,114.71	1,041.16	989.04
4.75%	4,126.52	3,083.68	2,759.07	2,306.65	1,711.23	1,421.69	1,254.26	1,147.62	1,075.48	1,024.67
5.00%	4,151.67	3,109.46	2,785.18	2,333.44	1,739.75	1,451.90	1,286.10	1,181.01	1,110.31	1,060.83
5.25%	4,176.92	3,135.37	2,811.44	2,360.42	1,768.53	1,482.46	1,318.34	1,214.85	1,145.63	1,097.51
5.50%	4,202.26	3,161.41	2,837.85	2,387.58	1,797.58	1,513.35	1,350.99	1,249.14	1,181.44	1,134.69
5.75%	4,227.69	3,187.58	2,864.41	2,414.92	1,826.90	1,544.58	1,384.03	1,283.86	1,217.70	1,172.35
6.00%	4,253.22	3,213.88	2,891.11	2,442.45	1,856.49	1,576.15	1,417.46	1,319.01	1,254.42	1,210.47
6.25%	4,278.84	3,240.31	2,917.97	2,470.16	1,886.33	1,608.04	1,451.27	1,354.58	1,291.57	1,249.03
6.50%	4,304.55	3,266.88	2,944.97	2,498.06	1,916.44	1,640.26	1,485.46	1,390.55	1,329.14	1,288.00
6.75%	4,330.36	3,293.57	2,972.12	2,526.13	1,946.80	1,672.80	1,520.01	1,426.92	1,367.12	1,327.39
7.00%	4,356.26	3,320.39	2,999.42	2,554.39	1,977.42	1,705.66	1,554.91	1,463.67	1,405.48	1,367.15
7.25%	4,382.26	3,347.34	3,026.86	2,582.82	2,008.30	1,738.83	1,590.18	1,500.79	1,444.23	1,407.28
7.50%	4,408.35	3,374.42	3,054.45	2,611.44	2,039.43	1,772.31	1,625.78	1,538.27	1,483.33	1,447.76
7.75%	4,434.53	3,401.63	3,082.19	2,640.23	2,070.81	1,806.09	1,661.72	1,576.11	1,522.79	1,488.56
8.00%	4,460.81	3,428.97	3,110.07	2,669.21	2,102.43	1,840.17	1,698.00	1,614.28	1,562.57	1,529.69
8.25%	4,487.18	3,456.43	3,138.10	2,698.36	2,134.31	1,874.54	1,734.59	1,652.79	1,602.68	1,571.11
8.50%	4,513.64	3,484.03	3,166.27	2,727.69	2,166.43	1,909.21	1,771.50	1,691.61	1,643.09	1,612.81
8.75%	4,540.19	3,511.75	3,194.58	2,757.19	2,198.79	1,944.16	1,808.72	1,730.74	1,683.80	1,654.78
9.00%	4,566.84	3,539.60	3,223.04	2,786.87	2,231.39	1,979.40	1,846.23	1,770.17	1,724.78	1,697.00
9.25%	4,593.58	3,567.57	3,251.65	2,816.72	2,264.22	2,014.91	1,884.04	1,809.89	1,766.04	1,739.45
9.50%	4,620.41	3,595.68	3,280.40	2,846.75	2,297.29	2,050.69	1,922.13	1,849.88	1,807.55	1,782.14
9.75%	4,647.33	3,623.91	3,309.28	2,876.95	2,330.60	2,086.74	1,960.50	1,890.14	1,849.30	1,825.03
10.00%	4,674.35	3,652.26	3,338.32	2,907.32	2,364.13	2,123.05	1,999.14	1,930.66	1,891.28	1,868.12
10.25%	4,701.46	3,680.74	3,367.49	2,937.86	2,397.89	2,159.62	2,038.04	1,971.42	1,933.48	1,911.40
10.50%	4,728.66	3,709.35	3,396.80	2,968.57	2,431.88	2,196.44	2,077.20	2,012.43	1,975.89	1,954.85
10.75%	4,755.95	3,738.08	3,426.26	2,999.45	2,466.09	2,233.50	2,116.60	2,053.66	2,018.51	1,998.47

$220,000   11.00 - 20.75%   5 - 40 Years

	5	7	8	10	15	20	25	30	35	40
11.00%	4,783.33	3,766.94	3,455.85	3,030.50	2,500.51	2,270.81	2,156.25	2,095.11	2,061.31	2,042.25
11.25%	4,810.81	3,795.92	3,485.59	3,061.72	2,535.16	2,308.36	2,196.13	2,136.78	2,104.29	2,086.17
11.50%	4,838.37	3,825.02	3,515.46	3,093.10	2,570.02	2,346.15	2,236.23	2,178.64	2,147.44	2,130.22
11.75%	4,866.03	3,854.25	3,545.47	3,124.65	2,605.09	2,384.16	2,276.56	2,220.70	2,190.75	2,174.40
12.00%	4,893.78	3,883.60	3,575.63	3,156.36	2,640.37	2,422.39	2,317.09	2,262.95	2,234.21	2,218.70
12.25%	4,921.62	3,913.08	3,605.91	3,188.24	2,675.86	2,460.84	2,357.84	2,305.37	2,277.82	2,263.11
12.50%	4,949.55	3,942.67	3,636.34	3,220.28	2,711.55	2,499.51	2,398.78	2,347.97	2,321.56	2,307.62
12.75%	4,977.57	3,972.39	3,666.90	3,252.48	2,747.44	2,538.39	2,439.91	2,390.73	2,365.43	2,352.23
13.00%	5,005.68	4,002.23	3,697.60	3,284.84	2,783.53	2,577.47	2,481.24	2,433.64	2,409.42	2,396.93
13.25%	5,033.88	4,032.19	3,728.43	3,317.36	2,819.82	2,616.75	2,522.74	2,476.70	2,453.53	2,441.71
13.50%	5,062.17	4,062.28	3,759.40	3,350.03	2,856.30	2,656.22	2,564.42	2,519.91	2,497.75	2,486.57
13.75%	5,090.55	4,092.48	3,790.50	3,382.87	2,892.97	2,695.89	2,606.27	2,563.25	2,542.07	2,531.51
14.00%	5,119.02	4,122.80	3,821.73	3,415.86	2,929.83	2,735.75	2,648.27	2,606.72	2,586.48	2,576.51
14.25%	5,147.57	4,153.25	3,853.10	3,449.01	2,966.88	2,775.78	2,690.44	2,650.31	2,630.99	2,621.57
14.50%	5,176.22	4,183.81	3,884.60	3,482.31	3,004.10	2,816.00	2,732.76	2,694.02	2,675.58	2,666.69
14.75%	5,204.96	4,214.49	3,916.23	3,515.76	3,041.51	2,856.38	2,775.22	2,737.85	2,720.24	2,711.87
15.00%	5,233.78	4,245.29	3,947.99	3,549.37	3,079.09	2,896.94	2,817.83	2,781.78	2,764.99	2,757.09
15.25%	5,262.70	4,276.20	3,979.88	3,583.13	3,116.85	2,937.66	2,860.57	2,825.81	2,809.80	2,802.36
15.50%	5,291.70	4,307.24	4,011.90	3,617.03	3,154.78	2,978.54	2,903.44	2,869.94	2,854.69	2,847.68
15.75%	5,320.79	4,338.39	4,044.05	3,651.09	3,192.88	3,019.57	2,946.44	2,914.16	2,899.63	2,893.03
16.00%	5,349.97	4,369.65	4,076.33	3,685.29	3,231.14	3,060.76	2,989.56	2,958.47	2,944.63	2,938.43
16.25%	5,379.24	4,401.04	4,108.74	3,719.64	3,269.57	3,102.10	3,032.79	3,002.86	2,989.69	2,983.85
16.50%	5,408.59	4,432.54	4,141.27	3,754.13	3,308.16	3,143.58	3,076.14	3,047.33	3,034.80	3,029.31
16.75%	5,438.04	4,464.15	4,173.93	3,788.77	3,346.91	3,185.20	3,119.59	3,091.87	3,079.96	3,074.80
17.00%	5,467.57	4,495.88	4,206.72	3,823.55	3,385.81	3,226.96	3,163.15	3,136.49	3,125.16	3,120.31
17.25%	5,497.18	4,527.72	4,239.63	3,858.47	3,424.87	3,268.85	3,206.81	3,181.17	3,170.40	3,165.85
17.50%	5,526.89	4,559.67	4,272.67	3,893.53	3,464.07	3,310.87	3,250.57	3,225.92	3,215.69	3,211.41
17.75%	5,556.68	4,591.74	4,305.83	3,928.73	3,503.43	3,353.02	3,294.41	3,270.72	3,261.01	3,257.00
18.00%	5,586.55	4,623.92	4,339.11	3,964.07	3,542.93	3,395.29	3,338.35	3,315.59	3,306.36	3,302.60
18.25%	5,616.52	4,656.22	4,372.51	3,999.55	3,582.57	3,437.67	3,382.36	3,360.51	3,351.75	3,348.22
18.50%	5,646.57	4,688.62	4,406.04	4,035.16	3,622.35	3,480.17	3,426.47	3,405.48	3,397.17	3,393.86
18.75%	5,676.70	4,721.14	4,439.68	4,070.91	3,662.27	3,522.79	3,470.64	3,450.50	3,442.62	3,439.52
19.00%	5,706.92	4,753.76	4,473.45	4,106.79	3,702.33	3,565.51	3,514.90	3,495.56	3,488.09	3,485.18
19.25%	5,737.23	4,786.50	4,507.34	4,142.80	3,742.52	3,608.33	3,559.22	3,540.67	3,533.59	3,530.87
19.50%	5,767.62	4,819.35	4,541.34	4,178.95	3,782.83	3,651.26	3,603.61	3,585.82	3,579.11	3,576.56
19.75%	5,798.09	4,852.30	4,575.46	4,215.22	3,823.28	3,694.29	3,648.07	3,631.01	3,624.65	3,622.27
20.00%	5,828.65	4,885.36	4,609.70	4,251.62	3,863.85	3,737.41	3,692.59	3,676.24	3,670.21	3,667.98
20.25%	5,859.30	4,918.53	4,644.06	4,288.15	3,904.55	3,780.63	3,737.18	3,721.50	3,715.79	3,713.71
20.50%	5,890.03	4,951.81	4,678.53	4,324.81	3,945.36	3,823.94	3,781.82	3,766.80	3,761.39	3,759.44
20.75%	5,920.84	4,985.20	4,713.12	4,361.59	3,986.30	3,867.33	3,826.51	3,812.12	3,807.01	3,805.18

	5	7	8	10	15	20	25	30	35	40
1.00%	3,846.09	2,774.53	2,439.73	1,971.09	1,346.61	1,034.76	847.96	723.69	635.14	568.93
1.25%	3,870.36	2,798.86	2,464.11	1,995.60	1,371.50	1,060.05	873.67	749.82	661.69	595.90
1.50%	3,894.72	2,823.33	2,488.65	2,020.31	1,396.67	1,085.73	899.86	776.52	688.91	623.64
1.75%	3,919.19	2,847.93	2,513.35	2,045.21	1,422.14	1,111.79	926.53	803.80	716.80	652.13
2.00%	3,943.75	2,872.67	2,538.20	2,070.30	1,447.89	1,138.24	953.67	831.64	745.34	681.36
2.25%	3,968.40	2,897.55	2,563.20	2,095.59	1,473.94	1,165.07	981.29	860.05	774.53	711.32
2.50%	3,993.16	2,922.56	2,588.36	2,121.07	1,500.28	1,192.28	1,009.39	889.02	804.36	742.00
2.75%	4,018.01	2,947.71	2,613.68	2,146.75	1,526.90	1,219.87	1,037.95	918.54	834.83	773.39
3.00%	4,042.96	2,972.99	2,639.15	2,172.62	1,553.81	1,247.84	1,066.98	948.61	865.91	805.46
3.25%	4,068.00	2,998.41	2,664.78	2,198.68	1,581.00	1,276.19	1,096.46	979.21	897.61	838.22
3.50%	4,093.14	3,023.97	2,690.56	2,224.93	1,608.49	1,304.91	1,126.40	1,010.35	929.90	871.63
3.75%	4,118.38	3,049.66	2,716.50	2,251.38	1,636.25	1,334.00	1,156.80	1,042.01	962.79	905.68
4.00%	4,143.72	3,075.48	2,742.59	2,278.02	1,664.30	1,363.46	1,187.63	1,074.18	996.24	940.36
4.25%	4,169.15	3,101.44	2,768.83	2,304.84	1,692.63	1,393.28	1,218.91	1,106.86	1,030.26	975.65
4.50%	4,194.68	3,127.54	2,795.23	2,331.86	1,721.23	1,423.46	1,250.62	1,140.04	1,064.83	1,011.52
4.75%	4,220.31	3,153.77	2,821.78	2,359.07	1,750.12	1,454.00	1,282.76	1,173.71	1,099.93	1,047.96
5.00%	4,246.03	3,180.13	2,848.48	2,386.47	1,779.29	1,484.90	1,315.33	1,207.85	1,135.55	1,084.94
5.25%	4,271.85	3,206.63	2,875.34	2,414.06	1,808.72	1,516.15	1,348.31	1,242.46	1,171.67	1,122.46
5.50%	4,297.76	3,233.26	2,902.35	2,441.84	1,838.44	1,547.75	1,381.70	1,277.53	1,208.29	1,160.48
5.75%	4,323.77	3,260.03	2,929.51	2,469.81	1,868.42	1,579.69	1,415.49	1,313.04	1,245.38	1,199.00
6.00%	4,349.88	3,286.92	2,956.82	2,497.96	1,898.68	1,611.97	1,449.68	1,348.99	1,282.93	1,237.98
6.25%	4,376.08	3,313.96	2,984.29	2,526.30	1,929.20	1,644.59	1,484.26	1,385.36	1,320.92	1,277.41
6.50%	4,402.38	3,341.12	3,011.90	2,554.83	1,959.99	1,677.54	1,519.22	1,422.15	1,359.35	1,317.28
6.75%	4,428.78	3,368.42	3,039.67	2,583.54	1,991.05	1,710.82	1,554.55	1,459.35	1,398.19	1,357.55
7.00%	4,455.27	3,395.85	3,067.59	2,612.44	2,022.36	1,744.42	1,590.25	1,496.93	1,437.43	1,398.22
7.25%	4,481.86	3,423.42	3,095.65	2,641.52	2,053.94	1,778.35	1,626.32	1,534.90	1,477.05	1,439.26
7.50%	4,508.54	3,451.11	3,123.87	2,670.79	2,085.78	1,812.58	1,662.73	1,573.23	1,517.05	1,480.66
7.75%	4,535.32	3,478.94	3,152.24	2,700.24	2,117.87	1,847.13	1,699.49	1,611.93	1,557.40	1,522.39
8.00%	4,562.19	3,506.90	3,180.75	2,729.87	2,150.22	1,881.99	1,736.59	1,650.97	1,598.09	1,564.45
8.25%	4,589.16	3,534.99	3,209.42	2,759.68	2,182.82	1,917.15	1,774.01	1,690.35	1,639.11	1,606.81
8.50%	4,616.22	3,563.21	3,238.23	2,789.68	2,215.66	1,952.60	1,811.76	1,730.06	1,680.44	1,649.46
8.75%	4,643.38	3,591.56	3,267.19	2,819.85	2,248.76	1,988.35	1,849.82	1,770.08	1,722.07	1,692.38
9.00%	4,670.63	3,620.04	3,296.30	2,850.20	2,282.10	2,024.38	1,888.19	1,810.40	1,763.98	1,735.56
9.25%	4,697.98	3,648.65	3,325.55	2,880.74	2,315.68	2,060.70	1,926.86	1,851.02	1,806.17	1,778.99
9.50%	4,725.42	3,677.40	3,354.95	2,911.45	2,349.51	2,097.30	1,965.82	1,891.92	1,848.63	1,822.64
9.75%	4,752.95	3,706.27	3,384.50	2,942.33	2,383.57	2,134.16	2,005.06	1,933.10	1,891.33	1,866.51
10.00%	4,780.59	3,735.27	3,414.19	2,973.39	2,417.86	2,171.30	2,044.58	1,974.54	1,934.26	1,910.58
10.25%	4,808.31	3,764.39	3,444.02	3,004.63	2,452.39	2,208.70	2,084.36	2,016.23	1,977.43	1,954.84
10.50%	4,836.13	3,793.65	3,474.00	3,036.04	2,487.15	2,246.35	2,124.41	2,058.16	2,020.80	1,999.28
10.75%	4,864.04	3,823.04	3,504.13	3,067.62	2,522.13	2,284.27	2,164.71	2,100.33	2,064.38	2,043.89

$225,000   11.00 - 20.75%   5 - 40 Years

	5	7	8	10	15	20	25	30	35	40
11.00%	4,892.05	3,852.55	3,534.40	3,099.38	2,557.34	2,322.42	2,205.25	2,142.73	2,108.15	2,088.66
11.25%	4,920.14	3,882.19	3,564.81	3,131.30	2,592.78	2,360.83	2,246.04	2,185.34	2,152.11	2,133.58
11.50%	4,948.34	3,911.95	3,595.36	3,163.40	2,628.43	2,399.47	2,287.06	2,228.16	2,196.24	2,178.63
11.75%	4,976.62	3,941.85	3,626.05	3,195.66	2,664.30	2,438.34	2,328.30	2,271.17	2,240.54	2,223.82
12.00%	5,005.00	3,971.86	3,656.89	3,228.10	2,700.38	2,477.44	2,369.75	2,314.38	2,284.99	2,269.12
12.25%	5,033.47	4,002.01	3,687.87	3,260.70	2,736.67	2,516.77	2,411.42	2,357.77	2,329.59	2,314.54
12.50%	5,062.04	4,032.28	3,718.98	3,293.46	2,773.17	2,556.32	2,453.30	2,401.33	2,374.32	2,360.07
12.75%	5,090.69	4,062.67	3,750.24	3,326.40	2,809.88	2,596.08	2,495.37	2,445.06	2,419.19	2,405.69
13.00%	5,119.44	4,093.19	3,781.63	3,359.49	2,846.79	2,636.05	2,537.63	2,488.95	2,464.18	2,451.41
13.25%	5,148.28	4,123.83	3,813.17	3,392.75	2,883.91	2,676.22	2,580.08	2,532.99	2,509.30	2,497.21
13.50%	5,177.22	4,154.60	3,844.84	3,426.17	2,921.22	2,716.59	2,622.70	2,577.18	2,554.52	2,543.09
13.75%	5,206.24	4,185.49	3,876.64	3,459.75	2,958.72	2,757.16	2,665.50	2,621.50	2,599.84	2,589.04
14.00%	5,235.36	4,216.50	3,908.59	3,493.49	2,996.42	2,797.92	2,708.46	2,665.96	2,645.26	2,635.07
14.25%	5,264.56	4,247.64	3,940.67	3,527.39	3,034.30	2,838.87	2,751.59	2,710.55	2,690.78	2,681.15
14.50%	5,293.86	4,278.89	3,972.88	3,561.45	3,072.38	2,879.99	2,794.87	2,755.25	2,736.38	2,727.30
14.75%	5,323.25	4,310.27	4,005.23	3,595.67	3,110.63	2,921.30	2,838.30	2,800.07	2,782.07	2,773.50
15.00%	5,352.73	4,341.77	4,037.72	3,630.04	3,149.07	2,962.78	2,881.87	2,845.00	2,827.83	2,819.75
15.25%	5,382.31	4,373.39	4,070.33	3,664.56	3,187.69	3,004.42	2,925.58	2,890.03	2,873.66	2,866.06
15.50%	5,411.97	4,405.13	4,103.08	3,699.24	3,226.48	3,046.23	2,969.43	2,935.16	2,919.57	2,912.40
15.75%	5,441.72	4,436.99	4,135.96	3,734.07	3,265.44	3,088.20	3,013.40	2,980.39	2,965.53	2,958.79
16.00%	5,471.56	4,468.96	4,168.98	3,769.05	3,304.58	3,130.33	3,057.50	3,025.70	3,011.56	3,005.21
16.25%	5,501.50	4,501.06	4,202.12	3,804.17	3,343.88	3,172.60	3,101.72	3,071.10	3,057.64	3,051.67
16.50%	5,531.52	4,533.28	4,235.39	3,839.45	3,383.34	3,215.03	3,146.05	3,116.58	3,103.77	3,098.16
16.75%	5,561.63	4,565.61	4,268.80	3,874.88	3,422.97	3,257.59	3,190.49	3,162.14	3,149.95	3,144.68
17.00%	5,591.83	4,598.06	4,302.33	3,910.45	3,462.76	3,300.30	3,235.04	3,207.77	3,196.18	3,191.23
17.25%	5,622.12	4,630.62	4,335.99	3,946.16	3,502.70	3,343.14	3,279.69	3,253.47	3,242.46	3,237.80
17.50%	5,652.50	4,663.30	4,369.77	3,982.02	3,542.80	3,386.12	3,324.44	3,299.23	3,288.77	3,284.40
17.75%	5,682.97	4,696.10	4,403.68	4,018.02	3,583.05	3,429.22	3,369.28	3,345.06	3,335.12	3,331.02
18.00%	5,713.52	4,729.01	4,437.72	4,054.17	3,623.45	3,472.45	3,414.22	3,390.94	3,381.51	3,377.66
18.25%	5,744.17	4,762.04	4,471.89	4,090.45	3,663.99	3,515.80	3,459.24	3,436.88	3,427.93	3,424.32
18.50%	5,774.90	4,795.18	4,506.17	4,126.87	3,704.68	3,559.27	3,504.34	3,482.88	3,474.38	3,470.99
18.75%	5,805.72	4,828.44	4,540.59	4,163.43	3,745.51	3,602.85	3,549.52	3,528.92	3,520.86	3,517.69
19.00%	5,836.62	4,861.80	4,575.12	4,200.13	3,786.47	3,646.54	3,594.78	3,575.01	3,567.36	3,564.39
19.25%	5,867.62	4,895.28	4,609.78	4,236.96	3,827.57	3,690.34	3,640.11	3,621.14	3,613.89	3,611.11
19.50%	5,898.70	4,928.88	4,644.55	4,273.92	3,868.81	3,734.25	3,685.51	3,667.32	3,660.45	3,657.85
19.75%	5,929.87	4,962.58	4,679.45	4,311.02	3,910.17	3,778.25	3,730.98	3,713.54	3,707.03	3,704.59
20.00%	5,961.12	4,996.39	4,714.47	4,348.25	3,951.67	3,822.36	3,776.52	3,759.79	3,753.63	3,751.34
20.25%	5,992.47	5,030.32	4,749.61	4,385.61	3,993.29	3,866.55	3,822.11	3,806.08	3,800.24	3,798.11
20.50%	6,023.89	5,064.35	4,784.86	4,423.10	4,035.03	3,910.85	3,867.77	3,852.41	3,846.88	3,844.88
20.75%	6,055.41	5,098.50	4,820.24	4,460.72	4,076.89	3,955.23	3,913.48	3,898.76	3,893.53	3,891.66

	5	7	8	10	15	20	25	30	35	40
1.00%	3,931.56	2,836.19	2,493.94	2,014.89	1,376.54	1,057.76	866.81	739.77	649.26	581.57
1.25%	3,956.37	2,861.06	2,518.87	2,039.95	1,401.97	1,083.61	893.08	766.48	676.40	609.14
1.50%	3,981.27	2,886.07	2,543.95	2,065.20	1,427.71	1,109.85	919.85	793.78	704.22	637.50
1.75%	4,006.28	2,911.22	2,569.20	2,090.66	1,453.74	1,136.50	947.11	821.66	732.73	666.62
2.00%	4,031.38	2,936.51	2,594.60	2,116.31	1,480.07	1,163.53	974.86	850.12	761.90	696.50
2.25%	4,056.59	2,961.94	2,620.16	2,142.16	1,506.69	1,190.96	1,003.10	879.17	791.74	727.13
2.50%	4,081.89	2,987.51	2,645.88	2,168.21	1,533.62	1,218.78	1,031.82	908.78	822.24	758.49
2.75%	4,107.30	3,013.21	2,671.76	2,194.45	1,560.83	1,246.98	1,061.01	938.95	853.38	790.57
3.00%	4,132.80	3,039.06	2,697.80	2,220.90	1,588.34	1,275.57	1,090.69	969.69	885.16	823.36
3.25%	4,158.40	3,065.04	2,724.00	2,247.54	1,616.14	1,304.55	1,120.83	1,000.97	917.56	856.84
3.50%	4,184.10	3,091.17	2,750.35	2,274.37	1,644.23	1,333.91	1,151.43	1,032.80	950.57	891.00
3.75%	4,209.90	3,117.43	2,776.86	2,301.41	1,672.61	1,363.64	1,182.50	1,065.17	984.18	925.81
4.00%	4,235.80	3,143.83	2,803.53	2,328.64	1,701.28	1,393.75	1,214.02	1,098.06	1,018.38	961.26
4.25%	4,261.80	3,170.36	2,830.36	2,356.06	1,730.24	1,424.24	1,246.00	1,131.46	1,053.16	997.33
4.50%	4,287.89	3,197.04	2,857.34	2,383.68	1,759.48	1,455.09	1,278.41	1,165.38	1,088.49	1,033.99
4.75%	4,314.09	3,223.85	2,884.48	2,411.50	1,789.01	1,486.31	1,311.27	1,199.79	1,124.37	1,071.24
5.00%	4,340.38	3,250.80	2,911.78	2,439.51	1,818.83	1,517.90	1,344.56	1,234.69	1,160.78	1,109.05
5.25%	4,366.78	3,277.89	2,939.23	2,467.71	1,848.92	1,549.84	1,378.27	1,270.07	1,197.71	1,147.40
5.50%	4,393.27	3,305.11	2,966.84	2,496.10	1,879.29	1,582.14	1,412.40	1,305.91	1,235.14	1,186.27
5.75%	4,419.86	3,332.47	2,994.61	2,524.69	1,909.94	1,614.79	1,446.94	1,342.22	1,273.05	1,225.64
6.00%	4,446.54	3,359.97	3,022.53	2,553.47	1,940.87	1,647.79	1,481.89	1,378.97	1,311.44	1,265.49
6.25%	4,473.33	3,387.60	3,050.60	2,582.44	1,972.07	1,681.13	1,517.24	1,416.15	1,350.28	1,305.80
6.50%	4,500.21	3,415.37	3,078.83	2,611.60	2,003.55	1,714.82	1,552.98	1,453.76	1,389.55	1,346.55
6.75%	4,527.20	3,443.28	3,107.22	2,640.95	2,035.29	1,748.84	1,589.10	1,491.78	1,429.26	1,387.72
7.00%	4,554.28	3,471.32	3,135.75	2,670.50	2,067.31	1,783.19	1,625.59	1,530.20	1,469.37	1,429.29
7.25%	4,581.45	3,499.49	3,164.45	2,700.22	2,099.58	1,817.86	1,662.46	1,569.01	1,509.87	1,471.25
7.50%	4,608.73	3,527.80	3,193.29	2,730.14	2,132.13	1,852.86	1,699.68	1,608.19	1,550.76	1,513.56
7.75%	4,636.10	3,556.25	3,222.29	2,760.24	2,164.93	1,888.18	1,737.26	1,647.75	1,592.00	1,556.23
8.00%	4,663.57	3,584.83	3,251.44	2,790.53	2,198.00	1,923.81	1,775.18	1,687.66	1,633.60	1,599.22
8.25%	4,691.14	3,613.54	3,280.74	2,821.01	2,231.32	1,959.75	1,813.44	1,727.91	1,675.53	1,642.52
8.50%	4,718.80	3,642.39	3,310.19	2,851.67	2,264.90	1,995.99	1,852.02	1,768.50	1,717.78	1,686.12
8.75%	4,746.56	3,671.37	3,339.79	2,882.52	2,298.73	2,032.53	1,890.93	1,809.41	1,760.34	1,729.99
9.00%	4,774.42	3,700.49	3,369.55	2,913.54	2,332.81	2,069.37	1,930.15	1,850.63	1,803.18	1,774.13
9.25%	4,802.38	3,729.74	3,399.45	2,944.75	2,367.14	2,106.49	1,969.68	1,892.15	1,846.31	1,818.52
9.50%	4,830.43	3,759.12	3,429.50	2,976.14	2,401.72	2,143.90	2,009.50	1,933.96	1,889.71	1,863.14
9.75%	4,858.58	3,788.63	3,459.71	3,007.72	2,436.53	2,181.59	2,049.62	1,976.06	1,933.36	1,907.98
10.00%	4,886.82	3,818.27	3,490.06	3,039.47	2,471.59	2,219.55	2,090.01	2,018.41	1,977.25	1,953.04
10.25%	4,915.16	3,848.05	3,520.56	3,071.40	2,506.89	2,257.78	2,130.68	2,061.03	2,021.37	1,998.28
10.50%	4,943.60	3,877.95	3,551.20	3,103.50	2,542.42	2,296.27	2,171.62	2,103.90	2,065.71	2,043.71
10.75%	4,972.13	3,907.99	3,582.00	3,135.79	2,578.18	2,335.03	2,212.81	2,147.01	2,110.26	2,089.31

$230,000 11.00 - 20.75% 5 - 40 Years

	5	7	8	10	15	20	25	30	35	40
11.00%	5,000.76	3,938.16	3,612.94	3,168.25	2,614.17	2,374.03	2,254.26	2,190.34	2,155.00	2,135.08
11.25%	5,029.48	3,968.46	3,644.02	3,200.89	2,650.39	2,413.29	2,295.95	2,233.90	2,199.94	2,180.99
11.50%	5,058.30	3,998.89	3,675.26	3,233.70	2,686.84	2,452.79	2,337.88	2,277.67	2,245.05	2,227.05
11.75%	5,087.21	4,029.44	3,706.63	3,266.68	2,723.50	2,492.53	2,380.04	2,321.64	2,290.33	2,273.24
12.00%	5,116.22	4,060.13	3,738.15	3,299.83	2,760.39	2,532.50	2,422.42	2,365.81	2,335.76	2,319.55
12.25%	5,145.33	4,090.94	3,769.82	3,333.16	2,797.49	2,572.70	2,465.01	2,410.16	2,381.35	2,365.98
12.50%	5,174.53	4,121.88	3,801.63	3,366.65	2,834.80	2,613.12	2,507.81	2,454.69	2,427.09	2,412.51
12.75%	5,203.82	4,152.95	3,833.58	3,400.32	2,872.33	2,653.77	2,550.82	2,499.39	2,472.95	2,459.15
13.00%	5,233.21	4,184.15	3,865.67	3,434.15	2,910.06	2,694.62	2,594.02	2,544.26	2,518.94	2,505.88
13.25%	5,262.69	4,215.48	3,897.90	3,468.15	2,947.99	2,735.69	2,637.41	2,589.28	2,565.06	2,552.70
13.50%	5,292.26	4,246.93	3,930.28	3,502.31	2,986.13	2,776.96	2,680.98	2,634.45	2,611.28	2,599.60
13.75%	5,321.93	4,278.50	3,962.79	3,536.64	3,024.47	2,818.43	2,724.73	2,679.76	2,657.62	2,646.58
14.00%	5,351.70	4,310.20	3,995.45	3,571.13	3,063.01	2,860.10	2,768.65	2,725.21	2,704.05	2,693.62
14.25%	5,381.55	4,342.03	4,028.24	3,605.78	3,101.73	2,901.95	2,812.73	2,770.78	2,750.58	2,740.73
14.50%	5,411.50	4,373.98	4,061.17	3,640.60	3,140.65	2,943.99	2,856.97	2,816.48	2,797.19	2,787.91
14.75%	5,441.55	4,406.05	4,094.24	3,675.57	3,179.76	2,986.22	2,901.37	2,862.29	2,843.89	2,835.13
15.00%	5,471.68	4,438.25	4,127.44	3,710.70	3,219.05	3,028.62	2,945.91	2,908.22	2,890.67	2,882.42
15.25%	5,501.91	4,470.58	4,160.78	3,745.99	3,258.52	3,071.19	2,990.59	2,954.25	2,937.52	2,929.75
15.50%	5,532.23	4,503.02	4,194.26	3,781.44	3,298.18	3,113.93	3,035.41	3,000.39	2,984.44	2,977.12
15.75%	5,562.65	4,535.59	4,227.87	3,817.05	3,338.01	3,156.83	3,080.37	3,046.62	3,031.43	3,024.54
16.00%	5,593.15	4,568.27	4,261.62	3,852.80	3,378.01	3,199.89	3,125.44	3,092.94	3,078.48	3,071.99
16.25%	5,623.75	4,601.08	4,295.50	3,888.71	3,418.19	3,243.10	3,170.64	3,139.35	3,125.58	3,119.48
16.50%	5,654.44	4,634.01	4,329.51	3,924.77	3,458.53	3,286.47	3,215.96	3,185.84	3,172.74	3,167.01
16.75%	5,685.22	4,667.06	4,363.66	3,960.98	3,499.04	3,329.98	3,261.39	3,232.41	3,219.95	3,214.56
17.00%	5,716.09	4,700.24	4,397.93	3,997.35	3,539.71	3,373.64	3,306.93	3,279.05	3,267.21	3,262.14
17.25%	5,747.06	4,733.52	4,432.34	4,033.86	3,580.54	3,417.44	3,352.58	3,325.77	3,314.51	3,309.75
17.50%	5,778.11	4,766.93	4,466.88	4,070.51	3,621.53	3,461.37	3,398.32	3,372.55	3,361.85	3,357.39
17.75%	5,809.25	4,800.46	4,501.54	4,107.31	3,662.67	3,505.43	3,444.16	3,419.39	3,409.23	3,405.04
18.00%	5,840.49	4,834.10	4,536.34	4,144.26	3,703.97	3,549.62	3,490.09	3,466.30	3,456.65	3,452.72
18.25%	5,871.81	4,867.86	4,571.26	4,181.35	3,745.41	3,593.93	3,536.11	3,513.26	3,504.10	3,500.41
18.50%	5,903.23	4,901.74	4,606.31	4,218.58	3,787.00	3,638.36	3,582.21	3,560.27	3,551.59	3,548.13
18.75%	5,934.73	4,935.74	4,641.49	4,255.95	3,828.74	3,682.91	3,628.40	3,607.34	3,599.10	3,595.86
19.00%	5,966.33	4,969.84	4,676.79	4,293.46	3,870.61	3,727.58	3,674.66	3,654.45	3,646.64	3,643.60
19.25%	5,998.01	5,004.07	4,712.22	4,331.11	3,912.63	3,772.35	3,721.00	3,701.61	3,694.20	3,691.36
19.50%	6,029.78	5,038.41	4,747.77	4,368.90	3,954.78	3,817.23	3,767.41	3,748.82	3,741.79	3,739.13
19.75%	6,061.64	5,072.86	4,783.44	4,406.82	3,997.07	3,862.21	3,813.89	3,796.06	3,789.41	3,786.91
20.00%	6,093.59	5,107.43	4,819.24	4,444.88	4,039.48	3,907.30	3,860.44	3,843.34	3,837.04	3,834.71
20.25%	6,125.63	5,142.10	4,855.15	4,483.07	4,082.03	3,952.48	3,907.05	3,890.66	3,884.69	3,882.51
20.50%	6,157.76	5,176.90	4,891.19	4,521.39	4,124.70	3,997.75	3,953.72	3,938.02	3,932.36	3,930.32
20.75%	6,189.97	5,211.80	4,927.35	4,559.85	4,167.49	4,043.12	4,000.44	3,985.40	3,980.05	3,978.14

	5	7	8	10	15	20	25	30	35	40
1.00%	4,017.03	2,897.84	2,548.16	2,058.70	1,406.46	1,080.75	885.65	755.85	663.37	594.21
1.25%	4,042.38	2,923.26	2,573.63	2,084.30	1,432.45	1,107.16	912.50	783.14	691.10	622.39
1.50%	4,067.82	2,948.81	2,599.26	2,110.10	1,458.75	1,133.98	939.85	811.03	719.53	651.36
1.75%	4,093.37	2,974.51	2,625.05	2,136.11	1,485.34	1,161.20	967.70	839.52	748.66	681.11
2.00%	4,119.02	3,000.35	2,651.01	2,162.32	1,512.25	1,188.83	996.06	868.61	778.47	711.64
2.25%	4,144.78	3,026.33	2,677.12	2,188.73	1,539.45	1,216.85	1,024.91	898.28	808.96	742.93
2.50%	4,170.63	3,052.45	2,703.40	2,215.34	1,566.95	1,245.27	1,054.25	928.53	840.11	774.98
2.75%	4,196.59	3,078.72	2,729.85	2,242.16	1,594.76	1,274.09	1,084.08	959.37	871.93	807.76
3.00%	4,222.64	3,105.13	2,756.45	2,269.18	1,622.87	1,303.30	1,114.40	990.77	904.40	841.26
3.25%	4,248.80	3,131.67	2,783.22	2,296.40	1,651.27	1,332.91	1,145.19	1,022.73	937.50	875.47
3.50%	4,275.06	3,158.36	2,810.14	2,323.82	1,679.97	1,362.91	1,176.47	1,055.26	971.23	910.37
3.75%	4,301.42	3,185.20	2,837.23	2,351.44	1,708.97	1,393.29	1,208.21	1,088.32	1,005.58	945.94
4.00%	4,327.88	3,212.17	2,864.48	2,379.26	1,738.27	1,424.05	1,240.42	1,121.93	1,040.52	982.16
4.25%	4,354.45	3,239.28	2,891.89	2,407.28	1,767.85	1,455.20	1,273.08	1,156.06	1,076.05	1,019.01
4.50%	4,381.11	3,266.54	2,919.46	2,435.50	1,797.73	1,486.73	1,306.21	1,190.71	1,112.15	1,056.47
4.75%	4,407.87	3,293.93	2,947.19	2,463.92	1,827.91	1,518.63	1,339.78	1,225.87	1,148.81	1,094.53
5.00%	4,434.74	3,321.47	2,975.08	2,492.54	1,858.37	1,550.90	1,373.79	1,261.53	1,186.02	1,133.16
5.25%	4,461.71	3,349.14	3,003.13	2,521.35	1,889.11	1,583.53	1,408.23	1,297.68	1,223.75	1,172.35
5.50%	4,488.77	3,376.96	3,031.34	2,550.37	1,920.15	1,616.54	1,443.11	1,334.30	1,261.99	1,212.06
5.75%	4,515.94	3,404.92	3,059.71	2,579.58	1,951.46	1,649.90	1,478.40	1,371.40	1,300.73	1,252.29
6.00%	4,543.21	3,433.01	3,088.24	2,608.98	1,983.06	1,683.61	1,514.11	1,408.94	1,339.95	1,293.00
6.25%	4,570.58	3,461.24	3,116.92	2,638.58	2,014.94	1,717.68	1,550.22	1,446.94	1,379.63	1,334.19
6.50%	4,598.04	3,489.62	3,145.76	2,668.38	2,047.10	1,752.10	1,586.74	1,485.36	1,419.76	1,375.82
6.75%	4,625.61	3,518.13	3,174.77	2,698.37	2,079.54	1,786.86	1,623.64	1,524.21	1,460.33	1,417.89
7.00%	4,653.28	3,546.78	3,203.92	2,728.55	2,112.25	1,821.95	1,660.93	1,563.46	1,501.31	1,460.36
7.25%	4,681.05	3,575.57	3,233.24	2,758.92	2,145.23	1,857.38	1,698.60	1,603.11	1,542.70	1,503.23
7.50%	4,708.92	3,604.49	3,262.71	2,789.49	2,178.48	1,893.14	1,736.63	1,643.15	1,584.47	1,546.47
7.75%	4,736.89	3,633.56	3,292.34	2,820.25	2,212.00	1,929.23	1,775.02	1,683.57	1,626.61	1,590.06
8.00%	4,764.95	3,662.76	3,322.12	2,851.20	2,245.78	1,965.63	1,813.77	1,724.35	1,669.11	1,633.98
8.25%	4,793.12	3,692.10	3,352.06	2,882.34	2,279.83	2,002.35	1,852.86	1,765.48	1,711.95	1,678.23
8.50%	4,821.38	3,721.57	3,382.15	2,913.66	2,314.14	2,039.38	1,892.28	1,806.95	1,755.12	1,722.77
8.75%	4,849.75	3,751.19	3,412.40	2,945.18	2,348.70	2,076.72	1,932.04	1,848.75	1,798.60	1,767.60
9.00%	4,878.21	3,780.93	3,442.80	2,976.88	2,383.53	2,114.36	1,972.11	1,890.86	1,842.38	1,812.70
9.25%	4,906.78	3,810.82	3,473.35	3,008.77	2,418.60	2,152.29	2,012.50	1,933.29	1,886.45	1,858.05
9.50%	4,935.44	3,840.84	3,504.06	3,040.84	2,453.93	2,190.51	2,053.19	1,976.01	1,930.79	1,903.64
9.75%	4,964.20	3,870.99	3,534.92	3,073.10	2,489.50	2,229.01	2,094.17	2,019.01	1,975.39	1,949.46
10.00%	4,993.06	3,901.28	3,565.93	3,105.54	2,525.32	2,267.80	2,135.45	2,062.29	2,020.23	1,995.49
10.25%	5,022.01	3,931.70	3,597.09	3,138.17	2,561.38	2,306.86	2,177.00	2,105.84	2,065.31	2,041.72
10.50%	5,051.07	3,962.26	3,628.40	3,170.97	2,597.69	2,346.19	2,218.83	2,149.64	2,110.61	2,088.14
10.75%	5,080.22	3,992.95	3,659.87	3,203.96	2,634.23	2,385.79	2,260.92	2,193.68	2,156.13	2,134.73

$235,000   11.00 - 20.75%   5 - 40 Years

	5	7	8	10	15	20	25	30	35	40
11.00%	5,109.47	4,023.77	3,691.48	3,237.13	2,671.00	2,425.64	2,303.27	2,237.96	2,201.85	2,181.49
11.25%	5,138.82	4,054.73	3,723.24	3,270.47	2,708.01	2,465.75	2,345.86	2,282.46	2,247.76	2,228.40
11.50%	5,168.26	4,085.82	3,755.15	3,303.99	2,745.25	2,506.11	2,388.70	2,327.18	2,293.85	2,275.46
11.75%	5,197.81	4,117.04	3,787.21	3,337.69	2,782.71	2,546.71	2,431.78	2,372.11	2,340.12	2,322.66
12.00%	5,227.45	4,148.39	3,819.42	3,371.57	2,820.39	2,587.55	2,475.08	2,417.24	2,386.54	2,369.80
12.25%	5,257.18	4,179.88	3,851.77	3,405.62	2,858.30	2,628.63	2,518.60	2,462.56	2,433.12	2,417.41
12.50%	5,287.02	4,211.49	3,884.27	3,439.84	2,896.43	2,669.93	2,562.33	2,508.06	2,479.85	2,464.96
12.75%	5,316.95	4,243.24	3,916.91	3,474.24	2,934.77	2,711.46	2,606.27	2,553.73	2,526.71	2,512.61
13.00%	5,346.97	4,275.11	3,949.70	3,508.80	2,973.32	2,753.20	2,650.41	2,599.57	2,573.70	2,560.36
13.25%	5,377.09	4,307.12	3,982.64	3,543.54	3,012.08	2,795.16	2,694.75	2,645.57	2,620.82	2,608.19
13.50%	5,407.31	4,339.25	4,015.72	3,578.45	3,051.05	2,837.33	2,739.27	2,691.72	2,668.05	2,656.11
13.75%	5,437.63	4,371.51	4,048.94	3,613.52	3,090.22	2,879.70	2,783.97	2,738.01	2,715.39	2,704.11
14.00%	5,468.04	4,403.90	4,082.30	3,648.76	3,129.59	2,922.27	2,828.84	2,784.45	2,762.83	2,752.18
14.25%	5,498.54	4,436.42	4,115.81	3,684.17	3,169.16	2,965.04	2,873.88	2,831.01	2,810.37	2,800.31
14.50%	5,529.15	4,469.07	4,149.46	3,719.74	3,208.93	3,007.99	2,919.08	2,877.71	2,858.00	2,848.51
14.75%	5,559.84	4,501.84	4,183.24	3,755.47	3,248.88	3,051.13	2,964.44	2,924.52	2,905.72	2,896.77
15.00%	5,590.63	4,534.74	4,217.17	3,791.37	3,289.03	3,094.46	3,009.95	2,971.44	2,953.51	2,945.08
15.25%	5,621.52	4,567.76	4,251.24	3,827.43	3,329.36	3,137.95	3,055.61	3,018.48	3,001.38	2,993.44
15.50%	5,652.50	4,600.91	4,285.44	3,863.65	3,369.88	3,181.62	3,101.40	3,065.61	3,049.32	3,041.84
15.75%	5,683.57	4,634.19	4,319.78	3,900.02	3,410.57	3,225.45	3,147.33	3,112.85	3,097.33	3,090.29
16.00%	5,714.74	4,667.59	4,354.26	3,936.56	3,451.45	3,269.45	3,193.39	3,160.18	3,145.40	3,138.77
16.25%	5,746.01	4,701.11	4,388.88	3,973.25	3,492.50	3,313.61	3,239.57	3,207.60	3,193.53	3,187.30
16.50%	5,777.36	4,734.75	4,423.63	4,010.09	3,533.72	3,357.92	3,285.87	3,255.10	3,241.72	3,235.85
16.75%	5,808.81	4,768.52	4,458.52	4,047.09	3,575.10	3,402.38	3,332.29	3,302.68	3,289.95	3,284.44
17.00%	5,840.36	4,802.41	4,493.54	4,084.24	3,616.66	3,446.98	3,378.82	3,350.34	3,338.24	3,333.06
17.25%	5,871.99	4,836.43	4,528.70	4,121.55	3,658.38	3,491.73	3,425.46	3,398.07	3,386.57	3,381.70
17.50%	5,903.72	4,870.56	4,563.98	4,159.00	3,700.26	3,536.61	3,472.19	3,445.86	3,434.94	3,430.37
17.75%	5,935.54	4,904.82	4,599.40	4,196.60	3,742.30	3,581.63	3,519.03	3,493.73	3,483.35	3,479.07
18.00%	5,967.46	4,939.19	4,634.96	4,234.35	3,784.49	3,626.78	3,565.96	3,541.65	3,531.80	3,527.78
18.25%	5,999.46	4,973.69	4,670.64	4,272.25	3,826.83	3,672.06	3,612.98	3,589.63	3,580.28	3,576.51
18.50%	6,031.56	5,008.30	4,706.45	4,310.29	3,869.33	3,717.46	3,660.09	3,637.67	3,628.79	3,625.26
18.75%	6,063.75	5,043.03	4,742.39	4,348.47	3,911.97	3,762.98	3,707.28	3,685.76	3,677.34	3,674.03
19.00%	6,096.03	5,077.88	4,778.46	4,386.80	3,954.76	3,808.61	3,754.55	3,733.90	3,725.91	3,722.81
19.25%	6,128.40	5,112.85	4,814.65	4,425.27	3,997.69	3,854.36	3,801.89	3,782.08	3,774.51	3,771.61
19.50%	6,160.86	5,147.94	4,850.98	4,463.88	4,040.75	3,900.21	3,849.31	3,830.31	3,823.14	3,820.42
19.75%	6,193.42	5,183.14	4,887.43	4,502.62	4,083.96	3,946.17	3,896.80	3,878.58	3,871.78	3,869.24
20.00%	6,226.06	5,218.46	4,924.00	4,541.51	4,127.30	3,992.24	3,944.36	3,926.89	3,920.45	3,918.07
20.25%	6,258.80	5,253.89	4,960.70	4,580.53	4,170.77	4,038.40	3,991.98	3,975.24	3,969.14	3,966.91
20.50%	6,291.62	5,289.44	4,997.52	4,619.68	4,214.36	4,084.66	4,039.67	4,023.63	4,017.85	4,015.77
20.75%	6,324.54	5,325.10	5,034.47	4,658.97	4,258.09	4,131.02	4,087.41	4,072.04	4,066.58	4,064.63

	5	7	8	10	15	20	25	30	35	40
1.00%	4,102.50	2,959.50	2,602.37	2,102.50	1,436.39	1,103.75	904.49	771.93	677.49	606.85
1.25%	4,128.38	2,985.45	2,628.38	2,128.64	1,462.93	1,130.72	931.91	799.80	705.81	635.63
1.50%	4,154.37	3,011.55	2,654.56	2,155.00	1,489.78	1,158.11	959.85	828.29	734.84	665.21
1.75%	4,180.47	3,037.80	2,680.90	2,181.56	1,516.95	1,185.91	988.29	857.38	764.59	695.60
2.00%	4,206.66	3,064.18	2,707.41	2,208.32	1,544.42	1,214.12	1,017.25	887.09	795.03	726.78
2.25%	4,232.96	3,090.72	2,734.08	2,235.30	1,572.20	1,242.74	1,046.71	917.39	826.17	758.74
2.50%	4,259.37	3,117.40	2,760.92	2,262.48	1,600.29	1,271.77	1,076.68	948.29	857.99	791.47
2.75%	4,285.87	3,144.22	2,787.93	2,289.86	1,628.69	1,301.20	1,107.15	979.78	890.48	824.95
3.00%	4,312.49	3,171.19	2,815.10	2,317.46	1,657.40	1,331.03	1,138.11	1,011.85	923.64	859.16
3.25%	4,339.20	3,198.31	2,842.43	2,345.26	1,686.41	1,361.27	1,169.56	1,044.50	957.45	894.10
3.50%	4,366.02	3,225.56	2,869.93	2,373.26	1,715.72	1,391.90	1,201.50	1,077.71	991.90	929.74
3.75%	4,392.94	3,252.97	2,897.60	2,401.47	1,745.33	1,422.93	1,233.91	1,111.48	1,026.97	966.06
4.00%	4,419.97	3,280.51	2,925.43	2,429.88	1,775.25	1,454.35	1,266.81	1,145.80	1,062.66	1,003.05
4.25%	4,447.09	3,308.20	2,953.42	2,458.50	1,805.47	1,486.16	1,300.17	1,180.66	1,098.95	1,040.69
4.50%	4,474.32	3,336.04	2,981.58	2,487.32	1,835.98	1,518.36	1,334.00	1,216.04	1,135.82	1,078.95
4.75%	4,501.66	3,364.02	3,009.90	2,516.35	1,866.80	1,550.94	1,368.28	1,251.95	1,173.26	1,117.82
5.00%	4,529.10	3,392.14	3,038.38	2,545.57	1,897.90	1,583.89	1,403.02	1,288.37	1,211.25	1,157.27
5.25%	4,556.64	3,420.40	3,067.03	2,575.00	1,929.31	1,617.23	1,438.19	1,325.29	1,249.78	1,197.29
5.50%	4,584.28	3,448.81	3,095.84	2,604.63	1,961.00	1,650.93	1,473.81	1,362.69	1,288.84	1,237.85
5.75%	4,612.02	3,477.36	3,124.81	2,634.46	1,992.98	1,685.00	1,509.86	1,400.57	1,328.40	1,278.93
6.00%	4,639.87	3,506.05	3,153.94	2,664.49	2,025.26	1,719.43	1,546.32	1,438.92	1,368.46	1,320.51
6.25%	4,667.82	3,534.89	3,183.24	2,694.72	2,057.81	1,754.23	1,583.21	1,477.72	1,408.98	1,362.57
6.50%	4,695.88	3,563.86	3,212.70	2,725.15	2,090.66	1,789.38	1,620.50	1,516.96	1,449.97	1,405.10
6.75%	4,724.03	3,592.98	3,242.31	2,755.78	2,123.78	1,824.87	1,658.19	1,556.64	1,491.40	1,448.06
7.00%	4,752.29	3,622.24	3,272.09	2,786.60	2,157.19	1,860.72	1,696.27	1,596.73	1,533.26	1,491.44
7.25%	4,780.65	3,651.64	3,302.03	2,817.62	2,190.87	1,896.90	1,734.74	1,637.22	1,575.52	1,535.21
7.50%	4,809.11	3,681.19	3,332.13	2,848.84	2,224.83	1,933.42	1,773.58	1,678.11	1,618.18	1,579.37
7.75%	4,837.67	3,710.87	3,362.39	2,880.26	2,259.06	1,970.28	1,812.79	1,719.39	1,661.22	1,623.89
8.00%	4,866.33	3,740.69	3,392.80	2,911.86	2,293.57	2,007.46	1,852.36	1,761.03	1,704.63	1,668.75
8.25%	4,895.10	3,770.65	3,423.38	2,943.66	2,328.34	2,044.96	1,892.28	1,803.04	1,748.38	1,713.93
8.50%	4,923.97	3,800.76	3,454.11	2,975.66	2,363.37	2,082.78	1,932.55	1,845.39	1,792.47	1,759.43
8.75%	4,952.94	3,831.00	3,485.00	3,007.84	2,398.68	2,120.91	1,973.14	1,888.08	1,836.87	1,805.21
9.00%	4,982.01	3,861.38	3,516.05	3,040.22	2,434.24	2,159.34	2,014.07	1,931.09	1,881.58	1,851.27
9.25%	5,011.18	3,891.90	3,547.25	3,072.79	2,470.06	2,198.08	2,055.32	1,974.42	1,926.59	1,897.59
9.50%	5,040.45	3,922.56	3,578.61	3,105.54	2,506.14	2,237.11	2,096.87	2,018.05	1,971.87	1,944.15
9.75%	5,069.82	3,953.35	3,610.13	3,138.49	2,542.47	2,276.44	2,138.73	2,061.97	2,017.41	1,990.94
10.00%	5,099.29	3,984.28	3,641.80	3,171.62	2,579.05	2,316.05	2,180.88	2,106.17	2,063.21	2,037.95
10.25%	5,128.86	4,015.35	3,673.62	3,204.94	2,615.88	2,355.94	2,223.32	2,150.64	2,109.25	2,085.16
10.50%	5,158.54	4,046.56	3,705.60	3,238.44	2,652.96	2,396.11	2,266.04	2,195.37	2,155.52	2,132.57
10.75%	5,188.31	4,077.91	3,737.74	3,272.13	2,690.28	2,436.55	2,309.02	2,240.36	2,202.01	2,180.15

$240,000   11.00 - 20.75%   5 - 40 Years

	5	7	8	10	15	20	25	30	35	40
11.00%	5,218.18	4,109.38	3,770.02	3,306.00	2,727.83	2,477.25	2,352.27	2,285.58	2,248.70	2,227.91
11.25%	5,248.15	4,141.00	3,802.46	3,340.05	2,765.63	2,518.21	2,395.77	2,331.03	2,295.59	2,275.82
11.50%	5,278.23	4,172.75	3,835.05	3,374.29	2,803.66	2,559.43	2,439.53	2,376.70	2,342.66	2,323.88
11.75%	5,308.40	4,204.64	3,867.79	3,408.71	2,841.92	2,600.90	2,483.52	2,422.58	2,389.91	2,372.07
12.00%	5,338.67	4,236.66	3,900.68	3,443.30	2,880.40	2,642.61	2,527.74	2,468.67	2,437.32	2,420.40
12.25%	5,369.04	4,268.81	3,933.72	3,478.08	2,919.12	2,684.56	2,572.19	2,514.95	2,484.89	2,468.85
12.50%	5,399.51	4,301.10	3,966.91	3,513.03	2,958.05	2,726.74	2,616.85	2,561.42	2,532.61	2,517.41
12.75%	5,430.07	4,333.52	4,000.25	3,548.16	2,997.21	2,769.15	2,661.73	2,608.06	2,580.47	2,566.07
13.00%	5,460.74	4,366.07	4,033.74	3,583.46	3,036.58	2,811.78	2,706.80	2,654.88	2,628.46	2,614.83
13.25%	5,491.50	4,398.76	4,067.38	3,618.93	3,076.17	2,854.63	2,752.08	2,701.86	2,676.58	2,663.69
13.50%	5,522.36	4,431.57	4,101.16	3,654.58	3,115.96	2,897.70	2,797.55	2,748.99	2,724.82	2,712.63
13.75%	5,553.32	4,464.52	4,135.09	3,690.40	3,155.97	2,940.97	2,843.20	2,796.27	2,773.16	2,761.64
14.00%	5,584.38	4,497.60	4,169.16	3,726.39	3,196.18	2,984.45	2,889.03	2,843.69	2,821.62	2,810.74
14.25%	5,615.54	4,530.81	4,203.38	3,762.55	3,236.59	3,028.13	2,935.03	2,891.25	2,870.17	2,859.90
14.50%	5,646.79	4,564.15	4,237.74	3,798.88	3,277.20	3,071.99	2,981.19	2,938.93	2,918.81	2,909.12
14.75%	5,678.14	4,597.62	4,272.25	3,835.38	3,318.01	3,116.05	3,027.52	2,986.74	2,967.54	2,958.40
15.00%	5,709.58	4,631.22	4,306.90	3,872.04	3,359.01	3,160.29	3,073.99	3,034.67	3,016.35	3,007.74
15.25%	5,741.13	4,664.95	4,341.69	3,908.86	3,400.20	3,204.72	3,120.62	3,082.70	3,065.24	3,057.13
15.50%	5,772.77	4,698.80	4,376.62	3,945.85	3,441.58	3,249.31	3,167.39	3,130.84	3,114.20	3,106.56
15.75%	5,804.50	4,732.79	4,411.70	3,983.00	3,483.14	3,294.08	3,214.29	3,179.08	3,163.23	3,156.04
16.00%	5,836.33	4,766.90	4,446.91	4,020.31	3,524.88	3,339.01	3,261.33	3,227.42	3,212.33	3,205.56
16.25%	5,868.26	4,801.13	4,482.26	4,057.79	3,566.80	3,384.11	3,308.50	3,275.84	3,261.48	3,255.11
16.50%	5,900.29	4,835.49	4,517.75	4,095.42	3,608.90	3,429.36	3,355.79	3,324.36	3,310.69	3,304.70
16.75%	5,932.40	4,869.98	4,553.38	4,133.20	3,651.17	3,474.77	3,403.19	3,372.95	3,359.95	3,354.32
17.00%	5,964.62	4,904.59	4,589.15	4,171.14	3,693.61	3,520.32	3,450.71	3,421.62	3,409.26	3,403.98
17.25%	5,996.93	4,939.33	4,625.05	4,209.24	3,736.22	3,566.02	3,498.34	3,470.37	3,458.62	3,453.66
17.50%	6,029.33	4,974.19	4,661.09	4,247.49	3,778.99	3,611.86	3,546.07	3,519.18	3,508.02	3,503.36
17.75%	6,061.83	5,009.17	4,697.26	4,285.89	3,821.92	3,657.84	3,593.90	3,568.06	3,557.46	3,553.09
18.00%	6,094.42	5,044.28	4,733.57	4,324.44	3,865.01	3,703.95	3,641.83	3,617.00	3,606.94	3,602.84
18.25%	6,127.11	5,079.51	4,770.01	4,363.15	3,908.26	3,750.19	3,689.85	3,666.01	3,656.45	3,652.61
18.50%	6,159.89	5,114.86	4,806.59	4,402.00	3,951.66	3,796.55	3,737.96	3,715.07	3,706.00	3,702.39
18.75%	6,192.76	5,150.33	4,843.29	4,440.99	3,995.21	3,843.04	3,786.16	3,764.18	3,755.58	3,752.20
19.00%	6,225.73	5,185.92	4,880.13	4,480.14	4,038.90	3,889.64	3,834.43	3,813.34	3,805.19	3,802.02
19.25%	6,258.79	5,221.64	4,917.09	4,519.42	4,082.74	3,936.36	3,882.79	3,862.55	3,854.82	3,851.85
19.50%	6,291.95	5,257.47	4,954.19	4,558.85	4,126.73	3,983.20	3,931.21	3,911.81	3,904.48	3,901.70
19.75%	6,325.19	5,293.42	4,991.42	4,598.42	4,170.85	4,030.13	3,979.72	3,961.11	3,954.16	3,951.56
20.00%	6,358.53	5,329.49	5,028.77	4,638.14	4,215.11	4,077.18	4,028.28	4,010.44	4,003.87	4,001.43
20.25%	6,391.96	5,365.67	5,066.25	4,677.99	4,259.51	4,124.33	4,076.92	4,059.82	4,053.59	4,051.32
20.50%	6,425.49	5,401.98	5,103.85	4,717.98	4,304.03	4,171.57	4,125.62	4,109.23	4,103.34	4,101.21
20.75%	6,459.10	5,438.40	5,141.59	4,758.10	4,348.69	4,218.91	4,174.38	4,158.68	4,153.10	4,151.11

$245,000 1.00 - 10.75% 5 - 40 Years

	5	7	8	10	15	20	25	30	35	40
1.00%	4,187.97	3,021.16	2,656.59	2,146.30	1,466.31	1,126.74	923.34	788.02	691.60	619.50
1.25%	4,214.39	3,047.65	2,683.14	2,172.99	1,493.41	1,154.28	951.33	816.47	720.51	648.87
1.50%	4,240.92	3,074.29	2,709.86	2,199.89	1,520.82	1,182.24	979.84	845.54	750.15	679.07
1.75%	4,267.56	3,101.08	2,736.75	2,227.00	1,548.55	1,210.62	1,008.88	875.25	780.52	710.09
2.00%	4,294.30	3,128.02	2,763.81	2,254.33	1,576.60	1,239.41	1,038.44	905.57	811.59	741.92
2.25%	4,321.15	3,155.11	2,791.04	2,281.87	1,604.96	1,268.63	1,068.52	936.50	843.38	774.55
2.50%	4,348.10	3,182.34	2,818.44	2,309.61	1,633.63	1,298.26	1,099.11	968.05	875.86	807.96
2.75%	4,375.16	3,209.73	2,846.01	2,337.57	1,662.62	1,328.31	1,130.21	1,000.19	909.03	842.13
3.00%	4,402.33	3,237.26	2,873.75	2,365.74	1,691.93	1,358.76	1,161.82	1,032.93	942.88	877.06
3.25%	4,429.60	3,264.94	2,901.65	2,394.12	1,721.54	1,389.63	1,193.92	1,066.26	977.40	912.73
3.50%	4,456.98	3,292.76	2,929.72	2,422.70	1,751.46	1,420.90	1,226.53	1,100.16	1,012.56	949.11
3.75%	4,484.46	3,320.74	2,957.96	2,451.50	1,781.69	1,452.58	1,259.62	1,134.63	1,048.37	986.19
4.00%	4,512.05	3,348.86	2,986.37	2,480.51	1,812.24	1,484.65	1,293.20	1,169.67	1,084.80	1,023.95
4.25%	4,539.74	3,377.13	3,014.95	2,509.72	1,843.08	1,517.12	1,327.26	1,205.25	1,121.84	1,062.37
4.50%	4,567.54	3,405.54	3,043.69	2,539.14	1,874.23	1,549.99	1,361.79	1,241.38	1,159.48	1,101.43
4.75%	4,595.44	3,434.10	3,072.60	2,568.77	1,905.69	1,583.25	1,396.79	1,278.04	1,197.70	1,141.11
5.00%	4,623.45	3,462.81	3,101.68	2,598.61	1,937.44	1,616.89	1,432.25	1,315.21	1,236.48	1,181.38
5.25%	4,651.57	3,491.66	3,130.92	2,628.65	1,969.50	1,650.92	1,468.16	1,352.90	1,275.82	1,222.23
5.50%	4,679.78	3,520.66	3,160.33	2,658.89	2,001.85	1,685.32	1,504.51	1,391.08	1,315.69	1,263.64
5.75%	4,708.11	3,549.81	3,189.91	2,689.35	2,034.50	1,720.10	1,541.31	1,429.75	1,356.08	1,305.57
6.00%	4,736.54	3,579.10	3,219.65	2,720.00	2,067.45	1,755.26	1,578.54	1,468.90	1,396.96	1,348.02
6.25%	4,765.07	3,608.53	3,249.56	2,750.86	2,100.69	1,790.77	1,616.19	1,508.51	1,438.34	1,390.96
6.50%	4,793.71	3,638.11	3,279.63	2,781.93	2,134.21	1,826.65	1,654.26	1,548.57	1,480.18	1,434.37
6.75%	4,822.45	3,667.84	3,309.86	2,813.19	2,168.03	1,862.89	1,692.73	1,589.07	1,522.47	1,478.22
7.00%	4,851.29	3,697.71	3,340.26	2,844.66	2,202.13	1,899.48	1,731.61	1,629.99	1,565.20	1,522.51
7.25%	4,880.24	3,727.72	3,370.82	2,876.33	2,236.51	1,936.42	1,770.88	1,671.33	1,608.34	1,567.20
7.50%	4,909.30	3,757.88	3,401.55	2,908.19	2,271.18	1,973.70	1,810.53	1,713.08	1,651.89	1,612.27
7.75%	4,938.46	3,788.18	3,432.44	2,940.26	2,306.13	2,011.32	1,850.56	1,755.21	1,695.83	1,657.72
8.00%	4,967.72	3,818.62	3,463.49	2,972.53	2,341.35	2,049.28	1,890.95	1,797.72	1,740.14	1,703.51
8.25%	4,997.08	3,849.21	3,494.70	3,004.99	2,376.84	2,087.56	1,931.70	1,840.60	1,784.80	1,749.64
8.50%	5,026.55	3,879.94	3,526.07	3,037.65	2,412.61	2,126.17	1,972.81	1,883.84	1,829.81	1,796.08
8.75%	5,056.12	3,910.81	3,557.61	3,070.51	2,448.65	2,165.09	2,014.25	1,927.42	1,875.14	1,842.82
9.00%	5,085.80	3,941.82	3,589.30	3,103.56	2,484.95	2,204.33	2,056.03	1,971.33	1,920.78	1,889.84
9.25%	5,115.58	3,972.98	3,621.15	3,136.80	2,521.52	2,243.87	2,098.14	2,015.55	1,966.72	1,937.12
9.50%	5,145.46	4,004.28	3,653.17	3,170.24	2,558.35	2,283.72	2,140.56	2,060.09	2,012.95	1,984.65
9.75%	5,175.44	4,035.71	3,685.34	3,203.87	2,595.44	2,323.87	2,183.29	2,104.93	2,059.44	2,032.42
10.00%	5,205.53	4,067.29	3,717.67	3,237.69	2,632.78	2,364.30	2,226.32	2,150.05	2,106.20	2,080.41
10.25%	5,235.71	4,099.01	3,750.16	3,271.71	2,670.38	2,405.03	2,269.64	2,195.45	2,153.20	2,128.60
10.50%	5,266.01	4,130.86	3,782.80	3,305.91	2,708.23	2,446.03	2,313.25	2,241.11	2,200.43	2,177.00
10.75%	5,296.40	4,162.86	3,815.61	3,340.30	2,746.32	2,487.31	2,357.13	2,287.03	2,247.88	2,225.57

$245,000　　11.00 - 20.75%　　5 - 40 Years

	5	7	8	10	15	20	25	30	35	40
11.00%	5,326.89	4,195.00	3,848.56	3,374.88	2,784.66	2,528.86	2,401.28	2,333.19	2,295.55	2,274.32
11.25%	5,357.49	4,227.27	3,881.68	3,409.64	2,823.24	2,570.68	2,445.69	2,379.59	2,343.41	2,323.23
11.50%	5,388.19	4,259.68	3,914.95	3,444.59	2,862.07	2,612.75	2,490.35	2,426.21	2,391.46	2,372.29
11.75%	5,418.99	4,292.23	3,948.37	3,479.72	2,901.12	2,655.08	2,535.26	2,473.05	2,439.70	2,421.49
12.00%	5,449.89	4,324.92	3,981.95	3,515.04	2,940.41	2,697.66	2,580.40	2,520.10	2,488.10	2,470.82
12.25%	5,480.89	4,357.74	4,015.68	3,550.54	2,979.93	2,740.48	2,625.77	2,567.35	2,536.66	2,520.28
12.50%	5,511.99	4,390.70	4,049.56	3,586.22	3,019.68	2,783.54	2,671.37	2,614.78	2,585.37	2,569.85
12.75%	5,543.20	4,423.80	4,083.59	3,622.08	3,059.65	2,826.84	2,717.18	2,662.40	2,634.23	2,619.53
13.00%	5,574.50	4,457.03	4,117.78	3,658.11	3,099.84	2,870.36	2,763.20	2,710.19	2,683.22	2,669.31
13.25%	5,605.91	4,490.40	4,152.11	3,694.33	3,140.25	2,914.11	2,809.42	2,758.15	2,732.34	2,719.18
13.50%	5,637.41	4,523.90	4,186.60	3,730.72	3,180.88	2,958.07	2,855.83	2,806.26	2,781.58	2,769.14
13.75%	5,669.02	4,557.53	4,221.23	3,767.29	3,221.72	3,002.24	2,902.43	2,854.53	2,830.94	2,819.18
14.00%	5,700.72	4,591.30	4,256.02	3,804.03	3,262.77	3,046.63	2,949.21	2,902.94	2,880.40	2,869.29
14.25%	5,732.53	4,625.20	4,290.95	3,840.94	3,304.02	3,091.21	2,996.17	2,951.48	2,929.96	2,919.48
14.50%	5,764.43	4,659.24	4,326.03	3,878.03	3,345.48	3,135.99	3,043.30	3,000.16	2,979.62	2,969.73
14.75%	5,796.43	4,693.41	4,361.25	3,915.28	3,387.13	3,180.97	3,090.59	3,048.97	3,029.36	3,020.03
15.00%	5,828.53	4,727.70	4,396.62	3,952.71	3,428.99	3,226.13	3,138.03	3,097.89	3,079.19	3,070.40
15.25%	5,860.73	4,762.13	4,432.14	3,990.30	3,471.04	3,271.48	3,185.63	3,146.92	3,129.10	3,120.82
15.50%	5,893.03	4,796.69	4,467.80	4,028.06	3,513.28	3,317.01	3,233.38	3,196.07	3,179.08	3,171.28
15.75%	5,925.43	4,831.39	4,503.61	4,065.98	3,555.70	3,362.71	3,281.26	3,245.31	3,229.13	3,221.79
16.00%	5,957.92	4,866.21	4,539.55	4,104.07	3,598.32	3,408.58	3,329.28	3,294.65	3,279.25	3,272.34
16.25%	5,990.52	4,901.15	4,575.64	4,142.32	3,641.11	3,454.61	3,377.43	3,344.09	3,329.43	3,322.93
16.50%	6,023.21	4,936.23	4,611.87	4,180.74	3,684.09	3,500.81	3,425.70	3,393.61	3,379.66	3,373.55
16.75%	6,056.00	4,971.44	4,648.24	4,219.31	3,727.24	3,547.16	3,474.09	3,443.22	3,429.95	3,424.21
17.00%	6,088.88	5,006.77	4,684.76	4,258.04	3,770.56	3,593.66	3,522.60	3,492.90	3,480.29	3,474.89
17.25%	6,121.86	5,042.23	4,721.41	4,296.93	3,814.05	3,640.31	3,571.22	3,542.67	3,530.67	3,525.61
17.50%	6,154.94	5,077.82	4,758.20	4,335.98	3,857.72	3,687.11	3,619.95	3,592.50	3,581.10	3,576.35
17.75%	6,188.12	5,113.53	4,795.12	4,375.18	3,901.54	3,734.04	3,668.78	3,642.40	3,631.58	3,627.11
18.00%	6,221.39	5,149.37	4,832.19	4,414.54	3,945.53	3,781.11	3,717.70	3,692.36	3,682.09	3,677.90
18.25%	6,254.76	5,185.33	4,869.39	4,454.05	3,989.68	3,828.32	3,766.72	3,742.38	3,732.63	3,728.70
18.50%	6,288.22	5,221.42	4,906.72	4,493.71	4,033.98	3,875.65	3,815.84	3,792.46	3,783.21	3,779.53
18.75%	6,321.78	5,257.63	4,944.19	4,533.51	4,078.44	3,923.10	3,865.03	3,842.60	3,833.82	3,830.37
19.00%	6,355.44	5,293.96	4,981.80	4,573.47	4,123.05	3,970.68	3,914.32	3,892.79	3,884.46	3,881.23
19.25%	6,389.18	5,330.42	5,019.53	4,613.58	4,167.80	4,018.37	3,963.68	3,943.02	3,935.13	3,932.10
19.50%	6,423.03	5,367.00	5,057.40	4,653.83	4,212.70	4,066.18	4,013.12	3,993.30	3,985.82	3,982.99
19.75%	6,456.97	5,403.70	5,095.40	4,694.22	4,257.74	4,114.10	4,062.63	4,043.63	4,036.54	4,033.89
20.00%	6,491.00	5,440.52	5,133.53	4,734.76	4,302.93	4,162.12	4,112.21	4,094.00	4,087.28	4,084.80
20.25%	6,525.13	5,477.46	5,171.79	4,775.44	4,348.25	4,210.25	4,161.85	4,144.40	4,138.04	4,135.72
20.50%	6,559.35	5,514.52	5,210.18	4,816.27	4,393.70	4,258.48	4,211.57	4,194.84	4,188.82	4,186.65
20.75%	6,593.67	5,551.70	5,248.70	4,857.23	4,439.29	4,306.80	4,261.34	4,245.32	4,239.62	4,237.59

	5	7	8	10	15	20	25	30	35	40
1.00%	4,273.44	3,082.81	2,710.81	2,190.10	1,496.24	1,149.74	942.18	804.10	705.71	632.14
1.25%	4,300.40	3,109.85	2,737.90	2,217.34	1,523.88	1,177.83	970.74	833.13	735.22	662.11
1.50%	4,327.47	3,137.03	2,765.17	2,244.79	1,551.86	1,206.36	999.84	862.80	765.46	692.93
1.75%	4,354.65	3,164.37	2,792.61	2,272.45	1,580.15	1,235.32	1,029.47	893.11	796.44	724.59
2.00%	4,381.94	3,191.86	2,820.22	2,300.34	1,608.77	1,264.71	1,059.64	924.05	828.16	757.06
2.25%	4,409.34	3,219.50	2,848.00	2,328.43	1,637.71	1,294.52	1,090.33	955.62	860.59	790.36
2.50%	4,436.84	3,247.29	2,875.96	2,356.75	1,666.97	1,324.76	1,121.54	987.80	893.74	824.45
2.75%	4,464.45	3,275.23	2,904.09	2,385.28	1,696.55	1,355.42	1,153.28	1,020.60	927.59	859.32
3.00%	4,492.17	3,303.33	2,932.39	2,414.02	1,726.45	1,386.49	1,185.53	1,054.01	962.13	894.96
3.25%	4,520.00	3,331.57	2,960.87	2,442.98	1,756.67	1,417.99	1,218.29	1,088.02	997.34	931.35
3.50%	4,547.94	3,359.96	2,989.51	2,472.15	1,787.21	1,449.90	1,251.56	1,122.61	1,033.23	968.48
3.75%	4,575.98	3,388.51	3,018.33	2,501.53	1,818.06	1,482.22	1,285.33	1,157.79	1,069.76	1,006.32
4.00%	4,604.13	3,417.20	3,047.32	2,531.13	1,849.22	1,514.95	1,319.59	1,193.54	1,106.94	1,044.85
4.25%	4,632.39	3,446.05	3,076.48	2,560.94	1,880.70	1,548.09	1,354.35	1,229.85	1,144.73	1,084.05
4.50%	4,660.75	3,475.04	3,105.81	2,590.96	1,912.48	1,581.62	1,389.58	1,266.71	1,183.14	1,123.91
4.75%	4,689.23	3,504.18	3,135.31	2,621.19	1,944.58	1,615.56	1,425.29	1,304.12	1,222.14	1,164.39
5.00%	4,717.81	3,533.48	3,164.98	2,651.64	1,976.98	1,649.89	1,461.48	1,342.05	1,261.72	1,205.49
5.25%	4,746.50	3,562.92	3,194.82	2,682.29	2,009.69	1,684.61	1,498.12	1,380.51	1,301.86	1,247.18
5.50%	4,775.29	3,592.51	3,224.83	2,713.16	2,042.71	1,719.72	1,535.22	1,419.47	1,342.54	1,289.43
5.75%	4,804.19	3,622.25	3,255.01	2,744.23	2,076.03	1,755.21	1,572.77	1,458.93	1,383.75	1,332.22
6.00%	4,833.20	3,652.14	3,285.36	2,775.51	2,109.64	1,791.08	1,610.75	1,498.88	1,425.47	1,375.53
6.25%	4,862.32	3,682.17	3,315.87	2,807.00	2,143.56	1,827.32	1,649.17	1,539.29	1,467.69	1,419.35
6.50%	4,891.54	3,712.36	3,346.56	2,838.70	2,177.77	1,863.93	1,688.02	1,580.17	1,510.39	1,463.64
6.75%	4,920.87	3,742.69	3,377.41	2,870.60	2,212.27	1,900.91	1,727.28	1,621.50	1,553.54	1,508.39
7.00%	4,950.30	3,773.17	3,408.43	2,902.71	2,247.07	1,938.25	1,766.95	1,663.26	1,597.14	1,553.58
7.25%	4,979.84	3,803.80	3,439.62	2,935.03	2,282.16	1,975.94	1,807.02	1,705.44	1,641.17	1,599.18
7.50%	5,009.49	3,834.57	3,470.97	2,967.54	2,317.53	2,013.98	1,847.48	1,748.04	1,685.61	1,645.18
7.75%	5,039.24	3,865.49	3,502.49	3,000.27	2,353.19	2,052.37	1,888.32	1,791.03	1,730.44	1,691.55
8.00%	5,069.10	3,896.55	3,534.17	3,033.19	2,389.13	2,091.10	1,929.54	1,834.41	1,775.65	1,738.28
8.25%	5,099.06	3,927.76	3,566.02	3,066.32	2,425.35	2,130.16	1,971.13	1,878.17	1,821.23	1,785.35
8.50%	5,129.13	3,959.12	3,598.03	3,099.64	2,461.85	2,169.56	2,013.07	1,922.28	1,867.15	1,832.74
8.75%	5,159.31	3,990.62	3,630.21	3,133.17	2,498.62	2,209.28	2,055.36	1,966.75	1,913.41	1,880.43
9.00%	5,189.59	4,022.27	3,662.55	3,166.89	2,535.67	2,249.31	2,097.99	2,011.56	1,959.98	1,928.40
9.25%	5,219.97	4,054.06	3,695.06	3,200.82	2,572.98	2,289.67	2,140.95	2,056.69	2,006.86	1,976.65
9.50%	5,250.47	4,086.00	3,727.72	3,234.94	2,610.56	2,330.33	2,184.24	2,102.14	2,054.03	2,025.15
9.75%	5,281.06	4,118.07	3,760.55	3,269.26	2,648.41	2,371.29	2,227.84	2,147.89	2,101.47	2,073.90
10.00%	5,311.76	4,150.30	3,793.54	3,303.77	2,686.51	2,412.55	2,271.75	2,193.93	2,149.18	2,122.86
10.25%	5,342.57	4,182.66	3,826.69	3,338.48	2,724.88	2,454.11	2,315.96	2,240.25	2,197.14	2,172.05
10.50%	5,373.48	4,215.17	3,860.00	3,373.37	2,763.50	2,495.95	2,360.45	2,286.85	2,245.34	2,221.43
10.75%	5,404.49	4,247.82	3,893.48	3,408.47	2,802.37	2,538.07	2,405.23	2,333.70	2,293.76	2,270.99

$250,000   11.00 - 20.75%   5 - 40 Years

	5	7	8	10	15	20	25	30	35	40
11.00%	5,435.61	4,280.61	3,927.11	3,443.75	2,841.49	2,580.47	2,450.28	2,380.81	2,342.39	2,320.74
11.25%	5,466.83	4,313.54	3,960.90	3,479.22	2,880.86	2,623.14	2,495.60	2,428.15	2,391.23	2,370.64
11.50%	5,498.15	4,346.62	3,994.84	3,514.89	2,920.47	2,666.07	2,541.17	2,475.73	2,440.27	2,420.70
11.75%	5,529.58	4,379.83	4,028.95	3,550.74	2,960.33	2,709.27	2,587.00	2,523.52	2,489.48	2,470.91
12.00%	5,561.11	4,413.18	4,063.21	3,586.77	3,000.42	2,752.72	2,633.06	2,571.53	2,538.87	2,521.25
12.25%	5,592.75	4,446.68	4,097.63	3,623.00	3,040.75	2,796.41	2,679.36	2,619.74	2,588.43	2,571.72
12.50%	5,624.48	4,480.31	4,132.20	3,659.40	3,081.31	2,840.35	2,725.89	2,668.14	2,638.14	2,622.30
12.75%	5,656.33	4,514.08	4,166.93	3,696.00	3,122.09	2,884.53	2,772.63	2,716.73	2,687.99	2,672.99
13.00%	5,688.27	4,547.99	4,201.81	3,732.77	3,163.11	2,928.94	2,819.59	2,765.50	2,737.98	2,723.79
13.25%	5,720.31	4,582.04	4,236.85	3,769.72	3,204.34	2,973.58	2,866.75	2,814.43	2,788.11	2,774.67
13.50%	5,752.46	4,616.22	4,272.04	3,806.86	3,245.80	3,018.44	2,914.11	2,863.53	2,838.35	2,825.65
13.75%	5,784.71	4,650.54	4,307.38	3,844.17	3,287.47	3,063.51	2,961.66	2,912.78	2,888.71	2,876.71
14.00%	5,817.06	4,685.00	4,342.88	3,881.66	3,329.35	3,108.80	3,009.40	2,962.18	2,939.18	2,927.85
14.25%	5,849.52	4,719.60	4,378.52	3,919.33	3,371.45	3,154.30	3,057.32	3,011.72	2,989.76	2,979.06
14.50%	5,882.07	4,754.33	4,414.31	3,957.17	3,413.75	3,199.99	3,105.41	3,061.39	3,040.43	3,030.33
14.75%	5,914.73	4,789.19	4,450.26	3,995.19	3,456.26	3,245.89	3,153.66	3,111.19	3,091.19	3,081.67
15.00%	5,947.48	4,824.19	4,486.35	4,033.37	3,498.97	3,291.97	3,202.08	3,161.11	3,142.03	3,133.06
15.25%	5,980.34	4,859.32	4,522.59	4,071.73	3,541.87	3,338.25	3,250.65	3,211.15	3,192.96	3,184.51
15.50%	6,013.30	4,894.59	4,558.98	4,110.26	3,584.98	3,384.70	3,299.36	3,261.29	3,243.96	3,236.00
15.75%	6,046.36	4,929.99	4,595.52	4,148.96	3,628.27	3,431.33	3,348.22	3,311.54	3,295.03	3,287.54
16.00%	6,079.51	4,965.52	4,632.20	4,187.83	3,671.75	3,478.14	3,397.22	3,361.89	3,346.17	3,339.12
16.25%	6,112.77	5,001.18	4,669.02	4,226.86	3,715.42	3,525.11	3,446.35	3,412.34	3,397.37	3,390.74
16.50%	6,146.13	5,036.97	4,705.99	4,266.06	3,759.27	3,572.25	3,495.61	3,462.87	3,448.63	3,442.40
16.75%	6,179.59	5,072.90	4,743.11	4,305.42	3,803.30	3,619.55	3,544.99	3,513.49	3,499.95	3,494.09
17.00%	6,213.14	5,108.95	4,780.36	4,344.94	3,847.51	3,667.00	3,594.49	3,564.19	3,551.32	3,545.81
17.25%	6,246.80	5,145.14	4,817.76	4,384.63	3,891.89	3,714.60	3,644.10	3,614.96	3,602.73	3,597.56
17.50%	6,280.55	5,181.45	4,855.30	4,424.47	3,936.45	3,762.35	3,693.82	3,665.81	3,654.19	3,649.33
17.75%	6,314.41	5,217.89	4,892.98	4,464.47	3,981.17	3,810.25	3,743.65	3,716.73	3,705.69	3,701.13
18.00%	6,348.36	5,254.46	4,930.80	4,504.63	4,026.05	3,858.28	3,793.57	3,767.71	3,757.23	3,752.96
18.25%	6,382.41	5,291.16	4,968.76	4,544.94	4,071.10	3,906.44	3,843.60	3,818.76	3,808.81	3,804.80
18.50%	6,416.55	5,327.98	5,006.86	4,585.41	4,116.31	3,954.74	3,893.71	3,869.86	3,860.42	3,856.66
18.75%	6,450.80	5,364.93	5,045.09	4,626.04	4,161.67	4,003.17	3,943.91	3,921.02	3,912.06	3,908.54
19.00%	6,485.14	5,402.00	5,083.47	4,666.81	4,207.19	4,051.71	3,994.20	3,972.23	3,963.74	3,960.44
19.25%	6,519.58	5,439.21	5,121.97	4,707.73	4,252.86	4,100.38	4,044.57	4,023.49	4,015.44	4,012.35
19.50%	6,554.11	5,476.53	5,160.62	4,748.81	4,298.68	4,149.16	4,095.02	4,074.80	4,067.17	4,064.27
19.75%	6,588.74	5,513.98	5,199.39	4,790.03	4,344.64	4,198.06	4,145.54	4,126.15	4,118.92	4,116.21
20.00%	6,623.47	5,551.55	5,238.30	4,831.39	4,390.74	4,247.06	4,196.13	4,177.55	4,170.70	4,168.16
20.25%	6,658.29	5,589.24	5,277.34	4,872.90	4,436.99	4,296.17	4,246.79	4,228.98	4,222.49	4,220.12
20.50%	6,693.21	5,627.06	5,316.51	4,914.56	4,483.37	4,345.39	4,297.52	4,280.45	4,274.31	4,272.09
20.75%	6,728.23	5,665.00	5,355.82	4,956.35	4,529.88	4,394.70	4,348.31	4,331.96	4,326.15	4,324.07

	5	7	8	10	15	20	25	30	35	40
1.00%	4,358.91	3,144.47	2,765.02	2,233.91	1,526.16	1,172.73	961.02	820.18	719.83	644.78
1.25%	4,386.41	3,172.04	2,792.66	2,261.68	1,554.36	1,201.39	990.16	849.79	749.92	675.36
1.50%	4,414.02	3,199.77	2,820.47	2,289.68	1,582.89	1,230.49	1,019.84	880.06	780.77	706.79
1.75%	4,441.74	3,227.66	2,848.46	2,317.90	1,611.76	1,260.03	1,050.06	910.97	812.37	739.08
2.00%	4,469.58	3,255.70	2,876.62	2,346.34	1,640.95	1,290.00	1,080.83	942.53	844.72	772.21
2.25%	4,497.52	3,283.89	2,904.96	2,375.00	1,670.47	1,320.41	1,112.13	974.73	877.80	806.16
2.50%	4,525.58	3,312.24	2,933.48	2,403.88	1,700.31	1,351.25	1,143.97	1,007.56	911.61	840.93
2.75%	4,553.74	3,340.74	2,962.17	2,432.98	1,730.49	1,382.52	1,176.34	1,041.02	946.14	876.51
3.00%	4,582.02	3,369.39	2,991.04	2,462.30	1,760.98	1,414.22	1,209.24	1,075.09	981.37	912.86
3.25%	4,610.40	3,398.20	3,020.08	2,491.84	1,791.81	1,446.35	1,242.66	1,109.78	1,017.29	949.98
3.50%	4,638.89	3,427.16	3,049.30	2,521.59	1,822.95	1,478.90	1,276.59	1,145.06	1,053.89	987.85
3.75%	4,667.50	3,456.28	3,078.70	2,551.56	1,854.42	1,511.87	1,311.03	1,180.94	1,091.16	1,026.44
4.00%	4,696.21	3,485.55	3,108.27	2,581.75	1,886.20	1,545.25	1,345.98	1,217.41	1,129.08	1,065.74
4.25%	4,725.04	3,514.97	3,138.01	2,612.16	1,918.31	1,579.05	1,381.43	1,254.45	1,167.63	1,105.73
4.50%	4,753.97	3,544.54	3,167.92	2,642.78	1,950.73	1,613.26	1,417.37	1,292.05	1,206.80	1,146.39
4.75%	4,783.01	3,574.27	3,198.02	2,673.62	1,983.47	1,647.87	1,453.80	1,330.20	1,246.58	1,187.68
5.00%	4,812.16	3,604.15	3,228.28	2,704.67	2,016.52	1,682.89	1,490.70	1,368.90	1,286.95	1,229.60
5.25%	4,841.43	3,634.18	3,258.72	2,735.94	2,049.89	1,718.30	1,528.08	1,408.12	1,327.89	1,272.12
5.50%	4,870.80	3,664.36	3,289.33	2,767.42	2,083.56	1,754.11	1,565.92	1,447.86	1,369.39	1,315.21
5.75%	4,900.28	3,694.70	3,320.11	2,799.12	2,117.55	1,790.31	1,604.22	1,488.11	1,411.43	1,358.86
6.00%	4,929.86	3,725.18	3,351.06	2,831.02	2,151.83	1,826.90	1,642.97	1,528.85	1,453.98	1,403.04
6.25%	4,959.56	3,755.82	3,382.19	2,863.14	2,186.43	1,863.87	1,682.16	1,570.08	1,497.05	1,447.74
6.50%	4,989.37	3,786.61	3,413.49	2,895.47	2,221.32	1,901.21	1,721.78	1,611.77	1,540.59	1,492.91
6.75%	5,019.28	3,817.54	3,444.96	2,928.01	2,256.52	1,938.93	1,761.82	1,653.93	1,584.61	1,538.56
7.00%	5,049.31	3,848.63	3,476.60	2,960.77	2,292.01	1,977.01	1,802.29	1,696.52	1,629.08	1,584.65
7.25%	5,079.44	3,879.87	3,508.41	2,993.73	2,327.80	2,015.46	1,843.16	1,739.55	1,673.99	1,631.16
7.50%	5,109.68	3,911.26	3,540.39	3,026.90	2,363.88	2,054.26	1,884.43	1,783.00	1,719.32	1,678.08
7.75%	5,140.02	3,942.80	3,572.54	3,060.27	2,400.25	2,093.42	1,926.09	1,826.85	1,765.05	1,725.38
8.00%	5,170.48	3,974.48	3,604.85	3,093.85	2,436.91	2,132.92	1,968.13	1,871.10	1,811.17	1,773.04
8.25%	5,201.04	4,006.32	3,637.34	3,127.64	2,473.86	2,172.77	2,010.55	1,915.73	1,857.65	1,821.05
8.50%	5,231.72	4,038.30	3,669.99	3,161.64	2,511.09	2,212.95	2,053.33	1,960.73	1,904.49	1,869.39
8.75%	5,262.49	4,070.44	3,702.81	3,195.83	2,548.59	2,253.46	2,096.47	2,006.09	1,951.68	1,918.03
9.00%	5,293.38	4,102.71	3,735.80	3,230.23	2,586.38	2,294.30	2,139.95	2,051.79	1,999.18	1,966.97
9.25%	5,324.37	4,135.14	3,768.96	3,264.83	2,624.44	2,335.46	2,183.77	2,097.82	2,047.00	2,016.18
9.50%	5,355.47	4,167.72	3,802.28	3,299.64	2,662.77	2,376.93	2,227.93	2,144.18	2,095.11	2,065.66
9.75%	5,386.68	4,200.44	3,835.76	3,334.64	2,701.37	2,418.72	2,272.40	2,190.84	2,143.50	2,115.37
10.00%	5,418.00	4,233.30	3,869.41	3,369.84	2,740.24	2,460.81	2,317.19	2,237.81	2,192.16	2,165.32
10.25%	5,449.42	4,266.31	3,903.23	3,405.24	2,779.37	2,503.19	2,362.28	2,285.06	2,241.08	2,215.49
10.50%	5,480.94	4,299.47	3,937.20	3,440.84	2,818.77	2,545.87	2,407.66	2,332.59	2,290.24	2,265.85
10.75%	5,512.58	4,332.77	3,971.35	3,476.64	2,858.42	2,588.83	2,453.34	2,380.38	2,339.63	2,316.41

$255,000   11.00 - 20.75%   5 - 40 Years

	5	7	8	10	15	20	25	30	35	40
11.00%	5,544.32	4,366.22	4,005.65	3,512.63	2,898.32	2,632.08	2,499.29	2,428.42	2,389.24	2,367.15
11.25%	5,576.16	4,399.81	4,040.11	3,548.81	2,938.48	2,675.60	2,545.51	2,476.72	2,439.06	2,418.06
11.50%	5,608.11	4,433.55	4,074.74	3,585.18	2,978.88	2,719.40	2,592.00	2,525.24	2,489.07	2,469.12
11.75%	5,640.17	4,467.43	4,109.53	3,621.75	3,019.53	2,763.45	2,638.74	2,573.99	2,539.27	2,520.33
12.00%	5,672.33	4,501.45	4,144.47	3,658.51	3,060.43	2,807.77	2,685.72	2,622.96	2,589.65	2,571.67
12.25%	5,704.60	4,535.61	4,179.58	3,695.46	3,101.56	2,852.34	2,732.95	2,672.14	2,640.20	2,623.15
12.50%	5,736.97	4,569.92	4,214.85	3,732.59	3,142.93	2,897.16	2,780.40	2,721.51	2,690.90	2,674.74
12.75%	5,769.45	4,604.36	4,250.27	3,769.92	3,184.53	2,942.22	2,828.08	2,771.07	2,741.75	2,726.45
13.00%	5,802.03	4,638.95	4,285.85	3,807.42	3,226.37	2,987.52	2,875.98	2,820.81	2,792.74	2,778.26
13.25%	5,834.72	4,673.68	4,321.59	3,845.12	3,268.43	3,033.05	2,924.09	2,870.72	2,843.87	2,830.17
13.50%	5,867.51	4,708.55	4,357.48	3,882.99	3,310.71	3,078.81	2,972.39	2,920.80	2,895.12	2,882.17
13.75%	5,900.41	4,743.56	4,393.53	3,921.05	3,353.22	3,124.78	3,020.90	2,971.04	2,946.49	2,934.25
14.00%	5,933.40	4,778.70	4,429.73	3,959.29	3,395.94	3,170.98	3,069.59	3,021.42	2,997.97	2,986.41
14.25%	5,966.51	4,813.99	4,466.09	3,997.71	3,438.88	3,217.38	3,118.47	3,071.95	3,049.55	3,038.64
14.50%	5,999.71	4,849.41	4,502.60	4,036.31	3,482.03	3,263.99	3,167.52	3,122.62	3,101.23	3,090.94
14.75%	6,033.02	4,884.97	4,539.26	4,075.09	3,525.38	3,310.81	3,216.74	3,173.41	3,153.01	3,143.30
15.00%	6,066.43	4,920.67	4,576.08	4,114.04	3,568.95	3,357.81	3,266.12	3,224.33	3,204.87	3,195.72
15.25%	6,099.95	4,956.51	4,613.04	4,153.17	3,612.71	3,405.01	3,315.66	3,275.37	3,256.82	3,248.20
15.50%	6,133.56	4,992.48	4,650.16	4,192.47	3,656.68	3,452.40	3,365.35	3,326.52	3,308.84	3,300.72
15.75%	6,167.28	5,028.58	4,687.43	4,231.94	3,700.83	3,499.96	3,415.19	3,377.77	3,360.94	3,353.29
16.00%	6,201.10	5,064.83	4,724.84	4,271.58	3,745.19	3,547.70	3,465.17	3,429.13	3,413.10	3,405.90
16.25%	6,235.03	5,101.20	4,762.40	4,311.40	3,789.73	3,595.62	3,515.28	3,480.58	3,465.32	3,458.56
16.50%	6,269.05	5,137.71	4,800.11	4,351.38	3,834.46	3,643.70	3,565.52	3,532.13	3,517.61	3,511.25
16.75%	6,303.18	5,174.35	4,837.97	4,391.53	3,879.37	3,691.94	3,615.89	3,583.76	3,569.95	3,563.97
17.00%	6,337.41	5,211.13	4,875.97	4,431.84	3,924.46	3,740.34	3,666.38	3,635.47	3,622.34	3,616.73
17.25%	6,371.74	5,248.04	4,914.12	4,472.32	3,969.73	3,788.90	3,716.99	3,687.26	3,674.78	3,669.51
17.50%	6,406.16	5,285.08	4,952.41	4,512.96	4,015.17	3,837.60	3,767.70	3,739.13	3,727.27	3,722.32
17.75%	6,440.69	5,322.25	4,990.84	4,553.76	4,060.79	3,886.45	3,818.52	3,791.07	3,779.80	3,775.16
18.00%	6,475.32	5,359.55	5,029.42	4,594.72	4,106.57	3,935.44	3,869.45	3,843.07	3,832.37	3,828.01
18.25%	6,510.05	5,396.98	5,068.14	4,635.84	4,152.52	3,984.57	3,920.47	3,895.13	3,884.98	3,880.89
18.50%	6,544.88	5,434.54	5,107.00	4,677.12	4,198.63	4,033.84	3,971.58	3,947.26	3,937.63	3,933.79
18.75%	6,579.81	5,472.23	5,146.00	4,718.56	4,244.91	4,083.23	4,022.79	3,999.44	3,990.30	3,986.71
19.00%	6,614.84	5,510.04	5,185.14	4,760.15	4,291.33	4,132.75	4,074.08	4,051.68	4,043.01	4,039.65
19.25%	6,649.97	5,547.99	5,224.41	4,801.89	4,337.92	4,182.39	4,125.46	4,103.96	4,095.75	4,092.60
19.50%	6,685.19	5,586.06	5,263.83	4,843.78	4,384.65	4,232.14	4,176.92	4,156.30	4,148.51	4,145.56
19.75%	6,720.52	5,624.26	5,303.38	4,885.83	4,431.53	4,282.02	4,228.45	4,208.68	4,201.30	4,198.53
20.00%	6,755.94	5,662.58	5,343.07	4,928.02	4,478.56	4,332.00	4,280.05	4,261.10	4,254.11	4,251.52
20.25%	6,791.46	5,701.03	5,382.89	4,970.36	4,525.73	4,382.10	4,331.73	4,313.56	4,306.94	4,304.52
20.50%	6,827.08	5,739.60	5,422.85	5,012.85	4,573.03	4,432.29	4,383.47	4,366.06	4,359.80	4,357.53
20.75%	6,862.79	5,778.30	5,462.94	5,055.48	4,620.48	4,482.59	4,435.27	4,418.60	4,412.67	4,410.55

$260,000   1.00 - 10.75%   5 - 40 Years

	5	7	8	10	15	20	25	30	35	40
1.00%	4,444.37	3,206.12	2,819.24	2,277.71	1,556.09	1,195.73	979.87	836.26	733.94	657.43
1.25%	4,472.42	3,234.24	2,847.42	2,306.03	1,584.84	1,224.95	1,009.57	866.45	764.62	688.60
1.50%	4,500.57	3,262.51	2,875.77	2,334.58	1,613.93	1,254.62	1,039.83	897.31	796.08	720.65
1.75%	4,528.84	3,290.94	2,904.31	2,363.35	1,643.36	1,284.73	1,070.65	928.83	828.30	753.57
2.00%	4,557.22	3,319.53	2,933.03	2,392.35	1,673.12	1,315.30	1,102.02	961.01	861.28	787.35
2.25%	4,585.71	3,348.28	2,961.92	2,421.57	1,703.22	1,346.30	1,133.94	993.84	895.02	821.97
2.50%	4,614.31	3,377.18	2,991.00	2,451.02	1,733.65	1,377.75	1,166.40	1,027.31	929.49	857.42
2.75%	4,643.03	3,406.24	3,020.25	2,480.69	1,764.42	1,409.63	1,199.41	1,061.43	964.69	893.69
3.00%	4,671.86	3,435.46	3,049.69	2,510.58	1,795.51	1,441.95	1,232.95	1,096.17	1,000.61	930.76
3.25%	4,700.80	3,464.83	3,079.30	2,540.69	1,826.94	1,474.71	1,267.02	1,131.54	1,037.24	968.61
3.50%	4,729.85	3,494.36	3,109.09	2,571.03	1,858.69	1,507.90	1,301.62	1,167.52	1,074.56	1,007.22
3.75%	4,759.02	3,524.05	3,139.06	2,601.59	1,890.78	1,541.51	1,336.74	1,204.10	1,112.55	1,046.57
4.00%	4,788.30	3,553.89	3,169.21	2,632.37	1,923.19	1,575.55	1,372.38	1,241.28	1,151.21	1,086.64
4.25%	4,817.68	3,583.89	3,199.54	2,663.38	1,955.92	1,610.01	1,408.52	1,279.04	1,190.52	1,127.41
4.50%	4,847.19	3,614.04	3,230.04	2,694.60	1,988.98	1,644.89	1,445.16	1,317.38	1,230.47	1,168.86
4.75%	4,876.80	3,644.35	3,260.72	2,726.04	2,022.36	1,680.18	1,482.31	1,356.28	1,271.03	1,210.97
5.00%	4,906.52	3,674.82	3,291.58	2,757.70	2,056.06	1,715.88	1,519.93	1,395.74	1,312.19	1,253.71
5.25%	4,936.36	3,705.44	3,322.61	2,789.58	2,090.08	1,751.99	1,558.04	1,435.73	1,353.93	1,297.06
5.50%	4,966.30	3,736.21	3,353.82	2,821.68	2,124.42	1,788.51	1,596.63	1,476.25	1,396.24	1,341.00
5.75%	4,996.36	3,767.14	3,385.21	2,854.00	2,159.07	1,825.42	1,635.68	1,517.29	1,439.10	1,385.51
6.00%	5,026.53	3,798.22	3,416.77	2,886.53	2,194.03	1,862.72	1,675.18	1,558.83	1,482.49	1,430.56
6.25%	5,056.81	3,829.46	3,448.51	2,919.28	2,229.30	1,900.41	1,715.14	1,600.86	1,526.40	1,476.12
6.50%	5,087.20	3,860.85	3,480.42	2,952.25	2,264.88	1,938.49	1,755.54	1,643.38	1,570.80	1,522.19
6.75%	5,117.70	3,892.40	3,512.51	2,985.43	2,300.76	1,976.95	1,796.37	1,686.36	1,615.68	1,568.73
7.00%	5,148.31	3,924.10	3,544.77	3,018.82	2,336.95	2,015.78	1,837.63	1,729.79	1,661.03	1,615.72
7.25%	5,179.03	3,955.95	3,577.20	3,052.43	2,373.44	2,054.98	1,879.30	1,773.66	1,706.81	1,663.15
7.50%	5,209.87	3,987.95	3,609.81	3,086.25	2,410.23	2,094.54	1,921.38	1,817.96	1,753.03	1,710.98
7.75%	5,240.81	4,020.11	3,642.59	3,120.28	2,447.32	2,134.47	1,963.85	1,862.67	1,799.66	1,759.21
8.00%	5,271.86	4,052.42	3,675.54	3,154.52	2,484.70	2,174.74	2,006.72	1,907.79	1,846.68	1,807.81
8.25%	5,303.03	4,084.88	3,708.66	3,188.97	2,522.36	2,215.37	2,049.97	1,953.29	1,894.08	1,856.76
8.50%	5,334.30	4,117.49	3,741.95	3,223.63	2,560.32	2,256.34	2,093.59	1,999.18	1,941.84	1,906.04
8.75%	5,365.68	4,150.25	3,775.42	3,258.50	2,598.57	2,297.65	2,137.57	2,045.42	1,989.94	1,955.64
9.00%	5,397.17	4,183.16	3,809.05	3,293.57	2,637.09	2,339.29	2,181.91	2,092.02	2,038.38	2,005.54
9.25%	5,428.77	4,216.22	3,842.86	3,328.85	2,675.90	2,381.25	2,226.59	2,138.96	2,087.14	2,055.72
9.50%	5,460.48	4,249.44	3,876.83	3,364.34	2,714.98	2,423.54	2,271.61	2,186.22	2,136.19	2,106.16
9.75%	5,492.30	4,282.80	3,910.97	3,400.03	2,754.34	2,466.14	2,316.96	2,233.80	2,185.53	2,156.85
10.00%	5,524.23	4,316.31	3,945.28	3,435.92	2,793.97	2,509.06	2,362.62	2,281.69	2,235.15	2,207.78
10.25%	5,556.27	4,349.97	3,979.76	3,472.01	2,833.87	2,552.27	2,408.60	2,329.86	2,285.02	2,258.93
10.50%	5,588.41	4,383.78	4,014.40	3,508.31	2,874.04	2,595.79	2,454.87	2,378.32	2,335.15	2,310.28
10.75%	5,620.67	4,417.73	4,049.21	3,544.81	2,914.46	2,639.60	2,501.44	2,427.05	2,385.51	2,361.83

$260,000   11.00 - 20.75%   5 - 40 Years

	5	7	8	10	15	20	25	30	35	40
11.00%	5,653.03	4,451.83	4,084.19	3,581.50	2,955.15	2,683.69	2,548.29	2,476.04	2,436.09	2,413.57
11.25%	5,685.50	4,486.08	4,119.33	3,618.39	2,996.10	2,728.07	2,595.42	2,525.28	2,486.88	2,465.47
11.50%	5,718.08	4,520.48	4,154.64	3,655.48	3,037.29	2,772.72	2,642.82	2,574.76	2,537.88	2,517.53
11.75%	5,750.76	4,555.02	4,190.11	3,692.77	3,078.74	2,817.64	2,690.48	2,624.47	2,589.06	2,569.75
12.00%	5,783.56	4,589.71	4,225.74	3,730.24	3,120.44	2,862.82	2,738.38	2,674.39	2,640.43	2,622.10
12.25%	5,816.46	4,624.54	4,261.53	3,767.92	3,162.38	2,908.27	2,786.53	2,724.53	2,691.96	2,674.58
12.50%	5,849.46	4,659.52	4,297.49	3,805.78	3,204.56	2,953.97	2,834.92	2,774.87	2,743.66	2,727.19
12.75%	5,882.58	4,694.64	4,333.61	3,843.84	3,246.98	2,999.91	2,883.54	2,825.40	2,795.51	2,779.91
13.00%	5,915.80	4,729.91	4,369.89	3,882.08	3,289.63	3,046.10	2,932.37	2,876.12	2,847.50	2,832.74
13.25%	5,949.13	4,765.32	4,406.32	3,920.51	3,332.51	3,092.52	2,981.42	2,927.01	2,899.63	2,885.66
13.50%	5,982.56	4,800.87	4,442.92	3,959.13	3,375.63	3,139.17	3,030.68	2,978.07	2,951.89	2,938.68
13.75%	6,016.10	4,836.57	4,479.68	3,997.94	3,418.97	3,186.05	3,080.13	3,029.29	3,004.26	2,991.78
14.00%	6,049.75	4,872.40	4,516.59	4,036.93	3,462.53	3,233.15	3,129.78	3,080.67	3,056.75	3,044.96
14.25%	6,083.50	4,908.38	4,553.66	4,076.10	3,506.31	3,280.47	3,179.61	3,132.19	3,109.35	3,098.22
14.50%	6,117.35	4,944.50	4,590.89	4,115.46	3,550.30	3,327.99	3,229.62	3,183.85	3,162.04	3,151.55
14.75%	6,151.31	4,980.76	4,628.27	4,154.99	3,594.51	3,375.72	3,279.81	3,235.64	3,214.83	3,204.93
15.00%	6,185.38	5,017.16	4,665.81	4,194.71	3,638.93	3,423.65	3,330.16	3,287.55	3,267.71	3,258.38
15.25%	6,219.55	5,053.69	4,703.50	4,234.60	3,683.55	3,471.78	3,380.67	3,339.59	3,320.68	3,311.89
15.50%	6,253.83	5,090.37	4,741.34	4,274.67	3,728.37	3,520.09	3,431.34	3,391.74	3,373.72	3,365.44
15.75%	6,288.21	5,127.18	4,779.34	4,314.92	3,773.40	3,568.59	3,482.15	3,444.00	3,426.84	3,419.04
16.00%	6,322.69	5,164.14	4,817.48	4,355.34	3,818.62	3,617.27	3,533.11	3,496.37	3,480.02	3,472.69
16.25%	6,357.28	5,201.23	4,855.78	4,395.93	3,864.04	3,666.12	3,584.21	3,548.83	3,533.27	3,526.37
16.50%	6,391.98	5,238.45	4,894.23	4,436.70	3,909.64	3,715.14	3,635.44	3,601.39	3,586.58	3,580.09
16.75%	6,426.77	5,275.81	4,932.83	4,477.63	3,955.43	3,764.33	3,686.79	3,654.03	3,639.95	3,633.85
17.00%	6,461.67	5,313.31	4,971.58	4,518.74	4,001.41	3,813.68	3,738.27	3,706.76	3,693.37	3,687.64
17.25%	6,496.67	5,350.94	5,010.47	4,560.01	4,047.57	3,863.19	3,789.87	3,759.56	3,746.84	3,741.46
17.50%	6,531.78	5,388.71	5,049.51	4,601.45	4,093.90	3,912.85	3,841.58	3,812.45	3,800.36	3,795.31
17.75%	6,566.98	5,426.61	5,088.70	4,643.05	4,140.41	3,962.66	3,893.40	3,865.40	3,853.92	3,849.18
18.00%	6,602.29	5,464.64	5,128.04	4,684.82	4,187.09	4,012.61	3,945.32	3,918.42	3,907.52	3,903.07
18.25%	6,637.70	5,502.80	5,167.51	4,726.74	4,233.94	4,062.70	3,997.34	3,971.51	3,961.16	3,956.99
18.50%	6,673.21	5,541.10	5,207.13	4,768.83	4,280.96	4,112.93	4,049.46	4,024.66	4,014.84	4,010.93
18.75%	6,708.83	5,579.53	5,246.90	4,811.08	4,328.14	4,163.29	4,101.67	4,077.86	4,068.55	4,064.88
19.00%	6,744.54	5,618.08	5,286.80	4,853.48	4,375.48	4,213.78	4,153.97	4,131.12	4,122.29	4,118.85
19.25%	6,780.36	5,656.77	5,326.85	4,896.04	4,422.97	4,264.39	4,206.35	4,184.43	4,176.06	4,172.84
19.50%	6,816.28	5,695.59	5,367.04	4,938.76	4,470.62	4,315.13	4,258.82	4,237.79	4,229.85	4,226.84
19.75%	6,852.29	5,734.54	5,407.37	4,981.63	4,518.42	4,365.98	4,311.36	4,291.20	4,283.68	4,280.86
20.00%	6,888.41	5,773.61	5,447.83	5,024.65	4,566.37	4,416.94	4,363.97	4,344.65	4,337.52	4,334.89
20.25%	6,924.63	5,812.81	5,488.44	5,067.82	4,614.46	4,468.02	4,416.66	4,398.14	4,391.39	4,388.93
20.50%	6,960.94	5,852.14	5,529.18	5,111.14	4,662.70	4,519.20	4,469.42	4,451.67	4,445.28	4,442.97
20.75%	6,997.36	5,891.60	5,570.05	5,154.61	4,711.08	4,570.49	4,522.24	4,505.24	4,499.19	4,497.03

	5	7	8	10	15	20	25	30	35	40
1.00%	4,529.84	3,267.78	2,873.45	2,321.51	1,586.01	1,218.72	998.71	852.34	748.06	670.07
1.25%	4,558.42	3,296.44	2,902.17	2,350.38	1,615.32	1,248.50	1,028.99	883.12	779.33	701.84
1.50%	4,587.12	3,325.25	2,931.08	2,379.47	1,644.97	1,278.75	1,059.83	914.57	811.39	734.51
1.75%	4,615.93	3,354.23	2,960.16	2,408.80	1,674.96	1,309.44	1,091.24	946.70	844.23	768.06
2.00%	4,644.86	3,383.37	2,989.43	2,438.36	1,705.30	1,340.59	1,123.21	979.49	877.85	802.49
2.25%	4,673.90	3,412.67	3,018.88	2,468.14	1,735.97	1,372.19	1,155.75	1,012.95	912.23	837.78
2.50%	4,703.05	3,442.13	3,048.52	2,498.15	1,766.99	1,404.24	1,188.83	1,047.07	947.36	873.91
2.75%	4,732.32	3,471.75	3,078.34	2,528.39	1,798.35	1,436.74	1,222.47	1,081.84	983.24	910.88
3.00%	4,761.70	3,501.52	3,108.34	2,558.86	1,830.04	1,469.68	1,256.66	1,117.25	1,019.85	948.66
3.25%	4,791.20	3,531.46	3,138.52	2,589.55	1,862.07	1,503.07	1,291.39	1,153.30	1,057.18	987.23
3.50%	4,820.81	3,561.56	3,168.88	2,620.48	1,894.44	1,536.89	1,326.65	1,189.97	1,095.22	1,026.59
3.75%	4,850.54	3,591.82	3,199.43	2,651.62	1,927.14	1,571.15	1,362.45	1,227.26	1,133.95	1,066.69
4.00%	4,880.38	3,622.23	3,230.16	2,683.00	1,960.17	1,605.85	1,398.77	1,265.15	1,173.35	1,107.54
4.25%	4,910.33	3,652.81	3,261.07	2,714.59	1,993.54	1,640.97	1,435.61	1,303.64	1,213.42	1,149.09
4.50%	4,940.40	3,683.54	3,292.16	2,746.42	2,027.23	1,676.52	1,472.96	1,342.72	1,254.13	1,191.34
4.75%	4,970.58	3,714.44	3,323.43	2,778.47	2,061.25	1,712.49	1,510.81	1,382.37	1,295.47	1,234.26
5.00%	5,000.88	3,745.49	3,354.88	2,810.74	2,095.60	1,748.88	1,549.16	1,422.58	1,337.42	1,277.82
5.25%	5,031.29	3,776.69	3,386.51	2,843.23	2,130.28	1,785.69	1,588.01	1,463.34	1,379.97	1,322.01
5.50%	5,061.81	3,808.06	3,418.32	2,875.95	2,165.27	1,822.90	1,627.33	1,504.64	1,423.09	1,366.79
5.75%	5,092.44	3,839.59	3,450.31	2,908.88	2,200.59	1,860.52	1,667.13	1,546.47	1,466.78	1,412.15
6.00%	5,123.19	3,871.27	3,482.48	2,942.04	2,236.22	1,898.54	1,707.40	1,588.81	1,511.00	1,458.07
6.25%	5,154.05	3,903.11	3,514.83	2,975.42	2,272.17	1,936.96	1,748.12	1,631.65	1,555.75	1,504.51
6.50%	5,185.03	3,935.10	3,547.35	3,009.02	2,308.43	1,975.77	1,789.30	1,674.98	1,601.01	1,551.46
6.75%	5,216.12	3,967.25	3,580.05	3,042.84	2,345.01	2,014.96	1,830.92	1,718.78	1,646.75	1,598.90
7.00%	5,247.32	3,999.56	3,612.94	3,076.87	2,381.89	2,054.54	1,872.96	1,763.05	1,692.97	1,646.79
7.25%	5,278.63	4,032.02	3,645.99	3,111.13	2,419.09	2,094.50	1,915.44	1,807.77	1,739.64	1,695.13
7.50%	5,310.06	4,064.64	3,679.23	3,145.60	2,456.58	2,134.82	1,958.33	1,852.92	1,786.74	1,743.89
7.75%	5,341.59	4,097.42	3,712.64	3,180.28	2,494.38	2,175.51	2,001.62	1,898.49	1,834.27	1,793.04
8.00%	5,373.24	4,130.35	3,746.22	3,215.18	2,532.48	2,216.57	2,045.31	1,944.48	1,882.19	1,842.58
8.25%	5,405.01	4,163.43	3,779.98	3,250.29	2,570.87	2,257.97	2,089.39	1,990.86	1,930.50	1,892.47
8.50%	5,436.88	4,196.67	3,813.91	3,285.62	2,609.56	2,299.73	2,133.85	2,037.62	1,979.18	1,942.70
8.75%	5,468.87	4,230.06	3,848.02	3,321.16	2,648.54	2,341.83	2,178.68	2,084.76	2,028.21	1,993.25
9.00%	5,500.96	4,263.61	3,882.30	3,356.91	2,687.81	2,384.27	2,223.87	2,132.25	2,077.58	2,044.11
9.25%	5,533.17	4,297.30	3,916.76	3,392.87	2,727.36	2,427.05	2,269.41	2,180.09	2,127.27	2,095.25
9.50%	5,565.49	4,331.16	3,951.39	3,429.04	2,767.20	2,470.15	2,315.30	2,228.26	2,177.27	2,146.66
9.75%	5,597.92	4,365.16	3,986.18	3,465.41	2,807.31	2,513.57	2,361.51	2,276.76	2,227.56	2,198.33
10.00%	5,630.47	4,399.31	4,021.15	3,501.99	2,847.70	2,557.31	2,408.06	2,325.56	2,278.13	2,250.24
10.25%	5,663.12	4,433.62	4,056.29	3,538.78	2,888.37	2,601.35	2,454.92	2,374.67	2,328.97	2,302.37
10.50%	5,695.88	4,468.08	4,091.60	3,575.78	2,929.31	2,645.71	2,502.08	2,424.06	2,380.06	2,354.71
10.75%	5,728.76	4,502.69	4,127.08	3,612.98	2,970.51	2,690.36	2,549.55	2,473.73	2,431.38	2,407.25

$265,000   11.00 - 20.75%   5 - 40 Years

	5	7	8	10	15	20	25	30	35	40
11.00%	5,761.74	4,537.45	4,162.73	3,650.38	3,011.98	2,735.30	2,597.30	2,523.66	2,482.94	2,459.98
11.25%	5,794.84	4,572.35	4,198.55	3,687.98	3,053.71	2,780.53	2,645.33	2,573.84	2,534.71	2,512.88
11.50%	5,828.04	4,607.41	4,234.53	3,725.78	3,095.70	2,826.04	2,693.64	2,624.27	2,586.68	2,565.95
11.75%	5,861.36	4,642.62	4,270.69	3,763.78	3,137.95	2,871.82	2,742.22	2,674.94	2,638.85	2,619.16
12.00%	5,894.78	4,677.97	4,307.00	3,801.98	3,180.45	2,917.88	2,791.04	2,725.82	2,691.21	2,672.52
12.25%	5,928.31	4,713.48	4,343.49	3,840.38	3,223.19	2,964.20	2,840.12	2,776.93	2,743.73	2,726.02
12.50%	5,961.95	4,749.13	4,380.13	3,878.97	3,266.18	3,010.77	2,889.44	2,828.23	2,796.42	2,779.64
12.75%	5,995.70	4,784.93	4,416.95	3,917.75	3,309.42	3,057.60	2,938.99	2,879.74	2,849.27	2,833.37
13.00%	6,029.56	4,820.87	4,453.92	3,956.73	3,352.89	3,104.68	2,988.76	2,931.43	2,902.26	2,887.21
13.25%	6,063.53	4,856.96	4,491.06	3,995.91	3,396.60	3,151.99	3,038.76	2,983.30	2,955.39	2,941.16
13.50%	6,097.61	4,893.20	4,528.36	4,035.27	3,440.54	3,199.54	3,088.96	3,035.34	3,008.65	2,995.19
13.75%	6,131.79	4,929.58	4,565.82	4,074.82	3,484.72	3,247.32	3,139.36	3,087.55	3,062.04	3,049.32
14.00%	6,166.09	4,966.10	4,603.45	4,114.56	3,529.11	3,295.33	3,189.97	3,139.91	3,115.53	3,103.52
14.25%	6,200.49	5,002.77	4,641.23	4,154.49	3,573.74	3,343.56	3,240.76	3,192.42	3,169.14	3,157.80
14.50%	6,234.99	5,039.59	4,679.17	4,194.60	3,618.58	3,391.99	3,291.73	3,245.07	3,222.85	3,212.15
14.75%	6,269.61	5,076.54	4,717.27	4,234.90	3,663.63	3,440.64	3,342.88	3,297.86	3,276.66	3,266.57
15.00%	6,304.33	5,113.64	4,755.53	4,275.38	3,708.91	3,489.49	3,394.20	3,350.78	3,330.56	3,321.04
15.25%	6,339.16	5,150.88	4,793.95	4,316.04	3,754.39	3,538.54	3,445.68	3,403.82	3,384.54	3,375.58
15.50%	6,374.10	5,188.26	4,832.52	4,356.88	3,800.07	3,587.78	3,497.32	3,456.97	3,438.60	3,430.16
15.75%	6,409.14	5,225.78	4,871.25	4,397.90	3,845.97	3,637.21	3,549.12	3,510.24	3,492.74	3,484.79
16.00%	6,444.29	5,263.45	4,910.13	4,439.10	3,892.06	3,686.83	3,601.06	3,563.61	3,546.94	3,539.47
16.25%	6,479.54	5,301.25	4,949.16	4,480.47	3,938.35	3,736.62	3,653.13	3,617.08	3,601.22	3,594.19
16.50%	6,514.90	5,339.19	4,988.35	4,522.02	3,984.83	3,786.59	3,705.35	3,670.64	3,655.55	3,648.94
16.75%	6,550.36	5,377.27	5,027.69	4,563.74	4,031.50	3,836.72	3,757.69	3,724.30	3,709.95	3,703.73
17.00%	6,585.93	5,415.49	5,067.19	4,605.64	4,078.36	3,887.02	3,810.16	3,778.04	3,764.39	3,758.56
17.25%	6,621.61	5,453.84	5,106.83	4,647.70	4,125.41	3,937.48	3,862.75	3,831.86	3,818.89	3,813.41
17.50%	6,657.39	5,492.34	5,146.62	4,689.94	4,172.63	3,988.10	3,915.45	3,885.76	3,873.44	3,868.29
17.75%	6,693.27	5,530.96	5,186.56	4,732.34	4,220.04	4,038.86	3,968.27	3,939.73	3,928.03	3,923.20
18.00%	6,729.26	5,569.73	5,226.65	4,774.91	4,267.62	4,089.78	4,021.19	3,993.78	3,982.66	3,978.13
18.25%	6,765.35	5,608.63	5,266.89	4,817.64	4,315.37	4,140.83	4,074.21	4,047.88	4,037.34	4,033.09
18.50%	6,801.55	5,647.66	5,307.27	4,860.54	4,363.29	4,192.03	4,127.33	4,102.05	4,092.04	4,088.06
18.75%	6,837.84	5,686.83	5,347.80	4,903.60	4,411.37	4,243.36	4,180.55	4,156.28	4,146.79	4,143.05
19.00%	6,874.25	5,726.13	5,388.47	4,946.82	4,459.62	4,294.81	4,233.85	4,210.57	4,201.56	4,198.06
19.25%	6,910.75	5,765.56	5,429.29	4,990.20	4,508.03	4,346.40	4,287.24	4,264.90	4,256.37	4,253.09
19.50%	6,947.36	5,805.12	5,470.25	5,033.73	4,556.60	4,398.11	4,340.72	4,319.29	4,311.20	4,308.13
19.75%	6,984.07	5,844.82	5,511.35	5,077.43	4,605.32	4,449.94	4,394.27	4,373.72	4,366.06	4,363.18
20.00%	7,020.88	5,884.64	5,552.60	5,121.28	4,654.19	4,501.89	4,447.90	4,428.20	4,420.94	4,418.25
20.25%	7,057.79	5,924.60	5,593.98	5,165.28	4,703.20	4,553.94	4,501.60	4,482.72	4,475.84	4,473.33
20.50%	7,094.81	5,964.68	5,635.51	5,209.43	4,752.37	4,606.11	4,555.37	4,537.28	4,530.77	4,528.42
20.75%	7,131.92	6,004.90	5,677.17	5,253.74	4,801.68	4,658.38	4,609.21	4,591.88	4,585.71	4,583.51

	5	7	8	10	15	20	25	30	35	40
1.00%	4,615.31	3,329.44	2,927.67	2,365.31	1,615.94	1,241.71	1,017.56	868.43	762.17	682.71
1.25%	4,644.43	3,358.63	2,956.93	2,394.72	1,645.80	1,272.06	1,048.40	899.78	794.03	715.08
1.50%	4,673.67	3,387.99	2,986.38	2,424.37	1,676.01	1,302.87	1,079.83	931.82	826.70	748.37
1.75%	4,703.02	3,417.52	3,016.01	2,454.25	1,706.57	1,334.15	1,111.83	964.56	860.16	782.55
2.00%	4,732.50	3,447.21	3,045.84	2,484.36	1,737.47	1,365.89	1,144.41	997.97	894.41	817.63
2.25%	4,762.08	3,477.06	3,075.84	2,514.71	1,768.73	1,398.08	1,177.55	1,032.06	929.44	853.58
2.50%	4,791.79	3,507.07	3,106.04	2,545.29	1,800.33	1,430.74	1,211.27	1,066.83	965.24	890.40
2.75%	4,821.61	3,537.25	3,136.42	2,576.10	1,832.28	1,463.85	1,245.54	1,102.25	1,001.79	928.07
3.00%	4,851.55	3,567.59	3,166.98	2,607.14	1,864.57	1,497.41	1,280.37	1,138.33	1,039.10	966.56
3.25%	4,881.60	3,598.09	3,197.74	2,638.41	1,897.21	1,531.43	1,315.75	1,175.06	1,077.13	1,005.86
3.50%	4,911.77	3,628.76	3,228.67	2,669.92	1,930.18	1,565.89	1,351.68	1,212.42	1,115.88	1,045.96
3.75%	4,942.06	3,659.59	3,259.80	2,701.65	1,963.50	1,600.80	1,388.15	1,250.41	1,155.34	1,086.82
4.00%	4,972.46	3,690.58	3,291.10	2,733.62	1,997.16	1,636.15	1,425.16	1,289.02	1,195.49	1,128.43
4.25%	5,002.98	3,721.73	3,322.60	2,765.81	2,031.15	1,671.93	1,462.69	1,328.24	1,236.31	1,170.77
4.50%	5,033.62	3,753.04	3,354.27	2,798.24	2,065.48	1,708.15	1,500.75	1,368.05	1,277.79	1,213.82
4.75%	5,064.37	3,784.52	3,386.13	2,830.89	2,100.15	1,744.80	1,539.32	1,408.45	1,319.91	1,257.55
5.00%	5,095.23	3,816.16	3,418.18	2,863.77	2,135.14	1,781.88	1,578.39	1,449.42	1,362.66	1,301.93
5.25%	5,126.22	3,847.95	3,450.41	2,896.88	2,170.47	1,819.38	1,617.97	1,490.95	1,406.01	1,346.95
5.50%	5,157.31	3,879.91	3,482.82	2,930.21	2,206.13	1,857.30	1,658.04	1,533.03	1,449.94	1,392.58
5.75%	5,188.53	3,912.03	3,515.41	2,963.77	2,242.11	1,895.63	1,698.59	1,575.65	1,494.45	1,438.80
6.00%	5,219.86	3,944.31	3,548.19	2,997.55	2,278.41	1,934.36	1,739.61	1,618.79	1,539.51	1,485.58
6.25%	5,251.30	3,976.75	3,581.14	3,031.56	2,315.04	1,973.51	1,781.11	1,662.44	1,585.11	1,532.90
6.50%	5,282.86	4,009.35	3,614.28	3,065.80	2,351.99	2,013.05	1,823.06	1,706.58	1,631.22	1,580.73
6.75%	5,314.53	4,042.11	3,647.60	3,100.25	2,389.26	2,052.98	1,865.46	1,751.21	1,677.82	1,629.06
7.00%	5,346.32	4,075.02	3,681.10	3,134.93	2,426.84	2,093.31	1,908.30	1,796.32	1,724.91	1,677.86
7.25%	5,378.23	4,108.10	3,714.78	3,169.83	2,464.73	2,134.02	1,951.58	1,841.88	1,772.46	1,727.11
7.50%	5,410.25	4,141.33	3,748.65	3,204.95	2,502.93	2,175.10	1,995.28	1,887.88	1,820.46	1,776.79
7.75%	5,442.38	4,174.73	3,782.68	3,240.29	2,541.44	2,216.56	2,039.39	1,934.31	1,868.88	1,826.87
8.00%	5,474.63	4,208.28	3,816.90	3,275.85	2,580.26	2,258.39	2,083.90	1,981.16	1,917.70	1,877.34
8.25%	5,506.99	4,241.99	3,851.30	3,311.62	2,619.38	2,300.58	2,128.82	2,028.42	1,966.93	1,928.17
8.50%	5,539.46	4,275.85	3,885.87	3,347.61	2,658.80	2,343.12	2,174.11	2,076.07	2,016.52	1,979.35
8.75%	5,572.05	4,309.87	3,920.63	3,383.82	2,698.51	2,386.02	2,219.79	2,124.09	2,066.48	2,030.86
9.00%	5,604.76	4,344.05	3,955.55	3,420.25	2,738.52	2,429.26	2,265.83	2,172.48	2,116.78	2,082.68
9.25%	5,637.57	4,378.39	3,990.66	3,456.88	2,778.82	2,472.84	2,312.23	2,221.22	2,167.41	2,134.78
9.50%	5,670.50	4,412.88	4,025.94	3,493.73	2,819.41	2,516.75	2,358.98	2,270.31	2,218.35	2,187.17
9.75%	5,703.55	4,447.52	4,061.39	3,530.80	2,860.28	2,561.00	2,406.07	2,319.72	2,269.59	2,239.81
10.00%	5,736.70	4,482.32	4,097.02	3,568.07	2,901.43	2,605.56	2,453.49	2,369.44	2,321.12	2,292.69
10.25%	5,769.97	4,517.27	4,132.83	3,605.55	2,942.87	2,650.44	2,501.23	2,419.47	2,372.91	2,345.81
10.50%	5,803.35	4,552.38	4,168.80	3,643.24	2,984.58	2,695.63	2,549.29	2,469.80	2,424.96	2,399.14
10.75%	5,836.85	4,587.64	4,204.95	3,681.14	3,026.56	2,741.12	2,597.65	2,520.40	2,477.26	2,452.67

$270,000　　11.00 - 20.75%　　5 - 40 Years

	5	7	8	10	15	20	25	30	35	40
11.00%	5,870.45	4,623.06	4,241.27	3,719.25	3,068.81	2,786.91	2,646.31	2,571.27	2,529.79	2,506.39
11.25%	5,904.17	4,658.63	4,277.77	3,757.56	3,111.33	2,832.99	2,695.25	2,622.41	2,582.53	2,560.29
11.50%	5,938.00	4,694.34	4,314.43	3,796.08	3,154.11	2,879.36	2,744.47	2,673.79	2,635.49	2,614.36
11.75%	5,971.95	4,730.22	4,351.26	3,834.80	3,197.15	2,926.01	2,793.96	2,725.41	2,688.64	2,668.58
12.00%	6,006.00	4,766.24	4,388.27	3,873.72	3,240.45	2,972.93	2,843.71	2,777.25	2,741.98	2,722.95
12.25%	6,040.17	4,802.41	4,425.44	3,912.84	3,284.01	3,020.12	2,893.71	2,829.32	2,795.50	2,777.45
12.50%	6,074.44	4,838.73	4,462.78	3,952.16	3,327.81	3,067.58	2,943.96	2,881.60	2,849.19	2,832.08
12.75%	6,108.83	4,875.21	4,500.29	3,991.67	3,371.86	3,115.29	2,994.44	2,934.07	2,903.03	2,886.83
13.00%	6,143.33	4,911.83	4,537.96	4,031.39	3,416.15	3,163.25	3,045.16	2,986.74	2,957.02	2,941.69
13.25%	6,177.94	4,948.60	4,575.80	4,071.30	3,460.69	3,211.46	3,096.09	3,039.59	3,011.15	2,996.65
13.50%	6,212.66	4,985.52	4,613.80	4,111.41	3,505.46	3,259.91	3,147.24	3,092.61	3,065.42	3,051.71
13.75%	6,247.49	5,022.59	4,651.97	4,151.70	3,550.47	3,308.59	3,198.60	3,145.80	3,119.81	3,106.85
14.00%	6,282.43	5,059.80	4,690.31	4,192.19	3,595.70	3,357.51	3,250.15	3,199.15	3,174.32	3,162.08
14.25%	6,317.48	5,097.16	4,728.80	4,232.87	3,641.17	3,406.64	3,301.90	3,252.66	3,228.94	3,217.38
14.50%	6,352.64	5,134.67	4,767.46	4,273.74	3,686.85	3,455.99	3,353.84	3,306.30	3,283.66	3,272.76
14.75%	6,387.90	5,172.33	4,806.28	4,314.80	3,732.76	3,505.56	3,405.95	3,360.08	3,338.48	3,328.20
15.00%	6,423.28	5,210.12	4,845.26	4,356.04	3,778.89	3,555.33	3,458.24	3,414.00	3,393.40	3,383.71
15.25%	6,458.77	5,248.07	4,884.40	4,397.47	3,825.22	3,605.31	3,510.70	3,468.04	3,448.40	3,439.27
15.50%	6,494.36	5,286.15	4,923.70	4,439.08	3,871.77	3,655.48	3,563.31	3,522.20	3,503.48	3,494.88
15.75%	6,530.06	5,324.38	4,963.16	4,480.88	3,918.53	3,705.84	3,616.08	3,576.47	3,558.64	3,550.54
16.00%	6,565.88	5,362.76	5,002.77	4,522.85	3,965.49	3,756.39	3,669.00	3,630.84	3,613.87	3,606.25
16.25%	6,601.79	5,401.27	5,042.54	4,565.01	4,012.65	3,807.12	3,722.06	3,685.32	3,669.16	3,662.00
16.50%	6,637.82	5,439.93	5,082.47	4,607.34	4,060.01	3,858.03	3,775.26	3,739.90	3,724.53	3,717.79
16.75%	6,673.95	5,478.73	5,122.56	4,649.85	4,107.57	3,909.11	3,828.59	3,794.57	3,779.95	3,773.62
17.00%	6,710.20	5,517.67	5,162.79	4,692.54	4,155.31	3,960.36	3,882.05	3,849.32	3,835.42	3,829.47
17.25%	6,746.54	5,556.75	5,203.18	4,735.40	4,203.24	4,011.77	3,935.63	3,904.16	3,890.95	3,885.36
17.50%	6,783.00	5,595.96	5,243.73	4,778.43	4,251.36	4,063.34	3,989.33	3,959.08	3,946.52	3,941.28
17.75%	6,819.56	5,635.32	5,284.42	4,821.63	4,299.66	4,115.07	4,043.14	4,014.07	4,002.14	3,997.22
18.00%	6,856.23	5,674.82	5,325.27	4,865.00	4,348.14	4,166.94	4,097.06	4,069.13	4,057.81	4,053.19
18.25%	6,893.00	5,714.45	5,366.26	4,908.54	4,396.79	4,218.96	4,151.08	4,124.26	4,113.51	4,109.18
18.50%	6,929.88	5,754.22	5,407.41	4,952.25	4,445.61	4,271.12	4,205.21	4,179.45	4,169.25	4,165.19
18.75%	6,966.86	5,794.12	5,448.70	4,996.12	4,494.61	4,323.42	4,259.43	4,234.70	4,225.03	4,221.22
19.00%	7,003.95	5,834.17	5,490.14	5,040.15	4,543.77	4,375.85	4,313.74	4,290.01	4,280.84	4,277.27
19.25%	7,041.14	5,874.34	5,531.73	5,084.35	4,593.09	4,428.41	4,368.13	4,345.37	4,336.67	4,333.34
19.50%	7,078.44	5,914.65	5,573.46	5,128.71	4,642.57	4,481.09	4,422.62	4,400.78	4,392.54	4,389.41
19.75%	7,115.84	5,955.10	5,615.34	5,173.23	4,692.21	4,533.90	4,477.18	4,456.24	4,448.43	4,445.51
20.00%	7,153.35	5,995.67	5,657.36	5,217.90	4,742.00	4,586.83	4,531.82	4,511.75	4,504.35	4,501.61
20.25%	7,190.96	6,036.38	5,699.53	5,262.74	4,791.94	4,639.87	4,586.53	4,567.30	4,560.29	4,557.73
20.50%	7,228.67	6,077.23	5,741.84	5,307.72	4,842.04	4,693.02	4,641.32	4,622.89	4,616.25	4,613.86
20.75%	7,266.49	6,118.20	5,784.28	5,352.86	4,892.27	4,746.27	4,696.17	4,678.52	4,672.24	4,670.00

	5	7	8	10	15	20	25	30	35	40
1.00%	4,700.78	3,391.09	2,981.89	2,409.11	1,645.86	1,264.71	1,036.40	884.51	776.29	695.35
1.25%	4,730.44	3,420.83	3,011.69	2,439.07	1,676.27	1,295.62	1,067.82	916.44	808.74	728.32
1.50%	4,760.22	3,450.74	3,041.68	2,469.27	1,707.04	1,327.00	1,099.82	949.08	842.01	762.22
1.75%	4,790.12	3,480.81	3,071.87	2,499.70	1,738.17	1,358.85	1,132.42	982.42	876.09	797.04
2.00%	4,820.13	3,511.04	3,102.24	2,530.37	1,769.65	1,391.18	1,165.60	1,016.45	910.97	832.77
2.25%	4,850.27	3,541.45	3,132.80	2,561.28	1,801.48	1,423.97	1,199.36	1,051.18	946.65	869.39
2.50%	4,880.52	3,572.02	3,163.56	2,592.42	1,833.67	1,457.23	1,233.70	1,086.58	983.11	906.89
2.75%	4,910.90	3,602.76	3,194.50	2,623.80	1,866.21	1,490.96	1,268.60	1,122.66	1,020.35	945.25
3.00%	4,941.39	3,633.66	3,225.63	2,655.42	1,899.10	1,525.14	1,304.08	1,159.41	1,058.34	984.46
3.25%	4,972.00	3,664.73	3,256.95	2,687.27	1,932.34	1,559.79	1,340.12	1,196.82	1,097.08	1,024.49
3.50%	5,002.73	3,695.96	3,288.46	2,719.36	1,965.93	1,594.89	1,376.71	1,234.87	1,136.55	1,065.33
3.75%	5,033.58	3,727.36	3,320.16	2,751.68	1,999.86	1,630.44	1,413.86	1,273.57	1,176.74	1,106.95
4.00%	5,064.54	3,758.92	3,352.05	2,784.24	2,034.14	1,666.45	1,451.55	1,312.89	1,217.63	1,149.33
4.25%	5,095.63	3,790.65	3,384.13	2,817.03	2,068.77	1,702.89	1,489.78	1,352.83	1,259.21	1,192.46
4.50%	5,126.83	3,822.54	3,416.39	2,850.06	2,103.73	1,739.79	1,528.54	1,393.38	1,301.46	1,236.30
4.75%	5,158.15	3,854.60	3,448.84	2,883.31	2,139.04	1,777.11	1,567.82	1,434.53	1,344.36	1,280.83
5.00%	5,189.59	3,886.82	3,481.48	2,916.80	2,174.68	1,814.88	1,607.62	1,476.26	1,387.89	1,326.04
5.25%	5,221.15	3,919.21	3,514.30	2,950.52	2,210.66	1,853.07	1,647.93	1,518.56	1,432.04	1,371.89
5.50%	5,252.82	3,951.76	3,547.31	2,984.47	2,246.98	1,891.69	1,688.74	1,561.42	1,476.79	1,418.37
5.75%	5,284.61	3,984.48	3,580.51	3,018.65	2,283.63	1,930.73	1,730.04	1,604.83	1,522.13	1,465.44
6.00%	5,316.52	4,017.35	3,613.89	3,053.06	2,320.61	1,970.19	1,771.83	1,648.76	1,568.02	1,513.09
6.25%	5,348.55	4,050.39	3,647.46	3,087.70	2,357.91	2,010.05	1,814.09	1,693.22	1,614.46	1,561.28
6.50%	5,380.69	4,083.60	3,681.21	3,122.57	2,395.55	2,050.33	1,856.82	1,738.19	1,661.42	1,610.01
6.75%	5,412.95	4,116.96	3,715.15	3,157.66	2,433.50	2,091.00	1,900.01	1,783.64	1,708.90	1,659.23
7.00%	5,445.33	4,150.49	3,749.27	3,192.98	2,471.78	2,132.07	1,943.64	1,829.58	1,756.85	1,708.94
7.25%	5,477.82	4,184.18	3,783.58	3,228.53	2,510.37	2,173.53	1,987.72	1,875.98	1,805.28	1,759.10
7.50%	5,510.44	4,218.03	3,818.06	3,264.30	2,549.28	2,215.38	2,032.23	1,922.84	1,854.17	1,809.69
7.75%	5,543.16	4,252.04	3,852.73	3,300.29	2,588.51	2,257.61	2,077.15	1,970.13	1,903.48	1,860.70
8.00%	5,576.01	4,286.21	3,887.59	3,336.51	2,628.04	2,300.21	2,122.49	2,017.85	1,953.22	1,912.11
8.25%	5,608.97	4,320.54	3,922.62	3,372.95	2,667.89	2,343.18	2,168.24	2,065.98	2,003.35	1,963.88
8.50%	5,642.05	4,355.03	3,957.84	3,409.61	2,708.03	2,386.51	2,214.37	2,114.51	2,053.87	2,016.01
8.75%	5,675.24	4,389.69	3,993.23	3,446.49	2,748.48	2,430.20	2,260.89	2,163.43	2,104.75	2,068.47
9.00%	5,708.55	4,424.50	4,028.81	3,483.58	2,789.23	2,474.25	2,307.79	2,212.71	2,155.98	2,121.24
9.25%	5,741.97	4,459.47	4,064.56	3,520.90	2,830.28	2,518.63	2,355.05	2,262.36	2,207.55	2,174.32
9.50%	5,775.51	4,494.59	4,100.49	3,558.43	2,871.62	2,563.36	2,402.67	2,312.35	2,259.43	2,227.67
9.75%	5,809.17	4,529.88	4,136.61	3,596.18	2,913.25	2,608.42	2,450.63	2,362.67	2,311.62	2,281.29
10.00%	5,842.94	4,565.33	4,172.90	3,634.15	2,955.16	2,653.81	2,498.93	2,413.32	2,364.10	2,335.15
10.25%	5,876.82	4,600.93	4,209.36	3,672.32	2,997.37	2,699.52	2,547.55	2,464.28	2,416.85	2,389.25
10.50%	5,910.82	4,636.69	4,246.00	3,710.71	3,039.85	2,745.54	2,596.50	2,515.53	2,469.87	2,443.57
10.75%	5,944.94	4,672.60	4,282.82	3,749.31	3,082.61	2,791.88	2,645.75	2,567.07	2,523.13	2,498.09

$275,000   11.00 - 20.75%   5 - 40 Years

	5	7	8	10	15	20	25	30	35	40
11.00%	5,979.17	4,708.67	4,319.82	3,788.13	3,125.64	2,838.52	2,695.31	2,618.89	2,576.63	2,552.81
11.25%	6,013.51	4,744.90	4,356.99	3,827.15	3,168.95	2,885.45	2,745.16	2,670.97	2,630.36	2,607.71
11.50%	6,047.97	4,781.28	4,394.33	3,866.37	3,212.52	2,932.68	2,795.29	2,723.30	2,684.30	2,662.78
11.75%	6,082.54	4,817.81	4,431.84	3,905.81	3,256.36	2,980.19	2,845.70	2,775.88	2,738.43	2,718.00
12.00%	6,117.22	4,854.50	4,469.53	3,945.45	3,300.46	3,027.99	2,896.37	2,828.68	2,792.76	2,773.37
12.25%	6,152.02	4,891.34	4,507.39	3,985.30	3,344.82	3,076.05	2,947.30	2,881.72	2,847.27	2,828.89
12.50%	6,186.93	4,928.34	4,545.42	4,025.34	3,389.44	3,124.39	2,998.47	2,934.96	2,901.95	2,884.53
12.75%	6,221.96	4,965.49	4,583.62	4,065.59	3,434.30	3,172.98	3,049.89	2,988.41	2,956.79	2,940.29
13.00%	6,257.10	5,002.79	4,622.00	4,106.05	3,479.42	3,221.83	3,101.55	3,042.05	3,011.78	2,996.16
13.25%	6,292.35	5,040.24	4,660.54	4,146.70	3,524.78	3,270.93	3,153.43	3,095.88	3,066.92	3,052.14
13.50%	6,327.71	5,077.85	4,699.24	4,187.54	3,570.38	3,320.28	3,205.52	3,149.88	3,122.19	3,108.22
13.75%	6,363.18	5,115.60	4,738.12	4,228.59	3,616.21	3,369.86	3,257.83	3,204.06	3,177.58	3,164.38
14.00%	6,398.77	5,153.50	4,777.16	4,269.83	3,662.29	3,419.68	3,310.34	3,258.40	3,233.10	3,220.64
14.25%	6,434.47	5,191.56	4,816.37	4,311.26	3,708.59	3,469.73	3,363.05	3,312.89	3,288.73	3,276.96
14.50%	6,470.28	5,229.76	4,855.75	4,352.89	3,755.13	3,519.99	3,415.95	3,367.53	3,344.47	3,333.37
14.75%	6,506.20	5,268.11	4,895.28	4,394.70	3,801.89	3,570.48	3,469.03	3,422.31	3,400.31	3,389.83
15.00%	6,542.23	5,306.61	4,934.99	4,436.71	3,848.86	3,621.17	3,522.28	3,477.22	3,456.24	3,446.37
15.25%	6,578.37	5,345.25	4,974.85	4,478.91	3,896.06	3,672.07	3,575.71	3,532.26	3,512.26	3,502.96
15.50%	6,614.63	5,384.05	5,014.88	4,521.29	3,943.47	3,723.17	3,629.30	3,587.42	3,568.36	3,559.60
15.75%	6,650.99	5,422.98	5,055.07	4,563.86	3,991.10	3,774.47	3,683.05	3,642.70	3,624.54	3,616.29
16.00%	6,687.47	5,462.07	5,095.42	4,606.61	4,038.93	3,825.95	3,736.94	3,698.08	3,680.79	3,673.03
16.25%	6,724.05	5,501.30	5,135.92	4,649.55	4,086.96	3,877.63	3,790.99	3,753.57	3,737.11	3,729.82
16.50%	6,760.74	5,540.67	5,176.59	4,692.66	4,135.20	3,929.48	3,845.17	3,809.16	3,793.50	3,786.64
16.75%	6,797.55	5,580.19	5,217.42	4,735.96	4,183.63	3,981.50	3,899.49	3,864.84	3,849.94	3,843.50
17.00%	6,834.46	5,619.85	5,258.40	4,779.44	4,232.26	4,033.70	3,953.94	3,920.61	3,906.45	3,900.39
17.25%	6,871.48	5,659.65	5,299.54	4,823.09	4,281.08	4,086.07	4,008.51	3,976.46	3,963.00	3,957.31
17.50%	6,908.61	5,699.59	5,340.83	4,866.92	4,330.09	4,138.59	4,063.21	4,032.39	4,019.61	4,014.27
17.75%	6,945.85	5,739.68	5,382.28	4,910.92	4,379.28	4,191.27	4,118.01	4,088.40	4,076.26	4,071.25
18.00%	6,983.19	5,779.91	5,423.88	4,955.09	4,428.66	4,244.11	4,172.93	4,144.48	4,132.95	4,128.25
18.25%	7,020.65	5,820.27	5,465.64	4,999.44	4,478.21	4,297.09	4,227.96	4,200.63	4,189.69	4,185.28
18.50%	7,058.21	5,860.78	5,507.55	5,043.95	4,527.94	4,350.22	4,283.08	4,256.85	4,246.46	4,242.33
18.75%	7,095.88	5,901.42	5,549.60	5,088.64	4,577.84	4,403.48	4,338.30	4,313.12	4,303.27	4,299.39
19.00%	7,133.65	5,942.21	5,591.81	5,133.49	4,627.91	4,456.88	4,393.62	4,369.45	4,360.11	4,356.48
19.25%	7,171.53	5,983.13	5,634.17	5,178.51	4,678.14	4,510.42	4,449.03	4,425.84	4,416.98	4,413.58
19.50%	7,209.52	6,024.18	5,676.68	5,223.69	4,728.54	4,564.08	4,504.52	4,482.28	4,473.88	4,470.70
19.75%	7,247.62	6,065.38	5,719.33	5,269.03	4,779.10	4,617.86	4,560.09	4,538.77	4,530.81	4,527.83
20.00%	7,285.82	6,106.70	5,762.13	5,314.53	4,829.82	4,671.77	4,615.74	4,595.30	4,587.77	4,584.98
20.25%	7,324.12	6,148.17	5,805.08	5,360.19	4,880.68	4,725.79	4,671.47	4,651.88	4,644.74	4,642.13
20.50%	7,362.54	6,189.77	5,848.17	5,406.01	4,931.70	4,779.92	4,727.27	4,708.50	4,701.74	4,699.30
20.75%	7,401.05	6,231.50	5,891.40	5,451.99	4,982.87	4,834.17	4,783.14	4,765.16	4,758.76	4,756.48

	5	7	8	10	15	20	25	30	35	40
1.00%	4,786.25	3,452.75	3,036.10	2,452.92	1,675.78	1,287.70	1,055.24	900.59	790.40	708.00
1.25%	4,816.45	3,483.03	3,066.45	2,483.42	1,706.75	1,319.17	1,087.23	933.10	823.44	741.57
1.50%	4,846.77	3,513.48	3,096.99	2,514.16	1,738.08	1,351.13	1,119.82	966.34	857.32	776.08
1.75%	4,877.21	3,544.09	3,127.72	2,545.15	1,769.77	1,383.56	1,153.01	1,000.28	892.02	811.54
2.00%	4,907.77	3,574.88	3,158.64	2,576.38	1,801.82	1,416.47	1,186.79	1,034.93	927.54	847.91
2.25%	4,938.46	3,605.84	3,189.76	2,607.85	1,834.24	1,449.86	1,221.17	1,070.29	963.86	885.20
2.50%	4,969.26	3,636.96	3,221.08	2,639.56	1,867.01	1,483.73	1,256.13	1,106.34	1,000.99	923.38
2.75%	5,000.19	3,668.26	3,252.58	2,671.51	1,900.14	1,518.07	1,291.67	1,143.08	1,038.90	962.44
3.00%	5,031.23	3,699.72	3,284.28	2,703.70	1,933.63	1,552.87	1,327.79	1,180.49	1,077.58	1,002.36
3.25%	5,062.40	3,731.36	3,316.17	2,736.13	1,967.47	1,588.15	1,364.49	1,218.58	1,117.02	1,043.12
3.50%	5,093.69	3,763.16	3,348.25	2,768.80	2,001.67	1,623.89	1,401.75	1,257.33	1,157.21	1,084.69
3.75%	5,125.10	3,795.13	3,380.53	2,801.71	2,036.22	1,660.09	1,439.57	1,296.72	1,198.13	1,127.07
4.00%	5,156.63	3,827.27	3,413.00	2,834.86	2,071.13	1,696.74	1,477.94	1,336.76	1,239.77	1,170.23
4.25%	5,188.28	3,859.57	3,445.66	2,868.25	2,106.38	1,733.86	1,516.87	1,377.43	1,282.10	1,214.14
4.50%	5,220.05	3,892.05	3,478.51	2,901.88	2,141.98	1,771.42	1,556.33	1,418.72	1,325.12	1,258.78
4.75%	5,251.94	3,924.69	3,511.55	2,935.74	2,177.93	1,809.43	1,596.33	1,460.61	1,368.80	1,304.12
5.00%	5,283.95	3,957.49	3,544.78	2,969.83	2,214.22	1,847.88	1,636.85	1,503.10	1,413.13	1,350.15
5.25%	5,316.08	3,990.47	3,578.20	3,004.17	2,250.86	1,886.76	1,677.89	1,546.17	1,458.08	1,396.84
5.50%	5,348.33	4,023.61	3,611.81	3,038.74	2,287.83	1,926.08	1,719.44	1,589.81	1,503.65	1,444.16
5.75%	5,380.70	4,056.92	3,645.61	3,073.54	2,325.15	1,965.83	1,761.50	1,634.00	1,549.80	1,492.09
6.00%	5,413.18	4,090.40	3,679.60	3,108.57	2,362.80	2,006.01	1,804.04	1,678.74	1,596.53	1,540.60
6.25%	5,445.79	4,124.04	3,713.78	3,143.84	2,400.78	2,046.60	1,847.07	1,724.01	1,643.81	1,589.67
6.50%	5,478.52	4,157.84	3,748.15	3,179.34	2,439.10	2,087.60	1,890.58	1,769.79	1,691.63	1,639.28
6.75%	5,511.37	4,191.81	3,782.70	3,215.08	2,477.75	2,129.02	1,934.55	1,816.07	1,739.97	1,689.40
7.00%	5,544.34	4,225.95	3,817.44	3,251.04	2,516.72	2,170.84	1,978.98	1,862.85	1,788.80	1,740.01
7.25%	5,577.42	4,260.25	3,852.37	3,287.23	2,556.02	2,213.05	2,023.86	1,910.09	1,838.11	1,791.08
7.50%	5,610.63	4,294.72	3,887.48	3,323.65	2,595.63	2,255.66	2,069.18	1,957.80	1,887.88	1,842.60
7.75%	5,643.95	4,329.35	3,922.78	3,360.30	2,635.57	2,298.66	2,114.92	2,005.95	1,938.09	1,894.54
8.00%	5,677.39	4,364.14	3,958.27	3,397.17	2,675.83	2,342.03	2,161.09	2,054.54	1,988.73	1,946.87
8.25%	5,710.95	4,399.10	3,993.94	3,434.27	2,716.39	2,385.78	2,207.66	2,103.55	2,039.78	1,999.59
8.50%	5,744.63	4,434.22	4,029.80	3,471.60	2,757.27	2,429.91	2,254.64	2,152.96	2,091.21	2,052.66
8.75%	5,778.43	4,469.50	4,065.83	3,509.15	2,798.46	2,474.39	2,302.00	2,202.76	2,143.02	2,106.08
9.00%	5,812.34	4,504.94	4,102.06	3,546.92	2,839.95	2,519.23	2,349.75	2,252.94	2,195.18	2,159.81
9.25%	5,846.37	4,540.55	4,138.46	3,584.92	2,881.74	2,564.43	2,397.87	2,303.49	2,247.68	2,213.85
9.50%	5,880.52	4,576.31	4,175.05	3,623.13	2,923.83	2,609.97	2,446.35	2,354.39	2,300.51	2,268.17
9.75%	5,914.79	4,612.24	4,211.82	3,661.57	2,966.22	2,655.85	2,495.18	2,405.63	2,353.65	2,322.76
10.00%	5,949.17	4,648.33	4,248.77	3,700.22	3,008.89	2,702.06	2,544.36	2,457.20	2,407.08	2,377.61
10.25%	5,983.67	4,684.58	4,285.90	3,739.09	3,051.86	2,748.60	2,593.87	2,509.08	2,460.80	2,432.69
10.50%	6,018.29	4,720.99	4,323.20	3,778.18	3,095.12	2,795.46	2,643.71	2,561.27	2,514.78	2,488.00
10.75%	6,053.03	4,757.56	4,360.69	3,817.48	3,138.65	2,842.64	2,693.86	2,613.75	2,569.01	2,543.51

$280,000   11.00 - 20.75%   5 - 40 Years

	5	7	8	10	15	20	25	30	35	40
11.00%	6,087.88	4,794.28	4,398.36	3,857.00	3,182.47	2,890.13	2,744.32	2,666.51	2,623.48	2,599.22
11.25%	6,122.85	4,831.17	4,436.20	3,896.73	3,226.56	2,937.92	2,795.07	2,719.53	2,678.18	2,655.12
11.50%	6,157.93	4,868.21	4,474.22	3,936.67	3,270.93	2,986.00	2,846.11	2,772.82	2,733.10	2,711.19
11.75%	6,193.13	4,905.41	4,512.42	3,976.82	3,315.57	3,034.38	2,897.43	2,826.35	2,788.22	2,767.42
12.00%	6,228.45	4,942.77	4,550.80	4,017.19	3,360.47	3,083.04	2,949.03	2,880.12	2,843.54	2,823.80
12.25%	6,263.88	4,980.28	4,589.34	4,057.76	3,405.64	3,131.98	3,000.88	2,934.11	2,899.04	2,880.32
12.50%	6,299.42	5,017.95	4,628.07	4,098.53	3,451.06	3,181.19	3,052.99	2,988.32	2,954.71	2,936.97
12.75%	6,335.08	5,055.77	4,666.96	4,139.51	3,496.74	3,230.67	3,105.35	3,042.74	3,010.55	2,993.75
13.00%	6,370.86	5,093.75	4,706.03	4,180.70	3,542.68	3,280.41	3,157.94	3,097.36	3,066.54	3,050.64
13.25%	6,406.75	5,131.88	4,745.27	4,222.09	3,588.86	3,330.41	3,210.76	3,152.17	3,122.68	3,107.64
13.50%	6,442.76	5,170.17	4,784.68	4,263.68	3,635.29	3,380.65	3,263.81	3,207.15	3,178.95	3,164.73
13.75%	6,478.88	5,208.61	4,824.27	4,305.47	3,681.96	3,431.14	3,317.06	3,262.32	3,235.36	3,221.92
14.00%	6,515.11	5,247.20	4,864.02	4,347.46	3,728.88	3,481.86	3,370.53	3,317.64	3,291.89	3,279.19
14.25%	6,551.46	5,285.95	4,903.94	4,389.65	3,776.02	3,532.81	3,424.20	3,373.12	3,348.53	3,336.55
14.50%	6,587.92	5,324.85	4,944.03	4,432.03	3,823.40	3,583.99	3,478.06	3,428.76	3,405.28	3,393.97
14.75%	6,624.49	5,363.89	4,984.29	4,474.61	3,871.01	3,635.39	3,532.10	3,484.53	3,462.13	3,451.47
15.00%	6,661.18	5,403.09	5,024.71	4,517.38	3,918.84	3,687.01	3,586.33	3,540.44	3,519.08	3,509.03
15.25%	6,697.98	5,442.44	5,065.30	4,560.34	3,966.90	3,738.84	3,640.72	3,596.48	3,576.11	3,566.65
15.50%	6,734.89	5,481.94	5,106.06	4,603.50	4,015.17	3,790.87	3,695.29	3,652.65	3,633.24	3,624.32
15.75%	6,771.92	5,521.58	5,146.98	4,646.84	4,063.66	3,843.09	3,750.01	3,708.93	3,690.44	3,682.04
16.00%	6,809.06	5,561.38	5,188.06	4,690.37	4,112.36	3,895.52	3,804.89	3,765.32	3,747.71	3,739.82
16.25%	6,846.31	5,601.32	5,229.31	4,734.08	4,161.27	3,948.13	3,859.92	3,821.82	3,805.06	3,797.63
16.50%	6,883.67	5,641.41	5,270.71	4,777.98	4,210.38	4,000.92	3,915.09	3,878.41	3,862.47	3,855.49
16.75%	6,921.14	5,681.64	5,312.28	4,822.07	4,259.70	4,053.89	3,970.39	3,935.11	3,919.94	3,913.38
17.00%	6,958.72	5,722.03	5,354.01	4,866.33	4,309.21	4,107.04	4,025.83	3,991.89	3,977.47	3,971.31
17.25%	6,996.42	5,762.55	5,395.89	4,910.78	4,358.92	4,160.36	4,081.40	4,048.76	4,035.06	4,029.27
17.50%	7,034.22	5,803.22	5,437.94	4,955.41	4,408.82	4,213.84	4,137.08	4,105.71	4,092.69	4,087.25
17.75%	7,072.13	5,844.04	5,480.14	5,000.21	4,458.91	4,267.48	4,192.89	4,162.74	4,150.37	4,145.27
18.00%	7,110.16	5,884.99	5,522.50	5,045.19	4,509.18	4,321.27	4,248.80	4,219.84	4,208.10	4,203.31
18.25%	7,148.29	5,926.10	5,565.01	5,090.34	4,559.63	4,375.22	4,304.83	4,277.01	4,265.86	4,261.37
18.50%	7,186.54	5,967.34	5,607.68	5,135.66	4,610.27	4,429.31	4,360.96	4,334.24	4,323.67	4,319.46
18.75%	7,224.89	6,008.72	5,650.51	5,181.16	4,661.07	4,483.54	4,417.18	4,391.54	4,381.51	4,377.57
19.00%	7,263.35	6,050.25	5,693.48	5,226.83	4,712.05	4,537.92	4,473.50	4,448.90	4,439.39	4,435.69
19.25%	7,301.93	6,091.91	5,736.61	5,272.66	4,763.20	4,592.42	4,529.92	4,506.31	4,497.29	4,493.83
19.50%	7,340.60	6,133.71	5,779.89	5,318.66	4,814.52	4,647.06	4,586.42	4,563.78	4,555.23	4,551.99
19.75%	7,379.39	6,175.66	5,823.32	5,364.83	4,865.99	4,701.82	4,643.00	4,621.29	4,613.19	4,610.16
20.00%	7,418.29	6,217.74	5,866.90	5,411.16	4,917.63	4,756.71	4,699.66	4,678.85	4,671.18	4,668.34
20.25%	7,457.29	6,259.95	5,910.62	5,457.65	4,969.42	4,811.71	4,756.41	4,736.46	4,729.19	4,726.54
20.50%	7,496.40	6,302.31	5,954.50	5,504.30	5,021.37	4,866.83	4,813.22	4,794.11	4,787.23	4,784.74
20.75%	7,535.62	6,344.80	5,998.52	5,551.12	5,073.47	4,922.06	4,870.10	4,851.79	4,845.28	4,842.96

	5	7	8	10	15	20	25	30	35	40
1.00%	4,871.72	3,514.41	3,090.32	2,496.72	1,705.71	1,310.70	1,074.09	916.67	804.51	720.64
1.25%	4,902.46	3,545.22	3,121.21	2,527.76	1,737.23	1,342.73	1,106.65	949.77	838.15	754.81
1.50%	4,933.32	3,576.22	3,152.29	2,559.06	1,769.12	1,375.25	1,139.82	983.59	872.63	789.94
1.75%	4,964.30	3,607.38	3,183.57	2,590.60	1,801.37	1,408.27	1,173.60	1,018.14	907.95	826.03
2.00%	4,995.41	3,638.72	3,215.05	2,622.38	1,834.00	1,441.77	1,207.98	1,053.42	944.10	863.05
2.25%	5,026.64	3,670.23	3,246.72	2,654.42	1,866.99	1,475.75	1,242.97	1,089.40	981.07	901.01
2.50%	5,058.00	3,701.91	3,278.60	2,686.69	1,900.35	1,510.22	1,278.56	1,126.09	1,018.86	939.87
2.75%	5,089.48	3,733.76	3,310.66	2,719.21	1,934.07	1,545.17	1,314.74	1,163.49	1,057.45	979.62
3.00%	5,121.08	3,765.79	3,342.93	2,751.98	1,968.16	1,580.60	1,351.50	1,201.57	1,096.82	1,020.26
3.25%	5,152.80	3,797.99	3,375.39	2,784.99	2,002.61	1,616.51	1,388.85	1,240.34	1,136.97	1,061.74
3.50%	5,184.65	3,830.36	3,408.04	2,818.25	2,037.42	1,652.89	1,426.78	1,279.78	1,177.88	1,104.06
3.75%	5,216.62	3,862.90	3,440.90	2,851.75	2,072.58	1,689.73	1,465.27	1,319.88	1,219.53	1,147.20
4.00%	5,248.71	3,895.61	3,473.94	2,885.49	2,108.11	1,727.04	1,504.33	1,360.63	1,261.91	1,191.12
4.25%	5,280.92	3,928.49	3,507.19	2,919.47	2,143.99	1,764.82	1,543.95	1,402.03	1,305.00	1,235.82
4.50%	5,313.26	3,961.55	3,540.62	2,953.69	2,180.23	1,803.05	1,584.12	1,444.05	1,348.78	1,281.25
4.75%	5,345.72	3,994.77	3,574.25	2,988.16	2,216.82	1,841.74	1,624.83	1,486.69	1,393.24	1,327.41
5.00%	5,378.30	4,028.16	3,608.08	3,022.87	2,253.76	1,880.87	1,666.08	1,529.94	1,438.36	1,374.26
5.25%	5,411.01	4,061.73	3,642.10	3,057.81	2,291.05	1,920.46	1,707.86	1,573.78	1,484.12	1,421.78
5.50%	5,443.83	4,095.46	3,676.31	3,093.00	2,328.69	1,960.48	1,750.15	1,618.20	1,530.50	1,469.95
5.75%	5,476.78	4,129.37	3,710.71	3,128.42	2,366.67	2,000.94	1,792.95	1,663.18	1,577.48	1,518.73
6.00%	5,509.85	4,163.44	3,745.31	3,164.08	2,404.99	2,041.83	1,836.26	1,708.72	1,625.04	1,568.11
6.25%	5,543.04	4,197.68	3,780.10	3,199.98	2,443.66	2,083.15	1,880.06	1,754.79	1,673.17	1,618.06
6.50%	5,576.35	4,232.09	3,815.08	3,236.12	2,482.66	2,124.88	1,924.34	1,801.39	1,721.84	1,668.55
6.75%	5,609.79	4,266.67	3,850.25	3,272.49	2,521.99	2,167.04	1,969.10	1,848.50	1,771.04	1,719.57
7.00%	5,643.34	4,301.41	3,885.61	3,309.09	2,561.66	2,209.60	2,014.32	1,896.11	1,820.74	1,771.08
7.25%	5,677.02	4,336.33	3,921.16	3,345.93	2,601.66	2,252.57	2,060.00	1,944.20	1,870.93	1,823.06
7.50%	5,710.82	4,371.41	3,956.90	3,383.00	2,641.99	2,295.94	2,106.12	1,992.76	1,921.59	1,875.50
7.75%	5,744.73	4,406.66	3,992.83	3,420.30	2,682.64	2,339.70	2,152.69	2,041.77	1,972.70	1,928.37
8.00%	5,778.77	4,442.07	4,028.95	3,457.84	2,723.61	2,383.85	2,199.68	2,091.23	2,024.24	1,981.64
8.25%	5,812.93	4,477.65	4,065.26	3,495.60	2,764.90	2,428.39	2,247.08	2,141.11	2,076.20	2,035.30
8.50%	5,847.21	4,513.40	4,101.76	3,533.59	2,806.51	2,473.30	2,294.90	2,191.40	2,128.55	2,089.32
8.75%	5,881.61	4,549.31	4,138.44	3,571.81	2,848.43	2,518.58	2,343.11	2,242.10	2,181.28	2,143.69
9.00%	5,916.13	4,585.39	4,175.31	3,610.26	2,890.66	2,564.22	2,391.71	2,293.17	2,234.38	2,198.38
9.25%	5,950.77	4,621.63	4,212.36	3,648.93	2,933.20	2,610.22	2,440.69	2,344.62	2,287.82	2,253.38
9.50%	5,985.53	4,658.03	4,249.60	3,687.83	2,976.04	2,656.57	2,490.04	2,396.43	2,341.59	2,308.68
9.75%	6,020.41	4,694.60	4,287.03	3,726.95	3,019.18	2,703.27	2,539.74	2,448.59	2,395.68	2,364.24
10.00%	6,055.41	4,731.34	4,324.64	3,766.30	3,062.62	2,750.31	2,589.80	2,501.08	2,450.07	2,420.07
10.25%	6,090.53	4,768.23	4,362.43	3,805.86	3,106.36	2,797.68	2,640.19	2,553.89	2,504.74	2,476.13
10.50%	6,125.76	4,805.29	4,400.40	3,845.65	3,150.39	2,845.38	2,690.92	2,607.01	2,559.68	2,532.43
10.75%	6,161.12	4,842.51	4,438.56	3,885.65	3,194.70	2,893.40	2,741.96	2,660.42	2,614.88	2,588.93

	5	7	8	10	15	20	25	30	35	40
11.00%	6,196.59	4,879.89	4,476.90	3,925.88	3,239.30	2,941.74	2,793.32	2,714.12	2,670.33	2,645.64
11.25%	6,232.18	4,917.44	4,515.42	3,966.31	3,284.18	2,990.38	2,844.98	2,768.09	2,726.01	2,702.53
11.50%	6,267.89	4,955.14	4,554.12	4,006.97	3,329.34	3,039.32	2,896.94	2,822.33	2,781.91	2,759.60
11.75%	6,303.72	4,993.01	4,593.00	4,047.84	3,374.77	3,088.57	2,949.17	2,876.82	2,838.01	2,816.84
12.00%	6,339.67	5,031.03	4,632.06	4,088.92	3,420.48	3,138.10	3,001.69	2,931.55	2,894.32	2,874.22
12.25%	6,375.73	5,069.21	4,671.30	4,130.22	3,466.45	3,187.91	3,054.47	2,986.50	2,950.81	2,931.76
12.50%	6,411.91	5,107.55	4,710.71	4,171.72	3,512.69	3,238.00	3,107.51	3,041.68	3,007.48	2,989.42
12.75%	6,448.21	5,146.05	4,750.30	4,213.43	3,559.19	3,288.36	3,160.80	3,097.08	3,064.31	3,047.21
13.00%	6,484.63	5,184.71	4,790.07	4,255.36	3,605.94	3,338.99	3,214.33	3,152.67	3,121.30	3,105.12
13.25%	6,521.16	5,223.52	4,830.01	4,297.48	3,652.95	3,389.88	3,268.10	3,208.45	3,178.44	3,163.13
13.50%	6,557.81	5,262.49	4,870.13	4,339.82	3,700.21	3,441.02	3,322.09	3,264.42	3,235.72	3,221.24
13.75%	6,594.57	5,301.62	4,910.42	4,382.35	3,747.71	3,492.41	3,376.30	3,320.57	3,293.13	3,279.45
14.00%	6,631.45	5,340.90	4,950.88	4,425.09	3,795.46	3,544.03	3,430.72	3,376.88	3,350.67	3,337.75
14.25%	6,668.45	5,380.34	4,991.51	4,468.03	3,843.45	3,595.90	3,485.34	3,433.36	3,408.32	3,396.13
14.50%	6,705.56	5,419.93	5,032.32	4,511.17	3,891.68	3,647.99	3,540.16	3,489.98	3,466.09	3,454.58
14.75%	6,742.79	5,459.68	5,073.29	4,554.51	3,940.14	3,700.31	3,595.17	3,546.76	3,523.95	3,513.10
15.00%	6,780.13	5,499.58	5,114.44	4,598.05	3,988.82	3,752.85	3,650.37	3,603.67	3,581.92	3,571.69
15.25%	6,817.59	5,539.63	5,155.76	4,641.78	4,037.74	3,805.60	3,705.74	3,660.71	3,639.97	3,630.34
15.50%	6,855.16	5,579.83	5,197.24	4,685.70	4,086.87	3,858.56	3,761.27	3,717.87	3,698.12	3,689.04
15.75%	6,892.85	5,620.18	5,238.89	4,729.82	4,136.23	3,911.72	3,816.98	3,775.16	3,756.34	3,747.80
16.00%	6,930.65	5,660.69	5,280.70	4,774.12	4,185.80	3,965.08	3,872.83	3,832.56	3,814.64	3,806.60
16.25%	6,968.56	5,701.34	5,322.69	4,818.62	4,235.58	4,018.63	3,928.84	3,890.06	3,873.01	3,865.45
16.50%	7,006.59	5,742.15	5,364.83	4,863.31	4,285.57	4,072.37	3,985.00	3,947.67	3,931.44	3,924.33
16.75%	7,044.73	5,783.10	5,407.14	4,908.18	4,335.77	4,126.29	4,041.29	4,005.38	3,989.94	3,983.26
17.00%	7,082.98	5,824.20	5,449.61	4,953.23	4,386.16	4,180.38	4,097.72	4,063.17	4,048.50	4,042.22
17.25%	7,121.35	5,865.45	5,492.25	4,998.47	4,436.76	4,234.65	4,154.28	4,121.06	4,107.11	4,101.22
17.50%	7,159.83	5,906.85	5,535.04	5,043.89	4,487.55	4,289.08	4,210.96	4,179.03	4,165.77	4,160.24
17.75%	7,198.42	5,948.39	5,578.00	5,089.50	4,538.53	4,343.68	4,267.76	4,237.07	4,224.49	4,219.29
18.00%	7,237.13	5,990.08	5,621.12	5,135.28	4,589.70	4,398.44	4,324.68	4,295.19	4,283.24	4,278.37
18.25%	7,275.94	6,031.92	5,664.39	5,181.24	4,641.05	4,453.35	4,381.70	4,353.38	4,342.04	4,337.47
18.50%	7,314.87	6,073.90	5,707.82	5,227.37	4,692.59	4,508.41	4,438.83	4,411.64	4,400.88	4,396.59
18.75%	7,353.91	6,116.02	5,751.41	5,273.68	4,744.31	4,563.61	4,496.06	4,469.96	4,459.75	4,455.74
19.00%	7,393.06	6,158.29	5,795.15	5,320.16	4,796.20	4,618.95	4,553.39	4,528.34	4,518.66	4,514.90
19.25%	7,432.32	6,200.69	5,839.05	5,366.82	4,848.26	4,674.43	4,610.81	4,586.78	4,577.60	4,574.08
19.50%	7,471.69	6,243.24	5,883.10	5,413.64	4,900.49	4,730.04	4,668.32	4,645.27	4,636.57	4,633.27
19.75%	7,511.17	6,285.94	5,927.31	5,460.63	4,952.89	4,785.78	4,725.91	4,703.81	4,695.57	4,692.48
20.00%	7,550.76	6,328.77	5,971.66	5,507.79	5,005.45	4,841.65	4,783.59	4,762.40	4,754.59	4,751.70
20.25%	7,590.46	6,371.74	6,016.17	5,555.11	5,058.16	4,897.64	4,841.34	4,821.04	4,813.64	4,810.94
20.50%	7,630.26	6,414.85	6,060.83	5,602.60	5,111.04	4,953.74	4,899.17	4,879.72	4,872.71	4,870.18
20.75%	7,670.18	6,458.10	6,105.63	5,650.24	5,164.07	5,009.96	4,957.07	4,938.43	4,931.81	4,929.44

	5	7	8	10	15	20	25	30	35	40
1.00%	4,957.19	3,576.06	3,144.54	2,540.52	1,735.63	1,333.69	1,092.93	932.75	818.63	733.28
1.25%	4,988.46	3,607.42	3,175.96	2,572.11	1,767.71	1,366.29	1,126.06	966.43	852.85	768.05
1.50%	5,019.87	3,638.96	3,207.59	2,603.95	1,800.15	1,399.38	1,159.82	1,000.85	887.93	803.80
1.75%	5,051.40	3,670.67	3,239.42	2,636.05	1,832.98	1,432.97	1,194.19	1,036.01	923.88	840.52
2.00%	5,083.05	3,702.56	3,271.45	2,668.39	1,866.18	1,467.06	1,229.18	1,071.90	960.66	878.19
2.25%	5,114.83	3,734.62	3,303.68	2,700.98	1,899.75	1,501.64	1,264.78	1,108.51	998.29	916.81
2.50%	5,146.73	3,766.86	3,336.11	2,733.83	1,933.69	1,536.72	1,300.99	1,145.85	1,036.74	956.36
2.75%	5,178.76	3,799.27	3,368.75	2,766.92	1,968.00	1,572.28	1,337.80	1,183.90	1,076.00	996.81
3.00%	5,210.92	3,831.86	3,401.58	2,800.26	2,002.69	1,608.33	1,375.21	1,222.65	1,116.07	1,038.15
3.25%	5,243.20	3,864.62	3,434.61	2,833.85	2,037.74	1,644.87	1,413.22	1,262.10	1,156.92	1,080.37
3.50%	5,275.61	3,897.56	3,467.84	2,867.69	2,073.16	1,681.88	1,451.81	1,302.23	1,198.54	1,123.43
3.75%	5,308.14	3,930.67	3,501.26	2,901.78	2,108.95	1,719.38	1,490.98	1,343.04	1,240.92	1,167.33
4.00%	5,340.79	3,963.95	3,534.89	2,936.11	2,145.09	1,757.34	1,530.73	1,384.50	1,284.05	1,212.02
4.25%	5,373.57	3,997.41	3,568.71	2,970.69	2,181.61	1,795.78	1,571.04	1,426.63	1,327.89	1,257.50
4.50%	5,406.48	4,031.05	3,602.74	3,005.51	2,218.48	1,834.68	1,611.91	1,469.39	1,372.44	1,303.73
4.75%	5,439.50	4,064.85	3,636.96	3,040.58	2,255.71	1,874.05	1,653.34	1,512.78	1,417.68	1,350.70
5.00%	5,472.66	4,098.83	3,671.38	3,075.90	2,293.30	1,913.87	1,695.31	1,556.78	1,463.59	1,398.37
5.25%	5,505.94	4,132.99	3,705.99	3,111.46	2,331.25	1,954.15	1,737.82	1,601.39	1,510.15	1,446.72
5.50%	5,539.34	4,167.31	3,740.80	3,147.26	2,369.54	1,994.87	1,780.85	1,646.59	1,557.35	1,495.73
5.75%	5,572.86	4,201.81	3,775.81	3,183.31	2,408.19	2,036.04	1,824.41	1,692.36	1,605.15	1,545.37
6.00%	5,606.51	4,236.48	3,811.01	3,219.59	2,447.18	2,077.65	1,868.47	1,738.70	1,653.55	1,595.62
6.25%	5,640.29	4,271.32	3,846.41	3,256.12	2,486.53	2,119.69	1,913.04	1,785.58	1,702.52	1,646.44
6.50%	5,674.18	4,306.34	3,882.01	3,292.89	2,526.21	2,162.16	1,958.10	1,833.00	1,752.05	1,697.82
6.75%	5,708.20	4,341.52	3,917.80	3,329.90	2,566.24	2,205.06	2,003.64	1,880.93	1,802.11	1,749.73
7.00%	5,742.35	4,376.88	3,953.78	3,367.15	2,606.60	2,248.37	2,049.66	1,929.38	1,852.68	1,802.15
7.25%	5,776.61	4,412.40	3,989.95	3,404.63	2,647.30	2,292.09	2,096.14	1,978.31	1,903.76	1,855.05
7.50%	5,811.01	4,448.10	4,026.32	3,442.35	2,688.34	2,336.22	2,143.07	2,027.72	1,955.30	1,908.41
7.75%	5,845.52	4,483.97	4,062.88	3,480.31	2,729.70	2,380.75	2,190.45	2,077.60	2,007.31	1,962.20
8.00%	5,880.15	4,520.00	4,099.64	3,518.50	2,771.39	2,425.68	2,238.27	2,127.92	2,059.76	2,016.40
8.25%	5,914.91	4,556.21	4,136.58	3,556.93	2,813.41	2,470.99	2,286.51	2,178.67	2,112.62	2,071.00
8.50%	5,949.79	4,592.58	4,173.72	3,595.58	2,855.74	2,516.69	2,335.16	2,229.85	2,165.90	2,125.97
8.75%	5,984.80	4,629.12	4,211.04	3,634.48	2,898.40	2,562.76	2,384.22	2,281.43	2,219.55	2,181.29
9.00%	6,019.92	4,665.83	4,248.56	3,673.60	2,941.37	2,609.21	2,433.67	2,333.41	2,273.58	2,236.95
9.25%	6,055.17	4,702.71	4,286.26	3,712.95	2,984.66	2,656.01	2,483.51	2,385.76	2,327.96	2,292.92
9.50%	6,090.54	4,739.75	4,324.16	3,752.53	3,028.25	2,703.18	2,533.72	2,438.48	2,382.67	2,349.18
9.75%	6,126.03	4,776.97	4,362.24	3,792.34	3,072.15	2,750.70	2,584.30	2,491.55	2,437.71	2,405.72
10.00%	6,161.64	4,814.34	4,400.51	3,832.37	3,116.35	2,798.56	2,635.23	2,544.96	2,493.05	2,462.52
10.25%	6,197.38	4,851.89	4,438.96	3,872.63	3,160.86	2,846.77	2,686.51	2,598.69	2,548.68	2,519.57
10.50%	6,233.23	4,889.60	4,477.60	3,913.11	3,205.66	2,895.30	2,738.13	2,652.74	2,604.59	2,576.85
10.75%	6,269.21	4,927.47	4,516.43	3,953.82	3,250.75	2,944.16	2,790.07	2,707.10	2,660.76	2,634.35

	5	7	8	10	15	20	25	30	35	40
11.00%	6,305.30	4,965.51	4,555.44	3,994.75	3,296.13	2,993.35	2,842.33	2,761.74	2,717.18	2,692.05
11.25%	6,341.52	5,003.71	4,594.64	4,035.90	3,341.80	3,042.84	2,894.89	2,816.66	2,773.83	2,749.95
11.50%	6,377.86	5,042.07	4,634.02	4,077.27	3,387.75	3,092.65	2,947.76	2,871.85	2,830.71	2,808.02
11.75%	6,414.31	5,080.60	4,673.58	4,118.85	3,433.98	3,142.75	3,000.91	2,927.29	2,887.80	2,866.26
12.00%	6,450.89	5,119.29	4,713.32	4,160.66	3,480.49	3,193.15	3,054.35	2,982.98	2,945.09	2,924.65
12.25%	6,487.59	5,158.15	4,753.25	4,202.68	3,527.27	3,243.84	3,108.06	3,038.90	3,002.58	2,983.19
12.50%	6,524.40	5,197.16	4,793.35	4,244.91	3,574.31	3,294.81	3,162.03	3,095.05	3,060.24	3,041.87
12.75%	6,561.34	5,236.33	4,833.64	4,287.35	3,621.63	3,346.05	3,216.25	3,151.41	3,118.07	3,100.67
13.00%	6,598.39	5,275.67	4,874.10	4,330.01	3,669.20	3,397.57	3,270.72	3,207.98	3,176.06	3,159.59
13.25%	6,635.56	5,315.16	4,914.75	4,372.88	3,717.04	3,449.35	3,325.43	3,264.74	3,234.20	3,218.62
13.50%	6,672.86	5,354.82	4,955.57	4,415.95	3,765.12	3,501.39	3,380.37	3,321.70	3,292.49	3,277.76
13.75%	6,710.27	5,394.63	4,996.56	4,459.24	3,813.46	3,553.68	3,435.53	3,378.83	3,350.91	3,336.99
14.00%	6,747.79	5,434.60	5,037.74	4,502.73	3,862.05	3,606.21	3,490.91	3,436.13	3,409.45	3,396.31
14.25%	6,785.44	5,474.73	5,079.08	4,546.42	3,910.88	3,658.98	3,546.49	3,493.59	3,468.12	3,455.71
14.50%	6,823.20	5,515.02	5,120.60	4,590.32	3,959.95	3,711.99	3,602.27	3,551.21	3,526.89	3,515.19
14.75%	6,861.08	5,555.46	5,162.30	4,634.42	4,009.26	3,765.23	3,658.25	3,608.98	3,585.78	3,574.73
15.00%	6,899.08	5,596.06	5,204.17	4,678.71	4,058.80	3,818.69	3,714.41	3,666.89	3,644.76	3,634.35
15.25%	6,937.19	5,636.81	5,246.21	4,723.21	4,108.57	3,872.37	3,770.75	3,724.93	3,703.83	3,694.03
15.50%	6,975.43	5,677.72	5,288.42	4,767.91	4,158.57	3,926.25	3,827.26	3,783.10	3,763.00	3,753.76
15.75%	7,013.77	5,718.78	5,330.80	4,812.80	4,208.79	3,980.35	3,883.94	3,841.39	3,822.24	3,813.55
16.00%	7,052.24	5,760.00	5,373.35	4,857.88	4,259.23	4,034.64	3,940.78	3,899.80	3,881.56	3,873.38
16.25%	7,090.82	5,801.37	5,416.07	4,903.16	4,309.89	4,089.13	3,997.77	3,958.31	3,940.95	3,933.26
16.50%	7,129.51	5,842.89	5,458.95	4,948.63	4,360.75	4,143.81	4,054.91	4,016.93	4,000.42	3,993.18
16.75%	7,168.32	5,884.56	5,502.00	4,994.29	4,411.83	4,198.68	4,112.19	4,075.65	4,059.94	4,053.14
17.00%	7,207.25	5,926.38	5,545.22	5,040.13	4,463.11	4,253.72	4,169.61	4,134.46	4,119.53	4,113.14
17.25%	7,246.29	5,968.36	5,588.60	5,086.17	4,514.60	4,308.94	4,227.16	4,193.36	4,179.17	4,173.17
17.50%	7,285.44	6,010.48	5,632.15	5,132.38	4,566.28	4,364.33	4,284.84	4,252.34	4,238.86	4,233.23
17.75%	7,324.71	6,052.75	5,675.86	5,178.79	4,618.15	4,419.89	4,342.63	4,311.41	4,298.60	4,293.31
18.00%	7,364.09	6,095.17	5,719.73	5,225.37	4,670.22	4,475.60	4,400.55	4,370.55	4,358.39	4,353.43
18.25%	7,403.59	6,137.74	5,763.76	5,272.14	4,722.48	4,531.48	4,458.57	4,429.76	4,418.22	4,413.57
18.50%	7,443.20	6,180.46	5,807.96	5,319.08	4,774.92	4,587.50	4,516.70	4,489.04	4,478.09	4,473.73
18.75%	7,482.92	6,223.32	5,852.31	5,366.20	4,827.54	4,643.67	4,574.94	4,548.38	4,537.99	4,533.91
19.00%	7,522.76	6,266.33	5,896.82	5,413.50	4,880.34	4,699.99	4,633.27	4,607.79	4,597.93	4,594.11
19.25%	7,562.71	6,309.48	5,941.49	5,460.97	4,933.32	4,756.44	4,691.70	4,667.25	4,657.91	4,654.32
19.50%	7,602.77	6,352.77	5,986.31	5,508.61	4,986.46	4,813.03	4,750.22	4,726.77	4,717.91	4,714.56
19.75%	7,642.94	6,396.21	6,031.29	5,556.43	5,039.78	4,869.75	4,808.82	4,786.34	4,777.95	4,774.80
20.00%	7,683.23	6,439.80	6,076.43	5,604.41	5,093.26	4,926.59	4,867.51	4,845.95	4,838.01	4,835.07
20.25%	7,723.62	6,483.52	6,121.72	5,652.57	5,146.90	4,983.56	4,926.28	4,905.62	4,898.09	4,895.34
20.50%	7,764.13	6,527.39	6,167.16	5,700.89	5,200.71	5,040.65	4,985.12	4,965.32	4,958.20	4,955.63
20.75%	7,804.75	6,571.40	6,212.75	5,749.37	5,254.66	5,097.85	5,044.04	5,025.07	5,018.33	5,015.92

	5	7	8	10	15	20	25	30	35	40
1.00%	5,042.66	3,637.72	3,198.75	2,584.32	1,765.56	1,356.69	1,111.77	948.84	832.74	745.93
1.25%	5,074.47	3,669.62	3,230.72	2,616.46	1,798.18	1,389.84	1,145.48	983.09	867.55	781.29
1.50%	5,106.42	3,701.70	3,262.90	2,648.85	1,831.19	1,423.51	1,179.81	1,018.10	903.24	817.66
1.75%	5,138.49	3,733.96	3,295.27	2,681.50	1,864.58	1,457.68	1,214.78	1,053.87	939.80	855.01
2.00%	5,170.69	3,766.39	3,327.86	2,714.40	1,898.35	1,492.36	1,250.37	1,090.38	977.23	893.34
2.25%	5,203.02	3,799.01	3,360.64	2,747.55	1,932.50	1,527.53	1,286.59	1,127.63	1,015.50	932.62
2.50%	5,235.47	3,831.80	3,393.63	2,780.96	1,967.03	1,563.21	1,323.42	1,165.61	1,054.61	972.85
2.75%	5,268.05	3,864.77	3,426.83	2,814.63	2,001.93	1,599.39	1,360.87	1,204.31	1,094.55	1,014.00
3.00%	5,300.76	3,897.92	3,460.22	2,848.54	2,037.22	1,636.06	1,398.92	1,243.73	1,135.31	1,056.05
3.25%	5,333.60	3,931.25	3,493.82	2,882.71	2,072.87	1,673.23	1,437.58	1,283.86	1,176.86	1,099.00
3.50%	5,366.56	3,964.76	3,527.63	2,917.13	2,108.90	1,710.88	1,476.84	1,324.68	1,219.21	1,142.80
3.75%	5,399.66	3,998.44	3,561.63	2,951.81	2,145.31	1,749.02	1,516.69	1,366.19	1,262.32	1,187.45
4.00%	5,432.87	4,032.30	3,595.84	2,986.73	2,182.08	1,787.64	1,557.12	1,408.38	1,306.19	1,232.92
4.25%	5,466.22	4,066.33	3,630.24	3,021.91	2,219.22	1,826.74	1,598.13	1,451.22	1,350.79	1,279.18
4.50%	5,499.69	4,100.55	3,664.85	3,057.33	2,256.73	1,866.32	1,639.71	1,494.72	1,396.11	1,326.21
4.75%	5,533.29	4,134.94	3,699.66	3,093.01	2,294.60	1,906.36	1,681.85	1,538.86	1,442.13	1,373.99
5.00%	5,567.01	4,169.50	3,734.68	3,128.93	2,332.84	1,946.87	1,724.54	1,583.62	1,488.83	1,422.48
5.25%	5,600.87	4,204.25	3,769.89	3,165.11	2,371.44	1,987.84	1,767.78	1,629.00	1,536.19	1,471.67
5.50%	5,634.84	4,239.16	3,805.30	3,201.53	2,410.40	2,029.27	1,811.56	1,674.98	1,584.20	1,521.52
5.75%	5,668.95	4,274.26	3,840.91	3,238.19	2,449.71	2,071.15	1,855.86	1,721.54	1,632.83	1,572.02
6.00%	5,703.18	4,309.52	3,876.72	3,275.10	2,489.38	2,113.47	1,900.69	1,768.67	1,682.06	1,623.13
6.25%	5,737.53	4,344.97	3,912.73	3,312.26	2,529.40	2,156.24	1,946.02	1,816.37	1,731.88	1,674.83
6.50%	5,772.01	4,380.58	3,948.94	3,349.67	2,569.77	2,199.44	1,991.86	1,864.60	1,782.26	1,727.10
6.75%	5,806.62	4,416.38	3,985.34	3,387.31	2,610.48	2,243.07	2,038.19	1,913.36	1,833.18	1,779.90
7.00%	5,841.35	4,452.34	4,021.95	3,425.20	2,651.54	2,287.13	2,085.00	1,962.64	1,884.63	1,833.22
7.25%	5,876.21	4,488.48	4,058.75	3,463.33	2,692.95	2,331.61	2,132.28	2,012.42	1,936.58	1,887.03
7.50%	5,911.19	4,524.79	4,095.74	3,501.70	2,734.69	2,376.50	2,180.02	2,062.68	1,989.02	1,941.31
7.75%	5,946.30	4,561.28	4,132.93	3,540.31	2,776.76	2,421.80	2,228.22	2,113.42	2,041.92	1,996.03
8.00%	5,981.54	4,597.93	4,170.32	3,579.16	2,819.17	2,467.50	2,276.86	2,164.61	2,095.27	2,051.17
8.25%	6,016.89	4,634.76	4,207.90	3,618.25	2,861.91	2,513.59	2,325.93	2,216.24	2,149.05	2,106.71
8.50%	6,052.38	4,671.76	4,245.68	3,657.58	2,904.98	2,560.08	2,375.42	2,268.29	2,203.24	2,162.63
8.75%	6,087.98	4,708.94	4,283.65	3,697.14	2,948.37	2,606.95	2,425.32	2,320.77	2,257.82	2,218.90
9.00%	6,123.71	4,746.28	4,321.81	3,736.94	2,992.09	2,654.19	2,475.63	2,373.64	2,312.78	2,275.52
9.25%	6,159.57	4,783.79	4,360.16	3,776.97	3,036.12	2,701.81	2,526.33	2,426.89	2,368.10	2,332.45
9.50%	6,195.55	4,821.47	4,398.71	3,817.23	3,080.46	2,749.79	2,577.41	2,480.52	2,423.75	2,389.68
9.75%	6,231.65	4,859.33	4,437.45	3,857.72	3,125.12	2,798.12	2,628.86	2,534.51	2,479.74	2,447.20
10.00%	6,267.88	4,897.35	4,476.38	3,898.45	3,170.09	2,846.81	2,680.67	2,588.84	2,536.03	2,504.98
10.25%	6,304.23	4,935.54	4,515.50	3,939.40	3,215.36	2,895.85	2,732.83	2,643.50	2,592.62	2,563.01
10.50%	6,340.70	4,973.90	4,554.80	3,980.58	3,260.93	2,945.22	2,785.34	2,698.48	2,649.50	2,621.28
10.75%	6,377.30	5,012.43	4,594.30	4,021.99	3,306.80	2,994.93	2,838.17	2,753.77	2,706.63	2,679.77

$295,000   11.00 - 20.75%   5 - 40 Years

	5	7	8	10	15	20	25	30	35	40
11.00%	6,414.01	5,051.12	4,633.99	4,063.63	3,352.96	3,044.96	2,891.33	2,809.35	2,764.03	2,738.47
11.25%	6,450.86	5,089.98	4,673.86	4,105.48	3,399.42	3,095.31	2,944.81	2,865.22	2,821.66	2,797.36
11.50%	6,487.82	5,129.01	4,713.92	4,147.57	3,446.16	3,145.97	2,998.58	2,921.36	2,879.52	2,856.43
11.75%	6,524.90	5,168.20	4,754.16	4,189.87	3,493.19	3,196.94	3,052.65	2,977.76	2,937.59	2,915.67
12.00%	6,562.11	5,207.56	4,794.59	4,232.39	3,540.50	3,248.20	3,107.01	3,034.41	2,995.87	2,975.07
12.25%	6,599.44	5,247.08	4,835.20	4,275.14	3,588.08	3,299.77	3,161.64	3,091.29	3,054.34	3,034.62
12.50%	6,636.89	5,286.77	4,876.00	4,318.10	3,635.94	3,351.61	3,216.54	3,148.41	3,113.00	3,094.31
12.75%	6,674.46	5,326.62	4,916.98	4,361.27	3,684.07	3,403.74	3,271.70	3,205.74	3,171.83	3,154.13
13.00%	6,712.16	5,366.63	4,958.14	4,404.67	3,732.46	3,456.15	3,327.11	3,263.29	3,230.82	3,214.07
13.25%	6,749.97	5,406.81	4,999.48	4,448.27	3,781.12	3,508.82	3,382.77	3,321.03	3,289.96	3,274.12
13.50%	6,787.90	5,447.14	5,041.01	4,492.09	3,830.04	3,561.76	3,438.65	3,378.97	3,349.25	3,334.27
13.75%	6,825.96	5,487.64	5,082.71	4,536.12	3,879.21	3,614.95	3,494.76	3,437.08	3,408.68	3,394.52
14.00%	6,864.13	5,528.30	5,124.59	4,580.36	3,928.64	3,668.39	3,551.10	3,495.37	3,468.24	3,454.86
14.25%	6,902.43	5,569.12	5,166.65	4,624.81	3,978.31	3,722.07	3,607.64	3,553.83	3,527.91	3,515.29
14.50%	6,940.84	5,610.10	5,208.89	4,669.46	4,028.23	3,775.99	3,664.38	3,612.44	3,587.70	3,575.79
14.75%	6,979.38	5,651.24	5,251.30	4,714.32	4,078.39	3,830.15	3,721.32	3,671.20	3,647.60	3,636.37
15.00%	7,018.03	5,692.54	5,293.89	4,759.38	4,128.78	3,884.53	3,778.45	3,730.11	3,707.60	3,697.01
15.25%	7,056.80	5,734.00	5,336.66	4,804.65	4,179.41	3,939.13	3,835.76	3,789.15	3,767.69	3,757.72
15.50%	7,095.69	5,775.61	5,379.60	4,850.11	4,230.27	3,993.95	3,893.25	3,848.32	3,827.87	3,818.48
15.75%	7,134.70	5,817.38	5,422.71	4,895.78	4,281.36	4,048.97	3,950.90	3,907.62	3,888.14	3,879.30
16.00%	7,173.83	5,859.31	5,465.99	4,941.64	4,332.67	4,104.21	4,008.72	3,967.03	3,948.48	3,940.16
16.25%	7,213.07	5,901.39	5,509.45	4,987.70	4,384.20	4,159.63	4,066.70	4,026.56	4,008.90	4,001.08
16.50%	7,252.43	5,943.63	5,553.07	5,033.95	4,435.94	4,215.26	4,124.82	4,086.19	4,069.39	4,062.03
16.75%	7,291.91	5,986.02	5,596.87	5,080.39	4,487.90	4,271.07	4,183.09	4,145.92	4,129.94	4,123.02
17.00%	7,331.51	6,028.56	5,640.83	5,127.03	4,540.06	4,327.06	4,241.50	4,205.74	4,190.55	4,184.05
17.25%	7,371.22	6,071.26	5,684.96	5,173.86	4,592.43	4,383.23	4,300.04	4,265.66	4,251.22	4,245.12
17.50%	7,411.05	6,114.11	5,729.26	5,220.87	4,645.01	4,439.58	4,358.71	4,325.66	4,311.94	4,306.21
17.75%	7,451.00	6,157.11	5,773.72	5,268.08	4,697.78	4,496.09	4,417.51	4,385.74	4,372.71	4,367.34
18.00%	7,491.06	6,200.26	5,818.35	5,315.46	4,750.74	4,552.77	4,476.42	4,445.90	4,433.53	4,428.49
18.25%	7,531.24	6,243.56	5,863.14	5,363.03	4,803.90	4,609.60	4,535.44	4,506.13	4,494.39	4,489.66
18.50%	7,571.53	6,287.02	5,908.10	5,410.79	4,857.24	4,666.59	4,594.58	4,566.44	4,555.29	4,550.86
18.75%	7,611.94	6,330.62	5,953.21	5,458.72	4,910.77	4,723.73	4,653.82	4,626.80	4,616.23	4,612.08
19.00%	7,652.46	6,374.37	5,998.49	5,506.83	4,964.48	4,781.02	4,713.16	4,687.23	4,677.21	4,673.32
19.25%	7,693.10	6,418.26	6,043.93	5,555.12	5,018.37	4,838.45	4,772.59	4,747.72	4,738.22	4,734.57
19.50%	7,733.85	6,462.31	6,089.53	5,603.59	5,072.44	4,896.01	4,832.12	4,808.26	4,799.26	4,795.84
19.75%	7,774.72	6,506.49	6,135.28	5,652.23	5,126.67	4,953.71	4,891.73	4,868.86	4,860.33	4,857.13
20.00%	7,815.70	6,550.83	6,181.19	5,701.04	5,181.07	5,011.53	4,951.43	4,929.51	4,921.42	4,918.43
20.25%	7,856.79	6,595.31	6,227.26	5,750.03	5,235.64	5,069.48	5,011.21	4,990.20	4,982.54	4,979.74
20.50%	7,897.99	6,639.93	6,273.49	5,799.18	5,290.37	5,127.55	5,071.07	5,050.93	5,043.69	5,041.07
20.75%	7,939.31	6,684.70	6,319.87	5,848.50	5,345.26	5,185.74	5,131.00	5,111.71	5,104.85	5,102.40

	5	7	8	10	15	20	25	30	35	40
1.00%	5,128.12	3,699.37	3,252.97	2,628.12	1,795.48	1,379.68	1,130.62	964.92	846.86	758.57
1.25%	5,160.48	3,731.82	3,285.48	2,660.80	1,828.66	1,413.40	1,164.89	999.76	882.26	794.54
1.50%	5,192.97	3,764.44	3,318.20	2,693.74	1,862.23	1,447.64	1,199.81	1,035.36	918.55	831.52
1.75%	5,225.58	3,797.24	3,351.13	2,726.94	1,896.18	1,482.39	1,235.37	1,071.73	955.73	869.50
2.00%	5,258.33	3,830.23	3,384.26	2,760.40	1,930.53	1,517.65	1,271.56	1,108.86	993.79	908.48
2.25%	5,291.20	3,863.40	3,417.60	2,794.12	1,965.25	1,553.42	1,308.39	1,146.74	1,032.71	948.43
2.50%	5,324.21	3,896.75	3,451.15	2,828.10	2,000.37	1,589.71	1,345.85	1,185.36	1,072.49	989.33
2.75%	5,357.34	3,930.28	3,484.91	2,862.33	2,035.86	1,626.50	1,383.93	1,224.72	1,113.10	1,031.18
3.00%	5,390.61	3,963.99	3,518.87	2,896.82	2,071.74	1,663.79	1,422.63	1,264.81	1,154.55	1,073.95
3.25%	5,424.00	3,997.88	3,553.04	2,931.57	2,108.01	1,701.59	1,461.95	1,305.62	1,196.81	1,117.62
3.50%	5,457.52	4,031.96	3,587.42	2,966.58	2,144.65	1,739.88	1,501.87	1,347.13	1,239.87	1,162.17
3.75%	5,491.18	4,066.21	3,622.00	3,001.84	2,181.67	1,778.66	1,542.39	1,389.35	1,283.72	1,207.58
4.00%	5,524.96	4,100.64	3,656.78	3,037.35	2,219.06	1,817.94	1,583.51	1,432.25	1,328.32	1,253.82
4.25%	5,558.87	4,135.26	3,691.77	3,073.13	2,256.84	1,857.70	1,625.21	1,475.82	1,373.68	1,300.86
4.50%	5,592.91	4,170.05	3,726.97	3,109.15	2,294.98	1,897.95	1,667.50	1,520.06	1,419.77	1,348.69
4.75%	5,627.07	4,205.02	3,762.37	3,145.43	2,333.50	1,938.67	1,710.35	1,564.94	1,466.57	1,397.27
5.00%	5,661.37	4,240.17	3,797.98	3,181.97	2,372.38	1,979.87	1,753.77	1,610.46	1,514.06	1,446.59
5.25%	5,695.80	4,275.50	3,833.78	3,218.75	2,411.63	2,021.53	1,797.74	1,656.61	1,562.23	1,496.61
5.50%	5,730.35	4,311.01	3,869.80	3,255.79	2,451.25	2,063.66	1,842.26	1,703.37	1,611.05	1,547.31
5.75%	5,765.03	4,346.70	3,906.01	3,293.08	2,491.23	2,106.25	1,887.32	1,750.72	1,660.50	1,598.66
6.00%	5,799.84	4,382.57	3,942.43	3,330.62	2,531.57	2,149.29	1,932.90	1,798.65	1,710.57	1,650.64
6.25%	5,834.78	4,418.61	3,979.05	3,368.40	2,572.27	2,192.78	1,979.01	1,847.15	1,761.23	1,703.22
6.50%	5,869.84	4,454.83	4,015.87	3,406.44	2,613.32	2,236.72	2,025.62	1,896.20	1,812.46	1,756.37
6.75%	5,905.04	4,491.23	4,052.89	3,444.72	2,654.73	2,281.09	2,072.73	1,945.79	1,864.25	1,810.07
7.00%	5,940.36	4,527.80	4,090.12	3,483.25	2,696.48	2,325.90	2,120.34	1,995.91	1,916.57	1,864.29
7.25%	5,975.81	4,564.56	4,127.54	3,522.03	2,738.59	2,371.13	2,168.42	2,046.53	1,969.40	1,919.02
7.50%	6,011.38	4,601.48	4,165.16	3,561.05	2,781.04	2,416.78	2,216.97	2,097.64	2,022.73	1,974.21
7.75%	6,047.09	4,638.59	4,202.98	3,600.32	2,823.83	2,462.85	2,265.99	2,149.24	2,076.53	2,029.86
8.00%	6,082.92	4,675.86	4,241.00	3,639.83	2,866.96	2,509.32	2,315.45	2,201.29	2,130.78	2,085.94
8.25%	6,118.88	4,713.32	4,279.22	3,679.58	2,910.42	2,556.20	2,365.35	2,253.80	2,185.47	2,142.42
8.50%	6,154.96	4,750.95	4,317.64	3,719.57	2,954.22	2,603.47	2,415.68	2,306.74	2,240.58	2,199.28
8.75%	6,191.17	4,788.75	4,356.25	3,759.80	2,998.35	2,651.13	2,466.43	2,360.10	2,296.09	2,256.51
9.00%	6,227.51	4,826.72	4,395.06	3,800.27	3,042.80	2,699.18	2,517.59	2,413.87	2,351.98	2,314.08
9.25%	6,263.97	4,864.87	4,434.07	3,840.98	3,087.58	2,747.60	2,569.15	2,468.03	2,408.23	2,371.98
9.50%	6,300.56	4,903.19	4,473.27	3,881.93	3,132.67	2,796.39	2,621.09	2,522.56	2,464.83	2,430.18
9.75%	6,337.27	4,941.69	4,512.66	3,923.11	3,178.09	2,845.55	2,673.41	2,577.46	2,521.77	2,488.68
10.00%	6,374.11	4,980.36	4,552.25	3,964.52	3,223.82	2,895.06	2,726.10	2,632.71	2,579.02	2,547.44
10.25%	6,411.08	5,019.19	4,592.03	4,006.17	3,269.85	2,944.93	2,779.15	2,688.30	2,636.57	2,606.45
10.50%	6,448.17	5,058.20	4,632.00	4,048.05	3,316.20	2,995.14	2,832.55	2,744.22	2,694.40	2,665.71
10.75%	6,485.39	5,097.38	4,672.17	4,090.16	3,362.84	3,045.69	2,886.28	2,800.44	2,752.51	2,725.19

$300,000   11.00 - 20.75%   5 - 40 Years

	5	7	8	10	15	20	25	30	35	40
11.00%	6,522.73	5,136.73	4,712.53	4,132.50	3,409.79	3,096.57	2,940.34	2,856.97	2,810.87	2,784.88
11.25%	6,560.19	5,176.25	4,753.08	4,175.07	3,457.03	3,147.77	2,994.72	2,913.78	2,869.48	2,844.77
11.50%	6,597.78	5,215.94	4,793.81	4,217.86	3,504.57	3,199.29	3,049.41	2,970.87	2,928.32	2,904.85
11.75%	6,635.50	5,255.80	4,834.74	4,260.88	3,552.39	3,251.12	3,104.39	3,028.23	2,987.38	2,965.09
12.00%	6,673.33	5,295.82	4,875.85	4,304.13	3,600.50	3,303.26	3,159.67	3,085.84	3,046.65	3,025.50
12.25%	6,711.30	5,336.01	4,917.15	4,347.60	3,648.90	3,355.69	3,215.23	3,143.69	3,106.11	3,086.06
12.50%	6,749.38	5,376.37	4,958.64	4,391.29	3,697.57	3,408.42	3,271.06	3,201.77	3,165.76	3,146.76
12.75%	6,787.59	5,416.90	5,000.32	4,435.19	3,746.51	3,461.43	3,327.16	3,260.08	3,225.59	3,207.59
13.00%	6,825.92	5,457.59	5,042.18	4,479.32	3,795.73	3,514.73	3,383.51	3,318.60	3,285.58	3,268.54
13.25%	6,864.38	5,498.45	5,084.22	4,523.67	3,845.21	3,568.29	3,440.10	3,377.32	3,345.73	3,329.61
13.50%	6,902.95	5,539.47	5,126.45	4,568.23	3,894.96	3,622.12	3,496.93	3,436.24	3,406.02	3,390.78
13.75%	6,941.65	5,580.65	5,168.86	4,613.00	3,944.96	3,676.22	3,554.00	3,495.34	3,466.46	3,452.06
14.00%	6,980.48	5,622.00	5,211.45	4,657.99	3,995.22	3,730.56	3,611.28	3,554.62	3,527.02	3,513.42
14.25%	7,019.42	5,663.52	5,254.22	4,703.19	4,045.74	3,785.16	3,668.78	3,614.06	3,587.71	3,574.87
14.50%	7,058.48	5,705.19	5,297.18	4,748.60	4,096.50	3,839.99	3,726.49	3,673.67	3,648.51	3,636.40
14.75%	7,097.67	5,747.03	5,340.31	4,794.22	4,147.51	3,895.07	3,784.39	3,733.43	3,709.42	3,698.00
15.00%	7,136.98	5,789.03	5,383.62	4,840.05	4,198.76	3,950.37	3,842.49	3,793.33	3,770.44	3,759.67
15.25%	7,176.41	5,831.19	5,427.11	4,886.08	4,250.25	4,005.90	3,900.77	3,853.38	3,831.55	3,821.41
15.50%	7,215.96	5,873.50	5,470.78	4,932.32	4,301.97	4,061.64	3,959.24	3,913.55	3,892.75	3,883.20
15.75%	7,255.63	5,915.98	5,514.62	4,978.75	4,353.92	4,117.60	4,017.87	3,973.85	3,954.04	3,945.05
16.00%	7,295.42	5,958.62	5,558.64	5,025.39	4,406.10	4,173.77	4,076.67	4,034.27	4,015.41	4,006.95
16.25%	7,335.33	6,001.41	5,602.83	5,072.23	4,458.50	4,230.14	4,135.62	4,094.80	4,076.85	4,068.89
16.50%	7,375.36	6,044.37	5,647.19	5,119.27	4,511.13	4,286.70	4,194.73	4,155.44	4,138.36	4,130.88
16.75%	7,415.51	6,087.48	5,691.73	5,166.50	4,563.96	4,343.46	4,253.99	4,216.19	4,199.94	4,192.91
17.00%	7,455.77	6,130.74	5,736.44	5,213.93	4,617.01	4,400.40	4,313.39	4,277.03	4,261.58	4,254.97
17.25%	7,496.16	6,174.16	5,781.31	5,261.55	4,670.27	4,457.53	4,372.92	4,337.96	4,323.28	4,317.07
17.50%	7,536.66	6,217.74	5,826.36	5,309.36	4,723.73	4,514.83	4,432.59	4,398.98	4,385.03	4,379.20
17.75%	7,577.29	6,261.47	5,871.58	5,357.37	4,777.40	4,572.30	4,492.38	4,460.08	4,446.83	4,441.36
18.00%	7,618.03	6,305.35	5,916.96	5,405.56	4,831.26	4,629.93	4,552.29	4,521.26	4,508.68	4,503.55
18.25%	7,658.89	6,349.39	5,962.52	5,453.93	4,885.32	4,687.73	4,612.32	4,582.51	4,570.57	4,565.76
18.50%	7,699.86	6,393.58	6,008.23	5,502.50	4,939.57	4,745.69	4,672.45	4,643.83	4,632.50	4,627.99
18.75%	7,740.96	6,437.92	6,054.11	5,551.24	4,994.01	4,803.80	4,732.70	4,705.22	4,694.48	4,690.25
19.00%	7,782.17	6,482.41	6,100.16	5,600.17	5,048.63	4,862.05	4,793.04	4,766.68	4,756.48	4,752.52
19.25%	7,823.49	6,527.05	6,146.37	5,649.28	5,103.43	4,920.45	4,853.48	4,828.19	4,818.53	4,814.82
19.50%	7,864.93	6,571.84	6,192.74	5,698.57	5,158.41	4,978.99	4,914.02	4,889.76	4,880.60	4,877.13
19.75%	7,906.49	6,616.77	6,239.27	5,748.03	5,213.56	5,037.67	4,974.64	4,951.38	4,942.70	4,939.45
20.00%	7,948.17	6,661.86	6,285.96	5,797.67	5,268.89	5,096.47	5,035.36	5,013.06	5,004.83	5,001.79
20.25%	7,989.95	6,707.09	6,332.81	5,847.48	5,324.38	5,155.41	5,096.15	5,074.78	5,066.99	5,064.14
20.50%	8,031.86	6,752.47	6,379.82	5,897.47	5,380.04	5,214.46	5,157.02	5,136.54	5,129.17	5,126.51
20.75%	8,073.88	6,798.00	6,426.98	5,947.63	5,435.86	5,273.64	5,217.97	5,198.35	5,191.37	5,188.88

	5	7	8	10	15	20	25	30	35	40
1.00%	5,213.59	3,761.03	3,307.18	2,671.93	1,825.41	1,402.68	1,149.46	981.00	860.97	771.21
1.25%	5,246.49	3,794.01	3,340.24	2,705.15	1,859.14	1,436.96	1,184.31	1,016.42	896.96	807.78
1.50%	5,279.52	3,827.18	3,373.50	2,738.64	1,893.27	1,471.76	1,219.81	1,052.62	933.86	845.38
1.75%	5,312.68	3,860.53	3,406.98	2,772.39	1,927.79	1,507.09	1,255.96	1,089.59	971.66	883.99
2.00%	5,345.97	3,894.07	3,440.67	2,806.41	1,962.70	1,542.94	1,292.76	1,127.34	1,010.35	923.62
2.25%	5,379.39	3,927.79	3,474.56	2,840.69	1,998.01	1,579.32	1,330.20	1,165.85	1,049.92	964.23
2.50%	5,412.95	3,961.69	3,508.67	2,875.23	2,033.71	1,616.20	1,368.28	1,205.12	1,090.36	1,005.82
2.75%	5,446.63	3,995.78	3,542.99	2,910.04	2,069.80	1,653.61	1,407.00	1,245.14	1,131.66	1,048.37
3.00%	5,480.45	4,030.06	3,577.52	2,945.10	2,106.27	1,691.52	1,446.34	1,285.89	1,173.79	1,091.85
3.25%	5,514.40	4,064.51	3,612.26	2,980.43	2,143.14	1,729.95	1,486.31	1,327.38	1,216.76	1,136.25
3.50%	5,548.48	4,099.15	3,647.21	3,016.02	2,180.39	1,768.88	1,526.90	1,369.59	1,260.54	1,181.54
3.75%	5,582.70	4,133.98	3,682.36	3,051.87	2,218.03	1,808.31	1,568.10	1,412.50	1,305.11	1,227.70
4.00%	5,617.04	4,168.99	3,717.73	3,087.98	2,256.05	1,848.24	1,609.90	1,456.12	1,350.46	1,274.71
4.25%	5,651.51	4,204.18	3,753.30	3,124.34	2,294.45	1,888.67	1,652.30	1,500.42	1,396.58	1,322.54
4.50%	5,686.12	4,239.55	3,789.09	3,160.97	2,333.23	1,929.58	1,695.29	1,545.39	1,443.43	1,371.17
4.75%	5,720.86	4,275.10	3,825.08	3,197.86	2,372.39	1,970.98	1,738.86	1,591.02	1,491.01	1,420.56
5.00%	5,755.73	4,310.84	3,861.28	3,235.00	2,411.92	2,012.87	1,783.00	1,637.31	1,539.30	1,470.70
5.25%	5,790.73	4,346.76	3,897.68	3,272.40	2,451.83	2,055.22	1,827.71	1,684.22	1,588.27	1,521.55
5.50%	5,825.85	4,382.86	3,934.29	3,310.05	2,492.10	2,098.06	1,872.97	1,731.76	1,637.90	1,573.10
5.75%	5,861.11	4,419.15	3,971.11	3,347.96	2,532.75	2,141.35	1,918.77	1,779.90	1,688.18	1,625.31
6.00%	5,896.50	4,455.61	4,008.14	3,386.13	2,573.76	2,185.11	1,965.12	1,828.63	1,739.08	1,678.15
6.25%	5,932.02	4,492.25	4,045.37	3,424.54	2,615.14	2,229.33	2,011.99	1,877.94	1,790.58	1,731.61
6.50%	5,967.68	4,529.08	4,082.80	3,463.21	2,656.88	2,274.00	2,059.38	1,927.81	1,842.67	1,785.64
6.75%	6,003.46	4,566.08	4,120.44	3,502.14	2,698.97	2,319.11	2,107.28	1,978.22	1,895.32	1,840.24
7.00%	6,039.37	4,603.27	4,158.28	3,541.31	2,741.43	2,364.66	2,155.68	2,029.17	1,948.51	1,895.37
7.25%	6,075.41	4,640.63	4,196.33	3,580.73	2,784.23	2,410.65	2,204.56	2,080.64	2,002.23	1,951.00
7.50%	6,111.57	4,678.17	4,234.58	3,620.40	2,827.39	2,457.06	2,253.92	2,132.60	2,056.44	2,007.12
7.75%	6,147.87	4,715.90	4,273.03	3,660.32	2,870.89	2,503.89	2,303.75	2,185.06	2,111.14	2,063.69
8.00%	6,184.30	4,753.80	4,311.69	3,700.49	2,914.74	2,551.14	2,354.04	2,237.98	2,166.30	2,120.70
8.25%	6,220.86	4,791.87	4,350.54	3,740.91	2,958.93	2,598.80	2,404.77	2,291.36	2,221.90	2,178.12
8.50%	6,257.54	4,830.13	4,389.60	3,781.56	3,003.46	2,646.86	2,455.94	2,345.19	2,277.92	2,235.94
8.75%	6,294.36	4,868.56	4,428.86	3,822.47	3,048.32	2,695.32	2,507.54	2,399.44	2,334.36	2,294.12
9.00%	6,331.30	4,907.17	4,468.31	3,863.61	3,093.51	2,744.16	2,559.55	2,454.10	2,391.18	2,352.65
9.25%	6,368.37	4,945.95	4,507.97	3,905.00	3,139.04	2,793.39	2,611.96	2,509.16	2,448.37	2,411.51
9.50%	6,405.57	4,984.91	4,547.82	3,946.63	3,184.89	2,843.00	2,664.77	2,564.61	2,505.92	2,470.69
9.75%	6,442.89	5,024.05	4,587.87	3,988.49	3,231.06	2,892.98	2,717.97	2,620.42	2,563.80	2,530.15
10.00%	6,480.35	5,063.36	4,628.12	4,030.60	3,277.55	2,943.32	2,771.54	2,676.59	2,622.00	2,589.90
10.25%	6,517.93	5,102.85	4,668.56	4,072.94	3,324.35	2,994.01	2,825.47	2,733.11	2,680.51	2,649.90
10.50%	6,555.64	5,142.51	4,709.20	4,115.52	3,371.47	3,045.06	2,879.75	2,789.95	2,739.31	2,710.14
10.75%	6,593.48	5,182.34	4,750.04	4,158.33	3,418.89	3,096.45	2,934.38	2,847.12	2,798.38	2,770.61

$305,000   11.00 - 20.75%   5 - 40 Years

	5	7	8	10	15	20	25	30	35	40
11.00%	6,631.44	5,222.34	4,791.07	4,201.38	3,466.62	3,148.17	2,989.34	2,904.59	2,857.72	2,831.30
11.25%	6,669.53	5,262.52	4,832.29	4,244.65	3,514.65	3,200.23	3,044.63	2,962.35	2,917.31	2,892.18
11.50%	6,707.75	5,302.87	4,873.71	4,288.16	3,562.98	3,252.61	3,100.23	3,020.39	2,977.13	2,953.26
11.75%	6,746.09	5,343.39	4,915.32	4,331.90	3,611.60	3,305.31	3,156.13	3,078.70	3,037.17	3,014.51
12.00%	6,784.56	5,384.08	4,957.12	4,375.86	3,660.51	3,358.31	3,212.33	3,137.27	3,097.43	3,075.92
12.25%	6,823.15	5,424.95	4,999.11	4,420.06	3,709.71	3,411.62	3,268.82	3,196.08	3,157.88	3,137.49
12.50%	6,861.87	5,465.98	5,041.29	4,464.47	3,759.19	3,465.23	3,325.58	3,255.14	3,218.53	3,199.20
12.75%	6,900.72	5,507.18	5,083.66	4,509.11	3,808.95	3,519.13	3,382.61	3,314.41	3,279.35	3,261.05
13.00%	6,939.69	5,548.55	5,126.21	4,553.98	3,858.99	3,573.31	3,439.90	3,373.91	3,340.34	3,323.02
13.25%	6,978.78	5,590.09	5,168.96	4,599.06	3,909.30	3,627.76	3,497.44	3,433.61	3,401.49	3,385.10
13.50%	7,018.00	5,631.79	5,211.89	4,644.37	3,959.87	3,682.49	3,555.22	3,493.51	3,462.79	3,447.30
13.75%	7,057.35	5,673.66	5,255.01	4,689.89	4,010.71	3,737.49	3,613.23	3,553.59	3,524.23	3,509.59
14.00%	7,096.82	5,715.70	5,298.31	4,735.63	4,061.81	3,792.74	3,671.47	3,613.86	3,585.80	3,571.98
14.25%	7,136.41	5,757.91	5,341.79	4,781.58	4,113.17	3,848.24	3,729.93	3,674.30	3,647.50	3,634.45
14.50%	7,176.13	5,800.28	5,385.46	4,827.75	4,164.78	3,903.99	3,788.60	3,734.90	3,709.32	3,697.01
14.75%	7,215.97	5,842.81	5,429.32	4,874.13	4,216.64	3,959.98	3,847.47	3,795.65	3,771.25	3,759.63
15.00%	7,255.93	5,885.51	5,473.35	4,920.72	4,268.74	4,016.21	3,906.53	3,856.55	3,833.28	3,822.33
15.25%	7,296.01	5,928.37	5,517.56	4,967.52	4,321.09	4,072.66	3,965.79	3,917.60	3,895.41	3,885.10
15.50%	7,336.22	5,971.40	5,561.96	5,014.52	4,373.67	4,129.34	4,025.22	3,978.78	3,957.63	3,947.92
15.75%	7,376.55	6,014.58	5,606.53	5,061.73	4,426.49	4,186.23	4,084.83	4,040.08	4,019.94	4,010.80
16.00%	7,417.01	6,057.93	5,651.28	5,109.15	4,479.54	4,243.33	4,144.61	4,101.51	4,082.33	4,073.73
16.25%	7,457.58	6,101.44	5,696.21	5,156.77	4,532.81	4,300.64	4,204.55	4,163.05	4,144.80	4,136.70
16.50%	7,498.28	6,145.11	5,741.31	5,204.59	4,586.31	4,358.15	4,264.65	4,224.70	4,207.33	4,199.73
16.75%	7,539.10	6,188.93	5,786.59	5,252.61	4,640.03	4,415.85	4,324.89	4,286.46	4,269.94	4,262.79
17.00%	7,580.04	6,232.92	5,832.04	5,300.83	4,693.96	4,473.74	4,385.28	4,348.31	4,332.60	4,325.89
17.25%	7,621.10	6,277.07	5,877.67	5,349.24	4,748.11	4,531.82	4,445.81	4,410.26	4,395.33	4,389.02
17.50%	7,662.28	6,321.37	5,923.47	5,397.85	4,802.46	4,590.07	4,506.47	4,472.29	4,458.11	4,452.19
17.75%	7,703.58	6,365.83	5,969.44	5,446.65	4,857.02	4,648.50	4,567.25	4,534.41	4,520.94	4,515.38
18.00%	7,745.00	6,410.44	6,015.58	5,495.65	4,911.78	4,707.10	4,628.16	4,596.61	4,583.82	4,578.61
18.25%	7,786.53	6,455.21	6,061.89	5,544.83	4,966.74	4,765.86	4,689.19	4,658.88	4,646.74	4,641.85
18.50%	7,828.19	6,500.14	6,108.37	5,594.20	5,021.90	4,824.78	4,750.33	4,721.23	4,709.71	4,705.13
18.75%	7,869.97	6,545.21	6,155.02	5,643.76	5,077.24	4,883.86	4,811.57	4,783.64	4,772.72	4,768.42
19.00%	7,911.87	6,590.45	6,201.83	5,693.51	5,132.77	4,943.09	4,872.92	4,846.12	4,835.76	4,831.73
19.25%	7,953.88	6,635.83	6,248.81	5,743.43	5,188.49	5,002.46	4,934.37	4,908.66	4,898.84	4,895.06
19.50%	7,996.02	6,681.37	6,295.95	5,793.54	5,244.38	5,061.98	4,995.92	4,971.26	4,961.94	4,958.41
19.75%	8,038.27	6,727.05	6,343.26	5,843.83	5,300.46	5,121.63	5,057.55	5,033.91	5,025.08	5,021.78
20.00%	8,080.63	6,772.89	6,390.73	5,894.30	5,356.70	5,181.42	5,119.28	5,096.61	5,088.25	5,085.16
20.25%	8,123.12	6,818.88	6,438.36	5,944.94	5,413.12	5,241.33	5,181.08	5,159.36	5,151.44	5,148.55
20.50%	8,165.72	6,865.01	6,486.15	5,995.76	5,469.71	5,301.37	5,242.97	5,222.15	5,214.66	5,211.95
20.75%	8,208.44	6,911.30	6,534.10	6,046.75	5,526.46	5,361.53	5,304.93	5,284.99	5,277.90	5,275.37

	5	7	8	10	15	20	25	30	35	40
1.00%	5,299.06	3,822.69	3,361.40	2,715.73	1,855.33	1,425.67	1,168.30	997.08	875.09	783.85
1.25%	5,332.50	3,856.21	3,395.00	2,749.50	1,889.62	1,460.51	1,203.72	1,033.08	911.67	821.02
1.50%	5,366.07	3,889.92	3,428.81	2,783.54	1,924.30	1,495.89	1,239.80	1,069.87	949.17	859.23
1.75%	5,399.77	3,923.82	3,462.83	2,817.84	1,959.39	1,531.80	1,276.55	1,107.45	987.59	898.49
2.00%	5,433.61	3,957.90	3,497.07	2,852.42	1,994.88	1,568.24	1,313.95	1,145.82	1,026.91	938.76
2.25%	5,467.58	3,992.18	3,531.52	2,887.26	2,030.76	1,605.21	1,352.01	1,184.96	1,067.13	980.04
2.50%	5,501.68	4,026.64	3,566.19	2,922.37	2,067.05	1,642.70	1,390.71	1,224.87	1,108.24	1,022.31
2.75%	5,535.92	4,061.29	3,601.07	2,957.74	2,103.73	1,680.72	1,430.06	1,265.55	1,150.21	1,065.56
3.00%	5,570.29	4,096.12	3,636.17	2,993.38	2,140.80	1,719.25	1,470.06	1,306.97	1,193.04	1,109.75
3.25%	5,604.80	4,131.15	3,671.48	3,029.29	2,178.27	1,758.31	1,510.68	1,349.14	1,236.71	1,154.88
3.50%	5,639.44	4,166.35	3,707.00	3,065.46	2,216.14	1,797.88	1,551.93	1,392.04	1,281.20	1,200.91
3.75%	5,674.21	4,201.75	3,742.73	3,101.90	2,254.39	1,837.95	1,593.81	1,435.66	1,326.51	1,247.83
4.00%	5,709.12	4,237.33	3,778.68	3,138.60	2,293.03	1,878.54	1,636.29	1,479.99	1,372.60	1,295.61
4.25%	5,744.16	4,273.10	3,814.83	3,175.56	2,332.06	1,919.63	1,679.39	1,525.01	1,419.47	1,344.22
4.50%	5,779.34	4,309.05	3,851.20	3,212.79	2,371.48	1,961.21	1,723.08	1,570.72	1,467.10	1,393.64
4.75%	5,814.64	4,345.19	3,887.78	3,250.28	2,411.28	2,003.29	1,767.36	1,617.11	1,515.46	1,443.85
5.00%	5,850.08	4,381.51	3,924.58	3,288.03	2,451.46	2,045.86	1,812.23	1,664.15	1,564.53	1,494.81
5.25%	5,885.65	4,418.02	3,961.58	3,326.04	2,492.02	2,088.92	1,857.67	1,711.83	1,614.30	1,546.50
5.50%	5,921.36	4,454.71	3,998.79	3,364.31	2,532.96	2,132.45	1,903.67	1,760.15	1,664.75	1,598.89
5.75%	5,957.20	4,491.59	4,036.21	3,402.85	2,574.27	2,176.46	1,950.23	1,809.08	1,715.85	1,651.95
6.00%	5,993.17	4,528.65	4,073.84	3,441.64	2,615.96	2,220.94	1,997.33	1,858.61	1,767.59	1,705.66
6.25%	6,029.27	4,565.90	4,111.68	3,480.68	2,658.01	2,265.88	2,044.98	1,908.72	1,819.94	1,759.99
6.50%	6,065.51	4,603.33	4,149.73	3,519.99	2,700.43	2,311.28	2,093.14	1,959.41	1,872.88	1,814.92
6.75%	6,101.87	4,640.94	4,187.99	3,559.55	2,743.22	2,357.13	2,141.83	2,010.65	1,926.39	1,870.41
7.00%	6,138.37	4,678.73	4,226.45	3,599.36	2,786.37	2,403.43	2,191.02	2,062.44	1,980.45	1,926.44
7.25%	6,175.00	4,716.71	4,265.12	3,639.43	2,829.87	2,450.17	2,240.70	2,114.75	2,035.05	1,982.98
7.50%	6,211.76	4,754.87	4,304.00	3,679.75	2,873.74	2,497.34	2,290.87	2,167.56	2,090.15	2,040.02
7.75%	6,248.66	4,793.21	4,343.08	3,720.33	2,917.95	2,544.94	2,341.52	2,220.88	2,145.75	2,097.52
8.00%	6,285.68	4,831.73	4,382.37	3,761.16	2,962.52	2,592.96	2,392.63	2,274.67	2,201.81	2,155.47
8.25%	6,322.84	4,870.43	4,421.86	3,802.23	3,007.44	2,641.40	2,444.20	2,328.93	2,258.32	2,213.83
8.50%	6,360.12	4,909.31	4,461.56	3,843.56	3,052.69	2,690.25	2,496.20	2,383.63	2,315.27	2,272.59
8.75%	6,397.54	4,948.37	4,501.46	3,885.13	3,098.29	2,739.50	2,548.65	2,438.77	2,372.63	2,331.73
9.00%	6,435.09	4,987.61	4,541.56	3,926.95	3,144.23	2,789.15	2,601.51	2,494.33	2,430.38	2,391.22
9.25%	6,472.77	5,027.03	4,581.87	3,969.01	3,190.50	2,839.19	2,654.78	2,550.29	2,488.51	2,451.05
9.50%	6,510.58	5,066.63	4,622.38	4,011.32	3,237.10	2,889.61	2,708.46	2,606.65	2,547.00	2,511.19
9.75%	6,548.52	5,106.41	4,663.08	4,053.88	3,284.02	2,940.40	2,762.53	2,663.38	2,605.83	2,571.63
10.00%	6,586.58	5,146.37	4,703.99	4,096.67	3,331.28	2,991.57	2,816.97	2,720.47	2,664.98	2,632.35
10.25%	6,624.78	5,186.50	4,745.10	4,139.71	3,378.85	3,043.09	2,871.79	2,777.91	2,724.45	2,693.34
10.50%	6,663.11	5,226.81	4,786.41	4,182.98	3,426.74	3,094.98	2,926.96	2,835.69	2,784.22	2,754.57
10.75%	6,701.57	5,267.29	4,827.91	4,226.50	3,474.94	3,147.21	2,982.49	2,893.79	2,844.26	2,816.03

$310,000   11.00 - 20.75%   5 - 40 Years

	5	7	8	10	15	20	25	30	35	40
11.00%	6,740.15	5,307.96	4,869.61	4,270.25	3,523.45	3,199.78	3,038.35	2,952.20	2,904.57	2,877.71
11.25%	6,778.87	5,348.79	4,911.51	4,314.24	3,572.27	3,252.69	3,094.54	3,010.91	2,965.13	2,939.60
11.50%	6,817.71	5,389.80	4,953.61	4,358.46	3,621.39	3,305.93	3,151.05	3,069.90	3,025.93	3,001.67
11.75%	6,856.68	5,430.99	4,995.90	4,402.91	3,670.81	3,359.49	3,207.87	3,129.17	3,086.96	3,063.93
12.00%	6,895.78	5,472.35	5,038.38	4,447.60	3,720.52	3,413.37	3,264.99	3,188.70	3,148.20	3,126.35
12.25%	6,935.01	5,513.88	5,081.06	4,492.52	3,770.53	3,467.55	3,322.41	3,248.48	3,209.65	3,188.93
12.50%	6,974.36	5,555.58	5,123.93	4,537.66	3,820.82	3,522.04	3,380.10	3,308.50	3,271.29	3,251.65
12.75%	7,013.84	5,597.46	5,166.99	4,583.03	3,871.39	3,576.82	3,438.06	3,368.75	3,333.11	3,314.51
13.00%	7,053.45	5,639.51	5,210.25	4,628.63	3,922.25	3,631.88	3,496.29	3,429.22	3,395.10	3,377.49
13.25%	7,093.19	5,681.73	5,253.69	4,674.46	3,973.38	3,687.24	3,554.77	3,489.90	3,457.25	3,440.60
13.50%	7,133.05	5,724.12	5,297.33	4,720.50	4,024.79	3,742.86	3,613.50	3,550.78	3,519.56	3,503.81
13.75%	7,173.04	5,766.68	5,341.15	4,766.77	4,076.46	3,798.76	3,672.46	3,611.85	3,582.00	3,567.12
14.00%	7,213.16	5,809.40	5,385.17	4,813.26	4,128.40	3,854.91	3,731.66	3,673.10	3,644.59	3,630.53
14.25%	7,253.40	5,852.30	5,429.36	4,859.97	4,180.60	3,911.33	3,791.08	3,734.53	3,707.30	3,694.03
14.50%	7,293.77	5,895.36	5,473.75	4,906.89	4,233.05	3,967.99	3,850.71	3,796.12	3,770.13	3,757.61
14.75%	7,334.26	5,938.60	5,518.32	4,954.03	4,285.76	4,024.90	3,910.54	3,857.87	3,833.07	3,821.27
15.00%	7,374.88	5,981.99	5,563.08	5,001.38	4,338.72	4,082.05	3,970.57	3,919.78	3,896.12	3,884.99
15.25%	7,415.62	6,025.56	5,608.01	5,048.95	4,391.92	4,139.43	4,030.80	3,981.82	3,959.27	3,948.79
15.50%	7,456.49	6,069.29	5,653.14	5,096.73	4,445.37	4,197.03	4,091.21	4,044.00	4,022.51	4,012.64
15.75%	7,497.48	6,113.18	5,698.44	5,144.71	4,499.05	4,254.85	4,151.80	4,106.31	4,085.84	4,076.55
16.00%	7,538.60	6,157.24	5,743.92	5,192.91	4,552.97	4,312.89	4,212.56	4,168.75	4,149.26	4,140.51
16.25%	7,579.84	6,201.46	5,789.59	5,241.31	4,607.12	4,371.14	4,273.48	4,231.30	4,212.74	4,204.52
16.50%	7,621.20	6,245.85	5,835.43	5,289.91	4,661.50	4,429.59	4,334.56	4,293.96	4,276.31	4,268.57
16.75%	7,662.69	6,290.39	5,881.45	5,338.72	4,716.10	4,488.24	4,395.79	4,356.73	4,339.94	4,332.67
17.00%	7,704.30	6,335.10	5,927.65	5,387.73	4,770.91	4,547.08	4,457.17	4,419.59	4,403.63	4,396.80
17.25%	7,746.03	6,379.97	5,974.03	5,436.94	4,825.95	4,606.11	4,518.69	4,482.56	4,467.38	4,460.97
17.50%	7,787.89	6,425.00	6,020.58	5,486.34	4,881.19	4,665.32	4,580.34	4,545.61	4,531.19	4,525.17
17.75%	7,829.86	6,470.18	6,067.30	5,535.94	4,936.65	4,724.71	4,642.13	4,608.75	4,595.05	4,589.41
18.00%	7,871.96	6,515.53	6,114.20	5,585.74	4,992.31	4,784.27	4,704.03	4,671.96	4,658.97	4,653.67
18.25%	7,914.18	6,561.03	6,161.27	5,635.73	5,048.17	4,843.99	4,766.06	4,735.26	4,722.92	4,717.95
18.50%	7,956.52	6,606.69	6,208.51	5,685.91	5,104.22	4,903.88	4,828.20	4,798.63	4,786.92	4,782.26
18.75%	7,998.99	6,652.51	6,255.92	5,736.28	5,160.47	4,963.92	4,890.45	4,862.06	4,850.96	4,846.59
19.00%	8,041.57	6,698.49	6,303.50	5,786.84	5,216.92	5,024.12	4,952.81	4,925.57	4,915.03	4,910.94
19.25%	8,084.27	6,744.61	6,351.25	5,837.59	5,273.54	5,084.47	5,015.27	4,989.13	4,979.14	4,975.31
19.50%	8,127.10	6,790.90	6,399.16	5,888.52	5,330.36	5,144.96	5,077.82	5,052.75	5,043.29	5,039.70
19.75%	8,170.04	6,837.33	6,447.24	5,939.63	5,387.35	5,205.59	5,140.47	5,116.43	5,107.46	5,104.10
20.00%	8,213.10	6,883.92	6,495.49	5,990.93	5,444.52	5,266.36	5,203.20	5,180.16	5,171.66	5,168.52
20.25%	8,256.29	6,930.66	6,543.90	6,042.40	5,501.86	5,327.25	5,266.02	5,243.94	5,235.89	5,232.95
20.50%	8,299.59	6,977.55	6,592.48	6,094.05	5,559.37	5,388.28	5,328.92	5,307.76	5,300.14	5,297.39
20.75%	8,343.00	7,024.60	6,641.22	6,145.88	5,617.05	5,449.43	5,391.90	5,371.63	5,364.42	5,361.85

	5	7	8	10	15	20	25	30	35	40
1.00%	5,384.53	3,884.34	3,415.62	2,759.53	1,885.26	1,448.67	1,187.15	1,013.16	889.20	796.50
1.25%	5,418.50	3,918.41	3,449.75	2,793.84	1,920.10	1,484.07	1,223.14	1,049.74	926.37	834.26
1.50%	5,452.61	3,952.66	3,484.11	2,828.43	1,955.34	1,520.02	1,259.80	1,087.13	964.48	873.09
1.75%	5,486.86	3,987.11	3,518.68	2,863.29	1,990.99	1,556.51	1,297.14	1,125.32	1,003.52	912.98
2.00%	5,521.24	4,021.74	3,553.47	2,898.42	2,027.05	1,593.53	1,335.14	1,164.30	1,043.48	953.90
2.25%	5,555.76	4,056.57	3,588.48	2,933.83	2,063.52	1,631.10	1,373.81	1,204.08	1,084.35	995.85
2.50%	5,590.42	4,091.59	3,623.71	2,969.50	2,100.39	1,669.19	1,413.14	1,244.63	1,126.11	1,038.80
2.75%	5,625.21	4,126.79	3,659.15	3,005.45	2,137.66	1,707.82	1,453.13	1,285.96	1,168.76	1,082.74
3.00%	5,660.14	4,162.19	3,694.82	3,041.66	2,175.33	1,746.98	1,493.77	1,328.05	1,212.28	1,127.65
3.25%	5,695.20	4,197.78	3,730.69	3,078.15	2,213.41	1,786.67	1,535.05	1,370.90	1,256.65	1,173.50
3.50%	5,730.40	4,233.55	3,766.79	3,114.90	2,251.88	1,826.87	1,576.96	1,414.49	1,301.87	1,220.28
3.75%	5,765.73	4,269.52	3,803.10	3,151.93	2,290.75	1,867.60	1,619.51	1,458.81	1,347.90	1,267.96
4.00%	5,801.20	4,305.67	3,839.62	3,189.22	2,330.02	1,908.84	1,662.69	1,503.86	1,394.74	1,316.51
4.25%	5,836.81	4,342.02	3,876.36	3,226.78	2,369.68	1,950.59	1,706.48	1,549.61	1,442.37	1,365.90
4.50%	5,872.55	4,378.55	3,913.32	3,264.61	2,409.73	1,992.85	1,750.87	1,596.06	1,490.76	1,416.12
4.75%	5,908.43	4,415.27	3,950.49	3,302.70	2,450.17	2,035.60	1,795.87	1,643.19	1,539.90	1,467.14
5.00%	5,944.44	4,452.18	3,987.87	3,341.06	2,491.00	2,078.86	1,841.46	1,690.99	1,589.77	1,518.92
5.25%	5,980.58	4,489.28	4,025.47	3,379.69	2,532.21	2,122.61	1,887.63	1,739.44	1,640.34	1,571.44
5.50%	6,016.87	4,526.56	4,063.29	3,418.58	2,573.81	2,166.85	1,934.38	1,788.54	1,691.60	1,624.68
5.75%	6,053.28	4,564.04	4,101.31	3,457.73	2,615.79	2,211.56	1,981.69	1,838.25	1,743.53	1,678.60
6.00%	6,089.83	4,601.69	4,139.55	3,497.15	2,658.15	2,256.76	2,029.55	1,888.58	1,796.10	1,733.17
6.25%	6,126.52	4,639.54	4,178.00	3,536.82	2,700.88	2,302.42	2,077.96	1,939.51	1,849.29	1,788.38
6.50%	6,163.34	4,677.57	4,216.66	3,576.76	2,743.99	2,348.56	2,126.90	1,991.01	1,903.09	1,844.19
6.75%	6,200.29	4,715.79	4,255.54	3,616.96	2,787.46	2,395.15	2,176.37	2,043.08	1,957.46	1,900.57
7.00%	6,237.38	4,754.19	4,294.62	3,657.42	2,831.31	2,442.19	2,226.35	2,095.70	2,012.40	1,957.51
7.25%	6,274.60	4,792.78	4,333.92	3,698.13	2,875.52	2,489.68	2,276.84	2,148.86	2,067.87	2,014.97
7.50%	6,311.95	4,831.56	4,373.42	3,739.11	2,920.09	2,537.62	2,327.82	2,202.53	2,123.86	2,072.92
7.75%	6,349.44	4,870.52	4,413.13	3,780.33	2,965.02	2,585.99	2,379.29	2,256.70	2,180.35	2,131.35
8.00%	6,387.06	4,909.66	4,453.05	3,821.82	3,010.30	2,634.79	2,431.22	2,311.36	2,237.32	2,190.23
8.25%	6,424.82	4,948.98	4,493.18	3,863.56	3,055.94	2,684.01	2,483.62	2,366.49	2,294.75	2,249.54
8.50%	6,462.71	4,988.49	4,533.52	3,905.55	3,101.93	2,733.64	2,536.47	2,422.08	2,352.61	2,309.25
8.75%	6,500.73	5,028.19	4,574.06	3,947.79	3,148.26	2,783.69	2,589.75	2,478.11	2,410.89	2,369.34
9.00%	6,538.88	5,068.06	4,614.81	3,990.29	3,194.94	2,834.14	2,643.47	2,534.56	2,469.58	2,429.79
9.25%	6,577.17	5,108.12	4,655.77	4,033.03	3,241.96	2,884.98	2,697.60	2,591.43	2,528.64	2,490.58
9.50%	6,615.59	5,148.35	4,696.93	4,076.02	3,289.31	2,936.21	2,752.14	2,648.69	2,588.08	2,551.69
9.75%	6,654.14	5,188.77	4,738.29	4,119.26	3,336.99	2,987.83	2,807.08	2,706.34	2,647.86	2,613.11
10.00%	6,692.82	5,229.37	4,779.86	4,162.75	3,385.01	3,039.82	2,862.41	2,764.35	2,707.97	2,674.81
10.25%	6,731.63	5,270.15	4,821.63	4,206.48	3,433.35	3,092.18	2,918.11	2,822.72	2,768.40	2,736.78
10.50%	6,770.58	5,311.11	4,863.61	4,250.45	3,482.01	3,144.90	2,974.17	2,881.43	2,829.12	2,799.00
10.75%	6,809.66	5,352.25	4,905.78	4,294.67	3,530.99	3,197.97	3,030.59	2,940.47	2,890.13	2,861.45

$315,000   11.00 - 20.75%   5 - 40 Years

	5	7	8	10	15	20	25	30	35	40
11.00%	6,848.86	5,393.57	4,948.15	4,339.13	3,580.28	3,251.39	3,087.36	2,999.82	2,951.42	2,924.13
11.25%	6,888.20	5,435.06	4,990.73	4,383.82	3,629.89	3,305.16	3,144.45	3,059.47	3,012.96	2,987.01
11.50%	6,927.67	5,476.74	5,033.50	4,428.76	3,679.80	3,359.25	3,201.88	3,119.42	3,074.74	3,050.09
11.75%	6,967.27	5,518.58	5,076.48	4,473.93	3,730.01	3,413.68	3,259.61	3,179.64	3,136.75	3,113.35
12.00%	7,007.00	5,560.61	5,119.65	4,519.33	3,780.53	3,468.42	3,317.66	3,240.13	3,198.98	3,176.77
12.25%	7,046.86	5,602.81	5,163.01	4,564.98	3,831.34	3,523.48	3,375.99	3,300.87	3,261.42	3,240.36
12.50%	7,086.85	5,645.19	5,206.57	4,610.85	3,882.44	3,578.84	3,434.62	3,361.86	3,324.05	3,304.10
12.75%	7,126.97	5,687.74	5,250.33	4,656.95	3,933.84	3,634.51	3,493.51	3,423.08	3,386.87	3,367.97
13.00%	7,167.22	5,730.47	5,294.29	4,703.29	3,985.51	3,690.46	3,552.68	3,484.53	3,449.86	3,431.97
13.25%	7,207.60	5,773.37	5,338.43	4,749.85	4,037.47	3,746.71	3,612.11	3,546.19	3,513.01	3,496.09
13.50%	7,248.10	5,816.44	5,382.77	4,796.64	4,089.70	3,803.23	3,671.78	3,608.05	3,576.32	3,560.32
13.75%	7,288.74	5,859.69	5,427.30	4,843.65	4,142.21	3,860.03	3,731.70	3,670.10	3,639.78	3,624.66
14.00%	7,329.50	5,903.10	5,472.02	4,890.89	4,194.99	3,917.09	3,791.85	3,732.35	3,703.37	3,689.09
14.25%	7,370.39	5,946.69	5,516.93	4,938.35	4,248.03	3,974.41	3,852.22	3,794.76	3,767.09	3,753.61
14.50%	7,411.41	5,990.45	5,562.04	4,986.03	4,301.33	4,031.99	3,912.81	3,857.35	3,830.94	3,818.22
14.75%	7,452.55	6,034.38	5,607.33	5,033.93	4,354.89	4,089.82	3,973.61	3,920.10	3,894.90	3,882.90
15.00%	7,493.83	6,078.48	5,652.80	5,082.05	4,408.70	4,147.89	4,034.62	3,983.00	3,958.96	3,947.66
15.25%	7,535.23	6,122.74	5,698.47	5,130.38	4,462.76	4,206.19	4,095.81	4,046.04	4,023.13	4,012.48
15.50%	7,576.76	6,167.18	5,744.32	5,178.93	4,517.07	4,264.72	4,157.20	4,109.23	4,087.39	4,077.36
15.75%	7,618.41	6,211.78	5,790.35	5,227.69	4,571.62	4,323.48	4,218.76	4,172.54	4,151.74	4,142.30
16.00%	7,660.19	6,256.55	5,836.57	5,276.66	4,626.41	4,382.46	4,280.50	4,235.98	4,216.18	4,207.29
16.25%	7,702.09	6,301.48	5,882.97	5,325.84	4,681.43	4,441.64	4,342.41	4,299.54	4,280.69	4,272.33
16.50%	7,744.12	6,346.59	5,929.55	5,375.23	4,736.68	4,501.04	4,404.47	4,363.22	4,345.28	4,337.42
16.75%	7,786.28	6,391.85	5,976.31	5,424.83	4,792.16	4,560.63	4,466.69	4,427.00	4,409.94	4,402.55
17.00%	7,828.56	6,437.28	6,023.26	5,474.63	4,847.86	4,620.42	4,529.06	4,490.88	4,474.66	4,467.72
17.25%	7,870.97	6,482.87	6,070.38	5,524.63	4,903.78	4,680.40	4,591.57	4,554.86	4,539.44	4,532.92
17.50%	7,913.50	6,528.63	6,117.68	5,574.83	4,959.92	4,740.57	4,654.22	4,618.92	4,604.28	4,598.16
17.75%	7,956.15	6,574.54	6,165.16	5,625.23	5,016.27	4,800.91	4,717.00	4,683.08	4,669.17	4,663.43
18.00%	7,998.93	6,620.62	6,212.81	5,675.83	5,072.83	4,861.43	4,779.90	4,747.32	4,734.11	4,728.72
18.25%	8,041.83	6,666.86	6,260.64	5,726.63	5,129.59	4,922.12	4,842.93	4,811.64	4,799.10	4,794.05
18.50%	8,084.86	6,713.25	6,308.64	5,777.62	5,186.55	4,982.97	4,906.08	4,876.03	4,864.13	4,859.39
18.75%	8,128.00	6,759.81	6,356.82	5,828.80	5,243.71	5,043.99	4,969.33	4,940.49	4,929.20	4,924.76
19.00%	8,171.27	6,806.53	6,405.17	5,880.18	5,301.06	5,105.16	5,032.69	5,005.01	4,994.31	4,990.15
19.25%	8,214.67	6,853.40	6,453.69	5,931.74	5,358.60	5,166.48	5,096.16	5,069.60	5,059.45	5,055.56
19.50%	8,258.18	6,900.43	6,502.37	5,983.49	5,416.33	5,227.94	5,159.72	5,134.25	5,124.63	5,120.98
19.75%	8,301.82	6,947.61	6,551.23	6,035.43	5,474.24	5,289.55	5,223.38	5,198.95	5,189.84	5,186.43
20.00%	8,345.57	6,994.95	6,600.26	6,087.55	5,532.33	5,351.30	5,287.12	5,263.71	5,255.08	5,251.88
20.25%	8,389.45	7,042.45	6,649.45	6,139.86	5,590.60	5,413.18	5,350.96	5,328.52	5,320.34	5,317.35
20.50%	8,433.45	7,090.10	6,698.81	6,192.34	5,649.04	5,475.19	5,414.87	5,393.37	5,385.63	5,382.83
20.75%	8,477.57	7,137.90	6,748.33	6,245.01	5,707.65	5,537.32	5,478.87	5,458.27	5,450.94	5,448.33

	5	7	8	10	15	20	25	30	35	40
1.00%	5,470.00	3,946.00	3,469.83	2,803.33	1,915.18	1,471.66	1,205.99	1,029.25	903.31	809.14
1.25%	5,504.51	3,980.60	3,504.51	2,838.19	1,950.57	1,507.63	1,242.55	1,066.41	941.08	847.50
1.50%	5,539.16	4,015.40	3,539.41	2,873.33	1,986.38	1,544.15	1,279.80	1,104.38	979.79	886.95
1.75%	5,573.95	4,050.39	3,574.54	2,908.74	2,022.60	1,581.21	1,317.73	1,143.18	1,019.45	927.47
2.00%	5,608.88	4,085.58	3,609.88	2,944.43	2,059.23	1,618.83	1,356.33	1,182.78	1,060.04	969.04
2.25%	5,643.95	4,120.96	3,645.44	2,980.40	2,096.27	1,656.99	1,395.62	1,223.19	1,101.56	1,011.65
2.50%	5,679.16	4,156.53	3,681.23	3,016.64	2,133.73	1,695.69	1,435.57	1,264.39	1,143.98	1,055.29
2.75%	5,714.50	4,192.30	3,717.24	3,053.15	2,171.59	1,734.93	1,476.19	1,306.37	1,187.31	1,099.93
3.00%	5,749.98	4,228.26	3,753.46	3,089.94	2,209.86	1,774.71	1,517.48	1,349.13	1,231.52	1,145.55
3.25%	5,785.60	4,264.41	3,789.91	3,127.01	2,248.54	1,815.03	1,559.41	1,392.66	1,276.60	1,192.13
3.50%	5,821.36	4,300.75	3,826.58	3,164.35	2,287.62	1,855.87	1,602.00	1,436.94	1,322.53	1,239.65
3.75%	5,857.25	4,337.29	3,863.46	3,201.96	2,327.11	1,897.24	1,645.22	1,481.97	1,369.30	1,288.08
4.00%	5,893.29	4,374.02	3,900.57	3,239.84	2,367.00	1,939.14	1,689.08	1,527.73	1,416.88	1,337.40
4.25%	5,929.46	4,410.94	3,937.89	3,278.00	2,407.29	1,981.55	1,733.56	1,574.21	1,465.26	1,387.58
4.50%	5,965.77	4,448.05	3,975.44	3,316.43	2,447.98	2,024.48	1,778.66	1,621.39	1,514.42	1,438.60
4.75%	6,002.21	4,485.36	4,013.20	3,355.13	2,489.06	2,067.92	1,824.38	1,669.27	1,564.34	1,490.43
5.00%	6,038.79	4,522.85	4,051.17	3,394.10	2,530.54	2,111.86	1,870.69	1,717.83	1,615.00	1,543.03
5.25%	6,075.51	4,560.54	4,089.37	3,433.33	2,572.41	2,156.30	1,917.59	1,767.05	1,666.38	1,596.39
5.50%	6,112.37	4,598.41	4,127.78	3,472.84	2,614.67	2,201.24	1,965.08	1,816.92	1,718.45	1,650.46
5.75%	6,149.37	4,636.48	4,166.41	3,512.62	2,657.31	2,246.67	2,013.14	1,867.43	1,771.20	1,705.24
6.00%	6,186.50	4,674.74	4,205.26	3,552.66	2,700.34	2,292.58	2,061.76	1,918.56	1,824.61	1,760.68
6.25%	6,223.76	4,713.18	4,244.32	3,592.96	2,743.75	2,338.97	2,110.94	1,970.30	1,878.64	1,816.77
6.50%	6,261.17	4,751.82	4,283.59	3,633.54	2,787.54	2,385.83	2,160.66	2,022.62	1,933.29	1,873.46
6.75%	6,298.71	4,790.64	4,323.08	3,674.37	2,831.71	2,433.16	2,210.92	2,075.51	1,988.53	1,930.74
7.00%	6,336.38	4,829.66	4,362.79	3,715.47	2,876.25	2,480.96	2,261.69	2,128.97	2,044.34	1,988.58
7.25%	6,374.20	4,868.86	4,402.71	3,756.83	2,921.16	2,529.20	2,312.98	2,182.96	2,100.70	2,046.95
7.50%	6,412.14	4,908.25	4,442.84	3,798.46	2,966.44	2,577.90	2,364.77	2,237.49	2,157.58	2,105.83
7.75%	6,450.23	4,947.82	4,483.18	3,840.34	3,012.08	2,627.04	2,417.05	2,292.52	2,214.96	2,165.18
8.00%	6,488.45	4,987.59	4,523.74	3,882.48	3,058.09	2,676.61	2,469.81	2,348.05	2,272.83	2,225.00
8.25%	6,526.80	5,027.54	4,564.50	3,924.88	3,104.45	2,726.61	2,523.04	2,404.05	2,331.17	2,285.24
8.50%	6,565.29	5,067.68	4,605.48	3,967.54	3,151.17	2,777.03	2,576.73	2,460.52	2,389.95	2,345.90
8.75%	6,603.91	5,108.00	4,646.67	4,010.46	3,198.24	2,827.87	2,630.86	2,517.44	2,449.16	2,406.95
9.00%	6,642.67	5,148.51	4,688.07	4,053.62	3,245.65	2,879.12	2,685.43	2,574.79	2,508.78	2,468.36
9.25%	6,681.57	5,189.20	4,729.67	4,097.05	3,293.42	2,930.77	2,740.42	2,632.56	2,568.78	2,530.11
9.50%	6,720.60	5,230.07	4,771.48	4,140.72	3,341.52	2,982.82	2,795.83	2,690.73	2,629.16	2,592.20
9.75%	6,759.76	5,271.13	4,813.50	4,184.65	3,389.96	3,035.25	2,851.64	2,749.29	2,689.89	2,654.59
10.00%	6,799.05	5,312.38	4,855.73	4,228.82	3,438.74	3,088.07	2,907.84	2,808.23	2,750.95	2,717.27
10.25%	6,838.48	5,353.81	4,898.17	4,273.25	3,487.84	3,141.26	2,964.43	2,867.52	2,812.34	2,780.22
10.50%	6,878.05	5,395.42	4,940.81	4,317.92	3,537.28	3,194.82	3,021.38	2,927.17	2,874.03	2,843.42
10.75%	6,917.75	5,437.21	4,983.65	4,362.84	3,587.03	3,248.73	3,078.70	2,987.14	2,936.01	2,906.87

$320,000   11.00 - 20.75%   5 - 40 Years

	5	7	8	10	15	20	25	30	35	40
11.00%	6,957.58	5,479.18	5,026.70	4,408.00	3,637.11	3,303.00	3,136.36	3,047.43	2,998.26	2,970.54
11.25%	6,997.54	5,521.33	5,069.95	4,453.41	3,687.50	3,357.62	3,194.37	3,108.04	3,060.78	3,034.42
11.50%	7,037.63	5,563.67	5,113.40	4,499.05	3,738.21	3,412.57	3,252.70	3,168.93	3,123.54	3,098.50
11.75%	7,077.86	5,606.18	5,157.05	4,544.94	3,789.22	3,467.86	3,311.35	3,230.11	3,186.54	3,162.76
12.00%	7,118.22	5,648.87	5,200.91	4,591.07	3,840.54	3,523.48	3,370.32	3,291.56	3,249.76	3,227.20
12.25%	7,158.72	5,691.75	5,244.96	4,637.44	3,892.16	3,579.41	3,429.58	3,353.27	3,313.19	3,291.80
12.50%	7,199.34	5,734.80	5,289.22	4,684.04	3,944.07	3,635.65	3,489.13	3,415.22	3,376.81	3,356.54
12.75%	7,240.10	5,778.02	5,333.67	4,730.87	3,996.28	3,692.20	3,548.97	3,477.42	3,440.63	3,421.43
13.00%	7,280.98	5,821.43	5,378.32	4,777.94	4,048.77	3,749.04	3,609.07	3,539.84	3,504.62	3,486.45
13.25%	7,322.00	5,865.01	5,423.17	4,825.25	4,101.56	3,806.18	3,669.44	3,602.48	3,568.78	3,551.58
13.50%	7,363.15	5,908.77	5,468.21	4,872.78	4,154.62	3,863.60	3,730.06	3,665.32	3,633.09	3,616.84
13.75%	7,404.43	5,952.70	5,513.45	4,920.54	4,207.96	3,921.30	3,790.93	3,728.36	3,697.55	3,682.19
14.00%	7,445.84	5,996.80	5,558.88	4,968.53	4,261.57	3,979.27	3,852.04	3,791.59	3,762.15	3,747.65
14.25%	7,487.38	6,041.08	5,604.51	5,016.74	4,315.45	4,037.50	3,913.37	3,855.00	3,826.89	3,813.19
14.50%	7,529.05	6,085.54	5,650.32	5,065.18	4,369.60	4,095.99	3,974.92	3,918.58	3,891.75	3,878.83
14.75%	7,570.85	6,130.16	5,696.33	5,113.84	4,424.01	4,154.74	4,036.69	3,982.32	3,956.72	3,944.53
15.00%	7,612.78	6,174.96	5,742.53	5,162.72	4,478.68	4,213.73	4,098.66	4,046.22	4,021.80	4,010.32
15.25%	7,654.84	6,219.93	5,788.92	5,211.82	4,533.60	4,272.96	4,160.83	4,110.27	4,086.99	4,076.17
15.50%	7,697.02	6,265.07	5,835.50	5,261.14	4,588.77	4,332.42	4,223.18	4,174.45	4,152.27	4,142.08
15.75%	7,739.34	6,310.38	5,882.26	5,310.67	4,644.18	4,392.11	4,285.73	4,238.77	4,217.64	4,208.00
16.00%	7,781.78	6,355.86	5,929.21	5,360.42	4,699.84	4,452.02	4,348.44	4,303.22	4,283.10	4,274.08
16.25%	7,824.35	6,401.51	5,976.35	5,410.38	4,755.74	4,512.15	4,411.33	4,367.79	4,348.64	4,340.15
16.50%	7,867.05	6,447.32	6,023.67	5,460.55	4,811.87	4,572.48	4,474.38	4,432.47	4,414.25	4,406.27
16.75%	7,909.87	6,493.31	6,071.18	5,510.94	4,868.23	4,633.02	4,537.59	4,497.27	4,479.94	4,472.43
17.00%	7,952.82	6,539.46	6,118.87	5,561.52	4,924.81	4,693.76	4,600.95	4,562.16	4,545.68	4,538.64
17.25%	7,995.90	6,585.77	6,166.74	5,612.32	4,981.62	4,754.69	4,664.45	4,627.15	4,611.49	4,604.87
17.50%	8,039.11	6,632.25	6,214.79	5,663.32	5,038.65	4,815.81	4,728.10	4,692.24	4,677.36	4,671.15
17.75%	8,082.44	6,678.90	6,263.02	5,714.52	5,095.89	4,877.12	4,791.87	4,757.42	4,743.28	4,737.45
18.00%	8,125.90	6,725.71	6,311.43	5,765.93	5,153.35	4,938.60	4,855.78	4,822.67	4,809.25	4,803.78
18.25%	8,169.48	6,772.68	6,360.02	5,817.53	5,211.01	5,000.25	4,919.80	4,888.01	4,875.27	4,870.14
18.50%	8,213.19	6,819.81	6,408.78	5,869.33	5,268.87	5,062.07	4,983.95	4,953.42	4,941.34	4,936.53
18.75%	8,257.02	6,867.11	6,457.72	5,921.33	5,326.94	5,124.05	5,048.21	5,018.91	5,007.44	5,002.93
19.00%	8,300.98	6,914.57	6,506.84	5,973.52	5,385.20	5,186.19	5,112.58	5,084.46	5,073.58	5,069.36
19.25%	8,345.06	6,962.18	6,556.13	6,025.90	5,443.66	5,248.48	5,177.05	5,150.07	5,139.76	5,135.81
19.50%	8,389.26	7,009.96	6,605.59	6,078.47	5,502.30	5,310.93	5,241.62	5,215.74	5,205.97	5,202.27
19.75%	8,433.59	7,057.89	6,655.22	6,131.23	5,561.14	5,373.51	5,306.29	5,281.47	5,272.22	5,268.75
20.00%	8,478.04	7,105.98	6,705.02	6,184.18	5,620.15	5,436.24	5,371.05	5,347.26	5,338.49	5,335.25
20.25%	8,522.62	7,154.23	6,755.00	6,237.32	5,679.34	5,499.10	5,435.89	5,413.10	5,404.79	5,401.75
20.50%	8,567.31	7,202.64	6,805.14	6,290.63	5,738.71	5,562.09	5,500.82	5,478.98	5,471.12	5,468.28
20.75%	8,612.13	7,251.20	6,855.45	6,344.13	5,798.25	5,625.21	5,565.83	5,544.91	5,537.47	5,534.81

	5	7	8	10	15	20	25	30	35	40
1.00%	5,555.47	4,007.66	3,524.05	2,847.13	1,945.11	1,494.66	1,224.84	1,045.33	917.43	821.78
1.25%	5,590.52	4,042.80	3,559.27	2,882.54	1,981.05	1,531.18	1,261.97	1,083.07	955.78	860.75
1.50%	5,625.71	4,078.14	3,594.72	2,918.22	2,017.41	1,568.27	1,299.79	1,121.64	995.10	900.81
1.75%	5,661.05	4,113.68	3,630.39	2,954.19	2,054.20	1,605.92	1,338.31	1,161.04	1,035.38	941.96
2.00%	5,696.52	4,149.42	3,666.28	2,990.44	2,091.40	1,644.12	1,377.53	1,201.26	1,076.60	984.18
2.25%	5,732.14	4,185.35	3,702.40	3,026.96	2,129.03	1,682.88	1,417.42	1,242.30	1,118.77	1,027.46
2.50%	5,767.89	4,221.48	3,738.75	3,063.77	2,167.06	1,722.18	1,458.00	1,284.14	1,161.86	1,071.78
2.75%	5,803.79	4,257.80	3,775.32	3,100.86	2,205.52	1,762.04	1,499.26	1,326.78	1,205.86	1,117.12
3.00%	5,839.82	4,294.32	3,812.11	3,138.22	2,244.39	1,802.44	1,541.19	1,370.21	1,250.76	1,163.45
3.25%	5,876.00	4,331.04	3,849.13	3,175.87	2,283.67	1,843.39	1,583.78	1,414.42	1,296.55	1,210.76
3.50%	5,912.32	4,367.95	3,886.37	3,213.79	2,323.37	1,884.87	1,627.03	1,459.40	1,343.19	1,259.02
3.75%	5,948.77	4,405.06	3,923.83	3,251.99	2,363.47	1,926.89	1,670.93	1,505.13	1,390.69	1,308.21
4.00%	5,985.37	4,442.36	3,961.51	3,290.47	2,403.99	1,969.44	1,715.47	1,551.60	1,439.02	1,358.30
4.25%	6,022.11	4,479.86	3,999.42	3,329.22	2,444.90	2,012.51	1,760.65	1,598.80	1,488.16	1,409.27
4.50%	6,058.98	4,517.55	4,037.55	3,368.25	2,486.23	2,056.11	1,806.46	1,646.73	1,538.08	1,461.08
4.75%	6,096.00	4,555.44	4,075.90	3,407.55	2,527.95	2,100.23	1,852.88	1,695.35	1,588.78	1,513.71
5.00%	6,133.15	4,593.52	4,114.47	3,447.13	2,570.08	2,144.86	1,899.92	1,744.67	1,640.23	1,567.14
5.25%	6,170.44	4,631.80	4,153.27	3,486.98	2,612.60	2,189.99	1,947.56	1,794.66	1,692.41	1,621.33
5.50%	6,207.88	4,670.26	4,192.28	3,527.10	2,655.52	2,235.63	1,995.78	1,845.31	1,745.30	1,676.25
5.75%	6,245.45	4,708.93	4,231.51	3,567.50	2,698.83	2,281.77	2,044.60	1,896.61	1,798.88	1,731.88
6.00%	6,283.16	4,747.78	4,270.96	3,608.17	2,742.53	2,328.40	2,093.98	1,948.54	1,853.12	1,788.19
6.25%	6,321.01	4,786.83	4,310.64	3,649.10	2,786.62	2,375.52	2,143.93	2,001.08	1,908.00	1,845.15
6.50%	6,359.00	4,826.07	4,350.53	3,690.31	2,831.10	2,423.11	2,194.42	2,054.22	1,963.50	1,902.73
6.75%	6,397.12	4,865.50	4,390.63	3,731.78	2,875.96	2,471.18	2,245.46	2,107.94	2,019.60	1,960.91
7.00%	6,435.39	4,905.12	4,430.96	3,773.53	2,921.19	2,519.72	2,297.03	2,162.23	2,076.28	2,019.65
7.25%	6,473.79	4,944.93	4,471.50	3,815.53	2,966.80	2,568.72	2,349.12	2,217.07	2,133.52	2,078.93
7.50%	6,512.33	4,984.94	4,512.26	3,857.81	3,012.79	2,618.18	2,401.72	2,272.45	2,191.29	2,138.73
7.75%	6,551.01	5,025.13	4,553.23	3,900.35	3,059.15	2,668.08	2,454.82	2,328.34	2,249.57	2,199.01
8.00%	6,589.83	5,065.52	4,594.42	3,943.15	3,105.87	2,718.43	2,508.40	2,384.73	2,308.35	2,259.76
8.25%	6,628.78	5,106.09	4,635.82	3,986.21	3,152.96	2,769.21	2,562.46	2,441.62	2,367.60	2,320.95
8.50%	6,667.87	5,146.86	4,677.44	4,029.53	3,200.40	2,820.43	2,616.99	2,498.97	2,427.30	2,382.56
8.75%	6,707.10	5,187.81	4,719.27	4,073.12	3,248.21	2,872.06	2,671.97	2,556.78	2,487.43	2,444.55
9.00%	6,746.47	5,228.95	4,761.32	4,116.96	3,296.37	2,924.11	2,727.39	2,615.02	2,547.98	2,506.92
9.25%	6,785.97	5,270.28	4,803.57	4,161.06	3,344.87	2,976.57	2,783.24	2,673.70	2,608.92	2,569.65
9.50%	6,825.60	5,311.79	4,846.04	4,205.42	3,393.73	3,029.43	2,839.51	2,732.78	2,670.24	2,632.70
9.75%	6,865.38	5,353.50	4,888.72	4,250.03	3,442.93	3,082.68	2,896.20	2,792.25	2,731.92	2,696.07
10.00%	6,905.29	5,395.38	4,931.60	4,294.90	3,492.47	3,136.32	2,953.28	2,852.11	2,793.94	2,759.72
10.25%	6,945.34	5,437.46	4,974.70	4,340.02	3,542.34	3,190.34	3,010.75	2,912.33	2,856.28	2,823.66
10.50%	6,985.52	5,479.72	5,018.01	4,385.39	3,592.55	3,244.73	3,068.59	2,972.90	2,918.94	2,887.85
10.75%	7,025.83	5,522.16	5,061.52	4,431.01	3,643.08	3,299.49	3,126.80	3,033.81	2,981.88	2,952.29

	5	7	8	10	15	20	25	30	35	40
11.00%	7,066.29	5,564.79	5,105.24	4,476.88	3,693.94	3,354.61	3,185.37	3,095.05	3,045.11	3,016.96
11.25%	7,106.88	5,607.60	5,149.16	4,522.99	3,745.12	3,410.08	3,244.28	3,156.60	3,108.61	3,081.84
11.50%	7,147.60	5,650.60	5,193.30	4,569.35	3,796.62	3,465.90	3,303.52	3,218.45	3,172.35	3,146.92
11.75%	7,188.45	5,693.78	5,237.63	4,615.96	3,848.43	3,522.05	3,363.09	3,280.58	3,236.33	3,212.18
12.00%	7,229.45	5,737.14	5,282.17	4,662.81	3,900.55	3,578.53	3,422.98	3,342.99	3,300.54	3,277.62
12.25%	7,270.57	5,780.68	5,326.92	4,709.90	3,952.97	3,635.34	3,483.17	3,405.66	3,364.96	3,343.23
12.50%	7,311.83	5,824.40	5,371.86	4,757.23	4,005.70	3,692.46	3,543.65	3,468.59	3,429.58	3,408.99
12.75%	7,353.22	5,868.31	5,417.01	4,804.79	4,058.72	3,749.89	3,604.42	3,531.75	3,494.39	3,474.89
13.00%	7,394.75	5,912.39	5,462.36	4,852.60	4,112.04	3,807.62	3,665.46	3,595.15	3,559.38	3,540.92
13.25%	7,436.41	5,956.65	5,507.91	4,900.64	4,165.64	3,865.65	3,726.78	3,658.76	3,624.54	3,607.08
13.50%	7,478.20	6,001.09	5,553.65	4,948.91	4,219.54	3,923.97	3,788.35	3,722.59	3,689.86	3,673.35
13.75%	7,520.12	6,045.71	5,599.60	4,997.42	4,273.71	3,982.57	3,850.16	3,786.62	3,755.33	3,739.73
14.00%	7,562.18	6,090.50	5,645.74	5,046.16	4,328.16	4,041.44	3,912.22	3,850.83	3,820.94	3,806.21
14.25%	7,604.37	6,135.48	5,692.08	5,095.13	4,382.88	4,100.59	3,974.51	3,915.23	3,886.68	3,872.78
14.50%	7,646.69	6,180.62	5,738.61	5,144.32	4,437.88	4,159.99	4,037.03	3,979.81	3,952.55	3,939.43
14.75%	7,689.14	6,225.95	5,785.34	5,193.74	4,493.14	4,219.65	4,099.76	4,044.55	4,018.54	4,006.17
15.00%	7,731.73	6,271.45	5,832.26	5,243.39	4,548.66	4,279.57	4,162.70	4,109.44	4,084.64	4,072.98
15.25%	7,774.44	6,317.12	5,879.37	5,293.25	4,604.44	4,339.72	4,225.84	4,174.49	4,150.85	4,139.86
15.50%	7,817.29	6,362.96	5,926.67	5,343.34	4,660.47	4,400.11	4,289.17	4,239.68	4,217.15	4,206.80
15.75%	7,860.26	6,408.98	5,974.17	5,393.65	4,716.75	4,460.73	4,352.69	4,305.01	4,283.54	4,273.80
16.00%	7,903.37	6,455.17	6,021.86	5,444.18	4,773.28	4,521.58	4,416.39	4,370.46	4,350.03	4,340.86
16.25%	7,946.60	6,501.53	6,069.73	5,494.92	4,830.05	4,582.65	4,480.26	4,436.04	4,416.59	4,407.96
16.50%	7,989.97	6,548.06	6,117.79	5,545.87	4,887.05	4,643.93	4,544.30	4,501.73	4,483.23	4,475.12
16.75%	8,033.46	6,594.77	6,166.04	5,597.04	4,944.29	4,705.41	4,608.49	4,567.54	4,549.93	4,542.31
17.00%	8,077.09	6,641.64	6,214.47	5,648.42	5,001.76	4,767.10	4,672.84	4,633.44	4,616.71	4,609.55
17.25%	8,120.84	6,688.68	6,263.09	5,700.01	5,059.46	4,828.99	4,737.33	4,699.45	4,683.55	4,676.83
17.50%	8,164.72	6,735.88	6,311.89	5,751.81	5,117.38	4,891.06	4,801.97	4,765.56	4,750.44	4,744.13
17.75%	8,208.73	6,783.26	6,360.88	5,803.81	5,175.52	4,953.32	4,866.74	4,831.75	4,817.40	4,811.47
18.00%	8,252.86	6,830.80	6,410.04	5,856.02	5,233.87	5,015.76	4,931.65	4,898.03	4,884.40	4,878.84
18.25%	8,297.13	6,878.50	6,459.39	5,908.43	5,292.43	5,078.38	4,996.68	4,964.39	4,951.45	4,946.24
18.50%	8,341.52	6,926.37	6,508.92	5,961.04	5,351.20	5,141.16	5,061.82	5,030.82	5,018.54	5,013.66
18.75%	8,386.04	6,974.41	6,558.62	6,013.85	5,410.17	5,204.11	5,127.09	5,097.33	5,085.68	5,081.10
19.00%	8,430.68	7,022.61	6,608.51	6,066.85	5,469.35	5,267.23	5,192.46	5,163.90	5,152.86	5,148.57
19.25%	8,475.45	7,070.97	6,658.57	6,120.05	5,528.72	5,330.49	5,257.94	5,230.54	5,220.07	5,216.05
19.50%	8,520.34	7,119.49	6,708.80	6,173.45	5,588.28	5,393.91	5,323.52	5,297.24	5,287.32	5,283.55
19.75%	8,565.37	7,168.17	6,759.21	6,227.03	5,648.03	5,457.47	5,389.20	5,364.00	5,354.60	5,351.07
20.00%	8,610.51	7,217.01	6,809.79	6,280.81	5,707.96	5,521.18	5,454.97	5,430.81	5,421.90	5,418.61
20.25%	8,655.78	7,266.02	6,860.54	6,334.77	5,768.08	5,585.02	5,520.83	5,497.68	5,489.24	5,486.16
20.50%	8,701.18	7,315.18	6,911.47	6,388.92	5,828.38	5,649.00	5,586.77	5,564.59	5,556.60	5,553.72
20.75%	8,746.70	7,364.50	6,962.56	6,443.26	5,888.85	5,713.11	5,652.80	5,631.55	5,623.99	5,621.29

	5	7	8	10	15	20	25	30	35	40
1.00%	5,640.94	4,069.31	3,578.26	2,890.94	1,975.03	1,517.65	1,243.68	1,061.41	931.54	834.42
1.25%	5,676.53	4,105.00	3,614.03	2,926.88	2,011.53	1,554.74	1,281.38	1,099.73	970.48	873.99
1.50%	5,712.26	4,140.88	3,650.02	2,963.12	2,048.45	1,592.40	1,319.79	1,138.90	1,010.41	914.67
1.75%	5,748.14	4,176.97	3,686.24	2,999.64	2,085.80	1,630.63	1,358.90	1,178.90	1,051.31	956.45
2.00%	5,784.16	4,213.25	3,722.69	3,036.44	2,123.58	1,669.42	1,398.72	1,219.74	1,093.17	999.32
2.25%	5,820.32	4,249.74	3,759.36	3,073.53	2,161.78	1,708.77	1,439.23	1,261.41	1,135.98	1,043.27
2.50%	5,856.63	4,286.42	3,796.27	3,110.91	2,200.40	1,748.68	1,480.44	1,303.90	1,179.73	1,088.27
2.75%	5,893.08	4,323.31	3,833.40	3,148.56	2,239.45	1,789.15	1,522.33	1,347.20	1,224.41	1,134.30
3.00%	5,929.67	4,360.39	3,870.76	3,186.50	2,278.92	1,830.17	1,564.90	1,391.29	1,270.01	1,181.35
3.25%	5,966.40	4,397.67	3,908.34	3,224.73	2,318.81	1,871.75	1,608.14	1,436.18	1,316.49	1,229.39
3.50%	6,003.28	4,435.15	3,946.16	3,263.23	2,359.11	1,913.87	1,652.06	1,481.85	1,363.86	1,278.39
3.75%	6,040.29	4,472.83	3,984.20	3,302.02	2,399.83	1,956.53	1,696.63	1,528.28	1,412.09	1,328.34
4.00%	6,077.45	4,510.71	4,022.46	3,341.09	2,440.97	1,999.74	1,741.86	1,575.47	1,461.16	1,379.20
4.25%	6,114.75	4,548.78	4,060.95	3,380.44	2,482.52	2,043.47	1,787.74	1,623.40	1,511.05	1,430.95
4.50%	6,152.20	4,587.05	4,099.67	3,420.07	2,524.48	2,087.74	1,834.25	1,672.06	1,561.75	1,483.56
4.75%	6,189.78	4,625.52	4,138.61	3,459.98	2,566.85	2,132.54	1,881.39	1,721.44	1,613.23	1,537.00
5.00%	6,227.51	4,664.19	4,177.77	3,500.16	2,609.62	2,177.85	1,929.15	1,771.51	1,665.47	1,591.25
5.25%	6,265.37	4,703.05	4,217.16	3,540.63	2,652.80	2,223.69	1,977.52	1,822.27	1,718.45	1,646.27
5.50%	6,303.38	4,742.11	4,256.78	3,581.37	2,696.38	2,270.03	2,026.49	1,873.70	1,772.15	1,702.04
5.75%	6,341.53	4,781.37	4,296.61	3,622.38	2,740.35	2,316.88	2,076.05	1,925.79	1,826.55	1,758.53
6.00%	6,379.82	4,820.82	4,336.67	3,663.68	2,784.73	2,364.22	2,126.19	1,978.52	1,881.63	1,815.71
6.25%	6,418.26	4,860.47	4,376.95	3,705.24	2,829.50	2,412.06	2,176.91	2,031.87	1,937.35	1,873.54
6.50%	6,456.83	4,900.31	4,417.46	3,747.08	2,874.65	2,460.39	2,228.18	2,085.82	1,993.71	1,932.01
6.75%	6,495.54	4,940.35	4,458.18	3,789.20	2,920.20	2,509.20	2,280.01	2,140.37	2,050.67	1,991.08
7.00%	6,534.40	4,980.58	4,499.13	3,831.58	2,966.13	2,558.49	2,332.37	2,195.50	2,108.23	2,050.72
7.25%	6,573.39	5,021.01	4,540.29	3,874.23	3,012.45	2,608.24	2,385.26	2,251.18	2,166.34	2,110.92
7.50%	6,612.52	5,061.63	4,581.68	3,917.16	3,059.14	2,658.46	2,438.67	2,307.41	2,225.00	2,171.63
7.75%	6,651.80	5,102.44	4,623.28	3,960.35	3,106.21	2,709.13	2,492.58	2,364.16	2,284.18	2,232.85
8.00%	6,691.21	5,143.45	4,665.10	4,003.81	3,153.65	2,760.25	2,546.99	2,421.42	2,343.86	2,294.53
8.25%	6,730.76	5,184.65	4,707.14	4,047.54	3,201.46	2,811.82	2,601.89	2,479.18	2,404.02	2,356.66
8.50%	6,770.46	5,226.04	4,749.40	4,091.53	3,249.64	2,863.82	2,657.25	2,537.41	2,464.64	2,419.21
8.75%	6,810.29	5,267.62	4,791.88	4,135.78	3,298.18	2,916.25	2,713.07	2,596.11	2,525.70	2,482.16
9.00%	6,850.26	5,309.40	4,834.57	4,180.30	3,347.08	2,969.10	2,769.35	2,655.25	2,587.18	2,545.49
9.25%	6,890.37	5,351.36	4,877.47	4,225.08	3,396.33	3,022.36	2,826.06	2,714.83	2,649.06	2,609.18
9.50%	6,930.61	5,393.51	4,920.59	4,270.12	3,445.94	3,076.03	2,883.20	2,774.82	2,711.32	2,673.20
9.75%	6,971.00	5,435.86	4,963.93	4,315.42	3,495.90	3,130.11	2,940.75	2,835.21	2,773.94	2,737.54
10.00%	7,011.52	5,478.39	5,007.47	4,360.97	3,546.20	3,184.57	2,998.71	2,895.99	2,836.92	2,802.18
10.25%	7,052.19	5,521.11	5,051.23	4,406.79	3,596.84	3,239.42	3,057.06	2,957.13	2,900.22	2,867.10
10.50%	7,092.99	5,564.02	5,095.21	4,452.85	3,647.82	3,294.65	3,115.80	3,018.64	2,963.84	2,932.28
10.75%	7,133.92	5,607.12	5,139.39	4,499.18	3,699.13	3,350.26	3,174.91	3,080.49	3,027.76	2,997.71

$330,000   11.00 - 20.75%   5 - 40 Years

	5	7	8	10	15	20	25	30	35	40
11.00%	7,175.00	5,650.40	5,183.78	4,545.75	3,750.77	3,406.22	3,234.37	3,142.67	3,091.96	3,063.37
11.25%	7,216.21	5,693.88	5,228.38	4,592.58	3,802.74	3,462.54	3,294.19	3,205.16	3,156.43	3,129.25
11.50%	7,257.56	5,737.53	5,273.19	4,639.65	3,855.03	3,519.22	3,354.35	3,267.96	3,221.15	3,195.33
11.75%	7,299.05	5,781.37	5,318.21	4,686.97	3,907.63	3,576.23	3,414.83	3,331.05	3,286.12	3,261.60
12.00%	7,340.67	5,825.40	5,363.44	4,734.54	3,960.55	3,633.58	3,475.64	3,394.42	3,351.31	3,328.05
12.25%	7,382.43	5,869.61	5,408.87	4,782.36	4,013.79	3,691.26	3,536.75	3,458.06	3,416.72	3,394.66
12.50%	7,424.32	5,914.01	5,454.51	4,830.41	4,067.32	3,749.26	3,598.17	3,521.95	3,482.34	3,461.43
12.75%	7,466.35	5,958.59	5,500.35	4,878.71	4,121.16	3,807.58	3,659.87	3,586.09	3,548.15	3,528.35
13.00%	7,508.51	6,003.35	5,546.39	4,927.25	4,175.30	3,866.20	3,721.86	3,650.46	3,614.14	3,595.40
13.25%	7,550.81	6,048.29	5,592.64	4,976.03	4,229.73	3,925.12	3,784.11	3,715.05	3,680.30	3,662.57
13.50%	7,593.25	6,093.41	5,639.09	5,025.05	4,284.45	3,984.34	3,846.63	3,779.86	3,746.62	3,729.86
13.75%	7,635.82	6,138.72	5,685.74	5,074.30	4,339.46	4,043.84	3,909.40	3,844.87	3,813.10	3,797.26
14.00%	7,678.52	6,184.20	5,732.60	5,123.79	4,394.75	4,103.62	3,972.41	3,910.08	3,879.72	3,864.76
14.25%	7,721.36	6,229.87	5,779.65	5,173.51	4,450.31	4,163.67	4,035.66	3,975.47	3,946.48	3,932.36
14.50%	7,764.33	6,275.71	5,826.89	5,223.46	4,506.15	4,223.99	4,099.14	4,041.03	4,013.36	4,000.04
14.75%	7,807.44	6,321.73	5,874.34	5,273.64	4,562.26	4,284.57	4,162.83	4,106.77	4,080.37	4,067.80
15.00%	7,850.68	6,367.93	5,921.98	5,324.05	4,618.64	4,345.41	4,226.74	4,172.67	4,147.48	4,135.64
15.25%	7,894.05	6,414.30	5,969.82	5,374.69	4,675.27	4,406.49	4,290.85	4,238.71	4,214.71	4,203.55
15.50%	7,937.55	6,460.85	6,017.85	5,425.55	4,732.17	4,467.81	4,355.16	4,304.91	4,282.03	4,271.52
15.75%	7,981.19	6,507.58	6,066.08	5,476.63	4,789.32	4,529.36	4,419.66	4,371.24	4,349.45	4,339.55
16.00%	8,024.96	6,554.48	6,114.50	5,527.93	4,846.71	4,591.14	4,484.33	4,437.70	4,416.95	4,407.64
16.25%	8,068.86	6,601.56	6,163.11	5,579.46	4,904.35	4,653.15	4,549.19	4,504.28	4,484.53	4,475.78
16.50%	8,112.89	6,648.80	6,211.91	5,631.20	4,962.24	4,715.37	4,614.21	4,570.99	4,552.20	4,543.97
16.75%	8,157.06	6,696.22	6,260.90	5,683.15	5,020.36	4,777.80	4,679.39	4,637.81	4,619.93	4,612.20
17.00%	8,201.35	6,743.82	6,310.08	5,735.32	5,078.71	4,840.44	4,744.73	4,704.73	4,687.74	4,680.47
17.25%	8,245.78	6,791.58	6,359.45	5,787.71	5,137.30	4,903.28	4,810.22	4,771.75	4,755.60	4,748.78
17.50%	8,290.33	6,839.51	6,409.00	5,840.30	5,196.11	4,966.31	4,875.85	4,838.87	4,823.53	4,817.12
17.75%	8,335.02	6,887.61	6,458.74	5,893.10	5,255.14	5,029.53	4,941.62	4,906.08	4,891.51	4,885.50
18.00%	8,379.83	6,935.89	6,508.66	5,946.11	5,314.39	5,092.93	5,007.52	4,973.38	4,959.54	4,953.90
18.25%	8,424.78	6,984.33	6,558.77	5,999.33	5,373.85	5,156.51	5,073.55	5,040.76	5,027.63	5,022.33
18.50%	8,469.85	7,032.93	6,609.06	6,052.75	5,433.53	5,220.26	5,139.70	5,108.22	5,095.75	5,090.79
18.75%	8,515.05	7,081.71	6,659.53	6,106.37	5,493.41	5,284.18	5,205.96	5,175.75	5,163.92	5,159.27
19.00%	8,560.38	7,130.65	6,710.18	6,160.19	5,553.49	5,348.26	5,272.34	5,243.35	5,232.13	5,227.78
19.25%	8,605.84	7,179.75	6,761.00	6,214.21	5,613.77	5,412.50	5,338.83	5,311.01	5,300.38	5,296.30
19.50%	8,651.43	7,229.02	6,812.01	6,268.42	5,674.25	5,476.89	5,405.42	5,378.74	5,368.66	5,364.84
19.75%	8,697.14	7,278.45	6,863.20	6,322.83	5,734.92	5,541.44	5,472.11	5,446.52	5,436.97	5,433.40
20.00%	8,742.98	7,328.05	6,914.56	6,377.44	5,795.78	5,606.12	5,538.89	5,514.36	5,505.32	5,501.97
20.25%	8,788.95	7,377.80	6,966.09	6,432.23	5,856.82	5,670.95	5,605.76	5,582.25	5,573.69	5,570.56
20.50%	8,835.04	7,427.72	7,017.80	6,487.22	5,918.04	5,735.91	5,672.72	5,650.20	5,642.09	5,639.16
20.75%	8,881.26	7,477.80	7,069.68	6,542.39	5,979.45	5,801.00	5,739.77	5,718.19	5,710.51	5,707.77

	5	7	8	10	15	20	25	30	35	40
1.00%	5,726.41	4,130.97	3,632.48	2,934.74	2,004.96	1,540.65	1,262.52	1,077.49	945.66	847.07
1.25%	5,762.54	4,167.19	3,668.79	2,971.23	2,042.01	1,578.30	1,300.80	1,116.39	985.19	887.23
1.50%	5,798.81	4,203.62	3,705.32	3,008.02	2,079.49	1,616.53	1,339.79	1,156.15	1,025.72	928.53
1.75%	5,835.23	4,240.26	3,742.09	3,045.09	2,117.41	1,655.33	1,379.49	1,196.77	1,067.23	970.94
2.00%	5,871.80	4,277.09	3,779.09	3,082.45	2,155.75	1,694.71	1,419.91	1,238.23	1,109.73	1,014.47
2.25%	5,908.51	4,314.13	3,816.32	3,120.10	2,194.53	1,734.66	1,461.04	1,280.52	1,153.19	1,059.08
2.50%	5,945.37	4,351.37	3,853.79	3,158.04	2,233.74	1,775.17	1,502.87	1,323.66	1,197.61	1,104.76
2.75%	5,982.37	4,388.81	3,891.48	3,196.27	2,273.38	1,816.26	1,545.39	1,367.61	1,242.97	1,151.49
3.00%	6,019.51	4,426.46	3,929.41	3,234.78	2,313.45	1,857.90	1,588.61	1,412.37	1,289.25	1,199.25
3.25%	6,056.80	4,464.30	3,967.56	3,273.59	2,353.94	1,900.11	1,632.51	1,457.94	1,336.44	1,248.01
3.50%	6,094.23	4,502.35	4,005.95	3,312.68	2,394.86	1,942.87	1,677.09	1,504.30	1,384.52	1,297.76
3.75%	6,131.81	4,540.60	4,044.56	3,352.05	2,436.20	1,986.18	1,722.34	1,551.44	1,433.48	1,348.46
4.00%	6,169.53	4,579.05	4,083.41	3,391.71	2,477.95	2,030.03	1,768.25	1,599.34	1,483.30	1,400.09
4.25%	6,207.40	4,617.70	4,122.48	3,431.66	2,520.13	2,074.44	1,814.82	1,648.00	1,533.94	1,452.63
4.50%	6,245.41	4,656.55	4,161.78	3,471.89	2,562.73	2,119.38	1,862.04	1,697.40	1,585.41	1,506.04
4.75%	6,283.57	4,695.61	4,201.31	3,512.40	2,605.74	2,164.85	1,909.89	1,747.52	1,637.67	1,560.29
5.00%	6,321.86	4,734.86	4,241.07	3,553.19	2,649.16	2,210.85	1,958.38	1,798.35	1,690.70	1,615.36
5.25%	6,360.30	4,774.31	4,281.06	3,594.27	2,692.99	2,257.38	2,007.48	1,849.88	1,744.49	1,671.22
5.50%	6,398.89	4,813.96	4,321.27	3,635.63	2,737.23	2,304.42	2,057.19	1,902.09	1,799.00	1,727.83
5.75%	6,437.62	4,853.82	4,361.71	3,677.27	2,781.87	2,351.98	2,107.51	1,954.97	1,854.23	1,785.17
6.00%	6,476.49	4,893.87	4,402.38	3,719.19	2,826.92	2,400.04	2,158.41	2,008.49	1,910.14	1,843.22
6.25%	6,515.50	4,934.11	4,443.27	3,761.38	2,872.37	2,448.61	2,209.89	2,062.65	1,966.71	1,901.93
6.50%	6,554.66	4,974.56	4,484.39	3,803.86	2,918.21	2,497.67	2,261.94	2,117.43	2,023.92	1,961.28
6.75%	6,593.96	5,015.21	4,525.73	3,846.61	2,964.45	2,547.22	2,314.55	2,172.80	2,081.75	2,021.25
7.00%	6,633.40	5,056.05	4,567.30	3,889.63	3,011.07	2,597.25	2,367.71	2,228.76	2,140.17	2,081.79
7.25%	6,672.99	5,097.09	4,609.08	3,932.93	3,058.09	2,647.76	2,421.40	2,285.29	2,199.17	2,142.90
7.50%	6,712.71	5,138.32	4,651.10	3,976.51	3,105.49	2,698.74	2,475.62	2,342.37	2,258.71	2,204.54
7.75%	6,752.58	5,179.75	4,693.33	4,020.36	3,153.27	2,750.18	2,530.35	2,399.98	2,318.79	2,266.68
8.00%	6,792.59	5,221.38	4,735.79	4,064.47	3,201.43	2,802.07	2,585.58	2,458.11	2,379.37	2,329.29
8.25%	6,832.74	5,263.20	4,778.47	4,108.86	3,249.97	2,854.42	2,641.31	2,516.74	2,440.45	2,392.37
8.50%	6,873.04	5,305.22	4,821.36	4,153.52	3,298.88	2,907.21	2,697.51	2,575.86	2,501.98	2,455.87
8.75%	6,913.47	5,347.43	4,864.48	4,198.45	3,348.15	2,960.43	2,754.18	2,635.45	2,563.97	2,519.77
9.00%	6,954.05	5,389.84	4,907.82	4,243.64	3,397.79	3,014.08	2,811.31	2,695.49	2,626.38	2,584.06
9.25%	6,994.77	5,432.44	4,951.37	4,289.10	3,447.79	3,068.15	2,868.88	2,755.96	2,689.19	2,648.71
9.50%	7,035.62	5,475.23	4,995.15	4,334.82	3,498.15	3,122.64	2,926.88	2,816.86	2,752.40	2,713.71
9.75%	7,076.62	5,518.22	5,039.14	4,380.80	3,548.86	3,177.53	2,985.31	2,878.17	2,815.97	2,779.02
10.00%	7,117.76	5,561.40	5,083.34	4,427.05	3,599.93	3,232.82	3,044.15	2,939.86	2,879.90	2,844.64
10.25%	7,159.04	5,604.77	5,127.77	4,473.56	3,651.34	3,288.51	3,103.38	3,001.94	2,944.17	2,910.54
10.50%	7,200.46	5,648.33	5,172.41	4,520.32	3,703.09	3,344.57	3,163.01	3,064.38	3,008.75	2,976.71
10.75%	7,242.01	5,692.08	5,217.26	4,567.35	3,755.18	3,401.02	3,223.01	3,127.16	3,073.63	3,043.13

	5	7	8	10	15	20	25	30	35	40
11.00%	7,283.71	5,736.02	5,262.32	4,614.63	3,807.60	3,457.83	3,283.38	3,190.28	3,138.81	3,109.79
11.25%	7,325.55	5,780.15	5,307.60	4,662.16	3,860.35	3,515.01	3,344.10	3,253.73	3,204.25	3,176.66
11.50%	7,367.52	5,824.46	5,353.09	4,709.95	3,913.44	3,572.54	3,405.17	3,317.48	3,269.96	3,243.74
11.75%	7,409.64	5,868.97	5,398.79	4,757.99	3,966.84	3,630.42	3,466.57	3,381.52	3,335.91	3,311.02
12.00%	7,451.89	5,913.67	5,444.70	4,806.28	4,020.56	3,688.64	3,528.30	3,445.85	3,402.09	3,378.47
12.25%	7,494.28	5,958.55	5,490.82	4,854.82	4,074.60	3,747.19	3,590.34	3,510.45	3,468.49	3,446.10
12.50%	7,536.81	6,003.61	5,537.15	4,903.60	4,128.95	3,806.07	3,652.69	3,575.31	3,535.10	3,513.88
12.75%	7,579.48	6,048.87	5,583.69	4,952.63	4,183.60	3,865.27	3,715.33	3,640.42	3,601.91	3,581.81
13.00%	7,622.28	6,094.31	5,630.43	5,001.91	4,238.56	3,924.78	3,778.25	3,705.77	3,668.90	3,649.87
13.25%	7,665.22	6,139.93	5,677.38	5,051.43	4,293.82	3,984.59	3,841.45	3,771.34	3,736.06	3,718.06
13.50%	7,708.30	6,185.74	5,724.53	5,101.19	4,349.37	4,044.71	3,904.91	3,837.13	3,803.39	3,786.37
13.75%	7,751.51	6,231.73	5,771.89	5,151.19	4,405.21	4,105.11	3,968.63	3,903.13	3,870.87	3,854.80
14.00%	7,794.86	6,277.90	5,819.45	5,201.43	4,461.33	4,165.79	4,032.60	3,969.32	3,938.51	3,923.32
14.25%	7,838.35	6,324.26	5,867.22	5,251.90	4,517.74	4,226.76	4,096.81	4,035.70	4,006.27	3,991.94
14.50%	7,881.97	6,370.80	5,915.18	5,302.61	4,574.43	4,287.99	4,161.25	4,102.26	4,074.17	4,060.65
14.75%	7,925.73	6,417.51	5,963.35	5,353.55	4,631.39	4,349.49	4,225.91	4,168.99	4,142.19	4,129.43
15.00%	7,969.63	6,464.41	6,011.71	5,404.72	4,688.62	4,411.25	4,290.78	4,235.89	4,210.32	4,198.30
15.25%	8,013.66	6,511.49	6,060.27	5,456.12	4,746.11	4,473.25	4,355.86	4,302.94	4,278.57	4,267.24
15.50%	8,057.82	6,558.75	6,109.03	5,507.75	4,803.87	4,535.50	4,421.15	4,370.13	4,346.91	4,336.24
15.75%	8,102.12	6,606.18	6,157.99	5,559.61	4,861.88	4,597.99	4,486.62	4,437.47	4,415.35	4,405.30
16.00%	8,146.55	6,653.79	6,207.14	5,611.69	4,920.15	4,660.71	4,552.28	4,504.94	4,483.87	4,474.42
16.25%	8,191.12	6,701.58	6,256.49	5,663.99	4,978.66	4,723.65	4,618.11	4,572.53	4,552.48	4,543.59
16.50%	8,235.81	6,749.54	6,306.03	5,716.52	5,037.42	4,786.82	4,684.12	4,640.25	4,621.17	4,612.81
16.75%	8,280.65	6,797.68	6,355.76	5,769.26	5,096.43	4,850.20	4,750.29	4,708.08	4,689.93	4,682.08
17.00%	8,325.61	6,845.99	6,405.69	5,822.22	5,155.66	4,913.78	4,816.62	4,776.01	4,758.76	4,751.38
17.25%	8,370.71	6,894.48	6,455.80	5,875.40	5,215.14	4,977.57	4,883.10	4,844.05	4,827.66	4,820.73
17.50%	8,415.94	6,943.14	6,506.11	5,928.79	5,274.84	5,041.56	4,949.72	4,912.19	4,896.61	4,890.11
17.75%	8,461.30	6,991.97	6,556.60	5,982.39	5,334.76	5,105.73	5,016.49	4,980.42	4,965.62	4,959.52
18.00%	8,506.80	7,040.98	6,607.28	6,036.20	5,394.91	5,170.09	5,083.39	5,048.74	5,034.69	5,028.96
18.25%	8,552.42	7,090.15	6,658.14	6,090.23	5,455.28	5,234.64	5,150.42	5,117.14	5,103.80	5,098.43
18.50%	8,598.18	7,139.49	6,709.19	6,144.45	5,515.85	5,299.35	5,217.57	5,185.61	5,172.96	5,167.93
18.75%	8,644.07	7,189.01	6,760.43	6,198.89	5,576.64	5,364.24	5,284.84	5,254.17	5,242.16	5,237.44
19.00%	8,690.08	7,238.69	6,811.84	6,253.52	5,637.63	5,429.29	5,352.23	5,322.79	5,311.41	5,306.99
19.25%	8,736.23	7,288.53	6,863.44	6,308.36	5,698.83	5,494.51	5,419.72	5,391.48	5,380.69	5,376.55
19.50%	8,782.51	7,338.55	6,915.22	6,363.40	5,760.22	5,559.88	5,487.32	5,460.23	5,450.00	5,446.13
19.75%	8,828.92	7,388.73	6,967.18	6,418.63	5,821.81	5,625.40	5,555.02	5,529.04	5,519.35	5,515.72
20.00%	8,875.45	7,439.08	7,019.32	6,474.07	5,883.59	5,691.06	5,622.81	5,597.91	5,588.73	5,585.33
20.25%	8,922.12	7,489.59	7,071.64	6,529.69	5,945.56	5,756.87	5,690.70	5,666.83	5,658.14	5,654.96
20.50%	8,968.91	7,540.26	7,124.13	6,585.51	6,007.71	5,822.82	5,758.67	5,735.81	5,727.57	5,724.60
20.75%	9,015.83	7,591.10	7,176.80	6,641.51	6,070.04	5,888.90	5,826.73	5,804.83	5,797.03	5,794.25

$340,000 1.00 - 10.75% 5 - 40 Years

	5	7	8	10	15	20	25	30	35	40
1.00%	5,811.87	4,192.62	3,686.70	2,978.54	2,034.88	1,563.64	1,281.37	1,093.57	959.77	859.71
1.25%	5,848.54	4,229.39	3,723.54	3,015.58	2,072.48	1,601.85	1,320.21	1,133.06	999.89	900.47
1.50%	5,885.36	4,266.36	3,760.63	3,052.91	2,110.53	1,640.65	1,359.78	1,173.41	1,041.03	942.39
1.75%	5,922.33	4,303.54	3,797.94	3,090.54	2,149.01	1,680.04	1,400.08	1,214.63	1,083.16	985.44
2.00%	5,959.44	4,340.93	3,835.50	3,128.46	2,187.93	1,720.00	1,441.10	1,256.71	1,126.29	1,029.61
2.25%	5,996.70	4,378.52	3,873.28	3,166.67	2,227.29	1,760.55	1,482.84	1,299.64	1,170.40	1,074.88
2.50%	6,034.10	4,416.31	3,911.31	3,205.18	2,267.08	1,801.67	1,525.30	1,343.41	1,215.48	1,121.25
2.75%	6,071.66	4,454.32	3,949.56	3,243.98	2,307.31	1,843.37	1,568.46	1,388.02	1,261.52	1,168.67
3.00%	6,109.35	4,492.52	3,988.05	3,283.07	2,347.98	1,885.63	1,612.32	1,433.45	1,308.49	1,217.15
3.25%	6,147.20	4,530.93	4,026.78	3,322.45	2,389.07	1,928.47	1,656.88	1,479.70	1,356.39	1,266.64
3.50%	6,185.19	4,569.55	4,065.74	3,362.12	2,430.60	1,971.86	1,702.12	1,526.75	1,405.19	1,317.13
3.75%	6,223.33	4,608.37	4,104.93	3,402.08	2,472.56	2,015.82	1,748.05	1,574.59	1,454.88	1,368.59
4.00%	6,261.62	4,647.39	4,144.35	3,442.33	2,514.94	2,060.33	1,794.65	1,623.21	1,505.43	1,420.99
4.25%	6,300.05	4,686.62	4,184.01	3,482.88	2,557.75	2,105.40	1,841.91	1,672.60	1,556.84	1,474.31
4.50%	6,338.63	4,726.05	4,223.90	3,523.71	2,600.98	2,151.01	1,889.83	1,722.73	1,609.07	1,528.51
4.75%	6,377.35	4,765.69	4,264.02	3,564.82	2,644.63	2,197.16	1,938.40	1,773.60	1,662.11	1,583.58
5.00%	6,416.22	4,805.53	4,304.37	3,606.23	2,688.70	2,243.85	1,987.61	1,825.19	1,715.94	1,639.47
5.25%	6,455.23	4,845.57	4,344.96	3,647.92	2,733.18	2,291.07	2,037.44	1,877.49	1,770.53	1,696.16
5.50%	6,494.40	4,885.81	4,385.77	3,689.89	2,778.08	2,338.82	2,087.90	1,930.48	1,825.86	1,753.62
5.75%	6,533.70	4,926.26	4,426.81	3,732.15	2,823.39	2,387.08	2,138.96	1,984.15	1,881.90	1,811.82
6.00%	6,573.15	4,966.91	4,468.09	3,774.70	2,869.11	2,435.87	2,190.62	2,038.47	1,938.65	1,870.73
6.25%	6,612.75	5,007.76	4,509.59	3,817.52	2,915.24	2,485.16	2,242.88	2,093.44	1,996.06	1,930.31
6.50%	6,652.49	5,048.81	4,551.32	3,860.63	2,961.77	2,534.95	2,295.70	2,149.03	2,054.12	1,990.55
6.75%	6,692.38	5,090.06	4,593.28	3,904.02	3,008.69	2,585.24	2,349.10	2,205.23	2,112.82	2,051.41
7.00%	6,732.41	5,131.51	4,635.46	3,947.69	3,056.02	2,636.02	2,403.05	2,262.03	2,172.11	2,112.87
7.25%	6,772.58	5,173.16	4,677.88	3,991.64	3,103.73	2,687.28	2,457.54	2,319.40	2,231.99	2,174.88
7.50%	6,812.90	5,215.01	4,720.52	4,035.86	3,151.84	2,739.02	2,512.57	2,377.33	2,292.42	2,237.44
7.75%	6,853.37	5,257.06	4,763.38	4,080.36	3,200.34	2,791.23	2,568.12	2,435.80	2,353.40	2,300.51
8.00%	6,893.97	5,299.31	4,806.47	4,125.14	3,249.22	2,843.90	2,624.18	2,494.80	2,414.89	2,364.06
8.25%	6,934.73	5,341.76	4,849.79	4,170.19	3,298.48	2,897.02	2,680.73	2,554.31	2,476.87	2,428.07
8.50%	6,975.62	5,384.41	4,893.32	4,215.51	3,348.11	2,950.60	2,737.77	2,614.31	2,539.33	2,492.52
8.75%	7,016.66	5,427.25	4,937.09	4,261.11	3,398.13	3,004.62	2,795.29	2,674.78	2,602.23	2,557.38
9.00%	7,057.84	5,470.29	4,981.07	4,306.98	3,448.51	3,059.07	2,853.27	2,735.72	2,665.58	2,622.63
9.25%	7,099.17	5,513.52	5,025.27	4,353.11	3,499.25	3,113.95	2,911.70	2,797.10	2,729.33	2,688.25
9.50%	7,140.63	5,556.95	5,069.70	4,399.52	3,550.36	3,169.25	2,970.57	2,858.90	2,793.48	2,754.21
9.75%	7,182.24	5,600.58	5,114.35	4,446.19	3,601.83	3,224.96	3,029.87	2,921.13	2,858.00	2,820.50
10.00%	7,224.00	5,644.40	5,159.22	4,493.13	3,653.66	3,281.07	3,089.58	2,983.74	2,922.89	2,887.10
10.25%	7,265.89	5,688.42	5,204.30	4,540.33	3,705.83	3,337.59	3,149.70	3,046.74	2,988.11	2,953.98
10.50%	7,307.93	5,732.63	5,249.61	4,587.79	3,758.36	3,394.49	3,210.22	3,110.11	3,053.66	3,021.14
10.75%	7,350.10	5,777.03	5,295.13	4,635.52	3,811.22	3,451.78	3,271.12	3,173.84	3,119.51	3,088.55

$340,000   11.00 - 20.75%   5 - 40 Years

	5	7	8	10	15	20	25	30	35	40
11.00%	7,392.42	5,821.63	5,340.86	4,683.50	3,864.43	3,509.44	3,332.38	3,237.90	3,185.66	3,156.20
11.25%	7,434.88	5,866.42	5,386.82	4,731.74	3,917.97	3,567.47	3,394.01	3,302.29	3,252.08	3,224.07
11.50%	7,477.49	5,911.40	5,432.99	4,780.25	3,971.85	3,625.86	3,455.99	3,366.99	3,318.76	3,292.16
11.75%	7,520.23	5,956.57	5,479.37	4,829.00	4,026.05	3,684.60	3,518.31	3,431.99	3,385.70	3,360.44
12.00%	7,563.11	6,001.93	5,525.97	4,878.01	4,080.57	3,743.69	3,580.96	3,497.28	3,452.87	3,428.90
12.25%	7,606.14	6,047.48	5,572.77	4,927.28	4,135.42	3,803.12	3,643.93	3,562.85	3,520.26	3,497.53
12.50%	7,649.30	6,093.22	5,619.79	4,976.79	4,190.58	3,862.88	3,707.20	3,628.68	3,587.86	3,566.33
12.75%	7,692.60	6,139.15	5,667.03	5,026.55	4,246.05	3,922.96	3,770.78	3,694.76	3,655.67	3,635.27
13.00%	7,736.04	6,185.27	5,714.47	5,076.57	4,301.82	3,983.36	3,834.64	3,761.08	3,723.66	3,704.35
13.25%	7,779.63	6,231.57	5,762.12	5,126.82	4,357.90	4,044.06	3,898.78	3,827.63	3,791.82	3,773.56
13.50%	7,823.35	6,278.06	5,809.97	5,177.33	4,414.28	4,105.07	3,963.19	3,894.40	3,860.16	3,842.89
13.75%	7,867.21	6,324.74	5,858.04	5,228.07	4,470.96	4,166.38	4,027.86	3,961.38	3,928.65	3,912.33
14.00%	7,911.21	6,371.60	5,906.31	5,279.06	4,527.92	4,227.97	4,092.79	4,028.56	3,997.29	3,981.88
14.25%	7,955.34	6,418.65	5,954.79	5,330.29	4,585.17	4,289.84	4,157.95	4,095.94	4,066.07	4,051.52
14.50%	7,999.62	6,465.88	6,003.47	5,381.75	4,642.70	4,351.99	4,223.35	4,163.49	4,134.98	4,121.25
14.75%	8,044.03	6,513.30	6,052.35	5,433.45	4,700.51	4,414.41	4,288.98	4,231.22	4,204.01	4,191.07
15.00%	8,088.58	6,560.90	6,101.44	5,485.39	4,758.60	4,477.08	4,354.82	4,299.11	4,273.17	4,260.96
15.25%	8,133.26	6,608.68	6,150.73	5,537.56	4,816.95	4,540.02	4,420.88	4,367.16	4,342.43	4,330.93
15.50%	8,178.08	6,656.64	6,200.21	5,589.96	4,875.57	4,603.19	4,487.13	4,435.36	4,411.79	4,400.96
15.75%	8,223.04	6,704.78	6,249.90	5,642.59	4,934.45	4,666.61	4,553.58	4,503.70	4,481.25	4,471.05
16.00%	8,268.14	6,753.10	6,299.79	5,695.45	4,993.58	4,730.27	4,620.22	4,572.17	4,550.80	4,541.20
16.25%	8,313.37	6,801.60	6,349.87	5,748.53	5,052.97	4,794.15	4,687.04	4,640.78	4,620.43	4,611.41
16.50%	8,358.74	6,850.28	6,400.15	5,801.84	5,112.61	4,858.26	4,754.03	4,709.50	4,690.14	4,681.66
16.75%	8,404.24	6,899.14	6,450.63	5,855.37	5,172.49	4,922.59	4,821.19	4,778.34	4,759.93	4,751.96
17.00%	8,449.88	6,948.17	6,501.29	5,909.12	5,232.61	4,987.12	4,888.51	4,847.30	4,829.79	4,822.30
17.25%	8,495.65	6,997.38	6,552.16	5,963.09	5,292.97	5,051.86	4,955.98	4,916.35	4,899.71	4,892.68
17.50%	8,541.55	7,046.77	6,603.21	6,017.28	5,353.57	5,116.80	5,023.60	4,985.51	4,969.70	4,963.09
17.75%	8,587.59	7,096.33	6,654.46	6,071.68	5,414.39	5,181.94	5,091.36	5,054.75	5,039.74	5,033.54
18.00%	8,633.77	7,146.06	6,705.89	6,126.30	5,475.43	5,247.26	5,159.26	5,124.09	5,109.83	5,104.02
18.25%	8,680.07	7,195.97	6,757.52	6,181.12	5,536.70	5,312.76	5,227.29	5,193.51	5,179.98	5,174.53
18.50%	8,726.51	7,246.05	6,809.33	6,236.16	5,598.18	5,378.45	5,295.45	5,263.01	5,250.17	5,245.06
18.75%	8,773.08	7,296.30	6,861.33	6,291.41	5,659.87	5,444.30	5,363.72	5,332.59	5,320.41	5,315.62
19.00%	8,819.79	7,346.73	6,913.51	6,346.86	5,721.78	5,510.33	5,432.11	5,402.23	5,390.68	5,386.19
19.25%	8,866.62	7,397.32	6,965.88	6,402.52	5,783.89	5,576.52	5,500.61	5,471.95	5,461.00	5,456.79
19.50%	8,913.59	7,448.08	7,018.44	6,458.38	5,846.20	5,642.86	5,569.22	5,541.73	5,531.35	5,527.41
19.75%	8,960.69	7,499.01	7,071.17	6,514.43	5,908.71	5,709.36	5,637.93	5,611.57	5,601.73	5,598.05
20.00%	9,007.92	7,550.11	7,124.09	6,570.69	5,971.41	5,776.00	5,706.74	5,681.46	5,672.15	5,668.70
20.25%	9,055.28	7,601.37	7,177.18	6,627.15	6,034.30	5,842.79	5,775.64	5,751.41	5,742.59	5,739.36
20.50%	9,102.77	7,652.80	7,230.46	6,683.80	6,097.38	5,909.72	5,844.62	5,821.42	5,813.06	5,810.04
20.75%	9,150.39	7,704.40	7,283.91	6,740.64	6,160.64	5,976.79	5,913.70	5,891.47	5,883.56	5,880.74

$345,000   1.00 - 10.75%   5 - 40 Years

	5	7	8	10	15	20	25	30	35	40
1.00%	5,897.34	4,254.28	3,740.91	3,022.34	2,064.81	1,586.64	1,300.21	1,109.66	973.89	872.35
1.25%	5,934.55	4,291.59	3,778.30	3,059.93	2,102.96	1,625.41	1,339.63	1,149.72	1,014.60	913.72
1.50%	5,971.91	4,329.10	3,815.93	3,097.81	2,141.56	1,664.78	1,379.78	1,190.66	1,056.34	956.25
1.75%	6,009.42	4,366.83	3,853.80	3,135.99	2,180.61	1,704.74	1,420.67	1,232.49	1,099.09	999.93
2.00%	6,047.08	4,404.77	3,891.90	3,174.46	2,220.11	1,745.30	1,462.30	1,275.19	1,142.86	1,044.75
2.25%	6,084.88	4,442.91	3,930.24	3,213.24	2,260.04	1,786.44	1,504.65	1,318.75	1,187.62	1,090.69
2.50%	6,122.84	4,481.26	3,968.83	3,252.31	2,300.42	1,828.16	1,547.73	1,363.17	1,233.36	1,137.73
2.75%	6,160.94	4,519.82	4,007.65	3,291.68	2,341.24	1,870.47	1,591.52	1,408.43	1,280.07	1,185.86
3.00%	6,199.20	4,558.59	4,046.70	3,331.35	2,382.51	1,913.36	1,636.03	1,454.53	1,327.73	1,235.05
3.25%	6,237.60	4,597.56	4,086.00	3,371.31	2,424.21	1,956.83	1,681.24	1,501.46	1,376.33	1,285.27
3.50%	6,276.15	4,636.75	4,125.53	3,411.56	2,466.34	2,000.86	1,727.15	1,549.20	1,425.85	1,336.50
3.75%	6,314.85	4,676.14	4,165.30	3,452.11	2,508.92	2,045.46	1,773.75	1,597.75	1,476.27	1,388.71
4.00%	6,353.70	4,715.74	4,205.30	3,492.96	2,551.92	2,090.63	1,821.04	1,647.08	1,527.57	1,441.89
4.25%	6,392.70	4,755.54	4,245.54	3,534.09	2,595.36	2,136.36	1,869.00	1,697.19	1,579.73	1,495.99
4.50%	6,431.84	4,795.56	4,286.02	3,575.53	2,639.23	2,182.64	1,917.62	1,748.06	1,632.74	1,550.99
4.75%	6,471.13	4,835.77	4,326.73	3,617.25	2,683.52	2,229.47	1,966.90	1,799.68	1,686.56	1,606.86
5.00%	6,510.58	4,876.20	4,367.67	3,659.26	2,728.24	2,276.85	2,016.84	1,852.03	1,741.17	1,663.58
5.25%	6,550.16	4,916.83	4,408.85	3,701.56	2,773.38	2,324.76	2,067.40	1,905.10	1,796.56	1,721.10
5.50%	6,589.90	4,957.66	4,450.27	3,744.16	2,818.94	2,373.21	2,118.60	1,958.87	1,852.71	1,779.41
5.75%	6,629.79	4,998.71	4,491.91	3,787.04	2,864.91	2,422.19	2,170.42	2,013.33	1,909.58	1,838.46
6.00%	6,669.82	5,039.95	4,533.79	3,830.21	2,911.31	2,471.69	2,222.84	2,068.45	1,967.15	1,898.24
6.25%	6,710.00	5,081.40	4,575.91	3,873.66	2,958.11	2,521.70	2,275.86	2,124.22	2,025.41	1,958.70
6.50%	6,750.32	5,123.06	4,618.25	3,917.41	3,005.32	2,572.23	2,329.46	2,180.63	2,084.33	2,019.83
6.75%	6,790.79	5,164.91	4,660.83	3,961.43	3,052.94	2,623.26	2,383.64	2,237.66	2,143.89	2,081.58
7.00%	6,831.41	5,206.97	4,703.63	4,005.74	3,100.96	2,674.78	2,438.39	2,295.29	2,204.05	2,143.94
7.25%	6,872.18	5,249.24	4,746.67	4,050.34	3,149.38	2,726.80	2,493.68	2,353.51	2,264.81	2,206.87
7.50%	6,913.09	5,291.71	4,789.94	4,095.21	3,198.19	2,779.30	2,549.52	2,412.29	2,326.14	2,270.34
7.75%	6,954.15	5,334.37	4,833.43	4,140.37	3,247.40	2,832.27	2,605.88	2,471.62	2,388.01	2,334.34
8.00%	6,995.36	5,377.24	4,877.15	4,185.80	3,297.00	2,885.72	2,662.77	2,531.49	2,450.40	2,398.83
8.25%	7,036.71	5,420.32	4,921.11	4,231.52	3,346.98	2,939.63	2,720.15	2,591.87	2,513.29	2,463.78
8.50%	7,078.20	5,463.59	4,965.28	4,277.51	3,397.35	2,993.99	2,778.03	2,652.75	2,576.67	2,529.17
8.75%	7,119.85	5,507.06	5,009.69	4,323.77	3,448.10	3,048.80	2,836.40	2,714.12	2,640.50	2,594.99
9.00%	7,161.63	5,550.73	5,054.32	4,370.31	3,499.22	3,104.05	2,895.23	2,775.95	2,704.78	2,661.20
9.25%	7,203.56	5,594.60	5,099.18	4,417.13	3,550.71	3,159.74	2,954.52	2,838.23	2,769.47	2,727.78
9.50%	7,245.64	5,638.67	5,144.26	4,464.22	3,602.58	3,215.85	3,014.25	2,900.95	2,834.56	2,794.71
9.75%	7,287.86	5,682.94	5,189.56	4,511.57	3,654.80	3,272.38	3,074.42	2,964.08	2,900.03	2,861.98
10.00%	7,330.23	5,727.41	5,235.09	4,559.20	3,707.39	3,329.32	3,135.02	3,027.62	2,965.87	2,929.55
10.25%	7,372.74	5,772.07	5,280.84	4,607.10	3,760.33	3,386.67	3,196.02	3,091.55	3,032.05	2,997.42
10.50%	7,415.40	5,816.93	5,326.81	4,655.26	3,813.63	3,444.41	3,257.43	3,155.85	3,098.56	3,065.57
10.75%	7,458.19	5,861.99	5,373.00	4,703.68	3,867.27	3,502.54	3,319.22	3,220.51	3,165.38	3,133.97

$345,000   11.00 - 20.75%   5 - 40 Years

	5	7	8	10	15	20	25	30	35	40
11.00%	7,501.14	5,907.24	5,419.41	4,752.38	3,921.26	3,561.05	3,381.39	3,285.52	3,232.50	3,202.62
11.25%	7,544.22	5,952.69	5,466.04	4,801.33	3,975.59	3,619.93	3,443.93	3,350.85	3,299.90	3,271.49
11.50%	7,587.45	5,998.33	5,512.88	4,850.54	4,030.25	3,679.18	3,506.82	3,416.51	3,367.57	3,340.57
11.75%	7,630.82	6,044.16	5,559.95	4,900.02	4,085.25	3,738.79	3,570.05	3,482.46	3,435.49	3,409.86
12.00%	7,674.33	6,090.19	5,607.23	4,949.75	4,140.58	3,798.75	3,633.62	3,548.71	3,503.65	3,479.32
12.25%	7,717.99	6,136.41	5,654.73	4,999.74	4,196.23	3,859.05	3,697.52	3,615.24	3,572.03	3,548.97
12.50%	7,761.79	6,182.83	5,702.44	5,049.98	4,252.20	3,919.68	3,761.72	3,682.04	3,640.63	3,618.77
12.75%	7,805.73	6,229.43	5,750.36	5,100.47	4,308.49	3,980.65	3,826.23	3,749.09	3,709.43	3,688.73
13.00%	7,849.81	6,276.23	5,798.50	5,151.22	4,365.09	4,041.94	3,891.03	3,816.39	3,778.42	3,758.82
13.25%	7,894.03	6,323.21	5,846.85	5,202.22	4,421.99	4,103.54	3,956.12	3,883.92	3,847.59	3,829.05
13.50%	7,938.40	6,370.39	5,895.42	5,253.46	4,479.20	4,165.44	4,021.47	3,951.67	3,916.92	3,899.40
13.75%	7,982.90	6,417.75	5,944.19	5,304.95	4,536.71	4,227.65	4,087.10	4,019.64	3,986.42	3,969.86
14.00%	8,027.55	6,465.30	5,993.17	5,356.69	4,594.51	4,290.15	4,152.98	4,087.81	4,056.07	4,040.43
14.25%	8,072.33	6,513.04	6,042.36	5,408.67	4,652.60	4,352.93	4,219.10	4,156.17	4,125.86	4,111.10
14.50%	8,117.26	6,560.97	6,091.75	5,460.89	4,710.98	4,415.99	4,285.46	4,224.72	4,195.79	4,181.86
14.75%	8,162.32	6,609.08	6,141.36	5,513.36	4,769.64	4,479.33	4,352.05	4,293.44	4,265.84	4,252.70
15.00%	8,207.53	6,657.38	6,191.16	5,566.06	4,828.58	4,542.92	4,418.87	4,362.33	4,336.01	4,323.62
15.25%	8,252.87	6,705.86	6,241.18	5,618.99	4,887.79	4,606.78	4,485.89	4,431.38	4,406.28	4,394.62
15.50%	8,298.35	6,754.53	6,291.39	5,672.16	4,947.27	4,670.89	4,553.12	4,500.58	4,476.67	4,465.68
15.75%	8,343.97	6,803.38	6,341.81	5,725.57	5,007.01	4,735.24	4,620.55	4,569.93	4,547.15	4,536.80
16.00%	8,389.73	6,852.41	6,392.43	5,779.20	5,067.02	4,799.83	4,688.17	4,639.41	4,617.72	4,607.99
16.25%	8,435.63	6,901.63	6,443.25	5,833.07	5,127.28	4,864.66	4,755.97	4,709.02	4,688.38	4,679.22
16.50%	8,481.66	6,951.02	6,494.27	5,887.16	5,187.79	4,929.71	4,823.94	4,778.76	4,759.12	4,750.51
16.75%	8,527.83	7,000.60	6,545.49	5,941.48	5,248.56	4,994.98	4,892.09	4,848.61	4,829.93	4,821.84
17.00%	8,574.14	7,050.35	6,596.90	5,996.02	5,309.56	5,060.46	4,960.40	4,918.58	4,900.82	4,893.22
17.25%	8,620.58	7,100.29	6,648.51	6,050.78	5,370.81	5,126.15	5,028.86	4,988.65	4,971.77	4,964.63
17.50%	8,667.16	7,150.40	6,700.32	6,105.77	5,432.29	5,192.05	5,097.48	5,058.82	5,042.78	5,036.08
17.75%	8,713.88	7,200.69	6,752.32	6,160.97	5,494.01	5,258.14	5,166.24	5,129.09	5,113.85	5,107.56
18.00%	8,760.73	7,251.15	6,804.51	6,216.39	5,555.95	5,324.42	5,235.13	5,199.44	5,184.98	5,179.08
18.25%	8,807.72	7,301.80	6,856.89	6,272.02	5,618.12	5,390.89	5,304.16	5,269.89	5,256.15	5,250.62
18.50%	8,854.84	7,352.61	6,909.47	6,327.87	5,680.51	5,457.54	5,373.32	5,340.41	5,327.38	5,322.19
18.75%	8,902.10	7,403.60	6,962.23	6,383.93	5,743.11	5,524.37	5,442.60	5,411.01	5,398.65	5,393.79
19.00%	8,949.49	7,454.77	7,015.18	6,440.20	5,805.92	5,591.36	5,512.00	5,481.68	5,469.96	5,465.40
19.25%	8,997.02	7,506.10	7,068.32	6,496.67	5,868.94	5,658.52	5,581.50	5,552.42	5,541.31	5,537.04
19.50%	9,044.67	7,557.61	7,121.65	6,553.35	5,932.17	5,725.84	5,651.12	5,623.22	5,612.69	5,608.70
19.75%	9,092.47	7,609.29	7,175.16	6,610.24	5,995.60	5,793.32	5,720.84	5,694.09	5,684.11	5,680.37
20.00%	9,140.39	7,661.14	7,228.85	6,667.32	6,059.22	5,860.94	5,790.66	5,765.01	5,755.56	5,752.06
20.25%	9,188.45	7,713.16	7,282.73	6,724.61	6,123.04	5,928.72	5,860.57	5,835.99	5,827.04	5,823.77
20.50%	9,236.64	7,765.34	7,336.79	6,782.09	6,187.05	5,996.63	5,930.57	5,907.02	5,898.55	5,895.49
20.75%	9,284.96	7,817.70	7,391.03	6,839.77	6,251.24	6,064.68	6,000.66	5,978.10	5,970.08	5,967.22

	5	7	8	10	15	20	25	30	35	40
1.00%	5,982.81	4,315.94	3,795.13	3,066.14	2,094.73	1,609.63	1,319.05	1,125.74	988.00	885.00
1.25%	6,020.56	4,353.78	3,833.06	3,104.27	2,133.44	1,648.97	1,359.04	1,166.38	1,029.30	926.96
1.50%	6,058.46	4,391.85	3,871.23	3,142.70	2,172.60	1,688.91	1,399.78	1,207.92	1,071.65	970.10
1.75%	6,096.51	4,430.12	3,909.65	3,181.44	2,212.21	1,729.45	1,441.26	1,250.35	1,115.02	1,014.42
2.00%	6,134.72	4,468.60	3,948.31	3,220.47	2,252.28	1,770.59	1,483.49	1,293.67	1,159.42	1,059.89
2.25%	6,173.07	4,507.30	3,987.20	3,259.81	2,292.80	1,812.33	1,526.46	1,337.86	1,204.83	1,106.50
2.50%	6,211.58	4,546.21	4,026.35	3,299.45	2,333.76	1,854.66	1,570.16	1,382.92	1,251.23	1,154.22
2.75%	6,250.23	4,585.32	4,065.73	3,339.39	2,375.18	1,897.58	1,614.59	1,428.84	1,298.62	1,203.05
3.00%	6,289.04	4,624.66	4,105.35	3,379.63	2,417.04	1,941.09	1,659.74	1,475.61	1,346.98	1,252.95
3.25%	6,328.00	4,664.20	4,145.21	3,420.17	2,459.34	1,985.19	1,705.61	1,523.22	1,396.28	1,303.89
3.50%	6,367.11	4,703.95	4,185.32	3,461.01	2,502.09	2,029.86	1,752.18	1,571.66	1,446.52	1,355.87
3.75%	6,406.37	4,743.91	4,225.66	3,502.14	2,545.28	2,075.11	1,799.46	1,620.90	1,497.67	1,408.84
4.00%	6,445.78	4,784.08	4,266.25	3,543.58	2,588.91	2,120.93	1,847.43	1,670.95	1,549.71	1,462.78
4.25%	6,485.34	4,824.46	4,307.07	3,585.31	2,632.97	2,167.32	1,896.08	1,721.79	1,602.63	1,517.67
4.50%	6,525.05	4,865.06	4,348.13	3,627.34	2,677.48	2,214.27	1,945.41	1,773.40	1,656.40	1,573.47
4.75%	6,564.92	4,905.86	4,389.43	3,669.67	2,722.41	2,261.78	1,995.41	1,825.77	1,711.00	1,630.15
5.00%	6,604.93	4,946.87	4,430.97	3,712.29	2,767.78	2,309.85	2,046.07	1,878.88	1,766.41	1,687.69
5.25%	6,645.09	4,988.09	4,472.75	3,755.21	2,813.57	2,358.45	2,097.37	1,932.71	1,822.60	1,746.05
5.50%	6,685.41	5,029.51	4,514.76	3,798.42	2,859.79	2,407.61	2,149.31	1,987.26	1,879.56	1,805.20
5.75%	6,725.87	5,071.15	4,557.01	3,841.92	2,906.44	2,457.29	2,201.87	2,042.50	1,937.25	1,865.11
6.00%	6,766.48	5,112.99	4,599.50	3,885.72	2,953.50	2,507.51	2,255.05	2,098.43	1,995.66	1,925.75
6.25%	6,807.24	5,155.04	4,642.22	3,929.80	3,000.98	2,558.25	2,308.84	2,155.01	2,054.77	1,987.09
6.50%	6,848.15	5,197.30	4,685.18	3,974.18	3,048.88	2,609.51	2,363.23	2,212.24	2,114.54	2,049.10
6.75%	6,889.21	5,239.77	4,728.37	4,018.84	3,097.18	2,661.27	2,418.19	2,270.09	2,174.96	2,111.75
7.00%	6,930.42	5,282.44	4,771.80	4,063.80	3,145.90	2,713.55	2,473.73	2,328.56	2,236.00	2,175.01
7.25%	6,971.78	5,325.31	4,815.46	4,109.04	3,195.02	2,766.32	2,529.82	2,387.62	2,297.64	2,238.85
7.50%	7,013.28	5,368.40	4,859.35	4,154.56	3,244.54	2,819.58	2,586.47	2,447.25	2,359.85	2,303.25
7.75%	7,054.94	5,411.68	4,903.48	4,200.37	3,294.47	2,873.32	2,643.65	2,507.44	2,422.62	2,368.17
8.00%	7,096.74	5,455.18	4,947.84	4,246.47	3,344.78	2,927.54	2,701.36	2,568.18	2,485.91	2,433.59
8.25%	7,138.69	5,498.87	4,992.43	4,292.84	3,395.49	2,982.23	2,759.58	2,629.43	2,549.72	2,499.49
8.50%	7,180.79	5,542.77	5,037.25	4,339.50	3,446.59	3,037.38	2,818.29	2,691.20	2,614.01	2,565.83
8.75%	7,223.03	5,586.87	5,082.29	4,386.44	3,498.07	3,092.99	2,877.50	2,753.45	2,678.77	2,632.60
9.00%	7,265.42	5,631.18	5,127.57	4,433.65	3,549.93	3,149.04	2,937.19	2,816.18	2,743.98	2,699.77
9.25%	7,307.96	5,675.68	5,173.08	4,481.15	3,602.17	3,205.53	2,997.34	2,879.36	2,809.61	2,767.31
9.50%	7,350.65	5,720.39	5,218.81	4,528.91	3,654.79	3,262.46	3,057.94	2,942.99	2,875.64	2,835.22
9.75%	7,393.49	5,765.30	5,264.77	4,576.96	3,707.77	3,319.81	3,118.98	3,007.04	2,942.06	2,903.45
10.00%	7,436.47	5,810.41	5,310.96	4,625.28	3,761.12	3,377.58	3,180.45	3,071.50	3,008.85	2,972.01
10.25%	7,479.59	5,855.73	5,357.37	4,673.87	3,814.83	3,435.75	3,242.34	3,136.35	3,075.99	3,040.86
10.50%	7,522.87	5,901.24	5,404.01	4,722.72	3,868.90	3,494.33	3,304.64	3,201.59	3,143.47	3,110.00
10.75%	7,566.28	5,946.94	5,450.87	4,771.85	3,923.32	3,553.30	3,367.32	3,267.18	3,211.26	3,179.39

$350,000   11.00 - 20.75%   5 - 40 Years

	5	7	8	10	15	20	25	30	35	40
11.00%	7,609.85	5,992.85	5,497.95	4,821.25	3,978.09	3,612.66	3,430.40	3,333.13	3,279.35	3,249.03
11.25%	7,653.56	6,038.96	5,545.25	4,870.91	4,033.21	3,672.40	3,493.84	3,399.41	3,347.73	3,318.90
11.50%	7,697.41	6,085.26	5,592.78	4,920.84	4,088.66	3,732.50	3,557.64	3,466.02	3,416.38	3,388.99
11.75%	7,741.41	6,131.76	5,640.53	4,971.03	4,144.46	3,792.97	3,621.79	3,532.93	3,485.28	3,459.27
12.00%	7,785.56	6,178.46	5,688.49	5,021.48	4,200.59	3,853.80	3,686.28	3,600.14	3,554.42	3,529.75
12.25%	7,829.85	6,225.35	5,736.68	5,072.20	4,257.05	3,914.98	3,751.10	3,667.64	3,623.80	3,600.40
12.50%	7,874.28	6,272.43	5,785.08	5,123.17	4,313.83	3,976.49	3,816.24	3,735.40	3,693.39	3,671.22
12.75%	7,918.86	6,319.71	5,833.70	5,174.39	4,370.93	4,038.34	3,881.68	3,803.43	3,763.19	3,742.19
13.00%	7,963.58	6,367.19	5,882.54	5,225.88	4,428.35	4,100.51	3,947.42	3,871.70	3,833.18	3,813.30
13.25%	8,008.44	6,414.85	5,931.59	5,277.61	4,486.08	4,163.01	4,013.45	3,940.21	3,903.35	3,884.54
13.50%	8,053.45	6,462.71	5,980.86	5,329.60	4,544.11	4,225.81	4,079.76	4,008.94	3,973.69	3,955.91
13.75%	8,098.60	6,510.76	6,030.33	5,381.84	4,602.46	4,288.92	4,146.33	4,077.89	4,044.20	4,027.40
14.00%	8,143.89	6,559.00	6,080.03	5,434.33	4,661.09	4,352.32	4,213.16	4,147.05	4,114.86	4,098.99
14.25%	8,189.32	6,607.44	6,129.93	5,487.06	4,720.03	4,416.02	4,280.25	4,216.40	4,185.66	4,170.60
14.50%	8,234.90	6,656.06	6,180.04	5,540.04	4,779.25	4,479.99	4,347.57	4,285.95	4,256.60	4,242.40
14.75%	8,280.62	6,704.87	6,230.36	5,593.26	4,838.76	4,544.24	4,415.13	4,355.67	4,327.66	4,314.34
15.00%	8,326.48	6,753.86	6,280.89	5,646.72	4,898.55	4,608.76	4,482.91	4,425.55	4,398.85	4,386.28
15.25%	8,372.48	6,803.05	6,331.63	5,700.43	4,958.62	4,673.55	4,550.90	4,495.60	4,470.14	4,458.31
15.50%	8,418.62	6,852.42	6,382.57	5,754.37	5,018.97	4,738.58	4,619.11	4,565.81	4,541.55	4,530.40
15.75%	8,464.90	6,901.98	6,433.72	5,808.55	5,079.58	4,803.87	4,687.51	4,636.16	4,613.05	4,602.56
16.00%	8,511.32	6,951.72	6,485.08	5,862.96	5,140.45	4,869.40	4,756.11	4,706.65	4,684.64	4,674.77
16.25%	8,557.88	7,001.65	6,536.63	5,917.60	5,201.59	4,935.16	4,824.89	4,777.27	4,756.32	4,747.04
16.50%	8,604.58	7,051.76	6,588.39	5,972.48	5,262.98	5,001.15	4,893.86	4,848.02	4,828.09	4,819.36
16.75%	8,651.42	7,102.06	6,640.35	6,027.59	5,324.62	5,067.37	4,962.99	4,918.88	4,899.93	4,891.72
17.00%	8,698.40	7,152.53	6,692.51	6,082.92	5,386.52	5,133.80	5,032.29	4,989.86	4,971.84	4,964.13
17.25%	8,745.52	7,203.19	6,744.87	6,138.48	5,448.65	5,200.45	5,101.74	5,060.95	5,043.82	5,036.58
17.50%	8,792.77	7,254.03	6,797.42	6,194.26	5,511.02	5,267.30	5,171.35	5,132.14	5,115.86	5,109.07
17.75%	8,840.17	7,305.05	6,850.18	6,250.26	5,573.63	5,334.35	5,241.11	5,203.42	5,187.97	5,181.59
18.00%	8,887.70	7,356.24	6,903.12	6,306.48	5,636.47	5,401.59	5,311.00	5,274.80	5,260.12	5,254.14
18.25%	8,935.37	7,407.62	6,956.27	6,362.92	5,699.54	5,469.02	5,381.04	5,346.26	5,332.33	5,326.72
18.50%	8,983.17	7,459.17	7,009.60	6,419.58	5,762.83	5,536.64	5,451.19	5,417.81	5,404.59	5,399.33
18.75%	9,031.11	7,510.90	7,063.13	6,476.45	5,826.34	5,604.43	5,521.48	5,489.43	5,476.89	5,471.96
19.00%	9,079.19	7,562.81	7,116.85	6,533.53	5,890.07	5,672.40	5,591.88	5,561.12	5,549.23	5,544.61
19.25%	9,127.41	7,614.89	7,170.76	6,590.83	5,954.00	5,740.53	5,662.40	5,632.89	5,621.61	5,617.29
19.50%	9,175.76	7,667.14	7,224.86	6,648.33	6,018.15	5,808.83	5,733.02	5,704.72	5,694.03	5,689.98
19.75%	9,224.24	7,719.57	7,279.15	6,706.04	6,082.49	5,877.28	5,803.75	5,776.61	5,766.49	5,762.70
20.00%	9,272.86	7,772.17	7,333.62	6,763.95	6,147.04	5,945.89	5,874.58	5,848.57	5,838.97	5,835.42
20.25%	9,321.61	7,824.94	7,388.28	6,822.06	6,211.78	6,014.64	5,945.51	5,920.57	5,911.49	5,908.17
20.50%	9,370.50	7,877.88	7,443.12	6,880.38	6,276.71	6,083.54	6,016.52	5,992.63	5,984.03	5,980.93
20.75%	9,419.52	7,931.00	7,498.15	6,938.90	6,341.84	6,152.58	6,087.63	6,064.74	6,056.60	6,053.70

	5	7	8	10	15	20	25	30	35	40
1.00%	6,068.28	4,377.59	3,849.35	3,109.95	2,124.66	1,632.62	1,337.90	1,141.82	1,002.11	897.64
1.25%	6,106.57	4,415.98	3,887.82	3,148.62	2,163.92	1,672.52	1,378.45	1,183.04	1,044.01	940.20
1.50%	6,145.01	4,454.59	3,926.54	3,187.60	2,203.64	1,713.04	1,419.77	1,225.18	1,086.95	983.96
1.75%	6,183.61	4,493.41	3,965.50	3,226.88	2,243.82	1,754.16	1,461.85	1,268.21	1,130.95	1,028.91
2.00%	6,222.35	4,532.44	4,004.71	3,266.48	2,284.46	1,795.89	1,504.68	1,312.15	1,175.98	1,075.03
2.25%	6,261.26	4,571.69	4,044.16	3,306.38	2,325.55	1,838.22	1,548.26	1,356.97	1,222.04	1,122.30
2.50%	6,300.31	4,611.15	4,083.86	3,346.58	2,367.10	1,881.16	1,592.59	1,402.68	1,269.11	1,170.71
2.75%	6,339.52	4,650.83	4,123.81	3,387.09	2,409.11	1,924.69	1,637.65	1,449.26	1,317.17	1,220.23
3.00%	6,378.89	4,690.72	4,164.00	3,427.91	2,451.56	1,968.82	1,683.45	1,496.69	1,366.22	1,270.84
3.25%	6,418.40	4,730.83	4,204.43	3,469.03	2,494.47	2,013.54	1,729.97	1,544.98	1,416.23	1,322.52
3.50%	6,458.07	4,771.15	4,245.11	3,510.45	2,537.83	2,058.86	1,777.21	1,594.11	1,467.18	1,375.24
3.75%	6,497.89	4,811.68	4,286.03	3,552.17	2,581.64	2,104.75	1,825.17	1,644.06	1,519.06	1,428.97
4.00%	6,537.87	4,852.43	4,327.19	3,594.20	2,625.89	2,151.23	1,873.82	1,694.82	1,571.85	1,483.68
4.25%	6,577.99	4,893.39	4,368.60	3,636.53	2,670.59	2,198.28	1,923.17	1,746.39	1,625.52	1,539.35
4.50%	6,618.27	4,934.56	4,410.25	3,679.16	2,715.73	2,245.91	1,973.21	1,798.73	1,680.06	1,595.95
4.75%	6,658.70	4,975.94	4,452.14	3,722.09	2,761.30	2,294.09	2,023.92	1,851.85	1,735.44	1,653.44
5.00%	6,699.29	5,017.54	4,494.27	3,765.33	2,807.32	2,342.84	2,075.29	1,905.72	1,791.64	1,711.80
5.25%	6,740.02	5,059.35	4,536.65	3,808.86	2,853.77	2,392.15	2,127.33	1,960.32	1,848.64	1,770.99
5.50%	6,780.91	5,101.37	4,579.26	3,852.68	2,900.65	2,442.00	2,180.01	2,015.65	1,906.41	1,830.98
5.75%	6,821.95	5,143.60	4,622.11	3,896.81	2,947.96	2,492.40	2,233.33	2,071.68	1,964.93	1,891.75
6.00%	6,863.14	5,186.04	4,665.21	3,941.23	2,995.69	2,543.33	2,287.27	2,128.40	2,024.17	1,953.26
6.25%	6,904.49	5,228.69	4,708.54	3,985.94	3,043.85	2,594.80	2,341.83	2,185.80	2,084.12	2,015.48
6.50%	6,945.98	5,271.55	4,752.11	4,030.95	3,092.43	2,646.78	2,396.99	2,243.84	2,144.75	2,078.37
6.75%	6,987.63	5,314.62	4,795.92	4,076.26	3,141.43	2,699.29	2,452.74	2,302.52	2,206.03	2,141.92
7.00%	7,029.43	5,357.90	4,839.97	4,121.85	3,190.84	2,752.31	2,509.07	2,361.82	2,267.94	2,206.08
7.25%	7,071.37	5,401.39	4,884.25	4,167.74	3,240.66	2,805.83	2,565.96	2,421.73	2,330.46	2,270.84
7.50%	7,113.47	5,445.09	4,928.77	4,213.91	3,290.89	2,859.86	2,623.42	2,482.21	2,393.56	2,336.15
7.75%	7,155.72	5,488.99	4,973.53	4,260.38	3,341.53	2,914.37	2,681.42	2,543.26	2,457.22	2,402.00
8.00%	7,198.12	5,533.11	5,018.52	4,307.13	3,392.56	2,969.36	2,739.95	2,604.86	2,521.43	2,468.36
8.25%	7,240.67	5,577.43	5,063.75	4,354.17	3,444.00	3,024.83	2,799.00	2,667.00	2,586.14	2,535.19
8.50%	7,283.37	5,621.95	5,109.21	4,401.49	3,495.83	3,080.77	2,858.56	2,729.64	2,651.36	2,602.48
8.75%	7,326.22	5,666.68	5,154.90	4,449.10	3,548.04	3,137.17	2,918.61	2,792.79	2,717.04	2,670.21
9.00%	7,369.22	5,711.62	5,200.82	4,496.99	3,600.65	3,194.03	2,979.15	2,856.41	2,783.18	2,738.33
9.25%	7,412.36	5,756.77	5,246.98	4,545.16	3,653.63	3,251.33	3,040.16	2,920.50	2,849.74	2,806.85
9.50%	7,455.66	5,802.11	5,293.37	4,593.61	3,707.00	3,309.07	3,101.62	2,985.03	2,916.72	2,875.72
9.75%	7,499.11	5,847.67	5,339.98	4,642.34	3,760.74	3,367.23	3,163.54	3,050.00	2,984.09	2,944.93
10.00%	7,542.70	5,893.42	5,386.83	4,691.35	3,814.85	3,425.83	3,225.89	3,115.38	3,051.84	3,014.47
10.25%	7,586.44	5,939.38	5,433.90	4,740.63	3,869.33	3,484.83	3,288.66	3,181.16	3,119.94	3,084.30
10.50%	7,630.33	5,985.54	5,481.21	4,790.19	3,924.17	3,544.25	3,351.85	3,247.32	3,188.38	3,154.42
10.75%	7,674.37	6,031.90	5,528.74	4,840.02	3,979.37	3,604.06	3,415.43	3,313.86	3,257.14	3,224.81

$355,000   11.00 - 20.75%   5 - 40 Years

	5	7	8	10	15	20	25	30	35	40
11.00%	7,718.56	6,078.46	5,576.49	4,890.13	4,034.92	3,664.27	3,479.40	3,380.75	3,326.20	3,295.45
11.25%	7,762.89	6,125.23	5,624.47	4,940.50	4,090.82	3,724.86	3,543.75	3,447.98	3,395.55	3,366.31
11.50%	7,807.38	6,172.19	5,672.68	4,991.14	4,147.07	3,785.83	3,608.46	3,515.53	3,465.18	3,437.40
11.75%	7,852.00	6,219.36	5,721.11	5,042.05	4,203.67	3,847.16	3,673.53	3,583.40	3,535.07	3,508.69
12.00%	7,896.78	6,266.72	5,769.76	5,093.22	4,260.60	3,908.86	3,738.95	3,651.57	3,605.20	3,580.17
12.25%	7,941.70	6,314.28	5,818.63	5,144.66	4,317.86	3,970.90	3,804.69	3,720.03	3,675.57	3,651.84
12.50%	7,986.77	6,362.04	5,867.73	5,196.35	4,375.45	4,033.30	3,870.76	3,788.77	3,746.15	3,723.66
12.75%	8,031.98	6,410.00	5,917.04	5,248.31	4,433.37	4,096.03	3,937.14	3,857.76	3,816.95	3,795.65
13.00%	8,077.34	6,458.15	5,966.58	5,300.53	4,491.61	4,159.09	4,003.82	3,927.01	3,887.94	3,867.78
13.25%	8,122.85	6,506.49	6,016.33	5,353.01	4,550.16	4,222.48	4,070.79	3,996.50	3,959.11	3,940.04
13.50%	8,168.50	6,555.04	6,066.30	5,405.74	4,609.03	4,286.18	4,138.04	4,066.21	4,030.46	4,012.43
13.75%	8,214.29	6,603.77	6,116.48	5,458.72	4,668.20	4,350.19	4,205.56	4,136.15	4,101.97	4,084.93
14.00%	8,260.23	6,652.70	6,166.88	5,511.96	4,727.68	4,414.50	4,273.35	4,206.29	4,173.64	4,157.55
14.25%	8,306.31	6,701.83	6,217.50	5,565.45	4,787.46	4,479.10	4,341.39	4,276.64	4,245.45	4,230.26
14.50%	8,352.54	6,751.14	6,268.33	5,619.18	4,847.53	4,543.99	4,409.68	4,347.17	4,317.41	4,303.07
14.75%	8,398.91	6,800.65	6,319.37	5,673.16	4,907.89	4,609.16	4,478.20	4,417.89	4,389.49	4,375.97
15.00%	8,445.43	6,850.35	6,370.62	5,727.39	4,968.53	4,674.60	4,546.95	4,488.78	4,461.69	4,448.95
15.25%	8,492.08	6,900.24	6,422.08	5,781.86	5,029.46	4,740.31	4,615.92	4,559.83	4,534.00	4,522.00
15.50%	8,538.88	6,950.31	6,473.75	5,836.57	5,090.67	4,806.28	4,685.10	4,631.04	4,606.43	4,595.12
15.75%	8,585.83	7,000.58	6,525.63	5,891.53	5,152.14	4,872.49	4,754.48	4,702.39	4,678.95	4,668.31
16.00%	8,632.91	7,051.03	6,577.72	5,946.72	5,213.89	4,938.96	4,824.06	4,773.89	4,751.57	4,741.55
16.25%	8,680.14	7,101.67	6,630.01	6,002.14	5,275.90	5,005.66	4,893.82	4,845.52	4,824.27	4,814.85
16.50%	8,727.50	7,152.50	6,682.51	6,057.80	5,338.17	5,072.60	4,963.77	4,917.28	4,897.06	4,888.21
16.75%	8,775.01	7,203.51	6,735.21	6,113.69	5,400.69	5,139.76	5,033.89	4,989.15	4,969.93	4,961.61
17.00%	8,822.66	7,254.71	6,788.12	6,169.82	5,463.47	5,207.14	5,104.18	5,061.15	5,042.87	5,035.05
17.25%	8,870.46	7,306.09	6,841.22	6,226.17	5,526.49	5,274.74	5,174.63	5,133.25	5,115.88	5,108.53
17.50%	8,918.39	7,357.66	6,894.53	6,282.75	5,589.75	5,342.54	5,245.23	5,205.45	5,188.95	5,182.05
17.75%	8,966.46	7,409.40	6,948.04	6,339.55	5,653.26	5,410.55	5,315.98	5,277.76	5,262.08	5,255.61
18.00%	9,014.67	7,461.33	7,001.74	6,396.57	5,716.99	5,478.76	5,386.88	5,350.15	5,335.27	5,329.20
18.25%	9,063.02	7,513.44	7,055.64	6,453.82	5,780.96	5,547.15	5,457.91	5,422.64	5,408.51	5,402.81
18.50%	9,111.50	7,565.73	7,109.74	6,511.29	5,845.16	5,615.73	5,529.07	5,495.20	5,481.79	5,476.46
18.75%	9,160.13	7,618.20	7,164.03	6,568.97	5,909.57	5,684.49	5,600.36	5,567.85	5,555.13	5,550.13
19.00%	9,208.90	7,670.85	7,218.52	6,626.87	5,974.21	5,753.43	5,671.76	5,640.57	5,628.51	5,623.82
19.25%	9,257.80	7,723.67	7,273.20	6,684.98	6,039.06	5,822.54	5,743.29	5,713.36	5,701.92	5,697.53
19.50%	9,306.84	7,776.67	7,328.07	6,743.30	6,104.12	5,891.81	5,814.92	5,786.22	5,775.38	5,771.27
19.75%	9,356.02	7,829.85	7,383.14	6,801.84	6,169.38	5,961.24	5,886.66	5,859.14	5,848.87	5,845.02
20.00%	9,405.33	7,883.20	7,438.39	6,860.58	6,234.85	6,030.83	5,958.50	5,932.12	5,922.39	5,918.79
20.25%	9,454.78	7,936.73	7,493.83	6,919.52	6,300.52	6,100.56	6,030.44	6,005.15	5,995.94	5,992.57
20.50%	9,504.36	7,990.43	7,549.45	6,978.67	6,366.38	6,170.45	6,102.48	6,078.24	6,069.52	6,066.37
20.75%	9,554.09	8,044.30	7,605.26	7,038.02	6,432.43	6,240.47	6,174.60	6,151.38	6,143.13	6,140.18

	5	7	8	10	15	20	25	30	35	40
1.00%	6,153.75	4,439.25	3,903.56	3,153.75	2,154.58	1,655.62	1,356.74	1,157.90	1,016.23	910.28
1.25%	6,192.58	4,478.18	3,942.58	3,192.97	2,194.39	1,696.08	1,397.81	1,199.71	1,058.71	953.44
1.50%	6,231.56	4,517.33	3,981.84	3,232.49	2,234.67	1,737.16	1,439.77	1,242.43	1,102.26	997.82
1.75%	6,270.70	4,556.69	4,021.35	3,272.33	2,275.42	1,778.86	1,482.44	1,286.08	1,146.88	1,043.40
2.00%	6,309.99	4,596.28	4,061.11	3,312.48	2,316.63	1,821.18	1,525.88	1,330.63	1,192.55	1,090.17
2.25%	6,349.44	4,636.08	4,101.12	3,352.95	2,358.31	1,864.11	1,570.07	1,376.09	1,239.25	1,138.11
2.50%	6,389.05	4,676.10	4,141.38	3,393.72	2,400.44	1,907.65	1,615.02	1,422.44	1,286.98	1,187.20
2.75%	6,428.81	4,716.33	4,181.89	3,434.80	2,443.04	1,951.80	1,660.72	1,469.67	1,335.72	1,237.42
3.00%	6,468.73	4,756.79	4,222.65	3,476.19	2,486.09	1,996.55	1,707.16	1,517.77	1,385.46	1,288.74
3.25%	6,508.80	4,797.46	4,263.65	3,517.89	2,529.61	2,041.90	1,754.34	1,566.74	1,436.17	1,341.15
3.50%	6,549.03	4,838.35	4,304.90	3,559.89	2,573.58	2,087.85	1,802.24	1,616.56	1,487.85	1,394.61
3.75%	6,589.41	4,879.45	4,346.40	3,602.20	2,618.00	2,134.40	1,850.87	1,667.22	1,540.46	1,449.09
4.00%	6,629.95	4,920.77	4,388.14	3,644.82	2,662.88	2,181.53	1,900.21	1,718.70	1,593.99	1,504.58
4.25%	6,670.64	4,962.31	4,430.13	3,687.75	2,708.20	2,229.24	1,950.26	1,770.98	1,648.42	1,561.03
4.50%	6,711.49	5,004.06	4,472.36	3,730.98	2,753.98	2,277.54	2,001.00	1,824.07	1,703.72	1,618.43
4.75%	6,752.49	5,046.03	4,514.85	3,774.52	2,800.19	2,326.41	2,052.42	1,877.93	1,759.88	1,676.73
5.00%	6,793.64	5,088.21	4,557.57	3,818.36	2,846.86	2,375.84	2,104.52	1,932.56	1,816.88	1,735.91
5.25%	6,834.95	5,130.60	4,600.54	3,862.50	2,893.96	2,425.84	2,157.29	1,987.93	1,874.67	1,795.93
5.50%	6,876.42	5,173.22	4,643.76	3,906.95	2,941.50	2,476.39	2,210.71	2,044.04	1,933.26	1,856.77
5.75%	6,918.04	5,216.04	4,687.21	3,951.69	2,989.48	2,527.50	2,264.78	2,100.86	1,992.60	1,918.40
6.00%	6,959.81	5,259.08	4,730.91	3,996.74	3,037.88	2,579.15	2,319.49	2,158.38	2,052.68	1,980.77
6.25%	7,001.73	5,302.33	4,774.86	4,042.08	3,086.72	2,631.34	2,374.81	2,216.58	2,113.48	2,043.86
6.50%	7,043.81	5,345.80	4,819.04	4,087.73	3,135.99	2,684.06	2,430.75	2,275.44	2,174.96	2,107.64
6.75%	7,086.05	5,389.47	4,863.47	4,133.67	3,185.67	2,737.31	2,487.28	2,334.95	2,237.10	2,172.08
7.00%	7,128.43	5,433.36	4,908.14	4,179.91	3,235.78	2,791.08	2,544.41	2,395.09	2,299.88	2,237.15
7.25%	7,170.97	5,477.47	4,953.05	4,226.44	3,286.31	2,845.35	2,602.10	2,455.83	2,363.28	2,302.82
7.50%	7,213.66	5,521.78	4,998.19	4,273.26	3,337.24	2,900.14	2,660.37	2,517.17	2,427.27	2,369.05
7.75%	7,256.51	5,566.30	5,043.58	4,320.38	3,388.59	2,955.41	2,719.18	2,579.08	2,491.83	2,435.83
8.00%	7,299.50	5,611.04	5,089.20	4,367.79	3,440.35	3,011.18	2,778.54	2,641.55	2,556.94	2,503.12
8.25%	7,342.65	5,655.98	5,135.07	4,415.49	3,492.51	3,067.44	2,838.42	2,704.56	2,622.57	2,570.90
8.50%	7,385.95	5,701.13	5,181.17	4,463.48	3,545.06	3,124.16	2,898.82	2,768.09	2,688.70	2,639.14
8.75%	7,429.40	5,746.50	5,227.50	4,511.76	3,598.02	3,181.36	2,959.72	2,832.12	2,755.31	2,707.81
9.00%	7,473.01	5,792.07	5,274.07	4,560.33	3,651.36	3,239.01	3,021.11	2,896.64	2,822.37	2,776.90
9.25%	7,516.76	5,837.85	5,320.88	4,609.18	3,705.09	3,297.12	3,082.97	2,961.63	2,889.88	2,846.38
9.50%	7,560.67	5,883.83	5,367.92	4,658.31	3,759.21	3,355.67	3,145.31	3,027.08	2,957.80	2,916.22
9.75%	7,604.73	5,930.03	5,415.19	4,707.73	3,813.71	3,414.66	3,208.09	3,092.96	3,026.12	2,986.41
10.00%	7,648.94	5,976.43	5,462.70	4,757.43	3,868.58	3,474.08	3,271.32	3,159.26	3,094.82	3,056.93
10.25%	7,693.29	6,023.03	5,510.44	4,807.40	3,923.82	3,533.92	3,334.98	3,225.96	3,163.88	3,127.75
10.50%	7,737.80	6,069.84	5,558.41	4,857.66	3,979.44	3,594.17	3,399.05	3,293.06	3,233.28	3,198.85
10.75%	7,782.46	6,116.86	5,606.60	4,908.19	4,035.41	3,654.82	3,463.53	3,360.53	3,303.01	3,270.23

$360,000   11.00 - 20.75%   5 - 40 Years

	5	7	8	10	15	20	25	30	35	40
11.00%	7,827.27	6,164.08	5,655.03	4,959.00	4,091.75	3,715.88	3,528.41	3,428.36	3,373.05	3,341.86
11.25%	7,872.23	6,211.50	5,703.69	5,010.08	4,148.44	3,777.32	3,593.66	3,496.54	3,443.38	3,413.73
11.50%	7,917.34	6,259.13	5,752.57	5,061.44	4,205.48	3,839.15	3,659.29	3,565.05	3,513.99	3,485.81
11.75%	7,962.60	6,306.95	5,801.69	5,113.06	4,262.87	3,901.35	3,725.27	3,633.88	3,584.86	3,558.11
12.00%	8,008.00	6,354.98	5,851.02	5,164.95	4,320.61	3,963.91	3,791.61	3,703.01	3,655.98	3,630.60
12.25%	8,053.56	6,403.21	5,900.58	5,217.12	4,378.68	4,026.83	3,858.28	3,772.43	3,727.34	3,703.27
12.50%	8,099.26	6,451.65	5,950.37	5,269.54	4,437.08	4,090.11	3,925.27	3,842.13	3,798.92	3,776.11
12.75%	8,145.11	6,500.28	6,000.38	5,322.23	4,495.81	4,153.72	3,992.59	3,912.10	3,870.71	3,849.11
13.00%	8,191.11	6,549.11	6,050.61	5,375.19	4,554.87	4,217.67	4,060.21	3,982.32	3,942.70	3,922.25
13.25%	8,237.25	6,598.14	6,101.06	5,428.40	4,614.25	4,281.95	4,128.12	4,052.78	4,014.87	3,995.53
13.50%	8,283.54	6,647.36	6,151.74	5,481.87	4,673.95	4,346.55	4,196.32	4,123.48	4,087.23	4,068.94
13.75%	8,329.98	6,696.78	6,202.63	5,535.61	4,733.95	4,411.46	4,264.80	4,194.41	4,159.75	4,142.47
14.00%	8,376.57	6,746.40	6,253.74	5,589.59	4,794.27	4,476.67	4,333.54	4,265.54	4,232.42	4,216.10
14.25%	8,423.30	6,796.22	6,305.07	5,643.83	4,854.89	4,542.19	4,402.54	4,336.87	4,305.25	4,289.84
14.50%	8,470.18	6,846.23	6,356.61	5,698.32	4,915.80	4,607.99	4,471.79	4,408.40	4,378.21	4,363.68
14.75%	8,517.21	6,896.43	6,408.37	5,753.07	4,977.01	4,674.08	4,541.27	4,480.11	4,451.31	4,437.60
15.00%	8,564.37	6,946.83	6,460.35	5,808.06	5,038.51	4,740.44	4,610.99	4,552.00	4,524.53	4,511.61
15.25%	8,611.69	6,997.42	6,512.53	5,863.30	5,100.30	4,807.08	4,680.93	4,624.05	4,597.86	4,585.69
15.50%	8,659.15	7,048.20	6,564.93	5,918.78	5,162.37	4,873.97	4,751.08	4,696.26	4,671.30	4,659.84
15.75%	8,706.75	7,099.18	6,617.54	5,974.51	5,224.71	4,941.12	4,821.44	4,768.62	4,744.85	4,734.06
16.00%	8,754.50	7,150.34	6,670.36	6,030.47	5,287.32	5,008.52	4,892.00	4,841.13	4,818.49	4,808.33
16.25%	8,802.39	7,201.70	6,723.39	6,086.68	5,350.21	5,076.16	4,962.75	4,913.76	4,892.22	4,882.67
16.50%	8,850.43	7,253.24	6,776.63	6,143.12	5,413.35	5,144.04	5,033.68	4,986.53	4,966.03	4,957.05
16.75%	8,898.61	7,304.97	6,830.07	6,199.80	5,476.76	5,212.15	5,104.79	5,059.42	5,039.93	5,031.49
17.00%	8,946.93	7,356.89	6,883.72	6,256.72	5,540.42	5,280.48	5,176.07	5,132.43	5,113.89	5,105.96
17.25%	8,995.39	7,408.99	6,937.58	6,313.86	5,604.33	5,349.03	5,247.51	5,205.55	5,187.93	5,180.48
17.50%	9,044.00	7,461.29	6,991.64	6,371.24	5,668.48	5,417.79	5,319.11	5,278.77	5,262.03	5,255.04
17.75%	9,092.74	7,513.76	7,045.90	6,428.84	5,732.88	5,486.76	5,390.86	5,352.09	5,336.19	5,329.63
18.00%	9,141.63	7,566.42	7,100.36	6,486.67	5,797.52	5,555.92	5,462.75	5,425.51	5,410.41	5,404.26
18.25%	9,190.66	7,619.27	7,155.02	6,544.72	5,862.39	5,625.28	5,534.78	5,499.01	5,484.68	5,478.91
18.50%	9,239.84	7,672.29	7,209.88	6,603.00	5,927.48	5,694.83	5,606.94	5,572.60	5,559.00	5,553.59
18.75%	9,289.15	7,725.50	7,264.94	6,661.49	5,992.81	5,764.56	5,679.23	5,646.27	5,633.37	5,628.30
19.00%	9,338.60	7,778.89	7,320.19	6,720.20	6,058.35	5,834.47	5,751.65	5,720.01	5,707.78	5,703.03
19.25%	9,388.19	7,832.46	7,375.64	6,779.13	6,124.12	5,904.55	5,824.18	5,793.83	5,782.23	5,777.78
19.50%	9,437.92	7,886.20	7,431.29	6,838.28	6,190.09	5,974.79	5,896.82	5,867.71	5,856.72	5,852.55
19.75%	9,487.79	7,940.13	7,487.12	6,897.64	6,256.28	6,045.20	5,969.57	5,941.66	5,931.24	5,927.34
20.00%	9,537.80	7,994.23	7,543.15	6,957.20	6,322.67	6,115.77	6,042.43	6,015.67	6,005.80	6,002.15
20.25%	9,587.94	8,048.51	7,599.37	7,016.98	6,389.26	6,186.49	6,115.38	6,089.73	6,080.39	6,076.97
20.50%	9,638.23	8,102.97	7,655.78	7,076.96	6,456.05	6,257.35	6,188.43	6,163.85	6,155.01	6,151.81
20.75%	9,688.65	8,157.60	7,712.38	7,137.15	6,523.03	6,328.37	6,261.56	6,238.02	6,229.65	6,226.66

	5	7	8	10	15	20	25	30	35	40
1.00%	6,239.22	4,500.91	3,957.78	3,197.55	2,184.50	1,678.61	1,375.58	1,173.98	1,030.34	922.92
1.25%	6,278.58	4,540.38	3,997.33	3,237.31	2,224.87	1,719.64	1,417.28	1,216.37	1,073.41	966.69
1.50%	6,318.11	4,580.07	4,037.14	3,277.39	2,265.71	1,761.29	1,459.77	1,259.69	1,117.57	1,011.68
1.75%	6,357.79	4,619.98	4,077.20	3,317.78	2,307.02	1,803.57	1,503.03	1,303.94	1,162.81	1,057.89
2.00%	6,397.63	4,660.11	4,117.52	3,358.49	2,348.81	1,846.47	1,547.07	1,349.11	1,209.11	1,105.31
2.25%	6,437.63	4,700.47	4,158.08	3,399.51	2,391.06	1,890.00	1,591.88	1,395.20	1,256.46	1,153.92
2.50%	6,477.79	4,741.04	4,198.90	3,440.85	2,433.78	1,934.15	1,637.45	1,442.19	1,304.86	1,203.69
2.75%	6,518.10	4,781.84	4,239.97	3,482.50	2,476.97	1,978.91	1,683.78	1,490.08	1,354.28	1,254.61
3.00%	6,558.57	4,822.85	4,281.29	3,524.47	2,520.62	2,024.28	1,730.87	1,538.85	1,404.70	1,306.64
3.25%	6,599.20	4,864.09	4,322.87	3,566.74	2,564.74	2,070.26	1,778.70	1,588.50	1,456.12	1,359.78
3.50%	6,639.99	4,905.55	4,364.69	3,609.33	2,609.32	2,116.85	1,827.28	1,639.01	1,508.51	1,413.98
3.75%	6,680.93	4,947.22	4,406.76	3,652.24	2,654.36	2,164.04	1,876.58	1,690.37	1,561.85	1,469.22
4.00%	6,722.03	4,989.11	4,449.09	3,695.45	2,699.86	2,211.83	1,926.60	1,742.57	1,616.13	1,525.48
4.25%	6,763.29	5,031.23	4,491.66	3,738.97	2,745.82	2,260.21	1,977.34	1,795.58	1,671.31	1,582.71
4.50%	6,804.70	5,073.56	4,534.48	3,782.80	2,792.23	2,309.17	2,028.79	1,849.40	1,727.39	1,640.90
4.75%	6,846.27	5,116.11	4,577.55	3,826.94	2,839.09	2,358.72	2,080.93	1,904.01	1,784.33	1,700.02
5.00%	6,888.00	5,158.88	4,620.87	3,871.39	2,886.40	2,408.84	2,133.75	1,959.40	1,842.11	1,760.02
5.25%	6,929.88	5,201.86	4,664.44	3,916.15	2,934.15	2,459.53	2,187.25	2,015.54	1,900.71	1,820.88
5.50%	6,971.92	5,245.07	4,708.25	3,961.21	2,982.35	2,510.79	2,241.42	2,072.43	1,960.11	1,882.56
5.75%	7,014.12	5,288.49	4,752.31	4,006.58	3,031.00	2,562.60	2,296.24	2,130.04	2,020.28	1,945.04
6.00%	7,056.47	5,332.12	4,796.62	4,052.25	3,080.08	2,614.97	2,351.70	2,188.36	2,081.19	2,008.28
6.25%	7,098.98	5,375.98	4,841.18	4,098.22	3,129.59	2,667.89	2,407.79	2,247.37	2,142.83	2,072.25
6.50%	7,141.64	5,420.04	4,885.97	4,144.50	3,179.54	2,721.34	2,464.51	2,307.05	2,205.16	2,136.92
6.75%	7,184.46	5,464.33	4,931.02	4,191.08	3,229.92	2,775.33	2,521.83	2,367.38	2,268.17	2,202.25
7.00%	7,227.44	5,508.83	4,976.31	4,237.96	3,280.72	2,829.84	2,579.74	2,428.35	2,331.83	2,268.22
7.25%	7,270.57	5,553.54	5,021.84	4,285.14	3,331.95	2,884.87	2,638.25	2,489.94	2,396.11	2,334.80
7.50%	7,313.85	5,598.47	5,067.61	4,332.61	3,383.60	2,940.42	2,697.32	2,552.13	2,460.99	2,401.96
7.75%	7,357.29	5,643.61	5,113.63	4,380.39	3,435.66	2,996.46	2,756.95	2,614.90	2,526.44	2,469.66
8.00%	7,400.88	5,688.97	5,159.89	4,428.46	3,488.13	3,053.01	2,817.13	2,678.24	2,592.45	2,537.89
8.25%	7,444.63	5,734.54	5,206.39	4,476.82	3,541.01	3,110.04	2,877.84	2,742.12	2,658.99	2,606.61
8.50%	7,488.53	5,780.32	5,253.13	4,525.48	3,594.30	3,167.55	2,939.08	2,806.53	2,726.04	2,675.79
8.75%	7,532.59	5,826.31	5,300.11	4,574.43	3,647.99	3,225.54	3,000.82	2,871.46	2,793.58	2,745.42
9.00%	7,576.80	5,872.51	5,347.32	4,623.67	3,702.07	3,284.00	3,063.07	2,936.87	2,861.57	2,815.47
9.25%	7,621.16	5,918.93	5,394.78	4,673.19	3,756.55	3,342.91	3,125.79	3,002.77	2,930.02	2,885.91
9.50%	7,665.68	5,965.55	5,442.47	4,723.01	3,811.42	3,402.28	3,188.99	3,069.12	2,998.88	2,956.72
9.75%	7,710.35	6,012.39	5,490.40	4,773.11	3,866.67	3,462.09	3,252.65	3,135.91	3,068.15	3,027.89
10.00%	7,755.17	6,059.43	5,538.57	4,823.50	3,922.31	3,522.33	3,316.76	3,203.14	3,137.80	3,099.38
10.25%	7,800.15	6,106.68	5,586.97	4,874.17	3,978.32	3,583.00	3,381.30	3,270.77	3,207.82	3,171.19
10.50%	7,845.27	6,154.15	5,635.61	4,925.13	4,034.71	3,644.09	3,446.26	3,338.80	3,278.19	3,243.28
10.75%	7,890.55	6,201.81	5,684.47	4,976.36	4,091.46	3,705.59	3,511.64	3,407.21	3,348.89	3,315.65

	5	7	8	10	15	20	25	30	35	40
11.00%	7,935.98	6,249.69	5,733.58	5,027.88	4,148.58	3,767.49	3,577.41	3,475.98	3,419.90	3,388.27
11.25%	7,981.57	6,297.77	5,782.91	5,079.67	4,206.06	3,829.78	3,643.57	3,545.10	3,491.20	3,461.14
11.50%	8,027.30	6,346.06	5,832.47	5,131.73	4,263.89	3,892.47	3,710.11	3,614.56	3,562.79	3,534.23
11.75%	8,073.19	6,394.55	5,882.26	5,184.08	4,322.08	3,955.53	3,777.01	3,684.35	3,634.65	3,607.53
12.00%	8,119.22	6,443.25	5,932.29	5,236.69	4,380.61	4,018.96	3,844.27	3,754.44	3,706.76	3,681.02
12.25%	8,165.41	6,492.15	5,982.54	5,289.58	4,439.49	4,082.76	3,911.86	3,824.82	3,779.10	3,754.70
12.50%	8,211.75	6,541.25	6,033.02	5,342.73	4,498.71	4,146.91	3,979.79	3,895.49	3,851.68	3,828.56
12.75%	8,258.23	6,590.56	6,083.72	5,396.15	4,558.25	4,211.41	4,048.04	3,966.43	3,924.47	3,902.57
13.00%	8,304.87	6,640.07	6,134.65	5,449.84	4,618.13	4,276.25	4,116.60	4,037.63	3,997.45	3,976.73
13.25%	8,351.66	6,689.78	6,185.80	5,503.80	4,678.34	4,341.42	4,185.46	4,109.07	4,070.63	4,051.03
13.50%	8,398.59	6,739.69	6,237.18	5,558.01	4,738.86	4,406.92	4,254.60	4,180.75	4,143.99	4,125.45
13.75%	8,445.68	6,789.80	6,288.78	5,612.49	4,799.70	4,472.73	4,324.03	4,252.66	4,217.52	4,200.00
14.00%	8,492.91	6,840.10	6,340.60	5,667.22	4,860.86	4,538.85	4,393.73	4,324.78	4,291.21	4,274.66
14.25%	8,540.29	6,890.61	6,392.64	5,722.22	4,922.32	4,605.27	4,463.69	4,397.11	4,365.04	4,349.42
14.50%	8,587.82	6,941.32	6,444.90	5,777.47	4,984.08	4,671.99	4,533.89	4,469.63	4,439.02	4,424.29
14.75%	8,635.50	6,992.22	6,497.38	5,832.97	5,046.14	4,739.00	4,604.35	4,542.34	4,513.13	4,499.24
15.00%	8,683.32	7,043.32	6,550.07	5,888.73	5,108.49	4,806.28	4,675.03	4,615.22	4,587.37	4,574.27
15.25%	8,731.30	7,094.61	6,602.98	5,944.73	5,171.14	4,873.84	4,745.94	4,688.27	4,661.72	4,649.38
15.50%	8,779.41	7,146.10	6,656.11	6,000.98	5,234.06	4,941.66	4,817.07	4,761.49	4,736.18	4,724.56
15.75%	8,827.68	7,197.78	6,709.45	6,057.48	5,297.27	5,009.75	4,888.41	4,834.85	4,810.75	4,799.81
16.00%	8,876.09	7,249.65	6,763.01	6,114.23	5,360.76	5,078.08	4,959.94	4,908.36	4,885.41	4,875.12
16.25%	8,924.65	7,301.72	6,816.77	6,171.22	5,424.51	5,146.67	5,031.68	4,982.01	4,960.17	4,950.48
16.50%	8,973.35	7,353.98	6,870.75	6,228.44	5,488.54	5,215.49	5,103.59	5,055.79	5,035.01	5,025.90
16.75%	9,022.20	7,406.43	6,924.94	6,285.91	5,552.82	5,284.54	5,175.69	5,129.69	5,109.93	5,101.37
17.00%	9,071.19	7,459.07	6,979.33	6,343.61	5,617.37	5,353.82	5,247.96	5,203.72	5,184.92	5,176.88
17.25%	9,120.33	7,511.90	7,033.93	6,401.55	5,682.16	5,423.32	5,320.39	5,277.85	5,259.98	5,252.43
17.50%	9,169.61	7,564.91	7,088.74	6,459.72	5,747.21	5,493.04	5,392.98	5,352.09	5,335.11	5,328.03
17.75%	9,219.03	7,618.12	7,143.76	6,518.13	5,812.50	5,562.96	5,465.73	5,426.43	5,410.31	5,403.65
18.00%	9,268.60	7,671.51	7,198.97	6,576.76	5,878.04	5,633.09	5,538.62	5,500.86	5,485.56	5,479.32
18.25%	9,318.31	7,725.09	7,254.39	6,635.62	5,943.81	5,703.41	5,611.65	5,575.39	5,560.86	5,555.01
18.50%	9,368.17	7,778.85	7,310.02	6,694.70	6,009.81	5,773.92	5,684.82	5,650.00	5,636.21	5,630.73
18.75%	9,418.16	7,832.80	7,365.84	6,754.01	6,076.04	5,844.62	5,758.11	5,724.69	5,711.61	5,706.47
19.00%	9,468.30	7,886.93	7,421.86	6,813.54	6,142.50	5,915.50	5,831.53	5,799.46	5,787.06	5,782.24
19.25%	9,518.58	7,941.24	7,478.08	6,873.29	6,209.17	5,986.55	5,905.07	5,874.30	5,862.54	5,858.03
19.50%	9,569.00	7,995.73	7,534.50	6,933.26	6,276.07	6,057.78	5,978.72	5,949.21	5,938.06	5,933.84
19.75%	9,619.56	8,050.41	7,591.11	6,993.44	6,343.17	6,129.16	6,052.48	6,024.18	6,013.62	6,009.67
20.00%	9,670.27	8,105.26	7,647.92	7,053.83	6,410.48	6,200.71	6,126.35	6,099.22	6,089.22	6,085.51
20.25%	9,721.11	8,160.30	7,704.92	7,114.44	6,478.00	6,272.41	6,200.31	6,174.31	6,164.84	6,161.38
20.50%	9,772.09	8,215.51	7,762.11	7,175.25	6,545.72	6,344.26	6,274.38	6,249.46	6,240.49	6,237.25
20.75%	9,823.22	8,270.90	7,819.50	7,236.28	6,613.63	6,416.26	6,348.53	6,324.66	6,316.17	6,313.14

	5	7	8	10	15	20	25	30	35	40
1.00%	6,324.69	4,562.56	4,011.99	3,241.35	2,214.43	1,701.61	1,394.43	1,190.07	1,044.46	935.57
1.25%	6,364.59	4,602.57	4,052.09	3,281.66	2,255.35	1,743.19	1,436.70	1,233.03	1,088.12	979.93
1.50%	6,404.66	4,642.81	4,092.45	3,322.29	2,296.75	1,785.42	1,479.76	1,276.94	1,132.88	1,025.54
1.75%	6,444.88	4,683.27	4,133.06	3,363.23	2,338.63	1,828.28	1,523.62	1,321.80	1,178.74	1,072.39
2.00%	6,485.27	4,723.95	4,173.92	3,404.50	2,380.98	1,871.77	1,568.26	1,367.59	1,225.67	1,120.45
2.25%	6,525.82	4,764.86	4,215.04	3,446.08	2,423.81	1,915.89	1,613.68	1,414.31	1,273.68	1,169.73
2.50%	6,566.52	4,805.99	4,256.42	3,487.99	2,467.12	1,960.64	1,659.88	1,461.95	1,322.73	1,220.18
2.75%	6,607.39	4,847.34	4,298.05	3,530.21	2,510.90	2,006.02	1,706.85	1,510.49	1,372.83	1,271.79
3.00%	6,648.42	4,888.92	4,339.94	3,572.75	2,555.15	2,052.01	1,754.58	1,559.93	1,423.95	1,324.54
3.25%	6,689.60	4,930.72	4,382.08	3,615.60	2,599.87	2,098.62	1,803.07	1,610.26	1,476.07	1,378.40
3.50%	6,730.95	4,972.74	4,424.48	3,658.78	2,645.07	2,145.85	1,852.31	1,661.47	1,529.18	1,433.35
3.75%	6,772.45	5,014.99	4,467.13	3,702.27	2,690.72	2,193.69	1,902.29	1,713.53	1,583.25	1,489.35
4.00%	6,814.11	5,057.46	4,510.03	3,746.07	2,736.85	2,242.13	1,953.00	1,766.44	1,638.27	1,546.37
4.25%	6,855.94	5,100.15	4,553.19	3,790.19	2,783.43	2,291.17	2,004.43	1,820.18	1,694.21	1,604.39
4.50%	6,897.92	5,143.06	4,596.60	3,834.62	2,830.48	2,340.80	2,056.58	1,874.74	1,751.05	1,663.38
4.75%	6,940.06	5,186.19	4,640.26	3,879.37	2,877.98	2,391.03	2,109.43	1,930.10	1,808.77	1,723.30
5.00%	6,982.36	5,229.55	4,684.17	3,924.42	2,925.94	2,441.84	2,162.98	1,986.24	1,867.34	1,784.13
5.25%	7,024.81	5,273.12	4,728.33	3,969.79	2,974.35	2,493.22	2,217.22	2,043.15	1,926.75	1,845.82
5.50%	7,067.43	5,316.92	4,772.75	4,015.47	3,023.21	2,545.18	2,272.12	2,100.82	1,986.96	1,908.35
5.75%	7,110.20	5,360.93	4,817.41	4,061.46	3,072.52	2,597.71	2,327.69	2,159.22	2,047.95	1,971.68
6.00%	7,153.14	5,405.17	4,862.33	4,107.76	3,122.27	2,650.79	2,383.92	2,218.34	2,109.70	2,035.79
6.25%	7,196.23	5,449.62	4,907.49	4,154.36	3,172.46	2,704.43	2,440.78	2,278.15	2,172.18	2,100.64
6.50%	7,239.47	5,494.29	4,952.91	4,201.28	3,223.10	2,758.62	2,498.27	2,338.65	2,235.37	2,166.19
6.75%	7,282.88	5,539.18	4,998.57	4,248.49	3,274.17	2,813.35	2,556.37	2,399.81	2,299.24	2,232.42
7.00%	7,326.44	5,584.29	5,044.48	4,296.01	3,325.66	2,868.61	2,615.08	2,461.62	2,363.77	2,299.30
7.25%	7,370.16	5,629.62	5,090.63	4,343.84	3,377.59	2,924.39	2,674.39	2,524.05	2,428.93	2,366.79
7.50%	7,414.04	5,675.16	5,137.03	4,391.97	3,429.95	2,980.69	2,734.27	2,587.09	2,494.70	2,434.86
7.75%	7,458.08	5,720.92	5,183.68	4,440.39	3,482.72	3,037.51	2,794.72	2,650.73	2,561.05	2,503.49
8.00%	7,502.27	5,766.90	5,230.57	4,489.12	3,535.91	3,094.83	2,855.72	2,714.93	2,627.97	2,572.65
8.25%	7,546.61	5,813.09	5,277.71	4,538.15	3,589.52	3,152.64	2,917.27	2,779.69	2,695.42	2,642.31
8.50%	7,591.12	5,859.50	5,325.09	4,587.47	3,643.54	3,210.95	2,979.34	2,844.98	2,763.38	2,712.45
8.75%	7,635.78	5,906.12	5,372.71	4,637.09	3,697.96	3,269.73	3,041.93	2,910.79	2,831.84	2,783.03
9.00%	7,680.59	5,952.96	5,420.58	4,687.00	3,752.79	3,328.99	3,105.03	2,977.10	2,900.77	2,854.04
9.25%	7,725.56	6,000.01	5,468.68	4,737.21	3,808.01	3,388.71	3,168.61	3,043.90	2,970.15	2,925.44
9.50%	7,770.69	6,047.27	5,517.03	4,787.71	3,863.63	3,448.89	3,232.68	3,111.16	3,039.96	2,997.23
9.75%	7,815.97	6,094.75	5,565.61	4,838.50	3,919.64	3,509.51	3,297.21	3,178.87	3,110.18	3,069.37
10.00%	7,861.41	6,142.44	5,614.44	4,889.58	3,976.04	3,570.58	3,362.19	3,247.01	3,180.79	3,141.84
10.25%	7,907.00	6,190.34	5,663.50	4,940.94	4,032.82	3,632.08	3,427.62	3,315.57	3,251.77	3,214.63
10.50%	7,952.74	6,238.45	5,712.81	4,992.59	4,089.98	3,694.01	3,493.47	3,384.54	3,323.10	3,287.71
10.75%	7,998.64	6,286.77	5,762.34	5,044.53	4,147.51	3,756.35	3,559.74	3,453.88	3,394.76	3,361.07

$370,000   11.00 - 20.75%   5 - 40 Years

	5	7	8	10	15	20	25	30	35	40
11.00%	8,044.70	6,335.30	5,812.12	5,096.75	4,205.41	3,819.10	3,626.42	3,523.60	3,466.74	3,434.69
11.25%	8,090.90	6,384.04	5,862.13	5,149.25	4,263.68	3,882.25	3,693.49	3,593.67	3,539.03	3,508.55
11.50%	8,137.26	6,432.99	5,912.37	5,202.03	4,322.30	3,945.79	3,760.94	3,664.08	3,611.60	3,582.64
11.75%	8,183.78	6,482.15	5,962.84	5,255.09	4,381.29	4,009.72	3,828.75	3,734.82	3,684.44	3,656.95
12.00%	8,230.45	6,531.51	6,013.55	5,308.43	4,440.62	4,074.02	3,896.93	3,805.87	3,757.53	3,731.45
12.25%	8,277.27	6,581.08	6,064.49	5,362.04	4,500.31	4,138.69	3,965.45	3,877.22	3,830.87	3,806.14
12.50%	8,324.24	6,630.86	6,115.66	5,415.92	4,560.33	4,203.72	4,034.31	3,948.85	3,904.44	3,881.00
12.75%	8,371.36	6,680.84	6,167.06	5,470.07	4,620.70	4,269.10	4,103.49	4,020.76	3,978.23	3,956.03
13.00%	8,418.64	6,731.03	6,218.68	5,524.50	4,681.40	4,334.83	4,172.99	4,092.94	4,052.21	4,031.20
13.25%	8,466.06	6,781.42	6,270.54	5,579.19	4,742.42	4,400.89	4,242.79	4,165.36	4,126.40	4,106.52
13.50%	8,513.64	6,832.01	6,322.62	5,634.15	4,803.78	4,467.29	4,312.89	4,238.03	4,200.76	4,181.97
13.75%	8,561.37	6,882.81	6,374.93	5,689.37	4,865.45	4,534.00	4,383.26	4,310.92	4,275.29	4,257.54
14.00%	8,609.25	6,933.80	6,427.46	5,744.86	4,927.44	4,601.03	4,453.92	4,384.03	4,349.99	4,333.22
14.25%	8,657.28	6,985.00	6,480.21	5,800.61	4,989.74	4,668.36	4,524.83	4,457.34	4,424.84	4,409.01
14.50%	8,705.46	7,036.40	6,533.19	5,856.61	5,052.35	4,735.99	4,596.00	4,530.86	4,499.83	4,484.89
14.75%	8,753.79	7,088.00	6,586.38	5,912.87	5,115.26	4,803.91	4,667.42	4,604.56	4,574.96	4,560.87
15.00%	8,802.27	7,139.80	6,639.80	5,969.39	5,178.47	4,872.12	4,739.07	4,678.44	4,650.21	4,636.93
15.25%	8,850.90	7,191.80	6,693.44	6,026.17	5,241.97	4,940.61	4,810.96	4,752.50	4,725.58	4,713.07
15.50%	8,899.68	7,243.99	6,747.29	6,083.19	5,305.76	5,009.36	4,883.06	4,826.71	4,801.06	4,789.28
15.75%	8,948.61	7,296.38	6,801.36	6,140.46	5,369.84	5,078.37	4,955.37	4,901.08	4,876.65	4,865.56
16.00%	8,997.68	7,348.96	6,855.65	6,197.99	5,434.19	5,147.65	5,027.89	4,975.60	4,952.34	4,941.90
16.25%	9,046.90	7,401.74	6,910.15	6,255.75	5,498.82	5,217.17	5,100.60	5,050.26	5,028.11	5,018.30
16.50%	9,096.27	7,454.72	6,964.87	6,313.77	5,563.72	5,286.93	5,173.51	5,125.05	5,103.98	5,094.75
16.75%	9,145.79	7,507.89	7,019.80	6,372.02	5,628.89	5,356.93	5,246.59	5,199.96	5,179.93	5,171.25
17.00%	9,195.45	7,561.25	7,074.94	6,430.51	5,694.32	5,427.16	5,319.85	5,275.00	5,255.95	5,247.80
17.25%	9,245.26	7,614.80	7,130.29	6,489.25	5,760.00	5,497.62	5,393.27	5,350.15	5,332.04	5,324.39
17.50%	9,295.22	7,668.54	7,185.85	6,548.21	5,825.94	5,568.29	5,466.86	5,425.40	5,408.20	5,401.01
17.75%	9,345.32	7,722.48	7,241.62	6,607.42	5,892.13	5,639.17	5,540.60	5,500.76	5,484.42	5,477.68
18.00%	9,395.57	7,776.60	7,297.59	6,666.85	5,958.56	5,710.25	5,614.49	5,576.22	5,560.70	5,554.37
18.25%	9,445.96	7,830.91	7,353.77	6,726.52	6,025.23	5,781.54	5,688.52	5,651.76	5,637.03	5,631.10
18.50%	9,496.50	7,885.41	7,410.15	6,786.41	6,092.14	5,853.02	5,762.69	5,727.39	5,713.42	5,707.86
18.75%	9,547.18	7,940.10	7,466.74	6,846.53	6,159.28	5,924.68	5,836.99	5,803.11	5,789.85	5,784.64
19.00%	9,598.00	7,994.97	7,523.53	6,906.88	6,226.64	5,996.53	5,911.42	5,878.90	5,866.33	5,861.45
19.25%	9,648.97	8,050.02	7,580.52	6,967.44	6,294.23	6,068.56	5,985.96	5,954.77	5,942.85	5,938.28
19.50%	9,700.08	8,105.26	7,637.71	7,028.23	6,362.04	6,140.76	6,060.62	6,030.70	6,019.41	6,015.12
19.75%	9,751.34	8,160.69	7,695.10	7,089.24	6,430.06	6,213.12	6,135.39	6,106.71	6,096.00	6,091.99
20.00%	9,802.74	8,216.29	7,752.68	7,150.46	6,498.30	6,285.65	6,210.27	6,182.77	6,172.63	6,168.88
20.25%	9,854.28	8,272.08	7,810.47	7,211.90	6,566.74	6,358.33	6,285.25	6,258.89	6,249.29	6,245.78
20.50%	9,905.96	8,328.05	7,868.44	7,273.55	6,635.38	6,431.17	6,360.33	6,335.07	6,325.98	6,322.69
20.75%	9,957.78	8,384.20	7,926.61	7,335.40	6,704.23	6,504.15	6,435.49	6,411.30	6,402.69	6,399.62

	5	7	8	10	15	20	25	30	35	40
1.00%	6,410.16	4,624.22	4,066.21	3,285.15	2,244.35	1,724.60	1,413.27	1,206.15	1,058.57	948.21
1.25%	6,450.60	4,664.77	4,106.85	3,326.01	2,285.83	1,766.75	1,456.11	1,249.69	1,102.82	993.17
1.50%	6,491.21	4,705.55	4,147.75	3,367.18	2,327.79	1,809.55	1,499.76	1,294.20	1,148.19	1,039.40
1.75%	6,531.98	4,746.55	4,188.91	3,408.68	2,370.23	1,852.98	1,544.21	1,339.66	1,194.67	1,086.88
2.00%	6,572.91	4,787.79	4,230.33	3,450.50	2,413.16	1,897.06	1,589.45	1,386.07	1,242.24	1,135.60
2.25%	6,614.00	4,829.25	4,272.00	3,492.65	2,456.57	1,941.78	1,635.49	1,433.42	1,290.89	1,185.53
2.50%	6,655.26	4,870.93	4,313.94	3,535.12	2,500.46	1,987.14	1,682.31	1,481.70	1,340.61	1,236.67
2.75%	6,696.68	4,912.85	4,356.14	3,577.91	2,544.83	2,033.12	1,729.92	1,530.90	1,391.38	1,288.98
3.00%	6,738.26	4,954.99	4,398.59	3,621.03	2,589.68	2,079.74	1,778.29	1,581.02	1,443.19	1,342.44
3.25%	6,780.00	4,997.35	4,441.30	3,664.46	2,635.01	2,126.98	1,827.44	1,632.02	1,496.01	1,397.03
3.50%	6,821.90	5,039.94	4,484.27	3,708.22	2,680.81	2,174.85	1,877.34	1,683.92	1,549.84	1,452.72
3.75%	6,863.97	5,082.76	4,527.50	3,752.30	2,727.08	2,223.33	1,927.99	1,736.68	1,604.64	1,509.47
4.00%	6,906.20	5,125.80	4,570.98	3,796.69	2,773.83	2,272.43	1,979.39	1,790.31	1,660.41	1,567.27
4.25%	6,948.58	5,169.07	4,614.72	3,841.41	2,821.04	2,322.13	2,031.52	1,844.77	1,717.10	1,626.08
4.50%	6,991.13	5,212.56	4,658.71	3,886.44	2,868.72	2,372.44	2,084.37	1,900.07	1,774.71	1,685.86
4.75%	7,033.84	5,256.28	4,702.96	3,931.79	2,916.87	2,423.34	2,137.94	1,956.18	1,833.21	1,746.59
5.00%	7,076.71	5,300.22	4,747.47	3,977.46	2,965.48	2,474.83	2,192.21	2,013.08	1,892.58	1,808.24
5.25%	7,119.74	5,344.38	4,792.23	4,023.44	3,014.54	2,526.92	2,247.18	2,070.76	1,952.79	1,870.76
5.50%	7,162.94	5,388.77	4,837.25	4,069.74	3,064.06	2,579.58	2,302.83	2,129.21	2,013.81	1,934.14
5.75%	7,206.29	5,433.38	4,882.51	4,116.35	3,114.04	2,632.81	2,359.15	2,188.40	2,075.63	1,998.33
6.00%	7,249.80	5,478.21	4,928.04	4,163.27	3,164.46	2,686.62	2,416.13	2,248.31	2,138.21	2,063.30
6.25%	7,293.47	5,523.26	4,973.81	4,210.50	3,215.34	2,740.98	2,473.76	2,308.94	2,201.54	2,129.02
6.50%	7,337.31	5,568.54	5,019.84	4,258.05	3,266.65	2,795.90	2,532.03	2,370.26	2,265.58	2,195.46
6.75%	7,381.30	5,614.04	5,066.12	4,305.90	3,318.41	2,851.37	2,590.92	2,432.24	2,330.31	2,262.59
7.00%	7,425.45	5,659.75	5,112.64	4,354.07	3,370.61	2,907.37	2,650.42	2,494.88	2,395.71	2,330.37
7.25%	7,469.76	5,705.69	5,159.42	4,402.54	3,423.24	2,963.91	2,710.53	2,558.16	2,461.75	2,398.77
7.50%	7,514.23	5,751.85	5,206.45	4,451.32	3,476.30	3,020.97	2,771.22	2,622.05	2,528.41	2,467.77
7.75%	7,558.86	5,798.23	5,253.73	4,500.40	3,529.78	3,078.56	2,832.48	2,686.55	2,595.66	2,537.32
8.00%	7,603.65	5,844.83	5,301.25	4,549.78	3,583.70	3,136.65	2,894.31	2,751.62	2,663.48	2,607.42
8.25%	7,648.59	5,891.65	5,349.03	4,599.47	3,638.03	3,195.25	2,956.69	2,817.25	2,731.84	2,678.02
8.50%	7,693.70	5,938.68	5,397.05	4,649.46	3,692.77	3,254.34	3,019.60	2,883.43	2,800.73	2,749.10
8.75%	7,738.96	5,985.93	5,445.31	4,699.75	3,747.93	3,313.92	3,083.04	2,950.13	2,870.11	2,820.64
9.00%	7,784.38	6,033.40	5,493.83	4,750.34	3,803.50	3,373.97	3,146.99	3,017.33	2,939.97	2,892.61
9.25%	7,829.96	6,081.09	5,542.58	4,801.23	3,859.47	3,434.50	3,211.43	3,085.03	3,010.29	2,964.98
9.50%	7,875.70	6,128.99	5,591.58	4,852.41	3,915.84	3,495.49	3,276.36	3,153.20	3,081.04	3,037.73
9.75%	7,921.59	6,177.11	5,640.83	4,903.88	3,972.61	3,556.94	3,341.77	3,221.83	3,152.21	3,110.84
10.00%	7,967.64	6,225.44	5,690.31	4,955.65	4,029.77	3,618.83	3,407.63	3,290.89	3,223.77	3,184.30
10.25%	8,013.85	6,273.99	5,740.04	5,007.71	4,087.32	3,681.16	3,473.94	3,360.38	3,295.71	3,258.07
10.50%	8,060.21	6,322.75	5,790.01	5,060.06	4,145.25	3,743.92	3,540.68	3,430.27	3,368.00	3,332.14
10.75%	8,106.73	6,371.73	5,840.21	5,112.70	4,203.55	3,807.11	3,607.85	3,500.56	3,440.64	3,406.49

$375,000   11.00 - 20.75%   5 - 40 Years

	5	7	8	10	15	20	25	30	35	40
11.00%	8,153.41	6,420.91	5,890.66	5,165.63	4,262.24	3,870.71	3,675.42	3,571.21	3,513.59	3,481.10
11.25%	8,200.24	6,470.31	5,941.34	5,218.84	4,321.29	3,934.71	3,743.40	3,642.23	3,586.85	3,555.97
11.50%	8,247.23	6,519.92	5,992.27	5,272.33	4,380.71	3,999.11	3,811.76	3,713.59	3,660.40	3,631.06
11.75%	8,294.37	6,569.74	6,043.42	5,326.10	4,440.49	4,063.90	3,880.49	3,785.29	3,734.23	3,706.36
12.00%	8,341.67	6,619.77	6,094.82	5,380.16	4,500.63	4,129.07	3,949.59	3,857.30	3,808.31	3,781.87
12.25%	8,389.12	6,670.02	6,146.44	5,434.49	4,561.12	4,194.62	4,019.04	3,929.61	3,882.64	3,857.57
12.50%	8,436.73	6,720.46	6,198.30	5,489.11	4,621.96	4,260.53	4,088.83	4,002.22	3,957.20	3,933.45
12.75%	8,484.49	6,771.12	6,250.40	5,543.99	4,683.14	4,326.79	4,158.95	4,075.10	4,031.99	4,009.49
13.00%	8,532.40	6,821.99	6,302.72	5,599.15	4,744.66	4,393.41	4,229.38	4,148.25	4,106.97	4,085.68
13.25%	8,580.47	6,873.06	6,355.28	5,654.58	4,806.51	4,460.37	4,300.13	4,221.65	4,182.16	4,162.01
13.50%	8,628.69	6,924.33	6,408.06	5,710.29	4,868.69	4,527.66	4,371.17	4,295.30	4,257.53	4,238.48
13.75%	8,677.07	6,975.82	6,461.07	5,766.26	4,931.20	4,595.27	4,442.50	4,369.17	4,333.07	4,315.07
14.00%	8,725.59	7,027.50	6,514.31	5,822.49	4,994.03	4,663.20	4,514.10	4,443.27	4,408.77	4,391.78
14.25%	8,774.27	7,079.40	6,567.78	5,878.99	5,057.17	4,731.45	4,585.98	4,517.58	4,484.63	4,468.59
14.50%	8,823.11	7,131.49	6,621.47	5,935.75	5,120.63	4,799.99	4,658.11	4,592.08	4,560.64	4,545.50
14.75%	8,872.09	7,183.79	6,675.39	5,992.78	5,184.39	4,868.83	4,730.49	4,666.78	4,636.78	4,622.50
15.00%	8,921.22	7,236.28	6,729.53	6,050.06	5,248.45	4,937.96	4,803.11	4,741.67	4,713.05	4,699.59
15.25%	8,970.51	7,288.98	6,783.89	6,107.60	5,312.81	5,007.37	4,875.97	4,816.72	4,789.44	4,776.76
15.50%	9,019.95	7,341.88	6,838.47	6,165.40	5,377.46	5,077.05	4,949.04	4,891.94	4,865.94	4,854.00
15.75%	9,069.53	7,394.98	6,893.27	6,223.44	5,442.40	5,147.00	5,022.34	4,967.31	4,942.55	4,931.31
16.00%	9,119.27	7,448.27	6,948.29	6,281.74	5,507.63	5,217.21	5,095.83	5,042.84	5,019.26	5,008.68
16.25%	9,169.16	7,501.77	7,003.53	6,340.29	5,573.13	5,287.67	5,169.53	5,118.50	5,096.06	5,086.11
16.50%	9,219.20	7,555.46	7,058.99	6,399.09	5,638.91	5,358.38	5,243.42	5,194.31	5,172.95	5,163.60
16.75%	9,269.38	7,609.35	7,114.66	6,458.13	5,704.95	5,429.32	5,317.49	5,270.23	5,249.92	5,241.13
17.00%	9,319.72	7,663.43	7,170.55	6,517.41	5,771.27	5,500.50	5,391.74	5,346.28	5,326.97	5,318.71
17.25%	9,370.20	7,717.70	7,226.64	6,576.94	5,837.84	5,571.91	5,466.16	5,422.45	5,404.09	5,396.34
17.50%	9,420.83	7,772.17	7,282.95	6,636.70	5,904.67	5,643.53	5,540.74	5,498.72	5,481.28	5,474.00
17.75%	9,471.61	7,826.84	7,339.47	6,696.71	5,971.75	5,715.37	5,615.47	5,575.10	5,558.53	5,551.70
18.00%	9,522.54	7,881.69	7,396.21	6,756.94	6,039.08	5,787.42	5,690.36	5,651.57	5,635.84	5,629.43
18.25%	9,573.61	7,936.73	7,453.14	6,817.42	6,106.65	5,859.67	5,765.39	5,728.14	5,713.21	5,707.20
18.50%	9,624.83	7,991.97	7,510.29	6,878.12	6,174.46	5,932.11	5,840.57	5,804.79	5,790.63	5,784.99
18.75%	9,676.19	8,047.39	7,567.64	6,939.05	6,242.51	6,004.75	5,915.87	5,881.53	5,868.09	5,862.81
19.00%	9,727.71	8,103.01	7,625.20	7,000.21	6,310.79	6,077.57	5,991.30	5,958.35	5,945.61	5,940.66
19.25%	9,779.36	8,158.81	7,682.96	7,061.60	6,379.29	6,150.57	6,066.85	6,035.24	6,023.16	6,018.52
19.50%	9,831.17	8,214.79	7,740.92	7,123.21	6,448.01	6,223.74	6,142.52	6,112.20	6,100.75	6,096.41
19.75%	9,883.11	8,270.97	7,799.09	7,185.04	6,516.96	6,297.09	6,218.30	6,189.23	6,178.38	6,174.32
20.00%	9,935.21	8,327.32	7,857.45	7,247.09	6,586.11	6,370.59	6,294.19	6,266.32	6,256.04	6,252.24
20.25%	9,987.44	8,383.87	7,916.01	7,309.35	6,655.48	6,444.26	6,370.19	6,343.47	6,333.74	6,330.18
20.50%	10,039.82	8,440.59	7,974.77	7,371.84	6,725.05	6,518.08	6,446.28	6,420.68	6,411.46	6,408.14
20.75%	10,092.34	8,497.50	8,033.73	7,434.53	6,794.82	6,592.05	6,522.46	6,497.94	6,489.22	6,486.11

	5	7	8	10	15	20	25	30	35	40
1.00%	6,495.62	4,685.87	4,120.43	3,328.96	2,274.28	1,747.60	1,432.12	1,222.23	1,072.69	960.85
1.25%	6,536.61	4,726.97	4,161.61	3,370.35	2,316.31	1,790.31	1,475.53	1,266.36	1,117.53	1,006.41
1.50%	6,577.76	4,768.29	4,203.05	3,412.08	2,358.82	1,833.67	1,519.76	1,311.46	1,163.50	1,053.26
1.75%	6,619.07	4,809.84	4,244.76	3,454.13	2,401.83	1,877.69	1,564.80	1,357.53	1,210.59	1,101.37
2.00%	6,660.55	4,851.63	4,286.73	3,496.51	2,445.33	1,922.36	1,610.65	1,404.55	1,258.80	1,150.74
2.25%	6,702.19	4,893.64	4,328.96	3,539.22	2,489.32	1,967.67	1,657.30	1,452.54	1,308.10	1,201.34
2.50%	6,744.00	4,935.88	4,371.46	3,582.26	2,533.80	2,013.63	1,704.74	1,501.46	1,358.48	1,253.16
2.75%	6,785.97	4,978.35	4,414.22	3,625.62	2,578.76	2,060.23	1,752.98	1,551.32	1,409.93	1,306.17
3.00%	6,828.10	5,021.05	4,457.24	3,669.31	2,624.21	2,107.47	1,802.00	1,602.10	1,462.43	1,360.34
3.25%	6,870.40	5,063.98	4,500.52	3,713.32	2,670.14	2,155.34	1,851.80	1,653.78	1,515.96	1,415.66
3.50%	6,912.86	5,107.14	4,544.06	3,757.66	2,716.55	2,203.85	1,902.37	1,706.37	1,570.50	1,472.09
3.75%	6,955.49	5,150.53	4,587.86	3,802.33	2,763.45	2,252.98	1,953.70	1,759.84	1,626.04	1,529.60
4.00%	6,998.28	5,194.15	4,631.92	3,847.32	2,810.81	2,302.73	2,005.78	1,814.18	1,682.54	1,588.17
4.25%	7,041.23	5,237.99	4,676.25	3,892.63	2,858.66	2,353.09	2,058.60	1,869.37	1,740.00	1,647.76
4.50%	7,084.35	5,282.06	4,720.83	3,938.26	2,906.97	2,404.07	2,112.16	1,925.40	1,798.38	1,708.34
4.75%	7,127.63	5,326.36	4,765.67	3,984.21	2,955.76	2,455.65	2,166.45	1,982.26	1,857.66	1,769.88
5.00%	7,171.07	5,370.89	4,810.77	4,030.49	3,005.02	2,507.83	2,221.44	2,039.92	1,917.81	1,832.35
5.25%	7,214.67	5,415.64	4,856.13	4,077.08	3,054.74	2,560.61	2,277.14	2,098.37	1,978.82	1,895.71
5.50%	7,258.44	5,460.62	4,901.74	4,124.00	3,104.92	2,613.97	2,333.53	2,157.60	2,040.66	1,959.93
5.75%	7,302.37	5,505.82	4,947.61	4,171.23	3,155.56	2,667.92	2,390.60	2,217.58	2,103.30	2,024.97
6.00%	7,346.46	5,551.25	4,993.74	4,218.78	3,206.66	2,722.44	2,448.35	2,278.29	2,166.72	2,090.81
6.25%	7,390.72	5,596.91	5,040.13	4,266.64	3,258.21	2,777.53	2,506.74	2,339.73	2,230.89	2,157.41
6.50%	7,435.14	5,642.79	5,086.77	4,314.82	3,310.21	2,833.18	2,565.79	2,401.86	2,295.79	2,224.74
6.75%	7,479.72	5,688.89	5,133.66	4,363.32	3,362.66	2,889.38	2,625.46	2,464.67	2,361.38	2,292.76
7.00%	7,524.46	5,735.22	5,180.81	4,412.12	3,415.55	2,946.14	2,685.76	2,528.15	2,427.65	2,361.44
7.25%	7,569.36	5,781.77	5,228.22	4,461.24	3,468.88	3,003.43	2,746.67	2,592.27	2,494.58	2,430.75
7.50%	7,614.42	5,828.54	5,275.87	4,510.67	3,522.65	3,061.25	2,808.17	2,657.02	2,562.12	2,500.67
7.75%	7,659.64	5,875.54	5,323.78	4,560.40	3,576.85	3,119.60	2,870.25	2,722.37	2,630.27	2,571.16
8.00%	7,705.03	5,922.76	5,371.94	4,610.45	3,631.48	3,178.47	2,932.90	2,788.31	2,698.99	2,642.18
8.25%	7,750.58	5,970.20	5,420.35	4,660.80	3,686.53	3,237.85	2,996.11	2,854.81	2,768.27	2,713.73
8.50%	7,796.28	6,017.86	5,469.01	4,711.46	3,742.01	3,297.73	3,059.86	2,921.87	2,838.07	2,785.76
8.75%	7,842.15	6,065.75	5,517.92	4,762.42	3,797.90	3,358.10	3,124.15	2,989.46	2,908.38	2,858.25
9.00%	7,888.17	6,113.85	5,567.08	4,813.68	3,854.21	3,418.96	3,188.95	3,057.57	2,979.17	2,931.17
9.25%	7,934.36	6,162.17	5,616.48	4,865.24	3,910.93	3,480.29	3,254.25	3,126.17	3,050.43	3,004.51
9.50%	7,980.71	6,210.71	5,666.14	4,917.11	3,968.05	3,542.10	3,320.05	3,195.25	3,122.12	3,078.23
9.75%	8,027.21	6,259.47	5,716.04	4,969.27	4,025.58	3,604.36	3,386.32	3,264.79	3,194.24	3,152.32
10.00%	8,073.88	6,308.45	5,766.18	5,021.73	4,083.50	3,667.08	3,453.06	3,334.77	3,266.76	3,226.75
10.25%	8,120.70	6,357.64	5,816.57	5,074.48	4,141.81	3,730.24	3,520.26	3,405.18	3,339.65	3,301.51
10.50%	8,167.68	6,407.06	5,867.21	5,127.53	4,200.52	3,793.84	3,587.89	3,476.01	3,412.91	3,376.57
10.75%	8,214.82	6,456.68	5,918.08	5,180.87	4,259.60	3,857.87	3,655.95	3,547.23	3,486.51	3,451.91

	5	7	8	10	15	20	25	30	35	40
11.00%	8,262.12	6,506.53	5,969.20	5,234.50	4,319.07	3,922.32	3,724.43	3,618.83	3,560.44	3,527.52
11.25%	8,309.58	6,556.58	6,020.56	5,288.42	4,378.91	3,987.17	3,793.31	3,690.79	3,634.68	3,603.38
11.50%	8,357.19	6,606.86	6,072.16	5,342.63	4,439.12	4,052.43	3,862.58	3,763.11	3,709.21	3,679.47
11.75%	8,404.96	6,657.34	6,124.00	5,397.12	4,499.70	4,118.09	3,932.23	3,835.76	3,784.02	3,755.78
12.00%	8,452.89	6,708.04	6,176.08	5,451.90	4,560.64	4,184.13	4,002.25	3,908.73	3,859.09	3,832.30
12.25%	8,500.98	6,758.95	6,228.40	5,506.95	4,621.94	4,250.55	4,072.63	3,982.01	3,934.41	3,909.01
12.50%	8,549.22	6,810.07	6,280.95	5,562.29	4,683.58	4,317.33	4,143.35	4,055.58	4,009.97	3,985.89
12.75%	8,597.61	6,861.40	6,333.73	5,617.91	4,745.58	4,384.48	4,214.40	4,129.43	4,085.75	4,062.95
13.00%	8,646.17	6,912.95	6,386.76	5,673.81	4,807.92	4,451.99	4,285.77	4,203.56	4,161.73	4,140.15
13.25%	8,694.88	6,964.70	6,440.01	5,729.98	4,870.60	4,519.84	4,357.46	4,277.94	4,237.92	4,217.51
13.50%	8,743.74	7,016.66	6,493.50	5,786.42	4,933.61	4,588.02	4,429.45	4,352.57	4,314.29	4,294.99
13.75%	8,792.76	7,068.83	6,547.22	5,843.14	4,996.95	4,656.54	4,501.73	4,427.43	4,390.84	4,372.60
14.00%	8,841.94	7,121.20	6,601.17	5,900.12	5,060.62	4,725.38	4,574.29	4,502.51	4,467.56	4,450.33
14.25%	8,891.26	7,173.79	6,655.35	5,957.38	5,124.60	4,794.53	4,647.12	4,577.81	4,544.43	4,528.17
14.50%	8,940.75	7,226.58	6,709.76	6,014.90	5,188.90	4,863.99	4,720.22	4,653.31	4,621.45	4,606.11
14.75%	8,990.38	7,279.57	6,764.39	6,072.68	5,253.51	4,933.75	4,793.57	4,729.01	4,698.60	4,684.14
15.00%	9,040.17	7,332.77	6,819.25	6,130.73	5,318.43	5,003.80	4,867.16	4,804.89	4,775.89	4,762.25
15.25%	9,090.12	7,386.17	6,874.34	6,189.04	5,383.65	5,074.13	4,940.98	4,880.94	4,853.30	4,840.45
15.50%	9,140.21	7,439.77	6,929.65	6,247.60	5,449.16	5,144.75	5,015.03	4,957.16	4,930.82	4,918.72
15.75%	9,190.46	7,493.58	6,985.18	6,306.42	5,514.97	5,215.63	5,089.30	5,033.54	5,008.45	4,997.06
16.00%	9,240.86	7,547.58	7,040.94	6,365.50	5,581.06	5,286.77	5,163.78	5,110.08	5,086.18	5,075.46
16.25%	9,291.41	7,601.79	7,096.91	6,424.83	5,647.44	5,358.17	5,238.46	5,186.75	5,164.01	5,153.93
16.50%	9,342.12	7,656.20	7,153.11	6,484.41	5,714.09	5,429.82	5,313.33	5,263.56	5,241.92	5,232.45
16.75%	9,392.97	7,710.80	7,209.52	6,544.24	5,781.02	5,501.71	5,388.39	5,340.50	5,319.92	5,311.01
17.00%	9,443.98	7,765.61	7,266.15	6,604.31	5,848.22	5,573.84	5,463.63	5,417.57	5,398.00	5,389.63
17.25%	9,495.13	7,820.61	7,323.00	6,664.63	5,915.68	5,646.20	5,539.04	5,494.75	5,476.15	5,468.29
17.50%	9,546.44	7,875.80	7,380.06	6,725.19	5,983.40	5,718.78	5,614.61	5,572.04	5,554.37	5,546.99
17.75%	9,597.90	7,931.19	7,437.33	6,786.00	6,051.37	5,791.58	5,690.35	5,649.43	5,632.65	5,625.72
18.00%	9,649.50	7,986.78	7,494.82	6,847.04	6,119.60	5,864.58	5,766.23	5,726.92	5,710.99	5,704.49
18.25%	9,701.26	8,042.56	7,552.52	6,908.32	6,188.07	5,937.80	5,842.27	5,804.51	5,789.39	5,783.29
18.50%	9,753.16	8,098.53	7,610.43	6,969.83	6,256.79	6,011.21	5,918.44	5,882.19	5,867.84	5,862.12
18.75%	9,805.21	8,154.69	7,668.54	7,031.57	6,325.74	6,084.81	5,994.75	5,959.95	5,946.34	5,940.98
19.00%	9,857.41	8,211.05	7,726.87	7,093.55	6,394.93	6,158.60	6,071.18	6,037.79	6,024.88	6,019.86
19.25%	9,909.76	8,267.59	7,785.40	7,155.75	6,464.35	6,232.58	6,147.74	6,115.71	6,103.47	6,098.77
19.50%	9,962.25	8,324.33	7,844.13	7,218.18	6,533.99	6,306.73	6,224.42	6,193.70	6,182.09	6,177.69
19.75%	10,014.89	8,381.25	7,903.07	7,280.84	6,603.85	6,381.05	6,301.22	6,271.75	6,260.76	6,256.64
20.00%	10,067.68	8,438.36	7,962.22	7,343.72	6,673.93	6,455.53	6,378.12	6,349.87	6,339.46	6,335.60
20.25%	10,120.61	8,495.65	8,021.56	7,406.81	6,744.22	6,530.18	6,455.12	6,428.05	6,418.19	6,414.58
20.50%	10,173.69	8,553.13	8,081.10	7,470.13	6,814.72	6,604.99	6,532.23	6,506.29	6,496.95	6,493.58
20.75%	10,226.91	8,610.80	8,140.84	7,533.66	6,885.42	6,679.94	6,609.43	6,584.58	6,575.74	6,572.59

	5	7	8	10	15	20	25	30	35	40
1.00%	6,581.09	4,747.53	4,174.64	3,372.76	2,304.20	1,770.59	1,450.96	1,238.31	1,086.80	973.50
1.25%	6,622.62	4,789.16	4,216.37	3,414.70	2,346.78	1,813.86	1,494.94	1,283.02	1,132.23	1,019.65
1.50%	6,664.31	4,831.03	4,258.36	3,456.97	2,389.86	1,857.80	1,539.75	1,328.71	1,178.81	1,067.11
1.75%	6,706.16	4,873.13	4,300.61	3,499.58	2,433.44	1,902.40	1,585.39	1,375.39	1,226.52	1,115.86
2.00%	6,748.19	4,915.46	4,343.14	3,542.52	2,477.51	1,947.65	1,631.84	1,423.03	1,275.36	1,165.88
2.25%	6,790.38	4,958.03	4,385.92	3,585.79	2,522.08	1,993.56	1,679.10	1,471.65	1,325.31	1,217.15
2.50%	6,832.73	5,000.83	4,428.98	3,629.39	2,567.14	2,040.13	1,727.17	1,521.22	1,376.36	1,269.65
2.75%	6,875.26	5,043.86	4,472.30	3,673.32	2,612.69	2,087.34	1,776.05	1,571.73	1,428.48	1,323.35
3.00%	6,917.95	5,087.12	4,515.89	3,717.59	2,658.74	2,135.20	1,825.71	1,623.18	1,481.67	1,378.24
3.25%	6,960.80	5,130.62	4,559.74	3,762.18	2,705.27	2,183.70	1,876.17	1,675.54	1,535.91	1,434.28
3.50%	7,003.82	5,174.34	4,603.85	3,807.11	2,752.30	2,232.84	1,927.40	1,728.82	1,591.17	1,491.46
3.75%	7,047.01	5,218.30	4,648.23	3,852.36	2,799.81	2,282.62	1,979.41	1,783.00	1,647.43	1,549.73
4.00%	7,090.36	5,262.49	4,692.87	3,897.94	2,847.80	2,333.02	2,032.17	1,838.05	1,704.68	1,609.06
4.25%	7,133.88	5,306.91	4,737.78	3,943.85	2,896.27	2,384.05	2,085.69	1,893.97	1,762.89	1,669.44
4.50%	7,177.56	5,351.56	4,782.95	3,990.08	2,945.22	2,435.70	2,139.96	1,950.74	1,822.04	1,730.82
4.75%	7,221.41	5,396.44	4,828.38	4,036.64	2,994.65	2,487.96	2,194.95	2,008.34	1,882.10	1,793.17
5.00%	7,265.42	5,441.55	4,874.07	4,083.52	3,044.56	2,540.83	2,250.67	2,066.76	1,943.05	1,856.46
5.25%	7,309.60	5,486.90	4,920.02	4,130.73	3,094.93	2,594.30	2,307.10	2,125.98	2,004.86	1,920.65
5.50%	7,353.95	5,532.47	4,966.24	4,178.26	3,145.77	2,648.37	2,364.24	2,185.99	2,067.51	1,985.72
5.75%	7,398.46	5,578.27	5,012.71	4,226.11	3,197.08	2,703.02	2,422.06	2,246.76	2,130.98	2,051.62
6.00%	7,443.13	5,624.29	5,059.45	4,274.29	3,248.85	2,758.26	2,480.56	2,308.27	2,195.23	2,118.32
6.25%	7,487.97	5,670.55	5,106.45	4,322.78	3,301.08	2,814.07	2,539.73	2,370.51	2,260.24	2,185.80
6.50%	7,532.97	5,717.03	5,153.70	4,371.60	3,353.76	2,870.46	2,599.55	2,433.46	2,325.99	2,254.01
6.75%	7,578.13	5,763.74	5,201.21	4,420.73	3,406.90	2,927.40	2,660.01	2,497.10	2,392.45	2,322.92
7.00%	7,623.46	5,810.68	5,248.98	4,470.18	3,460.49	2,984.90	2,721.10	2,561.41	2,459.60	2,392.51
7.25%	7,668.95	5,857.85	5,297.01	4,519.94	3,514.52	3,042.95	2,782.81	2,626.38	2,527.40	2,462.74
7.50%	7,714.61	5,905.24	5,345.29	4,570.02	3,569.00	3,101.53	2,845.12	2,691.98	2,595.83	2,533.57
7.75%	7,760.43	5,952.85	5,393.83	4,620.41	3,623.91	3,160.65	2,908.02	2,758.19	2,664.88	2,604.99
8.00%	7,806.41	6,000.69	5,442.62	4,671.11	3,679.26	3,220.29	2,971.49	2,824.99	2,734.50	2,676.95
8.25%	7,852.56	6,048.76	5,491.67	4,722.13	3,735.04	3,280.45	3,035.53	2,892.38	2,804.69	2,749.43
8.50%	7,898.86	6,097.05	5,540.97	4,773.45	3,791.25	3,341.12	3,100.12	2,960.32	2,875.41	2,822.41
8.75%	7,945.33	6,145.56	5,590.52	4,825.08	3,847.88	3,402.29	3,165.25	3,028.80	2,946.65	2,895.86
9.00%	7,991.97	6,194.30	5,640.33	4,877.02	3,904.93	3,463.94	3,230.91	3,097.80	3,018.37	2,969.74
9.25%	8,038.76	6,243.25	5,690.38	4,929.26	3,962.39	3,526.09	3,297.07	3,167.30	3,090.57	3,044.04
9.50%	8,085.72	6,292.43	5,740.69	4,981.81	4,020.27	3,588.71	3,363.73	3,237.29	3,163.20	3,118.74
9.75%	8,132.83	6,341.83	5,791.25	5,034.65	4,078.55	3,651.79	3,430.88	3,307.74	3,236.27	3,193.80
10.00%	8,180.11	6,391.46	5,842.05	5,087.80	4,137.23	3,715.33	3,498.50	3,378.65	3,309.74	3,269.21
10.25%	8,227.55	6,441.30	5,893.11	5,141.25	4,196.31	3,779.33	3,566.58	3,449.99	3,383.59	3,344.95
10.50%	8,275.15	6,491.36	5,944.41	5,195.00	4,255.79	3,843.76	3,635.10	3,521.75	3,457.82	3,421.00
10.75%	8,322.91	6,541.64	5,995.95	5,249.04	4,315.65	3,908.63	3,704.06	3,593.90	3,532.39	3,497.33

$385,000   11.00 - 20.75%   5 - 40 Years

	5	7	8	10	15	20	25	30	35	40
11.00%	8,370.83	6,592.14	6,047.74	5,303.38	4,375.90	3,973.93	3,773.44	3,666.45	3,607.29	3,573.93
11.25%	8,418.91	6,642.85	6,099.78	5,358.00	4,436.53	4,039.64	3,843.22	3,739.36	3,682.50	3,650.79
11.50%	8,467.15	6,693.79	6,152.06	5,412.92	4,497.53	4,105.75	3,913.41	3,812.62	3,758.01	3,727.89
11.75%	8,515.55	6,744.94	6,204.58	5,468.13	4,558.91	4,172.27	3,983.97	3,886.23	3,833.81	3,805.20
12.00%	8,564.11	6,796.30	6,257.34	5,523.63	4,620.65	4,239.18	4,054.91	3,960.16	3,909.87	3,882.72
12.25%	8,612.83	6,847.88	6,310.35	5,579.41	4,682.75	4,306.47	4,126.21	4,034.40	3,986.18	3,960.44
12.50%	8,661.71	6,899.68	6,363.59	5,635.48	4,745.21	4,374.14	4,197.86	4,108.94	4,062.73	4,038.34
12.75%	8,710.74	6,951.68	6,417.07	5,691.83	4,808.02	4,442.17	4,269.85	4,183.77	4,139.51	4,116.41
13.00%	8,759.93	7,003.91	6,470.79	5,748.46	4,871.18	4,510.57	4,342.17	4,258.87	4,216.49	4,194.63
13.25%	8,809.28	7,056.34	6,524.75	5,805.37	4,934.69	4,579.31	4,414.80	4,334.23	4,293.68	4,273.00
13.50%	8,858.79	7,108.98	6,578.94	5,862.56	4,998.53	4,648.39	4,487.73	4,409.84	4,371.06	4,351.51
13.75%	8,908.46	7,161.84	6,633.37	5,920.02	5,062.70	4,717.81	4,560.96	4,485.68	4,448.62	4,430.14
14.00%	8,958.28	7,214.90	6,688.03	5,977.76	5,127.20	4,787.56	4,634.48	4,561.76	4,526.34	4,508.89
14.25%	9,008.25	7,268.18	6,742.92	6,035.76	5,192.03	4,857.62	4,708.27	4,638.05	4,604.22	4,587.75
14.50%	9,058.39	7,321.66	6,798.04	6,094.04	5,257.18	4,927.99	4,782.33	4,714.54	4,682.26	4,666.71
14.75%	9,108.68	7,375.35	6,853.40	6,152.59	5,322.64	4,998.67	4,856.64	4,791.23	4,760.43	4,745.77
15.00%	9,159.12	7,429.25	6,908.98	6,211.40	5,388.41	5,069.64	4,931.20	4,868.11	4,838.73	4,824.91
15.25%	9,209.72	7,483.35	6,964.79	6,270.47	5,454.49	5,140.90	5,005.99	4,945.17	4,917.16	4,904.14
15.50%	9,260.48	7,537.66	7,020.83	6,329.81	5,520.86	5,212.44	5,081.02	5,022.39	4,995.70	4,983.44
15.75%	9,311.39	7,592.18	7,077.09	6,389.40	5,587.53	5,284.25	5,156.26	5,099.78	5,074.35	5,062.81
16.00%	9,362.45	7,646.89	7,133.58	6,449.26	5,654.50	5,356.34	5,231.72	5,177.31	5,153.11	5,142.25
16.25%	9,413.67	7,701.81	7,190.29	6,509.36	5,721.75	5,428.68	5,307.38	5,255.00	5,231.96	5,221.74
16.50%	9,465.04	7,756.94	7,247.23	6,569.73	5,789.28	5,501.27	5,383.24	5,332.82	5,310.90	5,301.29
16.75%	9,516.56	7,812.26	7,304.38	6,630.34	5,857.09	5,574.11	5,459.29	5,410.77	5,389.92	5,380.90
17.00%	9,568.24	7,867.78	7,361.76	6,691.21	5,925.17	5,647.18	5,535.52	5,488.85	5,469.03	5,460.55
17.25%	9,620.07	7,923.51	7,419.35	6,752.32	5,993.51	5,720.49	5,611.92	5,567.05	5,548.20	5,540.24
17.50%	9,672.05	7,979.43	7,477.17	6,813.68	6,062.13	5,794.03	5,688.49	5,645.35	5,627.45	5,619.97
17.75%	9,724.19	8,035.55	7,535.19	6,875.29	6,131.00	5,867.78	5,765.22	5,723.77	5,706.76	5,699.75
18.00%	9,776.47	8,091.87	7,593.44	6,937.13	6,200.12	5,941.75	5,842.11	5,802.28	5,786.13	5,779.55
18.25%	9,828.90	8,148.38	7,651.89	6,999.21	6,269.50	6,015.92	5,919.14	5,880.89	5,865.56	5,859.39
18.50%	9,881.49	8,205.09	7,710.56	7,061.54	6,339.11	6,090.30	5,996.31	5,959.59	5,945.05	5,939.26
18.75%	9,934.23	8,261.99	7,769.45	7,124.09	6,408.98	6,164.87	6,073.63	6,038.37	6,024.58	6,019.15
19.00%	9,987.11	8,319.09	7,828.54	7,186.89	6,479.07	6,239.64	6,151.07	6,117.24	6,104.15	6,099.07
19.25%	10,040.15	8,376.38	7,887.84	7,249.91	6,549.40	6,314.58	6,228.64	6,196.18	6,183.78	6,179.02
19.50%	10,093.33	8,433.86	7,947.35	7,313.16	6,619.96	6,389.71	6,306.32	6,275.19	6,263.44	6,258.98
19.75%	10,146.66	8,491.53	8,007.06	7,376.64	6,690.74	6,465.01	6,384.13	6,354.27	6,343.14	6,338.96
20.00%	10,200.15	8,549.39	8,066.98	7,440.34	6,761.74	6,540.47	6,462.04	6,433.42	6,422.87	6,418.97
20.25%	10,253.77	8,607.44	8,127.11	7,504.27	6,832.96	6,616.10	6,540.06	6,512.63	6,502.64	6,498.99
20.50%	10,307.55	8,665.67	8,187.43	7,568.42	6,904.38	6,691.89	6,618.18	6,591.90	6,582.44	6,579.02
20.75%	10,361.47	8,724.10	8,247.96	7,632.79	6,976.02	6,767.84	6,696.39	6,671.22	6,662.26	6,659.07

	5	7	8	10	15	20	25	30	35	40
1.00%	6,666.56	4,809.19	4,228.86	3,416.56	2,334.13	1,793.59	1,469.80	1,254.39	1,100.91	986.14
1.25%	6,708.62	4,851.36	4,271.12	3,459.05	2,377.26	1,837.42	1,514.36	1,299.68	1,146.94	1,032.90
1.50%	6,750.86	4,893.77	4,313.66	3,501.87	2,420.90	1,881.93	1,559.75	1,345.97	1,194.12	1,080.97
1.75%	6,793.26	4,936.42	4,356.46	3,545.03	2,465.04	1,927.10	1,605.98	1,393.25	1,242.45	1,130.35
2.00%	6,835.83	4,979.30	4,399.54	3,588.52	2,509.68	1,972.95	1,653.03	1,441.52	1,291.92	1,181.02
2.25%	6,878.56	5,022.42	4,442.88	3,632.36	2,554.83	2,019.45	1,700.91	1,490.76	1,342.52	1,232.95
2.50%	6,921.47	5,065.77	4,486.50	3,676.53	2,600.48	2,066.62	1,749.61	1,540.97	1,394.23	1,286.14
2.75%	6,964.55	5,109.36	4,530.38	3,721.03	2,646.62	2,114.45	1,799.11	1,592.14	1,447.03	1,340.54
3.00%	7,007.79	5,153.19	4,574.53	3,765.87	2,693.27	2,162.93	1,849.42	1,644.26	1,500.92	1,396.14
3.25%	7,051.20	5,197.25	4,618.95	3,811.04	2,740.41	2,212.06	1,900.53	1,697.30	1,555.86	1,452.91
3.50%	7,094.78	5,241.54	4,663.64	3,856.55	2,788.04	2,261.84	1,952.43	1,751.27	1,611.83	1,510.82
3.75%	7,138.53	5,286.07	4,708.60	3,902.39	2,836.17	2,312.26	2,005.11	1,806.15	1,668.83	1,569.85
4.00%	7,182.44	5,330.83	4,753.82	3,948.56	2,884.78	2,363.32	2,058.56	1,861.92	1,726.82	1,629.96
4.25%	7,226.53	5,375.83	4,799.31	3,995.06	2,933.89	2,415.01	2,112.78	1,918.57	1,785.79	1,691.12
4.50%	7,270.78	5,421.06	4,845.06	4,041.90	2,983.47	2,467.33	2,167.75	1,976.07	1,845.70	1,753.30
4.75%	7,315.20	5,466.53	4,891.08	4,089.06	3,033.54	2,520.27	2,223.46	2,034.42	1,906.54	1,816.46
5.00%	7,359.78	5,512.22	4,937.37	4,136.56	3,084.10	2,573.83	2,279.90	2,093.60	1,968.28	1,880.57
5.25%	7,404.53	5,558.15	4,983.92	4,184.38	3,135.12	2,627.99	2,337.07	2,153.59	2,030.90	1,945.59
5.50%	7,449.45	5,604.32	5,030.74	4,232.52	3,186.63	2,682.76	2,394.94	2,214.38	2,094.36	2,011.50
5.75%	7,494.54	5,650.71	5,077.82	4,281.00	3,238.60	2,738.13	2,453.51	2,275.93	2,158.65	2,078.26
6.00%	7,539.79	5,697.34	5,125.16	4,329.80	3,291.04	2,794.08	2,512.78	2,338.25	2,223.74	2,145.83
6.25%	7,585.21	5,744.19	5,172.76	4,378.92	3,343.95	2,850.62	2,572.71	2,401.30	2,289.60	2,214.18
6.50%	7,630.80	5,791.28	5,220.63	4,428.37	3,397.32	2,907.74	2,633.31	2,465.07	2,356.20	2,283.28
6.75%	7,676.55	5,838.60	5,268.76	4,478.14	3,451.15	2,965.42	2,694.55	2,529.53	2,423.52	2,353.09
7.00%	7,722.47	5,886.15	5,317.15	4,528.23	3,505.43	3,023.67	2,756.44	2,594.68	2,491.54	2,423.58
7.25%	7,768.55	5,933.92	5,365.80	4,578.64	3,560.17	3,082.47	2,818.95	2,660.49	2,560.22	2,494.72
7.50%	7,814.80	5,981.93	5,414.71	4,629.37	3,615.35	3,141.81	2,882.07	2,726.94	2,629.55	2,566.48
7.75%	7,861.21	6,030.16	5,463.88	4,680.41	3,670.98	3,201.70	2,945.78	2,794.01	2,699.49	2,638.82
8.00%	7,907.79	6,078.62	5,513.30	4,731.78	3,727.04	3,262.12	3,010.08	2,861.68	2,770.02	2,711.72
8.25%	7,954.54	6,127.31	5,562.99	4,783.45	3,783.55	3,323.06	3,074.96	2,929.94	2,841.12	2,785.14
8.50%	8,001.45	6,176.23	5,612.93	4,835.44	3,840.48	3,384.51	3,140.39	2,998.76	2,912.76	2,859.07
8.75%	8,048.52	6,225.37	5,663.13	4,887.74	3,897.85	3,446.47	3,206.36	3,068.13	2,984.92	2,933.47
9.00%	8,095.76	6,274.74	5,713.58	4,940.36	3,955.64	3,508.93	3,272.87	3,138.03	3,057.57	3,008.31
9.25%	8,143.16	6,324.33	5,764.29	4,993.28	4,013.85	3,571.88	3,339.89	3,208.43	3,130.70	3,083.58
9.50%	8,190.73	6,374.15	5,815.25	5,046.50	4,072.48	3,635.31	3,407.42	3,279.33	3,204.29	3,159.24
9.75%	8,238.46	6,424.20	5,866.46	5,100.04	4,131.51	3,699.22	3,475.44	3,350.70	3,278.30	3,235.28
10.00%	8,286.35	6,474.46	5,917.92	5,153.88	4,190.96	3,763.58	3,543.93	3,422.53	3,352.72	3,311.67
10.25%	8,334.40	6,524.95	5,969.64	5,208.02	4,250.81	3,828.41	3,612.89	3,494.80	3,427.54	3,388.39
10.50%	8,382.62	6,575.66	6,021.61	5,262.46	4,311.06	3,893.68	3,682.31	3,567.48	3,502.72	3,465.42
10.75%	8,431.00	6,626.60	6,073.82	5,317.21	4,371.70	3,959.39	3,752.16	3,640.58	3,578.26	3,542.75

	5	7	8	10	15	20	25	30	35	40
11.00%	8,479.54	6,677.75	6,126.29	5,372.25	4,432.73	4,025.53	3,822.44	3,714.06	3,654.13	3,620.35
11.25%	8,528.25	6,729.13	6,179.00	5,427.59	4,494.14	4,092.10	3,893.13	3,787.92	3,730.33	3,698.20
11.50%	8,577.12	6,780.72	6,231.96	5,483.22	4,555.94	4,159.08	3,964.23	3,862.14	3,806.82	3,776.30
11.75%	8,626.15	6,832.53	6,285.16	5,539.15	4,618.11	4,226.46	4,035.71	3,936.70	3,883.60	3,854.62
12.00%	8,675.33	6,884.57	6,338.61	5,595.37	4,680.66	4,294.24	4,107.57	4,011.59	3,960.64	3,933.15
12.25%	8,724.68	6,936.82	6,392.30	5,651.87	4,743.56	4,362.40	4,179.80	4,086.80	4,037.95	4,011.88
12.50%	8,774.20	6,989.28	6,446.24	5,708.67	4,806.84	4,430.95	4,252.38	4,162.31	4,115.49	4,090.79
12.75%	8,823.87	7,041.97	6,500.41	5,765.75	4,870.46	4,499.87	4,325.30	4,238.10	4,193.26	4,169.87
13.00%	8,873.70	7,094.87	6,554.83	5,823.12	4,934.44	4,569.15	4,398.56	4,314.18	4,271.25	4,249.11
13.25%	8,923.69	7,147.98	6,609.49	5,880.77	4,998.77	4,638.78	4,472.13	4,390.52	4,349.44	4,328.49
13.50%	8,973.84	7,201.31	6,664.38	5,938.70	5,063.44	4,708.76	4,546.02	4,467.11	4,427.83	4,408.02
13.75%	9,024.15	7,254.85	6,719.52	5,996.91	5,128.45	4,779.08	4,620.20	4,543.94	4,506.39	4,487.67
14.00%	9,074.62	7,308.60	6,774.89	6,055.39	5,193.79	4,849.73	4,694.67	4,621.00	4,585.13	4,567.45
14.25%	9,125.24	7,362.57	6,830.49	6,114.15	5,259.46	4,920.70	4,769.42	4,698.28	4,664.02	4,647.33
14.50%	9,176.03	7,416.75	6,886.33	6,173.18	5,325.45	4,991.99	4,844.44	4,775.77	4,743.06	4,727.32
14.75%	9,226.97	7,471.14	6,942.40	6,232.49	5,391.76	5,063.59	4,919.71	4,853.46	4,822.25	4,807.40
15.00%	9,278.07	7,525.73	6,998.71	6,292.06	5,458.39	5,135.48	4,995.24	4,931.33	4,901.57	4,887.57
15.25%	9,329.33	7,580.54	7,055.24	6,351.90	5,525.32	5,207.66	5,071.01	5,009.39	4,981.02	4,967.83
15.50%	9,380.74	7,635.56	7,112.01	6,412.01	5,592.56	5,280.13	5,147.01	5,087.62	5,060.58	5,048.16
15.75%	9,432.32	7,690.78	7,169.00	6,472.38	5,660.10	5,352.88	5,223.23	5,166.01	5,140.25	5,128.56
16.00%	9,484.04	7,746.20	7,226.23	6,533.01	5,727.93	5,425.90	5,299.67	5,244.55	5,220.03	5,209.03
16.25%	9,535.93	7,801.84	7,283.68	6,593.90	5,796.06	5,499.18	5,376.31	5,323.25	5,299.90	5,289.56
16.50%	9,587.96	7,857.68	7,341.35	6,655.05	5,864.46	5,572.71	5,453.15	5,402.08	5,379.87	5,370.14
16.75%	9,640.16	7,913.72	7,399.25	6,716.45	5,933.15	5,646.50	5,530.19	5,481.04	5,459.92	5,450.78
17.00%	9,692.50	7,969.96	7,457.37	6,778.11	6,002.12	5,720.52	5,607.41	5,560.13	5,540.05	5,531.46
17.25%	9,745.01	8,026.41	7,515.71	6,840.02	6,071.35	5,794.78	5,684.80	5,639.34	5,620.26	5,612.19
17.50%	9,797.66	8,083.06	7,574.27	6,902.17	6,140.86	5,869.27	5,762.37	5,718.67	5,700.53	5,692.96
17.75%	9,850.47	8,139.91	7,633.05	6,964.57	6,210.62	5,943.99	5,840.09	5,798.10	5,780.88	5,773.77
18.00%	9,903.44	8,196.96	7,692.05	7,027.22	6,280.64	6,018.91	5,917.98	5,877.63	5,861.28	5,854.61
18.25%	9,956.55	8,254.20	7,751.27	7,090.11	6,350.92	6,094.05	5,996.01	5,957.26	5,941.74	5,935.49
18.50%	10,009.82	8,311.65	7,810.70	7,153.25	6,421.44	6,169.40	6,074.19	6,036.98	6,022.25	6,016.39
18.75%	10,063.24	8,369.29	7,870.35	7,216.62	6,492.21	6,244.94	6,152.50	6,116.79	6,102.82	6,097.32
19.00%	10,116.81	8,427.13	7,930.21	7,280.22	6,563.22	6,320.67	6,230.95	6,196.68	6,183.43	6,178.28
19.25%	10,170.54	8,485.16	7,990.28	7,344.06	6,634.46	6,396.59	6,309.53	6,276.65	6,264.08	6,259.26
19.50%	10,224.41	8,543.39	8,050.56	7,408.14	6,705.93	6,472.69	6,388.22	6,356.69	6,344.78	6,340.27
19.75%	10,278.44	8,601.81	8,111.05	7,472.44	6,777.63	6,548.97	6,467.04	6,436.80	6,425.52	6,421.29
20.00%	10,332.61	8,660.42	8,171.75	7,536.97	6,849.56	6,625.42	6,545.96	6,516.97	6,506.29	6,502.33
20.25%	10,386.94	8,719.22	8,232.65	7,601.73	6,921.70	6,702.03	6,624.99	6,597.21	6,587.09	6,583.39
20.50%	10,441.41	8,778.21	8,293.76	7,666.71	6,994.05	6,778.80	6,704.13	6,677.51	6,667.92	6,664.46
20.75%	10,496.04	8,837.40	8,355.08	7,731.91	7,066.62	6,855.73	6,783.36	6,757.86	6,748.79	6,745.55

	5	7	8	10	15	20	25	30	35	40
1.00%	6,752.03	4,870.84	4,283.07	3,460.36	2,364.05	1,816.58	1,488.65	1,270.48	1,115.03	998.78
1.25%	6,794.63	4,913.56	4,325.88	3,503.39	2,407.74	1,860.98	1,533.77	1,316.34	1,161.64	1,046.14
1.50%	6,837.41	4,956.51	4,368.96	3,546.76	2,451.93	1,906.05	1,579.75	1,363.22	1,209.43	1,094.83
1.75%	6,880.35	4,999.70	4,412.32	3,590.48	2,496.64	1,951.81	1,626.57	1,411.11	1,258.38	1,144.84
2.00%	6,923.47	5,043.14	4,455.94	3,634.53	2,541.86	1,998.24	1,674.22	1,460.00	1,308.49	1,196.16
2.25%	6,966.75	5,086.81	4,499.85	3,678.93	2,587.58	2,045.34	1,722.72	1,509.87	1,359.73	1,248.76
2.50%	7,010.21	5,130.72	4,544.02	3,723.66	2,633.82	2,093.12	1,772.04	1,560.73	1,412.11	1,302.62
2.75%	7,053.84	5,174.87	4,588.46	3,768.74	2,680.56	2,141.56	1,822.18	1,612.55	1,465.59	1,357.72
3.00%	7,097.63	5,219.25	4,633.18	3,814.15	2,727.80	2,190.66	1,873.13	1,665.34	1,520.16	1,414.04
3.25%	7,141.60	5,263.88	4,678.17	3,859.90	2,775.54	2,240.42	1,924.90	1,719.06	1,575.80	1,471.54
3.50%	7,185.74	5,308.74	4,723.43	3,905.99	2,823.79	2,290.84	1,977.46	1,773.73	1,632.50	1,530.19
3.75%	7,230.05	5,353.84	4,768.96	3,952.42	2,872.53	2,341.91	2,030.82	1,829.31	1,690.22	1,589.98
4.00%	7,274.53	5,399.18	4,814.76	3,999.18	2,921.77	2,393.62	2,084.96	1,885.79	1,748.96	1,650.86
4.25%	7,319.17	5,444.75	4,860.84	4,046.28	2,971.50	2,445.98	2,139.87	1,943.16	1,808.68	1,712.80
4.50%	7,363.99	5,490.56	4,907.18	4,093.72	3,021.72	2,498.97	2,195.54	2,001.41	1,869.36	1,775.77
4.75%	7,408.98	5,536.61	4,953.79	4,141.49	3,072.44	2,552.58	2,251.96	2,060.51	1,930.98	1,839.74
5.00%	7,454.14	5,582.89	5,000.67	4,189.59	3,123.63	2,606.83	2,309.13	2,120.45	1,993.52	1,904.68
5.25%	7,499.46	5,629.41	5,047.82	4,238.02	3,175.32	2,661.68	2,367.03	2,181.20	2,056.94	1,970.54
5.50%	7,544.96	5,676.17	5,095.23	4,286.79	3,227.48	2,717.15	2,425.65	2,242.77	2,121.21	2,037.29
5.75%	7,590.62	5,723.16	5,142.92	4,335.88	3,280.12	2,773.23	2,484.97	2,305.11	2,186.33	2,104.91
6.00%	7,636.46	5,770.38	5,190.86	4,385.31	3,333.23	2,829.90	2,544.99	2,368.22	2,252.25	2,173.34
6.25%	7,682.46	5,817.84	5,239.08	4,435.06	3,386.82	2,887.17	2,605.69	2,432.08	2,318.95	2,242.57
6.50%	7,728.63	5,865.53	5,287.56	4,485.15	3,440.87	2,945.01	2,667.07	2,496.67	2,386.41	2,312.55
6.75%	7,774.97	5,913.45	5,336.31	4,535.55	3,495.39	3,003.44	2,729.10	2,561.96	2,454.60	2,383.26
7.00%	7,821.47	5,961.61	5,385.32	4,586.28	3,550.37	3,062.43	2,791.78	2,627.94	2,523.48	2,454.65
7.25%	7,868.15	6,010.00	5,434.59	4,637.34	3,605.81	3,121.99	2,855.09	2,694.60	2,593.05	2,526.70
7.50%	7,914.99	6,058.62	5,484.13	4,688.72	3,661.70	3,182.09	2,919.02	2,761.90	2,663.26	2,599.38
7.75%	7,962.00	6,107.47	5,533.93	4,740.42	3,718.04	3,242.75	2,983.55	2,829.83	2,734.09	2,672.65
8.00%	8,009.18	6,156.55	5,583.99	4,792.44	3,774.83	3,303.94	3,048.67	2,898.37	2,805.53	2,746.48
8.25%	8,056.52	6,205.87	5,634.31	4,844.78	3,832.05	3,365.66	3,114.38	2,967.50	2,877.54	2,820.85
8.50%	8,104.03	6,255.41	5,684.89	4,897.43	3,889.72	3,427.90	3,180.65	3,037.21	2,950.10	2,895.72
8.75%	8,151.71	6,305.18	5,735.73	4,950.41	3,947.82	3,490.66	3,247.47	3,107.47	3,023.18	2,971.07
9.00%	8,199.55	6,355.19	5,786.83	5,003.69	4,006.35	3,553.92	3,314.83	3,178.26	3,096.77	3,046.88
9.25%	8,247.56	6,405.42	5,838.19	5,057.29	4,065.31	3,617.67	3,382.71	3,249.57	3,170.84	3,123.11
9.50%	8,295.74	6,455.87	5,889.80	5,111.20	4,124.69	3,681.92	3,451.10	3,321.37	3,245.37	3,199.74
9.75%	8,344.08	6,506.56	5,941.67	5,165.42	4,184.48	3,746.64	3,519.99	3,393.66	3,320.33	3,276.76
10.00%	8,392.58	6,557.47	5,993.79	5,219.95	4,244.69	3,811.84	3,589.37	3,466.41	3,395.71	3,354.13
10.25%	8,441.25	6,608.60	6,046.17	5,274.79	4,305.31	3,877.49	3,659.21	3,539.60	3,471.48	3,431.83
10.50%	8,490.09	6,659.97	6,098.81	5,329.93	4,366.33	3,943.60	3,729.52	3,613.22	3,547.63	3,509.85
10.75%	8,539.09	6,711.55	6,151.69	5,385.38	4,427.74	4,010.15	3,800.27	3,687.25	3,624.14	3,588.17

$395,000 11.00 - 20.75% 5 - 40 Years

	5	7	8	10	15	20	25	30	35	40
11.00%	8,588.26	6,763.36	6,204.83	5,441.13	4,489.56	4,077.14	3,871.45	3,761.68	3,700.98	3,666.76
11.25%	8,637.59	6,815.40	6,258.22	5,497.17	4,551.76	4,144.56	3,943.05	3,836.48	3,778.15	3,745.62
11.50%	8,687.08	6,867.65	6,311.85	5,553.52	4,614.35	4,212.40	4,015.05	3,911.65	3,855.62	3,824.71
11.75%	8,736.74	6,920.13	6,365.74	5,610.16	4,677.32	4,280.64	4,087.45	3,987.17	3,933.39	3,904.04
12.00%	8,786.56	6,972.83	6,419.87	5,667.10	4,740.66	4,349.29	4,160.24	4,063.02	4,011.42	3,983.57
12.25%	8,836.54	7,025.75	6,474.25	5,724.33	4,804.38	4,418.33	4,233.39	4,139.19	4,089.72	4,063.31
12.50%	8,886.69	7,078.89	6,528.88	5,781.86	4,868.46	4,487.76	4,306.90	4,215.67	4,168.25	4,143.23
12.75%	8,936.99	7,132.25	6,583.75	5,839.67	4,932.91	4,557.56	4,380.76	4,292.44	4,247.02	4,223.33
13.00%	8,987.46	7,185.83	6,638.87	5,897.77	4,997.71	4,627.72	4,454.95	4,369.49	4,326.01	4,303.58
13.25%	9,038.10	7,239.62	6,694.22	5,956.16	5,062.86	4,698.25	4,529.47	4,446.81	4,405.21	4,383.99
13.50%	9,088.89	7,293.63	6,749.82	6,014.83	5,128.36	4,769.13	4,604.30	4,524.38	4,484.59	4,464.53
13.75%	9,139.84	7,347.86	6,805.66	6,073.79	5,194.20	4,840.35	4,679.43	4,602.19	4,564.17	4,545.21
14.00%	9,190.96	7,402.30	6,861.74	6,133.02	5,260.38	4,911.91	4,754.86	4,680.24	4,643.91	4,626.00
14.25%	9,242.23	7,456.96	6,918.06	6,192.54	5,326.89	4,983.79	4,830.56	4,758.51	4,723.82	4,706.91
14.50%	9,293.67	7,511.84	6,974.62	6,252.33	5,393.73	5,055.99	4,906.54	4,837.00	4,803.87	4,787.93
14.75%	9,345.27	7,566.92	7,031.41	6,312.39	5,460.89	5,128.50	4,982.79	4,915.68	4,884.08	4,869.04
15.00%	9,397.02	7,622.22	7,088.44	6,372.73	5,528.37	5,201.32	5,059.28	4,994.55	4,964.41	4,950.24
15.25%	9,448.94	7,677.73	7,145.70	6,433.34	5,596.16	5,274.43	5,136.02	5,073.61	5,044.88	5,031.52
15.50%	9,501.01	7,733.45	7,203.19	6,494.22	5,664.26	5,347.83	5,212.99	5,152.84	5,125.46	5,112.88
15.75%	9,553.24	7,789.38	7,260.91	6,555.36	5,732.67	5,421.51	5,290.19	5,232.24	5,206.15	5,194.31
16.00%	9,605.63	7,845.52	7,318.87	6,616.77	5,801.37	5,495.46	5,367.61	5,311.79	5,286.95	5,275.81
16.25%	9,658.18	7,901.86	7,377.06	6,678.44	5,870.36	5,569.68	5,445.24	5,391.49	5,367.85	5,357.37
16.50%	9,710.89	7,958.42	7,435.47	6,740.37	5,939.65	5,644.16	5,523.07	5,471.33	5,448.84	5,438.99
16.75%	9,763.75	8,015.18	7,494.11	6,802.56	6,009.22	5,718.89	5,601.09	5,551.31	5,529.92	5,520.66
17.00%	9,816.77	8,072.14	7,552.97	6,865.01	6,079.07	5,793.86	5,679.30	5,631.42	5,611.08	5,602.38
17.25%	9,869.94	8,129.31	7,612.06	6,927.71	6,149.19	5,869.08	5,757.68	5,711.64	5,692.31	5,684.14
17.50%	9,923.27	8,186.69	7,671.38	6,990.66	6,219.58	5,944.52	5,836.24	5,791.98	5,773.62	5,765.95
17.75%	9,976.76	8,244.27	7,730.91	7,053.86	6,290.24	6,020.19	5,914.97	5,872.43	5,854.99	5,847.79
18.00%	10,030.40	8,302.05	7,790.67	7,117.32	6,361.16	6,096.08	5,993.85	5,952.99	5,936.42	5,929.67
18.25%	10,084.20	8,360.03	7,850.65	7,181.01	6,432.34	6,172.18	6,072.88	6,033.64	6,017.92	6,011.58
18.50%	10,138.15	8,418.21	7,910.84	7,244.95	6,503.77	6,248.49	6,152.06	6,114.38	6,099.46	6,093.52
18.75%	10,192.26	8,476.59	7,971.25	7,309.14	6,575.44	6,325.00	6,231.38	6,195.21	6,181.06	6,175.49
19.00%	10,246.52	8,535.17	8,031.88	7,373.56	6,647.36	6,401.71	6,310.84	6,276.13	6,262.70	6,257.49
19.25%	10,300.93	8,593.94	8,092.72	7,438.22	6,719.52	6,478.60	6,390.42	6,357.12	6,344.39	6,339.51
19.50%	10,355.50	8,652.92	8,153.77	7,503.11	6,791.91	6,555.68	6,470.12	6,438.18	6,426.12	6,421.55
19.75%	10,410.21	8,712.09	8,215.04	7,568.24	6,864.53	6,632.93	6,549.95	6,519.32	6,507.89	6,503.61
20.00%	10,465.08	8,771.45	8,276.51	7,633.60	6,937.37	6,710.36	6,629.88	6,600.52	6,589.70	6,585.69
20.25%	10,520.11	8,831.01	8,338.20	7,699.19	7,010.44	6,787.95	6,709.93	6,681.79	6,671.54	6,667.79
20.50%	10,575.28	8,890.76	8,400.09	7,765.00	7,083.72	6,865.71	6,790.08	6,763.11	6,753.41	6,749.90
20.75%	10,630.60	8,950.70	8,462.19	7,831.04	7,157.21	6,943.62	6,870.33	6,844.50	6,835.31	6,832.03

	5	7	8	10	15	20	25	30	35	40
1.00%	6,837.50	4,932.50	4,337.29	3,504.16	2,393.98	1,839.58	1,507.49	1,286.56	1,129.14	1,011.42
1.25%	6,880.64	4,975.75	4,380.64	3,547.74	2,438.22	1,884.53	1,553.19	1,333.01	1,176.35	1,059.38
1.50%	6,923.96	5,019.25	4,424.27	3,591.66	2,482.97	1,930.18	1,599.75	1,380.48	1,224.74	1,108.69
1.75%	6,967.44	5,062.99	4,468.17	3,635.93	2,528.25	1,976.52	1,647.16	1,428.97	1,274.31	1,159.34
2.00%	7,011.10	5,106.97	4,512.35	3,680.54	2,574.03	2,023.53	1,695.42	1,478.48	1,325.05	1,211.30
2.25%	7,054.94	5,151.20	4,556.81	3,725.49	2,620.34	2,071.23	1,744.52	1,528.98	1,376.95	1,264.57
2.50%	7,098.94	5,195.66	4,601.54	3,770.80	2,667.16	2,119.61	1,794.47	1,580.48	1,429.98	1,319.11
2.75%	7,143.12	5,240.37	4,646.55	3,816.44	2,714.49	2,168.67	1,845.24	1,632.96	1,484.14	1,374.91
3.00%	7,187.48	5,285.32	4,691.83	3,862.43	2,762.33	2,218.39	1,896.85	1,686.42	1,539.40	1,431.94
3.25%	7,232.00	5,330.51	4,737.39	3,908.76	2,810.68	2,268.78	1,949.26	1,740.83	1,595.75	1,490.16
3.50%	7,276.70	5,375.94	4,783.22	3,955.43	2,859.53	2,319.84	2,002.49	1,796.18	1,653.16	1,549.56
3.75%	7,321.57	5,421.61	4,829.33	4,002.45	2,908.89	2,371.55	2,056.52	1,852.46	1,711.62	1,610.10
4.00%	7,366.61	5,467.52	4,875.71	4,049.81	2,958.75	2,423.92	2,111.35	1,909.66	1,771.10	1,671.75
4.25%	7,411.82	5,513.67	4,922.37	4,097.50	3,009.11	2,476.94	2,166.95	1,967.76	1,831.58	1,734.48
4.50%	7,457.21	5,560.06	4,969.29	4,145.54	3,059.97	2,530.60	2,223.33	2,026.74	1,893.03	1,798.25
4.75%	7,502.76	5,606.69	5,016.49	4,193.91	3,111.33	2,584.89	2,280.47	2,086.59	1,955.43	1,863.03
5.00%	7,548.49	5,653.56	5,063.97	4,242.62	3,163.17	2,639.82	2,338.36	2,147.29	2,018.75	1,928.79
5.25%	7,594.39	5,700.67	5,111.71	4,291.67	3,215.51	2,695.38	2,396.99	2,208.81	2,082.97	1,995.48
5.50%	7,640.46	5,748.02	5,159.73	4,341.05	3,268.33	2,751.55	2,456.35	2,271.16	2,148.07	2,063.08
5.75%	7,686.71	5,795.60	5,208.02	4,390.77	3,321.64	2,808.33	2,516.43	2,334.29	2,214.00	2,131.55
6.00%	7,733.12	5,843.42	5,256.57	4,440.82	3,375.43	2,865.72	2,577.21	2,398.20	2,280.76	2,200.85
6.25%	7,779.70	5,891.48	5,305.40	4,491.20	3,429.69	2,923.71	2,638.68	2,462.87	2,348.31	2,270.96
6.50%	7,826.46	5,939.77	5,354.49	4,541.92	3,484.43	2,982.29	2,700.83	2,528.27	2,416.62	2,341.83
6.75%	7,873.38	5,988.31	5,403.86	4,592.96	3,539.64	3,041.46	2,763.65	2,594.39	2,485.67	2,413.43
7.00%	7,920.48	6,037.07	5,453.49	4,644.34	3,595.31	3,101.20	2,827.12	2,661.21	2,555.43	2,485.73
7.25%	7,967.74	6,086.07	5,503.38	4,696.04	3,651.45	3,161.50	2,891.23	2,728.71	2,625.87	2,558.69
7.50%	8,015.18	6,135.31	5,553.55	4,748.07	3,708.05	3,222.37	2,955.96	2,796.86	2,696.97	2,632.28
7.75%	8,062.78	6,184.78	5,603.98	4,800.43	3,765.10	3,283.79	3,021.32	2,865.65	2,768.70	2,706.48
8.00%	8,110.56	6,234.49	5,654.67	4,853.10	3,822.61	3,345.76	3,087.26	2,935.06	2,841.04	2,781.25
8.25%	8,158.50	6,284.42	5,705.63	4,906.11	3,880.56	3,408.26	3,153.80	3,005.07	2,913.96	2,856.56
8.50%	8,206.61	6,334.59	5,756.85	4,959.43	3,938.96	3,471.29	3,220.91	3,075.65	2,987.44	2,932.38
8.75%	8,254.89	6,385.00	5,808.34	5,013.07	3,997.79	3,534.84	3,288.57	3,146.80	3,061.45	3,008.68
9.00%	8,303.34	6,435.63	5,860.08	5,067.03	4,057.07	3,598.90	3,356.79	3,218.49	3,135.97	3,085.45
9.25%	8,351.96	6,486.50	5,912.09	5,121.31	4,116.77	3,663.47	3,425.53	3,290.70	3,210.98	3,162.64
9.50%	8,400.74	6,537.59	5,964.35	5,175.90	4,176.90	3,728.52	3,494.79	3,363.42	3,286.45	3,240.25
9.75%	8,449.70	6,588.92	6,016.88	5,230.81	4,237.45	3,794.07	3,564.55	3,436.62	3,362.36	3,318.23
10.00%	8,498.82	6,640.47	6,069.67	5,286.03	4,298.42	3,860.09	3,634.80	3,510.29	3,438.69	3,396.58
10.25%	8,548.11	6,692.26	6,122.71	5,341.56	4,359.80	3,926.57	3,705.53	3,584.41	3,515.42	3,475.27
10.50%	8,597.56	6,744.27	6,176.01	5,397.40	4,421.60	3,993.52	3,776.73	3,658.96	3,592.54	3,554.28
10.75%	8,647.18	6,796.51	6,229.56	5,453.55	4,483.79	4,060.92	3,848.37	3,733.93	3,670.01	3,633.59

	5	7	8	10	15	20	25	30	35	40
11.00%	8,696.97	6,848.97	6,283.37	5,510.00	4,546.39	4,128.75	3,920.45	3,809.29	3,747.83	3,713.18
11.25%	8,746.92	6,901.67	6,337.43	5,566.76	4,609.38	4,197.02	3,992.96	3,885.05	3,825.98	3,793.03
11.50%	8,797.04	6,954.58	6,391.75	5,623.82	4,672.76	4,265.72	4,065.88	3,961.17	3,904.43	3,873.13
11.75%	8,847.33	7,007.73	6,446.32	5,681.18	4,736.53	4,334.83	4,139.19	4,037.64	3,983.18	3,953.46
12.00%	8,897.78	7,061.09	6,501.14	5,738.84	4,800.67	4,404.34	4,212.90	4,114.45	4,062.20	4,034.00
12.25%	8,948.39	7,114.68	6,556.21	5,796.79	4,865.19	4,474.26	4,286.98	4,191.59	4,141.48	4,114.74
12.50%	8,999.18	7,168.50	6,611.52	5,855.05	4,930.09	4,544.56	4,361.42	4,269.03	4,221.02	4,195.68
12.75%	9,050.12	7,222.53	6,667.09	5,913.59	4,995.35	4,615.25	4,436.21	4,346.77	4,300.78	4,276.79
13.00%	9,101.23	7,276.79	6,722.90	5,972.43	5,060.97	4,686.30	4,511.34	4,424.80	4,380.77	4,358.06
13.25%	9,152.50	7,331.26	6,778.96	6,031.56	5,126.95	4,757.72	4,586.80	4,503.09	4,460.97	4,439.48
13.50%	9,203.94	7,385.96	6,835.26	6,090.97	5,193.27	4,829.50	4,662.58	4,581.65	4,541.36	4,521.04
13.75%	9,255.54	7,440.87	6,891.81	6,150.67	5,259.95	4,901.62	4,738.66	4,660.45	4,621.94	4,602.74
14.00%	9,307.30	7,496.00	6,948.60	6,210.66	5,326.97	4,974.08	4,815.04	4,739.49	4,702.69	4,684.56
14.25%	9,359.23	7,551.35	7,005.63	6,270.92	5,394.32	5,046.88	4,891.71	4,818.75	4,783.61	4,766.49
14.50%	9,411.31	7,606.92	7,062.90	6,331.47	5,462.00	5,119.99	4,968.65	4,898.22	4,864.68	4,848.53
14.75%	9,463.56	7,662.70	7,120.41	6,392.30	5,530.02	5,193.42	5,045.86	4,977.90	4,945.90	4,930.67
15.00%	9,515.97	7,718.70	7,178.16	6,453.40	5,598.35	5,267.16	5,123.32	5,057.78	5,027.25	5,012.90
15.25%	9,568.54	7,774.91	7,236.15	6,514.77	5,667.00	5,341.19	5,201.03	5,137.83	5,108.74	5,095.21
15.50%	9,621.28	7,831.34	7,294.37	6,576.42	5,735.96	5,415.52	5,278.98	5,218.07	5,190.34	5,177.60
15.75%	9,674.17	7,887.98	7,352.83	6,638.34	5,805.23	5,490.13	5,357.16	5,298.47	5,272.05	5,260.06
16.00%	9,727.22	7,944.83	7,411.51	6,700.52	5,874.80	5,565.02	5,435.56	5,379.03	5,353.88	5,342.59
16.25%	9,780.44	8,001.89	7,470.44	6,762.98	5,944.67	5,640.18	5,514.17	5,459.74	5,435.80	5,425.19
16.50%	9,833.81	8,059.16	7,529.59	6,825.69	6,014.83	5,715.60	5,592.98	5,540.59	5,517.82	5,507.84
16.75%	9,887.34	8,116.63	7,588.97	6,888.67	6,085.28	5,791.28	5,671.99	5,621.58	5,599.92	5,590.54
17.00%	9,941.03	8,174.32	7,648.58	6,951.91	6,156.02	5,867.20	5,751.19	5,702.70	5,682.10	5,673.29
17.25%	9,994.88	8,232.22	7,708.42	7,015.40	6,227.03	5,943.37	5,830.57	5,783.94	5,764.37	5,756.09
17.50%	10,048.89	8,290.32	7,768.48	7,079.15	6,298.31	6,019.77	5,910.12	5,865.30	5,846.70	5,838.93
17.75%	10,103.05	8,348.62	7,828.77	7,143.15	6,369.87	6,096.40	5,989.84	5,946.77	5,929.10	5,921.81
18.00%	10,157.37	8,407.14	7,889.29	7,207.41	6,441.68	6,173.25	6,069.72	6,028.34	6,011.57	6,004.73
18.25%	10,211.85	8,465.85	7,950.02	7,271.91	6,513.76	6,250.31	6,149.75	6,110.01	6,094.09	6,087.68
18.50%	10,266.48	8,524.77	8,010.98	7,336.66	6,586.09	6,327.59	6,229.94	6,191.78	6,176.67	6,170.66
18.75%	10,321.27	8,583.89	8,072.15	7,401.66	6,658.68	6,405.06	6,310.26	6,273.63	6,259.30	6,253.67
19.00%	10,376.22	8,643.21	8,133.55	7,466.89	6,731.50	6,482.74	6,390.72	6,355.57	6,341.98	6,336.70
19.25%	10,431.32	8,702.73	8,195.16	7,532.37	6,804.57	6,560.61	6,471.31	6,437.59	6,424.70	6,419.76
19.50%	10,486.58	8,762.45	8,256.98	7,598.09	6,877.88	6,638.66	6,552.02	6,519.68	6,507.47	6,502.84
19.75%	10,541.99	8,822.37	8,319.03	7,664.04	6,951.42	6,716.89	6,632.86	6,601.84	6,590.27	6,585.94
20.00%	10,597.55	8,882.48	8,381.28	7,730.23	7,025.19	6,795.30	6,713.81	6,684.07	6,673.11	6,669.06
20.25%	10,653.27	8,942.79	8,443.75	7,796.64	7,099.18	6,873.88	6,794.87	6,766.37	6,755.99	6,752.19
20.50%	10,709.14	9,003.30	8,506.42	7,863.29	7,173.39	6,952.62	6,876.03	6,848.72	6,838.90	6,835.35
20.75%	10,765.17	9,064.00	8,569.31	7,930.17	7,247.81	7,031.52	6,957.29	6,931.14	6,921.83	6,918.51

	5	7	8	10	15	20	25	30	35	40
1.00%	6,922.97	4,994.15	4,391.51	3,547.97	2,423.90	1,862.57	1,526.33	1,302.64	1,143.26	1,024.07
1.25%	6,966.65	5,037.95	4,435.40	3,592.09	2,468.69	1,908.09	1,572.60	1,349.67	1,191.05	1,072.62
1.50%	7,010.50	5,081.99	4,479.57	3,636.56	2,514.01	1,954.31	1,619.74	1,397.74	1,240.05	1,122.55
1.75%	7,054.54	5,126.28	4,524.02	3,681.38	2,559.85	2,001.22	1,667.75	1,446.84	1,290.24	1,173.83
2.00%	7,098.74	5,170.81	4,568.75	3,726.54	2,606.21	2,048.83	1,716.61	1,496.96	1,341.61	1,226.44
2.25%	7,143.12	5,215.59	4,613.77	3,772.06	2,653.09	2,097.12	1,766.33	1,548.10	1,394.16	1,280.38
2.50%	7,187.68	5,260.61	4,659.06	3,817.93	2,700.50	2,146.11	1,816.90	1,600.24	1,447.86	1,335.60
2.75%	7,232.41	5,305.88	4,704.63	3,864.15	2,748.42	2,195.77	1,868.31	1,653.38	1,502.69	1,392.10
3.00%	7,277.32	5,351.39	4,750.48	3,910.71	2,796.86	2,246.12	1,920.56	1,707.50	1,558.64	1,449.84
3.25%	7,322.40	5,397.14	4,796.60	3,957.62	2,845.81	2,297.14	1,973.63	1,762.59	1,615.70	1,508.79
3.50%	7,367.66	5,443.14	4,843.01	4,004.88	2,895.27	2,348.84	2,027.53	1,818.63	1,673.83	1,568.93
3.75%	7,413.09	5,489.38	4,889.70	4,052.48	2,945.25	2,401.20	2,082.23	1,875.62	1,733.02	1,630.23
4.00%	7,458.69	5,535.87	4,936.66	4,100.43	2,995.74	2,454.22	2,137.74	1,933.53	1,793.24	1,692.65
4.25%	7,504.47	5,582.59	4,983.89	4,148.72	3,046.73	2,507.90	2,194.04	1,992.36	1,854.47	1,756.16
4.50%	7,550.42	5,629.57	5,031.41	4,197.36	3,098.22	2,562.23	2,251.12	2,052.08	1,916.69	1,820.73
4.75%	7,596.55	5,676.78	5,079.20	4,246.33	3,150.22	2,617.21	2,308.98	2,112.67	1,979.87	1,886.32
5.00%	7,642.85	5,724.23	5,127.27	4,295.65	3,202.71	2,672.82	2,367.59	2,174.13	2,043.99	1,952.90
5.25%	7,689.32	5,771.93	5,175.61	4,345.31	3,255.70	2,729.07	2,426.95	2,236.42	2,109.01	2,020.42
5.50%	7,735.97	5,819.87	5,224.23	4,395.31	3,309.19	2,785.94	2,487.05	2,299.55	2,174.92	2,088.87
5.75%	7,782.79	5,868.05	5,273.12	4,445.65	3,363.16	2,843.44	2,547.88	2,363.47	2,241.68	2,158.19
6.00%	7,829.78	5,916.46	5,322.28	4,496.33	3,417.62	2,901.55	2,609.42	2,428.18	2,309.27	2,228.37
6.25%	7,876.95	5,965.12	5,371.72	4,547.34	3,472.56	2,960.26	2,671.66	2,493.65	2,377.66	2,299.35
6.50%	7,924.29	6,014.02	5,421.42	4,598.69	3,527.98	3,019.57	2,734.59	2,559.88	2,446.82	2,371.10
6.75%	7,971.80	6,063.16	5,471.40	4,650.38	3,583.88	3,079.47	2,798.19	2,626.82	2,516.74	2,443.60
7.00%	8,019.49	6,112.54	5,521.66	4,702.39	3,640.25	3,139.96	2,862.46	2,694.48	2,587.37	2,516.80
7.25%	8,067.34	6,162.15	5,572.18	4,754.74	3,697.09	3,201.02	2,927.37	2,762.81	2,658.69	2,590.67
7.50%	8,115.37	6,212.00	5,622.97	4,807.42	3,754.40	3,262.65	2,992.91	2,831.82	2,730.68	2,665.19
7.75%	8,163.57	6,262.09	5,674.03	4,860.43	3,812.17	3,324.84	3,059.08	2,901.47	2,803.31	2,740.31
8.00%	8,211.94	6,312.42	5,725.36	4,913.77	3,870.39	3,387.58	3,125.86	2,971.75	2,876.56	2,816.01
8.25%	8,260.48	6,362.98	5,776.95	4,967.43	3,929.07	3,450.87	3,193.22	3,042.63	2,950.39	2,892.26
8.50%	8,309.20	6,413.78	5,828.81	5,021.42	3,988.20	3,514.68	3,261.17	3,114.10	3,024.79	2,969.03
8.75%	8,358.08	6,464.81	5,880.94	5,075.73	4,047.77	3,579.03	3,329.68	3,186.14	3,099.72	3,046.29
9.00%	8,407.13	6,516.08	5,933.33	5,130.37	4,107.78	3,643.89	3,398.75	3,258.72	3,175.17	3,124.01
9.25%	8,456.36	6,567.58	5,985.99	5,185.33	4,168.23	3,709.26	3,468.35	3,331.84	3,251.11	3,202.18
9.50%	8,505.75	6,619.31	6,038.91	5,240.60	4,229.11	3,775.13	3,538.47	3,405.46	3,327.53	3,280.75
9.75%	8,555.32	6,671.28	6,092.09	5,296.19	4,290.42	3,841.49	3,609.11	3,479.58	3,404.39	3,359.71
10.00%	8,605.05	6,723.48	6,145.54	5,352.10	4,352.15	3,908.34	3,680.24	3,554.16	3,481.67	3,439.04
10.25%	8,654.96	6,775.91	6,199.24	5,408.33	4,414.30	3,975.66	3,751.85	3,629.21	3,559.37	3,518.71
10.50%	8,705.03	6,828.57	6,253.21	5,464.87	4,476.87	4,043.44	3,823.94	3,704.69	3,637.44	3,598.71
10.75%	8,755.27	6,881.46	6,307.43	5,521.72	4,539.84	4,111.68	3,896.48	3,780.60	3,715.89	3,679.01

$405,000   11.00 - 20.75%   5 - 40 Years

	5	7	8	10	15	20	25	30	35	40
11.00%	8,805.68	6,934.59	6,361.91	5,578.88	4,603.22	4,180.36	3,969.46	3,856.91	3,794.68	3,759.59
11.25%	8,856.26	6,987.94	6,416.65	5,636.34	4,667.00	4,249.49	4,042.87	3,933.61	3,873.80	3,840.44
11.50%	8,907.01	7,041.52	6,471.65	5,694.12	4,731.17	4,319.04	4,116.70	4,010.68	3,953.23	3,921.54
11.75%	8,957.92	7,095.32	6,526.90	5,752.19	4,795.73	4,389.01	4,190.93	4,088.11	4,032.97	4,002.87
12.00%	9,009.00	7,149.36	6,582.40	5,810.57	4,860.68	4,459.40	4,265.56	4,165.88	4,112.98	4,084.42
12.25%	9,060.25	7,203.62	6,638.16	5,869.25	4,926.01	4,530.19	4,340.56	4,243.98	4,193.25	4,166.18
12.50%	9,111.66	7,258.10	6,694.17	5,928.23	4,991.71	4,601.37	4,415.93	4,322.39	4,273.78	4,248.12
12.75%	9,163.25	7,312.81	6,750.43	5,987.51	5,057.79	4,672.94	4,491.66	4,401.11	4,354.54	4,330.25
13.00%	9,214.99	7,367.75	6,806.94	6,047.08	5,124.23	4,744.88	4,567.73	4,480.11	4,435.53	4,412.53
13.25%	9,266.91	7,422.90	6,863.70	6,106.95	5,191.03	4,817.19	4,644.14	4,559.38	4,516.73	4,494.97
13.50%	9,318.99	7,478.28	6,920.70	6,167.11	5,258.19	4,889.87	4,720.86	4,638.92	4,598.13	4,577.56
13.75%	9,371.23	7,533.88	6,977.96	6,227.56	5,325.70	4,962.89	4,797.90	4,718.71	4,679.71	4,660.28
14.00%	9,423.64	7,589.70	7,035.46	6,288.29	5,393.55	5,036.26	4,875.23	4,798.73	4,761.48	4,743.12
14.25%	9,476.22	7,645.75	7,093.20	6,349.31	5,461.75	5,109.96	4,952.86	4,878.98	4,843.41	4,826.07
14.50%	9,528.95	7,702.01	7,151.19	6,410.61	5,530.28	5,183.99	5,030.76	4,959.45	4,925.49	4,909.14
14.75%	9,581.86	7,758.49	7,209.42	6,472.20	5,599.14	5,258.34	5,108.93	5,040.13	5,007.72	4,992.30
15.00%	9,634.92	7,815.19	7,267.89	6,534.07	5,668.33	5,333.00	5,187.36	5,121.00	5,090.09	5,075.56
15.25%	9,688.15	7,872.10	7,326.60	6,596.21	5,737.84	5,407.96	5,266.05	5,202.06	5,172.59	5,158.90
15.50%	9,741.54	7,929.23	7,385.55	6,658.63	5,807.66	5,483.22	5,344.97	5,283.29	5,255.22	5,242.32
15.75%	9,795.10	7,986.58	7,444.74	6,721.32	5,877.80	5,558.76	5,424.12	5,364.70	5,337.96	5,325.81
16.00%	9,848.81	8,044.14	7,504.16	6,784.28	5,948.24	5,634.59	5,503.50	5,446.27	5,420.80	5,409.38
16.25%	9,902.69	8,101.91	7,563.82	6,847.51	6,018.98	5,710.68	5,583.09	5,527.99	5,503.75	5,493.00
16.50%	9,956.73	8,159.90	7,623.71	6,911.01	6,090.02	5,787.05	5,662.89	5,609.85	5,586.79	5,576.69
16.75%	10,010.93	8,218.09	7,683.83	6,974.78	6,161.35	5,863.67	5,742.89	5,691.85	5,669.92	5,660.42
17.00%	10,065.29	8,276.50	7,744.19	7,038.80	6,232.97	5,940.54	5,823.08	5,773.99	5,753.13	5,744.21
17.25%	10,119.81	8,335.12	7,804.78	7,103.09	6,304.87	6,017.66	5,903.45	5,856.24	5,836.42	5,828.04
17.50%	10,174.50	8,393.95	7,865.59	7,167.64	6,377.04	6,095.01	5,984.00	5,938.62	5,919.79	5,911.92
17.75%	10,229.34	8,452.98	7,926.63	7,232.44	6,449.49	6,172.60	6,064.71	6,021.10	6,003.22	5,995.84
18.00%	10,284.34	8,512.22	7,987.90	7,297.50	6,522.21	6,250.41	6,145.59	6,103.70	6,086.71	6,079.79
18.25%	10,339.50	8,571.67	8,049.40	7,362.81	6,595.18	6,328.44	6,226.63	6,186.39	6,170.27	6,163.77
18.50%	10,394.81	8,631.33	8,111.11	7,428.37	6,668.42	6,406.68	6,307.81	6,269.18	6,253.88	6,247.79
18.75%	10,450.29	8,691.19	8,173.05	7,494.18	6,741.91	6,485.13	6,389.14	6,352.05	6,337.54	6,331.84
19.00%	10,505.92	8,751.25	8,235.22	7,560.23	6,815.65	6,563.77	6,470.60	6,435.01	6,421.25	6,415.91
19.25%	10,561.71	8,811.51	8,297.60	7,626.53	6,889.63	6,642.61	6,552.20	6,518.06	6,505.01	6,500.00
19.50%	10,617.66	8,871.98	8,360.20	7,693.06	6,963.85	6,721.64	6,633.92	6,601.18	6,588.81	6,584.12
19.75%	10,673.76	8,932.64	8,423.01	7,759.84	7,038.31	6,800.85	6,715.77	6,684.37	6,672.65	6,668.26
20.00%	10,730.02	8,993.51	8,486.05	7,826.85	7,113.00	6,880.24	6,797.73	6,767.63	6,756.53	6,752.42
20.25%	10,786.44	9,054.58	8,549.29	7,894.10	7,187.92	6,959.80	6,879.80	6,850.95	6,840.44	6,836.60
20.50%	10,843.01	9,115.84	8,612.75	7,961.58	7,263.05	7,039.52	6,961.98	6,934.33	6,924.38	6,920.79
20.75%	10,899.73	9,177.30	8,676.43	8,029.29	7,338.41	7,119.41	7,044.26	7,017.77	7,008.36	7,004.99

	5	7	8	10	15	20	25	30	35	40
1.00%	7,008.44	5,055.81	4,445.72	3,591.77	2,453.83	1,885.57	1,545.18	1,318.72	1,157.37	1,036.71
1.25%	7,052.66	5,100.15	4,490.16	3,636.43	2,499.17	1,931.65	1,592.02	1,366.33	1,205.75	1,085.87
1.50%	7,097.05	5,144.73	4,534.87	3,681.45	2,545.05	1,978.44	1,639.74	1,414.99	1,255.36	1,136.41
1.75%	7,141.63	5,189.57	4,579.87	3,726.82	2,591.45	2,025.93	1,688.34	1,464.70	1,306.17	1,188.32
2.00%	7,186.38	5,234.65	4,625.16	3,772.55	2,638.39	2,074.12	1,737.80	1,515.44	1,358.18	1,241.59
2.25%	7,231.31	5,279.98	4,670.73	3,818.63	2,685.85	2,123.01	1,788.14	1,567.21	1,411.37	1,296.18
2.50%	7,276.42	5,325.56	4,716.58	3,865.07	2,733.84	2,172.60	1,839.33	1,620.00	1,465.73	1,352.09
2.75%	7,321.70	5,371.38	4,762.71	3,911.85	2,782.35	2,222.88	1,891.37	1,673.79	1,521.24	1,409.28
3.00%	7,367.16	5,417.45	4,809.12	3,958.99	2,831.38	2,273.85	1,944.27	1,728.58	1,577.89	1,467.74
3.25%	7,412.80	5,463.77	4,855.82	4,006.48	2,880.94	2,325.50	1,998.00	1,784.35	1,635.64	1,527.42
3.50%	7,458.62	5,510.34	4,902.80	4,054.32	2,931.02	2,377.83	2,052.56	1,841.08	1,694.49	1,588.30
3.75%	7,504.61	5,557.15	4,950.06	4,102.51	2,981.61	2,430.84	2,107.94	1,898.77	1,754.41	1,650.36
4.00%	7,550.77	5,604.21	4,997.60	4,151.05	3,032.72	2,484.52	2,164.13	1,957.40	1,815.38	1,713.55
4.25%	7,597.12	5,651.52	5,045.42	4,199.94	3,084.34	2,538.86	2,221.13	2,016.95	1,877.37	1,777.84
4.50%	7,643.64	5,699.07	5,093.53	4,249.17	3,136.47	2,593.86	2,278.91	2,077.41	1,940.35	1,843.21
4.75%	7,690.33	5,746.86	5,141.91	4,298.76	3,189.11	2,649.52	2,337.48	2,138.75	2,004.31	1,909.61
5.00%	7,737.21	5,794.90	5,190.57	4,348.69	3,242.25	2,705.82	2,396.82	2,200.97	2,069.22	1,977.01
5.25%	7,784.25	5,843.19	5,239.51	4,398.96	3,295.90	2,762.76	2,456.92	2,264.04	2,135.05	2,045.37
5.50%	7,831.48	5,891.72	5,288.72	4,449.58	3,350.04	2,820.34	2,517.76	2,327.93	2,201.77	2,114.66
5.75%	7,878.87	5,940.49	5,338.22	4,500.54	3,404.68	2,878.54	2,579.34	2,392.65	2,269.35	2,184.84
6.00%	7,926.45	5,989.51	5,387.99	4,551.84	3,459.81	2,937.37	2,641.64	2,458.16	2,337.78	2,255.88
6.25%	7,974.20	6,038.77	5,438.03	4,603.48	3,515.43	2,996.81	2,704.64	2,524.44	2,407.01	2,327.73
6.50%	8,022.12	6,088.27	5,488.36	4,655.47	3,571.54	3,056.85	2,768.35	2,591.48	2,477.03	2,400.37
6.75%	8,070.22	6,138.01	5,538.95	4,707.79	3,628.13	3,117.49	2,832.74	2,659.25	2,547.81	2,473.76
7.00%	8,118.49	6,188.00	5,589.82	4,760.45	3,685.20	3,178.73	2,897.79	2,727.74	2,619.31	2,547.87
7.25%	8,166.94	6,238.23	5,640.97	4,813.44	3,742.74	3,240.54	2,963.51	2,796.92	2,691.52	2,622.65
7.50%	8,215.56	6,288.69	5,692.39	4,866.77	3,800.75	3,302.93	3,029.86	2,866.78	2,764.39	2,698.09
7.75%	8,264.35	6,339.40	5,744.08	4,920.44	3,859.23	3,365.89	3,096.85	2,937.29	2,837.92	2,774.14
8.00%	8,313.32	6,390.35	5,796.04	4,974.43	3,918.17	3,429.40	3,164.45	3,008.43	2,912.07	2,850.78
8.25%	8,362.46	6,441.53	5,848.27	5,028.76	3,977.58	3,493.47	3,232.65	3,080.19	2,986.81	2,927.97
8.50%	8,411.78	6,492.96	5,900.77	5,083.41	4,037.43	3,558.08	3,301.43	3,152.55	3,062.13	3,005.69
8.75%	8,461.27	6,544.62	5,953.54	5,138.40	4,097.74	3,623.21	3,370.79	3,225.47	3,137.99	3,083.90
9.00%	8,510.93	6,596.52	6,006.58	5,193.71	4,158.49	3,688.88	3,440.71	3,298.95	3,214.37	3,162.58
9.25%	8,560.76	6,648.66	6,059.89	5,249.34	4,219.69	3,755.05	3,511.17	3,372.97	3,291.25	3,241.71
9.50%	8,610.76	6,701.03	6,113.46	5,305.30	4,281.32	3,821.74	3,582.16	3,447.50	3,368.61	3,321.25
9.75%	8,660.94	6,753.64	6,167.30	5,361.58	4,343.39	3,888.92	3,653.66	3,522.53	3,446.42	3,401.19
10.00%	8,711.29	6,806.49	6,221.41	5,418.18	4,405.88	3,956.59	3,725.67	3,598.04	3,524.66	3,481.50
10.25%	8,761.81	6,859.56	6,275.78	5,475.10	4,468.80	4,024.74	3,798.17	3,674.02	3,603.31	3,562.15
10.50%	8,812.50	6,912.88	6,330.41	5,532.33	4,532.14	4,093.36	3,871.14	3,750.43	3,682.35	3,643.14
10.75%	8,863.36	6,966.42	6,385.30	5,589.89	4,595.89	4,162.44	3,944.58	3,827.27	3,761.76	3,724.43

$410,000   11.00 - 20.75%   5 - 40 Years

	5	7	8	10	15	20	25	30	35	40
11.00%	8,914.39	7,020.20	6,440.45	5,647.75	4,660.05	4,231.97	4,018.46	3,904.53	3,841.53	3,806.01
11.25%	8,965.60	7,074.21	6,495.87	5,705.93	4,724.61	4,301.95	4,092.78	3,982.17	3,921.62	3,887.86
11.50%	9,016.97	7,128.45	6,551.54	5,764.41	4,789.58	4,372.36	4,167.52	4,060.19	4,002.04	3,969.96
11.75%	9,068.51	7,182.92	6,607.48	5,823.21	4,854.94	4,443.20	4,242.67	4,138.58	4,082.76	4,052.29
12.00%	9,120.22	7,237.62	6,663.66	5,882.31	4,920.69	4,514.45	4,318.22	4,217.31	4,163.75	4,134.85
12.25%	9,172.10	7,292.55	6,720.11	5,941.71	4,986.82	4,586.12	4,394.15	4,296.38	4,245.02	4,217.61
12.50%	9,224.15	7,347.71	6,776.81	6,001.42	5,053.34	4,658.18	4,470.45	4,375.76	4,326.54	4,300.57
12.75%	9,276.37	7,403.09	6,833.77	6,061.43	5,120.23	4,730.63	4,547.11	4,455.44	4,408.30	4,383.71
13.00%	9,328.76	7,458.70	6,890.97	6,121.74	5,187.49	4,803.46	4,624.12	4,535.42	4,490.29	4,467.01
13.25%	9,381.31	7,514.54	6,948.43	6,182.35	5,255.12	4,876.67	4,701.47	4,615.67	4,572.49	4,550.47
13.50%	9,434.04	7,570.61	7,006.15	6,243.25	5,323.11	4,950.24	4,779.14	4,696.16	4,654.90	4,634.07
13.75%	9,486.93	7,626.89	7,064.11	6,304.44	5,391.45	5,024.16	4,857.13	4,776.96	4,737.49	4,717.81
14.00%	9,539.98	7,683.40	7,122.32	6,365.92	5,460.14	5,098.44	4,935.42	4,857.97	4,820.26	4,801.67
14.25%	9,593.21	7,740.14	7,180.77	6,427.70	5,529.18	5,173.05	5,014.00	4,939.22	4,903.20	4,885.66
14.50%	9,646.60	7,797.09	7,239.48	6,489.76	5,598.55	5,247.99	5,092.87	5,020.68	4,986.36	4,969.75
14.75%	9,700.15	7,854.27	7,298.42	6,552.10	5,668.27	5,323.26	5,172.01	5,102.35	5,069.55	5,053.94
15.00%	9,753.87	7,911.67	7,357.62	6,614.73	5,738.31	5,398.84	5,251.41	5,184.22	5,152.93	5,138.22
15.25%	9,807.76	7,969.29	7,417.05	6,677.64	5,808.67	5,474.72	5,331.06	5,266.28	5,236.45	5,222.59
15.50%	9,861.81	8,027.12	7,476.73	6,740.83	5,879.36	5,550.91	5,410.96	5,348.52	5,320.10	5,307.04
15.75%	9,916.02	8,085.18	7,536.65	6,804.30	5,950.36	5,627.39	5,491.09	5,430.93	5,403.86	5,391.56
16.00%	9,970.40	8,143.45	7,596.80	6,868.04	6,021.67	5,704.15	5,571.44	5,513.50	5,487.72	5,476.16
16.25%	10,024.95	8,201.93	7,657.20	6,932.05	6,093.29	5,781.19	5,652.02	5,596.23	5,571.69	5,560.82
16.50%	10,079.65	8,260.63	7,717.83	6,996.33	6,165.21	5,858.49	5,732.80	5,679.11	5,655.76	5,645.53
16.75%	10,134.52	8,319.55	7,778.70	7,060.89	6,237.42	5,936.06	5,813.79	5,762.12	5,739.92	5,730.30
17.00%	10,189.56	8,378.68	7,839.80	7,125.70	6,309.92	6,013.88	5,894.97	5,845.27	5,824.16	5,815.13
17.25%	10,244.75	8,438.02	7,901.13	7,190.79	6,382.70	6,091.95	5,976.33	5,928.54	5,908.48	5,900.00
17.50%	10,300.11	8,497.58	7,962.70	7,256.13	6,455.77	6,170.26	6,057.87	6,011.93	5,992.87	5,984.91
17.75%	10,355.63	8,557.34	8,024.49	7,321.73	6,529.11	6,248.81	6,139.59	6,095.44	6,077.33	6,069.86
18.00%	10,411.31	8,617.31	8,086.52	7,387.59	6,602.73	6,327.58	6,221.46	6,179.05	6,161.86	6,154.85
18.25%	10,467.15	8,677.50	8,148.77	7,453.71	6,676.61	6,406.57	6,303.50	6,262.76	6,246.44	6,239.87
18.50%	10,523.15	8,737.89	8,211.25	7,520.08	6,750.75	6,485.78	6,385.69	6,346.57	6,331.09	6,324.92
18.75%	10,579.31	8,798.48	8,273.96	7,586.70	6,825.14	6,565.19	6,468.02	6,430.47	6,415.78	6,410.01
19.00%	10,635.63	8,859.29	8,336.88	7,653.57	6,899.79	6,644.81	6,550.49	6,514.46	6,500.53	6,495.12
19.25%	10,692.10	8,920.30	8,400.04	7,720.68	6,974.69	6,724.62	6,633.09	6,598.53	6,585.32	6,580.25
19.50%	10,748.74	8,981.51	8,463.41	7,788.04	7,049.83	6,804.62	6,715.83	6,682.67	6,670.15	6,665.41
19.75%	10,805.54	9,042.92	8,527.00	7,855.64	7,125.20	6,884.81	6,798.68	6,766.89	6,755.03	6,750.59
20.00%	10,862.49	9,104.54	8,590.81	7,923.48	7,200.82	6,965.18	6,881.65	6,851.18	6,839.94	6,835.78
20.25%	10,919.60	9,166.36	8,654.84	7,991.56	7,276.66	7,045.72	6,964.74	6,935.53	6,924.89	6,921.00
20.50%	10,976.87	9,228.38	8,719.08	8,059.87	7,352.72	7,126.43	7,047.93	7,019.94	7,009.87	7,006.23
20.75%	11,034.30	9,290.60	8,783.54	8,128.42	7,429.01	7,207.30	7,131.22	7,104.41	7,094.88	7,091.48

	5	7	8	10	15	20	25	30	35	40
1.00%	7,093.91	5,117.47	4,499.94	3,635.57	2,483.75	1,908.56	1,564.02	1,334.80	1,171.49	1,049.35
1.25%	7,138.66	5,162.34	4,544.91	3,680.78	2,529.65	1,955.20	1,611.43	1,382.99	1,220.46	1,099.11
1.50%	7,183.60	5,207.47	4,590.18	3,726.35	2,576.08	2,002.56	1,659.74	1,432.25	1,270.67	1,150.27
1.75%	7,228.72	5,252.85	4,635.73	3,772.27	2,623.05	2,050.63	1,708.92	1,482.56	1,322.10	1,202.81
2.00%	7,274.02	5,298.49	4,681.56	3,818.56	2,670.56	2,099.42	1,759.00	1,533.92	1,374.74	1,256.73
2.25%	7,319.50	5,344.37	4,727.69	3,865.20	2,718.60	2,148.90	1,809.94	1,586.32	1,428.58	1,311.99
2.50%	7,365.16	5,390.50	4,774.09	3,912.20	2,767.18	2,199.10	1,861.76	1,639.75	1,483.61	1,368.58
2.75%	7,410.99	5,436.89	4,820.79	3,959.56	2,816.28	2,249.99	1,914.44	1,694.20	1,539.79	1,426.47
3.00%	7,457.01	5,483.52	4,867.77	4,007.27	2,865.91	2,301.58	1,967.98	1,749.66	1,597.13	1,485.64
3.25%	7,503.20	5,530.40	4,915.04	4,055.34	2,916.08	2,353.86	2,022.36	1,806.11	1,655.59	1,546.05
3.50%	7,549.57	5,577.54	4,962.59	4,103.76	2,966.76	2,406.83	2,077.59	1,863.54	1,715.16	1,607.67
3.75%	7,596.13	5,624.92	5,010.43	4,152.54	3,017.97	2,460.49	2,133.64	1,921.93	1,775.81	1,670.48
4.00%	7,642.86	5,672.55	5,058.55	4,201.67	3,069.70	2,514.82	2,190.52	1,981.27	1,837.52	1,734.44
4.25%	7,689.77	5,720.44	5,106.95	4,251.16	3,121.96	2,569.82	2,248.21	2,041.55	1,900.26	1,799.52
4.50%	7,736.85	5,768.57	5,155.64	4,300.99	3,174.72	2,625.49	2,306.70	2,102.74	1,964.02	1,865.69
4.75%	7,784.12	5,816.95	5,204.61	4,351.18	3,228.00	2,681.83	2,365.99	2,164.84	2,028.76	1,932.90
5.00%	7,831.56	5,865.57	5,253.87	4,401.72	3,281.79	2,738.82	2,426.05	2,227.81	2,094.45	2,001.12
5.25%	7,879.18	5,914.45	5,303.40	4,452.61	3,336.09	2,796.45	2,486.88	2,291.65	2,161.08	2,070.31
5.50%	7,926.98	5,963.57	5,353.22	4,503.84	3,390.90	2,854.73	2,548.46	2,356.32	2,228.62	2,140.45
5.75%	7,974.96	6,012.94	5,403.32	4,555.42	3,446.20	2,913.65	2,610.79	2,421.83	2,297.03	2,211.48
6.00%	8,023.11	6,062.55	5,453.69	4,607.35	3,502.01	2,973.19	2,673.85	2,488.13	2,366.29	2,283.39
6.25%	8,071.44	6,112.41	5,504.35	4,659.62	3,558.30	3,033.35	2,737.63	2,555.23	2,436.37	2,356.12
6.50%	8,119.95	6,162.52	5,555.29	4,712.24	3,615.10	3,094.13	2,802.11	2,623.08	2,507.24	2,429.65
6.75%	8,168.64	6,212.87	5,606.50	4,765.20	3,672.37	3,155.51	2,867.28	2,691.68	2,578.88	2,503.93
7.00%	8,217.50	6,263.46	5,657.99	4,818.50	3,730.14	3,217.49	2,933.13	2,761.01	2,651.25	2,578.94
7.25%	8,266.53	6,314.30	5,709.76	4,872.14	3,788.38	3,280.06	2,999.65	2,831.03	2,724.34	2,654.64
7.50%	8,315.75	6,365.38	5,761.81	4,926.12	3,847.10	3,343.21	3,066.81	2,901.74	2,798.11	2,730.99
7.75%	8,365.14	6,416.71	5,814.13	4,980.44	3,906.29	3,406.94	3,134.61	2,973.11	2,872.53	2,807.97
8.00%	8,414.70	6,468.28	5,866.72	5,035.10	3,965.96	3,471.23	3,203.04	3,045.12	2,947.58	2,885.54
8.25%	8,464.44	6,520.09	5,919.59	5,090.08	4,026.08	3,536.07	3,272.07	3,117.76	3,023.24	2,963.68
8.50%	8,514.36	6,572.14	5,972.73	5,145.41	4,086.67	3,601.47	3,341.69	3,190.99	3,099.47	3,042.34
8.75%	8,564.45	6,624.43	6,026.15	5,201.06	4,147.71	3,667.40	3,411.90	3,264.81	3,176.26	3,121.51
9.00%	8,614.72	6,676.97	6,079.83	5,257.04	4,209.21	3,733.86	3,482.66	3,339.18	3,253.57	3,201.15
9.25%	8,665.16	6,729.74	6,133.79	5,313.36	4,271.15	3,800.85	3,553.98	3,414.10	3,331.39	3,281.24
9.50%	8,715.77	6,782.75	6,188.02	5,370.00	4,333.53	3,868.34	3,625.84	3,489.54	3,409.69	3,361.76
9.75%	8,766.56	6,836.00	6,242.51	5,426.97	4,396.36	3,936.34	3,698.22	3,565.49	3,488.45	3,442.67
10.00%	8,817.52	6,889.49	6,297.28	5,484.26	4,459.61	4,004.84	3,771.11	3,641.92	3,567.64	3,523.96
10.25%	8,868.66	6,943.22	6,352.31	5,541.87	4,523.30	4,073.82	3,844.49	3,718.82	3,647.25	3,605.60
10.50%	8,919.97	6,997.18	6,407.61	5,599.80	4,587.41	4,143.28	3,918.35	3,796.17	3,727.26	3,687.57
10.75%	8,971.45	7,051.38	6,463.17	5,658.06	4,651.93	4,213.20	3,992.68	3,873.95	3,807.64	3,769.85

$415,000   11.00 - 20.75%   5 - 40 Years

	5	7	8	10	15	20	25	30	35	40
11.00%	9,023.11	7,105.81	6,519.00	5,716.63	4,716.88	4,283.58	4,067.47	3,952.14	3,888.37	3,852.42
11.25%	9,074.93	7,160.48	6,575.09	5,775.51	4,782.23	4,354.41	4,142.69	4,030.73	3,969.45	3,935.27
11.50%	9,126.93	7,215.38	6,631.44	5,834.71	4,847.99	4,425.68	4,218.35	4,109.71	4,050.85	4,018.37
11.75%	9,179.10	7,270.52	6,688.05	5,894.22	4,914.15	4,497.38	4,294.41	4,189.05	4,132.54	4,101.71
12.00%	9,231.45	7,325.88	6,744.93	5,954.04	4,980.70	4,569.51	4,370.88	4,268.74	4,214.53	4,185.27
12.25%	9,283.96	7,381.48	6,802.06	6,014.17	5,047.64	4,642.04	4,447.74	4,348.77	4,296.79	4,269.05
12.50%	9,336.64	7,437.31	6,859.46	6,074.61	5,114.97	4,714.98	4,524.97	4,429.12	4,379.31	4,353.02
12.75%	9,389.50	7,493.37	6,917.11	6,135.35	5,182.67	4,788.32	4,602.57	4,509.78	4,462.06	4,437.16
13.00%	9,442.53	7,549.66	6,975.01	6,196.40	5,250.75	4,862.04	4,680.52	4,590.73	4,545.05	4,521.48
13.25%	9,495.72	7,606.18	7,033.17	6,257.74	5,319.21	4,936.14	4,758.81	4,671.96	4,628.26	4,605.96
13.50%	9,549.09	7,662.93	7,091.59	6,319.38	5,388.02	5,010.60	4,837.43	4,753.46	4,711.66	4,690.58
13.75%	9,602.62	7,719.90	7,150.25	6,381.32	5,457.20	5,085.43	4,916.36	4,835.22	4,795.26	4,775.34
14.00%	9,656.32	7,777.10	7,209.17	6,443.56	5,526.73	5,160.61	4,995.61	4,917.22	4,879.04	4,860.23
14.25%	9,710.20	7,834.53	7,268.34	6,506.08	5,596.61	5,236.13	5,075.15	4,999.45	4,963.00	4,945.24
14.50%	9,764.24	7,892.18	7,327.76	6,568.90	5,666.83	5,311.99	5,154.98	5,081.91	5,047.11	5,030.35
14.75%	9,818.45	7,950.06	7,387.43	6,632.01	5,737.39	5,388.17	5,235.08	5,164.57	5,131.37	5,115.57
15.00%	9,872.82	8,008.15	7,447.34	6,695.40	5,808.29	5,464.68	5,315.45	5,247.44	5,215.78	5,200.88
15.25%	9,927.36	8,066.47	7,507.50	6,759.08	5,879.51	5,541.49	5,396.07	5,330.50	5,300.31	5,286.28
15.50%	9,982.07	8,125.01	7,567.91	6,823.04	5,951.06	5,618.60	5,476.94	5,413.75	5,384.98	5,371.76
15.75%	10,036.95	8,183.78	7,628.56	6,887.28	6,022.93	5,696.01	5,558.05	5,497.16	5,469.76	5,457.32
16.00%	10,091.99	8,242.76	7,689.45	6,951.79	6,095.11	5,773.71	5,639.39	5,580.74	5,554.65	5,542.94
16.25%	10,147.20	8,301.96	7,750.58	7,016.59	6,167.60	5,851.69	5,720.95	5,664.48	5,639.64	5,628.63
16.50%	10,202.58	8,361.37	7,811.95	7,081.66	6,240.39	5,929.94	5,802.72	5,748.36	5,724.73	5,714.38
16.75%	10,258.12	8,421.01	7,873.56	7,146.99	6,313.48	6,008.45	5,884.69	5,832.39	5,809.92	5,800.19
17.00%	10,313.82	8,480.86	7,935.40	7,212.60	6,386.87	6,087.22	5,966.86	5,916.55	5,895.18	5,886.04
17.25%	10,369.69	8,540.92	7,997.49	7,278.48	6,460.54	6,166.24	6,049.21	6,000.84	5,980.53	5,971.95
17.50%	10,425.72	8,601.20	8,059.80	7,344.62	6,534.50	6,245.51	6,131.75	6,085.25	6,065.95	6,057.89
17.75%	10,481.91	8,661.70	8,122.35	7,411.02	6,608.74	6,325.01	6,214.46	6,169.77	6,151.44	6,143.88
18.00%	10,538.27	8,722.40	8,185.13	7,477.69	6,683.25	6,404.74	6,297.33	6,254.40	6,237.00	6,229.91
18.25%	10,594.79	8,783.32	8,248.15	7,544.61	6,758.03	6,484.70	6,380.37	6,339.14	6,322.62	6,315.97
18.50%	10,651.48	8,844.45	8,311.39	7,611.79	6,833.07	6,564.87	6,463.56	6,423.97	6,408.30	6,402.06
18.75%	10,708.32	8,905.78	8,374.86	7,679.22	6,908.38	6,645.25	6,546.90	6,508.89	6,494.02	6,488.18
19.00%	10,765.33	8,967.33	8,438.55	7,746.90	6,983.94	6,725.84	6,630.37	6,593.90	6,579.80	6,574.33
19.25%	10,822.50	9,029.08	8,502.48	7,814.84	7,059.75	6,806.63	6,713.98	6,679.00	6,665.63	6,660.50
19.50%	10,879.82	9,091.04	8,566.62	7,883.02	7,135.80	6,887.61	6,797.73	6,764.17	6,751.50	6,746.69
19.75%	10,937.31	9,153.20	8,630.99	7,951.44	7,212.10	6,968.77	6,881.59	6,849.41	6,837.41	6,832.91
20.00%	10,994.96	9,215.57	8,695.58	8,020.11	7,288.63	7,050.12	6,965.57	6,934.73	6,923.35	6,919.15
20.25%	11,052.77	9,278.15	8,760.39	8,089.02	7,365.40	7,131.65	7,049.67	7,020.11	7,009.34	7,005.40
20.50%	11,110.74	9,340.92	8,825.41	8,158.17	7,442.39	7,213.34	7,133.88	7,105.55	7,095.35	7,091.67
20.75%	11,168.86	9,403.90	8,890.66	8,227.55	7,519.61	7,295.20	7,218.19	7,191.05	7,181.40	7,177.96

$420,000   1.00 - 10.75%   5 - 40 Years

	5	7	8	10	15	20	25	30	35	40
1.00%	7,179.37	5,179.12	4,554.15	3,679.37	2,513.68	1,931.56	1,582.86	1,350.89	1,185.60	1,062.00
1.25%	7,224.67	5,224.54	4,599.67	3,725.13	2,560.13	1,978.76	1,630.85	1,399.66	1,235.16	1,112.35
1.50%	7,270.15	5,270.21	4,645.48	3,771.24	2,607.12	2,026.69	1,679.73	1,449.50	1,285.97	1,164.12
1.75%	7,315.82	5,316.14	4,691.58	3,817.72	2,654.66	2,075.34	1,729.51	1,500.42	1,338.03	1,217.30
2.00%	7,361.66	5,362.32	4,737.97	3,864.57	2,702.74	2,124.71	1,780.19	1,552.40	1,391.30	1,271.87
2.25%	7,407.68	5,408.76	4,784.65	3,911.77	2,751.36	2,174.79	1,831.75	1,605.43	1,445.79	1,327.80
2.50%	7,453.89	5,455.45	4,831.61	3,959.34	2,800.51	2,225.59	1,884.19	1,659.51	1,501.48	1,385.07
2.75%	7,500.28	5,502.39	4,878.87	4,007.26	2,850.21	2,277.10	1,937.51	1,714.61	1,558.35	1,443.66
3.00%	7,546.85	5,549.59	4,926.42	4,055.55	2,900.44	2,329.31	1,991.69	1,770.74	1,616.37	1,503.53
3.25%	7,593.60	5,597.04	4,974.26	4,104.20	2,951.21	2,382.22	2,046.73	1,827.87	1,675.54	1,564.67
3.50%	7,640.53	5,644.74	5,022.38	4,153.21	3,002.51	2,435.83	2,102.62	1,885.99	1,735.82	1,627.04
3.75%	7,687.65	5,692.69	5,070.79	4,202.57	3,054.33	2,490.13	2,159.35	1,945.09	1,797.20	1,690.61
4.00%	7,734.94	5,740.90	5,119.50	4,252.30	3,106.69	2,545.12	2,216.91	2,005.14	1,859.65	1,755.34
4.25%	7,782.41	5,789.36	5,168.48	4,302.38	3,159.57	2,600.78	2,275.30	2,066.15	1,923.15	1,821.20
4.50%	7,830.07	5,838.07	5,217.76	4,352.81	3,212.97	2,657.13	2,334.50	2,128.08	1,987.68	1,888.16
4.75%	7,877.90	5,887.03	5,267.32	4,403.61	3,266.89	2,714.14	2,394.49	2,190.92	2,053.20	1,956.18
5.00%	7,925.92	5,936.24	5,317.17	4,454.75	3,321.33	2,771.81	2,455.28	2,254.65	2,119.69	2,025.23
5.25%	7,974.11	5,985.70	5,367.30	4,506.25	3,376.29	2,830.15	2,516.84	2,319.26	2,187.12	2,095.26
5.50%	8,022.49	6,035.42	5,417.72	4,558.10	3,431.75	2,889.13	2,579.17	2,384.71	2,255.47	2,166.24
5.75%	8,071.04	6,085.38	5,468.42	4,610.31	3,487.72	2,948.75	2,642.25	2,451.01	2,324.70	2,238.13
6.00%	8,119.78	6,135.59	5,519.40	4,662.86	3,544.20	3,009.01	2,706.07	2,518.11	2,394.80	2,310.90
6.25%	8,168.69	6,186.05	5,570.67	4,715.76	3,601.18	3,069.90	2,770.61	2,586.01	2,465.72	2,384.51
6.50%	8,217.78	6,236.76	5,622.22	4,769.02	3,658.65	3,131.41	2,835.87	2,654.69	2,537.45	2,458.92
6.75%	8,267.05	6,287.72	5,674.05	4,822.61	3,716.62	3,193.53	2,901.83	2,724.11	2,609.95	2,534.10
7.00%	8,316.50	6,338.93	5,726.16	4,876.56	3,775.08	3,256.26	2,968.47	2,794.27	2,683.20	2,610.01
7.25%	8,366.13	6,390.38	5,778.55	4,930.84	3,834.02	3,319.58	3,035.79	2,865.14	2,757.16	2,686.62
7.50%	8,415.94	6,442.08	5,831.23	4,985.47	3,893.45	3,383.49	3,103.76	2,936.70	2,831.82	2,763.90
7.75%	8,465.92	6,494.02	5,884.18	5,040.45	3,953.36	3,447.98	3,172.38	3,008.93	2,907.14	2,841.80
8.00%	8,516.09	6,546.21	5,937.41	5,095.76	4,013.74	3,513.05	3,241.63	3,081.81	2,983.10	2,920.31
8.25%	8,566.43	6,598.64	5,990.91	5,151.41	4,074.59	3,578.68	3,311.49	3,155.32	3,059.66	2,999.38
8.50%	8,616.94	6,651.32	6,044.69	5,207.40	4,135.91	3,644.86	3,381.95	3,229.44	3,136.81	3,079.00
8.75%	8,667.64	6,704.25	6,098.75	5,263.72	4,197.68	3,711.58	3,453.00	3,304.14	3,214.53	3,159.12
9.00%	8,718.51	6,757.41	6,153.09	5,320.38	4,259.92	3,778.85	3,524.62	3,379.41	3,292.77	3,239.72
9.25%	8,769.56	6,810.82	6,207.69	5,377.37	4,322.61	3,846.64	3,596.80	3,455.24	3,371.53	3,320.77
9.50%	8,820.78	6,864.47	6,262.57	5,434.70	4,385.74	3,914.95	3,669.53	3,531.59	3,450.77	3,402.26
9.75%	8,872.18	6,918.36	6,317.73	5,492.35	4,449.32	3,983.77	3,742.78	3,608.45	3,530.48	3,484.15
10.00%	8,923.76	6,972.50	6,373.15	5,550.33	4,513.34	4,053.09	3,816.54	3,685.80	3,610.62	3,566.41
10.25%	8,975.51	7,026.87	6,428.84	5,608.64	4,577.79	4,122.90	3,890.81	3,763.63	3,691.19	3,649.04
10.50%	9,027.44	7,081.48	6,484.81	5,667.27	4,642.68	4,193.20	3,965.56	3,841.91	3,772.16	3,732.00
10.75%	9,079.54	7,136.33	6,541.04	5,726.22	4,707.98	4,263.96	4,040.79	3,920.62	3,853.51	3,815.27

$420,000   11.00 - 20.75%   5 - 40 Years

	5	7	8	10	15	20	25	30	35	40
11.00%	9,131.82	7,191.42	6,597.54	5,785.50	4,773.71	4,335.19	4,116.47	3,999.76	3,935.22	3,898.84
11.25%	9,184.27	7,246.75	6,654.31	5,845.10	4,839.85	4,406.88	4,192.61	4,079.30	4,017.27	3,982.68
11.50%	9,236.90	7,302.31	6,711.34	5,905.01	4,906.40	4,479.00	4,269.17	4,159.22	4,099.65	4,066.78
11.75%	9,289.69	7,358.11	6,768.63	5,965.24	4,973.35	4,551.57	4,346.15	4,239.52	4,182.33	4,151.13
12.00%	9,342.67	7,414.15	6,826.19	6,025.78	5,040.71	4,624.56	4,423.54	4,320.17	4,265.31	4,235.70
12.25%	9,395.81	7,470.42	6,884.02	6,086.63	5,108.45	4,697.97	4,501.32	4,401.17	4,348.56	4,320.48
12.50%	9,449.13	7,526.92	6,942.10	6,147.80	5,176.59	4,771.79	4,579.49	4,482.48	4,432.07	4,405.46
12.75%	9,502.63	7,583.66	7,000.44	6,209.27	5,245.12	4,846.01	4,658.02	4,564.11	4,515.82	4,490.62
13.00%	9,556.29	7,640.62	7,059.05	6,271.05	5,314.02	4,920.62	4,736.91	4,646.04	4,599.81	4,575.96
13.25%	9,610.13	7,697.82	7,117.91	6,333.13	5,383.29	4,995.61	4,816.14	4,728.25	4,684.02	4,661.45
13.50%	9,664.14	7,755.25	7,177.03	6,395.52	5,452.94	5,070.97	4,895.71	4,810.73	4,768.43	4,747.10
13.75%	9,718.31	7,812.92	7,236.40	6,458.21	5,522.95	5,146.70	4,975.60	4,893.47	4,853.04	4,832.88
14.00%	9,772.67	7,870.80	7,296.03	6,521.19	5,593.31	5,222.79	5,055.80	4,976.46	4,937.83	4,918.79
14.25%	9,827.19	7,928.92	7,355.91	6,584.47	5,664.03	5,299.22	5,136.30	5,059.69	5,022.79	5,004.82
14.50%	9,881.88	7,987.27	7,416.05	6,648.05	5,735.10	5,375.99	5,217.08	5,143.13	5,107.92	5,090.96
14.75%	9,936.74	8,045.84	7,476.43	6,711.91	5,806.52	5,453.09	5,298.15	5,226.80	5,193.19	5,177.20
15.00%	9,991.77	8,104.64	7,537.07	6,776.07	5,878.27	5,530.52	5,379.49	5,310.66	5,278.62	5,263.54
15.25%	10,046.97	8,163.66	7,597.96	6,840.51	5,950.35	5,608.25	5,461.08	5,394.73	5,364.17	5,349.97
15.50%	10,102.34	8,222.91	7,659.09	6,905.24	6,022.76	5,686.30	5,542.93	5,478.97	5,449.86	5,436.48
15.75%	10,157.88	8,282.38	7,720.47	6,970.26	6,095.49	5,764.64	5,625.02	5,563.39	5,535.66	5,523.07
16.00%	10,213.58	8,342.07	7,782.09	7,035.55	6,168.54	5,843.27	5,707.33	5,647.98	5,621.57	5,609.72
16.25%	10,269.46	8,401.98	7,843.96	7,101.13	6,241.91	5,922.19	5,789.87	5,732.73	5,707.59	5,696.45
16.50%	10,325.50	8,462.11	7,906.07	7,166.98	6,315.58	6,001.38	5,872.63	5,817.62	5,793.71	5,783.23
16.75%	10,381.71	8,522.47	7,968.42	7,233.10	6,389.55	6,080.84	5,955.59	5,902.66	5,879.92	5,870.07
17.00%	10,438.08	8,583.04	8,031.01	7,299.50	6,463.82	6,160.56	6,038.75	5,987.84	5,966.21	5,956.96
17.25%	10,494.62	8,643.83	8,093.84	7,366.17	6,538.38	6,240.54	6,122.09	6,073.14	6,052.59	6,043.90
17.50%	10,551.33	8,704.83	8,156.91	7,433.11	6,613.23	6,320.76	6,205.62	6,158.57	6,139.04	6,130.88
17.75%	10,608.20	8,766.06	8,220.21	7,500.31	6,688.36	6,401.22	6,289.33	6,244.11	6,225.56	6,217.90
18.00%	10,665.24	8,827.49	8,283.75	7,567.78	6,763.77	6,481.91	6,373.21	6,329.76	6,312.15	6,304.97
18.25%	10,722.44	8,889.14	8,347.52	7,635.51	6,839.45	6,562.83	6,457.24	6,415.51	6,398.80	6,392.06
18.50%	10,779.81	8,951.01	8,411.53	7,703.49	6,915.40	6,643.97	6,541.43	6,501.37	6,485.50	6,479.19
18.75%	10,837.34	9,013.08	8,475.76	7,771.74	6,991.61	6,725.32	6,625.77	6,587.31	6,572.27	6,566.35
19.00%	10,895.03	9,075.37	8,540.22	7,840.24	7,068.08	6,806.88	6,710.26	6,673.35	6,659.08	6,653.53
19.25%	10,952.89	9,137.86	8,604.91	7,908.99	7,144.80	6,888.64	6,794.88	6,759.47	6,745.94	6,740.74
19.50%	11,010.91	9,200.57	8,669.83	7,977.99	7,221.77	6,970.59	6,879.63	6,845.66	6,832.84	6,827.98
19.75%	11,069.09	9,263.48	8,734.98	8,047.24	7,298.99	7,052.74	6,964.50	6,931.94	6,919.79	6,915.23
20.00%	11,127.43	9,326.60	8,800.34	8,116.74	7,376.45	7,135.06	7,049.50	7,018.28	7,006.77	7,002.51
20.25%	11,185.94	9,389.93	8,865.93	8,186.48	7,454.14	7,217.57	7,134.61	7,104.69	7,093.79	7,089.80
20.50%	11,244.60	9,453.46	8,931.74	8,256.46	7,532.06	7,300.25	7,219.83	7,191.16	7,180.84	7,177.11
20.75%	11,303.43	9,517.20	8,997.78	8,326.68	7,610.20	7,383.09	7,305.16	7,277.69	7,267.92	7,264.44

	5	7	8	10	15	20	25	30	35	40
1.00%	7,264.84	5,240.78	4,608.37	3,723.18	2,543.60	1,954.55	1,601.71	1,366.97	1,199.71	1,074.64
1.25%	7,310.68	5,286.74	4,654.43	3,769.47	2,590.60	2,002.32	1,650.26	1,416.32	1,249.87	1,125.59
1.50%	7,356.70	5,332.96	4,700.78	3,816.14	2,638.16	2,050.82	1,699.73	1,466.76	1,301.28	1,177.98
1.75%	7,402.91	5,379.43	4,747.43	3,863.17	2,686.26	2,100.05	1,750.10	1,518.28	1,353.95	1,231.79
2.00%	7,449.30	5,426.16	4,794.37	3,910.57	2,734.91	2,150.00	1,801.38	1,570.88	1,407.87	1,287.01
2.25%	7,495.87	5,473.15	4,841.61	3,958.34	2,784.11	2,200.69	1,853.56	1,624.55	1,463.01	1,343.60
2.50%	7,542.63	5,520.39	4,889.13	4,006.47	2,833.85	2,252.09	1,906.62	1,679.26	1,519.35	1,401.56
2.75%	7,589.57	5,567.89	4,936.95	4,054.97	2,884.14	2,304.21	1,960.57	1,735.03	1,576.90	1,460.84
3.00%	7,636.69	5,615.65	4,985.07	4,103.83	2,934.97	2,357.04	2,015.40	1,791.82	1,635.61	1,521.43
3.25%	7,684.00	5,663.67	5,033.47	4,153.06	2,986.34	2,410.58	2,071.09	1,849.63	1,695.48	1,583.30
3.50%	7,731.49	5,711.94	5,082.17	4,202.65	3,038.25	2,464.83	2,127.65	1,908.44	1,756.49	1,646.41
3.75%	7,779.17	5,760.46	5,131.16	4,252.60	3,090.70	2,519.78	2,185.06	1,968.24	1,818.60	1,710.74
4.00%	7,827.02	5,809.24	5,180.44	4,302.92	3,143.67	2,575.42	2,243.31	2,029.02	1,881.79	1,776.24
4.25%	7,875.06	5,858.28	5,230.01	4,353.60	3,197.18	2,631.75	2,302.39	2,090.74	1,946.05	1,842.89
4.50%	7,923.28	5,907.57	5,279.87	4,404.63	3,251.22	2,688.76	2,362.29	2,153.41	2,011.34	1,910.64
4.75%	7,971.69	5,957.11	5,330.03	4,456.03	3,305.79	2,746.45	2,423.00	2,217.00	2,077.64	1,979.47
5.00%	8,020.27	6,006.91	5,380.47	4,507.78	3,360.87	2,804.81	2,484.51	2,281.49	2,144.92	2,049.34
5.25%	8,069.04	6,056.96	5,431.19	4,559.90	3,416.48	2,863.84	2,546.80	2,346.87	2,213.16	2,120.20
5.50%	8,117.99	6,107.27	5,482.21	4,612.37	3,472.60	2,923.52	2,609.87	2,413.10	2,282.32	2,192.02
5.75%	8,167.13	6,157.83	5,533.52	4,665.19	3,529.24	2,983.85	2,673.70	2,480.18	2,352.38	2,264.77
6.00%	8,216.44	6,208.64	5,585.11	4,718.37	3,586.39	3,044.83	2,738.28	2,548.09	2,423.31	2,338.41
6.25%	8,265.94	6,259.70	5,636.99	4,771.90	3,644.05	3,106.44	2,803.59	2,616.80	2,495.08	2,412.89
6.50%	8,315.61	6,311.01	5,689.15	4,825.79	3,702.21	3,168.69	2,869.63	2,686.29	2,567.66	2,488.19
6.75%	8,365.47	6,362.57	5,741.60	4,880.02	3,760.87	3,231.55	2,936.37	2,756.54	2,641.02	2,564.27
7.00%	8,415.51	6,414.39	5,794.33	4,934.61	3,820.02	3,295.02	3,003.81	2,827.54	2,715.14	2,641.08
7.25%	8,465.73	6,466.45	5,847.35	4,989.54	3,879.67	3,359.10	3,071.93	2,899.25	2,789.99	2,718.61
7.50%	8,516.13	6,518.77	5,900.64	5,044.83	3,939.80	3,423.77	3,140.71	2,971.66	2,865.53	2,796.80
7.75%	8,566.71	6,571.33	5,954.23	5,100.45	4,000.42	3,489.03	3,210.15	3,044.75	2,941.75	2,875.63
8.00%	8,617.47	6,624.14	6,008.09	5,156.42	4,061.52	3,554.87	3,280.22	3,118.50	3,018.61	2,955.07
8.25%	8,668.41	6,677.20	6,062.23	5,212.74	4,123.10	3,621.28	3,350.91	3,192.88	3,096.09	3,035.09
8.50%	8,719.53	6,730.51	6,116.65	5,269.39	4,185.14	3,688.25	3,422.22	3,267.88	3,174.16	3,115.65
8.75%	8,770.82	6,784.06	6,171.36	5,326.39	4,247.66	3,755.77	3,494.11	3,343.48	3,252.79	3,196.72
9.00%	8,822.30	6,837.86	6,226.34	5,383.72	4,310.63	3,823.84	3,566.58	3,419.65	3,331.97	3,278.29
9.25%	8,873.96	6,891.90	6,281.59	5,441.39	4,374.07	3,892.43	3,639.62	3,496.37	3,411.66	3,360.31
9.50%	8,925.79	6,946.19	6,337.13	5,499.40	4,437.95	3,961.56	3,713.21	3,573.63	3,491.85	3,442.76
9.75%	8,977.80	7,000.73	6,392.94	5,557.74	4,502.29	4,031.20	3,787.33	3,651.41	3,572.50	3,525.62
10.00%	9,029.99	7,055.50	6,449.02	5,616.41	4,567.07	4,101.34	3,861.98	3,729.68	3,653.61	3,608.87
10.25%	9,082.36	7,110.52	6,505.38	5,675.41	4,632.29	4,171.98	3,937.13	3,808.43	3,735.14	3,692.48
10.50%	9,134.91	7,165.79	6,562.01	5,734.74	4,697.95	4,243.11	4,012.77	3,887.64	3,817.07	3,776.42
10.75%	9,187.63	7,221.29	6,618.91	5,794.39	4,764.03	4,314.72	4,088.89	3,967.30	3,899.39	3,860.69

$425,000   11.00 - 20.75%   5 - 40 Years

	5	7	8	10	15	20	25	30	35	40
11.00%	9,240.53	7,277.04	6,676.08	5,854.38	4,830.54	4,386.80	4,165.48	4,047.37	3,982.07	3,945.25
11.25%	9,293.61	7,333.02	6,733.52	5,914.68	4,897.46	4,459.34	4,242.52	4,127.86	4,065.10	4,030.09
11.50%	9,346.86	7,389.25	6,791.23	5,975.31	4,964.81	4,532.33	4,319.99	4,208.74	4,148.46	4,115.20
11.75%	9,400.29	7,445.71	6,849.21	6,036.25	5,032.56	4,605.76	4,397.89	4,289.99	4,232.12	4,200.55
12.00%	9,453.89	7,502.41	6,907.46	6,097.52	5,100.71	4,679.62	4,476.20	4,371.60	4,316.09	4,286.12
12.25%	9,507.67	7,559.35	6,965.97	6,159.09	5,169.27	4,753.90	4,554.91	4,453.56	4,400.33	4,371.92
12.50%	9,561.62	7,616.53	7,024.74	6,220.99	5,238.22	4,828.60	4,634.01	4,535.85	4,484.83	4,457.91
12.75%	9,615.75	7,673.94	7,083.78	6,283.19	5,307.56	4,903.70	4,713.47	4,618.45	4,569.58	4,544.08
13.00%	9,670.06	7,731.58	7,143.08	6,345.71	5,377.28	4,979.20	4,793.30	4,701.35	4,654.57	4,630.44
13.25%	9,724.53	7,789.47	7,202.65	6,408.53	5,447.38	5,055.08	4,873.48	4,784.54	4,739.78	4,716.95
13.50%	9,779.18	7,847.58	7,262.47	6,471.66	5,517.85	5,131.34	4,953.99	4,868.00	4,825.20	4,803.61
13.75%	9,834.01	7,905.93	7,322.55	6,535.09	5,588.70	5,207.97	5,034.83	4,951.73	4,910.81	4,890.41
14.00%	9,889.01	7,964.50	7,382.89	6,598.82	5,659.90	5,284.96	5,115.98	5,035.70	4,996.61	4,977.35
14.25%	9,944.18	8,023.31	7,443.48	6,662.86	5,731.46	5,362.31	5,197.44	5,119.92	5,082.59	5,064.40
14.50%	9,999.52	8,082.35	7,504.33	6,727.19	5,803.38	5,439.99	5,279.19	5,204.36	5,168.72	5,151.57
14.75%	10,055.03	8,141.62	7,565.44	6,791.82	5,875.64	5,518.01	5,361.23	5,289.02	5,255.02	5,238.84
15.00%	10,110.72	8,201.12	7,626.80	6,856.74	5,948.25	5,596.36	5,443.53	5,373.89	5,341.46	5,326.20
15.25%	10,166.58	8,260.85	7,688.41	6,921.95	6,021.19	5,675.02	5,526.10	5,458.95	5,428.03	5,413.66
15.50%	10,222.61	8,320.80	7,750.27	6,987.45	6,094.46	5,753.99	5,608.92	5,544.20	5,514.73	5,501.20
15.75%	10,278.81	8,380.97	7,812.38	7,053.24	6,168.06	5,833.27	5,691.98	5,629.62	5,601.56	5,588.82
16.00%	10,335.17	8,441.38	7,874.73	7,119.31	6,241.98	5,912.84	5,775.28	5,715.22	5,688.49	5,676.51
16.25%	10,391.71	8,502.00	7,937.34	7,185.66	6,316.21	5,992.69	5,858.80	5,800.97	5,775.54	5,764.26
16.50%	10,448.42	8,562.85	8,000.19	7,252.30	6,390.76	6,072.83	5,942.54	5,886.88	5,862.68	5,852.00
16.75%	10,505.30	8,623.92	8,063.28	7,319.21	6,465.61	6,153.23	6,026.49	5,972.93	5,949.91	5,939.95
17.00%	10,562.34	8,685.22	8,126.62	7,386.40	6,540.77	6,233.90	6,110.64	6,059.12	6,037.24	6,027.88
17.25%	10,619.56	8,746.73	8,190.20	7,453.86	6,616.22	6,314.83	6,194.98	6,145.44	6,124.64	6,115.85
17.50%	10,676.94	8,808.46	8,254.01	7,521.60	6,691.96	6,396.00	6,279.50	6,231.88	6,212.12	6,203.87
17.75%	10,734.49	8,870.41	8,318.07	7,589.60	6,767.98	6,477.42	6,364.20	6,318.44	6,299.67	6,291.93
18.00%	10,792.21	8,932.58	8,382.37	7,657.87	6,844.29	6,559.07	6,449.08	6,405.11	6,387.29	6,380.02
18.25%	10,850.09	8,994.97	8,446.90	7,726.41	6,920.87	6,640.96	6,534.11	6,491.89	6,474.97	6,468.16
18.50%	10,908.14	9,057.57	8,511.66	7,795.20	6,997.72	6,723.06	6,619.31	6,578.76	6,562.71	6,556.32
18.75%	10,966.35	9,120.38	8,576.66	7,864.26	7,074.84	6,805.38	6,704.65	6,665.73	6,650.51	6,644.52
19.00%	11,024.73	9,183.41	8,641.89	7,933.58	7,152.22	6,887.91	6,790.14	6,752.79	6,738.35	6,732.74
19.25%	11,083.28	9,246.65	8,707.35	8,003.15	7,229.86	6,970.64	6,875.77	6,839.94	6,826.25	6,820.99
19.50%	11,141.99	9,310.10	8,773.05	8,072.97	7,307.75	7,053.57	6,961.53	6,927.16	6,914.18	6,909.26
19.75%	11,200.86	9,373.76	8,838.96	8,143.04	7,385.88	7,136.70	7,047.41	7,014.46	7,002.16	6,997.56
20.00%	11,259.90	9,437.63	8,905.11	8,213.37	7,464.26	7,220.00	7,133.42	7,101.83	7,090.18	7,085.87
20.25%	11,319.10	9,501.71	8,971.48	8,283.94	7,542.88	7,303.49	7,219.54	7,189.27	7,178.24	7,174.20
20.50%	11,378.46	9,566.00	9,038.08	8,354.75	7,621.72	7,387.16	7,305.78	7,276.77	7,266.33	7,262.55
20.75%	11,437.99	9,630.50	9,104.89	8,425.80	7,700.80	7,470.99	7,392.12	7,364.33	7,354.45	7,350.92

	5	7	8	10	15	20	25	30	35	40
1.00%	7,350.31	5,302.44	4,662.59	3,766.98	2,573.53	1,977.55	1,620.55	1,383.05	1,213.83	1,087.28
1.25%	7,396.69	5,348.94	4,709.19	3,813.82	2,621.08	2,025.88	1,669.68	1,432.98	1,264.57	1,138.83
1.50%	7,443.25	5,395.70	4,756.09	3,861.03	2,669.19	2,074.95	1,719.73	1,484.02	1,316.59	1,191.84
1.75%	7,490.00	5,442.72	4,803.28	3,908.62	2,717.86	2,124.75	1,770.69	1,536.15	1,369.88	1,246.29
2.00%	7,536.94	5,490.00	4,850.78	3,956.58	2,767.09	2,175.30	1,822.57	1,589.36	1,424.43	1,302.15
2.25%	7,584.06	5,537.54	4,898.57	4,004.91	2,816.86	2,226.58	1,875.36	1,643.66	1,480.22	1,359.41
2.50%	7,631.37	5,585.34	4,946.65	4,053.61	2,867.19	2,278.58	1,929.05	1,699.02	1,537.23	1,418.05
2.75%	7,678.86	5,633.40	4,995.04	4,102.67	2,918.07	2,331.32	1,983.64	1,755.44	1,595.45	1,478.03
3.00%	7,726.54	5,681.72	5,043.72	4,152.11	2,969.50	2,384.77	2,039.11	1,812.90	1,654.86	1,539.33
3.25%	7,774.40	5,730.30	5,092.69	4,201.92	3,021.48	2,438.94	2,095.46	1,871.39	1,715.43	1,601.93
3.50%	7,822.45	5,779.14	5,141.96	4,252.09	3,073.99	2,493.83	2,152.68	1,930.89	1,777.15	1,665.78
3.75%	7,870.68	5,828.23	5,191.53	4,302.63	3,127.06	2,549.42	2,210.76	1,991.40	1,839.99	1,730.86
4.00%	7,919.10	5,877.59	5,241.39	4,353.54	3,180.66	2,605.72	2,269.70	2,052.89	1,903.93	1,797.14
4.25%	7,967.71	5,927.20	5,291.54	4,404.81	3,234.80	2,662.71	2,329.47	2,115.34	1,968.94	1,864.57
4.50%	8,016.50	5,977.07	5,341.99	4,456.45	3,289.47	2,720.39	2,390.08	2,178.75	2,035.00	1,933.12
4.75%	8,065.47	6,027.20	5,392.73	4,508.45	3,344.68	2,778.76	2,451.50	2,243.08	2,102.08	2,002.76
5.00%	8,114.63	6,077.58	5,443.77	4,560.82	3,400.41	2,837.81	2,513.74	2,308.33	2,170.16	2,073.45
5.25%	8,163.97	6,128.22	5,495.09	4,613.54	3,456.67	2,897.53	2,576.77	2,374.48	2,239.20	2,145.14
5.50%	8,213.50	6,179.12	5,546.71	4,666.63	3,513.46	2,957.92	2,640.58	2,441.49	2,309.17	2,217.81
5.75%	8,263.21	6,230.27	5,598.62	4,720.08	3,570.76	3,018.96	2,705.16	2,509.36	2,380.05	2,291.42
6.00%	8,313.10	6,281.68	5,650.81	4,773.88	3,628.58	3,080.65	2,770.50	2,578.07	2,451.82	2,365.92
6.25%	8,363.18	6,333.34	5,703.30	4,828.04	3,686.92	3,142.99	2,836.58	2,647.58	2,524.43	2,441.28
6.50%	8,413.44	6,385.26	5,756.08	4,882.56	3,745.76	3,205.96	2,903.39	2,717.89	2,597.86	2,517.46
6.75%	8,463.89	6,437.43	5,809.15	4,937.44	3,805.11	3,269.57	2,970.92	2,788.97	2,672.09	2,594.43
7.00%	8,514.52	6,489.85	5,862.50	4,992.66	3,864.96	3,333.79	3,039.15	2,860.80	2,747.08	2,672.15
7.25%	8,565.33	6,542.53	5,916.14	5,048.24	3,925.31	3,398.62	3,108.07	2,933.36	2,822.81	2,750.59
7.50%	8,616.32	6,595.46	5,970.06	5,104.18	3,986.15	3,464.05	3,177.66	3,006.62	2,899.24	2,829.70
7.75%	8,667.49	6,648.64	6,024.28	5,160.46	4,047.49	3,530.08	3,247.91	3,080.57	2,976.36	2,909.47
8.00%	8,718.85	6,702.07	6,078.77	5,217.09	4,109.30	3,596.69	3,318.81	3,155.19	3,054.12	2,989.84
8.25%	8,770.39	6,755.76	6,133.55	5,274.06	4,171.60	3,663.88	3,390.34	3,230.45	3,132.51	3,070.80
8.50%	8,822.11	6,809.69	6,188.62	5,331.38	4,234.38	3,731.64	3,462.48	3,306.33	3,211.50	3,152.30
8.75%	8,874.01	6,863.87	6,243.96	5,389.05	4,297.63	3,799.96	3,535.22	3,382.81	3,291.06	3,234.33
9.00%	8,926.09	6,918.30	6,299.59	5,447.06	4,361.35	3,868.82	3,608.54	3,459.88	3,371.17	3,316.85
9.25%	8,978.36	6,972.98	6,355.49	5,505.41	4,425.53	3,938.23	3,682.44	3,537.50	3,451.80	3,399.84
9.50%	9,030.80	7,027.91	6,411.68	5,564.09	4,490.17	4,008.16	3,756.90	3,615.67	3,532.93	3,483.26
9.75%	9,083.42	7,083.09	6,468.15	5,623.12	4,555.26	4,078.62	3,831.89	3,694.36	3,614.53	3,567.10
10.00%	9,136.23	7,138.51	6,524.89	5,682.48	4,620.80	4,149.59	3,907.41	3,773.56	3,696.59	3,651.33
10.25%	9,189.21	7,194.18	6,581.91	5,742.18	4,686.79	4,221.07	3,983.45	3,853.24	3,779.08	3,735.92
10.50%	9,242.38	7,250.09	6,639.21	5,802.20	4,753.22	4,293.03	4,059.98	3,933.38	3,861.98	3,820.85
10.75%	9,295.72	7,306.25	6,696.78	5,862.56	4,820.08	4,365.48	4,137.00	4,013.97	3,945.26	3,906.11

$430,000　　11.00 - 20.75%　　5 - 40 Years

	5	7	8	10	15	20	25	30	35	40
11.00%	9,349.24	7,362.65	6,754.62	5,923.25	4,887.37	4,438.41	4,214.49	4,094.99	4,028.92	3,991.67
11.25%	9,402.94	7,419.29	6,812.74	5,984.26	4,955.08	4,511.80	4,292.43	4,176.42	4,112.92	4,077.51
11.50%	9,456.82	7,476.18	6,871.13	6,045.60	5,023.22	4,585.65	4,370.82	4,258.25	4,197.26	4,163.61
11.75%	9,510.88	7,533.31	6,929.79	6,107.27	5,091.76	4,659.94	4,449.63	4,340.46	4,281.91	4,249.97
12.00%	9,565.11	7,590.68	6,988.72	6,169.25	5,160.72	4,734.67	4,528.86	4,423.03	4,366.86	4,336.55
12.25%	9,619.52	7,648.28	7,047.92	6,231.55	5,230.08	4,809.83	4,608.50	4,505.95	4,452.10	4,423.35
12.50%	9,674.11	7,706.13	7,107.39	6,294.18	5,299.84	4,885.40	4,688.52	4,589.21	4,537.59	4,510.35
12.75%	9,728.88	7,764.22	7,167.12	6,357.11	5,370.00	4,961.39	4,768.92	4,672.78	4,623.34	4,597.54
13.00%	9,783.82	7,822.54	7,227.12	6,420.36	5,440.54	5,037.78	4,849.69	4,756.66	4,709.33	4,684.91
13.25%	9,838.94	7,881.11	7,287.38	6,483.92	5,511.47	5,114.55	4,930.81	4,840.83	4,795.54	4,772.44
13.50%	9,894.23	7,939.90	7,347.91	6,547.79	5,582.77	5,191.71	5,012.27	4,925.27	4,881.96	4,860.12
13.75%	9,949.70	7,998.94	7,408.70	6,611.97	5,654.45	5,269.24	5,094.06	5,009.98	4,968.59	4,947.95
14.00%	10,005.35	8,058.20	7,469.75	6,676.46	5,726.49	5,347.14	5,176.17	5,094.95	5,055.40	5,035.90
14.25%	10,061.17	8,117.71	7,531.05	6,741.24	5,798.89	5,425.39	5,258.59	5,180.15	5,142.38	5,123.98
14.50%	10,117.16	8,177.44	7,592.62	6,806.33	5,871.65	5,503.99	5,341.30	5,265.59	5,229.53	5,212.17
14.75%	10,173.33	8,237.41	7,654.44	6,871.72	5,944.77	5,582.93	5,424.30	5,351.25	5,316.84	5,300.47
15.00%	10,229.67	8,297.60	7,716.52	6,937.40	6,018.22	5,662.20	5,507.57	5,437.11	5,404.30	5,388.86
15.25%	10,286.18	8,358.03	7,778.86	7,003.38	6,092.02	5,741.78	5,591.11	5,523.17	5,491.89	5,477.35
15.50%	10,342.87	8,418.69	7,841.45	7,069.65	6,166.16	5,821.69	5,674.90	5,609.42	5,579.61	5,565.92
15.75%	10,399.73	8,479.57	7,904.29	7,136.21	6,240.62	5,901.90	5,758.94	5,695.85	5,667.46	5,654.57
16.00%	10,456.76	8,540.69	7,967.38	7,203.06	6,315.41	5,982.40	5,843.22	5,782.46	5,755.42	5,743.29
16.25%	10,513.97	8,602.03	8,030.72	7,270.20	6,390.52	6,063.20	5,927.73	5,869.22	5,843.48	5,832.08
16.50%	10,571.34	8,663.59	8,094.31	7,337.62	6,465.95	6,144.27	6,012.45	5,956.14	5,931.65	5,920.93
16.75%	10,628.89	8,725.38	8,158.14	7,405.32	6,541.68	6,225.62	6,097.39	6,043.20	6,019.91	6,009.83
17.00%	10,686.61	8,787.40	8,222.23	7,473.30	6,617.72	6,307.24	6,182.53	6,130.40	6,108.26	6,098.79
17.25%	10,744.49	8,849.63	8,286.55	7,541.56	6,694.06	6,389.12	6,267.86	6,217.74	6,196.69	6,187.80
17.50%	10,802.55	8,912.09	8,351.12	7,610.09	6,770.69	6,471.25	6,353.38	6,305.20	6,285.20	6,276.85
17.75%	10,860.78	8,974.77	8,415.93	7,678.89	6,847.61	6,553.63	6,439.08	6,392.78	6,373.79	6,365.95
18.00%	10,919.17	9,037.67	8,480.98	7,747.96	6,924.81	6,636.24	6,524.95	6,480.47	6,462.44	6,455.08
18.25%	10,977.74	9,100.79	8,546.27	7,817.30	7,002.29	6,719.08	6,610.99	6,568.26	6,551.15	6,544.25
18.50%	11,036.47	9,164.13	8,611.80	7,886.91	7,080.05	6,802.16	6,697.18	6,656.16	6,639.92	6,633.46
18.75%	11,095.37	9,227.68	8,677.56	7,956.78	7,158.08	6,885.44	6,783.53	6,744.15	6,728.75	6,722.69
19.00%	11,154.44	9,291.45	8,743.56	8,026.91	7,236.37	6,968.94	6,870.02	6,832.24	6,817.63	6,811.95
19.25%	11,213.67	9,355.43	8,809.79	8,097.30	7,314.92	7,052.65	6,956.66	6,920.41	6,906.55	6,901.24
19.50%	11,273.07	9,419.63	8,876.26	8,167.95	7,393.72	7,136.56	7,043.43	7,008.66	6,995.53	6,990.55
19.75%	11,332.64	9,484.04	8,942.95	8,238.84	7,472.78	7,220.66	7,130.32	7,096.98	7,084.54	7,079.88
20.00%	11,392.37	9,548.67	9,009.88	8,309.99	7,552.07	7,304.95	7,217.34	7,185.38	7,173.60	7,169.24
20.25%	11,452.27	9,613.50	9,077.03	8,381.39	7,631.62	7,389.42	7,304.48	7,273.85	7,262.69	7,258.61
20.50%	11,512.33	9,678.54	9,144.41	8,453.04	7,711.39	7,474.06	7,391.73	7,362.38	7,351.81	7,348.00
20.75%	11,572.55	9,743.80	9,212.01	8,524.93	7,791.40	7,558.88	7,479.09	7,450.97	7,440.97	7,437.40

	5	7	8	10	15	20	25	30	35	40
1.00%	7,435.78	5,364.09	4,716.80	3,810.78	2,603.45	2,000.54	1,639.40	1,399.13	1,227.94	1,099.92
1.25%	7,482.70	5,411.13	4,763.95	3,858.17	2,651.56	2,049.43	1,689.09	1,449.64	1,279.28	1,152.08
1.50%	7,529.80	5,458.44	4,811.39	3,905.93	2,700.23	2,099.07	1,739.72	1,501.27	1,331.90	1,205.70
1.75%	7,577.09	5,506.00	4,859.13	3,954.07	2,749.47	2,149.46	1,791.28	1,554.01	1,385.81	1,260.78
2.00%	7,624.58	5,553.83	4,907.18	4,002.59	2,799.26	2,200.59	1,843.77	1,607.84	1,440.99	1,317.29
2.25%	7,672.24	5,601.93	4,955.53	4,051.48	2,849.62	2,252.47	1,897.17	1,662.77	1,497.43	1,375.22
2.50%	7,720.10	5,650.28	5,004.17	4,100.74	2,900.53	2,305.08	1,951.48	1,718.78	1,555.10	1,434.54
2.75%	7,768.15	5,698.90	5,053.12	4,150.38	2,952.00	2,358.42	2,006.70	1,775.85	1,614.00	1,495.22
3.00%	7,816.38	5,747.79	5,102.36	4,200.39	3,004.03	2,412.50	2,062.82	1,833.98	1,674.10	1,557.23
3.25%	7,864.80	5,796.93	5,151.91	4,250.78	3,056.61	2,467.30	2,119.83	1,893.15	1,735.38	1,620.55
3.50%	7,913.41	5,846.34	5,201.75	4,301.54	3,109.74	2,522.82	2,177.71	1,953.34	1,797.81	1,685.15
3.75%	7,962.20	5,896.00	5,251.89	4,352.66	3,163.42	2,579.06	2,236.47	2,014.55	1,861.39	1,750.99
4.00%	8,011.19	5,945.93	5,302.33	4,404.16	3,217.64	2,636.01	2,296.09	2,076.76	1,926.07	1,818.03
4.25%	8,060.36	5,996.12	5,353.07	4,456.03	3,272.41	2,693.67	2,356.56	2,139.94	1,991.84	1,886.25
4.50%	8,109.71	6,046.57	5,404.11	4,508.27	3,327.72	2,752.02	2,417.87	2,204.08	2,058.67	1,955.60
4.75%	8,159.26	6,097.28	5,455.44	4,560.88	3,383.57	2,811.07	2,480.01	2,269.17	2,126.53	2,026.05
5.00%	8,208.99	6,148.25	5,507.07	4,613.85	3,439.95	2,870.81	2,542.97	2,335.17	2,195.39	2,097.56
5.25%	8,258.90	6,199.48	5,558.99	4,667.19	3,496.87	2,931.22	2,606.73	2,402.09	2,265.23	2,170.09
5.50%	8,309.01	6,250.97	5,611.21	4,720.89	3,554.31	2,992.31	2,671.28	2,469.88	2,336.02	2,243.60
5.75%	8,359.29	6,302.72	5,663.72	4,774.96	3,612.28	3,054.06	2,736.61	2,538.54	2,407.73	2,318.06
6.00%	8,409.77	6,354.72	5,716.52	4,829.39	3,670.78	3,116.48	2,802.71	2,608.04	2,480.33	2,393.43
6.25%	8,460.43	6,406.98	5,769.62	4,884.18	3,729.79	3,179.54	2,869.56	2,678.37	2,553.78	2,469.67
6.50%	8,511.27	6,459.50	5,823.01	4,939.34	3,789.32	3,243.24	2,937.15	2,749.50	2,628.07	2,546.74
6.75%	8,562.31	6,512.28	5,876.69	4,994.85	3,849.36	3,307.58	3,005.47	2,821.40	2,703.16	2,624.60
7.00%	8,613.52	6,565.32	5,930.67	5,050.72	3,909.90	3,372.55	3,074.49	2,894.07	2,779.03	2,703.23
7.25%	8,664.92	6,618.61	5,984.93	5,106.95	3,970.95	3,438.14	3,144.21	2,967.47	2,855.63	2,782.57
7.50%	8,716.51	6,672.15	6,039.48	5,163.53	4,032.50	3,504.33	3,214.61	3,041.58	2,932.96	2,862.61
7.75%	8,768.28	6,725.95	6,094.33	5,220.46	4,094.55	3,571.13	3,285.68	3,116.39	3,010.97	2,943.30
8.00%	8,820.23	6,780.00	6,149.46	5,277.75	4,157.09	3,638.51	3,357.40	3,191.88	3,089.63	3,024.61
8.25%	8,872.37	6,834.31	6,204.87	5,335.39	4,220.11	3,706.49	3,429.76	3,268.01	3,168.94	3,106.50
8.50%	8,924.69	6,888.87	6,260.58	5,393.38	4,283.62	3,775.03	3,502.74	3,344.77	3,248.84	3,188.96
8.75%	8,977.20	6,943.68	6,316.56	5,451.71	4,347.60	3,844.14	3,576.32	3,422.15	3,329.33	3,271.94
9.00%	9,029.88	6,998.75	6,372.84	5,510.40	4,412.06	3,913.81	3,650.50	3,500.11	3,410.37	3,355.42
9.25%	9,082.76	7,054.07	6,429.40	5,569.42	4,476.99	3,984.02	3,725.26	3,578.64	3,491.94	3,439.37
9.50%	9,135.81	7,109.63	6,486.24	5,628.79	4,542.38	4,054.77	3,800.58	3,657.72	3,574.01	3,523.77
9.75%	9,189.05	7,165.45	6,543.36	5,688.51	4,608.23	4,126.05	3,876.45	3,737.32	3,656.56	3,608.58
10.00%	9,242.46	7,221.52	6,600.76	5,748.56	4,674.53	4,197.84	3,952.85	3,817.44	3,739.58	3,693.78
10.25%	9,296.06	7,277.83	6,658.44	5,808.95	4,741.29	4,270.15	4,029.77	3,898.04	3,823.02	3,779.36
10.50%	9,349.85	7,334.39	6,716.41	5,869.67	4,808.49	4,342.95	4,107.19	3,979.12	3,906.88	3,865.28
10.75%	9,403.81	7,391.20	6,774.65	5,930.73	4,876.12	4,416.25	4,185.10	4,060.64	3,991.14	3,951.53

$435,000   11.00 - 20.75%   5 - 40 Years

	5	7	8	10	15	20	25	30	35	40
11.00%	9,457.95	7,448.26	6,833.17	5,992.13	4,944.20	4,490.02	4,263.49	4,142.61	4,075.77	4,038.08
11.25%	9,512.28	7,505.56	6,891.96	6,053.85	5,012.70	4,564.26	4,342.34	4,224.99	4,160.75	4,124.92
11.50%	9,566.78	7,563.11	6,951.05	6,115.90	5,081.63	4,638.97	4,421.64	4,307.77	4,246.07	4,212.03
11.75%	9,621.47	7,620.90	7,010.37	6,178.28	5,150.97	4,714.13	4,501.37	4,390.93	4,331.70	4,299.38
12.00%	9,676.33	7,678.94	7,069.99	6,240.99	5,220.73	4,789.72	4,581.53	4,474.46	4,417.64	4,386.97
12.25%	9,731.38	7,737.22	7,129.87	6,304.01	5,290.90	4,865.76	4,662.09	4,558.35	4,503.86	4,474.78
12.50%	9,786.60	7,795.74	7,190.03	6,367.36	5,361.47	4,942.21	4,743.04	4,642.57	4,590.36	4,562.80
12.75%	9,842.01	7,854.50	7,250.46	6,431.03	5,432.44	5,019.08	4,824.38	4,727.12	4,677.10	4,651.00
13.00%	9,897.59	7,913.50	7,311.16	6,495.02	5,503.80	5,096.35	4,906.08	4,811.97	4,764.09	4,739.39
13.25%	9,953.35	7,972.75	7,372.12	6,559.32	5,575.55	5,174.02	4,988.15	4,897.11	4,851.30	4,827.93
13.50%	10,009.28	8,032.23	7,433.35	6,623.93	5,647.69	5,252.08	5,070.56	4,982.54	4,938.73	4,916.64
13.75%	10,065.40	8,091.95	7,494.84	6,688.86	5,720.19	5,330.51	5,153.30	5,068.24	5,026.36	5,005.48
14.00%	10,121.69	8,151.91	7,556.60	6,754.09	5,793.08	5,409.32	5,236.36	5,154.19	5,114.18	5,094.46
14.25%	10,178.16	8,212.10	7,618.62	6,819.63	5,866.32	5,488.48	5,319.73	5,240.39	5,202.18	5,183.56
14.50%	10,234.80	8,272.53	7,680.91	6,885.48	5,939.93	5,567.99	5,403.41	5,326.82	5,290.34	5,272.78
14.75%	10,291.62	8,333.19	7,743.45	6,951.62	6,013.89	5,647.85	5,487.37	5,413.47	5,378.67	5,362.10
15.00%	10,348.62	8,394.09	7,806.25	7,018.07	6,088.20	5,728.03	5,571.61	5,500.33	5,467.14	5,451.52
15.25%	10,405.79	8,455.22	7,869.31	7,084.82	6,162.86	5,808.55	5,656.12	5,587.39	5,555.75	5,541.04
15.50%	10,463.14	8,516.58	7,932.63	7,151.86	6,237.86	5,889.38	5,740.89	5,674.65	5,644.49	5,630.64
15.75%	10,520.66	8,578.17	7,996.20	7,219.19	6,313.19	5,970.52	5,825.91	5,762.08	5,733.36	5,720.32
16.00%	10,578.35	8,640.00	8,060.02	7,286.82	6,388.85	6,051.96	5,911.17	5,849.69	5,822.34	5,810.07
16.25%	10,636.22	8,702.05	8,124.10	7,354.74	6,464.83	6,133.70	5,996.65	5,937.47	5,911.43	5,899.89
16.50%	10,694.27	8,764.33	8,188.43	7,422.94	6,541.13	6,215.72	6,082.36	6,025.39	6,000.62	5,989.77
16.75%	10,752.48	8,826.84	8,253.01	7,491.43	6,617.75	6,298.02	6,168.29	6,113.47	6,089.91	6,079.71
17.00%	10,810.87	8,889.58	8,317.83	7,560.20	6,694.67	6,380.58	6,254.42	6,201.69	6,179.29	6,169.71
17.25%	10,869.43	8,952.54	8,382.91	7,629.25	6,771.89	6,463.41	6,340.74	6,290.04	6,268.75	6,259.75
17.50%	10,928.16	9,015.72	8,448.23	7,698.58	6,849.42	6,546.50	6,427.25	6,378.51	6,358.29	6,349.84
17.75%	10,987.07	9,079.13	8,513.79	7,768.18	6,927.23	6,629.83	6,513.95	6,467.11	6,447.90	6,439.97
18.00%	11,046.14	9,142.76	8,579.60	7,838.06	7,005.33	6,713.41	6,600.82	6,555.82	6,537.58	6,530.14
18.25%	11,105.39	9,206.61	8,645.65	7,908.20	7,083.72	6,797.21	6,687.86	6,644.64	6,627.32	6,620.35
18.50%	11,164.80	9,270.68	8,711.94	7,978.62	7,162.38	6,881.25	6,775.06	6,733.56	6,717.13	6,710.59
18.75%	11,224.39	9,334.98	8,778.47	8,049.30	7,241.31	6,965.51	6,862.41	6,822.57	6,806.99	6,800.86
19.00%	11,284.14	9,399.49	8,845.23	8,120.25	7,320.51	7,049.98	6,949.91	6,911.68	6,896.90	6,891.16
19.25%	11,344.06	9,464.22	8,912.23	8,191.45	7,399.97	7,134.66	7,037.55	7,000.88	6,986.86	6,981.49
19.50%	11,404.15	9,529.16	8,979.47	8,262.92	7,479.69	7,219.54	7,125.33	7,090.15	7,076.87	7,071.84
19.75%	11,464.41	9,594.32	9,046.94	8,334.64	7,559.67	7,304.62	7,213.23	7,179.51	7,166.92	7,162.21
20.00%	11,524.84	9,659.70	9,114.64	8,406.62	7,639.89	7,389.89	7,301.27	7,268.93	7,257.01	7,252.60
20.25%	11,585.43	9,725.28	9,182.57	8,478.85	7,720.35	7,475.34	7,389.42	7,358.43	7,347.14	7,343.01
20.50%	11,646.19	9,791.09	9,250.74	8,551.33	7,801.06	7,560.97	7,477.68	7,447.99	7,437.30	7,433.44
20.75%	11,707.12	9,857.10	9,319.12	8,624.06	7,882.00	7,646.77	7,566.05	7,537.61	7,527.49	7,523.88

	5	7	8	10	15	20	25	30	35	40
1.00%	7,521.25	5,425.75	4,771.02	3,854.58	2,633.38	2,023.53	1,658.24	1,415.21	1,242.06	1,112.57
1.25%	7,568.70	5,473.33	4,818.70	3,902.51	2,682.04	2,072.99	1,708.51	1,466.31	1,293.98	1,165.32
1.50%	7,616.35	5,521.18	4,866.69	3,950.83	2,731.27	2,123.20	1,759.72	1,518.53	1,347.21	1,219.56
1.75%	7,664.19	5,569.29	4,914.99	3,999.52	2,781.07	2,174.17	1,811.87	1,571.87	1,401.74	1,275.27
2.00%	7,712.21	5,617.67	4,963.58	4,048.59	2,831.44	2,225.89	1,864.96	1,626.33	1,457.56	1,332.43
2.25%	7,760.43	5,666.32	5,012.49	4,098.04	2,882.37	2,278.36	1,918.98	1,681.88	1,514.64	1,391.03
2.50%	7,808.84	5,715.23	5,061.69	4,147.88	2,933.87	2,331.57	1,973.91	1,738.53	1,572.98	1,451.02
2.75%	7,857.44	5,764.41	5,111.20	4,198.09	2,985.94	2,385.53	2,029.77	1,796.26	1,632.55	1,512.40
3.00%	7,906.22	5,813.85	5,161.01	4,248.67	3,038.56	2,440.23	2,086.53	1,855.06	1,693.34	1,575.13
3.25%	7,955.20	5,863.56	5,211.13	4,299.64	3,091.74	2,495.66	2,144.19	1,914.91	1,755.32	1,639.18
3.50%	8,004.37	5,913.53	5,261.54	4,350.98	3,145.48	2,551.82	2,202.74	1,975.80	1,818.48	1,704.52
3.75%	8,053.72	5,963.77	5,312.26	4,402.69	3,199.78	2,608.71	2,262.18	2,037.71	1,882.78	1,771.11
4.00%	8,103.27	6,014.27	5,363.28	4,454.79	3,254.63	2,666.31	2,322.48	2,100.63	1,948.21	1,838.93
4.25%	8,153.00	6,065.04	5,414.60	4,507.25	3,310.03	2,724.63	2,383.65	2,164.54	2,014.73	1,907.93
4.50%	8,202.93	6,116.07	5,466.22	4,560.09	3,365.97	2,783.66	2,445.66	2,229.42	2,082.33	1,978.08
4.75%	8,253.04	6,167.36	5,518.14	4,613.30	3,422.46	2,843.38	2,508.52	2,295.25	2,150.97	2,049.33
5.00%	8,303.34	6,218.92	5,570.36	4,666.88	3,479.49	2,903.81	2,572.20	2,362.02	2,220.63	2,121.67
5.25%	8,353.83	6,270.74	5,622.88	4,720.83	3,537.06	2,964.91	2,636.69	2,429.70	2,291.27	2,195.03
5.50%	8,404.51	6,322.82	5,675.70	4,775.16	3,595.17	3,026.70	2,701.98	2,498.27	2,362.87	2,269.39
5.75%	8,455.38	6,375.16	5,728.82	4,829.85	3,653.80	3,089.17	2,768.07	2,567.72	2,435.40	2,344.71
6.00%	8,506.43	6,427.76	5,782.25	4,884.90	3,712.97	3,152.30	2,834.93	2,638.02	2,508.83	2,420.94
6.25%	8,557.68	6,480.63	5,835.94	4,940.32	3,772.66	3,216.08	2,902.55	2,709.16	2,583.14	2,498.05
6.50%	8,609.11	6,533.75	5,889.94	4,996.11	3,832.87	3,280.52	2,970.91	2,781.10	2,658.28	2,576.01
6.75%	8,660.72	6,587.14	5,944.24	5,052.26	3,893.60	3,345.60	3,040.01	2,853.83	2,734.23	2,654.77
7.00%	8,712.53	6,640.78	5,998.84	5,108.77	3,954.84	3,411.32	3,109.83	2,927.33	2,810.97	2,734.30
7.25%	8,764.52	6,694.68	6,053.72	5,165.65	4,016.60	3,477.65	3,180.35	3,001.58	2,888.46	2,814.56
7.50%	8,816.70	6,748.84	6,108.90	5,222.88	4,078.85	3,544.61	3,251.56	3,076.54	2,966.67	2,895.51
7.75%	8,869.06	6,803.26	6,164.38	5,280.47	4,141.61	3,612.17	3,323.45	3,152.21	3,045.57	2,977.13
8.00%	8,921.61	6,857.93	6,220.14	5,338.41	4,204.87	3,680.34	3,395.99	3,228.56	3,125.15	3,059.37
8.25%	8,974.35	6,912.87	6,276.19	5,396.72	4,268.62	3,749.09	3,469.18	3,305.57	3,205.36	3,142.21
8.50%	9,027.27	6,968.05	6,332.54	5,455.37	4,332.85	3,818.42	3,543.00	3,383.22	3,286.19	3,225.61
8.75%	9,080.38	7,023.50	6,389.17	5,514.38	4,397.57	3,888.33	3,617.43	3,461.48	3,367.60	3,309.55
9.00%	9,133.68	7,079.19	6,446.09	5,573.73	4,462.77	3,958.79	3,692.46	3,540.34	3,449.57	3,393.99
9.25%	9,187.16	7,135.15	6,503.30	5,633.44	4,528.45	4,029.81	3,768.08	3,619.77	3,532.08	3,478.91
9.50%	9,240.82	7,191.35	6,560.79	5,693.49	4,594.59	4,101.38	3,844.27	3,699.76	3,615.09	3,564.27
9.75%	9,294.67	7,247.81	6,618.57	5,753.89	4,661.20	4,173.47	3,921.00	3,780.28	3,698.59	3,650.06
10.00%	9,348.70	7,304.52	6,676.63	5,814.63	4,728.26	4,246.10	3,998.28	3,861.31	3,782.56	3,736.24
10.25%	9,402.92	7,361.48	6,734.98	5,875.72	4,795.78	4,319.23	4,076.09	3,942.85	3,866.96	3,822.80
10.50%	9,457.32	7,418.70	6,793.61	5,937.14	4,863.76	4,392.87	4,154.40	4,024.85	3,951.79	3,909.71
10.75%	9,511.90	7,476.16	6,852.52	5,998.90	4,932.17	4,467.01	4,233.21	4,107.32	4,037.01	3,996.95

$440,000   11.00 - 20.75%   5 - 40 Years

	5	7	8	10	15	20	25	30	35	40
11.00%	9,566.67	7,533.87	6,911.71	6,061.00	5,001.03	4,541.63	4,312.50	4,190.22	4,122.61	4,084.50
11.25%	9,621.62	7,591.83	6,971.18	6,123.43	5,070.32	4,616.73	4,392.25	4,273.55	4,208.57	4,172.33
11.50%	9,676.75	7,650.04	7,030.92	6,186.20	5,140.04	4,692.29	4,472.46	4,357.28	4,294.87	4,260.44
11.75%	9,732.06	7,708.50	7,090.95	6,249.30	5,210.18	4,768.31	4,553.11	4,441.40	4,381.49	4,348.80
12.00%	9,787.56	7,767.20	7,151.25	6,312.72	5,280.74	4,844.78	4,634.19	4,525.90	4,468.42	4,437.40
12.25%	9,843.23	7,826.15	7,211.83	6,376.47	5,351.71	4,921.68	4,715.67	4,610.74	4,555.63	4,526.22
12.50%	9,899.09	7,885.34	7,272.68	6,440.55	5,423.10	4,999.02	4,797.56	4,695.93	4,643.12	4,615.25
12.75%	9,955.13	7,944.78	7,333.80	6,504.95	5,494.88	5,076.77	4,879.83	4,781.45	4,730.86	4,704.46
13.00%	10,011.35	8,004.46	7,395.19	6,569.67	5,567.07	5,154.93	4,962.48	4,867.28	4,818.85	4,793.86
13.25%	10,067.75	8,064.39	7,456.86	6,634.71	5,639.64	5,233.50	5,045.48	4,953.40	4,907.07	4,883.43
13.50%	10,124.33	8,124.55	7,518.79	6,700.07	5,712.60	5,312.45	5,128.84	5,039.81	4,995.50	4,973.15
13.75%	10,181.09	8,184.96	7,580.99	6,765.74	5,785.94	5,391.78	5,212.53	5,126.50	5,084.13	5,063.02
14.00%	10,238.03	8,245.61	7,643.46	6,831.72	5,859.66	5,471.49	5,296.55	5,213.44	5,172.96	5,153.02
14.25%	10,295.15	8,306.49	7,706.19	6,898.02	5,933.75	5,551.56	5,380.88	5,300.62	5,261.97	5,243.14
14.50%	10,352.44	8,367.61	7,769.19	6,964.62	6,008.20	5,631.99	5,465.52	5,388.05	5,351.15	5,333.38
14.75%	10,409.92	8,428.97	7,832.45	7,031.53	6,083.02	5,712.76	5,550.44	5,475.69	5,440.49	5,423.74
15.00%	10,467.57	8,490.57	7,895.98	7,098.74	6,158.18	5,793.87	5,635.65	5,563.55	5,529.98	5,514.19
15.25%	10,525.40	8,552.41	7,959.76	7,166.25	6,233.70	5,875.31	5,721.14	5,651.62	5,619.61	5,604.73
15.50%	10,583.40	8,614.47	8,023.81	7,234.06	6,309.56	5,957.08	5,806.88	5,739.87	5,709.37	5,695.36
15.75%	10,641.59	8,676.77	8,088.11	7,302.17	6,385.75	6,039.15	5,892.87	5,828.32	5,799.26	5,786.07
16.00%	10,699.95	8,739.31	8,152.67	7,370.58	6,462.28	6,121.53	5,979.11	5,916.93	5,889.27	5,876.85
16.25%	10,758.48	8,802.07	8,217.48	7,439.27	6,539.14	6,204.20	6,065.58	6,005.71	5,979.38	5,967.71
16.50%	10,817.19	8,865.07	8,282.55	7,508.26	6,616.32	6,287.16	6,152.28	6,094.65	6,069.60	6,058.62
16.75%	10,876.07	8,928.30	8,347.87	7,577.54	6,693.81	6,370.41	6,239.19	6,183.74	6,159.91	6,149.60
17.00%	10,935.13	8,991.75	8,413.44	7,647.10	6,771.62	6,453.92	6,326.30	6,272.97	6,250.32	6,240.62
17.25%	10,994.37	9,055.44	8,479.26	7,716.94	6,849.73	6,537.70	6,413.62	6,362.34	6,340.80	6,331.70
17.50%	11,053.77	9,119.35	8,545.33	7,787.07	6,928.14	6,621.74	6,501.13	6,451.83	6,431.37	6,422.83
17.75%	11,113.35	9,183.49	8,611.65	7,857.47	7,006.85	6,706.04	6,588.82	6,541.45	6,522.01	6,513.99
18.00%	11,173.11	9,247.85	8,678.21	7,928.15	7,085.85	6,790.57	6,676.69	6,631.18	6,612.72	6,605.20
18.25%	11,233.03	9,312.44	8,745.02	7,999.10	7,165.14	6,875.34	6,764.73	6,721.01	6,703.50	6,696.45
18.50%	11,293.13	9,377.24	8,812.07	8,070.33	7,244.70	6,960.34	6,852.93	6,810.96	6,794.34	6,787.72
18.75%	11,353.40	9,442.28	8,879.37	8,141.82	7,324.54	7,045.57	6,941.29	6,901.00	6,885.23	6,879.03
19.00%	11,413.84	9,507.53	8,946.90	8,213.58	7,404.65	7,131.01	7,029.79	6,991.13	6,976.18	6,970.37
19.25%	11,474.45	9,573.00	9,014.67	8,285.61	7,485.03	7,216.67	7,118.44	7,081.35	7,067.17	7,061.73
19.50%	11,535.24	9,638.69	9,082.68	8,357.90	7,565.67	7,302.52	7,207.23	7,171.65	7,158.21	7,153.12
19.75%	11,596.19	9,704.60	9,150.93	8,430.44	7,646.56	7,388.58	7,296.14	7,262.03	7,249.30	7,244.53
20.00%	11,657.31	9,770.73	9,219.41	8,503.25	7,727.70	7,474.83	7,385.19	7,352.48	7,340.42	7,335.96
20.25%	11,718.60	9,837.07	9,288.12	8,576.31	7,809.09	7,561.26	7,474.35	7,443.01	7,431.59	7,427.41
20.50%	11,780.06	9,903.63	9,357.07	8,649.62	7,890.73	7,647.88	7,563.63	7,533.60	7,522.78	7,518.88
20.75%	11,841.68	9,970.40	9,426.24	8,723.18	7,972.59	7,734.67	7,653.02	7,624.25	7,614.02	7,610.36

	5	7	8	10	15	20	25	30	35	40
1.00%	7,606.72	5,487.40	4,825.24	3,898.38	2,663.30	2,046.53	1,677.08	1,431.30	1,256.17	1,125.21
1.25%	7,654.71	5,535.53	4,873.46	3,946.86	2,712.52	2,096.55	1,727.92	1,482.97	1,308.68	1,178.56
1.50%	7,702.90	5,583.92	4,922.00	3,995.72	2,762.31	2,147.33	1,779.72	1,535.78	1,362.52	1,233.42
1.75%	7,751.28	5,632.58	4,970.84	4,044.97	2,812.67	2,198.87	1,832.46	1,589.73	1,417.67	1,289.76
2.00%	7,799.85	5,681.51	5,019.99	4,094.60	2,863.61	2,251.18	1,886.15	1,644.81	1,474.12	1,347.57
2.25%	7,848.62	5,730.71	5,069.45	4,144.61	2,915.13	2,304.25	1,940.78	1,701.00	1,531.85	1,406.83
2.50%	7,897.58	5,780.18	5,119.21	4,195.01	2,967.21	2,358.07	1,996.34	1,758.29	1,590.85	1,467.51
2.75%	7,946.73	5,829.91	5,169.28	4,245.79	3,019.87	2,412.64	2,052.83	1,816.67	1,651.10	1,529.59
3.00%	7,996.07	5,879.92	5,219.66	4,296.95	3,073.09	2,467.96	2,110.24	1,876.14	1,712.58	1,593.03
3.25%	8,045.60	5,930.19	5,270.34	4,348.50	3,126.88	2,524.02	2,168.56	1,936.67	1,775.27	1,657.81
3.50%	8,095.33	5,980.73	5,321.33	4,400.42	3,181.23	2,580.82	2,227.77	1,998.25	1,839.14	1,723.89
3.75%	8,145.24	6,031.54	5,372.63	4,452.73	3,236.14	2,638.35	2,287.88	2,060.86	1,904.18	1,791.24
4.00%	8,195.35	6,082.62	5,424.23	4,505.41	3,291.61	2,696.61	2,348.87	2,124.50	1,970.35	1,859.83
4.25%	8,245.65	6,133.96	5,476.13	4,558.47	3,347.64	2,755.59	2,410.73	2,189.13	2,037.63	1,929.61
4.50%	8,296.14	6,185.57	5,528.34	4,611.91	3,404.22	2,815.29	2,473.45	2,254.75	2,105.99	2,000.55
4.75%	8,346.83	6,237.45	5,580.85	4,665.72	3,461.35	2,875.70	2,537.02	2,321.33	2,175.41	2,072.62
5.00%	8,397.70	6,289.59	5,633.66	4,719.92	3,519.03	2,936.80	2,601.43	2,388.86	2,245.86	2,145.77
5.25%	8,448.76	6,342.00	5,686.78	4,774.48	3,577.26	2,998.61	2,666.65	2,457.31	2,317.31	2,219.97
5.50%	8,500.02	6,394.67	5,740.20	4,829.42	3,636.02	3,061.10	2,732.69	2,526.66	2,389.72	2,295.18
5.75%	8,551.46	6,447.61	5,793.92	4,884.73	3,695.32	3,124.27	2,799.52	2,596.90	2,463.08	2,371.35
6.00%	8,603.10	6,500.81	5,847.94	4,940.41	3,755.16	3,188.12	2,867.14	2,668.00	2,537.34	2,448.45
6.25%	8,654.92	6,554.27	5,902.26	4,996.46	3,815.53	3,252.63	2,935.53	2,739.94	2,612.49	2,526.44
6.50%	8,706.94	6,608.00	5,956.87	5,052.88	3,876.43	3,317.80	3,004.67	2,812.70	2,688.49	2,605.28
6.75%	8,759.14	6,661.99	6,011.79	5,109.67	3,937.85	3,383.62	3,074.56	2,886.26	2,765.30	2,684.94
7.00%	8,811.53	6,716.24	6,067.00	5,166.83	3,999.79	3,450.08	3,145.17	2,960.60	2,842.91	2,765.37
7.25%	8,864.12	6,770.76	6,122.52	5,224.35	4,062.24	3,517.17	3,216.49	3,035.68	2,921.28	2,846.54
7.50%	8,916.89	6,825.53	6,178.32	5,282.23	4,125.21	3,584.89	3,288.51	3,111.50	3,000.38	2,928.41
7.75%	8,969.85	6,880.57	6,234.43	5,340.47	4,188.68	3,653.22	3,361.21	3,188.03	3,080.18	3,010.96
8.00%	9,023.00	6,935.87	6,290.82	5,399.08	4,252.65	3,722.16	3,434.58	3,265.25	3,160.66	3,094.14
8.25%	9,076.33	6,991.42	6,347.51	5,458.04	4,317.12	3,791.69	3,508.60	3,343.14	3,241.79	3,177.92
8.50%	9,129.86	7,047.24	6,404.50	5,517.36	4,382.09	3,861.81	3,583.26	3,421.67	3,323.53	3,262.27
8.75%	9,183.57	7,103.31	6,461.77	5,577.04	4,447.55	3,932.51	3,658.54	3,500.82	3,405.87	3,347.16
9.00%	9,237.47	7,159.64	6,519.34	5,637.07	4,513.49	4,003.78	3,734.42	3,580.57	3,488.77	3,432.56
9.25%	9,291.55	7,216.23	6,577.20	5,697.46	4,579.91	4,075.61	3,810.90	3,660.91	3,572.21	3,518.44
9.50%	9,345.83	7,273.07	6,635.34	5,758.19	4,646.80	4,147.98	3,887.95	3,741.80	3,656.11	3,604.77
9.75%	9,400.29	7,330.17	6,693.78	5,819.28	4,714.16	4,220.90	3,965.56	3,823.24	3,740.62	3,691.54
10.00%	9,454.93	7,387.53	6,752.50	5,880.71	4,781.99	4,294.35	4,043.72	3,905.19	3,825.54	3,778.70
10.25%	9,509.77	7,445.14	6,811.51	5,942.49	4,850.28	4,368.31	4,122.41	3,987.65	3,910.91	3,866.24
10.50%	9,564.79	7,503.00	6,870.81	6,004.61	4,919.03	4,442.79	4,201.61	4,070.59	3,996.70	3,954.14
10.75%	9,619.99	7,561.12	6,930.39	6,067.07	4,988.22	4,517.77	4,281.31	4,153.99	4,082.89	4,042.37

$445,000   11.00 - 20.75%   5 - 40 Years

	5	7	8	10	15	20	25	30	35	40
11.00%	9,675.38	7,619.48	6,990.25	6,129.88	5,057.86	4,593.24	4,361.50	4,237.84	4,169.46	4,130.91
11.25%	9,730.95	7,678.10	7,050.39	6,193.02	5,127.93	4,669.19	4,442.17	4,322.11	4,256.40	4,219.75
11.50%	9,786.71	7,736.98	7,110.82	6,256.50	5,198.44	4,745.61	4,523.29	4,406.80	4,343.68	4,308.85
11.75%	9,842.65	7,796.10	7,171.53	6,320.31	5,269.38	4,822.50	4,604.85	4,491.87	4,431.28	4,398.22
12.00%	9,898.78	7,855.47	7,232.51	6,384.46	5,340.75	4,899.83	4,686.85	4,577.33	4,519.20	4,487.82
12.25%	9,955.09	7,915.08	7,293.78	6,448.93	5,412.53	4,977.61	4,769.26	4,663.14	4,607.40	4,577.65
12.50%	10,011.58	7,974.95	7,355.32	6,513.74	5,484.72	5,055.83	4,852.08	4,749.30	4,695.88	4,667.69
12.75%	10,068.26	8,035.06	7,417.14	6,578.87	5,557.32	5,134.46	4,935.28	4,835.78	4,784.62	4,757.92
13.00%	10,125.12	8,095.42	7,479.23	6,644.33	5,630.33	5,213.51	5,018.87	4,922.59	4,873.61	4,848.34
13.25%	10,182.16	8,156.03	7,541.59	6,710.11	5,703.73	5,292.97	5,102.82	5,009.69	4,962.83	4,938.92
13.50%	10,239.38	8,216.88	7,604.23	6,776.21	5,777.52	5,372.82	5,187.12	5,097.08	5,052.27	5,029.66
13.75%	10,296.79	8,277.97	7,667.14	6,842.62	5,851.69	5,453.05	5,271.76	5,184.75	5,141.91	5,120.55
14.00%	10,354.37	8,339.31	7,730.32	6,909.36	5,926.25	5,533.67	5,356.74	5,272.68	5,231.75	5,211.57
14.25%	10,412.14	8,400.88	7,793.76	6,976.40	6,001.18	5,614.65	5,442.03	5,360.86	5,321.77	5,302.72
14.50%	10,470.09	8,462.70	7,857.48	7,043.76	6,076.48	5,695.99	5,527.62	5,449.27	5,411.96	5,393.99
14.75%	10,528.21	8,524.76	7,921.46	7,111.43	6,152.14	5,777.68	5,613.52	5,537.92	5,502.31	5,485.37
15.00%	10,586.52	8,587.06	7,985.71	7,179.41	6,228.16	5,859.71	5,699.70	5,626.78	5,592.82	5,576.85
15.25%	10,645.00	8,649.59	8,050.21	7,247.69	6,304.54	5,942.08	5,786.15	5,715.84	5,683.47	5,668.42
15.50%	10,703.67	8,712.36	8,114.99	7,316.27	6,381.26	6,024.77	5,872.87	5,805.10	5,774.25	5,760.08
15.75%	10,762.51	8,775.37	8,180.02	7,385.15	6,458.32	6,107.78	5,959.84	5,894.55	5,865.16	5,851.82
16.00%	10,821.54	8,838.62	8,245.31	7,454.33	6,535.72	6,191.09	6,047.06	5,984.17	5,956.19	5,943.64
16.25%	10,880.73	8,902.10	8,310.86	7,523.81	6,613.45	6,274.70	6,134.51	6,073.96	6,047.33	6,035.52
16.50%	10,940.11	8,965.81	8,376.67	7,593.58	6,691.50	6,358.61	6,222.19	6,163.91	6,138.57	6,127.47
16.75%	10,999.67	9,029.76	8,442.73	7,663.64	6,769.88	6,442.80	6,310.09	6,254.01	6,229.91	6,219.48
17.00%	11,059.40	9,093.93	8,509.05	7,734.00	6,848.57	6,527.26	6,398.19	6,344.26	6,321.34	6,311.54
17.25%	11,119.30	9,158.34	8,575.62	7,804.63	6,927.57	6,612.00	6,486.50	6,434.64	6,412.86	6,403.65
17.50%	11,179.39	9,222.98	8,642.44	7,875.54	7,006.87	6,696.99	6,575.01	6,525.15	6,504.46	6,495.81
17.75%	11,239.64	9,287.84	8,709.51	7,946.76	7,086.48	6,782.24	6,663.70	6,615.78	6,596.13	6,588.02
18.00%	11,300.08	9,352.94	8,776.83	8,018.24	7,166.37	6,867.74	6,752.56	6,706.53	6,687.87	6,680.26
18.25%	11,360.68	9,418.26	8,844.40	8,090.00	7,246.56	6,953.47	6,841.60	6,797.39	6,779.68	6,772.54
18.50%	11,421.46	9,483.80	8,912.21	8,162.04	7,327.03	7,039.44	6,930.80	6,888.35	6,871.55	6,864.86
18.75%	11,482.42	9,549.57	8,980.27	8,234.34	7,407.78	7,125.63	7,020.16	6,979.42	6,963.47	6,957.20
19.00%	11,543.55	9,615.57	9,048.57	8,306.92	7,488.80	7,212.05	7,109.68	7,070.57	7,055.45	7,049.58
19.25%	11,604.85	9,681.78	9,117.11	8,379.76	7,570.09	7,298.67	7,199.33	7,161.82	7,147.48	7,141.98
19.50%	11,666.32	9,748.22	9,185.89	8,452.87	7,651.64	7,385.51	7,289.13	7,253.14	7,239.56	7,234.41
19.75%	11,727.96	9,814.88	9,254.92	8,526.25	7,733.45	7,472.54	7,379.06	7,344.55	7,331.68	7,326.86
20.00%	11,789.78	9,881.76	9,324.17	8,599.88	7,815.52	7,559.77	7,469.11	7,436.03	7,423.84	7,419.33
20.25%	11,851.76	9,948.85	9,393.67	8,673.77	7,897.83	7,647.19	7,559.29	7,527.59	7,516.04	7,511.81
20.50%	11,913.92	10,016.17	9,463.40	8,747.91	7,980.39	7,734.79	7,649.58	7,619.21	7,608.27	7,604.32
20.75%	11,976.25	10,083.70	9,533.36	8,822.31	8,063.19	7,822.56	7,739.99	7,710.89	7,700.54	7,696.85

$450,000　　1.00 - 10.75%　　5 - 40 Years

	5	7	8	10	15	20	25	30	35	40
1.00%	7,692.19	5,549.06	4,879.45	3,942.19	2,693.23	2,069.52	1,695.93	1,447.38	1,270.29	1,137.85
1.25%	7,740.72	5,597.72	4,928.22	3,991.21	2,742.99	2,120.10	1,747.34	1,499.63	1,323.39	1,191.80
1.50%	7,789.45	5,646.66	4,977.30	4,040.62	2,793.34	2,171.45	1,799.71	1,553.04	1,377.83	1,247.28
1.75%	7,838.37	5,695.87	5,026.69	4,090.42	2,844.28	2,223.58	1,853.05	1,607.60	1,433.60	1,304.25
2.00%	7,887.49	5,745.35	5,076.39	4,140.61	2,895.79	2,276.48	1,907.34	1,663.29	1,490.68	1,362.72
2.25%	7,936.81	5,795.10	5,126.41	4,191.18	2,947.88	2,330.14	1,962.59	1,720.11	1,549.06	1,422.64
2.50%	7,986.31	5,845.12	5,176.73	4,242.15	3,000.55	2,384.56	2,018.78	1,778.04	1,608.73	1,484.00
2.75%	8,036.01	5,895.42	5,227.36	4,293.50	3,053.80	2,439.75	2,075.90	1,837.09	1,669.66	1,546.78
3.00%	8,085.91	5,945.99	5,278.31	4,345.23	3,107.62	2,495.69	2,133.95	1,897.22	1,731.83	1,610.93
3.25%	8,136.00	5,996.82	5,329.56	4,397.36	3,162.01	2,552.38	2,192.92	1,958.43	1,795.22	1,676.44
3.50%	8,186.29	6,047.93	5,381.12	4,449.86	3,216.97	2,609.82	2,252.81	2,020.70	1,859.81	1,743.26
3.75%	8,236.76	6,099.31	5,432.99	4,502.76	3,272.50	2,668.00	2,313.59	2,084.02	1,925.57	1,811.37
4.00%	8,287.43	6,150.96	5,485.17	4,556.03	3,328.60	2,726.91	2,375.27	2,148.37	1,992.49	1,880.72
4.25%	8,338.30	6,202.88	5,537.66	4,609.69	3,385.25	2,786.56	2,437.82	2,213.73	2,060.52	1,951.29
4.50%	8,389.36	6,255.07	5,590.46	4,663.73	3,442.47	2,846.92	2,501.25	2,280.08	2,129.66	2,023.03
4.75%	8,440.61	6,307.53	5,643.56	4,718.15	3,500.24	2,908.01	2,565.53	2,347.41	2,199.86	2,095.91
5.00%	8,492.06	6,360.26	5,696.96	4,772.95	3,558.57	2,969.80	2,630.66	2,415.70	2,271.09	2,169.88
5.25%	8,543.69	6,413.26	5,750.68	4,828.13	3,617.45	3,032.30	2,696.61	2,484.92	2,343.34	2,244.92
5.50%	8,595.52	6,466.52	5,804.69	4,883.68	3,676.88	3,095.49	2,763.39	2,555.05	2,416.57	2,320.97
5.75%	8,647.55	6,520.05	5,859.02	4,939.61	3,736.85	3,159.38	2,830.98	2,626.08	2,490.75	2,397.99
6.00%	8,699.76	6,573.85	5,913.64	4,995.92	3,797.36	3,223.94	2,899.36	2,697.98	2,565.85	2,475.96
6.25%	8,752.17	6,627.91	5,968.57	5,052.60	3,858.40	3,289.18	2,968.51	2,770.73	2,641.84	2,554.83
6.50%	8,804.77	6,682.25	6,023.80	5,109.66	3,919.98	3,355.08	3,038.43	2,844.31	2,718.69	2,634.56
6.75%	8,857.56	6,736.84	6,079.34	5,167.09	3,982.09	3,421.64	3,109.10	2,918.69	2,796.37	2,715.11
7.00%	8,910.54	6,791.71	6,135.17	5,224.88	4,044.73	3,488.85	3,180.51	2,993.86	2,874.85	2,796.44
7.25%	8,963.71	6,846.83	6,191.31	5,283.05	4,107.88	3,556.69	3,252.63	3,069.79	2,954.10	2,878.52
7.50%	9,017.08	6,902.22	6,247.74	5,341.58	4,171.56	3,625.17	3,325.46	3,146.47	3,034.09	2,961.32
7.75%	9,070.63	6,957.88	6,304.47	5,400.48	4,235.74	3,694.27	3,398.98	3,223.86	3,114.79	3,044.79
8.00%	9,124.38	7,013.80	6,361.51	5,459.74	4,300.43	3,763.98	3,473.17	3,301.94	3,196.17	3,128.90
8.25%	9,178.31	7,069.98	6,418.83	5,519.37	4,365.63	3,834.30	3,548.03	3,380.70	3,278.21	3,213.62
8.50%	9,232.44	7,126.42	6,476.46	5,579.36	4,431.33	3,905.20	3,623.52	3,460.11	3,360.87	3,298.92
8.75%	9,286.75	7,183.12	6,534.38	5,639.70	4,497.52	3,976.70	3,699.65	3,540.15	3,444.13	3,384.77
9.00%	9,341.26	7,240.09	6,592.59	5,700.41	4,564.20	4,048.77	3,776.38	3,620.80	3,527.97	3,471.13
9.25%	9,395.95	7,297.31	6,651.10	5,761.47	4,631.37	4,121.40	3,853.72	3,702.04	3,612.35	3,557.97
9.50%	9,450.84	7,354.79	6,709.90	5,822.89	4,699.01	4,194.59	3,931.63	3,783.84	3,697.25	3,645.28
9.75%	9,505.91	7,412.53	6,768.99	5,884.66	4,767.13	4,268.33	4,010.12	3,866.19	3,782.65	3,733.01
10.00%	9,561.17	7,470.53	6,828.37	5,946.78	4,835.72	4,342.60	4,089.15	3,949.07	3,868.53	3,821.16
10.25%	9,616.62	7,528.79	6,888.05	6,009.26	4,904.78	4,417.40	4,168.72	4,032.46	3,954.85	3,909.68
10.50%	9,672.26	7,587.30	6,948.01	6,072.07	4,974.30	4,492.71	4,248.82	4,116.33	4,041.60	3,998.57
10.75%	9,728.08	7,646.07	7,008.26	6,135.24	5,044.27	4,568.53	4,329.42	4,200.67	4,128.76	4,087.79

$450,000   11.00 - 20.75%   5 - 40 Years

	5	7	8	10	15	20	25	30	35	40
11.00%	9,784.09	7,705.10	7,068.79	6,198.75	5,114.69	4,644.85	4,410.51	4,285.46	4,216.31	4,177.32
11.25%	9,840.29	7,764.38	7,129.61	6,262.60	5,185.55	4,721.65	4,492.08	4,370.68	4,304.22	4,267.16
11.50%	9,896.67	7,823.91	7,190.72	6,326.79	5,256.85	4,798.93	4,574.11	4,456.31	4,392.48	4,357.27
11.75%	9,953.24	7,883.69	7,252.11	6,391.33	5,328.59	4,876.68	4,656.59	4,542.34	4,481.07	4,447.64
12.00%	10,010.00	7,943.73	7,313.78	6,456.19	5,400.76	4,954.89	4,739.51	4,628.76	4,569.97	4,538.25
12.25%	10,066.94	8,004.02	7,375.73	6,521.39	5,473.34	5,033.54	4,822.85	4,715.53	4,659.17	4,629.09
12.50%	10,124.07	8,064.56	7,437.96	6,586.93	5,546.35	5,112.63	4,906.59	4,802.66	4,748.64	4,720.14
12.75%	10,181.39	8,125.35	7,500.48	6,652.79	5,619.77	5,192.15	4,990.74	4,890.12	4,838.38	4,811.38
13.00%	10,238.88	8,186.38	7,563.26	6,718.98	5,693.59	5,272.09	5,075.26	4,977.90	4,928.37	4,902.81
13.25%	10,296.56	8,247.67	7,626.33	6,785.50	5,767.81	5,352.44	5,160.15	5,065.98	5,018.59	4,994.41
13.50%	10,354.43	8,309.20	7,689.67	6,852.34	5,842.43	5,433.19	5,245.40	5,154.35	5,109.03	5,086.18
13.75%	10,412.48	8,370.98	7,753.29	6,919.51	5,917.44	5,514.32	5,331.00	5,243.01	5,199.68	5,178.08
14.00%	10,470.71	8,433.01	7,817.18	6,986.99	5,992.84	5,595.84	5,416.92	5,331.92	5,290.53	5,270.13
14.25%	10,529.13	8,495.27	7,881.34	7,054.79	6,068.61	5,677.74	5,503.17	5,421.09	5,381.56	5,362.30
14.50%	10,587.73	8,557.79	7,945.77	7,122.91	6,144.75	5,759.99	5,589.73	5,510.50	5,472.77	5,454.60
14.75%	10,646.51	8,620.54	8,010.47	7,191.33	6,221.27	5,842.60	5,676.59	5,600.14	5,564.14	5,547.00
15.00%	10,705.47	8,683.54	8,075.43	7,260.07	6,298.14	5,925.55	5,763.74	5,690.00	5,655.66	5,639.51
15.25%	10,764.61	8,746.78	8,140.67	7,329.12	6,375.37	6,008.84	5,851.16	5,780.06	5,747.33	5,732.11
15.50%	10,823.94	8,810.26	8,206.17	7,398.47	6,452.96	6,092.46	5,938.85	5,870.33	5,839.13	5,824.80
15.75%	10,883.44	8,873.97	8,271.93	7,468.13	6,530.88	6,176.40	6,026.80	5,960.78	5,931.06	5,917.57
16.00%	10,943.13	8,937.93	8,337.95	7,538.09	6,609.15	6,260.65	6,115.00	6,051.41	6,023.11	6,010.42
16.25%	11,002.99	9,002.12	8,404.24	7,608.35	6,687.76	6,345.20	6,203.44	6,142.21	6,115.27	6,103.34
16.50%	11,063.03	9,066.55	8,470.79	7,678.90	6,766.69	6,430.05	6,292.10	6,233.17	6,207.54	6,196.32
16.75%	11,123.26	9,131.21	8,537.59	7,749.75	6,845.94	6,515.19	6,380.99	6,324.28	6,299.91	6,289.36
17.00%	11,183.66	9,196.11	8,604.65	7,820.89	6,925.52	6,600.60	6,470.08	6,415.54	6,392.37	6,382.46
17.25%	11,244.24	9,261.24	8,671.97	7,892.33	7,005.41	6,686.29	6,559.39	6,506.94	6,484.91	6,475.60
17.50%	11,305.00	9,326.61	8,739.54	7,964.04	7,085.60	6,772.24	6,648.88	6,598.46	6,577.54	6,568.80
17.75%	11,365.93	9,392.20	8,807.37	8,036.05	7,166.10	6,858.45	6,738.57	6,690.12	6,670.24	6,662.04
18.00%	11,427.04	9,458.03	8,875.45	8,108.33	7,246.89	6,944.90	6,828.43	6,781.88	6,763.01	6,755.32
18.25%	11,488.33	9,524.08	8,943.77	8,180.90	7,327.98	7,031.60	6,918.47	6,873.76	6,855.85	6,848.64
18.50%	11,549.79	9,590.36	9,012.35	8,253.74	7,409.36	7,118.53	7,008.68	6,965.75	6,948.75	6,941.99
18.75%	11,611.43	9,656.87	9,081.17	8,326.86	7,491.01	7,205.70	7,099.04	7,057.84	7,041.71	7,035.37
19.00%	11,673.25	9,723.61	9,150.24	8,400.26	7,572.94	7,293.08	7,189.56	7,150.02	7,134.73	7,128.79
19.25%	11,735.24	9,790.57	9,219.55	8,473.92	7,655.15	7,380.68	7,280.22	7,242.29	7,227.79	7,222.23
19.50%	11,797.40	9,857.75	9,289.11	8,547.85	7,737.62	7,468.49	7,371.03	7,334.64	7,320.90	7,315.69
19.75%	11,859.74	9,925.16	9,358.90	8,622.05	7,820.35	7,556.50	7,461.97	7,427.07	7,414.06	7,409.18
20.00%	11,922.25	9,992.79	9,428.94	8,696.51	7,903.33	7,644.71	7,553.03	7,519.58	7,507.25	7,502.69
20.25%	11,984.93	10,060.64	9,499.21	8,771.23	7,986.57	7,733.11	7,644.22	7,612.17	7,600.49	7,596.22
20.50%	12,047.79	10,128.71	9,569.73	8,846.20	8,070.06	7,821.69	7,735.53	7,704.81	7,693.76	7,689.76
20.75%	12,110.81	10,197.00	9,640.47	8,921.44	8,153.79	7,910.46	7,826.95	7,797.53	7,787.06	7,783.33

	5	7	8	10	15	20	25	30	35	40
1.00%	7,777.66	5,610.72	4,933.67	3,985.99	2,723.15	2,092.52	1,714.77	1,463.46	1,284.40	1,150.50
1.25%	7,826.73	5,659.92	4,982.98	4,035.55	2,773.47	2,143.66	1,766.75	1,516.30	1,338.09	1,205.05
1.50%	7,876.00	5,709.40	5,032.60	4,085.51	2,824.38	2,195.58	1,819.71	1,570.30	1,393.14	1,261.13
1.75%	7,925.47	5,759.15	5,082.54	4,135.87	2,875.88	2,248.29	1,873.64	1,625.46	1,449.53	1,318.75
2.00%	7,975.13	5,809.18	5,132.80	4,186.61	2,927.96	2,301.77	1,928.54	1,681.77	1,507.25	1,377.86
2.25%	8,024.99	5,859.49	5,183.37	4,237.75	2,980.64	2,356.03	1,984.39	1,739.22	1,566.28	1,438.45
2.50%	8,075.05	5,910.07	5,234.25	4,289.28	3,033.89	2,411.06	2,041.21	1,797.80	1,626.60	1,500.49
2.75%	8,125.30	5,960.92	5,285.45	4,341.20	3,087.73	2,466.86	2,098.96	1,857.50	1,688.21	1,563.96
3.00%	8,175.75	6,012.05	5,336.96	4,393.51	3,142.15	2,523.42	2,157.66	1,918.30	1,751.07	1,628.83
3.25%	8,226.40	6,063.45	5,388.78	4,446.22	3,197.14	2,580.74	2,217.29	1,980.19	1,815.16	1,695.06
3.50%	8,277.24	6,115.13	5,440.91	4,499.31	3,252.72	2,638.82	2,277.84	2,043.15	1,880.47	1,762.63
3.75%	8,328.28	6,167.08	5,493.36	4,552.79	3,308.86	2,697.64	2,339.30	2,107.18	1,946.97	1,831.49
4.00%	8,379.52	6,219.31	5,546.12	4,606.65	3,365.58	2,757.21	2,401.66	2,172.24	2,014.63	1,901.62
4.25%	8,430.95	6,271.80	5,599.19	4,660.91	3,422.87	2,817.52	2,464.91	2,238.33	2,083.42	1,972.97
4.50%	8,482.57	6,324.57	5,652.57	4,715.55	3,480.72	2,878.55	2,529.04	2,305.42	2,153.32	2,045.51
4.75%	8,534.39	6,377.62	5,706.26	4,770.57	3,539.14	2,940.32	2,594.03	2,373.50	2,224.30	2,119.20
5.00%	8,586.41	6,430.93	5,760.26	4,825.98	3,598.11	3,002.80	2,659.88	2,442.54	2,296.33	2,193.99
5.25%	8,638.62	6,484.51	5,814.57	4,881.77	3,657.64	3,065.99	2,726.58	2,512.53	2,369.38	2,269.86
5.50%	8,691.03	6,538.37	5,869.19	4,937.95	3,717.73	3,129.89	2,794.10	2,583.44	2,443.42	2,346.75
5.75%	8,743.63	6,592.50	5,924.12	4,994.50	3,778.37	3,194.48	2,862.43	2,655.26	2,518.43	2,424.64
6.00%	8,796.42	6,646.89	5,979.35	5,051.43	3,839.55	3,259.76	2,931.57	2,727.95	2,594.36	2,503.47
6.25%	8,849.41	6,701.56	6,034.89	5,108.74	3,901.27	3,325.72	3,001.50	2,801.51	2,671.20	2,583.22
6.50%	8,902.60	6,756.49	6,090.74	5,166.43	3,963.54	3,392.36	3,072.19	2,875.91	2,748.90	2,663.83
6.75%	8,955.97	6,811.70	6,146.89	5,224.50	4,026.34	3,459.66	3,143.65	2,951.12	2,827.45	2,745.27
7.00%	9,009.55	6,867.17	6,203.34	5,282.94	4,089.67	3,527.61	3,215.85	3,027.13	2,906.80	2,827.51
7.25%	9,063.31	6,922.91	6,260.10	5,341.75	4,153.53	3,596.21	3,288.77	3,103.90	2,986.93	2,910.51
7.50%	9,117.27	6,978.92	6,317.16	5,400.93	4,217.91	3,665.45	3,362.41	3,181.43	3,067.80	2,994.22
7.75%	9,171.42	7,035.19	6,374.52	5,460.48	4,282.80	3,735.32	3,436.75	3,259.68	3,149.40	3,078.62
8.00%	9,225.76	7,091.73	6,432.19	5,520.41	4,348.22	3,805.80	3,511.76	3,338.63	3,231.69	3,163.67
8.25%	9,280.29	7,148.53	6,490.15	5,580.69	4,414.14	3,876.90	3,587.45	3,418.26	3,314.63	3,249.33
8.50%	9,335.02	7,205.60	6,548.42	5,641.35	4,480.56	3,948.60	3,663.78	3,498.56	3,398.22	3,335.58
8.75%	9,389.94	7,262.93	6,606.98	5,702.37	4,547.49	4,020.88	3,740.75	3,579.49	3,482.40	3,422.38
9.00%	9,445.05	7,320.53	6,665.84	5,763.75	4,614.91	4,093.75	3,818.34	3,661.03	3,567.17	3,509.69
9.25%	9,500.35	7,378.39	6,725.00	5,825.49	4,682.82	4,167.19	3,896.54	3,743.17	3,652.49	3,597.51
9.50%	9,555.85	7,436.51	6,784.45	5,887.59	4,751.22	4,241.20	3,975.32	3,825.89	3,738.33	3,685.78
9.75%	9,611.53	7,494.89	6,844.20	5,950.05	4,820.10	4,315.75	4,054.68	3,909.15	3,824.68	3,774.49
10.00%	9,667.41	7,553.54	6,904.24	6,012.86	4,889.45	4,390.85	4,134.59	3,992.95	3,911.51	3,863.61
10.25%	9,723.47	7,612.44	6,964.58	6,076.02	4,959.28	4,466.48	4,215.04	4,077.26	3,998.79	3,953.12
10.50%	9,779.72	7,671.61	7,025.21	6,139.54	5,029.57	4,542.63	4,296.03	4,162.06	4,086.51	4,042.99
10.75%	9,836.17	7,731.03	7,086.13	6,203.41	5,100.31	4,619.29	4,377.52	4,247.34	4,174.64	4,133.21

$455,000   11.00 - 20.75%   5 - 40 Years

	5	7	8	10	15	20	25	30	35	40
11.00%	9,892.80	7,790.71	7,147.33	6,267.63	5,171.52	4,696.46	4,459.51	4,333.07	4,263.16	4,223.74
11.25%	9,949.63	7,850.65	7,208.83	6,332.19	5,243.17	4,774.11	4,541.99	4,419.24	4,352.05	4,314.57
11.50%	10,006.64	7,910.84	7,270.62	6,397.09	5,315.26	4,852.25	4,624.93	4,505.83	4,441.29	4,405.68
11.75%	10,063.84	7,971.29	7,332.69	6,462.34	5,387.80	4,930.87	4,708.33	4,592.81	4,530.86	4,497.06
12.00%	10,121.22	8,031.99	7,395.04	6,527.93	5,460.76	5,009.94	4,792.17	4,680.19	4,620.75	4,588.67
12.25%	10,178.80	8,092.95	7,457.68	6,593.85	5,534.16	5,089.47	4,876.43	4,767.93	4,710.94	4,680.52
12.50%	10,236.56	8,154.16	7,520.61	6,660.12	5,607.98	5,169.44	4,961.11	4,856.02	4,801.41	4,772.58
12.75%	10,294.51	8,215.63	7,583.81	6,726.71	5,682.21	5,249.84	5,046.19	4,944.45	4,892.14	4,864.84
13.00%	10,352.65	8,277.34	7,647.30	6,793.64	5,756.85	5,330.67	5,131.65	5,033.21	4,983.13	4,957.29
13.25%	10,410.97	8,339.31	7,711.07	6,860.90	5,831.90	5,411.91	5,217.49	5,122.27	5,074.35	5,049.91
13.50%	10,469.48	8,401.53	7,775.11	6,928.48	5,907.35	5,493.55	5,303.68	5,211.63	5,165.80	5,142.69
13.75%	10,528.17	8,463.99	7,839.43	6,996.39	5,983.19	5,575.59	5,390.23	5,301.26	5,257.46	5,235.62
14.00%	10,587.05	8,526.71	7,904.03	7,064.62	6,059.42	5,658.02	5,477.11	5,391.17	5,349.31	5,328.69
14.25%	10,646.12	8,589.67	7,968.91	7,133.18	6,136.04	5,740.82	5,564.32	5,481.33	5,441.36	5,421.89
14.50%	10,705.37	8,652.87	8,034.05	7,202.05	6,213.03	5,823.99	5,651.84	5,571.73	5,533.58	5,515.20
14.75%	10,764.80	8,716.33	8,099.47	7,271.24	6,290.39	5,907.52	5,739.66	5,662.36	5,625.96	5,608.64
15.00%	10,824.42	8,780.02	8,165.16	7,340.74	6,368.12	5,991.39	5,827.78	5,753.22	5,718.50	5,702.17
15.25%	10,884.22	8,843.96	8,231.12	7,410.56	6,446.21	6,075.61	5,916.17	5,844.29	5,811.19	5,795.80
15.50%	10,944.20	8,908.15	8,297.34	7,480.68	6,524.66	6,160.16	6,004.84	5,935.55	5,904.01	5,889.52
15.75%	11,004.37	8,972.57	8,363.84	7,551.11	6,603.45	6,245.03	6,093.77	6,027.01	5,996.96	5,983.32
16.00%	11,064.72	9,037.24	8,430.60	7,621.85	6,682.59	6,330.21	6,182.94	6,118.64	6,090.04	6,077.20
16.25%	11,125.25	9,102.14	8,497.62	7,692.89	6,762.06	6,415.71	6,272.36	6,210.45	6,183.22	6,171.15
16.50%	11,185.96	9,167.29	8,564.91	7,764.22	6,841.87	6,501.50	6,362.01	6,302.42	6,276.52	6,265.16
16.75%	11,246.85	9,232.67	8,632.45	7,835.86	6,922.01	6,587.58	6,451.89	6,394.55	6,369.91	6,359.24
17.00%	11,307.92	9,298.29	8,700.26	7,907.79	7,002.47	6,673.94	6,541.97	6,486.82	6,463.39	6,453.37
17.25%	11,369.17	9,364.15	8,768.33	7,980.02	7,083.24	6,760.58	6,632.27	6,579.24	6,556.97	6,547.56
17.50%	11,430.61	9,430.24	8,836.65	8,052.53	7,164.33	6,847.49	6,722.76	6,671.78	6,650.62	6,641.79
17.75%	11,492.22	9,496.56	8,905.23	8,125.34	7,245.72	6,934.65	6,813.44	6,764.45	6,744.35	6,736.06
18.00%	11,554.01	9,563.12	8,974.06	8,198.43	7,327.42	7,022.07	6,904.31	6,857.24	6,838.16	6,830.38
18.25%	11,615.98	9,629.90	9,043.15	8,271.80	7,409.40	7,109.73	6,995.35	6,950.14	6,932.03	6,924.73
18.50%	11,678.13	9,696.92	9,112.49	8,345.45	7,491.68	7,197.63	7,086.55	7,043.15	7,025.96	7,019.12
18.75%	11,740.45	9,764.17	9,182.07	8,419.38	7,574.24	7,285.76	7,177.92	7,136.26	7,119.95	7,113.54
19.00%	11,802.95	9,831.65	9,251.91	8,493.59	7,657.09	7,374.12	7,269.44	7,229.46	7,214.00	7,208.00
19.25%	11,865.63	9,899.35	9,321.99	8,568.07	7,740.20	7,462.69	7,361.12	7,322.76	7,308.10	7,302.47
19.50%	11,928.48	9,967.28	9,392.32	8,642.83	7,823.59	7,551.47	7,452.93	7,416.14	7,402.24	7,396.98
19.75%	11,991.51	10,035.44	9,462.89	8,717.85	7,907.24	7,640.46	7,544.88	7,509.60	7,496.43	7,491.50
20.00%	12,054.72	10,103.82	9,533.71	8,793.13	7,991.15	7,729.65	7,636.96	7,603.14	7,590.67	7,586.05
20.25%	12,118.10	10,172.42	9,604.76	8,868.68	8,075.31	7,819.03	7,729.16	7,696.75	7,684.94	7,680.62
20.50%	12,181.65	10,241.25	9,676.06	8,944.49	8,159.73	7,908.60	7,821.48	7,790.42	7,779.24	7,775.21
20.75%	12,245.38	10,310.30	9,747.59	9,020.56	8,244.39	7,998.35	7,913.92	7,884.17	7,873.58	7,869.81

	5	7	8	10	15	20	25	30	35	40
1.00%	7,863.12	5,672.37	4,987.88	4,029.79	2,753.07	2,115.51	1,733.61	1,479.54	1,298.51	1,163.14
1.25%	7,912.74	5,722.12	5,037.74	4,079.90	2,803.95	2,167.22	1,786.17	1,532.96	1,352.80	1,218.29
1.50%	7,962.55	5,772.14	5,087.91	4,130.41	2,855.42	2,219.71	1,839.71	1,587.55	1,408.45	1,274.99
1.75%	8,012.56	5,822.44	5,138.39	4,181.32	2,907.48	2,272.99	1,894.23	1,643.32	1,465.46	1,333.24
2.00%	8,062.77	5,873.02	5,189.20	4,232.62	2,960.14	2,327.06	1,949.73	1,700.25	1,523.81	1,393.00
2.25%	8,113.18	5,923.88	5,240.33	4,284.32	3,013.39	2,381.92	2,006.20	1,758.33	1,583.49	1,454.25
2.50%	8,163.79	5,975.01	5,291.77	4,336.42	3,067.23	2,437.55	2,063.64	1,817.56	1,644.48	1,516.98
2.75%	8,214.59	6,026.43	5,343.53	4,388.91	3,121.66	2,493.97	2,122.03	1,877.91	1,706.76	1,581.15
3.00%	8,265.60	6,078.12	5,395.60	4,441.79	3,176.68	2,551.15	2,181.37	1,939.38	1,770.31	1,646.73
3.25%	8,316.80	6,130.09	5,448.00	4,495.08	3,232.28	2,609.10	2,241.65	2,001.95	1,835.11	1,713.69
3.50%	8,368.20	6,182.33	5,500.70	4,548.75	3,288.46	2,667.81	2,302.87	2,065.61	1,901.14	1,782.00
3.75%	8,419.80	6,234.85	5,553.73	4,602.82	3,345.22	2,727.29	2,365.00	2,130.33	1,968.36	1,851.62
4.00%	8,471.60	6,287.65	5,607.07	4,657.28	3,402.56	2,787.51	2,428.05	2,196.11	2,036.76	1,922.52
4.25%	8,523.60	6,340.72	5,660.72	4,712.13	3,460.48	2,848.48	2,492.00	2,262.92	2,106.31	1,994.65
4.50%	8,575.79	6,394.07	5,714.69	4,767.37	3,518.97	2,910.19	2,556.83	2,330.75	2,176.98	2,067.99
4.75%	8,628.18	6,447.70	5,768.97	4,823.00	3,578.03	2,972.63	2,622.54	2,399.58	2,248.74	2,142.49
5.00%	8,680.77	6,501.60	5,823.56	4,879.01	3,637.65	3,035.80	2,689.11	2,469.38	2,321.56	2,218.10
5.25%	8,733.55	6,555.77	5,878.47	4,935.42	3,697.84	3,099.68	2,756.54	2,540.14	2,395.42	2,294.80
5.50%	8,786.53	6,610.22	5,933.69	4,992.21	3,758.58	3,164.28	2,824.80	2,611.83	2,470.27	2,372.54
5.75%	8,839.71	6,664.94	5,989.22	5,049.38	3,819.89	3,229.58	2,893.89	2,684.44	2,546.10	2,451.28
6.00%	8,893.09	6,719.94	6,045.06	5,106.94	3,881.74	3,295.58	2,963.79	2,757.93	2,622.87	2,530.98
6.25%	8,946.66	6,775.20	6,101.21	5,164.88	3,944.15	3,362.27	3,034.48	2,832.30	2,700.55	2,611.60
6.50%	9,000.43	6,830.74	6,157.67	5,223.21	4,007.09	3,429.64	3,105.95	2,907.51	2,779.11	2,693.10
6.75%	9,054.39	6,886.55	6,214.43	5,281.91	4,070.58	3,497.67	3,178.19	2,983.55	2,858.52	2,775.44
7.00%	9,108.55	6,942.63	6,271.51	5,340.99	4,134.61	3,566.38	3,251.18	3,060.39	2,938.74	2,858.58
7.25%	9,162.91	6,998.98	6,328.89	5,400.45	4,199.17	3,635.73	3,324.91	3,138.01	3,019.75	2,942.49
7.50%	9,217.46	7,055.61	6,386.58	5,460.28	4,264.26	3,705.73	3,399.36	3,216.39	3,101.52	3,027.13
7.75%	9,272.20	7,112.50	6,444.57	5,520.49	4,329.87	3,776.36	3,474.51	3,295.50	3,184.01	3,112.45
8.00%	9,327.14	7,169.66	6,502.87	5,581.07	4,396.00	3,847.62	3,550.35	3,375.32	3,267.20	3,198.43
8.25%	9,382.28	7,227.09	6,561.47	5,642.02	4,462.65	3,919.50	3,626.87	3,455.83	3,351.06	3,285.04
8.50%	9,437.60	7,284.78	6,620.38	5,703.34	4,529.80	3,991.99	3,704.04	3,537.00	3,435.56	3,372.23
8.75%	9,493.13	7,342.75	6,679.59	5,765.03	4,597.46	4,065.07	3,781.86	3,618.82	3,520.67	3,459.98
9.00%	9,548.84	7,400.98	6,739.09	5,827.09	4,665.63	4,138.74	3,860.30	3,701.26	3,606.37	3,548.26
9.25%	9,604.75	7,459.47	6,798.90	5,889.51	4,734.28	4,212.99	3,939.36	3,784.31	3,692.62	3,637.04
9.50%	9,660.86	7,518.23	6,859.01	5,952.29	4,803.43	4,287.80	4,019.00	3,867.93	3,779.41	3,726.28
9.75%	9,717.15	7,577.26	6,919.41	6,015.43	4,873.07	4,363.18	4,099.23	3,952.11	3,866.71	3,815.97
10.00%	9,773.64	7,636.54	6,980.12	6,078.93	4,943.18	4,439.10	4,180.02	4,036.83	3,954.49	3,906.07
10.25%	9,830.32	7,696.10	7,041.11	6,142.79	5,013.77	4,515.56	4,261.36	4,122.07	4,042.74	3,996.56
10.50%	9,887.19	7,755.91	7,102.41	6,207.01	5,084.84	4,592.55	4,343.24	4,207.80	4,131.42	4,087.42
10.75%	9,944.26	7,815.98	7,164.00	6,271.58	5,156.36	4,670.05	4,425.63	4,294.01	4,220.51	4,178.63

$460,000   11.00 - 20.75%   5 - 40 Years

	5	7	8	10	15	20	25	30	35	40
11.00%	10,001.51	7,876.32	7,225.88	6,336.50	5,228.35	4,748.07	4,508.52	4,380.69	4,310.01	4,270.15
11.25%	10,058.96	7,936.92	7,288.05	6,401.77	5,300.79	4,826.58	4,591.90	4,467.80	4,399.87	4,361.98
11.50%	10,116.60	7,997.77	7,350.51	6,467.39	5,373.67	4,905.58	4,675.76	4,555.34	4,490.09	4,454.10
11.75%	10,174.43	8,058.89	7,413.27	6,533.36	5,447.00	4,985.05	4,760.07	4,643.28	4,580.65	4,546.47
12.00%	10,232.45	8,120.26	7,476.31	6,599.66	5,520.77	5,065.00	4,844.83	4,731.62	4,671.53	4,639.10
12.25%	10,290.65	8,181.89	7,539.64	6,666.31	5,594.97	5,145.40	4,930.02	4,820.32	4,762.71	4,731.96
12.50%	10,349.05	8,243.77	7,603.25	6,733.30	5,669.60	5,226.25	5,015.63	4,909.39	4,854.17	4,825.03
12.75%	10,407.64	8,305.91	7,667.15	6,800.63	5,744.65	5,307.53	5,101.64	4,998.79	4,945.90	4,918.30
13.00%	10,466.41	8,368.30	7,731.34	6,868.29	5,820.11	5,389.25	5,188.04	5,088.52	5,037.89	5,011.77
13.25%	10,525.38	8,430.95	7,795.80	6,936.29	5,895.99	5,471.38	5,274.82	5,178.56	5,130.11	5,105.40
13.50%	10,584.53	8,493.85	7,860.55	7,004.62	5,972.27	5,553.92	5,361.97	5,268.90	5,222.57	5,199.20
13.75%	10,643.87	8,557.00	7,925.58	7,073.27	6,048.94	5,636.86	5,449.46	5,359.52	5,315.23	5,293.15
14.00%	10,703.40	8,620.41	7,990.89	7,142.26	6,126.01	5,720.20	5,537.30	5,450.41	5,408.10	5,387.24
14.25%	10,763.11	8,684.06	8,056.48	7,211.56	6,203.47	5,803.91	5,625.47	5,541.56	5,501.15	5,481.47
14.50%	10,823.01	8,747.96	8,122.34	7,281.19	6,281.30	5,887.99	5,713.95	5,632.96	5,594.38	5,575.81
14.75%	10,883.10	8,812.11	8,188.48	7,351.14	6,359.52	5,972.43	5,802.74	5,724.59	5,687.78	5,670.27
15.00%	10,943.37	8,876.51	8,254.89	7,421.41	6,438.10	6,057.23	5,891.82	5,816.44	5,781.34	5,764.83
15.25%	11,003.83	8,941.15	8,321.57	7,491.99	6,517.05	6,142.37	5,981.19	5,908.51	5,875.05	5,859.49
15.50%	11,064.47	9,006.04	8,388.52	7,562.88	6,596.36	6,227.85	6,070.83	6,000.78	5,968.89	5,954.24
15.75%	11,125.29	9,071.17	8,455.75	7,634.09	6,676.02	6,313.66	6,160.73	6,093.24	6,062.86	6,049.07
16.00%	11,186.31	9,136.55	8,523.24	7,705.60	6,756.02	6,399.78	6,250.89	6,185.88	6,156.96	6,143.98
16.25%	11,247.50	9,202.17	8,591.00	7,777.42	6,836.37	6,486.21	6,341.29	6,278.70	6,251.17	6,238.96
16.50%	11,308.88	9,268.03	8,659.03	7,849.55	6,917.06	6,572.94	6,431.93	6,371.68	6,345.49	6,334.01
16.75%	11,370.44	9,334.13	8,727.32	7,921.97	6,998.08	6,659.97	6,522.79	6,464.82	6,439.91	6,429.12
17.00%	11,432.18	9,400.47	8,795.87	7,994.69	7,079.42	6,747.28	6,613.86	6,558.11	6,534.42	6,524.29
17.25%	11,494.11	9,467.05	8,864.68	8,067.71	7,161.08	6,834.87	6,705.15	6,651.53	6,629.02	6,619.51
17.50%	11,556.22	9,533.87	8,933.76	8,141.02	7,243.06	6,922.73	6,796.64	6,745.10	6,723.71	6,714.77
17.75%	11,618.51	9,600.92	9,003.09	8,214.63	7,325.35	7,010.86	6,888.31	6,838.78	6,818.47	6,810.09
18.00%	11,680.98	9,668.21	9,072.68	8,288.52	7,407.94	7,099.23	6,980.18	6,932.59	6,913.30	6,905.44
18.25%	11,743.63	9,735.73	9,142.52	8,362.70	7,490.83	7,187.86	7,072.22	7,026.51	7,008.21	7,000.83
18.50%	11,806.46	9,803.48	9,212.62	8,437.16	7,574.01	7,276.72	7,164.43	7,120.54	7,103.17	7,096.26
18.75%	11,869.47	9,871.47	9,282.97	8,511.91	7,657.48	7,365.82	7,256.80	7,214.68	7,198.20	7,191.72
19.00%	11,932.65	9,939.69	9,353.58	8,586.93	7,741.23	7,455.15	7,349.33	7,308.91	7,293.28	7,287.20
19.25%	11,996.02	10,008.14	9,424.43	8,662.23	7,825.26	7,544.70	7,442.01	7,403.23	7,388.41	7,382.72
19.50%	12,059.56	10,076.81	9,495.53	8,737.80	7,909.56	7,634.46	7,534.83	7,497.63	7,483.59	7,478.26
19.75%	12,123.29	10,145.72	9,566.88	8,813.65	7,994.13	7,724.42	7,627.79	7,592.12	7,578.81	7,573.83
20.00%	12,187.19	10,214.85	9,638.47	8,889.76	8,078.96	7,814.59	7,720.88	7,686.69	7,674.08	7,669.41
20.25%	12,251.26	10,284.21	9,710.31	8,966.14	8,164.05	7,904.96	7,814.09	7,781.32	7,769.39	7,765.02
20.50%	12,315.51	10,353.79	9,782.39	9,042.79	8,249.40	7,995.51	7,907.43	7,876.03	7,864.73	7,860.65
20.75%	12,379.94	10,423.60	9,854.71	9,119.69	8,334.98	8,086.24	8,000.89	7,970.81	7,960.11	7,956.29

$465,000   1.00 - 10.75%   5 - 40 Years

	5	7	8	10	15	20	25	30	35	40
1.00%	7,948.59	5,734.03	5,042.10	4,073.59	2,783.00	2,138.51	1,752.46	1,495.62	1,312.63	1,175.78
1.25%	7,998.74	5,784.31	5,092.49	4,124.25	2,834.43	2,190.77	1,805.58	1,549.62	1,367.50	1,231.53
1.50%	8,049.10	5,834.88	5,143.21	4,175.30	2,886.46	2,243.84	1,859.70	1,604.81	1,423.76	1,288.85
1.75%	8,099.65	5,885.73	5,194.25	4,226.76	2,939.09	2,297.70	1,914.82	1,661.18	1,481.39	1,347.73
2.00%	8,150.41	5,936.86	5,245.61	4,278.63	2,992.32	2,352.36	1,970.92	1,718.73	1,540.37	1,408.14
2.25%	8,201.37	5,988.27	5,297.29	4,330.89	3,046.14	2,407.81	2,028.01	1,777.44	1,600.70	1,470.06
2.50%	8,252.52	6,039.96	5,349.29	4,383.55	3,100.57	2,464.05	2,086.07	1,837.31	1,662.35	1,533.47
2.75%	8,303.88	6,091.93	5,401.61	4,436.61	3,155.59	2,521.07	2,145.10	1,898.32	1,725.31	1,598.33
3.00%	8,355.44	6,144.18	5,454.25	4,490.07	3,211.20	2,578.88	2,205.08	1,960.46	1,789.55	1,664.63
3.25%	8,407.20	6,196.72	5,507.21	4,543.93	3,267.41	2,637.46	2,266.02	2,023.71	1,855.06	1,732.32
3.50%	8,459.16	6,249.53	5,560.49	4,598.19	3,324.20	2,696.81	2,327.90	2,088.06	1,921.80	1,801.37
3.75%	8,511.32	6,302.62	5,614.09	4,652.85	3,381.58	2,756.93	2,390.71	2,153.49	1,989.76	1,871.75
4.00%	8,563.68	6,355.99	5,668.01	4,707.90	3,439.55	2,817.81	2,454.44	2,219.98	2,058.90	1,943.41
4.25%	8,616.24	6,409.65	5,722.25	4,763.35	3,498.09	2,879.44	2,519.08	2,287.52	2,129.21	2,016.33
4.50%	8,669.00	6,463.58	5,776.80	4,819.19	3,557.22	2,941.82	2,584.62	2,356.09	2,200.64	2,090.47
4.75%	8,721.96	6,517.78	5,831.68	4,875.42	3,616.92	3,004.94	2,651.05	2,425.66	2,273.18	2,165.77
5.00%	8,775.12	6,572.27	5,886.86	4,932.05	3,677.19	3,068.79	2,718.34	2,496.22	2,346.80	2,242.21
5.25%	8,828.48	6,627.03	5,942.37	4,989.06	3,738.03	3,133.38	2,786.50	2,567.75	2,421.46	2,319.75
5.50%	8,882.04	6,682.07	5,998.18	5,046.47	3,799.44	3,198.68	2,855.51	2,640.22	2,497.13	2,398.33
5.75%	8,935.80	6,737.39	6,054.32	5,104.27	3,861.41	3,264.69	2,925.34	2,713.61	2,573.78	2,477.93
6.00%	8,989.75	6,792.98	6,110.77	5,162.45	3,923.93	3,331.40	2,996.00	2,787.91	2,651.38	2,558.49
6.25%	9,043.91	6,848.85	6,167.53	5,221.02	3,987.02	3,398.82	3,067.46	2,863.08	2,729.91	2,639.99
6.50%	9,098.26	6,904.99	6,224.60	5,279.98	4,050.65	3,466.92	3,139.71	2,939.12	2,809.32	2,722.37
6.75%	9,152.81	6,961.41	6,281.98	5,339.32	4,114.83	3,535.69	3,212.74	3,015.98	2,889.59	2,805.61
7.00%	9,207.56	7,018.10	6,339.68	5,399.04	4,179.55	3,605.14	3,286.52	3,093.66	2,970.68	2,889.66
7.25%	9,262.50	7,075.06	6,397.68	5,459.15	4,244.81	3,675.25	3,361.05	3,172.12	3,052.57	2,974.47
7.50%	9,317.65	7,132.30	6,456.00	5,519.63	4,310.61	3,746.01	3,436.31	3,251.35	3,135.23	3,060.03
7.75%	9,372.99	7,189.81	6,514.62	5,580.49	4,376.93	3,817.41	3,512.28	3,331.32	3,218.62	3,146.28
8.00%	9,428.52	7,247.59	6,573.56	5,641.73	4,443.78	3,889.45	3,588.95	3,412.01	3,302.71	3,233.20
8.25%	9,484.26	7,305.64	6,632.79	5,703.35	4,511.15	3,962.11	3,666.29	3,493.39	3,387.48	3,320.75
8.50%	9,540.19	7,363.97	6,692.34	5,765.33	4,579.04	4,035.38	3,744.31	3,575.45	3,472.90	3,408.89
8.75%	9,596.31	7,422.56	6,752.19	5,827.69	4,647.44	4,109.25	3,822.97	3,658.16	3,558.94	3,497.59
9.00%	9,652.64	7,481.42	6,812.34	5,890.42	4,716.34	4,183.73	3,902.26	3,741.50	3,645.57	3,586.83
9.25%	9,709.15	7,540.55	6,872.80	5,953.52	4,785.74	4,258.78	3,982.18	3,825.44	3,732.76	3,676.57
9.50%	9,765.87	7,599.95	6,933.56	6,016.99	4,855.64	4,334.41	4,062.69	3,909.97	3,820.49	3,766.79
9.75%	9,822.77	7,659.62	6,994.62	6,080.82	4,926.04	4,410.60	4,143.79	3,995.07	3,908.74	3,857.45
10.00%	9,879.88	7,719.55	7,055.99	6,145.01	4,996.91	4,487.35	4,225.46	4,080.71	3,997.48	3,948.53
10.25%	9,937.17	7,779.75	7,117.65	6,209.56	5,068.27	4,564.64	4,307.68	4,166.87	4,086.68	4,040.00
10.50%	9,994.66	7,840.21	7,179.61	6,274.48	5,140.10	4,642.47	4,390.44	4,253.54	4,176.32	4,131.85
10.75%	10,052.35	7,900.94	7,241.86	6,339.75	5,212.41	4,720.81	4,473.73	4,340.69	4,266.39	4,224.05

$465,000   11.00 - 20.75%   5 - 40 Years

	5	7	8	10	15	20	25	30	35	40
11.00%	10,110.23	7,961.93	7,304.42	6,405.38	5,285.18	4,799.68	4,557.53	4,428.30	4,356.85	4,316.57
11.25%	10,168.30	8,023.19	7,367.27	6,471.36	5,358.40	4,879.04	4,641.81	4,516.37	4,447.70	4,409.40
11.50%	10,226.56	8,084.70	7,430.41	6,537.69	5,432.08	4,958.90	4,726.58	4,604.86	4,538.90	4,502.51
11.75%	10,285.02	8,146.48	7,493.84	6,604.37	5,506.21	5,039.24	4,811.81	4,693.76	4,630.44	4,595.89
12.00%	10,343.67	8,208.52	7,557.57	6,671.40	5,580.78	5,120.05	4,897.49	4,783.05	4,722.31	4,689.52
12.25%	10,402.51	8,270.82	7,621.59	6,738.77	5,655.79	5,201.33	4,983.61	4,872.72	4,814.48	4,783.39
12.50%	10,461.54	8,333.38	7,685.90	6,806.49	5,731.23	5,283.05	5,070.15	4,962.75	4,906.93	4,877.48
12.75%	10,520.76	8,396.19	7,750.49	6,874.55	5,807.09	5,365.22	5,157.09	5,053.12	4,999.66	4,971.76
13.00%	10,580.18	8,459.26	7,815.37	6,942.95	5,883.38	5,447.83	5,244.43	5,143.83	5,092.65	5,066.24
13.25%	10,639.78	8,522.59	7,880.54	7,011.68	5,960.07	5,530.85	5,332.16	5,234.85	5,185.88	5,160.90
13.50%	10,699.58	8,586.18	7,945.99	7,080.75	6,037.18	5,614.29	5,420.25	5,326.17	5,279.33	5,255.71
13.75%	10,759.56	8,650.01	8,011.73	7,150.16	6,114.69	5,698.14	5,508.70	5,417.77	5,373.01	5,350.69
14.00%	10,819.74	8,714.11	8,077.75	7,219.89	6,192.60	5,782.37	5,597.49	5,509.65	5,466.88	5,445.80
14.25%	10,880.10	8,778.45	8,144.05	7,289.95	6,270.90	5,866.99	5,686.61	5,601.79	5,560.95	5,541.05
14.50%	10,940.65	8,843.05	8,210.62	7,360.34	6,349.58	5,951.99	5,776.06	5,694.19	5,655.19	5,636.42
14.75%	11,001.39	8,907.89	8,277.48	7,431.05	6,428.64	6,037.35	5,865.81	5,786.81	5,749.61	5,731.90
15.00%	11,062.32	8,972.99	8,344.61	7,502.08	6,508.08	6,123.07	5,955.86	5,879.66	5,844.18	5,827.49
15.25%	11,123.43	9,038.34	8,412.02	7,573.42	6,587.89	6,209.14	6,046.20	5,972.73	5,938.91	5,923.18
15.50%	11,184.73	9,103.93	8,479.70	7,645.09	6,668.06	6,295.55	6,136.82	6,066.00	6,033.77	6,018.96
15.75%	11,246.22	9,169.77	8,547.66	7,717.07	6,748.58	6,382.28	6,227.70	6,159.47	6,128.76	6,114.82
16.00%	11,307.90	9,235.86	8,615.89	7,789.36	6,829.46	6,469.34	6,318.83	6,253.12	6,223.88	6,210.77
16.25%	11,369.76	9,302.19	8,684.38	7,861.96	6,910.68	6,556.71	6,410.22	6,346.95	6,319.12	6,306.78
16.50%	11,431.80	9,368.77	8,753.15	7,934.87	6,992.25	6,644.39	6,501.84	6,440.94	6,414.46	6,402.86
16.75%	11,494.03	9,435.59	8,822.18	8,008.08	7,074.14	6,732.36	6,593.69	6,535.09	6,509.91	6,499.00
17.00%	11,556.45	9,502.65	8,891.48	8,081.59	7,156.37	6,820.62	6,685.75	6,629.39	6,605.45	6,595.20
17.25%	11,619.05	9,569.95	8,961.04	8,155.40	7,238.92	6,909.16	6,778.03	6,723.83	6,701.08	6,691.46
17.50%	11,681.83	9,637.49	9,030.86	8,229.51	7,321.79	6,997.98	6,870.51	6,818.41	6,796.79	6,787.76
17.75%	11,744.80	9,705.28	9,100.95	8,303.92	7,404.97	7,087.06	6,963.19	6,913.12	6,892.58	6,884.11
18.00%	11,807.94	9,773.29	9,171.29	8,378.61	7,488.46	7,176.40	7,056.05	7,007.95	6,988.45	6,980.50
18.25%	11,871.27	9,841.55	9,241.90	8,453.60	7,572.25	7,265.99	7,149.09	7,102.89	7,084.38	7,076.93
18.50%	11,934.79	9,910.04	9,312.76	8,528.87	7,656.33	7,355.82	7,242.30	7,197.94	7,180.38	7,173.39
18.75%	11,998.48	9,978.77	9,383.88	8,604.43	7,740.71	7,445.89	7,335.68	7,293.10	7,276.44	7,269.89
19.00%	12,062.36	10,047.73	9,455.25	8,680.26	7,825.37	7,536.18	7,429.21	7,388.35	7,372.55	7,366.41
19.25%	12,126.41	10,116.92	9,526.87	8,756.38	7,910.32	7,626.70	7,522.90	7,483.70	7,468.72	7,462.97
19.50%	12,190.65	10,186.35	9,598.74	8,832.78	7,995.54	7,717.44	7,616.73	7,579.13	7,564.93	7,559.55
19.75%	12,255.06	10,256.00	9,670.87	8,909.45	8,081.02	7,808.39	7,710.70	7,674.64	7,661.19	7,656.15
20.00%	12,319.66	10,325.88	9,743.24	8,986.39	8,166.78	7,899.53	7,804.80	7,770.24	7,757.49	7,752.78
20.25%	12,384.43	10,395.99	9,815.86	9,063.60	8,252.79	7,990.88	7,899.03	7,865.90	7,853.84	7,849.42
20.50%	12,449.38	10,466.33	9,888.72	9,141.08	8,339.06	8,082.42	7,993.38	7,961.64	7,950.22	7,946.09
20.75%	12,514.51	10,536.90	9,961.82	9,218.82	8,425.58	8,174.14	8,087.85	8,057.44	8,046.63	8,042.77

	5	7	8	10	15	20	25	30	35	40
1.00%	8,034.06	5,795.69	5,096.32	4,117.39	2,812.92	2,161.50	1,771.30	1,511.71	1,326.74	1,188.42
1.25%	8,084.75	5,846.51	5,147.25	4,168.59	2,864.90	2,214.33	1,825.00	1,566.28	1,382.21	1,244.77
1.50%	8,135.65	5,897.62	5,198.51	4,220.20	2,917.49	2,267.96	1,879.70	1,622.06	1,439.07	1,302.71
1.75%	8,186.75	5,949.02	5,250.10	4,272.21	2,970.69	2,322.41	1,935.41	1,679.04	1,497.31	1,362.22
2.00%	8,238.05	6,000.69	5,302.01	4,324.63	3,024.49	2,377.65	1,992.12	1,737.21	1,556.94	1,423.28
2.25%	8,289.55	6,052.66	5,354.25	4,377.46	3,078.90	2,433.70	2,049.81	1,796.56	1,617.91	1,485.87
2.50%	8,341.26	6,104.91	5,406.81	4,430.69	3,133.91	2,490.54	2,108.50	1,857.07	1,680.23	1,549.96
2.75%	8,393.17	6,157.44	5,459.69	4,484.32	3,189.52	2,548.18	2,168.16	1,918.73	1,743.86	1,615.52
3.00%	8,445.28	6,210.25	5,512.90	4,538.36	3,245.73	2,606.61	2,228.79	1,981.54	1,808.80	1,682.53
3.25%	8,497.60	6,263.35	5,566.43	4,592.79	3,302.54	2,665.82	2,290.39	2,045.47	1,875.01	1,750.94
3.50%	8,550.12	6,316.73	5,620.28	4,647.64	3,359.95	2,725.81	2,352.93	2,110.51	1,942.47	1,820.74
3.75%	8,602.84	6,370.39	5,674.46	4,702.88	3,417.95	2,786.58	2,416.42	2,176.64	2,011.15	1,891.87
4.00%	8,655.77	6,424.34	5,728.96	4,758.52	3,476.53	2,848.11	2,480.83	2,243.85	2,081.04	1,964.31
4.25%	8,708.89	6,478.57	5,783.78	4,814.56	3,535.71	2,910.40	2,546.17	2,312.12	2,152.10	2,038.01
4.50%	8,762.22	6,533.08	5,838.92	4,871.01	3,595.47	2,973.45	2,612.41	2,381.42	2,224.31	2,112.95
4.75%	8,815.75	6,587.87	5,894.38	4,927.84	3,655.81	3,037.25	2,679.55	2,451.74	2,297.63	2,189.06
5.00%	8,869.48	6,642.94	5,950.16	4,985.08	3,716.73	3,101.79	2,747.57	2,523.06	2,372.03	2,266.32
5.25%	8,923.41	6,698.29	6,006.26	5,042.71	3,778.23	3,167.07	2,816.46	2,595.36	2,447.49	2,344.69
5.50%	8,977.55	6,753.92	6,062.68	5,100.74	3,840.29	3,233.07	2,886.21	2,668.61	2,523.98	2,424.12
5.75%	9,031.88	6,809.83	6,119.42	5,159.15	3,902.93	3,299.79	2,956.80	2,742.79	2,601.45	2,504.57
6.00%	9,086.42	6,866.02	6,176.47	5,217.96	3,966.13	3,367.23	3,028.22	2,817.89	2,679.89	2,586.00
6.25%	9,141.15	6,922.49	6,233.84	5,277.16	4,029.89	3,435.36	3,100.45	2,893.87	2,759.26	2,668.38
6.50%	9,196.09	6,979.24	6,291.53	5,336.75	4,094.20	3,504.19	3,173.47	2,970.72	2,839.53	2,751.65
6.75%	9,251.23	7,036.26	6,349.53	5,396.73	4,159.07	3,573.71	3,247.28	3,048.41	2,920.66	2,835.78
7.00%	9,306.56	7,093.56	6,407.85	5,457.10	4,224.49	3,643.90	3,321.86	3,126.92	3,002.62	2,920.73
7.25%	9,362.10	7,151.14	6,466.48	5,517.85	4,290.46	3,714.77	3,397.19	3,206.23	3,085.40	3,006.46
7.50%	9,417.84	7,208.99	6,525.42	5,578.98	4,356.96	3,786.29	3,473.26	3,286.31	3,168.94	3,092.93
7.75%	9,473.77	7,267.12	6,584.67	5,640.50	4,424.00	3,858.46	3,550.05	3,367.14	3,253.23	3,180.11
8.00%	9,529.91	7,325.52	6,644.24	5,702.40	4,491.56	3,931.27	3,627.54	3,448.69	3,338.23	3,267.96
8.25%	9,586.24	7,384.20	6,704.12	5,764.67	4,559.66	4,004.71	3,705.72	3,530.95	3,423.91	3,356.45
8.50%	9,642.77	7,443.15	6,764.30	5,827.33	4,628.28	4,078.77	3,784.57	3,613.89	3,510.24	3,445.54
8.75%	9,699.50	7,502.37	6,824.79	5,890.36	4,697.41	4,153.44	3,864.08	3,697.49	3,597.21	3,535.20
9.00%	9,756.43	7,561.87	6,885.60	5,953.76	4,767.05	4,228.71	3,944.22	3,781.73	3,684.77	3,625.40
9.25%	9,813.55	7,621.63	6,946.70	6,017.54	4,837.20	4,304.57	4,024.99	3,866.57	3,772.90	3,716.10
9.50%	9,870.87	7,681.67	7,008.12	6,081.69	4,907.86	4,381.02	4,106.37	3,952.01	3,861.57	3,807.29
9.75%	9,928.39	7,741.98	7,069.84	6,146.20	4,979.00	4,458.03	4,188.35	4,038.03	3,950.77	3,898.93
10.00%	9,986.11	7,802.56	7,131.86	6,211.08	5,050.64	4,535.60	4,270.89	4,124.59	4,040.46	3,990.99
10.25%	10,044.02	7,863.40	7,194.18	6,276.33	5,122.77	4,613.72	4,354.00	4,211.68	4,130.62	4,083.45
10.50%	10,102.13	7,924.52	7,256.81	6,341.94	5,195.37	4,692.39	4,437.65	4,299.27	4,221.23	4,176.28
10.75%	10,160.44	7,985.90	7,319.73	6,407.92	5,268.46	4,771.58	4,521.84	4,387.36	4,312.26	4,269.47

$470,000   11.00 - 20.75%   5 - 40 Years

	5	7	8	10	15	20	25	30	35	40
11.00%	10,218.94	8,047.55	7,382.96	6,474.25	5,342.01	4,851.29	4,606.53	4,475.92	4,403.70	4,362.98
11.25%	10,277.63	8,109.46	7,446.48	6,540.94	5,416.02	4,931.50	4,691.73	4,564.93	4,495.52	4,456.81
11.50%	10,336.53	8,171.64	7,510.31	6,607.99	5,490.49	5,012.22	4,777.40	4,654.37	4,587.70	4,550.92
11.75%	10,395.61	8,234.08	7,574.42	6,675.38	5,565.42	5,093.42	4,863.55	4,744.23	4,680.23	4,645.31
12.00%	10,454.89	8,296.78	7,638.84	6,743.13	5,640.79	5,175.10	4,950.15	4,834.48	4,773.08	4,739.95
12.25%	10,514.36	8,359.75	7,703.54	6,811.23	5,716.60	5,257.25	5,037.20	4,925.11	4,866.24	4,834.83
12.50%	10,574.03	8,422.98	7,768.54	6,879.68	5,792.85	5,339.86	5,124.66	5,016.11	4,959.70	4,929.92
12.75%	10,633.89	8,486.47	7,833.83	6,948.47	5,869.53	5,422.91	5,212.55	5,107.46	5,053.42	5,025.22
13.00%	10,693.94	8,550.22	7,899.41	7,017.60	5,946.64	5,506.41	5,300.83	5,199.14	5,147.41	5,120.72
13.25%	10,754.19	8,614.23	7,965.28	7,087.08	6,024.16	5,590.32	5,389.49	5,291.14	5,241.64	5,216.39
13.50%	10,814.63	8,678.50	8,031.44	7,156.89	6,102.10	5,674.66	5,478.53	5,383.44	5,336.10	5,312.23
13.75%	10,875.26	8,743.02	8,097.88	7,227.04	6,180.44	5,759.41	5,567.93	5,476.03	5,430.78	5,408.22
14.00%	10,936.08	8,807.81	8,164.61	7,297.52	6,259.18	5,844.55	5,657.68	5,568.90	5,525.66	5,504.36
14.25%	10,997.09	8,872.84	8,231.62	7,368.34	6,338.32	5,930.08	5,747.76	5,662.03	5,620.74	5,600.63
14.50%	11,058.29	8,938.13	8,298.91	7,439.48	6,417.85	6,015.99	5,838.17	5,755.41	5,716.00	5,697.02
14.75%	11,119.68	9,003.68	8,366.49	7,510.95	6,497.77	6,102.27	5,928.88	5,849.04	5,811.43	5,793.54
15.00%	11,181.27	9,069.47	8,434.34	7,582.74	6,578.06	6,188.91	6,019.90	5,942.89	5,907.02	5,890.15
15.25%	11,243.04	9,135.52	8,502.47	7,654.86	6,658.72	6,275.90	6,111.21	6,036.95	6,002.76	5,986.87
15.50%	11,305.00	9,201.82	8,570.88	7,727.30	6,739.75	6,363.24	6,202.80	6,131.23	6,098.65	6,083.68
15.75%	11,367.15	9,268.37	8,639.57	7,800.05	6,821.15	6,450.91	6,294.66	6,225.70	6,194.66	6,180.57
16.00%	11,429.49	9,335.17	8,708.53	7,873.12	6,902.89	6,538.90	6,386.78	6,320.36	6,290.81	6,277.55
16.25%	11,492.01	9,402.22	8,777.76	7,946.50	6,984.99	6,627.21	6,479.14	6,415.19	6,387.06	6,374.59
16.50%	11,554.72	9,469.51	8,847.27	8,020.19	7,067.43	6,715.83	6,571.75	6,510.20	6,483.43	6,471.71
16.75%	11,617.62	9,537.05	8,917.04	8,094.19	7,150.21	6,804.75	6,664.59	6,605.36	6,579.90	6,568.89
17.00%	11,680.71	9,604.83	8,987.08	8,168.49	7,233.32	6,893.96	6,757.64	6,700.67	6,676.47	6,666.12
17.25%	11,743.98	9,672.85	9,057.39	8,243.10	7,316.76	6,983.46	6,850.91	6,796.13	6,773.13	6,763.41
17.50%	11,807.44	9,741.12	9,127.97	8,318.00	7,400.52	7,073.23	6,944.39	6,891.73	6,869.87	6,860.75
17.75%	11,871.08	9,809.63	9,198.81	8,393.21	7,484.59	7,163.27	7,038.06	6,987.45	6,966.70	6,958.13
18.00%	11,934.91	9,878.38	9,269.91	8,468.70	7,568.98	7,253.56	7,131.92	7,083.30	7,063.59	7,055.56
18.25%	11,998.92	9,947.37	9,341.27	8,544.50	7,653.67	7,344.12	7,225.96	7,179.27	7,160.56	7,153.02
18.50%	12,063.12	10,016.60	9,412.90	8,620.58	7,738.66	7,434.91	7,320.18	7,275.34	7,257.59	7,250.52
18.75%	12,127.50	10,086.07	9,484.78	8,696.95	7,823.94	7,525.95	7,414.56	7,371.52	7,354.68	7,348.06
19.00%	12,192.06	10,155.77	9,556.92	8,773.60	7,909.52	7,617.22	7,509.10	7,467.79	7,451.83	7,445.62
19.25%	12,256.80	10,225.71	9,629.31	8,850.54	7,995.37	7,708.71	7,603.79	7,564.17	7,549.03	7,543.21
19.50%	12,321.73	10,295.88	9,701.96	8,927.75	8,081.51	7,800.42	7,698.63	7,660.62	7,646.27	7,640.83
19.75%	12,386.84	10,366.28	9,774.85	9,005.25	8,167.92	7,892.35	7,793.61	7,757.17	7,743.57	7,738.48
20.00%	12,452.13	10,436.91	9,848.00	9,083.02	8,254.59	7,984.48	7,888.72	7,853.79	7,840.91	7,836.14
20.25%	12,517.59	10,507.78	9,921.40	9,161.06	8,341.53	8,076.80	7,983.97	7,950.48	7,938.29	7,933.83
20.50%	12,583.24	10,578.87	9,995.05	9,239.37	8,428.73	8,169.32	8,079.33	8,047.25	8,035.70	8,031.53
20.75%	12,649.07	10,650.20	10,068.94	9,317.95	8,516.18	8,262.03	8,174.82	8,144.08	8,133.15	8,129.25

$475,000   1.00 - 10.75%   5 - 40 Years

	5	7	8	10	15	20	25	30	35	40
1.00%	8,119.53	5,857.34	5,150.53	4,161.20	2,842.85	2,184.50	1,790.14	1,527.79	1,340.86	1,201.07
1.25%	8,170.76	5,908.71	5,202.01	4,212.94	2,895.38	2,237.89	1,844.41	1,582.95	1,396.91	1,258.01
1.50%	8,222.20	5,960.36	5,253.82	4,265.10	2,948.53	2,292.09	1,899.70	1,639.32	1,454.38	1,316.57
1.75%	8,273.84	6,012.30	5,305.95	4,317.66	3,002.29	2,347.11	1,956.00	1,696.91	1,513.24	1,376.71
2.00%	8,325.69	6,064.53	5,358.41	4,370.64	3,056.67	2,402.95	2,013.31	1,755.69	1,573.50	1,438.42
2.25%	8,377.74	6,117.05	5,411.21	4,424.03	3,111.65	2,459.59	2,071.62	1,815.67	1,635.12	1,501.68
2.50%	8,430.00	6,169.85	5,464.33	4,477.82	3,167.25	2,517.04	2,130.93	1,876.82	1,698.10	1,566.45
2.75%	8,482.46	6,222.94	5,517.77	4,532.02	3,223.45	2,575.29	2,191.23	1,939.15	1,762.41	1,632.71
3.00%	8,535.13	6,276.32	5,571.55	4,586.64	3,280.26	2,634.34	2,252.50	2,002.62	1,828.04	1,700.43
3.25%	8,588.00	6,329.98	5,625.65	4,641.65	3,337.68	2,694.18	2,314.75	2,067.23	1,894.95	1,769.57
3.50%	8,641.08	6,383.93	5,680.07	4,697.08	3,395.69	2,754.81	2,377.96	2,132.96	1,963.13	1,840.11
3.75%	8,694.36	6,438.16	5,734.83	4,752.91	3,454.31	2,816.22	2,442.12	2,199.80	2,032.55	1,912.00
4.00%	8,747.85	6,492.68	5,789.91	4,809.14	3,513.52	2,878.41	2,507.22	2,267.72	2,103.18	1,985.21
4.25%	8,801.54	6,547.49	5,845.31	4,865.78	3,573.32	2,941.36	2,573.26	2,336.71	2,175.00	2,059.70
4.50%	8,855.43	6,602.58	5,901.04	4,922.82	3,633.72	3,005.08	2,640.20	2,406.76	2,247.97	2,135.42
4.75%	8,909.53	6,657.95	5,957.09	4,980.27	3,694.70	3,069.56	2,708.06	2,477.82	2,322.07	2,212.35
5.00%	8,963.84	6,713.61	6,013.46	5,038.11	3,756.27	3,134.79	2,776.80	2,549.90	2,397.27	2,290.43
5.25%	9,018.34	6,769.55	6,070.16	5,096.36	3,818.42	3,200.76	2,846.43	2,622.97	2,473.53	2,369.63
5.50%	9,073.05	6,825.77	6,127.18	5,155.00	3,881.15	3,267.46	2,916.92	2,697.00	2,550.83	2,449.91
5.75%	9,127.96	6,882.28	6,184.52	5,214.04	3,944.45	3,334.90	2,988.26	2,771.97	2,629.13	2,531.22
6.00%	9,183.08	6,939.06	6,242.18	5,273.47	4,008.32	3,403.05	3,060.43	2,847.86	2,708.40	2,613.51
6.25%	9,238.40	6,996.13	6,300.16	5,333.30	4,072.76	3,471.91	3,133.43	2,924.66	2,788.61	2,696.76
6.50%	9,293.92	7,053.48	6,358.46	5,393.53	4,137.76	3,541.47	3,207.23	3,002.32	2,869.73	2,780.92
6.75%	9,349.64	7,111.11	6,417.08	5,454.15	4,203.32	3,611.73	3,281.83	3,080.84	2,951.73	2,865.94
7.00%	9,405.57	7,169.02	6,476.02	5,515.15	4,269.43	3,682.67	3,357.20	3,160.19	3,034.57	2,951.80
7.25%	9,461.70	7,227.21	6,535.27	5,576.55	4,336.10	3,754.29	3,433.33	3,240.34	3,118.22	3,038.44
7.50%	9,518.03	7,285.68	6,594.84	5,638.33	4,403.31	3,826.57	3,510.21	3,321.27	3,202.65	3,125.84
7.75%	9,574.56	7,344.43	6,654.72	5,700.50	4,471.06	3,899.51	3,587.81	3,402.96	3,287.84	3,213.94
8.00%	9,631.29	7,403.45	6,714.92	5,763.06	4,539.35	3,973.09	3,666.13	3,485.38	3,373.74	3,302.73
8.25%	9,688.22	7,462.75	6,775.44	5,826.00	4,608.17	4,047.31	3,745.14	3,568.52	3,460.33	3,392.16
8.50%	9,745.35	7,522.33	6,836.26	5,889.32	4,677.51	4,122.16	3,824.83	3,652.34	3,547.59	3,482.20
8.75%	9,802.69	7,582.18	6,897.40	5,953.02	4,747.38	4,197.63	3,905.18	3,736.83	3,635.47	3,572.81
9.00%	9,860.22	7,642.31	6,958.85	6,017.10	4,817.77	4,273.70	3,986.18	3,821.96	3,723.97	3,663.97
9.25%	9,917.95	7,702.71	7,020.60	6,081.55	4,888.66	4,350.37	4,067.81	3,907.71	3,813.04	3,755.64
9.50%	9,975.88	7,763.39	7,082.67	6,146.38	4,960.07	4,427.62	4,150.06	3,994.06	3,902.66	3,847.79
9.75%	10,034.02	7,824.34	7,145.05	6,211.59	5,031.97	4,505.46	4,232.90	4,080.98	3,992.80	3,940.40
10.00%	10,092.35	7,885.56	7,207.73	6,277.16	5,104.37	4,583.85	4,316.33	4,168.46	4,083.44	4,033.44
10.25%	10,150.88	7,947.06	7,270.72	6,343.10	5,177.27	4,662.81	4,400.32	4,256.48	4,174.56	4,126.89
10.50%	10,209.60	8,008.82	7,334.01	6,409.41	5,250.64	4,742.30	4,484.86	4,345.01	4,266.14	4,220.71
10.75%	10,268.53	8,070.85	7,397.60	6,476.09	5,324.50	4,822.34	4,569.94	4,434.04	4,358.14	4,314.89

$475,000   11.00 - 20.75%   5 - 40 Years

	5	7	8	10	15	20	25	30	35	40
11.00%	10,327.65	8,133.16	7,461.50	6,543.13	5,398.84	4,902.89	4,655.54	4,523.54	4,450.55	4,409.40
11.25%	10,386.97	8,195.73	7,525.70	6,610.52	5,473.64	4,983.97	4,741.64	4,613.49	4,543.35	4,504.22
11.50%	10,446.49	8,258.57	7,590.20	6,678.28	5,548.90	5,065.54	4,828.23	4,703.88	4,636.51	4,599.34
11.75%	10,506.20	8,321.68	7,655.00	6,746.40	5,624.62	5,147.61	4,915.29	4,794.70	4,730.02	4,694.73
12.00%	10,566.11	8,385.05	7,720.10	6,814.87	5,700.80	5,230.16	5,002.81	4,885.91	4,823.86	4,790.37
12.25%	10,626.22	8,448.69	7,785.49	6,883.69	5,777.42	5,313.18	5,090.78	4,977.51	4,918.01	4,886.26
12.50%	10,686.52	8,512.59	7,851.18	6,952.87	5,854.48	5,396.67	5,179.18	5,069.47	5,012.46	4,982.37
12.75%	10,747.02	8,576.75	7,917.17	7,022.39	5,931.98	5,480.61	5,268.00	5,161.79	5,107.18	5,078.68
13.00%	10,807.71	8,641.18	7,983.45	7,092.26	6,009.90	5,564.98	5,357.22	5,254.45	5,202.17	5,175.19
13.25%	10,868.60	8,705.87	8,050.02	7,162.47	6,088.25	5,649.80	5,446.83	5,347.42	5,297.40	5,271.88
13.50%	10,929.68	8,770.82	8,116.88	7,233.03	6,167.01	5,735.03	5,536.81	5,440.71	5,392.87	5,368.74
13.75%	10,990.95	8,836.04	8,184.03	7,303.92	6,246.19	5,820.68	5,627.16	5,534.28	5,488.55	5,465.76
14.00%	11,052.42	8,901.51	8,251.46	7,375.16	6,325.77	5,906.72	5,717.86	5,628.14	5,584.45	5,562.92
14.25%	11,114.08	8,967.23	8,319.19	7,446.72	6,405.75	5,993.16	5,808.91	5,722.26	5,680.54	5,660.21
14.50%	11,175.93	9,033.22	8,387.20	7,518.62	6,486.13	6,079.99	5,900.27	5,816.64	5,776.81	5,757.63
14.75%	11,237.98	9,099.46	8,455.49	7,590.85	6,566.89	6,167.19	5,991.96	5,911.26	5,873.26	5,855.17
15.00%	11,300.22	9,165.96	8,524.07	7,663.41	6,648.04	6,254.75	6,083.95	6,006.11	5,969.86	5,952.81
15.25%	11,362.65	9,232.71	8,592.93	7,736.29	6,729.56	6,342.67	6,176.23	6,101.18	6,066.62	6,050.56
15.50%	11,425.27	9,299.71	8,662.06	7,809.50	6,811.45	6,430.93	6,268.79	6,196.46	6,163.53	6,148.40
15.75%	11,488.08	9,366.97	8,731.48	7,883.03	6,893.71	6,519.54	6,361.63	6,291.93	6,260.57	6,246.33
16.00%	11,551.08	9,434.48	8,801.17	7,956.87	6,976.33	6,608.47	6,454.72	6,387.60	6,357.73	6,344.33
16.25%	11,614.27	9,502.24	8,871.14	8,031.03	7,059.30	6,697.72	6,548.07	6,483.44	6,455.01	6,442.41
16.50%	11,677.65	9,570.25	8,941.39	8,105.51	7,142.62	6,787.28	6,641.66	6,579.45	6,552.41	6,540.56
16.75%	11,741.22	9,638.50	9,011.90	8,180.29	7,226.28	6,877.14	6,735.49	6,675.63	6,649.90	6,638.77
17.00%	11,804.97	9,707.01	9,082.69	8,255.39	7,310.27	6,967.30	6,829.53	6,771.96	6,747.50	6,737.04
17.25%	11,868.92	9,775.76	9,153.75	8,330.79	7,394.60	7,057.75	6,923.80	6,868.43	6,845.19	6,835.36
17.50%	11,933.05	9,844.75	9,225.07	8,406.49	7,479.25	7,148.47	7,018.27	6,965.04	6,942.96	6,933.73
17.75%	11,997.37	9,913.99	9,296.67	8,482.49	7,564.22	7,239.47	7,112.93	7,061.79	7,040.81	7,032.15
18.00%	12,061.88	9,983.47	9,368.53	8,558.80	7,649.50	7,330.73	7,207.79	7,158.66	7,138.74	7,130.62
18.25%	12,126.57	10,053.20	9,440.65	8,635.39	7,735.09	7,422.25	7,302.83	7,255.64	7,236.73	7,229.12
18.50%	12,191.45	10,123.16	9,513.03	8,712.29	7,820.99	7,514.01	7,398.05	7,352.74	7,334.80	7,327.66
18.75%	12,256.51	10,193.37	9,585.68	8,789.47	7,907.18	7,606.01	7,493.43	7,449.94	7,432.92	7,426.23
19.00%	12,321.76	10,263.81	9,658.59	8,866.94	7,993.66	7,698.25	7,588.98	7,547.24	7,531.10	7,524.83
19.25%	12,387.19	10,334.49	9,731.75	8,944.69	8,080.43	7,790.72	7,684.68	7,644.64	7,629.33	7,623.46
19.50%	12,452.81	10,405.41	9,805.17	9,022.73	8,167.48	7,883.41	7,780.53	7,742.12	7,727.62	7,722.12
19.75%	12,518.61	10,476.56	9,878.84	9,101.05	8,254.81	7,976.31	7,876.52	7,839.69	7,825.95	7,820.80
20.00%	12,584.59	10,547.94	9,952.77	9,179.64	8,342.41	8,069.42	7,972.65	7,937.34	7,924.32	7,919.50
20.25%	12,650.76	10,619.56	10,026.95	9,258.52	8,430.27	8,162.73	8,068.90	8,035.06	8,022.74	8,018.23
20.50%	12,717.11	10,691.41	10,101.38	9,337.66	8,518.40	8,256.23	8,165.28	8,132.86	8,121.19	8,116.97
20.75%	12,783.64	10,763.50	10,176.06	9,417.07	8,606.78	8,349.93	8,261.78	8,230.72	8,219.68	8,215.73

	5	7	8	10	15	20	25	30	35	40
1.00%	8,205.00	5,919.00	5,204.75	4,205.00	2,872.77	2,207.49	1,808.99	1,543.87	1,354.97	1,213.71
1.25%	8,256.77	5,970.90	5,256.77	4,257.29	2,925.86	2,261.44	1,863.83	1,599.61	1,411.61	1,271.26
1.50%	8,308.75	6,023.10	5,309.12	4,309.99	2,979.57	2,316.22	1,919.69	1,656.58	1,469.69	1,330.43
1.75%	8,360.93	6,075.59	5,361.80	4,363.11	3,033.89	2,371.82	1,976.59	1,714.77	1,529.17	1,391.20
2.00%	8,413.32	6,128.37	5,414.82	4,416.65	3,088.84	2,428.24	2,034.50	1,774.17	1,590.06	1,453.56
2.25%	8,465.93	6,181.44	5,468.17	4,470.59	3,144.41	2,485.48	2,093.43	1,834.78	1,652.34	1,517.48
2.50%	8,518.73	6,234.80	5,521.84	4,524.96	3,200.59	2,543.53	2,153.36	1,896.58	1,715.98	1,582.94
2.75%	8,571.75	6,288.45	5,575.85	4,579.73	3,257.38	2,602.40	2,214.29	1,959.56	1,780.97	1,649.89
3.00%	8,624.97	6,342.38	5,630.19	4,634.92	3,314.79	2,662.07	2,276.21	2,023.70	1,847.28	1,718.33
3.25%	8,678.40	6,396.61	5,684.86	4,690.51	3,372.81	2,722.54	2,339.12	2,088.99	1,914.90	1,788.20
3.50%	8,732.04	6,451.13	5,739.86	4,746.52	3,431.44	2,783.81	2,402.99	2,155.41	1,983.80	1,859.48
3.75%	8,785.88	6,505.93	5,795.19	4,802.94	3,490.67	2,845.86	2,467.83	2,222.95	2,053.94	1,932.12
4.00%	8,839.93	6,561.03	5,850.85	4,859.77	3,550.50	2,908.71	2,533.62	2,291.59	2,125.32	2,006.10
4.25%	8,894.19	6,616.41	5,906.84	4,917.00	3,610.94	2,972.33	2,600.34	2,361.31	2,197.89	2,081.38
4.50%	8,948.65	6,672.08	5,963.15	4,974.64	3,671.97	3,036.72	2,668.00	2,432.09	2,271.63	2,157.90
4.75%	9,003.32	6,728.03	6,019.79	5,032.69	3,733.59	3,101.87	2,736.56	2,503.91	2,346.51	2,235.64
5.00%	9,058.19	6,784.28	6,076.76	5,091.14	3,795.81	3,167.79	2,806.03	2,576.74	2,422.50	2,314.54
5.25%	9,113.27	6,840.81	6,134.06	5,150.00	3,858.61	3,234.45	2,876.39	2,650.58	2,499.57	2,394.58
5.50%	9,168.56	6,897.62	6,191.67	5,209.26	3,922.00	3,301.86	2,947.62	2,725.39	2,577.68	2,475.70
5.75%	9,224.05	6,954.72	6,249.62	5,268.92	3,985.97	3,370.00	3,019.71	2,801.15	2,656.80	2,557.86
6.00%	9,279.74	7,012.11	6,307.89	5,328.98	4,050.51	3,438.87	3,092.65	2,877.84	2,736.91	2,641.03
6.25%	9,335.65	7,069.78	6,366.48	5,389.44	4,115.63	3,508.46	3,166.41	2,955.44	2,817.97	2,725.15
6.50%	9,391.75	7,127.73	6,425.39	5,450.30	4,181.32	3,578.75	3,240.99	3,033.93	2,899.94	2,810.19
6.75%	9,448.06	7,185.97	6,484.63	5,511.56	4,247.57	3,649.75	3,316.38	3,113.27	2,982.80	2,896.11
7.00%	9,504.58	7,244.49	6,544.18	5,573.21	4,314.38	3,721.43	3,392.54	3,193.45	3,066.51	2,982.87
7.25%	9,561.29	7,303.29	6,604.06	5,635.25	4,381.74	3,793.80	3,469.47	3,274.45	3,151.04	3,070.43
7.50%	9,618.22	7,362.37	6,664.26	5,697.68	4,449.66	3,866.85	3,547.16	3,356.23	3,236.36	3,158.74
7.75%	9,675.34	7,421.74	6,724.77	5,760.51	4,518.12	3,940.55	3,625.58	3,438.78	3,322.44	3,247.78
8.00%	9,732.67	7,481.38	6,785.61	5,823.72	4,587.13	4,014.91	3,704.72	3,522.07	3,409.25	3,337.50
8.25%	9,790.20	7,541.31	6,846.76	5,887.33	4,656.67	4,089.92	3,784.56	3,606.08	3,496.76	3,427.87
8.50%	9,847.94	7,601.51	6,908.22	5,951.31	4,726.75	4,165.55	3,865.09	3,690.78	3,584.93	3,518.85
8.75%	9,905.87	7,662.00	6,970.00	6,015.68	4,797.35	4,241.81	3,946.29	3,776.16	3,673.74	3,610.42
9.00%	9,964.01	7,722.76	7,032.10	6,080.44	4,868.48	4,318.68	4,028.14	3,862.19	3,763.17	3,702.54
9.25%	10,022.35	7,783.80	7,094.51	6,145.57	4,940.12	4,396.16	4,110.63	3,948.84	3,853.17	3,795.17
9.50%	10,080.89	7,845.11	7,157.23	6,211.08	5,012.28	4,474.23	4,193.74	4,036.10	3,943.74	3,888.30
9.75%	10,139.64	7,906.70	7,220.26	6,276.97	5,084.94	4,552.88	4,277.46	4,123.94	4,034.83	3,981.88
10.00%	10,198.58	7,968.57	7,283.60	6,343.24	5,158.10	4,632.10	4,361.76	4,212.34	4,126.43	4,075.90
10.25%	10,257.73	8,030.71	7,347.25	6,409.87	5,231.76	4,711.89	4,446.64	4,301.29	4,218.51	4,170.33
10.50%	10,317.07	8,093.12	7,411.21	6,476.88	5,305.91	4,792.22	4,532.07	4,390.75	4,311.04	4,265.14
10.75%	10,376.62	8,155.81	7,475.47	6,544.26	5,380.55	4,873.10	4,618.05	4,480.71	4,404.01	4,360.31

	5	7	8	10	15	20	25	30	35	40
11.00%	10,436.36	8,218.77	7,540.04	6,612.00	5,455.67	4,954.50	4,704.54	4,571.15	4,497.40	4,455.81
11.25%	10,496.31	8,282.00	7,604.92	6,680.11	5,531.25	5,036.43	4,791.55	4,662.05	4,591.17	4,551.64
11.50%	10,556.45	8,345.50	7,670.10	6,748.58	5,607.31	5,118.86	4,879.05	4,753.40	4,685.32	4,647.75
11.75%	10,616.79	8,409.27	7,735.58	6,817.41	5,683.83	5,201.79	4,967.03	4,845.17	4,779.81	4,744.15
12.00%	10,677.33	8,473.31	7,801.36	6,886.61	5,760.81	5,285.21	5,055.48	4,937.34	4,874.64	4,840.80
12.25%	10,738.07	8,537.62	7,867.45	6,956.15	5,838.23	5,369.11	5,144.37	5,029.90	4,969.78	4,937.69
12.50%	10,799.01	8,602.19	7,933.83	7,026.06	5,916.11	5,453.47	5,233.70	5,122.84	5,065.22	5,034.81
12.75%	10,860.14	8,667.04	8,000.51	7,096.31	5,994.42	5,538.30	5,323.45	5,216.13	5,160.94	5,132.14
13.00%	10,921.48	8,732.14	8,067.48	7,166.92	6,073.16	5,623.56	5,413.61	5,309.76	5,256.93	5,229.67
13.25%	10,983.00	8,797.51	8,134.75	7,237.87	6,152.33	5,709.27	5,504.16	5,403.71	5,353.16	5,327.38
13.50%	11,044.73	8,863.15	8,202.32	7,309.17	6,231.93	5,795.40	5,595.10	5,497.98	5,449.63	5,425.25
13.75%	11,106.65	8,929.05	8,270.17	7,380.81	6,311.94	5,881.95	5,686.40	5,592.54	5,546.33	5,523.29
14.00%	11,168.76	8,995.21	8,338.32	7,452.79	6,392.36	5,968.90	5,778.05	5,687.38	5,643.23	5,621.47
14.25%	11,231.07	9,061.63	8,406.76	7,525.11	6,473.18	6,056.25	5,870.05	5,782.50	5,740.33	5,719.79
14.50%	11,293.57	9,128.31	8,475.48	7,597.77	6,554.40	6,143.99	5,962.38	5,877.87	5,837.62	5,818.24
14.75%	11,356.27	9,195.25	8,544.50	7,670.76	6,636.02	6,232.11	6,055.03	5,973.48	5,935.08	5,916.80
15.00%	11,419.17	9,262.44	8,613.79	7,744.08	6,718.02	6,320.59	6,147.99	6,069.33	6,032.70	6,015.48
15.25%	11,482.25	9,329.90	8,683.38	7,817.73	6,800.40	6,409.43	6,241.24	6,165.40	6,130.48	6,114.25
15.50%	11,545.53	9,397.61	8,753.24	7,891.71	6,883.15	6,498.63	6,334.78	6,261.68	6,228.41	6,213.12
15.75%	11,609.00	9,465.57	8,823.39	7,966.01	6,966.28	6,588.16	6,428.59	6,358.16	6,326.47	6,312.08
16.00%	11,672.67	9,533.79	8,893.82	8,040.63	7,049.76	6,678.03	6,522.67	6,454.83	6,424.65	6,411.11
16.25%	11,736.52	9,602.26	8,964.52	8,115.57	7,133.61	6,768.22	6,617.00	6,551.69	6,522.96	6,510.22
16.50%	11,800.57	9,670.99	9,035.51	8,190.83	7,217.80	6,858.72	6,711.57	6,648.71	6,621.38	6,609.40
16.75%	11,864.81	9,739.96	9,106.76	8,266.40	7,302.34	6,949.53	6,806.39	6,745.90	6,719.90	6,708.65
17.00%	11,929.24	9,809.19	9,178.30	8,342.29	7,387.22	7,040.64	6,901.42	6,843.24	6,818.53	6,807.95
17.25%	11,993.85	9,878.66	9,250.10	8,418.48	7,472.43	7,132.04	6,996.68	6,940.73	6,917.24	6,907.31
17.50%	12,058.66	9,948.38	9,322.18	8,494.98	7,557.98	7,223.72	7,092.14	7,038.36	7,016.04	7,006.72
17.75%	12,123.66	10,018.35	9,394.53	8,571.78	7,643.84	7,315.68	7,187.81	7,136.12	7,114.92	7,106.18
18.00%	12,188.85	10,088.56	9,467.14	8,648.89	7,730.02	7,407.90	7,283.66	7,234.01	7,213.88	7,205.68
18.25%	12,254.22	10,159.02	9,540.02	8,726.29	7,816.51	7,500.37	7,379.71	7,332.02	7,312.91	7,305.21
18.50%	12,319.78	10,229.72	9,613.17	8,803.99	7,903.31	7,593.10	7,475.92	7,430.13	7,412.00	7,404.79
18.75%	12,385.53	10,300.66	9,686.58	8,881.99	7,990.41	7,686.08	7,572.31	7,528.36	7,511.16	7,504.40
19.00%	12,451.46	10,371.85	9,760.26	8,960.27	8,077.80	7,779.29	7,668.86	7,626.68	7,610.37	7,604.04
19.25%	12,517.59	10,443.27	9,834.19	9,038.85	8,165.49	7,872.73	7,765.57	7,725.10	7,709.64	7,703.71
19.50%	12,583.89	10,514.94	9,908.39	9,117.71	8,253.46	7,966.39	7,862.43	7,823.62	7,808.96	7,803.40
19.75%	12,650.39	10,586.84	9,982.83	9,196.85	8,341.70	8,060.27	7,959.43	7,922.21	7,908.33	7,903.12
20.00%	12,717.06	10,658.98	10,057.54	9,276.27	8,430.22	8,154.36	8,056.57	8,020.89	8,007.74	8,002.87
20.25%	12,783.93	10,731.35	10,132.50	9,355.97	8,519.01	8,248.65	8,153.84	8,119.64	8,107.19	8,102.63
20.50%	12,850.97	10,803.96	10,207.71	9,435.95	8,608.06	8,343.14	8,251.23	8,218.47	8,206.67	8,202.41
20.75%	12,918.20	10,876.80	10,283.17	9,516.20	8,697.38	8,437.82	8,348.75	8,317.36	8,306.20	8,302.21

	5	7	8	10	15	20	25	30	35	40
1.00%	8,290.47	5,980.65	5,258.96	4,248.80	2,902.70	2,230.49	1,827.83	1,559.95	1,369.09	1,226.35
1.25%	8,342.78	6,033.10	5,311.53	4,301.63	2,956.34	2,285.00	1,883.24	1,616.27	1,426.32	1,284.50
1.50%	8,395.30	6,085.84	5,364.42	4,354.89	3,010.60	2,340.35	1,939.69	1,673.83	1,484.99	1,344.29
1.75%	8,448.02	6,138.88	5,417.66	4,408.56	3,065.50	2,396.52	1,997.18	1,732.63	1,545.10	1,405.70
2.00%	8,500.96	6,192.21	5,471.22	4,462.65	3,121.02	2,453.53	2,055.69	1,792.65	1,606.62	1,468.70
2.25%	8,554.11	6,245.83	5,525.13	4,517.16	3,177.16	2,511.37	2,115.23	1,853.89	1,669.55	1,533.29
2.50%	8,607.47	6,299.74	5,579.36	4,572.09	3,233.93	2,570.03	2,175.79	1,916.34	1,733.85	1,599.42
2.75%	8,661.04	6,353.95	5,633.94	4,627.43	3,291.31	2,629.51	2,237.36	1,979.97	1,799.52	1,667.08
3.00%	8,714.81	6,408.45	5,688.84	4,683.20	3,349.32	2,689.80	2,299.92	2,044.78	1,866.52	1,736.22
3.25%	8,768.80	6,463.24	5,744.08	4,739.37	3,407.94	2,750.90	2,363.48	2,110.75	1,934.85	1,806.82
3.50%	8,823.00	6,518.33	5,799.66	4,795.96	3,467.18	2,812.80	2,428.02	2,177.87	2,004.46	1,878.85
3.75%	8,877.40	6,573.70	5,855.56	4,852.97	3,527.03	2,875.51	2,493.54	2,246.11	2,075.34	1,952.25
4.00%	8,932.01	6,629.37	5,911.80	4,910.39	3,587.49	2,939.00	2,560.01	2,315.46	2,147.46	2,027.00
4.25%	8,986.83	6,685.33	5,968.37	4,968.22	3,648.55	3,003.29	2,627.43	2,385.91	2,220.79	2,103.06
4.50%	9,041.86	6,741.58	6,025.27	5,026.46	3,710.22	3,068.35	2,695.79	2,457.42	2,295.30	2,180.38
4.75%	9,097.10	6,798.12	6,082.50	5,085.12	3,772.48	3,134.18	2,765.07	2,529.99	2,370.96	2,258.93
5.00%	9,152.55	6,854.95	6,140.06	5,144.18	3,835.35	3,200.79	2,835.26	2,603.58	2,447.74	2,338.65
5.25%	9,208.20	6,912.06	6,197.95	5,203.65	3,898.81	3,268.14	2,906.35	2,678.19	2,525.60	2,419.52
5.50%	9,264.06	6,969.47	6,256.17	5,263.52	3,962.85	3,336.25	2,978.32	2,753.78	2,604.53	2,501.49
5.75%	9,320.13	7,027.17	6,314.72	5,323.81	4,027.49	3,405.11	3,051.17	2,830.33	2,684.48	2,584.51
6.00%	9,376.41	7,085.15	6,373.59	5,384.49	4,092.71	3,474.69	3,124.86	2,907.82	2,765.42	2,668.54
6.25%	9,432.89	7,143.42	6,432.80	5,445.58	4,158.50	3,545.00	3,199.40	2,986.23	2,847.32	2,753.54
6.50%	9,489.58	7,201.98	6,492.32	5,507.08	4,224.87	3,616.03	3,274.75	3,065.53	2,930.15	2,839.47
6.75%	9,546.48	7,260.82	6,552.18	5,568.97	4,291.81	3,687.77	3,350.92	3,145.70	3,013.87	2,926.28
7.00%	9,603.58	7,319.95	6,612.35	5,631.26	4,359.32	3,760.20	3,427.88	3,226.72	3,098.45	3,013.94
7.25%	9,660.89	7,379.36	6,672.85	5,693.95	4,427.38	3,833.32	3,505.61	3,308.55	3,183.87	3,102.41
7.50%	9,718.41	7,439.06	6,733.68	5,757.04	4,496.01	3,907.13	3,584.11	3,391.19	3,270.08	3,191.64
7.75%	9,776.13	7,499.05	6,794.82	5,820.52	4,565.19	3,981.60	3,663.34	3,474.60	3,357.05	3,281.61
8.00%	9,834.05	7,559.31	6,856.29	5,884.39	4,634.91	4,056.73	3,743.31	3,558.76	3,444.77	3,372.26
8.25%	9,892.18	7,619.86	6,918.08	5,948.65	4,705.18	4,132.52	3,823.98	3,643.64	3,533.18	3,463.57
8.50%	9,950.52	7,680.70	6,980.18	6,013.31	4,775.99	4,208.94	3,905.35	3,729.23	3,622.27	3,555.51
8.75%	10,009.06	7,741.81	7,042.61	6,078.35	4,847.33	4,286.00	3,987.40	3,815.50	3,712.01	3,648.03
9.00%	10,067.80	7,803.20	7,105.35	6,143.78	4,919.19	4,363.67	4,070.10	3,902.42	3,802.37	3,741.10
9.25%	10,126.75	7,864.88	7,168.41	6,209.59	4,991.58	4,441.95	4,153.45	3,989.98	3,893.31	3,834.70
9.50%	10,185.90	7,926.83	7,231.78	6,275.78	5,064.49	4,520.84	4,237.43	4,078.14	3,984.82	3,928.80
9.75%	10,245.26	7,989.06	7,295.47	6,342.36	5,137.91	4,600.31	4,322.02	4,166.90	4,076.86	4,023.36
10.00%	10,304.82	8,051.57	7,359.47	6,409.31	5,211.83	4,680.35	4,407.20	4,256.22	4,169.41	4,118.36
10.25%	10,364.58	8,114.36	7,423.78	6,476.64	5,286.26	4,760.97	4,492.96	4,346.09	4,262.45	4,213.77
10.50%	10,424.54	8,177.43	7,488.41	6,544.35	5,361.18	4,842.14	4,579.28	4,436.49	4,355.95	4,309.57
10.75%	10,484.71	8,240.77	7,553.34	6,612.43	5,436.60	4,923.86	4,666.15	4,527.38	4,449.89	4,405.73

$485,000　　11.00 - 20.75%　　5 - 40 Years

	5	7	8	10	15	20	25	30	35	40
11.00%	10,545.08	8,304.38	7,618.59	6,680.88	5,512.50	5,006.11	4,753.55	4,618.77	4,544.24	4,502.23
11.25%	10,605.64	8,368.27	7,684.14	6,749.69	5,588.87	5,088.89	4,841.46	4,710.62	4,639.00	4,599.05
11.50%	10,666.41	8,432.43	7,750.00	6,818.88	5,665.72	5,172.18	4,929.87	4,802.91	4,734.12	4,696.17
11.75%	10,727.39	8,496.87	7,816.16	6,888.43	5,743.04	5,255.98	5,018.77	4,895.64	4,829.60	4,793.57
12.00%	10,788.56	8,561.58	7,882.63	6,958.34	5,820.82	5,340.27	5,108.14	4,988.77	4,925.42	4,891.22
12.25%	10,849.93	8,626.55	7,949.40	7,028.61	5,899.05	5,425.04	5,197.96	5,082.30	5,021.55	4,989.13
12.50%	10,911.50	8,691.80	8,016.47	7,099.24	5,977.73	5,510.28	5,288.22	5,176.20	5,117.98	5,087.26
12.75%	10,973.27	8,757.32	8,083.85	7,170.23	6,056.86	5,595.99	5,378.90	5,270.46	5,214.70	5,185.60
13.00%	11,035.24	8,823.10	8,151.52	7,241.57	6,136.42	5,682.14	5,470.00	5,365.07	5,311.69	5,284.14
13.25%	11,097.41	8,889.15	8,219.49	7,313.26	6,216.42	5,768.74	5,561.50	5,460.00	5,408.92	5,382.87
13.50%	11,159.78	8,955.47	8,287.76	7,385.30	6,296.84	5,855.77	5,653.38	5,555.25	5,506.40	5,481.77
13.75%	11,222.34	9,022.06	8,356.32	7,457.69	6,377.69	5,943.22	5,745.63	5,650.80	5,604.10	5,580.82
14.00%	11,285.10	9,088.91	8,425.18	7,530.42	6,458.95	6,031.08	5,838.24	5,746.63	5,702.02	5,680.03
14.25%	11,348.06	9,156.02	8,494.33	7,603.50	6,540.61	6,119.34	5,931.20	5,842.73	5,800.13	5,779.37
14.50%	11,411.22	9,223.39	8,563.77	7,676.91	6,622.68	6,207.99	6,024.49	5,939.10	5,898.43	5,878.84
14.75%	11,474.57	9,291.03	8,633.50	7,750.66	6,705.14	6,297.02	6,118.10	6,035.71	5,996.90	5,978.44
15.00%	11,538.12	9,358.93	8,703.52	7,824.75	6,788.00	6,386.43	6,212.03	6,132.55	6,095.54	6,078.14
15.25%	11,601.86	9,427.08	8,773.83	7,899.16	6,871.24	6,476.20	6,306.25	6,229.62	6,194.34	6,177.94
15.50%	11,665.80	9,495.50	8,844.42	7,973.91	6,954.85	6,566.32	6,400.76	6,326.91	6,293.29	6,277.84
15.75%	11,729.93	9,564.17	8,915.30	8,048.99	7,038.84	6,656.79	6,495.55	6,424.39	6,392.37	6,377.83
16.00%	11,794.26	9,633.10	8,986.46	8,124.39	7,123.20	6,747.59	6,590.61	6,522.07	6,491.58	6,477.90
16.25%	11,858.78	9,702.29	9,057.90	8,200.11	7,207.92	6,838.72	6,685.93	6,619.93	6,590.91	6,578.04
16.50%	11,923.49	9,771.73	9,129.63	8,276.15	7,292.99	6,930.17	6,781.49	6,717.97	6,690.35	6,678.25
16.75%	11,988.40	9,841.42	9,201.63	8,352.51	7,378.41	7,021.92	6,877.29	6,816.17	6,789.90	6,778.53
17.00%	12,053.50	9,911.37	9,273.91	8,429.19	7,464.17	7,113.98	6,973.31	6,914.53	6,889.55	6,878.87
17.25%	12,118.79	9,981.56	9,346.46	8,506.17	7,550.27	7,206.33	7,069.56	7,013.03	6,989.29	6,979.26
17.50%	12,184.27	10,052.01	9,419.29	8,583.47	7,636.70	7,298.97	7,166.02	7,111.68	7,089.13	7,079.71
17.75%	12,249.95	10,122.71	9,492.39	8,661.07	7,723.46	7,391.88	7,262.68	7,210.46	7,189.04	7,180.20
18.00%	12,315.81	10,193.65	9,565.76	8,738.98	7,810.54	7,485.06	7,359.54	7,309.36	7,289.03	7,280.73
18.25%	12,381.87	10,264.84	9,639.40	8,817.19	7,897.94	7,578.50	7,456.58	7,408.39	7,389.09	7,381.31
18.50%	12,448.11	10,336.28	9,713.31	8,895.70	7,985.64	7,672.20	7,553.80	7,507.53	7,489.21	7,481.92
18.75%	12,514.55	10,407.96	9,787.48	8,974.51	8,073.64	7,766.14	7,651.19	7,606.78	7,589.40	7,582.57
19.00%	12,581.17	10,479.89	9,861.92	9,053.61	8,161.95	7,860.32	7,748.75	7,706.13	7,689.65	7,683.25
19.25%	12,647.98	10,552.06	9,936.63	9,133.00	8,250.55	7,954.73	7,846.46	7,805.57	7,789.95	7,783.96
19.50%	12,714.98	10,624.47	10,011.59	9,212.68	8,339.43	8,049.37	7,944.33	7,905.11	7,890.30	7,884.69
19.75%	12,782.16	10,697.12	10,086.82	9,292.65	8,428.60	8,144.23	8,042.34	8,004.74	7,990.70	7,985.45
20.00%	12,849.53	10,770.01	10,162.30	9,372.90	8,518.04	8,239.30	8,140.49	8,104.44	8,091.15	8,086.23
20.25%	12,917.09	10,843.13	10,238.04	9,453.43	8,607.75	8,334.57	8,238.77	8,204.22	8,191.64	8,187.03
20.50%	12,984.84	10,916.50	10,314.04	9,534.24	8,697.73	8,430.05	8,337.18	8,304.08	8,292.16	8,287.86
20.75%	13,052.77	10,990.10	10,390.29	9,615.33	8,787.97	8,525.71	8,435.72	8,404.00	8,392.72	8,388.70

	5	7	8	10	15	20	25	30	35	40
1.00%	8,375.94	6,042.31	5,313.18	4,292.60	2,932.62	2,253.48	1,846.68	1,576.03	1,383.20	1,238.99
1.25%	8,428.78	6,095.30	5,366.28	4,345.98	2,986.81	2,308.56	1,902.66	1,632.93	1,441.02	1,297.74
1.50%	8,481.85	6,148.58	5,419.73	4,399.78	3,041.64	2,364.47	1,959.69	1,691.09	1,500.30	1,358.15
1.75%	8,535.12	6,202.17	5,473.51	4,454.01	3,097.10	2,421.23	2,017.77	1,750.49	1,561.03	1,420.19
2.00%	8,588.60	6,256.04	5,527.63	4,508.66	3,153.19	2,478.83	2,076.89	1,811.14	1,623.19	1,483.85
2.25%	8,642.30	6,310.22	5,582.09	4,563.73	3,209.92	2,537.26	2,137.04	1,873.01	1,686.76	1,549.10
2.50%	8,696.21	6,364.69	5,636.88	4,619.23	3,267.27	2,596.52	2,198.22	1,936.09	1,751.73	1,615.91
2.75%	8,750.33	6,419.45	5,692.02	4,675.14	3,325.25	2,656.61	2,260.42	2,000.38	1,818.07	1,684.27
3.00%	8,804.66	6,474.52	5,747.49	4,731.48	3,383.85	2,717.53	2,323.64	2,065.86	1,885.77	1,754.12
3.25%	8,859.20	6,529.87	5,803.30	4,788.23	3,443.08	2,779.26	2,387.85	2,132.51	1,954.79	1,825.45
3.50%	8,913.96	6,585.53	5,859.45	4,845.41	3,502.92	2,841.80	2,453.06	2,200.32	2,025.12	1,898.22
3.75%	8,968.92	6,641.47	5,915.93	4,903.00	3,563.39	2,905.15	2,519.24	2,269.27	2,096.73	1,972.38
4.00%	9,024.10	6,697.72	5,972.74	4,961.01	3,624.47	2,969.30	2,586.40	2,339.33	2,169.60	2,047.90
4.25%	9,079.48	6,754.25	6,029.90	5,019.44	3,686.16	3,034.25	2,654.52	2,410.51	2,243.68	2,124.74
4.50%	9,135.08	6,811.08	6,087.38	5,078.28	3,748.47	3,099.98	2,723.58	2,482.76	2,318.96	2,202.86
4.75%	9,190.89	6,868.20	6,145.21	5,137.54	3,811.38	3,166.50	2,793.58	2,556.07	2,395.40	2,282.21
5.00%	9,246.90	6,925.62	6,203.36	5,197.21	3,874.89	3,233.78	2,864.49	2,630.43	2,472.97	2,362.76
5.25%	9,303.13	6,983.32	6,261.85	5,257.29	3,939.00	3,301.84	2,936.31	2,705.80	2,551.64	2,444.46
5.50%	9,359.57	7,041.32	6,320.67	5,317.79	4,003.71	3,370.65	3,009.03	2,782.17	2,631.38	2,527.27
5.75%	9,416.22	7,099.61	6,379.82	5,378.69	4,069.01	3,440.21	3,082.62	2,859.51	2,712.15	2,611.15
6.00%	9,473.07	7,158.19	6,439.30	5,440.00	4,134.90	3,510.51	3,157.08	2,937.80	2,793.93	2,696.05
6.25%	9,530.14	7,217.06	6,499.11	5,501.72	4,201.37	3,581.55	3,232.38	3,017.01	2,876.67	2,781.92
6.50%	9,587.41	7,276.22	6,559.25	5,563.85	4,268.43	3,653.31	3,308.52	3,097.13	2,960.36	2,868.74
6.75%	9,644.90	7,335.67	6,619.72	5,626.38	4,336.06	3,725.78	3,385.47	3,178.13	3,044.94	2,956.45
7.00%	9,702.59	7,395.41	6,680.52	5,689.32	4,404.26	3,798.96	3,463.22	3,259.98	3,130.40	3,045.01
7.25%	9,760.49	7,455.44	6,741.65	5,752.65	4,473.03	3,872.84	3,541.75	3,342.66	3,216.69	3,134.39
7.50%	9,818.59	7,515.76	6,803.10	5,816.39	4,542.36	3,947.41	3,621.06	3,426.15	3,303.79	3,224.55
7.75%	9,876.91	7,576.36	6,864.87	5,880.52	4,612.25	4,022.65	3,701.11	3,510.42	3,391.66	3,315.44
8.00%	9,935.43	7,637.25	6,926.97	5,945.05	4,682.70	4,098.56	3,781.90	3,595.45	3,480.28	3,407.03
8.25%	9,994.16	7,698.42	6,989.40	6,009.98	4,753.69	4,175.12	3,863.41	3,681.21	3,569.61	3,499.28
8.50%	10,053.10	7,759.88	7,052.14	6,075.30	4,825.22	4,252.33	3,945.61	3,767.68	3,659.62	3,592.16
8.75%	10,112.24	7,821.62	7,115.21	6,141.01	4,897.30	4,330.18	4,028.50	3,854.83	3,750.28	3,685.64
9.00%	10,171.59	7,883.65	7,178.60	6,207.11	4,969.91	4,408.66	4,112.06	3,942.65	3,841.57	3,779.67
9.25%	10,231.15	7,945.96	7,242.31	6,273.60	5,043.04	4,487.75	4,196.27	4,031.11	3,933.45	3,874.24
9.50%	10,290.91	8,008.55	7,306.33	6,340.48	5,116.70	4,567.44	4,281.11	4,120.19	4,025.90	3,969.30
9.75%	10,350.88	8,071.43	7,370.68	6,407.74	5,190.88	4,647.73	4,366.57	4,209.86	4,118.89	4,064.84
10.00%	10,411.05	8,134.58	7,435.34	6,475.39	5,265.57	4,728.61	4,452.63	4,300.10	4,212.39	4,160.81
10.25%	10,471.43	8,198.02	7,500.32	6,543.41	5,340.76	4,810.05	4,539.28	4,390.90	4,306.39	4,257.21
10.50%	10,532.01	8,261.73	7,565.61	6,611.81	5,416.45	4,892.06	4,626.49	4,482.22	4,400.86	4,353.99
10.75%	10,592.80	8,325.72	7,631.21	6,680.60	5,492.65	4,974.62	4,714.25	4,574.06	4,495.76	4,451.15

$490,000   11.00 - 20.75%   5 - 40 Years

	5	7	8	10	15	20	25	30	35	40
11.00%	10,653.79	8,389.99	7,697.13	6,749.75	5,569.32	5,057.72	4,802.55	4,666.38	4,591.09	4,548.64
11.25%	10,714.98	8,454.54	7,763.36	6,819.28	5,646.49	5,141.35	4,891.37	4,759.18	4,686.82	4,646.46
11.50%	10,776.38	8,519.37	7,829.89	6,889.18	5,724.13	5,225.51	4,980.70	4,852.43	4,782.93	4,744.58
11.75%	10,837.98	8,584.47	7,896.74	6,959.44	5,802.24	5,310.16	5,070.51	4,946.11	4,879.39	4,842.98
12.00%	10,899.78	8,649.84	7,963.89	7,030.08	5,880.82	5,395.32	5,160.80	5,040.20	4,976.19	4,941.65
12.25%	10,961.78	8,715.49	8,031.35	7,101.07	5,959.86	5,480.97	5,251.54	5,134.69	5,073.32	5,040.56
12.50%	11,023.99	8,781.41	8,099.12	7,172.43	6,039.36	5,567.09	5,342.74	5,229.56	5,170.75	5,139.71
12.75%	11,086.40	8,847.60	8,167.18	7,244.15	6,119.30	5,653.68	5,434.36	5,324.80	5,268.46	5,239.06
13.00%	11,149.01	8,914.06	8,235.55	7,316.23	6,199.69	5,740.72	5,526.39	5,420.38	5,366.45	5,338.62
13.25%	11,211.82	8,980.80	8,304.23	7,388.66	6,280.51	5,828.21	5,618.83	5,516.29	5,464.69	5,438.36
13.50%	11,274.82	9,047.80	8,373.20	7,461.44	6,361.76	5,916.14	5,711.66	5,612.52	5,563.17	5,538.28
13.75%	11,338.03	9,115.07	8,442.47	7,534.57	6,443.44	6,004.49	5,804.86	5,709.05	5,661.88	5,638.36
14.00%	11,401.44	9,182.61	8,512.04	7,608.06	6,525.53	6,093.25	5,898.43	5,805.87	5,760.80	5,738.59
14.25%	11,465.05	9,250.41	8,581.90	7,681.88	6,608.04	6,182.42	5,992.34	5,902.97	5,859.92	5,838.95
14.50%	11,528.86	9,318.48	8,652.06	7,756.05	6,690.95	6,271.99	6,086.60	6,000.32	5,959.24	5,939.45
14.75%	11,592.86	9,386.81	8,722.51	7,830.56	6,774.27	6,361.94	6,181.18	6,097.93	6,058.73	6,040.07
15.00%	11,657.07	9,455.41	8,793.25	7,905.41	6,857.98	6,452.27	6,276.07	6,195.78	6,158.39	6,140.80
15.25%	11,721.47	9,524.27	8,864.28	7,980.60	6,942.07	6,542.96	6,371.27	6,293.85	6,258.20	6,241.63
15.50%	11,786.06	9,593.39	8,935.60	8,056.12	7,026.55	6,634.02	6,466.75	6,392.13	6,358.16	6,342.56
15.75%	11,850.86	9,662.77	9,007.21	8,131.97	7,111.41	6,725.42	6,562.52	6,490.62	6,458.27	6,443.58
16.00%	11,915.85	9,732.41	9,079.11	8,208.14	7,196.63	6,817.15	6,658.56	6,589.31	6,558.50	6,544.68
16.25%	11,981.03	9,802.31	9,151.28	8,284.65	7,282.22	6,909.22	6,754.85	6,688.18	6,658.85	6,645.85
16.50%	12,046.42	9,872.47	9,223.75	8,361.47	7,368.17	7,001.61	6,851.40	6,787.23	6,759.32	6,747.10
16.75%	12,111.99	9,942.88	9,296.49	8,438.62	7,454.47	7,094.32	6,948.19	6,886.44	6,859.90	6,848.41
17.00%	12,177.76	10,013.54	9,369.51	8,516.08	7,541.12	7,187.32	7,045.20	6,985.81	6,960.58	6,949.79
17.25%	12,243.73	10,084.47	9,442.81	8,593.87	7,628.11	7,280.63	7,142.44	7,085.33	7,061.35	7,051.21
17.50%	12,309.88	10,155.64	9,516.39	8,671.96	7,715.43	7,374.22	7,239.90	7,184.99	7,162.21	7,152.69
17.75%	12,376.24	10,227.06	9,590.25	8,750.36	7,803.09	7,468.09	7,337.55	7,284.79	7,263.15	7,254.22
18.00%	12,442.78	10,298.74	9,664.37	8,829.07	7,891.06	7,562.23	7,435.41	7,384.72	7,364.17	7,355.79
18.25%	12,509.52	10,370.67	9,738.78	8,908.09	7,979.36	7,656.63	7,533.45	7,484.77	7,465.26	7,457.41
18.50%	12,576.44	10,442.84	9,813.45	8,987.41	8,067.96	7,751.29	7,631.67	7,584.93	7,566.42	7,559.06
18.75%	12,643.56	10,515.26	9,888.39	9,067.03	8,156.88	7,846.20	7,730.07	7,685.20	7,667.64	7,660.74
19.00%	12,710.87	10,587.93	9,963.59	9,146.95	8,246.09	7,941.36	7,828.63	7,785.57	7,768.92	7,762.46
19.25%	12,778.37	10,660.84	10,039.07	9,227.16	8,335.60	8,036.74	7,927.35	7,886.04	7,870.26	7,864.20
19.50%	12,846.06	10,734.00	10,114.81	9,307.66	8,425.40	8,132.36	8,026.23	7,986.61	7,971.65	7,965.98
19.75%	12,913.94	10,807.40	10,190.81	9,388.45	8,515.49	8,228.19	8,125.25	8,087.26	8,073.08	8,067.77
20.00%	12,982.00	10,881.04	10,267.07	9,469.53	8,605.85	8,324.24	8,224.41	8,187.99	8,174.56	8,169.59
20.25%	13,050.26	10,954.92	10,343.59	9,550.89	8,696.49	8,420.50	8,323.71	8,288.80	8,276.09	8,271.44
20.50%	13,118.70	11,029.04	10,420.37	9,632.53	8,787.40	8,516.96	8,423.13	8,389.69	8,377.65	8,373.30
20.75%	13,187.33	11,103.40	10,497.40	9,714.45	8,878.57	8,613.61	8,522.68	8,490.64	8,479.24	8,475.18

$495,000   1.00 - 10.75%   5 - 40 Years

	5	7	8	10	15	20	25	30	35	40
1.00%	8,461.40	6,103.97	5,367.40	4,336.40	2,962.55	2,276.48	1,865.52	1,592.12	1,397.31	1,251.64
1.25%	8,514.79	6,157.50	5,421.04	4,390.33	3,017.29	2,332.11	1,922.07	1,649.60	1,455.73	1,310.98
1.50%	8,568.39	6,211.32	5,475.04	4,444.68	3,072.68	2,388.60	1,979.68	1,708.35	1,515.61	1,372.00
1.75%	8,622.21	6,265.45	5,529.36	4,499.46	3,128.70	2,445.94	2,038.36	1,768.36	1,576.96	1,434.68
2.00%	8,676.24	6,319.88	5,584.03	4,554.67	3,185.37	2,504.12	2,098.08	1,829.62	1,639.75	1,498.99
2.25%	8,730.49	6,374.61	5,639.05	4,610.30	3,242.67	2,563.15	2,158.85	1,892.12	1,703.97	1,564.90
2.50%	8,784.94	6,429.63	5,694.40	4,666.36	3,300.61	2,623.02	2,220.65	1,955.85	1,769.60	1,632.40
2.75%	8,839.62	6,484.96	5,750.10	4,722.85	3,359.18	2,683.72	2,283.49	2,020.79	1,836.62	1,701.45
3.00%	8,894.50	6,540.58	5,806.14	4,779.76	3,418.38	2,745.26	2,347.35	2,086.94	1,905.01	1,772.02
3.25%	8,949.60	6,596.51	5,862.52	4,837.09	3,478.21	2,807.62	2,412.22	2,154.27	1,974.74	1,844.08
3.50%	9,004.91	6,652.73	5,919.24	4,894.85	3,538.67	2,870.80	2,478.09	2,222.77	2,045.79	1,917.59
3.75%	9,060.44	6,709.24	5,976.29	4,953.03	3,599.75	2,934.80	2,544.95	2,292.42	2,118.13	1,992.50
4.00%	9,116.18	6,766.06	6,033.69	5,011.63	3,661.46	2,999.60	2,612.79	2,363.21	2,191.73	2,068.80
4.25%	9,172.13	6,823.17	6,091.43	5,070.66	3,723.78	3,065.21	2,681.60	2,435.10	2,266.58	2,146.42
4.50%	9,228.29	6,880.58	6,149.50	5,130.10	3,786.72	3,131.61	2,751.37	2,508.09	2,342.62	2,225.34
4.75%	9,284.67	6,938.28	6,207.91	5,189.96	3,850.27	3,198.81	2,822.08	2,582.15	2,419.84	2,305.50
5.00%	9,341.26	6,996.28	6,266.66	5,250.24	3,914.43	3,266.78	2,893.72	2,657.27	2,498.20	2,386.87
5.25%	9,398.06	7,054.58	6,325.74	5,310.94	3,979.19	3,335.53	2,966.28	2,733.41	2,577.68	2,469.41
5.50%	9,455.08	7,113.17	6,385.16	5,372.05	4,044.56	3,405.04	3,039.73	2,810.56	2,658.23	2,553.06
5.75%	9,512.30	7,172.06	6,444.92	5,433.58	4,110.53	3,475.31	3,114.08	2,888.69	2,739.83	2,637.79
6.00%	9,569.74	7,231.23	6,505.01	5,495.51	4,177.09	3,546.33	3,189.29	2,967.78	2,822.44	2,723.56
6.25%	9,627.38	7,290.71	6,565.43	5,557.86	4,244.24	3,618.09	3,265.36	3,047.80	2,906.03	2,810.31
6.50%	9,685.24	7,350.47	6,626.19	5,620.62	4,311.98	3,690.59	3,342.28	3,128.74	2,990.56	2,898.01
6.75%	9,743.31	7,410.53	6,687.27	5,683.79	4,380.30	3,763.80	3,420.01	3,210.56	3,076.01	2,986.62
7.00%	9,801.59	7,470.88	6,748.69	5,747.37	4,449.20	3,837.73	3,498.56	3,293.25	3,162.34	3,076.08
7.25%	9,860.08	7,531.52	6,810.44	5,811.35	4,518.67	3,912.36	3,577.89	3,376.77	3,249.51	3,166.38
7.50%	9,918.78	7,592.45	6,872.52	5,875.74	4,588.71	3,987.69	3,658.01	3,461.11	3,337.50	3,257.45
7.75%	9,977.70	7,653.67	6,934.92	5,940.53	4,659.31	4,063.70	3,738.88	3,546.24	3,426.27	3,349.27
8.00%	10,036.82	7,715.18	6,997.66	6,005.72	4,730.48	4,140.38	3,820.49	3,632.13	3,515.79	3,441.79
8.25%	10,096.14	7,776.97	7,060.72	6,071.30	4,802.19	4,217.72	3,902.83	3,718.77	3,606.03	3,534.99
8.50%	10,155.68	7,839.06	7,124.10	6,137.29	4,874.46	4,295.73	3,985.87	3,806.12	3,696.96	3,628.82
8.75%	10,215.43	7,901.43	7,187.82	6,203.67	4,947.27	4,374.37	4,069.61	3,894.17	3,788.55	3,723.24
9.00%	10,275.39	7,964.09	7,251.85	6,270.45	5,020.62	4,453.64	4,154.02	3,982.88	3,880.77	3,818.24
9.25%	10,335.55	8,027.04	7,316.21	6,337.62	5,094.50	4,533.54	4,239.09	4,072.24	3,973.58	3,913.77
9.50%	10,395.92	8,090.27	7,380.89	6,405.18	5,168.91	4,614.05	4,324.80	4,162.23	4,066.98	4,009.80
9.75%	10,456.50	8,153.79	7,445.89	6,473.13	5,243.85	4,695.16	4,411.13	4,252.81	4,160.92	4,106.31
10.00%	10,517.29	8,217.59	7,511.21	6,541.46	5,319.30	4,776.86	4,498.07	4,343.98	4,255.38	4,203.27
10.25%	10,578.28	8,281.67	7,576.85	6,610.18	5,395.26	4,859.13	4,585.60	4,435.70	4,350.34	4,300.65
10.50%	10,639.48	8,346.03	7,642.81	6,679.28	5,471.72	4,941.98	4,673.70	4,527.96	4,445.76	4,398.42
10.75%	10,700.89	8,410.68	7,709.08	6,748.76	5,548.69	5,025.38	4,762.36	4,620.73	4,541.64	4,496.57

$495,000   11.00 - 20.75%   5 - 40 Years

	5	7	8	10	15	20	25	30	35	40
11.00%	10,762.50	8,475.61	7,775.67	6,818.63	5,626.15	5,109.33	4,851.56	4,714.00	4,637.94	4,595.06
11.25%	10,824.32	8,540.81	7,842.57	6,888.86	5,704.11	5,193.82	4,941.29	4,807.74	4,734.64	4,693.87
11.50%	10,886.34	8,606.30	7,909.79	6,959.47	5,782.54	5,278.83	5,031.52	4,901.94	4,831.73	4,793.00
11.75%	10,948.57	8,672.06	7,977.32	7,030.46	5,861.45	5,364.35	5,122.25	4,996.58	4,929.18	4,892.40
12.00%	11,011.00	8,738.10	8,045.16	7,101.81	5,940.83	5,450.38	5,213.46	5,091.63	5,026.97	4,992.07
12.25%	11,073.64	8,804.42	8,113.30	7,173.53	6,020.68	5,536.90	5,305.13	5,187.09	5,125.09	5,092.00
12.50%	11,136.48	8,871.01	8,181.76	7,245.62	6,100.98	5,623.90	5,397.25	5,282.93	5,223.51	5,192.15
12.75%	11,199.52	8,937.88	8,250.52	7,318.07	6,181.74	5,711.37	5,489.81	5,379.13	5,322.22	5,292.52
13.00%	11,262.77	9,005.02	8,319.59	7,390.88	6,262.95	5,799.30	5,582.78	5,475.69	5,421.21	5,393.10
13.25%	11,326.22	9,072.44	8,388.96	7,464.05	6,344.60	5,887.68	5,676.17	5,572.58	5,520.45	5,493.86
13.50%	11,389.87	9,140.12	8,458.64	7,537.58	6,426.68	5,976.50	5,769.94	5,669.79	5,619.94	5,594.79
13.75%	11,453.73	9,208.08	8,528.62	7,611.46	6,509.19	6,065.76	5,864.10	5,767.31	5,719.65	5,695.89
14.00%	11,517.78	9,276.31	8,598.89	7,685.69	6,592.12	6,155.43	5,958.62	5,865.12	5,819.58	5,797.14
14.25%	11,582.04	9,344.80	8,669.47	7,760.27	6,675.47	6,245.51	6,053.49	5,963.20	5,919.72	5,898.54
14.50%	11,646.50	9,413.57	8,740.34	7,835.20	6,759.23	6,335.99	6,148.71	6,061.55	6,020.04	6,000.06
14.75%	11,711.16	9,482.60	8,811.51	7,910.47	6,843.39	6,426.86	6,244.25	6,160.15	6,120.55	6,101.70
15.00%	11,776.02	9,551.89	8,882.98	7,986.08	6,927.96	6,518.11	6,340.11	6,259.00	6,221.23	6,203.46
15.25%	11,841.07	9,621.46	8,954.73	8,062.03	7,012.91	6,609.73	6,436.28	6,358.07	6,322.06	6,305.32
15.50%	11,906.33	9,691.28	9,026.78	8,138.32	7,098.25	6,701.71	6,532.74	6,457.36	6,423.04	6,407.28
15.75%	11,971.78	9,761.37	9,099.12	8,214.94	7,183.97	6,794.04	6,629.48	6,556.85	6,524.17	6,509.33
16.00%	12,037.44	9,831.72	9,171.75	8,291.90	7,270.07	6,886.72	6,726.50	6,656.55	6,625.42	6,611.46
16.25%	12,103.29	9,902.33	9,244.66	8,369.18	7,356.53	6,979.73	6,823.78	6,756.43	6,726.80	6,713.67
16.50%	12,169.34	9,973.21	9,317.87	8,446.79	7,443.36	7,073.06	6,921.31	6,856.48	6,828.30	6,815.95
16.75%	12,235.58	10,044.34	9,391.35	8,524.73	7,530.54	7,166.71	7,019.09	6,956.71	6,929.90	6,918.29
17.00%	12,302.03	10,115.72	9,465.12	8,602.98	7,618.07	7,260.66	7,117.09	7,057.09	7,031.60	7,020.70
17.25%	12,368.66	10,187.37	9,539.17	8,681.56	7,705.95	7,354.92	7,215.32	7,157.63	7,133.40	7,123.17
17.50%	12,435.50	10,259.27	9,613.50	8,760.45	7,794.16	7,449.46	7,313.77	7,258.31	7,235.29	7,225.68
17.75%	12,502.52	10,331.42	9,688.11	8,839.65	7,882.71	7,544.29	7,412.43	7,359.13	7,337.27	7,328.24
18.00%	12,569.75	10,403.83	9,762.99	8,919.17	7,971.58	7,639.39	7,511.28	7,460.07	7,439.32	7,430.85
18.25%	12,637.16	10,476.49	9,838.15	8,998.99	8,060.78	7,734.76	7,610.32	7,561.14	7,541.44	7,533.50
18.50%	12,704.77	10,549.40	9,913.58	9,079.12	8,150.29	7,830.39	7,709.55	7,662.33	7,643.63	7,636.19
18.75%	12,772.58	10,622.56	9,989.29	9,159.55	8,240.11	7,926.27	7,808.95	7,763.62	7,745.88	7,738.91
19.00%	12,840.57	10,695.97	10,065.26	9,240.28	8,330.24	8,022.39	7,908.52	7,865.02	7,848.20	7,841.67
19.25%	12,908.76	10,769.63	10,141.51	9,321.31	8,420.66	8,118.75	8,008.25	7,966.51	7,950.57	7,944.45
19.50%	12,977.14	10,843.53	10,218.02	9,402.63	8,511.38	8,215.34	8,108.13	8,068.10	8,052.99	8,047.26
19.75%	13,045.71	10,917.68	10,294.79	9,484.25	8,602.38	8,312.15	8,208.16	8,169.78	8,155.46	8,150.10
20.00%	13,114.47	10,992.07	10,371.83	9,566.16	8,693.67	8,409.18	8,308.34	8,271.54	8,257.98	8,252.96
20.25%	13,183.42	11,066.70	10,449.14	9,648.35	8,785.23	8,506.42	8,408.65	8,373.38	8,360.54	8,355.84
20.50%	13,252.56	11,141.58	10,526.70	9,730.82	8,877.07	8,603.86	8,509.08	8,475.30	8,463.13	8,458.74
20.75%	13,321.89	11,216.70	10,604.52	9,813.58	8,969.17	8,701.50	8,609.65	8,577.28	8,565.77	8,561.66

	5	7	8	10	15	20	25	30	35	40
1.00%	8,546.87	6,165.62	5,421.61	4,380.21	2,992.47	2,299.47	1,884.36	1,608.20	1,411.43	1,264.28
1.25%	8,600.80	6,219.69	5,475.80	4,434.67	3,047.77	2,355.67	1,941.49	1,666.26	1,470.43	1,324.23
1.50%	8,654.94	6,274.06	5,530.33	4,489.57	3,103.72	2,412.73	1,999.68	1,725.60	1,530.92	1,385.86
1.75%	8,709.30	6,328.74	5,585.21	4,544.91	3,160.15	2,470.64	2,058.95	1,786.22	1,592.89	1,449.17
2.00%	8,763.88	6,383.72	5,640.44	4,600.67	3,217.54	2,529.42	2,119.27	1,848.10	1,656.31	1,514.13
2.25%	8,818.67	6,439.00	5,696.01	4,656.87	3,275.42	2,589.04	2,180.65	1,911.23	1,721.18	1,580.71
2.50%	8,873.68	6,494.58	5,751.92	4,713.50	3,333.95	2,649.51	2,243.08	1,975.60	1,787.48	1,648.89
2.75%	8,928.91	6,550.46	5,808.18	4,770.55	3,393.11	2,710.83	2,306.55	2,041.21	1,855.17	1,718.64
3.00%	8,984.35	6,606.65	5,864.79	4,828.04	3,452.91	2,772.99	2,371.06	2,108.02	1,924.25	1,789.92
3.25%	9,040.00	6,663.14	5,921.73	4,885.95	3,513.34	2,835.98	2,436.58	2,176.03	1,994.69	1,862.71
3.50%	9,095.87	6,719.93	5,979.03	4,944.29	3,574.41	2,899.80	2,503.12	2,245.22	2,066.45	1,936.95
3.75%	9,151.96	6,777.01	6,036.66	5,003.06	3,636.11	2,964.44	2,570.66	2,315.58	2,139.53	2,012.63
4.00%	9,208.26	6,834.40	6,094.64	5,062.26	3,698.44	3,029.90	2,639.18	2,387.08	2,213.87	2,089.69
4.25%	9,264.78	6,892.09	6,152.96	5,121.88	3,761.39	3,096.17	2,708.69	2,459.70	2,289.47	2,168.10
4.50%	9,321.51	6,950.08	6,211.62	5,181.92	3,824.97	3,163.25	2,779.16	2,533.43	2,366.28	2,247.81
4.75%	9,378.46	7,008.37	6,270.62	5,242.39	3,889.16	3,231.12	2,850.59	2,608.24	2,444.28	2,328.79
5.00%	9,435.62	7,066.95	6,329.96	5,303.28	3,953.97	3,299.78	2,922.95	2,684.11	2,523.44	2,410.98
5.25%	9,492.99	7,125.84	6,389.64	5,364.59	4,019.39	3,369.22	2,996.24	2,761.02	2,603.72	2,494.35
5.50%	9,550.58	7,185.02	6,449.66	5,426.31	4,085.42	3,439.44	3,070.44	2,838.95	2,685.08	2,578.85
5.75%	9,608.38	7,244.50	6,510.02	5,488.46	4,152.05	3,510.42	3,145.53	2,917.86	2,767.50	2,664.44
6.00%	9,666.40	7,304.28	6,570.72	5,551.03	4,219.28	3,582.16	3,221.51	2,997.75	2,850.95	2,751.07
6.25%	9,724.63	7,364.35	6,631.75	5,614.00	4,287.11	3,654.64	3,298.35	3,078.59	2,935.38	2,838.70
6.50%	9,783.07	7,424.72	6,693.12	5,677.40	4,355.54	3,727.87	3,376.04	3,160.34	3,020.77	2,927.28
6.75%	9,841.73	7,485.38	6,754.82	5,741.21	4,424.55	3,801.82	3,454.56	3,242.99	3,107.08	3,016.78
7.00%	9,900.60	7,546.34	6,816.86	5,805.42	4,494.14	3,876.49	3,533.90	3,326.51	3,194.28	3,107.16
7.25%	9,959.68	7,607.59	6,879.23	5,870.05	4,564.31	3,951.88	3,614.03	3,410.88	3,282.34	3,198.36
7.50%	10,018.97	7,669.14	6,941.94	5,935.09	4,635.06	4,027.97	3,694.96	3,496.07	3,371.21	3,290.35
7.75%	10,078.48	7,730.98	7,004.97	6,000.53	4,706.38	4,104.74	3,776.64	3,582.06	3,460.88	3,383.10
8.00%	10,138.20	7,793.11	7,068.34	6,066.38	4,778.26	4,182.20	3,859.08	3,668.82	3,551.30	3,476.56
8.25%	10,198.13	7,855.53	7,132.04	6,132.63	4,850.70	4,260.33	3,942.25	3,756.33	3,642.46	3,570.69
8.50%	10,258.27	7,918.24	7,196.06	6,199.28	4,923.70	4,339.12	4,026.14	3,844.57	3,734.30	3,665.47
8.75%	10,318.62	7,981.25	7,260.42	6,266.34	4,997.24	4,418.55	4,110.72	3,933.50	3,826.82	3,760.85
9.00%	10,379.18	8,044.54	7,325.10	6,333.79	5,071.33	4,498.63	4,195.98	4,023.11	3,919.96	3,856.81
9.25%	10,439.95	8,108.12	7,390.11	6,401.64	5,145.96	4,579.33	4,281.91	4,113.38	4,013.72	3,953.30
9.50%	10,500.93	8,171.99	7,455.44	6,469.88	5,221.12	4,660.66	4,368.48	4,204.27	4,108.06	4,050.31
9.75%	10,562.12	8,236.15	7,521.10	6,538.51	5,296.81	4,742.58	4,455.69	4,295.77	4,202.95	4,147.79
10.00%	10,623.52	8,300.59	7,587.08	6,607.54	5,373.03	4,825.11	4,543.50	4,387.86	4,298.36	4,245.73
10.25%	10,685.13	8,365.32	7,653.38	6,676.95	5,449.75	4,908.22	4,631.92	4,480.51	4,394.28	4,344.09
10.50%	10,746.95	8,430.34	7,720.01	6,746.75	5,526.99	4,991.90	4,720.91	4,573.70	4,490.67	4,442.85
10.75%	10,808.98	8,495.64	7,786.95	6,816.93	5,604.74	5,076.14	4,810.46	4,667.41	4,587.51	4,541.99

$500,000   11.00 - 20.75%   5 - 40 Years

	5	7	8	10	15	20	25	30	35	40
11.00%	10,871.21	8,561.22	7,854.21	6,887.50	5,682.98	5,160.94	4,900.57	4,761.62	4,684.79	4,641.47
11.25%	10,933.65	8,627.08	7,921.79	6,958.45	5,761.72	5,246.28	4,991.20	4,856.31	4,782.47	4,741.29
11.50%	10,996.30	8,693.23	7,989.69	7,029.77	5,840.95	5,332.15	5,082.34	4,951.46	4,880.54	4,841.41
11.75%	11,059.16	8,759.66	8,057.90	7,101.47	5,920.66	5,418.54	5,173.99	5,047.05	4,978.97	4,941.82
12.00%	11,122.22	8,826.37	8,126.42	7,173.55	6,000.84	5,505.43	5,266.12	5,143.06	5,077.75	5,042.50
12.25%	11,185.49	8,893.35	8,195.26	7,245.99	6,081.49	5,592.82	5,358.72	5,239.48	5,176.86	5,143.43
12.50%	11,248.97	8,960.62	8,264.40	7,318.81	6,162.61	5,680.70	5,451.77	5,336.29	5,276.27	5,244.60
12.75%	11,312.65	9,028.16	8,333.86	7,391.99	6,244.18	5,769.06	5,545.26	5,433.47	5,375.98	5,345.98
13.00%	11,376.54	9,095.98	8,403.63	7,465.54	6,326.21	5,857.88	5,639.18	5,531.00	5,475.97	5,447.57
13.25%	11,440.63	9,164.08	8,473.70	7,539.45	6,408.68	5,947.15	5,733.50	5,628.87	5,576.21	5,549.35
13.50%	11,504.92	9,232.45	8,544.08	7,613.71	6,491.59	6,036.87	5,828.22	5,727.06	5,676.70	5,651.31
13.75%	11,569.42	9,301.09	8,614.76	7,688.34	6,574.94	6,127.03	5,923.33	5,825.56	5,777.43	5,753.43
14.00%	11,634.13	9,370.01	8,685.75	7,763.32	6,658.71	6,217.60	6,018.81	5,924.36	5,878.37	5,855.70
14.25%	11,699.03	9,439.19	8,757.04	7,838.66	6,742.90	6,308.59	6,114.64	6,023.44	5,979.51	5,958.12
14.50%	11,764.14	9,508.65	8,828.63	7,914.34	6,827.50	6,399.99	6,210.81	6,122.78	6,080.85	6,060.66
14.75%	11,829.45	9,578.38	8,900.52	7,990.37	6,912.52	6,491.78	6,307.32	6,222.38	6,182.37	6,163.34
15.00%	11,894.97	9,648.38	8,972.70	8,066.75	6,997.94	6,583.95	6,404.15	6,322.22	6,284.07	6,266.12
15.25%	11,960.68	9,718.64	9,045.18	8,143.47	7,083.75	6,676.49	6,501.29	6,422.29	6,385.92	6,369.01
15.50%	12,026.60	9,789.17	9,117.96	8,220.53	7,169.95	6,769.40	6,598.73	6,522.58	6,487.92	6,472.00
15.75%	12,092.71	9,859.97	9,191.03	8,297.92	7,256.54	6,862.67	6,696.45	6,623.09	6,590.07	6,575.08
16.00%	12,159.03	9,931.03	9,264.39	8,375.66	7,343.50	6,956.28	6,794.44	6,723.78	6,692.35	6,678.24
16.25%	12,225.54	10,002.36	9,338.04	8,453.72	7,430.84	7,050.23	6,892.71	6,824.67	6,794.75	6,781.48
16.50%	12,292.26	10,073.94	9,411.99	8,532.11	7,518.54	7,144.50	6,991.22	6,925.74	6,897.27	6,884.80
16.75%	12,359.18	10,145.79	9,486.21	8,610.84	7,606.61	7,239.10	7,089.99	7,026.98	6,999.90	6,988.18
17.00%	12,426.29	10,217.90	9,560.73	8,689.88	7,695.02	7,334.00	7,188.98	7,128.38	7,102.63	7,091.62
17.25%	12,493.60	10,290.27	9,635.52	8,769.25	7,783.79	7,429.21	7,288.21	7,229.93	7,205.46	7,195.12
17.50%	12,561.11	10,362.90	9,710.61	8,848.94	7,872.89	7,524.71	7,387.65	7,331.63	7,308.38	7,298.67
17.75%	12,628.81	10,435.78	9,785.97	8,928.94	7,962.33	7,620.50	7,487.30	7,433.46	7,411.38	7,402.27
18.00%	12,696.71	10,508.92	9,861.61	9,009.26	8,052.11	7,716.56	7,587.15	7,535.43	7,514.46	7,505.91
18.25%	12,764.81	10,582.31	9,937.53	9,089.89	8,142.20	7,812.89	7,687.19	7,637.52	7,617.61	7,609.60
18.50%	12,833.10	10,655.96	10,013.72	9,170.83	8,232.62	7,909.48	7,787.42	7,739.72	7,720.84	7,713.32
18.75%	12,901.59	10,729.86	10,090.19	9,252.07	8,323.34	8,006.33	7,887.83	7,842.04	7,824.13	7,817.08
19.00%	12,970.28	10,804.01	10,166.93	9,333.62	8,414.38	8,103.42	7,988.40	7,944.46	7,927.47	7,920.87
19.25%	13,039.15	10,878.41	10,243.95	9,415.47	8,505.72	8,200.76	8,089.14	8,046.98	8,030.88	8,024.70
19.50%	13,108.22	10,953.06	10,321.23	9,497.61	8,597.35	8,298.32	8,190.03	8,149.60	8,134.33	8,128.55
19.75%	13,177.49	11,027.96	10,398.78	9,580.05	8,689.27	8,396.11	8,291.07	8,252.30	8,237.84	8,232.42
20.00%	13,246.94	11,103.10	10,476.60	9,662.78	8,781.48	8,494.12	8,392.26	8,355.09	8,341.39	8,336.32
20.25%	13,316.59	11,178.49	10,554.68	9,745.81	8,873.97	8,592.34	8,493.58	8,457.96	8,444.99	8,440.24
20.50%	13,386.43	11,254.12	10,633.03	9,829.12	8,966.73	8,690.77	8,595.04	8,560.90	8,548.62	8,544.18
20.75%	13,456.46	11,330.00	10,711.64	9,912.71	9,059.77	8,789.40	8,696.61	8,663.92	8,652.29	8,648.14

	5	7	8	10	15	20	25	30	35	40
1.00%	8,717.81	6,288.94	5,530.05	4,467.81	3,052.32	2,345.46	1,922.05	1,640.36	1,439.66	1,289.57
1.25%	8,772.82	6,344.09	5,585.32	4,523.37	3,108.73	2,402.78	1,980.32	1,699.58	1,499.84	1,350.71
1.50%	8,828.04	6,399.55	5,640.94	4,579.37	3,165.79	2,460.98	2,039.68	1,760.11	1,561.54	1,413.58
1.75%	8,883.49	6,455.31	5,696.92	4,635.81	3,223.51	2,520.06	2,100.12	1,821.94	1,624.75	1,478.15
2.00%	8,939.16	6,511.39	5,753.24	4,692.69	3,281.89	2,580.01	2,161.66	1,885.06	1,689.44	1,544.41
2.25%	8,995.05	6,567.78	5,809.93	4,750.01	3,340.93	2,640.82	2,224.27	1,949.46	1,755.61	1,612.33
2.50%	9,051.15	6,624.47	5,866.96	4,807.76	3,400.62	2,702.50	2,287.95	2,015.12	1,823.23	1,681.87
2.75%	9,107.48	6,681.47	5,924.35	4,865.96	3,460.97	2,765.05	2,352.69	2,082.03	1,892.28	1,753.01
3.00%	9,164.03	6,738.78	5,982.08	4,924.60	3,521.97	2,828.45	2,418.48	2,150.18	1,962.74	1,825.72
3.25%	9,220.80	6,796.40	6,040.17	4,983.67	3,583.61	2,892.70	2,485.31	2,219.55	2,034.58	1,899.96
3.50%	9,277.79	6,854.32	6,098.61	5,043.18	3,645.90	2,957.79	2,553.18	2,290.13	2,107.78	1,975.69
3.75%	9,335.00	6,912.55	6,157.39	5,103.12	3,708.83	3,023.73	2,622.07	2,361.89	2,182.32	2,052.88
4.00%	9,392.43	6,971.09	6,216.53	5,163.50	3,772.41	3,090.50	2,691.97	2,434.82	2,258.15	2,131.49
4.25%	9,450.07	7,029.93	6,276.02	5,224.31	3,836.62	3,158.10	2,762.86	2,508.89	2,335.26	2,211.46
4.50%	9,507.94	7,089.08	6,335.85	5,285.56	3,901.47	3,226.51	2,834.75	2,584.10	2,413.61	2,292.77
4.75%	9,566.03	7,148.54	6,396.03	5,347.23	3,966.94	3,295.74	2,907.60	2,660.40	2,493.17	2,375.37
5.00%	9,624.33	7,208.29	6,456.56	5,409.34	4,033.05	3,365.77	2,981.41	2,737.79	2,573.91	2,459.20
5.25%	9,682.85	7,268.36	6,517.43	5,471.88	4,099.78	3,436.61	3,056.16	2,816.24	2,655.79	2,544.24
5.50%	9,741.59	7,328.72	6,578.65	5,534.84	4,167.13	3,508.23	3,131.85	2,895.72	2,738.78	2,630.43
5.75%	9,800.55	7,389.39	6,640.22	5,598.23	4,235.09	3,580.63	3,208.44	2,976.22	2,822.85	2,717.73
6.00%	9,859.73	7,450.36	6,702.13	5,662.05	4,303.67	3,653.80	3,285.94	3,057.71	2,907.97	2,806.09
6.25%	9,919.12	7,511.64	6,764.38	5,726.28	4,372.86	3,727.73	3,364.31	3,140.16	2,994.09	2,895.47
6.50%	9,978.74	7,573.21	6,826.98	5,790.95	4,442.65	3,802.42	3,443.56	3,223.55	3,081.19	2,985.83
6.75%	10,038.56	7,635.09	6,889.92	5,856.03	4,513.04	3,877.86	3,523.65	3,307.85	3,169.22	3,077.12
7.00%	10,098.61	7,697.27	6,953.20	5,921.53	4,584.02	3,954.02	3,604.57	3,393.04	3,258.17	3,169.30
7.25%	10,158.87	7,759.74	7,016.82	5,987.45	4,655.60	4,030.92	3,686.32	3,479.10	3,347.98	3,262.33
7.50%	10,219.35	7,822.52	7,080.77	6,053.79	4,727.76	4,108.53	3,768.86	3,565.99	3,438.64	3,356.16
7.75%	10,280.05	7,885.60	7,145.07	6,120.54	4,800.51	4,186.84	3,852.18	3,653.70	3,530.10	3,450.76
8.00%	10,340.96	7,948.97	7,209.71	6,187.71	4,873.83	4,265.84	3,936.26	3,742.20	3,622.33	3,546.09
8.25%	10,402.09	8,012.64	7,274.68	6,255.28	4,947.72	4,345.53	4,021.10	3,831.46	3,715.30	3,642.11
8.50%	10,463.43	8,076.61	7,339.99	6,323.27	5,022.17	4,425.90	4,106.66	3,921.46	3,808.99	3,738.78
8.75%	10,524.99	8,140.87	7,405.63	6,391.66	5,097.19	4,506.92	4,192.93	4,012.17	3,903.35	3,836.07
9.00%	10,586.76	8,205.43	7,471.60	6,460.46	5,172.76	4,588.60	4,279.90	4,103.58	3,998.36	3,933.94
9.25%	10,648.75	8,270.28	7,537.91	6,529.67	5,248.88	4,670.92	4,367.55	4,195.64	4,094.00	4,032.37
9.50%	10,710.95	8,335.43	7,604.55	6,599.28	5,325.55	4,753.87	4,455.85	4,288.36	4,190.22	4,131.31
9.75%	10,773.36	8,400.87	7,671.52	6,669.28	5,402.75	4,837.44	4,544.80	4,381.69	4,287.01	4,230.75
10.00%	10,835.99	8,466.60	7,738.82	6,739.69	5,480.49	4,921.61	4,634.37	4,475.62	4,384.33	4,330.64
10.25%	10,898.83	8,532.63	7,806.45	6,810.49	5,558.75	5,006.38	4,724.55	4,570.12	4,482.16	4,430.97
10.50%	10,961.89	8,598.94	7,874.41	6,881.68	5,637.53	5,091.74	4,815.33	4,665.17	4,580.48	4,531.71
10.75%	11,025.16	8,665.55	7,942.69	6,953.27	5,716.83	5,177.67	4,906.67	4,760.75	4,679.26	4,632.83

$510,000   11.00 - 20.75%   5 - 40 Years

	5	7	8	10	15	20	25	30	35	40
11.00%	11,088.64	8,732.44	8,011.30	7,025.25	5,796.64	5,264.16	4,998.58	4,856.85	4,778.48	4,734.30
11.25%	11,152.33	8,799.63	8,080.23	7,097.62	5,876.96	5,351.21	5,091.02	4,953.43	4,878.12	4,836.11
11.50%	11,216.23	8,867.10	8,149.48	7,170.37	5,957.77	5,438.79	5,183.99	5,050.49	4,978.15	4,938.24
11.75%	11,280.34	8,934.85	8,219.05	7,243.50	6,039.07	5,526.91	5,277.47	5,147.99	5,078.55	5,040.66
12.00%	11,344.67	9,002.89	8,288.95	7,317.02	6,120.86	5,615.54	5,371.44	5,245.92	5,179.30	5,143.35
12.25%	11,409.20	9,071.22	8,359.16	7,390.91	6,203.12	5,704.68	5,465.89	5,344.27	5,280.39	5,246.30
12.50%	11,473.95	9,139.83	8,429.69	7,465.18	6,285.86	5,794.32	5,560.81	5,443.01	5,381.80	5,349.49
12.75%	11,538.90	9,208.73	8,500.54	7,539.83	6,369.07	5,884.44	5,656.17	5,542.14	5,483.50	5,452.90
13.00%	11,604.07	9,277.90	8,571.70	7,614.85	6,452.74	5,975.04	5,751.96	5,641.62	5,585.49	5,556.52
13.25%	11,669.44	9,347.36	8,643.17	7,690.23	6,536.86	6,066.10	5,848.17	5,741.44	5,687.74	5,660.34
13.50%	11,735.02	9,417.10	8,714.96	7,765.99	6,621.42	6,157.61	5,944.79	5,841.60	5,790.24	5,764.33
13.75%	11,800.81	9,487.11	8,787.06	7,842.11	6,706.44	6,249.57	6,041.80	5,942.07	5,892.97	5,868.50
14.00%	11,866.81	9,557.41	8,859.47	7,918.59	6,791.88	6,341.96	6,139.18	6,042.85	5,995.93	5,972.81
14.25%	11,933.01	9,627.98	8,932.18	7,995.43	6,877.76	6,434.77	6,236.93	6,143.90	6,099.10	6,077.28
14.50%	11,999.42	9,698.83	9,005.20	8,072.63	6,964.05	6,527.99	6,335.03	6,245.24	6,202.47	6,181.88
14.75%	12,066.04	9,769.95	9,078.53	8,150.18	7,050.77	6,621.61	6,433.47	6,346.83	6,306.02	6,286.60
15.00%	12,132.86	9,841.34	9,152.16	8,228.08	7,137.89	6,715.63	6,532.24	6,448.66	6,409.75	6,391.44
15.25%	12,199.89	9,913.01	9,226.09	8,306.34	7,225.42	6,810.02	6,631.32	6,550.74	6,513.64	6,496.39
15.50%	12,267.13	9,984.96	9,300.32	8,384.94	7,313.35	6,904.79	6,730.70	6,653.04	6,617.68	6,601.44
15.75%	12,334.57	10,057.17	9,374.85	8,463.88	7,401.67	6,999.92	6,830.38	6,755.55	6,721.87	6,706.58
16.00%	12,402.21	10,129.65	9,449.68	8,543.17	7,490.37	7,095.41	6,930.33	6,858.26	6,826.19	6,811.81
16.25%	12,470.06	10,202.40	9,524.81	8,622.80	7,579.46	7,191.23	7,030.56	6,961.17	6,930.64	6,917.11
16.50%	12,538.11	10,275.42	9,600.23	8,702.76	7,668.91	7,287.39	7,131.05	7,064.26	7,035.22	7,022.49
16.75%	12,606.36	10,348.71	9,675.94	8,783.05	7,758.74	7,383.88	7,231.78	7,167.52	7,139.90	7,127.94
17.00%	12,674.81	10,422.26	9,751.94	8,863.68	7,848.92	7,480.68	7,332.76	7,270.94	7,244.68	7,233.45
17.25%	12,743.47	10,496.08	9,828.24	8,944.64	7,939.46	7,577.79	7,433.97	7,374.53	7,349.57	7,339.02
17.50%	12,812.33	10,570.15	9,904.82	9,025.92	8,030.35	7,675.20	7,535.40	7,478.26	7,454.54	7,444.64
17.75%	12,881.39	10,644.50	9,981.69	9,107.52	8,121.58	7,772.90	7,637.04	7,582.13	7,559.61	7,550.31
18.00%	12,950.65	10,719.10	10,058.84	9,189.45	8,213.15	7,870.89	7,738.89	7,686.14	7,664.75	7,656.03
18.25%	13,020.11	10,793.96	10,136.28	9,271.69	8,305.05	7,969.15	7,840.94	7,790.27	7,769.97	7,761.79
18.50%	13,089.77	10,869.08	10,213.99	9,354.24	8,397.27	8,067.67	7,943.17	7,894.52	7,875.25	7,867.59
18.75%	13,159.62	10,944.46	10,291.99	9,437.11	8,489.81	8,166.46	8,045.58	7,998.88	7,980.61	7,973.42
19.00%	13,229.68	11,020.09	10,370.27	9,520.29	8,582.67	8,265.49	8,148.17	8,103.35	8,086.02	8,079.29
19.25%	13,299.94	11,095.98	10,448.83	9,603.77	8,675.83	8,364.77	8,250.92	8,207.92	8,191.50	8,185.19
19.50%	13,370.39	11,172.12	10,527.65	9,687.56	8,769.30	8,464.29	8,353.83	8,312.59	8,297.02	8,291.12
19.75%	13,441.04	11,248.52	10,606.76	9,771.65	8,863.06	8,564.04	8,456.89	8,417.35	8,402.60	8,397.07
20.00%	13,511.88	11,325.16	10,686.13	9,856.04	8,957.11	8,664.01	8,560.10	8,522.20	8,508.22	8,503.05
20.25%	13,582.92	11,402.06	10,765.78	9,940.72	9,051.45	8,764.19	8,663.45	8,627.12	8,613.89	8,609.05
20.50%	13,654.16	11,479.20	10,845.69	10,025.70	9,146.07	8,864.59	8,766.94	8,732.12	8,719.59	8,715.07
20.75%	13,725.59	11,556.60	10,925.87	10,110.96	9,240.96	8,965.18	8,870.55	8,837.20	8,825.34	8,821.10

	5	7	8	10	15	20	25	30	35	40
1.00%	8,888.75	6,412.25	5,638.48	4,555.41	3,112.17	2,391.45	1,959.74	1,672.53	1,467.89	1,314.85
1.25%	8,944.83	6,468.48	5,694.83	4,612.06	3,169.68	2,449.90	2,019.14	1,732.91	1,529.25	1,377.20
1.50%	9,001.14	6,525.03	5,751.55	4,669.16	3,227.86	2,509.24	2,079.67	1,794.63	1,592.16	1,441.30
1.75%	9,057.68	6,581.89	5,808.62	4,726.70	3,286.72	2,569.47	2,141.30	1,857.67	1,656.60	1,507.14
2.00%	9,114.44	6,639.07	5,866.05	4,784.70	3,346.25	2,630.59	2,204.04	1,922.02	1,722.57	1,574.69
2.25%	9,171.42	6,696.56	5,923.85	4,843.14	3,406.44	2,692.60	2,267.88	1,987.68	1,790.03	1,643.94
2.50%	9,228.63	6,754.36	5,982.00	4,902.03	3,467.30	2,755.50	2,332.81	2,054.63	1,858.98	1,714.85
2.75%	9,286.06	6,812.48	6,040.51	4,961.37	3,528.83	2,819.26	2,398.82	2,122.85	1,929.38	1,787.38
3.00%	9,343.72	6,870.92	6,099.38	5,021.16	3,591.02	2,883.91	2,465.90	2,192.34	2,001.22	1,861.52
3.25%	9,401.60	6,929.66	6,158.60	5,081.39	3,653.88	2,949.42	2,534.04	2,263.07	2,074.47	1,937.21
3.50%	9,459.71	6,988.72	6,218.19	5,142.07	3,717.39	3,015.79	2,603.24	2,335.03	2,149.11	2,014.43
3.75%	9,518.04	7,048.09	6,278.13	5,203.18	3,781.56	3,083.02	2,673.48	2,408.20	2,225.11	2,093.14
4.00%	9,576.59	7,107.78	6,338.42	5,264.75	3,846.38	3,151.10	2,744.75	2,482.56	2,302.43	2,173.28
4.25%	9,635.37	7,167.78	6,399.08	5,326.75	3,911.85	3,220.02	2,817.04	2,558.09	2,381.05	2,254.83
4.50%	9,694.37	7,228.08	6,460.08	5,389.20	3,977.97	3,289.78	2,890.33	2,634.76	2,460.94	2,337.73
4.75%	9,753.59	7,288.70	6,521.44	5,452.08	4,044.73	3,360.36	2,964.61	2,712.57	2,542.06	2,421.94
5.00%	9,813.04	7,349.63	6,583.16	5,515.41	4,112.13	3,431.77	3,039.87	2,791.47	2,624.38	2,507.42
5.25%	9,872.71	7,410.87	6,645.23	5,579.17	4,180.16	3,503.99	3,116.09	2,871.46	2,707.86	2,594.13
5.50%	9,932.60	7,472.42	6,707.65	5,643.37	4,248.83	3,577.01	3,193.25	2,952.50	2,792.48	2,682.01
5.75%	9,992.72	7,534.28	6,770.42	5,708.00	4,318.13	3,650.83	3,271.35	3,034.58	2,878.20	2,771.02
6.00%	10,053.06	7,596.45	6,833.54	5,773.07	4,388.06	3,725.44	3,350.37	3,117.66	2,964.99	2,861.11
6.25%	10,113.62	7,658.92	6,897.02	5,838.57	4,458.60	3,800.83	3,430.28	3,201.73	3,052.80	2,952.25
6.50%	10,174.40	7,721.71	6,960.84	5,904.49	4,529.76	3,876.98	3,511.08	3,286.75	3,141.60	3,044.38
6.75%	10,235.40	7,784.80	7,025.01	5,970.85	4,601.53	3,953.89	3,592.74	3,372.71	3,231.37	3,137.46
7.00%	10,296.62	7,848.19	7,089.53	6,037.64	4,673.91	4,031.55	3,675.25	3,459.57	3,322.05	3,231.44
7.25%	10,358.07	7,911.90	7,154.40	6,104.85	4,746.89	4,109.96	3,758.60	3,547.32	3,413.63	3,326.29
7.50%	10,419.73	7,975.90	7,219.61	6,172.49	4,820.46	4,189.08	3,842.75	3,635.92	3,506.06	3,421.97
7.75%	10,481.62	8,040.22	7,285.17	6,240.55	4,894.63	4,268.93	3,927.71	3,725.34	3,599.31	3,518.42
8.00%	10,543.73	8,104.83	7,351.07	6,309.03	4,969.39	4,349.49	4,013.44	3,815.58	3,693.36	3,615.62
8.25%	10,606.05	8,169.75	7,417.32	6,377.94	5,044.73	4,430.74	4,099.94	3,906.59	3,788.15	3,713.52
8.50%	10,668.60	8,234.97	7,483.91	6,447.26	5,120.65	4,512.68	4,187.18	3,998.35	3,883.67	3,812.09
8.75%	10,731.36	8,300.50	7,550.84	6,516.99	5,197.13	4,595.30	4,275.15	4,090.84	3,979.89	3,911.29
9.00%	10,794.34	8,366.32	7,618.11	6,587.14	5,274.19	4,678.57	4,363.82	4,184.04	4,076.76	4,011.08
9.25%	10,857.55	8,432.45	7,685.71	6,657.70	5,351.80	4,762.51	4,453.19	4,277.91	4,174.27	4,111.43
9.50%	10,920.97	8,498.87	7,753.66	6,728.67	5,429.97	4,847.08	4,543.22	4,372.44	4,272.38	4,212.32
9.75%	10,984.61	8,565.59	7,821.95	6,800.05	5,508.69	4,932.29	4,633.91	4,467.60	4,371.06	4,313.70
10.00%	11,048.46	8,632.62	7,890.57	6,871.84	5,587.95	5,018.11	4,725.24	4,563.37	4,470.30	4,415.56
10.25%	11,112.54	8,699.93	7,959.52	6,944.03	5,667.74	5,104.55	4,817.19	4,659.73	4,570.05	4,517.85
10.50%	11,176.83	8,767.55	8,028.81	7,016.62	5,748.07	5,191.58	4,909.74	4,756.64	4,670.30	4,620.57
10.75%	11,241.34	8,835.46	8,098.43	7,089.61	5,828.93	5,279.19	5,002.88	4,854.10	4,771.02	4,723.67

	5	7	8	10	15	20	25	30	35	40
11.00%	11,306.06	8,903.67	8,168.38	7,163.00	5,910.30	5,367.38	5,096.59	4,952.08	4,872.18	4,827.13
11.25%	11,371.00	8,972.17	8,238.66	7,236.79	5,992.19	5,456.13	5,190.85	5,050.56	4,973.77	4,930.94
11.50%	11,436.16	9,040.96	8,309.27	7,310.96	6,074.59	5,545.43	5,285.64	5,149.52	5,075.76	5,035.07
11.75%	11,501.53	9,110.04	8,380.21	7,385.53	6,157.48	5,635.28	5,380.95	5,248.93	5,178.13	5,139.49
12.00%	11,567.11	9,179.42	8,451.48	7,460.49	6,240.87	5,725.65	5,476.77	5,348.79	5,280.86	5,244.20
12.25%	11,632.91	9,249.09	8,523.07	7,535.83	6,324.75	5,816.54	5,573.07	5,449.06	5,383.93	5,349.17
12.50%	11,698.93	9,319.04	8,594.98	7,611.56	6,409.11	5,907.93	5,669.84	5,549.74	5,487.32	5,454.38
12.75%	11,765.16	9,389.29	8,667.22	7,687.67	6,493.95	5,999.82	5,767.07	5,650.80	5,591.02	5,559.82
13.00%	11,831.60	9,459.82	8,739.77	7,764.16	6,579.26	6,092.19	5,864.74	5,752.24	5,695.00	5,665.47
13.25%	11,898.25	9,530.64	8,812.65	7,841.02	6,665.03	6,185.04	5,962.84	5,854.02	5,799.26	5,771.32
13.50%	11,965.12	9,601.74	8,885.84	7,918.26	6,751.26	6,278.35	6,061.35	5,956.14	5,903.77	5,877.36
13.75%	12,032.20	9,673.13	8,959.35	7,995.87	6,837.93	6,372.11	6,160.26	6,058.59	6,008.52	5,983.56
14.00%	12,099.49	9,744.81	9,033.18	8,073.85	6,925.06	6,466.31	6,259.56	6,161.33	6,113.50	6,089.93
14.25%	12,166.99	9,816.76	9,107.32	8,152.20	7,012.61	6,560.94	6,359.22	6,264.37	6,218.69	6,196.44
14.50%	12,234.71	9,889.00	9,181.77	8,230.91	7,100.60	6,655.99	6,459.25	6,367.69	6,324.09	6,303.09
14.75%	12,302.63	9,961.52	9,256.54	8,309.99	7,189.02	6,751.45	6,559.62	6,471.27	6,429.67	6,409.87
15.00%	12,370.76	10,034.31	9,331.61	8,389.42	7,277.85	6,847.31	6,660.32	6,575.11	6,535.43	6,516.77
15.25%	12,439.11	10,107.39	9,406.99	8,469.21	7,367.10	6,943.55	6,761.34	6,679.18	6,641.36	6,623.77
15.50%	12,507.66	10,180.74	9,482.68	8,549.35	7,456.75	7,040.18	6,862.68	6,783.49	6,747.44	6,730.88
15.75%	12,576.42	10,254.37	9,558.67	8,629.84	7,546.80	7,137.18	6,964.31	6,888.01	6,853.67	6,838.08
16.00%	12,645.39	10,328.27	9,634.97	8,710.68	7,637.24	7,234.53	7,066.22	6,992.74	6,960.04	6,945.37
16.25%	12,714.57	10,402.45	9,711.57	8,791.87	7,728.07	7,332.24	7,168.41	7,097.66	7,066.54	7,052.74
16.50%	12,783.95	10,476.90	9,788.47	8,873.40	7,819.28	7,430.28	7,270.87	7,202.77	7,173.16	7,160.19
16.75%	12,853.54	10,551.63	9,865.66	8,955.27	7,910.87	7,528.66	7,373.58	7,308.06	7,279.89	7,267.70
17.00%	12,923.34	10,626.62	9,943.16	9,037.48	8,002.82	7,627.36	7,476.54	7,413.51	7,386.74	7,375.28
17.25%	12,993.34	10,701.88	10,020.95	9,120.02	8,095.14	7,726.38	7,579.74	7,519.13	7,493.68	7,482.92
17.50%	13,063.55	10,777.41	10,099.03	9,202.90	8,187.81	7,825.70	7,683.15	7,624.89	7,600.71	7,590.61
17.75%	13,133.96	10,853.21	10,177.40	9,286.10	8,280.83	7,925.31	7,786.79	7,730.80	7,707.83	7,698.36
18.00%	13,204.58	10,929.28	10,256.07	9,369.63	8,374.19	8,025.22	7,890.64	7,836.84	7,815.04	7,806.15
18.25%	13,275.40	11,005.61	10,335.03	9,453.48	8,467.89	8,125.41	7,994.68	7,943.02	7,922.32	7,913.98
18.50%	13,346.43	11,082.20	10,414.27	9,537.66	8,561.92	8,225.86	8,098.92	8,049.31	8,029.67	8,021.85
18.75%	13,417.66	11,159.05	10,493.80	9,622.15	8,656.28	8,326.58	8,203.34	8,155.72	8,137.09	8,129.76
19.00%	13,489.09	11,236.17	10,573.61	9,706.96	8,750.96	8,427.56	8,307.94	8,262.24	8,244.57	8,237.71
19.25%	13,560.72	11,313.55	10,653.70	9,792.08	8,845.95	8,528.79	8,412.70	8,368.86	8,352.11	8,345.68
19.50%	13,632.55	11,391.18	10,734.08	9,877.51	8,941.24	8,630.26	8,517.63	8,475.58	8,459.71	8,453.69
19.75%	13,704.59	11,469.07	10,814.73	9,963.25	9,036.84	8,731.96	8,622.72	8,582.40	8,567.35	8,561.72
20.00%	13,776.82	11,547.22	10,895.66	10,049.29	9,132.74	8,833.89	8,727.95	8,689.30	8,675.05	8,669.77
20.25%	13,849.25	11,625.63	10,976.87	10,135.64	9,228.93	8,936.04	8,833.32	8,796.28	8,782.78	8,777.85
20.50%	13,921.89	11,704.29	11,058.35	10,222.28	9,325.40	9,038.40	8,938.84	8,903.34	8,890.56	8,885.95
20.75%	13,994.72	11,783.20	11,140.10	10,309.22	9,422.16	9,140.97	9,044.48	9,010.48	8,998.38	8,994.07

	5	7	8	10	15	20	25	30	35	40
1.00%	9,059.69	6,535.56	5,746.91	4,643.02	3,172.02	2,437.44	1,997.42	1,704.69	1,496.11	1,340.14
1.25%	9,116.85	6,592.87	5,804.35	4,700.75	3,230.64	2,497.01	2,057.97	1,766.23	1,558.66	1,403.68
1.50%	9,174.24	6,650.51	5,862.15	4,758.95	3,289.94	2,557.49	2,119.66	1,829.14	1,622.78	1,469.01
1.75%	9,231.86	6,708.46	5,920.32	4,817.60	3,349.93	2,618.88	2,182.48	1,893.39	1,688.46	1,536.12
2.00%	9,289.71	6,766.74	5,978.86	4,876.71	3,410.60	2,681.18	2,246.43	1,958.98	1,755.69	1,604.98
2.25%	9,347.79	6,825.34	6,037.77	4,936.28	3,471.95	2,744.38	2,311.49	2,025.90	1,824.45	1,675.55
2.50%	9,406.10	6,884.25	6,097.04	4,996.30	3,533.98	2,808.49	2,377.67	2,094.14	1,894.72	1,747.82
2.75%	9,464.64	6,943.49	6,156.67	5,056.78	3,596.69	2,873.48	2,444.95	2,163.68	1,966.48	1,821.76
3.00%	9,523.41	7,003.05	6,216.67	5,117.72	3,660.08	2,939.37	2,513.32	2,234.50	2,039.71	1,897.32
3.25%	9,582.40	7,062.93	6,277.04	5,179.11	3,724.14	3,006.14	2,582.78	2,306.59	2,114.37	1,974.47
3.50%	9,641.62	7,123.12	6,337.77	5,240.95	3,788.88	3,073.79	2,653.30	2,379.94	2,190.44	2,053.17
3.75%	9,701.08	7,183.63	6,398.86	5,303.25	3,854.28	3,142.31	2,724.90	2,454.51	2,267.90	2,133.39
4.00%	9,760.76	7,244.47	6,460.32	5,365.99	3,920.35	3,211.70	2,797.54	2,530.30	2,346.71	2,215.07
4.25%	9,820.66	7,305.62	6,522.13	5,429.19	3,987.08	3,281.94	2,871.21	2,607.28	2,426.84	2,298.19
4.50%	9,880.80	7,367.09	6,584.31	5,492.84	4,054.46	3,353.04	2,945.91	2,685.43	2,508.26	2,382.68
4.75%	9,941.16	7,428.87	6,646.86	5,556.93	4,122.51	3,424.99	3,021.62	2,764.73	2,590.94	2,468.52
5.00%	10,001.75	7,490.97	6,709.76	5,621.47	4,191.21	3,497.77	3,098.33	2,845.15	2,674.84	2,555.64
5.25%	10,062.57	7,553.39	6,773.02	5,686.46	4,260.55	3,571.37	3,176.01	2,926.68	2,759.94	2,644.01
5.50%	10,123.62	7,616.12	6,836.64	5,751.89	4,330.54	3,645.80	3,254.66	3,009.28	2,846.19	2,733.58
5.75%	10,184.89	7,679.17	6,900.62	5,817.77	4,401.17	3,721.04	3,334.26	3,092.94	2,933.55	2,824.30
6.00%	10,246.38	7,742.53	6,964.96	5,884.09	4,472.44	3,797.08	3,414.80	3,177.62	3,022.01	2,916.13
6.25%	10,308.11	7,806.21	7,029.65	5,950.85	4,544.34	3,873.92	3,496.25	3,263.30	3,111.51	3,009.02
6.50%	10,370.06	7,870.20	7,094.70	6,018.04	4,616.87	3,951.54	3,578.60	3,349.96	3,202.02	3,102.92
6.75%	10,432.23	7,934.50	7,160.11	6,085.68	4,690.02	4,029.93	3,661.83	3,437.57	3,293.51	3,197.79
7.00%	10,494.62	7,999.12	7,225.87	6,153.75	4,763.79	4,109.08	3,745.93	3,526.10	3,385.94	3,293.59
7.25%	10,557.26	8,064.05	7,291.98	6,222.26	4,838.17	4,188.99	3,830.88	3,615.53	3,479.28	3,390.26
7.50%	10,620.11	8,129.29	7,358.45	6,291.19	4,913.17	4,269.64	3,916.65	3,705.84	3,573.49	3,487.77
7.75%	10,683.19	8,194.84	7,425.27	6,360.56	4,988.76	4,351.03	4,003.24	3,796.98	3,668.53	3,586.09
8.00%	10,746.49	8,260.69	7,492.44	6,430.36	5,064.96	4,433.13	4,090.63	3,888.95	3,764.38	3,685.15
8.25%	10,810.01	8,326.86	7,559.96	6,500.59	5,141.74	4,515.95	4,178.79	3,981.71	3,861.00	3,784.94
8.50%	10,873.76	8,393.34	7,627.83	6,571.24	5,219.12	4,599.46	4,267.70	4,075.24	3,958.36	3,885.40
8.75%	10,937.73	8,460.12	7,696.04	6,642.32	5,297.08	4,683.67	4,357.36	4,169.51	4,056.42	3,986.50
9.00%	11,001.93	8,527.21	7,764.61	6,713.82	5,375.61	4,768.55	4,447.74	4,264.50	4,155.16	4,088.22
9.25%	11,066.35	8,594.61	7,833.52	6,785.73	5,454.72	4,854.09	4,538.82	4,360.18	4,254.54	4,190.50
9.50%	11,130.99	8,662.31	7,902.77	6,858.07	5,534.39	4,940.30	4,630.59	4,456.53	4,354.54	4,293.33
9.75%	11,195.85	8,730.32	7,972.37	6,930.82	5,614.62	5,027.14	4,723.03	4,553.52	4,455.12	4,396.66
10.00%	11,260.93	8,798.63	8,042.31	7,003.99	5,695.41	5,114.61	4,816.11	4,651.13	4,556.26	4,500.47
10.25%	11,326.24	8,867.24	8,112.59	7,077.57	5,776.74	5,202.71	4,909.83	4,749.34	4,657.93	4,604.74
10.50%	11,391.77	8,936.16	8,183.21	7,151.55	5,858.61	5,291.41	5,004.16	4,848.12	4,760.11	4,709.42
10.75%	11,457.52	9,005.37	8,254.17	7,225.95	5,941.02	5,380.71	5,099.09	4,947.45	4,862.77	4,814.51

$530,000   11.00 - 20.75%   5 - 40 Years

	5	7	8	10	15	20	25	30	35	40
11.00%	11,523.48	9,074.89	8,325.47	7,300.75	6,023.96	5,470.60	5,194.60	5,047.31	4,965.88	4,919.96
11.25%	11,589.67	9,144.71	8,397.10	7,375.95	6,107.43	5,561.06	5,290.67	5,147.69	5,069.42	5,025.76
11.50%	11,656.08	9,214.82	8,469.07	7,451.56	6,191.41	5,652.08	5,387.29	5,248.54	5,173.37	5,131.89
11.75%	11,722.71	9,285.24	8,541.37	7,527.56	6,275.90	5,743.65	5,484.43	5,349.87	5,277.71	5,238.33
12.00%	11,789.56	9,355.95	8,614.01	7,603.96	6,360.89	5,835.76	5,582.09	5,451.65	5,382.41	5,345.05
12.25%	11,856.62	9,426.95	8,686.97	7,680.75	6,446.38	5,928.39	5,680.24	5,553.85	5,487.47	5,452.04
12.50%	11,923.91	9,498.26	8,760.27	7,757.94	6,532.37	6,021.54	5,778.88	5,656.47	5,592.85	5,559.27
12.75%	11,991.41	9,569.85	8,833.89	7,835.51	6,618.84	6,115.20	5,877.98	5,759.47	5,698.54	5,666.74
13.00%	12,059.13	9,641.74	8,907.85	7,913.47	6,705.78	6,209.35	5,977.53	5,862.86	5,804.52	5,774.43
13.25%	12,127.07	9,713.92	8,982.12	7,991.81	6,793.20	6,303.98	6,077.51	5,966.60	5,910.78	5,882.31
13.50%	12,195.22	9,786.39	9,056.72	8,070.54	6,881.09	6,399.09	6,177.92	6,070.68	6,017.30	5,990.38
13.75%	12,263.59	9,859.16	9,131.65	8,149.64	6,969.43	6,494.65	6,278.73	6,175.10	6,124.07	6,098.63
14.00%	12,332.17	9,932.21	9,206.90	8,229.12	7,058.23	6,590.66	6,379.93	6,279.82	6,231.07	6,207.04
14.25%	12,400.97	10,005.55	9,282.46	8,308.97	7,147.47	6,687.11	6,481.52	6,384.84	6,338.28	6,315.60
14.50%	12,469.99	10,079.17	9,358.35	8,389.20	7,237.15	6,783.99	6,583.46	6,490.15	6,445.70	6,424.30
14.75%	12,539.22	10,153.08	9,434.55	8,469.79	7,327.27	6,881.28	6,685.76	6,595.72	6,553.32	6,533.14
15.00%	12,608.66	10,227.28	9,511.06	8,550.75	7,417.81	6,978.98	6,788.40	6,701.55	6,661.11	6,642.09
15.25%	12,678.32	10,301.76	9,587.90	8,632.08	7,508.77	7,077.08	6,891.37	6,807.63	6,769.07	6,751.15
15.50%	12,748.19	10,376.52	9,665.04	8,713.76	7,600.15	7,175.57	6,994.65	6,913.94	6,877.20	6,860.32
15.75%	12,818.27	10,451.57	9,742.49	8,795.80	7,691.93	7,274.43	7,098.23	7,020.47	6,985.47	6,969.58
16.00%	12,888.57	10,526.89	9,820.26	8,878.20	7,784.11	7,373.66	7,202.11	7,127.21	7,093.89	7,078.94
16.25%	12,959.08	10,602.50	9,898.33	8,960.94	7,876.69	7,473.24	7,306.27	7,234.15	7,202.43	7,188.37
16.50%	13,029.80	10,678.38	9,976.70	9,044.04	7,969.66	7,573.17	7,410.70	7,341.28	7,311.11	7,297.88
16.75%	13,100.73	10,754.54	10,055.39	9,127.49	8,063.00	7,673.44	7,515.38	7,448.60	7,419.89	7,407.47
17.00%	13,171.87	10,830.98	10,134.37	9,211.28	8,156.72	7,774.04	7,620.32	7,556.08	7,528.79	7,517.11
17.25%	13,243.21	10,907.69	10,213.66	9,295.41	8,250.81	7,874.96	7,725.50	7,663.72	7,637.79	7,626.82
17.50%	13,314.77	10,984.67	10,293.24	9,379.87	8,345.26	7,976.19	7,830.91	7,771.52	7,746.88	7,736.59
17.75%	13,386.54	11,061.93	10,373.12	9,464.68	8,440.07	8,077.72	7,936.54	7,879.47	7,856.06	7,846.40
18.00%	13,458.52	11,139.45	10,453.30	9,549.82	8,535.23	8,179.55	8,042.38	7,987.55	7,965.33	7,956.27
18.25%	13,530.70	11,217.25	10,533.78	9,635.28	8,630.73	8,281.66	8,148.42	8,095.77	8,074.67	8,066.17
18.50%	13,603.09	11,295.32	10,614.54	9,721.08	8,726.57	8,384.05	8,254.67	8,204.11	8,184.09	8,176.12
18.75%	13,675.69	11,373.65	10,695.60	9,807.20	8,822.75	8,486.71	8,361.10	8,312.56	8,293.57	8,286.11
19.00%	13,748.49	11,452.25	10,776.95	9,893.63	8,919.24	8,589.63	8,467.70	8,421.13	8,403.12	8,396.13
19.25%	13,821.50	11,531.11	10,858.58	9,980.39	9,016.06	8,692.80	8,574.49	8,529.80	8,512.73	8,506.18
19.50%	13,894.72	11,610.24	10,940.50	10,067.47	9,113.19	8,796.22	8,681.43	8,638.58	8,622.39	8,616.26
19.75%	13,968.14	11,689.63	11,022.71	10,154.85	9,210.63	8,899.88	8,788.54	8,747.44	8,732.11	8,726.37
20.00%	14,041.76	11,769.29	11,105.20	10,242.55	9,308.37	9,003.77	8,895.79	8,856.40	8,841.87	8,836.50
20.25%	14,115.59	11,849.20	11,187.96	10,330.55	9,406.41	9,107.88	9,003.20	8,965.44	8,951.68	8,946.66
20.50%	14,189.61	11,929.37	11,271.01	10,418.86	9,504.74	9,212.22	9,110.74	9,074.56	9,061.54	9,056.83
20.75%	14,263.85	12,009.80	11,354.34	10,507.47	9,603.35	9,316.76	9,218.41	9,183.75	9,171.43	9,167.03

$540,000   1.00 - 10.75%   5 - 40 Years

	5	7	8	10	15	20	25	30	35	40
1.00%	9,230.62	6,658.87	5,855.34	4,730.62	3,231.87	2,483.43	2,035.11	1,736.85	1,524.34	1,365.42
1.25%	9,288.86	6,717.27	5,913.86	4,789.45	3,291.59	2,544.12	2,096.80	1,799.56	1,588.07	1,430.16
1.50%	9,347.34	6,775.99	5,972.76	4,848.74	3,352.01	2,605.75	2,159.66	1,863.65	1,653.40	1,496.73
1.75%	9,406.05	6,835.04	6,032.03	4,908.50	3,413.13	2,668.30	2,223.66	1,929.11	1,720.32	1,565.10
2.00%	9,464.99	6,894.41	6,091.67	4,968.73	3,474.95	2,731.77	2,288.81	1,995.95	1,788.82	1,635.26
2.25%	9,524.17	6,954.12	6,151.69	5,029.42	3,537.46	2,796.16	2,355.11	2,064.13	1,858.88	1,707.17
2.50%	9,583.58	7,014.15	6,212.08	5,090.57	3,600.66	2,861.48	2,422.53	2,133.65	1,930.47	1,780.80
2.75%	9,643.22	7,074.50	6,272.84	5,152.20	3,664.56	2,927.70	2,491.08	2,204.50	2,003.59	1,856.13
3.00%	9,703.09	7,135.18	6,333.97	5,214.28	3,729.14	2,994.83	2,560.74	2,276.66	2,078.19	1,933.12
3.25%	9,763.20	7,196.19	6,395.47	5,276.83	3,794.41	3,062.86	2,631.51	2,350.11	2,154.26	2,011.72
3.50%	9,823.54	7,257.52	6,457.35	5,339.84	3,860.37	3,131.78	2,703.37	2,424.84	2,231.77	2,091.91
3.75%	9,884.12	7,319.18	6,519.59	5,403.31	3,927.00	3,201.60	2,776.31	2,500.82	2,310.69	2,173.64
4.00%	9,944.92	7,381.16	6,582.21	5,467.24	3,994.31	3,272.29	2,850.32	2,578.04	2,390.98	2,256.87
4.25%	10,005.96	7,443.46	6,645.19	5,531.63	4,062.30	3,343.87	2,925.39	2,656.48	2,472.63	2,341.55
4.50%	10,067.23	7,506.09	6,708.55	5,596.47	4,130.96	3,416.31	3,001.50	2,736.10	2,555.59	2,427.64
4.75%	10,128.73	7,569.04	6,772.27	5,661.78	4,200.29	3,489.61	3,078.63	2,816.90	2,639.83	2,515.09
5.00%	10,190.47	7,632.31	6,836.36	5,727.54	4,270.29	3,563.76	3,156.79	2,898.84	2,725.31	2,603.86
5.25%	10,252.43	7,695.91	6,900.81	5,793.75	4,340.94	3,638.76	3,235.94	2,981.90	2,812.01	2,693.90
5.50%	10,314.63	7,759.82	6,965.63	5,860.42	4,412.25	3,714.59	3,316.07	3,066.06	2,899.89	2,785.16
5.75%	10,377.05	7,824.06	7,030.82	5,927.54	4,484.21	3,791.25	3,397.17	3,151.29	2,988.90	2,877.59
6.00%	10,439.71	7,888.62	7,096.37	5,995.11	4,556.83	3,868.73	3,479.23	3,237.57	3,079.02	2,971.15
6.25%	10,502.60	7,953.50	7,162.29	6,063.13	4,630.08	3,947.01	3,562.21	3,324.87	3,170.21	3,065.79
6.50%	10,565.72	8,018.70	7,228.57	6,131.59	4,703.98	4,026.09	3,646.12	3,413.17	3,262.43	3,161.47
6.75%	10,629.07	8,084.21	7,295.21	6,200.50	4,778.51	4,105.97	3,730.92	3,502.43	3,355.65	3,258.13
7.00%	10,692.65	8,150.05	7,362.21	6,269.86	4,853.67	4,186.61	3,816.61	3,592.63	3,449.82	3,355.73
7.25%	10,756.46	8,216.20	7,429.57	6,339.66	4,929.46	4,268.03	3,903.16	3,683.75	3,544.92	3,454.23
7.50%	10,820.49	8,282.67	7,497.29	6,409.90	5,005.87	4,350.20	3,990.55	3,775.76	3,640.91	3,553.58
7.75%	10,884.76	8,349.45	7,565.37	6,480.57	5,082.89	4,433.12	4,078.78	3,868.63	3,737.75	3,653.75
8.00%	10,949.25	8,416.56	7,633.81	6,551.69	5,160.52	4,516.78	4,167.81	3,962.33	3,835.41	3,754.68
8.25%	11,013.98	8,483.97	7,702.60	6,623.24	5,238.76	4,601.15	4,257.63	4,056.84	3,933.85	3,856.35
8.50%	11,078.93	8,551.70	7,771.75	6,695.23	5,317.59	4,686.25	4,348.23	4,152.13	4,033.05	3,958.71
8.75%	11,144.11	8,619.75	7,841.25	6,767.64	5,397.02	4,772.04	4,439.58	4,248.18	4,132.96	4,061.72
9.00%	11,209.51	8,688.10	7,911.11	6,840.49	5,477.04	4,858.52	4,531.66	4,344.96	4,233.56	4,165.35
9.25%	11,275.15	8,756.77	7,981.32	6,913.77	5,557.64	4,945.68	4,624.46	4,442.45	4,334.82	4,269.57
9.50%	11,341.01	8,825.75	8,051.88	6,987.47	5,638.81	5,033.51	4,717.96	4,540.61	4,436.70	4,374.33
9.75%	11,407.09	8,895.04	8,122.79	7,061.59	5,720.56	5,121.99	4,812.14	4,639.43	4,539.18	4,479.62
10.00%	11,473.40	8,964.64	8,194.05	7,136.14	5,802.87	5,211.12	4,906.98	4,738.89	4,642.23	4,585.39
10.25%	11,539.94	9,034.55	8,265.66	7,211.11	5,885.73	5,300.87	5,002.47	4,838.95	4,745.82	4,691.62
10.50%	11,606.71	9,104.76	8,337.61	7,286.49	5,969.15	5,391.25	5,098.58	4,939.59	4,849.92	4,798.28
10.75%	11,673.69	9,175.29	8,409.91	7,362.29	6,053.12	5,482.24	5,195.30	5,040.80	4,954.52	4,905.35

$540,000   11.00 - 20.75%   5 - 40 Years

	5	7	8	10	15	20	25	30	35	40
11.00%	11,740.91	9,246.12	8,482.55	7,438.50	6,137.62	5,573.82	5,292.61	5,142.55	5,059.57	5,012.79
11.25%	11,808.35	9,317.25	8,555.54	7,515.12	6,222.66	5,665.98	5,390.49	5,244.81	5,165.07	5,120.59
11.50%	11,876.01	9,388.69	8,628.86	7,592.15	6,308.22	5,758.72	5,488.93	5,347.57	5,270.98	5,228.72
11.75%	11,943.89	9,460.43	8,702.53	7,669.59	6,394.31	5,852.02	5,587.91	5,450.81	5,377.29	5,337.17
12.00%	12,012.00	9,532.48	8,776.53	7,747.43	6,480.91	5,945.87	5,687.41	5,554.51	5,483.97	5,445.90
12.25%	12,080.33	9,604.82	8,850.88	7,825.67	6,568.01	6,040.25	5,787.42	5,658.64	5,591.00	5,554.91
12.50%	12,148.89	9,677.47	8,925.56	7,904.31	6,655.62	6,135.16	5,887.91	5,763.19	5,698.37	5,664.16
12.75%	12,217.66	9,750.42	9,000.57	7,983.35	6,743.72	6,230.58	5,988.88	5,868.14	5,806.06	5,773.66
13.00%	12,286.66	9,823.66	9,075.92	8,062.78	6,832.31	6,326.51	6,090.31	5,973.48	5,914.04	5,883.38
13.25%	12,355.88	9,897.20	9,151.60	8,142.60	6,921.38	6,422.93	6,192.18	6,079.18	6,022.31	5,993.30
13.50%	12,425.32	9,971.04	9,227.61	8,222.81	7,010.92	6,519.82	6,294.48	6,185.23	6,130.84	6,103.41
13.75%	12,494.98	10,045.18	9,303.94	8,303.41	7,100.93	6,617.19	6,397.20	6,291.61	6,239.62	6,213.70
14.00%	12,564.86	10,119.61	9,380.61	8,384.39	7,191.40	6,715.01	6,500.31	6,398.31	6,348.64	6,324.16
14.25%	12,634.95	10,194.33	9,457.60	8,465.75	7,282.33	6,813.28	6,603.81	6,505.31	6,457.87	6,434.77
14.50%	12,705.27	10,269.34	9,534.92	8,547.49	7,373.70	6,911.99	6,707.68	6,612.60	6,567.32	6,545.52
14.75%	12,775.81	10,344.65	9,612.56	8,629.60	7,465.52	7,011.12	6,811.91	6,720.17	6,676.96	6,656.40
15.00%	12,846.56	10,420.25	9,690.52	8,712.09	7,557.77	7,110.66	6,916.49	6,828.00	6,786.79	6,767.41
15.25%	12,917.53	10,496.13	9,768.80	8,794.94	7,650.45	7,210.61	7,021.39	6,936.08	6,896.79	6,878.53
15.50%	12,988.72	10,572.31	9,847.40	8,878.17	7,743.55	7,310.96	7,126.62	7,044.39	7,006.96	6,989.76
15.75%	13,060.13	10,648.77	9,926.31	8,961.76	7,837.06	7,411.68	7,232.16	7,152.93	7,117.27	7,101.09
16.00%	13,131.75	10,725.51	10,005.54	9,045.71	7,930.98	7,512.78	7,338.00	7,261.69	7,227.73	7,212.50
16.25%	13,203.59	10,802.55	10,085.09	9,130.02	8,025.31	7,614.25	7,444.12	7,370.65	7,338.33	7,324.00
16.50%	13,275.64	10,879.86	10,164.94	9,214.68	8,120.03	7,716.06	7,550.52	7,479.80	7,449.05	7,435.58
16.75%	13,347.91	10,957.46	10,245.11	9,299.70	8,215.13	7,818.23	7,657.18	7,589.14	7,559.89	7,547.23
17.00%	13,420.39	11,035.33	10,325.59	9,385.07	8,310.62	7,920.72	7,764.10	7,698.65	7,670.84	7,658.95
17.25%	13,493.09	11,113.49	10,406.37	9,470.79	8,406.49	8,023.55	7,871.26	7,808.32	7,781.90	7,770.73
17.50%	13,566.00	11,191.93	10,487.45	9,556.85	8,502.72	8,126.69	7,978.66	7,918.16	7,893.05	7,882.56
17.75%	13,639.12	11,270.64	10,568.84	9,643.26	8,599.32	8,230.13	8,086.28	8,028.14	8,004.29	7,994.45
18.00%	13,712.45	11,349.63	10,650.54	9,730.00	8,696.27	8,333.88	8,194.12	8,138.26	8,115.62	8,106.38
18.25%	13,786.00	11,428.90	10,732.53	9,817.08	8,793.58	8,437.92	8,302.17	8,248.52	8,227.02	8,218.37
18.50%	13,859.75	11,508.44	10,814.82	9,904.49	8,891.23	8,542.24	8,410.41	8,358.90	8,338.50	8,330.39
18.75%	13,933.72	11,588.25	10,897.41	9,992.24	8,989.21	8,646.84	8,518.85	8,469.40	8,450.06	8,442.45
19.00%	14,007.90	11,668.33	10,980.29	10,080.31	9,087.53	8,751.70	8,627.47	8,580.02	8,561.67	8,554.54
19.25%	14,082.28	11,748.68	11,063.46	10,168.70	9,186.17	8,856.82	8,736.27	8,690.74	8,673.35	8,666.67
19.50%	14,156.88	11,829.30	11,146.93	10,257.42	9,285.14	8,962.19	8,845.23	8,801.57	8,785.08	8,778.83
19.75%	14,231.68	11,910.19	11,230.68	10,346.45	9,384.42	9,067.80	8,954.36	8,912.49	8,896.87	8,891.00
20.00%	14,306.70	11,991.35	11,314.73	10,435.81	9,484.00	9,173.65	9,063.64	9,023.50	9,008.70	9,003.23
20.25%	14,381.92	12,072.77	11,399.06	10,525.47	9,583.89	9,279.73	9,173.07	9,134.60	9,120.58	9,115.46
20.50%	14,457.34	12,154.45	11,483.67	10,615.44	9,684.07	9,386.03	9,282.64	9,245.78	9,232.51	9,227.72
20.75%	14,532.98	12,236.40	11,568.57	10,705.73	9,784.55	9,492.55	9,392.34	9,357.03	9,344.47	9,339.99

	5	7	8	10	15	20	25	30	35	40
1.00%	9,401.56	6,782.19	5,963.77	4,818.23	3,291.72	2,529.42	2,072.80	1,769.02	1,552.57	1,390.71
1.25%	9,460.88	6,841.66	6,023.38	4,878.14	3,352.55	2,591.24	2,135.63	1,832.88	1,617.47	1,456.65
1.50%	9,520.44	6,901.47	6,083.37	4,938.53	3,414.09	2,654.00	2,199.65	1,898.16	1,684.01	1,524.45
1.75%	9,580.23	6,961.61	6,143.73	4,999.40	3,476.34	2,717.71	2,264.84	1,964.84	1,752.18	1,594.09
2.00%	9,640.27	7,022.09	6,204.48	5,060.74	3,539.30	2,782.36	2,331.20	2,032.91	1,821.95	1,665.54
2.25%	9,700.54	7,082.90	6,265.61	5,122.56	3,602.97	2,847.95	2,398.72	2,102.35	1,893.30	1,738.78
2.50%	9,761.05	7,144.04	6,327.11	5,184.84	3,667.34	2,914.47	2,467.39	2,173.16	1,966.22	1,813.78
2.75%	9,821.80	7,205.51	6,389.00	5,247.61	3,732.42	2,981.91	2,537.21	2,245.33	2,040.69	1,890.50
3.00%	9,882.78	7,267.32	6,451.26	5,310.84	3,798.20	3,050.29	2,608.16	2,318.82	2,116.68	1,968.91
3.25%	9,944.00	7,329.45	6,513.91	5,374.55	3,864.68	3,119.58	2,680.24	2,393.63	2,194.15	2,048.98
3.50%	10,005.46	7,391.92	6,576.93	5,438.72	3,931.85	3,189.78	2,753.43	2,469.75	2,273.10	2,130.65
3.75%	10,067.16	7,454.72	6,640.33	5,503.37	3,999.72	3,260.89	2,827.72	2,547.14	2,353.48	2,213.89
4.00%	10,129.09	7,517.84	6,704.10	5,568.48	4,068.28	3,332.89	2,903.10	2,625.78	2,435.26	2,298.66
4.25%	10,191.26	7,581.30	6,768.25	5,634.06	4,137.53	3,405.79	2,979.56	2,705.67	2,518.42	2,384.91
4.50%	10,253.66	7,645.09	6,832.78	5,700.11	4,207.46	3,479.57	3,057.08	2,786.77	2,602.91	2,472.60
4.75%	10,316.30	7,709.21	6,897.68	5,766.63	4,278.08	3,554.23	3,135.65	2,869.06	2,688.71	2,561.67
5.00%	10,379.18	7,773.65	6,962.96	5,833.60	4,349.36	3,629.76	3,215.25	2,952.52	2,775.78	2,652.08
5.25%	10,442.29	7,838.42	7,028.61	5,901.04	4,421.33	3,706.14	3,295.86	3,037.12	2,864.09	2,743.79
5.50%	10,505.64	7,903.52	7,094.63	5,968.95	4,493.96	3,783.38	3,377.48	3,122.84	2,953.59	2,836.74
5.75%	10,569.22	7,968.95	7,161.02	6,037.31	4,567.26	3,861.46	3,460.09	3,209.65	3,044.25	2,930.88
6.00%	10,633.04	8,034.70	7,227.79	6,106.13	4,641.21	3,940.37	3,543.66	3,297.53	3,136.04	3,026.18
6.25%	10,697.09	8,100.78	7,294.92	6,175.41	4,715.83	4,020.11	3,628.18	3,386.44	3,228.92	3,122.57
6.50%	10,761.38	8,167.19	7,362.43	6,245.14	4,791.09	4,100.65	3,713.64	3,476.37	3,322.85	3,220.01
6.75%	10,825.90	8,233.92	7,430.30	6,315.33	4,867.00	4,182.00	3,800.01	3,567.29	3,417.79	3,318.46
7.00%	10,890.66	8,300.97	7,498.54	6,385.97	4,943.56	4,264.14	3,887.29	3,659.16	3,513.71	3,417.87
7.25%	10,955.65	8,368.35	7,567.15	6,457.06	5,020.75	4,347.07	3,975.44	3,751.97	3,610.57	3,518.20
7.50%	11,020.87	8,436.05	7,636.13	6,528.60	5,098.57	4,430.76	4,064.45	3,845.68	3,708.33	3,619.39
7.75%	11,086.33	8,504.07	7,705.47	6,600.58	5,177.02	4,515.22	4,154.31	3,940.27	3,806.97	3,721.41
8.00%	11,152.02	8,572.42	7,775.17	6,673.02	5,256.09	4,600.42	4,244.99	4,035.71	3,906.43	3,824.21
8.25%	11,217.94	8,641.08	7,845.24	6,745.89	5,335.77	4,686.36	4,336.48	4,131.97	4,006.70	3,927.76
8.50%	11,284.09	8,710.07	7,915.67	6,819.21	5,416.07	4,773.03	4,428.75	4,229.02	4,107.73	4,032.02
8.75%	11,350.48	8,779.37	7,986.46	6,892.97	5,496.97	4,860.41	4,521.79	4,326.85	4,209.50	4,136.94
9.00%	11,417.10	8,848.99	8,057.61	6,967.17	5,578.47	4,948.49	4,615.58	4,425.42	4,311.96	4,242.49
9.25%	11,483.94	8,918.93	8,129.12	7,041.80	5,660.56	5,037.27	4,710.10	4,524.71	4,415.09	4,348.63
9.50%	11,551.02	8,989.19	8,200.99	7,116.87	5,743.24	5,126.72	4,805.33	4,624.70	4,518.86	4,455.34
9.75%	11,618.33	9,059.76	8,273.21	7,192.36	5,826.49	5,216.84	4,901.26	4,725.35	4,623.24	4,562.57
10.00%	11,685.87	9,130.65	8,345.79	7,268.29	5,910.33	5,307.62	4,997.85	4,826.64	4,728.20	4,670.30
10.25%	11,753.65	9,201.85	8,418.72	7,344.65	5,994.73	5,399.04	5,095.11	4,928.56	4,833.71	4,778.50
10.50%	11,821.65	9,273.37	8,492.01	7,421.42	6,079.69	5,491.09	5,193.00	5,031.07	4,939.74	4,887.14
10.75%	11,889.87	9,345.20	8,565.65	7,498.63	6,165.21	5,583.76	5,291.51	5,134.15	5,046.27	4,996.18

$550,000   11.00 - 20.75%   5 - 40 Years

	5	7	8	10	15	20	25	30	35	40
11.00%	11,958.33	9,417.34	8,639.63	7,576.25	6,251.28	5,677.04	5,390.62	5,237.78	5,153.27	5,105.62
11.25%	12,027.02	9,489.79	8,713.97	7,654.29	6,337.90	5,770.91	5,490.32	5,341.94	5,260.72	5,215.42
11.50%	12,095.93	9,562.55	8,788.66	7,732.75	6,425.04	5,865.36	5,590.58	5,446.60	5,368.59	5,325.55
11.75%	12,165.08	9,635.62	8,863.69	7,811.62	6,512.72	5,960.39	5,691.39	5,551.75	5,476.87	5,436.00
12.00%	12,234.45	9,709.00	8,939.06	7,890.90	6,600.92	6,055.97	5,792.73	5,657.37	5,585.52	5,546.75
12.25%	12,304.04	9,782.69	9,014.78	7,970.59	6,689.64	6,152.11	5,894.59	5,763.43	5,694.54	5,657.77
12.50%	12,373.87	9,856.68	9,090.84	8,050.69	6,778.87	6,248.77	5,996.95	5,869.92	5,803.90	5,769.06
12.75%	12,443.92	9,930.98	9,167.25	8,131.19	6,868.60	6,345.96	6,099.79	5,976.81	5,913.58	5,880.58
13.00%	12,514.19	10,005.58	9,243.99	8,212.09	6,958.83	6,443.67	6,203.09	6,084.10	6,023.56	5,992.33
13.25%	12,584.69	10,080.48	9,321.07	8,293.39	7,049.55	6,541.87	6,306.85	6,191.75	6,133.83	6,104.28
13.50%	12,655.42	10,155.69	9,398.49	8,375.09	7,140.75	6,640.56	6,411.05	6,299.77	6,244.37	6,216.44
13.75%	12,726.36	10,231.20	9,476.24	8,457.17	7,232.43	6,739.73	6,515.66	6,408.12	6,355.17	6,328.77
14.00%	12,797.54	10,307.01	9,554.33	8,539.65	7,324.58	6,839.36	6,620.69	6,516.79	6,466.20	6,441.27
14.25%	12,868.93	10,383.11	9,632.74	8,622.52	7,417.19	6,939.45	6,726.10	6,625.78	6,577.46	6,553.93
14.50%	12,940.55	10,459.52	9,711.49	8,705.77	7,510.25	7,039.99	6,831.90	6,735.06	6,688.94	6,666.73
14.75%	13,012.40	10,536.22	9,790.57	8,789.41	7,603.77	7,140.95	6,938.06	6,844.62	6,800.61	6,779.67
15.00%	13,084.46	10,613.22	9,869.97	8,873.42	7,697.73	7,242.34	7,044.57	6,954.44	6,912.47	6,892.73
15.25%	13,156.75	10,690.51	9,949.70	8,957.81	7,792.12	7,344.14	7,151.42	7,064.52	7,024.51	7,005.91
15.50%	13,229.26	10,768.09	10,029.76	9,042.58	7,886.95	7,446.34	7,258.60	7,174.84	7,136.72	7,119.20
15.75%	13,301.98	10,845.97	10,110.13	9,127.72	7,982.19	7,548.94	7,366.09	7,285.39	7,249.08	7,232.59
16.00%	13,374.93	10,924.14	10,190.83	9,213.22	8,077.85	7,651.91	7,473.89	7,396.16	7,361.58	7,346.07
16.25%	13,448.10	11,002.59	10,271.85	9,299.09	8,173.92	7,755.25	7,581.98	7,507.14	7,474.22	7,459.63
16.50%	13,521.49	11,081.34	10,353.18	9,385.33	8,270.40	7,858.95	7,690.35	7,618.31	7,587.00	7,573.28
16.75%	13,595.09	11,160.37	10,434.83	9,471.92	8,367.27	7,963.01	7,798.98	7,729.68	7,699.89	7,686.99
17.00%	13,668.92	11,239.69	10,516.80	9,558.87	8,464.52	8,067.40	7,907.88	7,841.21	7,812.89	7,800.78
17.25%	13,742.96	11,319.30	10,599.08	9,646.18	8,562.16	8,172.13	8,017.03	7,952.92	7,926.00	7,914.63
17.50%	13,817.22	11,399.19	10,681.67	9,733.83	8,660.18	8,277.18	8,126.41	8,064.79	8,039.21	8,028.53
17.75%	13,891.69	11,479.36	10,764.56	9,821.84	8,758.57	8,382.54	8,236.03	8,176.81	8,152.52	8,142.49
18.00%	13,966.39	11,559.81	10,847.77	9,910.19	8,857.32	8,488.21	8,345.86	8,288.97	8,265.91	8,256.50
18.25%	14,041.29	11,640.54	10,931.28	9,998.88	8,956.42	8,594.18	8,455.91	8,401.27	8,379.38	8,370.56
18.50%	14,116.42	11,721.56	11,015.09	10,087.91	9,055.88	8,700.43	8,566.16	8,513.69	8,492.92	8,484.65
18.75%	14,191.75	11,802.84	11,099.21	10,177.28	9,155.68	8,806.96	8,676.61	8,626.24	8,606.54	8,598.79
19.00%	14,267.30	11,884.41	11,183.63	10,266.98	9,255.82	8,913.77	8,787.24	8,738.91	8,720.22	8,712.96
19.25%	14,343.07	11,966.25	11,268.34	10,357.01	9,356.29	9,020.83	8,898.05	8,851.68	8,833.97	8,827.17
19.50%	14,419.04	12,048.37	11,353.35	10,447.37	9,457.09	9,128.16	9,009.03	8,964.56	8,947.77	8,941.40
19.75%	14,495.23	12,130.75	11,438.66	10,538.06	9,558.20	9,235.73	9,120.18	9,077.54	9,061.62	9,055.66
20.00%	14,571.64	12,213.41	11,524.26	10,629.06	9,659.63	9,343.54	9,231.48	9,190.60	9,175.53	9,169.95
20.25%	14,648.25	12,296.34	11,610.15	10,720.39	9,761.37	9,451.58	9,342.94	9,303.76	9,289.48	9,284.27
20.50%	14,725.07	12,379.53	11,696.33	10,812.03	9,863.41	9,559.85	9,454.54	9,417.00	9,403.48	9,398.60
20.75%	14,802.11	12,463.00	11,782.80	10,903.98	9,965.74	9,668.34	9,566.28	9,530.31	9,517.52	9,512.95

	5	7	8	10	15	20	25	30	35	40
1.00%	9,572.50	6,905.50	6,072.21	4,905.83	3,351.57	2,575.41	2,110.49	1,801.18	1,580.80	1,415.99
1.25%	9,632.90	6,966.06	6,132.90	4,966.84	3,413.50	2,638.35	2,174.46	1,866.21	1,646.88	1,483.13
1.50%	9,693.54	7,026.95	6,193.97	5,028.32	3,476.16	2,702.25	2,239.64	1,932.67	1,714.63	1,552.17
1.75%	9,754.42	7,088.19	6,255.44	5,090.30	3,539.54	2,767.12	2,306.02	2,000.56	1,784.03	1,623.07
2.00%	9,815.55	7,149.76	6,317.29	5,152.75	3,603.65	2,832.95	2,373.58	2,069.87	1,855.07	1,695.82
2.25%	9,876.91	7,211.68	6,379.53	5,215.69	3,668.47	2,899.73	2,442.33	2,140.58	1,927.72	1,770.40
2.50%	9,938.52	7,273.93	6,442.15	5,279.11	3,734.02	2,967.46	2,512.25	2,212.68	2,001.97	1,846.76
2.75%	10,000.37	7,336.52	6,505.16	5,343.02	3,800.28	3,036.13	2,583.34	2,286.15	2,077.79	1,924.88
3.00%	10,062.47	7,399.45	6,568.56	5,407.40	3,867.26	3,105.75	2,655.58	2,360.98	2,155.16	2,004.71
3.25%	10,124.80	7,462.71	6,632.34	5,472.27	3,934.95	3,176.30	2,728.97	2,437.16	2,234.05	2,086.23
3.50%	10,187.38	7,526.32	6,696.51	5,537.61	4,003.34	3,247.77	2,803.49	2,514.65	2,314.43	2,169.39
3.75%	10,250.19	7,590.26	6,761.06	5,603.43	4,072.45	3,320.17	2,879.13	2,593.45	2,396.27	2,254.15
4.00%	10,313.25	7,654.53	6,825.99	5,669.73	4,142.25	3,393.49	2,955.89	2,673.53	2,479.54	2,340.46
4.25%	10,376.55	7,719.14	6,891.31	5,736.50	4,212.76	3,467.71	3,033.73	2,754.86	2,564.21	2,428.27
4.50%	10,440.09	7,784.09	6,957.01	5,803.75	4,283.96	3,542.84	3,112.66	2,837.44	2,650.24	2,517.55
4.75%	10,503.87	7,849.37	7,023.09	5,871.47	4,355.86	3,618.85	3,192.66	2,921.23	2,737.60	2,608.24
5.00%	10,567.89	7,914.99	7,089.56	5,939.67	4,428.44	3,695.75	3,273.70	3,006.20	2,826.25	2,700.30
5.25%	10,632.15	7,980.94	7,156.40	6,008.34	4,501.72	3,773.53	3,355.79	3,092.34	2,916.16	2,793.67
5.50%	10,696.65	8,047.22	7,223.62	6,077.47	4,575.67	3,852.17	3,438.89	3,179.62	3,007.29	2,888.31
5.75%	10,761.39	8,113.84	7,291.22	6,147.08	4,650.30	3,931.67	3,523.00	3,268.01	3,099.60	2,984.17
6.00%	10,826.37	8,180.79	7,359.20	6,217.15	4,725.60	4,012.01	3,608.09	3,357.48	3,193.06	3,081.20
6.25%	10,891.59	8,248.07	7,427.56	6,287.69	4,801.57	4,093.20	3,694.15	3,448.02	3,287.63	3,179.34
6.50%	10,957.04	8,315.68	7,496.29	6,358.69	4,878.20	4,175.21	3,781.16	3,539.58	3,383.26	3,278.56
6.75%	11,022.74	8,383.63	7,565.40	6,430.15	4,955.49	4,258.04	3,869.10	3,632.15	3,479.93	3,378.80
7.00%	11,088.67	8,451.90	7,634.88	6,502.07	5,033.44	4,341.67	3,957.96	3,725.69	3,577.60	3,480.02
7.25%	11,154.84	8,520.50	7,704.74	6,574.46	5,112.03	4,426.11	4,047.72	3,820.19	3,676.22	3,582.16
7.50%	11,221.25	8,589.43	7,774.97	6,647.30	5,191.27	4,511.32	4,138.35	3,915.60	3,775.76	3,685.20
7.75%	11,287.90	8,658.69	7,845.57	6,720.60	5,271.14	4,597.31	4,229.84	4,011.91	3,876.19	3,789.07
8.00%	11,354.78	8,728.28	7,916.54	6,794.35	5,351.65	4,684.06	4,322.17	4,109.08	3,977.46	3,893.75
8.25%	11,421.90	8,798.19	7,987.88	6,868.55	5,432.79	4,771.57	4,415.32	4,207.09	4,079.55	3,999.18
8.50%	11,489.26	8,868.43	8,059.59	6,943.20	5,514.54	4,859.81	4,509.27	4,305.92	4,182.42	4,105.33
8.75%	11,556.85	8,939.00	8,131.67	7,018.30	5,596.91	4,948.78	4,604.00	4,405.52	4,286.03	4,212.15
9.00%	11,624.68	9,009.88	8,204.11	7,093.84	5,679.89	5,038.47	4,699.50	4,505.89	4,390.36	4,319.62
9.25%	11,692.74	9,081.10	8,276.92	7,169.83	5,763.48	5,128.85	4,795.74	4,606.98	4,495.37	4,427.70
9.50%	11,761.04	9,152.63	8,350.10	7,246.26	5,847.66	5,219.93	4,892.70	4,708.78	4,601.02	4,536.34
9.75%	11,829.58	9,224.49	8,423.63	7,323.13	5,932.43	5,311.69	4,990.37	4,811.26	4,707.30	4,645.53
10.00%	11,898.35	9,296.66	8,497.53	7,400.44	6,017.79	5,404.12	5,088.72	4,914.40	4,814.17	4,755.22
10.25%	11,967.35	9,369.16	8,571.79	7,478.18	6,103.73	5,497.20	5,187.75	5,018.17	4,921.59	4,865.38
10.50%	12,036.58	9,441.98	8,646.41	7,556.36	6,190.23	5,590.93	5,287.42	5,122.54	5,029.55	4,975.99
10.75%	12,106.05	9,515.11	8,721.39	7,634.97	6,277.31	5,685.28	5,387.72	5,227.50	5,138.02	5,087.02

$560,000   11.00 - 20.75%   5 - 40 Years

	5	7	8	10	15	20	25	30	35	40
11.00%	12,175.76	9,588.56	8,796.72	7,714.00	6,364.94	5,780.25	5,488.63	5,333.01	5,246.96	5,198.45
11.25%	12,245.69	9,662.33	8,872.41	7,793.46	6,453.13	5,875.83	5,590.14	5,439.06	5,356.37	5,310.24
11.50%	12,315.86	9,736.42	8,948.45	7,873.34	6,541.86	5,972.01	5,692.23	5,545.63	5,466.20	5,422.38
11.75%	12,386.26	9,810.82	9,024.84	7,953.65	6,631.14	6,068.76	5,794.87	5,652.69	5,576.45	5,534.84
12.00%	12,456.89	9,885.53	9,101.59	8,034.37	6,720.94	6,166.08	5,898.06	5,760.23	5,687.08	5,647.60
12.25%	12,527.75	9,960.56	9,178.69	8,115.51	6,811.27	6,263.96	6,001.77	5,868.22	5,798.08	5,760.64
12.50%	12,598.85	10,035.89	9,256.13	8,197.07	6,902.12	6,362.39	6,105.98	5,976.64	5,909.42	5,873.95
12.75%	12,670.17	10,111.54	9,333.93	8,279.03	6,993.49	6,461.34	6,210.69	6,085.48	6,021.10	5,987.50
13.00%	12,741.72	10,187.50	9,412.06	8,361.40	7,085.36	6,560.82	6,315.88	6,194.72	6,133.08	6,101.28
13.25%	12,813.50	10,263.77	9,490.54	8,444.18	7,177.72	6,660.81	6,421.52	6,304.33	6,245.36	6,215.27
13.50%	12,885.51	10,340.34	9,569.37	8,527.36	7,270.58	6,761.30	6,527.61	6,414.31	6,357.91	6,329.46
13.75%	12,957.75	10,417.22	9,648.54	8,610.94	7,363.93	6,862.27	6,634.13	6,524.63	6,470.72	6,443.84
14.00%	13,030.22	10,494.41	9,728.04	8,694.92	7,457.75	6,963.72	6,741.06	6,635.28	6,583.77	6,558.38
14.25%	13,102.92	10,571.90	9,807.88	8,779.29	7,552.05	7,065.63	6,848.39	6,746.25	6,697.05	6,673.09
14.50%	13,175.84	10,649.69	9,888.06	8,864.06	7,646.80	7,167.99	6,956.11	6,857.51	6,810.55	6,787.94
14.75%	13,248.99	10,727.79	9,968.58	8,949.22	7,742.02	7,270.79	7,064.20	6,969.06	6,924.26	6,902.94
15.00%	13,322.36	10,806.18	10,049.43	9,034.76	7,837.69	7,374.02	7,172.65	7,080.89	7,038.15	7,018.06
15.25%	13,395.96	10,884.88	10,130.61	9,120.68	7,933.80	7,477.67	7,281.45	7,192.97	7,152.23	7,133.29
15.50%	13,469.79	10,963.87	10,212.12	9,206.99	8,030.35	7,581.73	7,390.57	7,305.29	7,266.47	7,248.64
15.75%	13,543.84	11,043.17	10,293.96	9,293.67	8,127.32	7,686.19	7,500.02	7,417.86	7,380.88	7,364.09
16.00%	13,618.11	11,122.76	10,376.12	9,380.73	8,224.72	7,791.03	7,609.78	7,530.64	7,495.43	7,479.63
16.25%	13,692.61	11,202.64	10,458.61	9,468.17	8,322.54	7,896.25	7,719.83	7,643.63	7,610.12	7,595.26
16.50%	13,767.33	11,282.82	10,541.42	9,555.97	8,420.77	8,001.84	7,830.17	7,756.83	7,724.94	7,710.97
16.75%	13,842.28	11,363.29	10,624.56	9,644.14	8,519.40	8,107.79	7,940.78	7,870.22	7,839.89	7,826.76
17.00%	13,917.44	11,444.05	10,708.01	9,732.67	8,618.42	8,214.08	8,051.66	7,983.78	7,954.95	7,942.61
17.25%	13,992.83	11,525.10	10,791.79	9,821.56	8,717.84	8,320.71	8,162.79	8,097.52	8,070.11	8,058.53
17.50%	14,068.44	11,606.44	10,875.88	9,910.81	8,817.64	8,427.67	8,274.17	8,211.42	8,185.38	8,174.51
17.75%	14,144.27	11,688.07	10,960.28	10,000.42	8,917.81	8,534.95	8,385.77	8,325.48	8,300.74	8,290.54
18.00%	14,220.32	11,769.99	11,045.00	10,090.37	9,018.36	8,642.54	8,497.61	8,439.68	8,416.19	8,406.62
18.25%	14,296.59	11,852.19	11,130.03	10,180.68	9,119.27	8,750.44	8,609.66	8,554.02	8,531.73	8,522.75
18.50%	14,373.08	11,934.67	11,215.37	10,271.33	9,220.53	8,858.62	8,721.91	8,668.49	8,647.34	8,638.92
18.75%	14,449.78	12,017.44	11,301.01	10,362.32	9,322.15	8,967.09	8,834.36	8,783.08	8,763.02	8,755.13
19.00%	14,526.71	12,100.49	11,386.96	10,453.65	9,424.11	9,075.84	8,947.01	8,897.80	8,878.77	8,871.38
19.25%	14,603.85	12,183.82	11,473.22	10,545.32	9,526.40	9,184.85	9,059.83	9,012.62	8,994.58	8,987.66
19.50%	14,681.21	12,267.43	11,559.78	10,637.32	9,629.03	9,294.12	9,172.83	9,127.55	9,110.45	9,103.97
19.75%	14,758.78	12,351.31	11,646.64	10,729.66	9,731.99	9,403.65	9,286.00	9,242.58	9,226.38	9,220.31
20.00%	14,836.57	12,435.47	11,733.79	10,822.32	9,835.26	9,513.42	9,399.33	9,357.70	9,342.36	9,336.68
20.25%	14,914.58	12,519.91	11,821.25	10,915.30	9,938.85	9,623.43	9,512.81	9,472.92	9,458.38	9,453.07
20.50%	14,992.80	12,604.62	11,908.99	11,008.61	10,042.74	9,733.66	9,626.44	9,588.21	9,574.45	9,569.48
20.75%	15,071.23	12,689.60	11,997.03	11,102.23	10,146.94	9,844.12	9,740.21	9,703.59	9,690.57	9,685.92

	5	7	8	10	15	20	25	30	35	40
1.00%	9,743.44	7,028.81	6,180.64	4,993.43	3,411.42	2,621.40	2,148.17	1,833.35	1,609.03	1,441.28
1.25%	9,804.91	7,090.45	6,242.41	5,055.53	3,474.46	2,685.46	2,213.29	1,899.53	1,676.29	1,509.62
1.50%	9,866.64	7,152.43	6,304.58	5,118.12	3,538.24	2,750.51	2,279.64	1,967.19	1,745.25	1,579.88
1.75%	9,928.61	7,214.76	6,367.14	5,181.20	3,602.75	2,816.53	2,347.20	2,036.29	1,815.89	1,652.05
2.00%	9,990.82	7,277.44	6,430.10	5,244.77	3,668.00	2,883.54	2,415.97	2,106.83	1,888.20	1,726.11
2.25%	10,053.29	7,340.46	6,493.45	5,308.83	3,733.98	2,951.51	2,485.94	2,178.80	1,962.15	1,802.01
2.50%	10,116.00	7,403.82	6,557.19	5,373.38	3,800.70	3,020.45	2,557.12	2,252.19	2,037.72	1,879.74
2.75%	10,178.95	7,467.53	6,621.33	5,438.43	3,868.14	3,090.35	2,629.47	2,326.97	2,114.90	1,959.25
3.00%	10,242.15	7,531.58	6,685.86	5,503.96	3,936.32	3,161.21	2,703.00	2,403.14	2,193.65	2,040.51
3.25%	10,305.60	7,595.98	6,750.78	5,569.98	4,005.21	3,233.02	2,777.70	2,480.68	2,273.94	2,123.49
3.50%	10,369.29	7,660.71	6,816.09	5,636.49	4,074.83	3,305.77	2,853.55	2,559.55	2,355.76	2,208.13
3.75%	10,433.23	7,725.80	6,881.79	5,703.49	4,145.17	3,379.46	2,930.55	2,639.76	2,439.06	2,294.40
4.00%	10,497.42	7,791.22	6,947.89	5,770.97	4,216.22	3,454.09	3,008.67	2,721.27	2,523.82	2,382.25
4.25%	10,561.85	7,856.99	7,014.37	5,838.94	4,287.99	3,529.64	3,087.91	2,804.06	2,610.00	2,471.64
4.50%	10,626.52	7,923.09	7,081.24	5,907.39	4,360.46	3,606.10	3,168.25	2,888.11	2,697.56	2,562.51
4.75%	10,691.44	7,989.54	7,148.51	5,976.32	4,433.64	3,683.47	3,249.67	2,973.39	2,786.48	2,654.82
5.00%	10,756.60	8,056.33	7,216.15	6,045.73	4,507.52	3,761.75	3,332.16	3,059.88	2,876.72	2,748.52
5.25%	10,822.01	8,123.46	7,284.19	6,115.63	4,582.10	3,840.91	3,415.71	3,147.56	2,968.24	2,843.56
5.50%	10,887.66	8,190.92	7,352.61	6,186.00	4,657.38	3,920.96	3,500.30	3,236.40	3,060.99	2,939.89
5.75%	10,953.56	8,258.73	7,421.42	6,256.85	4,733.34	4,001.88	3,585.91	3,326.37	3,154.95	3,037.46
6.00%	11,019.70	8,326.88	7,490.62	6,328.17	4,809.98	4,083.66	3,672.52	3,417.44	3,250.08	3,136.22
6.25%	11,086.08	8,395.36	7,560.19	6,399.97	4,887.31	4,166.29	3,760.12	3,509.59	3,346.34	3,236.12
6.50%	11,152.70	8,464.18	7,630.15	6,472.23	4,965.31	4,249.77	3,848.68	3,602.79	3,443.68	3,337.10
6.75%	11,219.57	8,533.34	7,700.50	6,544.97	5,043.98	4,334.07	3,938.20	3,697.01	3,542.07	3,439.13
7.00%	11,286.68	8,602.83	7,771.22	6,618.18	5,123.32	4,419.20	4,028.64	3,792.22	3,641.48	3,542.16
7.25%	11,354.04	8,672.66	7,842.32	6,691.86	5,203.32	4,505.14	4,120.00	3,888.40	3,741.86	3,646.13
7.50%	11,421.63	8,742.82	7,913.81	6,766.00	5,283.97	4,591.88	4,212.25	3,985.52	3,843.18	3,751.00
7.75%	11,489.47	8,813.31	7,985.67	6,840.61	5,365.27	4,679.41	4,305.37	4,083.55	3,945.40	3,856.73
8.00%	11,557.54	8,884.14	8,057.91	6,915.67	5,447.22	4,767.71	4,399.35	4,182.46	4,048.49	3,963.28
8.25%	11,625.86	8,955.30	8,130.52	6,991.20	5,529.80	4,856.77	4,494.17	4,282.22	4,152.40	4,070.59
8.50%	11,694.42	9,026.80	8,203.51	7,067.18	5,613.02	4,946.59	4,589.79	4,382.81	4,257.11	4,178.64
8.75%	11,763.22	9,098.62	8,276.88	7,143.62	5,696.86	5,037.15	4,686.22	4,484.19	4,362.57	4,287.37
9.00%	11,832.26	9,170.77	8,350.62	7,220.52	5,781.32	5,128.44	4,783.42	4,586.35	4,468.76	4,396.76
9.25%	11,901.54	9,243.26	8,424.73	7,297.87	5,866.40	5,220.44	4,881.38	4,689.25	4,575.64	4,506.77
9.50%	11,971.06	9,316.07	8,499.21	7,375.66	5,952.08	5,313.15	4,980.07	4,792.87	4,683.19	4,617.35
9.75%	12,040.82	9,389.21	8,574.06	7,453.90	6,038.37	5,406.55	5,079.48	4,897.18	4,791.36	4,728.48
10.00%	12,110.82	9,462.67	8,649.27	7,532.59	6,125.25	5,500.62	5,179.59	5,002.16	4,900.13	4,840.13
10.25%	12,181.05	9,536.47	8,724.86	7,611.72	6,212.72	5,595.37	5,280.38	5,107.78	5,009.48	4,952.26
10.50%	12,251.52	9,610.58	8,800.81	7,691.29	6,300.77	5,690.77	5,381.84	5,214.01	5,119.36	5,064.85
10.75%	12,322.23	9,685.02	8,877.12	7,771.30	6,389.40	5,786.81	5,483.93	5,320.84	5,229.77	5,177.86

$570,000   11.00 - 20.75%   5 - 40 Years

	5	7	8	10	15	20	25	30	35	40
11.00%	12,393.18	9,759.79	8,953.80	7,851.75	6,478.60	5,883.47	5,586.64	5,428.24	5,340.66	5,291.28
11.25%	12,464.37	9,834.88	9,030.84	7,932.63	6,568.36	5,980.76	5,689.97	5,536.19	5,452.02	5,405.07
11.50%	12,535.79	9,910.28	9,108.24	8,013.94	6,658.68	6,078.65	5,793.87	5,644.66	5,563.81	5,519.21
11.75%	12,607.44	9,986.01	9,186.00	8,095.68	6,749.55	6,177.13	5,898.35	5,753.64	5,676.03	5,633.67
12.00%	12,679.34	10,062.06	9,264.12	8,177.84	6,840.96	6,276.19	6,003.38	5,863.09	5,788.63	5,748.45
12.25%	12,751.46	10,138.42	9,342.59	8,260.43	6,932.90	6,375.82	6,108.94	5,973.01	5,901.62	5,863.51
12.50%	12,823.82	10,215.11	9,421.42	8,343.44	7,025.38	6,476.00	6,215.02	6,083.37	6,014.95	5,978.84
12.75%	12,896.42	10,292.10	9,500.60	8,426.87	7,118.37	6,576.73	6,321.60	6,194.15	6,128.62	6,094.42
13.00%	12,969.25	10,369.42	9,580.14	8,510.71	7,211.88	6,677.98	6,428.66	6,305.34	6,242.60	6,210.23
13.25%	13,042.32	10,447.05	9,660.02	8,594.97	7,305.90	6,779.76	6,536.19	6,416.91	6,356.88	6,326.26
13.50%	13,115.61	10,524.99	9,740.25	8,679.63	7,400.42	6,882.04	6,644.18	6,528.85	6,471.44	6,442.49
13.75%	13,189.14	10,603.24	9,820.83	8,764.71	7,495.43	6,984.81	6,752.60	6,641.14	6,586.26	6,558.91
14.00%	13,262.90	10,681.81	9,901.76	8,850.19	7,590.93	7,088.07	6,861.44	6,753.77	6,701.34	6,675.50
14.25%	13,336.90	10,760.68	9,983.02	8,936.07	7,686.90	7,191.80	6,970.69	6,866.72	6,816.64	6,792.25
14.50%	13,411.12	10,839.86	10,064.64	9,022.35	7,783.35	7,295.99	7,080.33	6,979.97	6,932.17	6,909.16
14.75%	13,485.58	10,919.35	10,146.59	9,109.02	7,880.27	7,400.63	7,190.35	7,093.51	7,047.91	7,026.20
15.00%	13,560.26	10,999.15	10,228.88	9,196.09	7,977.65	7,505.70	7,300.73	7,207.33	7,163.84	7,143.38
15.25%	13,635.17	11,079.25	10,311.51	9,283.55	8,075.47	7,611.20	7,411.47	7,321.41	7,279.95	7,260.67
15.50%	13,710.32	11,159.66	10,394.48	9,371.40	8,173.74	7,717.12	7,522.55	7,435.75	7,396.23	7,378.08
15.75%	13,785.69	11,240.37	10,477.78	9,459.63	8,272.45	7,823.44	7,633.95	7,550.32	7,512.68	7,495.59
16.00%	13,861.29	11,321.38	10,561.41	9,548.25	8,371.59	7,930.16	7,745.67	7,665.11	7,629.28	7,613.20
16.25%	13,937.12	11,402.69	10,645.37	9,637.24	8,471.16	8,037.26	7,857.69	7,780.13	7,746.01	7,730.89
16.50%	14,013.18	11,484.30	10,729.66	9,726.61	8,571.14	8,144.73	7,969.99	7,895.34	7,862.89	7,848.67
16.75%	14,089.46	11,566.20	10,814.28	9,816.35	8,671.53	8,252.57	8,082.58	8,010.75	7,979.88	7,966.52
17.00%	14,165.97	11,648.41	10,899.23	9,906.47	8,772.32	8,360.76	8,195.44	8,126.35	8,097.00	8,084.44
17.25%	14,242.70	11,730.91	10,984.50	9,996.95	8,873.52	8,469.30	8,308.56	8,242.12	8,214.22	8,202.43
17.50%	14,319.66	11,813.70	11,070.09	10,087.79	8,975.10	8,578.17	8,421.92	8,358.05	8,331.55	8,320.48
17.75%	14,396.85	11,896.79	11,156.00	10,178.99	9,077.06	8,687.36	8,535.52	8,474.15	8,448.97	8,438.58
18.00%	14,474.25	11,980.17	11,242.23	10,270.56	9,179.40	8,796.88	8,649.35	8,590.39	8,566.48	8,556.74
18.25%	14,551.88	12,063.84	11,328.78	10,362.47	9,282.11	8,906.69	8,763.40	8,706.77	8,684.08	8,674.94
18.50%	14,629.74	12,147.79	11,415.64	10,454.74	9,385.18	9,016.81	8,877.66	8,823.28	8,801.76	8,793.19
18.75%	14,707.82	12,232.04	11,502.82	10,547.36	9,488.61	9,127.22	8,992.12	8,939.93	8,919.50	8,911.47
19.00%	14,786.11	12,316.57	11,590.30	10,640.32	9,592.39	9,237.90	9,106.78	9,056.69	9,037.32	9,029.80
19.25%	14,864.63	12,401.39	11,678.10	10,733.63	9,696.52	9,348.86	9,221.62	9,173.56	9,155.20	9,148.15
19.50%	14,943.37	12,486.49	11,766.20	10,827.28	9,800.98	9,460.09	9,336.63	9,290.54	9,273.14	9,266.54
19.75%	15,022.33	12,571.87	11,854.61	10,921.26	9,905.77	9,571.57	9,451.82	9,407.63	9,391.14	9,384.96
20.00%	15,101.51	12,657.53	11,943.32	11,015.57	10,010.89	9,683.30	9,567.18	9,524.81	9,509.19	9,503.41
20.25%	15,180.91	12,743.48	12,032.34	11,110.22	10,116.33	9,795.27	9,682.68	9,642.08	9,627.28	9,621.87
20.50%	15,260.53	12,829.70	12,121.65	11,205.19	10,222.08	9,907.48	9,798.34	9,759.43	9,745.43	9,740.37
20.75%	15,340.36	12,916.20	12,211.27	11,300.49	10,328.13	10,019.91	9,914.14	9,876.87	9,863.61	9,858.88

	5	7	8	10	15	20	25	30	35	40
1.00%	9,914.37	7,152.12	6,289.07	5,081.04	3,471.27	2,667.39	2,185.86	1,865.51	1,637.26	1,466.57
1.25%	9,976.93	7,214.84	6,351.93	5,144.22	3,535.41	2,732.58	2,252.12	1,932.86	1,705.70	1,536.10
1.50%	10,039.74	7,277.92	6,415.19	5,207.91	3,600.31	2,798.76	2,319.63	2,001.70	1,775.87	1,607.60
1.75%	10,102.79	7,341.34	6,478.85	5,272.09	3,665.96	2,865.95	2,388.38	2,072.01	1,847.75	1,681.04
2.00%	10,166.10	7,405.11	6,542.91	5,336.78	3,732.35	2,934.12	2,458.36	2,143.79	1,921.32	1,756.39
2.25%	10,229.66	7,469.24	6,607.37	5,401.97	3,799.49	3,003.29	2,529.56	2,217.03	1,996.57	1,833.62
2.50%	10,293.47	7,533.71	6,672.23	5,467.65	3,867.38	3,073.44	2,601.98	2,291.70	2,073.47	1,912.71
2.75%	10,357.53	7,598.54	6,737.49	5,533.84	3,936.01	3,144.56	2,675.60	2,367.80	2,152.00	1,993.62
3.00%	10,421.84	7,663.71	6,803.15	5,600.52	4,005.37	3,216.67	2,750.43	2,445.30	2,232.13	2,076.31
3.25%	10,486.40	7,729.24	6,869.21	5,667.70	4,075.48	3,289.74	2,826.43	2,524.20	2,313.84	2,160.74
3.50%	10,551.21	7,795.11	6,935.67	5,735.38	4,146.32	3,363.77	2,903.62	2,604.46	2,397.09	2,246.87
3.75%	10,616.27	7,861.34	7,002.53	5,803.55	4,217.89	3,438.75	2,981.96	2,686.07	2,481.85	2,334.65
4.00%	10,681.58	7,927.91	7,069.78	5,872.22	4,290.19	3,514.69	3,061.45	2,769.01	2,568.09	2,424.04
4.25%	10,747.14	7,994.83	7,137.43	5,941.38	4,363.21	3,591.56	3,142.08	2,853.25	2,655.79	2,515.00
4.50%	10,812.95	8,062.09	7,205.48	6,011.03	4,436.96	3,669.37	3,223.83	2,938.77	2,744.89	2,607.46
4.75%	10,879.01	8,129.71	7,273.92	6,081.17	4,511.43	3,748.10	3,306.68	3,025.55	2,835.37	2,701.40
5.00%	10,945.32	8,197.67	7,342.75	6,151.80	4,586.60	3,827.74	3,390.62	3,113.57	2,927.19	2,796.74
5.25%	11,011.87	8,265.97	7,411.98	6,222.92	4,662.49	3,908.30	3,475.64	3,202.78	3,020.31	2,893.45
5.50%	11,078.67	8,334.62	7,481.61	6,294.52	4,739.08	3,989.75	3,561.71	3,293.18	3,114.69	2,991.47
5.75%	11,145.73	8,403.62	7,551.62	6,366.61	4,816.38	4,072.08	3,648.82	3,384.72	3,210.30	3,090.75
6.00%	11,213.02	8,472.96	7,622.03	6,439.19	4,894.37	4,155.30	3,736.95	3,477.39	3,307.10	3,191.24
6.25%	11,280.57	8,542.65	7,692.83	6,512.25	4,973.05	4,239.38	3,826.08	3,571.16	3,405.04	3,292.89
6.50%	11,348.37	8,612.67	7,764.01	6,585.78	5,052.42	4,324.32	3,916.20	3,665.99	3,504.10	3,395.65
6.75%	11,416.41	8,683.04	7,835.59	6,659.80	5,132.47	4,410.11	4,007.29	3,761.87	3,604.22	3,499.47
7.00%	11,484.70	8,753.75	7,907.56	6,734.29	5,213.20	4,496.73	4,099.32	3,858.75	3,705.37	3,604.30
7.25%	11,553.23	8,824.81	7,979.91	6,809.26	5,294.60	4,584.18	4,192.28	3,956.62	3,807.51	3,710.10
7.50%	11,622.01	8,896.20	8,052.64	6,884.70	5,376.67	4,672.44	4,286.15	4,055.44	3,910.61	3,816.81
7.75%	11,691.04	8,967.93	8,125.77	6,960.62	5,459.40	4,761.50	4,380.91	4,155.19	4,014.62	3,924.40
8.00%	11,760.31	9,040.00	8,199.27	7,037.00	5,542.78	4,851.35	4,476.53	4,255.83	4,119.51	4,032.81
8.25%	11,829.83	9,112.41	8,273.16	7,113.85	5,626.81	4,941.98	4,573.01	4,357.35	4,225.25	4,142.01
8.50%	11,899.59	9,185.16	8,347.43	7,191.17	5,711.49	5,033.37	4,670.32	4,459.70	4,331.79	4,251.95
8.75%	11,969.59	9,258.25	8,422.09	7,268.95	5,796.80	5,125.52	4,768.43	4,562.86	4,439.11	4,362.59
9.00%	12,039.85	9,331.67	8,497.12	7,347.19	5,882.75	5,218.41	4,867.34	4,666.81	4,547.16	4,473.90
9.25%	12,110.34	9,405.42	8,572.53	7,425.90	5,969.32	5,312.03	4,967.01	4,771.52	4,655.92	4,585.83
9.50%	12,181.08	9,479.51	8,648.31	7,505.06	6,056.50	5,406.36	5,067.44	4,876.95	4,765.35	4,698.36
9.75%	12,252.06	9,553.93	8,724.48	7,584.67	6,144.30	5,501.40	5,168.60	4,983.10	4,875.42	4,811.44
10.00%	12,323.29	9,628.69	8,801.02	7,664.74	6,232.71	5,597.13	5,270.46	5,089.92	4,986.10	4,925.05
10.25%	12,394.75	9,703.77	8,877.93	7,745.26	6,321.72	5,693.53	5,373.02	5,197.39	5,097.36	5,039.15
10.50%	12,466.46	9,779.19	8,955.21	7,826.23	6,411.31	5,790.60	5,476.25	5,305.49	5,209.18	5,153.71
10.75%	12,538.41	9,854.94	9,032.86	7,907.64	6,501.50	5,888.33	5,580.14	5,414.19	5,321.52	5,268.70

$580,000   11.00 - 20.75%   5 - 40 Years

	5	7	8	10	15	20	25	30	35	40
11.00%	12,610.61	9,931.01	9,110.89	7,989.50	6,592.26	5,986.69	5,684.66	5,523.48	5,434.35	5,384.11
11.25%	12,683.04	10,007.42	9,189.28	8,071.80	6,683.60	6,085.68	5,789.79	5,633.32	5,547.66	5,499.89
11.50%	12,755.71	10,084.15	9,268.04	8,154.54	6,775.50	6,185.29	5,895.52	5,743.69	5,661.42	5,616.03
11.75%	12,828.63	10,161.20	9,347.16	8,237.71	6,867.96	6,285.50	6,001.83	5,854.58	5,775.60	5,732.51
12.00%	12,901.78	10,238.59	9,426.65	8,321.32	6,960.97	6,386.30	6,108.70	5,965.95	5,890.19	5,849.30
12.25%	12,975.17	10,316.29	9,506.50	8,405.35	7,054.53	6,487.68	6,216.11	6,077.80	6,005.15	5,966.38
12.50%	13,048.80	10,394.32	9,586.71	8,489.82	7,148.63	6,589.62	6,324.05	6,190.10	6,120.48	6,083.73
12.75%	13,122.67	10,472.67	9,667.28	8,574.71	7,243.25	6,692.11	6,432.50	6,302.82	6,236.14	6,201.34
13.00%	13,196.78	10,551.34	9,748.21	8,660.02	7,338.40	6,795.14	6,541.44	6,415.96	6,352.12	6,319.18
13.25%	13,271.13	10,630.33	9,829.49	8,745.76	7,434.07	6,898.70	6,650.86	6,529.49	6,468.41	6,437.25
13.50%	13,345.71	10,709.64	9,911.13	8,831.91	7,530.25	7,002.77	6,760.74	6,643.39	6,584.97	6,555.51
13.75%	13,420.53	10,789.26	9,993.13	8,918.48	7,626.93	7,107.35	6,871.06	6,757.65	6,701.81	6,673.97
14.00%	13,495.59	10,869.21	10,075.47	9,005.45	7,724.10	7,212.42	6,981.81	6,872.26	6,818.91	6,792.61
14.25%	13,570.88	10,949.46	10,158.17	9,092.84	7,821.76	7,317.97	7,092.98	6,987.19	6,936.23	6,911.42
14.50%	13,646.40	11,030.04	10,241.21	9,180.63	7,919.90	7,423.99	7,204.54	7,102.42	7,053.79	7,030.37
14.75%	13,722.16	11,110.92	10,324.60	9,268.83	8,018.52	7,530.46	7,316.50	7,217.96	7,171.55	7,149.47
15.00%	13,798.16	11,192.12	10,408.34	9,357.43	8,117.61	7,637.38	7,428.82	7,333.78	7,289.52	7,268.70
15.25%	13,874.39	11,273.62	10,492.41	9,446.42	8,217.15	7,744.73	7,541.50	7,449.86	7,407.67	7,388.05
15.50%	13,950.85	11,355.44	10,576.84	9,535.81	8,317.14	7,852.51	7,654.52	7,566.20	7,525.99	7,507.52
15.75%	14,027.55	11,437.57	10,661.60	9,625.59	8,417.58	7,960.70	7,767.88	7,682.78	7,644.48	7,627.09
16.00%	14,104.47	11,520.00	10,746.70	9,715.76	8,518.46	8,069.28	7,881.56	7,799.59	7,763.12	7,746.76
16.25%	14,181.63	11,602.73	10,832.13	9,806.32	8,619.77	8,178.26	7,995.54	7,916.62	7,881.91	7,866.52
16.50%	14,259.02	11,685.78	10,917.90	9,897.25	8,721.51	8,287.62	8,109.82	8,033.86	8,000.83	7,986.36
16.75%	14,336.64	11,769.12	11,004.01	9,988.57	8,823.66	8,397.35	8,224.38	8,151.29	8,119.88	8,106.28
17.00%	14,414.49	11,852.77	11,090.44	10,080.26	8,926.22	8,507.44	8,339.22	8,268.92	8,239.05	8,226.28
17.25%	14,492.57	11,936.71	11,177.21	10,172.33	9,029.19	8,617.88	8,454.32	8,386.72	8,358.33	8,346.33
17.50%	14,570.88	12,020.96	11,264.30	10,264.77	9,132.55	8,728.66	8,569.67	8,504.69	8,477.72	8,466.45
17.75%	14,649.42	12,105.50	11,351.72	10,357.57	9,236.31	8,839.77	8,685.27	8,622.82	8,597.20	8,586.63
18.00%	14,728.19	12,190.35	11,439.46	10,450.74	9,340.44	8,951.21	8,801.09	8,741.10	8,716.77	8,706.86
18.25%	14,807.18	12,275.48	11,527.53	10,544.27	9,444.95	9,062.95	8,917.14	8,859.52	8,836.43	8,827.13
18.50%	14,886.40	12,360.91	11,615.92	10,638.16	9,549.84	9,175.00	9,033.41	8,978.08	8,956.17	8,947.45
18.75%	14,965.85	12,446.64	11,704.62	10,732.40	9,655.08	9,287.34	9,149.88	9,096.77	9,075.99	9,067.81
19.00%	15,045.52	12,532.65	11,793.64	10,827.00	9,760.68	9,399.97	9,266.54	9,215.58	9,195.87	9,188.21
19.25%	15,125.42	12,618.96	11,882.98	10,921.94	9,866.63	9,512.88	9,383.40	9,334.50	9,315.82	9,308.65
19.50%	15,205.54	12,705.55	11,972.63	11,017.23	9,972.93	9,626.05	9,500.44	9,453.54	9,435.83	9,429.11
19.75%	15,285.88	12,792.43	12,062.59	11,112.86	10,079.56	9,739.49	9,617.64	9,572.67	9,555.89	9,549.61
20.00%	15,366.45	12,879.60	12,152.86	11,208.83	10,186.52	9,853.18	9,735.02	9,691.91	9,676.01	9,670.13
20.25%	15,447.24	12,967.05	12,243.43	11,305.13	10,293.81	9,967.12	9,852.55	9,811.24	9,796.18	9,790.68
20.50%	15,528.26	13,054.78	12,334.31	11,401.77	10,401.41	10,081.29	9,970.24	9,930.65	9,916.40	9,911.25
20.75%	15,609.49	13,142.80	12,425.50	11,498.74	10,509.33	10,195.70	10,088.07	10,050.15	10,036.66	10,031.84

	5	7	8	10	15	20	25	30	35	40
1.00%	10,085.31	7,275.44	6,397.50	5,168.64	3,531.12	2,713.38	2,223.55	1,897.67	1,665.49	1,491.85
1.25%	10,148.94	7,339.24	6,461.44	5,232.92	3,596.37	2,779.69	2,290.95	1,966.18	1,735.11	1,562.59
1.50%	10,212.83	7,403.40	6,525.79	5,297.70	3,662.38	2,847.02	2,359.62	2,036.21	1,806.49	1,635.32
1.75%	10,276.98	7,467.91	6,590.55	5,362.99	3,729.16	2,915.36	2,429.56	2,107.74	1,879.61	1,710.02
2.00%	10,341.38	7,532.79	6,655.71	5,428.79	3,796.70	2,984.71	2,500.74	2,180.75	1,954.45	1,786.67
2.25%	10,406.03	7,598.02	6,721.29	5,495.10	3,865.00	3,055.07	2,573.17	2,255.25	2,031.00	1,865.24
2.50%	10,470.94	7,663.60	6,787.27	5,561.92	3,934.06	3,126.43	2,646.84	2,331.21	2,109.22	1,945.69
2.75%	10,536.11	7,729.55	6,853.65	5,629.25	4,003.87	3,198.78	2,721.73	2,408.62	2,189.10	2,027.99
3.00%	10,601.53	7,795.85	6,920.45	5,697.08	4,074.43	3,272.13	2,797.85	2,487.46	2,270.62	2,112.11
3.25%	10,667.20	7,862.50	6,987.65	5,765.42	4,145.75	3,346.45	2,875.17	2,567.72	2,353.73	2,197.99
3.50%	10,733.13	7,929.51	7,055.25	5,834.27	4,217.81	3,421.76	2,953.68	2,649.36	2,438.41	2,285.61
3.75%	10,799.31	7,996.88	7,123.26	5,903.61	4,290.61	3,498.04	3,033.37	2,732.38	2,524.64	2,374.90
4.00%	10,865.75	8,064.60	7,191.67	5,973.46	4,364.16	3,575.28	3,114.24	2,816.75	2,612.37	2,465.84
4.25%	10,932.44	8,132.67	7,260.49	6,043.81	4,438.44	3,653.48	3,196.25	2,902.45	2,701.57	2,558.36
4.50%	10,999.38	8,201.10	7,329.71	6,114.67	4,513.46	3,732.63	3,279.41	2,989.44	2,792.21	2,652.42
4.75%	11,066.58	8,269.87	7,399.33	6,186.02	4,589.21	3,812.72	3,363.69	3,077.72	2,884.25	2,747.97
5.00%	11,134.03	8,339.01	7,469.35	6,257.87	4,665.68	3,893.74	3,449.08	3,167.25	2,977.66	2,844.96
5.25%	11,201.73	8,408.49	7,539.78	6,330.21	4,742.88	3,975.68	3,535.56	3,258.00	3,072.38	2,943.33
5.50%	11,269.69	8,478.33	7,610.60	6,403.05	4,820.79	4,058.54	3,623.12	3,349.96	3,168.40	3,043.04
5.75%	11,337.89	8,548.51	7,681.82	6,476.38	4,899.42	4,142.29	3,711.73	3,443.08	3,265.65	3,144.04
6.00%	11,406.35	8,619.05	7,753.44	6,550.21	4,978.76	4,226.94	3,801.38	3,537.35	3,364.12	3,246.26
6.25%	11,475.06	8,689.93	7,825.46	6,624.53	5,058.79	4,312.48	3,892.05	3,632.73	3,463.75	3,349.66
6.50%	11,544.03	8,761.17	7,897.88	6,699.33	5,139.53	4,398.88	3,983.72	3,729.20	3,564.51	3,454.20
6.75%	11,613.24	8,832.75	7,970.69	6,774.62	5,220.97	4,486.15	4,076.38	3,826.73	3,666.36	3,559.81
7.00%	11,682.71	8,904.68	8,043.89	6,850.40	5,303.09	4,574.26	4,170.00	3,925.28	3,769.25	3,666.44
7.25%	11,752.42	8,976.96	8,117.49	6,926.66	5,385.89	4,663.22	4,264.56	4,024.84	3,873.16	3,774.06
7.50%	11,822.39	9,049.58	8,191.48	7,003.40	5,469.37	4,753.00	4,360.05	4,125.37	3,978.03	3,882.62
7.75%	11,892.61	9,122.55	8,265.87	7,080.63	5,553.53	4,843.60	4,456.44	4,226.83	4,083.84	3,992.06
8.00%	11,963.07	9,195.87	8,340.64	7,158.33	5,638.35	4,935.00	4,553.72	4,329.21	4,190.54	4,102.34
8.25%	12,033.79	9,269.52	8,415.80	7,236.50	5,723.83	5,027.19	4,651.86	4,432.47	4,298.10	4,213.42
8.50%	12,104.75	9,343.53	8,491.36	7,315.16	5,809.96	5,120.16	4,750.84	4,536.59	4,406.48	4,325.26
8.75%	12,175.97	9,417.87	8,567.29	7,394.28	5,896.75	5,213.89	4,850.65	4,641.53	4,515.64	4,437.81
9.00%	12,247.43	9,492.56	8,643.62	7,473.87	5,984.17	5,308.38	4,951.26	4,747.27	4,625.56	4,551.03
9.25%	12,319.14	9,567.58	8,720.33	7,553.93	6,072.23	5,403.61	5,052.65	4,853.79	4,736.19	4,664.90
9.50%	12,391.10	9,642.95	8,797.42	7,634.46	6,160.93	5,499.57	5,154.81	4,961.04	4,847.51	4,779.36
9.75%	12,463.30	9,718.65	8,874.90	7,715.44	6,250.24	5,596.25	5,257.71	5,069.01	4,959.48	4,894.40
10.00%	12,535.76	9,794.70	8,952.76	7,796.89	6,340.17	5,693.63	5,361.33	5,177.67	5,072.07	5,009.96
10.25%	12,608.46	9,871.08	9,030.99	7,878.80	6,430.71	5,791.70	5,465.66	5,287.00	5,185.25	5,126.03
10.50%	12,681.40	9,947.80	9,109.61	7,961.16	6,521.85	5,890.44	5,570.67	5,396.96	5,298.99	5,242.56
10.75%	12,754.59	10,024.85	9,188.60	8,043.98	6,613.59	5,989.85	5,676.35	5,507.54	5,413.27	5,359.54

$590,000   11.00 - 20.75%   5 - 40 Years

	5	7	8	10	15	20	25	30	35	40
11.00%	12,828.03	10,102.24	9,267.97	8,127.25	6,705.92	6,089.91	5,782.67	5,618.71	5,528.05	5,476.94
11.25%	12,901.71	10,179.96	9,347.71	8,210.97	6,798.83	6,190.61	5,889.61	5,730.44	5,643.31	5,594.72
11.50%	12,975.64	10,258.01	9,427.83	8,295.13	6,892.32	6,291.93	5,997.17	5,842.72	5,759.03	5,712.86
11.75%	13,049.81	10,336.40	9,508.32	8,379.74	6,986.38	6,393.87	6,105.31	5,955.52	5,875.18	5,831.35
12.00%	13,124.22	10,415.11	9,589.18	8,464.79	7,080.99	6,496.41	6,214.02	6,068.81	5,991.74	5,950.15
12.25%	13,198.88	10,494.16	9,670.40	8,550.27	7,176.16	6,599.53	6,323.29	6,182.59	6,108.69	6,069.25
12.50%	13,273.78	10,573.53	9,752.00	8,636.19	7,271.88	6,703.23	6,433.09	6,296.82	6,226.00	6,188.62
12.75%	13,348.93	10,653.23	9,833.96	8,722.55	7,368.14	6,807.49	6,543.41	6,411.49	6,343.66	6,308.26
13.00%	13,424.31	10,733.26	9,916.28	8,809.33	7,464.93	6,912.30	6,654.23	6,526.58	6,461.64	6,428.13
13.25%	13,499.94	10,813.61	9,998.97	8,896.55	7,562.24	7,017.64	6,765.53	6,642.06	6,579.93	6,548.23
13.50%	13,575.81	10,894.29	10,082.01	8,984.18	7,660.08	7,123.51	6,877.30	6,757.93	6,698.51	6,668.54
13.75%	13,651.92	10,975.29	10,165.42	9,072.24	7,758.42	7,229.89	6,989.53	6,874.16	6,817.36	6,789.04
14.00%	13,728.27	11,056.61	10,249.19	9,160.72	7,857.27	7,336.77	7,102.19	6,990.74	6,936.47	6,909.73
14.25%	13,804.86	11,138.25	10,333.31	9,249.61	7,956.62	7,444.14	7,215.27	7,107.65	7,055.83	7,030.58
14.50%	13,881.69	11,220.21	10,417.78	9,338.92	8,056.46	7,551.99	7,328.76	7,224.88	7,175.41	7,151.58
14.75%	13,958.75	11,302.49	10,502.61	9,428.64	8,156.77	7,660.30	7,442.64	7,342.41	7,295.20	7,272.74
15.00%	14,036.06	11,385.09	10,587.79	9,518.76	8,257.56	7,769.06	7,556.90	7,460.22	7,415.20	7,394.02
15.25%	14,113.60	11,468.00	10,673.32	9,609.29	8,358.82	7,878.26	7,671.52	7,578.31	7,535.38	7,515.43
15.50%	14,191.38	11,551.22	10,759.19	9,700.22	8,460.54	7,987.90	7,786.50	7,696.65	7,655.75	7,636.96
15.75%	14,269.40	11,634.77	10,845.42	9,791.55	8,562.72	8,097.95	7,901.81	7,815.24	7,776.28	7,758.59
16.00%	14,347.65	11,718.62	10,931.98	9,883.27	8,665.33	8,208.41	8,017.44	7,934.07	7,896.97	7,880.33
16.25%	14,426.14	11,802.78	11,018.89	9,975.39	8,768.39	8,319.27	8,133.39	8,053.11	8,017.80	8,002.15
16.50%	14,504.87	11,887.25	11,106.14	10,067.90	8,871.88	8,430.51	8,249.64	8,172.37	8,138.78	8,124.06
16.75%	14,583.83	11,972.04	11,193.73	10,160.79	8,975.79	8,542.14	8,366.18	8,291.83	8,259.88	8,246.05
17.00%	14,663.02	12,057.12	11,281.66	10,254.06	9,080.13	8,654.12	8,483.00	8,411.48	8,381.10	8,368.11
17.25%	14,742.45	12,142.52	11,369.92	10,347.72	9,184.87	8,766.47	8,600.08	8,531.32	8,502.44	8,490.24
17.50%	14,822.11	12,228.22	11,458.51	10,441.75	9,290.01	8,879.16	8,717.43	8,651.32	8,623.88	8,612.43
17.75%	14,902.00	12,314.22	11,547.44	10,536.15	9,395.55	8,992.18	8,835.01	8,771.48	8,745.43	8,734.68
18.00%	14,982.12	12,400.52	11,636.70	10,630.93	9,501.48	9,105.54	8,952.84	8,891.80	8,867.06	8,856.98
18.25%	15,062.48	12,487.13	11,726.28	10,726.07	9,607.80	9,219.21	9,070.89	9,012.27	8,988.78	8,979.33
18.50%	15,143.06	12,574.03	11,816.19	10,821.58	9,714.49	9,333.19	9,189.16	9,132.87	9,110.59	9,101.72
18.75%	15,223.88	12,661.23	11,906.42	10,917.44	9,821.55	9,447.47	9,307.63	9,253.61	9,232.47	9,224.16
19.00%	15,304.93	12,748.73	11,996.98	11,013.67	9,928.97	9,562.04	9,426.31	9,374.47	9,354.42	9,346.63
19.25%	15,386.20	12,836.52	12,087.86	11,110.25	10,036.75	9,676.89	9,545.18	9,495.44	9,476.44	9,469.14
19.50%	15,467.70	12,924.61	12,179.05	11,207.18	10,144.87	9,792.02	9,664.24	9,616.53	9,598.51	9,591.68
19.75%	15,549.43	13,012.99	12,270.56	11,304.46	10,253.34	9,907.41	9,783.47	9,737.72	9,720.65	9,714.26
20.00%	15,631.39	13,101.66	12,362.39	11,402.08	10,362.15	10,023.07	9,902.87	9,859.01	9,842.84	9,836.90
20.25%	15,713.58	13,190.62	12,454.53	11,500.05	10,471.29	10,138.97	10,022.43	9,980.39	9,965.08	9,959.48
20.50%	15,795.99	13,279.86	12,546.97	11,598.36	10,580.75	10,255.11	10,142.14	10,101.87	10,087.37	10,082.13
20.75%	15,878.62	13,369.40	12,639.73	11,697.00	10,690.52	10,371.49	10,262.01	10,223.42	10,209.70	10,204.81

	5	7	8	10	15	20	25	30	35	40
1.00%	10,256.25	7,398.75	6,505.94	5,256.25	3,590.97	2,759.37	2,261.23	1,929.84	1,693.71	1,517.14
1.25%	10,320.96	7,463.63	6,570.96	5,321.61	3,657.32	2,826.80	2,329.78	1,999.51	1,764.52	1,589.07
1.50%	10,385.93	7,528.88	6,636.40	5,387.49	3,724.46	2,895.27	2,399.62	2,070.72	1,837.11	1,663.03
1.75%	10,451.16	7,594.49	6,702.25	5,453.89	3,792.37	2,964.77	2,470.73	2,143.46	1,911.47	1,739.00
2.00%	10,516.66	7,660.46	6,768.52	5,520.81	3,861.05	3,035.30	2,543.13	2,217.72	1,987.58	1,816.95
2.25%	10,582.41	7,726.80	6,835.21	5,588.24	3,930.51	3,106.85	2,616.78	2,293.48	2,065.42	1,896.85
2.50%	10,648.42	7,793.50	6,902.31	5,656.19	4,000.74	3,179.42	2,691.70	2,370.73	2,144.97	1,978.67
2.75%	10,714.69	7,860.56	6,969.82	5,724.66	4,071.73	3,253.00	2,767.87	2,449.45	2,226.21	2,062.37
3.00%	10,781.21	7,927.98	7,037.74	5,793.64	4,143.49	3,327.59	2,845.22	2,529.62	2,309.10	2,147.91
3.25%	10,848.00	7,995.76	7,106.08	5,863.14	4,216.01	3,403.17	2,923.90	2,611.24	2,393.62	2,235.25
3.50%	10,915.05	8,063.91	7,174.83	5,933.15	4,289.30	3,479.76	3,003.74	2,694.27	2,479.74	2,324.35
3.75%	10,982.35	8,132.42	7,243.99	6,003.67	4,363.33	3,557.33	3,084.79	2,778.69	2,567.43	2,415.16
4.00%	11,049.91	8,201.28	7,313.57	6,074.71	4,438.13	3,635.88	3,167.02	2,864.49	2,656.65	2,507.63
4.25%	11,117.73	8,270.51	7,383.55	6,146.25	4,513.67	3,715.41	3,250.43	2,951.64	2,747.36	2,601.72
4.50%	11,185.81	8,340.10	7,453.94	6,218.30	4,589.96	3,795.90	3,334.99	3,040.11	2,839.54	2,697.38
4.75%	11,254.15	8,410.04	7,524.74	6,290.86	4,666.99	3,877.34	3,420.70	3,129.88	2,933.14	2,794.55
5.00%	11,322.74	8,480.35	7,595.95	6,363.93	4,744.76	3,959.73	3,507.54	3,220.93	3,028.13	2,893.18
5.25%	11,391.59	8,551.01	7,667.57	6,437.50	4,823.27	4,043.06	3,595.49	3,313.22	3,124.46	2,993.22
5.50%	11,460.70	8,622.03	7,739.59	6,511.58	4,902.50	4,127.32	3,684.52	3,406.73	3,222.10	3,094.62
5.75%	11,530.06	8,693.40	7,812.02	6,586.15	4,982.46	4,212.50	3,774.64	3,501.44	3,321.00	3,197.33
6.00%	11,599.68	8,765.13	7,884.86	6,661.23	5,063.14	4,298.59	3,865.81	3,597.30	3,421.14	3,301.28
6.25%	11,669.56	8,837.22	7,958.10	6,736.81	5,144.54	4,385.57	3,958.02	3,694.30	3,522.46	3,406.44
6.50%	11,739.69	8,909.66	8,031.74	6,812.88	5,226.64	4,473.44	4,051.24	3,792.41	3,624.93	3,512.74
6.75%	11,810.08	8,982.46	8,105.78	6,889.45	5,309.46	4,562.18	4,145.47	3,891.59	3,728.50	3,620.14
7.00%	11,880.72	9,055.61	8,180.23	6,966.51	5,392.97	4,651.79	4,240.68	3,991.81	3,833.14	3,728.59
7.25%	11,951.62	9,129.11	8,255.08	7,044.06	5,477.18	4,742.26	4,336.84	4,093.06	3,938.80	3,838.03
7.50%	12,022.77	9,202.97	8,330.32	7,122.11	5,562.07	4,833.56	4,433.95	4,195.29	4,045.46	3,948.42
7.75%	12,094.18	9,277.17	8,405.97	7,200.64	5,647.65	4,925.69	4,531.97	4,298.47	4,153.06	4,059.72
8.00%	12,165.84	9,351.73	8,482.01	7,279.66	5,733.91	5,018.64	4,630.90	4,402.59	4,261.57	4,171.87
8.25%	12,237.75	9,426.64	8,558.44	7,359.16	5,820.84	5,112.39	4,730.70	4,507.60	4,370.95	4,284.83
8.50%	12,309.92	9,501.89	8,635.28	7,439.14	5,908.44	5,206.94	4,831.36	4,613.48	4,481.16	4,398.56
8.75%	12,382.34	9,577.50	8,712.50	7,519.61	5,996.69	5,302.26	4,932.86	4,720.20	4,592.18	4,513.02
9.00%	12,455.01	9,653.45	8,790.12	7,600.55	6,085.60	5,398.36	5,035.18	4,827.74	4,703.96	4,628.17
9.25%	12,527.94	9,729.75	8,868.13	7,681.96	6,175.15	5,495.20	5,138.29	4,936.05	4,816.47	4,743.96
9.50%	12,601.12	9,806.39	8,946.53	7,763.85	6,265.35	5,592.79	5,242.18	5,045.13	4,929.67	4,860.37
9.75%	12,674.55	9,883.38	9,025.32	7,846.21	6,356.18	5,691.10	5,346.82	5,154.93	5,043.54	4,977.35
10.00%	12,748.23	9,960.71	9,104.50	7,929.04	6,447.63	5,790.13	5,452.20	5,265.43	5,158.03	5,094.88
10.25%	12,822.16	10,038.39	9,184.06	8,012.34	6,539.71	5,889.86	5,558.30	5,376.61	5,273.13	5,212.91
10.50%	12,896.34	10,116.40	9,264.01	8,096.10	6,632.39	5,990.28	5,665.09	5,488.44	5,388.80	5,331.42
10.75%	12,970.77	10,194.76	9,344.34	8,180.32	6,725.69	6,091.37	5,772.56	5,600.89	5,505.02	5,450.38

$600,000   11.00 - 20.75%   5 - 40 Years

	5	7	8	10	15	20	25	30	35	40
11.00%	13,045.45	10,273.46	9,425.06	8,265.00	6,819.58	6,193.13	5,880.68	5,713.94	5,621.75	5,569.77
11.25%	13,120.38	10,352.50	9,506.15	8,350.14	6,914.07	6,295.54	5,989.44	5,827.57	5,738.96	5,689.54
11.50%	13,195.56	10,431.88	9,587.62	8,435.73	7,009.14	6,398.58	6,098.81	5,941.75	5,856.64	5,809.69
11.75%	13,270.97	10,511.59	9,669.48	8,521.77	7,104.79	6,502.24	6,208.79	6,056.46	5,974.76	5,930.18
12.00%	13,346.67	10,591.64	9,751.70	8,608.26	7,201.01	6,606.52	6,319.34	6,171.68	6,093.30	6,051.00
12.25%	13,422.59	10,672.02	9,834.31	8,695.19	7,297.79	6,711.39	6,430.46	6,287.38	6,212.23	6,172.12
12.50%	13,498.76	10,752.74	9,917.29	8,782.57	7,395.13	6,816.84	6,542.12	6,403.55	6,331.53	6,293.52
12.75%	13,575.18	10,833.79	10,000.63	8,870.39	7,493.02	6,922.87	6,654.31	6,520.16	6,451.18	6,415.18
13.00%	13,651.84	10,915.18	10,084.35	8,958.64	7,591.45	7,029.45	6,767.01	6,637.20	6,571.16	6,537.08
13.25%	13,728.75	10,996.89	10,168.44	9,047.33	7,690.42	7,136.58	6,880.20	6,754.64	6,691.45	6,659.22
13.50%	13,805.91	11,078.94	10,252.90	9,136.46	7,789.91	7,244.25	6,993.87	6,872.47	6,812.04	6,781.57
13.75%	13,883.31	11,161.31	10,337.72	9,226.01	7,889.92	7,352.43	7,108.00	6,990.68	6,932.91	6,904.11
14.00%	13,960.95	11,244.01	10,422.90	9,315.99	7,990.45	7,461.12	7,222.57	7,109.23	7,054.04	7,026.84
14.25%	14,038.84	11,327.03	10,508.45	9,406.39	8,091.48	7,570.31	7,337.57	7,228.12	7,175.42	7,149.74
14.50%	14,116.97	11,410.38	10,594.35	9,497.21	8,193.01	7,679.99	7,452.98	7,347.34	7,297.02	7,272.85
14.75%	14,195.34	11,494.06	10,680.62	9,588.45	8,295.02	7,790.13	7,568.79	7,466.85	7,418.85	7,396.00
15.00%	14,273.96	11,578.05	10,767.24	9,680.10	8,397.52	7,900.74	7,684.98	7,586.66	7,540.88	7,519.34
15.25%	14,352.82	11,662.37	10,854.22	9,772.16	8,500.50	8,011.79	7,801.55	7,706.75	7,663.10	7,642.81
15.50%	14,431.91	11,747.01	10,941.55	9,864.63	8,603.94	8,123.28	7,918.47	7,827.10	7,785.51	7,766.40
15.75%	14,511.25	11,831.96	11,029.24	9,957.51	8,707.85	8,235.20	8,035.74	7,947.70	7,908.08	7,890.09
16.00%	14,590.83	11,917.24	11,117.27	10,050.79	8,812.20	8,347.54	8,153.33	8,068.54	8,030.82	8,013.89
16.25%	14,670.65	12,002.83	11,205.65	10,144.46	8,917.01	8,460.27	8,271.25	8,189.61	8,153.70	8,137.78
16.50%	14,750.71	12,088.73	11,294.38	10,238.54	9,022.25	8,573.40	8,389.47	8,310.89	8,276.72	8,261.76
16.75%	14,831.01	12,174.95	11,383.46	10,333.00	9,127.93	8,686.92	8,507.98	8,432.37	8,399.88	8,385.81
17.00%	14,911.55	12,261.48	11,472.87	10,427.86	9,234.03	8,800.80	8,626.78	8,554.05	8,523.16	8,509.94
17.25%	14,992.32	12,348.32	11,562.63	10,523.10	9,340.54	8,915.05	8,745.85	8,675.91	8,646.55	8,634.14
17.50%	15,073.33	12,435.48	11,652.73	10,618.73	9,447.47	9,029.65	8,865.18	8,797.95	8,770.05	8,758.40
17.75%	15,154.57	12,522.94	11,743.16	10,714.73	9,554.80	9,144.59	8,984.76	8,920.15	8,893.65	8,882.72
18.00%	15,236.06	12,610.70	11,833.93	10,811.11	9,662.53	9,259.87	9,104.58	9,042.51	9,017.35	9,007.09
18.25%	15,317.77	12,698.78	11,925.03	10,907.87	9,770.64	9,375.47	9,224.63	9,165.02	9,141.14	9,131.52
18.50%	15,399.73	12,787.15	12,016.46	11,004.99	9,879.14	9,491.38	9,344.90	9,287.67	9,265.01	9,255.99
18.75%	15,481.91	12,875.83	12,108.23	11,102.48	9,988.01	9,607.60	9,465.39	9,410.45	9,388.95	9,380.50
19.00%	15,564.33	12,964.81	12,200.32	11,200.34	10,097.26	9,724.11	9,586.08	9,533.35	9,512.97	9,505.05
19.25%	15,646.98	13,054.09	12,292.74	11,298.56	10,206.86	9,840.91	9,706.96	9,656.38	9,637.05	9,629.64
19.50%	15,729.87	13,143.67	12,385.48	11,397.13	10,316.82	9,957.99	9,828.04	9,779.52	9,761.20	9,754.26
19.75%	15,812.98	13,233.55	12,478.54	11,496.06	10,427.13	10,075.34	9,949.29	9,902.77	9,885.41	9,878.91
20.00%	15,896.33	13,323.72	12,571.92	11,595.34	10,537.78	10,192.95	10,070.71	10,026.11	10,009.67	10,003.58
20.25%	15,979.91	13,414.19	12,665.62	11,694.97	10,648.77	10,310.81	10,192.30	10,149.55	10,133.98	10,128.29
20.50%	16,063.71	13,504.94	12,759.64	11,794.94	10,760.08	10,428.92	10,314.04	10,273.09	10,258.34	10,253.02
20.75%	16,147.75	13,596.00	12,853.96	11,895.25	10,871.72	10,547.28	10,435.94	10,396.70	10,382.75	10,377.77

	5	7	8	10	15	20	25	30	35	40
1.00%	10,427.19	7,522.06	6,614.37	5,343.85	3,650.82	2,805.36	2,298.92	1,962.00	1,721.94	1,542.42
1.25%	10,492.98	7,588.02	6,680.48	5,410.30	3,718.28	2,873.92	2,368.61	2,032.84	1,793.93	1,615.56
1.50%	10,559.03	7,654.36	6,747.01	5,477.28	3,786.53	2,943.53	2,439.61	2,105.23	1,867.73	1,690.75
1.75%	10,625.35	7,721.06	6,813.96	5,544.79	3,855.57	3,014.19	2,511.91	2,179.19	1,943.32	1,767.99
2.00%	10,691.93	7,788.14	6,881.33	5,612.82	3,925.40	3,085.89	2,585.51	2,254.68	2,020.70	1,847.24
2.25%	10,758.78	7,855.58	6,949.13	5,681.38	3,996.02	3,158.63	2,660.40	2,331.70	2,099.84	1,928.47
2.50%	10,825.89	7,923.39	7,017.34	5,750.46	4,067.41	3,232.41	2,736.56	2,410.24	2,180.72	2,011.65
2.75%	10,893.26	7,991.57	7,085.98	5,820.07	4,139.59	3,307.21	2,814.00	2,490.27	2,263.31	2,096.74
3.00%	10,960.90	8,060.11	7,155.04	5,890.21	4,212.55	3,383.05	2,892.69	2,571.78	2,347.59	2,183.70
3.25%	11,028.80	8,129.03	7,224.52	5,960.86	4,286.28	3,459.89	2,972.63	2,654.76	2,433.52	2,272.50
3.50%	11,096.96	8,198.31	7,294.41	6,032.04	4,360.78	3,537.75	3,053.80	2,739.17	2,521.07	2,363.08
3.75%	11,165.39	8,267.96	7,364.73	6,103.74	4,436.06	3,616.62	3,136.20	2,825.01	2,610.22	2,455.41
4.00%	11,234.08	8,337.97	7,435.46	6,175.95	4,512.10	3,696.48	3,219.80	2,912.23	2,700.93	2,549.42
4.25%	11,303.03	8,408.35	7,506.61	6,248.69	4,588.90	3,777.33	3,304.60	3,000.83	2,793.15	2,645.08
4.50%	11,372.24	8,479.10	7,578.17	6,321.94	4,666.46	3,859.16	3,390.58	3,090.78	2,886.87	2,742.33
4.75%	11,441.72	8,550.21	7,650.15	6,395.71	4,744.77	3,941.96	3,477.72	3,182.05	2,982.03	2,841.12
5.00%	11,511.45	8,621.68	7,722.55	6,470.00	4,823.84	4,025.73	3,566.00	3,274.61	3,078.59	2,941.40
5.25%	11,581.45	8,693.52	7,795.36	6,544.79	4,903.65	4,110.45	3,655.41	3,368.44	3,176.53	3,043.11
5.50%	11,651.71	8,765.73	7,868.59	6,620.10	4,984.21	4,196.11	3,745.93	3,463.51	3,275.80	3,146.20
5.75%	11,722.23	8,838.29	7,942.22	6,695.92	5,065.50	4,282.71	3,837.55	3,559.79	3,376.35	3,250.61
6.00%	11,793.01	8,911.22	8,016.27	6,772.25	5,147.53	4,370.23	3,930.24	3,657.26	3,478.16	3,356.30
6.25%	11,864.05	8,984.51	8,090.73	6,849.09	5,230.28	4,458.66	4,023.98	3,755.87	3,581.17	3,463.21
6.50%	11,935.35	9,058.16	8,165.60	6,926.43	5,313.75	4,548.00	4,118.76	3,855.61	3,685.34	3,571.29
6.75%	12,006.91	9,132.17	8,240.88	7,004.27	5,397.95	4,638.22	4,214.56	3,956.45	3,790.64	3,680.48
7.00%	12,078.73	9,206.53	8,316.57	7,082.62	5,482.85	4,729.32	4,311.35	4,058.35	3,897.02	3,790.73
7.25%	12,150.81	9,281.26	8,392.66	7,161.46	5,568.46	4,821.29	4,409.12	4,161.28	4,004.45	3,902.00
7.50%	12,223.15	9,356.35	8,469.16	7,240.81	5,654.78	4,914.12	4,507.85	4,265.21	4,112.88	4,014.23
7.75%	12,295.75	9,431.79	8,546.07	7,320.65	5,741.78	5,007.79	4,607.51	4,370.11	4,222.27	4,127.38
8.00%	12,368.60	9,507.59	8,623.37	7,400.98	5,829.48	5,102.28	4,708.08	4,475.96	4,332.59	4,241.40
8.25%	12,441.71	9,583.75	8,701.09	7,481.81	5,917.86	5,197.60	4,809.55	4,582.73	4,443.80	4,356.25
8.50%	12,515.08	9,660.26	8,779.20	7,563.13	6,006.91	5,293.72	4,911.89	4,690.37	4,555.85	4,471.87
8.75%	12,588.71	9,737.12	8,857.71	7,644.93	6,096.64	5,390.64	5,015.08	4,798.87	4,668.72	4,588.24
9.00%	12,662.60	9,814.34	8,936.62	7,727.22	6,187.03	5,488.33	5,119.10	4,908.20	4,782.36	4,705.31
9.25%	12,736.74	9,891.91	9,015.93	7,810.00	6,278.07	5,586.79	5,223.93	5,018.32	4,896.74	4,823.03
9.50%	12,811.14	9,969.83	9,095.64	7,893.25	6,369.77	5,686.00	5,329.55	5,129.21	5,011.83	4,941.38
9.75%	12,885.79	10,048.10	9,175.74	7,976.98	6,462.11	5,785.95	5,435.94	5,240.84	5,127.60	5,060.31
10.00%	12,960.70	10,126.72	9,256.24	8,061.19	6,555.09	5,886.63	5,543.07	5,353.19	5,244.00	5,179.79
10.25%	13,035.86	10,205.69	9,337.13	8,145.88	6,648.70	5,988.02	5,650.94	5,466.22	5,361.02	5,299.79
10.50%	13,111.28	10,285.01	9,418.41	8,231.03	6,742.93	6,090.12	5,759.51	5,579.91	5,478.62	5,420.28
10.75%	13,186.95	10,364.68	9,500.08	8,316.66	6,837.78	6,192.90	5,868.77	5,694.24	5,596.77	5,541.22

$610,000   11.00 - 20.75%   5 - 40 Years

	5	7	8	10	15	20	25	30	35	40
11.00%	13,262.88	10,444.69	9,582.14	8,402.75	6,933.24	6,296.35	5,978.69	5,809.17	5,715.44	5,662.60
11.25%	13,339.06	10,525.04	9,664.59	8,489.31	7,029.30	6,400.46	6,089.26	5,924.69	5,834.61	5,784.37
11.50%	13,415.49	10,605.74	9,747.42	8,576.32	7,125.96	6,505.22	6,200.46	6,040.78	5,954.25	5,906.52
11.75%	13,492.18	10,686.78	9,830.63	8,663.80	7,223.20	6,610.61	6,312.27	6,157.40	6,074.34	6,029.02
12.00%	13,569.11	10,768.17	9,914.23	8,751.73	7,321.03	6,716.63	6,424.67	6,274.54	6,194.85	6,151.85
12.25%	13,646.30	10,849.89	9,998.21	8,840.11	7,419.42	6,823.24	6,537.64	6,392.17	6,315.76	6,274.99
12.50%	13,723.74	10,931.96	10,082.57	8,928.95	7,518.38	6,930.46	6,651.16	6,510.27	6,437.05	6,398.41
12.75%	13,801.43	11,014.36	10,167.31	9,018.23	7,617.91	7,038.25	6,765.22	6,628.83	6,558.70	6,522.10
13.00%	13,879.37	11,097.10	10,252.43	9,107.96	7,717.98	7,146.61	6,879.80	6,747.82	6,680.68	6,646.04
13.25%	13,957.57	11,180.17	10,337.91	9,198.12	7,818.59	7,255.53	6,994.87	6,867.22	6,802.98	6,770.21
13.50%	14,036.01	11,263.58	10,423.78	9,288.73	7,919.74	7,364.99	7,110.43	6,987.01	6,925.58	6,894.59
13.75%	14,114.70	11,347.33	10,510.01	9,379.78	8,021.42	7,474.97	7,226.46	7,107.19	7,048.46	7,019.18
14.00%	14,193.63	11,431.41	10,596.62	9,471.25	8,123.62	7,585.48	7,342.94	7,227.72	7,171.61	7,143.95
14.25%	14,272.82	11,515.82	10,683.59	9,563.16	8,226.34	7,696.49	7,459.86	7,348.59	7,295.01	7,268.90
14.50%	14,352.25	11,600.56	10,770.93	9,655.49	8,329.56	7,807.99	7,577.19	7,469.79	7,418.64	7,394.01
14.75%	14,431.93	11,685.62	10,858.63	9,748.25	8,433.27	7,919.97	7,694.93	7,591.30	7,542.50	7,519.27
15.00%	14,511.86	11,771.02	10,946.70	9,841.43	8,537.48	8,032.42	7,813.07	7,713.11	7,666.56	7,644.67
15.25%	14,592.03	11,856.74	11,035.13	9,935.03	8,642.17	8,145.32	7,931.58	7,835.20	7,790.82	7,770.19
15.50%	14,672.45	11,942.79	11,123.91	10,029.04	8,747.34	8,258.67	8,050.45	7,957.55	7,915.27	7,895.84
15.75%	14,753.11	12,029.16	11,213.06	10,123.47	8,852.98	8,372.46	8,169.67	8,080.16	8,039.88	8,021.60
16.00%	14,834.01	12,115.86	11,302.56	10,218.30	8,959.07	8,486.66	8,289.22	8,203.02	8,164.66	8,147.46
16.25%	14,915.16	12,202.88	11,392.41	10,313.54	9,065.63	8,601.28	8,409.10	8,326.10	8,289.59	8,273.41
16.50%	14,996.56	12,290.21	11,482.62	10,409.18	9,172.62	8,716.29	8,529.29	8,449.40	8,414.67	8,399.45
16.75%	15,078.19	12,377.87	11,573.18	10,505.22	9,280.06	8,831.70	8,649.78	8,572.91	8,539.88	8,525.58
17.00%	15,160.07	12,465.84	11,664.09	10,601.66	9,387.93	8,947.48	8,770.56	8,696.62	8,665.21	8,651.77
17.25%	15,242.19	12,554.13	11,755.34	10,698.49	9,496.22	9,063.64	8,891.61	8,820.51	8,790.66	8,778.04
17.50%	15,324.55	12,642.73	11,846.94	10,795.70	9,604.93	9,180.15	9,012.93	8,944.58	8,916.22	8,904.37
17.75%	15,407.15	12,731.65	11,938.88	10,893.31	9,714.05	9,297.00	9,134.50	9,068.82	9,041.88	9,030.77
18.00%	15,489.99	12,820.88	12,031.16	10,991.30	9,823.57	9,414.20	9,256.32	9,193.22	9,167.64	9,157.21
18.25%	15,573.07	12,910.42	12,123.78	11,089.66	9,933.49	9,531.73	9,378.38	9,317.77	9,293.49	9,283.71
18.50%	15,656.39	13,000.27	12,216.74	11,188.41	10,043.79	9,649.57	9,500.65	9,442.46	9,419.42	9,410.25
18.75%	15,739.94	13,090.43	12,310.03	11,287.53	10,154.48	9,767.72	9,623.15	9,567.29	9,545.43	9,536.84
19.00%	15,823.74	13,180.89	12,403.66	11,387.01	10,265.54	9,886.18	9,745.85	9,692.24	9,671.52	9,663.47
19.25%	15,907.77	13,271.66	12,497.61	11,486.87	10,376.97	10,004.92	9,868.75	9,817.32	9,797.67	9,790.13
19.50%	15,992.03	13,362.73	12,591.90	11,587.08	10,488.77	10,123.95	9,991.84	9,942.51	9,923.89	9,916.83
19.75%	16,076.53	13,454.11	12,686.51	11,687.66	10,600.91	10,243.26	10,115.11	10,067.81	10,050.16	10,043.55
20.00%	16,161.27	13,545.78	12,781.45	11,788.60	10,713.41	10,362.83	10,238.56	10,193.21	10,176.50	10,170.31
20.25%	16,246.24	13,637.76	12,876.71	11,889.88	10,826.24	10,482.66	10,362.17	10,318.71	10,302.88	10,297.09
20.50%	16,331.44	13,730.03	12,972.30	11,991.52	10,939.42	10,602.74	10,485.94	10,444.30	10,429.32	10,423.90
20.75%	16,416.88	13,822.60	13,068.20	12,093.50	11,052.91	10,723.06	10,609.87	10,569.98	10,555.79	10,550.73

	5	7	8	10	15	20	25	30	35	40
1.00%	10,598.12	7,645.37	6,722.80	5,431.46	3,710.67	2,851.34	2,336.61	1,994.17	1,750.17	1,567.71
1.25%	10,664.99	7,712.42	6,789.99	5,499.00	3,779.23	2,921.03	2,407.44	2,066.16	1,823.33	1,642.04
1.50%	10,732.13	7,779.84	6,857.61	5,567.07	3,848.61	2,991.78	2,479.61	2,139.75	1,898.34	1,718.47
1.75%	10,799.54	7,847.64	6,925.66	5,635.69	3,918.78	3,063.60	2,553.09	2,214.91	1,975.18	1,796.97
2.00%	10,867.21	7,915.81	6,994.14	5,704.83	3,989.75	3,136.48	2,627.90	2,291.64	2,053.83	1,877.52
2.25%	10,935.15	7,984.36	7,063.05	5,774.52	4,061.53	3,210.41	2,704.01	2,369.93	2,134.27	1,960.08
2.50%	11,003.36	8,053.28	7,132.38	5,844.73	4,134.09	3,285.40	2,781.42	2,449.75	2,216.47	2,044.63
2.75%	11,071.84	8,122.58	7,202.15	5,915.48	4,207.45	3,361.43	2,860.13	2,531.10	2,300.41	2,131.11
3.00%	11,140.59	8,192.25	7,272.33	5,986.77	4,281.61	3,438.51	2,940.11	2,613.95	2,386.07	2,219.50
3.25%	11,209.60	8,262.29	7,342.95	6,058.58	4,356.55	3,516.61	3,021.36	2,698.28	2,473.41	2,309.76
3.50%	11,278.88	8,332.71	7,413.99	6,130.92	4,432.27	3,595.75	3,103.87	2,784.08	2,562.40	2,401.82
3.75%	11,348.43	8,403.50	7,485.46	6,203.80	4,508.78	3,675.91	3,187.61	2,871.32	2,653.01	2,495.66
4.00%	11,418.24	8,474.66	7,557.35	6,277.20	4,586.07	3,757.08	3,272.59	2,959.97	2,745.20	2,591.22
4.25%	11,488.32	8,546.19	7,629.67	6,351.13	4,664.13	3,839.25	3,358.78	3,050.03	2,838.94	2,688.45
4.50%	11,558.67	8,618.10	7,702.41	6,425.58	4,742.96	3,922.43	3,446.16	3,141.45	2,934.19	2,787.29
4.75%	11,629.29	8,690.38	7,775.57	6,500.56	4,822.56	4,006.59	3,534.73	3,234.21	3,030.91	2,887.70
5.00%	11,700.16	8,763.02	7,849.15	6,576.06	4,902.92	4,091.73	3,624.46	3,328.29	3,129.06	2,989.62
5.25%	11,771.31	8,836.04	7,923.15	6,652.09	4,984.04	4,177.83	3,715.34	3,423.66	3,228.61	3,093.00
5.50%	11,842.72	8,909.43	7,997.58	6,728.63	5,065.92	4,264.90	3,807.34	3,520.29	3,329.50	3,197.78
5.75%	11,914.40	8,983.18	8,072.42	6,805.69	5,148.54	4,352.92	3,900.46	3,618.15	3,431.70	3,303.90
6.00%	11,986.34	9,057.30	8,147.69	6,883.27	5,231.91	4,441.87	3,994.67	3,717.21	3,535.18	3,411.32
6.25%	12,058.54	9,131.79	8,223.37	6,961.37	5,316.02	4,531.75	4,089.95	3,817.45	3,639.87	3,519.99
6.50%	12,131.01	9,206.65	8,299.46	7,039.97	5,400.87	4,622.55	4,186.28	3,918.82	3,745.76	3,629.83
6.75%	12,203.75	9,281.87	8,375.98	7,119.10	5,486.44	4,714.26	4,283.65	4,021.31	3,852.78	3,740.81
7.00%	12,276.74	9,357.46	8,452.90	7,198.73	5,572.74	4,806.85	4,382.03	4,124.88	3,960.91	3,852.87
7.25%	12,350.00	9,433.41	8,530.25	7,278.86	5,659.75	4,900.33	4,481.40	4,229.49	4,070.10	3,965.97
7.50%	12,423.53	9,509.73	8,608.00	7,359.51	5,747.48	4,994.68	4,581.75	4,335.13	4,180.30	4,080.04
7.75%	12,497.32	9,586.41	8,686.17	7,440.66	5,835.91	5,089.88	4,683.04	4,441.76	4,291.49	4,195.04
8.00%	12,571.36	9,663.45	8,764.74	7,522.31	5,925.04	5,185.93	4,785.26	4,549.34	4,403.62	4,310.93
8.25%	12,645.68	9,740.86	8,843.73	7,604.46	6,014.87	5,282.81	4,888.39	4,657.85	4,516.65	4,427.66
8.50%	12,720.25	9,818.62	8,923.12	7,687.11	6,105.39	5,380.50	4,992.41	4,767.26	4,630.54	4,545.18
8.75%	12,795.08	9,896.75	9,002.92	7,770.26	6,196.58	5,479.01	5,097.29	4,877.54	4,745.25	4,663.46
9.00%	12,870.18	9,975.23	9,083.13	7,853.90	6,288.45	5,578.30	5,203.02	4,988.66	4,860.76	4,782.44
9.25%	12,945.54	10,054.07	9,163.74	7,938.03	6,380.99	5,678.37	5,309.57	5,100.59	4,977.01	4,902.10
9.50%	13,021.15	10,133.27	9,244.75	8,022.65	6,474.19	5,779.21	5,416.92	5,213.30	5,093.99	5,022.38
9.75%	13,097.03	10,212.82	9,326.17	8,107.76	6,568.05	5,880.80	5,525.05	5,326.76	5,211.65	5,143.26
10.00%	13,173.17	10,292.73	9,407.98	8,193.35	6,662.55	5,983.13	5,633.94	5,440.94	5,329.97	5,264.70
10.25%	13,249.56	10,373.00	9,490.20	8,279.42	6,757.70	6,086.19	5,743.58	5,555.83	5,448.90	5,386.67
10.50%	13,326.22	10,453.62	9,572.81	8,365.97	6,853.47	6,189.96	5,853.93	5,671.38	5,568.43	5,509.14
10.75%	13,403.13	10,534.59	9,655.82	8,453.00	6,949.88	6,294.42	5,964.97	5,787.58	5,688.52	5,632.06

$620,000   11.00 - 20.75%   5 - 40 Years

	5	7	8	10	15	20	25	30	35	40
11.00%	13,480.30	10,615.91	9,739.22	8,540.50	7,046.90	6,399.57	6,076.70	5,904.41	5,809.14	5,755.43
11.25%	13,557.73	10,697.58	9,823.02	8,628.47	7,144.54	6,505.39	6,189.09	6,021.82	5,930.26	5,879.20
11.50%	13,635.42	10,779.61	9,907.21	8,716.92	7,242.78	6,611.86	6,302.11	6,139.81	6,051.87	6,003.35
11.75%	13,713.36	10,861.98	9,991.79	8,805.83	7,341.61	6,718.98	6,415.75	6,258.34	6,173.92	6,127.86
12.00%	13,791.56	10,944.69	10,076.76	8,895.20	7,441.04	6,826.73	6,529.99	6,377.40	6,296.41	6,252.70
12.25%	13,870.01	11,027.76	10,162.12	8,985.03	7,541.05	6,935.10	6,644.81	6,496.96	6,419.30	6,377.85
12.50%	13,948.72	11,111.17	10,247.86	9,075.32	7,641.64	7,044.07	6,760.20	6,617.00	6,542.58	6,503.30
12.75%	14,027.69	11,194.92	10,333.99	9,166.07	7,742.79	7,153.63	6,876.12	6,737.50	6,666.22	6,629.02
13.00%	14,106.91	11,279.02	10,420.50	9,257.27	7,844.50	7,263.77	6,992.58	6,858.44	6,790.20	6,754.99
13.25%	14,186.38	11,363.46	10,507.39	9,348.91	7,946.77	7,374.47	7,109.54	6,979.80	6,914.50	6,881.19
13.50%	14,266.10	11,448.23	10,594.66	9,441.00	8,049.57	7,485.72	7,227.00	7,101.56	7,039.11	7,007.62
13.75%	14,346.08	11,533.35	10,682.31	9,533.54	8,152.92	7,597.51	7,344.93	7,223.70	7,164.01	7,134.25
14.00%	14,426.32	11,618.81	10,770.33	9,626.52	8,256.80	7,709.83	7,463.32	7,346.20	7,289.17	7,261.07
14.25%	14,506.80	11,704.60	10,858.73	9,719.93	8,361.19	7,822.66	7,582.15	7,469.06	7,414.60	7,388.06
14.50%	14,587.53	11,790.73	10,947.50	9,813.78	8,466.11	7,935.99	7,701.41	7,592.25	7,540.26	7,515.22
14.75%	14,668.52	11,877.19	11,036.64	9,908.06	8,571.52	8,049.80	7,821.08	7,715.75	7,666.14	7,642.54
15.00%	14,749.76	11,963.99	11,126.15	10,002.77	8,677.44	8,164.10	7,941.15	7,839.55	7,792.24	7,769.99
15.25%	14,831.24	12,051.12	11,216.03	10,097.90	8,783.85	8,278.85	8,061.60	7,963.64	7,918.54	7,897.57
15.50%	14,912.98	12,138.58	11,306.27	10,193.45	8,890.74	8,394.06	8,182.42	8,088.00	8,045.02	8,025.28
15.75%	14,994.96	12,226.36	11,396.88	10,289.43	8,998.11	8,509.71	8,303.59	8,212.63	8,171.69	8,153.10
16.00%	15,077.20	12,314.48	11,487.85	10,385.81	9,105.94	8,625.79	8,425.11	8,337.49	8,298.51	8,281.02
16.25%	15,159.68	12,402.92	11,579.18	10,482.61	9,214.24	8,742.28	8,546.96	8,462.59	8,425.49	8,409.04
16.50%	15,242.40	12,491.69	11,670.86	10,579.82	9,322.99	8,859.18	8,669.12	8,587.92	8,552.61	8,537.15
16.75%	15,325.38	12,580.78	11,762.90	10,677.44	9,432.19	8,976.48	8,791.58	8,713.45	8,679.87	8,665.34
17.00%	15,408.60	12,670.20	11,855.30	10,775.45	9,541.83	9,094.16	8,914.34	8,839.19	8,807.26	8,793.61
17.25%	15,492.06	12,759.94	11,948.05	10,873.87	9,651.89	9,212.22	9,037.38	8,965.11	8,934.77	8,921.94
17.50%	15,575.77	12,849.99	12,041.15	10,972.68	9,762.39	9,330.64	9,160.68	9,091.22	9,062.39	9,050.35
17.75%	15,659.73	12,940.37	12,134.60	11,071.89	9,873.29	9,449.41	9,284.25	9,217.49	9,190.11	9,178.81
18.00%	15,743.93	13,031.06	12,228.39	11,171.48	9,984.61	9,568.53	9,408.07	9,343.93	9,317.93	9,307.33
18.25%	15,828.37	13,122.07	12,322.53	11,271.46	10,096.33	9,687.98	9,532.12	9,470.52	9,445.84	9,435.90
18.50%	15,913.05	13,213.39	12,417.01	11,371.83	10,208.44	9,807.76	9,656.40	9,597.26	9,573.84	9,564.52
18.75%	15,997.98	13,305.03	12,511.84	11,472.57	10,320.95	9,927.85	9,780.90	9,724.13	9,701.92	9,693.18
19.00%	16,083.14	13,396.97	12,607.00	11,573.69	10,433.83	10,048.25	9,905.62	9,851.13	9,830.07	9,821.88
19.25%	16,168.55	13,489.23	12,702.49	11,675.18	10,547.09	10,168.94	10,030.53	9,978.26	9,958.29	9,950.62
19.50%	16,254.20	13,581.79	12,798.33	11,777.04	10,660.71	10,289.92	10,155.64	10,105.50	10,086.57	10,079.40
19.75%	16,340.08	13,674.67	12,894.49	11,879.26	10,774.70	10,411.18	10,280.93	10,232.86	10,214.92	10,208.20
20.00%	16,426.21	13,767.84	12,990.98	11,981.85	10,889.04	10,532.71	10,406.40	10,360.32	10,343.33	10,337.04
20.25%	16,512.57	13,861.33	13,087.81	12,084.80	11,003.72	10,654.51	10,532.04	10,487.87	10,471.78	10,465.90
20.50%	16,599.17	13,955.11	13,184.96	12,188.10	11,118.75	10,776.56	10,657.84	10,615.52	10,600.29	10,594.79
20.75%	16,686.01	14,049.20	13,282.43	12,291.76	11,234.11	10,898.85	10,783.80	10,743.26	10,728.84	10,723.69

$630,000   1.00 - 10.75%   5 - 40 Years

	5	7	8	10	15	20	25	30	35	40
1.00%	10,769.06	7,768.69	6,831.23	5,519.06	3,770.52	2,897.33	2,374.30	2,026.33	1,778.40	1,592.99
1.25%	10,837.01	7,836.81	6,899.51	5,587.69	3,840.19	2,968.14	2,446.27	2,099.49	1,852.74	1,668.52
1.50%	10,905.23	7,905.32	6,968.22	5,656.86	3,910.68	3,040.04	2,519.60	2,174.26	1,928.96	1,746.19
1.75%	10,973.72	7,974.21	7,037.37	5,726.58	3,981.99	3,113.01	2,594.27	2,250.63	2,007.04	1,825.95
2.00%	11,042.49	8,043.48	7,106.95	5,796.85	4,054.10	3,187.07	2,670.28	2,328.60	2,086.96	1,907.80
2.25%	11,111.53	8,113.14	7,176.97	5,867.65	4,127.03	3,262.19	2,747.62	2,408.15	2,168.69	1,991.70
2.50%	11,180.84	8,183.17	7,247.42	5,939.00	4,200.77	3,338.39	2,826.29	2,489.26	2,252.22	2,077.60
2.75%	11,250.42	8,253.58	7,318.31	6,010.89	4,275.32	3,415.65	2,906.26	2,571.92	2,337.52	2,165.49
3.00%	11,320.28	8,324.38	7,389.63	6,083.33	4,350.66	3,493.96	2,987.53	2,656.11	2,424.56	2,255.30
3.25%	11,390.40	8,395.55	7,461.39	6,156.30	4,426.81	3,573.33	3,070.09	2,741.80	2,513.30	2,347.01
3.50%	11,460.80	8,467.11	7,533.57	6,229.81	4,503.76	3,653.75	3,153.93	2,828.98	2,603.73	2,440.56
3.75%	11,531.47	8,539.04	7,606.19	6,303.86	4,581.50	3,735.20	3,239.03	2,917.63	2,695.80	2,535.91
4.00%	11,602.41	8,611.35	7,679.24	6,378.44	4,660.03	3,817.68	3,325.37	3,007.72	2,789.48	2,633.01
4.25%	11,673.62	8,684.04	7,752.73	6,453.56	4,739.35	3,901.18	3,412.95	3,099.22	2,884.73	2,731.81
4.50%	11,745.10	8,757.10	7,826.64	6,529.22	4,819.46	3,985.69	3,501.74	3,192.12	2,981.52	2,832.25
4.75%	11,816.85	8,830.54	7,900.98	6,605.41	4,900.34	4,071.21	3,591.74	3,286.38	3,079.80	2,934.27
5.00%	11,888.88	8,904.36	7,975.75	6,682.13	4,982.00	4,157.72	3,682.92	3,381.98	3,179.53	3,037.84
5.25%	11,961.17	8,978.56	8,050.95	6,759.38	5,064.43	4,245.22	3,775.26	3,478.88	3,280.68	3,142.88
5.50%	12,033.73	9,053.13	8,126.57	6,837.16	5,147.63	4,333.69	3,868.75	3,577.07	3,383.20	3,249.35
5.75%	12,106.56	9,128.07	8,202.62	6,915.46	5,231.58	4,423.13	3,963.37	3,676.51	3,487.05	3,357.19
6.00%	12,179.66	9,203.39	8,279.10	6,994.29	5,316.30	4,513.52	4,059.10	3,777.17	3,592.20	3,466.35
6.25%	12,253.03	9,279.08	8,356.00	7,073.65	5,401.76	4,604.85	4,155.92	3,879.02	3,698.58	3,576.76
6.50%	12,326.67	9,355.14	8,433.33	7,153.52	5,487.98	4,697.11	4,253.81	3,982.03	3,806.17	3,688.38
6.75%	12,400.58	9,431.58	8,511.07	7,233.92	5,574.93	4,790.29	4,352.74	4,086.17	3,914.92	3,801.15
7.00%	12,474.76	9,508.39	8,589.24	7,314.83	5,662.62	4,884.38	4,452.71	4,191.41	4,024.80	3,915.02
7.25%	12,549.20	9,585.57	8,667.83	7,396.27	5,751.04	4,979.37	4,553.68	4,297.71	4,135.74	4,029.93
7.50%	12,623.91	9,663.11	8,746.84	7,478.21	5,840.18	5,075.24	4,655.64	4,405.05	4,247.73	4,145.85
7.75%	12,698.88	9,741.03	8,826.26	7,560.67	5,930.04	5,171.98	4,758.57	4,513.40	4,360.71	4,262.71
8.00%	12,774.13	9,819.32	8,906.11	7,643.64	6,020.61	5,269.57	4,862.44	4,622.72	4,474.64	4,380.46
8.25%	12,849.64	9,897.97	8,986.37	7,727.12	6,111.88	5,368.01	4,967.24	4,732.98	4,589.49	4,499.07
8.50%	12,925.41	9,976.99	9,067.04	7,811.10	6,203.86	5,467.29	5,072.93	4,844.15	4,705.22	4,618.49
8.75%	13,001.46	10,056.37	9,148.13	7,895.59	6,296.53	5,567.38	5,179.50	4,956.21	4,821.79	4,738.67
9.00%	13,077.76	10,136.12	9,229.63	7,980.57	6,389.88	5,668.27	5,286.94	5,069.12	4,939.16	4,859.58
9.25%	13,154.34	10,216.23	9,311.54	8,066.06	6,483.91	5,769.96	5,395.21	5,182.86	5,057.29	4,981.16
9.50%	13,231.17	10,296.71	9,393.86	8,152.05	6,578.62	5,872.43	5,504.29	5,297.38	5,176.15	5,103.39
9.75%	13,308.27	10,377.55	9,476.59	8,238.53	6,673.98	5,975.66	5,614.17	5,412.67	5,295.71	5,226.22
10.00%	13,385.64	10,458.75	9,559.72	8,325.50	6,770.01	6,079.64	5,724.81	5,528.70	5,415.94	5,349.62
10.25%	13,463.27	10,540.31	9,643.26	8,412.96	6,866.69	6,184.35	5,836.21	5,645.44	5,536.79	5,473.55
10.50%	13,541.16	10,622.22	9,727.21	8,500.90	6,964.01	6,289.79	5,948.34	5,762.86	5,658.24	5,597.99
10.75%	13,619.31	10,704.50	9,811.56	8,589.34	7,061.97	6,395.94	6,061.18	5,880.93	5,780.27	5,722.90

$630,000   11.00 - 20.75%   5 - 40 Years

	5	7	8	10	15	20	25	30	35	40
11.00%	13,697.73	10,787.13	9,896.31	8,678.25	7,160.56	6,502.79	6,174.71	5,999.64	5,902.83	5,848.25
11.25%	13,776.40	10,870.13	9,981.46	8,767.64	7,259.77	6,610.31	6,288.91	6,118.95	6,025.91	5,974.02
11.50%	13,855.34	10,953.47	10,067.01	8,857.51	7,359.60	6,718.51	6,403.75	6,238.84	6,149.48	6,100.18
11.75%	13,934.54	11,037.17	10,152.95	8,947.86	7,460.03	6,827.35	6,519.23	6,359.28	6,273.50	6,226.69
12.00%	14,014.00	11,121.22	10,239.29	9,038.67	7,561.06	6,936.84	6,635.31	6,480.26	6,397.96	6,353.55
12.25%	14,093.72	11,205.63	10,326.02	9,129.95	7,662.68	7,046.96	6,751.99	6,601.75	6,522.84	6,480.72
12.50%	14,173.70	11,290.38	10,413.15	9,221.70	7,764.89	7,157.69	6,869.23	6,723.72	6,648.10	6,608.19
12.75%	14,253.94	11,375.48	10,500.67	9,313.91	7,867.67	7,269.01	6,987.03	6,846.17	6,773.74	6,735.94
13.00%	14,334.44	11,460.94	10,588.57	9,406.58	7,971.03	7,380.93	7,105.36	6,969.06	6,899.72	6,863.94
13.25%	14,415.19	11,546.74	10,676.86	9,499.70	8,074.94	7,493.41	7,224.21	7,092.37	7,026.03	6,992.18
13.50%	14,496.20	11,632.88	10,765.54	9,593.28	8,179.41	7,606.46	7,343.56	7,216.10	7,152.65	7,120.65
13.75%	14,577.47	11,719.37	10,854.60	9,687.31	8,284.42	7,720.05	7,463.40	7,340.21	7,279.56	7,249.32
14.00%	14,659.00	11,806.21	10,944.05	9,781.79	8,389.97	7,834.18	7,583.69	7,464.69	7,406.74	7,378.18
14.25%	14,740.78	11,893.38	11,033.87	9,876.71	8,496.05	7,948.83	7,704.44	7,589.53	7,534.19	7,507.23
14.50%	14,822.82	11,980.90	11,124.07	9,972.07	8,602.66	8,063.99	7,825.63	7,714.70	7,661.87	7,636.44
14.75%	14,905.11	12,068.76	11,214.65	10,067.87	8,709.77	8,179.64	7,947.23	7,840.20	7,789.79	7,765.80
15.00%	14,987.66	12,156.96	11,305.61	10,164.10	8,817.40	8,295.77	8,069.23	7,966.00	7,917.92	7,895.31
15.25%	15,070.46	12,245.49	11,396.93	10,260.77	8,925.52	8,412.38	8,191.63	8,092.09	8,046.26	8,024.95
15.50%	15,153.51	12,334.36	11,488.63	10,357.86	9,034.14	8,529.45	8,314.39	8,218.46	8,174.78	8,154.72
15.75%	15,236.82	12,423.56	11,580.70	10,455.38	9,143.24	8,646.96	8,437.52	8,345.09	8,303.49	8,284.60
16.00%	15,320.38	12,513.10	11,673.14	10,553.33	9,252.81	8,764.91	8,561.00	8,471.97	8,432.36	8,414.59
16.25%	15,404.19	12,602.97	11,765.94	10,651.69	9,362.86	8,883.29	8,684.81	8,599.09	8,561.38	8,544.67
16.50%	15,488.25	12,693.17	11,859.10	10,750.46	9,473.36	9,002.07	8,808.94	8,726.43	8,690.56	8,674.84
16.75%	15,572.56	12,783.70	11,952.63	10,849.65	9,584.32	9,121.26	8,933.38	8,853.99	8,819.87	8,805.10
17.00%	15,657.12	12,874.56	12,046.52	10,949.25	9,695.73	9,240.84	9,058.12	8,981.75	8,949.31	8,935.44
17.25%	15,741.93	12,965.74	12,140.76	11,049.26	9,807.57	9,360.80	9,183.14	9,109.71	9,078.88	9,065.85
17.50%	15,826.99	13,057.25	12,235.36	11,149.66	9,919.84	9,481.13	9,308.44	9,237.85	9,208.55	9,196.32
17.75%	15,912.30	13,149.08	12,330.32	11,250.47	10,032.54	9,601.82	9,434.00	9,366.16	9,338.34	9,326.86
18.00%	15,997.86	13,241.24	12,425.62	11,351.67	10,145.65	9,722.86	9,559.81	9,494.64	9,468.22	9,457.45
18.25%	16,083.66	13,333.71	12,521.28	11,453.26	10,259.17	9,844.24	9,685.86	9,623.27	9,598.19	9,588.09
18.50%	16,169.71	13,426.51	12,617.29	11,555.24	10,373.10	9,965.95	9,812.15	9,752.05	9,728.26	9,718.79
18.75%	16,256.01	13,519.62	12,713.64	11,657.61	10,487.41	10,087.98	9,938.66	9,880.97	9,858.40	9,849.52
19.00%	16,342.55	13,613.05	12,810.33	11,760.36	10,602.12	10,210.31	10,065.38	10,010.02	9,988.62	9,980.30
19.25%	16,429.33	13,706.80	12,907.37	11,863.49	10,717.20	10,332.95	10,192.31	10,139.20	10,118.91	10,111.12
19.50%	16,516.36	13,800.85	13,004.75	11,966.99	10,832.66	10,455.89	10,319.44	10,268.50	10,249.26	10,241.97
19.75%	16,603.63	13,895.22	13,102.47	12,070.86	10,948.48	10,579.10	10,446.75	10,397.90	10,379.68	10,372.85
20.00%	16,691.15	13,989.91	13,200.52	12,175.11	11,064.67	10,702.60	10,574.25	10,527.42	10,510.15	10,503.76
20.25%	16,778.90	14,084.90	13,298.90	12,279.72	11,181.20	10,826.35	10,701.91	10,657.03	10,640.68	10,634.70
20.50%	16,866.90	14,180.19	13,397.62	12,384.69	11,298.08	10,950.37	10,829.74	10,786.74	10,771.26	10,765.67
20.75%	16,955.14	14,275.80	13,496.66	12,490.01	11,415.30	11,074.64	10,957.73	10,916.54	10,901.89	10,896.66

$640,000 1.00 - 10.75% 5 - 40 Years

	5	7	8	10	15	20	25	30	35	40
1.00%	10,940.00	7,892.00	6,939.66	5,606.66	3,830.36	2,943.32	2,411.98	2,058.49	1,806.63	1,618.28
1.25%	11,009.02	7,961.21	7,009.02	5,676.38	3,901.15	3,015.26	2,485.10	2,132.81	1,882.15	1,695.01
1.50%	11,078.33	8,030.80	7,078.83	5,746.66	3,972.76	3,088.29	2,559.59	2,208.77	1,959.58	1,773.90
1.75%	11,147.91	8,100.79	7,149.07	5,817.48	4,045.19	3,162.42	2,635.45	2,286.36	2,038.90	1,854.94
2.00%	11,217.77	8,171.16	7,219.76	5,888.86	4,118.46	3,237.65	2,712.67	2,365.56	2,120.08	1,938.08
2.25%	11,287.90	8,241.92	7,290.89	5,960.79	4,192.54	3,313.97	2,791.24	2,446.38	2,203.11	2,023.31
2.50%	11,358.31	8,313.06	7,362.46	6,033.27	4,267.45	3,391.38	2,871.15	2,528.77	2,287.97	2,110.58
2.75%	11,429.00	8,384.59	7,434.47	6,106.31	4,343.18	3,469.86	2,952.39	2,612.74	2,374.62	2,199.86
3.00%	11,499.96	8,456.51	7,506.93	6,179.89	4,419.72	3,549.42	3,034.95	2,698.27	2,463.04	2,291.10
3.25%	11,571.20	8,528.82	7,579.82	6,254.02	4,497.08	3,630.05	3,118.82	2,785.32	2,553.20	2,384.26
3.50%	11,642.72	8,601.50	7,653.15	6,328.70	4,575.25	3,711.74	3,203.99	2,873.89	2,645.06	2,479.30
3.75%	11,714.51	8,674.58	7,726.93	6,403.92	4,654.22	3,794.49	3,290.44	2,963.94	2,738.59	2,576.17
4.00%	11,786.57	8,748.04	7,801.14	6,479.69	4,734.00	3,878.27	3,378.16	3,055.46	2,833.76	2,674.81
4.25%	11,858.92	8,821.88	7,875.78	6,556.00	4,814.58	3,963.10	3,467.12	3,148.42	2,930.52	2,775.17
4.50%	11,931.53	8,896.10	7,950.87	6,632.86	4,895.96	4,048.96	3,557.33	3,242.79	3,028.84	2,877.20
4.75%	12,004.42	8,970.71	8,026.39	6,710.26	4,978.12	4,135.83	3,648.75	3,338.54	3,128.68	2,980.85
5.00%	12,077.59	9,045.70	8,102.35	6,788.19	5,061.08	4,223.72	3,741.38	3,435.66	3,230.00	3,086.06
5.25%	12,151.03	9,121.07	8,178.74	6,866.67	5,144.82	4,312.60	3,835.19	3,534.10	3,332.76	3,192.77
5.50%	12,224.74	9,196.83	8,255.57	6,945.68	5,229.33	4,402.48	3,930.16	3,633.85	3,436.90	3,300.93
5.75%	12,298.73	9,272.96	8,332.82	7,025.23	5,314.62	4,493.33	4,026.28	3,734.87	3,542.40	3,410.48
6.00%	12,372.99	9,349.47	8,410.52	7,105.31	5,400.68	4,585.16	4,123.53	3,837.12	3,649.21	3,521.37
6.25%	12,447.53	9,426.37	8,488.64	7,185.93	5,487.51	4,677.94	4,221.88	3,940.59	3,757.29	3,633.53
6.50%	12,522.33	9,503.64	8,567.19	7,267.07	5,575.09	4,771.67	4,321.33	4,045.24	3,866.59	3,746.92
6.75%	12,597.41	9,581.29	8,646.17	7,348.74	5,663.42	4,866.33	4,421.83	4,151.03	3,977.07	3,861.48
7.00%	12,672.77	9,659.32	8,725.58	7,430.94	5,752.50	4,961.91	4,523.39	4,257.94	4,088.68	3,977.16
7.25%	12,748.39	9,737.72	8,805.42	7,513.67	5,842.32	5,058.41	4,625.96	4,365.93	4,201.39	4,093.90
7.50%	12,824.29	9,816.50	8,885.68	7,596.91	5,932.88	5,155.80	4,729.54	4,474.97	4,315.15	4,211.65
7.75%	12,900.45	9,895.65	8,966.36	7,680.68	6,024.16	5,254.07	4,834.10	4,585.04	4,429.93	4,330.37
8.00%	12,976.89	9,975.18	9,047.47	7,764.97	6,116.17	5,353.22	4,939.62	4,696.09	4,545.67	4,449.99
8.25%	13,053.60	10,055.08	9,129.01	7,849.77	6,208.90	5,453.22	5,046.08	4,808.11	4,662.34	4,570.49
8.50%	13,130.58	10,135.35	9,210.96	7,935.08	6,302.33	5,554.07	5,153.45	4,921.05	4,779.91	4,691.80
8.75%	13,207.83	10,216.00	9,293.34	8,020.91	6,396.47	5,655.75	5,261.72	5,034.88	4,898.32	4,813.89
9.00%	13,285.35	10,297.01	9,376.13	8,107.25	6,491.31	5,758.25	5,370.86	5,149.58	5,017.56	4,936.71
9.25%	13,363.13	10,378.39	9,459.34	8,194.09	6,586.83	5,861.55	5,480.84	5,265.12	5,137.56	5,060.23
9.50%	13,441.19	10,460.15	9,542.97	8,281.44	6,683.04	5,965.64	5,591.66	5,381.47	5,258.31	5,184.39
9.75%	13,519.52	10,542.27	9,627.01	8,369.30	6,779.92	6,070.51	5,703.28	5,498.59	5,379.77	5,309.17
10.00%	13,598.11	10,624.76	9,711.47	8,457.65	6,877.47	6,176.14	5,815.68	5,616.46	5,501.90	5,434.53
10.25%	13,676.97	10,707.61	9,796.33	8,546.50	6,975.69	6,282.52	5,928.85	5,735.05	5,624.68	5,560.44
10.50%	13,756.10	10,790.83	9,881.61	8,635.84	7,074.55	6,389.63	6,042.76	5,854.33	5,748.06	5,686.85
10.75%	13,835.49	10,874.41	9,967.30	8,725.68	7,174.07	6,497.47	6,157.39	5,974.28	5,872.02	5,813.74

$640,000   11.00 - 20.75%   5 - 40 Years

	5	7	8	10	15	20	25	30	35	40
11.00%	13,915.15	10,958.36	10,053.39	8,816.00	7,274.22	6,606.01	6,272.72	6,094.87	5,996.53	5,941.08
11.25%	13,995.08	11,042.67	10,139.89	8,906.81	7,375.01	6,715.24	6,388.73	6,216.07	6,121.56	6,068.85
11.50%	14,075.27	11,127.33	10,226.80	8,998.11	7,476.41	6,825.15	6,505.40	6,337.87	6,247.09	6,197.00
11.75%	14,155.73	11,212.36	10,314.11	9,089.89	7,578.44	6,935.73	6,622.71	6,460.22	6,373.08	6,325.53
12.00%	14,236.45	11,297.75	10,401.82	9,182.14	7,681.08	7,046.95	6,740.63	6,583.12	6,499.52	6,454.40
12.25%	14,317.43	11,383.49	10,489.93	9,274.87	7,784.31	7,158.81	6,859.16	6,706.54	6,626.38	6,583.59
12.50%	14,398.68	11,469.59	10,578.44	9,368.07	7,888.14	7,271.30	6,978.27	6,830.45	6,753.63	6,713.08
12.75%	14,480.19	11,556.05	10,667.34	9,461.75	7,992.56	7,384.39	7,097.93	6,954.84	6,881.26	6,842.86
13.00%	14,561.97	11,642.86	10,756.64	9,555.89	8,097.55	7,498.08	7,218.15	7,079.68	7,009.24	6,972.89
13.25%	14,644.00	11,730.02	10,846.34	9,650.49	8,203.11	7,612.36	7,338.88	7,204.95	7,137.55	7,103.17
13.50%	14,726.30	11,817.53	10,936.42	9,745.55	8,309.24	7,727.20	7,460.13	7,330.64	7,266.18	7,233.67
13.75%	14,808.86	11,905.39	11,026.90	9,841.08	8,415.92	7,842.59	7,581.86	7,456.72	7,395.10	7,364.39
14.00%	14,891.68	11,993.61	11,117.76	9,937.05	8,523.14	7,958.53	7,704.07	7,583.18	7,524.31	7,495.30
14.25%	14,974.76	12,082.17	11,209.01	10,033.48	8,630.91	8,075.00	7,826.74	7,710.00	7,653.78	7,626.39
14.50%	15,058.10	12,171.07	11,300.64	10,130.35	8,739.21	8,191.99	7,949.84	7,837.16	7,783.49	7,757.65
14.75%	15,141.70	12,260.33	11,392.66	10,227.67	8,848.02	8,309.47	8,073.37	7,964.64	7,913.44	7,889.07
15.00%	15,225.56	12,349.92	11,485.06	10,325.44	8,957.36	8,427.45	8,197.32	8,092.44	8,043.61	8,020.63
15.25%	15,309.67	12,439.86	11,577.84	10,423.64	9,067.20	8,545.91	8,321.65	8,220.53	8,173.98	8,152.33
15.50%	15,394.04	12,530.14	11,670.99	10,522.27	9,177.54	8,664.84	8,446.37	8,348.91	8,304.54	8,284.16
15.75%	15,478.67	12,620.76	11,764.52	10,621.34	9,288.37	8,784.22	8,571.45	8,477.55	8,435.29	8,416.10
16.00%	15,563.56	12,711.72	11,858.42	10,720.84	9,399.68	8,904.04	8,696.89	8,606.44	8,566.20	8,548.15
16.25%	15,648.70	12,803.02	11,952.70	10,820.76	9,511.48	9,024.29	8,822.66	8,735.58	8,697.28	8,680.30
16.50%	15,734.09	12,894.65	12,047.34	10,921.11	9,623.74	9,144.96	8,948.77	8,864.95	8,828.51	8,812.54
16.75%	15,819.74	12,986.62	12,142.35	11,021.87	9,736.45	9,266.05	9,075.18	8,994.53	8,959.87	8,944.87
17.00%	15,905.65	13,078.92	12,237.73	11,123.05	9,849.63	9,387.52	9,201.90	9,124.32	9,091.37	9,077.27
17.25%	15,991.81	13,171.55	12,333.47	11,224.64	9,963.25	9,509.39	9,328.90	9,254.31	9,222.99	9,209.75
17.50%	16,078.22	13,264.51	12,429.57	11,326.64	10,077.30	9,631.63	9,456.19	9,384.48	9,354.72	9,342.29
17.75%	16,164.88	13,357.80	12,526.04	11,429.05	10,191.79	9,754.23	9,583.74	9,514.83	9,486.56	9,474.90
18.00%	16,251.79	13,451.42	12,622.86	11,531.85	10,306.69	9,877.19	9,711.55	9,645.35	9,618.51	9,607.57
18.25%	16,338.96	13,545.36	12,720.03	11,635.06	10,422.02	10,000.50	9,839.61	9,776.02	9,750.55	9,740.28
18.50%	16,426.37	13,639.63	12,817.56	11,738.66	10,537.75	10,124.14	9,967.90	9,906.84	9,882.67	9,873.05
18.75%	16,514.04	13,734.22	12,915.44	11,842.65	10,653.88	10,248.10	10,096.42	10,037.81	10,014.88	10,005.86
19.00%	16,601.95	13,829.13	13,013.67	11,947.03	10,770.41	10,372.38	10,225.15	10,168.91	10,147.17	10,138.72
19.25%	16,690.12	13,924.36	13,112.25	12,051.80	10,887.32	10,496.97	10,354.10	10,300.14	10,279.52	10,271.61
19.50%	16,778.53	14,019.92	13,211.17	12,156.94	11,004.61	10,621.85	10,483.24	10,431.49	10,411.95	10,404.54
19.75%	16,867.18	14,115.78	13,310.44	12,262.47	11,122.27	10,747.03	10,612.57	10,562.95	10,544.44	10,537.50
20.00%	16,956.09	14,211.97	13,410.05	12,368.36	11,240.30	10,872.48	10,742.09	10,694.52	10,676.98	10,670.49
20.25%	17,045.23	14,308.46	13,509.99	12,474.63	11,358.68	10,998.20	10,871.78	10,826.19	10,809.58	10,803.51
20.50%	17,134.63	14,405.27	13,610.28	12,581.27	11,477.42	11,124.19	11,001.65	10,957.96	10,942.23	10,936.55
20.75%	17,224.27	14,502.40	13,710.90	12,688.27	11,596.50	11,250.43	11,131.67	11,089.82	11,074.93	11,069.62

	5	7	8	10	15	20	25	30	35	40
1.00%	11,110.94	8,015.31	7,048.10	5,694.27	3,890.21	2,989.31	2,449.67	2,090.66	1,834.86	1,643.56
1.25%	11,181.04	8,085.60	7,118.54	5,765.08	3,962.10	3,062.37	2,523.93	2,166.14	1,911.56	1,721.49
1.50%	11,251.43	8,156.28	7,189.43	5,836.45	4,034.83	3,136.55	2,599.59	2,243.28	1,990.20	1,801.62
1.75%	11,322.10	8,227.36	7,260.77	5,908.38	4,108.40	3,211.84	2,676.63	2,322.08	2,070.75	1,883.92
2.00%	11,393.04	8,298.83	7,332.57	5,980.87	4,182.81	3,288.24	2,755.05	2,402.53	2,153.21	1,968.37
2.25%	11,464.27	8,370.70	7,404.81	6,053.93	4,258.05	3,365.75	2,834.85	2,484.60	2,237.54	2,054.92
2.50%	11,535.79	8,442.95	7,477.50	6,127.54	4,334.13	3,444.37	2,916.01	2,568.29	2,323.72	2,143.56
2.75%	11,607.58	8,515.60	7,550.64	6,201.72	4,411.04	3,524.08	2,998.52	2,653.57	2,411.72	2,234.23
3.00%	11,679.65	8,588.65	7,624.22	6,276.45	4,488.78	3,604.88	3,082.37	2,740.43	2,501.53	2,326.90
3.25%	11,752.00	8,662.08	7,698.25	6,351.74	4,567.35	3,686.77	3,167.56	2,828.84	2,593.09	2,421.52
3.50%	11,824.63	8,735.90	7,772.73	6,427.58	4,646.74	3,769.74	3,254.05	2,918.79	2,686.39	2,518.04
3.75%	11,897.55	8,810.12	7,847.66	6,503.98	4,726.95	3,853.77	3,341.85	3,010.25	2,781.38	2,616.42
4.00%	11,970.74	8,884.72	7,923.03	6,580.93	4,807.97	3,938.87	3,430.94	3,103.20	2,878.04	2,716.60
4.25%	12,044.21	8,959.72	7,998.84	6,658.44	4,889.81	4,025.02	3,521.30	3,197.61	2,976.31	2,818.53
4.50%	12,117.96	9,035.10	8,075.10	6,736.50	4,972.46	4,112.22	3,612.91	3,293.45	3,076.17	2,922.16
4.75%	12,191.99	9,110.88	8,151.80	6,815.10	5,055.91	4,200.45	3,705.76	3,390.71	3,177.57	3,027.43
5.00%	12,266.30	9,187.04	8,228.95	6,894.26	5,140.16	4,289.71	3,799.84	3,489.34	3,280.47	3,134.28
5.25%	12,340.89	9,263.59	8,306.53	6,973.96	5,225.21	4,379.99	3,895.11	3,589.32	3,384.83	3,242.66
5.50%	12,415.76	9,340.53	8,384.56	7,054.21	5,311.04	4,471.27	3,991.57	3,690.63	3,490.61	3,352.51
5.75%	12,490.90	9,417.85	8,463.03	7,135.00	5,397.67	4,563.54	4,089.19	3,793.22	3,597.75	3,463.77
6.00%	12,566.32	9,495.56	8,541.93	7,216.33	5,485.07	4,656.80	4,187.96	3,897.08	3,706.23	3,576.39
6.25%	12,642.02	9,573.65	8,621.27	7,298.21	5,573.25	4,751.03	4,287.85	4,002.16	3,816.00	3,690.31
6.50%	12,718.00	9,652.13	8,701.05	7,380.62	5,662.20	4,846.23	4,388.85	4,108.44	3,927.00	3,805.47
6.75%	12,794.25	9,731.00	8,781.27	7,463.57	5,751.91	4,942.37	4,490.92	4,215.89	4,039.21	3,921.82
7.00%	12,870.78	9,810.24	8,861.92	7,547.05	5,842.38	5,039.44	4,594.06	4,324.47	4,152.57	4,039.30
7.25%	12,947.58	9,889.87	8,943.00	7,631.07	5,933.61	5,137.44	4,698.24	4,434.15	4,267.04	4,157.87
7.50%	13,024.67	9,969.88	9,024.52	7,715.61	6,025.58	5,236.36	4,803.44	4,544.89	4,382.58	4,277.46
7.75%	13,102.02	10,050.27	9,106.46	7,800.69	6,118.29	5,336.17	4,909.64	4,656.68	4,499.14	4,398.03
8.00%	13,179.66	10,131.04	9,188.84	7,886.29	6,211.74	5,436.86	5,016.81	4,769.47	4,616.70	4,519.53
8.25%	13,257.56	10,212.19	9,271.65	7,972.42	6,305.91	5,538.43	5,124.93	4,883.23	4,735.19	4,641.90
8.50%	13,335.75	10,293.72	9,354.88	8,059.07	6,400.81	5,640.85	5,233.98	4,997.94	4,854.59	4,765.11
8.75%	13,414.20	10,375.62	9,438.55	8,146.24	6,496.42	5,744.12	5,343.93	5,113.55	4,974.86	4,889.11
9.00%	13,492.93	10,457.90	9,522.63	8,233.93	6,592.73	5,848.22	5,454.78	5,230.05	5,095.95	5,013.85
9.25%	13,571.93	10,540.56	9,607.14	8,322.13	6,689.75	5,953.13	5,566.48	5,347.39	5,217.84	5,139.29
9.50%	13,651.21	10,623.59	9,692.08	8,410.84	6,787.46	6,058.85	5,679.03	5,465.55	5,340.48	5,265.40
9.75%	13,730.76	10,706.99	9,777.43	8,500.07	6,885.86	6,165.36	5,792.39	5,584.50	5,463.83	5,392.13
10.00%	13,810.58	10,790.77	9,863.21	8,589.80	6,984.93	6,272.64	5,906.55	5,704.22	5,587.87	5,519.45
10.25%	13,890.67	10,874.92	9,949.40	8,680.04	7,084.68	6,380.68	6,021.49	5,824.66	5,712.56	5,647.32
10.50%	13,971.04	10,959.44	10,036.01	8,770.77	7,185.09	6,489.47	6,137.18	5,945.81	5,837.87	5,775.71
10.75%	14,051.67	11,044.33	10,123.04	8,862.01	7,286.16	6,598.99	6,253.60	6,067.63	5,963.77	5,904.58

$650,000   11.00 - 20.75%   5 - 40 Years

	5	7	8	10	15	20	25	30	35	40
11.00%	14,132.57	11,129.58	10,210.48	8,953.75	7,387.88	6,709.22	6,370.73	6,190.10	6,090.22	6,033.91
11.25%	14,213.75	11,215.21	10,298.33	9,045.98	7,490.24	6,820.16	6,488.56	6,313.20	6,217.21	6,163.67
11.50%	14,295.19	11,301.20	10,386.59	9,138.70	7,593.23	6,931.79	6,607.05	6,436.89	6,344.70	6,293.83
11.75%	14,376.91	11,387.56	10,475.27	9,231.91	7,696.85	7,044.10	6,726.19	6,561.16	6,472.66	6,424.37
12.00%	14,458.89	11,474.28	10,564.35	9,325.61	7,801.09	7,157.06	6,845.96	6,685.98	6,601.07	6,555.25
12.25%	14,541.14	11,561.36	10,653.83	9,419.79	7,905.94	7,270.67	6,966.33	6,811.33	6,729.91	6,686.46
12.50%	14,623.66	11,648.80	10,743.73	9,514.45	8,011.39	7,384.91	7,087.30	6,937.18	6,859.15	6,817.98
12.75%	14,706.45	11,736.61	10,834.02	9,609.59	8,117.44	7,499.78	7,208.84	7,063.51	6,988.77	6,949.78
13.00%	14,789.50	11,824.78	10,924.72	9,705.20	8,224.07	7,615.24	7,330.93	7,190.30	7,118.76	7,081.84
13.25%	14,872.82	11,913.30	11,015.81	9,801.28	8,331.29	7,731.30	7,453.55	7,317.53	7,249.07	7,214.15
13.50%	14,956.40	12,002.18	11,107.30	9,897.83	8,439.07	7,847.94	7,576.69	7,445.18	7,379.71	7,346.70
13.75%	15,040.25	12,091.42	11,199.19	9,994.84	8,547.42	7,965.13	7,700.33	7,573.23	7,510.65	7,479.45
14.00%	15,124.36	12,181.01	11,291.48	10,092.32	8,656.32	8,082.89	7,824.45	7,701.67	7,641.88	7,612.41
14.25%	15,208.74	12,270.95	11,384.15	10,190.25	8,765.77	8,201.17	7,949.03	7,830.47	7,773.37	7,745.55
14.50%	15,293.38	12,361.25	11,477.22	10,288.64	8,875.76	8,319.99	8,074.06	7,959.61	7,905.11	7,878.86
14.75%	15,378.29	12,451.89	11,570.67	10,387.48	8,986.27	8,439.31	8,199.52	8,089.09	8,037.09	8,012.34
15.00%	15,463.45	12,542.89	11,664.51	10,486.77	9,097.32	8,559.13	8,325.40	8,218.89	8,169.29	8,145.96
15.25%	15,548.88	12,634.23	11,758.74	10,586.51	9,208.87	8,679.44	8,451.68	8,348.98	8,301.70	8,279.71
15.50%	15,634.57	12,725.93	11,853.35	10,686.68	9,320.94	8,800.22	8,578.34	8,479.36	8,434.30	8,413.60
15.75%	15,720.53	12,817.96	11,948.34	10,787.30	9,433.50	8,921.47	8,705.38	8,610.01	8,567.09	8,547.60
16.00%	15,806.74	12,910.34	12,043.71	10,888.35	9,546.55	9,043.16	8,832.78	8,740.92	8,700.05	8,681.71
16.25%	15,893.21	13,003.06	12,139.46	10,989.84	9,660.09	9,165.30	8,960.52	8,872.08	8,833.17	8,815.93
16.50%	15,979.94	13,096.13	12,235.58	11,091.75	9,774.11	9,287.85	9,088.59	9,003.46	8,966.45	8,950.24
16.75%	16,066.93	13,189.53	12,332.08	11,194.09	9,888.59	9,410.83	9,216.98	9,135.07	9,099.87	9,084.63
17.00%	16,154.17	13,283.27	12,428.95	11,296.85	10,003.53	9,534.20	9,345.68	9,266.89	9,233.42	9,219.10
17.25%	16,241.68	13,377.35	12,526.18	11,400.03	10,118.92	9,657.97	9,474.67	9,398.91	9,367.10	9,353.65
17.50%	16,329.44	13,471.77	12,623.79	11,503.62	10,234.76	9,782.12	9,603.94	9,531.11	9,500.89	9,488.27
17.75%	16,417.46	13,566.51	12,721.76	11,607.62	10,351.03	9,906.64	9,733.49	9,663.50	9,634.79	9,622.95
18.00%	16,505.73	13,661.59	12,820.09	11,712.04	10,467.74	10,031.52	9,863.29	9,796.05	9,768.80	9,757.69
18.25%	16,594.25	13,757.01	12,918.78	11,816.86	10,584.86	10,156.76	9,993.35	9,928.77	9,902.90	9,892.48
18.50%	16,683.04	13,852.75	13,017.84	11,922.08	10,702.40	10,282.33	10,123.65	10,061.64	10,037.09	10,027.32
18.75%	16,772.07	13,948.82	13,117.25	12,027.69	10,820.35	10,408.23	10,254.17	10,194.65	10,171.36	10,162.21
19.00%	16,861.36	14,045.21	13,217.01	12,133.70	10,938.69	10,534.45	10,384.92	10,327.80	10,305.72	10,297.14
19.25%	16,950.90	14,141.93	13,317.13	12,240.10	11,057.43	10,660.98	10,515.88	10,461.08	10,440.14	10,432.10
19.50%	17,040.69	14,238.98	13,417.60	12,346.89	11,176.56	10,787.82	10,647.04	10,594.48	10,574.63	10,567.11
19.75%	17,130.73	14,336.34	13,518.42	12,454.07	11,296.06	10,914.95	10,778.40	10,728.00	10,709.19	10,702.15
20.00%	17,221.02	14,434.03	13,619.58	12,561.62	11,415.93	11,042.36	10,909.94	10,861.62	10,843.81	10,837.22
20.25%	17,311.57	14,532.03	13,721.09	12,669.55	11,536.16	11,170.05	11,041.66	10,995.35	10,978.48	10,972.31
20.50%	17,402.36	14,630.36	13,822.94	12,777.85	11,656.75	11,298.00	11,173.55	11,129.18	11,113.21	11,107.44
20.75%	17,493.40	14,729.00	13,925.13	12,886.52	11,777.70	11,426.22	11,305.60	11,263.09	11,247.98	11,242.58

	5	7	8	10	15	20	25	30	35	40
1.00%	11,281.87	8,138.62	7,156.53	5,781.87	3,950.06	3,035.30	2,487.36	2,122.82	1,863.09	1,668.85
1.25%	11,353.06	8,209.99	7,228.06	5,853.77	4,023.06	3,109.48	2,562.76	2,199.46	1,940.97	1,747.98
1.50%	11,424.53	8,281.77	7,300.04	5,926.24	4,096.90	3,184.80	2,639.58	2,277.79	2,020.82	1,829.34
1.75%	11,496.28	8,353.94	7,372.48	5,999.28	4,171.60	3,261.25	2,717.81	2,357.81	2,102.61	1,912.91
2.00%	11,568.32	8,426.51	7,445.38	6,072.89	4,247.16	3,338.83	2,797.44	2,439.49	2,186.33	1,998.65
2.25%	11,640.65	8,499.48	7,518.73	6,147.07	4,323.56	3,417.53	2,878.46	2,522.82	2,271.96	2,086.54
2.50%	11,713.26	8,572.85	7,592.54	6,221.81	4,400.81	3,497.36	2,960.87	2,607.80	2,359.47	2,176.54
2.75%	11,786.15	8,646.61	7,666.80	6,297.13	4,478.90	3,578.30	3,044.65	2,694.39	2,448.83	2,268.60
3.00%	11,859.34	8,720.78	7,741.52	6,373.01	4,557.84	3,660.34	3,129.79	2,782.59	2,540.01	2,362.70
3.25%	11,932.80	8,795.34	7,816.69	6,449.46	4,637.61	3,743.49	3,216.29	2,872.36	2,632.99	2,458.77
3.50%	12,006.55	8,870.30	7,892.31	6,526.47	4,718.22	3,827.73	3,304.12	2,963.69	2,727.72	2,556.78
3.75%	12,080.59	8,945.66	7,968.39	6,604.04	4,799.67	3,913.06	3,393.27	3,056.56	2,824.17	2,656.67
4.00%	12,154.90	9,021.41	8,044.92	6,682.18	4,881.94	3,999.47	3,483.72	3,150.94	2,922.31	2,758.39
4.25%	12,229.51	9,097.56	8,121.90	6,760.88	4,965.04	4,086.95	3,575.47	3,246.80	3,022.10	2,861.89
4.50%	12,304.39	9,174.11	8,199.33	6,840.13	5,048.96	4,175.49	3,668.49	3,344.12	3,123.49	2,967.11
4.75%	12,379.56	9,251.05	8,277.22	6,919.95	5,133.69	4,265.08	3,762.77	3,442.87	3,226.45	3,074.00
5.00%	12,455.01	9,328.38	8,355.55	7,000.32	5,219.24	4,355.71	3,858.29	3,543.02	3,330.94	3,182.50
5.25%	12,530.75	9,406.11	8,434.33	7,081.25	5,305.59	4,447.37	3,955.03	3,644.54	3,436.90	3,292.54
5.50%	12,606.77	9,484.23	8,513.55	7,162.73	5,392.75	4,540.06	4,052.98	3,747.41	3,544.31	3,404.08
5.75%	12,683.07	9,562.74	8,593.23	7,244.77	5,480.71	4,633.75	4,152.10	3,851.58	3,653.10	3,517.06
6.00%	12,759.65	9,641.65	8,673.34	7,327.35	5,569.46	4,728.44	4,252.39	3,957.03	3,763.25	3,631.41
6.25%	12,836.51	9,720.94	8,753.91	7,410.49	5,658.99	4,824.13	4,353.82	4,063.73	3,874.70	3,747.08
6.50%	12,913.66	9,800.63	8,834.91	7,494.17	5,749.31	4,920.78	4,456.37	4,171.65	3,987.42	3,864.01
6.75%	12,991.08	9,880.70	8,916.36	7,578.39	5,840.40	5,018.40	4,560.02	4,280.75	4,101.35	3,982.16
7.00%	13,068.79	9,961.17	8,998.25	7,663.16	5,932.27	5,116.97	4,664.74	4,391.00	4,216.45	4,101.45
7.25%	13,146.78	10,042.02	9,080.58	7,748.47	6,024.90	5,216.48	4,770.53	4,502.36	4,332.68	4,221.83
7.50%	13,225.05	10,123.26	9,163.35	7,834.32	6,118.28	5,316.92	4,877.34	4,614.82	4,450.00	4,343.27
7.75%	13,303.59	10,204.89	9,246.56	7,920.70	6,212.42	5,418.26	4,985.17	4,728.32	4,568.36	4,465.69
8.00%	13,382.42	10,286.90	9,330.21	8,007.62	6,307.30	5,520.50	5,093.99	4,842.85	4,687.72	4,589.06
8.25%	13,461.53	10,369.30	9,414.29	8,095.07	6,402.93	5,623.63	5,203.77	4,958.36	4,808.04	4,713.32
8.50%	13,540.91	10,452.08	9,498.80	8,183.06	6,499.28	5,727.63	5,314.50	5,074.83	4,929.28	4,838.42
8.75%	13,620.57	10,535.24	9,583.75	8,271.57	6,596.36	5,832.49	5,426.15	5,192.22	5,051.40	4,964.33
9.00%	13,700.51	10,618.79	9,669.13	8,360.60	6,694.16	5,938.19	5,538.70	5,310.51	5,174.35	5,090.99
9.25%	13,780.73	10,702.72	9,754.95	8,450.16	6,792.67	6,044.72	5,652.12	5,429.66	5,298.11	5,218.36
9.50%	13,861.23	10,787.03	9,841.19	8,540.24	6,891.88	6,152.07	5,766.40	5,549.64	5,422.64	5,346.41
9.75%	13,942.00	10,871.72	9,927.85	8,630.84	6,991.79	6,260.21	5,881.51	5,670.42	5,547.89	5,475.09
10.00%	14,023.05	10,956.78	10,014.95	8,721.95	7,092.39	6,369.14	5,997.42	5,791.97	5,673.84	5,604.36
10.25%	14,104.37	11,042.22	10,102.47	8,813.57	7,193.68	6,478.85	6,114.13	5,914.27	5,800.45	5,734.20
10.50%	14,185.97	11,128.04	10,190.41	8,905.71	7,295.63	6,589.31	6,231.60	6,037.28	5,927.68	5,864.56
10.75%	14,267.85	11,214.24	10,278.78	8,998.35	7,398.26	6,700.51	6,349.81	6,160.98	6,055.52	5,995.42

$660,000   11.00 - 20.75%   5 - 40 Years

	5	7	8	10	15	20	25	30	35	40
11.00%	14,350.00	11,300.81	10,367.56	9,091.50	7,501.54	6,812.44	6,468.75	6,285.33	6,183.92	6,126.74
11.25%	14,432.42	11,387.75	10,456.77	9,185.15	7,605.47	6,925.09	6,588.38	6,410.33	6,312.86	6,258.50
11.50%	14,515.12	11,475.06	10,546.39	9,279.30	7,710.05	7,038.44	6,708.70	6,535.92	6,442.31	6,390.66
11.75%	14,598.09	11,562.75	10,636.42	9,373.94	7,815.27	7,152.47	6,829.67	6,662.10	6,572.24	6,523.20
12.00%	14,681.34	11,650.80	10,726.88	9,469.08	7,921.11	7,267.17	6,951.28	6,788.84	6,702.63	6,656.10
12.25%	14,764.85	11,739.23	10,817.74	9,564.71	8,027.57	7,382.53	7,073.51	6,916.12	6,833.45	6,789.33
12.50%	14,848.64	11,828.02	10,909.01	9,660.83	8,134.65	7,498.53	7,196.34	7,043.90	6,964.68	6,922.87
12.75%	14,932.70	11,917.17	11,000.70	9,757.43	8,242.32	7,615.16	7,319.74	7,172.18	7,096.29	7,056.70
13.00%	15,017.03	12,006.70	11,092.79	9,854.51	8,350.60	7,732.40	7,443.71	7,300.92	7,228.27	7,190.79
13.25%	15,101.63	12,096.58	11,185.28	9,952.07	8,459.46	7,850.24	7,568.22	7,430.11	7,360.60	7,325.14
13.50%	15,186.50	12,186.83	11,278.19	10,050.10	8,568.90	7,968.67	7,693.26	7,559.72	7,493.25	7,459.72
13.75%	15,271.64	12,277.44	11,371.49	10,148.61	8,678.92	8,087.68	7,818.80	7,689.74	7,626.20	7,594.52
14.00%	15,357.05	12,368.41	11,465.19	10,247.58	8,789.49	8,207.24	7,944.82	7,820.15	7,759.44	7,729.52
14.25%	15,442.72	12,459.74	11,559.29	10,347.03	8,900.63	8,327.35	8,071.32	7,950.93	7,892.96	7,864.71
14.50%	15,528.67	12,551.42	11,653.79	10,446.93	9,012.31	8,447.99	8,198.28	8,082.07	8,026.73	8,000.08
14.75%	15,614.88	12,643.46	11,748.68	10,547.29	9,124.52	8,569.14	8,325.67	8,213.54	8,160.73	8,135.60
15.00%	15,701.35	12,735.86	11,843.97	10,648.11	9,237.27	8,690.81	8,453.48	8,345.33	8,294.97	8,271.28
15.25%	15,788.10	12,828.61	11,939.64	10,749.38	9,350.55	8,812.97	8,581.70	8,477.43	8,429.41	8,407.09
15.50%	15,875.11	12,921.71	12,035.71	10,851.10	9,464.34	8,935.61	8,710.32	8,609.81	8,564.06	8,543.04
15.75%	15,962.38	13,015.16	12,132.16	10,953.26	9,578.63	9,058.72	8,839.31	8,742.47	8,698.89	8,679.10
16.00%	16,049.92	13,108.96	12,229.00	11,055.87	9,693.42	9,182.29	8,968.67	8,875.40	8,833.90	8,815.28
16.25%	16,137.72	13,203.11	12,326.22	11,158.91	9,808.71	9,306.30	9,098.37	9,008.57	8,969.07	8,951.56
16.50%	16,225.78	13,297.61	12,423.82	11,262.39	9,924.48	9,430.74	9,228.41	9,141.98	9,104.40	9,087.93
16.75%	16,314.11	13,392.45	12,521.80	11,366.30	10,040.72	9,555.61	9,358.78	9,275.61	9,239.87	9,224.39
17.00%	16,402.70	13,487.63	12,620.16	11,470.65	10,157.43	9,680.88	9,489.46	9,409.46	9,375.47	9,360.94
17.25%	16,491.55	13,583.16	12,718.89	11,575.41	10,274.60	9,806.56	9,620.43	9,543.51	9,511.21	9,497.55
17.50%	16,580.66	13,679.02	12,818.00	11,680.60	10,392.22	9,932.62	9,751.70	9,677.75	9,647.06	9,634.24
17.75%	16,670.03	13,775.23	12,917.48	11,786.20	10,510.28	10,059.05	9,883.23	9,812.17	9,783.02	9,770.99
18.00%	16,759.66	13,871.77	13,017.32	11,892.22	10,628.78	10,185.86	10,015.04	9,946.76	9,919.09	9,907.80
18.25%	16,849.55	13,968.65	13,117.53	11,998.65	10,747.71	10,313.01	10,147.09	10,081.52	10,055.25	10,044.67
18.50%	16,939.70	14,065.87	13,218.11	12,105.49	10,867.05	10,440.52	10,279.40	10,216.43	10,191.51	10,181.59
18.75%	17,030.10	14,163.41	13,319.05	12,212.73	10,986.82	10,568.36	10,411.93	10,351.49	10,327.85	10,318.55
19.00%	17,120.76	14,261.29	13,420.35	12,320.38	11,106.98	10,696.52	10,544.69	10,486.69	10,464.27	10,455.55
19.25%	17,211.68	14,359.50	13,522.01	12,428.41	11,227.55	10,825.00	10,677.66	10,622.02	10,600.76	10,592.60
19.50%	17,302.85	14,458.04	13,624.02	12,536.85	11,348.50	10,953.79	10,810.84	10,757.47	10,737.32	10,729.68
19.75%	17,394.28	14,556.90	13,726.39	12,645.67	11,469.84	11,082.87	10,944.22	10,893.04	10,873.95	10,866.80
20.00%	17,485.96	14,656.09	13,829.11	12,754.87	11,591.56	11,212.24	11,077.78	11,028.72	11,010.64	11,003.94
20.25%	17,577.90	14,755.60	13,932.18	12,864.46	11,713.64	11,341.89	11,211.53	11,164.51	11,147.38	11,141.12
20.50%	17,670.09	14,855.44	14,035.60	12,974.43	11,836.09	11,471.82	11,345.45	11,300.39	11,284.18	11,278.32
20.75%	17,762.53	14,955.59	14,139.36	13,084.78	11,958.89	11,602.00	11,479.53	11,436.37	11,421.02	11,415.55

	5	7	8	10	15	20	25	30	35	40
1.00%	11,452.81	8,261.94	7,264.96	5,869.48	4,009.91	3,081.29	2,525.05	2,154.98	1,891.31	1,694.14
1.25%	11,525.07	8,334.39	7,337.57	5,942.46	4,084.01	3,156.60	2,601.59	2,232.79	1,970.38	1,774.46
1.50%	11,597.62	8,407.25	7,410.65	6,016.03	4,158.98	3,233.05	2,679.57	2,312.31	2,051.44	1,857.06
1.75%	11,670.47	8,480.51	7,484.18	6,090.18	4,234.81	3,310.66	2,758.99	2,393.53	2,134.47	1,941.89
2.00%	11,743.60	8,554.18	7,558.18	6,164.90	4,311.51	3,389.42	2,839.82	2,476.45	2,219.46	2,028.93
2.25%	11,817.02	8,628.26	7,632.65	6,240.20	4,389.07	3,469.32	2,922.08	2,561.05	2,306.38	2,118.15
2.50%	11,890.73	8,702.74	7,707.58	6,316.08	4,467.49	3,550.35	3,005.73	2,647.31	2,395.22	2,209.51
2.75%	11,964.73	8,777.62	7,782.96	6,392.54	4,546.76	3,632.51	3,090.78	2,735.22	2,485.93	2,302.98
3.00%	12,039.02	8,852.91	7,858.81	6,469.57	4,626.90	3,715.80	3,177.22	2,824.75	2,578.50	2,398.50
3.25%	12,113.60	8,928.60	7,935.12	6,547.17	4,707.88	3,800.21	3,265.02	2,915.88	2,672.88	2,496.03
3.50%	12,188.47	9,004.70	8,011.89	6,625.35	4,789.71	3,885.73	3,354.18	3,008.60	2,769.05	2,595.52
3.75%	12,263.63	9,081.20	8,089.13	6,704.10	4,872.39	3,972.35	3,444.68	3,102.87	2,866.96	2,696.92
4.00%	12,339.07	9,158.10	8,166.81	6,783.42	4,955.91	4,060.07	3,536.51	3,198.68	2,966.59	2,800.19
4.25%	12,414.80	9,235.40	8,244.96	6,863.31	5,040.27	4,148.87	3,629.65	3,296.00	3,067.89	2,905.26
4.50%	12,490.82	9,313.11	8,323.57	6,943.77	5,125.46	4,238.75	3,724.08	3,394.79	3,170.82	3,012.07
4.75%	12,567.13	9,391.21	8,402.63	7,024.80	5,211.47	4,329.70	3,819.79	3,495.04	3,275.34	3,120.58
5.00%	12,643.73	9,469.72	8,482.15	7,106.39	5,298.32	4,421.70	3,916.75	3,596.70	3,381.41	3,230.72
5.25%	12,720.61	9,548.62	8,562.12	7,188.54	5,385.98	4,514.76	4,014.96	3,699.76	3,488.98	3,342.43
5.50%	12,797.78	9,627.93	8,642.55	7,271.26	5,474.46	4,608.84	4,114.39	3,804.19	3,598.01	3,455.66
5.75%	12,875.23	9,707.63	8,723.43	7,354.54	5,563.75	4,703.96	4,215.01	3,909.94	3,708.45	3,570.35
6.00%	12,952.98	9,787.73	8,804.76	7,438.37	5,653.84	4,800.09	4,316.82	4,016.99	3,820.27	3,686.43
6.25%	13,031.01	9,868.23	8,886.54	7,522.77	5,744.73	4,897.22	4,419.78	4,125.31	3,933.41	3,803.86
6.50%	13,109.32	9,949.12	8,968.78	7,607.71	5,836.42	4,995.34	4,523.89	4,234.86	4,047.83	3,922.56
6.75%	13,187.92	10,030.41	9,051.46	7,693.22	5,928.89	5,094.44	4,629.11	4,345.61	4,163.49	4,042.49
7.00%	13,266.80	10,112.10	9,134.59	7,779.27	6,022.15	5,194.50	4,735.42	4,457.53	4,280.34	4,163.59
7.25%	13,345.97	10,194.17	9,218.17	7,865.87	6,116.18	5,295.52	4,842.81	4,570.58	4,398.33	4,285.80
7.50%	13,425.43	10,276.64	9,302.19	7,953.02	6,210.98	5,397.47	4,951.24	4,684.74	4,517.43	4,409.07
7.75%	13,505.16	10,359.51	9,386.66	8,040.71	6,306.55	5,500.36	5,060.70	4,799.96	4,637.58	4,533.35
8.00%	13,585.18	10,442.76	9,471.58	8,128.95	6,402.87	5,604.15	5,171.17	4,916.22	4,758.75	4,658.59
8.25%	13,665.49	10,526.41	9,556.93	8,217.73	6,499.94	5,708.84	5,282.62	5,033.49	4,880.89	4,784.73
8.50%	13,746.08	10,610.45	9,642.73	8,307.04	6,597.76	5,814.42	5,395.02	5,151.72	5,003.97	4,911.73
8.75%	13,826.95	10,694.87	9,728.96	8,396.89	6,696.31	5,920.86	5,508.36	5,270.89	5,127.93	5,039.54
9.00%	13,908.10	10,779.68	9,815.64	8,487.28	6,795.59	6,028.16	5,622.62	5,390.97	5,252.75	5,168.12
9.25%	13,989.53	10,864.88	9,902.75	8,578.19	6,895.59	6,136.31	5,737.76	5,511.93	5,378.39	5,297.43
9.50%	14,071.25	10,950.47	9,990.29	8,669.64	6,996.31	6,245.28	5,853.77	5,633.72	5,504.80	5,427.41
9.75%	14,153.24	11,036.44	10,078.28	8,761.61	7,097.73	6,355.06	5,970.62	5,756.33	5,631.95	5,558.04
10.00%	14,235.52	11,122.79	10,166.69	8,854.10	7,199.85	6,465.65	6,088.29	5,879.73	5,759.81	5,689.28
10.25%	14,318.08	11,209.53	10,255.54	8,947.11	7,302.67	6,577.01	6,206.77	6,003.88	5,888.33	5,821.08
10.50%	14,400.91	11,296.65	10,344.81	9,040.64	7,406.17	6,689.15	6,326.02	6,128.75	6,017.50	5,953.42
10.75%	14,484.03	11,384.15	10,434.51	9,134.69	7,510.35	6,802.03	6,446.02	6,254.33	6,147.27	6,086.26

$670,000   11.00 - 20.75%   5 - 40 Years

	5	7	8	10	15	20	25	30	35	40
11.00%	14,567.42	11,472.03	10,524.65	9,229.25	7,615.20	6,915.66	6,566.76	6,380.57	6,277.62	6,219.57
11.25%	14,651.10	11,560.29	10,615.20	9,324.32	7,720.71	7,030.02	6,688.20	6,507.45	6,408.51	6,353.32
11.50%	14,735.05	11,648.93	10,706.18	9,419.89	7,826.87	7,145.08	6,810.34	6,634.95	6,539.92	6,487.49
11.75%	14,819.27	11,737.94	10,797.58	9,515.97	7,933.68	7,260.84	6,933.15	6,763.05	6,671.82	6,622.04
12.00%	14,903.78	11,827.33	10,889.40	9,612.55	8,041.13	7,377.28	7,056.60	6,891.70	6,804.18	6,756.95
12.25%	14,988.56	11,917.09	10,981.64	9,709.63	8,149.20	7,494.38	7,180.68	7,020.91	6,936.99	6,892.20
12.50%	15,073.62	12,007.23	11,074.30	9,807.20	8,257.90	7,612.14	7,305.37	7,150.63	7,070.20	7,027.76
12.75%	15,158.95	12,097.74	11,167.37	9,905.27	8,367.21	7,730.54	7,430.65	7,280.84	7,203.81	7,163.62
13.00%	15,244.56	12,188.62	11,260.86	10,003.82	8,477.12	7,849.56	7,556.50	7,411.54	7,337.79	7,299.74
13.25%	15,330.44	12,279.86	11,354.76	10,102.86	8,587.63	7,969.19	7,682.89	7,542.68	7,472.12	7,436.13
13.50%	15,416.60	12,371.48	11,449.07	10,202.38	8,698.73	8,089.41	7,809.82	7,674.26	7,606.78	7,572.75
13.75%	15,503.03	12,463.46	11,543.78	10,302.38	8,810.41	8,210.22	7,937.26	7,806.25	7,741.75	7,709.59
14.00%	15,589.73	12,555.81	11,638.91	10,402.85	8,922.67	8,331.59	8,065.20	7,938.64	7,877.01	7,846.64
14.25%	15,676.70	12,648.52	11,734.43	10,503.80	9,035.48	8,453.52	8,193.61	8,071.40	8,012.55	7,983.88
14.50%	15,763.95	12,741.59	11,830.36	10,605.21	9,148.86	8,575.99	8,322.49	8,204.52	8,148.34	8,121.29
14.75%	15,851.47	12,835.03	11,926.69	10,707.10	9,262.78	8,698.98	8,451.81	8,337.99	8,284.38	8,258.87
15.00%	15,939.25	12,928.83	12,023.42	10,809.44	9,377.23	8,822.49	8,581.57	8,471.77	8,420.65	8,396.60
15.25%	16,027.31	13,022.98	12,120.55	10,912.25	9,492.22	8,946.50	8,711.73	8,605.87	8,557.13	8,534.48
15.50%	16,115.64	13,117.49	12,218.07	11,015.51	9,607.74	9,071.00	8,842.29	8,740.26	8,693.82	8,672.48
15.75%	16,204.23	13,212.36	12,315.98	11,119.22	9,723.76	9,195.98	8,973.24	8,874.93	8,830.69	8,810.61
16.00%	16,293.10	13,307.58	12,414.29	11,223.38	9,840.29	9,321.41	9,104.56	9,009.87	8,967.74	8,948.84
16.25%	16,382.23	13,403.16	12,512.98	11,327.99	9,957.33	9,447.30	9,236.23	9,145.06	9,104.96	9,087.19
16.50%	16,471.63	13,499.09	12,612.06	11,433.03	10,074.85	9,573.63	9,368.24	9,280.49	9,242.34	9,225.63
16.75%	16,561.29	13,595.36	12,711.53	11,538.52	10,192.85	9,700.39	9,500.58	9,416.15	9,379.86	9,364.16
17.00%	16,651.23	13,691.99	12,811.37	11,644.44	10,311.33	9,827.56	9,633.24	9,552.02	9,517.53	9,502.77
17.25%	16,741.42	13,788.96	12,911.60	11,750.80	10,430.27	9,955.14	9,766.20	9,688.10	9,655.31	9,641.46
17.50%	16,831.88	13,886.28	13,012.21	11,857.58	10,549.67	10,083.11	9,899.45	9,824.38	9,793.22	9,780.21
17.75%	16,922.61	13,983.95	13,113.19	11,964.78	10,669.53	10,211.46	10,032.98	9,960.84	9,931.25	9,919.04
18.00%	17,013.60	14,081.95	13,214.55	12,072.41	10,789.82	10,340.19	10,166.78	10,097.47	10,069.38	10,057.92
18.25%	17,104.85	14,180.30	13,316.28	12,180.45	10,910.55	10,469.27	10,300.84	10,234.27	10,207.60	10,196.86
18.50%	17,196.36	14,278.99	13,418.39	12,288.91	11,031.71	10,598.71	10,435.14	10,371.23	10,345.92	10,335.85
18.75%	17,288.13	14,378.01	13,520.85	12,397.77	11,153.28	10,728.48	10,569.69	10,508.33	10,484.33	10,474.89
19.00%	17,380.17	14,477.37	13,623.69	12,507.05	11,275.27	10,858.59	10,704.46	10,645.58	10,622.81	10,613.97
19.25%	17,472.46	14,577.07	13,726.89	12,616.72	11,397.66	10,989.02	10,839.44	10,782.96	10,761.38	10,753.09
19.50%	17,565.02	14,677.10	13,830.45	12,726.80	11,520.45	11,119.75	10,974.64	10,920.46	10,900.01	10,892.25
19.75%	17,657.83	14,777.46	13,934.37	12,837.27	11,643.63	11,250.79	11,110.04	11,058.09	11,038.71	11,031.44
20.00%	17,750.90	14,878.15	14,038.64	12,948.13	11,767.19	11,382.12	11,245.63	11,195.83	11,177.46	11,170.67
20.25%	17,844.23	14,979.17	14,143.28	13,059.38	11,891.12	11,513.74	11,381.40	11,333.67	11,316.28	11,309.92
20.50%	17,937.81	15,080.52	14,248.26	13,171.01	12,015.42	11,645.63	11,517.35	11,471.61	11,455.15	11,449.20
20.75%	18,031.66	15,182.19	14,353.59	13,283.03	12,140.09	11,777.79	11,653.46	11,609.65	11,594.07	11,588.51

	5	7	8	10	15	20	25	30	35	40
1.00%	11,623.75	8,385.25	7,373.39	5,957.08	4,069.76	3,127.28	2,562.73	2,187.15	1,919.54	1,719.42
1.25%	11,697.09	8,458.78	7,447.09	6,031.16	4,144.97	3,203.71	2,640.42	2,266.11	1,999.79	1,800.95
1.50%	11,770.72	8,532.73	7,521.25	6,105.82	4,221.05	3,281.31	2,719.57	2,346.82	2,082.05	1,884.77
1.75%	11,844.65	8,607.09	7,595.89	6,181.07	4,298.02	3,360.08	2,800.17	2,429.26	2,166.33	1,970.87
2.00%	11,918.88	8,681.86	7,670.99	6,256.91	4,375.86	3,440.01	2,882.21	2,513.41	2,252.59	2,059.21
2.25%	11,993.39	8,757.04	7,746.57	6,333.34	4,454.58	3,521.10	2,965.69	2,599.27	2,340.81	2,149.77
2.50%	12,068.21	8,832.63	7,822.61	6,410.35	4,534.17	3,603.34	3,050.59	2,686.82	2,430.97	2,242.49
2.75%	12,143.31	8,908.63	7,899.13	6,487.95	4,614.63	3,686.73	3,136.91	2,776.04	2,523.04	2,337.35
3.00%	12,218.71	8,985.04	7,976.11	6,566.13	4,695.96	3,771.26	3,224.64	2,866.91	2,616.98	2,434.29
3.25%	12,294.40	9,061.87	8,053.56	6,644.89	4,778.15	3,856.93	3,313.75	2,959.40	2,712.77	2,533.28
3.50%	12,370.39	9,139.10	8,131.48	6,724.24	4,861.20	3,943.73	3,404.24	3,053.50	2,810.38	2,634.26
3.75%	12,446.66	9,216.74	8,209.86	6,804.16	4,945.11	4,031.64	3,496.09	3,149.19	2,909.75	2,737.18
4.00%	12,523.23	9,294.79	8,288.71	6,884.67	5,029.88	4,120.67	3,589.29	3,246.42	3,010.87	2,841.98
4.25%	12,600.10	9,373.25	8,368.02	6,965.75	5,115.49	4,210.79	3,683.82	3,345.19	3,113.68	2,948.62
4.50%	12,677.25	9,452.11	8,447.80	7,047.41	5,201.95	4,302.02	3,779.66	3,445.46	3,218.15	3,057.03
4.75%	12,754.70	9,531.38	8,528.04	7,129.65	5,289.26	4,394.32	3,876.80	3,547.20	3,324.23	3,167.15
5.00%	12,832.44	9,611.06	8,608.75	7,212.46	5,377.40	4,487.70	3,975.21	3,650.39	3,431.88	3,278.94
5.25%	12,910.47	9,691.14	8,689.91	7,295.84	5,466.37	4,582.14	4,074.88	3,754.99	3,541.05	3,392.32
5.50%	12,988.79	9,771.63	8,771.54	7,379.79	5,556.17	4,677.63	4,175.79	3,860.97	3,651.71	3,507.24
5.75%	13,067.40	9,852.52	8,853.63	7,464.31	5,646.79	4,774.17	4,277.92	3,968.30	3,763.80	3,623.64
6.00%	13,146.31	9,933.82	8,936.17	7,549.39	5,738.23	4,871.73	4,381.25	4,076.94	3,877.29	3,741.45
6.25%	13,225.50	10,015.52	9,019.18	7,635.05	5,830.48	4,970.31	4,485.75	4,186.88	3,992.12	3,860.63
6.50%	13,304.98	10,097.62	9,102.64	7,721.26	5,923.53	5,069.90	4,591.41	4,298.06	4,108.25	3,981.11
6.75%	13,384.75	10,180.12	9,186.56	7,808.04	6,017.38	5,170.48	4,698.20	4,410.47	4,225.63	4,102.83
7.00%	13,464.82	10,263.02	9,270.93	7,895.38	6,112.03	5,272.03	4,806.10	4,524.06	4,344.22	4,225.73
7.25%	13,545.17	10,346.33	9,355.75	7,983.27	6,207.47	5,374.56	4,915.09	4,638.80	4,463.98	4,349.77
7.50%	13,625.81	10,430.03	9,441.03	8,071.72	6,303.68	5,478.03	5,025.14	4,754.66	4,584.85	4,474.88
7.75%	13,706.73	10,514.13	9,526.76	8,160.72	6,400.68	5,582.45	5,136.24	4,871.60	4,706.80	4,601.02
8.00%	13,787.95	10,598.63	9,612.94	8,250.28	6,498.43	5,687.79	5,248.35	4,989.60	4,829.77	4,728.12
8.25%	13,869.45	10,683.52	9,699.57	8,340.38	6,596.95	5,794.05	5,361.46	5,108.61	4,953.74	4,856.14
8.50%	13,951.24	10,768.81	9,786.65	8,431.03	6,696.23	5,901.20	5,475.54	5,228.61	5,078.65	4,985.04
8.75%	14,033.32	10,854.49	9,874.17	8,522.22	6,796.25	6,009.23	5,590.58	5,349.56	5,204.47	5,114.76
9.00%	14,115.68	10,940.57	9,962.14	8,613.95	6,897.01	6,118.14	5,706.54	5,471.43	5,331.15	5,245.26
9.25%	14,198.33	11,027.04	10,050.55	8,706.23	6,998.51	6,227.89	5,823.40	5,594.19	5,458.66	5,376.49
9.50%	14,281.27	11,113.91	10,139.40	8,799.03	7,100.73	6,338.49	5,941.14	5,717.81	5,586.96	5,508.42
9.75%	14,364.49	11,201.16	10,228.70	8,892.38	7,203.67	6,449.91	6,059.73	5,842.25	5,716.01	5,641.00
10.00%	14,447.99	11,288.81	10,318.43	8,986.25	7,307.31	6,562.15	6,179.17	5,967.49	5,845.77	5,774.19
10.25%	14,531.78	11,376.84	10,408.60	9,080.65	7,411.67	6,675.18	6,299.41	6,093.49	5,976.22	5,907.96
10.50%	14,615.85	11,465.26	10,499.21	9,175.58	7,516.71	6,788.98	6,420.44	6,220.23	6,107.31	6,042.28
10.75%	14,700.21	11,554.06	10,590.25	9,271.03	7,622.45	6,903.56	6,542.23	6,347.67	6,239.02	6,177.10

$680,000   11.00 - 20.75%   5 - 40 Years

	5	7	8	10	15	20	25	30	35	40
11.00%	14,784.85	11,643.26	10,681.73	9,367.00	7,728.86	7,018.88	6,664.77	6,475.80	6,371.31	6,312.40
11.25%	14,869.77	11,732.83	10,773.64	9,463.49	7,835.94	7,134.94	6,788.03	6,604.58	6,504.16	6,448.15
11.50%	14,954.97	11,822.79	10,865.97	9,560.49	7,943.69	7,251.72	6,911.99	6,733.98	6,637.53	6,584.32
11.75%	15,040.46	11,913.14	10,958.74	9,658.00	8,052.09	7,369.21	7,036.63	6,863.99	6,771.40	6,720.88
12.00%	15,126.22	12,003.86	11,051.93	9,756.02	8,161.14	7,487.39	7,161.92	6,994.57	6,905.74	6,857.80
12.25%	15,212.27	12,094.96	11,145.55	9,854.55	8,270.83	7,606.24	7,287.86	7,125.70	7,040.52	6,995.07
12.50%	15,298.60	12,186.44	11,239.59	9,953.58	8,381.15	7,725.76	7,414.41	7,257.35	7,175.73	7,132.65
12.75%	15,385.20	12,278.30	11,334.05	10,053.11	8,492.09	7,845.92	7,541.56	7,389.51	7,311.33	7,270.54
13.00%	15,472.09	12,370.54	11,428.93	10,153.13	8,603.65	7,966.71	7,669.28	7,522.16	7,447.31	7,408.70
13.25%	15,559.25	12,463.14	11,524.23	10,253.65	8,715.81	8,088.13	7,797.56	7,655.26	7,583.65	7,547.12
13.50%	15,646.70	12,556.13	11,619.95	10,354.65	8,828.57	8,210.15	7,926.39	7,788.80	7,720.32	7,685.78
13.75%	15,734.41	12,649.48	11,716.08	10,456.14	8,941.91	8,332.76	8,055.73	7,922.77	7,857.30	7,824.66
14.00%	15,822.41	12,743.21	11,812.62	10,558.12	9,055.84	8,455.94	8,185.58	8,057.13	7,994.58	7,963.75
14.25%	15,910.68	12,837.30	11,909.57	10,660.57	9,170.34	8,579.69	8,315.91	8,191.87	8,132.14	8,103.04
14.50%	15,999.23	12,931.77	12,006.93	10,763.50	9,285.41	8,703.98	8,446.71	8,326.98	8,269.96	8,242.50
14.75%	16,088.05	13,026.60	12,104.70	10,866.90	9,401.03	8,828.82	8,577.96	8,462.43	8,408.03	8,382.14
15.00%	16,177.15	13,121.79	12,202.88	10,970.78	9,517.19	8,954.17	8,709.65	8,598.22	8,546.33	8,521.92
15.25%	16,266.52	13,217.35	12,301.45	11,075.12	9,633.90	9,080.03	8,841.76	8,734.32	8,684.85	8,661.86
15.50%	16,356.17	13,313.28	12,400.43	11,179.92	9,751.13	9,206.39	8,974.27	8,870.72	8,823.58	8,801.92
15.75%	16,446.09	13,409.56	12,499.80	11,285.18	9,868.89	9,333.23	9,107.17	9,007.40	8,962.49	8,942.11
16.00%	16,536.28	13,506.20	12,599.57	11,390.89	9,987.17	9,460.54	9,240.44	9,144.35	9,101.59	9,082.41
16.25%	16,626.74	13,603.21	12,699.74	11,497.06	10,105.94	9,588.31	9,374.08	9,281.56	9,240.86	9,222.82
16.50%	16,717.47	13,700.56	12,800.30	11,603.68	10,225.22	9,716.52	9,508.06	9,419.01	9,380.29	9,363.32
16.75%	16,808.48	13,798.28	12,901.25	11,710.74	10,344.98	9,845.17	9,642.38	9,556.69	9,519.86	9,503.92
17.00%	16,899.75	13,896.35	13,002.59	11,818.24	10,465.23	9,974.24	9,777.02	9,694.59	9,659.58	9,644.60
17.25%	16,991.29	13,994.77	13,104.31	11,926.18	10,585.95	10,103.72	9,911.96	9,832.70	9,799.42	9,785.36
17.50%	17,083.11	14,093.54	13,206.42	12,034.56	10,707.13	10,233.61	10,047.20	9,971.01	9,939.39	9,926.19
17.75%	17,175.18	14,192.66	13,308.91	12,143.36	10,828.77	10,363.87	10,182.73	10,109.51	10,079.48	10,067.08
18.00%	17,267.53	14,292.13	13,411.79	12,252.59	10,950.86	10,494.52	10,318.52	10,248.18	10,219.67	10,208.04
18.25%	17,360.14	14,391.95	13,515.03	12,362.25	11,073.39	10,625.53	10,454.58	10,387.02	10,359.96	10,349.05
18.50%	17,453.02	14,492.11	13,618.66	12,472.32	11,196.36	10,756.90	10,590.89	10,526.02	10,500.34	10,490.12
18.75%	17,546.17	14,592.61	13,722.66	12,582.82	11,319.75	10,888.61	10,727.44	10,665.17	10,640.81	10,631.23
19.00%	17,639.57	14,693.45	13,827.03	12,693.72	11,443.56	11,020.66	10,864.22	10,804.47	10,781.36	10,772.39
19.25%	17,733.25	14,794.64	13,931.77	12,805.03	11,567.78	11,153.03	11,001.23	10,943.90	10,921.99	10,913.59
19.50%	17,827.18	14,896.16	14,036.87	12,916.75	11,692.40	11,285.72	11,138.44	11,083.46	11,062.69	11,054.82
19.75%	17,921.38	14,998.02	14,142.34	13,028.87	11,817.41	11,418.71	11,275.86	11,223.13	11,203.46	11,196.09
20.00%	18,015.84	15,100.22	14,248.18	13,141.39	11,942.82	11,552.01	11,413.47	11,362.93	11,344.29	11,337.40
20.25%	18,110.56	15,202.74	14,354.37	13,254.30	12,068.60	11,685.59	11,551.27	11,502.83	11,485.18	11,478.73
20.50%	18,205.54	15,305.60	14,460.92	13,367.60	12,194.76	11,819.45	11,689.25	11,642.83	11,626.12	11,620.09
20.75%	18,300.78	15,408.79	14,567.83	13,481.28	12,321.28	11,953.58	11,827.40	11,782.93	11,767.11	11,761.47

	5	7	8	10	15	20	25	30	35	40
1.00%	11,794.69	8,508.56	7,481.83	6,044.68	4,129.61	3,173.27	2,600.42	2,219.31	1,947.77	1,744.71
1.25%	11,869.10	8,583.18	7,556.60	6,119.85	4,205.92	3,250.82	2,679.25	2,299.44	2,029.20	1,827.43
1.50%	11,943.82	8,658.21	7,631.86	6,195.61	4,283.13	3,329.56	2,759.56	2,381.33	2,112.67	1,912.49
1.75%	12,018.84	8,733.66	7,707.59	6,271.97	4,361.22	3,409.49	2,841.34	2,464.98	2,198.19	1,999.86
2.00%	12,094.15	8,809.53	7,783.80	6,348.93	4,440.21	3,490.60	2,924.59	2,550.37	2,285.71	2,089.50
2.25%	12,169.77	8,885.82	7,860.49	6,426.48	4,520.08	3,572.88	3,009.30	2,637.50	2,375.23	2,181.38
2.50%	12,245.68	8,962.52	7,937.65	6,504.62	4,600.85	3,656.33	3,095.46	2,726.33	2,466.72	2,275.47
2.75%	12,321.89	9,039.64	8,015.29	6,583.36	4,682.49	3,740.95	3,183.04	2,816.86	2,560.14	2,371.72
3.00%	12,398.40	9,117.18	8,093.40	6,662.69	4,765.01	3,826.72	3,272.06	2,909.07	2,655.47	2,470.09
3.25%	12,475.20	9,195.13	8,171.99	6,742.61	4,848.41	3,913.65	3,362.48	3,002.92	2,752.67	2,570.53
3.50%	12,552.30	9,273.50	8,251.06	6,823.12	4,932.69	4,001.72	3,454.30	3,098.41	2,851.71	2,673.00
3.75%	12,629.70	9,352.28	8,330.59	6,904.23	5,017.83	4,090.93	3,547.51	3,195.50	2,952.54	2,777.43
4.00%	12,707.40	9,431.48	8,410.60	6,985.91	5,103.85	4,181.26	3,642.07	3,294.17	3,055.15	2,883.78
4.25%	12,785.39	9,511.09	8,491.08	7,068.19	5,190.72	4,272.72	3,737.99	3,394.39	3,159.47	2,991.98
4.50%	12,863.68	9,591.11	8,572.03	7,151.05	5,278.45	4,365.28	3,835.24	3,496.13	3,265.47	3,101.98
4.75%	12,942.27	9,671.55	8,653.45	7,234.49	5,367.04	4,458.94	3,933.81	3,599.37	3,373.11	3,213.73
5.00%	13,021.15	9,752.40	8,735.34	7,318.52	5,456.48	4,553.69	4,033.67	3,704.07	3,482.34	3,327.16
5.25%	13,100.33	9,833.66	8,817.70	7,403.13	5,546.76	4,649.52	4,134.81	3,810.21	3,593.13	3,442.21
5.50%	13,179.80	9,915.33	8,900.53	7,488.31	5,637.88	4,746.42	4,237.20	3,917.74	3,705.41	3,558.81
5.75%	13,259.57	9,997.41	8,983.83	7,574.08	5,729.83	4,844.38	4,340.83	4,026.65	3,819.16	3,676.92
6.00%	13,339.63	10,079.90	9,067.59	7,660.41	5,822.61	4,943.37	4,445.68	4,136.90	3,934.31	3,796.47
6.25%	13,419.99	10,162.80	9,151.81	7,747.33	5,916.22	5,043.40	4,551.72	4,248.45	4,050.83	3,917.40
6.50%	13,500.64	10,246.11	9,236.50	7,834.81	6,010.64	5,144.45	4,658.93	4,361.27	4,168.66	4,039.65
6.75%	13,581.59	10,329.83	9,321.65	7,922.86	6,105.88	5,246.51	4,767.29	4,475.33	4,287.77	4,163.16
7.00%	13,662.83	10,413.95	9,407.26	8,011.49	6,201.92	5,349.56	4,876.78	4,590.59	4,408.11	4,287.88
7.25%	13,744.36	10,498.48	9,493.34	8,100.67	6,298.75	5,453.59	4,987.37	4,707.02	4,529.62	4,413.74
7.50%	13,826.18	10,583.41	9,579.87	8,190.42	6,396.39	5,558.59	5,099.04	4,824.58	4,652.27	4,540.69
7.75%	13,908.30	10,668.75	9,666.86	8,280.73	6,494.80	5,664.55	5,211.77	4,943.24	4,776.01	4,668.68
8.00%	13,990.71	10,754.49	9,754.31	8,371.60	6,594.00	5,771.44	5,325.53	5,062.98	4,900.80	4,797.65
8.25%	14,073.41	10,840.63	9,842.21	8,463.03	6,693.97	5,879.25	5,440.31	5,183.74	5,026.59	4,927.56
8.50%	14,156.41	10,927.17	9,930.57	8,555.01	6,794.70	5,987.98	5,556.07	5,305.50	5,153.34	5,058.35
8.75%	14,239.69	11,014.12	10,019.38	8,647.55	6,896.20	6,097.60	5,672.79	5,428.23	5,281.01	5,189.98
9.00%	14,323.27	11,101.46	10,108.64	8,740.63	6,998.44	6,208.11	5,790.45	5,551.90	5,409.55	5,322.39
9.25%	14,407.13	11,189.21	10,198.35	8,834.26	7,101.43	6,319.48	5,909.03	5,676.46	5,538.94	5,455.56
9.50%	14,491.28	11,277.35	10,288.51	8,928.43	7,205.15	6,431.71	6,028.51	5,801.89	5,669.12	5,589.42
9.75%	14,575.73	11,365.88	10,379.12	9,023.15	7,309.60	6,544.77	6,148.85	5,928.17	5,800.07	5,723.95
10.00%	14,660.46	11,454.82	10,470.17	9,118.40	7,414.78	6,658.65	6,270.04	6,055.24	5,931.74	5,859.11
10.25%	14,745.48	11,544.14	10,561.67	9,214.19	7,520.66	6,773.34	6,392.04	6,183.10	6,064.10	5,994.85
10.50%	14,830.79	11,633.86	10,653.61	9,310.51	7,627.25	6,888.82	6,514.85	6,311.70	6,197.12	6,131.13
10.75%	14,916.39	11,723.98	10,745.99	9,407.37	7,734.54	7,005.08	6,638.44	6,441.02	6,330.77	6,267.94

$690,000   11.00 - 20.75%   5 - 40 Years

	5	7	8	10	15	20	25	30	35	40
11.00%	15,002.27	11,814.48	10,838.81	9,504.75	7,842.52	7,122.10	6,762.78	6,571.03	6,465.01	6,405.23
11.25%	15,088.44	11,905.38	10,932.07	9,602.66	7,951.18	7,239.87	6,887.85	6,701.70	6,599.81	6,542.98
11.50%	15,174.90	11,996.66	11,025.77	9,701.09	8,060.51	7,358.36	7,013.64	6,833.01	6,735.14	6,681.14
11.75%	15,261.64	12,088.33	11,119.90	9,800.03	8,170.51	7,477.58	7,140.11	6,964.93	6,870.98	6,819.71
12.00%	15,348.67	12,180.39	11,214.46	9,899.50	8,281.16	7,597.49	7,267.25	7,097.43	7,007.29	6,958.65
12.25%	15,435.98	12,272.83	11,309.45	9,999.47	8,392.46	7,718.10	7,395.03	7,230.49	7,144.06	7,097.93
12.50%	15,523.58	12,365.65	11,404.88	10,099.96	8,504.40	7,839.37	7,523.44	7,364.08	7,281.26	7,237.54
12.75%	15,611.46	12,458.86	11,500.73	10,200.95	8,616.98	7,961.30	7,652.46	7,498.18	7,418.85	7,377.45
13.00%	15,699.62	12,552.45	11,597.01	10,302.44	8,730.17	8,083.87	7,782.06	7,632.78	7,556.83	7,517.65
13.25%	15,788.07	12,646.43	11,693.71	10,404.44	8,843.98	8,207.07	7,912.23	7,767.84	7,695.17	7,658.10
13.50%	15,876.79	12,740.78	11,790.83	10,506.93	8,958.40	8,330.89	8,042.95	7,903.34	7,833.85	7,798.80
13.75%	15,965.80	12,835.50	11,888.37	10,609.91	9,073.41	8,455.30	8,174.20	8,039.28	7,972.85	7,939.73
14.00%	16,055.09	12,930.61	11,986.34	10,713.38	9,189.02	8,580.29	8,305.95	8,175.62	8,112.15	8,080.87
14.25%	16,144.66	13,026.09	12,084.71	10,817.34	9,305.20	8,705.86	8,438.20	8,312.34	8,251.73	8,222.20
14.50%	16,234.51	13,121.94	12,183.51	10,921.79	9,421.96	8,831.98	8,570.92	8,449.44	8,391.58	8,363.72
14.75%	16,324.64	13,218.16	12,282.71	11,026.71	9,539.28	8,958.65	8,704.11	8,586.88	8,531.68	8,505.40
15.00%	16,415.05	13,314.76	12,382.33	11,132.11	9,657.15	9,085.85	8,837.73	8,724.66	8,672.01	8,647.25
15.25%	16,505.74	13,411.73	12,482.35	11,237.98	9,775.57	9,213.56	8,971.78	8,862.76	8,812.57	8,789.24
15.50%	16,596.70	13,509.06	12,582.79	11,344.33	9,894.53	9,341.78	9,106.24	9,001.17	8,953.33	8,931.36
15.75%	16,687.94	13,606.76	12,683.62	11,451.14	10,014.02	9,470.48	9,241.10	9,139.86	9,094.29	9,073.61
16.00%	16,779.46	13,704.82	12,784.86	11,558.41	10,134.04	9,599.67	9,376.33	9,278.82	9,235.44	9,215.97
16.25%	16,871.25	13,803.25	12,886.50	11,666.13	10,254.56	9,729.31	9,511.93	9,418.05	9,376.75	9,358.45
16.50%	16,963.32	13,902.04	12,988.54	11,774.32	10,375.59	9,859.41	9,647.89	9,557.52	9,518.23	9,501.02
16.75%	17,055.66	14,001.19	13,090.97	11,882.95	10,497.12	9,989.95	9,784.18	9,697.23	9,659.86	9,643.68
17.00%	17,148.28	14,100.71	13,193.80	11,992.04	10,619.13	10,120.92	9,920.80	9,837.16	9,801.63	9,786.43
17.25%	17,241.17	14,200.57	13,297.02	12,101.57	10,741.62	10,252.31	10,057.73	9,977.30	9,943.53	9,929.26
17.50%	17,334.33	14,300.80	13,400.63	12,211.53	10,864.59	10,384.10	10,194.95	10,117.64	10,085.56	10,072.16
17.75%	17,427.76	14,401.38	13,504.63	12,321.94	10,988.02	10,516.28	10,332.47	10,258.18	10,227.70	10,215.13
18.00%	17,521.46	14,502.31	13,609.02	12,432.78	11,111.91	10,648.85	10,470.27	10,398.89	10,369.95	10,358.16
18.25%	17,615.44	14,603.59	13,713.79	12,544.05	11,236.24	10,781.79	10,608.33	10,539.77	10,512.31	10,501.24
18.50%	17,709.68	14,705.22	13,818.93	12,655.74	11,361.01	10,915.09	10,746.64	10,680.82	10,654.76	10,644.38
18.75%	17,804.20	14,807.21	13,924.46	12,767.86	11,486.22	11,048.74	10,885.20	10,822.02	10,797.29	10,787.57
19.00%	17,898.98	14,909.53	14,030.37	12,880.39	11,611.84	11,182.73	11,023.99	10,963.36	10,939.91	10,930.81
19.25%	17,994.03	15,012.21	14,136.65	12,993.34	11,737.89	11,317.05	11,163.01	11,104.84	11,082.61	11,074.08
19.50%	18,089.35	15,115.22	14,243.30	13,106.70	11,864.34	11,451.69	11,302.24	11,246.45	11,225.38	11,217.39
19.75%	18,184.93	15,218.58	14,350.32	13,220.47	11,991.20	11,586.64	11,441.68	11,388.18	11,368.22	11,360.74
20.00%	18,280.78	15,322.28	14,457.71	13,334.64	12,118.45	11,721.89	11,581.32	11,530.03	11,511.12	11,504.12
20.25%	18,376.89	15,426.31	14,565.46	13,449.21	12,246.08	11,857.43	11,721.14	11,671.99	11,654.08	11,647.53
20.50%	18,473.27	15,530.69	14,673.58	13,564.18	12,374.09	11,993.26	11,861.15	11,814.05	11,797.09	11,790.97
20.75%	18,569.91	15,635.39	14,782.06	13,679.54	12,502.48	12,129.37	12,001.33	11,956.21	11,940.16	11,934.43

	5	7	8	10	15	20	25	30	35	40
1.00%	11,965.62	8,631.87	7,590.26	6,132.29	4,189.46	3,219.26	2,638.11	2,251.48	1,976.00	1,769.99
1.25%	12,041.12	8,707.57	7,666.12	6,208.54	4,266.88	3,297.94	2,718.08	2,332.76	2,058.60	1,853.92
1.50%	12,116.92	8,783.69	7,742.47	6,285.40	4,345.20	3,377.82	2,799.55	2,415.84	2,143.29	1,940.21
1.75%	12,193.03	8,860.24	7,819.30	6,362.87	4,424.43	3,458.90	2,882.52	2,500.70	2,230.04	2,028.84
2.00%	12,269.43	8,937.20	7,896.61	6,440.94	4,504.56	3,541.18	2,966.98	2,587.34	2,318.84	2,119.78
2.25%	12,346.14	9,014.60	7,974.41	6,519.62	4,585.59	3,624.66	3,052.91	2,675.72	2,409.66	2,213.00
2.50%	12,423.15	9,092.41	8,052.69	6,598.89	4,667.52	3,709.32	3,140.32	2,765.85	2,502.47	2,308.45
2.75%	12,500.47	9,170.65	8,131.45	6,678.77	4,750.35	3,795.16	3,229.18	2,857.69	2,597.24	2,406.09
3.00%	12,578.08	9,249.31	8,210.70	6,759.25	4,834.07	3,882.18	3,319.48	2,951.23	2,693.95	2,505.89
3.25%	12,656.00	9,328.39	8,290.43	6,840.33	4,918.68	3,970.37	3,411.21	3,046.44	2,792.56	2,607.79
3.50%	12,734.22	9,407.90	8,370.64	6,922.01	5,004.18	4,059.72	3,504.36	3,143.31	2,893.03	2,711.74
3.75%	12,812.74	9,487.82	8,451.32	7,004.29	5,090.56	4,150.22	3,598.92	3,241.81	2,995.34	2,817.68
4.00%	12,891.57	9,568.16	8,532.49	7,087.16	5,177.82	4,241.86	3,694.86	3,341.91	3,099.42	2,925.57
4.25%	12,970.69	9,648.93	8,614.14	7,170.63	5,265.95	4,334.64	3,792.17	3,443.58	3,205.26	3,035.34
4.50%	13,050.11	9,730.11	8,696.26	7,254.69	5,354.95	4,428.55	3,890.83	3,546.80	3,312.80	3,146.94
4.75%	13,129.84	9,811.72	8,778.87	7,339.34	5,444.82	4,523.57	3,990.82	3,651.53	3,422.00	3,260.30
5.00%	13,209.86	9,893.74	8,861.94	7,424.59	5,535.56	4,619.69	4,092.13	3,757.75	3,532.81	3,375.38
5.25%	13,290.19	9,976.17	8,945.50	7,510.42	5,627.14	4,716.91	4,194.73	3,865.43	3,645.20	3,492.09
5.50%	13,370.81	10,059.03	9,029.53	7,596.84	5,719.58	4,815.21	4,298.61	3,974.52	3,759.11	3,610.39
5.75%	13,451.74	10,142.30	9,114.03	7,683.85	5,812.87	4,914.58	4,403.74	4,085.01	3,874.51	3,730.21
6.00%	13,532.96	10,225.99	9,199.00	7,771.44	5,907.00	5,015.02	4,510.11	4,196.85	3,991.33	3,851.50
6.25%	13,614.48	10,310.09	9,284.45	7,859.61	6,001.96	5,116.50	4,617.69	4,310.02	4,109.54	3,974.18
6.50%	13,696.30	10,394.61	9,370.36	7,948.36	6,097.75	5,219.01	4,726.45	4,424.48	4,229.08	4,098.20
6.75%	13,778.42	10,479.53	9,456.75	8,037.69	6,194.37	5,322.55	4,836.38	4,540.19	4,349.92	4,223.50
7.00%	13,860.84	10,564.88	9,543.60	8,127.59	6,291.80	5,427.09	4,947.45	4,657.12	4,471.99	4,350.02
7.25%	13,943.55	10,650.63	9,630.92	8,218.07	6,390.04	5,532.63	5,059.65	4,775.23	4,595.27	4,477.70
7.50%	14,026.56	10,736.79	9,718.71	8,309.12	6,489.09	5,639.15	5,172.94	4,894.50	4,719.70	4,606.50
7.75%	14,109.87	10,823.37	9,806.96	8,400.74	6,588.93	5,746.64	5,287.30	5,014.89	4,845.23	4,736.34
8.00%	14,193.48	10,910.35	9,895.68	8,492.93	6,689.56	5,855.08	5,402.71	5,136.35	4,971.83	4,867.18
8.25%	14,277.38	10,997.74	9,984.85	8,585.68	6,790.98	5,964.46	5,519.15	5,258.87	5,099.44	4,998.97
8.50%	14,361.57	11,085.54	10,074.49	8,679.00	6,893.18	6,074.76	5,636.59	5,382.39	5,228.02	5,131.66
8.75%	14,446.06	11,173.74	10,164.59	8,772.87	6,996.14	6,185.97	5,755.01	5,506.90	5,357.54	5,265.19
9.00%	14,530.84	11,262.35	10,255.14	8,867.30	7,099.87	6,298.08	5,874.37	5,632.36	5,487.95	5,399.53
9.25%	14,615.93	11,351.37	10,346.15	8,962.29	7,204.35	6,411.07	5,994.67	5,758.73	5,619.21	5,534.62
9.50%	14,701.30	11,440.79	10,437.62	9,057.83	7,309.57	6,524.92	6,115.88	5,885.98	5,751.28	5,670.43
9.75%	14,786.97	11,530.61	10,529.54	9,153.92	7,415.54	6,639.62	6,237.96	6,014.08	5,884.13	5,806.91
10.00%	14,872.93	11,620.83	10,621.91	9,250.55	7,522.24	6,755.15	6,360.91	6,143.00	6,017.71	5,944.02
10.25%	14,959.18	11,711.45	10,714.74	9,347.73	7,629.66	6,871.50	6,484.68	6,272.71	6,151.99	6,081.73
10.50%	15,045.73	11,802.47	10,808.01	9,445.45	7,737.79	6,988.66	6,609.27	6,403.18	6,286.94	6,219.99
10.75%	15,132.57	11,893.89	10,901.73	9,543.71	7,846.64	7,106.60	6,734.65	6,534.37	6,422.52	6,358.78

$700,000   11.00 - 20.75%   5 - 40 Years

	5	7	8	10	15	20	25	30	35	40
11.00%	15,219.70	11,985.71	10,995.90	9,642.50	7,956.18	7,225.32	6,860.79	6,666.26	6,558.70	6,498.06
11.25%	15,307.12	12,077.92	11,090.51	9,741.83	8,066.41	7,344.79	6,987.68	6,798.83	6,695.46	6,637.80
11.50%	15,394.83	12,170.52	11,185.56	9,841.68	8,177.33	7,465.01	7,115.28	6,932.04	6,832.75	6,777.97
11.75%	15,482.82	12,263.52	11,281.06	9,942.06	8,288.92	7,585.95	7,243.59	7,065.87	6,970.56	6,918.55
12.00%	15,571.11	12,356.91	11,376.99	10,042.97	8,401.18	7,707.60	7,372.57	7,200.29	7,108.85	7,059.50
12.25%	15,659.69	12,450.70	11,473.36	10,144.39	8,514.09	7,829.95	7,502.21	7,335.28	7,247.60	7,200.80
12.50%	15,748.56	12,544.87	11,570.17	10,246.33	8,627.65	7,952.98	7,632.48	7,470.80	7,386.78	7,342.44
12.75%	15,837.71	12,639.43	11,667.41	10,348.79	8,741.86	8,076.68	7,763.37	7,606.85	7,526.37	7,484.37
13.00%	15,927.15	12,734.37	11,765.08	10,451.75	8,856.70	8,201.03	7,894.85	7,743.40	7,666.35	7,626.60
13.25%	16,016.88	12,829.71	11,863.18	10,555.22	8,972.16	8,326.02	8,026.90	7,880.41	7,806.70	7,769.09
13.50%	16,106.89	12,925.42	11,961.71	10,659.20	9,088.23	8,451.62	8,159.51	8,017.89	7,947.38	7,911.83
13.75%	16,197.19	13,021.53	12,060.67	10,763.68	9,204.91	8,577.84	8,292.66	8,155.79	8,088.40	8,054.80
14.00%	16,287.78	13,118.01	12,160.05	10,868.65	9,322.19	8,704.65	8,426.33	8,294.10	8,229.71	8,197.98
14.25%	16,378.64	13,214.87	12,259.86	10,974.12	9,440.06	8,832.03	8,560.49	8,432.81	8,371.32	8,341.36
14.50%	16,469.80	13,312.11	12,360.08	11,080.08	9,558.51	8,959.98	8,695.14	8,571.89	8,513.19	8,484.93
14.75%	16,561.23	13,409.73	12,460.72	11,186.52	9,677.53	9,088.49	8,830.25	8,711.33	8,655.32	8,628.67
15.00%	16,652.95	13,507.73	12,561.78	11,293.45	9,797.11	9,217.53	8,965.81	8,851.11	8,797.69	8,772.57
15.25%	16,744.95	13,606.10	12,663.26	11,400.85	9,917.25	9,347.09	9,101.81	8,991.21	8,940.29	8,916.62
15.50%	16,837.23	13,704.84	12,765.15	11,508.74	10,037.93	9,477.16	9,238.22	9,131.62	9,083.09	9,060.80
15.75%	16,929.80	13,803.96	12,867.44	11,617.09	10,159.15	9,607.74	9,375.03	9,272.32	9,226.10	9,205.11
16.00%	17,022.64	13,903.44	12,970.15	11,725.92	10,280.91	9,738.79	9,512.22	9,413.30	9,369.29	9,349.54
16.25%	17,115.76	14,003.30	13,073.26	11,835.21	10,403.18	9,870.32	9,649.79	9,554.54	9,512.65	9,494.08
16.50%	17,209.16	14,103.52	13,176.78	11,944.96	10,525.96	10,002.30	9,787.71	9,696.04	9,656.18	9,638.72
16.75%	17,302.85	14,204.11	13,280.70	12,055.17	10,649.25	10,134.74	9,925.98	9,837.77	9,799.86	9,783.45
17.00%	17,396.80	14,305.06	13,385.02	12,165.84	10,773.03	10,267.60	10,064.58	9,979.73	9,943.68	9,928.26
17.25%	17,491.04	14,406.38	13,489.73	12,276.95	10,897.30	10,400.89	10,203.49	10,121.90	10,087.64	10,073.16
17.50%	17,585.55	14,508.06	13,594.85	12,388.51	11,022.05	10,534.59	10,342.71	10,264.28	10,231.73	10,218.13
17.75%	17,680.34	14,610.09	13,700.35	12,500.52	11,147.27	10,668.69	10,482.22	10,406.85	10,375.93	10,363.17
18.00%	17,775.40	14,712.49	13,806.25	12,612.96	11,272.95	10,803.18	10,622.01	10,549.60	10,520.24	10,508.28
18.25%	17,870.74	14,815.24	13,912.54	12,725.84	11,399.08	10,938.05	10,762.07	10,692.52	10,664.66	10,653.44
18.50%	17,966.35	14,918.34	14,019.21	12,839.16	11,525.66	11,073.28	10,902.39	10,835.61	10,809.17	10,798.65
18.75%	18,062.23	15,021.80	14,126.27	12,952.90	11,652.68	11,208.86	11,042.96	10,978.86	10,953.78	10,943.91
19.00%	18,158.39	15,125.61	14,233.71	13,067.06	11,780.13	11,344.79	11,183.76	11,122.25	11,098.46	11,089.22
19.25%	18,254.81	15,229.77	14,341.52	13,181.65	11,908.00	11,481.06	11,324.79	11,265.78	11,243.23	11,234.57
19.50%	18,351.51	15,334.28	14,449.72	13,296.65	12,036.29	11,617.65	11,466.04	11,409.44	11,388.07	11,379.96
19.75%	18,448.48	15,439.14	14,558.29	13,412.07	12,164.98	11,754.56	11,607.50	11,553.23	11,532.98	11,525.39
20.00%	18,545.72	15,544.34	14,667.24	13,527.90	12,294.08	11,891.77	11,749.16	11,697.13	11,677.95	11,670.85
20.25%	18,643.23	15,649.88	14,776.56	13,644.13	12,423.56	12,029.28	11,891.01	11,841.15	11,822.98	11,816.34
20.50%	18,741.00	15,755.77	14,886.24	13,760.76	12,553.43	12,167.08	12,033.05	11,985.27	11,968.07	11,961.85
20.75%	18,839.04	15,861.99	14,996.29	13,877.79	12,683.67	12,305.15	12,175.26	12,129.49	12,113.21	12,107.40

$710,000   1.00 - 10.75%   5 - 40 Years

	5	7	8	10	15	20	25	30	35	40
1.00%	12,136.56	8,755.19	7,698.69	6,219.89	4,249.31	3,265.25	2,675.79	2,283.64	2,004.23	1,795.28
1.25%	12,213.14	8,831.96	7,775.64	6,297.24	4,327.83	3,345.05	2,756.91	2,366.09	2,088.01	1,880.40
1.50%	12,290.02	8,909.17	7,853.07	6,375.20	4,407.28	3,426.07	2,839.55	2,450.35	2,173.91	1,967.92
1.75%	12,367.21	8,986.81	7,931.00	6,453.77	4,487.64	3,508.31	2,923.70	2,536.43	2,261.90	2,057.82
2.00%	12,444.71	9,064.88	8,009.42	6,532.96	4,568.91	3,591.77	3,009.37	2,624.30	2,351.97	2,150.06
2.25%	12,522.51	9,143.38	8,088.33	6,612.75	4,651.10	3,676.44	3,096.53	2,713.95	2,444.08	2,244.61
2.50%	12,600.63	9,222.30	8,167.73	6,693.16	4,734.20	3,762.31	3,185.18	2,805.36	2,538.22	2,341.43
2.75%	12,679.05	9,301.66	8,247.62	6,774.18	4,818.21	3,849.38	3,275.31	2,898.51	2,634.35	2,440.47
3.00%	12,757.77	9,381.44	8,328.00	6,855.81	4,903.13	3,937.64	3,366.90	2,993.39	2,732.44	2,541.69
3.25%	12,836.80	9,461.65	8,408.86	6,938.05	4,988.95	4,027.09	3,459.95	3,089.96	2,832.45	2,645.04
3.50%	12,916.14	9,542.29	8,490.22	7,020.90	5,075.67	4,117.71	3,554.43	3,188.22	2,934.36	2,750.48
3.75%	12,995.78	9,623.36	8,572.06	7,104.35	5,163.28	4,209.51	3,650.33	3,288.12	3,038.13	2,857.93
4.00%	13,075.73	9,704.85	8,654.39	7,188.40	5,251.78	4,302.46	3,747.64	3,389.65	3,143.70	2,967.36
4.25%	13,155.98	9,786.77	8,737.20	7,273.06	5,341.18	4,396.56	3,846.34	3,492.77	3,251.05	3,078.70
4.50%	13,236.54	9,869.11	8,820.50	7,358.33	5,431.45	4,491.81	3,946.41	3,597.47	3,360.12	3,191.90
4.75%	13,317.41	9,951.88	8,904.28	7,444.19	5,522.61	4,588.19	4,047.83	3,703.70	3,470.88	3,306.88
5.00%	13,398.58	10,035.08	8,988.54	7,530.65	5,614.63	4,685.69	4,150.59	3,811.43	3,583.28	3,423.60
5.25%	13,480.05	10,118.69	9,073.29	7,617.71	5,707.53	4,784.29	4,254.66	3,920.65	3,697.28	3,541.98
5.50%	13,561.83	10,202.73	9,158.52	7,705.37	5,801.29	4,884.00	4,360.02	4,031.30	3,812.82	3,661.97
5.75%	13,643.91	10,287.19	9,244.23	7,793.61	5,895.91	4,984.79	4,466.66	4,143.37	3,929.86	3,783.50
6.00%	13,726.29	10,372.07	9,330.42	7,882.46	5,991.38	5,086.66	4,574.54	4,256.81	4,048.35	3,906.52
6.25%	13,808.98	10,457.38	9,417.08	7,971.89	6,087.70	5,189.59	4,683.65	4,371.59	4,168.24	4,030.95
6.50%	13,891.97	10,543.10	9,504.23	8,061.91	6,184.86	5,293.57	4,793.97	4,487.68	4,289.50	4,156.74
6.75%	13,975.26	10,629.24	9,591.84	8,152.51	6,282.86	5,398.58	4,905.47	4,605.05	4,412.06	4,283.83
7.00%	14,058.85	10,715.80	9,679.94	8,243.70	6,381.68	5,504.62	5,018.13	4,723.65	4,535.88	4,412.16
7.25%	14,142.75	10,802.78	9,768.51	8,335.47	6,481.33	5,611.67	5,131.93	4,843.45	4,660.92	4,541.67
7.50%	14,226.94	10,890.18	9,857.55	8,427.83	6,581.79	5,719.71	5,246.84	4,964.42	4,787.12	4,672.30
7.75%	14,311.44	10,977.99	9,947.06	8,520.75	6,683.06	5,828.73	5,362.83	5,086.53	4,914.45	4,804.00
8.00%	14,396.24	11,066.21	10,037.04	8,614.26	6,785.13	5,938.72	5,479.90	5,209.73	5,042.85	4,936.71
8.25%	14,481.34	11,154.85	10,127.49	8,708.34	6,888.00	6,049.67	5,598.00	5,333.99	5,172.29	5,070.39
8.50%	14,566.74	11,243.90	10,218.41	8,802.98	6,991.65	6,161.54	5,717.11	5,459.29	5,302.71	5,204.97
8.75%	14,652.44	11,333.37	10,309.80	8,898.20	7,096.09	6,274.35	5,837.22	5,585.57	5,434.08	5,340.41
9.00%	14,738.43	11,423.25	10,401.64	8,993.98	7,201.29	6,388.05	5,958.29	5,712.82	5,566.35	5,476.67
9.25%	14,824.73	11,513.53	10,493.96	9,090.32	7,307.27	6,502.65	6,080.31	5,841.00	5,699.48	5,613.69
9.50%	14,911.32	11,604.23	10,586.73	9,187.23	7,414.00	6,618.13	6,203.25	5,970.06	5,833.44	5,751.44
9.75%	14,998.21	11,695.33	10,679.96	9,284.69	7,521.47	6,734.47	6,327.08	6,100.00	5,968.18	5,889.87
10.00%	15,085.40	11,786.84	10,773.66	9,382.70	7,629.70	6,851.65	6,451.78	6,230.76	6,103.67	6,028.94
10.25%	15,172.89	11,878.76	10,867.81	9,481.27	7,738.65	6,969.67	6,577.32	6,362.32	6,239.87	6,168.61
10.50%	15,260.67	11,971.08	10,962.41	9,580.38	7,848.33	7,088.50	6,703.69	6,494.65	6,376.75	6,308.85
10.75%	15,348.75	12,063.80	11,057.47	9,680.05	7,958.73	7,208.13	6,830.86	6,627.72	6,514.27	6,449.62

$710,000   11.00 - 20.75%   5 - 40 Years

	5	7	8	10	15	20	25	30	35	40
11.00%	15,437.12	12,156.93	11,152.98	9,780.25	8,069.84	7,328.54	6,958.80	6,761.50	6,652.40	6,590.89
11.25%	15,525.79	12,250.46	11,248.94	9,881.00	8,181.65	7,449.72	7,087.50	6,895.96	6,791.11	6,732.63
11.50%	15,614.75	12,344.39	11,345.36	9,982.28	8,294.15	7,571.65	7,216.93	7,031.07	6,930.36	6,874.80
11.75%	15,704.01	12,438.71	11,442.21	10,084.09	8,407.33	7,694.32	7,347.07	7,166.81	7,070.14	7,017.38
12.00%	15,793.56	12,533.44	11,539.52	10,186.44	8,521.19	7,817.71	7,477.89	7,303.15	7,210.40	7,160.35
12.25%	15,883.40	12,628.56	11,637.26	10,289.31	8,635.72	7,941.81	7,609.38	7,440.06	7,351.13	7,303.67
12.50%	15,973.54	12,724.08	11,735.45	10,392.71	8,750.91	8,066.60	7,741.51	7,577.53	7,492.31	7,447.33
12.75%	16,063.96	12,819.99	11,834.08	10,496.63	8,866.74	8,192.06	7,874.27	7,715.52	7,633.89	7,591.29
13.00%	16,154.68	12,916.29	11,933.15	10,601.06	8,983.22	8,318.19	8,007.63	7,854.02	7,775.87	7,735.55
13.25%	16,245.69	13,012.99	12,032.66	10,706.01	9,100.33	8,444.96	8,141.57	7,992.99	7,918.22	7,880.08
13.50%	16,336.99	13,110.07	12,132.59	10,811.47	9,218.06	8,572.36	8,276.08	8,132.43	8,060.92	8,024.85
13.75%	16,428.58	13,207.55	12,232.96	10,917.44	9,336.41	8,700.38	8,411.13	8,272.30	8,203.94	8,169.87
14.00%	16,520.46	13,305.41	12,333.77	11,023.92	9,455.36	8,829.00	8,546.70	8,412.59	8,347.28	8,315.09
14.25%	16,612.62	13,403.65	12,435.00	11,130.89	9,574.92	8,958.20	8,682.79	8,553.28	8,490.91	8,460.53
14.50%	16,705.08	13,502.29	12,536.65	11,238.36	9,695.06	9,087.98	8,819.36	8,694.35	8,634.81	8,606.14
14.75%	16,797.82	13,601.30	12,638.73	11,346.33	9,815.78	9,218.32	8,956.40	8,835.78	8,778.97	8,751.94
15.00%	16,890.85	13,700.70	12,741.24	11,454.78	9,937.07	9,349.21	9,093.90	8,977.55	8,923.37	8,897.89
15.25%	16,984.17	13,800.47	12,844.16	11,563.72	10,058.92	9,480.62	9,231.83	9,119.66	9,068.01	9,044.00
15.50%	17,077.77	13,900.63	12,947.51	11,673.15	10,181.33	9,612.55	9,370.19	9,262.07	9,212.85	9,190.24
15.75%	17,171.65	14,001.16	13,051.26	11,783.05	10,304.29	9,744.99	9,508.96	9,404.78	9,357.90	9,336.61
16.00%	17,265.82	14,102.07	13,155.44	11,893.43	10,427.78	9,877.92	9,648.11	9,547.77	9,503.13	9,483.10
16.25%	17,360.27	14,203.35	13,260.02	12,004.28	10,551.79	10,011.32	9,787.64	9,691.04	9,648.54	9,629.71
16.50%	17,455.01	14,305.00	13,365.02	12,115.60	10,676.33	10,145.19	9,927.54	9,834.55	9,794.12	9,776.41
16.75%	17,550.03	14,407.03	13,470.42	12,227.39	10,801.38	10,279.52	10,067.78	9,978.31	9,939.86	9,923.21
17.00%	17,645.33	14,509.42	13,576.23	12,339.63	10,926.93	10,414.28	10,208.36	10,122.29	10,085.74	10,070.10
17.25%	17,740.91	14,612.18	13,682.45	12,452.34	11,052.98	10,549.48	10,349.25	10,266.50	10,231.75	10,217.07
17.50%	17,836.77	14,715.31	13,789.06	12,565.49	11,179.51	10,685.09	10,490.46	10,410.91	10,377.89	10,364.11
17.75%	17,932.91	14,818.81	13,896.07	12,679.10	11,306.51	10,821.10	10,631.96	10,555.51	10,524.16	10,511.22
18.00%	18,029.33	14,922.66	14,003.48	12,793.15	11,433.99	10,957.51	10,773.75	10,700.31	10,670.53	10,658.39
18.25%	18,126.03	15,026.88	14,111.29	12,907.64	11,561.93	11,094.30	10,915.81	10,845.27	10,817.01	10,805.63
18.50%	18,223.01	15,131.46	14,219.48	13,022.57	11,690.32	11,231.47	11,058.14	10,990.41	10,963.59	10,952.92
18.75%	18,320.26	15,236.40	14,328.07	13,137.94	11,819.15	11,368.99	11,200.71	11,135.70	11,110.26	11,100.26
19.00%	18,417.79	15,341.69	14,437.04	13,253.74	11,948.42	11,506.86	11,343.53	11,281.14	11,257.01	11,247.64
19.25%	18,515.60	15,447.34	14,546.40	13,369.96	12,078.12	11,645.08	11,486.58	11,426.72	11,403.85	11,395.07
19.50%	18,613.68	15,553.34	14,656.15	13,486.61	12,208.24	11,783.62	11,629.84	11,572.43	11,550.75	11,542.54
19.75%	18,712.03	15,659.70	14,766.27	13,603.67	12,338.77	11,922.48	11,773.32	11,718.27	11,697.73	11,690.04
20.00%	18,810.66	15,766.40	14,876.77	13,721.15	12,469.71	12,061.65	11,917.01	11,864.23	11,844.78	11,837.58
20.25%	18,909.56	15,873.45	14,987.65	13,839.04	12,601.04	12,201.13	12,060.89	12,010.31	11,991.88	11,985.14
20.50%	19,008.73	15,980.85	15,098.90	13,957.34	12,732.76	12,340.89	12,204.95	12,156.49	12,139.04	12,132.74
20.75%	19,108.17	16,088.59	15,210.53	14,076.05	12,864.87	12,480.94	12,349.19	12,302.77	12,286.25	12,280.36

	5	7	8	10	15	20	25	30	35	40
1.00%	12,307.50	8,878.50	7,807.12	6,307.50	4,309.16	3,311.24	2,713.48	2,315.80	2,032.46	1,820.56
1.25%	12,385.15	8,956.36	7,885.15	6,385.93	4,388.79	3,392.16	2,795.74	2,399.41	2,117.42	1,906.89
1.50%	12,463.12	9,034.65	7,963.68	6,464.99	4,469.35	3,474.33	2,879.54	2,484.87	2,204.53	1,995.64
1.75%	12,541.40	9,113.39	8,042.70	6,544.67	4,550.84	3,557.73	2,964.88	2,572.15	2,293.76	2,086.81
2.00%	12,619.99	9,192.55	8,122.23	6,624.97	4,633.26	3,642.36	3,051.75	2,661.26	2,385.09	2,180.34
2.25%	12,698.89	9,272.16	8,202.25	6,705.89	4,716.61	3,728.22	3,140.14	2,752.17	2,478.50	2,276.22
2.50%	12,778.10	9,352.20	8,282.77	6,787.43	4,800.88	3,815.30	3,230.04	2,844.87	2,573.97	2,374.40
2.75%	12,857.62	9,432.67	8,363.78	6,869.59	4,886.08	3,903.60	3,321.44	2,939.34	2,671.45	2,474.84
3.00%	12,937.46	9,513.58	8,445.29	6,952.37	4,972.19	3,993.10	3,414.32	3,035.55	2,770.92	2,577.49
3.25%	13,017.60	9,594.92	8,527.30	7,035.77	5,059.22	4,083.81	3,508.68	3,133.49	2,872.35	2,682.30
3.50%	13,098.06	9,676.69	8,609.80	7,119.78	5,147.15	4,175.71	3,604.49	3,233.12	2,975.69	2,789.21
3.75%	13,178.82	9,758.90	8,692.79	7,204.41	5,236.00	4,268.80	3,701.74	3,334.43	3,080.92	2,898.19
4.00%	13,259.90	9,841.54	8,776.28	7,289.65	5,325.75	4,363.06	3,800.43	3,437.39	3,187.98	3,009.16
4.25%	13,341.28	9,924.61	8,860.26	7,375.50	5,416.40	4,458.49	3,900.51	3,541.97	3,296.84	3,122.07
4.50%	13,422.97	10,008.12	8,944.73	7,461.97	5,507.95	4,555.08	4,001.99	3,648.13	3,407.45	3,236.85
4.75%	13,504.98	10,092.05	9,029.69	7,549.04	5,600.39	4,652.81	4,104.85	3,755.86	3,519.77	3,353.46
5.00%	13,587.29	10,176.41	9,115.14	7,636.72	5,693.71	4,751.68	4,209.05	3,865.12	3,633.75	3,471.82
5.25%	13,669.91	10,261.21	9,201.08	7,725.00	5,787.92	4,851.68	4,314.58	3,975.87	3,749.35	3,591.87
5.50%	13,752.84	10,346.43	9,287.51	7,813.89	5,883.00	4,952.79	4,421.43	4,088.08	3,866.52	3,713.55
5.75%	13,836.07	10,432.08	9,374.43	7,903.38	5,978.95	5,055.00	4,529.57	4,201.72	3,985.21	3,836.79
6.00%	13,919.62	10,518.16	9,461.83	7,993.48	6,075.77	5,158.30	4,638.97	4,316.76	4,105.37	3,961.54
6.25%	14,003.47	10,604.66	9,549.72	8,084.17	6,173.44	5,262.68	4,749.62	4,433.16	4,226.95	4,087.72
6.50%	14,087.63	10,691.59	9,638.09	8,175.45	6,271.97	5,368.13	4,861.49	4,550.89	4,349.91	4,215.29
6.75%	14,172.09	10,778.95	9,726.94	8,267.34	6,371.35	5,474.62	4,974.56	4,669.91	4,474.20	4,344.17
7.00%	14,256.86	10,866.73	9,816.28	8,359.81	6,471.56	5,582.15	5,088.81	4,790.18	4,599.77	4,474.31
7.25%	14,341.94	10,954.93	9,906.09	8,452.87	6,572.61	5,690.71	5,204.21	4,911.67	4,726.56	4,605.64
7.50%	14,427.32	11,043.56	9,996.39	8,546.53	6,674.49	5,800.27	5,320.74	5,034.34	4,854.55	4,738.11
7.75%	14,513.01	11,132.61	10,087.16	8,640.77	6,777.19	5,910.83	5,438.37	5,158.17	4,983.67	4,871.66
8.00%	14,599.00	11,222.07	10,178.41	8,735.59	6,880.70	6,022.37	5,557.08	5,283.10	5,113.88	5,006.24
8.25%	14,685.30	11,311.96	10,270.13	8,830.99	6,985.01	6,134.87	5,676.84	5,409.12	5,245.14	5,141.80
8.50%	14,771.90	11,402.27	10,362.33	8,926.97	7,090.12	6,248.33	5,797.64	5,536.18	5,377.40	5,278.28
8.75%	14,858.81	11,492.99	10,455.00	9,023.53	7,196.03	6,362.72	5,919.43	5,664.24	5,510.61	5,415.63
9.00%	14,946.02	11,584.14	10,548.15	9,120.66	7,302.72	6,478.03	6,042.21	5,793.28	5,644.75	5,553.80
9.25%	15,033.53	11,675.69	10,641.76	9,218.36	7,410.18	6,594.24	6,165.95	5,923.26	5,779.76	5,692.76
9.50%	15,121.34	11,767.67	10,735.84	9,316.62	7,518.42	6,711.34	6,290.62	6,054.15	5,915.60	5,832.44
9.75%	15,209.46	11,860.05	10,830.39	9,415.46	7,627.41	6,829.32	6,416.19	6,185.91	6,052.24	5,972.82
10.00%	15,297.87	11,952.85	10,925.40	9,514.85	7,737.16	6,948.16	6,542.65	6,318.52	6,189.64	6,113.85
10.25%	15,386.59	12,046.06	11,020.87	9,614.81	7,847.65	7,067.83	6,669.96	6,451.93	6,327.76	6,255.49
10.50%	15,475.61	12,139.68	11,116.81	9,715.32	7,958.87	7,188.34	6,798.11	6,586.12	6,466.56	6,397.71
10.75%	15,564.93	12,233.72	11,213.21	9,816.38	8,070.83	7,309.65	6,927.07	6,721.07	6,606.02	6,540.46

$720,000   11.00 - 20.75%   5 - 40 Years

	5	7	8	10	15	20	25	30	35	40
11.00%	15,654.54	12,328.15	11,310.07	9,918.00	8,183.50	7,431.76	7,056.81	6,856.73	6,746.10	6,683.72
11.25%	15,744.46	12,423.00	11,407.38	10,020.16	8,296.88	7,554.64	7,187.32	6,993.08	6,886.76	6,827.45
11.50%	15,834.68	12,518.25	11,505.15	10,122.87	8,410.97	7,678.29	7,318.58	7,130.10	7,027.97	6,971.63
11.75%	15,925.19	12,613.91	11,603.37	10,226.12	8,525.75	7,802.69	7,450.55	7,267.75	7,169.72	7,116.22
12.00%	16,016.00	12,709.97	11,702.05	10,329.91	8,641.21	7,927.82	7,583.21	7,406.01	7,311.96	7,261.20
12.25%	16,107.11	12,806.43	11,801.17	10,434.23	8,757.35	8,053.67	7,716.56	7,544.85	7,454.67	7,406.54
12.50%	16,198.52	12,903.29	11,900.74	10,539.08	8,874.16	8,180.21	7,850.55	7,684.26	7,597.83	7,552.22
12.75%	16,290.22	13,000.55	12,000.76	10,644.47	8,991.63	8,307.44	7,985.18	7,824.19	7,741.41	7,698.21
13.00%	16,382.21	13,098.21	12,101.22	10,750.37	9,109.74	8,435.35	8,120.41	7,964.64	7,885.39	7,844.50
13.25%	16,474.50	13,196.27	12,202.13	10,856.80	9,228.50	8,563.90	8,256.24	8,105.57	8,029.74	7,991.06
13.50%	16,567.09	13,294.72	12,303.47	10,963.75	9,347.89	8,693.10	8,392.64	8,246.97	8,174.45	8,137.88
13.75%	16,659.97	13,393.57	12,405.26	11,071.21	9,467.91	8,822.92	8,529.59	8,388.81	8,319.49	8,284.93
14.00%	16,753.14	13,492.81	12,507.48	11,179.18	9,588.54	8,953.35	8,667.08	8,531.08	8,464.85	8,432.21
14.25%	16,846.61	13,592.44	12,610.14	11,287.66	9,709.77	9,084.38	8,805.08	8,673.75	8,610.50	8,579.69
14.50%	16,940.36	13,692.46	12,713.23	11,396.65	9,831.61	9,215.98	8,943.57	8,816.80	8,756.43	8,727.36
14.75%	17,034.41	13,792.87	12,816.74	11,506.13	9,954.03	9,348.16	9,082.55	8,960.23	8,902.62	8,875.20
15.00%	17,128.75	13,893.66	12,920.69	11,616.12	10,077.03	9,480.88	9,221.98	9,104.00	9,049.06	9,023.21
15.25%	17,223.38	13,994.84	13,025.07	11,726.59	10,200.60	9,614.15	9,361.86	9,248.10	9,195.72	9,171.38
15.50%	17,318.30	14,096.41	13,129.86	11,837.56	10,324.73	9,747.94	9,502.17	9,392.52	9,342.61	9,319.68
15.75%	17,413.51	14,198.36	13,235.09	11,949.01	10,449.42	9,882.24	9,642.88	9,537.24	9,489.70	9,468.11
16.00%	17,509.00	14,300.69	13,340.73	12,060.94	10,574.65	10,017.04	9,784.00	9,682.25	9,636.98	9,616.67
16.25%	17,604.78	14,403.39	13,446.78	12,173.36	10,700.41	10,152.33	9,925.50	9,827.53	9,784.44	9,765.34
16.50%	17,700.86	14,506.48	13,553.26	12,286.25	10,826.70	10,288.08	10,067.36	9,973.07	9,932.07	9,914.11
16.75%	17,797.21	14,609.94	13,660.15	12,399.60	10,953.51	10,424.30	10,209.58	10,118.85	10,079.85	10,062.97
17.00%	17,893.85	14,713.78	13,767.45	12,513.43	11,080.83	10,560.96	10,352.14	10,264.86	10,227.79	10,211.93
17.25%	17,990.78	14,817.99	13,875.16	12,627.72	11,208.65	10,698.06	10,495.02	10,411.10	10,375.86	10,360.97
17.50%	18,087.99	14,922.57	13,983.27	12,742.47	11,336.96	10,835.58	10,638.21	10,557.54	10,524.06	10,510.08
17.75%	18,185.49	15,027.52	14,091.79	12,857.68	11,465.76	10,973.51	10,781.71	10,704.18	10,672.39	10,659.26
18.00%	18,283.27	15,132.84	14,200.71	12,973.33	11,595.03	11,111.84	10,925.50	10,851.01	10,820.82	10,808.51
18.25%	18,381.33	15,238.53	14,310.04	13,089.44	11,724.77	11,250.56	11,069.56	10,998.02	10,969.36	10,957.82
18.50%	18,479.67	15,344.58	14,419.76	13,205.99	11,854.97	11,389.66	11,213.89	11,145.20	11,118.01	11,107.18
18.75%	18,578.29	15,451.00	14,529.87	13,322.98	11,985.62	11,529.12	11,358.47	11,292.54	11,266.74	11,256.60
19.00%	18,677.20	15,557.77	14,640.38	13,440.41	12,116.71	11,668.93	11,503.30	11,440.03	11,415.56	11,406.06
19.25%	18,776.38	15,664.91	14,751.28	13,558.27	12,248.23	11,809.09	11,648.36	11,587.66	11,564.46	11,555.56
19.50%	18,875.84	15,772.41	14,862.57	13,676.56	12,380.18	11,949.59	11,793.64	11,735.42	11,713.44	11,705.11
19.75%	18,975.58	15,880.26	14,974.25	13,795.27	12,512.55	12,090.40	11,939.15	11,883.32	11,862.49	11,854.69
20.00%	19,075.60	15,988.46	15,086.30	13,914.41	12,645.33	12,231.54	12,084.85	12,031.33	12,011.60	12,004.30
20.25%	19,175.89	16,097.02	15,198.74	14,033.96	12,778.52	12,372.98	12,230.76	12,179.46	12,160.78	12,153.95
20.50%	19,276.46	16,205.93	15,311.56	14,153.93	12,912.10	12,514.71	12,376.85	12,327.70	12,310.01	12,303.62
20.75%	19,377.30	16,315.19	15,424.76	14,274.30	13,046.06	12,656.73	12,523.13	12,476.04	12,459.30	12,453.32

	5	7	8	10	15	20	25	30	35	40
1.00%	12,478.44	9,001.81	7,915.55	6,395.10	4,369.01	3,357.23	2,751.17	2,347.97	2,060.69	1,845.85
1.25%	12,557.17	9,080.75	7,994.67	6,474.62	4,449.74	3,439.28	2,834.57	2,432.74	2,146.83	1,933.37
1.50%	12,636.22	9,160.13	8,074.29	6,554.78	4,531.42	3,522.58	2,919.54	2,519.38	2,235.15	2,023.36
1.75%	12,715.58	9,239.96	8,154.41	6,635.57	4,614.05	3,607.14	3,006.06	2,607.88	2,325.62	2,115.79
2.00%	12,795.26	9,320.23	8,235.04	6,716.98	4,697.61	3,692.95	3,094.14	2,698.22	2,418.22	2,210.63
2.25%	12,875.26	9,400.94	8,316.17	6,799.03	4,782.12	3,780.00	3,183.75	2,790.40	2,512.93	2,307.84
2.50%	12,955.57	9,482.09	8,397.81	6,881.70	4,867.56	3,868.29	3,274.90	2,884.38	2,609.72	2,407.38
2.75%	13,036.20	9,563.68	8,479.95	6,965.01	4,953.94	3,957.81	3,367.57	2,980.16	2,708.55	2,509.21
3.00%	13,117.14	9,645.71	8,562.59	7,048.93	5,041.25	4,048.56	3,461.74	3,077.71	2,809.41	2,613.29
3.25%	13,198.40	9,728.18	8,645.73	7,133.49	5,129.48	4,140.53	3,557.41	3,177.01	2,912.24	2,719.55
3.50%	13,279.97	9,811.09	8,729.38	7,218.67	5,218.64	4,233.71	3,654.55	3,278.03	3,017.02	2,827.95
3.75%	13,361.86	9,894.44	8,813.52	7,304.47	5,308.72	4,328.08	3,753.16	3,380.74	3,123.71	2,938.44
4.00%	13,444.06	9,978.23	8,898.17	7,390.90	5,399.72	4,423.66	3,853.21	3,485.13	3,232.26	3,050.95
4.25%	13,526.58	10,062.45	8,983.32	7,477.94	5,491.63	4,520.41	3,954.69	3,591.16	3,342.63	3,165.43
4.50%	13,609.40	10,147.12	9,068.96	7,565.60	5,584.45	4,618.34	4,057.58	3,698.80	3,454.77	3,281.81
4.75%	13,692.55	10,232.22	9,155.10	7,653.89	5,678.17	4,717.43	4,161.86	3,808.03	3,568.65	3,400.03
5.00%	13,776.00	10,317.75	9,241.74	7,742.78	5,772.79	4,817.68	4,267.51	3,918.80	3,684.22	3,520.04
5.25%	13,859.77	10,403.73	9,328.88	7,832.29	5,868.31	4,919.06	4,374.51	4,031.09	3,801.42	3,641.75
5.50%	13,943.85	10,490.13	9,416.51	7,922.42	5,964.71	5,021.58	4,482.84	4,144.86	3,920.22	3,765.12
5.75%	14,028.24	10,576.97	9,504.63	8,013.15	6,061.99	5,125.21	4,592.48	4,260.08	4,040.56	3,890.08
6.00%	14,112.95	10,664.24	9,593.24	8,104.50	6,160.15	5,229.95	4,703.40	4,376.72	4,162.38	4,016.56
6.25%	14,197.96	10,751.95	9,682.35	8,196.45	6,259.19	5,335.78	4,815.59	4,494.74	4,285.66	4,144.50
6.50%	14,283.29	10,840.09	9,771.95	8,289.00	6,359.08	5,442.68	4,929.01	4,614.10	4,410.33	4,273.83
6.75%	14,368.93	10,928.66	9,862.04	8,382.16	6,459.84	5,550.66	5,043.65	4,734.77	4,536.34	4,404.50
7.00%	14,454.87	11,017.66	9,952.61	8,475.92	6,561.45	5,659.68	5,159.49	4,856.71	4,663.65	4,536.45
7.25%	14,541.13	11,107.08	10,043.68	8,570.28	6,663.90	5,769.74	5,276.49	4,979.89	4,792.21	4,669.61
7.50%	14,627.70	11,196.94	10,135.23	8,665.23	6,767.19	5,880.83	5,394.64	5,104.27	4,921.97	4,803.92
7.75%	14,714.58	11,287.23	10,227.26	8,760.78	6,871.31	5,992.92	5,513.90	5,229.81	5,052.88	4,939.32
8.00%	14,801.77	11,377.94	10,319.78	8,856.91	6,976.26	6,106.01	5,634.26	5,356.48	5,184.90	5,075.78
8.25%	14,889.26	11,469.07	10,412.77	8,953.64	7,082.02	6,220.08	5,755.69	5,484.25	5,317.99	5,213.21
8.50%	14,977.07	11,560.63	10,506.25	9,050.96	7,188.60	6,335.11	5,878.16	5,613.07	5,452.08	5,351.59
8.75%	15,065.18	11,652.62	10,600.21	9,148.85	7,295.98	6,451.09	6,001.65	5,742.91	5,587.15	5,490.84
9.00%	15,153.60	11,745.03	10,694.65	9,247.33	7,404.15	6,568.00	6,126.13	5,873.75	5,723.15	5,630.94
9.25%	15,242.33	11,837.86	10,789.56	9,346.39	7,513.10	6,685.83	6,251.59	6,005.53	5,860.03	5,771.82
9.50%	15,331.36	11,931.11	10,884.95	9,446.02	7,622.84	6,804.56	6,377.99	6,138.24	5,997.76	5,913.45
9.75%	15,420.70	12,024.78	10,980.81	9,546.23	7,733.35	6,924.17	6,505.30	6,271.83	6,136.30	6,055.78
10.00%	15,510.34	12,118.86	11,077.14	9,647.00	7,844.62	7,044.66	6,633.52	6,406.27	6,275.61	6,198.77
10.25%	15,600.29	12,213.37	11,173.94	9,748.35	7,956.64	7,166.00	6,762.60	6,541.54	6,415.65	6,342.37
10.50%	15,690.55	12,308.29	11,271.21	9,850.25	8,069.41	7,288.17	6,892.53	6,677.60	6,556.38	6,486.56
10.75%	15,781.11	12,403.63	11,368.95	9,952.72	8,182.92	7,411.17	7,023.28	6,814.41	6,697.77	6,631.30

$730,000   11.00 - 20.75%   5 - 40 Years

	5	7	8	10	15	20	25	30	35	40
11.00%	15,871.97	12,499.38	11,467.15	10,055.75	8,297.16	7,534.98	7,154.83	6,951.96	6,839.79	6,776.55
11.25%	15,963.13	12,595.54	11,565.82	10,159.33	8,412.12	7,659.57	7,287.15	7,090.21	6,982.41	6,922.28
11.50%	16,054.60	12,692.12	11,664.94	10,263.47	8,527.79	7,784.94	7,420.22	7,229.13	7,125.58	7,068.46
11.75%	16,146.37	12,789.10	11,764.53	10,368.15	8,644.16	7,911.06	7,554.03	7,368.69	7,269.30	7,215.06
12.00%	16,238.45	12,886.49	11,864.57	10,473.38	8,761.23	8,037.93	7,688.54	7,508.87	7,413.51	7,362.05
12.25%	16,330.82	12,984.30	11,965.08	10,579.15	8,878.98	8,165.52	7,823.73	7,649.64	7,558.21	7,509.41
12.50%	16,423.49	13,082.50	12,066.03	10,685.46	8,997.41	8,293.83	7,959.59	7,790.98	7,703.36	7,657.11
12.75%	16,516.47	13,181.12	12,167.44	10,792.31	9,116.51	8,422.82	8,096.08	7,932.86	7,848.93	7,805.13
13.00%	16,609.74	13,280.13	12,269.30	10,899.68	9,236.27	8,552.50	8,233.20	8,075.26	7,994.91	7,953.45
13.25%	16,703.32	13,379.55	12,371.60	11,007.59	9,356.68	8,682.84	8,370.91	8,218.15	8,141.27	8,102.05
13.50%	16,797.19	13,479.37	12,474.36	11,116.02	9,477.73	8,813.84	8,509.21	8,361.51	8,287.99	8,250.91
13.75%	16,891.36	13,579.59	12,577.55	11,224.98	9,599.41	8,945.46	8,648.06	8,505.32	8,435.04	8,400.00
14.00%	16,985.82	13,680.21	12,681.20	11,334.45	9,721.71	9,077.70	8,787.46	8,649.56	8,582.41	8,549.32
14.25%	17,080.59	13,781.22	12,785.28	11,444.44	9,844.63	9,210.55	8,927.37	8,794.22	8,730.09	8,698.85
14.50%	17,175.65	13,882.63	12,889.80	11,554.94	9,968.16	9,343.98	9,067.79	8,939.26	8,878.04	8,848.57
14.75%	17,271.00	13,984.44	12,994.75	11,665.94	10,092.28	9,477.99	9,208.69	9,084.67	9,026.27	8,998.47
15.00%	17,366.65	14,086.63	13,100.15	11,777.45	10,216.99	9,612.56	9,350.06	9,230.44	9,174.74	9,148.54
15.25%	17,462.59	14,189.22	13,205.97	11,889.46	10,342.27	9,747.68	9,491.88	9,376.55	9,323.44	9,298.76
15.50%	17,558.83	14,292.19	13,312.22	12,001.97	10,468.13	9,883.33	9,634.14	9,522.97	9,472.37	9,449.12
15.75%	17,655.36	14,395.56	13,418.91	12,114.97	10,594.55	10,019.50	9,776.81	9,669.70	9,621.50	9,599.62
16.00%	17,752.18	14,499.31	13,526.01	12,228.46	10,721.52	10,156.17	9,919.89	9,816.73	9,770.83	9,750.23
16.25%	17,849.30	14,603.44	13,633.55	12,342.43	10,849.03	10,293.33	10,063.35	9,964.02	9,920.33	9,900.97
16.50%	17,946.70	14,707.96	13,741.50	12,456.89	10,977.07	10,430.97	10,207.19	10,111.58	10,070.01	10,051.80
16.75%	18,044.40	14,812.86	13,849.87	12,571.82	11,105.64	10,569.08	10,351.38	10,259.39	10,219.85	10,202.74
17.00%	18,142.38	14,918.14	13,958.66	12,687.23	11,234.73	10,707.64	10,495.92	10,407.43	10,369.84	10,353.76
17.25%	18,240.65	15,023.80	14,067.87	12,803.11	11,364.33	10,846.65	10,640.78	10,555.70	10,519.97	10,504.87
17.50%	18,339.22	15,129.83	14,177.48	12,919.45	11,494.42	10,986.08	10,785.97	10,704.17	10,670.23	10,656.05
17.75%	18,438.07	15,236.24	14,287.51	13,036.26	11,625.01	11,125.92	10,931.46	10,852.85	10,820.61	10,807.31
18.00%	18,537.20	15,343.02	14,397.95	13,153.52	11,756.07	11,266.17	11,077.24	11,001.72	10,971.11	10,958.63
18.25%	18,636.62	15,450.18	14,508.79	13,271.24	11,887.61	11,406.82	11,223.30	11,150.77	11,121.72	11,110.01
18.50%	18,736.33	15,557.70	14,620.03	13,389.41	12,019.62	11,547.85	11,369.63	11,300.00	11,272.42	11,261.45
18.75%	18,836.33	15,665.59	14,731.68	13,508.02	12,152.08	11,689.24	11,516.23	11,449.38	11,423.22	11,412.94
19.00%	18,936.60	15,773.85	14,843.72	13,627.08	12,285.00	11,831.00	11,663.06	11,598.92	11,574.11	11,564.48
19.25%	19,037.16	15,882.48	14,956.16	13,746.58	12,418.35	11,973.11	11,810.14	11,748.60	11,725.08	11,716.06
19.50%	19,138.01	15,991.47	15,069.00	13,866.51	12,552.13	12,115.55	11,957.44	11,898.42	11,876.13	11,867.68
19.75%	19,239.13	16,100.82	15,182.22	13,986.87	12,686.34	12,258.33	12,104.97	12,048.36	12,027.25	12,019.34
20.00%	19,340.54	16,210.53	15,295.84	14,107.66	12,820.96	12,401.42	12,252.70	12,198.44	12,178.43	12,171.03
20.25%	19,442.22	16,320.59	15,409.84	14,228.88	12,956.00	12,544.82	12,400.63	12,348.62	12,329.68	12,322.75
20.50%	19,544.19	16,431.02	15,524.22	14,350.51	13,091.43	12,688.53	12,548.75	12,498.92	12,480.98	12,474.51
20.75%	19,646.43	16,541.79	15,638.99	14,472.55	13,227.26	12,832.52	12,697.06	12,649.32	12,632.34	12,626.29

$740,000   1.00 - 10.75%   5 - 40 Years

	5	7	8	10	15	20	25	30	35	40
1.00%	12,649.37	9,125.12	8,023.99	6,482.70	4,428.86	3,403.22	2,788.86	2,380.13	2,088.91	1,871.13
1.25%	12,729.18	9,205.14	8,104.18	6,563.32	4,510.70	3,486.39	2,873.40	2,466.06	2,176.24	1,959.85
1.50%	12,809.32	9,285.62	8,184.89	6,644.57	4,593.50	3,570.84	2,959.53	2,553.89	2,265.76	2,051.08
1.75%	12,889.77	9,366.53	8,266.11	6,726.46	4,677.25	3,656.55	3,047.24	2,643.60	2,357.47	2,144.77
2.00%	12,970.54	9,447.90	8,347.85	6,809.00	4,761.96	3,743.54	3,136.52	2,735.18	2,451.34	2,240.91
2.25%	13,051.64	9,529.72	8,430.09	6,892.17	4,847.63	3,831.78	3,227.37	2,828.62	2,547.35	2,339.45
2.50%	13,133.05	9,611.98	8,512.84	6,975.97	4,934.24	3,921.28	3,319.76	2,923.89	2,645.46	2,440.36
2.75%	13,214.78	9,694.69	8,596.11	7,060.42	5,021.80	4,012.03	3,413.70	3,020.98	2,745.66	2,543.59
3.00%	13,296.83	9,777.84	8,679.88	7,145.50	5,110.30	4,104.02	3,509.16	3,119.87	2,847.89	2,649.08
3.25%	13,379.20	9,861.44	8,764.17	7,231.21	5,199.75	4,197.25	3,606.14	3,220.53	2,952.14	2,756.81
3.50%	13,461.89	9,945.49	8,848.96	7,317.55	5,290.13	4,291.70	3,704.61	3,322.93	3,058.35	2,866.69
3.75%	13,544.90	10,029.98	8,934.26	7,404.53	5,381.45	4,387.37	3,804.57	3,427.06	3,166.50	2,978.69
4.00%	13,628.23	10,114.92	9,020.06	7,492.14	5,473.69	4,484.25	3,905.99	3,532.87	3,276.53	3,092.74
4.25%	13,711.87	10,200.30	9,106.38	7,580.38	5,566.86	4,582.34	4,008.86	3,640.36	3,388.42	3,208.79
4.50%	13,795.83	10,286.12	9,193.19	7,669.24	5,660.95	4,681.61	4,113.16	3,749.47	3,502.10	3,326.76
4.75%	13,880.11	10,372.39	9,280.52	7,758.73	5,755.96	4,782.05	4,218.87	3,860.19	3,617.54	3,446.61
5.00%	13,964.71	10,459.09	9,368.34	7,848.85	5,851.87	4,883.67	4,325.97	3,972.48	3,734.69	3,568.25
5.25%	14,049.63	10,546.24	9,456.67	7,939.59	5,948.70	4,986.45	4,434.43	4,086.31	3,853.50	3,691.64
5.50%	14,134.86	10,633.83	9,545.50	8,030.94	6,046.42	5,090.37	4,544.25	4,201.64	3,973.92	3,816.70
5.75%	14,220.41	10,721.86	9,634.83	8,122.92	6,145.03	5,195.42	4,655.39	4,318.44	4,095.91	3,943.37
6.00%	14,306.27	10,810.33	9,724.66	8,215.52	6,244.54	5,301.59	4,767.83	4,436.67	4,219.40	4,071.58
6.25%	14,392.45	10,899.24	9,814.99	8,308.73	6,344.93	5,408.87	4,881.55	4,556.31	4,344.37	4,201.27
6.50%	14,478.95	10,988.58	9,905.81	8,402.55	6,446.19	5,517.24	4,996.53	4,677.30	4,470.74	4,332.38
6.75%	14,565.76	11,078.37	9,997.13	8,496.98	6,548.33	5,626.69	5,112.75	4,799.63	4,598.48	4,464.84
7.00%	14,652.89	11,168.58	10,088.95	8,592.03	6,651.33	5,737.21	5,230.17	4,923.24	4,727.54	4,598.59
7.25%	14,740.33	11,259.24	10,181.26	8,687.68	6,755.19	5,848.78	5,348.77	5,048.10	4,857.86	4,733.57
7.50%	14,828.08	11,350.32	10,274.06	8,783.93	6,859.89	5,961.39	5,468.53	5,174.19	4,989.40	4,869.72
7.75%	14,916.15	11,441.85	10,367.36	8,880.79	6,965.44	6,075.02	5,589.43	5,301.45	5,122.10	5,006.99
8.00%	15,004.53	11,533.80	10,461.14	8,978.24	7,071.83	6,189.66	5,711.44	5,429.86	5,255.93	5,145.31
8.25%	15,093.20	11,626.18	10,555.42	9,076.29	7,179.04	6,305.29	5,834.53	5,559.37	5,390.83	5,284.63
8.50%	15,182.20	11,719.00	10,650.18	9,174.94	7,287.07	6,421.89	5,958.68	5,689.96	5,526.77	5,424.90
8.75%	15,271.59	11,812.24	10,745.42	9,274.18	7,395.92	6,539.46	6,083.86	5,821.58	5,663.69	5,566.06
9.00%	15,361.18	11,905.92	10,841.15	9,374.01	7,505.57	6,657.97	6,210.05	5,954.21	5,801.55	5,708.08
9.25%	15,451.12	12,000.02	10,937.36	9,474.42	7,616.02	6,777.41	6,337.23	6,087.80	5,940.31	5,850.89
9.50%	15,541.38	12,094.55	11,034.06	9,575.42	7,727.26	6,897.77	6,465.36	6,222.32	6,079.93	5,994.46
9.75%	15,631.94	12,189.50	11,131.23	9,677.00	7,839.28	7,019.02	6,594.42	6,357.74	6,220.36	6,138.73
10.00%	15,722.81	12,284.88	11,228.88	9,779.15	7,952.08	7,141.16	6,724.39	6,494.03	6,361.58	6,283.68
10.25%	15,814.00	12,380.68	11,327.01	9,881.89	8,065.64	7,264.16	6,855.24	6,631.15	6,503.53	6,429.25
10.50%	15,905.49	12,476.90	11,425.61	9,985.19	8,179.95	7,388.01	6,986.94	6,769.07	6,646.19	6,575.42
10.75%	15,997.29	12,573.54	11,524.69	10,089.06	8,295.02	7,512.69	7,119.49	6,907.76	6,789.52	6,722.14

$740,000   11.00 - 20.75%   5 - 40 Years

	5	7	8	10	15	20	25	30	35	40
11.00%	16,089.39	12,670.60	11,624.23	10,193.50	8,410.82	7,638.19	7,252.84	7,047.19	6,933.49	6,869.38
11.25%	16,181.81	12,768.08	11,724.25	10,298.50	8,527.35	7,764.49	7,386.97	7,187.33	7,078.05	7,017.10
11.50%	16,274.53	12,865.98	11,824.74	10,404.06	8,644.60	7,891.58	7,521.87	7,328.16	7,223.19	7,165.29
11.75%	16,367.56	12,964.29	11,925.69	10,510.18	8,762.57	8,019.43	7,657.51	7,469.63	7,368.88	7,313.89
12.00%	16,460.89	13,063.02	12,027.10	10,616.85	8,881.24	8,148.04	7,793.86	7,611.73	7,515.07	7,462.90
12.25%	16,554.53	13,162.16	12,128.98	10,724.07	9,000.61	8,277.38	7,930.90	7,754.43	7,661.75	7,612.28
12.50%	16,648.47	13,261.72	12,231.32	10,831.84	9,120.66	8,407.44	8,068.62	7,897.71	7,808.88	7,762.00
12.75%	16,742.72	13,361.68	12,334.12	10,940.15	9,241.39	8,538.21	8,206.99	8,041.53	7,956.45	7,912.05
13.00%	16,837.27	13,462.05	12,437.37	11,048.99	9,362.79	8,669.66	8,345.98	8,185.88	8,104.43	8,062.40
13.25%	16,932.13	13,562.83	12,541.08	11,158.38	9,484.85	8,801.79	8,485.58	8,330.72	8,252.79	8,213.04
13.50%	17,027.29	13,664.02	12,645.24	11,268.30	9,607.56	8,934.57	8,625.77	8,476.05	8,401.52	8,363.93
13.75%	17,122.75	13,765.61	12,749.85	11,378.74	9,730.91	9,068.00	8,766.53	8,621.83	8,550.59	8,515.00
14.00%	17,218.51	13,867.61	12,854.91	11,489.72	9,854.89	9,202.05	8,907.83	8,768.05	8,699.98	8,666.44
14.25%	17,314.57	13,970.01	12,960.42	11,601.21	9,979.49	9,336.72	9,049.66	8,914.68	8,849.68	8,818.01
14.50%	17,410.93	14,072.81	13,066.37	11,713.22	10,104.71	9,471.98	9,192.01	9,061.71	8,999.66	8,969.78
14.75%	17,507.59	14,176.00	13,172.76	11,825.75	10,230.53	9,607.83	9,334.84	9,209.12	9,149.91	9,121.74
15.00%	17,604.55	14,279.60	13,279.60	11,938.79	10,356.94	9,744.24	9,478.15	9,356.89	9,300.42	9,273.86
15.25%	17,701.81	14,383.59	13,386.87	12,052.33	10,483.95	9,881.21	9,621.91	9,504.99	9,451.16	9,426.14
15.50%	17,799.36	14,487.98	13,494.58	12,166.38	10,611.53	10,018.72	9,766.11	9,653.43	9,602.13	9,578.56
15.75%	17,897.21	14,592.76	13,602.73	12,280.93	10,739.68	10,156.75	9,910.74	9,802.17	9,753.30	9,731.12
16.00%	17,995.36	14,697.93	13,711.30	12,395.97	10,868.39	10,295.29	10,055.78	9,951.20	9,904.67	9,883.80
16.25%	18,093.81	14,803.49	13,820.31	12,511.51	10,997.64	10,434.34	10,201.21	10,100.52	10,056.23	10,036.60
16.50%	18,192.55	14,909.44	13,929.74	12,627.53	11,127.44	10,573.86	10,347.01	10,250.10	10,207.96	10,189.50
16.75%	18,291.58	15,015.77	14,039.60	12,744.04	11,257.78	10,713.86	10,493.18	10,399.93	10,359.85	10,342.50
17.00%	18,390.91	15,122.50	14,149.88	12,861.03	11,388.63	10,854.32	10,639.69	10,550.00	10,511.89	10,495.59
17.25%	18,490.53	15,229.60	14,260.58	12,978.49	11,520.00	10,995.23	10,786.55	10,700.29	10,664.08	10,648.77
17.50%	18,590.44	15,337.09	14,371.70	13,096.43	11,651.88	11,136.57	10,933.72	10,850.81	10,816.40	10,802.03
17.75%	18,690.64	15,444.95	14,483.23	13,214.83	11,784.25	11,278.33	11,081.20	11,001.52	10,968.84	10,955.36
18.00%	18,791.14	15,553.20	14,595.18	13,333.70	11,917.12	11,420.51	11,228.98	11,152.43	11,121.40	11,108.75
18.25%	18,891.92	15,661.82	14,707.54	13,453.04	12,050.46	11,563.08	11,377.05	11,303.52	11,274.07	11,262.20
18.50%	18,992.99	15,770.82	14,820.31	13,572.82	12,184.27	11,706.03	11,525.38	11,454.79	11,426.84	11,415.72
18.75%	19,094.36	15,880.19	14,933.48	13,693.06	12,318.55	11,849.37	11,673.98	11,606.22	11,579.71	11,569.28
19.00%	19,196.01	15,989.93	15,047.06	13,813.75	12,453.28	11,993.07	11,822.83	11,757.80	11,732.66	11,722.89
19.25%	19,297.95	16,100.05	15,161.04	13,934.89	12,588.46	12,137.12	11,971.92	11,909.54	11,885.70	11,876.55
19.50%	19,400.17	16,210.53	15,275.42	14,056.46	12,724.08	12,281.52	12,121.25	12,061.41	12,038.81	12,030.25
19.75%	19,502.68	16,321.38	15,390.20	14,178.48	12,860.13	12,426.25	12,270.79	12,213.41	12,192.00	12,183.98
20.00%	19,605.47	16,432.59	15,505.37	14,300.92	12,996.59	12,571.30	12,420.54	12,365.54	12,345.26	12,337.75
20.25%	19,708.55	16,544.16	15,620.93	14,423.79	13,133.48	12,716.67	12,570.50	12,517.78	12,498.58	12,491.56
20.50%	19,811.91	16,656.10	15,736.88	14,547.09	13,270.77	12,862.34	12,720.65	12,670.14	12,651.96	12,645.39
20.75%	19,915.56	16,768.39	15,853.22	14,670.81	13,408.45	13,008.31	12,870.99	12,822.60	12,805.39	12,799.25

	5	7	8	10	15	20	25	30	35	40
1.00%	12,820.31	9,248.44	8,132.42	6,570.31	4,488.71	3,449.21	2,826.54	2,412.30	2,117.14	1,896.42
1.25%	12,901.20	9,329.54	8,213.70	6,652.01	4,571.65	3,533.50	2,912.23	2,499.39	2,205.65	1,986.34
1.50%	12,982.42	9,411.10	8,295.50	6,734.36	4,655.57	3,619.09	2,999.52	2,588.40	2,296.38	2,078.79
1.75%	13,063.96	9,493.11	8,377.82	6,817.36	4,740.46	3,705.97	3,088.42	2,679.33	2,389.33	2,173.76
2.00%	13,145.82	9,575.58	8,460.65	6,901.01	4,826.32	3,794.13	3,178.91	2,772.15	2,484.47	2,271.19
2.25%	13,228.01	9,658.50	8,544.01	6,985.30	4,913.14	3,883.56	3,270.98	2,866.85	2,581.77	2,371.07
2.50%	13,310.52	9,741.87	8,627.88	7,070.24	5,000.92	3,974.27	3,364.63	2,963.41	2,681.21	2,473.34
2.75%	13,393.36	9,825.70	8,712.27	7,155.83	5,089.66	4,066.25	3,459.83	3,061.81	2,782.76	2,577.96
3.00%	13,476.52	9,909.98	8,797.18	7,242.06	5,179.36	4,159.48	3,556.58	3,162.03	2,886.38	2,684.88
3.25%	13,560.00	9,994.71	8,882.60	7,328.93	5,270.02	4,253.97	3,654.87	3,264.05	2,992.03	2,794.06
3.50%	13,643.81	10,079.89	8,968.54	7,416.44	5,361.62	4,349.70	3,754.68	3,367.84	3,099.68	2,905.43
3.75%	13,727.94	10,165.52	9,054.99	7,504.59	5,454.17	4,446.66	3,855.98	3,473.37	3,209.29	3,018.95
4.00%	13,812.39	10,251.60	9,141.96	7,593.39	5,547.66	4,544.85	3,958.78	3,580.61	3,320.81	3,134.54
4.25%	13,897.17	10,338.14	9,229.44	7,682.82	5,642.09	4,644.26	4,063.04	3,689.55	3,434.20	3,252.15
4.50%	13,982.26	10,425.12	9,317.43	7,772.88	5,737.45	4,744.87	4,168.74	3,800.14	3,549.43	3,371.72
4.75%	14,067.68	10,512.55	9,405.93	7,863.58	5,833.74	4,846.68	4,275.88	3,912.36	3,666.43	3,493.18
5.00%	14,153.43	10,600.43	9,494.94	7,954.91	5,930.95	4,949.67	4,384.43	4,026.16	3,785.16	3,616.47
5.25%	14,239.49	10,688.76	9,584.46	8,046.88	6,029.08	5,053.83	4,494.36	4,141.53	3,905.57	3,741.53
5.50%	14,325.87	10,777.53	9,674.49	8,139.47	6,128.13	5,159.15	4,605.66	4,258.42	4,027.62	3,868.28
5.75%	14,412.58	10,866.75	9,765.03	8,232.69	6,228.08	5,265.63	4,718.30	4,376.80	4,151.26	3,996.66
6.00%	14,499.60	10,956.42	9,856.07	8,326.54	6,328.93	5,373.23	4,832.26	4,496.63	4,276.42	4,126.60
6.25%	14,586.95	11,046.52	9,947.62	8,421.01	6,430.67	5,481.96	4,947.52	4,617.88	4,403.07	4,258.05
6.50%	14,674.61	11,137.08	10,039.67	8,516.10	6,533.31	5,591.80	5,064.05	4,740.51	4,531.16	4,390.93
6.75%	14,762.60	11,228.07	10,132.23	8,611.81	6,636.82	5,702.73	5,181.84	4,864.49	4,660.62	4,525.18
7.00%	14,850.90	11,319.51	10,225.29	8,708.14	6,741.21	5,814.74	5,300.84	4,989.77	4,791.42	4,660.73
7.25%	14,939.52	11,411.39	10,318.85	8,805.08	6,846.47	5,927.82	5,421.05	5,116.32	4,923.50	4,797.54
7.50%	15,028.46	11,503.71	10,412.90	8,902.63	6,952.59	6,041.95	5,542.43	5,244.11	5,056.82	4,935.53
7.75%	15,117.72	11,596.46	10,507.46	9,000.80	7,059.57	6,157.11	5,664.97	5,373.09	5,191.32	5,074.65
8.00%	15,207.30	11,689.66	10,602.51	9,099.57	7,167.39	6,273.30	5,788.62	5,503.23	5,326.96	5,214.84
8.25%	15,297.19	11,783.29	10,698.06	9,198.95	7,276.05	6,390.49	5,913.38	5,634.50	5,463.68	5,356.04
8.50%	15,387.40	11,877.36	10,794.10	9,298.93	7,385.55	6,508.67	6,039.20	5,766.85	5,601.45	5,498.21
8.75%	15,477.92	11,971.87	10,890.63	9,399.51	7,495.86	6,627.83	6,166.08	5,900.25	5,740.22	5,641.28
9.00%	15,568.77	12,066.81	10,987.65	9,500.68	7,607.00	6,747.94	6,293.97	6,034.67	5,879.95	5,785.21
9.25%	15,659.92	12,162.18	11,085.17	9,602.45	7,718.94	6,869.00	6,422.86	6,170.07	6,020.58	5,929.95
9.50%	15,751.40	12,257.99	11,183.17	9,704.82	7,831.69	6,990.98	6,552.72	6,306.41	6,162.09	6,075.46
9.75%	15,843.18	12,354.22	11,281.65	9,807.77	7,945.22	7,113.88	6,683.53	6,443.66	6,304.42	6,221.69
10.00%	15,935.28	12,450.89	11,380.62	9,911.31	8,059.54	7,237.66	6,815.26	6,581.79	6,447.54	6,368.59
10.25%	16,027.70	12,547.98	11,480.08	10,015.43	8,174.63	7,362.33	6,947.87	6,720.76	6,591.42	6,516.14
10.50%	16,120.43	12,645.50	11,580.01	10,120.12	8,290.49	7,487.85	7,081.36	6,860.54	6,736.01	6,664.28
10.75%	16,213.47	12,743.45	11,680.43	10,225.40	8,407.11	7,614.22	7,215.70	7,001.11	6,881.27	6,812.98

$750,000   11.00 - 20.75%   5 - 40 Years

	5	7	8	10	15	20	25	30	35	40
11.00%	16,306.82	12,841.83	11,781.32	10,331.25	8,524.48	7,741.41	7,350.85	7,142.43	7,027.18	6,962.21
11.25%	16,400.48	12,940.63	11,882.69	10,437.67	8,642.58	7,869.42	7,486.80	7,284.46	7,173.70	7,111.93
11.50%	16,494.46	13,039.85	11,984.53	10,544.66	8,761.42	7,998.22	7,623.52	7,427.19	7,320.80	7,262.11
11.75%	16,588.74	13,139.49	12,086.85	10,652.21	8,880.99	8,127.80	7,760.99	7,570.57	7,468.45	7,412.73
12.00%	16,683.34	13,239.55	12,189.63	10,760.32	9,001.26	8,258.15	7,899.18	7,714.59	7,616.62	7,563.75
12.25%	16,778.24	13,340.03	12,292.89	10,868.99	9,122.24	8,389.24	8,038.08	7,859.22	7,765.28	7,715.15
12.50%	16,873.45	13,440.93	12,396.61	10,978.21	9,243.92	8,521.05	8,177.66	8,004.43	7,914.41	7,866.90
12.75%	16,968.98	13,542.24	12,500.79	11,087.99	9,366.28	8,653.59	8,317.89	8,150.20	8,063.97	8,018.97
13.00%	17,064.80	13,643.97	12,605.44	11,198.31	9,489.32	8,786.82	8,458.76	8,296.50	8,213.95	8,171.36
13.25%	17,160.94	13,746.12	12,710.55	11,309.17	9,613.02	8,920.73	8,600.25	8,443.30	8,364.32	8,324.02
13.50%	17,257.38	13,848.67	12,816.12	11,420.57	9,737.39	9,055.31	8,742.34	8,590.59	8,515.05	8,476.96
13.75%	17,354.13	13,951.63	12,922.15	11,532.51	9,862.40	9,190.54	8,884.99	8,738.34	8,666.14	8,630.14
14.00%	17,451.19	14,055.01	13,028.63	11,644.98	9,988.06	9,326.41	9,028.21	8,886.54	8,817.55	8,783.55
14.25%	17,548.55	14,158.79	13,135.56	11,757.98	10,114.35	9,462.89	9,171.96	9,035.15	8,969.27	8,937.17
14.50%	17,646.21	14,262.98	13,242.94	11,871.51	10,241.26	9,599.98	9,316.22	9,184.17	9,121.28	9,091.00
14.75%	17,744.18	14,367.57	13,350.78	11,985.56	10,368.78	9,737.66	9,460.99	9,333.57	9,273.56	9,245.00
15.00%	17,842.45	14,472.57	13,459.05	12,100.12	10,496.90	9,875.92	9,606.23	9,483.33	9,426.10	9,399.18
15.25%	17,941.02	14,577.96	13,567.78	12,215.20	10,625.62	10,014.74	9,751.94	9,633.44	9,578.88	9,553.52
15.50%	18,039.89	14,683.76	13,676.94	12,330.79	10,754.93	10,154.11	9,898.09	9,783.88	9,731.88	9,708.00
15.75%	18,139.07	14,789.96	13,786.55	12,446.89	10,884.81	10,294.00	10,044.67	9,934.63	9,885.10	9,862.62
16.00%	18,238.54	14,896.55	13,896.59	12,563.48	11,015.26	10,434.42	10,191.67	10,085.68	10,038.52	10,017.36
16.25%	18,338.32	15,003.54	14,007.07	12,680.58	11,146.26	10,575.34	10,339.06	10,237.01	10,192.12	10,172.23
16.50%	18,438.39	15,110.92	14,117.98	12,798.17	11,277.81	10,716.75	10,486.83	10,388.61	10,345.90	10,327.19
16.75%	18,538.76	15,218.69	14,229.32	12,916.25	11,409.91	10,858.65	10,634.98	10,540.47	10,499.85	10,482.26
17.00%	18,639.43	15,326.85	14,341.09	13,034.82	11,542.53	11,001.00	10,783.47	10,692.57	10,653.95	10,637.43
17.25%	18,740.40	15,435.41	14,453.29	13,153.88	11,675.68	11,143.81	10,932.31	10,844.89	10,808.19	10,792.67
17.50%	18,841.66	15,544.35	14,565.91	13,273.41	11,809.34	11,287.06	11,081.47	10,997.44	10,962.57	10,948.00
17.75%	18,943.22	15,653.64	14,678.95	13,393.41	11,943.50	11,430.74	11,230.95	11,150.19	11,117.07	11,103.40
18.00%	19,045.07	15,763.38	14,792.41	13,513.89	12,078.16	11,574.84	11,380.72	11,303.14	11,271.69	11,258.87
18.25%	19,147.22	15,873.47	14,906.29	13,634.82	12,213.30	11,719.33	11,530.79	11,456.27	11,426.42	11,414.40
18.50%	19,249.66	15,983.94	15,020.58	13,756.24	12,348.93	11,864.22	11,681.13	11,609.58	11,581.26	11,569.98
18.75%	19,352.39	16,094.79	15,135.28	13,878.11	12,485.02	12,009.50	11,831.74	11,763.06	11,736.19	11,725.62
19.00%	19,455.41	16,206.01	15,250.40	14,000.43	12,621.57	12,155.14	11,982.60	11,916.69	11,891.21	11,881.31
19.25%	19,558.73	16,317.62	15,365.92	14,123.20	12,758.58	12,301.14	12,133.71	12,070.48	12,046.32	12,037.04
19.50%	19,662.33	16,429.59	15,481.85	14,246.42	12,896.03	12,447.48	12,285.05	12,224.40	12,201.50	12,192.82
19.75%	19,766.23	16,541.93	15,598.17	14,370.08	13,033.91	12,594.17	12,436.61	12,378.46	12,356.76	12,348.63
20.00%	19,870.41	16,654.65	15,714.90	14,494.18	13,172.22	12,741.18	12,588.39	12,532.64	12,512.09	12,504.48
20.25%	19,974.88	16,767.73	15,832.02	14,618.71	13,310.96	12,888.52	12,740.37	12,686.94	12,667.48	12,660.36
20.50%	20,079.64	16,881.18	15,949.54	14,743.67	13,450.10	13,036.16	12,892.55	12,841.36	12,822.93	12,816.27
20.75%	20,184.69	16,994.99	16,067.46	14,869.06	13,589.65	13,184.09	13,044.92	12,995.88	12,978.44	12,972.21

	5	7	8	10	15	20	25	30	35	40
1.00%	12,991.25	9,371.75	8,240.85	6,657.91	4,548.56	3,495.20	2,864.23	2,444.46	2,145.37	1,921.71
1.25%	13,073.22	9,453.93	8,323.22	6,740.70	4,632.61	3,580.62	2,951.06	2,532.71	2,235.06	2,012.82
1.50%	13,155.51	9,536.58	8,406.11	6,824.15	4,717.65	3,667.35	3,039.52	2,622.91	2,327.00	2,106.51
1.75%	13,238.14	9,619.68	8,489.52	6,908.26	4,803.67	3,755.38	3,129.60	2,715.05	2,421.19	2,202.74
2.00%	13,321.10	9,703.25	8,573.46	6,993.02	4,890.67	3,844.71	3,221.29	2,809.11	2,517.60	2,301.47
2.25%	13,404.38	9,787.28	8,657.93	7,078.44	4,978.64	3,935.34	3,314.59	2,905.07	2,616.20	2,402.68
2.50%	13,487.99	9,871.76	8,742.92	7,164.51	5,067.60	4,027.26	3,409.49	3,002.92	2,716.96	2,506.31
2.75%	13,571.94	9,956.71	8,828.44	7,251.24	5,157.52	4,120.46	3,505.96	3,102.63	2,819.86	2,612.33
3.00%	13,656.20	10,042.11	8,914.47	7,338.62	5,248.42	4,214.94	3,604.01	3,204.19	2,924.86	2,720.68
3.25%	13,740.80	10,127.97	9,001.04	7,426.65	5,340.28	4,310.69	3,703.60	3,307.57	3,031.92	2,831.31
3.50%	13,825.73	10,214.29	9,088.12	7,515.33	5,433.11	4,407.69	3,804.74	3,412.74	3,141.01	2,944.17
3.75%	13,910.98	10,301.06	9,175.72	7,604.65	5,526.89	4,505.95	3,907.40	3,519.68	3,252.08	3,059.20
4.00%	13,996.56	10,388.29	9,263.85	7,694.63	5,621.63	4,605.45	4,011.56	3,628.36	3,365.09	3,176.33
4.25%	14,082.46	10,475.98	9,352.49	7,785.25	5,717.32	4,706.18	4,117.21	3,738.74	3,479.99	3,295.51
4.50%	14,168.69	10,564.12	9,441.66	7,876.52	5,813.95	4,808.14	4,224.33	3,850.81	3,596.75	3,416.68
4.75%	14,255.25	10,652.72	9,531.34	7,968.43	5,911.52	4,911.30	4,332.89	3,964.52	3,715.31	3,539.76
5.00%	14,342.14	10,741.77	9,621.54	8,060.98	6,010.03	5,015.66	4,442.88	4,079.84	3,835.63	3,664.69
5.25%	14,429.35	10,831.28	9,712.25	8,154.17	6,109.47	5,121.22	4,554.28	4,196.75	3,957.65	3,791.41
5.50%	14,516.88	10,921.23	9,803.48	8,248.00	6,209.83	5,227.94	4,667.06	4,315.20	4,081.32	3,919.85
5.75%	14,604.74	11,011.64	9,895.23	8,342.46	6,311.12	5,335.83	4,781.21	4,435.15	4,206.61	4,049.95
6.00%	14,692.93	11,102.50	9,987.49	8,437.56	6,413.31	5,444.88	4,896.69	4,556.58	4,333.44	4,181.62
6.25%	14,781.44	11,193.81	10,080.26	8,533.29	6,516.41	5,555.05	5,013.49	4,679.45	4,461.78	4,314.82
6.50%	14,870.27	11,285.57	10,173.54	8,629.65	6,620.42	5,666.36	5,131.57	4,803.72	4,591.57	4,449.47
6.75%	14,959.43	11,377.78	10,267.33	8,726.63	6,725.31	5,778.77	5,250.93	4,929.35	4,722.77	4,585.51
7.00%	15,048.91	11,470.44	10,361.62	8,824.24	6,831.09	5,892.27	5,371.52	5,056.30	4,855.31	4,722.88
7.25%	15,138.71	11,563.54	10,456.43	8,922.48	6,937.76	6,006.86	5,493.33	5,184.54	4,989.15	4,861.51
7.50%	15,228.84	11,657.09	10,551.74	9,021.33	7,045.29	6,122.51	5,616.33	5,314.03	5,124.24	5,001.34
7.75%	15,319.29	11,751.08	10,647.56	9,120.81	7,153.70	6,239.21	5,740.50	5,444.73	5,260.54	5,142.31
8.00%	15,410.06	11,845.52	10,743.88	9,220.90	7,262.96	6,356.94	5,865.80	5,576.61	5,397.98	5,284.37
8.25%	15,501.15	11,940.40	10,840.70	9,321.60	7,373.07	6,475.70	5,992.22	5,709.63	5,536.53	5,427.45
8.50%	15,592.56	12,035.73	10,938.02	9,422.91	7,484.02	6,595.46	6,119.73	5,843.74	5,676.14	5,571.51
8.75%	15,684.30	12,131.49	11,035.84	9,524.83	7,595.81	6,716.20	6,248.29	5,978.92	5,816.76	5,716.50
9.00%	15,776.35	12,227.70	11,134.15	9,627.36	7,708.43	6,837.92	6,377.89	6,115.13	5,958.35	5,862.35
9.25%	15,868.72	12,324.34	11,232.97	9,730.49	7,821.86	6,960.59	6,508.50	6,252.33	6,100.86	6,009.02
9.50%	15,961.41	12,421.43	11,332.27	9,834.21	7,936.11	7,084.20	6,640.09	6,390.49	6,244.25	6,156.47
9.75%	16,054.43	12,518.95	11,432.07	9,938.54	8,051.16	7,208.73	6,772.64	6,529.57	6,388.48	6,304.65
10.00%	16,147.75	12,616.90	11,532.36	10,043.46	8,167.00	7,334.16	6,906.13	6,669.54	6,533.51	6,453.51
10.25%	16,241.40	12,715.29	11,633.14	10,148.96	8,283.63	7,460.49	7,040.51	6,810.37	6,679.30	6,603.02
10.50%	16,335.36	12,814.11	11,734.41	10,255.06	8,401.03	7,587.69	7,175.78	6,952.02	6,825.82	6,753.13
10.75%	16,429.64	12,913.37	11,836.17	10,361.74	8,519.20	7,715.74	7,311.90	7,094.46	6,973.02	6,903.82

$760,000   11.00 - 20.75%   5 - 40 Years

	5	7	8	10	15	20	25	30	35	40
11.00%	16,524.24	13,013.05	11,938.40	10,469.00	8,638.14	7,844.63	7,448.86	7,237.66	7,120.88	7,055.04
11.25%	16,619.15	13,113.17	12,041.12	10,576.84	8,757.82	7,974.35	7,586.62	7,381.59	7,269.35	7,206.76
11.50%	16,714.38	13,213.71	12,144.32	10,685.25	8,878.24	8,104.87	7,725.16	7,526.21	7,418.42	7,358.94
11.75%	16,809.92	13,314.68	12,248.00	10,794.24	8,999.40	8,236.17	7,864.47	7,671.51	7,568.03	7,511.57
12.00%	16,905.78	13,416.08	12,352.16	10,903.79	9,121.28	8,368.25	8,004.50	7,817.46	7,718.18	7,664.60
12.25%	17,001.95	13,517.90	12,456.79	11,013.91	9,243.87	8,501.09	8,145.25	7,964.01	7,868.82	7,818.00
12.50%	17,098.43	13,620.14	12,561.89	11,124.59	9,367.17	8,634.67	8,286.69	8,111.16	8,019.93	7,971.79
12.75%	17,195.23	13,722.81	12,667.47	11,235.83	9,491.16	8,768.97	8,428.80	8,258.87	8,171.49	8,125.89
13.00%	17,292.34	13,825.89	12,773.51	11,347.62	9,615.84	8,903.98	8,571.55	8,407.12	8,323.47	8,280.31
13.25%	17,389.75	13,929.40	12,880.03	11,459.96	9,741.20	9,039.67	8,714.92	8,555.88	8,475.84	8,435.01
13.50%	17,487.48	14,033.32	12,987.00	11,572.85	9,867.22	9,176.05	8,858.90	8,705.13	8,628.59	8,589.98
13.75%	17,585.52	14,137.66	13,094.44	11,686.28	9,993.90	9,313.08	9,003.46	8,854.86	8,781.69	8,745.21
14.00%	17,683.87	14,242.41	13,202.34	11,800.25	10,121.23	9,450.76	9,148.58	9,005.03	8,935.12	8,900.66
14.25%	17,782.53	14,347.57	13,310.70	11,914.76	10,249.21	9,589.06	9,294.25	9,155.62	9,088.86	9,056.34
14.50%	17,881.49	14,453.15	13,419.52	12,029.80	10,377.81	9,727.98	9,440.44	9,306.63	9,242.90	9,212.21
14.75%	17,980.77	14,559.14	13,528.79	12,145.36	10,507.03	9,867.50	9,587.13	9,458.02	9,397.21	9,368.27
15.00%	18,080.35	14,665.53	13,638.51	12,261.46	10,636.86	10,007.60	9,734.31	9,609.77	9,551.78	9,524.50
15.25%	18,180.23	14,772.34	13,748.68	12,378.07	10,767.30	10,148.27	9,881.96	9,761.88	9,706.60	9,680.90
15.50%	18,280.43	14,879.54	13,859.30	12,495.20	10,898.33	10,289.49	10,030.06	9,914.33	9,861.64	9,837.44
15.75%	18,380.92	14,987.16	13,970.37	12,612.84	11,029.94	10,431.26	10,178.60	10,067.09	10,016.90	9,994.12
16.00%	18,481.72	15,095.17	14,081.88	12,731.00	11,162.13	10,573.55	10,327.56	10,220.15	10,172.37	10,150.93
16.25%	18,582.83	15,203.58	14,193.83	12,849.66	11,294.88	10,716.35	10,476.91	10,373.50	10,328.02	10,307.85
16.50%	18,684.24	15,312.40	14,306.22	12,968.81	11,428.19	10,859.64	10,626.66	10,527.13	10,483.85	10,464.89
16.75%	18,785.95	15,421.61	14,419.04	13,088.47	11,562.04	11,003.43	10,776.78	10,681.01	10,639.85	10,622.03
17.00%	18,887.96	15,531.21	14,532.31	13,208.62	11,696.43	11,147.68	10,927.25	10,835.13	10,796.00	10,779.26
17.25%	18,990.27	15,641.21	14,646.00	13,329.26	11,831.35	11,292.40	11,078.07	10,989.49	10,952.30	10,936.58
17.50%	19,092.88	15,751.60	14,760.12	13,450.39	11,966.79	11,437.56	11,229.23	11,144.07	11,108.73	11,093.97
17.75%	19,195.79	15,862.39	14,874.67	13,571.99	12,102.75	11,583.15	11,380.69	11,298.86	11,265.30	11,251.45
18.00%	19,299.00	15,973.56	14,989.64	13,694.08	12,239.20	11,729.17	11,532.47	11,453.85	11,421.98	11,408.99
18.25%	19,402.51	16,085.12	15,105.04	13,816.63	12,376.15	11,875.59	11,684.53	11,609.02	11,578.77	11,566.59
18.50%	19,506.32	16,197.06	15,220.86	13,939.66	12,513.58	12,022.41	11,836.88	11,764.38	11,735.67	11,724.25
18.75%	19,610.42	16,309.39	15,337.09	14,063.15	12,651.48	12,169.62	11,989.49	11,919.90	11,892.67	11,881.96
19.00%	19,714.82	16,422.09	15,453.74	14,187.10	12,789.86	12,317.20	12,142.37	12,075.58	12,049.76	12,039.73
19.25%	19,819.51	16,535.18	15,570.80	14,311.51	12,928.69	12,465.15	12,295.49	12,231.42	12,206.93	12,197.54
19.50%	19,924.50	16,648.65	15,688.27	14,436.37	13,067.97	12,613.45	12,448.85	12,387.39	12,364.19	12,355.39
19.75%	20,029.78	16,762.49	15,806.15	14,561.68	13,207.70	12,762.09	12,602.43	12,543.50	12,521.52	12,513.28
20.00%	20,135.35	16,876.71	15,924.43	14,687.43	13,347.85	12,911.07	12,756.23	12,699.74	12,678.91	12,671.21
20.25%	20,241.22	16,991.30	16,043.12	14,813.63	13,488.44	13,060.36	12,910.24	12,856.10	12,836.38	12,829.17
20.50%	20,347.37	17,106.26	16,162.20	14,940.26	13,629.44	13,209.97	13,064.45	13,012.58	12,993.90	12,987.16
20.75%	20,453.82	17,221.59	16,281.69	15,067.32	13,770.84	13,359.88	13,218.85	13,169.16	13,151.48	13,145.17

	5	7	8	10	15	20	25	30	35	40
1.00%	13,162.19	9,495.06	8,349.28	6,745.52	4,608.41	3,541.19	2,901.92	2,476.62	2,173.60	1,946.99
1.25%	13,245.23	9,578.33	8,432.73	6,829.40	4,693.57	3,627.73	2,989.89	2,566.04	2,264.46	2,039.31
1.50%	13,328.61	9,662.06	8,516.71	6,913.95	4,779.72	3,715.60	3,079.51	2,657.43	2,357.62	2,134.23
1.75%	13,412.33	9,746.26	8,601.23	6,999.16	4,866.87	3,804.79	3,170.78	2,750.77	2,453.05	2,231.72
2.00%	13,496.38	9,830.92	8,686.27	7,085.04	4,955.02	3,895.30	3,263.68	2,846.07	2,550.72	2,331.76
2.25%	13,580.76	9,916.06	8,771.85	7,171.58	5,044.15	3,987.12	3,358.21	2,943.29	2,650.62	2,434.29
2.50%	13,665.47	10,001.65	8,857.96	7,258.78	5,134.28	4,080.25	3,454.35	3,042.43	2,752.71	2,539.29
2.75%	13,750.51	10,087.71	8,944.60	7,346.65	5,225.39	4,174.68	3,552.09	3,143.46	2,856.97	2,646.70
3.00%	13,835.89	10,174.24	9,031.77	7,435.18	5,317.48	4,270.40	3,651.43	3,246.35	2,963.35	2,756.48
3.25%	13,921.60	10,261.23	9,119.47	7,524.37	5,410.55	4,367.41	3,752.33	3,351.09	3,071.82	2,868.57
3.50%	14,007.64	10,348.68	9,207.70	7,614.21	5,504.60	4,465.69	3,854.80	3,457.64	3,182.34	2,982.91
3.75%	14,094.02	10,436.60	9,296.46	7,704.72	5,599.61	4,565.24	3,958.81	3,565.99	3,294.87	3,099.45
4.00%	14,180.72	10,524.98	9,385.74	7,795.88	5,695.60	4,666.05	4,064.34	3,676.10	3,409.37	3,218.13
4.25%	14,267.76	10,613.82	9,475.55	7,887.69	5,792.54	4,768.11	4,171.38	3,787.94	3,525.78	3,338.88
4.50%	14,355.12	10,703.12	9,565.89	7,980.16	5,890.45	4,871.40	4,279.91	3,901.48	3,644.08	3,461.63
4.75%	14,442.82	10,792.89	9,656.75	8,073.28	5,989.31	4,975.92	4,389.90	4,016.68	3,764.20	3,586.34
5.00%	14,530.85	10,883.11	9,748.14	8,167.04	6,089.11	5,081.66	4,501.34	4,133.53	3,886.10	3,712.91
5.25%	14,619.21	10,973.79	9,840.05	8,261.46	6,189.86	5,188.60	4,614.21	4,251.97	4,009.72	3,841.30
5.50%	14,707.89	11,064.93	9,932.48	8,356.52	6,291.54	5,296.73	4,728.47	4,371.98	4,135.03	3,971.43
5.75%	14,796.91	11,156.53	10,025.43	8,452.23	6,394.16	5,406.04	4,844.12	4,493.51	4,261.96	4,103.23
6.00%	14,886.26	11,248.59	10,118.90	8,548.58	6,497.70	5,516.52	4,961.12	4,616.54	4,390.46	4,236.65
6.25%	14,975.93	11,341.10	10,212.89	8,645.57	6,602.16	5,628.15	5,079.45	4,741.02	4,520.49	4,371.59
6.50%	15,065.93	11,434.07	10,307.40	8,743.19	6,707.53	5,740.91	5,199.10	4,866.92	4,651.99	4,508.02
6.75%	15,156.26	11,527.49	10,402.42	8,841.46	6,813.80	5,854.80	5,320.02	4,994.21	4,784.91	4,645.85
7.00%	15,246.92	11,621.36	10,497.96	8,940.35	6,920.98	5,969.80	5,442.20	5,122.83	4,919.19	4,785.02
7.25%	15,337.91	11,715.69	10,594.02	9,039.88	7,029.04	6,085.90	5,565.61	5,252.76	5,054.80	4,925.47
7.50%	15,429.22	11,810.47	10,690.58	9,140.04	7,138.00	6,203.07	5,690.23	5,383.95	5,191.67	5,067.14
7.75%	15,520.86	11,905.70	10,787.66	9,240.82	7,247.82	6,321.30	5,816.03	5,516.37	5,329.75	5,209.97
8.00%	15,612.82	12,001.39	10,885.24	9,342.22	7,358.52	6,440.59	5,942.98	5,649.99	5,469.01	5,353.90
8.25%	15,705.11	12,097.52	10,983.34	9,444.25	7,470.08	6,560.91	6,071.07	5,784.75	5,609.38	5,498.87
8.50%	15,797.73	12,194.09	11,081.94	9,546.90	7,582.49	6,682.24	6,200.25	5,920.63	5,750.83	5,644.82
8.75%	15,890.67	12,291.12	11,181.05	9,650.16	7,695.75	6,804.57	6,330.51	6,057.59	5,893.30	5,791.71
9.00%	15,983.93	12,388.59	11,280.66	9,754.03	7,809.85	6,927.89	6,461.81	6,195.59	6,036.75	5,939.48
9.25%	16,077.52	12,486.51	11,380.77	9,858.52	7,924.78	7,052.17	6,594.14	6,334.60	6,181.13	6,088.09
9.50%	16,171.43	12,584.87	11,481.38	9,963.61	8,040.53	7,177.41	6,727.46	6,474.58	6,326.41	6,237.47
9.75%	16,265.67	12,683.67	11,582.50	10,069.31	8,157.09	7,303.58	6,861.76	6,615.49	6,472.54	6,387.60
10.00%	16,360.22	12,782.91	11,684.11	10,175.61	8,274.46	7,430.67	6,997.00	6,757.30	6,619.48	6,538.42
10.25%	16,455.10	12,882.60	11,786.21	10,282.50	8,392.62	7,558.65	7,133.15	6,899.98	6,767.19	6,689.90
10.50%	16,550.30	12,982.72	11,888.81	10,389.99	8,511.57	7,687.53	7,270.20	7,043.49	6,915.63	6,841.99
10.75%	16,645.82	13,083.28	11,991.90	10,498.08	8,631.30	7,817.26	7,408.11	7,187.81	7,064.77	6,994.66

$770,000   11.00 - 20.75%   5 - 40 Years

	5	7	8	10	15	20	25	30	35	40
11.00%	16,741.67	13,184.28	12,095.49	10,606.75	8,751.80	7,947.85	7,546.87	7,332.89	7,214.57	7,147.87
11.25%	16,837.83	13,285.71	12,199.56	10,716.01	8,873.05	8,079.27	7,686.44	7,478.71	7,365.00	7,301.58
11.50%	16,934.31	13,387.57	12,304.12	10,825.85	8,995.06	8,211.51	7,826.81	7,625.24	7,516.03	7,455.77
11.75%	17,031.11	13,489.87	12,409.16	10,936.27	9,117.81	8,344.54	7,967.95	7,772.45	7,667.61	7,610.40
12.00%	17,128.22	13,592.60	12,514.69	11,047.26	9,241.29	8,478.36	8,109.83	7,920.32	7,819.73	7,765.45
12.25%	17,225.66	13,695.76	12,620.70	11,158.83	9,365.50	8,612.95	8,252.43	8,068.80	7,972.36	7,920.88
12.50%	17,323.41	13,799.35	12,727.18	11,270.96	9,490.42	8,748.28	8,395.73	8,217.88	8,125.46	8,076.68
12.75%	17,421.48	13,903.37	12,834.15	11,383.67	9,616.04	8,884.35	8,539.70	8,367.54	8,279.01	8,232.81
13.00%	17,519.87	14,007.81	12,941.59	11,496.93	9,742.36	9,021.13	8,684.33	8,517.74	8,432.99	8,389.26
13.25%	17,618.57	14,112.68	13,049.50	11,610.75	9,869.37	9,158.62	8,829.59	8,668.46	8,587.37	8,546.00
13.50%	17,717.58	14,217.97	13,157.88	11,725.12	9,997.05	9,296.79	8,975.47	8,819.67	8,742.12	8,703.01
13.75%	17,816.91	14,323.68	13,266.74	11,840.04	10,125.40	9,435.62	9,121.93	8,971.37	8,897.24	8,860.28
14.00%	17,916.55	14,429.81	13,376.06	11,955.52	10,254.41	9,575.11	9,268.96	9,123.51	9,052.68	9,017.78
14.25%	18,016.51	14,536.36	13,485.84	12,071.53	10,384.06	9,715.24	9,416.54	9,276.09	9,208.45	9,175.50
14.50%	18,116.78	14,643.32	13,596.09	12,188.08	10,514.36	9,855.98	9,564.65	9,429.08	9,364.51	9,333.42
14.75%	18,217.36	14,750.71	13,706.80	12,305.17	10,645.28	9,997.34	9,713.28	9,582.46	9,520.86	9,491.54
15.00%	18,318.25	14,858.50	13,817.96	12,422.79	10,776.82	10,139.28	9,862.40	9,736.22	9,677.46	9,649.83
15.25%	18,419.45	14,966.71	13,929.58	12,540.94	10,908.97	10,281.80	10,011.99	9,890.33	9,834.32	9,808.28
15.50%	18,520.96	15,075.33	14,041.66	12,659.61	11,041.73	10,424.88	10,162.04	10,044.78	9,991.40	9,966.88
15.75%	18,622.78	15,184.35	14,154.19	12,778.80	11,175.07	10,568.51	10,312.53	10,199.55	10,148.71	10,125.62
16.00%	18,724.90	15,293.79	14,267.17	12,898.51	11,309.00	10,712.67	10,463.44	10,354.63	10,306.21	10,284.49
16.25%	18,827.34	15,403.63	14,380.59	13,018.73	11,443.49	10,857.35	10,614.77	10,510.00	10,463.91	10,443.48
16.50%	18,930.08	15,513.87	14,494.46	13,139.46	11,578.56	11,002.53	10,766.48	10,665.64	10,621.80	10,602.59
16.75%	19,033.13	15,624.52	14,608.77	13,260.69	11,714.17	11,148.21	10,918.58	10,821.55	10,779.84	10,761.79
17.00%	19,136.48	15,735.54	14,723.52	13,382.42	11,850.33	11,294.36	11,071.03	10,977.70	10,938.05	10,921.09
17.25%	19,240.14	15,847.02	14,838.71	13,504.65	11,987.03	11,440.98	11,223.84	11,134.09	11,096.41	11,080.48
17.50%	19,344.10	15,958.86	14,954.33	13,627.36	12,124.25	11,588.05	11,376.98	11,290.70	11,254.90	11,239.95
17.75%	19,448.37	16,071.10	15,070.39	13,750.57	12,261.99	11,735.56	11,530.44	11,447.53	11,413.52	11,399.49
18.00%	19,552.94	16,183.74	15,186.87	13,874.26	12,400.24	11,883.50	11,684.21	11,604.56	11,572.27	11,559.10
18.25%	19,657.81	16,296.76	15,303.79	13,998.43	12,538.99	12,031.85	11,838.28	11,761.77	11,731.13	11,718.78
18.50%	19,762.98	16,410.18	15,421.13	14,123.07	12,678.23	12,180.60	11,992.63	11,919.17	11,890.09	11,878.52
18.75%	19,868.45	16,523.98	15,538.89	14,248.19	12,817.95	12,329.75	12,147.25	12,076.74	12,049.15	12,038.31
19.00%	19,974.22	16,638.17	15,657.08	14,373.77	12,958.15	12,479.27	12,302.14	12,234.47	12,208.31	12,198.15
19.25%	20,080.29	16,752.75	15,775.68	14,499.82	13,098.80	12,629.17	12,457.27	12,392.36	12,367.55	12,358.03
19.50%	20,186.66	16,867.71	15,894.69	14,626.32	13,239.92	12,779.42	12,612.65	12,550.38	12,526.88	12,517.96
19.75%	20,293.33	16,983.05	16,014.12	14,753.28	13,381.48	12,930.02	12,768.25	12,708.55	12,686.27	12,677.93
20.00%	20,400.29	17,098.77	16,133.96	14,880.69	13,523.48	13,080.95	12,924.08	12,866.84	12,845.74	12,837.93
20.25%	20,507.55	17,214.87	16,254.21	15,008.54	13,665.92	13,232.21	13,080.12	13,025.26	13,005.28	12,997.97
20.50%	20,615.10	17,331.35	16,374.87	15,136.84	13,808.77	13,383.79	13,236.35	13,183.79	13,164.87	13,158.04
20.75%	20,722.95	17,448.19	16,495.92	15,265.57	13,952.04	13,535.67	13,392.79	13,342.44	13,324.53	13,318.14

$780,000   1.00 - 10.75%   5 - 40 Years

	5	7	8	10	15	20	25	30	35	40
1.00%	13,333.12	9,618.37	8,457.72	6,833.12	4,668.26	3,587.18	2,939.61	2,508.79	2,201.83	1,972.28
1.25%	13,417.25	9,702.72	8,542.25	6,918.09	4,754.52	3,674.84	3,028.72	2,599.36	2,293.87	2,065.79
1.50%	13,501.71	9,787.54	8,627.32	7,003.74	4,841.80	3,763.85	3,119.50	2,691.94	2,388.24	2,161.95
1.75%	13,586.51	9,872.83	8,712.93	7,090.06	4,930.08	3,854.20	3,211.96	2,786.50	2,484.91	2,260.71
2.00%	13,671.65	9,958.60	8,799.08	7,177.05	5,019.37	3,945.89	3,306.06	2,883.03	2,583.85	2,362.04
2.25%	13,757.13	10,044.84	8,885.77	7,264.72	5,109.66	4,038.90	3,401.82	2,981.52	2,685.05	2,465.91
2.50%	13,842.94	10,131.54	8,973.00	7,353.05	5,200.96	4,133.24	3,499.21	3,081.94	2,788.46	2,572.27
2.75%	13,929.09	10,218.72	9,060.76	7,442.06	5,293.25	4,228.90	3,598.22	3,184.28	2,894.07	2,681.08
3.00%	14,015.58	10,306.37	9,149.07	7,531.74	5,386.54	4,325.86	3,698.85	3,288.51	3,001.83	2,792.28
3.25%	14,102.40	10,394.49	9,237.91	7,622.08	5,480.82	4,424.13	3,801.07	3,394.61	3,111.71	2,905.82
3.50%	14,189.56	10,483.08	9,327.28	7,713.10	5,576.08	4,523.69	3,904.86	3,502.55	3,223.67	3,021.65
3.75%	14,277.06	10,572.14	9,417.19	7,804.78	5,672.34	4,624.53	4,010.22	3,612.30	3,337.66	3,139.70
4.00%	14,364.89	10,661.67	9,507.63	7,897.12	5,769.57	4,726.65	4,117.13	3,723.84	3,453.64	3,259.92
4.25%	14,453.05	10,751.66	9,598.61	7,990.13	5,867.57	4,830.03	4,225.56	3,837.13	3,571.57	3,382.24
4.50%	14,541.56	10,842.13	9,690.12	8,083.80	5,966.95	4,934.67	4,335.49	3,952.15	3,691.40	3,506.59
4.75%	14,630.39	10,933.05	9,782.16	8,178.12	6,067.09	5,040.54	4,446.92	4,068.85	3,813.08	3,632.91
5.00%	14,719.56	11,024.45	9,874.74	8,273.11	6,168.19	5,147.65	4,559.80	4,187.21	3,936.56	3,761.13
5.25%	14,809.07	11,116.31	9,967.84	8,368.75	6,270.25	5,255.98	4,674.13	4,307.19	4,061.80	3,891.19
5.50%	14,898.91	11,208.63	10,061.47	8,465.05	6,373.25	5,365.52	4,789.88	4,428.75	4,188.73	4,023.01
5.75%	14,989.08	11,301.42	10,155.63	8,562.00	6,477.20	5,476.25	4,907.03	4,551.87	4,317.31	4,156.52
6.00%	15,079.59	11,394.67	10,250.32	8,659.60	6,582.08	5,588.16	5,025.55	4,676.49	4,447.48	4,291.67
6.25%	15,170.42	11,488.39	10,345.53	8,757.85	6,687.90	5,701.24	5,145.42	4,802.59	4,579.20	4,428.37
6.50%	15,261.60	11,582.56	10,441.26	8,856.74	6,794.64	5,815.47	5,266.62	4,930.13	4,712.40	4,566.56
6.75%	15,353.10	11,677.20	10,537.52	8,956.28	6,902.29	5,930.84	5,389.11	5,059.07	4,847.05	4,706.18
7.00%	15,444.93	11,772.29	10,634.30	9,056.46	7,010.86	6,047.33	5,512.88	5,189.36	4,983.08	4,847.16
7.25%	15,537.10	11,867.84	10,731.60	9,157.28	7,120.33	6,164.93	5,637.89	5,320.97	5,120.44	4,989.44
7.50%	15,629.60	11,963.86	10,829.42	9,258.74	7,230.70	6,283.63	5,764.13	5,453.87	5,259.09	5,132.95
7.75%	15,722.43	12,060.32	10,927.76	9,360.83	7,341.95	6,403.40	5,891.56	5,588.02	5,398.97	5,277.63
8.00%	15,815.59	12,157.25	11,026.61	9,463.55	7,454.09	6,524.23	6,020.17	5,723.36	5,540.03	5,423.43
8.25%	15,909.08	12,254.63	11,125.98	9,566.90	7,567.09	6,646.11	6,149.91	5,859.88	5,682.23	5,570.28
8.50%	16,002.89	12,352.46	11,225.86	9,670.88	7,680.97	6,769.02	6,280.77	5,997.53	5,825.51	5,718.13
8.75%	16,097.04	12,450.74	11,326.25	9,775.49	7,795.70	6,892.94	6,412.72	6,136.26	5,969.83	5,866.93
9.00%	16,191.52	12,549.48	11,427.16	9,880.71	7,911.28	7,017.86	6,545.73	6,276.06	6,115.15	6,016.62
9.25%	16,286.32	12,648.67	11,528.57	9,986.55	8,027.70	7,143.76	6,679.78	6,416.87	6,261.41	6,167.15
9.50%	16,381.45	12,748.31	11,630.49	10,093.01	8,144.95	7,270.62	6,814.83	6,558.66	6,408.57	6,318.48
9.75%	16,476.91	12,848.39	11,732.92	10,200.08	8,263.03	7,398.43	6,950.87	6,701.40	6,556.60	6,470.56
10.00%	16,572.69	12,948.92	11,835.85	10,307.76	8,381.92	7,527.17	7,087.87	6,845.06	6,705.44	6,623.34
10.25%	16,668.81	13,049.90	11,939.28	10,416.04	8,501.62	7,656.82	7,225.79	6,989.59	6,855.07	6,776.78
10.50%	16,765.24	13,151.33	12,043.21	10,524.93	8,622.11	7,787.36	7,364.62	7,134.97	7,005.45	6,930.85
10.75%	16,862.00	13,253.19	12,147.64	10,634.42	8,743.39	7,918.79	7,504.32	7,281.15	7,156.52	7,085.50

$780,000   11.00 - 20.75%   5 - 40 Years

	5	7	8	10	15	20	25	30	35	40
11.00%	16,959.09	13,355.50	12,252.57	10,744.50	8,865.46	8,051.07	7,644.88	7,428.12	7,308.27	7,240.70
11.25%	17,056.50	13,458.25	12,358.00	10,855.18	8,988.29	8,184.20	7,786.27	7,575.84	7,460.65	7,396.41
11.50%	17,154.23	13,561.44	12,463.91	10,966.44	9,111.88	8,318.15	7,928.46	7,724.27	7,613.64	7,552.60
11.75%	17,252.29	13,665.07	12,570.32	11,078.30	9,236.22	8,452.92	8,071.43	7,873.40	7,767.19	7,709.24
12.00%	17,350.67	13,769.13	12,677.22	11,190.73	9,361.31	8,588.47	8,215.15	8,023.18	7,921.29	7,866.30
12.25%	17,449.37	13,873.63	12,784.60	11,303.75	9,487.13	8,724.80	8,359.60	8,173.59	8,075.89	8,023.75
12.50%	17,548.39	13,978.57	12,892.47	11,417.34	9,613.67	8,861.90	8,504.76	8,324.61	8,230.98	8,181.57
12.75%	17,647.73	14,083.93	13,000.82	11,531.51	9,740.93	8,999.73	8,650.61	8,476.21	8,386.53	8,339.73
13.00%	17,747.40	14,189.73	13,109.66	11,646.24	9,868.89	9,138.29	8,797.12	8,628.36	8,542.51	8,498.21
13.25%	17,847.38	14,295.96	13,218.97	11,761.54	9,997.54	9,277.56	8,944.26	8,781.03	8,698.89	8,656.99
13.50%	17,947.68	14,402.62	13,328.76	11,877.39	10,126.88	9,417.52	9,092.03	8,934.21	8,855.66	8,816.04
13.75%	18,048.30	14,509.70	13,439.03	11,993.81	10,256.90	9,558.16	9,240.39	9,087.88	9,012.78	8,975.35
14.00%	18,149.24	14,617.21	13,549.77	12,110.78	10,387.58	9,699.46	9,389.34	9,242.00	9,170.25	9,134.89
14.25%	18,250.49	14,725.14	13,660.98	12,228.30	10,518.92	9,841.41	9,538.83	9,396.56	9,328.04	9,294.66
14.50%	18,352.06	14,833.50	13,772.66	12,346.37	10,650.91	9,983.98	9,688.87	9,551.54	9,486.13	9,454.64
14.75%	18,453.94	14,942.27	13,884.81	12,464.98	10,783.53	10,127.17	9,839.42	9,706.91	9,644.50	9,614.80
15.00%	18,556.15	15,051.47	13,997.42	12,584.13	10,916.78	10,270.96	9,990.48	9,862.66	9,803.14	9,775.15
15.25%	18,658.66	15,161.08	14,110.49	12,703.81	11,050.65	10,415.33	10,142.01	10,018.78	9,962.03	9,935.66
15.50%	18,761.49	15,271.11	14,224.02	12,824.02	11,185.12	10,560.27	10,294.01	10,175.23	10,121.16	10,096.32
15.75%	18,864.63	15,381.55	14,338.01	12,944.76	11,320.20	10,705.76	10,446.46	10,332.01	10,280.51	10,257.12
16.00%	18,968.08	15,492.41	14,452.45	13,066.02	11,455.87	10,851.80	10,599.33	10,489.10	10,440.06	10,418.06
16.25%	19,071.85	15,603.68	14,567.35	13,187.80	11,592.11	10,998.35	10,752.62	10,646.49	10,599.81	10,579.11
16.50%	19,175.93	15,715.35	14,682.70	13,310.10	11,728.93	11,145.42	10,906.31	10,804.16	10,759.74	10,740.28
16.75%	19,280.31	15,827.44	14,798.49	13,432.90	11,866.30	11,292.99	11,060.38	10,962.09	10,919.84	10,901.56
17.00%	19,385.01	15,939.93	14,914.73	13,556.22	12,004.23	11,441.04	11,214.81	11,120.27	11,080.10	11,062.92
17.25%	19,490.01	16,052.82	15,031.42	13,680.03	12,142.71	11,589.57	11,369.60	11,278.69	11,240.52	11,224.38
17.50%	19,595.33	16,166.12	15,148.54	13,804.34	12,281.71	11,738.55	11,524.73	11,437.34	11,401.07	11,385.92
17.75%	19,700.95	16,279.82	15,266.11	13,929.15	12,421.24	11,887.97	11,680.19	11,596.20	11,561.75	11,547.54
18.00%	19,806.87	16,393.91	15,384.11	14,054.45	12,561.28	12,037.83	11,835.95	11,755.27	11,722.56	11,709.22
18.25%	19,913.11	16,508.41	15,502.54	14,180.23	12,701.83	12,188.11	11,992.02	11,914.53	11,883.48	11,870.97
18.50%	20,019.64	16,623.30	15,621.40	14,306.49	12,842.88	12,338.79	12,148.38	12,073.97	12,044.51	12,032.78
18.75%	20,126.48	16,738.58	15,740.70	14,433.23	12,984.42	12,489.88	12,305.01	12,233.58	12,205.64	12,194.65
19.00%	20,233.63	16,854.25	15,860.41	14,560.44	13,126.43	12,641.34	12,461.90	12,393.36	12,366.86	12,356.56
19.25%	20,341.08	16,970.32	15,980.56	14,688.13	13,268.92	12,793.18	12,619.05	12,553.30	12,528.17	12,518.53
19.50%	20,448.83	17,086.77	16,101.12	14,816.27	13,411.87	12,945.38	12,776.45	12,713.38	12,689.56	12,680.53
19.75%	20,556.88	17,203.61	16,222.10	14,944.88	13,555.27	13,097.94	12,934.07	12,873.60	12,851.03	12,842.58
20.00%	20,665.23	17,320.84	16,343.50	15,073.94	13,699.11	13,250.83	13,091.92	13,033.95	13,012.57	13,004.66
20.25%	20,773.88	17,438.44	16,465.31	15,203.46	13,843.39	13,404.06	13,249.99	13,194.42	13,174.18	13,166.78
20.50%	20,882.83	17,556.43	16,587.53	15,333.42	13,988.10	13,557.60	13,408.26	13,355.01	13,335.85	13,328.92
20.75%	20,992.08	17,674.79	16,710.15	15,463.83	14,133.23	13,711.46	13,566.72	13,515.71	13,497.57	13,491.10

	5	7	8	10	15	20	25	30	35	40
1.00%	13,504.06	9,741.69	8,566.15	6,920.73	4,728.11	3,633.17	2,977.29	2,540.95	2,230.06	1,997.56
1.25%	13,589.26	9,827.11	8,651.76	7,006.79	4,815.48	3,721.96	3,067.55	2,632.69	2,323.28	2,092.28
1.50%	13,674.81	9,913.02	8,737.93	7,093.53	4,903.87	3,812.11	3,159.50	2,726.45	2,418.86	2,189.66
1.75%	13,760.70	9,999.41	8,824.63	7,180.95	4,993.28	3,903.62	3,253.13	2,822.22	2,516.76	2,289.69
2.00%	13,846.93	10,086.27	8,911.89	7,269.06	5,083.72	3,996.48	3,348.45	2,919.99	2,616.98	2,392.32
2.25%	13,933.50	10,173.62	8,999.69	7,357.85	5,175.17	4,090.69	3,445.43	3,019.74	2,719.47	2,497.52
2.50%	14,020.42	10,261.44	9,088.04	7,447.32	5,267.63	4,186.23	3,544.07	3,121.46	2,824.21	2,605.25
2.75%	14,107.67	10,349.73	9,176.93	7,537.47	5,361.11	4,283.11	3,644.36	3,225.11	2,931.17	2,715.45
3.00%	14,195.27	10,438.51	9,266.36	7,628.30	5,455.59	4,381.32	3,746.27	3,330.67	3,040.32	2,828.08
3.25%	14,283.20	10,527.76	9,356.34	7,719.80	5,551.08	4,480.85	3,849.80	3,438.13	3,151.60	2,943.08
3.50%	14,371.48	10,617.48	9,446.86	7,811.98	5,647.57	4,581.68	3,954.93	3,547.45	3,265.00	3,060.39
3.75%	14,460.10	10,707.68	9,537.92	7,904.84	5,745.06	4,683.82	4,061.64	3,658.61	3,380.45	3,179.96
4.00%	14,549.05	10,798.36	9,629.53	7,998.37	5,843.53	4,787.24	4,169.91	3,771.58	3,497.92	3,301.71
4.25%	14,638.35	10,889.51	9,721.67	8,092.57	5,943.00	4,891.95	4,279.73	3,886.33	3,617.36	3,425.60
4.50%	14,727.99	10,981.13	9,814.36	8,187.43	6,043.45	4,997.93	4,391.08	4,002.81	3,738.73	3,551.55
4.75%	14,817.96	11,073.22	9,907.58	8,282.97	6,144.87	5,105.17	4,503.93	4,121.01	3,861.97	3,679.49
5.00%	14,908.27	11,165.79	10,001.34	8,379.18	6,247.27	5,213.65	4,618.26	4,240.89	3,987.03	3,809.35
5.25%	14,998.93	11,258.83	10,095.63	8,476.04	6,350.63	5,323.37	4,734.06	4,362.41	4,113.87	3,941.08
5.50%	15,089.92	11,352.33	10,190.46	8,573.58	6,454.96	5,434.31	4,851.29	4,485.53	4,242.43	4,074.59
5.75%	15,181.25	11,446.31	10,285.83	8,671.77	6,560.24	5,546.46	4,969.94	4,610.23	4,372.66	4,209.81
6.00%	15,272.91	11,540.76	10,381.73	8,770.62	6,666.47	5,659.81	5,089.98	4,736.45	4,504.50	4,346.69
6.25%	15,364.92	11,635.67	10,478.16	8,870.13	6,773.64	5,774.33	5,211.39	4,864.17	4,637.90	4,485.14
6.50%	15,457.26	11,731.05	10,575.12	8,970.29	6,881.75	5,890.03	5,334.14	4,993.34	4,772.82	4,625.11
6.75%	15,549.93	11,826.90	10,672.62	9,071.11	6,990.78	6,006.88	5,458.20	5,123.92	4,909.19	4,766.52
7.00%	15,642.95	11,923.22	10,770.64	9,172.57	7,100.74	6,124.86	5,583.56	5,255.89	5,046.97	4,909.31
7.25%	15,736.30	12,020.00	10,869.18	9,274.68	7,211.62	6,243.97	5,710.17	5,389.19	5,186.09	5,053.41
7.50%	15,829.98	12,117.24	10,968.26	9,377.44	7,323.40	6,364.19	5,838.03	5,523.79	5,326.52	5,198.76
7.75%	15,924.00	12,214.94	11,067.86	9,480.84	7,436.08	6,485.49	5,967.10	5,659.66	5,468.19	5,345.30
8.00%	16,018.35	12,313.11	11,167.98	9,584.88	7,549.65	6,607.88	6,097.35	5,796.74	5,611.06	5,492.96
8.25%	16,113.04	12,411.74	11,268.62	9,689.56	7,664.11	6,731.32	6,228.76	5,935.01	5,755.08	5,641.70
8.50%	16,208.06	12,510.82	11,369.78	9,794.87	7,779.44	6,855.80	6,361.29	6,074.42	5,900.20	5,791.44
8.75%	16,303.41	12,610.37	11,471.46	9,900.81	7,895.64	6,981.31	6,494.93	6,214.93	6,046.37	5,942.15
9.00%	16,399.10	12,710.37	11,573.66	10,007.39	8,012.71	7,107.84	6,629.65	6,356.52	6,193.54	6,093.76
9.25%	16,495.12	12,810.83	11,676.37	10,114.59	8,130.62	7,235.35	6,765.42	6,499.14	6,341.68	6,246.22
9.50%	16,591.47	12,911.75	11,779.60	10,222.41	8,249.37	7,363.84	6,902.20	6,642.75	6,490.73	6,399.49
9.75%	16,688.15	13,013.11	11,883.34	10,330.85	8,368.97	7,493.28	7,039.99	6,787.32	6,640.66	6,553.51
10.00%	16,785.17	13,114.94	11,987.59	10,439.91	8,489.38	7,623.67	7,178.74	6,932.82	6,791.41	6,708.25
10.25%	16,882.51	13,217.21	12,092.35	10,549.58	8,610.61	7,754.98	7,318.43	7,079.20	6,942.96	6,863.66
10.50%	16,980.18	13,319.93	12,197.61	10,659.86	8,732.65	7,887.20	7,459.04	7,226.44	7,095.26	7,019.71
10.75%	17,078.18	13,423.10	12,303.38	10,770.76	8,855.49	8,020.31	7,600.53	7,374.50	7,248.27	7,176.34

$790,000   11.00 - 20.75%   5 - 40 Years

	5	7	8	10	15	20	25	30	35	40
11.00%	17,176.51	13,526.72	12,409.66	10,882.25	8,979.12	8,154.29	7,742.89	7,523.35	7,401.97	7,333.53
11.25%	17,275.17	13,630.79	12,516.43	10,994.35	9,103.52	8,289.12	7,886.09	7,672.96	7,556.30	7,491.23
11.50%	17,374.16	13,735.30	12,623.71	11,107.04	9,228.70	8,424.79	8,030.10	7,823.30	7,711.25	7,649.43
11.75%	17,473.47	13,840.26	12,731.48	11,220.33	9,354.64	8,561.29	8,174.91	7,974.34	7,866.77	7,808.08
12.00%	17,573.11	13,945.66	12,839.74	11,334.20	9,481.33	8,698.58	8,320.47	8,126.04	8,022.84	7,967.15
12.25%	17,673.08	14,051.50	12,948.51	11,448.67	9,608.76	8,836.66	8,466.78	8,278.38	8,179.43	8,126.62
12.50%	17,773.37	14,157.78	13,057.76	11,563.72	9,736.92	8,975.51	8,613.80	8,431.34	8,336.51	8,286.46
12.75%	17,873.99	14,264.50	13,167.50	11,679.34	9,865.81	9,115.11	8,761.51	8,584.88	8,494.05	8,446.65
13.00%	17,974.93	14,371.65	13,277.73	11,795.55	9,995.41	9,255.45	8,909.90	8,738.98	8,652.03	8,607.16
13.25%	18,076.19	14,479.24	13,388.45	11,912.32	10,125.72	9,396.50	9,058.93	8,893.61	8,810.41	8,767.97
13.50%	18,177.78	14,587.27	13,499.65	12,029.67	10,256.72	9,538.26	9,208.59	9,048.76	8,969.19	8,929.06
13.75%	18,279.69	14,695.72	13,611.33	12,147.58	10,388.40	9,680.70	9,358.86	9,204.39	9,128.33	9,090.41
14.00%	18,381.92	14,804.61	13,723.49	12,266.05	10,520.76	9,823.81	9,509.71	9,360.49	9,287.82	9,252.01
14.25%	18,484.47	14,913.93	13,836.12	12,385.08	10,653.78	9,967.58	9,661.13	9,517.03	9,447.63	9,413.82
14.50%	18,587.34	15,023.67	13,949.23	12,504.66	10,787.46	10,111.98	9,813.09	9,673.99	9,607.75	9,575.85
14.75%	18,690.53	15,133.84	14,062.82	12,624.79	10,921.78	10,257.01	9,965.57	9,831.36	9,768.15	9,738.07
15.00%	18,794.04	15,244.44	14,176.87	12,745.46	11,056.74	10,402.64	10,118.56	9,989.11	9,928.83	9,900.47
15.25%	18,897.87	15,355.45	14,291.39	12,866.68	11,192.32	10,548.86	10,272.04	10,147.22	10,089.75	10,063.04
15.50%	19,002.02	15,466.89	14,406.38	12,988.43	11,328.52	10,695.66	10,425.99	10,305.68	10,250.92	10,225.76
15.75%	19,106.48	15,578.75	14,521.83	13,110.72	11,465.33	10,843.02	10,580.39	10,464.48	10,412.31	10,388.62
16.00%	19,211.27	15,691.03	14,637.74	13,233.54	11,602.74	10,990.92	10,735.22	10,623.58	10,573.91	10,551.62
16.25%	19,316.36	15,803.72	14,754.11	13,356.88	11,740.73	11,139.36	10,890.48	10,782.98	10,735.70	10,714.74
16.50%	19,421.77	15,916.83	14,870.94	13,480.74	11,879.30	11,288.32	11,046.13	10,942.67	10,897.69	10,877.98
16.75%	19,527.50	16,030.35	14,988.22	13,605.12	12,018.44	11,437.77	11,202.18	11,102.62	11,059.84	11,041.32
17.00%	19,633.53	16,144.29	15,105.95	13,730.01	12,158.13	11,587.72	11,358.59	11,262.84	11,222.16	11,204.76
17.25%	19,739.89	16,258.63	15,224.13	13,855.42	12,298.38	11,738.15	11,515.37	11,423.29	11,384.62	11,368.28
17.50%	19,846.55	16,373.38	15,342.76	13,981.32	12,439.17	11,889.04	11,672.48	11,583.97	11,547.24	11,531.89
17.75%	19,953.52	16,488.53	15,461.83	14,107.73	12,580.49	12,040.38	11,829.93	11,744.87	11,709.98	11,695.58
18.00%	20,060.81	16,604.09	15,581.34	14,234.63	12,722.33	12,192.16	11,987.70	11,905.97	11,872.85	11,859.34
18.25%	20,168.40	16,720.05	15,701.29	14,362.02	12,864.68	12,344.37	12,145.76	12,067.28	12,035.83	12,023.16
18.50%	20,276.31	16,836.42	15,821.68	14,489.91	13,007.53	12,496.98	12,304.12	12,228.76	12,198.92	12,187.05
18.75%	20,384.52	16,953.18	15,942.50	14,618.27	13,150.88	12,650.00	12,462.76	12,390.42	12,362.12	12,350.99
19.00%	20,493.04	17,070.34	16,063.75	14,747.12	13,294.72	12,803.41	12,621.67	12,552.25	12,525.41	12,514.98
19.25%	20,601.86	17,187.89	16,185.44	14,876.44	13,439.03	12,957.20	12,780.84	12,714.24	12,688.79	12,679.02
19.50%	20,710.99	17,305.83	16,307.54	15,006.22	13,583.81	13,111.35	12,940.25	12,876.37	12,852.25	12,843.10
19.75%	20,820.43	17,424.17	16,430.08	15,136.48	13,729.05	13,265.86	13,099.90	13,038.64	13,015.79	13,007.23
20.00%	20,930.17	17,542.90	16,553.03	15,267.20	13,874.74	13,420.71	13,259.77	13,201.05	13,179.40	13,171.39
20.25%	21,040.21	17,662.01	16,676.40	15,398.37	14,020.87	13,575.90	13,419.86	13,363.58	13,343.08	13,335.58
20.50%	21,150.56	17,781.51	16,800.19	15,530.00	14,167.44	13,731.42	13,580.16	13,526.23	13,506.82	13,499.81
20.75%	21,261.21	17,901.39	16,924.39	15,662.08	14,314.43	13,887.25	13,740.65	13,688.99	13,670.62	13,664.06

	5	7	8	10	15	20	25	30	35	40
1.00%	13,675.00	9,865.00	8,674.58	7,008.33	4,787.96	3,679.15	3,014.98	2,573.12	2,258.29	2,022.85
1.25%	13,761.28	9,951.51	8,761.28	7,095.48	4,876.43	3,769.07	3,106.38	2,666.01	2,352.69	2,118.76
1.50%	13,847.91	10,038.50	8,848.53	7,183.32	4,965.94	3,860.36	3,199.49	2,760.96	2,449.48	2,217.38
1.75%	13,934.89	10,125.98	8,936.34	7,271.85	5,056.49	3,953.03	3,294.31	2,857.95	2,548.62	2,318.67
2.00%	14,022.21	10,213.95	9,024.70	7,361.08	5,148.07	4,047.07	3,390.83	2,956.96	2,650.10	2,422.61
2.25%	14,109.88	10,302.40	9,113.61	7,450.99	5,240.68	4,142.47	3,489.05	3,057.97	2,753.89	2,529.14
2.50%	14,197.89	10,391.33	9,203.07	7,541.59	5,334.31	4,239.22	3,588.93	3,160.97	2,859.96	2,638.23
2.75%	14,286.25	10,480.74	9,293.09	7,632.88	5,428.97	4,337.33	3,690.49	3,265.93	2,968.28	2,749.82
3.00%	14,374.95	10,570.64	9,383.66	7,724.86	5,524.65	4,436.78	3,793.69	3,372.83	3,078.80	2,863.88
3.25%	14,464.00	10,661.02	9,474.77	7,817.52	5,621.35	4,537.57	3,898.53	3,481.65	3,191.50	2,980.33
3.50%	14,553.40	10,751.88	9,566.44	7,910.87	5,719.06	4,639.68	4,004.99	3,592.36	3,306.33	3,099.13
3.75%	14,643.13	10,843.22	9,658.66	8,004.90	5,817.78	4,743.11	4,113.05	3,704.92	3,423.24	3,220.21
4.00%	14,733.22	10,935.05	9,751.42	8,099.61	5,917.50	4,847.84	4,222.69	3,819.32	3,542.20	3,343.51
4.25%	14,823.64	11,027.35	9,844.73	8,195.00	6,018.23	4,953.88	4,333.90	3,935.52	3,663.15	3,468.96
4.50%	14,914.42	11,120.13	9,938.59	8,291.07	6,119.95	5,061.20	4,446.66	4,053.48	3,786.05	3,596.50
4.75%	15,005.53	11,213.39	10,032.99	8,387.82	6,222.66	5,169.79	4,560.94	4,173.18	3,910.85	3,726.06
5.00%	15,096.99	11,307.13	10,127.94	8,485.24	6,326.35	5,279.65	4,676.72	4,294.57	4,037.50	3,857.57
5.25%	15,188.79	11,401.34	10,223.43	8,583.34	6,431.02	5,390.75	4,793.98	4,417.63	4,165.94	3,990.96
5.50%	15,280.93	11,496.03	10,319.46	8,682.10	6,536.67	5,503.10	4,912.70	4,542.31	4,296.13	4,126.16
5.75%	15,373.41	11,591.20	10,416.03	8,781.54	6,643.28	5,616.67	5,032.85	4,668.58	4,428.01	4,263.10
6.00%	15,466.24	11,686.84	10,513.14	8,881.64	6,750.85	5,731.45	5,154.41	4,796.40	4,561.52	4,401.71
6.25%	15,559.41	11,782.96	10,610.80	8,982.41	6,859.38	5,847.43	5,277.36	4,925.74	4,696.61	4,541.92
6.50%	15,652.92	11,879.55	10,708.99	9,083.84	6,968.86	5,964.59	5,401.66	5,056.54	4,833.23	4,683.65
6.75%	15,746.77	11,976.61	10,807.71	9,185.93	7,079.28	6,082.91	5,527.29	5,188.78	4,971.33	4,826.85
7.00%	15,840.96	12,074.14	10,906.97	9,288.68	7,190.63	6,202.39	5,654.23	5,322.42	5,110.85	4,971.45
7.25%	15,935.49	12,172.15	11,006.77	9,392.08	7,302.90	6,323.01	5,782.45	5,457.41	5,251.74	5,117.38
7.50%	16,030.36	12,270.62	11,107.10	9,496.14	7,416.10	6,444.75	5,911.93	5,593.72	5,393.94	5,264.57
7.75%	16,125.57	12,369.56	11,207.96	9,600.85	7,530.21	6,567.59	6,042.63	5,731.30	5,537.41	5,412.96
8.00%	16,221.12	12,468.97	11,309.34	9,706.21	7,645.22	6,691.52	6,174.53	5,870.12	5,682.09	5,562.49
8.25%	16,317.00	12,568.85	11,411.26	9,812.21	7,761.12	6,816.53	6,307.60	6,010.13	5,827.93	5,713.11
8.50%	16,413.22	12,669.19	11,513.70	9,918.86	7,877.92	6,942.59	6,441.82	6,151.31	5,974.88	5,864.75
8.75%	16,509.79	12,769.99	11,616.67	10,026.14	7,995.59	7,069.69	6,577.15	6,293.60	6,122.91	6,017.36
9.00%	16,606.68	12,871.26	11,720.16	10,134.06	8,114.13	7,197.81	6,713.57	6,436.98	6,271.94	6,170.89
9.25%	16,703.92	12,972.99	11,824.18	10,242.62	8,233.54	7,326.93	6,851.05	6,581.40	6,421.95	6,325.28
9.50%	16,801.49	13,075.19	11,928.71	10,351.80	8,353.80	7,457.05	6,989.57	6,726.83	6,572.89	6,480.49
9.75%	16,899.39	13,177.84	12,033.76	10,461.62	8,474.90	7,588.13	7,129.10	6,873.24	6,724.72	6,636.47
10.00%	16,997.64	13,280.95	12,139.33	10,572.06	8,596.84	7,720.17	7,269.61	7,020.57	6,877.38	6,793.17
10.25%	17,096.21	13,384.51	12,245.42	10,683.12	8,719.61	7,853.15	7,411.07	7,168.81	7,030.84	6,950.55
10.50%	17,195.12	13,488.54	12,352.01	10,794.80	8,843.19	7,987.04	7,553.45	7,317.91	7,185.07	7,108.56
10.75%	17,294.36	13,593.02	12,459.12	10,907.09	8,967.58	8,121.83	7,696.74	7,467.85	7,340.02	7,267.18

	5	7	8	10	15	20	25	30	35	40
11.00%	17,393.94	13,697.95	12,566.74	11,020.00	9,092.78	8,257.51	7,840.90	7,618.59	7,495.66	7,426.36
11.25%	17,493.85	13,803.33	12,674.87	11,133.52	9,218.76	8,394.05	7,985.92	7,770.09	7,651.95	7,586.06
11.50%	17,594.09	13,909.17	12,783.50	11,247.64	9,345.52	8,531.44	8,131.75	7,922.33	7,808.86	7,746.25
11.75%	17,694.66	14,015.45	12,892.64	11,362.36	9,473.05	8,669.66	8,278.39	8,075.28	7,966.35	7,906.91
12.00%	17,795.56	14,122.19	13,002.27	11,477.68	9,601.34	8,808.69	8,425.79	8,228.90	8,124.40	8,068.00
12.25%	17,896.79	14,229.37	13,112.41	11,593.59	9,730.39	8,948.52	8,573.95	8,383.17	8,282.97	8,229.49
12.50%	17,998.35	14,336.99	13,223.05	11,710.09	9,860.18	9,089.12	8,722.83	8,538.06	8,442.04	8,391.36
12.75%	18,100.24	14,445.06	13,334.18	11,827.18	9,990.70	9,230.49	8,872.42	8,693.55	8,601.57	8,553.57
13.00%	18,202.46	14,553.57	13,445.80	11,944.86	10,121.94	9,372.61	9,022.68	8,849.60	8,761.55	8,716.11
13.25%	18,305.00	14,662.52	13,557.92	12,063.11	10,253.89	9,515.45	9,173.60	9,006.19	8,921.94	8,878.96
13.50%	18,407.88	14,771.91	13,670.53	12,181.94	10,386.55	9,659.00	9,325.16	9,163.30	9,082.72	9,042.09
13.75%	18,511.08	14,881.74	13,783.62	12,301.34	10,519.90	9,803.24	9,477.33	9,320.90	9,243.88	9,205.48
14.00%	18,614.60	14,992.01	13,897.20	12,421.31	10,653.93	9,948.17	9,630.09	9,478.97	9,405.39	9,369.12
14.25%	18,718.45	15,102.71	14,011.26	12,541.85	10,788.64	10,093.75	9,783.42	9,637.50	9,567.22	9,532.99
14.50%	18,822.62	15,213.84	14,125.81	12,662.94	10,924.01	10,239.98	9,937.30	9,796.45	9,729.36	9,697.06
14.75%	18,927.12	15,325.41	14,240.83	12,784.59	11,060.03	10,386.84	10,091.72	9,955.81	9,891.80	9,861.34
15.00%	19,031.94	15,437.40	14,356.32	12,906.80	11,196.70	10,534.32	10,246.64	10,115.55	10,054.51	10,025.79
15.25%	19,137.09	15,549.83	14,472.30	13,029.55	11,334.00	10,682.39	10,402.07	10,275.67	10,217.47	10,190.42
15.50%	19,242.55	15,662.68	14,588.74	13,152.84	11,471.92	10,831.05	10,557.96	10,436.14	10,380.68	10,355.20
15.75%	19,348.34	15,775.95	14,705.65	13,276.68	11,610.46	10,980.27	10,714.32	10,596.94	10,544.11	10,520.13
16.00%	19,454.45	15,889.65	14,823.03	13,401.05	11,749.61	11,130.05	10,871.11	10,758.06	10,707.76	10,685.19
16.25%	19,560.87	16,003.77	14,940.87	13,525.95	11,889.34	11,280.36	11,028.33	10,919.48	10,871.60	10,850.37
16.50%	19,667.62	16,118.31	15,059.18	13,651.38	12,029.67	11,431.21	11,185.96	11,081.18	11,035.63	11,015.67
16.75%	19,774.68	16,233.27	15,177.94	13,777.34	12,170.57	11,582.56	11,343.98	11,243.16	11,199.84	11,181.08
17.00%	19,882.06	16,348.64	15,297.16	13,903.81	12,312.03	11,734.40	11,502.37	11,405.40	11,364.21	11,346.59
17.25%	19,989.76	16,464.43	15,416.84	14,030.80	12,454.06	11,886.74	11,661.13	11,567.89	11,528.73	11,512.19
17.50%	20,097.77	16,580.64	15,536.97	14,158.30	12,596.63	12,039.54	11,820.24	11,730.60	11,693.40	11,677.87
17.75%	20,206.10	16,697.25	15,657.55	14,286.31	12,739.73	12,192.79	11,979.68	11,893.54	11,858.21	11,843.63
18.00%	20,314.74	16,814.27	15,778.57	14,414.82	12,883.37	12,346.49	12,139.44	12,056.68	12,023.14	12,009.46
18.25%	20,423.70	16,931.70	15,900.04	14,543.82	13,027.52	12,500.62	12,299.51	12,220.03	12,188.18	12,175.36
18.50%	20,532.97	17,049.54	16,021.95	14,673.32	13,172.19	12,655.17	12,459.87	12,383.56	12,353.34	12,341.32
18.75%	20,642.55	17,167.77	16,144.30	14,803.31	13,317.35	12,810.13	12,620.52	12,547.26	12,518.60	12,507.33
19.00%	20,752.44	17,286.42	16,267.09	14,933.79	13,463.01	12,965.48	12,781.44	12,711.14	12,683.96	12,673.40
19.25%	20,862.64	17,405.46	16,390.31	15,064.74	13,609.15	13,121.21	12,942.62	12,875.17	12,849.40	12,839.50
19.50%	20,973.16	17,524.89	16,513.97	15,196.18	13,755.76	13,277.32	13,104.05	13,039.36	13,014.94	13,005.67
19.75%	21,083.98	17,644.73	16,638.05	15,328.08	13,902.84	13,433.78	13,265.72	13,203.69	13,180.54	13,171.87
20.00%	21,195.11	17,764.96	16,762.56	15,460.45	14,050.37	13,590.60	13,427.61	13,368.15	13,346.23	13,338.11
20.25%	21,306.54	17,885.58	16,887.49	15,593.29	14,198.35	13,747.75	13,589.73	13,532.74	13,511.98	13,504.39
20.50%	21,418.29	18,006.59	17,012.85	15,726.58	14,346.77	13,905.23	13,752.06	13,697.45	13,677.79	13,670.69
20.75%	21,530.33	18,127.99	17,138.62	15,860.33	14,495.63	14,063.03	13,914.58	13,862.27	13,843.66	13,837.02

	5	7	8	10	15	20	25	30	35	40
1.00%	13,845.94	9,988.31	8,783.01	7,095.93	4,847.81	3,725.14	3,052.67	2,605.28	2,286.51	2,048.13
1.25%	13,933.30	10,075.90	8,870.80	7,184.17	4,937.39	3,816.18	3,145.21	2,699.34	2,382.10	2,145.25
1.50%	14,021.01	10,163.98	8,959.14	7,273.11	5,028.02	3,908.62	3,239.48	2,795.47	2,480.09	2,245.10
1.75%	14,109.07	10,252.56	9,048.04	7,362.75	5,119.70	4,002.44	3,335.49	2,893.67	2,580.48	2,347.66
2.00%	14,197.49	10,341.62	9,137.51	7,453.09	5,212.42	4,097.66	3,433.22	2,993.92	2,683.23	2,452.89
2.25%	14,286.25	10,431.18	9,227.53	7,544.13	5,306.19	4,194.25	3,532.66	3,096.19	2,788.32	2,560.75
2.50%	14,375.36	10,521.22	9,318.11	7,635.86	5,400.99	4,292.21	3,633.80	3,200.48	2,895.71	2,671.20
2.75%	14,464.83	10,611.75	9,409.25	7,728.29	5,496.84	4,391.55	3,736.62	3,306.75	3,005.38	2,784.20
3.00%	14,554.64	10,702.77	9,500.95	7,821.42	5,593.71	4,492.24	3,841.11	3,414.99	3,117.29	2,899.67
3.25%	14,644.80	10,794.28	9,593.21	7,915.24	5,691.62	4,594.29	3,947.26	3,525.17	3,231.39	3,017.58
3.50%	14,735.31	10,886.28	9,686.02	8,009.76	5,790.55	4,697.67	4,055.05	3,637.26	3,347.65	3,137.87
3.75%	14,826.17	10,978.76	9,779.39	8,104.96	5,890.50	4,802.40	4,164.46	3,751.24	3,466.03	3,260.46
4.00%	14,917.38	11,071.73	9,873.31	8,200.86	5,991.47	4,908.44	4,275.48	3,867.06	3,586.48	3,385.30
4.25%	15,008.94	11,165.19	9,967.79	8,297.44	6,093.46	5,015.80	4,388.08	3,984.71	3,708.94	3,512.32
4.50%	15,100.85	11,259.13	10,062.82	8,394.71	6,196.45	5,124.46	4,502.24	4,104.15	3,833.38	3,641.46
4.75%	15,193.10	11,353.56	10,158.40	8,492.67	6,300.44	5,234.41	4,617.95	4,225.34	3,959.74	3,772.64
5.00%	15,285.70	11,448.47	10,254.54	8,591.31	6,405.43	5,345.64	4,735.18	4,348.26	4,087.97	3,905.79
5.25%	15,378.65	11,543.86	10,351.22	8,690.63	6,511.41	5,458.14	4,853.91	4,472.85	4,218.02	4,040.85
5.50%	15,471.94	11,639.73	10,448.45	8,790.63	6,618.38	5,571.89	4,974.11	4,599.09	4,349.83	4,177.74
5.75%	15,565.58	11,736.09	10,546.23	8,891.31	6,726.32	5,686.88	5,095.76	4,726.94	4,483.36	4,316.39
6.00%	15,659.57	11,832.93	10,644.56	8,992.66	6,835.24	5,803.09	5,218.84	4,856.36	4,618.54	4,456.73
6.25%	15,753.90	11,930.25	10,743.43	9,094.69	6,945.13	5,920.52	5,343.32	4,987.31	4,755.32	4,598.69
6.50%	15,848.58	12,028.04	10,842.85	9,197.39	7,055.97	6,039.14	5,469.18	5,119.75	4,893.65	4,742.20
6.75%	15,943.60	12,126.32	10,942.81	9,300.75	7,167.77	6,158.95	5,596.38	5,253.64	5,033.47	4,887.19
7.00%	16,038.97	12,225.07	11,043.31	9,404.79	7,280.51	6,279.92	5,724.91	5,388.95	5,174.74	5,033.59
7.25%	16,134.68	12,324.30	11,144.35	9,509.48	7,394.19	6,402.05	5,854.74	5,525.63	5,317.38	5,181.34
7.50%	16,230.74	12,424.00	11,245.94	9,614.84	7,508.80	6,525.30	5,985.83	5,663.64	5,461.37	5,330.37
7.75%	16,327.14	12,524.18	11,348.05	9,720.86	7,624.33	6,649.68	6,118.16	5,802.94	5,606.63	5,480.62
8.00%	16,423.88	12,624.83	11,450.71	9,827.54	7,740.78	6,775.16	6,251.71	5,943.49	5,753.11	5,632.02
8.25%	16,520.96	12,725.96	11,553.90	9,934.86	7,858.14	6,901.73	6,386.45	6,085.26	5,900.78	5,784.52
8.50%	16,618.39	12,827.55	11,657.62	10,042.84	7,976.39	7,029.37	6,522.34	6,228.20	6,049.57	5,938.06
8.75%	16,716.16	12,929.62	11,761.88	10,151.47	8,095.53	7,158.06	6,659.36	6,372.27	6,199.44	6,092.58
9.00%	16,814.27	13,032.15	11,866.66	10,260.74	8,215.56	7,287.78	6,797.49	6,517.44	6,350.34	6,248.03
9.25%	16,912.72	13,135.16	11,971.98	10,370.65	8,336.46	7,418.52	6,936.69	6,663.67	6,502.23	6,404.35
9.50%	17,011.51	13,238.63	12,077.82	10,481.20	8,458.22	7,550.26	7,076.94	6,810.92	6,655.05	6,561.50
9.75%	17,110.64	13,342.56	12,184.18	10,592.39	8,580.84	7,682.99	7,218.21	6,959.15	6,808.77	6,719.42
10.00%	17,210.11	13,446.96	12,291.07	10,704.21	8,704.30	7,816.68	7,360.48	7,108.33	6,963.35	6,878.08
10.25%	17,309.91	13,551.82	12,398.48	10,816.66	8,828.60	7,951.31	7,503.70	7,258.42	7,118.73	7,037.43
10.50%	17,410.06	13,657.15	12,506.41	10,929.73	8,953.73	8,086.88	7,647.87	7,409.39	7,274.89	7,197.44
10.75%	17,510.54	13,762.93	12,614.86	11,043.43	9,079.68	8,223.35	7,792.95	7,561.20	7,431.77	7,358.02

$810,000   11.00 - 20.75%   5 - 40 Years

	5	7	8	10	15	20	25	30	35	40
11.00%	17,611.36	13,869.17	12,723.82	11,157.75	9,206.44	8,360.73	7,938.92	7,713.82	7,589.36	7,519.18
11.25%	17,712.52	13,975.88	12,833.30	11,272.68	9,333.99	8,498.97	8,085.74	7,867.22	7,747.60	7,680.88
11.50%	17,814.01	14,083.03	12,943.29	11,388.23	9,462.34	8,638.08	8,233.40	8,021.36	7,906.47	7,843.08
11.75%	17,915.84	14,190.65	13,053.79	11,504.39	9,591.46	8,778.03	8,381.87	8,176.22	8,065.93	8,005.75
12.00%	18,018.00	14,298.71	13,164.80	11,621.15	9,721.36	8,918.80	8,531.12	8,331.76	8,225.95	8,168.85
12.25%	18,120.50	14,407.23	13,276.32	11,738.51	9,852.02	9,060.37	8,681.12	8,487.96	8,386.51	8,332.36
12.50%	18,223.33	14,516.20	13,388.34	11,856.47	9,983.43	9,202.74	8,831.87	8,644.79	8,547.56	8,496.25
12.75%	18,326.49	14,625.62	13,500.86	11,975.02	10,115.58	9,345.87	8,983.32	8,802.22	8,709.09	8,660.49
13.00%	18,429.99	14,735.49	13,613.88	12,094.17	10,248.46	9,489.76	9,135.47	8,960.22	8,871.06	8,825.06
13.25%	18,533.82	14,845.80	13,727.40	12,213.90	10,382.05	9,634.39	9,288.27	9,118.77	9,033.46	8,989.95
13.50%	18,637.98	14,956.56	13,841.41	12,334.22	10,516.38	9,779.73	9,441.72	9,277.84	9,196.26	9,155.12
13.75%	18,742.46	15,067.77	13,955.92	12,455.11	10,651.40	9,925.78	9,595.79	9,437.41	9,359.43	9,320.55
14.00%	18,847.28	15,179.41	14,070.92	12,576.58	10,787.11	10,072.52	9,750.46	9,597.46	9,522.95	9,486.23
14.25%	18,952.43	15,291.49	14,186.40	12,698.62	10,923.50	10,219.92	9,905.71	9,757.97	9,686.81	9,652.15
14.50%	19,057.91	15,404.02	14,302.38	12,821.23	11,060.56	10,367.98	10,061.52	9,918.90	9,850.98	9,818.28
14.75%	19,163.71	15,516.98	14,418.84	12,944.40	11,198.28	10,516.68	10,217.86	10,080.25	10,015.45	9,984.60
15.00%	19,269.84	15,630.37	14,535.78	13,068.13	11,336.66	10,666.00	10,374.73	10,242.00	10,180.19	10,151.12
15.25%	19,376.30	15,744.20	14,653.20	13,192.42	11,475.67	10,815.92	10,532.09	10,404.11	10,345.19	10,317.80
15.50%	19,483.08	15,858.46	14,771.10	13,317.25	11,615.32	10,966.43	10,689.94	10,566.59	10,510.44	10,484.64
15.75%	19,590.19	15,973.15	14,889.47	13,442.64	11,755.59	11,117.52	10,848.25	10,729.40	10,675.91	10,651.63
16.00%	19,697.63	16,088.27	15,008.32	13,568.56	11,896.48	11,269.17	11,007.00	10,892.53	10,841.60	10,818.75
16.25%	19,805.38	16,203.82	15,127.63	13,695.03	12,037.96	11,421.37	11,166.18	11,055.97	11,007.49	10,986.00
16.50%	19,913.46	16,319.79	15,247.42	13,822.03	12,180.04	11,574.10	11,325.78	11,219.70	11,173.58	11,153.37
16.75%	20,021.86	16,436.19	15,367.67	13,949.56	12,322.70	11,727.34	11,485.78	11,383.70	11,339.84	11,320.85
17.00%	20,130.59	16,553.00	15,488.38	14,077.61	12,465.93	11,881.08	11,646.15	11,547.97	11,506.26	11,488.42
17.25%	20,239.63	16,670.24	15,609.55	14,206.19	12,609.73	12,035.32	11,806.90	11,712.48	11,672.84	11,656.09
17.50%	20,348.99	16,787.89	15,731.18	14,335.28	12,754.08	12,190.03	11,967.99	11,877.23	11,839.57	11,823.84
17.75%	20,458.68	16,905.96	15,853.27	14,464.89	12,898.98	12,345.20	12,129.42	12,042.21	12,006.43	11,991.67
18.00%	20,568.68	17,024.45	15,975.80	14,595.00	13,044.41	12,500.82	12,291.18	12,207.39	12,173.42	12,159.58
18.25%	20,678.99	17,143.35	16,098.79	14,725.62	13,190.37	12,656.88	12,453.25	12,372.78	12,340.54	12,327.55
18.50%	20,789.63	17,262.65	16,222.23	14,856.74	13,336.84	12,813.36	12,615.62	12,538.35	12,507.76	12,495.58
18.75%	20,900.58	17,382.37	16,346.11	14,988.35	13,483.82	12,970.26	12,778.28	12,704.10	12,675.08	12,663.67
19.00%	21,011.85	17,502.50	16,470.43	15,120.46	13,631.30	13,127.55	12,941.21	12,870.03	12,842.51	12,831.82
19.25%	21,123.43	17,623.02	16,595.19	15,253.05	13,779.26	13,285.23	13,104.40	13,036.11	13,010.02	13,000.01
19.50%	21,235.32	17,743.96	16,720.39	15,386.13	13,927.71	13,443.28	13,267.85	13,202.35	13,177.62	13,168.24
19.75%	21,347.53	17,865.29	16,846.03	15,519.68	14,076.62	13,601.70	13,431.54	13,368.73	13,345.30	13,336.52
20.00%	21,460.05	17,987.02	16,972.09	15,653.71	14,226.00	13,760.48	13,595.46	13,535.25	13,513.05	13,504.84
20.25%	21,572.88	18,109.15	17,098.59	15,788.21	14,375.83	13,919.60	13,759.60	13,701.90	13,680.88	13,673.19
20.50%	21,686.01	18,231.68	17,225.51	15,923.17	14,526.11	14,079.05	13,923.96	13,868.67	13,848.76	13,841.57
20.75%	21,799.46	18,354.59	17,352.85	16,058.59	14,676.82	14,238.82	14,088.52	14,035.55	14,016.71	14,009.99

$820,000   1.00 - 10.75%   5 - 40 Years

	5	7	8	10	15	20	25	30	35	40
1.00%	14,016.87	10,111.62	8,891.45	7,183.54	4,907.66	3,771.13	3,090.35	2,637.44	2,314.74	2,073.42
1.25%	14,105.31	10,200.30	8,980.31	7,272.87	4,998.34	3,863.30	3,184.04	2,732.66	2,411.51	2,171.73
1.50%	14,194.11	10,289.47	9,069.75	7,362.90	5,090.09	3,956.87	3,279.48	2,829.99	2,510.71	2,272.81
1.75%	14,283.26	10,379.13	9,159.75	7,453.65	5,182.90	4,051.86	3,376.67	2,929.40	2,612.34	2,376.64
2.00%	14,372.76	10,469.30	9,250.32	7,545.10	5,276.77	4,148.24	3,475.61	3,030.88	2,716.35	2,483.17
2.25%	14,462.62	10,559.96	9,341.45	7,637.26	5,371.70	4,246.03	3,576.27	3,134.42	2,822.74	2,592.37
2.50%	14,552.84	10,651.11	9,433.15	7,730.13	5,467.67	4,345.20	3,678.66	3,239.99	2,931.46	2,704.18
2.75%	14,643.40	10,742.76	9,525.42	7,823.70	5,564.70	4,445.76	3,782.75	3,347.58	3,042.48	2,818.57
3.00%	14,734.33	10,834.91	9,618.25	7,917.98	5,662.77	4,547.70	3,888.53	3,457.15	3,155.77	2,935.47
3.25%	14,825.60	10,927.54	9,711.64	8,012.96	5,761.88	4,651.01	3,995.99	3,568.69	3,271.29	3,054.84
3.50%	14,917.23	11,020.68	9,805.60	8,108.64	5,862.04	4,755.67	4,105.11	3,682.17	3,388.98	3,176.61
3.75%	15,009.21	11,114.30	9,900.12	8,205.02	5,963.22	4,861.68	4,215.88	3,797.55	3,508.82	3,300.71
4.00%	15,101.55	11,208.42	9,995.21	8,302.10	6,065.44	4,969.04	4,328.26	3,914.81	3,630.75	3,427.10
4.25%	15,194.24	11,303.03	10,090.85	8,399.88	6,168.68	5,077.72	4,442.25	4,033.91	3,754.73	3,555.69
4.50%	15,287.28	11,398.13	10,187.05	8,498.35	6,272.94	5,187.72	4,557.83	4,154.82	3,880.71	3,686.42
4.75%	15,380.67	11,493.72	10,283.81	8,597.51	6,378.22	5,299.03	4,674.96	4,277.51	4,008.63	3,819.21
5.00%	15,474.41	11,589.81	10,381.13	8,697.37	6,484.51	5,411.64	4,793.64	4,401.94	4,138.44	3,954.01
5.25%	15,568.51	11,686.38	10,479.01	8,797.92	6,591.80	5,525.52	4,913.83	4,528.07	4,270.09	4,090.74
5.50%	15,662.95	11,783.43	10,577.44	8,899.15	6,700.08	5,640.68	5,035.52	4,655.87	4,403.53	4,229.32
5.75%	15,757.75	11,880.98	10,676.43	9,001.08	6,809.36	5,757.08	5,158.67	4,785.30	4,538.71	4,369.68
6.00%	15,852.90	11,979.01	10,775.97	9,103.68	6,919.63	5,874.73	5,283.27	4,916.31	4,675.56	4,511.75
6.25%	15,948.39	12,077.53	10,876.07	9,206.97	7,030.87	5,993.61	5,409.29	5,048.88	4,814.03	4,655.46
6.50%	16,044.24	12,176.54	10,976.71	9,310.93	7,143.08	6,113.70	5,536.70	5,182.96	4,954.07	4,800.75
6.75%	16,140.44	12,276.03	11,077.91	9,415.58	7,256.26	6,234.98	5,665.47	5,318.50	5,095.62	4,947.53
7.00%	16,236.98	12,376.00	11,179.65	9,520.90	7,370.39	6,357.45	5,795.59	5,455.48	5,238.62	5,095.74
7.25%	16,333.88	12,476.45	11,281.94	9,626.89	7,485.48	6,481.08	5,927.02	5,593.85	5,383.03	5,245.31
7.50%	16,431.12	12,577.39	11,384.77	9,733.55	7,601.50	6,605.86	6,059.73	5,733.56	5,528.79	5,396.18
7.75%	16,528.71	12,678.80	11,488.15	9,840.87	7,718.46	6,731.78	6,193.70	5,874.58	5,675.84	5,548.28
8.00%	16,626.64	12,780.70	11,592.08	9,948.86	7,836.35	6,858.81	6,328.89	6,016.87	5,824.14	5,701.56
8.25%	16,724.93	12,883.07	11,696.54	10,057.52	7,955.15	6,986.94	6,465.29	6,160.39	5,973.63	5,855.94
8.50%	16,823.56	12,985.92	11,801.55	10,166.83	8,074.86	7,116.15	6,602.86	6,305.09	6,124.26	6,011.37
8.75%	16,922.53	13,089.24	11,907.09	10,276.79	8,195.48	7,246.43	6,741.58	6,450.94	6,275.98	6,167.80
9.00%	17,021.85	13,193.04	12,013.17	10,387.41	8,316.99	7,377.75	6,881.41	6,597.91	6,428.74	6,325.16
9.25%	17,121.52	13,297.32	12,119.78	10,498.68	8,439.38	7,510.11	7,022.33	6,745.94	6,582.50	6,483.42
9.50%	17,221.53	13,402.06	12,226.93	10,610.60	8,562.64	7,643.48	7,164.31	6,895.00	6,737.22	6,642.50
9.75%	17,321.88	13,507.28	12,334.61	10,723.16	8,686.77	7,777.84	7,307.33	7,045.07	6,892.83	6,802.38
10.00%	17,422.58	13,612.97	12,442.81	10,836.36	8,811.76	7,913.18	7,451.35	7,196.09	7,049.31	6,963.00
10.25%	17,523.62	13,719.13	12,551.55	10,950.20	8,937.60	8,049.48	7,596.34	7,348.03	7,206.62	7,124.31
10.50%	17,625.00	13,825.75	12,660.81	11,064.67	9,064.27	8,186.72	7,742.29	7,500.86	7,364.70	7,286.28
10.75%	17,726.72	13,932.84	12,770.60	11,179.77	9,191.77	8,324.88	7,889.16	7,654.55	7,523.52	7,448.86

$820,000   11.00 - 20.75%   5 - 40 Years

	5	7	8	10	15	20	25	30	35	40
11.00%	17,828.79	14,040.40	12,880.91	11,295.50	9,320.09	8,463.94	8,036.93	7,809.05	7,683.05	7,612.01
11.25%	17,931.19	14,148.42	12,991.74	11,411.85	9,449.23	8,603.90	8,185.56	7,964.34	7,843.25	7,775.71
11.50%	18,033.94	14,256.90	13,103.09	11,528.83	9,579.16	8,744.72	8,335.05	8,120.39	8,004.08	7,939.91
11.75%	18,137.02	14,365.84	13,214.95	11,646.42	9,709.88	8,886.40	8,485.35	8,277.16	8,165.51	8,104.58
12.00%	18,240.45	14,475.24	13,327.33	11,764.62	9,841.38	9,028.91	8,636.44	8,434.62	8,327.51	8,269.70
12.25%	18,344.21	14,585.10	13,440.22	11,883.43	9,973.65	9,172.23	8,788.30	8,592.75	8,490.04	8,435.23
12.50%	18,448.31	14,695.42	13,553.62	12,002.85	10,106.68	9,316.35	8,940.90	8,751.51	8,653.09	8,601.14
12.75%	18,552.75	14,806.19	13,667.53	12,122.86	10,240.46	9,461.26	9,094.23	8,910.88	8,816.61	8,767.41
13.00%	18,657.52	14,917.41	13,781.95	12,243.48	10,374.99	9,606.92	9,248.25	9,070.84	8,980.58	8,934.02
13.25%	18,762.63	15,029.09	13,896.87	12,364.69	10,510.24	9,753.33	9,402.94	9,231.34	9,144.99	9,100.93
13.50%	18,868.07	15,141.21	14,012.29	12,486.49	10,646.21	9,900.47	9,558.29	9,392.38	9,309.79	9,268.14
13.75%	18,973.85	15,253.79	14,128.21	12,608.88	10,782.90	10,048.32	9,714.26	9,553.92	9,474.98	9,435.62
14.00%	19,079.97	15,366.81	14,244.63	12,731.85	10,920.28	10,196.87	9,870.84	9,715.95	9,640.52	9,603.35
14.25%	19,186.41	15,480.28	14,361.54	12,855.40	11,058.35	10,346.10	10,028.01	9,878.43	9,806.40	9,771.31
14.50%	19,293.19	15,594.19	14,478.95	12,979.52	11,197.11	10,495.98	10,185.74	10,041.36	9,972.60	9,939.49
14.75%	19,400.30	15,708.54	14,596.85	13,104.21	11,336.53	10,646.51	10,344.01	10,204.70	10,139.09	10,107.87
15.00%	19,507.74	15,823.34	14,715.23	13,229.47	11,476.61	10,797.67	10,502.81	10,368.44	10,305.87	10,276.44
15.25%	19,615.51	15,938.57	14,834.10	13,355.29	11,617.35	10,949.45	10,662.12	10,532.56	10,472.91	10,445.18
15.50%	19,723.62	16,054.24	14,953.46	13,481.66	11,758.72	11,101.82	10,821.91	10,697.04	10,640.19	10,614.08
15.75%	19,832.05	16,170.35	15,073.29	13,608.60	11,900.72	11,254.78	10,982.17	10,861.86	10,807.71	10,783.13
16.00%	19,940.81	16,286.89	15,193.60	13,736.08	12,043.35	11,408.30	11,142.89	11,027.01	10,975.45	10,952.32
16.25%	20,049.89	16,403.87	15,314.39	13,864.10	12,186.58	11,562.37	11,304.04	11,192.46	11,143.39	11,121.63
16.50%	20,159.31	16,521.27	15,435.66	13,992.67	12,330.41	11,716.99	11,465.61	11,358.21	11,311.52	11,291.07
16.75%	20,269.05	16,639.10	15,557.39	14,121.77	12,474.83	11,872.12	11,627.58	11,524.24	11,479.83	11,460.61
17.00%	20,379.11	16,757.36	15,679.59	14,251.41	12,619.84	12,027.76	11,789.93	11,690.54	11,648.31	11,630.25
17.25%	20,489.50	16,876.04	15,802.26	14,381.57	12,765.41	12,183.90	11,952.66	11,857.08	11,816.95	11,799.99
17.50%	20,600.22	16,995.15	15,925.39	14,512.26	12,911.54	12,340.52	12,115.74	12,023.87	11,985.74	11,969.81
17.75%	20,711.25	17,114.68	16,048.98	14,643.46	13,058.23	12,497.61	12,279.17	12,190.88	12,154.66	12,139.72
18.00%	20,822.61	17,234.63	16,173.04	14,775.19	13,205.45	12,655.15	12,442.93	12,358.10	12,323.71	12,309.69
18.25%	20,934.29	17,354.99	16,297.54	14,907.42	13,353.21	12,813.14	12,607.00	12,525.53	12,492.89	12,479.74
18.50%	21,046.29	17,475.77	16,422.50	15,040.16	13,501.49	12,971.55	12,771.37	12,693.15	12,662.17	12,649.85
18.75%	21,158.61	17,596.97	16,547.91	15,173.40	13,650.29	13,130.38	12,936.03	12,860.95	12,831.57	12,820.01
19.00%	21,271.25	17,718.58	16,673.77	15,307.13	13,799.58	13,289.62	13,100.98	13,028.92	13,001.06	12,990.23
19.25%	21,384.21	17,840.59	16,800.07	15,441.36	13,949.38	13,449.24	13,266.19	13,197.05	13,170.64	13,160.50
19.50%	21,497.49	17,963.02	16,926.82	15,576.08	14,099.65	13,609.25	13,431.65	13,365.34	13,340.31	13,330.82
19.75%	21,611.08	18,085.85	17,054.00	15,711.28	14,250.41	13,769.63	13,597.36	13,533.78	13,510.06	13,501.17
20.00%	21,724.98	18,209.08	17,181.62	15,846.97	14,401.63	13,930.36	13,763.30	13,702.35	13,679.88	13,671.57
20.25%	21,839.21	18,332.72	17,309.68	15,983.12	14,553.31	14,091.44	13,929.47	13,871.06	13,849.78	13,842.00
20.50%	21,953.74	18,456.76	17,438.17	16,119.75	14,705.44	14,252.86	14,095.86	14,039.88	14,019.74	14,012.46
20.75%	22,068.59	18,581.19	17,567.09	16,256.84	14,858.02	14,414.61	14,262.45	14,208.83	14,189.76	14,182.95

	5	7	8	10	15	20	25	30	35	40
1.00%	14,187.81	10,234.93	8,999.88	7,271.14	4,967.50	3,817.12	3,128.04	2,669.61	2,342.97	2,098.71
1.25%	14,277.33	10,324.69	9,089.83	7,361.56	5,059.30	3,910.41	3,222.87	2,765.99	2,440.92	2,198.22
1.50%	14,367.21	10,414.95	9,180.35	7,452.69	5,152.17	4,005.13	3,319.47	2,864.50	2,541.33	2,300.53
1.75%	14,457.44	10,505.71	9,271.45	7,544.55	5,246.11	4,101.27	3,417.85	2,965.12	2,644.19	2,405.62
2.00%	14,548.04	10,596.97	9,363.12	7,637.12	5,341.12	4,198.83	3,517.99	3,067.84	2,749.48	2,513.45
2.25%	14,639.00	10,688.74	9,455.37	7,730.40	5,437.20	4,297.81	3,619.88	3,172.64	2,857.16	2,623.98
2.50%	14,730.31	10,781.00	9,548.19	7,824.40	5,534.35	4,398.19	3,723.52	3,279.50	2,967.21	2,737.16
2.75%	14,821.98	10,873.77	9,641.58	7,919.12	5,632.56	4,499.98	3,828.88	3,388.40	3,079.59	2,852.94
3.00%	14,914.01	10,967.04	9,735.54	8,014.54	5,731.83	4,603.16	3,935.95	3,499.31	3,194.26	2,971.27
3.25%	15,006.40	11,060.81	9,830.08	8,110.68	5,832.15	4,707.72	4,044.72	3,612.21	3,311.18	3,092.09
3.50%	15,099.15	11,155.08	9,925.18	8,207.53	5,933.53	4,813.67	4,155.18	3,727.07	3,430.31	3,215.34
3.75%	15,192.25	11,249.84	10,020.86	8,305.08	6,035.95	4,920.97	4,267.29	3,843.86	3,551.61	3,340.97
4.00%	15,285.71	11,345.11	10,117.10	8,403.35	6,139.41	5,029.64	4,381.05	3,962.55	3,675.03	3,468.89
4.25%	15,379.53	11,440.87	10,213.91	8,502.32	6,243.91	5,139.65	4,496.43	4,083.10	3,800.52	3,599.05
4.50%	15,473.71	11,537.13	10,311.28	8,601.99	6,349.44	5,250.99	4,613.41	4,205.49	3,928.03	3,731.37
4.75%	15,568.24	11,633.89	10,409.23	8,702.36	6,456.00	5,363.66	4,731.97	4,329.67	4,057.51	3,865.79
5.00%	15,663.12	11,731.14	10,507.73	8,803.44	6,563.59	5,477.63	4,852.10	4,455.62	4,188.91	4,002.23
5.25%	15,758.37	11,828.89	10,606.80	8,905.21	6,672.19	5,592.91	4,973.76	4,583.29	4,322.17	4,140.62
5.50%	15,853.96	11,927.14	10,706.44	9,007.68	6,781.79	5,709.46	5,096.93	4,712.65	4,457.24	4,280.89
5.75%	15,949.92	12,025.87	10,806.63	9,110.85	6,892.40	5,827.29	5,221.58	4,843.65	4,594.06	4,422.97
6.00%	16,046.23	12,125.10	10,907.39	9,214.70	7,004.01	5,946.38	5,347.70	4,976.27	4,732.57	4,566.77
6.25%	16,142.89	12,224.82	11,008.70	9,319.25	7,116.61	6,066.70	5,475.26	5,110.45	4,872.73	4,712.24
6.50%	16,239.90	12,325.03	11,110.57	9,424.48	7,230.19	6,188.26	5,604.22	5,246.16	5,014.48	4,859.29
6.75%	16,337.27	12,425.73	11,213.00	9,530.40	7,344.75	6,311.02	5,734.57	5,383.36	5,157.76	5,007.86
7.00%	16,434.99	12,526.92	11,315.99	9,637.00	7,460.27	6,434.98	5,866.27	5,522.01	5,302.51	5,157.88
7.25%	16,533.07	12,628.60	11,419.52	9,744.29	7,576.76	6,560.12	5,999.30	5,662.06	5,448.68	5,309.28
7.50%	16,631.50	12,730.77	11,523.61	9,852.25	7,694.20	6,686.42	6,133.63	5,803.48	5,596.21	5,461.99
7.75%	16,730.28	12,833.42	11,628.25	9,960.88	7,812.59	6,813.87	6,269.23	5,946.22	5,745.06	5,615.94
8.00%	16,829.41	12,936.56	11,733.44	10,070.19	7,931.91	6,942.45	6,406.07	6,090.25	5,895.17	5,771.09
8.25%	16,928.89	13,040.18	11,839.18	10,180.17	8,052.16	7,072.14	6,544.14	6,235.51	6,046.48	5,927.35
8.50%	17,028.72	13,144.28	11,945.47	10,290.81	8,173.34	7,202.93	6,683.38	6,381.98	6,198.94	6,084.68
8.75%	17,128.90	13,248.87	12,052.30	10,402.12	8,295.42	7,334.80	6,823.79	6,529.61	6,352.51	6,243.02
9.00%	17,229.43	13,353.93	12,159.67	10,514.09	8,418.41	7,467.73	6,965.33	6,678.37	6,507.14	6,402.30
9.25%	17,330.32	13,459.48	12,267.58	10,626.72	8,542.30	7,601.69	7,107.97	6,828.21	6,662.78	6,562.48
9.50%	17,431.54	13,565.50	12,376.04	10,740.00	8,667.06	7,736.69	7,251.68	6,979.09	6,819.38	6,723.51
9.75%	17,533.12	13,672.01	12,485.03	10,853.93	8,792.71	7,872.69	7,396.44	7,130.98	6,976.89	6,885.34
10.00%	17,635.05	13,778.98	12,594.56	10,968.51	8,919.22	8,009.68	7,542.22	7,283.84	7,135.28	7,047.91
10.25%	17,737.32	13,886.43	12,704.62	11,083.74	9,046.59	8,147.64	7,688.98	7,437.64	7,294.50	7,211.19
10.50%	17,839.94	13,994.36	12,815.21	11,199.60	9,174.81	8,286.55	7,836.71	7,592.34	7,454.51	7,375.13
10.75%	17,942.90	14,102.76	12,926.34	11,316.11	9,303.87	8,426.40	7,985.37	7,747.90	7,615.27	7,539.70

$830,000   11.00 - 20.75%   5 - 40 Years

	5	7	8	10	15	20	25	30	35	40
11.00%	18,046.21	14,211.62	13,037.99	11,433.25	9,433.75	8,567.16	8,134.94	7,904.28	7,776.75	7,704.84
11.25%	18,149.87	14,320.96	13,150.17	11,551.02	9,564.46	8,708.82	8,285.39	8,061.47	7,938.90	7,870.54
11.50%	18,253.86	14,430.76	13,262.88	11,669.42	9,695.98	8,851.37	8,436.69	8,219.42	8,101.69	8,036.74
11.75%	18,358.21	14,541.03	13,376.11	11,788.45	9,828.29	8,994.77	8,588.82	8,378.10	8,265.09	8,203.42
12.00%	18,462.89	14,651.77	13,489.86	11,908.09	9,961.39	9,139.01	8,741.76	8,537.48	8,429.06	8,370.55
12.25%	18,567.92	14,762.97	13,604.13	12,028.35	10,095.28	9,284.09	8,895.47	8,697.54	8,593.58	8,538.10
12.50%	18,673.29	14,874.63	13,718.91	12,149.22	10,229.93	9,429.97	9,049.94	8,858.24	8,758.61	8,706.03
12.75%	18,779.00	14,986.75	13,834.21	12,270.70	10,365.35	9,576.64	9,205.13	9,019.55	8,924.13	8,874.33
13.00%	18,885.05	15,099.33	13,950.02	12,392.79	10,501.51	9,724.08	9,361.03	9,181.46	9,090.10	9,042.97
13.25%	18,991.44	15,212.37	14,066.34	12,515.48	10,638.41	9,872.28	9,517.61	9,343.92	9,256.51	9,211.92
13.50%	19,098.17	15,325.86	14,183.17	12,638.77	10,776.04	10,021.21	9,674.85	9,506.92	9,423.33	9,381.15
13.75%	19,205.24	15,439.81	14,300.51	12,762.65	10,914.39	10,170.86	9,832.73	9,670.43	9,590.53	9,550.69
14.00%	19,312.65	15,554.21	14,418.35	12,887.11	11,053.45	10,321.22	9,991.22	9,834.44	9,758.09	9,720.46
14.25%	19,420.39	15,669.06	14,536.69	13,012.17	11,193.21	10,472.27	10,150.30	9,998.90	9,925.99	9,890.47
14.50%	19,528.47	15,784.36	14,655.52	13,137.80	11,333.66	10,623.98	10,309.95	10,163.81	10,094.22	10,060.70
14.75%	19,636.89	15,900.11	14,774.86	13,264.02	11,474.78	10,776.35	10,470.16	10,329.15	10,262.74	10,231.14
15.00%	19,745.64	16,016.31	14,894.69	13,390.80	11,616.57	10,929.35	10,630.89	10,494.89	10,431.55	10,401.76
15.25%	19,854.73	16,132.95	15,015.01	13,518.16	11,759.02	11,082.98	10,792.14	10,661.01	10,600.63	10,572.56
15.50%	19,964.15	16,250.03	15,135.82	13,646.07	11,902.12	11,237.21	10,953.89	10,827.49	10,769.95	10,743.52
15.75%	20,073.90	16,367.55	15,257.11	13,774.55	12,045.85	11,392.03	11,116.10	10,994.32	10,939.51	10,914.63
16.00%	20,183.99	16,485.51	15,378.89	13,903.59	12,190.22	11,547.42	11,278.78	11,161.48	11,109.30	11,085.88
16.25%	20,294.40	16,603.91	15,501.15	14,033.18	12,335.20	11,703.38	11,441.89	11,328.96	11,279.28	11,257.26
16.50%	20,405.15	16,722.75	15,623.90	14,163.31	12,480.78	11,859.88	11,605.43	11,496.73	11,449.47	11,428.76
16.75%	20,516.23	16,842.02	15,747.11	14,293.99	12,626.96	12,016.90	11,769.38	11,664.78	11,619.83	11,600.37
17.00%	20,627.64	16,961.72	15,870.81	14,425.21	12,773.74	12,174.44	11,933.71	11,833.11	11,790.37	11,772.09
17.25%	20,739.37	17,081.85	15,994.97	14,556.96	12,921.08	12,332.49	12,098.42	12,001.68	11,961.06	11,943.89
17.50%	20,851.44	17,202.41	16,119.60	14,689.24	13,069.00	12,491.02	12,263.50	12,170.50	12,131.91	12,115.79
17.75%	20,963.83	17,323.39	16,244.70	14,822.04	13,217.47	12,650.02	12,428.92	12,339.55	12,302.89	12,287.76
18.00%	21,076.54	17,444.81	16,370.27	14,955.37	13,366.49	12,809.49	12,594.67	12,508.81	12,474.00	12,459.81
18.25%	21,189.59	17,566.64	16,496.29	15,089.22	13,516.05	12,969.40	12,760.74	12,678.28	12,645.24	12,631.93
18.50%	21,302.95	17,688.89	16,622.78	15,223.57	13,666.14	13,129.74	12,927.12	12,847.94	12,816.59	12,804.11
18.75%	21,416.64	17,811.57	16,749.72	15,358.44	13,816.75	13,290.51	13,093.79	13,017.79	12,988.05	12,976.36
19.00%	21,530.66	17,934.66	16,877.11	15,493.81	13,967.87	13,451.68	13,260.74	13,187.81	13,159.61	13,148.65
19.25%	21,644.99	18,058.16	17,004.95	15,629.67	14,119.49	13,613.26	13,427.97	13,357.99	13,331.26	13,321.00
19.50%	21,759.65	18,182.08	17,133.24	15,766.03	14,271.60	13,775.22	13,595.45	13,528.34	13,503.00	13,493.39
19.75%	21,874.63	18,306.41	17,261.98	15,902.88	14,424.19	13,937.55	13,763.18	13,698.83	13,674.81	13,665.82
20.00%	21,989.92	18,431.15	17,391.16	16,040.22	14,577.26	14,100.24	13,931.15	13,869.46	13,846.71	13,838.29
20.25%	22,105.54	18,556.29	17,520.77	16,178.04	14,730.79	14,263.29	14,099.35	14,040.22	14,018.68	14,010.80
20.50%	22,221.47	18,681.84	17,650.83	16,316.33	14,884.78	14,426.68	14,267.76	14,211.10	14,190.71	14,183.34
20.75%	22,337.72	18,807.79	17,781.32	16,455.10	15,039.21	14,590.40	14,436.38	14,382.11	14,362.80	14,355.91

	5	7	8	10	15	20	25	30	35	40
1.00%	14,358.75	10,358.25	9,108.31	7,358.75	5,027.35	3,863.11	3,165.73	2,701.77	2,371.20	2,123.99
1.25%	14,449.35	10,449.08	9,199.34	7,450.25	5,120.25	3,957.52	3,261.70	2,799.31	2,470.32	2,224.70
1.50%	14,540.31	10,540.43	9,290.96	7,542.49	5,214.24	4,053.38	3,359.47	2,899.01	2,571.95	2,328.25
1.75%	14,631.63	10,632.28	9,383.16	7,635.45	5,309.32	4,150.68	3,459.03	3,000.84	2,676.05	2,434.61
2.00%	14,723.32	10,724.65	9,475.93	7,729.13	5,405.47	4,249.42	3,560.38	3,104.80	2,782.61	2,543.74
2.25%	14,815.37	10,817.52	9,569.29	7,823.54	5,502.71	4,349.59	3,663.50	3,210.87	2,891.59	2,655.59
2.50%	14,907.78	10,910.89	9,663.23	7,918.67	5,601.03	4,451.18	3,768.38	3,319.02	3,002.96	2,770.14
2.75%	15,000.56	11,004.78	9,757.75	8,014.53	5,700.42	4,554.20	3,875.01	3,429.23	3,116.69	2,887.31
3.00%	15,093.70	11,099.17	9,852.84	8,111.10	5,800.89	4,658.62	3,983.38	3,541.47	3,232.74	3,007.07
3.25%	15,187.20	11,194.07	9,948.51	8,208.40	5,902.42	4,764.44	4,093.46	3,655.73	3,351.07	3,129.35
3.50%	15,281.07	11,289.47	10,044.76	8,306.41	6,005.01	4,871.66	4,205.24	3,771.98	3,471.64	3,254.08
3.75%	15,375.29	11,385.38	10,141.59	8,405.14	6,108.67	4,980.26	4,318.70	3,890.17	3,594.40	3,381.22
4.00%	15,469.88	11,481.80	10,238.99	8,504.59	6,213.38	5,090.23	4,433.83	4,010.29	3,719.31	3,510.68
4.25%	15,564.83	11,578.71	10,336.97	8,604.75	6,319.14	5,201.57	4,550.60	4,132.30	3,846.31	3,642.41
4.50%	15,660.14	11,676.14	10,435.52	8,705.63	6,425.94	5,314.25	4,668.99	4,256.16	3,975.36	3,776.33
4.75%	15,755.81	11,774.06	10,534.64	8,807.21	6,533.79	5,428.28	4,788.99	4,381.84	4,106.40	3,912.37
5.00%	15,851.84	11,872.48	10,634.33	8,909.50	6,642.67	5,543.63	4,910.56	4,509.30	4,239.38	4,050.45
5.25%	15,948.23	11,971.41	10,734.60	9,012.50	6,752.57	5,660.29	5,033.68	4,638.51	4,374.24	4,190.51
5.50%	16,044.98	12,070.84	10,835.43	9,116.21	6,863.50	5,778.25	5,158.33	4,769.43	4,510.94	4,332.47
5.75%	16,142.09	12,170.76	10,936.83	9,220.61	6,975.44	5,897.50	5,284.49	4,902.01	4,649.41	4,476.26
6.00%	16,239.55	12,271.19	11,038.80	9,325.72	7,088.40	6,018.02	5,412.13	5,036.22	4,789.59	4,621.79
6.25%	16,337.38	12,372.11	11,141.34	9,431.53	7,202.35	6,139.80	5,541.22	5,172.02	4,931.44	4,769.01
6.50%	16,435.56	12,473.53	11,244.44	9,538.03	7,317.30	6,262.81	5,671.74	5,309.37	5,074.90	4,917.84
6.75%	16,534.11	12,575.44	11,348.10	9,645.23	7,433.24	6,387.06	5,803.66	5,448.22	5,219.90	5,068.20
7.00%	16,633.01	12,677.85	11,452.32	9,753.11	7,550.16	6,512.51	5,936.95	5,588.54	5,366.39	5,220.02
7.25%	16,732.26	12,780.75	11,557.11	9,861.69	7,668.05	6,639.16	6,071.58	5,730.28	5,514.32	5,373.24
7.50%	16,831.88	12,884.15	11,662.45	9,970.95	7,786.90	6,766.98	6,207.53	5,873.40	5,663.64	5,527.79
7.75%	16,931.85	12,988.04	11,768.35	10,080.89	7,906.72	6,895.97	6,344.76	6,017.86	5,814.28	5,683.61
8.00%	17,032.17	13,092.42	11,874.81	10,191.52	8,027.48	7,026.10	6,483.26	6,163.62	5,966.19	5,840.62
8.25%	17,132.85	13,197.29	11,981.82	10,302.82	8,149.18	7,157.35	6,622.98	6,310.64	6,119.33	5,998.77
8.50%	17,233.89	13,302.65	12,089.39	10,414.80	8,271.81	7,289.72	6,763.91	6,458.87	6,273.63	6,157.99
8.75%	17,335.28	13,408.49	12,197.50	10,527.45	8,395.37	7,423.17	6,906.01	6,608.28	6,429.05	6,318.23
9.00%	17,437.02	13,514.83	12,306.17	10,640.76	8,519.84	7,557.70	7,049.25	6,758.83	6,585.54	6,479.44
9.25%	17,539.11	13,621.64	12,415.38	10,754.75	8,645.22	7,693.28	7,193.61	6,910.47	6,743.05	6,641.55
9.50%	17,641.56	13,728.94	12,525.15	10,869.39	8,771.49	7,829.90	7,339.05	7,063.18	6,901.54	6,804.52
9.75%	17,744.36	13,836.73	12,635.45	10,984.70	8,898.65	7,967.54	7,485.55	7,216.90	7,060.95	6,968.29
10.00%	17,847.52	13,944.99	12,746.30	11,100.66	9,026.68	8,106.18	7,633.09	7,371.60	7,221.25	7,132.83
10.25%	17,951.02	14,053.74	12,857.69	11,217.28	9,155.59	8,245.80	7,781.62	7,527.25	7,382.39	7,298.07
10.50%	18,054.88	14,162.97	12,969.61	11,334.54	9,285.35	8,386.39	7,931.13	7,683.81	7,544.33	7,463.99
10.75%	18,159.08	14,272.67	13,082.08	11,452.45	9,415.96	8,527.92	8,081.58	7,841.24	7,707.02	7,630.54

$840,000   11.00 - 20.75%   5 - 40 Years

	5	7	8	10	15	20	25	30	35	40
11.00%	18,263.64	14,382.85	13,195.08	11,571.00	9,547.41	8,670.38	8,232.95	7,999.52	7,870.44	7,797.67
11.25%	18,368.54	14,493.50	13,308.61	11,690.19	9,679.69	8,813.75	8,385.21	8,158.60	8,034.55	7,965.36
11.50%	18,473.79	14,604.63	13,422.67	11,810.02	9,812.79	8,958.01	8,538.34	8,318.45	8,199.30	8,133.57
11.75%	18,579.39	14,716.23	13,537.27	11,930.47	9,946.70	9,103.14	8,692.30	8,479.04	8,364.67	8,302.26
12.00%	18,685.34	14,828.30	13,652.39	12,051.56	10,081.41	9,249.12	8,847.08	8,640.35	8,530.62	8,471.40
12.25%	18,791.63	14,940.83	13,768.03	12,173.27	10,216.91	9,395.94	9,002.65	8,802.33	8,697.12	8,640.96
12.50%	18,898.27	15,053.84	13,884.20	12,295.60	10,353.19	9,543.58	9,158.97	8,964.97	8,864.14	8,810.92
12.75%	19,005.25	15,167.31	14,000.89	12,418.54	10,490.23	9,692.02	9,316.04	9,128.22	9,031.65	8,981.25
13.00%	19,112.58	15,281.25	14,118.09	12,542.10	10,628.03	9,841.24	9,473.82	9,292.08	9,199.62	9,151.92
13.25%	19,220.25	15,395.65	14,235.82	12,666.27	10,766.59	9,991.22	9,632.28	9,456.50	9,368.03	9,322.91
13.50%	19,328.27	15,510.51	14,354.05	12,791.04	10,905.88	10,141.95	9,791.42	9,621.46	9,536.86	9,494.19
13.75%	19,436.63	15,625.83	14,472.80	12,916.41	11,045.89	10,293.41	9,951.19	9,786.95	9,706.07	9,665.76
14.00%	19,545.33	15,741.61	14,592.06	13,042.38	11,186.63	10,445.57	10,111.59	9,952.92	9,875.66	9,837.58
14.25%	19,654.37	15,857.85	14,711.83	13,168.94	11,328.07	10,598.44	10,272.59	10,119.37	10,045.58	10,009.64
14.50%	19,763.76	15,974.54	14,832.10	13,296.09	11,470.21	10,751.98	10,434.17	10,286.27	10,215.83	10,181.92
14.75%	19,873.48	16,091.68	14,952.87	13,423.82	11,613.03	10,906.18	10,596.30	10,453.60	10,386.39	10,354.40
15.00%	19,983.54	16,209.27	15,074.14	13,552.14	11,756.53	11,061.05	10,758.98	10,621.33	10,557.23	10,527.08
15.25%	20,093.94	16,327.32	15,195.91	13,681.03	11,900.70	11,216.55	10,922.17	10,789.45	10,728.34	10,699.94
15.50%	20,204.68	16,445.81	15,318.18	13,810.49	12,045.52	11,372.60	11,085.86	10,957.94	10,899.71	10,872.96
15.75%	20,315.76	16,564.75	15,440.93	13,940.51	12,190.99	11,529.28	11,250.03	11,126.78	11,071.32	11,046.13
16.00%	20,427.17	16,684.13	15,564.18	14,071.10	12,337.09	11,686.55	11,414.67	11,295.96	11,243.14	11,219.45
16.25%	20,538.92	16,803.96	15,687.92	14,202.25	12,483.81	11,844.38	11,579.75	11,465.45	11,415.18	11,392.89
16.50%	20,651.00	16,924.23	15,812.14	14,333.95	12,631.15	12,002.77	11,745.26	11,635.24	11,587.41	11,566.46
16.75%	20,763.41	17,044.93	15,936.84	14,466.21	12,779.10	12,161.68	11,911.18	11,805.32	11,759.83	11,740.14
17.00%	20,876.16	17,166.08	16,062.02	14,599.00	12,927.64	12,321.12	12,077.49	11,975.67	11,932.42	11,913.92
17.25%	20,989.25	17,287.65	16,187.68	14,732.34	13,076.76	12,481.07	12,244.19	12,146.28	12,105.17	12,087.80
17.50%	21,102.66	17,409.67	16,313.82	14,866.22	13,226.46	12,641.51	12,411.25	12,317.13	12,278.07	12,261.76
17.75%	21,216.40	17,532.11	16,440.42	15,000.62	13,376.72	12,802.43	12,578.66	12,488.21	12,451.12	12,435.81
18.00%	21,330.48	17,654.98	16,567.50	15,135.56	13,527.54	12,963.82	12,746.41	12,659.52	12,624.29	12,609.93
18.25%	21,444.88	17,778.29	16,695.04	15,271.01	13,678.90	13,125.65	12,914.48	12,831.03	12,797.59	12,784.12
18.50%	21,559.62	17,902.01	16,823.05	15,406.99	13,830.80	13,287.93	13,082.87	13,002.73	12,971.01	12,958.38
18.75%	21,674.68	18,026.16	16,951.52	15,543.48	13,983.22	13,450.63	13,251.55	13,174.63	13,144.53	13,132.70
19.00%	21,790.06	18,150.74	17,080.45	15,680.48	14,136.16	13,613.75	13,420.51	13,346.70	13,318.16	13,307.07
19.25%	21,905.78	18,275.73	17,209.83	15,817.98	14,289.60	13,777.27	13,589.75	13,518.93	13,491.87	13,481.49
19.50%	22,021.81	18,401.14	17,339.67	15,955.99	14,443.55	13,941.18	13,759.25	13,691.33	13,665.68	13,655.96
19.75%	22,138.18	18,526.97	17,469.95	16,094.49	14,597.98	14,105.47	13,929.00	13,863.87	13,839.57	13,830.47
20.00%	22,254.86	18,653.21	17,600.69	16,233.48	14,752.89	14,270.13	14,098.99	14,036.56	14,013.54	14,005.02
20.25%	22,371.87	18,779.86	17,731.87	16,372.95	14,908.27	14,435.14	14,269.22	14,209.38	14,187.58	14,179.61
20.50%	22,489.20	18,906.92	17,863.49	16,512.91	15,064.11	14,600.49	14,439.66	14,382.32	14,361.68	14,354.23
20.75%	22,606.85	19,034.39	17,995.55	16,653.35	15,220.41	14,766.19	14,610.31	14,555.38	14,535.85	14,528.88

	5	7	8	10	15	20	25	30	35	40
1.00%	14,529.69	10,481.56	9,216.74	7,446.35	5,087.20	3,909.10	3,203.42	2,733.94	2,399.43	2,149.28
1.25%	14,621.36	10,573.48	9,308.86	7,538.95	5,181.21	4,004.64	3,300.53	2,832.64	2,499.73	2,251.18
1.50%	14,713.40	10,665.91	9,401.57	7,632.28	5,276.32	4,101.64	3,399.46	2,933.52	2,602.57	2,355.97
1.75%	14,805.82	10,758.86	9,494.86	7,726.34	5,372.52	4,200.09	3,500.21	3,036.57	2,707.91	2,463.59
2.00%	14,898.60	10,852.32	9,588.74	7,821.14	5,469.82	4,300.01	3,602.76	3,141.77	2,815.73	2,574.02
2.25%	14,991.74	10,946.30	9,683.21	7,916.68	5,568.22	4,401.37	3,707.11	3,249.09	2,926.01	2,687.21
2.50%	15,085.26	11,040.79	9,778.27	8,012.94	5,667.71	4,504.17	3,813.24	3,358.53	3,038.71	2,803.11
2.75%	15,179.14	11,135.79	9,873.91	8,109.94	5,768.28	4,608.41	3,921.14	3,470.05	3,153.79	2,921.69
3.00%	15,273.39	11,231.31	9,970.14	8,207.66	5,869.94	4,714.08	4,030.80	3,583.63	3,271.23	3,042.87
3.25%	15,368.00	11,327.33	10,066.95	8,306.12	5,972.68	4,821.16	4,142.19	3,699.25	3,390.97	3,166.60
3.50%	15,462.98	11,423.87	10,164.34	8,405.30	6,076.50	4,929.66	4,255.30	3,816.88	3,512.97	3,292.82
3.75%	15,558.33	11,520.92	10,262.32	8,505.21	6,181.39	5,039.55	4,370.12	3,936.48	3,637.19	3,421.47
4.00%	15,654.04	11,618.49	10,360.88	8,605.84	6,287.35	5,150.83	4,486.61	4,058.03	3,763.59	3,552.48
4.25%	15,750.12	11,716.56	10,460.03	8,707.19	6,394.37	5,263.49	4,604.77	4,181.49	3,892.10	3,685.77
4.50%	15,846.57	11,815.14	10,559.75	8,809.26	6,502.44	5,377.52	4,724.58	4,306.83	4,022.68	3,821.28
4.75%	15,943.38	11,914.23	10,660.05	8,912.06	6,611.57	5,492.90	4,846.00	4,434.00	4,155.28	3,958.94
5.00%	16,040.55	12,013.82	10,760.93	9,015.57	6,721.75	5,609.62	4,969.02	4,562.98	4,289.85	4,098.67
5.25%	16,138.09	12,113.93	10,862.39	9,119.79	6,832.96	5,727.68	5,093.61	4,693.73	4,426.32	4,240.40
5.50%	16,235.99	12,214.54	10,964.42	9,224.73	6,945.21	5,847.04	5,219.74	4,826.21	4,564.64	4,384.05
5.75%	16,334.25	12,315.65	11,067.03	9,330.38	7,058.49	5,967.71	5,347.40	4,960.37	4,704.76	4,529.54
6.00%	16,432.88	12,417.27	11,170.22	9,436.74	7,172.78	6,089.66	5,476.56	5,096.18	4,846.61	4,676.82
6.25%	16,531.87	12,519.39	11,273.97	9,543.81	7,288.09	6,212.89	5,607.19	5,233.60	4,990.15	4,825.79
6.50%	16,631.23	12,622.02	11,378.30	9,651.58	7,404.41	6,337.37	5,739.26	5,372.58	5,135.31	4,976.38
6.75%	16,730.94	12,725.15	11,483.19	9,760.05	7,521.73	6,463.09	5,872.75	5,513.08	5,282.04	5,128.53
7.00%	16,831.02	12,828.78	11,588.66	9,869.22	7,640.04	6,590.04	6,007.62	5,655.07	5,430.28	5,282.17
7.25%	16,931.46	12,932.91	11,694.69	9,979.09	7,759.33	6,718.20	6,143.86	5,798.50	5,579.97	5,437.21
7.50%	17,032.26	13,037.53	11,801.29	10,089.65	7,879.61	6,847.54	6,281.43	5,943.32	5,731.06	5,593.60
7.75%	17,133.42	13,142.66	11,908.45	10,200.90	8,000.84	6,978.06	6,420.29	6,089.50	5,883.50	5,751.27
8.00%	17,234.94	13,248.28	12,016.18	10,312.85	8,123.04	7,109.74	6,560.44	6,237.00	6,037.22	5,910.15
8.25%	17,336.81	13,354.40	12,124.46	10,425.47	8,246.19	7,242.56	6,701.83	6,385.77	6,192.17	6,070.18
8.50%	17,439.05	13,461.01	12,233.31	10,538.78	8,370.29	7,376.50	6,844.43	6,535.76	6,348.31	6,231.30
8.75%	17,541.65	13,568.12	12,342.71	10,652.77	8,495.31	7,511.54	6,988.22	6,686.95	6,505.59	6,393.45
9.00%	17,644.60	13,675.72	12,452.67	10,767.44	8,621.27	7,647.67	7,133.17	6,839.29	6,663.94	6,556.57
9.25%	17,747.91	13,783.81	12,563.19	10,882.78	8,748.13	7,784.87	7,279.25	6,992.74	6,823.33	6,720.61
9.50%	17,851.58	13,892.38	12,674.25	10,998.79	8,875.91	7,923.12	7,426.42	7,147.26	6,983.70	6,885.52
9.75%	17,955.61	14,001.45	12,785.87	11,115.47	9,004.58	8,062.39	7,574.67	7,302.81	7,145.01	7,051.25
10.00%	18,059.99	14,111.01	12,898.04	11,232.81	9,134.14	8,202.68	7,723.96	7,459.36	7,307.22	7,217.74
10.25%	18,164.72	14,221.05	13,010.75	11,350.82	9,264.58	8,343.97	7,874.26	7,616.86	7,470.27	7,384.95
10.50%	18,269.82	14,331.57	13,124.01	11,469.47	9,395.89	8,486.23	8,025.54	7,775.28	7,634.14	7,552.85
10.75%	18,375.26	14,442.58	13,237.82	11,588.79	9,528.06	8,629.45	8,177.79	7,934.59	7,798.77	7,721.38

$850,000   11.00 - 20.75%   5 - 40 Years

	5	7	8	10	15	20	25	30	35	40
11.00%	18,481.06	14,554.07	13,352.16	11,708.75	9,661.07	8,773.60	8,330.96	8,094.75	7,964.14	7,890.50
11.25%	18,587.21	14,666.04	13,467.05	11,829.36	9,794.93	8,918.68	8,485.04	8,255.72	8,130.20	8,060.19
11.50%	18,693.72	14,778.49	13,582.47	11,950.61	9,929.61	9,064.65	8,639.99	8,417.48	8,296.91	8,230.40
11.75%	18,800.57	14,891.42	13,698.42	12,072.50	10,065.12	9,211.51	8,795.78	8,579.98	8,464.25	8,401.09
12.00%	18,907.78	15,004.82	13,814.92	12,195.03	10,201.43	9,359.23	8,952.41	8,743.21	8,632.17	8,572.25
12.25%	19,015.34	15,118.70	13,931.94	12,318.19	10,338.54	9,507.80	9,109.82	8,907.12	8,800.65	8,743.83
12.50%	19,123.25	15,233.05	14,049.49	12,441.97	10,476.44	9,657.19	9,268.01	9,071.69	8,969.66	8,915.81
12.75%	19,231.51	15,347.88	14,167.56	12,566.38	10,615.11	9,807.40	9,426.94	9,236.89	9,139.17	9,088.17
13.00%	19,340.11	15,463.17	14,286.17	12,691.41	10,754.56	9,958.39	9,586.60	9,402.70	9,309.14	9,260.87
13.25%	19,449.07	15,578.93	14,405.29	12,817.06	10,894.76	10,110.16	9,746.95	9,569.07	9,479.56	9,433.89
13.50%	19,558.37	15,695.16	14,524.94	12,943.31	11,035.71	10,262.68	9,907.98	9,736.00	9,650.39	9,607.22
13.75%	19,668.02	15,811.85	14,645.10	13,070.18	11,177.39	10,415.95	10,069.66	9,903.46	9,821.62	9,780.83
14.00%	19,778.01	15,929.01	14,765.78	13,197.65	11,319.80	10,569.93	10,231.97	10,071.41	9,993.22	9,954.69
14.25%	19,888.35	16,046.63	14,886.97	13,325.71	11,462.93	10,724.61	10,394.88	10,239.84	10,165.17	10,128.80
14.50%	19,999.04	16,164.71	15,008.67	13,454.38	11,606.76	10,879.98	10,558.38	10,408.73	10,337.45	10,303.13
14.75%	20,110.07	16,283.25	15,130.88	13,583.63	11,751.28	11,036.02	10,722.45	10,578.04	10,510.04	10,477.67
15.00%	20,221.44	16,402.24	15,253.59	13,713.47	11,896.49	11,192.71	10,887.06	10,747.77	10,682.91	10,652.41
15.25%	20,333.16	16,521.69	15,376.81	13,843.89	12,042.37	11,350.04	11,052.19	10,917.90	10,856.06	10,827.32
15.50%	20,445.21	16,641.59	15,500.53	13,974.90	12,188.92	11,507.99	11,217.83	11,088.39	11,029.47	11,002.40
15.75%	20,557.61	16,761.95	15,624.75	14,106.47	12,336.12	11,666.54	11,383.96	11,259.25	11,203.12	11,177.63
16.00%	20,670.35	16,882.75	15,749.47	14,238.62	12,483.96	11,825.68	11,550.56	11,430.43	11,376.99	11,353.01
16.25%	20,783.43	17,004.01	15,874.68	14,371.33	12,632.43	11,985.39	11,717.60	11,601.94	11,551.07	11,528.52
16.50%	20,896.84	17,125.71	16,000.38	14,504.60	12,781.52	12,145.66	11,885.08	11,773.76	11,725.36	11,704.15
16.75%	21,010.60	17,247.85	16,126.56	14,638.42	12,931.23	12,306.47	12,052.97	11,945.86	11,899.83	11,879.90
17.00%	21,124.69	17,370.43	16,253.24	14,772.80	13,081.54	12,467.80	12,221.27	12,118.24	12,074.47	12,055.75
17.25%	21,239.12	17,493.46	16,380.39	14,907.73	13,232.44	12,629.66	12,389.95	12,290.88	12,249.28	12,231.70
17.50%	21,353.88	17,616.92	16,508.03	15,043.19	13,383.92	12,792.01	12,559.00	12,463.76	12,424.24	12,407.73
17.75%	21,468.98	17,740.83	16,636.14	15,179.20	13,535.97	12,954.84	12,728.41	12,636.88	12,599.34	12,583.85
18.00%	21,584.41	17,865.16	16,764.73	15,315.74	13,688.58	13,118.15	12,898.15	12,810.23	12,774.58	12,760.05
18.25%	21,700.18	17,989.93	16,893.79	15,452.81	13,841.74	13,281.91	13,068.23	12,983.78	12,949.94	12,936.32
18.50%	21,816.28	18,115.13	17,023.32	15,590.41	13,995.45	13,446.12	13,238.62	13,157.53	13,125.42	13,112.65
18.75%	21,932.71	18,240.76	17,153.32	15,728.52	14,149.69	13,610.76	13,409.30	13,331.47	13,301.01	13,289.04
19.00%	22,049.47	18,366.82	17,283.79	15,867.15	14,304.45	13,775.82	13,580.28	13,505.59	13,476.71	13,465.49
19.25%	22,166.56	18,493.30	17,414.71	16,006.29	14,459.72	13,941.29	13,751.53	13,679.87	13,652.49	13,641.98
19.50%	22,283.98	18,620.20	17,546.09	16,145.94	14,615.50	14,107.15	13,923.05	13,854.32	13,828.37	13,818.53
19.75%	22,401.73	18,747.53	17,677.93	16,286.09	14,771.77	14,273.39	14,094.82	14,028.92	14,004.33	13,995.12
20.00%	22,519.80	18,875.27	17,810.22	16,426.73	14,928.52	14,440.01	14,266.84	14,203.66	14,180.37	14,171.74
20.25%	22,638.20	19,003.43	17,942.96	16,567.87	15,085.75	14,606.99	14,439.09	14,378.53	14,356.48	14,348.41
20.50%	22,756.93	19,132.01	18,076.15	16,709.50	15,243.45	14,774.31	14,611.56	14,553.54	14,532.65	14,525.11
20.75%	22,875.98	19,260.99	18,209.78	16,851.60	15,401.60	14,941.97	14,784.24	14,728.66	14,708.89	14,701.84

	5	7	8	10	15	20	25	30	35	40
1.00%	14,700.62	10,604.87	9,325.17	7,533.95	5,147.05	3,955.09	3,241.10	2,766.10	2,427.66	2,174.56
1.25%	14,793.38	10,697.87	9,418.38	7,627.64	5,242.16	4,051.75	3,339.36	2,865.96	2,529.14	2,277.67
1.50%	14,886.50	10,791.39	9,512.17	7,722.07	5,338.39	4,149.89	3,439.45	2,968.03	2,633.19	2,383.68
1.75%	14,980.00	10,885.43	9,606.56	7,817.24	5,435.73	4,249.51	3,541.39	3,072.29	2,739.77	2,492.57
2.00%	15,073.87	10,979.99	9,701.55	7,913.16	5,534.17	4,350.60	3,645.15	3,178.73	2,848.86	2,604.30
2.25%	15,168.12	11,075.08	9,797.13	8,009.81	5,633.73	4,453.15	3,750.72	3,287.32	2,960.43	2,718.82
2.50%	15,262.73	11,170.68	9,893.31	8,107.21	5,734.39	4,557.16	3,858.10	3,398.04	3,074.46	2,836.09
2.75%	15,357.72	11,266.80	9,990.07	8,205.35	5,836.15	4,662.63	3,967.27	3,510.87	3,190.90	2,956.06
3.00%	15,453.07	11,363.44	10,087.43	8,304.22	5,939.00	4,769.54	4,078.22	3,625.79	3,309.71	3,078.67
3.25%	15,548.80	11,460.60	10,185.38	8,403.84	6,042.95	4,877.88	4,190.92	3,742.77	3,430.86	3,203.85
3.50%	15,644.90	11,558.27	10,283.92	8,504.18	6,147.99	4,987.65	4,305.36	3,861.78	3,554.30	3,331.56
3.75%	15,741.37	11,656.46	10,383.06	8,605.27	6,254.11	5,098.84	4,421.53	3,982.79	3,679.98	3,461.72
4.00%	15,838.21	11,755.17	10,482.78	8,707.08	6,361.32	5,211.43	4,539.40	4,105.77	3,807.86	3,594.27
4.25%	15,935.42	11,854.40	10,583.09	8,809.63	6,469.59	5,325.42	4,658.95	4,230.68	3,937.89	3,729.13
4.50%	16,033.00	11,954.14	10,683.98	8,912.90	6,578.94	5,440.78	4,780.16	4,357.49	4,070.01	3,866.24
4.75%	16,130.94	12,054.39	10,785.46	9,016.91	6,689.35	5,557.52	4,903.01	4,486.17	4,204.17	4,005.52
5.00%	16,229.26	12,155.16	10,887.53	9,121.63	6,800.83	5,675.62	5,027.47	4,616.67	4,340.31	4,146.89
5.25%	16,327.95	12,256.44	10,990.18	9,227.09	6,913.35	5,795.06	5,153.53	4,748.95	4,478.39	4,290.28
5.50%	16,427.00	12,358.24	11,093.42	9,333.26	7,026.92	5,915.83	5,281.15	4,882.99	4,618.34	4,435.62
5.75%	16,526.42	12,460.54	11,197.23	9,440.15	7,141.53	6,037.92	5,410.32	5,018.73	4,760.11	4,582.83
6.00%	16,626.21	12,563.36	11,301.63	9,547.76	7,257.17	6,161.31	5,540.99	5,156.13	4,903.63	4,731.84
6.25%	16,726.37	12,666.68	11,406.61	9,656.09	7,373.84	6,285.98	5,673.16	5,295.17	5,048.86	4,882.56
6.50%	16,826.89	12,770.52	11,512.16	9,765.13	7,491.52	6,411.93	5,806.78	5,435.79	5,195.73	5,034.93
6.75%	16,927.78	12,874.86	11,618.29	9,874.87	7,610.22	6,539.13	5,941.84	5,577.94	5,344.18	5,188.87
7.00%	17,029.03	12,979.70	11,725.00	9,985.33	7,729.92	6,667.57	6,078.30	5,721.60	5,494.16	5,344.31
7.25%	17,130.65	13,085.06	11,832.28	10,096.49	7,850.62	6,797.23	6,216.14	5,866.72	5,645.62	5,501.18
7.50%	17,232.64	13,190.92	11,940.13	10,208.35	7,972.31	6,928.10	6,355.32	6,013.24	5,798.49	5,659.41
7.75%	17,334.99	13,297.28	12,048.55	10,320.91	8,094.97	7,060.16	6,495.83	6,161.15	5,952.71	5,818.93
8.00%	17,437.70	13,404.14	12,157.54	10,434.17	8,218.61	7,193.38	6,637.62	6,310.38	6,108.24	5,979.68
8.25%	17,540.78	13,511.51	12,267.10	10,548.13	8,343.21	7,327.76	6,780.67	6,460.89	6,265.02	6,141.59
8.50%	17,644.22	13,619.38	12,377.23	10,662.77	8,468.76	7,463.28	6,924.95	6,612.66	6,423.00	6,304.61
8.75%	17,748.02	13,727.74	12,487.92	10,778.10	8,595.26	7,599.91	7,070.44	6,765.62	6,582.12	6,468.67
9.00%	17,852.19	13,836.61	12,599.17	10,894.12	8,722.69	7,737.64	7,217.09	6,919.75	6,742.34	6,633.71
9.25%	17,956.71	13,945.97	12,710.99	11,010.81	8,851.05	7,876.45	7,364.88	7,075.01	6,903.60	6,799.68
9.50%	18,061.60	14,055.82	12,823.36	11,128.19	8,980.33	8,016.33	7,513.79	7,231.35	7,065.86	6,966.53
9.75%	18,166.85	14,166.17	12,936.29	11,246.24	9,110.52	8,157.24	7,663.78	7,388.73	7,229.07	7,134.20
10.00%	18,272.46	14,277.02	13,049.78	11,364.96	9,241.60	8,299.19	7,814.83	7,547.12	7,393.18	7,302.65
10.25%	18,378.43	14,388.35	13,163.82	11,484.35	9,373.58	8,442.13	7,966.90	7,706.47	7,558.16	7,471.84
10.50%	18,484.75	14,500.18	13,278.41	11,604.41	9,506.43	8,586.07	8,119.96	7,866.76	7,723.95	7,641.70
10.75%	18,591.44	14,612.49	13,393.56	11,725.13	9,640.15	8,730.97	8,274.00	8,027.94	7,890.52	7,812.22

$860,000   11.00 - 20.75%   5 - 40 Years

	5	7	8	10	15	20	25	30	35	40
11.00%	18,698.48	14,725.30	13,509.25	11,846.50	9,774.73	8,876.82	8,428.97	8,189.98	8,057.84	7,983.33
11.25%	18,805.88	14,838.58	13,625.48	11,968.53	9,910.16	9,023.60	8,584.86	8,352.85	8,225.85	8,155.01
11.50%	18,913.64	14,952.36	13,742.26	12,091.21	10,046.43	9,171.29	8,741.63	8,516.51	8,394.52	8,327.22
11.75%	19,021.76	15,066.61	13,859.58	12,214.53	10,183.53	9,319.88	8,899.26	8,680.92	8,563.83	8,499.93
12.00%	19,130.23	15,181.35	13,977.44	12,338.50	10,321.45	9,469.34	9,057.73	8,846.07	8,733.73	8,673.10
12.25%	19,239.05	15,296.57	14,095.84	12,463.11	10,460.17	9,619.66	9,217.00	9,011.91	8,904.19	8,846.70
12.50%	19,348.23	15,412.27	14,214.78	12,588.35	10,599.69	9,770.81	9,377.05	9,178.42	9,075.19	9,020.71
12.75%	19,457.76	15,528.44	14,334.24	12,714.22	10,740.00	9,922.78	9,537.85	9,345.56	9,246.69	9,195.09
13.00%	19,567.64	15,645.09	14,454.24	12,840.72	10,881.08	10,075.55	9,699.38	9,513.32	9,418.66	9,369.82
13.25%	19,677.88	15,762.21	14,574.77	12,967.85	11,022.93	10,229.10	9,861.62	9,681.65	9,591.08	9,544.88
13.50%	19,788.47	15,879.81	14,695.82	13,095.59	11,165.54	10,383.42	10,024.55	9,850.54	9,763.93	9,720.25
13.75%	19,899.41	15,997.87	14,817.39	13,223.95	11,308.89	10,538.49	10,188.13	10,019.97	9,937.17	9,895.89
14.00%	20,010.70	16,116.41	14,939.49	13,352.91	11,452.98	10,694.28	10,352.34	10,189.90	10,110.79	10,071.80
14.25%	20,122.33	16,235.41	15,062.11	13,482.49	11,597.79	10,850.78	10,517.18	10,360.31	10,284.76	10,247.96
14.50%	20,234.32	16,354.88	15,185.24	13,612.66	11,743.31	11,007.98	10,682.60	10,531.18	10,459.07	10,424.34
14.75%	20,346.66	16,474.81	15,308.89	13,743.44	11,889.53	11,165.86	10,848.60	10,702.49	10,633.68	10,600.94
15.00%	20,459.34	16,595.21	15,433.05	13,874.81	12,036.45	11,324.39	11,015.14	10,874.22	10,808.59	10,777.73
15.25%	20,572.37	16,716.06	15,557.72	14,006.76	12,184.05	11,483.57	11,182.22	11,046.34	10,983.78	10,954.70
15.50%	20,685.74	16,837.38	15,682.89	14,139.31	12,332.32	11,643.37	11,349.81	11,218.85	11,159.23	11,131.84
15.75%	20,799.46	16,959.15	15,808.57	14,272.43	12,481.25	11,803.79	11,517.89	11,391.71	11,334.92	11,309.14
16.00%	20,913.53	17,081.37	15,934.76	14,406.13	12,630.83	11,964.80	11,686.44	11,564.91	11,510.84	11,486.58
16.25%	21,027.94	17,204.05	16,061.44	14,540.40	12,781.05	12,126.39	11,855.45	11,738.44	11,686.97	11,664.15
16.50%	21,142.69	17,327.18	16,188.62	14,675.24	12,931.89	12,288.55	12,024.90	11,912.27	11,863.30	11,841.85
16.75%	21,257.78	17,450.76	16,316.29	14,810.64	13,083.36	12,451.25	12,194.77	12,086.40	12,039.83	12,019.66
17.00%	21,373.22	17,574.79	16,444.45	14,946.60	13,235.44	12,614.48	12,365.05	12,260.81	12,216.52	12,197.58
17.25%	21,488.99	17,699.27	16,573.10	15,083.11	13,388.11	12,778.24	12,535.72	12,435.48	12,393.39	12,375.60
17.50%	21,605.10	17,824.18	16,702.24	15,220.17	13,541.37	12,942.50	12,706.76	12,610.40	12,570.41	12,553.71
17.75%	21,721.56	17,949.54	16,831.86	15,357.78	13,695.21	13,107.25	12,878.15	12,785.55	12,747.57	12,731.90
18.00%	21,838.35	18,075.34	16,961.96	15,495.93	13,849.62	13,272.48	13,049.90	12,960.93	12,924.87	12,910.17
18.25%	21,955.48	18,201.58	17,092.54	15,634.61	14,004.59	13,438.17	13,221.97	13,136.53	13,102.30	13,088.51
18.50%	22,072.94	18,328.25	17,223.60	15,773.82	14,160.10	13,604.31	13,394.36	13,312.32	13,279.84	13,266.91
18.75%	22,190.74	18,455.36	17,355.13	15,913.56	14,316.15	13,770.89	13,567.06	13,488.31	13,457.50	13,445.38
19.00%	22,308.87	18,582.90	17,487.12	16,053.82	14,472.73	13,937.89	13,740.05	13,664.48	13,635.25	13,623.90
19.25%	22,427.34	18,710.87	17,619.59	16,194.60	14,629.83	14,105.30	13,913.32	13,840.81	13,813.11	13,802.48
19.50%	22,546.14	18,839.26	17,752.52	16,335.89	14,787.44	14,273.12	14,086.85	14,017.31	13,991.06	13,981.10
19.75%	22,665.28	18,968.08	17,885.90	16,477.69	14,945.55	14,441.32	14,260.65	14,193.96	14,169.08	14,159.76
20.00%	22,784.74	19,097.33	18,019.75	16,619.99	15,104.15	14,609.89	14,434.69	14,370.76	14,347.19	14,338.47
20.25%	22,904.53	19,227.00	18,154.06	16,762.79	15,263.23	14,778.83	14,608.96	14,547.69	14,525.38	14,517.21
20.50%	23,024.66	19,357.09	18,288.81	16,906.08	15,422.78	14,948.13	14,783.46	14,724.76	14,703.63	14,695.99
20.75%	23,145.11	19,487.59	18,424.02	17,049.86	15,582.80	15,117.76	14,958.18	14,901.94	14,881.94	14,874.80

$870,000   1.00 - 10.75%   5 - 40 Years

	5	7	8	10	15	20	25	30	35	40
1.00%	14,871.56	10,728.18	9,433.61	7,621.56	5,206.90	4,001.08	3,278.79	2,798.26	2,455.89	2,199.85
1.25%	14,965.39	10,822.27	9,527.89	7,716.33	5,303.12	4,098.86	3,378.18	2,899.29	2,558.55	2,304.15
1.50%	15,059.60	10,916.87	9,622.78	7,811.86	5,400.46	4,198.15	3,479.45	3,002.55	2,663.80	2,411.40
1.75%	15,154.19	11,012.01	9,718.27	7,908.14	5,498.93	4,298.92	3,582.57	3,108.02	2,771.63	2,521.56
2.00%	15,249.15	11,107.67	9,814.36	8,005.17	5,598.53	4,401.19	3,687.53	3,215.69	2,881.99	2,634.58
2.25%	15,344.49	11,203.86	9,911.05	8,102.95	5,699.24	4,504.93	3,794.34	3,325.54	2,994.86	2,750.44
2.50%	15,440.20	11,300.57	10,008.34	8,201.48	5,801.07	4,610.16	3,902.97	3,437.55	3,110.21	2,869.07
2.75%	15,536.29	11,397.81	10,106.24	8,300.76	5,904.01	4,716.85	4,013.40	3,551.70	3,228.00	2,990.43
3.00%	15,632.76	11,495.57	10,204.73	8,400.78	6,008.06	4,825.00	4,125.64	3,667.96	3,348.20	3,114.46
3.25%	15,729.60	11,593.86	10,303.82	8,501.56	6,113.22	4,934.60	4,239.65	3,786.29	3,470.75	3,241.11
3.50%	15,826.82	11,692.67	10,403.51	8,603.07	6,219.48	5,045.65	4,355.43	3,906.69	3,595.63	3,370.30
3.75%	15,924.41	11,792.00	10,503.79	8,705.33	6,326.84	5,158.13	4,472.94	4,029.11	3,722.77	3,501.98
4.00%	16,022.37	11,891.86	10,604.67	8,808.33	6,435.28	5,272.03	4,592.18	4,153.51	3,852.14	3,636.06
4.25%	16,120.71	11,992.24	10,706.14	8,912.07	6,544.82	5,387.34	4,713.12	4,279.88	3,983.68	3,772.50
4.50%	16,219.43	12,093.14	10,808.21	9,016.54	6,655.44	5,504.05	4,835.74	4,408.16	4,117.33	3,911.20
4.75%	16,318.51	12,194.56	10,910.88	9,121.75	6,767.14	5,622.15	4,960.02	4,538.33	4,253.05	4,052.09
5.00%	16,417.97	12,296.50	11,014.13	9,227.70	6,879.90	5,741.61	5,085.93	4,670.35	4,390.78	4,195.11
5.25%	16,517.81	12,398.96	11,117.98	9,334.38	6,993.74	5,862.44	5,213.46	4,804.17	4,530.46	4,340.17
5.50%	16,618.01	12,501.94	11,222.41	9,441.79	7,108.63	5,984.62	5,342.56	4,939.76	4,672.04	4,487.20
5.75%	16,718.59	12,605.43	11,327.43	9,549.92	7,224.57	6,108.13	5,473.23	5,077.08	4,815.46	4,636.12
6.00%	16,819.54	12,709.44	11,433.04	9,658.78	7,341.55	6,232.95	5,605.42	5,216.09	4,960.65	4,786.86
6.25%	16,920.86	12,813.97	11,539.24	9,768.37	7,459.58	6,359.08	5,739.12	5,356.74	5,107.57	4,939.33
6.50%	17,022.55	12,919.01	11,646.02	9,878.67	7,578.63	6,486.49	5,874.30	5,498.99	5,256.14	5,093.47
6.75%	17,124.61	13,024.56	11,753.39	9,989.70	7,698.71	6,615.17	6,010.93	5,642.80	5,406.32	5,249.20
7.00%	17,227.04	13,130.63	11,861.33	10,101.44	7,819.81	6,745.10	6,148.98	5,788.13	5,558.05	5,406.45
7.25%	17,329.84	13,237.21	11,969.86	10,213.89	7,941.91	6,876.27	6,288.42	5,934.93	5,711.27	5,565.15
7.50%	17,433.02	13,344.30	12,078.97	10,327.05	8,065.01	7,008.66	6,429.22	6,083.17	5,865.91	5,725.22
7.75%	17,536.55	13,451.90	12,188.65	10,440.92	8,189.10	7,142.25	6,571.36	6,232.79	6,021.93	5,886.59
8.00%	17,640.46	13,560.01	12,298.91	10,555.50	8,314.17	7,277.03	6,714.80	6,383.75	6,179.27	6,049.21
8.25%	17,744.74	13,668.62	12,409.75	10,670.78	8,440.22	7,412.97	6,859.52	6,536.02	6,337.87	6,213.01
8.50%	17,849.38	13,777.74	12,521.15	10,786.75	8,567.23	7,550.06	7,005.48	6,689.55	6,497.69	6,377.92
8.75%	17,954.39	13,887.37	12,633.13	10,903.43	8,695.20	7,688.28	7,152.65	6,844.29	6,658.66	6,543.88
9.00%	18,059.77	13,997.50	12,745.68	11,020.79	8,824.12	7,827.62	7,301.01	7,000.22	6,820.74	6,710.85
9.25%	18,165.51	14,108.13	12,858.79	11,138.85	8,953.97	7,968.04	7,450.52	7,157.28	6,983.88	6,878.75
9.50%	18,271.62	14,219.26	12,972.47	11,257.59	9,084.75	8,109.54	7,601.16	7,315.43	7,148.02	7,047.54
9.75%	18,378.09	14,330.90	13,086.72	11,377.01	9,216.46	8,252.10	7,752.90	7,474.64	7,313.13	7,217.16
10.00%	18,484.93	14,443.03	13,201.52	11,497.11	9,349.06	8,395.69	7,905.70	7,634.87	7,479.15	7,387.57
10.25%	18,592.13	14,555.66	13,316.89	11,617.89	9,482.57	8,540.30	8,059.53	7,796.08	7,646.04	7,558.72
10.50%	18,699.69	14,668.79	13,432.81	11,739.34	9,616.97	8,685.91	8,214.38	7,958.23	7,813.77	7,730.56
10.75%	18,807.62	14,782.41	13,549.30	11,861.47	9,752.25	8,832.49	8,370.21	8,121.29	7,982.28	7,903.06

$870,000   11.00 - 20.75%   5 - 40 Years

	5	7	8	10	15	20	25	30	35	40
11.00%	18,915.91	14,896.52	13,666.33	11,984.25	9,888.39	8,980.04	8,526.98	8,285.21	8,151.53	8,076.16
11.25%	19,024.56	15,011.13	13,783.92	12,107.70	10,025.40	9,128.53	8,684.68	8,449.97	8,321.50	8,249.84
11.50%	19,133.57	15,126.22	13,902.06	12,231.80	10,163.25	9,277.94	8,843.28	8,615.54	8,492.13	8,424.05
11.75%	19,242.94	15,241.81	14,020.74	12,356.56	10,301.94	9,428.25	9,002.74	8,781.86	8,663.41	8,598.77
12.00%	19,352.67	15,357.88	14,139.97	12,481.97	10,441.46	9,579.45	9,163.05	8,948.93	8,835.28	8,773.95
12.25%	19,462.76	15,474.44	14,259.75	12,608.03	10,581.80	9,731.51	9,324.17	9,116.70	9,007.73	8,949.57
12.50%	19,573.21	15,591.48	14,380.06	12,734.73	10,722.94	9,884.42	9,486.08	9,285.14	9,180.71	9,125.60
12.75%	19,684.01	15,709.00	14,500.92	12,862.06	10,864.88	10,038.16	9,648.75	9,454.23	9,354.21	9,302.01
13.00%	19,795.17	15,827.01	14,622.31	12,990.03	11,007.61	10,192.71	9,812.17	9,623.94	9,528.18	9,478.77
13.25%	19,906.69	15,945.49	14,744.24	13,118.64	11,151.11	10,348.05	9,976.29	9,794.23	9,702.61	9,655.87
13.50%	20,018.57	16,064.46	14,866.70	13,247.86	11,295.37	10,504.16	10,141.11	9,965.09	9,877.46	9,833.27
13.75%	20,130.80	16,183.90	14,989.69	13,377.71	11,440.39	10,661.03	10,306.59	10,136.48	10,052.72	10,010.96
14.00%	20,243.38	16,303.81	15,113.21	13,508.18	11,586.15	10,818.63	10,472.72	10,308.38	10,228.36	10,188.92
14.25%	20,356.31	16,424.20	15,237.25	13,639.26	11,732.64	10,976.95	10,639.47	10,480.78	10,404.35	10,367.12
14.50%	20,469.60	16,545.05	15,361.81	13,770.95	11,879.86	11,135.98	10,806.82	10,653.64	10,580.68	10,545.56
14.75%	20,583.25	16,666.38	15,486.90	13,903.25	12,027.78	11,295.69	10,974.74	10,826.94	10,757.33	10,724.20
15.00%	20,697.24	16,788.18	15,612.50	14,036.14	12,176.41	11,456.07	11,143.23	11,000.66	10,934.28	10,903.05
15.25%	20,811.58	16,910.44	15,738.62	14,169.63	12,325.72	11,617.10	11,312.25	11,174.79	11,111.50	11,082.08
15.50%	20,926.28	17,033.16	15,865.25	14,303.72	12,475.72	11,778.76	11,481.78	11,349.30	11,288.99	11,261.28
15.75%	21,041.32	17,156.35	15,992.39	14,438.39	12,626.38	11,941.04	11,651.82	11,524.17	11,466.72	11,440.64
16.00%	21,156.71	17,280.00	16,120.04	14,573.64	12,777.70	12,103.93	11,822.33	11,699.39	11,644.68	11,620.14
16.25%	21,272.45	17,404.10	16,248.20	14,709.47	12,929.66	12,267.40	11,993.31	11,874.93	11,822.86	11,799.78
16.50%	21,388.53	17,528.66	16,376.85	14,845.88	13,082.26	12,431.44	12,164.73	12,050.79	12,001.25	11,979.55
16.75%	21,504.96	17,653.68	16,506.01	14,982.86	13,235.49	12,596.03	12,336.57	12,226.94	12,179.82	12,159.43
17.00%	21,621.74	17,779.15	16,635.67	15,120.40	13,389.34	12,761.16	12,508.83	12,403.38	12,358.58	12,339.42
17.25%	21,738.86	17,905.07	16,765.81	15,258.50	13,543.79	12,926.82	12,681.48	12,580.08	12,537.50	12,519.50
17.50%	21,856.33	18,031.44	16,896.45	15,397.15	13,698.83	13,092.99	12,854.51	12,757.03	12,716.58	12,699.68
17.75%	21,974.13	18,158.26	17,027.58	15,536.36	13,854.46	13,259.66	13,027.90	12,934.22	12,895.80	12,879.94
18.00%	22,092.28	18,285.52	17,159.20	15,676.11	14,010.66	13,426.81	13,201.64	13,111.64	13,075.16	13,060.29
18.25%	22,210.77	18,413.22	17,291.29	15,816.41	14,167.43	13,594.43	13,375.72	13,289.28	13,254.65	13,240.70
18.50%	22,329.60	18,541.37	17,423.87	15,957.24	14,324.75	13,762.50	13,550.11	13,467.12	13,434.26	13,421.18
18.75%	22,448.77	18,669.95	17,556.93	16,098.60	14,482.62	13,931.01	13,724.82	13,645.15	13,613.98	13,601.72
19.00%	22,568.28	18,798.98	17,690.46	16,240.49	14,641.02	14,099.96	13,899.82	13,823.36	13,793.80	13,782.32
19.25%	22,688.13	18,928.43	17,824.47	16,382.91	14,799.95	14,269.32	14,075.10	14,001.75	13,973.73	13,962.97
19.50%	22,808.31	19,058.32	17,958.94	16,525.84	14,959.39	14,439.08	14,250.65	14,180.30	14,153.74	14,143.67
19.75%	22,928.83	19,188.64	18,093.88	16,669.29	15,119.34	14,609.24	14,426.47	14,359.01	14,333.84	14,324.41
20.00%	23,049.68	19,319.39	18,229.28	16,813.24	15,279.78	14,779.77	14,602.53	14,537.86	14,514.02	14,505.20
20.25%	23,170.87	19,450.57	18,365.15	16,957.70	15,440.71	14,950.68	14,778.83	14,716.85	14,694.27	14,686.02
20.50%	23,292.39	19,582.17	18,501.47	17,102.66	15,602.12	15,121.94	14,955.36	14,895.97	14,874.60	14,866.88
20.75%	23,414.24	19,714.19	18,638.25	17,248.11	15,763.99	15,293.55	15,132.11	15,075.22	15,054.99	15,047.76

	5	7	8	10	15	20	25	30	35	40
1.00%	15,042.50	10,851.50	9,542.04	7,709.16	5,266.75	4,047.07	3,316.48	2,830.43	2,484.11	2,225.13
1.25%	15,137.41	10,946.66	9,637.41	7,805.03	5,364.08	4,145.98	3,417.01	2,932.61	2,587.96	2,330.64
1.50%	15,232.70	11,042.35	9,733.39	7,901.65	5,462.54	4,246.40	3,519.44	3,037.06	2,694.42	2,439.12
1.75%	15,328.37	11,138.58	9,829.97	7,999.04	5,562.14	4,348.33	3,623.74	3,143.74	2,803.48	2,550.54
2.00%	15,424.43	11,235.34	9,927.17	8,097.18	5,662.88	4,451.77	3,729.92	3,252.65	2,915.11	2,664.87
2.25%	15,520.86	11,332.64	10,024.97	8,196.09	5,764.75	4,556.71	3,837.95	3,363.77	3,029.28	2,782.05
2.50%	15,617.68	11,430.46	10,123.38	8,295.75	5,867.75	4,663.15	3,947.83	3,477.06	3,145.96	2,902.05
2.75%	15,714.87	11,528.82	10,222.40	8,396.17	5,971.87	4,771.06	4,059.54	3,592.52	3,265.10	3,024.80
3.00%	15,812.45	11,627.70	10,322.02	8,497.35	6,077.12	4,880.46	4,173.06	3,710.12	3,386.68	3,150.26
3.25%	15,910.40	11,727.12	10,422.25	8,599.27	6,183.49	4,991.32	4,288.38	3,829.82	3,510.65	3,278.36
3.50%	16,008.74	11,827.07	10,523.09	8,701.96	6,290.97	5,103.65	4,405.49	3,951.59	3,636.96	3,409.04
3.75%	16,107.45	11,927.54	10,624.52	8,805.39	6,399.56	5,217.42	4,524.35	4,075.42	3,765.56	3,542.23
4.00%	16,206.54	12,028.55	10,726.56	8,909.57	6,509.25	5,332.63	4,644.96	4,201.25	3,896.42	3,677.86
4.25%	16,306.01	12,130.08	10,829.20	9,014.50	6,620.05	5,449.26	4,767.30	4,329.07	4,029.47	3,815.86
4.50%	16,405.86	12,232.14	10,932.45	9,120.18	6,731.94	5,567.31	4,891.33	4,458.83	4,164.66	3,956.15
4.75%	16,506.08	12,334.73	11,036.29	9,226.60	6,844.92	5,686.77	5,017.03	4,590.50	4,301.94	4,098.67
5.00%	16,606.69	12,437.84	11,140.73	9,333.77	6,958.98	5,807.61	5,144.39	4,724.03	4,441.25	4,243.33
5.25%	16,707.67	12,541.48	11,245.77	9,441.67	7,074.12	5,929.83	5,273.38	4,859.39	4,582.54	4,390.06
5.50%	16,809.02	12,645.64	11,351.40	9,550.31	7,190.33	6,053.41	5,403.97	4,996.54	4,725.74	4,538.78
5.75%	16,910.76	12,750.32	11,457.63	9,659.69	7,307.61	6,178.33	5,536.14	5,135.44	4,870.81	4,689.41
6.00%	17,012.87	12,855.53	11,564.46	9,769.80	7,425.94	6,304.59	5,669.85	5,276.04	5,017.67	4,841.88
6.25%	17,115.35	12,961.26	11,671.88	9,880.65	7,545.32	6,432.17	5,805.09	5,418.31	5,166.27	4,996.11
6.50%	17,218.21	13,067.50	11,779.88	9,992.22	7,665.74	6,561.04	5,941.82	5,562.20	5,316.56	5,152.02
6.75%	17,321.45	13,174.27	11,888.48	10,104.52	7,787.20	6,691.20	6,080.02	5,707.66	5,468.47	5,309.54
7.00%	17,425.05	13,281.56	11,997.67	10,217.55	7,909.69	6,822.63	6,219.66	5,854.66	5,621.94	5,468.60
7.25%	17,529.04	13,389.36	12,107.45	10,331.29	8,033.19	6,955.31	6,360.70	6,003.15	5,776.91	5,629.11
7.50%	17,633.39	13,497.68	12,217.81	10,445.76	8,157.71	7,089.22	6,503.12	6,153.09	5,933.33	5,791.02
7.75%	17,738.12	13,606.52	12,328.75	10,560.94	8,283.23	7,224.35	6,646.89	6,304.43	6,091.15	5,954.25
8.00%	17,843.23	13,715.87	12,440.28	10,676.83	8,409.74	7,360.67	6,791.98	6,457.13	6,250.30	6,118.74
8.25%	17,948.70	13,825.73	12,552.39	10,793.43	8,537.24	7,498.18	6,938.36	6,611.15	6,410.72	6,284.42
8.50%	18,054.55	13,936.11	12,665.07	10,910.74	8,665.71	7,636.84	7,086.00	6,766.44	6,572.37	6,451.23
8.75%	18,160.76	14,046.99	12,778.34	11,028.75	8,795.15	7,776.65	7,234.86	6,922.96	6,735.20	6,619.10
9.00%	18,267.35	14,158.39	12,892.18	11,147.47	8,925.55	7,917.59	7,384.93	7,080.68	6,899.14	6,787.98
9.25%	18,374.31	14,270.29	13,006.59	11,266.88	9,056.89	8,059.63	7,536.16	7,239.54	7,064.15	6,957.81
9.50%	18,481.64	14,382.70	13,121.58	11,386.99	9,189.18	8,202.75	7,688.53	7,399.52	7,230.18	7,128.54
9.75%	18,589.33	14,495.62	13,237.14	11,507.78	9,322.39	8,346.95	7,842.01	7,560.56	7,397.19	7,300.12
10.00%	18,697.40	14,609.04	13,353.26	11,629.26	9,456.53	8,492.19	7,996.57	7,722.63	7,565.12	7,472.48
10.25%	18,805.83	14,722.97	13,469.96	11,751.43	9,591.57	8,638.46	8,152.17	7,885.69	7,733.93	7,645.60
10.50%	18,914.63	14,837.39	13,587.21	11,874.28	9,727.51	8,785.74	8,308.80	8,049.71	7,903.58	7,819.42
10.75%	19,023.80	14,952.32	13,705.03	11,997.80	9,864.34	8,934.01	8,466.42	8,214.64	8,074.03	7,993.90

$880,000   11.00 - 20.75%   5 - 40 Years

	5	7	8	10	15	20	25	30	35	40
11.00%	19,133.33	15,067.74	13,823.41	12,122.00	10,002.05	9,083.26	8,625.00	8,380.45	8,245.23	8,168.99
11.25%	19,243.23	15,183.67	13,942.35	12,246.87	10,140.63	9,233.45	8,784.51	8,547.10	8,417.15	8,344.66
11.50%	19,353.49	15,300.09	14,061.85	12,372.40	10,280.07	9,384.58	8,944.93	8,714.56	8,589.74	8,520.88
11.75%	19,464.12	15,417.00	14,181.90	12,498.59	10,420.36	9,536.62	9,106.22	8,882.81	8,762.99	8,697.60
12.00%	19,575.11	15,534.40	14,302.50	12,625.44	10,561.48	9,689.56	9,268.37	9,051.79	8,936.84	8,874.80
12.25%	19,686.47	15,652.30	14,423.65	12,752.95	10,703.43	9,843.37	9,431.35	9,221.49	9,111.27	9,052.44
12.50%	19,798.19	15,770.69	14,545.35	12,881.10	10,846.19	9,998.04	9,595.12	9,391.87	9,286.24	9,230.49
12.75%	19,910.26	15,889.57	14,667.60	13,009.90	10,989.77	10,153.54	9,759.66	9,562.90	9,461.73	9,408.93
13.00%	20,022.70	16,008.93	14,790.38	13,139.35	11,134.13	10,309.87	9,924.95	9,734.56	9,637.70	9,587.72
13.25%	20,135.50	16,128.78	14,913.71	13,269.42	11,279.28	10,466.99	10,090.96	9,906.81	9,814.13	9,766.86
13.50%	20,248.66	16,249.11	15,037.58	13,400.14	11,425.20	10,624.90	10,257.67	10,079.63	9,991.00	9,946.30
13.75%	20,362.18	16,369.92	15,161.98	13,531.48	11,571.89	10,783.57	10,425.06	10,252.99	10,168.27	10,126.03
14.00%	20,476.06	16,491.21	15,286.92	13,663.45	11,719.32	10,942.98	10,593.10	10,426.87	10,345.92	10,306.03
14.25%	20,590.30	16,612.98	15,412.39	13,796.03	11,867.50	11,103.13	10,761.76	10,601.25	10,523.94	10,486.28
14.50%	20,704.89	16,735.23	15,538.39	13,929.24	12,016.41	11,263.98	10,931.03	10,776.09	10,702.30	10,666.77
14.75%	20,819.84	16,857.95	15,664.91	14,063.05	12,166.03	11,425.53	11,100.89	10,951.39	10,880.98	10,847.47
15.00%	20,935.14	16,981.14	15,791.96	14,197.48	12,316.37	11,587.75	11,271.31	11,127.11	11,059.96	11,028.37
15.25%	21,050.80	17,104.81	15,919.53	14,332.50	12,467.40	11,750.63	11,442.27	11,303.23	11,239.22	11,209.46
15.50%	21,166.81	17,228.95	16,047.61	14,468.13	12,619.11	11,914.15	11,613.76	11,479.75	11,418.75	11,390.72
15.75%	21,283.17	17,353.55	16,176.22	14,604.35	12,771.51	12,078.30	11,785.75	11,656.63	11,598.52	11,572.14
16.00%	21,399.89	17,478.62	16,305.33	14,741.15	12,924.57	12,243.05	11,958.22	11,833.86	11,778.53	11,753.71
16.25%	21,516.96	17,604.15	16,434.96	14,878.55	13,078.28	12,408.40	12,131.16	12,011.42	11,958.76	11,935.41
16.50%	21,634.38	17,730.14	16,565.09	15,016.52	13,232.64	12,574.33	12,304.55	12,189.30	12,139.19	12,117.24
16.75%	21,752.15	17,856.60	16,695.74	15,155.07	13,387.63	12,740.81	12,478.37	12,367.48	12,319.82	12,299.19
17.00%	21,870.27	17,983.51	16,826.88	15,294.19	13,543.24	12,907.84	12,652.61	12,545.94	12,500.63	12,481.25
17.25%	21,988.73	18,110.88	16,958.52	15,433.88	13,699.46	13,075.41	12,827.24	12,724.67	12,681.61	12,663.40
17.50%	22,107.55	18,238.70	17,090.66	15,574.13	13,856.29	13,243.49	13,002.26	12,903.66	12,862.74	12,845.65
17.75%	22,226.71	18,366.97	17,223.30	15,714.94	14,013.71	13,412.07	13,177.65	13,082.89	13,044.03	13,027.99
18.00%	22,346.22	18,495.70	17,356.43	15,856.30	14,171.71	13,581.14	13,353.38	13,262.35	13,225.45	13,210.40
18.25%	22,466.07	18,624.87	17,490.05	15,998.20	14,330.27	13,750.69	13,529.46	13,442.03	13,407.00	13,392.89
18.50%	22,586.26	18,754.49	17,624.15	16,140.66	14,489.41	13,920.69	13,705.86	13,621.91	13,588.67	13,575.45
18.75%	22,706.80	18,884.55	17,758.73	16,283.64	14,649.09	14,091.14	13,882.57	13,801.99	13,770.46	13,758.06
19.00%	22,827.69	19,015.06	17,893.80	16,427.17	14,809.31	14,262.03	14,059.58	13,982.25	13,952.35	13,940.74
19.25%	22,948.91	19,146.00	18,029.35	16,571.22	14,970.06	14,433.33	14,236.88	14,162.69	14,134.34	14,123.47
19.50%	23,070.47	19,277.38	18,165.36	16,715.79	15,131.34	14,605.05	14,414.45	14,343.30	14,316.43	14,306.24
19.75%	23,192.38	19,409.20	18,301.86	16,860.89	15,293.12	14,777.16	14,592.29	14,524.06	14,498.60	14,489.06
20.00%	23,314.62	19,541.46	18,438.82	17,006.50	15,455.41	14,949.66	14,770.38	14,704.96	14,680.85	14,671.92
20.25%	23,437.20	19,674.14	18,576.24	17,152.62	15,618.19	15,122.53	14,948.70	14,886.01	14,863.17	14,854.82
20.50%	23,560.12	19,807.25	18,714.13	17,299.24	15,781.45	15,295.76	15,127.26	15,067.19	15,045.57	15,037.76
20.75%	23,683.37	19,940.79	18,852.48	17,446.37	15,945.19	15,469.34	15,306.04	15,248.50	15,228.03	15,220.73

$890,000   1.00 - 10.75%   5 - 40 Years

	5	7	8	10	15	20	25	30	35	40
1.00%	15,213.44	10,974.81	9,650.47	7,796.77	5,326.60	4,093.06	3,354.16	2,862.59	2,512.34	2,250.42
1.25%	15,309.43	11,071.05	9,746.92	7,893.72	5,425.03	4,193.09	3,455.84	2,965.94	2,617.37	2,357.12
1.50%	15,405.80	11,167.84	9,843.99	7,991.44	5,524.61	4,294.65	3,559.43	3,071.57	2,725.04	2,466.84
1.75%	15,502.56	11,265.16	9,941.68	8,089.94	5,625.35	4,397.75	3,664.92	3,179.47	2,835.34	2,579.52
2.00%	15,599.71	11,363.02	10,039.98	8,189.20	5,727.23	4,502.36	3,772.30	3,289.61	2,948.24	2,695.15
2.25%	15,697.24	11,461.42	10,138.89	8,289.23	5,830.25	4,608.49	3,881.56	3,401.99	3,063.71	2,813.67
2.50%	15,795.15	11,560.35	10,238.42	8,390.02	5,934.42	4,716.14	3,992.69	3,516.58	3,181.71	2,935.03
2.75%	15,893.45	11,659.83	10,338.56	8,491.58	6,039.73	4,825.28	4,105.67	3,633.35	3,302.21	3,059.18
3.00%	15,992.13	11,759.84	10,439.32	8,593.91	6,146.18	4,935.92	4,220.48	3,752.28	3,425.17	3,186.06
3.25%	16,091.20	11,860.38	10,540.69	8,696.99	6,253.75	5,048.04	4,337.11	3,873.34	3,550.54	3,315.62
3.50%	16,190.65	11,961.47	10,642.67	8,800.84	6,362.45	5,161.64	4,455.55	3,996.50	3,678.29	3,447.78
3.75%	16,290.49	12,063.09	10,745.26	8,905.45	6,472.28	5,276.71	4,575.77	4,121.73	3,808.35	3,582.48
4.00%	16,390.70	12,165.24	10,848.46	9,010.82	6,583.22	5,393.22	4,697.75	4,249.00	3,940.70	3,719.65
4.25%	16,491.30	12,267.92	10,952.26	9,116.94	6,695.28	5,511.19	4,821.47	4,378.27	4,075.26	3,859.22
4.50%	16,592.29	12,371.14	11,056.68	9,223.82	6,808.44	5,630.58	4,946.91	4,509.50	4,211.98	4,001.11
4.75%	16,693.65	12,474.90	11,161.70	9,331.45	6,922.70	5,751.39	5,074.04	4,642.66	4,350.83	4,145.24
5.00%	16,795.40	12,579.18	11,267.33	9,439.83	7,038.06	5,873.61	5,202.85	4,777.71	4,491.72	4,291.55
5.25%	16,897.53	12,683.99	11,373.56	9,548.96	7,154.51	5,997.21	5,333.30	4,914.61	4,634.61	4,439.95
5.50%	17,000.03	12,789.34	11,480.40	9,658.84	7,272.04	6,122.20	5,465.38	5,053.32	4,779.44	4,590.36
5.75%	17,102.92	12,895.21	11,587.83	9,769.46	7,390.65	6,248.54	5,599.05	5,193.80	4,926.16	4,742.70
6.00%	17,206.19	13,001.61	11,695.87	9,880.82	7,510.33	6,376.24	5,734.28	5,336.00	5,074.69	4,896.90
6.25%	17,309.84	13,108.54	11,804.51	9,992.93	7,631.06	6,505.26	5,871.06	5,479.88	5,224.98	5,052.88
6.50%	17,413.87	13,216.00	11,913.75	10,105.77	7,752.86	6,635.60	6,009.34	5,625.41	5,376.97	5,210.57
6.75%	17,518.28	13,323.98	12,023.58	10,219.35	7,875.69	6,767.24	6,149.11	5,772.52	5,530.61	5,369.88
7.00%	17,623.07	13,432.49	12,134.01	10,333.65	7,999.57	6,900.16	6,290.33	5,921.19	5,685.82	5,530.74
7.25%	17,728.23	13,541.51	12,245.03	10,448.69	8,124.48	7,034.35	6,432.98	6,071.37	5,842.56	5,693.08
7.50%	17,833.77	13,651.07	12,356.64	10,564.46	8,250.41	7,169.78	6,577.02	6,223.01	6,000.76	5,856.83
7.75%	17,939.69	13,761.14	12,468.85	10,680.95	8,377.35	7,306.44	6,722.43	6,376.07	6,160.37	6,021.92
8.00%	18,045.99	13,871.73	12,581.64	10,798.16	8,505.30	7,444.32	6,869.16	6,530.50	6,321.32	6,188.27
8.25%	18,152.66	13,982.84	12,695.03	10,916.08	8,634.25	7,583.38	7,017.21	6,686.27	6,483.57	6,355.84
8.50%	18,259.71	14,094.47	12,808.99	11,034.73	8,764.18	7,723.63	7,166.52	6,843.33	6,647.06	6,524.54
8.75%	18,367.14	14,206.62	12,923.55	11,154.08	8,895.09	7,865.03	7,317.08	7,001.63	6,811.73	6,694.32
9.00%	18,474.94	14,319.28	13,038.68	11,274.14	9,026.97	8,007.56	7,468.85	7,161.14	6,977.54	6,865.12
9.25%	18,583.11	14,432.46	13,154.40	11,394.91	9,159.81	8,151.21	7,621.80	7,321.81	7,144.42	7,036.88
9.50%	18,691.66	14,546.14	13,270.69	11,516.38	9,293.60	8,295.97	7,775.90	7,483.60	7,312.34	7,209.55
9.75%	18,800.58	14,660.34	13,387.56	11,638.55	9,428.33	8,441.80	7,931.12	7,646.47	7,481.25	7,383.07
10.00%	18,909.87	14,775.05	13,505.01	11,761.42	9,563.99	8,588.69	8,087.44	7,810.39	7,651.08	7,557.40
10.25%	19,019.53	14,890.27	13,623.02	11,884.97	9,700.56	8,736.63	8,244.81	7,975.30	7,821.81	7,732.48
10.50%	19,129.57	15,006.00	13,741.61	12,009.21	9,838.05	8,885.58	8,403.22	8,141.18	7,993.39	7,908.28
10.75%	19,239.98	15,122.23	13,860.77	12,134.14	9,976.44	9,035.54	8,562.63	8,307.98	8,165.78	8,084.74

	5	7	8	10	15	20	25	30	35	40
11.00%	19,350.76	15,238.97	13,980.50	12,259.75	10,115.71	9,186.48	8,723.01	8,475.68	8,338.92	8,261.82
11.25%	19,461.90	15,356.21	14,100.79	12,386.04	10,255.87	9,338.38	8,884.33	8,644.23	8,512.80	8,439.49
11.50%	19,573.42	15,473.95	14,221.64	12,512.99	10,396.89	9,491.22	9,046.57	8,813.59	8,687.36	8,617.71
11.75%	19,685.31	15,592.19	14,343.06	12,640.62	10,538.77	9,644.99	9,209.70	8,983.75	8,862.57	8,796.44
12.00%	19,797.56	15,710.93	14,465.03	12,768.91	10,681.50	9,799.67	9,373.69	9,154.65	9,038.39	8,975.65
12.25%	19,910.18	15,830.17	14,587.56	12,897.87	10,825.06	9,955.23	9,538.52	9,326.28	9,214.80	9,155.31
12.50%	20,023.17	15,949.90	14,710.64	13,027.48	10,969.45	10,111.65	9,704.15	9,498.59	9,391.76	9,335.38
12.75%	20,136.52	16,070.13	14,834.27	13,157.74	11,114.65	10,268.92	9,870.57	9,671.57	9,569.25	9,515.85
13.00%	20,250.24	16,190.85	14,958.46	13,288.66	11,260.66	10,427.02	10,037.73	9,845.18	9,747.22	9,696.68
13.25%	20,364.32	16,312.06	15,083.19	13,420.21	11,407.45	10,585.93	10,205.63	10,019.38	9,925.66	9,877.84
13.50%	20,478.76	16,433.75	15,208.46	13,552.41	11,555.04	10,745.63	10,374.24	10,194.17	10,104.53	10,059.32
13.75%	20,593.57	16,555.94	15,334.28	13,685.25	11,703.39	10,906.11	10,543.53	10,369.50	10,283.82	10,241.10
14.00%	20,708.74	16,678.61	15,460.64	13,818.71	11,852.50	11,067.34	10,713.47	10,545.36	10,463.49	10,423.15
14.25%	20,824.28	16,801.76	15,587.53	13,952.81	12,002.36	11,229.30	10,884.06	10,721.72	10,643.53	10,605.45
14.50%	20,940.17	16,925.40	15,714.96	14,087.52	12,152.96	11,391.98	11,055.25	10,898.55	10,823.92	10,787.98
14.75%	21,056.42	17,049.52	15,842.92	14,222.86	12,304.28	11,555.36	11,227.04	11,075.83	11,004.63	10,970.74
15.00%	21,173.04	17,174.11	15,971.41	14,358.81	12,456.33	11,719.43	11,399.39	11,253.55	11,185.64	11,153.69
15.25%	21,290.01	17,299.18	16,100.43	14,495.37	12,609.07	11,884.16	11,572.30	11,431.68	11,366.94	11,336.84
15.50%	21,407.34	17,424.73	16,229.97	14,632.54	12,762.51	12,049.54	11,745.73	11,610.20	11,548.50	11,520.16
15.75%	21,525.03	17,550.75	16,360.04	14,770.30	12,916.64	12,215.55	11,919.68	11,789.09	11,730.32	11,703.64
16.00%	21,643.07	17,677.24	16,490.62	14,908.67	13,071.44	12,382.18	12,094.11	11,968.34	11,912.38	11,887.27
16.25%	21,761.47	17,804.20	16,621.72	15,047.62	13,226.90	12,549.41	12,269.02	12,147.92	12,094.65	12,071.04
16.50%	21,880.22	17,931.62	16,753.33	15,187.16	13,383.01	12,717.22	12,444.38	12,327.82	12,277.14	12,254.94
16.75%	21,999.33	18,059.51	16,885.46	15,327.29	13,539.76	12,885.59	12,620.17	12,508.02	12,459.82	12,438.95
17.00%	22,118.79	18,187.87	17,018.09	15,467.99	13,697.14	13,054.52	12,796.39	12,688.51	12,642.68	12,623.08
17.25%	22,238.61	18,316.68	17,151.23	15,609.27	13,855.14	13,223.99	12,973.01	12,869.27	12,825.72	12,807.31
17.50%	22,358.77	18,445.96	17,284.88	15,751.11	14,013.75	13,393.98	13,150.01	13,050.29	13,008.91	12,991.63
17.75%	22,479.29	18,575.69	17,419.02	15,893.52	14,172.95	13,564.48	13,327.39	13,231.56	13,192.25	13,176.04
18.00%	22,600.15	18,705.88	17,553.66	16,036.48	14,332.75	13,735.47	13,505.13	13,413.06	13,375.74	13,360.52
18.25%	22,721.36	18,836.52	17,688.80	16,180.00	14,493.12	13,906.94	13,683.20	13,594.78	13,559.35	13,545.08
18.50%	22,842.93	18,967.61	17,824.42	16,324.07	14,654.06	14,078.88	13,861.61	13,776.71	13,743.09	13,729.71
18.75%	22,964.84	19,099.15	17,960.54	16,468.69	14,815.55	14,251.27	14,040.33	13,958.83	13,926.94	13,914.41
19.00%	23,087.09	19,231.14	18,097.14	16,613.84	14,977.60	14,424.10	14,219.35	14,141.14	14,110.90	14,099.16
19.25%	23,209.69	19,363.57	18,234.22	16,759.53	15,140.18	14,597.35	14,398.66	14,323.63	14,294.96	14,283.96
19.50%	23,332.64	19,496.45	18,371.79	16,905.75	15,303.28	14,771.01	14,578.25	14,506.29	14,479.12	14,468.81
19.75%	23,455.93	19,629.76	18,509.83	17,052.49	15,466.91	14,945.08	14,758.11	14,689.10	14,663.36	14,653.71
20.00%	23,579.56	19,763.52	18,648.35	17,199.75	15,631.04	15,119.54	14,938.22	14,872.07	14,847.68	14,838.65
20.25%	23,703.53	19,897.71	18,787.34	17,347.53	15,795.67	15,294.37	15,118.58	15,055.17	15,032.07	15,023.63
20.50%	23,827.84	20,032.34	18,926.79	17,495.83	15,960.79	15,469.57	15,299.16	15,238.41	15,216.54	15,208.64
20.75%	23,952.50	20,167.39	19,066.71	17,644.62	16,126.38	15,645.13	15,479.97	15,421.78	15,401.08	15,393.69

	5	7	8	10	15	20	25	30	35	40
1.00%	15,384.37	11,098.12	9,758.90	7,884.37	5,386.45	4,139.05	3,391.85	2,894.76	2,540.57	2,275.70
1.25%	15,481.44	11,195.45	9,856.44	7,982.41	5,485.99	4,240.20	3,494.67	2,999.27	2,646.78	2,383.61
1.50%	15,578.90	11,293.32	9,954.60	8,081.23	5,586.69	4,342.91	3,599.43	3,106.08	2,755.66	2,494.55
1.75%	15,676.75	11,391.73	10,053.38	8,180.83	5,688.55	4,447.16	3,706.10	3,215.19	2,867.20	2,608.51
2.00%	15,774.98	11,490.69	10,152.79	8,281.21	5,791.58	4,552.95	3,814.69	3,326.58	2,981.36	2,725.43
2.25%	15,873.61	11,590.20	10,252.81	8,382.36	5,895.76	4,660.27	3,925.18	3,440.21	3,098.13	2,845.28
2.50%	15,972.63	11,690.24	10,353.46	8,484.29	6,001.10	4,769.13	4,037.55	3,556.09	3,217.46	2,968.00
2.75%	16,072.03	11,790.84	10,454.73	8,586.99	6,107.59	4,879.50	4,151.80	3,674.17	3,339.31	3,093.55
3.00%	16,171.82	11,891.97	10,556.61	8,690.47	6,215.23	4,991.38	4,267.90	3,794.44	3,463.65	3,221.86
3.25%	16,272.00	11,993.65	10,659.12	8,794.71	6,324.02	5,104.76	4,385.85	3,916.86	3,590.44	3,352.87
3.50%	16,372.57	12,095.87	10,762.25	8,899.73	6,433.94	5,219.64	4,505.61	4,041.40	3,719.62	3,486.52
3.75%	16,473.53	12,198.63	10,865.99	9,005.51	6,545.00	5,335.99	4,627.18	4,168.04	3,851.15	3,622.73
4.00%	16,574.87	12,301.93	10,970.35	9,112.06	6,657.19	5,453.82	4,750.53	4,296.74	3,984.97	3,761.45
4.25%	16,676.60	12,405.77	11,075.32	9,219.38	6,770.51	5,573.11	4,875.64	4,427.46	4,121.05	3,902.58
4.50%	16,778.72	12,510.15	11,180.91	9,327.46	6,884.94	5,693.84	5,002.49	4,560.17	4,259.31	4,046.07
4.75%	16,881.22	12,615.06	11,287.11	9,436.30	7,000.49	5,816.01	5,131.06	4,694.83	4,399.71	4,191.82
5.00%	16,984.11	12,720.52	11,393.93	9,545.90	7,117.14	5,939.60	5,261.31	4,831.39	4,542.19	4,339.77
5.25%	17,087.39	12,826.51	11,501.35	9,656.25	7,234.90	6,064.60	5,393.23	4,969.83	4,686.69	4,489.83
5.50%	17,191.05	12,933.04	11,609.39	9,767.37	7,353.75	6,190.99	5,526.79	5,110.10	4,833.15	4,641.93
5.75%	17,295.09	13,040.10	11,718.03	9,879.23	7,473.69	6,318.75	5,661.96	5,252.16	4,981.51	4,795.99
6.00%	17,399.52	13,147.70	11,827.29	9,991.85	7,594.71	6,447.88	5,798.71	5,395.95	5,131.71	4,951.92
6.25%	17,504.34	13,255.83	11,937.15	10,105.21	7,716.81	6,578.35	5,937.02	5,541.45	5,283.69	5,109.66
6.50%	17,609.53	13,364.49	12,047.61	10,219.32	7,839.97	6,710.16	6,076.86	5,688.61	5,437.39	5,269.11
6.75%	17,715.11	13,473.69	12,158.68	10,334.17	7,964.19	6,843.28	6,218.20	5,837.38	5,592.75	5,430.21
7.00%	17,821.08	13,583.41	12,270.35	10,449.76	8,089.45	6,977.69	6,361.01	5,987.72	5,749.71	5,592.88
7.25%	17,927.43	13,693.67	12,382.61	10,566.09	8,215.77	7,113.38	6,505.26	6,139.59	5,908.21	5,757.05
7.50%	18,034.15	13,804.45	12,495.48	10,683.16	8,343.11	7,250.34	6,650.92	6,292.93	6,068.18	5,922.64
7.75%	18,141.26	13,915.76	12,608.95	10,800.96	8,471.48	7,388.54	6,797.96	6,447.71	6,229.58	6,089.58
8.00%	18,248.75	14,027.59	12,723.01	10,919.48	8,600.87	7,527.96	6,946.35	6,603.88	6,392.35	6,257.81
8.25%	18,356.63	14,139.95	12,837.67	11,038.74	8,731.26	7,668.59	7,096.05	6,761.40	6,556.42	6,427.25
8.50%	18,464.88	14,252.84	12,952.92	11,158.71	8,862.66	7,810.41	7,247.04	6,920.22	6,721.75	6,597.85
8.75%	18,573.51	14,366.24	13,068.75	11,279.41	8,995.04	7,953.40	7,399.29	7,080.30	6,888.27	6,769.53
9.00%	18,682.52	14,480.17	13,185.18	11,400.82	9,128.40	8,097.53	7,552.77	7,241.60	7,055.94	6,942.25
9.25%	18,791.91	14,594.62	13,302.20	11,522.94	9,262.73	8,242.80	7,707.44	7,404.08	7,224.70	7,115.95
9.50%	18,901.68	14,709.58	13,419.80	11,645.78	9,398.02	8,389.18	7,863.27	7,567.69	7,394.50	7,290.55
9.75%	19,011.82	14,825.07	13,537.98	11,769.32	9,534.26	8,536.65	8,020.24	7,732.39	7,565.30	7,466.03
10.00%	19,122.34	14,941.07	13,656.75	11,893.57	9,671.45	8,685.19	8,178.31	7,898.14	7,737.05	7,642.31
10.25%	19,233.24	15,057.58	13,776.09	12,018.51	9,809.56	8,834.79	8,337.45	8,064.91	7,909.70	7,819.36
10.50%	19,344.51	15,174.61	13,896.01	12,144.15	9,948.59	8,985.42	8,497.64	8,232.65	8,083.21	7,997.13
10.75%	19,456.16	15,292.14	14,016.51	12,270.48	10,088.53	9,137.06	8,658.83	8,401.33	8,257.53	8,175.58

$900,000   11.00 - 20.75%   5 - 40 Years

	5	7	8	10	15	20	25	30	35	40
11.00%	19,568.18	15,410.19	14,137.58	12,397.50	10,229.37	9,289.70	8,821.02	8,570.91	8,432.62	8,354.65
11.25%	19,680.58	15,528.75	14,259.23	12,525.21	10,371.10	9,443.30	8,984.16	8,741.35	8,608.44	8,534.32
11.50%	19,793.35	15,647.81	14,381.44	12,653.59	10,513.71	9,597.87	9,148.22	8,912.62	8,784.97	8,714.54
11.75%	19,906.49	15,767.39	14,504.21	12,782.65	10,657.18	9,753.36	9,313.18	9,084.69	8,962.15	8,895.28
12.00%	20,020.00	15,887.46	14,627.56	12,912.39	10,801.51	9,909.78	9,479.02	9,257.51	9,139.95	9,076.50
12.25%	20,133.89	16,008.04	14,751.46	13,042.79	10,946.69	10,067.08	9,645.69	9,431.07	9,318.34	9,258.18
12.50%	20,248.14	16,129.11	14,875.93	13,173.86	11,092.70	10,225.26	9,813.19	9,605.32	9,497.29	9,440.27
12.75%	20,362.77	16,250.69	15,000.95	13,305.58	11,239.53	10,384.30	9,981.47	9,780.24	9,676.77	9,622.77
13.00%	20,477.77	16,372.77	15,126.53	13,437.97	11,387.18	10,544.18	10,150.52	9,955.80	9,856.74	9,805.63
13.25%	20,593.13	16,495.34	15,252.66	13,571.00	11,535.63	10,704.88	10,320.30	10,131.96	10,037.18	9,988.83
13.50%	20,708.86	16,618.40	15,379.34	13,704.69	11,684.87	10,866.37	10,490.80	10,308.71	10,218.06	10,172.35
13.75%	20,824.96	16,741.96	15,506.57	13,839.01	11,834.89	11,028.65	10,661.99	10,486.01	10,399.37	10,356.17
14.00%	20,941.43	16,866.01	15,634.35	13,973.98	11,985.67	11,191.69	10,833.85	10,663.85	10,581.06	10,540.26
14.25%	21,058.26	16,990.55	15,762.67	14,109.58	12,137.22	11,355.47	11,006.35	10,842.18	10,763.12	10,724.61
14.50%	21,175.45	17,115.57	15,891.53	14,245.81	12,289.51	11,519.98	11,179.47	11,021.00	10,945.53	10,909.20
14.75%	21,293.01	17,241.08	16,020.93	14,382.67	12,442.53	11,685.20	11,353.18	11,200.28	11,128.27	11,094.00
15.00%	21,410.94	17,367.08	16,150.86	14,520.15	12,596.28	11,851.11	11,527.48	11,380.00	11,311.32	11,279.02
15.25%	21,529.22	17,493.56	16,281.33	14,658.24	12,750.75	12,017.69	11,702.32	11,560.13	11,494.66	11,464.22
15.50%	21,647.87	17,620.51	16,412.33	14,796.95	12,905.91	12,184.93	11,877.71	11,740.65	11,678.26	11,649.60
15.75%	21,766.88	17,747.95	16,543.86	14,936.26	13,061.77	12,352.80	12,053.61	11,921.55	11,862.12	11,835.14
16.00%	21,886.25	17,875.86	16,675.91	15,076.18	13,218.31	12,521.30	12,230.00	12,102.81	12,046.22	12,020.84
16.25%	22,005.98	18,004.24	16,808.48	15,216.70	13,375.51	12,690.41	12,406.87	12,284.41	12,230.55	12,206.67
16.50%	22,126.07	18,133.10	16,941.57	15,357.81	13,533.38	12,860.11	12,584.20	12,466.33	12,415.09	12,392.63
16.75%	22,246.52	18,262.43	17,075.18	15,499.51	13,691.89	13,030.38	12,761.97	12,648.56	12,599.82	12,578.72
17.00%	22,367.32	18,392.22	17,209.31	15,641.79	13,851.04	13,201.20	12,940.17	12,831.08	12,784.74	12,764.91
17.25%	22,488.48	18,522.49	17,343.94	15,784.65	14,010.81	13,372.58	13,118.77	13,013.87	12,969.83	12,951.21
17.50%	22,609.99	18,653.21	17,479.09	15,928.09	14,171.20	13,544.48	13,297.77	13,196.93	13,155.08	13,137.60
17.75%	22,731.86	18,784.40	17,614.74	16,072.10	14,332.20	13,716.89	13,477.14	13,380.23	13,340.48	13,324.08
18.00%	22,854.08	18,916.05	17,750.89	16,216.67	14,493.79	13,889.80	13,656.87	13,563.77	13,526.03	13,510.64
18.25%	22,976.66	19,048.16	17,887.55	16,361.80	14,655.96	14,063.20	13,836.95	13,747.53	13,711.71	13,697.28
18.50%	23,099.59	19,180.73	18,024.70	16,507.49	14,818.71	14,237.07	14,017.36	13,931.50	13,897.51	13,883.98
18.75%	23,222.87	19,313.75	18,162.34	16,653.73	14,982.02	14,411.39	14,198.09	14,115.67	14,083.43	14,070.75
19.00%	23,346.50	19,447.22	18,300.48	16,800.51	15,145.88	14,586.16	14,379.12	14,300.03	14,269.45	14,257.57
19.25%	23,470.47	19,581.14	18,439.10	16,947.84	15,310.29	14,761.36	14,560.45	14,484.57	14,455.58	14,444.45
19.50%	23,594.80	19,715.51	18,578.21	17,095.70	15,475.23	14,936.98	14,742.06	14,669.28	14,641.80	14,631.38
19.75%	23,719.47	19,850.32	18,717.81	17,244.09	15,640.69	15,113.00	14,923.93	14,854.15	14,828.11	14,818.36
20.00%	23,844.50	19,985.58	18,857.88	17,393.01	15,806.67	15,289.42	15,106.07	15,039.17	15,014.50	15,005.38
20.25%	23,969.86	20,121.28	18,998.43	17,542.45	15,973.15	15,466.22	15,288.45	15,224.33	15,200.97	15,192.43
20.50%	24,095.57	20,257.42	19,139.45	17,692.41	16,140.12	15,643.39	15,471.06	15,409.63	15,387.51	15,379.53
20.75%	24,221.63	20,393.99	19,280.95	17,842.88	16,307.58	15,820.91	15,653.91	15,595.05	15,574.12	15,566.65

	5	7	8	10	15	20	25	30	35	40
1.00%	15,555.31	11,221.43	9,867.34	7,971.98	5,446.30	4,185.04	3,429.54	2,926.92	2,568.80	2,300.99
1.25%	15,653.46	11,319.84	9,965.96	8,071.11	5,546.94	4,287.32	3,533.50	3,032.59	2,676.19	2,410.09
1.50%	15,752.00	11,418.80	10,065.21	8,171.03	5,648.76	4,391.16	3,639.42	3,140.59	2,786.28	2,522.27
1.75%	15,850.93	11,518.31	10,165.08	8,271.73	5,751.76	4,496.57	3,747.28	3,250.92	2,899.06	2,637.49
2.00%	15,950.26	11,618.37	10,265.59	8,373.22	5,855.93	4,603.54	3,857.07	3,363.54	3,014.49	2,755.71
2.25%	16,049.98	11,718.98	10,366.73	8,475.50	5,961.27	4,712.06	3,968.79	3,478.44	3,132.55	2,876.89
2.50%	16,150.10	11,820.14	10,468.50	8,578.56	6,067.78	4,822.12	4,082.41	3,595.60	3,253.21	3,000.98
2.75%	16,250.61	11,921.84	10,570.89	8,682.40	6,175.46	4,933.71	4,197.93	3,714.99	3,376.41	3,127.92
3.00%	16,351.51	12,024.10	10,673.91	8,787.03	6,284.29	5,046.84	4,315.32	3,836.60	3,502.14	3,257.66
3.25%	16,452.80	12,126.91	10,777.56	8,892.43	6,394.29	5,161.48	4,434.58	3,960.38	3,630.33	3,390.13
3.50%	16,554.49	12,230.26	10,881.83	8,998.61	6,505.43	5,277.63	4,555.67	4,086.31	3,760.94	3,525.26
3.75%	16,656.57	12,334.17	10,986.72	9,105.57	6,617.72	5,395.28	4,678.59	4,214.35	3,893.94	3,662.99
4.00%	16,759.04	12,438.61	11,092.24	9,213.31	6,731.16	5,514.42	4,803.32	4,344.48	4,029.25	3,803.24
4.25%	16,861.90	12,543.61	11,198.38	9,321.82	6,845.73	5,635.03	4,929.82	4,476.65	4,166.84	3,945.94
4.50%	16,965.15	12,649.15	11,305.14	9,431.10	6,961.44	5,757.11	5,058.08	4,610.84	4,306.64	4,091.02
4.75%	17,068.79	12,755.23	11,412.53	9,541.14	7,078.27	5,880.64	5,188.07	4,746.99	4,448.60	4,238.40
5.00%	17,172.82	12,861.86	11,520.53	9,651.96	7,196.22	6,005.60	5,319.77	4,885.08	4,592.66	4,387.99
5.25%	17,277.25	12,969.03	11,629.15	9,763.54	7,315.29	6,131.98	5,453.15	5,025.05	4,738.76	4,539.72
5.50%	17,382.06	13,076.74	11,738.38	9,875.89	7,435.46	6,259.77	5,588.20	5,166.88	4,886.85	4,693.51
5.75%	17,487.26	13,184.99	11,848.24	9,989.00	7,556.73	6,388.96	5,724.87	5,310.51	5,036.86	4,849.28
6.00%	17,592.85	13,293.78	11,958.70	10,102.87	7,679.10	6,519.52	5,863.14	5,455.91	5,188.73	5,006.94
6.25%	17,698.83	13,403.12	12,069.78	10,217.49	7,802.55	6,651.45	6,002.99	5,603.03	5,342.40	5,166.43
6.50%	17,805.19	13,512.99	12,181.47	10,332.87	7,927.08	6,784.72	6,144.39	5,751.82	5,497.80	5,327.66
6.75%	17,911.95	13,623.39	12,293.77	10,448.99	8,052.68	6,919.31	6,287.29	5,902.24	5,654.89	5,490.55
7.00%	18,019.09	13,734.34	12,406.68	10,565.87	8,179.34	7,055.22	6,431.69	6,054.25	5,813.59	5,655.02
7.25%	18,126.62	13,845.82	12,520.20	10,683.49	8,307.05	7,192.42	6,577.54	6,207.80	5,973.85	5,821.01
7.50%	18,234.53	13,957.83	12,634.32	10,801.86	8,435.81	7,330.90	6,724.82	6,362.85	6,135.61	5,988.44
7.75%	18,342.83	14,070.38	12,749.05	10,920.97	8,565.61	7,470.63	6,873.49	6,519.35	6,298.80	6,157.24
8.00%	18,451.52	14,183.46	12,864.38	11,040.81	8,696.43	7,611.60	7,023.53	6,677.26	6,463.37	6,327.34
8.25%	18,560.59	14,297.06	12,980.31	11,161.39	8,828.28	7,753.80	7,174.90	6,836.53	6,629.27	6,498.66
8.50%	18,670.04	14,411.20	13,096.84	11,282.70	8,961.13	7,897.19	7,327.57	6,997.11	6,796.43	6,671.16
8.75%	18,779.88	14,525.87	13,213.96	11,404.73	9,094.98	8,041.77	7,481.51	7,158.97	6,964.80	6,844.75
9.00%	18,890.10	14,641.06	13,331.68	11,527.50	9,229.83	8,187.51	7,636.69	7,322.07	7,134.34	7,019.39
9.25%	19,000.71	14,756.78	13,450.00	11,650.98	9,365.65	8,334.39	7,793.07	7,486.35	7,304.97	7,195.01
9.50%	19,111.69	14,873.02	13,568.91	11,775.18	9,502.44	8,482.39	7,950.64	7,651.77	7,476.67	7,371.56
9.75%	19,223.06	14,989.79	13,688.40	11,900.09	9,640.20	8,631.50	8,109.35	7,818.31	7,649.36	7,548.98
10.00%	19,334.81	15,107.08	13,808.49	12,025.72	9,778.91	8,781.70	8,269.18	7,985.90	7,823.02	7,727.23
10.25%	19,446.94	15,224.89	13,929.16	12,152.05	9,918.55	8,932.95	8,430.09	8,154.52	7,997.59	7,906.25
10.50%	19,559.45	15,343.21	14,050.41	12,279.08	10,059.13	9,085.26	8,592.05	8,324.13	8,173.02	8,085.99
10.75%	19,672.34	15,462.06	14,172.25	12,406.82	10,200.63	9,238.58	8,755.04	8,494.68	8,349.28	8,266.41

$910,000   11.00 - 20.75%   5 - 40 Years

	5	7	8	10	15	20	25	30	35	40
11.00%	19,785.60	15,581.42	14,294.67	12,535.25	10,343.03	9,392.91	8,919.03	8,666.14	8,526.31	8,447.48
11.25%	19,899.25	15,701.29	14,417.66	12,664.37	10,486.34	9,548.23	9,083.98	8,838.48	8,704.09	8,629.14
11.50%	20,013.27	15,821.68	14,541.23	12,794.19	10,630.53	9,704.51	9,249.87	9,011.65	8,882.58	8,811.36
11.75%	20,127.67	15,942.58	14,665.37	12,924.68	10,775.60	9,861.73	9,416.66	9,185.63	9,061.72	8,994.11
12.00%	20,242.45	16,063.99	14,790.09	13,055.86	10,921.53	10,019.88	9,584.34	9,360.37	9,241.50	9,177.35
12.25%	20,357.60	16,185.90	14,915.37	13,187.71	11,068.32	10,178.94	9,752.87	9,535.86	9,421.88	9,361.04
12.50%	20,473.12	16,308.33	15,041.22	13,320.23	11,215.95	10,338.88	9,922.22	9,712.05	9,602.81	9,545.17
12.75%	20,589.02	16,431.26	15,167.63	13,453.42	11,364.42	10,499.69	10,092.38	9,888.91	9,784.28	9,729.69
13.00%	20,705.30	16,554.69	15,294.60	13,587.28	11,513.70	10,661.34	10,263.30	10,066.42	9,966.26	9,914.58
13.25%	20,821.94	16,678.62	15,422.14	13,721.79	11,663.80	10,823.82	10,434.97	10,244.54	10,148.70	10,099.82
13.50%	20,938.96	16,803.05	15,550.23	13,856.96	11,814.70	10,987.11	10,607.37	10,423.25	10,331.60	10,285.38
13.75%	21,056.35	16,927.98	15,678.87	13,992.78	11,966.38	11,151.19	10,780.46	10,602.52	10,514.91	10,471.24
14.00%	21,174.11	17,053.41	15,808.07	14,129.25	12,118.85	11,316.04	10,954.23	10,782.33	10,698.63	10,657.37
14.25%	21,292.24	17,179.33	15,937.81	14,266.35	12,272.07	11,481.64	11,128.64	10,962.65	10,882.71	10,843.77
14.50%	21,410.74	17,305.75	16,068.10	14,404.10	12,426.06	11,647.98	11,303.68	11,143.46	11,067.15	11,030.41
14.75%	21,529.60	17,432.65	16,198.94	14,542.48	12,580.78	11,815.03	11,479.33	11,324.73	11,251.92	11,217.27
15.00%	21,648.84	17,560.05	16,330.32	14,681.48	12,736.24	11,982.79	11,655.56	11,506.44	11,437.00	11,404.34
15.25%	21,768.44	17,687.93	16,462.24	14,821.11	12,892.42	12,151.22	11,832.35	11,688.57	11,622.37	11,591.60
15.50%	21,888.40	17,816.30	16,594.69	14,961.36	13,049.31	12,320.31	12,009.68	11,871.10	11,808.02	11,779.04
15.75%	22,008.74	17,945.15	16,727.68	15,102.22	13,206.90	12,490.06	12,187.53	12,054.02	11,993.93	11,966.64
16.00%	22,129.43	18,074.48	16,861.20	15,243.69	13,365.18	12,660.43	12,365.89	12,237.29	12,180.07	12,154.40
16.25%	22,250.49	18,204.29	16,995.24	15,385.77	13,524.13	12,831.41	12,544.73	12,420.91	12,366.44	12,342.30
16.50%	22,371.91	18,334.58	17,129.81	15,528.45	13,683.75	13,003.00	12,724.03	12,604.85	12,553.03	12,530.33
16.75%	22,493.70	18,465.34	17,264.91	15,671.72	13,844.02	13,175.16	12,903.77	12,789.10	12,739.82	12,718.48
17.00%	22,615.84	18,596.58	17,400.52	15,815.59	14,004.94	13,347.88	13,083.95	12,973.65	12,926.79	12,906.74
17.25%	22,738.35	18,728.29	17,536.66	15,960.04	14,166.49	13,521.16	13,264.54	13,158.47	13,113.93	13,095.11
17.50%	22,861.21	18,860.47	17,673.30	16,105.07	14,328.66	13,694.97	13,445.52	13,343.56	13,301.25	13,283.57
17.75%	22,984.44	18,993.12	17,810.46	16,250.67	14,491.45	13,869.30	13,626.88	13,528.90	13,488.71	13,472.13
18.00%	23,108.02	19,126.23	17,948.12	16,396.85	14,654.83	14,044.13	13,808.61	13,714.48	13,676.32	13,660.76
18.25%	23,231.96	19,259.81	18,086.30	16,543.60	14,818.81	14,219.46	13,990.69	13,900.28	13,864.06	13,849.47
18.50%	23,356.25	19,393.85	18,224.97	16,690.91	14,983.36	14,395.26	14,173.11	14,086.30	14,051.92	14,038.25
18.75%	23,480.90	19,528.34	18,364.15	16,838.77	15,148.49	14,571.52	14,355.84	14,272.51	14,239.91	14,227.09
19.00%	23,605.90	19,663.30	18,503.82	16,987.18	15,314.17	14,748.23	14,538.89	14,458.92	14,428.00	14,415.99
19.25%	23,731.26	19,798.71	18,643.98	17,136.15	15,480.41	14,925.38	14,722.23	14,645.51	14,616.20	14,604.95
19.50%	23,856.97	19,934.57	18,784.64	17,285.65	15,647.18	15,102.95	14,905.86	14,832.27	14,804.49	14,793.95
19.75%	23,983.02	20,070.88	18,925.78	17,435.69	15,814.48	15,280.93	15,089.75	15,019.19	14,992.87	14,983.01
20.00%	24,109.43	20,207.64	19,067.41	17,586.27	15,982.30	15,459.30	15,273.91	15,206.27	15,181.33	15,172.10
20.25%	24,236.19	20,344.85	19,209.52	17,737.37	16,150.63	15,638.07	15,458.32	15,393.49	15,369.87	15,361.24
20.50%	24,363.30	20,482.50	19,352.11	17,888.99	16,319.46	15,817.20	15,642.96	15,580.85	15,558.49	15,550.41
20.75%	24,490.76	20,620.59	19,495.18	18,041.13	16,488.77	15,996.70	15,827.84	15,768.33	15,747.17	15,739.62

$920,000

1.00 - 10.75% 5 - 40 Years

	5	7	8	10	15	20	25	30	35	40
1.00%	15,726.25	11,344.75	9,975.77	8,059.58	5,506.15	4,231.03	3,467.23	2,959.08	2,597.03	2,326.28
1.25%	15,825.47	11,444.23	10,075.47	8,159.80	5,607.90	4,334.43	3,572.33	3,065.92	2,705.59	2,436.58
1.50%	15,925.10	11,544.28	10,175.81	8,260.82	5,710.84	4,439.42	3,679.41	3,175.11	2,816.90	2,549.99
1.75%	16,025.12	11,644.88	10,276.79	8,362.63	5,814.96	4,545.99	3,788.46	3,286.64	2,930.91	2,666.47
2.00%	16,125.54	11,746.04	10,378.40	8,465.24	5,920.28	4,654.13	3,899.46	3,400.50	3,047.62	2,786.00
2.25%	16,226.36	11,847.76	10,480.65	8,568.64	6,026.78	4,763.84	4,012.40	3,516.66	3,166.98	2,908.51
2.50%	16,327.57	11,950.03	10,583.54	8,672.83	6,134.46	4,875.11	4,127.27	3,635.11	3,288.96	3,033.96
2.75%	16,429.19	12,052.85	10,687.05	8,777.81	6,243.32	4,987.93	4,244.06	3,755.82	3,413.52	3,162.30
3.00%	16,531.20	12,156.24	10,791.21	8,883.59	6,353.35	5,102.30	4,362.74	3,878.76	3,540.62	3,293.46
3.25%	16,633.60	12,260.17	10,895.99	8,990.15	6,464.55	5,218.20	4,483.31	4,003.90	3,670.22	3,427.38
3.50%	16,736.41	12,364.66	11,001.41	9,097.50	6,576.92	5,335.63	4,605.74	4,131.21	3,802.27	3,564.00
3.75%	16,839.60	12,469.71	11,107.46	9,205.63	6,690.45	5,454.57	4,730.01	4,260.66	3,936.73	3,703.24
4.00%	16,943.20	12,575.30	11,214.13	9,314.55	6,805.13	5,575.02	4,856.10	4,392.20	4,073.53	3,845.03
4.25%	17,047.19	12,681.45	11,321.44	9,424.25	6,920.96	5,696.96	4,983.99	4,525.85	4,212.62	3,989.31
4.50%	17,151.58	12,788.15	11,429.38	9,534.73	7,037.94	5,820.37	5,113.66	4,661.50	4,353.96	4,135.98
4.75%	17,256.36	12,895.40	11,537.94	9,645.99	7,156.05	5,945.26	5,245.08	4,799.16	4,497.48	4,284.97
5.00%	17,361.53	13,003.20	11,647.13	9,758.03	7,275.30	6,071.59	5,378.23	4,938.76	4,643.13	4,436.21
5.25%	17,467.11	13,111.54	11,756.94	9,870.84	7,395.67	6,199.37	5,513.08	5,080.27	4,790.84	4,589.61
5.50%	17,573.07	13,220.44	11,867.38	9,984.42	7,517.17	6,328.56	5,649.60	5,223.66	4,940.55	4,745.09
5.75%	17,679.43	13,329.88	11,978.44	10,098.77	7,639.77	6,459.17	5,787.78	5,368.87	5,092.21	4,902.57
6.00%	17,786.18	13,439.87	12,090.12	10,213.89	7,763.48	6,591.17	5,927.57	5,515.86	5,245.75	5,061.97
6.25%	17,893.32	13,550.40	12,202.42	10,329.77	7,888.29	6,724.54	6,068.96	5,664.60	5,401.10	5,223.20
6.50%	18,000.86	13,661.48	12,315.33	10,446.41	8,014.19	6,859.27	6,211.91	5,815.03	5,558.22	5,386.20
6.75%	18,108.78	13,773.10	12,428.87	10,563.82	8,141.17	6,995.35	6,356.39	5,967.10	5,717.03	5,550.88
7.00%	18,217.10	13,885.27	12,543.02	10,681.98	8,269.22	7,132.75	6,502.37	6,120.78	5,877.48	5,717.17
7.25%	18,325.81	13,997.97	12,657.78	10,800.90	8,398.34	7,271.46	6,649.82	6,276.02	6,039.50	5,884.98
7.50%	18,434.91	14,111.21	12,773.16	10,920.56	8,528.51	7,411.46	6,798.72	6,432.77	6,203.03	6,054.25
7.75%	18,544.40	14,225.00	12,889.15	11,040.98	8,659.74	7,552.73	6,949.02	6,590.99	6,368.02	6,224.90
8.00%	18,654.28	14,339.32	13,005.74	11,162.14	8,792.00	7,695.25	7,100.71	6,750.63	6,534.40	6,396.87
8.25%	18,764.55	14,454.17	13,122.95	11,284.04	8,925.29	7,839.00	7,253.74	6,911.65	6,702.12	6,570.08
8.50%	18,875.21	14,569.57	13,240.76	11,406.68	9,059.60	7,983.97	7,408.09	7,074.00	6,871.12	6,744.47
8.75%	18,986.25	14,685.49	13,359.17	11,530.06	9,194.93	8,130.14	7,563.72	7,237.64	7,041.34	6,919.97
9.00%	19,097.69	14,801.95	13,478.19	11,654.17	9,331.25	8,277.48	7,720.61	7,402.53	7,212.74	7,096.53
9.25%	19,209.51	14,918.94	13,597.80	11,779.01	9,468.57	8,425.97	7,878.71	7,568.61	7,385.25	7,274.08
9.50%	19,321.71	15,036.46	13,718.02	11,904.58	9,606.87	8,575.61	8,038.01	7,735.86	7,558.83	7,452.57
9.75%	19,434.30	15,154.51	13,838.83	12,030.86	9,746.14	8,726.36	8,198.46	7,904.22	7,733.42	7,631.94
10.00%	19,547.28	15,273.09	13,960.23	12,157.87	9,886.37	8,878.20	8,360.05	8,073.66	7,908.99	7,812.14
10.25%	19,660.64	15,392.19	14,082.23	12,285.59	10,027.55	9,031.12	8,522.73	8,244.13	8,085.47	7,993.13
10.50%	19,774.39	15,511.82	14,204.81	12,414.02	10,169.67	9,185.09	8,686.47	8,415.60	8,262.83	8,174.85
10.75%	19,888.52	15,631.97	14,327.99	12,543.16	10,312.72	9,340.11	8,851.25	8,588.03	8,441.03	8,357.25

$920,000   11.00 - 20.75%   5 - 40 Years

	5	7	8	10	15	20	25	30	35	40
11.00%	20,003.03	15,752.64	14,451.75	12,673.00	10,456.69	9,496.13	9,017.04	8,761.38	8,620.01	8,540.31
11.25%	20,117.92	15,873.83	14,576.10	12,803.54	10,601.57	9,653.16	9,183.80	8,935.60	8,799.74	8,723.97
11.50%	20,233.20	15,995.54	14,701.02	12,934.78	10,747.35	9,811.15	9,351.51	9,110.68	8,980.19	8,908.19
11.75%	20,348.86	16,117.77	14,826.53	13,066.71	10,894.01	9,970.10	9,520.14	9,286.57	9,161.30	9,092.95
12.00%	20,464.89	16,240.51	14,952.61	13,199.33	11,041.55	10,129.99	9,689.66	9,463.24	9,343.06	9,278.20
12.25%	20,581.31	16,363.77	15,079.27	13,332.63	11,189.95	10,290.80	9,860.04	9,640.65	9,525.41	9,463.91
12.50%	20,698.10	16,487.54	15,206.50	13,466.61	11,339.20	10,452.49	10,031.26	9,818.77	9,708.34	9,650.06
12.75%	20,815.28	16,611.82	15,334.31	13,601.26	11,489.30	10,615.07	10,203.28	9,997.58	9,891.80	9,836.61
13.00%	20,932.83	16,736.61	15,462.67	13,736.59	11,640.23	10,778.50	10,376.08	10,177.04	10,075.78	10,023.53
13.25%	21,050.75	16,861.90	15,591.61	13,872.58	11,791.98	10,942.76	10,549.64	10,357.12	10,260.23	10,210.80
13.50%	21,169.06	16,987.70	15,721.11	14,009.23	11,944.53	11,107.85	10,723.93	10,537.79	10,445.13	10,398.40
13.75%	21,287.74	17,114.01	15,851.16	14,146.55	12,097.88	11,273.73	10,898.93	10,719.04	10,630.46	10,586.30
14.00%	21,406.79	17,240.81	15,981.78	14,284.51	12,252.02	11,440.39	11,074.60	10,900.82	10,816.19	10,774.49
14.25%	21,526.22	17,368.12	16,112.95	14,423.13	12,406.93	11,607.81	11,250.93	11,083.12	11,002.30	10,962.93
14.50%	21,646.02	17,495.92	16,244.68	14,562.38	12,562.61	11,775.98	11,427.90	11,265.91	11,188.77	11,151.62
14.75%	21,766.19	17,624.22	16,376.95	14,702.28	12,719.03	11,944.87	11,605.48	11,449.18	11,375.57	11,340.54
15.00%	21,886.74	17,753.01	16,509.77	14,842.82	12,876.20	12,114.46	11,783.64	11,632.88	11,562.68	11,529.66
15.25%	22,007.65	17,882.30	16,643.14	14,983.98	13,034.10	12,284.75	11,962.38	11,817.02	11,750.09	11,718.98
15.50%	22,128.94	18,012.08	16,777.05	15,125.77	13,192.71	12,455.70	12,141.66	12,001.56	11,937.78	11,908.48
15.75%	22,250.59	18,142.35	16,911.50	15,268.18	13,352.03	12,627.31	12,321.46	12,186.48	12,125.73	12,098.15
16.00%	22,372.61	18,273.10	17,046.48	15,411.21	13,512.05	12,799.55	12,501.78	12,371.76	12,313.92	12,287.97
16.25%	22,495.00	18,404.34	17,182.00	15,554.85	13,672.75	12,972.42	12,682.58	12,557.40	12,502.34	12,477.93
16.50%	22,617.76	18,536.06	17,318.05	15,699.09	13,834.12	13,145.89	12,863.85	12,743.36	12,690.98	12,668.03
16.75%	22,740.88	18,668.26	17,454.63	15,843.94	13,996.15	13,319.94	13,045.57	12,929.64	12,879.81	12,858.24
17.00%	22,864.37	18,800.94	17,591.74	15,989.38	14,158.84	13,494.57	13,227.73	13,116.21	13,068.84	13,048.58
17.25%	22,988.22	18,934.10	17,729.37	16,135.42	14,322.17	13,669.75	13,410.30	13,303.07	13,258.04	13,239.01
17.50%	23,112.44	19,067.73	17,867.51	16,282.05	14,486.12	13,845.47	13,593.27	13,490.19	13,447.41	13,429.55
17.75%	23,237.01	19,201.84	18,006.18	16,429.25	14,650.69	14,021.71	13,776.63	13,677.57	13,636.94	13,620.17
18.00%	23,361.95	19,336.41	18,145.36	16,577.04	14,815.87	14,198.47	13,960.36	13,865.19	13,826.61	13,810.88
18.25%	23,487.25	19,471.46	18,285.05	16,725.40	14,981.65	14,375.72	14,144.44	14,053.03	14,016.41	14,001.66
18.50%	23,612.91	19,606.97	18,425.25	16,874.32	15,148.01	14,553.45	14,328.85	14,241.09	14,206.34	14,192.51
18.75%	23,738.93	19,742.94	18,565.95	17,023.81	15,314.95	14,731.65	14,513.60	14,429.35	14,396.39	14,383.43
19.00%	23,865.31	19,879.38	18,707.16	17,173.86	15,482.46	14,910.30	14,698.66	14,617.81	14,586.55	14,574.41
19.25%	23,992.04	20,016.27	18,848.86	17,324.46	15,650.52	15,089.39	14,884.01	14,806.45	14,776.82	14,765.44
19.50%	24,119.13	20,153.63	18,991.06	17,475.60	15,819.12	15,268.91	15,069.66	14,995.26	14,967.18	14,956.52
19.75%	24,246.57	20,291.44	19,133.76	17,627.29	15,988.26	15,448.85	15,255.57	15,184.24	15,157.63	15,147.66
20.00%	24,374.37	20,429.70	19,276.94	17,779.52	16,157.93	15,629.19	15,441.76	15,373.37	15,348.16	15,338.83
20.25%	24,502.53	20,568.42	19,420.62	17,932.28	16,328.11	15,809.91	15,628.19	15,562.65	15,538.77	15,530.04
20.50%	24,631.03	20,707.58	19,564.77	18,085.57	16,498.79	15,991.02	15,814.87	15,752.07	15,729.46	15,721.29
20.75%	24,759.89	20,847.19	19,709.41	18,239.38	16,669.97	16,172.49	16,001.77	15,941.61	15,920.21	15,912.58

	5	7	8	10	15	20	25	30	35	40
1.00%	15,897.19	11,468.06	10,084.20	8,147.18	5,566.00	4,277.02	3,504.91	2,991.25	2,625.26	2,351.56
1.25%	15,997.49	11,568.63	10,184.99	8,248.49	5,668.85	4,381.54	3,611.16	3,099.24	2,735.00	2,463.06
1.50%	16,098.20	11,669.76	10,286.42	8,350.61	5,772.91	4,487.67	3,719.41	3,209.62	2,847.52	2,577.70
1.75%	16,199.31	11,771.46	10,388.49	8,453.53	5,878.17	4,595.40	3,829.64	3,322.36	2,962.77	2,695.46
2.00%	16,300.82	11,873.71	10,491.21	8,557.25	5,984.63	4,704.72	3,941.85	3,437.46	3,080.74	2,816.28
2.25%	16,402.73	11,976.54	10,594.57	8,661.78	6,092.29	4,815.62	4,056.02	3,554.89	3,201.40	2,940.12
2.50%	16,505.05	12,079.92	10,698.57	8,767.10	6,201.14	4,928.10	4,172.14	3,674.62	3,324.71	3,066.94
2.75%	16,607.76	12,183.86	10,803.22	8,873.23	6,311.18	5,042.15	4,290.19	3,796.64	3,450.62	3,196.67
3.00%	16,710.88	12,288.37	10,908.50	8,980.15	6,422.41	5,157.76	4,410.17	3,920.92	3,579.11	3,329.26
3.25%	16,814.40	12,393.44	11,014.43	9,087.87	6,534.82	5,274.92	4,532.04	4,047.42	3,710.12	3,464.63
3.50%	16,918.32	12,499.06	11,120.99	9,196.39	6,648.41	5,393.63	4,655.80	4,176.12	3,843.60	3,602.74
3.75%	17,022.64	12,605.25	11,228.19	9,305.70	6,763.17	5,513.86	4,781.42	4,306.98	3,979.52	3,743.49
4.00%	17,127.37	12,711.99	11,336.03	9,415.80	6,879.10	5,635.62	4,908.88	4,439.96	4,117.81	3,886.83
4.25%	17,232.49	12,819.29	11,444.50	9,526.69	6,996.19	5,758.88	5,038.16	4,575.04	4,258.41	4,032.67
4.50%	17,338.01	12,927.15	11,553.61	9,638.37	7,114.44	5,883.64	5,169.24	4,712.17	4,401.29	4,180.93
4.75%	17,443.93	13,035.56	11,663.35	9,750.84	7,233.84	6,009.88	5,302.09	4,851.32	4,546.37	4,331.55
5.00%	17,550.25	13,144.54	11,773.73	9,864.09	7,354.38	6,137.59	5,436.69	4,992.44	4,693.60	4,484.43
5.25%	17,656.96	13,254.06	11,884.73	9,978.13	7,476.06	6,266.75	5,573.00	5,135.49	4,842.91	4,639.49
5.50%	17,764.08	13,364.14	11,996.37	10,092.94	7,598.88	6,397.35	5,711.01	5,280.44	4,994.25	4,796.66
5.75%	17,871.59	13,474.77	12,108.64	10,208.54	7,722.81	6,529.38	5,850.69	5,427.23	5,147.56	4,955.86
6.00%	17,979.51	13,585.96	12,221.53	10,324.91	7,847.87	6,662.81	5,992.00	5,575.82	5,302.76	5,116.99
6.25%	18,087.81	13,697.69	12,335.05	10,442.05	7,974.03	6,797.63	6,134.93	5,726.17	5,459.81	5,279.98
6.50%	18,196.52	13,809.98	12,449.20	10,559.96	8,101.30	6,933.83	6,279.43	5,878.23	5,618.64	5,444.75
6.75%	18,305.62	13,922.81	12,563.97	10,678.64	8,229.66	7,071.39	6,425.48	6,031.96	5,779.17	5,611.22
7.00%	18,415.11	14,036.19	12,679.36	10,798.09	8,359.10	7,210.28	6,573.05	6,187.31	5,941.36	5,779.31
7.25%	18,525.01	14,150.12	12,795.37	10,918.30	8,489.62	7,350.50	6,722.10	6,344.24	6,105.15	5,948.95
7.50%	18,635.29	14,264.60	12,912.00	11,039.26	8,621.21	7,492.02	6,872.62	6,502.69	6,270.46	6,120.06
7.75%	18,745.97	14,379.62	13,029.25	11,160.99	8,753.86	7,634.82	7,024.56	6,662.63	6,437.24	6,292.56
8.00%	18,857.05	14,495.18	13,147.11	11,283.47	8,887.56	7,778.89	7,177.89	6,824.01	6,605.43	6,466.40
8.25%	18,968.51	14,611.28	13,265.59	11,406.69	9,022.31	7,924.21	7,332.59	6,986.78	6,774.97	6,641.49
8.50%	19,080.37	14,727.93	13,384.68	11,530.67	9,158.08	8,070.76	7,488.61	7,150.90	6,945.80	6,817.77
8.75%	19,192.63	14,845.12	13,504.38	11,655.39	9,294.87	8,218.51	7,645.94	7,316.31	7,117.88	6,995.19
9.00%	19,305.27	14,962.84	13,624.69	11,780.85	9,432.68	8,367.45	7,804.53	7,482.99	7,291.13	7,173.66
9.25%	19,418.31	15,081.10	13,745.60	11,907.04	9,571.49	8,517.56	7,964.35	7,650.88	7,465.52	7,353.14
9.50%	19,531.73	15,199.90	13,867.13	12,033.97	9,711.29	8,668.82	8,125.38	7,819.94	7,640.99	7,533.57
9.75%	19,645.55	15,319.24	13,989.25	12,161.63	9,852.07	8,821.21	8,287.58	7,990.14	7,817.48	7,714.89
10.00%	19,759.75	15,439.10	14,111.97	12,290.02	9,993.83	8,974.70	8,450.92	8,161.42	7,994.95	7,897.06
10.25%	19,874.35	15,559.50	14,235.30	12,419.13	10,136.54	9,129.28	8,615.36	8,333.74	8,173.36	8,080.01
10.50%	19,989.33	15,680.43	14,359.22	12,548.95	10,280.21	9,284.93	8,780.89	8,507.08	8,352.65	8,263.70
10.75%	20,104.70	15,801.88	14,483.73	12,679.50	10,424.82	9,441.63	8,947.46	8,681.38	8,532.78	8,448.09

$930,000   11.00 - 20.75%   5 - 40 Years

	5	7	8	10	15	20	25	30	35	40
11.00%	20,220.45	15,923.87	14,608.84	12,810.75	10,570.35	9,599.35	9,115.05	8,856.61	8,713.71	8,633.14
11.25%	20,336.60	16,046.38	14,734.53	12,942.71	10,716.80	9,758.08	9,283.63	9,032.73	8,895.39	8,818.79
11.50%	20,453.12	16,169.41	14,860.82	13,075.38	10,864.17	9,917.80	9,453.16	9,209.71	9,077.80	9,005.02
11.75%	20,570.04	16,292.96	14,987.69	13,208.74	11,012.42	10,078.48	9,623.62	9,387.51	9,260.88	9,191.79
12.00%	20,687.34	16,417.04	15,115.14	13,342.80	11,161.56	10,240.10	9,794.98	9,566.10	9,444.61	9,379.05
12.25%	20,805.02	16,541.64	15,243.18	13,477.55	11,311.58	10,402.65	9,967.22	9,745.44	9,628.95	9,566.78
12.50%	20,923.08	16,666.75	15,371.79	13,612.98	11,462.46	10,566.11	10,140.29	9,925.50	9,813.87	9,754.95
12.75%	21,041.53	16,792.38	15,500.98	13,749.10	11,614.18	10,730.45	10,314.19	10,106.25	9,999.32	9,943.53
13.00%	21,160.36	16,918.53	15,630.75	13,885.90	11,766.75	10,895.65	10,488.87	10,287.66	10,185.30	10,132.48
13.25%	21,279.57	17,045.18	15,761.08	14,023.37	11,920.15	11,061.71	10,664.31	10,469.69	10,371.75	10,321.79
13.50%	21,399.16	17,172.35	15,891.99	14,161.51	12,074.36	11,228.58	10,840.50	10,652.33	10,558.67	10,511.43
13.75%	21,519.13	17,300.03	16,023.46	14,300.31	12,229.38	11,396.27	11,017.39	10,835.55	10,746.01	10,701.37
14.00%	21,639.47	17,428.21	16,155.50	14,439.78	12,385.19	11,564.74	11,194.98	11,019.31	10,933.76	10,891.60
14.25%	21,760.20	17,556.90	16,288.09	14,579.90	12,541.79	11,733.99	11,373.23	11,203.59	11,121.89	11,082.10
14.50%	21,881.30	17,686.09	16,421.25	14,720.67	12,699.16	11,903.98	11,552.12	11,388.37	11,310.39	11,272.84
14.75%	22,002.78	17,815.79	16,554.96	14,862.09	12,857.28	12,074.70	11,731.62	11,573.62	11,499.22	11,463.80
15.00%	22,124.63	17,945.98	16,689.23	15,004.15	13,016.16	12,246.14	11,911.72	11,759.33	11,688.36	11,654.98
15.25%	22,246.86	18,076.67	16,824.04	15,146.85	13,175.77	12,418.28	12,092.40	11,945.46	11,877.81	11,846.36
15.50%	22,369.47	18,207.86	16,959.41	15,290.18	13,336.11	12,591.09	12,273.63	12,132.01	12,067.54	12,037.92
15.75%	22,492.44	18,339.54	17,095.32	15,434.14	13,497.16	12,764.56	12,455.39	12,318.94	12,257.53	12,229.65
16.00%	22,615.79	18,471.72	17,231.77	15,578.72	13,658.92	12,938.68	12,637.67	12,506.24	12,447.77	12,421.53
16.25%	22,739.51	18,604.38	17,368.76	15,723.92	13,821.36	13,113.42	12,820.43	12,693.89	12,638.23	12,613.56
16.50%	22,863.60	18,737.54	17,506.29	15,869.73	13,984.49	13,288.78	13,003.68	12,881.88	12,828.92	12,805.72
16.75%	22,988.07	18,871.18	17,644.36	16,016.16	14,148.29	13,464.72	13,187.37	13,070.18	13,019.81	12,998.01
17.00%	23,112.90	19,005.30	17,782.95	16,163.18	14,312.74	13,641.25	13,371.51	13,258.78	13,210.89	13,190.41
17.25%	23,238.09	19,139.90	17,922.08	16,310.81	14,477.84	13,818.33	13,556.06	13,447.67	13,402.15	13,382.92
17.50%	23,363.66	19,274.99	18,061.73	16,459.02	14,643.58	13,995.96	13,741.03	13,636.82	13,593.58	13,575.52
17.75%	23,489.59	19,410.55	18,201.90	16,607.83	14,809.94	14,174.12	13,926.38	13,826.24	13,785.16	13,768.22
18.00%	23,615.89	19,546.59	18,342.59	16,757.22	14,976.92	14,352.80	14,112.10	14,015.89	13,976.90	13,961.00
18.25%	23,742.55	19,683.10	18,483.80	16,907.19	15,144.50	14,531.97	14,298.18	14,205.78	14,168.76	14,153.85
18.50%	23,869.57	19,820.08	18,625.52	17,057.74	15,312.67	14,711.64	14,484.60	14,395.88	14,360.76	14,346.78
18.75%	23,996.96	19,957.54	18,767.75	17,208.85	15,481.42	14,891.77	14,671.36	14,586.19	14,552.87	14,539.77
19.00%	24,124.71	20,095.46	18,910.49	17,360.53	15,650.75	15,072.37	14,858.42	14,776.70	14,745.10	14,732.83
19.25%	24,252.82	20,233.84	19,053.74	17,512.77	15,820.63	15,253.41	15,045.80	14,967.39	14,937.43	14,925.93
19.50%	24,381.29	20,372.69	19,197.49	17,665.56	15,991.07	15,434.88	15,233.46	15,158.26	15,129.86	15,119.10
19.75%	24,510.12	20,512.00	19,341.73	17,818.89	16,162.05	15,616.77	15,421.40	15,349.29	15,322.38	15,312.30
20.00%	24,639.31	20,651.77	19,486.48	17,972.78	16,333.56	15,799.07	15,609.60	15,540.47	15,514.99	15,505.56
20.25%	24,768.86	20,791.99	19,631.71	18,127.20	16,505.59	15,981.76	15,798.06	15,731.81	15,707.67	15,698.85
20.50%	24,898.76	20,932.66	19,777.44	18,282.15	16,678.12	16,164.83	15,986.77	15,923.28	15,900.43	15,892.18
20.75%	25,029.01	21,073.79	19,923.65	18,437.64	16,851.16	16,348.28	16,175.70	16,114.89	16,093.26	16,085.54

$940,000   1.00 - 10.75%   5 - 40 Years

	5	7	8	10	15	20	25	30	35	40
1.00%	16,068.12	11,591.37	10,192.63	8,234.79	5,625.85	4,323.01	3,542.60	3,023.41	2,653.49	2,376.85
1.25%	16,169.51	11,693.02	10,294.50	8,337.19	5,729.81	4,428.66	3,649.99	3,132.57	2,764.41	2,489.55
1.50%	16,271.29	11,795.24	10,397.03	8,440.40	5,834.98	4,535.93	3,759.40	3,244.13	2,878.13	2,605.42
1.75%	16,373.49	11,898.03	10,500.20	8,544.43	5,941.38	4,644.81	3,870.82	3,358.09	2,994.63	2,724.44
2.00%	16,476.09	12,001.39	10,604.02	8,649.26	6,048.98	4,755.30	3,984.23	3,474.42	3,113.87	2,846.56
2.25%	16,579.10	12,105.32	10,708.49	8,754.91	6,157.80	4,867.40	4,099.63	3,593.11	3,235.82	2,971.74
2.50%	16,682.52	12,209.81	10,813.61	8,861.37	6,267.82	4,981.09	4,217.00	3,714.14	3,360.46	3,099.92
2.75%	16,786.34	12,314.87	10,919.38	8,968.64	6,379.04	5,096.36	4,336.32	3,837.47	3,487.73	3,231.04
3.00%	16,890.57	12,420.50	11,025.80	9,076.71	6,491.47	5,213.22	4,457.59	3,963.08	3,617.59	3,365.05
3.25%	16,995.20	12,526.70	11,132.86	9,185.59	6,605.09	5,331.64	4,580.77	4,090.94	3,750.01	3,501.89
3.50%	17,100.24	12,633.46	11,240.57	9,295.27	6,719.90	5,451.62	4,705.86	4,221.02	3,884.93	3,641.48
3.75%	17,205.68	12,740.79	11,348.92	9,405.76	6,835.89	5,573.15	4,832.83	4,353.29	4,022.31	3,783.74
4.00%	17,311.53	12,848.68	11,457.92	9,517.04	6,953.07	5,696.22	4,961.67	4,487.70	4,162.08	3,928.62
4.25%	17,417.78	12,957.13	11,567.56	9,629.13	7,071.42	5,820.80	5,092.34	4,624.23	4,304.20	4,076.03
4.50%	17,524.44	13,066.15	11,677.84	9,742.01	7,190.94	5,946.90	5,224.83	4,762.84	4,448.61	4,225.89
4.75%	17,631.50	13,175.73	11,788.76	9,855.69	7,311.62	6,074.50	5,359.10	4,903.48	4,595.25	4,378.12
5.00%	17,738.96	13,285.87	11,900.32	9,970.16	7,433.46	6,203.58	5,495.15	5,046.12	4,744.06	4,532.65
5.25%	17,846.82	13,396.58	12,012.53	10,085.42	7,556.45	6,334.14	5,632.93	5,190.71	4,894.98	4,689.38
5.50%	17,955.09	13,507.84	12,125.36	10,201.47	7,680.58	6,466.14	5,772.42	5,337.22	5,047.95	4,848.24
5.75%	18,063.76	13,619.66	12,238.84	10,318.31	7,805.85	6,599.58	5,913.60	5,485.58	5,202.91	5,009.14
6.00%	18,172.83	13,732.04	12,352.94	10,435.93	7,932.25	6,734.45	6,056.43	5,635.77	5,359.78	5,172.01
6.25%	18,282.31	13,844.98	12,467.69	10,554.33	8,059.77	6,870.73	6,200.89	5,787.74	5,518.52	5,336.75
6.50%	18,392.18	13,958.47	12,583.06	10,673.51	8,188.41	7,008.39	6,346.95	5,941.44	5,679.05	5,503.29
6.75%	18,502.45	14,072.52	12,699.06	10,793.47	8,318.15	7,147.42	6,494.57	6,096.82	5,841.32	5,671.55
7.00%	18,613.13	14,187.12	12,815.69	10,914.20	8,448.99	7,287.81	6,643.72	6,253.84	6,005.25	5,841.45
7.25%	18,724.20	14,302.27	12,932.95	11,035.70	8,580.91	7,429.53	6,794.38	6,412.46	6,170.79	6,012.92
7.50%	18,835.67	14,417.98	13,050.84	11,157.97	8,713.92	7,572.58	6,946.52	6,572.62	6,337.88	6,185.86
7.75%	18,947.54	14,534.24	13,169.35	11,281.00	8,847.99	7,716.92	7,100.09	6,734.28	6,506.45	6,360.23
8.00%	19,059.81	14,651.04	13,288.48	11,404.79	8,983.13	7,862.54	7,255.07	6,897.39	6,676.45	6,535.93
8.25%	19,172.48	14,768.40	13,408.23	11,529.35	9,119.32	8,009.42	7,411.43	7,061.91	6,847.82	6,712.90
8.50%	19,285.54	14,886.30	13,528.60	11,654.65	9,256.55	8,157.54	7,569.13	7,227.79	7,020.49	6,891.08
8.75%	19,399.00	15,004.74	13,649.59	11,780.71	9,394.82	8,306.88	7,728.15	7,394.98	7,194.41	7,070.40
9.00%	19,512.85	15,123.73	13,771.19	11,907.52	9,534.11	8,457.42	7,888.45	7,563.45	7,369.53	7,250.80
9.25%	19,627.10	15,243.27	13,893.41	12,035.08	9,674.41	8,609.15	8,049.99	7,733.15	7,545.80	7,432.21
9.50%	19,741.75	15,363.34	14,016.23	12,163.37	9,815.71	8,762.03	8,212.75	7,904.03	7,723.15	7,614.58
9.75%	19,856.79	15,483.96	14,139.67	12,292.40	9,958.01	8,916.06	8,376.69	8,076.05	7,901.54	7,797.85
10.00%	19,972.22	15,605.11	14,263.71	12,422.17	10,101.29	9,071.20	8,541.79	8,249.17	8,080.92	7,981.97
10.25%	20,088.05	15,726.80	14,388.36	12,552.67	10,245.54	9,227.45	8,708.00	8,423.35	8,261.24	8,166.89
10.50%	20,204.27	15,849.03	14,513.62	12,683.89	10,390.75	9,384.77	8,875.31	8,598.55	8,442.46	8,352.56
10.75%	20,320.88	15,971.80	14,639.47	12,815.84	10,536.91	9,543.15	9,043.67	8,774.72	8,624.53	8,538.93

$940,000   11.00 - 20.75%   5 - 40 Years

	5	7	8	10	15	20	25	30	35	40
11.00%	20,437.88	16,095.09	14,765.92	12,948.50	10,684.01	9,702.57	9,213.06	8,951.84	8,807.40	8,725.97
11.25%	20,555.27	16,218.92	14,892.97	13,081.88	10,832.04	9,863.01	9,383.45	9,129.86	8,991.04	8,913.62
11.50%	20,673.05	16,343.27	15,020.61	13,215.97	10,980.98	10,024.44	9,554.81	9,308.74	9,175.41	9,101.85
11.75%	20,791.22	16,468.16	15,148.85	13,350.77	11,130.83	10,186.85	9,727.10	9,488.45	9,360.46	9,290.62
12.00%	20,909.78	16,593.57	15,277.67	13,486.27	11,281.58	10,350.21	9,900.31	9,668.96	9,546.17	9,479.90
12.25%	21,028.73	16,719.50	15,407.08	13,622.47	11,433.21	10,514.51	10,074.39	9,850.23	9,732.49	9,669.65
12.50%	21,148.06	16,845.96	15,537.08	13,759.36	11,585.71	10,679.72	10,249.33	10,032.22	9,919.39	9,859.84
12.75%	21,267.78	16,972.94	15,667.66	13,896.94	11,739.07	10,845.83	10,425.09	10,214.92	10,106.84	10,050.45
13.00%	21,387.89	17,100.45	15,798.82	14,035.21	11,893.28	11,012.81	10,601.65	10,398.28	10,294.82	10,241.43
13.25%	21,508.38	17,228.46	15,930.56	14,174.16	12,048.32	11,180.65	10,778.98	10,582.27	10,483.28	10,432.78
13.50%	21,629.26	17,357.00	16,062.87	14,313.78	12,204.19	11,349.32	10,957.06	10,766.87	10,672.20	10,624.45
13.75%	21,750.51	17,486.05	16,195.76	14,454.08	12,360.88	11,518.81	11,135.86	10,952.06	10,861.56	10,816.44
14.00%	21,872.16	17,615.61	16,329.21	14,595.04	12,518.37	11,689.10	11,315.35	11,137.79	11,051.33	11,008.72
14.25%	21,994.18	17,745.68	16,463.23	14,736.67	12,676.65	11,860.16	11,495.52	11,324.06	11,241.48	11,201.26
14.50%	22,116.58	17,876.27	16,597.82	14,878.96	12,835.71	12,031.98	11,676.33	11,510.83	11,432.00	11,394.05
14.75%	22,239.37	18,007.36	16,732.97	15,021.90	12,995.54	12,204.54	11,857.77	11,698.07	11,622.86	11,587.07
15.00%	22,362.53	18,138.95	16,868.68	15,165.49	13,156.12	12,377.82	12,039.81	11,885.77	11,814.04	11,780.31
15.25%	22,486.08	18,271.05	17,004.95	15,309.72	13,317.45	12,551.81	12,222.43	12,073.91	12,005.53	11,973.74
15.50%	22,610.00	18,403.65	17,141.77	15,454.59	13,479.51	12,726.48	12,405.61	12,262.46	12,197.30	12,167.36
15.75%	22,734.30	18,536.74	17,279.14	15,600.10	13,642.29	12,901.82	12,589.32	12,451.40	12,389.33	12,361.15
16.00%	22,858.97	18,670.34	17,417.06	15,746.23	13,805.79	13,077.81	12,773.56	12,640.72	12,581.61	12,555.10
16.25%	22,984.02	18,804.43	17,555.52	15,892.99	13,969.98	13,254.43	12,958.29	12,830.39	12,774.13	12,749.19
16.50%	23,109.45	18,939.02	17,694.53	16,040.38	14,134.86	13,431.67	13,143.50	13,020.39	12,966.87	12,943.42
16.75%	23,235.25	19,074.09	17,834.08	16,188.37	14,300.42	13,609.50	13,329.17	13,210.72	13,159.81	13,137.77
17.00%	23,361.42	19,209.66	17,974.17	16,336.98	14,466.64	13,787.93	13,515.29	13,401.35	13,352.95	13,332.24
17.25%	23,487.97	19,345.71	18,114.79	16,486.19	14,633.52	13,966.91	13,701.83	13,592.27	13,546.26	13,526.82
17.50%	23,614.88	19,482.25	18,255.94	16,636.00	14,801.04	14,146.45	13,888.78	13,783.46	13,739.75	13,721.49
17.75%	23,742.17	19,619.27	18,397.62	16,786.41	14,969.19	14,326.53	14,076.12	13,974.91	13,933.39	13,916.26
18.00%	23,869.82	19,756.77	18,539.82	16,937.41	15,137.96	14,507.13	14,263.84	14,166.60	14,127.18	14,111.11
18.25%	23,997.85	19,894.75	18,682.55	17,088.99	15,307.34	14,688.23	14,451.92	14,358.53	14,321.11	14,306.04
18.50%	24,126.24	20,033.20	18,825.79	17,241.15	15,477.32	14,869.83	14,640.35	14,550.68	14,515.17	14,501.05
18.75%	24,254.99	20,172.13	18,969.56	17,393.89	15,647.89	15,051.90	14,829.11	14,743.04	14,709.36	14,696.11
19.00%	24,384.12	20,311.54	19,113.83	17,547.20	15,819.03	15,234.44	15,018.19	14,935.59	14,903.65	14,891.24
19.25%	24,513.61	20,451.41	19,258.62	17,701.07	15,990.75	15,417.42	15,207.58	15,128.33	15,098.05	15,086.43
19.50%	24,643.46	20,591.75	19,403.91	17,855.51	16,163.02	15,600.85	15,397.26	15,321.25	15,292.55	15,281.67
19.75%	24,773.67	20,732.56	19,549.71	18,010.50	16,335.83	15,784.69	15,587.22	15,514.33	15,487.14	15,476.95
20.00%	24,904.25	20,873.83	19,696.01	18,166.03	16,509.19	15,968.95	15,777.45	15,707.58	15,681.82	15,672.28
20.25%	25,035.19	21,015.56	19,842.80	18,322.12	16,683.07	16,153.61	15,967.93	15,900.97	15,876.57	15,867.65
20.50%	25,166.49	21,157.75	19,990.10	18,478.74	16,857.46	16,338.65	16,158.67	16,094.50	16,071.40	16,063.06
20.75%	25,298.14	21,300.39	20,137.88	18,635.89	17,032.36	16,524.06	16,349.64	16,288.17	16,266.31	16,258.50

	5	7	8	10	15	20	25	30	35	40
1.00%	16,239.06	11,714.68	10,301.06	8,322.39	5,685.70	4,369.00	3,580.29	3,055.58	2,681.71	2,402.13
1.25%	16,341.52	11,817.42	10,404.02	8,425.88	5,790.76	4,475.77	3,688.82	3,165.89	2,793.82	2,516.03
1.50%	16,444.39	11,920.72	10,507.63	8,530.19	5,897.06	4,584.18	3,799.40	3,278.64	2,908.75	2,633.14
1.75%	16,547.68	12,024.61	10,611.90	8,635.33	6,004.58	4,694.22	3,912.00	3,393.81	3,026.49	2,753.42
2.00%	16,651.37	12,129.06	10,716.83	8,741.28	6,113.33	4,805.89	4,026.62	3,511.38	3,147.00	2,876.84
2.25%	16,755.48	12,234.10	10,822.41	8,848.05	6,223.31	4,919.18	4,143.24	3,631.34	3,270.25	3,003.35
2.50%	16,859.99	12,339.70	10,928.65	8,955.64	6,334.50	5,034.08	4,261.86	3,753.65	3,396.20	3,132.89
2.75%	16,964.92	12,445.88	11,035.55	9,064.05	6,446.91	5,150.58	4,382.45	3,878.29	3,524.83	3,265.41
3.00%	17,070.26	12,552.64	11,143.09	9,173.27	6,560.53	5,268.68	4,505.01	4,005.24	3,656.08	3,400.85
3.25%	17,176.00	12,659.96	11,251.29	9,283.31	6,675.35	5,388.36	4,629.50	4,134.46	3,789.90	3,539.14
3.50%	17,282.16	12,767.86	11,360.15	9,394.16	6,791.38	5,509.62	4,755.92	4,265.92	3,926.26	3,680.21
3.75%	17,388.72	12,876.33	11,469.65	9,505.82	6,908.61	5,632.44	4,884.25	4,399.60	4,065.10	3,824.00
4.00%	17,495.70	12,985.37	11,579.81	9,618.29	7,027.04	5,756.81	5,014.45	4,535.45	4,206.36	3,970.42
4.25%	17,603.08	13,094.98	11,690.62	9,731.57	7,146.64	5,882.73	5,146.51	4,673.43	4,349.99	4,119.39
4.50%	17,710.87	13,205.15	11,802.07	9,845.65	7,267.44	6,010.17	5,280.41	4,813.51	4,495.94	4,270.85
4.75%	17,819.07	13,315.90	11,914.18	9,960.54	7,389.40	6,139.12	5,416.11	4,955.65	4,644.14	4,424.70
5.00%	17,927.67	13,427.21	12,026.92	10,076.22	7,512.54	6,269.58	5,553.61	5,099.81	4,794.53	4,580.87
5.25%	18,036.68	13,539.09	12,140.32	10,192.71	7,636.84	6,401.52	5,692.85	5,245.94	4,947.06	4,739.27
5.50%	18,146.10	13,651.54	12,254.36	10,310.00	7,762.29	6,534.93	5,833.83	5,394.00	5,101.65	4,899.82
5.75%	18,255.93	13,764.55	12,369.04	10,428.08	7,888.90	6,669.79	5,976.51	5,543.94	5,258.26	5,062.43
6.00%	18,366.16	13,878.13	12,484.36	10,546.95	8,016.64	6,806.10	6,120.86	5,695.73	5,416.80	5,227.03
6.25%	18,476.80	13,992.26	12,600.32	10,666.61	8,145.52	6,943.82	6,266.86	5,849.31	5,577.23	5,393.53
6.50%	18,587.84	14,106.96	12,716.92	10,787.06	8,275.52	7,082.94	6,414.47	6,004.65	5,739.47	5,561.84
6.75%	18,699.29	14,222.23	12,834.16	10,908.29	8,406.64	7,223.46	6,563.66	6,161.68	5,903.46	5,731.89
7.00%	18,811.14	14,338.05	12,952.03	11,030.31	8,538.87	7,365.34	6,714.40	6,320.37	6,069.14	5,903.60
7.25%	18,923.39	14,454.43	13,070.54	11,153.10	8,672.20	7,508.57	6,866.67	6,480.67	6,236.44	6,076.88
7.50%	19,036.05	14,571.36	13,189.68	11,276.67	8,806.62	7,653.14	7,020.42	6,642.54	6,405.30	6,251.67
7.75%	19,149.11	14,688.86	13,309.45	11,401.01	8,942.12	7,799.01	7,175.62	6,805.92	6,575.67	6,427.89
8.00%	19,262.57	14,806.90	13,429.85	11,526.12	9,078.69	7,946.18	7,332.25	6,970.76	6,747.48	6,605.46
8.25%	19,376.44	14,925.51	13,550.87	11,652.00	9,216.33	8,094.62	7,490.28	7,137.03	6,920.67	6,784.32
8.50%	19,490.70	15,044.66	13,672.52	11,778.64	9,355.03	8,244.32	7,649.66	7,304.68	7,095.18	6,964.39
8.75%	19,605.37	15,164.37	13,794.80	11,906.04	9,494.76	8,395.25	7,810.36	7,473.65	7,270.95	7,145.62
9.00%	19,720.44	15,284.62	13,917.69	12,034.20	9,635.53	8,547.40	7,972.37	7,643.91	7,447.93	7,327.93
9.25%	19,835.90	15,405.43	14,041.21	12,163.11	9,777.33	8,700.73	8,135.63	7,815.42	7,626.07	7,511.28
9.50%	19,951.77	15,526.78	14,165.34	12,292.77	9,920.13	8,855.25	8,300.12	7,988.11	7,805.31	7,695.58
9.75%	20,068.03	15,648.68	14,290.09	12,423.17	10,063.95	9,010.91	8,465.81	8,161.97	7,985.60	7,880.81
10.00%	20,184.69	15,771.12	14,415.46	12,554.32	10,208.75	9,167.71	8,632.66	8,336.93	8,166.89	8,066.89
10.25%	20,301.75	15,894.11	14,541.43	12,686.21	10,354.53	9,325.61	8,800.64	8,512.96	8,349.13	8,253.77
10.50%	20,419.21	16,017.64	14,668.02	12,818.82	10,501.29	9,484.61	8,969.73	8,690.02	8,532.27	8,441.42
10.75%	20,537.06	16,141.71	14,795.21	12,952.17	10,649.01	9,644.68	9,139.88	8,868.07	8,716.28	8,629.77

$950,000

11.00 - 20.75%

5 - 40 Years

	5	7	8	10	15	20	25	30	35	40
11.00%	20,655.30	16,266.31	14,923.00	13,086.25	10,797.67	9,805.79	9,311.07	9,047.07	8,901.10	8,818.80
11.25%	20,773.94	16,391.46	15,051.40	13,221.05	10,947.27	9,967.93	9,483.28	9,226.98	9,086.69	9,008.44
11.50%	20,892.98	16,517.14	15,180.41	13,356.57	11,097.80	10,131.08	9,656.46	9,407.77	9,273.02	9,198.68
11.75%	21,012.40	16,643.35	15,310.00	13,492.80	11,249.25	10,295.22	9,830.58	9,589.39	9,460.04	9,389.46
12.00%	21,132.23	16,770.10	15,440.20	13,629.74	11,401.60	10,460.32	10,005.63	9,771.82	9,647.72	9,580.75
12.25%	21,252.44	16,897.37	15,570.99	13,767.39	11,554.84	10,626.36	10,181.57	9,955.02	9,836.03	9,772.52
12.50%	21,373.04	17,025.18	15,702.37	13,905.74	11,708.96	10,793.34	10,358.36	10,138.95	10,024.92	9,964.73
12.75%	21,494.04	17,153.51	15,834.34	14,044.78	11,863.95	10,961.21	10,536.00	10,323.59	10,214.36	10,157.37
13.00%	21,615.42	17,282.37	15,966.89	14,184.52	12,019.80	11,129.97	10,714.44	10,508.90	10,404.33	10,350.38
13.25%	21,737.19	17,411.75	16,100.03	14,324.95	12,176.50	11,299.59	10,893.65	10,694.85	10,594.80	10,543.76
13.50%	21,859.35	17,541.65	16,233.75	14,466.06	12,334.03	11,470.06	11,073.63	10,881.42	10,785.73	10,737.48
13.75%	21,981.90	17,672.07	16,368.05	14,607.85	12,492.38	11,641.35	11,254.33	11,068.57	10,977.11	10,931.51
14.00%	22,104.84	17,803.01	16,502.93	14,750.31	12,651.54	11,813.45	11,435.73	11,256.28	11,168.90	11,125.83
14.25%	22,228.16	17,934.47	16,638.37	14,893.45	12,811.51	11,986.33	11,617.81	11,444.53	11,361.07	11,320.42
14.50%	22,351.87	18,066.44	16,774.39	15,037.24	12,972.26	12,159.98	11,800.55	11,633.28	11,553.62	11,515.26
14.75%	22,475.96	18,198.92	16,910.98	15,181.71	13,133.79	12,334.38	11,983.92	11,822.52	11,746.51	11,710.34
15.00%	22,600.43	18,331.92	17,048.14	15,326.82	13,296.08	12,509.50	12,167.89	12,012.22	11,939.73	11,905.63
15.25%	22,725.29	18,465.42	17,185.85	15,472.59	13,459.12	12,685.34	12,352.45	12,202.36	12,133.25	12,101.12
15.50%	22,850.53	18,599.43	17,324.13	15,619.00	13,622.91	12,861.87	12,537.58	12,392.91	12,327.05	12,296.80
15.75%	22,976.15	18,733.94	17,462.96	15,766.06	13,787.42	13,039.07	12,723.25	12,583.86	12,521.13	12,492.65
16.00%	23,102.15	18,868.96	17,602.35	15,913.75	13,952.66	13,216.93	12,909.44	12,775.19	12,715.46	12,688.66
16.25%	23,228.54	19,004.48	17,742.29	16,062.07	14,118.60	13,395.43	13,096.14	12,966.88	12,910.02	12,884.82
16.50%	23,355.30	19,140.49	17,882.77	16,211.02	14,285.23	13,574.56	13,283.32	13,158.91	13,104.81	13,081.11
16.75%	23,482.43	19,277.01	18,023.81	16,360.59	14,452.55	13,754.29	13,470.97	13,351.26	13,299.81	13,277.54
17.00%	23,609.95	19,414.01	18,165.38	16,510.78	14,620.54	13,934.61	13,659.07	13,543.92	13,495.00	13,474.07
17.25%	23,737.84	19,551.51	18,307.50	16,661.58	14,789.19	14,115.50	13,847.59	13,736.86	13,690.37	13,670.72
17.50%	23,866.10	19,689.50	18,450.15	16,812.98	14,958.49	14,296.95	14,036.53	13,930.09	13,885.92	13,867.47
17.75%	23,994.74	19,827.98	18,593.34	16,964.99	15,128.43	14,478.94	14,225.87	14,123.58	14,081.62	14,064.31
18.00%	24,123.76	19,966.95	18,737.05	17,117.59	15,299.00	14,661.46	14,415.58	14,317.31	14,277.47	14,261.23
18.25%	24,253.14	20,106.39	18,881.30	17,270.79	15,470.18	14,844.49	14,605.67	14,511.28	14,473.47	14,458.24
18.50%	24,382.90	20,246.32	19,026.07	17,424.57	15,641.97	15,028.02	14,796.10	14,705.47	14,669.59	14,655.31
18.75%	24,513.03	20,386.73	19,171.36	17,578.93	15,814.36	15,212.03	14,986.87	14,899.88	14,865.84	14,852.46
19.00%	24,643.52	20,527.62	19,317.17	17,733.87	15,987.32	15,396.51	15,177.96	15,094.48	15,062.20	15,049.66
19.25%	24,774.39	20,668.98	19,463.50	17,889.38	16,160.86	15,581.44	15,369.36	15,289.27	15,258.67	15,246.92
19.50%	24,905.62	20,810.81	19,610.34	18,045.46	16,334.97	15,766.81	15,561.06	15,484.24	15,455.24	15,444.24
19.75%	25,037.22	20,953.12	19,757.69	18,202.10	16,509.62	15,952.62	15,753.04	15,679.38	15,651.90	15,641.60
20.00%	25,169.19	21,095.89	19,905.54	18,359.29	16,684.82	16,138.83	15,945.29	15,874.68	15,848.64	15,839.01
20.25%	25,301.52	21,239.13	20,053.90	18,517.03	16,860.54	16,325.45	16,137.80	16,070.13	16,045.47	16,036.46
20.50%	25,434.22	21,382.83	20,202.76	18,675.32	17,036.79	16,512.46	16,330.57	16,265.72	16,242.38	16,233.95
20.75%	25,567.27	21,526.99	20,352.11	18,834.15	17,213.55	16,699.85	16,523.57	16,461.45	16,439.35	16,431.47

	5	7	8	10	15	20	25	30	35	40
1.00%	16,410.00	11,838.00	10,409.50	8,410.00	5,745.55	4,414.99	3,617.98	3,087.74	2,709.94	2,427.42
1.25%	16,513.54	11,941.81	10,513.54	8,514.57	5,851.72	4,522.88	3,727.65	3,199.22	2,823.23	2,542.51
1.50%	16,617.49	12,046.20	10,618.24	8,619.98	5,959.13	4,632.44	3,839.39	3,313.15	2,939.37	2,660.86
1.75%	16,721.86	12,151.18	10,723.61	8,726.22	6,067.79	4,743.64	3,953.18	3,429.54	3,058.34	2,782.41
2.00%	16,826.65	12,256.74	10,829.64	8,833.29	6,177.68	4,856.48	4,069.00	3,548.35	3,180.12	2,907.13
2.25%	16,931.85	12,362.88	10,936.33	8,941.19	6,288.81	4,970.96	4,186.85	3,669.56	3,304.67	3,034.96
2.50%	17,037.47	12,469.59	11,043.69	9,049.91	6,401.18	5,087.07	4,306.72	3,793.16	3,431.95	3,165.87
2.75%	17,143.50	12,576.89	11,151.71	9,159.46	6,514.77	5,204.80	4,428.58	3,919.12	3,561.93	3,299.79
3.00%	17,249.94	12,684.77	11,260.39	9,269.83	6,629.58	5,324.14	4,552.43	4,047.40	3,694.56	3,436.65
3.25%	17,356.80	12,793.22	11,369.73	9,381.03	6,745.62	5,445.08	4,678.24	4,177.98	3,829.80	3,576.40
3.50%	17,464.08	12,902.26	11,479.73	9,493.04	6,862.87	5,567.61	4,805.99	4,310.83	3,967.59	3,718.95
3.75%	17,571.76	13,011.87	11,590.39	9,605.88	6,981.34	5,691.73	4,935.66	4,445.91	4,107.89	3,864.25
4.00%	17,679.86	13,122.05	11,701.70	9,719.53	7,101.00	5,817.41	5,067.23	4,583.19	4,250.64	4,012.21
4.25%	17,788.37	13,232.82	11,813.68	9,834.00	7,221.87	5,944.65	5,200.69	4,722.62	4,395.78	4,162.75
4.50%	17,897.30	13,344.15	11,926.31	9,949.29	7,343.94	6,073.43	5,335.99	4,864.18	4,543.26	4,315.80
4.75%	18,006.64	13,456.07	12,039.59	10,065.38	7,467.19	6,203.75	5,473.13	5,007.81	4,693.02	4,471.28
5.00%	18,116.38	13,568.55	12,153.52	10,182.29	7,591.62	6,335.58	5,612.06	5,153.49	4,845.00	4,629.09
5.25%	18,226.54	13,681.61	12,268.11	10,300.00	7,717.23	6,468.90	5,752.78	5,301.16	4,999.13	4,789.16
5.50%	18,337.12	13,795.24	12,383.35	10,418.52	7,844.00	6,603.72	5,895.24	5,450.77	5,155.36	4,951.39
5.75%	18,448.10	13,909.44	12,499.24	10,537.85	7,971.94	6,740.00	6,039.42	5,602.30	5,313.61	5,115.72
6.00%	18,559.49	14,024.21	12,615.77	10,657.97	8,101.03	6,877.74	6,185.29	5,755.69	5,473.82	5,282.05
6.25%	18,671.29	14,139.55	12,732.96	10,778.89	8,231.26	7,016.91	6,332.83	5,910.89	5,635.93	5,450.30
6.50%	18,783.50	14,255.46	12,850.78	10,900.61	8,362.63	7,157.50	6,481.99	6,067.85	5,799.88	5,620.39
6.75%	18,896.12	14,371.93	12,969.25	11,023.11	8,495.13	7,299.49	6,632.75	6,226.54	5,965.60	5,792.23
7.00%	19,009.15	14,488.97	13,088.37	11,146.41	8,628.75	7,442.87	6,785.08	6,386.90	6,133.02	5,965.74
7.25%	19,122.59	14,606.58	13,208.12	11,270.50	8,763.48	7,587.61	6,938.95	6,548.89	6,302.09	6,140.85
7.50%	19,236.43	14,724.74	13,328.52	11,395.37	8,899.32	7,733.69	7,094.32	6,712.46	6,472.73	6,317.48
7.75%	19,350.68	14,843.47	13,449.55	11,521.02	9,036.25	7,881.11	7,251.16	6,877.56	6,644.89	6,495.55
8.00%	19,465.34	14,962.77	13,571.21	11,647.45	9,174.26	8,029.82	7,409.44	7,044.14	6,818.50	6,674.99
8.25%	19,580.40	15,082.62	13,693.51	11,774.65	9,313.35	8,179.83	7,569.12	7,212.16	6,993.51	6,855.73
8.50%	19,695.87	15,203.03	13,816.44	11,902.63	9,453.50	8,331.10	7,730.18	7,381.57	7,169.86	7,037.70
8.75%	19,811.74	15,323.99	13,940.01	12,031.37	9,594.71	8,483.62	7,892.58	7,552.32	7,347.49	7,220.84
9.00%	19,928.02	15,445.52	14,064.20	12,160.87	9,736.96	8,637.37	8,056.29	7,724.38	7,526.33	7,405.07
9.25%	20,044.70	15,567.59	14,189.01	12,291.14	9,880.25	8,792.32	8,221.27	7,897.68	7,706.35	7,590.34
9.50%	20,161.79	15,690.22	14,314.45	12,422.17	10,024.56	8,948.46	8,387.49	8,072.20	7,887.47	7,776.59
9.75%	20,279.27	15,813.40	14,440.51	12,553.94	10,169.88	9,105.76	8,554.92	8,247.88	8,069.66	7,963.76
10.00%	20,397.16	15,937.14	14,567.20	12,686.47	10,316.21	9,264.21	8,723.53	8,424.69	8,252.86	8,151.80
10.25%	20,515.45	16,061.42	14,694.50	12,819.74	10,463.53	9,423.78	8,893.28	8,602.57	8,437.01	8,340.65
10.50%	20,634.14	16,186.25	14,822.42	12,953.76	10,611.83	9,584.45	9,064.14	8,781.50	8,622.09	8,530.27
10.75%	20,753.24	16,311.62	14,950.95	13,088.51	10,761.10	9,746.20	9,236.09	8,961.42	8,808.03	8,720.61

$960,000   11.00 - 20.75%   5 - 40 Years

	5	7	8	10	15	20	25	30	35	40
11.00%	20,872.73	16,437.54	15,080.09	13,224.00	10,911.33	9,909.01	9,409.09	9,142.30	8,994.79	8,911.63
11.25%	20,992.62	16,564.00	15,209.84	13,360.22	11,062.51	10,072.86	9,583.10	9,324.11	9,182.34	9,103.27
11.50%	21,112.90	16,691.00	15,340.20	13,497.16	11,214.62	10,237.72	9,758.10	9,506.80	9,370.63	9,295.51
11.75%	21,233.59	16,818.54	15,471.16	13,634.83	11,367.66	10,403.59	9,934.06	9,690.33	9,559.62	9,488.29
12.00%	21,354.67	16,946.62	15,602.73	13,773.21	11,521.61	10,570.43	10,110.95	9,874.68	9,749.28	9,681.60
12.25%	21,476.15	17,075.24	15,734.89	13,912.31	11,676.47	10,738.22	10,288.74	10,059.81	9,939.56	9,875.43
12.50%	21,598.02	17,204.39	15,867.66	14,052.11	11,832.21	10,906.95	10,467.40	10,245.67	10,130.44	10,069.63
12.75%	21,720.29	17,334.07	16,001.01	14,192.62	11,988.83	11,076.59	10,646.90	10,432.25	10,321.88	10,264.29
13.00%	21,842.95	17,464.28	16,134.96	14,333.83	12,146.32	11,247.13	10,827.22	10,619.52	10,513.85	10,459.34
13.25%	21,966.00	17,595.03	16,269.51	14,475.74	12,304.67	11,418.54	11,008.32	10,807.43	10,706.33	10,654.75
13.50%	22,089.45	17,726.30	16,404.63	14,618.33	12,463.86	11,590.80	11,190.19	10,995.96	10,899.27	10,850.51
13.75%	22,213.29	17,858.09	16,540.35	14,761.61	12,623.88	11,763.89	11,372.79	11,185.08	11,092.66	11,046.58
14.00%	22,337.52	17,990.41	16,676.64	14,905.58	12,784.72	11,937.80	11,556.11	11,374.77	11,286.46	11,242.94
14.25%	22,462.14	18,123.25	16,813.52	15,050.22	12,946.36	12,112.50	11,740.10	11,565.00	11,480.66	11,439.58
14.50%	22,587.15	18,256.61	16,950.97	15,195.53	13,108.81	12,287.98	11,924.76	11,755.74	11,675.24	11,636.48
14.75%	22,712.55	18,390.49	17,088.99	15,341.51	13,272.04	12,464.21	12,110.06	11,946.97	11,870.16	11,833.60
15.00%	22,838.33	18,524.88	17,227.59	15,488.16	13,436.04	12,641.18	12,295.97	12,138.66	12,065.41	12,030.95
15.25%	22,964.51	18,659.79	17,366.75	15,635.46	13,600.80	12,818.87	12,482.48	12,330.80	12,260.97	12,228.50
15.50%	23,091.06	18,795.21	17,506.49	15,783.41	13,766.31	12,997.25	12,669.55	12,523.36	12,456.81	12,426.24
15.75%	23,218.01	18,931.14	17,646.78	15,932.01	13,932.55	13,176.32	12,857.18	12,716.32	12,652.93	12,624.15
16.00%	23,345.33	19,067.58	17,787.63	16,081.26	14,099.53	13,356.06	13,045.33	12,909.67	12,849.31	12,822.23
16.25%	23,473.05	19,204.53	17,929.05	16,231.14	14,267.21	13,536.44	13,234.00	13,103.37	13,045.92	13,020.45
16.50%	23,601.14	19,341.97	18,071.01	16,381.66	14,435.60	13,717.45	13,423.15	13,297.42	13,242.76	13,218.81
16.75%	23,729.62	19,479.92	18,213.53	16,532.81	14,604.68	13,899.07	13,612.77	13,491.80	13,439.81	13,417.30
17.00%	23,858.47	19,618.37	18,356.60	16,684.57	14,774.44	14,081.29	13,802.85	13,686.48	13,637.05	13,615.91
17.25%	23,987.71	19,757.32	18,500.21	16,836.96	14,944.87	14,264.08	13,993.36	13,881.46	13,834.48	13,814.62
17.50%	24,117.33	19,896.76	18,644.36	16,989.96	15,115.95	14,447.44	14,184.29	14,076.72	14,032.08	14,013.44
17.75%	24,247.32	20,036.70	18,789.06	17,143.57	15,287.68	14,631.35	14,375.61	14,272.25	14,229.85	14,212.35
18.00%	24,377.69	20,177.12	18,934.29	17,297.78	15,460.04	14,815.79	14,567.33	14,468.02	14,427.76	14,411.35
18.25%	24,508.44	20,318.04	19,080.05	17,452.59	15,633.03	15,000.75	14,759.41	14,664.03	14,625.82	14,610.43
18.50%	24,639.56	20,459.44	19,226.34	17,607.99	15,806.62	15,186.21	14,951.85	14,860.27	14,824.01	14,809.58
18.75%	24,771.06	20,601.33	19,373.16	17,763.98	15,980.82	15,372.15	15,144.63	15,056.72	15,022.32	15,008.80
19.00%	24,902.93	20,743.70	19,520.51	17,920.55	16,155.61	15,558.57	15,337.73	15,253.37	15,220.75	15,208.08
19.25%	25,035.17	20,886.55	19,668.38	18,077.69	16,330.98	15,745.45	15,531.14	15,450.21	15,419.29	15,407.42
19.50%	25,167.79	21,029.87	19,816.76	18,235.41	16,506.91	15,932.78	15,724.86	15,647.23	15,617.92	15,606.81
19.75%	25,300.77	21,173.68	19,965.66	18,393.70	16,683.41	16,120.54	15,918.86	15,844.42	15,816.65	15,806.25
20.00%	25,434.13	21,317.95	20,115.07	18,552.54	16,860.45	16,308.72	16,113.14	16,041.78	16,015.47	16,005.74
20.25%	25,567.85	21,462.70	20,264.99	18,711.95	17,038.02	16,497.30	16,307.68	16,239.29	16,214.37	16,205.26
20.50%	25,701.94	21,607.91	20,415.42	18,871.90	17,216.13	16,686.28	16,502.47	16,436.94	16,413.35	16,404.83
20.75%	25,836.40	21,753.59	20,566.34	19,032.40	17,394.75	16,875.64	16,697.50	16,634.72	16,612.40	16,604.43

$970,000   1.00 - 10.75%   5 - 40 Years

	5	7	8	10	15	20	25	30	35	40
1.00%	16,580.94	11,961.31	10,517.93	8,497.60	5,805.40	4,460.97	3,655.66	3,119.90	2,738.17	2,452.70
1.25%	16,685.55	12,066.20	10,623.05	8,603.27	5,912.67	4,570.00	3,766.48	3,232.54	2,852.64	2,569.00
1.50%	16,790.59	12,171.69	10,728.84	8,709.78	6,021.21	4,680.69	3,879.38	3,347.67	2,969.99	2,688.57
1.75%	16,896.05	12,277.76	10,835.31	8,817.12	6,131.00	4,793.05	3,994.35	3,465.26	3,090.20	2,811.39
2.00%	17,001.93	12,384.41	10,942.45	8,925.31	6,242.03	4,907.07	4,111.39	3,585.31	3,213.25	2,937.41
2.25%	17,108.22	12,491.66	11,050.25	9,034.33	6,354.32	5,022.74	4,230.47	3,707.79	3,339.09	3,066.58
2.50%	17,214.94	12,599.49	11,158.73	9,144.18	6,467.86	5,140.06	4,351.58	3,832.67	3,467.70	3,198.85
2.75%	17,322.08	12,707.90	11,267.87	9,254.87	6,582.63	5,259.01	4,474.72	3,959.94	3,599.04	3,334.16
3.00%	17,429.63	12,816.90	11,377.68	9,366.39	6,698.64	5,379.60	4,599.85	4,089.56	3,733.05	3,472.45
3.25%	17,537.60	12,926.49	11,488.16	9,478.75	6,815.89	5,501.80	4,726.97	4,221.50	3,869.69	3,613.65
3.50%	17,645.99	13,036.66	11,599.31	9,591.93	6,934.36	5,625.61	4,856.05	4,355.73	4,008.92	3,757.69
3.75%	17,754.80	13,147.41	11,711.12	9,705.94	7,054.06	5,751.02	4,987.07	4,492.22	4,150.68	3,904.50
4.00%	17,864.03	13,258.74	11,823.60	9,820.78	7,174.97	5,878.01	5,120.02	4,630.93	4,294.91	4,054.00
4.25%	17,973.67	13,370.66	11,936.74	9,936.44	7,297.10	6,006.57	5,254.86	4,771.82	4,441.57	4,206.12
4.50%	18,083.73	13,483.16	12,050.54	10,052.93	7,420.43	6,136.70	5,391.58	4,914.85	4,590.59	4,360.76
4.75%	18,194.20	13,596.23	12,165.00	10,170.23	7,544.97	6,268.37	5,530.14	5,059.98	4,741.91	4,517.85
5.00%	18,305.10	13,709.89	12,280.12	10,288.35	7,670.70	6,401.57	5,670.52	5,207.17	4,895.47	4,677.31
5.25%	18,416.40	13,824.13	12,395.90	10,407.30	7,797.61	6,536.29	5,812.70	5,356.38	5,051.21	4,839.04
5.50%	18,528.13	13,938.94	12,512.34	10,527.05	7,925.71	6,672.51	5,956.65	5,507.55	5,209.06	5,002.97
5.75%	18,640.27	14,054.33	12,629.44	10,647.61	8,054.98	6,810.21	6,102.33	5,660.66	5,368.96	5,169.01
6.00%	18,752.82	14,170.30	12,747.19	10,768.99	8,185.41	6,949.38	6,249.72	5,815.64	5,530.84	5,337.07
6.25%	18,865.78	14,286.84	12,865.59	10,891.17	8,317.00	7,090.00	6,398.79	5,972.46	5,694.64	5,507.07
6.50%	18,979.16	14,403.95	12,984.65	11,014.15	8,449.74	7,232.06	6,549.51	6,131.06	5,860.30	5,678.93
6.75%	19,092.96	14,521.64	13,104.35	11,137.94	8,583.62	7,375.53	6,701.84	6,291.40	6,027.74	5,852.56
7.00%	19,207.16	14,639.90	13,224.71	11,262.52	8,718.63	7,520.40	6,855.76	6,453.43	6,196.91	6,027.88
7.25%	19,321.78	14,758.73	13,345.71	11,387.90	8,854.77	7,666.65	7,011.23	6,617.11	6,367.73	6,204.82
7.50%	19,436.81	14,878.13	13,467.35	11,514.07	8,992.02	7,814.25	7,168.21	6,782.38	6,540.15	6,383.29
7.75%	19,552.25	14,998.09	13,589.65	11,641.03	9,130.37	7,963.20	7,326.69	6,949.20	6,714.11	6,563.21
8.00%	19,668.10	15,118.63	13,712.58	11,768.78	9,269.83	8,113.47	7,486.62	7,117.52	6,889.53	6,744.52
8.25%	19,784.36	15,239.73	13,836.15	11,897.30	9,410.36	8,265.04	7,647.97	7,287.29	7,066.36	6,927.15
8.50%	19,901.04	15,361.39	13,960.36	12,026.61	9,551.97	8,417.89	7,810.70	7,458.46	7,244.55	7,111.01
8.75%	20,018.12	15,483.62	14,085.21	12,156.69	9,694.65	8,571.99	7,974.79	7,630.99	7,424.02	7,296.05
9.00%	20,135.60	15,606.41	14,210.70	12,287.55	9,838.39	8,727.34	8,140.20	7,804.84	7,604.73	7,482.21
9.25%	20,253.50	15,729.75	14,336.81	12,419.17	9,983.17	8,883.91	8,306.90	7,979.95	7,786.62	7,669.41
9.50%	20,371.81	15,853.66	14,463.56	12,551.56	10,128.98	9,041.67	8,474.86	8,156.29	7,969.63	7,857.60
9.75%	20,490.52	15,978.13	14,590.94	12,684.71	10,275.82	9,200.61	8,644.03	8,333.80	8,153.72	8,046.72
10.00%	20,609.63	16,103.15	14,718.94	12,818.62	10,423.67	9,360.71	8,814.40	8,512.44	8,338.82	8,236.72
10.25%	20,729.16	16,228.72	14,847.57	12,953.28	10,572.52	9,521.94	8,985.92	8,692.18	8,524.90	8,427.54
10.50%	20,849.08	16,354.85	14,976.82	13,088.69	10,722.37	9,684.28	9,158.56	8,872.97	8,711.90	8,619.13
10.75%	20,969.42	16,481.53	15,106.69	13,224.85	10,873.20	9,847.72	9,332.30	9,054.77	8,899.78	8,811.45

$970,000   11.00 - 20.75%   5 - 40 Years

	5	7	8	10	15	20	25	30	35	40
11.00%	21,090.15	16,608.76	15,237.17	13,361.75	11,024.99	10,012.23	9,507.10	9,237.54	9,088.49	9,004.46
11.25%	21,211.29	16,736.54	15,368.28	13,499.39	11,177.74	10,177.78	9,682.92	9,421.24	9,277.99	9,198.10
11.50%	21,332.83	16,864.87	15,499.99	13,637.76	11,331.44	10,344.37	9,859.75	9,605.83	9,468.24	9,392.33
11.75%	21,454.77	16,993.74	15,632.32	13,776.86	11,486.07	10,511.96	10,037.54	9,791.27	9,659.20	9,587.13
12.00%	21,577.11	17,123.15	15,765.26	13,916.68	11,641.63	10,680.54	10,216.27	9,977.54	9,850.83	9,782.45
12.25%	21,699.86	17,253.11	15,898.80	14,057.23	11,798.10	10,850.08	10,395.91	10,164.60	10,043.10	9,978.26
12.50%	21,823.00	17,383.60	16,032.94	14,198.49	11,955.46	11,020.56	10,576.44	10,352.40	10,235.97	10,174.52
12.75%	21,946.54	17,514.63	16,167.69	14,340.46	12,113.72	11,191.97	10,757.81	10,540.92	10,429.40	10,371.20
13.00%	22,070.48	17,646.20	16,303.04	14,483.14	12,272.85	11,364.28	10,940.00	10,730.14	10,623.37	10,568.29
13.25%	22,194.82	17,778.31	16,438.98	14,626.52	12,432.84	11,537.48	11,122.99	10,920.00	10,817.85	10,765.74
13.50%	22,319.55	17,910.95	16,575.51	14,770.61	12,593.69	11,711.53	11,306.76	11,110.50	11,012.80	10,963.53
13.75%	22,444.68	18,044.11	16,712.64	14,915.38	12,755.38	11,886.43	11,491.26	11,301.59	11,208.21	11,161.65
14.00%	22,570.20	18,177.81	16,850.36	15,060.84	12,917.89	12,062.15	11,676.48	11,493.26	11,404.03	11,360.06
14.25%	22,696.12	18,312.04	16,988.66	15,206.99	13,081.22	12,238.67	11,862.40	11,685.46	11,600.25	11,558.75
14.50%	22,822.43	18,446.79	17,127.54	15,353.82	13,245.36	12,415.98	12,048.98	11,878.19	11,796.85	11,757.69
14.75%	22,949.14	18,582.06	17,267.00	15,501.32	13,410.29	12,594.05	12,236.21	12,071.41	11,993.81	11,956.87
15.00%	23,076.23	18,717.85	17,407.04	15,649.49	13,576.00	12,772.86	12,424.06	12,265.11	12,191.09	12,156.27
15.25%	23,203.72	18,854.17	17,547.66	15,798.33	13,742.47	12,952.40	12,612.50	12,459.25	12,388.68	12,355.88
15.50%	23,331.60	18,991.00	17,688.85	15,947.82	13,909.71	13,132.64	12,801.53	12,653.81	12,586.57	12,555.68
15.75%	23,459.86	19,128.34	17,830.60	16,097.97	14,077.69	13,313.58	12,991.11	12,848.79	12,784.73	12,755.65
16.00%	23,588.52	19,266.20	17,972.92	16,248.77	14,246.40	13,495.18	13,181.22	13,044.14	12,983.15	12,955.79
16.25%	23,717.56	19,404.57	18,115.81	16,400.22	14,415.83	13,677.44	13,371.85	13,239.87	13,181.81	13,156.08
16.50%	23,846.99	19,543.45	18,259.25	16,552.30	14,585.97	13,860.34	13,562.97	13,435.94	13,380.70	13,356.51
16.75%	23,976.80	19,682.84	18,403.25	16,705.02	14,756.81	14,043.85	13,754.57	13,632.34	13,579.80	13,557.06
17.00%	24,107.00	19,822.73	18,547.81	16,858.37	14,928.34	14,227.97	13,946.63	13,829.05	13,779.10	13,757.74
17.25%	24,237.58	19,963.13	18,692.92	17,012.35	15,100.54	14,412.67	14,139.12	14,026.06	13,978.59	13,958.53
17.50%	24,368.55	20,104.02	18,838.57	17,166.94	15,273.41	14,597.94	14,332.04	14,223.35	14,178.25	14,159.41
17.75%	24,499.90	20,245.41	18,984.77	17,322.15	15,446.93	14,783.76	14,525.36	14,420.91	14,378.07	14,360.40
18.00%	24,631.62	20,387.30	19,131.52	17,477.96	15,621.08	14,970.12	14,719.07	14,618.73	14,578.05	14,561.47
18.25%	24,763.73	20,529.69	19,278.80	17,634.39	15,795.87	15,157.01	14,913.15	14,816.78	14,778.17	14,762.62
18.50%	24,896.22	20,672.56	19,426.62	17,791.40	15,971.28	15,344.40	15,107.60	15,015.06	14,978.43	14,963.84
18.75%	25,029.09	20,815.93	19,574.97	17,949.02	16,147.29	15,532.28	15,302.38	15,213.56	15,178.80	15,165.14
19.00%	25,162.33	20,959.78	19,723.85	18,107.22	16,323.90	15,720.64	15,497.50	15,412.26	15,379.30	15,366.50
19.25%	25,295.96	21,104.12	19,873.26	18,266.00	16,501.09	15,909.47	15,692.93	15,611.15	15,579.90	15,567.91
19.50%	25,429.95	21,248.94	20,023.19	18,425.36	16,678.86	16,098.75	15,888.66	15,810.22	15,780.61	15,769.38
19.75%	25,564.32	21,394.24	20,173.64	18,585.30	16,857.19	16,288.46	16,084.68	16,009.47	15,981.41	15,970.90
20.00%	25,699.07	21,540.01	20,324.60	18,745.80	17,036.08	16,478.60	16,280.98	16,208.88	16,182.30	16,172.46
20.25%	25,834.18	21,686.27	20,476.09	18,906.86	17,215.50	16,669.15	16,477.55	16,408.45	16,383.27	16,374.07
20.50%	25,969.67	21,832.99	20,628.08	19,068.48	17,395.46	16,860.10	16,674.37	16,608.16	16,584.32	16,575.71
20.75%	26,105.53	21,980.19	20,780.58	19,230.66	17,575.95	17,051.43	16,871.43	16,808.00	16,785.44	16,777.39

	5	7	8	10	15	20	25	30	35	40
1.00%	16,751.87	12,084.62	10,626.36	8,585.20	5,865.25	4,506.96	3,693.35	3,152.07	2,766.40	2,477.99
1.25%	16,857.57	12,190.60	10,732.57	8,691.96	5,973.63	4,617.11	3,805.31	3,265.87	2,882.05	2,595.48
1.50%	16,963.69	12,297.17	10,839.45	8,799.57	6,083.28	4,728.95	3,919.38	3,382.18	3,000.61	2,716.29
1.75%	17,070.24	12,404.33	10,947.01	8,908.02	6,194.20	4,842.46	4,035.53	3,500.99	3,122.06	2,840.37
2.00%	17,177.20	12,512.09	11,055.25	9,017.32	6,306.39	4,957.66	4,153.77	3,622.27	3,246.38	2,967.69
2.25%	17,284.60	12,620.44	11,164.17	9,127.46	6,419.83	5,074.52	4,274.08	3,746.01	3,373.52	3,098.19
2.50%	17,392.41	12,729.38	11,273.77	9,238.45	6,534.53	5,193.05	4,396.44	3,872.18	3,503.45	3,231.83
2.75%	17,500.65	12,838.91	11,384.04	9,350.28	6,650.49	5,313.23	4,520.85	4,000.76	3,636.14	3,368.53
3.00%	17,609.32	12,949.03	11,494.98	9,462.95	6,767.70	5,435.06	4,647.27	4,131.72	3,771.53	3,508.25
3.25%	17,718.40	13,059.75	11,606.60	9,576.46	6,886.15	5,558.52	4,775.70	4,265.02	3,909.58	3,650.90
3.50%	17,827.91	13,171.05	11,718.89	9,690.82	7,005.85	5,683.61	4,906.11	4,400.64	4,050.25	3,796.43
3.75%	17,937.84	13,282.95	11,831.85	9,806.00	7,126.78	5,810.31	5,038.49	4,538.53	4,193.47	3,944.75
4.00%	18,048.19	13,395.43	11,945.49	9,922.02	7,248.94	5,938.61	5,172.80	4,678.67	4,339.19	4,095.80
4.25%	18,158.96	13,508.50	12,059.80	10,038.88	7,372.33	6,068.50	5,309.03	4,821.01	4,487.36	4,249.48
4.50%	18,270.16	13,622.16	12,174.77	10,156.56	7,496.93	6,199.96	5,447.16	4,965.52	4,637.92	4,405.72
4.75%	18,381.77	13,736.40	12,290.41	10,275.08	7,622.75	6,332.99	5,587.15	5,112.14	4,790.80	4,564.43
5.00%	18,493.81	13,851.23	12,406.72	10,394.42	7,749.78	6,467.57	5,728.98	5,260.85	4,945.94	4,725.53
5.25%	18,606.26	13,966.64	12,523.70	10,514.59	7,878.00	6,603.67	5,872.63	5,411.60	5,103.28	4,888.93
5.50%	18,719.14	14,082.64	12,641.34	10,635.58	8,007.42	6,741.30	6,018.06	5,564.33	5,262.76	5,054.55
5.75%	18,832.43	14,199.22	12,759.64	10,757.38	8,138.02	6,880.42	6,165.24	5,719.01	5,424.31	5,222.30
6.00%	18,946.15	14,316.38	12,878.60	10,880.01	8,269.80	7,021.02	6,314.15	5,875.60	5,587.86	5,392.09
6.25%	19,060.28	14,434.13	12,998.23	11,003.45	8,402.74	7,163.10	6,464.76	6,034.03	5,753.35	5,563.85
6.50%	19,174.83	14,552.45	13,118.51	11,127.70	8,536.85	7,306.62	6,617.03	6,194.27	5,920.71	5,737.48
6.75%	19,289.79	14,671.35	13,239.45	11,252.76	8,672.11	7,451.57	6,770.93	6,356.26	6,089.88	5,912.90
7.00%	19,405.17	14,790.83	13,361.04	11,378.63	8,808.52	7,597.93	6,926.44	6,519.96	6,260.79	6,090.03
7.25%	19,520.97	14,910.88	13,483.29	11,505.30	8,946.06	7,745.68	7,083.51	6,685.33	6,433.38	6,268.78
7.50%	19,637.19	15,031.51	13,606.19	11,632.77	9,084.72	7,894.81	7,242.11	6,852.30	6,607.58	6,449.09
7.75%	19,753.82	15,152.71	13,729.75	11,761.04	9,224.50	8,045.30	7,402.22	7,020.84	6,783.32	6,630.87
8.00%	19,870.87	15,274.49	13,853.95	11,890.10	9,365.39	8,197.11	7,563.80	7,190.89	6,960.56	6,814.05
8.25%	19,988.33	15,396.84	13,978.79	12,019.96	9,507.38	8,350.24	7,726.81	7,362.41	7,139.21	6,998.56
8.50%	20,106.20	15,519.76	14,104.29	12,150.60	9,650.45	8,504.67	7,891.23	7,535.35	7,319.23	7,184.32
8.75%	20,224.49	15,643.24	14,230.42	12,282.02	9,794.60	8,660.36	8,057.01	7,709.66	7,500.56	7,371.27
9.00%	20,343.19	15,767.30	14,357.20	12,414.23	9,939.81	8,817.31	8,224.12	7,885.30	7,683.13	7,559.34
9.25%	20,462.30	15,891.92	14,484.62	12,547.21	10,086.08	8,975.49	8,392.54	8,062.22	7,866.89	7,748.47
9.50%	20,581.82	16,017.10	14,612.67	12,680.96	10,233.40	9,134.89	8,562.23	8,240.37	8,051.79	7,938.60
9.75%	20,701.76	16,142.85	14,741.36	12,815.48	10,381.75	9,295.47	8,733.15	8,419.71	8,237.78	8,129.67
10.00%	20,822.10	16,269.16	14,870.68	12,950.77	10,531.13	9,457.21	8,905.27	8,600.20	8,424.79	8,321.63
10.25%	20,942.86	16,396.03	15,000.63	13,086.82	10,681.52	9,620.11	9,078.56	8,781.79	8,612.78	8,514.42
10.50%	21,064.02	16,523.46	15,131.22	13,223.63	10,832.91	9,784.12	9,252.98	8,964.45	8,801.71	8,707.99
10.75%	21,185.59	16,651.45	15,262.42	13,361.19	10,985.29	9,949.24	9,428.51	9,148.12	8,991.53	8,902.29

$980,000   11.00 - 20.75%   5 - 40 Years

	5	7	8	10	15	20	25	30	35	40
11.00%	21,307.57	16,779.99	15,394.26	13,499.50	11,138.65	10,115.45	9,605.11	9,332.77	9,182.19	9,097.29
11.25%	21,429.96	16,909.08	15,526.71	13,638.56	11,292.98	10,282.71	9,782.75	9,518.36	9,373.64	9,292.92
11.50%	21,552.76	17,038.73	15,659.79	13,778.35	11,448.26	10,451.01	9,961.40	9,704.86	9,565.85	9,489.16
11.75%	21,675.95	17,168.93	15,793.48	13,918.89	11,604.49	10,620.33	10,141.02	9,892.22	9,758.78	9,685.97
12.00%	21,799.56	17,299.68	15,927.78	14,060.15	11,761.65	10,790.64	10,321.60	10,080.40	9,952.39	9,883.30
12.25%	21,923.57	17,430.97	16,062.70	14,202.15	11,919.73	10,961.93	10,503.09	10,269.39	10,146.64	10,081.12
12.50%	22,047.98	17,562.81	16,198.23	14,344.86	12,078.72	11,134.18	10,685.47	10,459.13	10,341.49	10,279.41
12.75%	22,172.79	17,695.20	16,334.37	14,488.30	12,238.60	11,307.35	10,868.71	10,649.59	10,536.92	10,478.12
13.00%	22,298.01	17,828.12	16,471.11	14,632.45	12,399.37	11,481.44	11,052.79	10,840.76	10,732.89	10,677.24
13.25%	22,423.63	17,961.59	16,608.45	14,777.31	12,561.02	11,656.42	11,237.66	11,032.58	10,929.37	10,876.73
13.50%	22,549.65	18,095.59	16,746.40	14,922.88	12,723.52	11,832.27	11,423.32	11,225.04	11,126.34	11,076.56
13.75%	22,676.07	18,230.14	16,884.94	15,069.15	12,886.88	12,008.97	11,609.73	11,418.10	11,323.75	11,276.72
14.00%	22,802.89	18,365.21	17,024.07	15,216.11	13,051.07	12,186.50	11,796.86	11,611.74	11,521.60	11,477.17
14.25%	22,930.10	18,500.82	17,163.80	15,363.76	13,216.08	12,364.85	11,984.69	11,805.93	11,719.85	11,677.91
14.50%	23,057.72	18,636.96	17,304.11	15,512.11	13,381.91	12,543.98	12,173.20	12,000.65	11,918.47	11,878.90
14.75%	23,185.73	18,773.63	17,445.01	15,661.13	13,548.54	12,723.88	12,362.35	12,195.86	12,117.45	12,080.14
15.00%	23,314.13	18,910.82	17,586.50	15,810.83	13,715.95	12,904.54	12,552.14	12,391.55	12,316.77	12,281.60
15.25%	23,442.93	19,048.54	17,728.56	15,961.20	13,884.15	13,085.93	12,742.53	12,587.69	12,516.40	12,483.26
15.50%	23,572.13	19,186.78	17,871.20	16,112.23	14,053.11	13,268.03	12,933.50	12,784.27	12,716.33	12,685.12
15.75%	23,701.72	19,325.54	18,014.42	16,263.93	14,222.82	13,450.83	13,125.04	12,981.25	12,916.53	12,887.15
16.00%	23,831.70	19,464.82	18,158.21	16,416.29	14,393.27	13,634.31	13,317.11	13,178.62	13,117.00	13,089.35
16.25%	23,962.07	19,604.62	18,302.57	16,569.29	14,564.45	13,818.45	13,509.70	13,376.36	13,317.71	13,291.71
16.50%	24,092.83	19,744.93	18,447.49	16,722.95	14,736.34	14,003.23	13,702.80	13,574.45	13,518.65	13,494.20
16.75%	24,223.98	19,885.75	18,592.98	16,877.24	14,908.95	14,188.63	13,896.37	13,772.88	13,719.80	13,696.83
17.00%	24,355.52	20,027.09	18,739.02	17,032.17	15,082.24	14,374.65	14,090.41	13,971.62	13,921.16	13,899.57
17.25%	24,487.45	20,168.93	18,885.63	17,187.73	15,256.22	14,561.25	14,284.89	14,170.66	14,122.70	14,102.43
17.50%	24,619.77	20,311.28	19,032.79	17,343.92	15,430.87	14,748.43	14,479.79	14,369.99	14,324.42	14,305.39
17.75%	24,752.47	20,454.13	19,180.49	17,500.73	15,606.17	14,936.17	14,675.11	14,569.58	14,526.30	14,508.44
18.00%	24,885.56	20,597.48	19,328.75	17,658.15	15,782.13	15,124.45	14,870.81	14,769.44	14,728.34	14,711.59
18.25%	25,019.03	20,741.33	19,477.55	17,816.18	15,958.72	15,313.26	15,066.90	14,969.53	14,930.52	14,914.81
18.50%	25,152.88	20,885.68	19,626.89	17,974.82	16,135.93	15,502.59	15,263.34	15,169.86	15,132.84	15,118.11
18.75%	25,287.12	21,030.52	19,776.77	18,134.06	16,313.76	15,692.41	15,460.14	15,370.40	15,335.29	15,321.48
19.00%	25,421.74	21,175.86	19,927.19	18,293.89	16,492.19	15,882.71	15,657.26	15,571.15	15,537.85	15,524.91
19.25%	25,556.74	21,321.68	20,078.13	18,454.31	16,671.21	16,073.48	15,854.71	15,772.09	15,740.52	15,728.40
19.50%	25,692.12	21,468.00	20,229.61	18,615.32	16,850.81	16,264.71	16,052.46	15,973.22	15,943.30	15,931.95
19.75%	25,827.87	21,614.79	20,381.61	18,776.90	17,030.98	16,456.38	16,250.50	16,174.52	16,146.17	16,135.55
20.00%	25,964.01	21,762.08	20,534.14	18,939.06	17,211.71	16,648.48	16,448.83	16,375.98	16,349.13	16,339.19
20.25%	26,100.52	21,909.84	20,687.18	19,101.78	17,392.98	16,840.99	16,647.42	16,577.60	16,552.17	16,542.87
20.50%	26,237.40	22,058.08	20,840.74	19,265.07	17,574.80	17,033.91	16,846.27	16,779.37	16,755.29	16,746.60
20.75%	26,374.66	22,206.79	20,994.81	19,428.91	17,757.14	17,227.22	17,045.36	16,981.28	16,958.49	16,950.36

	5	7	8	10	15	20	25	30	35	40
1.00%	16,922.81	12,207.93	10,734.79	8,672.81	5,925.10	4,552.95	3,731.04	3,184.23	2,794.63	2,503.27
1.25%	17,029.59	12,314.99	10,842.08	8,780.65	6,034.58	4,664.22	3,844.14	3,299.19	2,911.45	2,621.97
1.50%	17,136.79	12,422.65	10,950.06	8,889.36	6,145.36	4,777.20	3,959.37	3,416.69	3,031.23	2,744.01
1.75%	17,244.42	12,530.90	11,058.72	8,998.92	6,257.41	4,891.88	4,076.71	3,536.71	3,153.92	2,869.36
2.00%	17,352.48	12,639.76	11,168.06	9,109.33	6,370.74	5,008.25	4,196.16	3,659.23	3,279.50	2,997.97
2.25%	17,460.97	12,749.22	11,278.09	9,220.60	6,485.34	5,126.30	4,317.69	3,784.24	3,407.94	3,129.81
2.50%	17,569.89	12,859.27	11,388.80	9,332.72	6,601.21	5,246.04	4,441.31	3,911.70	3,539.20	3,264.80
2.75%	17,679.23	12,969.92	11,500.20	9,445.69	6,718.35	5,367.45	4,566.98	4,041.59	3,673.24	3,402.91
3.00%	17,789.00	13,081.17	11,612.28	9,559.51	6,836.76	5,490.52	4,694.69	4,173.88	3,810.02	3,544.05
3.25%	17,899.20	13,193.01	11,725.03	9,674.18	6,956.42	5,615.24	4,824.43	4,308.54	3,949.48	3,688.16
3.50%	18,009.83	13,305.45	11,838.47	9,789.70	7,077.34	5,741.60	4,956.17	4,445.54	4,091.58	3,835.17
3.75%	18,120.88	13,418.49	11,952.59	9,906.06	7,199.50	5,869.59	5,089.90	4,584.84	4,236.26	3,985.01
4.00%	18,232.36	13,532.12	12,067.38	10,023.27	7,322.91	5,999.21	5,225.58	4,726.41	4,383.47	4,137.59
4.25%	18,344.26	13,646.34	12,182.85	10,141.32	7,447.56	6,130.42	5,363.21	4,870.20	4,533.15	4,292.84
4.50%	18,456.59	13,761.16	12,299.00	10,260.20	7,573.43	6,263.23	5,502.74	5,016.18	4,685.24	4,450.67
4.75%	18,569.34	13,876.57	12,415.82	10,379.93	7,700.54	6,397.61	5,644.16	5,164.31	4,839.68	4,611.00
5.00%	18,682.52	13,992.57	12,533.32	10,500.49	7,828.86	6,533.56	5,787.44	5,314.53	4,996.41	4,773.75
5.25%	18,796.12	14,109.16	12,651.49	10,621.88	7,958.39	6,671.06	5,932.55	5,466.82	5,155.36	4,938.82
5.50%	18,910.15	14,226.34	12,770.33	10,744.10	8,089.13	6,810.08	6,079.47	5,621.11	5,316.46	5,106.13
5.75%	19,024.60	14,344.11	12,889.84	10,867.15	8,221.06	6,950.63	6,228.15	5,777.37	5,479.66	5,275.59
6.00%	19,139.47	14,462.47	13,010.02	10,991.03	8,354.18	7,092.67	6,378.58	5,935.55	5,644.88	5,447.12
6.25%	19,254.77	14,581.41	13,130.86	11,115.73	8,488.49	7,236.19	6,530.73	6,095.60	5,812.06	5,620.62
6.50%	19,370.49	14,700.94	13,252.37	11,241.25	8,623.96	7,381.17	6,684.55	6,257.47	5,981.13	5,796.02
6.75%	19,486.63	14,821.06	13,374.54	11,367.59	8,760.60	7,527.60	6,840.02	6,421.12	6,152.02	5,973.23
7.00%	19,603.19	14,941.75	13,497.38	11,494.74	8,898.40	7,675.46	6,997.11	6,586.49	6,324.68	6,152.17
7.25%	19,720.17	15,063.03	13,620.88	11,622.70	9,037.34	7,824.72	7,155.79	6,753.55	6,499.03	6,332.75
7.50%	19,837.57	15,184.89	13,745.03	11,751.48	9,177.42	7,975.37	7,316.01	6,922.22	6,675.00	6,514.90
7.75%	19,955.39	15,307.33	13,869.84	11,881.05	9,318.63	8,127.39	7,477.75	7,092.48	6,852.54	6,698.54
8.00%	20,073.63	15,430.35	13,995.31	12,011.43	9,460.96	8,280.76	7,640.98	7,264.27	7,031.58	6,883.59
8.25%	20,192.29	15,553.95	14,121.43	12,142.61	9,604.39	8,435.45	7,805.66	7,437.54	7,212.06	7,069.97
8.50%	20,311.37	15,678.12	14,248.21	12,274.58	9,748.92	8,591.45	7,971.75	7,612.24	7,393.92	7,257.63
8.75%	20,430.86	15,802.87	14,375.63	12,407.35	9,894.54	8,748.74	8,139.22	7,788.33	7,577.10	7,446.49
9.00%	20,550.77	15,928.19	14,503.70	12,540.90	10,041.24	8,907.29	8,308.04	7,965.76	7,761.53	7,636.48
9.25%	20,671.10	16,054.08	14,632.42	12,675.24	10,189.00	9,067.08	8,478.18	8,144.49	7,947.17	7,827.54
9.50%	20,791.84	16,180.54	14,761.78	12,810.36	10,337.82	9,228.10	8,649.60	8,324.46	8,133.95	8,019.61
9.75%	20,913.00	16,307.57	14,891.78	12,946.25	10,487.69	9,390.32	8,822.26	8,505.63	8,321.83	8,212.63
10.00%	21,034.57	16,435.17	15,022.42	13,082.92	10,638.59	9,553.71	8,996.14	8,687.96	8,510.76	8,406.54
10.25%	21,156.56	16,563.34	15,153.70	13,220.36	10,790.51	9,718.27	9,171.19	8,871.40	8,700.67	8,601.30
10.50%	21,278.96	16,692.07	15,285.62	13,358.56	10,943.45	9,883.96	9,347.40	9,055.92	8,891.53	8,796.85
10.75%	21,401.77	16,821.36	15,418.16	13,497.53	11,097.39	10,050.77	9,524.72	9,241.47	9,083.28	8,993.13

$990,000   11.00 - 20.75%   5 - 40 Years

	5	7	8	10	15	20	25	30	35	40
11.00%	21,525.00	16,951.21	15,551.34	13,637.25	11,252.31	10,218.67	9,703.12	9,428.00	9,275.88	9,190.11
11.25%	21,648.63	17,081.63	15,685.15	13,777.73	11,408.21	10,387.63	9,882.57	9,615.49	9,469.29	9,387.75
11.50%	21,772.68	17,212.60	15,819.58	13,918.95	11,565.08	10,557.65	10,063.04	9,803.89	9,663.46	9,585.99
11.75%	21,897.14	17,344.12	15,954.64	14,060.92	11,722.90	10,728.70	10,244.50	9,993.16	9,858.36	9,784.80
12.00%	22,022.00	17,476.21	16,090.31	14,203.62	11,881.66	10,900.75	10,426.92	10,183.26	10,053.94	9,984.15
12.25%	22,147.28	17,608.84	16,226.61	14,347.07	12,041.36	11,073.79	10,610.26	10,374.17	10,250.17	10,183.99
12.50%	22,272.96	17,742.03	16,363.52	14,491.24	12,201.97	11,247.79	10,794.51	10,565.85	10,447.02	10,384.30
12.75%	22,399.05	17,875.76	16,501.05	14,636.14	12,363.49	11,422.73	10,979.62	10,758.26	10,644.44	10,585.04
13.00%	22,525.54	18,010.04	16,639.18	14,781.76	12,525.90	11,598.60	11,165.57	10,951.38	10,842.41	10,786.19
13.25%	22,652.44	18,144.87	16,777.93	14,928.10	12,689.19	11,775.36	11,352.33	11,145.16	11,040.90	10,987.71
13.50%	22,779.75	18,280.24	16,917.28	15,075.15	12,853.35	11,953.01	11,539.88	11,339.58	11,239.87	11,189.59
13.75%	22,907.46	18,416.16	17,057.23	15,222.91	13,018.37	12,131.51	11,728.19	11,534.61	11,439.30	11,391.78
14.00%	23,035.57	18,552.61	17,197.79	15,371.38	13,184.24	12,310.86	11,917.23	11,730.23	11,639.17	11,594.29
14.25%	23,164.08	18,689.60	17,338.94	15,520.54	13,350.94	12,491.02	12,106.98	11,926.40	11,839.44	11,797.07
14.50%	23,293.00	18,827.13	17,480.68	15,670.39	13,518.46	12,671.98	12,297.41	12,123.10	12,040.09	12,000.12
14.75%	23,422.31	18,965.19	17,623.02	15,820.93	13,686.79	12,853.72	12,488.50	12,320.31	12,241.10	12,203.40
15.00%	23,552.03	19,103.79	17,765.95	15,972.16	13,855.91	13,036.22	12,680.22	12,518.00	12,442.45	12,406.92
15.25%	23,682.15	19,242.91	17,909.47	16,124.07	14,025.82	13,219.46	12,872.56	12,716.14	12,644.12	12,610.64
15.50%	23,812.66	19,382.56	18,053.56	16,276.64	14,196.50	13,403.42	13,065.48	12,914.72	12,846.09	12,814.56
15.75%	23,943.57	19,522.74	18,198.24	16,429.89	14,367.95	13,588.08	13,258.97	13,113.71	13,048.34	13,018.66
16.00%	24,074.88	19,663.44	18,343.50	16,583.80	14,540.14	13,773.43	13,453.00	13,313.09	13,250.85	13,222.92
16.25%	24,206.58	19,804.67	18,489.33	16,738.37	14,713.06	13,959.45	13,647.56	13,512.85	13,453.60	13,427.34
16.50%	24,338.68	19,946.41	18,635.73	16,893.59	14,886.72	14,146.12	13,842.62	13,712.97	13,656.59	13,631.90
16.75%	24,471.17	20,088.67	18,782.70	17,049.46	15,061.08	14,333.41	14,038.17	13,913.42	13,859.80	13,836.59
17.00%	24,604.05	20,231.45	18,930.24	17,205.97	15,236.14	14,521.33	14,234.19	14,114.19	14,063.21	14,041.40
17.25%	24,737.33	20,374.74	19,078.34	17,363.12	15,411.90	14,709.83	14,430.65	14,315.26	14,266.81	14,246.33
17.50%	24,870.99	20,518.54	19,227.00	17,520.90	15,588.32	14,898.93	14,627.54	14,516.62	14,470.59	14,451.36
17.75%	25,005.05	20,662.84	19,376.21	17,679.31	15,765.42	15,088.58	14,824.85	14,718.25	14,674.53	14,656.49
18.00%	25,139.49	20,807.66	19,525.98	17,838.33	15,943.17	15,278.78	15,022.56	14,920.15	14,878.63	14,861.70
18.25%	25,274.33	20,952.98	19,676.30	17,997.98	16,121.56	15,469.52	15,220.64	15,122.28	15,082.88	15,067.00
18.50%	25,409.55	21,098.80	19,827.17	18,158.24	16,300.58	15,660.78	15,419.09	15,324.65	15,287.26	15,272.38
18.75%	25,545.15	21,245.12	19,978.58	18,319.10	16,480.22	15,852.53	15,617.89	15,527.24	15,491.77	15,477.82
19.00%	25,681.15	21,391.94	20,130.53	18,480.56	16,660.47	16,044.78	15,817.03	15,730.04	15,696.40	15,683.33
19.25%	25,817.52	21,539.25	20,283.01	18,642.62	16,841.32	16,237.50	16,016.49	15,933.03	15,901.14	15,888.90
19.50%	25,954.28	21,687.06	20,436.04	18,805.27	17,022.75	16,430.68	16,216.26	16,136.21	16,105.98	16,094.52
19.75%	26,091.42	21,835.35	20,589.59	18,968.50	17,204.76	16,624.31	16,416.32	16,339.56	16,310.92	16,300.19
20.00%	26,228.94	21,984.14	20,743.67	19,132.31	17,387.34	16,818.36	16,616.67	16,543.08	16,515.96	16,505.91
20.25%	26,366.85	22,133.41	20,898.27	19,296.70	17,570.46	17,012.84	16,817.29	16,746.76	16,721.07	16,711.68
20.50%	26,505.13	22,283.16	21,053.40	19,461.65	17,754.13	17,207.73	17,018.17	16,950.59	16,926.27	16,917.48
20.75%	26,643.79	22,433.39	21,209.04	19,627.16	17,938.34	17,403.00	17,219.30	17,154.56	17,131.53	17,123.32

$1,000,000   1.00 - 10.75%   5 - 40 Years

	5	7	8	10	15	20	25	30	35	40
1.00%	17,093.75	12,331.25	10,843.23	8,760.41	5,984.95	4,598.94	3,768.72	3,216.40	2,822.86	2,528.56
1.25%	17,201.60	12,439.39	10,951.60	8,869.35	6,095.54	4,711.34	3,882.97	3,332.52	2,940.86	2,648.45
1.50%	17,309.89	12,548.13	11,060.66	8,979.15	6,207.43	4,825.45	3,999.36	3,451.20	3,061.84	2,771.72
1.75%	17,418.61	12,657.48	11,170.42	9,089.82	6,320.61	4,941.29	4,117.89	3,572.43	3,185.78	2,898.34
2.00%	17,527.76	12,767.44	11,280.87	9,201.35	6,435.09	5,058.83	4,238.54	3,696.19	3,312.63	3,028.26
2.25%	17,637.34	12,878.00	11,392.01	9,313.74	6,550.85	5,178.08	4,361.31	3,822.46	3,442.37	3,161.42
2.50%	17,747.36	12,989.16	11,503.84	9,426.99	6,667.89	5,299.03	4,486.17	3,951.21	3,574.95	3,297.78
2.75%	17,857.81	13,100.93	11,616.36	9,541.10	6,786.22	5,421.66	4,613.11	4,082.41	3,710.35	3,437.28
3.00%	17,968.69	13,213.30	11,729.57	9,656.07	6,905.82	5,545.98	4,742.11	4,216.04	3,848.50	3,579.84
3.25%	18,080.00	13,326.27	11,843.47	9,771.90	7,026.69	5,671.96	4,873.16	4,352.06	3,989.37	3,725.41
3.50%	18,191.74	13,439.85	11,958.05	9,888.59	7,148.83	5,799.60	5,006.24	4,490.45	4,132.91	3,873.91
3.75%	18,303.92	13,554.03	12,073.32	10,006.12	7,272.22	5,928.88	5,141.31	4,631.16	4,279.05	4,025.26
4.00%	18,416.52	13,668.81	12,189.28	10,124.51	7,396.88	6,059.80	5,278.37	4,774.15	4,427.75	4,179.38
4.25%	18,529.56	13,784.18	12,305.91	10,243.75	7,522.78	6,192.34	5,417.38	4,919.40	4,578.94	4,336.20
4.50%	18,643.02	13,900.16	12,423.23	10,363.84	7,649.93	6,326.49	5,558.32	5,066.85	4,732.57	4,495.63
4.75%	18,756.91	14,016.74	12,541.24	10,484.77	7,778.32	6,462.24	5,701.17	5,216.47	4,888.57	4,657.58
5.00%	18,871.23	14,133.91	12,659.92	10,606.55	7,907.94	6,599.56	5,845.90	5,368.22	5,046.88	4,821.97
5.25%	18,985.98	14,251.68	12,779.28	10,729.17	8,038.78	6,738.44	5,992.48	5,522.04	5,207.43	4,988.70
5.50%	19,101.16	14,370.04	12,899.32	10,852.63	8,170.83	6,878.87	6,140.87	5,677.89	5,370.16	5,157.70
5.75%	19,216.77	14,489.00	13,020.04	10,976.92	8,304.10	7,020.84	6,291.06	5,835.73	5,535.01	5,328.88
6.00%	19,332.80	14,608.55	13,141.43	11,102.05	8,438.57	7,164.31	6,443.01	5,995.51	5,701.90	5,502.14
6.25%	19,449.26	14,728.70	13,263.50	11,228.01	8,574.23	7,309.28	6,596.69	6,157.17	5,870.76	5,677.40
6.50%	19,566.15	14,849.44	13,386.23	11,354.80	8,711.07	7,455.73	6,752.07	6,320.68	6,041.54	5,854.57
6.75%	19,683.46	14,970.76	13,509.64	11,482.41	8,849.09	7,603.64	6,909.12	6,485.98	6,214.17	6,033.57
7.00%	19,801.20	15,092.68	13,633.72	11,610.85	8,988.28	7,752.99	7,067.79	6,653.02	6,388.56	6,214.31
7.25%	19,919.36	15,215.18	13,758.46	11,740.10	9,128.63	7,903.76	7,228.07	6,821.76	6,564.67	6,396.72
7.50%	20,037.95	15,338.28	13,883.87	11,870.18	9,270.12	8,055.93	7,389.91	6,992.15	6,742.43	6,580.71
7.75%	20,156.96	15,461.95	14,009.94	12,001.06	9,412.76	8,209.49	7,553.29	7,164.12	6,921.76	6,766.20
8.00%	20,276.39	15,586.21	14,136.68	12,132.76	9,556.52	8,364.40	7,718.16	7,337.65	7,102.61	6,953.12
8.25%	20,396.25	15,711.06	14,264.07	12,265.26	9,701.40	8,520.66	7,884.50	7,512.67	7,284.91	7,141.39
8.50%	20,516.53	15,836.49	14,392.13	12,398.57	9,847.40	8,678.23	8,052.27	7,689.13	7,468.61	7,330.94
8.75%	20,637.23	15,962.49	14,520.84	12,532.68	9,994.49	8,837.11	8,221.44	7,867.00	7,653.63	7,521.71
9.00%	20,758.36	16,089.08	14,650.20	12,667.58	10,142.67	8,997.26	8,391.96	8,046.23	7,839.93	7,713.61
9.25%	20,879.90	16,216.24	14,780.22	12,803.27	10,291.92	9,158.67	8,563.82	8,226.75	8,027.44	7,906.61
9.50%	21,001.86	16,343.98	14,910.89	12,939.76	10,442.25	9,321.31	8,736.97	8,408.54	8,216.12	8,100.62
9.75%	21,124.24	16,472.30	15,042.20	13,077.02	10,593.63	9,485.17	8,911.37	8,591.54	8,405.89	8,295.59
10.00%	21,247.04	16,601.18	15,174.16	13,215.07	10,746.05	9,650.22	9,087.01	8,775.72	8,596.72	8,491.46
10.25%	21,370.26	16,730.64	15,306.77	13,353.90	10,899.51	9,816.43	9,263.83	8,961.01	8,788.56	8,688.18
10.50%	21,493.90	16,860.67	15,440.02	13,493.50	11,053.99	9,983.80	9,441.82	9,147.39	8,981.34	8,885.70
10.75%	21,617.95	16,991.27	15,573.90	13,633.87	11,209.48	10,152.29	9,620.93	9,334.81	9,175.03	9,083.97

$1,000,000   11.00 - 20.75%   5 - 40 Years

	5	7	8	10	15	20	25	30	35	40
11.00%	21,742.42	17,122.44	15,708.43	13,775.00	11,365.97	10,321.88	9,801.13	9,523.23	9,369.58	9,282.94
11.25%	21,867.31	17,254.17	15,843.58	13,916.89	11,523.45	10,492.56	9,982.40	9,712.61	9,564.94	9,482.57
11.50%	21,992.61	17,386.46	15,979.37	14,059.54	11,681.90	10,664.30	10,164.69	9,902.91	9,761.07	9,682.82
11.75%	22,118.32	17,519.32	16,115.79	14,202.95	11,841.31	10,837.07	10,347.98	10,094.10	9,957.94	9,883.64
12.00%	22,244.45	17,652.73	16,252.84	14,347.09	12,001.68	11,010.86	10,532.24	10,286.13	10,155.50	10,085.00
12.25%	22,370.99	17,786.71	16,390.51	14,491.99	12,162.99	11,185.65	10,717.44	10,478.96	10,353.71	10,286.86
12.50%	22,497.94	17,921.24	16,528.81	14,637.62	12,325.22	11,361.41	10,903.54	10,672.58	10,552.54	10,489.19
12.75%	22,625.30	18,056.32	16,667.72	14,783.98	12,488.37	11,538.12	11,090.52	10,866.93	10,751.96	10,691.96
13.00%	22,753.07	18,191.96	16,807.26	14,931.07	12,652.42	11,715.76	11,278.35	11,062.00	10,951.93	10,895.14
13.25%	22,881.26	18,328.15	16,947.40	15,078.89	12,817.36	11,894.31	11,467.00	11,257.74	11,152.42	11,098.70
13.50%	23,009.85	18,464.89	17,088.16	15,227.43	12,983.19	12,073.75	11,656.45	11,454.12	11,353.41	11,302.61
13.75%	23,138.84	18,602.18	17,229.53	15,376.68	13,149.87	12,254.05	11,846.66	11,651.13	11,554.85	11,506.85
14.00%	23,268.25	18,740.01	17,371.50	15,526.64	13,317.41	12,435.21	12,037.61	11,848.72	11,756.73	11,711.40
14.25%	23,398.06	18,878.39	17,514.08	15,677.31	13,485.80	12,617.19	12,229.28	12,046.87	11,959.03	11,916.23
14.50%	23,528.28	19,017.30	17,657.26	15,828.68	13,655.01	12,799.98	12,421.63	12,245.56	12,161.71	12,121.33
14.75%	23,658.90	19,156.76	17,801.03	15,980.74	13,825.04	12,983.55	12,614.65	12,444.76	12,364.75	12,326.67
15.00%	23,789.93	19,296.75	17,945.41	16,133.50	13,995.87	13,167.90	12,808.31	12,644.44	12,568.13	12,532.24
15.25%	23,921.36	19,437.28	18,090.37	16,286.93	14,167.50	13,352.99	13,002.58	12,844.59	12,771.84	12,738.02
15.50%	24,053.19	19,578.35	18,235.92	16,441.05	14,339.90	13,538.81	13,197.45	13,045.17	12,975.85	12,944.00
15.75%	24,185.42	19,719.94	18,382.06	16,595.85	14,513.08	13,725.34	13,392.90	13,246.17	13,180.14	13,150.16
16.00%	24,318.06	19,862.06	18,528.79	16,751.31	14,687.01	13,912.56	13,588.89	13,447.57	13,384.69	13,356.48
16.25%	24,451.09	20,004.71	18,676.09	16,907.44	14,861.68	14,100.46	13,785.41	13,649.35	13,589.50	13,562.97
16.50%	24,584.52	20,147.89	18,823.97	17,064.23	15,037.09	14,289.01	13,982.45	13,851.48	13,794.54	13,769.59
16.75%	24,718.35	20,291.59	18,972.43	17,221.67	15,213.21	14,478.20	14,179.97	14,053.96	13,999.80	13,976.35
17.00%	24,852.58	20,435.80	19,121.45	17,379.77	15,390.04	14,668.01	14,377.97	14,256.75	14,205.26	14,183.24
17.25%	24,987.20	20,580.54	19,271.05	17,538.50	15,567.57	14,858.42	14,576.41	14,459.86	14,410.92	14,390.23
17.50%	25,122.21	20,725.79	19,421.21	17,697.88	15,745.78	15,049.42	14,775.30	14,663.25	14,616.75	14,597.33
17.75%	25,257.62	20,871.56	19,571.93	17,857.88	15,924.67	15,240.99	14,974.60	14,866.92	14,822.76	14,804.53
18.00%	25,393.43	21,017.84	19,723.21	18,018.52	16,104.21	15,433.12	15,174.30	15,070.85	15,028.92	15,011.82
18.25%	25,529.62	21,164.63	19,875.05	18,179.78	16,284.40	15,625.78	15,374.39	15,275.03	15,235.23	15,219.20
18.50%	25,666.21	21,311.92	20,027.44	18,341.65	16,465.23	15,818.97	15,574.84	15,479.45	15,441.68	15,426.64
18.75%	25,803.19	21,459.72	20,180.38	18,504.14	16,646.69	16,012.66	15,775.65	15,684.08	15,648.25	15,634.16
19.00%	25,940.55	21,608.02	20,333.86	18,667.24	16,828.76	16,206.85	15,976.80	15,888.92	15,854.95	15,841.75
19.25%	26,078.30	21,756.82	20,487.89	18,830.93	17,011.43	16,401.52	16,178.27	16,093.97	16,061.76	16,049.39
19.50%	26,216.45	21,906.12	20,642.46	18,995.22	17,194.70	16,596.65	16,380.06	16,299.20	16,268.67	16,257.09
19.75%	26,354.97	22,055.91	20,797.56	19,160.10	17,378.55	16,792.23	16,582.15	16,504.61	16,475.68	16,464.84
20.00%	26,493.88	22,206.20	20,953.20	19,325.57	17,562.97	16,988.25	16,784.52	16,710.19	16,682.78	16,672.64
20.25%	26,633.18	22,356.98	21,109.37	19,491.61	17,747.94	17,184.69	16,987.16	16,915.92	16,889.97	16,880.48
20.50%	26,772.86	22,508.24	21,266.06	19,658.23	17,933.47	17,381.54	17,190.07	17,121.81	17,097.24	17,088.36
20.75%	26,912.92	22,659.99	21,423.27	19,825.42	18,119.53	17,578.79	17,393.23	17,327.84	17,304.58	17,296.28

	5	7	8	10	15	20	25	30	35	40
11.00%	21,742.42	17,122.44	15,708.43	13,775.00	11,365.97	10,321.88	9,801.13	9,523.23	9,369.58	9,282.94
11.25%	21,867.31	17,254.17	15,843.58	13,916.89	11,523.45	10,492.56	9,982.40	9,712.61	9,564.94	9,482.57
11.50%	21,992.61	17,386.46	15,979.37	14,059.54	11,681.90	10,664.30	10,164.69	9,902.91	9,761.07	9,682.82
11.75%	22,118.32	17,519.32	16,115.79	14,202.95	11,841.31	10,837.07	10,347.98	10,094.10	9,957.94	9,883.64
12.00%	22,244.45	17,652.73	16,252.84	14,347.09	12,001.68	11,010.86	10,532.24	10,286.13	10,155.50	10,085.00
12.25%	22,370.99	17,786.71	16,390.51	14,491.99	12,162.99	11,185.65	10,717.44	10,478.96	10,353.71	10,286.86
12.50%	22,497.94	17,921.24	16,528.81	14,637.62	12,325.22	11,361.41	10,903.54	10,672.58	10,552.54	10,489.19
12.75%	22,625.30	18,056.32	16,667.72	14,783.98	12,488.37	11,538.12	11,090.52	10,866.93	10,751.96	10,691.96
13.00%	22,753.07	18,191.96	16,807.26	14,931.07	12,652.42	11,715.76	11,278.35	11,062.00	10,951.93	10,895.14
13.25%	22,881.26	18,328.15	16,947.40	15,078.89	12,817.36	11,894.31	11,467.00	11,257.74	11,152.42	11,098.70
13.50%	23,009.85	18,464.89	17,088.16	15,227.43	12,983.19	12,073.75	11,656.45	11,454.12	11,353.41	11,302.61
13.75%	23,138.84	18,602.18	17,229.53	15,376.68	13,149.87	12,254.05	11,846.66	11,651.13	11,554.85	11,506.85
14.00%	23,268.25	18,740.01	17,371.50	15,526.64	13,317.41	12,435.21	12,037.61	11,848.72	11,756.73	11,711.40
14.25%	23,398.06	18,878.39	17,514.08	15,677.31	13,485.80	12,617.19	12,229.28	12,046.87	11,959.03	11,916.23
14.50%	23,528.28	19,017.30	17,657.26	15,828.68	13,655.01	12,799.98	12,421.63	12,245.56	12,161.71	12,121.33
14.75%	23,658.90	19,156.76	17,801.03	15,980.74	13,825.04	12,983.55	12,614.65	12,444.76	12,364.75	12,326.67
15.00%	23,789.93	19,296.75	17,945.41	16,133.50	13,995.87	13,167.90	12,808.31	12,644.44	12,568.13	12,532.24
15.25%	23,921.36	19,437.28	18,090.37	16,286.93	14,167.50	13,352.99	13,002.58	12,844.59	12,771.84	12,738.02
15.50%	24,053.19	19,578.35	18,235.92	16,441.05	14,339.90	13,538.81	13,197.45	13,045.17	12,975.85	12,944.00
15.75%	24,185.42	19,719.94	18,382.06	16,595.85	14,513.08	13,725.34	13,392.90	13,246.17	13,180.14	13,150.16
16.00%	24,318.06	19,862.06	18,528.79	16,751.31	14,687.01	13,912.56	13,588.89	13,447.57	13,384.69	13,356.48
16.25%	24,451.09	20,004.71	18,676.09	16,907.44	14,861.68	14,100.46	13,785.41	13,649.35	13,589.50	13,562.97
16.50%	24,584.52	20,147.89	18,823.97	17,064.23	15,037.09	14,289.01	13,982.45	13,851.48	13,794.54	13,769.59
16.75%	24,718.35	20,291.59	18,972.43	17,221.67	15,213.21	14,478.20	14,179.97	14,053.96	13,999.80	13,976.35
17.00%	24,852.58	20,435.80	19,121.45	17,379.77	15,390.04	14,668.01	14,377.97	14,256.75	14,205.26	14,183.24
17.25%	24,987.20	20,580.54	19,271.05	17,538.50	15,567.57	14,858.42	14,576.41	14,459.86	14,410.92	14,390.23
17.50%	25,122.21	20,725.79	19,421.21	17,697.88	15,745.78	15,049.42	14,775.30	14,663.25	14,616.75	14,597.33
17.75%	25,257.62	20,871.56	19,571.93	17,857.88	15,924.67	15,240.99	14,974.60	14,866.92	14,822.76	14,804.53
18.00%	25,393.43	21,017.84	19,723.21	18,018.52	16,104.21	15,433.12	15,174.30	15,070.85	15,028.92	15,011.82
18.25%	25,529.62	21,164.63	19,875.05	18,179.78	16,284.40	15,625.78	15,374.39	15,275.03	15,235.23	15,219.20
18.50%	25,666.21	21,311.92	20,027.44	18,341.65	16,465.23	15,818.97	15,574.84	15,479.45	15,441.68	15,426.64
18.75%	25,803.19	21,459.72	20,180.38	18,504.14	16,646.69	16,012.66	15,775.65	15,684.08	15,648.25	15,634.16
19.00%	25,940.55	21,608.02	20,333.86	18,667.24	16,828.76	16,206.85	15,976.80	15,888.92	15,854.95	15,841.75
19.25%	26,078.30	21,756.82	20,487.89	18,830.93	17,011.43	16,401.52	16,178.27	16,093.97	16,061.76	16,049.39
19.50%	26,216.45	21,906.12	20,642.46	18,995.22	17,194.70	16,596.65	16,380.06	16,299.20	16,268.67	16,257.09
19.75%	26,354.97	22,055.91	20,797.56	19,160.10	17,378.55	16,792.23	16,582.15	16,504.61	16,475.68	16,464.84
20.00%	26,493.88	22,206.20	20,953.20	19,325.57	17,562.97	16,988.25	16,784.52	16,710.19	16,682.78	16,672.64
20.25%	26,633.18	22,356.98	21,109.37	19,491.61	17,747.94	17,184.69	16,987.16	16,915.92	16,889.97	16,880.48
20.50%	26,772.86	22,508.24	21,266.06	19,658.23	17,933.47	17,381.54	17,190.07	17,121.81	17,097.24	17,088.36
20.75%	26,912.92	22,659.99	21,423.27	19,825.42	18,119.53	17,578.79	17,393.23	17,327.84	17,304.58	17,296.28

Notes

Notes

Made in the USA
Middletown, DE
31 December 2020